FEB 1 2 2018

Historical Dictionary of
the Olympic Movement

HISTORICAL DICTIONARIES OF SPORTS

Jon Woronoff, Series Editor

HISTORICAL DICTIONARY

The historical dictionaries present essential information on a broad range of subjects, including American and world history, art, business, cities, countries, cultures, customs, film, global conflicts, international relations, literature, music, philosophy, religion, sports, and theater. Written by experts, all contain highly informative introductory essays of the topic and detailed chronologies that, in some cases, cover vast historical time periods but still manage to heavily feature more recent events.

Brief A–Z entries describe the main people, events, politics, social issues, institutions, and policies that make the topic unique, and entries are cross-referenced for ease of browsing. Extensive bibliographies are divided into several general subject areas, providing excellent access points for students, researchers, and anyone wanting to know more. Additionally, maps, photographs, and appendixes of supplemental information aid high school and college students doing term papers or introductory research projects. In short, the historical dictionaries are the perfect starting point for anyone looking to research in these fields.

Historical Dictionary of the Olympic Movement

Fifth Edition

John Grasso, Bill Mallon,
and Jeroen Heijmans

ROWMAN & LITTLEFIELD
Lanham • Boulder • New York • London

Published by Rowman & Littlefield
A wholly owned subsidary of The Rowman & Littlefield Publishing Group, Inc.
4501 Forbes Boulevard, Suite 200, Lanham, Maryland 20706
www.rowman.com

Unit A, Whitacre Mews, 26-34 Stannary Street, London SE11 4AB

British Library Cataloguing in Publication Information Available

Library of Congress Cataloging-in-Publication Data

Grasso, John.
  Historical dictionary of the Olympic movement / John Grasso, Bill Mallon,
and Jeroen Heijmans. — Fifth edition.
     pages cm. — (Historical dictionaries of sports)
  Includes bibliographical references.
  ISBN 978-1-4422-4859-5 (cloth : alk. paper) — ISBN 978-1-4422-4860-1 (ebook)
  1. Olympics—History—Dictionaries. 2. Olympics—Records. I. Mallon, Bill.
II. Heijmans, Jeroen. III. Title.
  GV721.5.B83 2015
  796.48'03—dc23

                                                                    2014043744

♾️ᵀᴹ The paper used in this publication meets the minimum requirements of
American National Standard for Information Sciences—Permanence of Paper
for Printed Library Materials, ANSI/NISO Z39.48-1992.

Printed in the United States of America

In memory of Ian Buchanan and Karl Lennartz

Contents

Editor's Foreword

The love of sports is worldwide, and at virtually any moment of the day or night, some major match is going on somewhere in the world, viewed by large audiences who enjoy the sport passively and sometimes actively. But there are two times every four years when sports lovers are fixated on the most extraordinary show on earth, the Olympic Games in the summer and the Olympic Winter Games, where the best athletes from all countries contend in one competition after the other. With thousands of participants and millions of viewers, these games outshine anything else of the sort. They vastly dwarf the original Olympics, going back to the ancient Greeks, and also the early attempts at re-creating them, first in various aborted projects, and then as fashioned single-mindedly by Pierre de Coubertin and other pioneers. Today, a whole "machine" produces Olympic Games, starting with the International Olympic Committee, the National Olympic Committees, the various International Federations, and countless other bodies. Although this "machine" is absolutely necessary to keep the Olympic Movement going, it does generate problems. And these, too, are part of the present world of sports.

This makes the task of the *Historical Dictionary of the Olympic Movement* a genuine challenge, but one that is accomplished periodically as more and more material is collected and added. This time, once again, the chronology of the Olympic Movement is somewhat longer, as is the chronology of the Summer and Winter Games, while remaining essential for those who want to survey the long course of events. The list of acronyms is even denser, but necessary to identify the organizational players. The introduction discusses more achievements and also more problems. The most important part, the dictionary section, has more entries than ever before, on the major organizations, the various sports, the numerous participating countries, and especially the outstanding athletes. For those who want the precious details, there is nothing like the multiple appendixes, covering presidents of the International Olympic Committee, games, awards, medal winners, and much more. This is already an excellent starting point but those who want to know more can check with the bibliography.

This is now the fifth edition of the *Historical Dictionary of the Olympic Movement*, whose appearance every four years has become a custom. This time, however, the main author is John Grasso, who is building on the earlier work of Bill Mallon and Jeroen Heijmans. Bill Mallon, who has been with the book from the beginning, is probably the best historian in the field, having helped found the International Society of Olympic Historians (ISOH) and long serving as its president. He is also a former editor of the ISOH's *Journal of Olympic History* and has written two dozen books on the Olympics. Jeroen Heijmans has also followed the Olympics very closely for several decades and written for the Dutch sports history website as well as being the webmaster of the ISOH. John Grasso, a lifetime member of the ISOH and currently its treasurer, has written widely on sports, including those in the Olympics, and has authored five historical dictionaries and co-authored a sixth. For this, now his seventh historical dictionary, he has provided considerable new information, which readers will greatly appreciate.

Jon Woronoff
Series Editor

Preface

I've followed the Olympic Games for the better part of my life. One of my earliest Olympic memories was watching the enthusiasm of the Pakistani hockey team following their upset of India in the 1960 Games. Announcer Bud Palmer asked the team's captain how the team felt after their victory, and the entire team went into a wild celebration in the television studio in response to his question. Since that time, I watched television coverage of every Summer and Winter Games and in 1976 decided to attend the Montreal Games. At that time I calculated that it would cost me and my wife about $2,000 to attend the two-week celebration, and that was quite a bit more than my budget at that time would allow. But then it dawned on me that if we just went for one week it would only cost $1,000 and that was manageable. Ticket prices in that era were much more reasonable, and we were able to attend the Opening Ceremonies and two events a day for seven additional days. We drove from New York to Montreal, stayed with a family there (arranged by the Montreal Organizing Committee), and had the most memorable vacation in my life. Being present at the Opening Ceremony was a thrill beyond belief. Over the next four decades I've been fortunate to attend the Summer Games in Los Angeles, Seoul, Atlanta, Athens, Beijing, and London and the Winter Games in Calgary and Sochi, and each one carries its own story as to my attendance as well as the experiences during the Games.

In 1988, for example, after watching the first weekend of the Winter Games in Calgary on television and being upset by the amount of commercial interruptions, I visited a local travel agent on Monday and inquired about the possibility of getting a flight to Calgary, a vehicle while there, accommodations in Calgary, and tickets for a few events. On Tuesday, I asked my boss for a few days' vacation. On Wednesday night, my wife and I were on our way and we spent the next five days at the Winter Olympics—arriving in Calgary at about 3 a.m. Thursday morning, driving the last available rental vehicle (a pickup truck), staying at the home of a local Calgaryite who was able to acquire tickets for us to see one event a day for the next five days, and departing on Monday (actually Tuesday on a 2 a.m. flight). Never having been to a Winter Olympics, we dressed as if we were going to the North Pole and were greatly surprised by the weather, which was between 40°F and 50°F

(4–10°C) during our stay. One strong memory from that trip was pulling up at a stop light in our pickup truck and looking at the pickup truck in the next lane, which was that of the Jamaican bobsled team.

During the 1980s, while doing some boxing writing, I was a co-founder of the International Boxing Research Organization (IBRO) and self-published an *Olympic Games Boxing Record Book* via IBRO. Bill Mallon found out about it and ordered a few copies. We corresponded off and on over the next decade, and in 1991, after he founded the International Society of Olympic Historians (ISOH), he invited me to join. A decade later, he asked if I wanted to run for treasurer of ISOH, and I've held that position since 2004 (mainly because no one else is interested in doing that job).

In 2013, Jon Woronoff asked if I would be interested in updating Bill's *Historical Dictionary of the Olympic Movement* and I was thrilled to accept the offer. Most of this edition is still the work of Bill and his co-authors, Ian Buchanan and later, Jeroen Heijmans, but I have added more than 150 new entries, expanded all the country entries with geographic data as well as describing their notable Olympic Games performances, and provided summaries of their Olympic results. I also added five appendices and brought the bibliography up to date with the inclusion of significant works published since the previous edition, also including several additional photographs.

Since the previous edition, the Olympic Movement has not stood still, and you will find this reflected in entries on Viktor An, Oscar Pistorius, Bode Miller, Ian Millar, Serena Williams, and Roger Federer, just to mention a few. In addition, I have added a few topics, such as terms used within Olympic sports (like *repêchage*) as well as brief biographies of several leading Olympic historians.

Major thanks to Dr. Bill Mallon, who got me involved in these historical dictionaries and who was the primary author of the first four editions of the *Historical Dictionary of the Olympic Movement.* Much of his statistical research now resides on the Sports Reference website (www.sports-reference.com/olympics) and served as the basis for many of the entries in this fifth edition.

Also special thanks to ISOH member Peter Lovesey, who helped clarify the difference between Great Britain, the U.K., and the British Isles, and to international sports expert Dr. Tomasz Malolepszy (who attended the 2004 Games with me), who reviewed the section on Poland and Polish Olympians. A big thank you goes to Volker Kluge, who provided many of the photos. Also thanks to editor Jon Woronoff and the staff at Rowman & Littlefield for helping to bring this book to fruition.

Acronyms and Abbreviations

THREE-LETTER SPORT ABBREVIATIONS

ARC	Archery
ASK	Alpine Skiing
ATH	Athletics (Track and Field)
BAS	Basketball
BDM	Badminton
BIA	Biathlon
BOB	Bobsledding
BOX	Boxing
BSB	Baseball
BVO	Beach Volleyball
CAN	Canoe and Kayaking
CCS	Cross-country Skiing
CRI	Cricket
CRO	Croquet
CUR	Curling
CYC	Cycling
DIV	Diving
EQU	Equestrian Events
FEN	Fencing
FRS	Freestyle Skiing
FSK	Figure Skating
FTB	Football, Association (Soccer)
GOL	Golf
GYM	Gymnastics
HAN	Team Handball
HOK	Hockey (Field)
ICH	Ice Hockey
JDP	Jeu de Paume
JUD	Judo
LAX	Lacrosse
LUG	Luge
MOP	Modern Pentathlon

MTB   Motorboating
MSP   Military Ski Patrol
NCO   Nordic Combined
PEL   Pelota Basque
POL   Polo
RAQ   Racquets
RGY   Rhythmic Gymnastics
ROW   Rowing
RUG   Rugby
SAI   Sailing
SHO   Shooting
SKE   Skeleton
SKJ   Ski Jumping
SNB   Snowboarding
SOF   Softball
SSK   Speed Skating
STK   Short-track Speed Skating
SWI   Swimming
SYN   Synchronized Swimming
TEN   Tennis (Lawn Tennis)
TKW   Taekwondo
TMP   Trampoline
TOW   Tug-of-War
TRI   Triathlon
TTN   Table Tennis
VOL   Volleyball
WAP   Water Polo
WLT   Weightlifting
WRE   Wrestling

THREE-LETTER NATIONAL ABBREVIATIONS

AFG   Afghanistan
AHO   Netherlands Antilles
ALB   Albania
ALG   Algeria
AND   Andorra
ANG   Angola
ANL   Antilles (West Indies)
ANT   Antigua and Barbuda
ANZ   Australasia
ARG   Argentina

ARM	Armenia
ARU	Aruba
ASA	American Samoa
AUS	Australia
AUT	Austria
AZE	Azerbaijan
BAH	The Bahamas
BAN	Bangladesh
BAR	Barbados
BDI	Burundi
BEL	Belgium
BEN	Benin
BER	Bermuda
BHU	Bhutan
BIH	Bosnia-Herzegovina
BIZ	Belize
BLR	Belarus
BOH	Bohemia
BOL	Bolivia
BOT	Botswana
BRA	Brazil
BRN	Bahrain
BRU	Brunei
BUL	Bulgaria
BUR	Burkina Faso
CAF	Central African Republic
CAM	Cambodia
CAN	Canada
CAY	Cayman Islands
CEY	Ceylon
CGO	Congo
CHA	Chad
CHI	Chile
CHN	China
CIV	Côte d'Ivoire (Ivory Coast)
CMR	Cameroon
COD	Democratic Republic of the Congo (Zaire)
COK	Cook Islands
COL	Colombia
COM	Comoros Islands
CPV	Cape Verde
CRC	Costa Rica
CRO	Croatia

CRT	Crete
CUB	Cuba
CYP	Cyprus
CZE	Czech Republic
DEN	Denmark
DJI	Djibouti
DMA	Dominica
DOM	Dominican Republic
ECU	Ecuador
EGY	Egypt
ERI	Eritrea
ESA	El Salvador
ESP	Spain
EST	Estonia
ETH	Ethiopia
EUN	Unified Team
FIJ	Fiji
FIN	Finland
FRA	France
FRG	Federal Republic of Germany
FSM	Federated States of Micronesia
GAB	Gabon
GAM	The Gambia
GBR	Great Britain
GBS	Guinea-Bissau
GDR	German Democratic Republic
GEO	Georgia
GEQ	Equatorial Guinea
GER	Germany
GHA	Ghana
GRE	Greece
GRN	Grenada
GUA	Guatemala
GUI	Guinea
GUM	Guam
GUY	Guyana
HAI	Haiti
HKG	Hong Kong
HON	Honduras
HUN	Hungary
INA	Indonesia
IND	India
IOA	Independent Olympic Athlete

IOP	Independent Olympic Participant
IRI	Iran
IRL	Ireland
IRQ	Iraq
ISL	Iceland
ISR	Israel
ISV	U.S. Virgin Islands
ITA	Italy
IVB	British Virgin Islands
JAM	Jamaica
JOR	Jordan
JPN	Japan
KAZ	Kazakhstan
KEN	Kenya
KGZ	Kyrgyzstan
KIR	Kiribati
KOR	Korea (South)
KSA	Saudi Arabia
KUW	Kuwait
LAO	Laos
LAT	Latvia
LBA	Libya
LBR	Liberia
LCA	Saint Lucia
LES	Lesotho
LIB	Lebanon
LIE	Liechtenstein
LTU	Lithuania
LUX	Luxembourg
MAD	Madagascar
MAL	Malaya
MAR	Morocco
MAS	Malaysia
MAW	Malawi
MDA	Moldova
MDV	Maldives
MEX	Mexico
MGL	Mongolia
MHL	Marshall Islands
MIX	mixed team
MKD	Macedonia
MLI	Mali
MLT	Malta

MNE	Montenegro
MON	Monaco
MOZ	Mozambique
MRI	Mauritius
MTN	Mauritania
MYA	Myanmar
NAM	Namibia
NBO	North Borneo
NCA	Nicaragua
NED	The Netherlands
NEP	Nepal
NFL	Newfoundland
NGR	Nigeria
NIG	Niger
NOR	Norway
NRU	Nauru
NZL	New Zealand
OMA	Oman
PAK	Pakistan
PAN	Panama
PAR	Paraguay
PER	Peru
PHI	The Philippines
PLE	Palestine
PLW	Palau
PNG	Papua-New Guinea
POL	Poland
POR	Portugal
PRK	Democratic People's Republic of Korea (North)
PUR	Puerto Rico
QAT	Qatar
ROU	Romania
RSA	South Africa
RUS	Russia
RWA	Rwanda
SAA	Saar
SAM	Samoa (Western)
SCG	Serbia and Montenegro
SCO	Scotland
SEN	Senegal
SEY	Seychelles
SIN	Singapore
SKN	St. Kitts and Nevis

SLE	Sierra Leone
SLO	Slovenia
SMR	San Marino
SOL	Solomon Islands
SOM	Somalia
SRB	Serbia
SRI	Sri Lanka
STP	São Tomé and Princípe
SUD	The Sudan
SUI	Switzerland
SUR	Suriname
SVK	Slovakia
SWE	Sweden
SWZ	Swaziland
SYR	Syria
TAN	Tanzania
TCH	Czechoslovakia
TGA	Tonga
THA	Thailand
TJK	Tajikistan
TKM	Turkmenistan
TLS	Timor Leste (East Timor)
TOG	Togo
TPE	Chinese Taipei
TRI	Trinidad and Tobago
TUN	Tunisia
TUR	Turkey
TUV	Tuvalu
UAE	United Arab Emirates
UAR	United Arab Republic
UGA	Uganda
UKR	The Ukraine
URS	Soviet Union
URU	Uruguay
USA	United States of America
UZB	Uzbekistan
VAN	Vanuatu
VAT	Vatican City
VEN	Venezuela
VIE	Vietnam
VIN	St. Vincent and the Grenadines
VNM	South Vietnam
WIF	West Indies Federation

YAR   Yemen Arab Republic (North)
YEM   Yemen
YMD   Yemen Democratic Republic (South)
YUG   Yugoslavia
ZAI   Zaire
ZAM   Zambia
ZIM   Zimbabwe

OTHER NATIONAL ABBREVIATIONS

BRD   Bundesrepublik Deutschland
DPRK   Democratic People's Republic of Korea (North)
FYROM   Former Yugoslav Republic of Macedonia
PLO   Palestine Liberation Organization
USSR   Union of Soviet Socialist Republics (Soviet Union)

SPORTS AND GAMES ORGANIZATIONS

AAU   Amateur Athletic Union
ACNO   Association des Comités Nationaux Olympiques
ACNOA   Association des Comités Nationaux Olympiques d'Afrique
ACNOE   Association des Comités Nationaux Olympiques d'Europe
           (former name)
AGFIS   Association Générale des Fédérations Internationales de Sports
AIBA   Association Internationale de Boxe Amateur
AIOWF   Association of International Olympic Winter Sports
           Federations
ANOC   Association of National Olympic Committees
ANOCA   Association of National Olympic Committees of Africa
APAO   Asociación Panibérica de Academias Olímpicas
APFA   American Professional Football Association
ARISF   Association of the IOC-Recognized International Sports
           Federations
ASO   Amaury Sport Organization
ASOIF   Association of Summer Olympic International Federations
ATHOC   Athens Organizing Committee
ATP   Association of Tennis Professionals
BOB   Beijing Olympic Broadcasting
BOCOG   Beijing Organizing Committee
BWF   Badminton World Federation (present name)

CACSO	Central American and Caribbean Sports Association (former name)
CAS	Court of Arbitration for Sport
CGF	Commonwealth Games Federation
CIFP	Comité International pour le Fair Play
CIJM	International Committee of the Mediterranean Games
CIPS	Confédération Internationale de la Pêche Sportive
CISM	Conseil Internationale du Sport Militaire
CISS	Comité International des Sports des Sourds
CISU	International Workers and Amateurs in Sports Confederation
CMAS	Confédération Mondiale des Activités Subaquatiques
CMSB	Confédération Mondiale des Sports de Boules
COJO	Comité d'Organisation des Jeux Olympiques
CP-ISRA	Cerebral Palsy International Sports and Recreation Association
CSIT	Comité Sportif International du Travail (formerly)
CSIT	Confédération Sportive Internationale du Travailliste et Amateur (now)
CWHL	Canadian Women's Hockey League
EOC	European Olympic Committees (present name)
FAI	Fédération Aéronautique Internationale
FEI	Fédération Équestre Internationale
FIA	Fédération Internationale de l'Automobile
FIAS	Fédération Internationale de Sambo
FIB	Federation of International Bandy
FIBA	Fédération Internationale de Basketball
FIBT	Fédération Internationale de Bobsleigh et de Tobogganing
FIBV	Federacion Internacional de Pelota Vasca
FIC	Fédération Internationale de Canoë
FICS	Fédération Internationale de Chiropractique du Sport
FIDE	Fédération Internationale des Échecs
FIE	Fédération Internationale d'Éscrime
FIFA	Fédération Internationale de Football Association
FIG	Fédération Internationale de Gymnastique
FIH	Fédération Internationale de Hockey
FIK	International Kendo Federation
FIL	Fédération Internationale de Luge de Course
FIL	Federation of International Lacrosse
FILA	Fédération Internationale de Luttes Associées
FILx	Federation of International Lacrosse
FIM	Fédération Internationale de Motocyclisme
FIMS	International Federation of Sports Medicine
FINA	Fédération Internationale de Natation

FINO	Fédération Internationale de Numismatic Olympique
FIP	Fédération Internationale de Polo
FIPO	Fédération International de Philately Olympique
FIPV	Federación Internacional de Pelota Vasca
FIQ	Fédération Internationale de Quilleurs
FIRS	Fédération Internationale de Roller Sports
FIS	Fédération Internationale de Ski
FISA	Fédération Internationale des Sociétés d'Aviron
FISav	Fédération Internationale de Savate
FISU	Fédération Internationale du Sport Universitaire
FIT	Fédération Internationale de Trampoline
FITA	Fédération Internationale de Tir à l'Arc
FIVB	Fédération Internationale de Volleyball
FMJD	Fédération Mondiale de Jeu de Dames
FSFI	Fédération Sportive Feminine Internationale
GAIF	General Assembly of International Federations (formerly)
GAISF	General Association of International Sports Federations (present)
GANEFO	Games of the New Emerging Forces
IAAF	International Amateur Athletic Federation (originally)
IAAF	International Association of Athletics Federations (present)
IAF	International Aikido Federation
IAKS	International Association for Sports and Leisure Facilities
IBAF	International Baseball Federation
IBC	International Broadcast Centre
IBF	International Badminton Federation (originally)
IBF	International Bandy Federation
IBF	International Boxing Federation
IBRO	International Boxing Research Organization
IBSA	International Blind Sports Federation
IBU	International Biathlon Union
ICC	International Cricket Council
ICF	International Canoe Federation
ICFP	International Committee for Fair Play
ICSF	International Casting Sport Federation
ICU	The International Cheer Union
IDBF	International Dragon Boat Federation
IDSF	International Dance Sport Federation (former name)
IF	International Federation
IFA	International Fistball Association
IFAF	International Federation of American Football
IFBB	International Federation of Body Building and Fitness
IFF	International Floorball Federation

IFI	International Federation Icestocksport
IFMA	International Federation of Muaythai Amateur
IFNA	International Federation of Netball Associations
IFRS	International Financial Reporting Standards
IFS	International Sumo Federation
IFSA	International Federation of Sports Acrobatics
IFSC	International Federation of Sport Climbing
IFSS	International Federation of Sleddog Sports
IGF	International Go Federation
IGF	International Golf Federation
IHF	International Handball Federation
IIHF	International Ice Hockey Federation
IJF	International Judo Federation
IKF	International Korfball Federation
ILO	International Labour Organization
ILSF	International Life Saving Federation
IMGA	International Masters Games Association
IMSA	International Mind Sports Association
INAS-FID	International Sports Federation for Persons with an Intellectual Disability
INF	International Netball Federation
IOA	International Olympic Academy
IOC	International Olympic Committee
IOF	International Orienteering Federation
IOTC	International Olympic Truce Centre
IOTF	International Olympic Truce Foundation
IPC	Institut Pierre de Coubertin
IPC	International Paralympic Committee
IPF	International Powerlifting Federation
IRB	International Rugby Board
IRB	Institutional Revue Board
IRF	International Racquetball Federation
ISA	International Surfing Association
ISAF	International Sailing Federation (current name)
ISF	International School Sport Federation
ISF	International Snowboard Federation
ISF	International Softball Federation
ISMF	International Ski Mountaineering Federation
ISMWSF	International Stoke Mandeville Wheelchair Sports Federation
ISOD	International Sports Organization of the Disabled
ISOH	International Society of Olympic Historians
ISSF	International Shooting Sport Federation
ISTAF	International Sepaktakraw Federation

ISTF	International Soft Tennis Federation
ISU	International Skating Union
ITF	International Tennis Federation
ITTF	International Table Tennis Federation
ITU	International Triathlon Union
IWF	International Weightlifting Federation
IWGA	International World Games Association
IWSF	International Water Ski Federation (former name to 2010)
IWUF	International Wushu Federation
IWWF	International Waterski and Wakeboard Federation (name since 2011)
IYRU	International Yacht Racing Union (formerly)
JJIF	Ju-Jitsu International Federation
LAOOC	Los Angeles Olympic Organizing Committee
LPGA	Ladies Professional Golf Association
MLB	Major League Baseball
NBA	National Basketball Association
NCAA	National Collegiate Athletic Association
NFL	National Football League
NGB	national governing body
NGO	nongovernmental organization
NHL	National Hockey League
NOA	National Olympic Academy
NOA	National Olympian Association
NOC	National Olympic Committee
NRA	National Rifle Association
NWHL	National Women's Hockey League
OBS	Olympic Broadcast Services
OBSV	Olympic Broadcasting Services Vancouver
OCA	Olympic Council of Asia
OCOG	Organizing Committee of the Olympic Games
ODECABE	Organización Deportiva Centroamericana y del Caribe
ODEPA	Organización Deportiva Panamericana
ODESUR	Organización Deportiva Sudamericana
OGKS	Olympic Games Knowledge Services
OHCHR	Office of the High Commissioner for Human Rights
ONOC	Oceania National Olympic Committees
PASO	PanAmerican Sports Organization
PGA	Permanent General Assembly of National Olympic Committees
PGA	Professional Golf Association
PI	Panathlon International
RSI	Red Sport International

SANOC	South Africa National Olympic Committee
SASI	Sozialistische Arbeiter Sport Internationale
SCSA	Supreme Council for Sport in Africa
SEGAS	Hellenic Association of Amateur Athletics
SLOC	Salt Lake Olympic Organizing Committee
SOI	Special Olympics
TOP	The Olympic Partners
TWIF	Tug of War International Federation
UCI	Union Cycliste Internationale
UIAA	Union Internationale des Associations d'Alpinisme
UIM	Union Internationale Motonautique
UIPM	Union Internationale de Pentathlon Moderne (current)
UIPMB	Union Internationale de Pentathlon Moderne et Biathlon (formerly)
UIT	Union Internationale de Tir (formerly)
USATF	USA Track and Field
USFSA	Union des Sociétés Françaises de Sports Athlétiques
USOC	United States Olympic Committee
WA	World Archery Federation
WADA	World Anti-Doping Agency
WADC	World Anti-Doping Code
WAKO	World Association of Kickboxing Organizations
WBA	World Boxing Association
WBC	World Boxing Council
WBF	World Bridge Federation
WBSC	World Baseball Softball Confederation
WCBS	World Confederation of Billiards Sports
WCF	World Curling Federation
WDF	World Darts Federation
WDSF	World Dance Sport Federation (since 2011)
WFDF	World Flying Disc Federation
WHC	World Handball Council
WHO	World Health Organization
WKF	World Karate Federation
WMF	World Minigolf Federation
WNBA	Women's National Basketball Association
WOA	World Olympians Association
WPS	Women's Professional Soccer
WSF	World Squash Federation
WTA	Women's Tennis Association
WTF	World Taekwondo Federation
WUSA	Women's United Soccer Association

OTHER ABBREVIATIONS

ABC	American Broadcasting Company
ACOM	Association of Collectors of Olympic Memorabilia
BALCO	Bay Area Laboratory Co-Operative
CBS	Columbia Broadcasting System
CEO	Chief Executive Officer
CNN	Cable News Network
DNA	Deoxyribonucleic acid
EBU	European Broadcasting Union
EPO	Erythropoietin (illegal drug)
EPOR	Erythropoietin receptor
ESPN	Entertainment and Sports Programming Network
FAO	Food and Agriculture Organization
FBI	Federal Bureau of Investigation
MVP	most valuable player
NBC	National Broadcasting Company
RCT	randomized controlled trial
RTV	radio and television
RSC	Referee Stops Contest
SPCA	Society for the Prevention of Cruelty to Animals
UCLA	University of California, Los Angeles
UN	United Nations
UNDP	United Nations Development Programme
UNEP	United Nations Environment Programme
UNESCO	United Nations Educational, Scientific and Cultural Organization
UNHCR	United Nations High Commissioner for Refugees
UNODCCP	United Nations Office for Drug Control and Crime Prevention
YMCA	Young Men's Christian Association

Chronology

1100s B.C. Classics scholars consider that the Ancient Olympic Games may have been held as early as this century, although no definite evidence of the competitions exists until 776 B.C.

776 B.C. First recorded Ancient Olympiad is celebrated in Olympia on the Peloponnesus peninsula in ancient Greece. The Olympic Games initially consist of a single race of about 190 meters in length, termed a *stadion* race. The first winner is Coroebus, a cook from the city-state of Elis.

582 B.C. The first Pythian Games are held at Delphi in ancient Greece. The first Isthmian Games are held at the Isthmus of Corinth in ancient Greece, possibly in 581 B.C.

573 B.C. The first Nemean Games are held at Nemea in ancient Greece.

A.D. 393 The Ancient Olympic Games end after 12 centuries, when they are prohibited by the imperial decree of Roman Emperor Theodosius I.

1612–1642 Robert Dover's Games, an early attempt at revival (often called the Cotswold Olimpick Games), are held annually in Cotswolds (England) on Thursday and Friday of Whitsun Week. They stop shortly after Dover's death in 1641, but are revived during the reign of King Charles II in the 1660s.

1850 22 October: The Much Wenlock Olympian Games, the brainchild of British sports enthusiast Dr. William Penny Brookes (1809–95), are held for the first time in Much Wenlock, England, a small town in rural Shropshire. The Much Wenlock "Olympics" are a major influence on Pierre de Coubertin, who visits them in 1889.

1859 15 November: The 1st Zappas Olympic Games, an early attempt at a revival of the Olympics, are held in Athens. The Games are initiated and financed by a wealthy grain dealer, Evangelis Zappas (1800–65).

1863 **1 January:** Pierre Frédy, the Baron de Coubertin, is born in Paris, France, to Charles Louis Frédy, the Baron de Coubertin, and the former Agathe Marie Marcelle Gabrielle de Grisenoy de Mirville.

1870 **15 November:** The 2nd Zappas Olympic Games are held in Athens. They are considered the most successful of the Zappas Olympics.

1875 **18 May:** The 3rd Zappas Olympic Games are held in Athens.

1889 **18 May:** The 4th Zappas Olympic Games are held in Athens.

1891 The 1st Panhellenic Gymnastic Society Games, modeled after the Zappas Olympics, are held in Athens.

1892 **25 November:** A meeting of sports dignitaries is held at the Sorbonne, celebrating the fifth anniversary of the Union des Sociétés Françaises de Sports Athlétiques (USFSA), at which Coubertin first broaches the idea of the revival of the Olympic Games. His speech ends with the now-famous summons, "Let us export rowers, runners, and fencers; there is the free trade of the future, and on the day when it is introduced within the walls of old Europe the cause of peace will have received a new and mighty stay. This is enough to encourage your servant to dream now about the second part of his program; he hopes that you will help him as you have helped him hitherto, and that with you he will be able to continue and complete, on a basis suited to the conditions of modern life, this grandiose and salutary task, the restoration of the Olympic Games."

1893 The 2nd Panhellenic Gymnastic Society Games, modeled after the Zappas Olympics, are held in Athens.

1894 **4–23 June:** The International Olympic Committee is formed at the end of the Sorbonne Congress; it consists mostly of sports dignitaries who had attended the Congress. Athens, Greece, is selected as host of the Games of the Ist Olympiad (1896), and Paris, France, is selected as host of the Games of the IInd Olympiad (1900). Demetrios Vikelas of Greece is elected as the first president of the International Olympic Committee (IOC) at the end of the 1st Session of the IOC. **16–24 June:** The Paris International Athletic Congress is organized by Coubertin at the Palais de la Sorbonne in Paris. Although purported to be a congress with amateurism as its main theme, the program lists 10 points to be discussed, the last three of which concern the reestablishment of the Olympic Games. This is later regarded as the 1st Olympic Congress.

1896   6–15 April: Athens, Greece—celebration of the Games of the Ist Olympiad of the modern era. **10 April:** Baron Pierre de Coubertin of France is elected as the second president of the International Olympic Committee at the 2nd Session of the IOC.

1897   23–31 July: Le Havre, France—the 2nd Olympic Congress is celebrated at the town hall of Le Havre, with "Sports Hygiene and Pedagogy" as the theme.

1900   14 May–28 October: Paris, France—celebration of the Games of the IInd Olympiad.

1901   22 May: Chicago, Illinois, USA, is selected as the host of the Games of the IIIrd Olympiad (1904) at the 4th IOC Session in Paris.

1902   February: Host city duties for the 1904 Olympic Games are transferred from Chicago, Illinois, to St. Louis, Missouri, USA.

1904   22 June: Rome, Italy, is selected as host of the Games of the IVth Olympiad (1908) at the 6th IOC Session in London. **1 July–23 November:** St. Louis, Missouri, USA—celebration of the Games of the IIIrd Olympiad.

1905   9–14 June: Brussels, Belgium—the 3rd Olympic Congress is celebrated at the Palais des Académies, with "Sport and Physical Education" as the theme.

1906   22 April–2 May: Athens, Greece—the Intercalated Olympic Games are held in Athens during the interim between the celebrations of the Olympiad. No longer officially recognized by the IOC, they are nonetheless the best Olympic Games to date and may have helped save the Olympic Games after the debacles of 1900 and 1904. **23–25 May:** Paris, France—the 4th Olympic Congress is celebrated at the Comédie Française et Touring Club, with "Art, Literature, and Sport" as the theme. **9 November:** After Rome turns down the invitation, London, England, is selected as host of the Games of the IVth Olympiad (1908) at the 8th IOC Session in Athens.

1908   27 April–31 October: London, England—celebration of the Games of the IVth Olympiad.

1909   28 May: Stockholm, Sweden, is selected as host of the Games of the Vth Olympiad (1912) at the 11th IOC Session in Berlin.

1912 5 May–27 July: Stockholm, Sweden—celebration of the Games of the Vth Olympiad. **4 July:** Berlin, Germany, is selected as host of the Games of the VIth Olympiad (1916) at the 15th IOC Session in Stockholm.

1913 7–11 May: Lausanne, Switzerland—the 5th Olympic Congress is celebrated at the Palais de l'Université, with "Sports Psychology and Physiology" as the theme.

1914 15–23 June: Paris, France—the 6th Olympic Congress is celebrated at the Palais de la Sorbonne, with "Olympic Regulations" as the theme.

1915 December (1915)–February (1917): Baron Godefroy de Blonay of Switzerland is appointed interim IOC president by Coubertin, who enlists to help the French war effort. Coubertin felt that the IOC should not be headed by a soldier.

1916 Summer: The Games of the VIth Olympiad, scheduled to be held in Berlin, Germany, are canceled due to World War I.

1917 February: Coubertin resumes his post as president of the IOC.

1919 5 April: Antwerp, Belgium, is selected as host of the Games of the VIIth Olympiad (1920) at the 17th IOC Session in Paris.

1920 23 April–12 September: Antwerp, Belgium—celebration of the Games of the VIIth Olympiad.

1921 2–7 June: Lausanne, Switzerland—the 7th Olympic Congress is celebrated at the Casino de Montbenon, with "Olympic Regulations" as the theme. Paris, France, is selected as host of the Games of the VIIIth Olympiad (1924), and Amsterdam, Netherlands, is selected as host of the Games of the IXth Olympiad (1928).

1923 8 April: Los Angeles, California, USA, is selected as host of the Games of the Xth Olympiad (1932) at the 22nd IOC Session in Rome.

1924 24 January–5 February: Chamonix, France—celebration of the "Semaine internationale des sports d'hiver" (International Winter Sports Week), which is later designated retroactively as the 1st Olympic Winter Games. **4 May–27 July:** Paris, France—celebration of the Games of the VIIIth Olympiad.

1925   28 May: Count Henry de Baillet-Latour of Belgium is elected as the third president of the International Olympic Committee at the 24th Session of the IOC in Prague. **29 May–4 June:** Prague, Czechoslovakia—the 8th Olympic Congress is celebrated at the Prague town hall, with "Sports Pedagogy and Olympic Regulations" as the theme. The Congress is notable for Coubertin's retirement as IOC president.

1926   6 May: St. Moritz, Switzerland, is selected as host of the 2nd Olympic Winter Games (1928) at the 25th IOC Session in Lisbon.

1928   11–19 February: St. Moritz, Switzerland—celebration of the 2nd Olympic Winter Games. **17 May–12 August:** Amsterdam, the Netherlands—celebration of the Games of the IXth Olympiad.

1929   10 April: Lake Placid, New York, USA, is selected as host of the 3rd Olympic Winter Games (1932) at the 28th IOC Session in Lausanne.

1930   25–30 May: Berlin, Germany—the 9th Olympic Congress is celebrated at the Aula of the Friedrich Wilhelm University, with "Olympic Regulations" as the theme.

1931   April–May: Berlin, Germany, is selected as host of the Games of the XIth Olympiad (1936) by a postal vote.

1932   4–15 February: Lake Placid, New York, USA—celebration of the 3rd Olympic Winter Games. **30 July–14 August:** Los Angeles, California, USA—celebration of the Games of the Xth Olympiad.

1933   13 May: Garmisch-Partenkirchen, Germany, is selected as host of the 4th Olympic Winter Games (1936) at the 32nd IOC Session in Vienna.

1935   15 September: At a rally in Nuremburg, Adolf Hitler announces the enactment of the Nuremburg Laws, stripping Jews of their German citizenship and their rights under German law. This gives new impetus to consideration to boycott the 1936 Olympics, both to be based in Germany.

1936   6–16 February: Garmisch-Partenkirchen, Germany—celebration of the 4th Olympic Winter Games. **7 March:** Hitler orders three battalions of the German army into the Rhineland, violating the Treaty of Versailles. In response, France considers the possibility of a boycott of the 1936 Olympics. **31 July:** Tokyo, Japan, is selected as host of the Games of the XIIth

Olympiad (1940) at the 35th IOC Session in Berlin. **1–16 August:** Berlin, Germany—celebration of the Games of the XIth Olympiad. Despite calls for a boycott from many nations, almost all IOC member nations participate at Berlin.

1937 **9 June:** Sapporo, Japan, is selected as host of the 1940 Olympic Winter Games at the 37th IOC Session in Warsaw. **2 September:** Coubertin dies while walking through Lagrange Park in Geneva, Switzerland.

1938 **26 March:** At a ceremony in Ancient Olympia, the heart of Coubertin, which had been removed from his body shortly after his death, is placed for perpetuity in a marble stele at the base of the Kronos Hill, near the Ancient Olympic stadium. **3 September:** After Sapporo, Japan, turned down the invitation, St. Moritz, Switzerland, was selected as host of the 1940 Olympic Winter Games at the IOC Executive Board Meeting in Brussels. At the same meeting, Helsinki, Finland, was selected as host of the Games of the XIIth Olympiad (1940).

1939 **9 June:** At the 39th IOC Session in London, Cortina d'Ampezzo, Italy, is selected as host of the 1944 Olympic Winter Games, and London, England, is selected as host of the Games of the XIIIth Olympiad (1944).

1940 **Winter:** The 5th Olympic Winter Games are canceled due to World War II. The Games were originally awarded to Sapporo, Japan, which withdrew on 16 July 1938. They were reassigned to St. Moritz, Switzerland, which withdrew as host on 9 June 1939. The Games were then reassigned to Garmisch-Partenkirchen, Germany. **Summer:** The Games of the XIIth Olympiad, originally scheduled to be held in Tokyo, Japan, and later (after the withdrawal of Tokyo on 16 July 1938) awarded to Helsinki, Finland (awarded 3 September 1938), are canceled due to World War II.

1942 **6 January:** IOC President Count Baillet-Latour dies. The International Olympic Committee presidency will remain vacant during the remainder of World War II, although Sweden's J. Sigfrid Edström assumes the position of de facto president.

1944 **Winter:** The 5th Olympic Winter Games, tentatively scheduled for Cortina d'Ampezzo, Italy, are canceled due to World War II. **Summer:** The Games of the XIIIth Olympiad, originally scheduled to be held in London, England, are canceled due to World War II.

1946   4 September: J[ohannes] Sigfrid Edström of Sweden is elected as the fourth president of the International Olympic Committee at the 40th Session of the IOC in Lausanne. London, England, is selected as host of the Games of the XIVth Olympiad (1948) at the 40th IOC Session in Lausanne. **6 September:** St. Moritz, Switzerland, is selected as host of the 5th Olympic Winter Games (1948) at the 40th IOC Session in Lausanne.

1947   21 June: At the 41st IOC Session in Stockholm, Oslo, Norway, is selected as host of the 6th Olympic Winter Games (1952), and Helsinki, Finland, is selected as host of the Games of the XVth Olympiad (1952).

1948   30 January–8 February: St. Moritz, Switzerland—celebration of the 5th Olympic Winter Games. **29 July–14 August:** London, England—celebration of the Games of the XIVth Olympiad.

1952   14–25 February: Oslo, Norway—celebration of the 6th Olympic Winter Games. **16 July:** Avery Brundage of the United States is elected as the fifth president of the International Olympic Committee at the 48th Session of the IOC in Helsinki. **19 July–3 August:** Helsinki, Finland—celebration of the Games of the XVth Olympiad.

1954   13 May: After Melbourne decides it cannot host the equestrian events of the 1956 Olympic Games because of Australian quarantine laws, Stockholm, Sweden, is selected as host of the 1956 Equestrian Games at the 44th IOC Session in Rome.

1955   14 June: Squaw Valley, California, USA, is selected as host of the 8th Olympic Winter Games (1960) at the 51st IOC Session in Paris. **16 June:** Rome, Italy, is selected as host of the Games of the XVIIth Olympiad (1960) at the 51st IOC Session in Paris.

1956   26 January–5 February: Cortina d'Ampezzo, Italy—celebration of the 7th Olympic Winter Games. **10–17 June:** Stockholm, Sweden—celebration of the Equestrian Games of the XVIth Olympiad. The separate Equestrian Games were necessary because of Australia's highly restrictive animal quarantine regulations. **29 October:** Israel invades the Sinai Peninsula, a part of Egypt. Egypt, Lebanon, and Iraq withdraw from the Melbourne Olympics in protest. **4 November:** Soviet troops enter Budapest, Hungary, in an effort to stop rising political insurgency. This eventually leads to boycotts of the Melbourne Olympics by Spain, Switzerland, and the Netherlands, protesting the Soviet action.

22 November–8 December: Melbourne, Victoria, Australia—celebration of the Games of the XVIth Olympiad. In an attempt to solve the problem of the two Germanys, a unified German team representing both East (GDR) and West (FRG) Germany competes at the International Olympic Committee's behest.

1959 25 May: Innsbruck, Austria, is selected as host of the 9th Olympic Winter Games (1964) at the 56th IOC Session in Munich. **26 May:** Tokyo, Japan, is selected as host of the Games of the XVIIIth Olympiad (1964) at the 56th IOC Session in Munich.

1960 18–28 February: Squaw Valley, California, USA—celebration of the 8th Olympic Winter Games. **25 August–11 September:** Rome, Italy—celebration of the Games of the XVIIth Olympiad.

1963 18 October: Mexico City, Mexico, is selected as host of the Games of the XIXth Olympiad (1968) at the 61st IOC Session in Baden-Baden. **10–22 November:** GANEFO—the Games of the New Emerging Forces—are held in Djakarta, Indonesia. GANEFO refuses to admit athletes from Israel or Taiwan (Chinese Taipei), and the International Federations for track and field athletics, swimming, and shooting ban all athletes who competed at GANEFO from competing at the Tokyo Olympics in 1964. The IOC does not support this blanket ban.

1964 28 January: Grenoble, France, is selected as host of the 10th Olympic Winter Games (1968) at the 62nd IOC Session in Innsbruck. **29 January–9 February:** Innsbruck, Austria—celebration of the 9th Olympic Winter Games. **10–24 October:** Tokyo, Japan—celebration of the Games of the XVIIIth Olympiad.

1966 26 April: At the 65th IOC Session in Rome, Sapporo, Japan, is selected as host of the 11th Olympic Winter Games (1972), and Munich, Federal Republic of Germany (FRG), is selected as host of the Games of the XXth Olympiad (1972).

1968 6–18 February: Grenoble, France—celebration of the 10th Olympic Winter Games. **2 October:** Student protests against the Mexico City Olympics come to a head in the capital city. On this day, student protesters hold a rally in the Plaza of Three Cultures, and government troops open fire, killing more than 250, with thousands injured and imprisoned. **12–27 October:** Mexico City, Mexico—celebration of the Games of the XIXth Olympiad.

1970 13 May: At the 70th IOC Session in Amsterdam, Denver, Colorado, USA, is selected as host of the 12th Olympic Winter Games (1976), and Montréal, Quebec, Canada, is selected as host of the Games of the XXIst Olympiad (1976).

1972 3–13 February: Sapporo, Japan—celebration of the 11th Olympic Winter Games. **21 August:** Sir Michael Morris, Lord Killanin of Dublin and Spiddal (Ireland), is elected as the sixth president of the International Olympic Committee at the 73rd Session of the International Olympic Committee in Munich. **26 August–11 September:** Munich, Federal Republic of Germany—celebration of the Games of the XXth Olympiad. **5 September:** Terrorists representing the Black September group forever change the Olympic Games when they take hostage and then savagely murder 11 members of the Israeli Olympic team. The deaths occur at Fürstenfeldbruck airport on the outskirts of Munich. **12 November:** Denver, Colorado, USA, withdraws as host of the 12th Olympic Winter Games (1976) after a citizen's referendum votes down the responsibility to serve as host city.

1973 4 February: After Denver turns down the invitation to host the 1976 Olympic Winter Games, Innsbruck, Austria, is selected as host of the 12th Olympic Winter Games (1976) at the IOC Executive Board Meeting in Lausanne. **30 September–4 October:** Varna, Bulgaria—the 10th Olympic Congress, the first in 43 years, is celebrated at the Sports Palace, with the theme of "Sport for a World of Peace—The Olympic Movement and Its Future."

1974 23 October: At the 75th IOC Session in Vienna, Lake Placid, New York, USA, is selected as host of the 13th Olympic Winter Games (1980), and Moscow, Russia, USSR, is selected as host of the Games of the XXIInd Olympiad (1980).

1976 4–15 February: Innsbruck, Austria—celebration of the 12th Olympic Winter Games. **17 July–1 August:** Montréal, Quebec, Canada—celebration of the Games of the XXIst Olympiad.

1978 18 May: Sarajevo, Yugoslavia, is selected as host of the 14th Olympic Winter Games (1984) at the 80th IOC Session in Athens. **7 October:** As the only candidate city, Los Angeles, California, USA, is selected as host of the Games of the XXIIIrd Olympiad (1984) at the 80th IOC Session in Athens in May, but the vote is not confirmed until an IOC Executive Board Session in October.

1979   25–26 November: The two-China question is finally resolved. On 25 November 1979, mainland China, the People's Republic of China, is officially recognized by the IOC. The next day, the Chinese Taipei Olympic Committee is given official International Olympic Committee recognition under that name, agreeing to compete using only that name, and not as the Republic of China. This clears the way for both Chinese Olympic Committees to compete together at the Olympic Games. **25–27 December:** The Soviet Union invades Afghanistan, precipitating an eventual boycott of the Moscow Olympics.

1980   4 January: In retaliation for the Soviet invasion of Afghanistan, U.S. President Jimmy Carter announces, for the first time, the possibility of a U.S. boycott of the 1980 Moscow Olympics. **13–24 February:** Lake Placid, New York, USA—celebration of the 13th Olympic Winter Games. **16 July:** Juan Antonio Samaranch (Torello) is elected as the seventh president of the International Olympic Committee at the 83rd Session of the IOC in Moscow. **19 July–3 August:** Moscow, USSR—celebration of the Games of the XXIInd Olympiad. Approximately 60 countries boycott the Olympics in protest of the Soviet Union's invasion of Afghanistan.

1981   23–28 September: Baden-Baden, Federal Republic of Germany— the 11th Olympic Congress is celebrated at Baden-Baden's Kurhaus, with "United by and for Sport" as the theme, with three subthemes: (1) "The Future of the Olympic Games," (2) "International Cooperation," and (3) "The Future Olympic Movement." **30 September:** At the 84th IOC Session in Baden-Baden, Calgary, Alberta, Canada, is selected as host of the 15th Olympic Winter Games (1988), and Seoul, Republic of Korea, is selected as host of the Games of the XXIVth Olympiad (1988).

1984   8–19 February: Sarajevo, Yugoslavia—celebration of the 14th Olympic Winter Games. **8 May:** The Soviet Union announces it will not attend the Los Angeles Olympic Games, citing concerns over the safety of its athletes in Los Angeles and because of "anti-Communist activities" in the United States. **28 July–12 August:** Los Angeles, California, USA—celebration of the Games of the XXIIIrd Olympiad. Fourteen invited countries join the Soviet-inspired boycott. Of the Soviet bloc nations, only Romania defies the boycott and competes.

1986   17 October: At the 91st IOC Session in Lausanne, Albertville, France, is selected as host of the 16th Olympic Winter Games (1992), and Barcelona, Spain, is selected as host of the Games of the XXVth Olympiad

(1992). At this IOC Session, the decision is also made to change the dates of the Olympic Winter Games, so that it will not be held in the same year as the Games of the Olympiad, with the first change to occur in 1994.

1988   13–28 February: Calgary, Alberta, Canada—celebration of the 15th Olympic Winter Games. **15 September:** Lillehammer, Norway, is selected as host of the 17th Olympic Winter Games (1994) at the 94th IOC Session in Seoul. **17 September–5 October:** Seoul, Republic of Korea—celebration of the Games of the XXIVth Olympiad. A small boycott of six nations occurs, because certain countries support only North Korea (Democratic People's Republic of Korea) and do not recognize South Korea (Republic of Korea), refusing to compete in that nation.

1990   18 September: Atlanta, Georgia, USA, is selected as host of the Games of the XXVIth Olympiad (1996) at the 96th IOC Session in Tokyo.

1991   15 June: Nagano, Japan, is selected as host of the 18th Olympic Winter Games (1998) at the 97th IOC Session in Birmingham.

1992   8–23 February: Albertville, France—celebration of the 16th Olympic Winter Games. **25 July–9 August:** Barcelona, Spain—celebration of the Games of the XXVth Olympiad. For the first Olympics since 1960, no politically inspired boycott or other serious political problems mar the Games.

1993   23 September: Sydney, New South Wales, Australia, is selected as host of the Games of the XXVIIth Olympiad (2000) at the 101st IOC Session in Monte Carlo.

1994   12–27 February: Lillehammer, Norway—celebration of the 17th Olympic Winter Games. **23 June:** The 100th anniversary of the founding of the modern Olympic Games is celebrated with a ceremony at the Sorbonne, where Coubertin held the 1st Olympic Congress that reestablished the modern Olympic Games. **29 August–3 September:** Paris, France—the 12th Olympic Congress is celebrated, with four main themes: (1) "The Olympic Movement's Contribution to Modern Society," (2) "The Contemporary Athlete," (3) "Sport in Its Social Context," and (4) "Sport and the Media." The 12th Olympic Congress is held in celebration of the 100th anniversary of the Olympic Movement.

1995   16 June: Salt Lake City, Utah, USA, is selected as host of the 19th Olympic Winter Games (2002) at the 104th IOC Session in Budapest.

1996   6 April: The 100th anniversary of the opening of the Games of the Ist Olympiad, the first Olympic Games of the modern era, is celebrated. **19 July–4 August:** Atlanta, Georgia, USA—celebration of the Games of the XXVIth Olympiad, the Centennial Olympic Games. **27 July:** During the Atlanta Olympics, a bomb explodes in Centennial Olympic Park, killing two people and injuring many more.

1997   5 September: Athens, Greece, is selected as host of the Games of the XXVIIIth Olympiad (2004) at the 106th IOC Session in Lausanne.

1998   7–22 February: Nagano, Japan—celebration of the 18th Olympic Winter Games. **24 November:** Salt Lake City television station KTVX reveals that the Salt Lake Bid Committee had been paying tuition and expenses for the daughter of an IOC member. The Olympic bribery scandal begins.

1999   8 February: The first report related to the Olympic bribery scandal is released by the Board of Ethics of the Salt Lake Organizing Committee for the Olympic Winter Games of 2002. **1 March:** Release of the Mitchell Commission Report. **17–18 March:** An Extraordinary Session of the IOC is held relating to the Olympic bribery scandal. The Pound Commission Report is released during this meeting. At the end of the session, 10 IOC members either resign or are expelled because of findings of the various commissions. **19 June:** Torino (Turin), Italy, is selected as host of the 20th Olympic Winter Games (2006) at the 109th IOC Session in Seoul. **10 November:** The World Anti-Doping Agency (WADA) is created, with its original headquarters in Lausanne, Switzerland. **11–12 December:** The 110th IOC Session is held in Lausanne, Switzerland, at which the 50 recommendations of the IOC 2000 Commission are discussed and, eventually, implemented in full.

2000   14 September–1 October: Sydney, New South Wales, Australia—celebration of the Games of the XXVIIth Olympiad.

2001   13 July: Beijing, China, is selected as host of the Games of the XXIXth Olympiad (2008) at the 112th IOC Session in Moscow. **16 July:** Dr. Jacques Rogge is elected as the eighth president of the International Olympic Committee at the 112th IOC Session in Moscow.

2002   8–24 February: Salt Lake City, Utah, USA—celebration of the19th Olympic Winter Games.

2003   2 July: Vancouver, British Columbia, Canada, is selected as host of the 21st Olympic Winter Games (2010) at the 115th IOC Session in Prague.

2004   13–29 August: Athens, Greece—celebration of the Games of the XXVIIIth Olympiad.

2005   6 July: London, England, is selected as host of the Games of the XXXth Olympiad (2012) at the 117th IOC Session in Singapore.

2006   10–26 February: Torino, Italy—celebration of the 20th Olympic Winter Games.

2007   4 July: Sochi, Russia, is selected as host of the 22nd Olympic Winter Games (2014) at the 119st IOC Session in Guatemala City.

2008   8–24 August: Beijing, China—celebration of the Games of the XXIXth Olympiad.

2009   2 October: Rio de Janeiro, Brazil, is selected as host of the Games of the XXXIst Olympiad (2016) at the 13th IOC Congress in Copenhagen. **3–5 October:** The 13th Olympic Congress is held in Copenhagen, Denmark. There are five themes: (1) "The Athletes," (2) "The Olympic Games," (3) "The Structure of the Olympic Movement," (4) "Olympism and Youth," and (5) "The Digital Revolution."

2010   12–28 February: Vancouver, British Columbia, Canada—celebration of the 20th Olympic Winter Games. **14–26 August:** Singapore, Singapore—1st Youth Olympic Games are held.

2011   6 July: Durban, South Africa, is selected as the host city for the 22nd Olympic Winter Games (Pyeongchang, South Korea) at the 123rd IOC Session.

2012   13–22 January: Innsbruck, Austria—celebration of the 1st Winter Youth Olympic Games. **27 July–12 August:** London, England—celebration of the Games of the XXXth Olympiad.

2013   11 February: In Lausanne, Switzerland, the IOC announces that wrestling will be dropped from the list of 25 core sports for the 2020 Olympic Games. **7–10 September:** In Buenos Aires, Argentina, at the 125th IOC Session, Thomas Bach is elected for an eight-year term as the ninth IOC president. Wrestling is reinstated for the 2020 Games, and Tokyo, Japan, is selected as the site of the Games of the XXXIInd Olympiad in 2020.

2014   7–23 February: Sochi, Russia—celebration of the 21st Olympic Winter Games. **16–28 August:** Nanjing, China—celebration of the 2nd Youth

Olympic Games. **December:** The 127th IOC Session is scheduled to be held in Monte Carlo, Monaco.

2015   July: The 128th IOC Session is scheduled to be held in Kuala Lumpur, Malaysia. Items on the agenda include selection of the host city for the 23rd Olympic Winter Games to be held in 2022.

2016   12–21 February: Scheduled celebration of the 2nd Winter Youth Olympic Games in Lillehammer, Norway. **5–21 August:** Rio de Janeiro, Brazil—scheduled celebration of the Games of the XXXIst Olympiad.

2018   9–25 February: Scheduled celebration of the 22nd Olympic Winter Games in Pyeongchang, Korea. **11–23 September:** Scheduled celebration of the 3rd Youth Olympic Games in Buenos Aires, Argentina.

2020   February: Site to be determined on 23 May 2015 for the scheduled celebration of the 3rd Winter Youth Olympic Games. **24 July–9 August:** Scheduled celebration of the Games of the XXXIInd Olympiad in Tokyo, Japan.

The Olympic Games and Olympic Winter Games

The Games of the Ist Olympiad (1896): The Games of the Ist Olympiad were held in Athens, Greece, from 6 through 15 April 1896. (At the time, Greece recognized the Julian calendar, not the Gregorian calendar then used by much of the world and now used universally. In Greek terms, the Games were held from 25 March to 3 April 1896.) London was initially to have been the site, but the Sorbonne Congress of 1894 elected Athens as the host city by acclamation. The only other city seriously considered was Paris.

From 12 to 14 nations (reports vary) competed in nine sports (athletics, cycling, fencing, gymnastics, shooting, swimming, tennis, weightlifting, wrestling) at Athens with approximately 235 to 255 athletes—it cannot be determined with certainty—only 176 have been definitively identified. No women competed. The first Olympic champion of the modern era was James Connolly of the United States, who won the hop, step, and jump in track and field athletics (now called the triple jump). Greece won the most medals with 50, while the United States won the most gold medals with 11, including most of the track and field athletics events. The highlight of the Games was the marathon victory of Spiridon Loues of Greece. When he neared the stadium, messengers came into the ancient stadium and cried out, "Hellas! Hellas!" ("A Greek! A Greek!"), sending the crowd into a frenzy. The Olympic pride based on millennia of Olympic tradition was then realized by the home crowd, which had been rather disappointed by the results of the Greek athletes. Loues won the race and became a hero, being offered gifts and riches by many Greek merchants. But he asked only for a cart to help him carry and sell his water, and he returned to being a shepherd in his small town of Amarousi.

Many people wanted the Games to remain permanently in Athens, and in 1896 the American athletes wrote a letter to the *New York Times* asking that this be done. But Pierre de Coubertin insisted that the Games be spread among various countries to emphasize the international flavor of the Olympic Games.

The Games of the IInd Olympiad (1900): The Games of the IInd Olympiad were held in Paris, France, from 14 May through 28 October 1900. They were a disaster. If one had to nominate the "worst modern Olympics" ever, 1900 and 1904 would surely lead the voting. In 1900, Paris hosted a great world's fair, the Exposition Universelle Internationale de 1900 à Paris. Coubertin made plans to hold the Olympics as part of the fair and planned to organize the events. But the organizers of the fair relegated Coubertin to a relatively minor administrative position and took over the organization of the sporting events connected with it. Most of the events we today consider "Olympic" were not even labeled as such in 1900, often being called the "Championnats d'Exposition" or "Championnats Internationaux." Years later, many athletes did not know that they had competed in the Olympic Games, believing that their sport had been only a part of the world's fair. Only the athletic (track and field) events were really publicized in the media as being part of the Olympics.

The Games were stretched out over five months (May–October), and formal opening and closing ceremonies were not held. Because of the confusion over titles and the many, many events held at the fair, it is difficult to know which events should actually be considered "Olympic" and which should not. The International Olympic Committee (IOC) had no real control over this, and thus one sees various listings. Many unusual sports and events were contested, such as motor boating, balloon racing, underwater swimming, and an obstacle swimming race. As a result, the number of nations and athletes competing is completely conjectural. (The Sports Reference website [www.sports-reference.com/olympics] identifies 1,200 men and 23 women from 31 countries in 20 sports.) Weightlifting and wrestling, both contested in Athens in 1896, were not included in Paris although archery, cricket, croquet, equestrianism, football, golf, pelota, polo, rowing, rugby, sailing, tug-of-war, and water polo were. Some of these sports were never again contested at the Olympic Games (cricket, croquet, pelota), while others (equestrianism, football, rowing, sailing, water polo) have appeared in nearly every Games since 1900.

Women made their Olympic debut, with the first known competitors being a yachtswoman Countess Hélène de Pourtalès of Switzerland, and three croquet players, Jeanne Filleaul-Brohy, Marie Ohnier, and Mme. Desprès. Charlotte Cooper (GBR) won the first championships by a woman in tennis singles and mixed doubles. Margaret Abbott (USA) won the "Olympic" golf championship in early October. Neither of those two sports was labeled as Olympic by the organizers. Years later, Abbott's relatives did not know for certain that the title she won that day had been for the Olympic championship. In many sports, medals were not awarded. Most of the listed prizes were cups and other similar trophies. In several sports, notably fencing and shooting, professional events were held and yet were considered later by the IOC to be of "Olympic" stature.

The Games of the IIIrd Olympiad (1904): The Games of the IIIrd Olympiad were held in St. Louis, Missouri, USA, from 1 July through 23 November 1904. After the debacle of 1900, Coubertin was hoping for better from the United States in 1904, but his hopes were not realized. The Games had been awarded to Chicago, but St. Louis was to host a major world's fair in 1904, the Louisiana Purchase International Exposition, and the St. Louis organizers wanted the Olympics as part of the fair. They threatened to hold competing Olympics if Chicago did not allow them to have the Games. Chicago eventually acquiesced.

The Games were very similar to those held in 1900. They lasted almost five months, and many of the events were not labeled as Olympic but only as championships of the fair (although the Games director, James E. Sullivan, considered everything an Olympic event). It is difficult to know which sports and events were definitely on the Olympic program, a number of unusual sports and events found their way onto the program, and the Games were mostly an afterthought to the fair. Again, the number of competing nations and athletes cannot be accurately determined and the Sports Reference website lists 644 men and six women from 15 countries in 18 sports, with boxing included for the first time. Also new to the Olympic program were diving, lacrosse, and roque, and weightlifting and wrestling returned. Sports that were not contested were cricket, croquet, equestrianism, pelota, polo, rugby, sailing, and shooting.

Coubertin vowed after 1904 that he would never again hold the Olympics as a sideshow to a fair. Notably, he did not even attend the Olympics in 1904, sending two IOC delegates from Hungary and Germany in his place. He was appalled when he heard of the happenings in St. Louis, but never more so than when he heard about the "Anthropological Days." The fair organizers included several days of "Olympic" competitions among several so-called primitive tribes that were being exhibited at the Exposition. Among these were pygmies, Patagonians, Filipinos, Native American tribes, Japanese Ainus, and certain Asian tribes. Events included throwing bolos, mud fighting, and climbing a greased pole.

Again, only the athletics (track and field) received any great publicity as being an Olympic sport. These events were virtually an American club championship, and in fact, Albert Spalding donated a trophy to be awarded to the American club scoring the most points in the event. Though surpassed by athletes in other sports, the American foursome of Archie Hahn, Harry Hillman, James Lightbody, and Ray Ewry won three gold medals each in track and field and received the bulk of the media attention. In other sports, American dominance was almost as complete, owing to the fact that only a few other countries attended the Games, and very few foreign athletes competed.

Two black Tswana tribesmen who were part of the Boer War exhibition at the fair, Len Tau (Taunyane) and Yamasani (Jan Mashiani), also competed in the marathon. Ironically, they are considered to be among the first Olympic competitors from South Africa.

The Intercalated Olympic Games of 1906: The Olympic Games of 1906 were held in Athens, Greece, from 22 April through 2 May 1906. Twenty-one nations attended, with 841 athletes competing (835 men and six women) in just 13 sports—athletics, cycling, diving, fencing, football, gymnastics, rowing, shooting, swimming, tennis, tug-of-war, weightlifting, and wrestling. All of these sports, except tug-of-war, are still contested in the 21st-century Olympic Games. Fifteen Danish women also gave a gymnastics exhibition in 1906.

Today, the IOC and some historians do not consider the 1906 Intercalated Olympics to be "true" Olympic Games. By doing so, they neglect the Games that may have helped save the Olympic Movement. After the debacles of 1900 and 1904, the Olympics were in desperate straits. The Greeks had wanted to host more Olympics, and they proposed holding "interim" Olympics, every four years in the even-numbered years between the Olympics. The first of these was scheduled in 1906. The Greeks later scheduled interim Olympics for 1910 and 1914, but political and economic events in Greece prevented those from being held.

The Games of 1906 were not of the caliber of many Olympics of later years, but they were the best Olympics to that date. Again, many of the facilities were not of the highest quality. However, as in 1896, the Greeks approached their responsibility with enthusiasm and the most international field to date competed in these Olympics. A true opening ceremony was conducted for the first time, with the athletes marching with their teams following flag bearers from their own countries.

The newspapers considered these Games to be the Olympics and labeled them as such. Coubertin, at first opposed to the idea, subsequently embraced them as Olympics when he saw that the Greeks were organizing the best "Olympics" of the modern era. The IOC made no official determination of the status of these events at first, but in 1948 declared them not to be official, based on the findings of the Brundage Commission. The Olympics of 1906 deserve that title much more so than do the farces held in 1900 and 1904. They resurrected the flagging Olympic Movement.

The Games of the IVth Olympiad (1908): The Games of the IVth Olympiad were held in London, England, from 27 April through 31 October 1908. Twenty-two nations attended, with 2,024 athletes competing (1,980 men and 44 women) in 24 sports. Sports that made their Olympic debut at the London

1908 Games were figure skating, field hockey, *jeu de paume*, motorboating, and racquets. Of these five sports, only field hockey remains on the Summer Games program. The Games were originally awarded to Rome, Italy, which was chosen over Berlin, Germany, at the 6th IOC Session in London on 22 June 1904. Historically, it has usually been stated that the Italians relinquished the 1908 Olympics because of the 1906 explosion of Mt. Vesuvius, which erupted near Naples, and the Italians felt that they needed the money to rebuild the area around the volcano. However, it is now established that the Italians were preparing to give up their rights to the IVth Olympiad, for financial reasons, even before the explosion. London gladly agreed to host the 1908 Olympics after the Italians told the IOC of their plans.

These Olympics were easily the best organized to date. They also had the most international flavor of any Olympics yet held. By now the Olympics were becoming "known" to the world, and athletes everywhere wanted to compete and managed to find ways to do so. Still, the Games, though superbly run, are best known for multiple political arguments and other bickering that occurred. For the first time, all nations competed with official teams, rather than with individual or club entries. Another innovation was that a winter sport made its Olympic debut, with figure skating being added to the Olympic program.

The problems began at the opening ceremony. The Swedish and U.S. flags did not fly over the stadium, as the organizers stated they could not find them. This so infuriated the Swedes that when a dispute arose over wrestling rules later in the Games, they threatened to withdraw from the competition. The Finns marched in the ceremony without a flag. Finland was a territory of Russia in 1908, but Russia allowed it to compete separately, provided it did so under the Russian flag. The Finns, in protest, marched under no flag. The United States later protested the officiating in multiple track and field athletic events.

Two of the best-known controversies involved the 400 meter race and the marathon. In the 400 meters, American John Carpenter won the initial running of the final, but was disqualified when it was ruled that he had run out of his lane in the final straight to impede Britain's Wyndham Halswelle. The other two Americans in the final, William Robbins and John Taylor, refused to run in the second final, and Halswelle walked over to the gold medal. In the tug-of-war, the Americans pulled a team of London policeman in the first round and were easily defeated. But the Americans protested the footwear of the London constables, stating that they were specially prepared to give them better traction during the pull. The protest was disallowed.

The final controversy and the most memorable event of the 1908 Olympics was the marathon. The race was to start at Windsor Castle so that Queen

Alexandra's grandchildren could watch the beginning. The distance from there to the finish line at the Shepherd's Bush stadium was 26 miles, 385 yards. This was the first time this distance was chosen for a marathon, and it later became the standard.

The leader for most of the second half of the race was Dorando Pietri, a candy maker from Capri, Italy. But when Pietri entered the stadium, he was totally exhausted. Like a drunken sailor, he staggered and fell several times before the finish line. He also turned in the wrong direction twice during the last lap. Officials, urged on by sympathetic fans, helped him to his feet and directed him to the finish line. He finished the race first and was declared the winner. Johnny Hayes of the United States finished a few hundred meters behind him. An immediate protest was lodged, and Pietri was disqualified, with Hayes winning the gold medal.

The Games of the Vth Olympiad (1912): The Games of the Vth Olympiad were held in Stockholm, Sweden, from 5 May through 27 July 1912. After the problems and controversies of 1908, the pseudo-Olympics of 1900 and 1904, and the meager international participation of 1896 and 1906, Stockholm should be credited with the first truly modern Games of Olympic proportions. No other city was seriously considered as host for 1912, and Stockholm was elected by acclamation at the 10th IOC Session in Berlin, Germany, on 28 May 1909. Art competitions in architecture, literature, music, painting, and sculpture were held for the first time as part of the Olympic Games. Including the art competitions, 29 nations attended, with 2,409 entrants (2,356 men and 53 women). Of these totals there were 33 men from 11 nations (including two whose nations are unknown) who entered the art competitions. One man entered both the art competitions and the shooting event, and one nation (Poland) did not enter the sporting events, resulting in a net total of 2,377 athletes (2,324 men, 53 women) from 28 nations who competed in 16 sporting events. Modern pentathlon was added to the Olympic program, equestrianism returned, and boxing (illegal in Sweden then) was dropped. Other sports contested in London 1908 that were dropped were archery, figure skating, hockey, *jeu de paume*, lacrosse, motorboating, polo, racquets, and rugby.

The Games were marvelously organized. The only significant political problems concerned the entries of Finland and Bohemia. Both nations wished to compete as independent nations, but in 1912 Finland was still a part of Russia, and Bohemia was a part of the Austro–Hungarian Empire. As in 1908, both were allowed to compete but were not allowed to use their own flags.

Probably more than any other Olympics, the 1912 Games belonged to one person, Jim Thorpe. Jim Thorpe was a Sac and Fox Indian from Oklahoma who had attended the Carlisle Indian School. In 1912, Thorpe decided to compete in the two new Olympic events testing the all-around abilities of the track and field athletes: the decathlon of 10 events and the pentathlon of five events. He won by enormous margins. When Thorpe was awarded his prizes by King Gustav V, the king reportedly said, "Sir, you are the greatest athlete in the world." Thorpe's reply was supposedly, "Thanks, King." But in 1913, it was discovered that Thorpe had played minor league professional baseball in 1909 and 1910, and he was stripped of his medals. This violated the rules as published by the 1912 Organizing Committee, as the discovery of his having played professional baseball was made after the statute of limitations had run out. Seventy years later, in 1982, the IOC finally relented and restored the medals to Thorpe's family—he had died in 1953.

Hannes Kolehmainen of Finland, the first of the great Flying Finn distance runners, also made his debut at the 1912 Olympics. He won four medals: three gold in the 5,000 meter, 10,000 meter, and individual cross-country, and a silver in the team cross-country. When Kolehmainen won, the Russian flag was raised because of Finland's subjugation to the Russians at that time. "I would almost rather not have won, than see that flag up there," he said (Lord Killanin and John Rodda, *The Olympic Games 1984,* 77 [Salem, N.H.: Michael Joseph, 1983]).

A tragedy occurred at the 1912 Olympic Games when the Portuguese marathoner Francisco Lazaro collapsed during the race and died early the next morning. He was the first Olympic athlete to die during the competition. This has occurred only one other time, in 1960, when the Danish cyclist Knut Enemark Jensen died during the cycling road race.

The 1912 Olympics were also noteworthy for the first swimming events for women. Previously, women had competed at the Olympics to any degree only in tennis, with minor appearances in archery, golf, yachting, and croquet in 1900, 1904, and 1908 and motorboating in 1908. There were only two swim events for women in 1912, a 100 meter freestyle and a freestyle relay, as well as a high diving event, but they were important as they were the first truly "athletic" events in which women were allowed to compete at the Olympics. The list of events in which women compete would increase with each Olympiad.

The Games of the VIth Olympiad (1916): The Games of the VIth Olympiad were originally awarded to Berlin, Germany, which was chosen at the 15th IOC Session in Stockholm on 4 July 1912 over Budapest, Hungary. Other cities that expressed an interest in hosting the 1916 Olympics were Alexandria, Egypt; Amsterdam, the Netherlands; Brussels, Belgium; Budapest, Hungary; and Cleveland, Ohio, USA. Because of World War I, the Games were not celebrated. Winter sports on snow and ice, skiing, and skating were also on the original program of the 1916 Olympics.

The Games of the VIIth Olympiad (1920): The Games of the VIIth Olympiad were held in Antwerp, Belgium, from 23 April through 12 September 1920. Other cities that had expressed an interest in hosting the 1920 Olympic Games were Amsterdam, the Netherlands; Atlanta, Georgia, USA; Budapest, Hungary; Cleveland, Ohio, USA; Havana, Cuba; and Philadelphia, Pennsylvania, USA. An offer from Lyon was seriously considered during World War I, when Belgium was being ravaged by the effects of the war, but Antwerp was officially chosen at the 18th IOC Session in Lausanne on 5 April 1919. Eventually, 29 nations attended the Games in Antwerp, with 2,674 entrants (2,596 men and 78 women), including those in the art competitions. Details of the art competitions are unknown and only the names of the winners have been recorded. The 11 winners (10 men, one woman) represented five nations. All five nations also had other entries in sporting events. The total athletes were 2,663 (2,586 men, 77 women) who took part in 24 sports. Most of the sports dropped in 1920 were restored and ice hockey was added.

The war was barely over when the 1920 Olympics were finally awarded to war-ravaged Belgium. Coubertin decided that, although the war would be over less than two years, the VIIth Olympiad should be celebrated as scheduled. Although the Games were decidedly austere, the Belgian people and the Organizing Committee did an amazing job in preparing for the Games on such short notice.

The opening ceremonies were notable for the first use of the Olympic flag at the Olympics, the first time the Olympic oath was taken by a competitor (Belgian fencer Victor Boin), and the first release of homing pigeons as a symbol of peace. Of the 29 countries competing, Germany, Austria, Hungary, and Bulgaria were missing, as the IOC barred them because they were aggressor nations in World War I, although this was opposed by IOC President Pierre de Coubertin.

The Olympics were most notable for the début of Paavo Nurmi of Finland, possibly the greatest distance runner ever. Nurmi competed in four events, losing only in the 5,000 meter race. His countryman, Hannes Kolehmainen, returned eight years after his Stockholm victories in the 5,000 and 10,000 meter races and won the marathon. The shooting program contained 20 events, including 10 team events, allowing Willis Lee and Lloyd Spooner of the United States to win seven medals, and Carl Osburn (USA) to win six. Nedo Nadi (ITA) was also much decorated, winning five gold medals in fencing.

One unusual aspect of the games occurred in the yachting (sailing) competition. In the 12-foot dinghy class, there were only two entrants, both from the Netherlands. After a controversy regarding the course, the final two races of the event were held in the Netherlands nearly two months after the first races.

The Antwerp Olympics helped the world recover from the Great War. Coubertin summarized them in the Antwerp town hall when he addressed the IOC in the presence of King Albert of Belgium:

> This is what the seventh Olympiad has brought us: general comprehension; the certainty of being henceforward understood by all. . . . These festivals . . . are above all festivals of human unity. In an incomparable synthesis the effort of muscles and of mind, mutual help and competition, lofty patriotism and intelligent cosmopolitanism, the personal interest in the champion and the abnegation of the team-member, are bound in a sheaf for a common task.

The 1st Olympic Winter Games (1924): The 1st Olympic Winter Games were held in Chamonix, France, from 24 January through 5 February 1924. Sixteen nations attended, with 292 athletes competing (279 men and 13 women) in nine sports—bobsledding, cross-country skiing, curling, figure skating, ice hockey, military ski patrol, Nordic combined, ski jumping, and speed skating. In addition, 21 men were honored under the category of alpinism for their attempt to scale Mount Everest. They represented Great Britain, Nepal, Australia, and India, and thus some sources include the latter three nations and state that 19 nations participated in the Games.

In June 1922, the French Olympic Committee held a congress at which representatives of skiing, skating, and ice hockey were present. They arranged to hold an International Winter Sports Week in Chamonix in early 1924. The contests were not originally called the Olympic Games, but the opening speech, though not using the word *Olympic* in their title, did state that they were under the "High Patronage of the International Olympic Committee." (Of note, however, is that all newspaper coverage called them the Olympic Winter Games.) Their original official title was the *Semaine internationale des sports d'hiver* (International Winter Sports Week). On 27 May 1925, the IOC amended its charter to begin a cycle of Olympic Winter Games. The Chamonix events were never officially mentioned as the 1st Olympic Winter Games in this proclamation. It is felt, however, that this was an error of the secretary taking the minutes, as the IOC has long since recognized the 1924 Chamonix events as the 1st Olympic Winter Games.

The politics of declaring these as Olympic Games may have been more interesting than the Games themselves. The 1924 Winter Olympics saw Clas Thunberg and Thorleif Haug crowned as multiple champions in skating and skiing, respectively. Gillis Grafström repeated his title in men's figure skating, which he had won at the Summer Games in Antwerp in 1920. In women's figure skating, Herma Planck-Szabó of Austria won the title, but the eighth, and last, place finisher (only 11 years old in 1924) would later become the greatest women's figure skater ever, Sonja Henie.

The Games of the VIIIth Olympiad (1924): The Games of the VIIIth Olympiad were held in Paris, France, from 4 May through 27 July 1924. Other cities considered as hosts were Amsterdam, the Netherlands; Barcelona, Spain; Los Angeles, California, USA; Prague, Czechoslovakia; and Rome, Italy. Including the art competitions, 45 nations attended the 1924 Olympics, with 3,256 athletes competing (3,104 men and 152 women). The art competitions attracted 189 entrants (172 men, 17 women) from 24 nations. Russia was the only nation to enter the art competitions but not the sporting events. A total of 3,067 athletes (2,932 men, 135 women) from 44 nations competed in sporting events in 19 sports. The program was reduced somewhat from the Antwerp Games with the removal of archery, field hockey, figure skating, ice hockey, and tug-of-war. After the difficulties of the 1900 Olympics in Paris, Coubertin fervently desired to see his home city host another Olympics. Paris was chosen to host the 1924 Olympics at the 20th IOC Session in Lausanne on 2 June 1921 and redeemed itself nicely.

The 1924 Olympics are today most famous as the Olympics of Harold Abrahams and Eric Liddell, the Olympics that served as the theme of the movie *Chariots of Fire*, which was made in 1981 to celebrate the lives of Abrahams and Liddell and their route to the 1924 Olympic Games. The movie won the Academy Award for Best Picture of the Year. It was an excellent movie, but much of the story was apocryphal, with ample use of poetic license.

Besides its heralded stars, the 1924 Olympics unveiled several other notable firsts. The Olympic motto—"Citius, Altius, Fortius"—was used for the first time at the Olympic Games themselves, although Coubertin had used it as early as 1894 in the *Revue Olympique*. And at the closing ceremony, the practice of raising three flags—one for the IOC, one for the host nation, and one for the succeeding host nation—was instituted for the first time. For the first time there was also a small Olympic Village at Paris.

In swimming, Johnny Weissmuller (USA) made his first Olympic appearance and showed why he would someday become known as the world's greatest swimmer. He later competed in the 1928 Olympics as well, and then turned to Hollywood, where he became famous as Tarzan, portraying that character in 19 movies.

The Games themselves were the personal playground of Paavo Nurmi, who took up where he left off in 1920. Nurmi won five gold medals and could have won more had the schedule allowed him time to compete in more events.

The 2nd Olympic Winter Games (1928): The 2nd Olympic Winter Games were held in St. Moritz, Switzerland, from 11 through 19 February 1928.

Other cities considered by the IOC as possible hosts were Davos, Switzerland, and Engelberg, Switzerland, but St. Moritz was awarded the Games at the 28th IOC Session in Lausanne on 10 April 1929. Twenty-five nations attended, with 461 athletes competing (433 men and 28 women) in eight sports. Curling and the military ski patrol were dropped and skeleton was added. The 1928 Olympic Winter Games were highly successful, but the organizers had to contend with poor weather. The *föhn*, a strong wind coming down the leeward side of a mountain and carrying warm weather with it, postponed several events and forced the cancellation of one. On the morning of the 50 km cross-country skiing, the temperature was about 0°C (32°F), but during the competition, the *föhn* came in, and temperatures rose to 25°C (77°F) by mid-day, playing havoc with the snow and waxing conditions.

Later that night, the warm weather brought rain, which poured down and ruined the ski courses. Fortunately, snow and frost over the next few days rescued the organizers. But the *föhn* affected several other events as well. In the 10,000 meter speed skating, Irving Jaffee (USA) had the best time after the first few runs. But the *föhn* was bringing in warm weather and melting the rink, so the event was halted because of the conditions, and it was never restarted. Jaffee is listed by some American sources, incorrectly, as having won the event, but it actually was never contested to a conclusion. The five-man bobsled race also suffered from the wrath of the *föhn*, when the course thawed and the four-run contest was shortened to only two runs.

The individual stars of the Games were Clas Thunberg, who won two more golds in speed skating; Johan Grøttumsbråten, who won two Nordic skiing golds; Gillis Grafström, who won his third consecutive figure skating title; and Sonja Henie, who won her first of three Olympic figure skating championships. But perhaps the real star of the 1928 Winter Olympics was the Canadian ice hockey leviathan, which in the absence of American participation was unchallenged in winning the title, with a goal margin of 38–0.

The Games of the IXth Olympiad (1928): The Games of the IXth Olympiad were held in Amsterdam, the Netherlands, from 17 May through 12 August 1928. The only other city seriously considered as a host was Los Angeles, California, USA. Amsterdam was chosen as host of the 1928 Olympics at the 19th IOC Session in Lausanne on 2 June 1921. Including the art competitions, 46 nations attended, with 3,248 competitors (2,937 men and 311 women). The art competitions produced 370 entrants (333 men, 37 women) from 19 nations. All nations with entrants in the art competitions also competed in the sporting events. There were a total of 2,878 athletes (2,604 men, 274 women) from 46 nations who took part in the sports events in 16 sports. Polo, shooting, and tennis were not held.

liv • THE OLYMPIC GAMES AND OLYMPIC WINTER GAMES

The 1928 Olympic Games were remarkable for the return of Germany to the Olympic Games for the first time since 1912, after the country had not been invited in 1920 or 1924. In addition, an Olympic flame burned at the Olympic stadium for the first time ever. It burned atop the marathon tower, although it was not lit at the end of a torch relay.

The 1928 Olympics were an unusual event in that no single athlete dominated. Paavo Nurmi was back and won three more medals, but only one was gold. Johnny Weissmuller was back and again won two gold medals. But the biggest story of the 1928 Olympics was probably the emergence of women.

The Ancient Olympic Games did not allow women as competitors, or even as spectators. If they were found to be watching, they were supposedly put to death. Coubertin did not want women in the Olympics, and he explicitly said so several times in his writings. In the modern Olympics, probably because of Coubertin's opposition, women were admitted slowly and only grudgingly.

Women had competed at the Olympics since 1900, but in small numbers and never in the showcase sport of track and field athletics. Women were not allowed to compete in this sport until the 1928 Olympics. Track and field is governed by the International Amateur Athletic Federation (IAAF), and it did not initially support the admission of women's track and field to the Olympics. So the women formed a separate organization, the Fédération Sportive Féminine Internationale (FSFI). The FSFI held its own events, the Women's "Olympics" in 1922 in Paris, and the 1926 "2nd International Ladies' Games" in Göteborg, Sweden.

It was only after these games proved the success of women's athletics that the IAAF acquiesced and allowed the sport into the Olympics. However, in 1928 only five events were held for women. The 1928 Olympic track and field events were so few and in such varied disciplines that no single woman could dominate. They were marred when several women finalists were on the verge of collapse after the 800 meter race, which was also a common sight among men. The IOC reacted by barring women from running distances over 200 meters, and this was not changed until 1960. Women also competed in Amsterdam in gymnastics for the first time at the Olympics.

The 1928 Olympics were one of the last truly peaceful and fully attended Olympics. The Great Depression had not yet occurred, which would mar the 1932 Olympics. Hitler was still in prison, and the post–World War II boycotts were yet to come. They were missing a single standout athlete and one other thing. Because of illness, Coubertin missed his first Olympics since 1906. He did not get to see women compete in track and field.

The 3rd Olympic Winter Games (1932): The 3rd Olympic Winter Games were held in Lake Placid, New York, USA, from 4 through 15 February 1932.

Seventeen nations attended, with 252 athletes competing (231 men and 21 women) in just seven sports, as skeleton was dropped. Five other U.S. cities also submitted candidatures to the IOC, as well as Montreal, Quebec, Canada, and Oslo, Norway, but Lake Placid was chosen to host at the 27th IOC Session in Lausanne on 10 April 1929.

The biggest news of these Games was the controversy over the manner in which the speed skating events were contested. For the first time in Olympic history, the European method of skating time trials in pairs was not used. Instead, the American method of pack racing was used to determine the Olympic champions. (It became a separate indoor discipline of the sport again in 1992 at Albertville.) The Europeans, unaccustomed to the style, fared badly, and the great Clas Thunberg, still a viable competitor at age 39, refused to compete, somewhat in protest of the change but also because he did not give himself much chance to win in that style. Norway's Ivar Ballangrud did compete, but managed only a silver medal in the unfamiliar style.

One innovation that debuted at the Olympics in 1932 was the use of the three-level victory podium for presentation of the medals. It had first been used at the 1930 British Empire Games in Hamilton, Ontario, Canada.

The pack style did make heroes of two U.S. skaters. Hometown boy Jack Shea returned from Dartmouth College and won the 500 and 1,500 meter races. He also delivered the oath of the athletes, and in 1980 would be a member of the Organizing Committee when the Winter Olympics returned to Lake Placid. His grandson, Jim Shea, would take the athletes' oath 70 years later at the Salt Lake City Games. Irving Jaffee won the other two events, the 5,000 and 10,000 meter races. A few years later, during the depths of the Great Depression, he pawned the gold medals and never saw them again.

In figure skating, Gillis Grafström competed again, but was finally defeated as Austrian Karl Schäfer won the title, with Grafström second. Sonja Henie repeated in the women's competition. In bobsledding, U.S. teammates Billy Fiske and Clifford Grey repeated as gold medalists from 1928.

The Games of the Xth Olympiad (1932): The Games of the Xth Olympiad were held in Los Angeles, California, USA, from 30 July through 14 August 1932. It was the only city that applied to host the Olympics. Los Angeles was awarded the Games by acclamation at the 22nd IOC Session on 8 April 1923. Although officially there were 1,921 competitors (1,720 men, 201 women) from 47 nations, 586 of them were entrants in the art competitions and two others were recognized for alpinism. In the athletic endeavors, there were 16 sports and disciplines contested (football was not held but shooting was) and only 37 nations attended, the first time the number of competing nations had not increased at an Olympics. There were 1,333 athletes (1,207 men and 126 women) who competed in sports. The Depression and the travel distance kept the international turnout low. Fewer than half as many athletes competed as in 1928, as many nations sent only small squads.

The 1932 Olympics also saw the unveiling of a woman to rival the feats of Jim Thorpe. Mildred Ella "Babe" Didrikson was a 21-year-old Texas tomboy in 1932. She was from Dallas and was heralded even before the Olympics. Restrictions on women's participation prevented Babe from showing her true colors. She was allowed to enter only three events, though no such restriction existed for men. She won the javelin throw and the 80 meter hurdles, but in a virtual dead heat with Evelyne Hall (USA). Babe was second in the high jump, losing in a jump-off after she tied for first with Jean Shiley. Had she been able to compete in more events, it is likely that Didrikson could have won several more medals. After the Olympics, Babe Didrikson took up golf and became the greatest women's player in that sport.

Paavo Nurmi also attempted to compete at the 1932 Olympics but was not allowed to do so. Shortly before the Games, the IOC declared him a professional for having received money for a tour of Germany. He had planned to run the marathon in 1932, and it is almost certain that he would have won that race had he been allowed to compete.

The United States dominated what was close to a domestic Olympics, winning 41 gold medals and 103 medals in all. This was more than the winning totals of the four next best nations combined.

The 4th Olympic Winter Games (1936): The 4th Olympic Winter Games were held in Garmisch-Partenkirchen, Germany, from 6 through 16 February 1936. Garmisch-Partenkirchen was chosen by the IOC at its 32nd Session in Vienna on 8 June 1933. Other candidate cities were Montreal, Quebec, Canada, and St. Moritz, Switzerland. Twenty-eight nations attended, with 668 athletes competing (588 men and 80 women) in eight sports, as Alpine skiing was added.

The 1936 Olympic Winter Games were held under the Nazi regime of Adolf Hitler. When IOC President Henry de Baillet-Latour was traveling to Garmisch to see the Games, he was astonished to see road signs en route declaring "Dogs and Jews not allowed." Baillet-Latour requested an audience with Der Führer and demanded that the signs be taken down. Hitler replied that he thought it usual, when a guest entered a person's home, that the guest followed the wishes of the host. Baillet-Latour responded that when the flag of Olympia flew over the area, he became the host, and Hitler was only an invited guest. Hitler acquiesced and had the signs removed.

The Games were opened in a blinding snowstorm. They ended with the ski jump being watched by a record attendance of 150,000 people. Ivar Ballangrud won three more gold medals in speed skating. Sonja Henie won her third consecutive gold medal in figure skating, but the victory was a bit controversial. Henie had become a favorite of Der Führer, and it was thought that he wished her to win. She was not undeserving, but Britain's Cecilia Colledge was much improved, and some thought that her second place finish was less than it could have been.

The biggest upset of the 1936 Olympic Winter Games occurred in ice hockey, when the British team defeated the Canadians. The victory was aided by the scheming of J. F. "Bunny" Ahearne, general secretary of the British Ice Hockey Federation. Ahearne had a "mole" working in the Canadian Amateur Hockey Association and by 1934 had a complete list of all Canadian registered players who had been born in the British Isles. He contacted many of them, and the team that won in Garmisch was led by eight ersatz Brits, several of whom had been imported from Canada. The Canadians howled in protest, but to no avail.

The Games of the XIth Olympiad (1936): The Games of the XIth Olympiad were held in Berlin, Germany, from 1 through 16 August 1936. The IOC considered at least 12 other cities as possible hosts, but Berlin was chosen in a postal vote over Barcelona, Spain, by 43–16 at the 30th IOC Session in Barcelona on 26 April 1931. Forty-nine nations attended, and 3,954 entrants (3,625 men and 329 women) took part in 21 sports and disciplines including basketball, canoeing, and handball for the first time. Football and polo also returned. There were also 527 entrants (496 men, 31 women) from 24 nations in the art competitions; also one Swiss man, honored for aeronautics and a Swiss man and his wife honored for alpinism. A total of 4,484 entrants (4,123 men and 361 women) from 49 nations took part in the Games, by far the largest assemblage for an Olympic Games.

Because of Nazi policies against Jews and their aggressive national tendencies, there were many protests against the Olympics being held in Berlin in 1936. The Americans came the closest to boycotting in protest, although the British and French both considered the option. At the IOC Session in Vienna on 7 June 1933, the membership discussed the discrepancy between Nazi doctrine and Olympic principles, with two American members questioning the German members about their country's policies. At the 33rd IOC Session in Athens on 15 May 1934, Lord Aberdare, a British member, then expressed concerns about reports from Germany. He pointedly asked the German IOC members if their government's pledges were trustworthy. In September 1934, future IOC president Avery Brundage traveled to Germany to inspect the country and its policies. He later recommended that the Games go on in Germany, but calls for a boycott continued, although they were never realized.

One U.S. IOC member, Ernest Lee Jahncke, supported the boycott and was removed from the IOC.

The Games were magnificently staged, as Hitler spared no expense and used them as a propaganda tool to demonstrate the beauty and efficiency of the Third Reich. He had Leni Riefenstahl, a renowned German filmmaker, produce a wondrous movie, *Olympia*, to ensure that the propaganda would not end at the closing ceremonies.

No other Olympics belonged to a single noncompetitor as much as the 1936 Olympics with Adolf Hitler. But these Olympics were actually dominated by Jesse Owens. He showed up Hitler's Aryan supremacy theories and ruled the Berlin Olympic Games. Owens, a black American, won four gold medals in track and field athletics, winning the 100 meters, the 200 meters, the long (broad) jump, and the 4x100 meter relay. He was the most heralded and popular athlete of the 1936 Olympics.

The greatest innovation of the 1936 Olympics was conceived by Dr. Carl Diem, head of the Organizing Committee. He proposed that a torch relay be instituted to carry a flame from ancient Olympia to the Berlin Stadium and then to light the Olympic flame at the stadium. On 20 July 1936, 15 Greek maidens clad in short, belted smocks, representing the robes of priestesses, gathered on the plain at ancient Olympia, and the flame was lit there by the rays of the Greek sun off a reflector. The high priestess presented the flame to Kyril Kondylis, the first Greek runner, to begin a torch relay. After being carried several thousand miles, the flame arrived in Berlin, where it was lit in the stadium by Fritz Schilgen. It is sad to think that the flame of Olympia burned over a reich that later used flames to incinerate millions of Jews and other "undesirables" in World War II.

The 1940 Olympic Winter Games: The 5th Olympic Winter Games, scheduled for 3–14 February 1940, were originally awarded to Sapporo, Japan, at the 37th IOC Session in Warsaw on 9 June 1937. Sapporo withdrew on 16 July 1938, and the Games were awarded to St. Moritz at the IOC Executive Board Meeting in Brussels on 3 September 1938. St. Moritz was removed by the IOC on 9 June 1939 at the 39th IOC Session in London, and the 1940 Olympic Winter Games were then awarded to Garmisch-Partenkirchen, which eventually also withdrew. The Games were not held because of World War II.

The Games of the XIIth Olympiad (1940): The Games of the XIIth Olympiad were to have been held 22 September–6 October 1940, but did not take place because of the onset of World War II. At the 36th IOC Session in Berlin on 31 July 1936, the Games were awarded to Tokyo, Japan, in a vote of 36–27 over Helsinki, Finland. Other cities that had expressed interest in hosting the 1940 Olympics were Alexandria, Egypt; Buenos Aires, Argentina; Dublin, Ireland; Athens, Greece; Rio de Janeiro, Brazil; Barcelona, Spain; Budapest, Hungary; and either Toronto or Montreal, Canada. On 16 July 1938, Tokyo withdrew as host. On 3 September 1938, at the IOC Executive Board Meeting in Brussels, the Games were awarded to Helsinki, but the Games were canceled late in 1939.

The 1944 Olympic Winter Games: Although the 1940 Olympic Winter Games were not held, the 5th Olympic Winter Games were scheduled for 1944 and were awarded to Cortina d'Ampezzo, Italy, which was chosen over Montreal, Quebec, Canada, and Oslo, Norway, at the 39th IOC Session in London on 9 June 1939. The Games were not celebrated because of World War II.

Bid Voting	Round 1	Round 2
Cortina d'Ampezzo, Italy	16	16
Montreal, Quebec, Canada	11	12
Oslo, Norway	7	2
Abstentions	1	5

The Games of the XIIIth Olympiad (1944): The Games of the XIIIth Olympiad were to have been held in 1944, but did not take place because of World War II. The Games had been awarded to London, England, which won the IOC nomination with 20 votes over Rome, Italy (11 votes); Detroit, Michigan, USA (2 votes); and Lausanne, Switzerland (1 vote), at the 39th IOC Session in London on 9 June 1939.

The 5th Olympic Winter Games (1948): The 5th Olympic Winter Games were held in St. Moritz, Switzerland, from 30 January through 8 February. Twenty-eight nations attended, with 668 athletes competing (591 men and 77 women) in nine sports, as skeleton was added because St. Moritz had a skeleton track. The only candidate that opposed St. Moritz for 1948 was Lake Placid, New York, USA. After a postal vote, St. Moritz was chosen by the IOC Executive Board, which met in Lausanne on 4 September 1946 and made its decision.

St. Moritz hurriedly put together excellent arrangements for the Games, which were again disturbed, though less severely, by the *föhn*. Several ice hockey matches (held outdoors) were postponed, and the 10,000 meter speed skating was hampered by softening ice during the event, but no events were canceled this time.

Alpine skiing made its true Olympic debut. Combined events for men and women had been held in 1936, but this time there were three events for both men and women. Two athletes won a second "St. Moritz" Olympic medal, as "Bibi" Torriani played on the Swiss ice hockey team to match his bronze from 1928, and John Heaton (USA) also repeated his silver medal from the skeleton race in 1928. The skeleton race, a form of tobogganing then unique to the St. Moritz resort, was held at the Olympics for the second time. Skeleton then did not return to the Olympic program until 2002 at Salt Lake City, Utah, USA.

The Games of the XIVth Olympiad (1948): The Games of the XIVth Olympiad were held in London, England, from 29 July through 14 August 1948. The Games were awarded by a postal vote after the IOC recommended London as the site to its members. The vote was confirmed by the IOC membership at its 40th Session in Lausanne on 4 September 1946. Other candidate cities were Baltimore, Maryland, USA; Lausanne, Switzerland; Los Angeles, California, USA; Minneapolis, Minnesota, USA; and Philadelphia, Pennsylvania, USA. Fifty-nine nations attended, with 4,373 entrants (3,933 men and 440 women) including the art competitions in which there were 301 entrants (254 men, 47 women) from 27 nations. There were 4,072 athletes (3,679 men, 393 women) from 59 nations who took part in sporting competition in 20 sports and disciplines. Handball and polo were dropped and lacrosse returned.

As in 1920, the IOC decided that it was necessary to resurrect the Olympic Movement at the earliest scheduled time. Thus, although England had been ravaged by Hitler's air raids, the Games of the XIVth Olympiad were awarded to London in 1948. In spite of years of difficulties caused by rationing of food, clothes, and other essential materials, the English Organizing Committee did an outstanding job.

No great innovations accompanied the Games themselves, as most of the protocols of the opening, closing, and victory ceremonies were by now established. However, these Games were significant because they were televised for the first time, although only to small local audiences. Television sets were still quite rare.

One country that was missed was the Soviet Union. The USSR had competed in 1946 at the European Championships in track and field athletics, and it was thought that perhaps it would return to the Olympics in 1948. This was not to be, and the reasons for its failure to compete have never been fully revealed. Germany and Japan were not invited because they were considered aggressor nations during World War II.

As a very popular sport in England, track and field was truly the focus of these Olympics, as it so often is. Three athletes stood out in the athletics stadium. "Fanny" Blankers-Koen (NED), a 30-year-old mother of three children in 1948, won the 100 meter, 200 meter, and 80 meter high hurdles and helped win gold in the 4 by 100 meter relay. Bob Mathias (USA), a 17-year-old schoolboy, won the decathlon despite a torrential downpour throughout much of the two-day event. In the next few years, he would prove that it was not a fluke. He would win again in 1952 at Helsinki and was never defeated in his decathlon career. Finally, Emil Zátopek (TCH) won the 10,000 meter race and finished second in the 5,000 meter race. It was only a prelude to his heroics in 1952.

The 6th Olympic Winter Games (1952): The 6th Olympic Winter Games were held in Oslo, Norway, from 14 through 25 February 1952. Thirty nations attended, with 694 athletes competing (585 men and 109 women) in eight sports as skeleton was again dropped. At the 41st IOC Session in Stockholm on 21 June 1947, Oslo was chosen by the IOC over Cortina d'Ampezzo, Italy, and Lake Placid, New York, USA.

Bid Voting	Round 1
Oslo, Norway	18
Cortina d'Ampezzo, Italy	9
Lake Placid, New York, USA	1

The Olympic Winter Games were finally held in a Nordic country, and an Olympic flame was first lit at the Olympic Winter Games. Unlike the Summer flame, however, this flame was originally lit from the hearth of the house in Morgedal, Norway, where Sondre Norheim, the pioneer of modern skiing, was born. At the end of a ski relay, Eigil Nansen, grandson of the explorer Fridtjof Nansen, lit the flame in the Bislett Stadium.

Norway's athletes dominated the events, especially Hjalmar Andersen, who won three gold medals in speed skating. In Alpine skiing, the handsome Stein Eriksen of Norway seemed the embodiment of a modern ski hero. He won the giant slalom and was second in the slalom. Dick Button (USA) won his second consecutive men's figure skating championship. In women's skiing, Andrea Mead-Lawrence (USA) won two events by upsetting the European women.

In bobsledding, Germany won both the two-man and four-man events. Its "athletes" in this event were so large that their momentum helped them win by increasing their speed. This caused the International Bobsleigh Federation to change its rules to place a weight limit on bobsled teams.

The Games of the XVth Olympiad (1952): The Games of the XVth Olympiad were held in Helsinki, Finland, from 19 July through 3 August

1952. Sixty-nine nations attended, with 4,932 athletes competing (4,411 men and 521 women) in 19 sports. The art competitions were no longer held and lacrosse was dropped. At the 41st IOC Session in Stockholm on 21 June 1947, Helsinki won the vote in the second round over Los Angeles, California, USA; Minneapolis, Minnesota, USA; Amsterdam, the Netherlands; Detroit, Michigan, USA; Chicago, Illinois, USA; and Philadelphia, Pennsylvania, USA.

Bid Voting	Round 1	Round 2
Helsinki, Finland	14	15
Los Angeles, California, USA	4	5
Minneapolis, Minnesota, USA	4	5
Amsterdam, The Netherlands	3	3
Detroit, Michigan, USA	2	—
Chicago, Illinois, USA	1	—
Philadelphia, Pennsylvania, USA	0	—

In 1952, the biggest news from Helsinki was that the Soviets were there. After the Bolshevik Revolution of 1917, the USSR had not competed in the Olympics until the Helsinki Games. The world braced for the athletic battles between the Soviet Union and the United States—in effect, a Cold War Olympics. The Soviets were accorded one rather unusual allowance. They were housed in a separate Olympic Village and stayed only with athletes from the Eastern Bloc countries of Hungary, Poland, Bulgaria, Romania, and Czechoslovakia.

It is always an exciting moment when the Olympic torch enters the stadium. In 1952, the excitement was palpable when the Finnish crowd realized that the torchbearer was the Finnish hero of heroes, Paavo Nurmi. Although by then 55 years old, Nurmi carried the torch on high and still had his very familiar stride. Not only the crowd, but even the athletes, were excited. They broke ranks to run to the side of the track to get closer to the distance running legend. Some Finnish football players then brought the torch from the track to the top of the tower, handing it to Hannes Kolehmainen, second only to Nurmi in the Finnish pantheon of sporting heroes. The 62-year-old Kolehmainen lit the Olympic flame at the top of the tower.

Given that the Games were opened by two of the greatest distance runners ever, it was fitting that the 1952 Olympics were dominated by a distance runner who even surpassed a few of their feats. Emil Zátopek, the Czech who had won the 10,000 meter race in 1948, was by now the greatest distance runner in the world. He entered the 5,000 and 10,000 meter races and won both of them rather easily. He then entered the marathon, a race he had never before run. Still, the extra distance did not deter Zátopek. He was running with the favored Jim Peters of Great Britain for the first half of the race, when he turned to Peters and asked him if the pace wasn't a bit slow. With no reply, Zátopek took off and was never seen again by Peters. Zátopek won the race by over two and a half minutes, while Peters failed to finish.

The Americans and the Soviets met several times in these Olympics, most notably in the boxing ring and basketball court. In the basketball final, the USSR played a stalling game to minimize the score, but the United States still prevailed, 36–25. In 1952, the Americans had the best of it, though the Soviets would improve in the coming years. The press made a big thing out of the medal counts, which were led early by the Soviet Union, although the United States eventually won the most medals and gold medals. This too would change in later Olympics. Two other nations returned to the Olympic fold, as both Germany and Japan were invited to compete in 1952.

The 7th Olympic Winter Games (1956): The 7th Olympic Winter Games were held in Cortina d'Ampezzo, Italy, from 26 January through 5 February 1956. Thirty-two nations attended, with 821 athletes competing (689 men and 132 women) in eight sports. Cortina d'Ampezzo was chosen at the 44th IOC Session in Rome on 28 April 1949 over Montreal, Quebec, Canada; Colorado Springs, Colorado, USA; and Lake Placid, New York, USA.

Bid Voting	Round 1
Cortina d'Ampezzo, Italy	31
Montreal, Quebec, Canada	7
Colorado Springs, Colorado, USA	2
Lake Placid, New York, USA	1

The Cortina Olympics began ominously when the torchbearer at the opening ceremony, speed skater Guido Caroli, tripped over a microphone wire and fell. However, he was not harmed, and the torch did not go out. After that initial difficulty, the Games were a wonder.

The big news was the entrance of the Soviets into the Winter Olympics. The Soviet Union immediately excelled at speed skating and, in an upset, began its domination of ice hockey when its team defeated the Canadians.

The hero of the Cortina Olympics was movie-idol handsome Toni Sailer of Austria, "The Blitz from Kitz" (Kitzbühel). Sailer won all three Alpine skiing events by large margins each time. In ski jumping, the Finns introduced a new aerodynamic style when they placed their arms against their sides rather than forward in front of their heads. With the new method, Antti Hyvirinen and Aulis Kallakorpi took first and second, respectively. The figure skating competitions saw two very close contests, as Americans swept the men's medals, with Hayes Alan Jenkins winning. Among the women, Tenley Albright narrowly defeated Carol Heiss. Heiss and Jenkins would later marry.

The 1956 Equestrian Olympic Games: After the IOC awarded the Games of the XVIth Olympiad to Melbourne, Australia, it learned that Australian quarantine laws would not allow the importation of horses for the equestrian events without an extended quarantine period. This precluded Melbourne from being able to host the equestrian events at the 1956 Olympic Games. It was decided, actually in violation of the *Olympic Charter*, to hold separate Equestrian Olympic Games in Stockholm, Sweden, from 10 through 17 June 1956. At the 50th IOC Session in Athens on 13 May 1954, Stockholm was chosen, with 25 votes, over Paris, France (10 votes); Rio de Janeiro, Brazil (8 votes); Berlin, Germany (2 votes); and Los Angeles, California, USA (2 votes).

The Equestrian Games of 1956 were held without major incidents and were contested by 29 nations and 158 athletes (145 men and 13 women). The opening ceremony was quite unusual, as all competitors came in on their mounts, including the flag bearers. Hans Wikne brought the Olympic flame into the stadium on horseback and lit the main torch. Karin Lindberg and Henry Eriksson held lighted torches, ran toward the stadium tower with the torches, and lit flames there. Sweden's Henri Saint Cyr recited the oath of the athletes while on his horse and later won two gold medals in individual and team dressage. This was matched by Germany's Hans Günter Winkler, who won gold medals in the individual and team show jumping events. The only controversy of the 1956 Equestrian Games occurred in the three-day event, when one horse broke his leg and had to be put down. The Society for the Prevention of Cruelty to Animals was very upset, and a lengthy debate followed.

The Games of the XVIth Olympiad (1956): The Games of the XVIth Olympiad were held in Melbourne, Victoria, Australia, from 22 November through 8 December 1956. Sixty-seven nations and 3,189 athletes eventually competed in Melbourne (2,818 men and 371 women) in 18 sports—the same as in Helsinki with the exception of equestrianism, which had been held earlier in the year in Stockholm. At the 44th IOC Session in Rome on 28 April 1949, Melbourne was awarded the Olympics by a single vote in the fourth round over Buenos Aires, Argentina. Other candidate cities were Los Angeles, California, USA (third round); Detroit, Michigan, USA (third round); Mexico City, Mexico (second round); Chicago, Illinois, USA (first round); Minneapolis, Minnesota, USA (first round); and Philadelphia, Pennsylvania, USA (first round).

Bid Voting	Round 1	Round 2	Round 3	Round 4
Melbourne, Australia	14	18	19	21
Buenos Aires, Argentina	9	12	13	20
Los Angeles, California, USA	5	4	5	—
Detroit, Michigan, USA	2	4	4	—
Mexico City, Mexico	9	3	—	—
Chicago, Illinois, USA	1	—	—	—
Minneapolis, Minnesota, USA	1	—	—	—
Philadelphia, Pennsylvania, USA	1	—	—	—

This was the first time that the Games were held in the Southern Hemisphere and necessitated the Olympic Games being held very late in the year to take advantage of the early part of the Australian summer. Because of Australian quarantine laws, it was decided, in violation of the *Olympic Charter*, to hold separate Olympic Equestrian Games in Stockholm, Sweden, from 10 to 17 June 1956. (*See* "The 1956 Equestrian Olympic Games," above.)

But between June and the Melbourne Olympics, the world was thrown into turmoil. On 29 October, Israel invaded Egypt's Sinai peninsula. Then on 4 November 1956, 200,000 Soviet troops entered Budapest, Hungary, to quell political uprisings in that country. Egypt, Lebanon, and Iraq withdrew in protest of Israel's action. The Netherlands, Spain, and, somewhat surprisingly, Switzerland withdrew in protest at the Soviet action. (Switzerland later retracted its boycott, but too late for its athletes to reach Melbourne.) Switzerland kept alive its record of competing in every modern Olympics only because it had already been represented by athletes in Stockholm. These protests constituted the first true boycott in modern Olympic history, though the scene would be repeated many times in the coming decades.

With that background, water polo had the unusual distinction of being perhaps the most awaited event of the Olympics. In a final round match, the Soviet Union met the Hungarians, usually a water polo power. The athletes from both countries wasted no time in breaking all known rules and niceties of water polo. The water was literally blood red several times during the match, and several players had to be helped out of the water because of injuries. Hungary achieved some measure of revenge for the invasion of its country when it won, 4–0.

The Games were less well attended than those of other years because of the travel distance to Australia. Still, all the major sporting countries were represented. In a precursor of problems to come, the People's Republic of China (Beijing, then Peking) withdrew because the Republic of China (Taiwan) was allowed to compete. The question of the two countries' representation would not be resolved for 28 years. However, Germany competed as a unified team, with athletes from both the Federal Republic of Germany (West) and the German Democratic Republic (East).

The 8th Olympic Winter Games (1960): The 8th Olympic Winter Games were held in Squaw Valley, California, USA, from 18 through 28 February 1960. Thirty nations attended, with 665 athletes competing (521 men and 144 women) in eight sports. Biathlon was added and bobsleigh was dropped. At the 51st IOC Session in Paris on 14 June 1955, Squaw Valley won a close contest by two votes over Innsbruck, Austria. Garmisch-Partenkirchen, Germany, and St. Moritz, Switzerland, were also candidate cities, but were eliminated in the first round of voting.

Bid Voting	Round 1	Round 2
Squaw Valley, California, USA	30	32
Innsbruck, Austria	24	30
Garmisch-Partenkirchen, FRG	5	—
St. Moritz, Switzerland	3	—

When the 1960 Olympic Winter Games were awarded to Squaw Valley, all that existed there was a hotel. The ski village was the dream of Alexander Cushing, and he succeeded in convincing the IOC to hold the Olympics based on his dream. After the award, the Europeans verbally attacked the site for various reasons. The ski courses were not up to Fédération Internationale de Ski (FIS) caliber in the Alpine competitions, while in the Nordic races, the altitude (2,000 meters [6,650 feet]) was felt to be too stressful for the competitors. The Squaw Valley organizers polled the Winter Olympic nations and found that only nine would send a bobsled team, so they elected to save the expense by not building a run and not contesting the sport. In all, despite the initial misgivings about the site, the Games were well run, with few problems. And U.S. television crews were present, showing the events to the American people for the first time.

Biathlon was introduced as a sport for the first time. Women's speed skating also made its Olympic debut and saw the arrival of Lidiya Skoblikova (URS), who won two gold medals. In figure skating, Hayes Alan Jenkins's brother, David Jenkins, won the men's titles, while David Jenkins's future sister-in-law, Carol Heiss, avenged her 1956 defeat to easily win the women's title. In the Nordic combined event, Georg Thoma (FRG) became the first non-Scandinavian to win a Nordic Olympic event. In ice hockey, the United States pulled a major upset when it defeated the Soviet Union in the semifinal match. The United States went on to defeat Czechoslovakia in the final and win the gold medal. Not as well publicized as the "Miracle on Ice" of 1980, the U.S. victory in 1960 was equally astonishing.

The Games of the XVIIth Olympiad (1960): The Games of the XVIIth Olympiad were held in Rome, Italy, from 25 August through 11 September 1960. Eighty-three nations attended the Games, with 5,350 athletes competing (4,738 men and 612 women) in 19 sports—the same program as the previous two Summer Games. At the 51st IOC Session in Paris on 16 June 1955, Rome was awarded the Games in the third round over Lausanne, Switzerland, by a vote of 35–24. The other candidate cities were Detroit, Michigan, USA (second round); Budapest, Hungary (second round); Brussels, Belgium (first round); Mexico City, Mexico (first round); and Tokyo, Japan (first round).

Bid Voting	Round 1	Round 2	Round 3
Rome, Italy	15	26	35
Lausanne, Switzerland	14	21	24
Detroit, Michigan, USA	6	11	—
Budapest, Hungary	8	1	—
Brussels, Belgium	6	—	—
Mexico City, Mexico	6	—	—
Tokyo, Japan	4	—	—

Rome had been awarded the 1908 Olympics, but eventually relinquished its right to host them. Fifty-two years later, the Olympics would return to the eternal city. Never before were the ancient and modern civilizations so intertwined at an Olympics. The 1960 Olympics were a wonder. With the boycotts, massacres, and political problems that were to come, many Olympic aficionados would later yearn for the glory that was ancient Greece and the grandeur that was modern Rome.

Many of the events took place in settings thousands of years old. Wrestling was held in the Basilica of Maxentius, where similar competitions had taken place two millennia previously. Gymnastics events were contested in the Terme di Caracalla. The marathon began in front of the ancient Roman capitol, on Capitoline Hill, and finished along the Appian Way beneath the Arch of Constantine. For modern facilities, the Italians provided Stadio Olimpico, a beautiful track and field complex, the Sports Palace for boxing, and the velodrome for cycling.

A number of heroes emerged from the Games. In women's athletics, the Italians and the world thrilled to the feats of Wilma Rudolph, an American sprinter from Tennessee. Long-legged and attractive, she was dubbed by the European press as "La Gazelle Noire"—the black gazelle. She won the women's 100 meter and 200 meter races and anchored the sprint relay.

In basketball and boxing, two of the greatest ever practitioners of those sports were on display. In basketball, the U.S. men's team won very easily, as the team was led by Oscar Robertson, Jerry West, Jerry Lucas, Walt Bellamy, and Terry Dischinger. Certainly the greatest amateur team ever, it rivals many of the great NBA teams. In boxing, the light-heavyweight gold medal was won by Cassius Marcellus Clay, who as Muhammad Ali would thrill the world for the next two decades as "The Greatest."

The 1960 Olympics were the first Summer Olympics televised in the United States, although all events were shown on tape delay after the film was flown from Rome to New York. And also for the first time since the 1912 marathon (Portuguese runner Francisco Lazaro), the Olympics saw the death of a competitor. In the cycling road race, Knut Enemark Jensen (DEN) collapsed and later died. He was found to have taken amphetamines, and his death was partially responsible for the institution of drug testing in the mid-1960s.

The 9th Olympic Winter Games (1964): The 9th Olympic Winter Games were held in Innsbruck, Austria, from 29 January through 9 February 1964. Thirty-six nations attended, with 1,094 athletes competing (894 men and 200 women) in 10 sports. Bobsleigh returned and luge was added. At the 56th IOC Session in Munich, Germany, on 26 May 1959, Innsbruck (49 votes) was chosen in the first round over Calgary, Alberta, Canada (nine votes), and Lahti, Finland (no votes).

Innsbruck was an overwhelming choice to host the 1964 Olympic Winter Games, and the IOC has made few better choices. Innsbruck became the first Olympic host city since World War II, winter or summer, to spread the Olympic events around a bit, with some events being held 30 km (20 miles) from Innsbruck's center. Because of this and the central location of the city, well over a million spectators saw these Olympics. In addition, television now transmitted them to over a billion viewers. Computers were also present for the first time at the Olympics, as the electronic age came to Olympia.

With all this, there were a few problems. The Organizing Committee forgot to order snow for the events. In the last few days before the Games, the Austrian army hauled 20,000 cubic meters of snow to the ski courses so they would be well packed. In practice before the Games, two athletes were killed—Ross Milne, an Australian skier, and Kazimierz Skrzypecki, a Polish-born British luger. Soviet women were the biggest winners at Innsbruck. Lidiya Skoblikova produced one of the great performances of the Olympic Winter Games when she won all four women's speed skating gold medals in four days. In women's cross-country skiing, Klavdiya Boyarskikh won gold medals in all three women's events. The Soviets also ensured there would be no repeat of 1960 and won the ice hockey title easily. But in bobsledding, both events produced big upsets. Britain's Tony Nash and Robin Dixon won the two-man title, while Vic Emery drove the four-man champion sled from Canada. Neither country had a bobsled run in 1964.

The Games of the XVIIIth Olympiad (1964): The Games of the XVIIIth Olympiad were held in Tokyo, Japan, from 10 through 24 October 1964. Ninety-three nations attended, with 5,137 athletes competing (4,457 men and 680 women) in 21 sports as judo and volleyball were contested for the first time. At the 56th IOC Session in Munich, Germany, on 26 May 1959, Tokyo (34 votes) won the final vote in the first round over Detroit, Michigan, USA (10 votes); Vienna, Austria (nine votes); and Brussels, Belgium (five votes).

For the first time, the Olympic Games were celebrated in an Asian country. The Japanese were eager to prove they had recovered from the horrors of World War II and, to emphasize the point, they chose as the final torch bearer Yoshinori Sakai, who had been born in Hiroshima on the day the atomic bomb immolated that city.

Before the Games began, there was a minor controversy when Indonesia and North Korea withdrew because several of their athletes were declared ineligible. The affected athletes had competed in the Games of the New Emerging Forces (GANEFO) in Jakarta, Indonesia, in November 1963. Indonesia did not allow Taiwan or Israel to compete at those Games, so the International Federations for athletics, swimming, and shooting banned any athlete from the Tokyo Olympics who had competed at GANEFO. Because this affected several of their athletes, Indonesia and North Korea withdrew from Tokyo in protest. The only significant athlete missing was Dan Sin-Kim of North Korea, the women's world record holder in the 400 and 800 meter races.

In athletics, Billy Mills of the United States pulled off one of the biggest upsets in Olympic history when he won the 10,000 meter run. The most decorated hero of the Games was swimmer Don Schollander, who won four gold medals in men's swimming. Schollander could have won a fifth gold medal, but the U.S. coaches left him off the medley relay team, although he was America's fastest freestyler.

The Japanese were gracious hosts, and they were helped in their own efforts by two new Olympic sports, judo and volleyball. In volleyball, the Japanese women, coached by the martinet-like Hirofumi Daimatsu, were easily victorious. In judo, the Japanese won three of the four gold medals. But the one they lost, in the open class to Holland's Anton Geesink, was a crushing blow to the hosts, as it was considered the blue ribbon event of the sport at the time.

The Games were beautifully run, and the minor boycott had no effect. The 1964 Olympics was the last Olympics to be held for 28 years without major political overtones and boycotts.

The 10th Olympic Winter Games (1968): The 10th Olympic Winter Games were held in Grenoble, France, from 6 through 18 February 1968. Thirty-seven nations attended, with 1,160 athletes competing (949 men and 211 women) in 10 sports. At the 62nd IOC Session in Innsbruck on 28 January 1964, Grenoble was chosen on the third ballot over a large field of candidate cities that included Calgary, Alberta, Canada; Lahti, Finland; Sapporo, Japan; Oslo, Norway; and Lake Placid, New York, USA.

Bid Voting	Round 1	Round 2	Round 3
Grenoble, France	15	18	27
Calgary, Alberta, Canada	12	19	24
Lahti, Sweden	11	14	—
Sapporo, Japan	6	—	—
Oslo, Norway	4	—	—
Lake Placid, New York, USA	3	—	—

The controversy so often associated with the Olympic Games began to reach Winter Olympia in 1968 at Grenoble. Though the Games went fairly well, there were many problems. Trouble began before the Olympics, when the IOC decided it wished to curb advertising on skis and clothing by the Alpine skiers. The IOC threatened to expel certain skiers, while the skiers threatened to withdraw en masse in revolt if that were done. A compromise was eventually reached in which the skiers agreed to remove all equipment with advertising prior to being photographed or interviewed.

The 1968 Winter Games' hero of heroes was Jean-Claude Killy, who had grown up and learned to ski in the neighboring mountains. He was favored in all three Alpine events, and all of France expected Killy to duplicate Toni Sailer's 1956 feat and win the three Alpine skiing gold medals. He succeeded, but not without a major controversy in the slalom. The race was held in fog, and both Karl Schranz (AUT) and Håkon Mjøn (NOR) initially posted faster times, but both were disqualified for missing gates. Schranz appealed, stating that he had been interfered with, and replays showed that he had. He was allowed a restart and again posted a winning time. But he was then disqualified when further investigation revealed that the interference on the first run occurred after Schranz had missed his gates. Killy had his third gold medal, and France had its hero.

In the bobsled events, held on l'Alpe d'Huez, the site of so much heroism and suffering during the Tour de France, Eugenio Monti of Italy, multiple world champion who had failed to win at the 1956 and 1964 Winter Olympics, finally succeeded in winning an Olympic gold medal. In fact, he won two. In pairs figure skating, the almost lyrical team of Lyudmila Belousova and Oleg Protopopov won their second consecutive championship.

The Games of the XIXth Olympiad (1968): The Games of the XIXth Olympiad were held from 12 through 27 October 1968 in Mexico City,

Mexico. At the 61st IOC Session in Baden-Baden, Germany, on 18 October 1963, Mexico City had been awarded the Games on the first ballot, with 30 votes, over Detroit, Michigan, USA (14 votes); Lyon, France (12 votes); and Buenos Aires, Argentina (two votes). One hundred twelve nations attended, with 5,557 athletes competing (4,774 men and 783 women) in 20 sports with judo not contested.

In 1963, the IOC awarded the Olympics to Mexico, despite warnings about the effects of competing at the altitude (2,134 meters [7,001 feet]) of Mexico City. The warnings would prove prophetic, both for good and bad, but also prominent because Mexico City was the first large-scale incursion of politics into the Olympic scene since 1936.

Political problems first manifested themselves as protests by Mexican students before the Games. The students were upset that so much money was being spent on the Olympics in the face of widespread poverty in their own country. As the protest movement gathered momentum leading up to the Games, the Mexican army took charge on the night of 2 October. When 10,000 people demonstrated in the Square of the Three Cultures in Mexico City, the army surrounded the crowd and opened fire. More than 250 people were killed and over a thousand were injured.

In the United States, Harry Edwards, a professor at San Jose State University, urged American blacks to boycott the Olympics to protest the rampant racism of American society. The boycott never materialized. However, his efforts came to fruition in the victory ceremony of the 200 meter race. The race was won by Tommie Smith (USA), with the bronze medal going to John Carlos (USA). On the victory platform, as "The Star-Spangled Banner" played in the background almost unheard, the two black Americans stood barefoot, heads bowed, and raised a single black-gloved fist in their own form of protest. The IOC banned the two from future Olympic participation and ordered them to leave the Olympic Village immediately.

On a positive political note, the Federal Republic of Germany (West Germany) and the German Democratic Republic (East Germany) entered separate national teams for the first time, although they competed wearing the same emblems and flag and used a joint anthem for medal ceremonies.

The altitude severely affected many track and field events. Bob Beamon used the lesser gravity to set a stunning world record in the long jump of 8.90 meters (29 feet 2.5 inches). It would not be broken for 23 years. In the 100, 200, and 400 meter races; 400 meter hurdles; 4x100 and 4x400 relays; and the triple jump—all sprint events not requiring much oxygen and aided by the lessened pull of gravity—new world records were set by the men. Many of these records would last for years. But the distance running events saw very slow times, as the runners gasped for oxygen that was in short supply.

The 11th Olympic Winter Games (1972): The 11th Olympic Winter Games were held in Sapporo, Japan, from 3 through 13 February 1972. Thirty-five nations attended, with 1,008 athletes competing (802 men and 206 women) in 10 sports. At the 65th IOC Session in Rome on 26 April 1966, Sapporo was chosen on the first ballot (32 votes) over Banff, Alberta, Canada (16 votes); Lahti, Finland (seven votes); and Salt Lake City, Utah, USA (seven votes).

The controversy that had started in Grenoble four years earlier continued and erupted at the beginning of the Games. Avery Brundage insisted on ending commercialization by skiers and singled out Austrian star Karl Schranz, who was expelled from the Games.

Another controversy occurred when Canada refused to send its ice hockey team, protesting professionalism by the Soviets. The USSR won that gold medal quite easily, though it is unlikely the Canadians would have made a difference, as by 1972 the Soviets were showing that they could now play well against the National Hockey League (NHL).

Ard Schenk (NED) was the most publicized athlete at these Olympics, winning three championships in speed skating. His triple was matched in women's cross-country skiing by Galina Kulakova (URS). The Japanese, not usually a winter sports power, were exultant when three of their ski jumpers, led by Yukio Kasaya, swept the medals in the 70 meter ski jumping.

The Games of the XXth Olympiad (1972): The Games of the XXth Olympiad were held in Munich, Germany (Federal Republic/West), from 26 August through 11 September 1972. One hundred twenty-one nations attended, with 7,113 athletes competing (6,053 men and 1,060 women) in 23 sports, as archery, handball, and judo all were returned to the Olympic program. At the 65th IOC Session in Rome in 1966, Munich had been awarded the Games on the second ballot over Montreal, Quebec, Canada; Madrid, Spain; and Detroit, Michigan, USA.

The Munich Olympics began as "The Games of Joy," in which the West German government attempted to atone for the militaristic Nazi image so associated with the 1936 Berlin Games. They ended as "The Games of Terror and Tragedy."

Bid Voting	Round 1	Round 2
Munich, FRG	21	31
Montreal, Quebec, Canada	16	15
Madrid, Spain	16	13
Detroit, Michigan, USA	6	—

The first 11 days of the 1972 Olympics were beautiful. But on the morning of 5 September, stark reality hit when the Games were interrupted by eight Arab terrorists, representing the militant Black September group. They entered the Olympic Village and took 11 members of the Israeli Olympic team as hostages. While the world watched on television and waited, the terrorists occupied the building of 31 Connollystraße and demanded freedom for several Arabs held in Israeli prisons. The Israeli government refused this, and a day of tense negotiations ensued.

Late in the evening of 5 September, the terrorists took their hostages to Fürstenfeldbruck, an army air base near Munich. There, in a few quick minutes of fighting as the Germans tried to save them, all the Israelis were murdered by a bomb the terrorists had set in the helicopter that was to take them to freedom. Several of the terrorists were killed, but most escaped. A few were later captured, but none ever came to trial.

The murdered Israeli athletes and coaches were David Marc Berger, Zeev Friedman, Yossef Gutfreund, Eliezer Halfin, Yossef Romano, Amitzur Shapira, Kehat Shorr, Mark Slavin, Andrei Spitzer, Yacov Springer, and Moshe Weinberg.

The day after the murders, a memorial service was held in the Olympic Stadium, and the Olympic Games were halted for a single day. Many people called for the cancellation of the remainder of the Olympics in memoriam. At the memorial service, International Olympic Committee President Avery Brundage incensed many when he compared the Israeli murders to the political problems that the International Olympic Committee had had with the African nations who wished to expel Rhodesia prior to the Olympics. During the service, Brundage made the now famous statement, "The Games must go on." There were some marvelous athletic performances at the 1972 Olympics, notably Mark Spitz winning seven gold medals and setting seven world records, but they seemed of little consequence. The Olympic Games would never be the same again.

The 12th Olympic Winter Games (1976): The 12th Olympic Winter Games were held in Innsbruck, Austria, from 4 through 15 February 1976. Thirty-seven nations attended, with 1,129 athletes competing (898 men and 231 women) in 10 sports. Innsbruck was not originally even a candidate city for the 1976 Olympic Winter Games. At the 70th IOC Session in Amsterdam on 13 May 1970, the original choice of the IOC was Denver, Colorado, USA, which won on the third ballot over Sion, Switzerland; Tampere, Finland; and Vancouver, British Columbia, Canada. In November 1972, the citizens of Colorado, in a referendum, indicated that they did not want the Olympics to be held in Denver, fearing a negative impact on the environment. Denver officially withdrew as host on 12 November 1972. Innsbruck, which had held the Games so successfully in 1964, was able to step in on short notice, after being selected over hastily arranged bids from Lake Placid, New York, USA,

Chamonix, France, and Tampere, Finland. Once again, Innsbruck demonstrated how well an Olympic Winter Games could be staged.

Original Bid Voting	Round 1	Round 2	Round 3
Denver, Colorado, USA	29	29	39
Sion, Switzerland	18	31	30
Tampere, Finland	12	8	—
Vancouver, BC, Canada	9	—	—

The competitions were well contested, though no single athlete could be said to dominate, as in years past. Rosi Mittermaier (FRG) was perhaps the best publicized Olympian in 1976. She won the downhill and slalom early in the Games and had a chance to equal the feats of Toni Sailer and Jean-Claude Killy by winning the giant slalom. Older than many of the competitors, close to retirement, and born nearby, just across the German border at Reit im Winkl, she was a heavy sentimental favorite. But it was not to be. Canada's Kathy Kreiner defeated Mittermaier by 12/100 of a second in the giant slalom. In men's skiing, Austria's Franz Klammer electrified fans and the television audience with a spectacular run, in which he skied to the edge and was on the verge of falling several times, to win the downhill gold medal over Switzerland's Bernhard Russi.

In figure skating, Irina Rodnina (URS) again won a pairs gold medal, but with a different partner than in 1972. In men's figure skating, Britain's John Curry and Canada's Toller Cranston introduced a more balletic style than in years past. Among the women, Dorothy Hamill of the United States became a media favorite with her ability and style, her wholesome looks, and her pixie-like hairdo.

The Games of the XXIst Olympiad (1976): The Games of the XXIst Olympiad were held in Montreal, Quebec, Canada, from 17 July through 1 August 1976. Ninety-two nations eventually competed in the Montreal Games, with 6,073 athletes participating (4,812 men and 1,261 women) in 23 sports—the same program as at Munich. At the 70th IOC Session on 13 May 1970, Montreal had been awarded the Games in the second round of balloting by the IOC over Moscow, USSR, and Los Angeles, California, USA.

Bid Voting	Round 1	Round 2
Montreal, Quebec, Canada	25	41
Moscow, Russia, USSR	28	28
Los Angeles, California, USA	17	—

The city of Montreal spent extravagantly to host the Games, leaving the citizens of Canada and Quebec with a tax debt they would be repaying for years, and the Games were dubbed the billion-dollar circus by the Canadian press. In 1994, the debt still remaining to the Quebec citizenry was estimated at $304 million (U.S. dollars). Much of the debt, however, was incurred to finance infrastructure that Montreal eventually would have needed anyway. Construction problems led to the main Olympic Stadium not being fully finished until after the Olympics ended.

Shortly before the 1976 Olympics were to start, they were marred by a boycott of 22 African countries, Guyana, and Chinese Taipei (then Taiwan). The African/Guyanan boycott was in protest of a recent tour of South Africa by the New Zealand national rugby team. As South Africa was ostracized from international sporting competition, the African nations demanded that New Zealand not be allowed to compete at Montreal. But the IOC had little control over this problem, as rugby had no current affiliation with the Olympic Movement. New Zealand competed, and most of Africa did not.

The Taiwan boycott occurred when Canada at first considered refusing to allow the team to enter the country, as the Canadian government did not recognize the island nation. This was in direct violation of its agreement as host country to admit all eligible nations in honoring the *Olympic Charter*. The Canadians acquiesced and were going to allow the Taiwanese to compete, but they refused to allow them to do so under the title of the Republic of China, their official national name. Several other countries protested and threatened withdrawal, notably the United States, if the Taiwanese athletes were not allowed to compete. However, these protests were short-lived, and the IOC finally gave in to the Canadian government. Taiwan withdrew and did not compete.

Twenty-seven nations eventually boycotted the Montreal Olympics. Twenty-three of these did not compete at all: Algeria, Central African Republic, Chad, People's Republic of the Congo, Ethiopia, the Gambia, Ghana, Guyana, Iraq, Kenya, Libya, Malawi, Mali, Niger, Nigeria, Sudan, Swaziland, Taiwan, Tanzania, Togo, Uganda, Upper Volta, and Zambia. In addition, Egypt, Cameroon, Morocco, and Tunisia also boycotted, although they are listed as competing nations because some of their athletes competed on the first two days of the Olympics before they officially withdrew.

After all this, the Olympics began. Despite the absence of some top African track athletes, they were well run, and the boycotts had minimal effect on competition. The fans thrilled to the exploits of Romania's Nadia Comăneci in gymnastics as she dominated the competition, scoring the first perfect 10s ever awarded at the Olympics. The major effect of the boycott on track and field athletics was felt in the 1,500 meter race, in which John Walker (ironically of New Zealand) and Filbert Bayi (Tanzania) were to compete. They were the two best milers in the world by far, but in Bayi's absence, Walker had only himself to beat, and he managed a comfortable gold medal victory. Probably the most spectacular athlete on the track was Cuba's Alberto Juantorena, who won the 400 and 800 meter runs.

The 13th Olympic Winter Games (1980): The 13th Olympic Winter Games were held in Lake Placid, New York, USA, from 13 through 24 February 1980. Thirty-seven nations attended, with 1,072 athletes competing (837 men and 235 women) in 10 sports. Lake Placid was unopposed in its bid and was chosen by the IOC at its 75th Session in Vienna on 23 October 1974.

Lake Placid, like St. Moritz and Innsbruck before it, was given a second chance to host the Olympic Winter Games. In an era of spiraling costs, Lake Placid promised a simpler Olympics. But the complexity of television and millions of spectators proved almost too much for the small upstate New York village. Transportation and communication were difficult, and the IOC vowed never to return the Games to such a small venue.

As if these were not enough problems, shortly before the Olympics, the Soviet Union invaded Afghanistan. President Jimmy Carter promptly called for a U.S.-led boycott of the Moscow Olympics. And he used Secretary of State Cyrus Vance to lecture the IOC at its session in Lake Placid days before the Games started, which greatly offended the IOC.

But Lake Placid had two great redeeming features: Eric Heiden and the U.S. ice hockey team. In speed skating, Heiden was the greatest skater in the world, and pre-Games predictions had him possibly winning five gold medals, though few believed he could actually win all five. But he did. He ended his Olympic dominance with a gold medal in the 10,000 meter race. Racing in the second pair with Viktor Lyoskin (URS), Heiden set a world record by six seconds and earned his fifth gold medal.

In ice hockey, the Soviet Union was by now conceded the gold medal at all Olympics. A week before the Olympics, the United States and the USSR played an exhibition game in Madison Square Garden, and the Soviets won, 10–3. But the U.S. team had more fortitude than anyone suspected and were led by a coach, Herb Brooks, who brought more out of them than they knew they had. The Americans could not, and would not, be intimidated.

In the semifinals, they faced the Soviets. The score was tied in the third period when captain Mike Eruzione scored to put the United States ahead, 4–3. As time ran out with that same score, Al Michaels, an ABC television announcer, echoed every American's thoughts when he asked, "Do you believe in miracles?" Two nights later, the Americans came from behind to defeat Finland and win the gold medal.

The Games of the XXIInd Olympiad (1980): The Games of the XXIInd Olympiad were held in Moscow, USSR, from 19 July through 3 August 1980. At the 75th IOC Session in Vienna on 22 October 1974, Moscow was awarded the Games by a vote of 39–20 over Los Angeles, the only other city that bid for the Olympics. Eighty countries eventually competed in Moscow, with 5,259 athletes competing (4,136 men and 1,123 women) in the same 23 sports as in the previous two Summer Games.

In late December 1979, Soviet tanks invaded Afghanistan. After the Soviet invasion of Afghanistan, U.S. President Jimmy Carter called for a boycott of the Moscow Olympics if the Soviets did not withdraw before 20 February 1980. They did not. Carter pressed his efforts, attempting to enlist other countries to join his boycott. But American allies Britain, Finland, France, Ireland, Italy, New Zealand, Spain, and Sweden all competed at Moscow as well as the U.S. Commonwealth of Puerto Rico. Carter made his announcement public to the IOC via Secretary of State Cyrus Vance, who rather rudely addressed the IOC at the Lake Placid Games in February.

Approximately 63 countries eventually boycotted the Moscow Olympics. Notable among these were the United States, Canada, West Germany, Japan, China, Kenya, and Norway (a full list follows at the end of this section). Several countries that did not boycott protested at the Olympic ceremonies in various ways. Ten countries elected not to march at the opening ceremonies, while six other nations marched behind flags of their National Olympic Committees, or the Olympic flag, rather than their national flags. Several countries chose not to have their national anthems played at victory ceremonies, substituting instead the Olympic Hymn. Finally, at the closing ceremony President Carter refused to allow the American flag to be raised as the host country of the next Olympics. The flag of Los Angeles was raised instead.

The Games suffered in the level of competition, but they were marvelously run, although spectators spoke often of the military atmosphere, as Soviet soldiers were on every street corner with automatic weapons. The most awaited races matched two British athletes in the 800 and 1,500 meter races in the track, and the boycott had no effect on them. Sebastian Coe was favored in the 800 meter race and Steve Ovett in the 1,500 meter race. They each won a gold medal, but in the "other man's" event. The athlete winning the most medals at Moscow was Soviet gymnast Aleksandr Dityatin, who won medals in all eight gymnastic events, three of them gold, setting a record for the most medals won at a single Olympics.

It is almost impossible to be certain how many nations boycotted or chose not to attend the 1980 Olympic Games in response to the Soviet invasion of Afghanistan. The U.S. government dogmatically stated numerous times that 65 nations joined the U.S.-led boycott, but that number is almost certainly overstated. Because of political repercussions, many nations simply stated they could not attend because of financial or other reasons, when in likelihood they were joining the boycott. On the other hand, among the nonparticipating nations, it is likely that a few were not boycotting, but did not compete for other reasons. No definitive conclusions can be drawn concerning the number of boycotting nations.

For the record, the following 63 nations did not compete in Moscow but were IOC members and eligible to compete in the Olympics, as of 27 May 1980, the due date for acceptance of invitations to the 1980 Olympic Games: Albania, Antigua, Argentina, Bahamas, Bahrain, Bangladesh, Barbados, Belize, Bermuda, Bolivia, Canada, Cayman Islands, Central African Republic, Chad, Chile, China, Egypt, El Salvador, Federal Republic of Germany, Fiji, Gabon, the Gambia, Ghana, Haiti, Honduras, Hong Kong, Indonesia, Israel, Ivory Coast, Japan, Kenya, Korea, Liberia, Liechtenstein, Malawi, Malaysia, Mauritania, Mauritius, Monaco, Morocco, Netherlands Antilles, Niger, Norway, Pakistan, Panama, Papua-New Guinea, Paraguay, Philippines, Saudi Arabia, Singapore, Somalia, Sudan, Suriname, Swaziland, Thailand, Togo, Tunisia, Turkey, United States, U.S. Virgin Islands, Upper Volta, Uruguay, and Zaire.

As stated, the deadline for responding to the Moscow invitation to compete at the Olympic Games was 27 May 1980. The nations listed can be separated into three categories based on this deadline: (1) declined the invitation, (2) did not respond to the invitation, and (3) accepted the invitation but eventually did not compete.

Twenty-eight nations declined the invitation to compete: Albania, Argentina, Bahrain, Bermuda, Canada, Cayman Islands, China, Federal Republic of Germany, the Gambia, Honduras, Hong Kong, Indonesia, Israel, Kenya, Liechtenstein, Malawi, Malaysia, Mauritania, Pakistan, Paraguay, the Philippines, Saudi Arabia, Singapore, Thailand, Tunisia, Turkey, United States, and Uruguay.

Twenty-nine nations did not respond to the invitation to compete by 27 May 1980: Antigua, Bahamas, Bangladesh, Barbados, Belize, Bolivia, Central African Republic, Chad, Chile, Egypt, El Salvador, Fiji, Ghana, Haiti, Ivory Coast, Japan, Korea, Liberia, Monaco, Morocco, Netherlands Antilles, Norway, Papua-New Guinea, Somalia, Sudan, Swaziland, Togo, U.S. Virgin Islands, and Zaire.

Six nations accepted the invitation to compete, but eventually chose not to: Gabon, Mauritius, Niger, Panama, Suriname, and Upper Volta. The reasons for these nations eventually choosing not to participate are not clear.

There were two further categories of "IOC member" nations in 1980. Both Chinese Taipei and Iran had been member nations of the IOC, but at the time of the Moscow invitation, they were in suspension and were not eligible to compete at the 1980 Olympic Games.

Finally, three nations were accepted into IOC membership at the IOC Executive Board Meeting in Lausanne on 9–10 June 1980, after the due date for acceptances to the Moscow invitation. These were Mozambique, Qatar, and the United Arab Emirates. These nations were therefore not technically eligible to compete at Moscow. However, Mozambique did compete, although Qatar and the United Arab Emirates did not. It is likely that, because of the boycott, late invitations were extended to these three nations to fill out the list of competing nations in Moscow, and Mozambique was able to field a team in time and chose to do so.

The 14th Olympic Winter Games (1984): The 14th Olympic Winter Games were held in Sarajevo, Bosnia-Herzegovina Province, Yugoslavia, from 8 through 19 February 1984. Forty-nine nations attended, with 1,273 athletes competing (996 men and 277 women) in 10 sports. At the 80th IOC Session in Athens on 18 May 1978, Sarajevo was chosen in the second round of balloting over Sapporo, Japan, and Göteburg, Sweden.

Bid Voting	Round 1	Round 2
Sarajevo, Bosnia-Herzegovina, Yugoslavia	31	39
Sapporo, Japan	33	36
Göteburg, Sweden	10	—

After the controversy, problems, and excitement at Lake Placid, Sarajevo's Winter Olympics were much quieter, in marked contrast to the Yugoslavian Civil War that would come to Sarajevo within the next decade. The only difficulties were early weather problems. An initial concern about lack of snow was alleviated when a blizzard hit shortly after the opening ceremonies, forcing the men's downhill to be postponed three times.

In Nordic skiing, Marja-Liisa Hämäläinen (FIN) won three cross-country skiing gold medals. But Nordic skiing rarely captures the press notices of figure skating, Alpine skiing, or ice hockey, and Hämäläinen's feat was noted with little fanfare outside Finland.

In ice hockey, the Soviets restored the status quo when they easily won the gold medal. The Canadians, having returned to Olympic ice hockey in 1980, were thought to have a chance, as some professionals could now be used, though no NHL players could be included. But the USSR played seven games, won all of them, and won the gold medal.

In ice dancing, the British couple Jayne Torvill and Christopher Dean were heavily favored based on past performances. Their final program was quite controversial, however, as it probably violated ice dancing protocol by being based on a single piece of music, Ravel's "Bolero." Their performance to "Bolero" was mesmerizing, building to an almost orgiastic finish that brought the crowd to a frenzy. The judges awarded the British pair the highest scores ever seen in figure skating, with 12 perfect 6s out of 18 marks.

In singles figure skating, Scott Hamilton (USA) and Katarina Witt (GDR) won gold medals. Hamilton was expected to win, as he had been nonpareil since the 1980 Olympics. Witt was not as well known and was not favored, but her stunning beauty helped to make her a crowd favorite.

Sarajevo had been a beautiful Olympic city, but within a decade it would lie in ruins, as would many of the sports facilities destroyed by the senseless war in the Balkans, and become a victim, along with many innocent people, of ethnic cleansing.

The Games of the XXIIIrd Olympiad (1984): The Games of the XXIIIrd Olympiad were held in Los Angeles, California, USA, from 28 July through 12 August 1984. Los Angeles was awarded the Olympics by acclamation at the 80th IOC Session in Athens on 18 May 1978. No other candidate city bid for these Olympics. One hundred forty nations attended the Los Angeles Olympics, with 6,798 athletes competing (5,229 men and 1,569 women) in 25 sports. Two new sports were added, rhythmic gymnastics and synchronized swimming, both solely for women.

In May 1984, the Soviet Union announced that it would not attend the Olympics in Los Angeles, citing concerns over the safety of its athletes because of "anti-Soviet and anti-Communist activities" in the Los Angeles area. Most people considered the boycott retribution for the U.S. refusal to compete in Moscow. Most of the Eastern European countries joined in the Soviet bloc boycott, notably East Germany (GDR), and it was joined by Cuba. Although only 14 invited countries did not compete in Los Angeles, the absence of the USSR, Cuba, and East Germany made many of the events mere shadows of what was anticipated.

Still, more countries and athletes competed at Los Angeles than in any previous Olympics. However, what the 1984 boycott lacked in numbers relative to the 1980 boycott it made up for in its impact on the competition. Boxing, weightlifting, wrestling, gymnastics, and, to a certain extent, track and field would have been dominated by the boycotting nations. The nations that did not compete were Afghanistan, Bulgaria, Cuba, Czechoslovakia, Ethiopia, German Democratic Republic, Hungary, Laos, Mongolia, North Korea, Poland, South Yemen, Vietnam, and the USSR. Bravely, Romania defied the boycott and competed at the Olympics, receiving an ovation at the opening ceremonies second only to that of the United States. Yugoslavia, not Soviet dominated, was the only other country from Eastern Europe to compete.

China also returned to the Olympic Games at Los Angeles in 1984, after an absence of 32 years. (China had competed at the Olympic Games of 1932, 1936, 1948, and 1952.) It had competed at the 1980 Olympic Winter Games in Lake Placid, and its appearance at the opening ceremonies was greeted warmly by the American crowd, especially in light of the Soviet boycott.

After all that, the Olympics were very well run, although the Europeans had numerous complaints, mostly about customary American methods of doing business. American television concentrated on U.S. athletes, which infuriated the Europeans. For the first time ever, the Games were managed in an entrepreneurial fashion. Organizing Committee President Peter Ueberroth insisted that the Olympics be designed to break even or even make a profit. Again, the Europeans, used to the idealistic image of the Olympics for the Olympics' sake, rebelled against this philosophy. But Ueberroth was determined that the Games would be financially independent, and he succeeded admirably in that regard. Ueberroth's marketing methods, though initially vilified by the Europeans, have since been copied by all Organizing Committees and even the IOC itself.

As to the sports themselves, the competition was good, though diluted in many ways because of the boycott. Carl Lewis emerged as the American men's star, equaling Jesse Owens's 1936 feat of winning four gold medals in track and field. But Lewis did not have Owens's appeal to the American public, and his image, almost obsequiously nurtured by his manager, failed to live up to his deeds on the track.

Failing Lewis, the American public focused instead on Mary Lou Retton, who became the first American gymnast to win the all-around individual gold. To win, she needed a perfect 10 on her last event, the horse vault. Given two vaults, she achieved the 10, not once, but twice.

After the difficulties of Munich and Montreal, Los Angeles had been the only bidder for the Games of 1984. But Los Angeles, despite its problems, revitalized the Olympic Movement to some degree. Having shown that the Olympics did not need to be a "loss leader" and could, in fact, produce an operating profit, many cities now were interested in hosting the Olympics.

Shortly after the 1984 Olympics, six cities would submit official bids to host the 1992 Games.

The 15th Olympic Winter Games (1988): The 15th Olympic Winter Games were held in Calgary, Alberta, Canada, from 13 through 28 February 1988. Fifty-seven nations attended, with 1,425 athletes competing (1,110 men and

315 women) in 10 sports. At the 84th IOC Session in Baden-Baden, Germany, on 30 September 1981, Calgary was chosen on the second round over Falun, Sweden, and Cortina d'Ampezzo, Italy.

Bid Voting	Round 1	Round 2
Calgary, Alberta, Canada	35	48
Falun, Sweden	25	31
Cortina d'Ampezzo, Italy	18	—

In ice hockey, the Soviets again were dominant. The speed skating hero was the unlikely Yvonne van Gennip of the Netherlands. All attention was focused on the GDR's quartet of Karin Kania, Andrea Ehrig, Christa Rothenburger, and Gabi Zange, and American Bonnie Blair. They skated well, with Blair winning the 500 meter and Rothenburger the 1,000 meter, and among them, those five won 12 of the available 15 medals. But the other three were won by van Gennip, who won the 1,500, 3,000, and 5,000 meter races, defeating the favored Ehrig and Zange in the long-distance races.

One of the media heroes was Italian Alpine skier Alberto Tomba, who won two gold medals and delighted the press with his nightly antics. He attempted to date the GDR's Katarina Witt, who won her second consecutive figure skating gold medal, but he got nowhere, which further delighted the media. Witt's top competitor was the American Debi Thomas, who had been World Champion in 1987, but Thomas skated relatively poorly and finished third. Her bronze medal was the first ever won by a black athlete at the Olympic Winter Games.

In men's speed skating, the real hero was probably a man who never finished a race at Calgary. Dan Jansen was a favorite in the 500 meter race, and in the 1,000 meter race, he was thought to have a chance to win. But on the morning of the first race, the 500 meter, he found out that his sister, who had been ill with leukemia, had died. He elected to skate that night, but fell on the first turn. A few days later, he hoped to redeem himself in the 1,000 meter race, and through 600 meters, he had the fastest pace. But he fell again. The world watched and suffered with him, but Dan Jansen offered no excuses. He was gracious and magnanimous throughout. Years of effort were lost, certainly by the emotions of the moment, but he responded with the grace so often requested of our athletes and yet so rarely offered.

The Games of the XXIVth Olympiad (1988): The Games of the XXIVth Olympiad were held in Seoul, Republic of Korea, from 17 September through 2 October 1988. One hundred fifty-nine nations attended the Olympics, with 8,453 athletes competing (6,251 men and 2,202 women) in 27 sports. Tennis and table tennis were added to the program. On 30 September 1981, the IOC elected Seoul as the host city over Nagoya, Japan, by a vote of 52–27 at the 84th IOC Session in Baden-Baden, Germany. The choice was highly controversial, as many prominent nations in the Olympic Movement, notably the Soviet bloc nations, did not have diplomatic relations with the Seoul government. There was widespread concern that another boycott would ensue because of this.

The problem became more complicated in July 1985, when North Korea demanded that it be allowed to cohost the Games with the Republic of Korea. Over the next three years, the IOC negotiated with North Korea and offered to allow it to stage several events. However, no IOC concession was ever enough for the North, which wanted equal cohost status and an equal number of events. It demanded this despite the fact that the Games were close at hand, and it had no possible hope of building the necessary facilities in time. When the IOC would not acquiesce further to the North's demands, North Korea announced that it would definitely boycott the Seoul Olympics.

By then, however, most of the Soviet bloc countries had agreed to compete in Seoul, making 1988 the first Summer Olympic competition in 12 years between the United States, the Soviet Union, and the German Democratic Republic. After the North Koreans' official boycott announcement, Cuba and Ethiopia also made it official that they would not attend the Olympics, out of solidarity with North Korea. Nicaragua, Albania, and the Seychelles also did not attend the Olympics, although their reasons were less clear and may not have been directly related to any boycott.

Thus, although there was a boycott of the 1988 Olympics, it encompassed only six nations and had minimal effect on the Games themselves. The Seoul Games went on and saw the largest participation in Olympic history. There were more nations and athletes represented than ever before. The Games themselves were excellent and were very well run. Controversies and political intrusions, unlike in the Games of the past 20 years, were relatively few and comparatively minor.

Three swimmers and one female track and field athlete dominated the sporting events. In the pool, Kristin Otto (GDR) broke many records by winning six gold medals, an unmatched performance by a woman at the Olympics. Her only rival for swimming supremacy was America's Janet Evans, who won three distance swimming gold medals. On the men's side, Matt Biondi was attempting to equal Mark Spitz's record of seven gold medals. He failed in his first two events, taking a silver and a bronze, but won gold medals in his last five events.

On the track, the world was stunned by the performances of sprinter Florence Griffith Joyner. At the Olympics, she won the 100 and 200 meter races, setting a world record in the 200 meter finals, and helped the American women win a gold medal in the 4x100 relay. She also ran anchor on the 4x400 relay team, adding a silver medal to her three golds, in the best race of the 1988 Olympics, as the Soviet Union narrowly defeated the American relay team.

The biggest media event of the 1988 Olympic Games was the disqualification of sprinter Ben Johnson, after he had won the 100 meter race in a world record time of 9.79 minutes, defeating Carl Lewis. Johnson tested positive for an anabolic steroid (stanozolol) and was disqualified, with Lewis receiving the gold medal. After the uproar of the scandal, the Canadians organized an investigation into drug use in international athletics, known as the Dubin Inquiry. At the inquiry, Johnson admitted that he had used steroids for several years.

The 16th Olympic Winter Games (1992): The 16th Olympic Winter Games were held in Albertville, France, from 8 through 23 February 1992. Sixty-four nations attended, with 1,801 athletes competing (1,313 men and 488 women) in 12 sports as both freestyle skiing and short track speed skating were added to the Olympic program. At the 91st IOC Session in Lausanne on 17 October 1986, Albertville was chosen by the IOC on the fifth round of voting over a large field of candidate cities: Sofia, Bulgaria; Falun, Sweden; Lillehammer, Norway; Cortina d'Ampezzo, Italy; Anchorage, Alaska, USA; and Berchtesgaden, Germany.

Bid Voting	Round 1	Round 2	Round 3	Round 4	Tie Breaker	Round 5
Albertville, France	19	26	29	42	—	51
Sofia, Bulgaria	25	25	28	24	—	25
Falun, Sweden	10	11	11	9	41	9
Lillehammer, Norway	10	11	9	9	40	—
Cortina d'Ampezzo, Italy	7	6	7	—	—	—
Anchorage, Alaska, USA	7	5	—	—	—	—
Berchtesgaden, Germany	6	—	—	—	—	—

This was the third Olympic Winter Games to be held in France and the second to be held in the French Savoie, after the 1924 Games in Chamonix in the Haute-Savoie. The 1968 Games in Grenoble (Isère) were in the Dauphiné area of the French Alps. The Games were awarded to Albertville, but they were actually spread over several small towns and villages of the French Savoie in the French Alps. Expected problems with transportation between the villages did not materialize, and the Games were extremely well run.

Another innovation was the introduction of a number of new Olympic sports and events to the Winter Games. Women competed in the biathlon for the first time. Men and women competed in short-track speed skating, skated indoors as pack racing. Freestyle skiing, which had been a demonstration sport in 1988, returned, with moguls debuting as a full medal sport. Speed skiing and the other two freestyle disciplines, ballet and aerials, were demonstration events.

The biggest news was the Olympic appearance of several new teams because of the political upheavals that had occurred in the past two years. Germany competed as a single team and independent nation for the first time since 1936. Because of the breakup of the Soviet Union, the Baltic states of Estonia and Latvia competed for the first time since 1936, and Lithuania for the first time since 1928. Two newly independent nations that had been former states of Yugoslavia, Croatia and Slovenia, competed at the Olympics as independent nations. The Soviet Union, which no longer existed, was represented instead by the Unified Team (Équipe Unifée), representing a portion of the Commonwealth of Independent States. Russia, Belarus (formerly Byelorussia), the Ukraine, Kazakhstan, and Uzbekistan made up the states of the Unified Team at Albertville.

Athletically, the biggest winners were two male cross-country skiers from Norway and two female cross-country skiers from the Unified Team. Yelena Välbe and Lyubov Yegorova each won five medals in the women's events, while Vegard Ulvang and Bjørn Dæhlie won four medals in the men's events.

The Games of the XXVth Olympiad (1992): The Games of the XXVth Olympiad were held in Barcelona, Spain, from 25 July through 9 August 1992. One hundred sixty-nine nations attended the Games, with 9,386 athletes competing (6,663 men and 2,723 women) in 29 sports. Badminton and baseball were added as full medal sports. At the 91st IOC Session in Lausanne on 17 October 1986, Barcelona was awarded the Games on the third ballot over Paris, France; Brisbane, Australia; and Belgrade, Yugoslavia. Other candidate cities that were eliminated earlier in the voting were Birmingham, England, and Amsterdam, the Netherlands.

Bid Voting	Round 1	Round 2	Round 3
Barcelona, Spain	29	37	47
Paris, France	19	20	23
Brisbane, Australia	11	9	10
Belgrade, Yugoslavia	13	11	5
Birmingham, England	8	8	—
Amsterdam, the Netherlands	5	—	—

The Barcelona Olympics were the Games of the "New World Order." They were the most highly attended Olympics in history, both in terms of countries and athletes attending. After four consecutive Olympics with some form of protest or boycott, the Barcelona Olympics were boycott-free.

Since Seoul in 1988, the world had taken on a new face. The Soviet Union no longer existed, but the Commonwealth of Independent States did. Estonia, Latvia, and Lithuania were once again free countries. East and West Germany were no more, replaced again by a unified Germany; Yugoslavia was now split into several republics; and North and South Yemen had merged into one. All of these new national groupings appeared at Barcelona. South Africa had eliminated apartheid, at least constitutionally, and competed at the Olympics for the first time since 1960. The Commonwealth of Independent States competed as a "Unified Team" for the last time, representing all the former republics of the Soviet Union, save for the Baltic states.

Yugoslavia was not allowed to compete as an independent nation, because it was under United Nations' sanction due to the Balkan War. Its athletes were allowed to compete in individual events under the new IOC category of Individual Olympic Participants (IOP).

The Games were opened beautifully and dramatically as archer Antônio Rebollo lit the Olympic flame via bow and arrow. The drama and beauty of Catalonia continued onstage throughout the 16 days of the Olympics. There was concern about terrorist activity, because the area was home to some terrorist groups, but heightened security and vigilance helped avoid any problems.

The competition was excellent. For the first time since 1972, all the major nations of the world attended. The most publicized athletes were the American basketball players. The United States was allowed to use professional players from the National Basketball Association (NBA), because all the other nations were by now using professionals. The NBA All-Star team, nicknamed "The Dream Team," did not disappoint, putting on a clinic for all nations and winning the gold medal unchallenged. It was led by professional greats Earvin "Magic" Johnson, Michael Jordan, and Larry Bird.

Many East European countries and the former Soviets continued to dominate certain sports, such as gymnastics and weightlifting. There were many great athletic performances but, other than The Dream Team, no one athlete seemed to capture these Games as so many had in the past. It was probably fitting, for then no athlete seemed larger than the Games themselves; Barcelona was possibly the finest manifestation yet seen of the Olympic Movement.

The 17th Olympic Winter Games (1994): The 17th Olympic Winter Games were held in Lillehammer, Norway, from 12 through 27 February 1994. Sixty-seven nations attended, with 1,738 athletes competing (1,216 men and 522 women) in 12 sports. At the 94th IOC Session in Seoul on 15 September 1988, Lillehammer was chosen on the third round over Östersund, Sweden; Anchorage, Alaska, USA; and Sofia, Bulgaria.

Bid Voting	Round 1	Round 2	Round 3
Lillehammer, Norway	25	30	45
Östersund, Sweden	19	33	39
Anchorage, Alaska, USA	23	22	—
Sofia, Bulgaria	17	—	—

For the first time, the Olympic Winter Games were not scheduled for the same year as the Games of the Olympiad. The International Olympic Committee had decided to hold the Olympic Winter Games in the second year after the Olympic Games, thus shortening the cycle so that an Olympic Games or Olympic Winter Games would be held in a rotation every two years. The reason was ostensibly that this would result in greater advertising and sponsorship money, as well as allowing the media and public to focus their attention more on the Winter Games.

Before the Lillehammer Olympics began, they were haunted by the Nancy Kerrigan–Tonya Harding scandal. Harding's bodyguard and ex-husband admitted to attacking Kerrigan prior to the U.S. Olympic Trials, a story that was ubiquitous in the U.S. press and television. Eventually, both Kerrigan and Harding made the U.S. Olympic figure skating team. Kerrigan skated well, winning a silver medal behind the Ukraine's Oksana Baiul. Harding eventually pleaded to having knowledge of the attack on Kerrigan, and her figure skating career effectively ended after her eighth-place finish at Lillehammer.

But even the "Kardigansaga" would not mar what was a fairytale-like two weeks, which ended all thoughts of the problems that had preceded them, reminding us again of what the Olympics and sport can bring to the world. There were many great athletic feats at the Lillehammer Games. Manuela Di

Centa won five medals in cross-country skiing. Norway's Johann Olav Koss won three speed skating gold medals in world record time. Dan Jansen won the hearts of sports fans everywhere when he finally won a gold medal in the 1,000 meter speed skating. But through it all, the champions seemed to be the small town of Lillehammer and the people of Norway.

There were also many poignant memories of Sarajevo, which had hosted the 1984 Olympic Winter Games, which then lay in ruins because of the senseless war in the Balkans. Katarina Witt skated her long program to "Where Have All the Flowers Gone?" in memory of the citizens who had lost their lives in that war. On the next-to-last night, at the figure skating exhibition, Jayne Torvill and Christopher Dean skated "Bolero" as they had done so hauntingly in 1984 at Sarajevo. Koss donated a major portion of his Olympic bonus (about $33,000 U.S. dollars) to Olympic Aid for the citizens of Sarajevo. And during the Lillehammer Olympics, IOC President Juan Antonio Samaranch visited Sarajevo, seeing in person the stark contrast between the Olympic City and the Sarajevo of 1994. At the closing ceremonies, Samaranch also spoke movingly about the war-torn city.

It was said of the Lillehammer Olympics: "The XVII Winter Olympics did not exist. Norway did not exist. These were the fairy-tale Games, drawn from the imagination, staged in the pages of a children's book. They could not exist. Reality cannot be this good" (Leigh Montville, *Sports Illustrated,* 7 March 1994, 90).

The Games of the XXVIth Olympiad (1996): The Games of the XXVIth Olympiad were held in Atlanta, Georgia, USA, from 19 July through 4 August 1996. For the first time in recent memory, all IOC member nations competed at the Olympics, with 197 nations present, and 10,341 athletes competing (6,821 men and 3,520 women) in 31 sports. Beach volleyball and softball (women only) were added. Atlanta won the IOC nomination at the 96th IOC Session on 18 September 1990 in the fifth round over Athens, Greece. Other candidate cities were Toronto, Ontario, Canada; Melbourne, Australia; Manchester, England; and Belgrade, Yugoslavia.

Bid Voting	Round 1	Round 2	Round 3	Round 4	Round 5
Atlanta, Georgia, USA	19	20	26	34	51
Athens, Greece	23	23	26	30	35
Toronto, Ontario, Canada	14	17	18	22	—
Melbourne, Australia	12	21	16	—	—
Manchester, England	11	5	—	—	—
Belgrade, Yugoslavia	7	—	—	—	—

Atlanta was a highly controversial choice, as Athens was favored. Athens had not been an Olympic host since 1906, or officially 1896, and the Greeks seemed to feel that the 1996 Olympics belonged to them as a birthright. When they lost the bid, the Greeks were irate, feeling that the games had been stolen from them, and accused Atlanta of having stolen the Games through the largesse of Coca-Cola, one of the main IOC sponsors, with its headquarters in Atlanta.

The 1996 Olympics presented a chance for Atlanta to demonstrate itself as a major international city. However, Atlanta was inundated with vendors and salespeople selling Olympic-related merchandise and attempting to make a fast buck off the Olympics. The atmosphere was unsavory and commercialized and not appreciated by many foreign visitors. The major problem occurred on Saturday, 27 July, shortly after midnight, when a bomb exploded in the Centennial Olympic Park, where many spectators and fans congregated and partied throughout the night. The bomb killed two people and injured several more.

The biggest medal winner at Atlanta was American swimmer Amy Van Dyken, who won four gold medals. She was challenged in the pool by the Irish swimmer Michelle Smith, who won three gold medals. But Smith was dogged by doping rumors because her times had improved so dramatically. In track and field athletics, Michael Johnson was expected to be the most publicized athlete; he did win the 200 meter race in world record time and added a second gold medal in the 400 meter race. But he was overshadowed by Carl Lewis, competing in his fourth Olympics, who came through as he had done so often, winning a fourth long jump gold medal in his last Olympics.

The 18th Olympic Winter Games (1998): The 18th Olympic Winter Games were held in Nagano, Japan, from 7 through 22 February 1998. At the 97th IOC Session in Birmingham, England, on 15 June 1991, Nagano won the nomination in the fourth round over Salt Lake City, Utah, USA; Östersund, Sweden; Aosta, Italy; and Jaca, Spain. Nagano had been an "upset" choice over the more favored selections of Salt Lake City and Östersund.

Bid Voting	Round 1	Tie Breaker	Round 2	Round 3	Round 4
Nagano, Japan	21	—	30	36	46
Salt Lake City, USA	15	59	27	29	42
Östersund, Sweden	18	—	25	23	—
Jaca, Spain	19	—	5	—	—
Aosta, Italy	15	29	—	—	—

A number of new events made their Olympic debut in Nagano, probably foremost among these being women's ice hockey, which was won by the U.S.

team in a mild upset over the favored Canadians. Snowboarding was new to the program, and curling returned for the first time as an official sport since the 1924 Olympic Winter Games. Snowboarding had four events: men's and women's half pipe and giant slalom. There were 72 nations present at Nagano, a record for the Olympic Winter Games, with 2,180 athletes competing (1,391 men and 789 women) in 14 sports.

In men's ice hockey, the big story was the presence of the top professional players in the world for the first time ever. The National Hockey League (NHL) closed down its mid-season schedule for two weeks to allow all the pros to represent their countries, reminiscent of the The Dream Team of NBA players at Barcelona. The difference in ice hockey, however, was that the top players were not solely from one nation, but were spread among several hockey powers—Canada, the United States, Russia, Sweden, Finland, and the Czech Republic. The two favorites, the United States and Canada, went out early, and neither won a medal. The final came down to Russia against the Czech Republic, and the Czechs won in a slight upset, aided by the superb goaltending of Dominik Hašek of the Buffalo Sabres of the NHL. The Czech team defeated successively the three greatest hockey nations in Olympic history: Canada, Russia, and the United States.

Norway's Bjørn Dæhlie added to his list of Olympic records by winning four medals and three golds, to bring his overall Olympic total to 12 medals and eight gold medals, all Olympic Winter Games' records. Russia's Larisa Lazutina won the most medals at Nagano, with five in women's Nordic skiing. She and Dæhlie were the only athletes to win three gold medals at Nagano.

Also dominant at Nagano were the Dutch speed skaters, whose men won nine of 15 Olympic medals and three of five events. Marianne Timmer also added two golds in the women's 1,000 and 1,500 meter races. Germany's Gunda Niemann won three medals in speed skating, bringing her Olympic career total to eight, equaling the Olympic speed skating record.

The Games of the XXVIIth Olympiad (2000): The Games of the XXVIIth Olympiad were held in Sydney, New South Wales, Australia, from 16 September to 1 October 2000, with preliminary football (soccer) matches actually opening the Games on 14 September. At Sydney, 199 nations competed, along with East Timor, not yet an IOC member, but whose athletes (three men and one woman) competed at the invitation of the IOC as Independent Olympic Athletes (IOA). There were 10,647 competitors (6,579 men and 4,068 women) in 34 sports. Additions to the Olympic program were three "t" sports—taekwondo, trampoline, and triathlon. In a closely fought contest, Sydney was awarded the 2000 Olympics during the 101st IOC Session in Monte Carlo on 23 September 1993 over Beijing, China, by only two votes in the fourth round. Other candidate cities participating in the voting were Manchester, England; Berlin, Germany; and Istanbul, Turkey. Brasilia, Brazil; Milan, Italy; and Tashkent, Uzbekistan; also made bids to the IOC but withdrew before the final vote.

Bid Voting	Round 1	Round 2	Round 3	Round 4
Sydney, New South Wales, Australia	30	30	37	45
Beijing, China	32	37	40	43
Manchester, England, Great Britain	11	13	11	—
Berlin, Germany	9	9	—	—
Istanbul, Turkey	7	—	—	—

The 2000 Olympic Games began on a Sydney evening in which the Olympic torch was lit by Australian 400 meter runner Cathy Freeman. Freeman was a decidedly political choice, as she was of aboriginal origin, and the country had effectively adopted her in keeping with their recent policy of making amends to the aboriginal peoples for years of mistreatment. If Freeman, who went on to win the 400 meter race, could be considered a perfect choice for the final torchbearer, as many felt she was, it was only the beginning of many perfect choices made by the Australian hosts.

The venues were centered around Sydney Olympic Park, built on the site of an old cattle yard. This one relatively small region contained virtually all the major venues for the Olympic events. The park served as an international collegial meeting place, while providing easy access for all spectators to the venues. And the venues met with uniform raves from the athletes, fans, and media alike.

Strangely, no single athlete dominated the 2000 Olympic Games, though several tried. Marion Jones (USA) tried to win five gold medals in track and field. She won three and added two bronzes, but it seemed almost anticlimactic. Years later, in 2007, she would confess to engaging in systematic use of performance-enhancing drugs, and all of her medals were removed.

Australia's Ian Thorpe was predicted to dominate the pool, but he won only one individual event and added another gold in a relay. In cycling, the Dutchwoman Leontien Zijlaard-van Moorsel won three gold medals and four medals in all. But no athlete seemed bigger than the host city itself. Sydney was the star of the 2000 Olympic Games.

Were the Sydney Olympic Games a perfect Olympics? No, because nothing of that sort could ever exist. But they came close, and at the closing ceremony, there were few who had attended who would not be willing to cede all future Olympic Games to the New South Wales capital. As he has done several times before, IOC President Samaranch declared the Sydney Olympics "the best ever." This time, there were no dissenters.

The 19th Olympic Winter Games (2002): The 19th Olympic Winter Games were held in Salt Lake City, Utah, USA, from 8 to 24 February 2002. At the 104th IOC Session in Budapest, Hungary, on 16 June 1995, Salt Lake City was chosen as the host city in round one over three other finalist cities, with 55 votes. The other cities were Östersund, Sweden; Sion, Switzerland; and Quebec City, Quebec, Canada. Ten cities made preliminary bids; the other six candidate cities were Almaty, Kazakhstan; Graz, Austria; Jaca, Spain; Poprad-Tatry, Slovakia; Sochi, Russia; and Tarvisio, Italy. On 24 January 1995, the IOC Evaluation Commission eliminated all but four bidding cities in a new effort to decrease time, effort, and costs for so many bid candidates.

Bid Voting	Round 1
Salt Lake City, Utah, USA	54
Östersund, Sweden	14
Sion, Switzerland	14
Quebec City, Quebec, Canada	7

In late 1998 to early 1999, the Salt Lake City bid was rocked by rumors of rampant bribery of IOC members in an attempt to secure the bid. This led to the Olympic bribery scandal and multiple investigations of the IOC, the Salt Lake City Bid Committee, and the Olympic Movement in general. (Full details of this can be found in the entry for the "Olympic Bribery Scandal.") After the withdrawal of several administrators who were implicated in the scandal, the Olympic Winter Games were only two years away and without leadership. Worse still was that several sponsors were making noise about withdrawing financial support, threatening a fiscal disaster. And as the stock market began to fall from its raging bull status in 1999–2000, new money to support the Salt Lake City Olympics could not easily be found. The Salt Lake City Organizing Committee reached out to Mitt Romney as their new chief. Romney was the son of George Romney, a former U.S. presidential candidate, and he was a financial wizard, having made a fortune as the leader of Bain Capital, a venture capital firm. He quickly righted the ship and all seemed well again on the banks of the Great Salt Lake.

Then on 11 September 2001, a scant five months before the opening ceremony, Arab terrorists savagely and cowardly attacked American soil, hijacking four airplanes and crashing two of them into the twin towers of the World Trade Center and another into the Pentagon. The United States responded by launching a war on terrorism and within weeks was waging war on Arab terrorists and the Al-Qaeda organization in Afghanistan. A larger war seemed imminent. Now the question was not if Salt Lake City could fund Olympic Games in February 2002, but whether there would be any Games at all.

Security concerns would have to be ramped up an order of magnitude. But federal security forces, which were to be used at the Winter Olympics, could be diverted to fight the war, and it was not known if they would be available for the Olympics. And if the United States waged an all-out war, would other nations attend peaceful Olympic Games? Remember, the United States had boycotted the Moscow 1980 Olympics specifically because they thought it was wrong to attend Olympic Games while the host nation was fighting a war.

But somehow the 2002 Olympic Winter Games were held, and they were Olympic Games to remember. Mitt Romney and the Salt Lake Organizing Committee (SLOC) overcame all the obstacles. Security was tight, but not much more intrusive than that which was seen at Sydney. The American public embraced the Winter Olympics as "our" Games, a chance to heal the wounds from the assault on its shores. The Europeans, often critical of American Olympic Games, made a few by now standard grumblings about too much television coverage of American athletes, but much less so than at Los Angeles in 1984. And there were none of the organizational problems of the 1996 Atlanta Olympics. The weather cooperated as well, with plenty of snow before the Games, but clear, cold weather in the first week, and then almost spring like conditions in the second week. There were 77 nations competing at Salt Lake City, with 2,399 athletes (1,513 men and 886 women) in 15 sports as skeleton returned to the program.

The biggest news of the 2002 Olympic Winter Games was the controversy surrounding the pairs figure skating event. On the night of the free skate, the leaders were the Russians, Yelena Berezhnaya and Anton Sikharulidze, with the Canadian pair, Jamie Salé and David Pelletier, close behind in second. Whoever won the free skate would win the gold medal, and to the audience and many figure skating experts, that appeared to be the Canadians, who skated cleanly, while the Russians had made several errors. But the judges voted 5–4 in favor of the Russians, giving them the gold medal. The audience and media howled in protest, and within 24 hours rumors of vote-fixing were rampant, focusing on the French skating judge, Marie Reine LeGougne. Eventually, IOC President Jacques Rogge ordered the International Skating Union (ISU) to hold emergency meetings to investigate the rumors. Within three days, the ISU and IOC announced that the two pairs would be considered co-champions, and Salé and Pelletier were also given gold medals. The controversy reached even further, calling for a complete overhaul of figure skating judging.

The two biggest medal winners at Salt Lake City received them in seeming obscurity, as the American media focused on the figure skating furor. Ole Einar Bjørndalen of Norway won four gold medals in the four biathlon events, sweeping the competition. In women's Alpine skiing, Croatia's Janica

Kostelić won three gold medals and four medals in all. She became the first Olympic Alpine skier to win four medals at one Games.

The Games of the XXVIIIth Olympiad (2004): The Games of the XX-VIIIth Olympiad were held in Athens, Greece, from 13 to 29 August 2004. There were 10,561 competitors in Athens (6,257 men and 4,304 women) in 34 sports (as at Sydney), with 201 nations attending. (The press usually states that there were 202 nations, but Djibouti, which entered four athletes, two in track and field athletics and two in tennis, had no athletes actually compete.)

Athens was awarded the 2004 Olympics during the 106th IOC Session in Lausanne on 5 September 1997 over Rome, Italy; Cape Town, South Africa; Stockholm, Sweden; and Buenos Aires, Argentina. There were originally 11 candidate cities. Because of the number of candidate cities, the IOC Evaluation Commission eliminated all but the above five cities prior to the voting. The other candidate cities, which did not advance to the voting round, were Istanbul, Turkey; Lille, France; Rio de Janeiro, Brazil; San Juan, Puerto Rico; Seville, Spain; and St. Petersburg, Russia.

Bid Voting	Round 1	Tie Breaker	Round 2	Round 3	Round 4
Athens, Greece	32	—	38	52	66
Rome, Italy	23	—	28	35	41
Cape Town, South Africa	16	62	22	20	—
Stockholm, Sweden	20	—	19	—	—
Buenos Aires, Argentina	16	44	—	—	—

The Athens Olympic Games were a return of the Olympic Movement to its roots, as the Ancient Olympic Games were held in Greece, in ancient Olympia, on the Peloponnesus peninsula. The first modern Olympic Games were held in Athens, and in 1906, Athens again hosted an Olympic Games. In 1990, Athens bid to host the 1996 Olympic Games, the Centennial Olympics, but lost out to Atlanta. The Greeks and Athenians were bitter that they had not been awarded the right to host the 100th anniversary of the modern Olympics, but regrouped to bid successfully for the 2004 Olympic Games, narrowly defeating the favorite, Rome.

But all was not well with the Athens organization. In early 2001, IOC President Samaranch visited Athens with the Coordination Commission for the Games of the XXVIIIth Olympiad and was alarmed that, only three years prior to the Olympics, construction had not been started on many of the venues, and much of the infrastructure needed to host this huge international celebration was not to be found. Samaranch told the media that he was giving a yellow light to Athens, as the Games would be held in the smallest Olympic host country since Helsinki in 1952, and many people wondered if the Greeks could actually host a 21st-century Olympic Games. There was conjecture in the media that the IOC might try to move the site to another city at the figurative last minute.

Around the time of Samaranch's announcement, the Athens Organizing Committee (ATHOC) hired Gianna Angelopoulos-Daskalaki to return as president of the Organizing Committee. Angelopoulos-Daskalaki had been the leader of the successful bid to host the 2004 Olympic Games, but originally stepped down from leading the ATHOC. Her return was heralded as the best chance the Greeks had to pull off what was becoming by early 2002 an organizational miracle.

Further complicating matters for the Greeks and the IOC was the international situation. After the Twin Towers attack of 11 September 2001, the United States waged war on Afghanistan and in late 2002 invaded Iraq. The Middle East, which sits contiguous to the Greek peninsula, was a firecracker waiting to be lit. Security in Greece was considered to be almost impossibly difficult because of the geography. In addition to being next to the site of an ongoing war, Greece's northern border is mountainous, which made securing it difficult at best. In addition, the Greek coastline is ragged and surrounds 80 percent of the nation. The cost of increasing security, in light of the world situation, became a major economic drag to the ATHOC.

But in the end, the Greeks pulled it off. The venues were all completed. The new airport and access roads to and from Athens were finished in plenty of time. Train routes around Athens and to the port city of Piraeus were upgraded and functioned well during the Olympics. There were almost no organizational difficulties once the Games began. The security worries never fully materialized. The only significant breach occurred during the men's marathon race, on the last day of the Olympics. The Brazilian Vanderlei Lima had a comfortable lead at 20 miles, when he was assaulted by a man who burst onto the race course and knocked Lima into the crowd. Lima recovered but lost his rhythm and was eventually passed, and he finished third. The assailant was an Irish priest who had made similar disruptions at previous sporting events, notably a Formula One car race.

The most publicized athlete in Greece was the American swimmer Michael Phelps. Phelps was trying to better Mark Spitz's performance in 1972 by winning eight gold medals. He "failed," although he did win eight medals, "only" six of them gold, missing the seven won by Spitz. Phelps won the 100 meter butterfly, the 200 meter butterfly, the 200 meter individual medley, the 400 meter individual medley, and relay gold medals in the 4x200 freestyle and 4x100 medley relays. In the 4x100 freestyle, the South Africans pulled off an improbable upset, and the favored U.S. team, led by Phelps, took only a bronze. In the 200 meter freestyle, Phelps finished third, with Australia's Ian Thorpe winning the race. Thorpe, the swimming star of the 2000 Olympics, also won the 400 meter freestyle and added a silver in the 4 by 100 free relay and a bronze in the 100 meter freestyle.

On the track, the biggest star was Great Britain's Kelly Holmes, who became only the third woman to win the Olympic 800 meter/1,500 meter double (also won in 1976 by Tatyana Kazankina [URS] and in 1996 by Svetlana Masterkova [RUS]). But the highlights of the track and field competition did not take place within the main Olympic stadium. The men's and women's marathons ran the original marathon course, beginning in the village of Marathon, and finished in the original Panathenaic Stadium, site of the 1896 and 1906 Olympics. Archery competition was also held at the Panathenaic Stadium.

For the first time since the end of the Ancient Olympic Games in 393 B.C., the Olympics returned to ancient Olympia. The men's and women's shot put competitions were held in the ancient Olympic Stadium, with no seats. As at the ancient Games, the spectators sat on the side of a hill, with no cover from the brilliant Greek summer sun. The Olympic Games had come home.

The 20th Olympic Winter Games (2006): The 20th Olympic Winter Games were held in Torino, Turin, Italy, from 10 to 26 February 2006. There were eventually 2,494 competitors in 15 sports in Torino (1,539 men and 955 women), representing 79 nations. At the 109th IOC Session in Seoul, Korea, on 19 June 1999, Torino was chosen as the host city in round one over Sion, Switzerland, the only other city that advanced to the voting round. There were other candidate cities, but the IOC Evaluation Commission eliminated all but Torino and Sion prior to the vote. The other candidate cities were Helsinki, Finland (with Lillehammer, Norway); Klagenfurt, Austria (with Cortina d'Ampezzo, Italy, and Ješnice, Slovenia); Poprad-Tatry, Slovakia; and Zakopane, Poland.

Bid Voting	Round 1
Torino (Turin), Italy	53
Sion, Switzerland	36

By all accounts, there was nothing wrong with the Torino Winter Olympics. But neither was there anything special about them. Prior to the Games, there were reports of apathy about the Games in Italy, with significant cost over-runs and the government at first refusing to help the Organizing Committee, although it finally came to their aid. The Italian government also raised ath-letes' hackles by proposing to enforce Italian criminal laws against doping at the Torino Olympics. Even the hyperstrict antidoping gods of the World Anti-Doping Agency did not want criminal charges against the athletes, and eventually a compromise was reached. Finally, the 20th Olympic Winter Games were held in Torino, but the apathy continued, with many venues lacking for spectators and many tickets going unsold.

There was nothing wrong inherently with Torino as a host city, nor was there anything significantly lacking in these Olympic Winter Games. They were just burdened throughout by a sense of ennui. After the Games had ended, the world's sporting press, in an unofficial poll, lumped the Torino Olympics with Atlanta in 1996 as their least memorable Olympic Games—hardly stirring company.

To the hometown fans, the big hero was their speed skater Enrico Fabris, who won three medals, including two gold. The biggest medal winner at Torino was another speed skater, Canadian Cindy Klassen, who won medals in five of the six speed skating events for women. On the snow, Croatia's Janica Kostelić won two Alpine skiing medals. Added to her four medals from Salt Lake City, this made her the first Alpine skier to win six Olympic medals. To add to the family sideboard, her brother, Ivica, also won a medal in men's Alpine skiing. Perhaps the biggest surprise of the Torino results was in cross-country skiing, where Norway, normally the dominant nation in this sport, won no gold medals. Norway did manage four medals in cross-country skiing, but only three silver and a bronze.

The Olympic athletes in Torino gave their usual superb performances. But there was no star at Torino—nobody stood out, and one could not identify these Games with a single athlete, as so often happens. This seemed to be the perfect eulogy for the Torino Winter Olympics: nobody came, nobody watched, nobody starred, nobody cared.

The Games of the XXIXth Olympiad (2008): The Games of the XXIXth Olympiad were held in Beijing, China, from 8 to 24 August 2008. There were eventually 10,901 competitors in Beijing (6,290 men and 4,611 women) in 34 sports (as in the previous two Summer Games), representing 204 nations. At the 112th IOC Session in Moscow, Russia, in July 2001, Beijing was chosen as the host city in round two, with 56 votes to 22 for Toronto, 18 for Paris, and nine for Istanbul, after Osaka, Japan, was eliminated in the first round of voting. Ten cities made application to the IOC to host the 2008 Olympic Games: Bangkok, Thailand; Beijing, China; Cairo, Egypt; Havana, Cuba; Istanbul, Turkey; Kuala Lumpur, Malaysia; Osaka, Japan; Paris, France; Seville, Spain; and Toronto, Ontario, Canada. At the first cut, Bangkok, Cairo, Havana, Kuala Lumpur, and Seville were eliminated.

Bid Voting	Round 1	Round 2
Beijing, China	44	56
Toronto, Canada	20	22
Paris, France	15	18
Istanbul, Turkey	17	9
Osaka, Japan	6	—

Via Beijing as candidate city, China bid for the 2000 Olympic Games and considered itself the favorite. The Chinese were quite upset when the bid went instead to Sydney, which put on a nonpareil Olympic Games. China returned to bid again for the 2008 Olympic Games and this time was successful. China hoped to use the Olympics as Tokyo had in 1964 and Seoul in 1988 to prove itself to the international community. The IOC awarded the bid to Beijing despite political pressures about human rights abuses and media censorship within the nation. The international community noted this and did not forget.

Other problems arose with the bid as the Olympics came closer to fruition. The athletes' biggest concern was the atmosphere in Beijing itself. On a typical day, the Beijing sky made a London pea-souper seem like minestrone. Distance athletes, such as marathoners and cyclists, were particularly concerned, and a few even declined to compete in those events. The Chinese government noted that it was taking steps to improve air quality, but it seemed like whistling into the wind.

The Chinese planned the most international ever torch relay, even planning on taking the torch to the top of Mount Everest, which is partially in Tibet. What they did not plan on was the response of the international community, which found in the torch relay a way to express displeasure with China's woeful record on human rights, its refusal to consider Tibetan independence, and its turning a blind eye to the tragedies in Darfur while supporting that regime financially and politically. Multiple protests enveloped the torch relay, the Olympic flame had to be closely guarded because the runners were physically attacked, and the route was changed several times, as the flame passed through nations and regions often unseen by the public.

Due to the concerns about human rights, Tibet, and Darfur, Mia Farrow, a former American actress, and many other prominent people started calls for a boycott of the Beijing Olympics. Although these found few ears, Steven Spielberg and Ang Lee, who were orchestrating the opening ceremony, withdrew in protest. Several heads of state stated that they did not support a boycott, but that they personally would not attend the 2008 Olympics nor the opening ceremony, although eventually many did, including U.S. President George W. Bush and French President Nicolas Sarkozy.

The media were also unhappy with the Chinese and with the Beijing Olympic Organizing Committee. The broadcast media were initially told they could not telecast anything from Tiananmen Square, scene of student protests in 1989, though this was later rescinded to a degree. The Internet was censored in several different ways, which greatly limited the print media in the 21st century. The Beijing Organizing Committee had promised the media uncensored Internet access, but one week before the Olympics started, they announced that the media would have only "sufficient" access to the Internet, although the sufficiency was defined by the Chinese government and not the media. As a result, as the August start of the Beijing Olympics approached, almost nothing positive was written about it in the world media.

The Chinese government did in a sense allow protesting. It set up a protest zone in Beijing, although it was far from the Olympic venues, but also required that any protesters obtain a permit. Over 70 applications were received during the Olympics, but none were allowed. Two older women, both grandmothers, applied several times for permits; for their impertinence, they were sentenced to hard labor in prison, though this was later rescinded after worldwide protests.

But then the Games began with a magical opening ceremony, and the world's press significantly changed its tune. Although the background problems were still around, they were somewhat ignored once the Olympics began. The opening ceremony was considered the most spectacular ever presented, although it came with a price tag rumored at $300 million (U.S. dollars)—for the ceremony alone. The venues were first-rate as well, highlighted by the track and field main stadium—the National Stadium, but called the Bird's Nest for its appearance—and the aquatics main stadium, called the Water Cube. Also spectacular were the equestrian venues in Hong Kong. The equestrian events were held in Hong Kong because of quarantine restrictions in mainland China, similar to what occurred in 1956 with Melbourne and Stockholm.

It was in the Water Cube that the highlight of the sports occurred. American swimmer Michael Phelps, who had won six gold medals in Athens, entered eight events and won eight gold medals. He won in almost every way possible—smashing world records and winning easily, such as in the 400 meter individual medley, having his teammate Jason Lezak pull out a narrow 4x100 freestyle relay upset victory on the anchor leg, and narrowly outtouching silver medalist Milorad Cavić of Serbia in the 100 meter butterfly, winning by only 1/100 of a second. His medal haul brought his overall Olympic total to 14 gold medals and 16 medals in all—the most ever gold medals by any athlete and the most ever medals by a man at the Olympics. His eight gold medals at a single Olympics surpassed the mark of seven set by Mark Spitz in 1972 at Munich.

On the track, the individual star was Jamaica's young sprinter Usain Bolt. Bolt was only 22 years old and had first come to international prominence in 2002 at the World Junior Championships. Considered primarily a 200 meter runner until 2008, in May of the Olympic year he had broken the world record for 100 meters. His first event was the 100 meter race, which he won with a world record time of 9.69 minutes. But more notable was the manner in which he won. Well ahead by 70 meters, he shut down at 80 meters, looking back, waving his arms in celebration, and virtually jogging in. He still won the race by two meters and broke the world record. A few days later, he won the 200 meter gold medal in 19.30 minutes, breaking the supposedly inviolable world record of 19.32 minutes set by Michael Johnson at the 1996 Olympics. Finally, Bolt helped his Jamaican teammates win gold in the 4x100, again breaking the world record. Following in the footsteps of triple Olympic sprint gold medalists Jesse Owens, Bobby Morrow, and Carl Lewis, only "The Lightning Bolt" could claim to have won all three golds with world records.

As a group, the story of track and field was the Jamaican sprinters. In addition to Bolt and the Jamaican men's 4x100 relay, Shelly-Ann Fraser won the women's 100 meter race, leading a Jamaican medal sweep; Veronica Campbell-Brown won the women's 200 meter race, followed by Kerron Stewart, who won a bronze; Shericka Williams took bronze in the women's 400 meter race; and Melanie Walker won the women's 400 meter hurdles. Their only stumbling block was the women's 4x100, which they were heavily favored to win until they dropped the baton during an exchange in the final and did not finish.

Great Britain dominated cycling. Making a nationalized effort to win medals in track cycling, they won five of seven gold medals in men's track cycling and two of four in women's track cycling. The star of the velodrome was Britain's Chris Hoy, who won the match sprint, the keirin, and led his British teammates to gold in the Olympic team sprint.

Overall, the Chinese had made a huge effort, as do most host countries, to improve their medal standings. For the Chinese, this worked, as they led the gold medal table with 51 gold medals to the 36 won by the United States. The United States won the most medals, 110, but the Chinese improved to second, with 100 medals.

In the end, the Beijing Olympics were considered one of the most beautifully conducted Olympic Games ever. The IOC had always stated that it hoped bringing the Olympics to China would help open up the country politically, as the 1988 Seoul Olympics had done. Whether or not this will occur cannot be determined. The final legacy of the Beijing Olympics will only be known years from now.

The 21st Olympic Winter Games (2010): The 21st Olympic Winter Games were held in Vancouver, British Columbia, Canada, from 12 to 28 February 2010. There were 2,536 athletes who competed in Vancouver (1,503 men and 1,033 women) in 15 sports, representing 82 nations. Eight cities applied to host the 2010 Olympic Winter Games. One of these, Bern, Switzerland, withdrew shortly after the application, when the citizens of its canton voted in a referendum to withdraw the bid. This left Andorra la Vella, Andorra; Harbin, China; Jaca, Spain; Pyeongchang, Korea; Salzburg, Austria; Sarajevo, Bosnia and Herzegovina; and Vancouver. The final cities that advanced to voting by the IOC were Vancouver, Salzburg, and Pyeongchang, with Vancouver defeating Pyeongchang in the second round to win the right to host the 2010 Winter Olympics.

Bid Voting	Round 1	Round 2
Vancouver, British Columbia, Canada	40	56
Pyeongchang, Korea	51	53
Salzburg, Austria	16	—

The Vancouver Olympic Winter Games could not have started any worse. On the day of the opening ceremony, tragedy struck. While taking a training run, Georgian luger Nodar Kumaritashvili went off the track, his body crashing against a post along the track. Kumaritashvili died shortly after the accident, casting a pall over the opening ceremony that evening.

January and February 2010 was the warmest winter in Vancouver history, and at Cypress Mountain, north of Vancouver, where the freestyle skiing and snowboarding were to be held, there was no snow. The courses could only be maintained by trucking in snow from distant sites. It was so warm in Vancouver that one Olympian, Shaun White, would later call them "The Spring Olympics." The jinx that seemed to be affecting the Vancouver Olympics was later manifested at the opening ceremony, when the lighting of the torch was supposed to be done by four Canadian sports heroes, led by "The Great One," Wayne Gretzky. The four lightings were to be done on four separate long cauldrons that were to rise from the floor of BC Place. But Catriona LeMay Doan could not light her flame, as one cauldron would not rise. However, the Vancouver Olympics soon overcame this very shaky start.

Canada had twice before hosted Olympic Games, at Montreal in 1976 and Calgary in 1988. No Canadian had won a gold medal at either Games. The Canadians set up a sports training program, funded both privately and by the government, called "Own the Podium," and they made plans to do just that.

There had been complaints that Canadian athletes monopolized training time on the sites, and after Kumaritashvili's death, this was mentioned. The seeming embargo on Canadian Olympic gold medals ended on the third day of the Games, when Alexandre Bilodeau mounted the top step of the podium with a gold medal in men's moguls freestyle skiing. Canada cheered—and breathed a sigh of relief.

After that there was little that was not sublime about the Vancouver Winter Olympics. The weather stayed warm in downtown Vancouver, but freestyle and snowboarding were held without major problems, and up at Whistler, where Alpine and Nordic events were contested, there was plenty of snow. Each day seemed to see another Canadian own the podium, and by the end of the 2010 Olympic Winter Games, Canada had won 14 gold medals, the most ever in Olympic history for one nation at a Winter Olympics. It also won one bronze, which shone just as brightly. In women's figure skating, Joannie Rochette was expected to challenge for a medal, though she was not expected to win gold. Her parents traveled from their small town in Quebec to watch her compete. Arriving shortly before her event started, her mother developed chest pains and died later that day in a Vancouver hospital. Rochette did not have to compete, but she did and won a bronze medal; to most who watched her, it sparkled like a gold in the warm Vancouver sun.

There were other outstanding performances in 2010. In cross-country skiing, Norway's Marit Bjørgen won five medals, three of them gold. Her teammate in biathlon, Ole Einar Bjørndalen, won two medals to bring his Winter Olympic total to 11, second in Olympic history only to cross-country legend Bjørn Dæhlie. On the Alpine slopes, Germany's Maria Riesch won two gold medals, surpassing her best friend, American Lindsey Vonn, whom the American press had built up before the Games, causing some to call them the Vonn-couver Olympics. Vonn was injured just before the Games and was not at her best, but became the first American woman to win the downhill and added a bronze in the super giant slalom.

Canadians live and die for one sport, ice hockey (just hockey to them), which they call simply "Our Game." And although the Canadian women dominated and would win their third consecutive gold medal in a tight final game against the United States, it was the Canadian men's team that was watched by most of the nation, who longed for them to win gold. Things did not start well, as after an initial win, Canada was forced to a shootout to defeat Switzerland in pool play and then lost the final pool game against the United States, 5–3. The team still advanced, and in the elimination rounds, began to play better, moving on to a final rematch against the Americans. The game was the most watched television event in Canadian history, and Canada led almost throughout, until the U.S. team pulled their goalie late and scored with only 25 seconds left, sending the game into overtime. Then, 7:40 into that overtime, Canada's new hockey hero, Sidney Crosby, came through with the winning goal, sending the nation, and the crowds in Vancouver, into a frenzy of patriotic fervor. Seemingly all of Canada spilled out onto the Vancouver streets to celebrate, but the celebration was restrained and only joyous, with no untoward incidents. The Games had begun under the worst of circumstances, with the loss of an athlete's life. They would end, for Canada, under the best of circumstances, with victory in its national game, in overtime, on home soil, against its archrival, with the goal scored by its national hero. Only fairy tales end like that. In between, Canada had indeed owned the podium, with 14 gold medals. At the closing ceremony, Canadians mocked themselves when an attendant walked out to the center of BC Place, held up a power cord, looked at it puzzled, then plugged it in, and up rose the fourth cauldron. Catriona Le May Doan was indeed able to honor the Olympic flame, as Canada and Vancouver had done so well for the previous two weeks.

The Games of the XXXth Olympiad (2012): The Games of the XXXth Olympiad were held in London, England, from 27 July to 12 August 2012. There were eventually 10,519 entrants in London (5,864 men and 4,655 women), representing 204 nations and competing in 32 sports. Both baseball and softball were removed from the Olympic program. Four of those entrants competed as Independent Olympic Athletes. At the 117th IOC Session in Singapore, on 6 July 2005, London was chosen as the host city in round four, with 54–50 votes for Paris, France. Madrid, Spain, was eliminated after the third round of voting, New York, New York, USA, was eliminated after the second round, and Moscow, Russia, was eliminated after the first round. The original nine candidate cities were Havana, Cuba; Istanbul, Turkey; Leipzig, Germany; London, England; Madrid, Spain; Moscow, Russia; New York, New York, USA; Paris, France; and Rio de Janeiro, Brazil. At the first cut, Havana, Istanbul, Leipzig, and Rio de Janeiro were eliminated.

Bid Voting	Round 1	Round 2	Round 3	Round 4
London, England	22	32	39	54
Paris, France	21	27	33	50
Madrid, Spain	20	25	31	—
New York, New York, USA	19	16	—	—
Moscow, Russia	15	—	—	—

The London Olympic Games were held efficiently without any significant controversy save a relatively minor one in badminton and an embarrassing mistake at the football venue. As has been the case with several recent Games, the first event actually took place prior to the opening ceremony.

The preliminary rounds of the women's football game were held in Cardiff, Wales, and Glasgow, Scotland, on 25 July, two days before the official start. The women's game in Glasgow between North Korea and Colombia produced an embarrassment for the hosts as the flag of South Korea was mistakenly displayed on the scoreboard next to the announcement of the North Korean team. This caused the North Koreans to walk off the pitch. The match finally resumed one hour later after the problem was corrected and apologies had been made.

The Games were officially opened by Queen Elizabeth II, who had previously opened the 1976 Games in Montreal. She also appeared as herself in a filmed vignette with Daniel Craig as James Bond. The Olympic flame arrived via a motorboat on the Thames piloted by British soccer star David Beckham and was passed to British Olympic champion rower Steve Redgrave who then passed it to a group of seven young British athletes, each nominated by a former British Olympic champion, who then lit the Olympic cauldron. The opening ceremony concluded with former Beatle's singer Sir Paul McCartney singing "Hey Jude."

Several firsts occurred mainly in the area of gender equity—women's boxing was held for the first time and the predominantly Islamic nations of Saudi Arabia, Qatar, and Brunei entered female athletes for the first time in their Olympic histories. Brunei had competed in 1996, 2000, and 2004 with three male athletes and in 2012 entered two other males and one female. Maziah Mahusin, a 400 meter runner, was not only Brunei's first female Olympian, but she was also the country's flag bearer in the opening ceremony. Qatar, which had competed in every Summer Games since 1984 and had sent 97 male athletes, had a contingent of eight men and four women in 2012. They also allowed one of the four females, Bahya Al-Hamad, a shooter, to carry their flag. Saudi Arabia had competed in nine previous Summer Games since 1972 with more than 120 men and no women. In 2012, they entered a team of 16 men and two women. With these three additions, every country that is now a member of the IOC has entered both male and female athletes in Olympic competition.

In addition to the 204 nations that were represented, there were four athletes who competed as Independent Olympic Athletes. Three were from the Netherlands Antilles, whose National Olympic Committee (NOC) was no longer recognized by the IOC, and one was from the new nation of South Sudan, which did not yet have an NOC. There were 85 different nations that won at least one medal and 54 of them won gold medals. The nations of Bahrain, Botswana, Cyprus, Gabon, Grenada, Guatemala, and Montenegro won Olympic medals for the first time, with Grenada's being a gold medal won by Kirani James in the men's 400 meter run. The United States won the most total medals, 104, as well as the most gold medals, 46, and silver medals, 29. Russia won the most bronze medals with 32. The top 10 nations in terms of medals won were the United States (104), China (88), Russia (82), Great Britain (65), Germany (44), Japan (38), Australia (35), France (34), Korea (28), and Italy (28).

The athletic stars of the Games included Usain Bolt of Jamaica, who, as in 2008, again won the 100 and 200 meter races and anchored the winning 4x100 Jamaican relay team. To the delight of the British fans, Mo Farah won both the 5,000 and 10,000 meter runs, Greg Rutherford won the men's long jump, and Jessica Ennis won the heptathlon. In archery, Korea showed their dominance by winning three of the four events and taking the bronze in the fourth in the contests that were held at the famed Lord's Cricket Ground. The sport of badminton produced one of the Games' low points as eight players (four from Korea, two from China, and two from Indonesia) were disqualified from the tournament for not playing their best in preliminary round matches and attempting to lose to better their overall position for the playoff rounds.

Basketball was won by the United States in both men's and women's tournaments, with the country again showing its superiority in the sport. The venue for beach volleyball was unique as it was held at the Horse Guards Parade with Buckingham Palace in the background. The American pair of Misty May-Treanor and Kerri Walsh won their third consecutive women's title, while a German team won its first men's gold medal in beach volleyball. Boxing saw three women's classes for the first time in addition to 10 men's weight classes. Britain won three gold medals including one by a woman. In cycling, Britain's Chris Hoy won gold medals in the men's keirin and team sprint, and his total of six gold and seven overall medals from 2000 to 2012 established him as Britain's most decorated Olympic medalist. In diving, China won six of eight gold medals and two silver medals to continue their dominance. In equestrianism, Canadian Ian Millar became the first Olympian to compete in 10 different Games.

The modern pentathlon underwent a major change. Previously, five separate events were contested (fencing, swimming, shooting, riding, and running). But in 2012, the shooting and running were combined into one contest similar to a biathlon. In sailing, the highlight was Britain's Ben Ainslie, winning his fourth gold medal in the Finn class (one man heavyweight dinghy).

The shooting competition was notable in that some of the weapons used are illegal in 21st-century England, and a special dispensation was required by the government to allow them to be brought into the country. In swimming, Michael Phelps established an all-time Olympic record by winning four gold and two silver medals, to bring his total to 22 medals and 18 gold medals—both Olympic records. His total of 22 surpassed former leader Larysa Latynina of the Soviet Union, who had won a total of 18. China also dominated table tennis, as usual, winning all four events and also two silver medals.

But the athletic highlight for the British people had to be Scotsman Andy Murray's defeat of Roger Federer for the men's singles tennis title contested at the historic All-England Tennis Club in Wimbledon. Only a few weeks prior, Federer had defeated Murray in the finals of the annual Wimbledon tournament. Murray also teamed with Laura Robson to win the silver medal in mixed doubles. American sisters Venus and Serena Williams won the women's doubles for the third time, and Serena won her first women's singles.

The 22nd Olympic Winter Games (2014): The 22nd Olympic Winter Games were held in Sochi, Russia, from 7 to 23 February 2014. Eventually, 2,748 athletes competed in 15 sports in Sochi (1,643 men and 1,105 women), representing 88 nations. In addition, there was one athlete from India who participated as an Independent Olympic Athlete since the Indian NOC had lost its recognition from the IOC shortly before the Games, although it regained it during the Games, which allowed two other Indian athletes to represent India. The host city for the 22nd Olympic Winter Games was chosen at the 119th IOC Session in Guatemala City in July 2007. The original seven candidate cities were Sochi, Russia; Pyeongchang, Korea; Salzburg, Austria; Almaty, Kazakhstan; Borjomi, Georgia; Jaca, Spain; and Sofia, Bulgaria. Four cities were eliminated, and the three remaining cities advancing to the final vote were Sochi, Pyeongchang, and Salzburg. Sochi was selected as the host city on the second round of voting, over Pyeongchang.

Bid Voting	Round 1	Round 2
Sochi, Russia	34	51
Pyeongchang, Korea	36	47
Salzburg, Austria	25	—

Sochi was one of the more unusual sites for an Olympic Winter Games, as the area was a summer resort on the Black Sea and all the facilities for winter sports had to be built from scratch. The entire infrastructure of roads between the mountain venues and the skating venues, a public transportation system, and hotels for spectators were built, with the total cost of $51 billion (U.S. dollars) far exceeded that of any prior Games—Winter or Summer. (The Beijing Summer Games had held the record at about $33 billion [U.S. dollars].) A second concern was the weather, and the Games organizers stockpiled snow for the mountain venues. The weather during the Games was quite pleasant, with temperatures often around 50°F (10°C), but it did not negatively impact any of the events. Another situation that caused negative publicity was a controversial Russian law that prohibited the promotion of nontraditional sexual relationships to minors. It was widely interpreted by the Western media as an antigay law. Although it caused much negative publicity prior to the Games and the United States responded by sending a delegation to the Games that included several outspoken gay individuals, there were no significant incidents.

The venues were actually outside the city of Sochi, with the main Olympic park that housed several stadia for the skating and curling events as well as the Olympic Village located in nearby Adler and the mountain sports (skiing, sliding, ski jumping) about an hour away in the Krasnaya Polyana region. An excellent train system brought attendees to the mountains.

Among the 88 nations present there were several nations that had not previously competed in the Olympic Winter Games that entered teams in 2014 in Sochi—Dominica, Malta, Paraguay, Timor-Leste, Togo, Tonga, and Zimbabwe. Dominica's team was quite controversial as it consisted of a husband and wife who entered cross-country skiing, although they had purchased their Dominican citizenship and were not born there or resided there. Additionally, the man dropped out of his event after skiing just a short distance and the woman did not even appear for the start of her event. They did, however, march in the opening ceremony.

The host nation, Russia, won the most medals (33), as well as the most gold (13) and silver medals (11). The United States had the second-most total medals (28) and the most bronze medals (12). Other nations that did well were Norway (26 total medals), Canada (25), the Netherlands (24—all in speed skating and short-track speed skating), Germany (19), Austria (17), France (15), Sweden (15), and Switzerland (11).

The same 15 sports were contested as in the three previous Winter Games, but several new team events were added. Biathlon, figure skating, and luge all added team events and women's ski jumping was held for the first time. Ski halfpipe, ski slopestyle, snowboard slopestyle, and snowboard parallel special slalom were also added.

Among the individual stars of the Games were Irene Wust of the Netherlands, who won five medals (two gold, three silver) in five women's speed skating events, and short track speed skater Viktor An, who switched allegiance from his native Korea to Russia following a dispute with Korean officials. An won four medals to bring his total to a record eight in his sport. Norwegian cross-country skier Marit Bjørgen won three gold medals and now has 10 total medals, tying her with Stefania Belmondo and Raisa Smetanina for the most total cross-country skiing medals among female skiers. Marit's total of six gold medals ties her with Lyubov Yegarova for the most women's cross-country skiing gold medals. Biathlete Ole Einar Bjørndalen of Norway won two gold medals and now has more total medals at the Olympic Winter Games than anyone else, regardless of sport.

In Alpine skiing, there were two shared medals, with athletes having identical times to the nearest one-hundredth of a second. Tina Maze of Slovenia and Dominique Gisin of Switzerland had identical times in the women's downhill and both received gold medals. In the men's super giant slalom, Bode Miller of the United States and Jan Hudec of Canada tied for third place. This was Miller's sixth Olympic medal, more than any other U.S. skier.

The Netherlands completely dominated speed skating, winning eight of 12 events and 23 of 32 available medals. In the men's 500, 5,000, and 10,000 meter races, they won gold, silver, and bronze in each race. In the bobsleigh competition, the U.S. women's team finished second by just one-tenth of a second, winning silver, and team member Lauryn Williams just missed being the first female athlete to win gold medals in both Summer and Winter Games as she had won a gold medal with the U.S. 4x100 meter relay track race in London in 2012. Canada won both men's and women's ice hockey and both men's and women's curling.

Despite the worries prior to the start, the Sochi Olympic Winter Games were quite successful, although the spectre of the facilities becoming white elephants still exists.

The Games of the XXXIst Olympiad (2016): The host city for the Games of the XXXIst Olympiad was chosen at the IOC Session preceding the 13th Olympic Congress in Copenhagen on 2 October 2009. The original seven candidate cities were Rio de Janeiro, Brazil; Chicago, Illinois, USA; Madrid, Spain; Tokyo, Japan; Baku, Azerbaijan; Doha, Qatar; and Prague, Czech Republic. Baku, Doha, and Prague were eliminated by the Evaluation Commission, with Rio de Janeiro, Chicago, Madrid, and Tokyo advancing to the final vote. Chicago was eliminated in the first round of voting, while Tokyo went out in the second round, with Rio de Janeiro selected to host the 2016 Olympic Games in the third round, over Madrid. The 2016 Olympics are scheduled to be held from 5 to 21 August 2016. This will be the first Olympic Games held in South America.

Bid Voting	Round 1	Round 2	Round 3
Rio de Janeiro, Brazil	26	46	66
Madrid, Spain	28	29	32
Tokyo, Japan	22	20	—
Chicago, Illinois, USA	18	—	—

The 23rd Olympic Winter Games (2018): The host city for the 23rd Olympic Winter Games was chosen at the 123rd IOC Session in Durban, South Africa, on 6 July 2011. Only three cities bid for these Games, the smallest number since the 1988 Olympic Games, which were awarded to Seoul. The three bidding cities were Annecy, France; Munich, Germany; and Pyeongchang, Korea. In its third attempt, Pyeongchang was awarded the Games.

Bid Voting	Round 1
Pyeongchang, Korea	63
Munich, Germany	25
Annecy, France	7

The Games of the XXXIInd Olympiad (2020): The host city for the Games of the XXXIInd Olympiad was chosen at the 125th IOC Session in Buenos Aires, Argentina, on 13 September 2013. The original six candidate cities were Rome, Italy; Istanbul, Turkey; Madrid, Spain; Tokyo, Japan; Baku, Azerbaijan; and Doha, Qatar. Baku and Doha were eliminated by the Evaluation Commission, and Rome withdrew its bid. Madrid, Istanbul, and Tokyo advanced to the final vote. The first round of voting resulted in a tie for second place between Istanbul and Madrid, with Tokyo receiving the most votes. A runoff ballot was held between Istanbul and Madrid, and Istanbul received just four more votes and advanced to the next round. In the final round, Tokyo again was a clear favorite and will be the host for the 2020 Olympic Games, which are scheduled to be held from 24 July to 9 August 2020. These will be the second Olympic Games to be held in Tokyo.

Bid Voting	Round 1	Runoff	Round 2
Tokyo, Japan	42	—	60
Istanbul, Turkey	26	49	36
Madrid, Spain	26	45	—

Introduction

Nearly everyone has heard of the Olympic Games, as they arc the most watched sporting event on the planet. But the term *Olympic Movement* is foreign to all but devoted followers of the Olympic Games and Olympic Movement. Basically, the Olympic Movement is an attempt to bring all the nations of the world together in a series of multisport festivals, the Olympic Games, seeking to use sport as a means to promote internationalism and peace. But in reality, it is much more complex than that, and one must examine its origins to fully understand the concept.

The Olympic Movement began with the Ancient Olympic Games, which were held in Greece on the Peloponnesus peninsula at Olympia, Greece. It is not clear why the Greeks instituted this quadrennial celebration in the form of an athletic festival. The recorded history of the Ancient Olympic Games begins in 776 B.C., although it is suspected that the Games had been held for several centuries by that time. The Games were conducted as religious celebrations in honor of the god Zeus, and it is known that Olympia was a shrine to Zeus from about 1000 B.C. They were a simple event, especially in comparison to the modern Olympic Games. In their heyday, they lasted for five days, with only one day given to the competitions and the other four days devoted to the religious ceremonies. In the beginning, the Ancient Olympic Games consisted of only one competition; a foot race of about 190 meters, called the *stadion*.[1]

The origins of the Ancient Olympic Games are also obscure. Some classicists state that they began to honor Hercules, and he founded them after his victory over Augeas. Hercules declared the Games to be in honor of his father, Zeus. Another legend connects the Games to Pelops, a Phrygian after whom the Peloponnesus was named. He defeated Oenomaus, king of Pisa, in a chariot race, which Oenomaus had ordered as a race in which Pelops could win the hand of his daughter, Hippodameia. Oenomaus was thrown from his chariot and killed, and Pelops was worshiped as a hero. He took over the kingdom, and the Games were supposedly held at his tomb and in his honor.

Many legends surround the Ancient Olympic Games, most of which are untrue. One concerns the Olympic truce. It is often stated that the ancient

Greeks proclaimed a truce during the Olympic Games, and all wars were stopped. In actuality, the Olympic truce only guaranteed safe passage for athletes and spectators traveling to and from Olympia to witness or participate in the Olympic Games. The Ancient Olympic Games never stopped any wars. Another popular legend is that the ancient Greek athletes were amateurs. But in truth, the term *amateur* did not even exist in the Greek language in that era. All of the greatest Greek Olympians were professionals, most of whom made their living by traveling from one athletic contest to the next, winning prizes at these events that provided their income.[2]

The Ancient Olympic Games were held through A.D. 393, when they were stopped by imperial decree of the Roman Emperor Theodosius I. By that time, they had degenerated into more of a circus atmosphere, popularized in the Roman Empire, but far from the original Olympic ideal that had inspired the Greeks.[3]

For almost 15 centuries, the world did not have Olympic Games, although they were not forgotten and were often mentioned in literature. The first attempts to restore the Olympic Games came in the 17th century with Robert Dover's Games, which were not much more than a series of country fair athletic contests held in the Cotswolds of England. In the 19th century, a series of attempted revivals of the Olympic Games were held in various parts of the world. The most prominent of these were the Much Wenlock Olympian Games, held in Shropshire, England, beginning in 1850, and the Zappas Olympic Games, held in Athens, Greece, which were first conducted in 1859. The Zappas Olympic Games were held four times and were strictly Greek national sporting festivals. The Much Wenlock Olympian Games were the brainchild of Dr. William Penny Brookes. Modern scholars of the Olympic Movement give much credit to Brookes as one of the men who originated the idea of reviving the Ancient Olympic Games.[4]

However, full credit for the renovation of the Olympic Games is usually given to the Frenchman Baron Pierre de Coubertin. To Coubertin, in particular, should be given credit for instituting the modern Olympic Movement, and for his efforts, Coubertin has been termed *le rénovateur.* Pierre de Coubertin was a French aristocrat born in 1863, who in the 1880s became interested in education and the French educational system and sought ways to improve it. He traveled to Great Britain, the United States, and Canada to study their educational systems and became fascinated with the fact that their educational systems emphasized physical education as being an important part of their overall development. In England, he was especially entranced by the teachings of Thomas Arnold, the former headmaster at Rugby School, who developed the philosophy of "muscular Christianity," a concept whereby athletic endeavors supposedly made one a better person spiritually.[5]

Coubertin's studies led him to the study of the ancient Greeks and the Ancient Olympic Games. The ancient Greeks also believed in a philosophy similar to muscular Christianity, epitomized by the well-known saying "*Mens sana in corpore sano*," or in English, "A sound mind in a sound body." The Greek philosophy was actually called *kalokagathia*, or the harmonic combination of beauty and goodness. In concert with his study of the ancient Greek philosophy of *kalokagathia*, Coubertin became enamored of the idea of the Ancient Olympic Games.

In Coubertin's mind, all of this seemed to fit together into one coherent goal. He would develop a movement that would emphasize international sports and athletics as a way of furthering the education of young men (but not women). This movement would have as its finest hour an international gathering of these young men in a great sporting festival reminiscent of the Ancient Olympics—the modern Olympic Games. Coubertin had also visited William Penny Brookes and the Much Wenlock Olympian Games at one point, giving him further impetus for his idea. What could be more perfect?

Coubertin first publicly suggested the idea of modern Olympic Games at a meeting of sports dignitaries at the Sorbonne in 1892, but nothing came of this. At this meeting, however, he first uttered his now famous plea, "Let us export rowers, runners, and fencers; there is the free trade of the future, and on the day when it is introduced within the walls of old Europe the cause of peace will have received a new and mighty stay. This is enough to encourage your servant to dream now about the second part of his program; he hopes that you will help him as you have helped him hitherto, and that with you he will be able to continue and complete, on a basis suited to the conditions of modern life, this grandiose and salutary task, the restoration of the Olympic Games." In 1894, he arranged another conference, the Paris International Athletic Congress, which was held ostensibly to discuss amateurism. However, Coubertin had different ideas. He began with a seven-point program on amateurism, but appended to it three further points, all to discuss the resurrection of the Olympic Games. His idea met with favor among the candidates, and the modern Olympic Games began two years later in Athens, Greece.[6]

The early years of the Olympic Movement were difficult, and it was not at all certain that the idea would survive. In 1896, the Greeks actually resisted Coubertin's efforts and were not necessarily enthralled with the idea of holding modern Olympic Games. Theirs was a poor country, and the effort was a difficult one for them financially. But Coubertin and the Greeks persisted and worked together, and the 1896 Olympic Games were successful, although they looked nothing like the more modern festivals. In both 1900 and 1904, the Olympic Games were held in conjunction with world fairs, virtually as sideshows to those fairs. In 1900, the French concurrently held the Exposition Universelle in Paris, and the 1900 Olympic Games suffered for the lack of attention. A similar fate awaited the 1904 Olympic Games, held in concert with the Louisiana Purchase International Exposition.[7]

Although the Greeks had not been keen on holding the 1896 Olympics, they quickly warmed to the Olympic Idea. In 1906, the Greeks held another Olympics, outside of the normal quadrennial cycle, usually termed Intercalated or Interim Olympics. The International Olympic Committee (IOC) still does not recognize these Games, which is unfortunate, because, after the debacles of 1900 and 1904, the 1906 Olympic Games were the best held to date and probably saved the nascent Olympic Movement. The Greeks actually planned to hold "Greek Olympic Games" every four years, spaced in between the "International" Olympic Games, but because of Greek political and financial troubles, this never came about.[8]

In 1908, the Olympic Games were held in London, and all that could be heard was bickering between the British hosts and the American officials, who protested multiple events and acted every bit like "ugly Americans." But the Games were actually the most international to date and were well run—even if U.S. officials thought otherwise. In addition, the 1908 Olympics forced many sports to form International Federations (IFs) to govern their sports on a worldwide basis and set up standard sets of rules in order to prevent future repeats of the many rules controversies in 1908.[9]

After 1908, the Olympic Games simply took off as the most successful international sporting event in the world. Since 1896, the Olympic Games have been held every four years, with the exception of 1916, 1940, and 1944, when they were not held because of world wars. In 1924, what would later be declared as the first Olympic Winter Games were held in Chamonix, France. These Winter Olympics have since been contested every four years, save 1940 and 1944, until 1992. In that year, the cycle for Olympic Winter Games changed, and the next ones were contested in 1994, with a new four-year cycle to ensue, so that the next Winter Olympics were held in 1998. This ensures that the Olympic Games and the Olympic Winter Games are not held in the same year.

In 1894, Coubertin was responsible not simply for suggesting the revival of the Olympic Games, but also for the formation of the IOC. The first president of the IOC was Demetrios Vikelas, who was established in the office by Coubertin, who felt that the IOC president should come from the host country of the Olympic Games. But Coubertin took over as president just after the 1896 Olympics and held the post until 1924. The IOC has existed since 1894 as an international nongovernmental organization (NGO), whose responsibilities include the planning and staging of the Olympic Games, overseeing the Olympic Movement, and spreading its philosophy, termed Olympism.

The IOC and its responsibilities and philosophy have evolved greatly over its first century of existence. Originally, the IOC basically consisted of a group run by Coubertin. Although there were other members, he was in charge, and the ideas and plans he espoused were usually accepted without argument by the other members of the IOC. Coubertin initially ran the IOC out of his home in Paris at 20 rue Oudinot. In April 1915, he moved to Lausanne, Switzerland, and established the IOC headquarters in that city, where it has remained to this day.

Through World War II, and even until the early 1960s, the IOC, the Olympic Games, and the Olympic Movement did not change a great deal, although they became a bit larger and better known. However, the IOC was still basically run by its president and a small headquarters staff, with relatively small financial backing. In fact, through the late 1950s the financial backing to run the IOC came from membership dues assessed to the IOC members.

In the 1960s, television began to realize the benefits of broadcasting the Olympic Games, and since that time, things have changed greatly. Network telecasts of the Olympic Games eventually engendered huge fees paid by the networks for that right. The money generated gave the IOC and the Olympic Movement significant financial freedom. This enabled the IOC to expand its horizons in an effort to spread its philosophy of Olympism and also to lend financial support to various structures within the Olympic Movement via Olympic solidarity.[10]

In the 1980s, the IOC began to seek other sources of financing its operations, via a commission of the IOC, originally called the Commission for New Sources of Financing, and now simply the Finance Commission. The purpose of this effort was to counteract the fact that by the 1980s, the IOC and even more so, the various Organizing Committees, had become completely dependent financially on the American television network televising the Olympic Games. Held hostage by this arrangement, the IOC realized it had to expand its financial sources and did so with the formation of the Olympic Programme (TOP), later called the Olympic Partners, discussed in greater detail below. This has served to strengthen the financial situation of the IOC and allow it to pursue its purpose even more aggressively.

The increasing economic independence, however, also engendered great problems. The Olympic Games became so highly publicized that they became subject to political manipulation, ending in several boycotts. In 1968, when political activists in Mexico City protested the Mexican government's staging of the Olympic Games, the Mexican army and police intervened, killing several hundred protesters. In 1972, Arab terrorists kidnapped most of the Israeli Olympic team in the Olympic Village and, after hours of negotiations, savagely murdered 11 of the Israelis. Between 1968 and 1988, all the Olympic Games saw some form of protest or boycott.[11]

Coubertin hated politics, stating, "We have not worked, my friends and I, to restore the Olympic Games to have them made a museum piece or a movie, nor for commercial or political interests to take over."[12] So initially, the IOC attempted to remain nonpolitical. However, this has been difficult, is probably not realistic, and is no longer an accurate description.

The IOC, via its seventh president, Juan Antonio Samaranch, was once quoted as saying that the mere act of declaring the group nonpolitical is, in itself, a political statement. The IOC realizes it cannot operate in a vacuum, attempting to divorce itself from all the political problems of a world that, superficially at least, appears to have no desire to pursue freedom for all people and more internationalism. Samaranch's philosophy of not allowing the IOC to be politically isolated is best exemplified by his negotiations with respect to the 1988 Seoul Olympics, in which he attempted to negotiate with Democratic People's Republic of Korea (DPR Korea) in an effort to allow it to host several Olympic events.[13] In fact, the IOC has now formed a Commission on International Relations to deal specifically with the changing political world.

The recent Olympic Games in Beijing in 2008 were also a controversial choice, with the selection embroiled in political overtones. Beijing bid for the 2000 Olympics and thought it was a lock to receive that bid, but the bid eventually went to Sydney, Australia, mostly because of concerns over China's record on human rights. When it came time to select the 2008 host city in 2001, the same concerns were present, but the IOC elected to send the Games to the most populous country in the world, which had never before hosted an Olympics. Although China's human rights record was not significantly better in 2001 than it was in 1993, and this was an issue leading up to and even during the Games, the 2008 Olympic Games went off largely without incident, and most attendees lauded the Beijing organizers for the manner in which they hosted the Olympics. The IOC has stated that it hoped that bringing the Games to China might open up the country to a better record on human rights, but that is still to be seen.

The 2010 Vancouver Olympic Winter Games and 2012 London Olympic Games were relatively free from controversy, but the 2014 Sochi Olympic Winter Games had several issues. First, the site was a summer resort, not a winter one, and facilities for all the events had to be built as well as transportation facilities and hotels. The price tag for this new construction came high and the estimated $51 billion spent was nearly double that of the previous high amount of $33 billion spent in Beijing—and that was for a Summer Olympics. A second controversial area was the passage of a law in Russia that prohibited the promotion of nontraditional sexual relationships to minors. It was widely interpreted by the Western media as an anti-gay law and generated much negative publicity prior to the Games. Fortunately for all concerned, there were no significant incidents during the Games in this regard. During the Games Russia's activities in the Crimean section of the Ukraine became cause for concern, although it did not directly impact the Games.

The purpose of the IOC may seem to the rest of the world to be to stage Olympic Games. But the IOC would state that its primary reason for existence is to spread the philosophy of Olympism via the Olympic Movement. It is not easy to define either Olympism or the Olympic Movement. Both are defined in the *Olympic Charter*, basically the constitution of the IOC, and fuller definitions are given in this dictionary.

The *Olympic Charter* states simply that "The Olympic Movement, led by the IOC, stems from modern Olympism."[14] The IOC has, however, defined the concept more fully in some of its press releases. It has stated that the Olympic Movement encompasses the IOC, the International Federations, and the National Olympic Committees (NOCs) and that the IOC is the supreme authority of the Olympic Movement. The Olympic Movement should also include the Organizing Committees of the Olympic Games (OCOGs or COJOs), which are groups formed in the host cities, whose only purpose is the staging of the Olympic Games and which usually disband within the year after their Olympic Games close. The main criterion for belonging to the Olympic Movement, per the *Olympic Charter*, is as follows: "Belonging to the Olympic Movement requires compliance with the *Olympic Charter* and recognition by the IOC."[15]

The IFs are the international governing bodies of the individual sports on the Olympic Program and also of the IOC-affiliated sports. The IOC gives the IFs almost complete autonomy in designing, organizing, and regulating the Olympic competitions under their aegis. The IFs have in the past defined amateurism for each sport and thus Olympic eligibility, although the concept of amateurism is mostly now a memory for many sports. The IFs provide the international officials who conduct the Olympic events. The IFs also set qualifying regulations for the Olympic sports, as it would not be possible for all athletes who wish to compete at the Olympic Games to do so.

National Olympic Committees are the governing bodies of Olympic sports in their respective countries or regions. (This is an important distinction, as not all NOCs represent autonomous nations. However, the *Olympic Charter* now states that, in the future, the IOC will only recognize nations with international standing as member NOCs.) The NOCs are responsible for fielding Olympic teams to represent their nation or NOC. The NOCs and IFs also work closely with groups called National Governing Bodies (NGBs), which

are the national governing organizations for individual sports. They come un-
der the umbrella of both their own NOC and their own IF. Thus, for example,
U.S.A. Track and Field (USATF), which governs track and field in the United
States, is a member of its NOC, the U.S. Olympic Committee, and its IF, the
International Amateur Athletic Federation (IAAF).

The philosophy of Olympism is quite difficult to define with precision, but
certainly stems from the writings and philosophy of Coubertin. This is the official definition of Olympism, as given in the *Olympic Charter*: "Olympism is
a philosophy of life, exalting and combining in a balanced whole the qualities
of body, will and mind. Blending sport with culture and education, Olympism
seeks to create a way of life based on the joy of effort, the educational value
of good example and respect for universal fundamental ethical principles."[16]
It further states that "The goal of Olympism is to place everywhere sport at
the service of the harmonious development of man, with a view to promoting
a peaceful society concerned with the preservation of human dignity."[17]

However, scholars of the Olympic Movement would have one believe
that Olympism is even more encompassing than this rather broad definition.
Coubertin considered sport a method of education and stated that it "is not a
luxury activity, or an activity for the idle, or even a physical compensation for
cerebral work. It is, on the contrary, a possible source of inner improvement
for everyone. Sport is part of every man and woman's heritage and its absence
can never be compensated for."[18]

This basically outlined Coubertin's philosophy of "sport for all," a cornerstone of the modern Olympic Movement. In 1919, Coubertin defined
this philosophy thus: "All sports for all people. This motto will no doubt be
criticized as utopian lunacy, but that doesn't worry me. I have given it considerable thought and I believe its realization is just and possible."[19] He also
noted, "Class distinctions should have no place in sport."[20]

Coubertin defined Olympism as "not a system but a state of mind. It may
be applied to the most diverse situations and is not the exclusive monopoly
of any one race or time. The Olympic spirit is a state of mind created by the
cultivation of both effort and eurhythmy . . . which in a paradoxical sense are
the basis of all absolute virility."[21]

Coubertin was not a great classics scholar, but he understood a great deal
about the religious and philosophical aspects of the Ancient Olympic Games.
His philosophy of Olympism was based on the ancient Greek ideal of *kalokagathia*, or the harmonic combination of beauty and goodness. Certainly his
philosophy of sport for all is also based somewhat on the Latin motto *Mens
sana in corpore sano*, or "a sound mind in a sound body."

To the bulk of the world, the Olympic Movement is the Olympic Games
and nothing else. Certainly they are the best publicized aspect of the Olympic

Movement, and the Games themselves now see politicians, philosophers, and the IOC itself wrestling with several controversial issues.

One is the commercialization of the Games. Although the IOC has become financially independent, this is not always considered a good thing, and as noted above, Coubertin himself never wanted this to occur. Many sports historians and philosophers of sport yearn for the days when Avery Brundage was IOC president and the IOC was run on a financial shoestring. Though it was less glamorous, Brundage simply did not allow commercialism and fought its encroachment on the Olympic Games to his dying day.

Commercialism has become a much bigger problem for the IOC now that financial riches have befallen the Olympic Movement. In the 1980s, IOC President Juan Antonio Samaranch stated that one of his goals was to bring the IOC financial freedom. In the 1970s, although television rights fees for the Olympic Games were increasing dramatically, bringing significant income to the IOC, the IOC was fully dependent on the largesse of the television networks, notably the American network hosting the Olympic Games. Samaranch was assisted by IOC member Dick Pound, a Canadian tax lawyer, in devising the Olympic Program (TOP), later renamed the Olympic Partners. TOP enlists major international corporations to support the Olympic Movement. Membership in TOP is very expensive, with fees now more than $50 million per quadrennium, and it is also very exclusive. Pound and the IOC made the exclusivity important, but demanded that corporations pay dearly for it. Via TOP, and television rights fees, which continued to increase dramatically throughout the 1980s, the IOC was awash with riches by the 1990s.

At Atlanta in 1996, many people thought that these riches had gone overboard in an orgiastic display of commercialism. Downtown Atlanta was plastered with marketing and merchants, with every corporation, and seemingly every person, trying to sell something related to the Olympic Games. Even the IOC was taken aback, stating that something would have to be done in the future to control this and prevent such gross spectacles at future Olympic Games.[22] One thing that the IOC still insists on is that Olympic venues are not allowed to carry advertising for specific products. If such advertising is in a venue prior to the Olympics, it is removed during the Games.

Another debate that has enveloped the Olympic Movement has been about the concept of amateurism, which has engendered multiple philosophical imbroglios since its inception in 19th-century England. English rowers of that era began to protest the inclusion of competitors who worked on the docks or rowed boats for a living, stating that it gave them an unfair advantage. Eventually, the concept was expanded by the British to exclude anybody who worked at manual labor, believing that the work strengthened them unfairly.

Thus, an amateur was somebody who either worked a desk job or was a member of the leisure class.

In the 20th century, the arguments concerning amateurism became more complex. Athletes who were given paid time off from work to compete or train, termed *broken-time payments*, were considered to be violating the rules of amateur status. But after World War II, when the Eastern bloc nations began competing at the Olympics, it was known that most of their athletes were essentially state-supported amateurs who had no other job except to train and compete in sports. Many of the countries placed these athletes in their military, although they were far from typical soldiers. This gave an unfair advantage to the Soviet bloc athletes compared to Western athletes, who were required to either work for a living or be declared a professional. But the IOC never drew the line against state-supported athletes, even while it was stringently opposed to any type of financial support for Western athletes.

Coubertin actually tired of debating the concepts of amateurism, finally declaring, "All I ask of the athlete . . . is loyalty to sport."[23] The Ancient Olympic Games are considered by many journalists and the lay public to have been contested by "amateur" athletes, but that is almost certainly not true. In fact, the ancient Greeks did not even have a word for the modern term *amateur*, and all of the greatest Greek athletes were paid, and paid well, for their efforts.[24]

Amateurism with respect to the Olympic Games has died out in many sports. Each IF is now responsible for providing its own definition of amateurism. The IOC leaves Olympic eligibility requirements to the IFs, and this situation has allowed professionals to compete in the Olympic Games in many sports, among them track and field athletics, basketball, cycling, football (soccer), figure skating, and volleyball, although football limits teams to just three players over the age of 23. In fact, boxing may be the only sport that prohibits professionals from competing at the Olympic Games.

Some sporting purists demur, stating that the Olympics should remain an amateur festival, but they usually have only a neophyte's understanding of the original meaning of the Olympic Games and the Olympic Movement. In today's world, many of the top international athletes are highly paid for their performances, and to exclude them would prevent the world's greatest athletes from competing in the world's greatest sporting event, the Olympic Games. It is very unlikely, however, that prize money will be given at the Olympic Games. (Some countries though, reward their athletes for superior Olympic performances with cash bonuses.) It is offered at many of the International Federation's World Championships, but Samaranch once noted, "I think the Olympic Games are different."[25]

The term *gigantism* has been applied to the increasing size of the Olympic Games and the commensurate increase in costs. This concept is interwoven with the commercialism of the Olympic Games, because as the Games increase in size and thus become more expensive, increased financial resources must be generated via commercialism to conduct the Olympic Games and run the Olympic Movement.

Gigantism of the Olympic Games is a very difficult problem to solve. To make the Olympic Games smaller, only two real solutions exist: decrease the number of sports and events or decrease the number of competitors in each sport. Decreasing the number of competitors also raises difficult philosophical questions. The simple solution would be to limit each event to the top-rated athletes in the world in that event. But this would virtually eliminate many of the world's sporting nations. Of the 204 NOCs currently recognized by the IOC, only a few can be considered sporting powers. Sports facilities and training techniques are simply not available to many of the world's athletes. To limit events to only the top competitors would prevent many of the world's NOCs from competing in the Olympic Games. This completely violates the IOC's ideals of sport for all and of promoting internationalism and international goodwill by bringing together the youth of all nations in a great sporting festival.

Further, the IOC has now mandated that any sport wishing to be represented on the Olympic Program must present an equal program for men and women. Though this is certainly desirable, it adds twice the number of athletes in the Olympic Games every time a sport is added. In a few cases, those women's sports may not be fully qualified according to the *Olympic Charter*. Prior to major revisions of the *Olympic Charter* in 2003, to be eligible for a spot in the Olympic Games, a sport was supposed to be practiced in 75 nations and on four continents for men, and in 40 nations and on three continents for women. At the Olympic Winter Games, the rule was 25 nations and three continents. Women's bobsled and skeleton racing was added to the program of the 2002 Winter Olympics in Salt Lake City, but a few critics noted at the time that there were not close to 25 nations in the world in which women competed in these two sports; at Salt Lake City, women from 11 nations competed in bobsledding and women from 10 nations in skeleton. Further, the same critics in the media have also questioned whether there are actually 25 nations that compete in skeleton racing for men—there were only 18 nations represented in the 2002 men's skeleton event.

With the revision of the *Olympic Charter*, the rules have changed and are no longer specifically spelled out in terms of sports being practiced in a certain number of nations or continents. A Program Commission evaluates the Olympic Program after each Olympic Games and Olympic Winter Games. The *Charter* notes that there is a core of 25 sports that are supposed to be included on the program, chosen from those that have historically been contested at the Olympics. Oddly, for the Summer Olympics, these are to be chosen from the following 28 sports: aquatics (swimming, diving, open water swimming, water polo, synchronized swimming), archery, athletics (track and field), badminton, baseball, basketball, boxing, canoe, cycling, equestrian, fencing, football (soccer), gymnastic, handball, hockey, judo, modern pentathlon, rowing, sailing, shooting, softball, table tennis, taekwondo, tennis, triathlon, volleyball, weightlifting, and wrestling. For the Winter Games, seven sports are considered core sports: biathlon, bobsledding and tobogganing, curling, ice hockey, luge, skating, and skiing. After the Program Commission makes its post-Olympic evaluations, its recommendations are forwarded to the IOC Session, which makes the final decision about future revisions to the program.

When women attempted to have ski jumping placed on the 2010 Olympic Program, the IOC balked, quoting the original rules requiring significant international representation in the sport, and the sport was not approved for inclusion. In 2014, it was added to the Olympic Program with one event from the normal hill for women. Women still do not compete in the Nordic combined—a two-pronged event consisting of cross-country skiing and ski jumping. The decision about the 2010 Games was an unusual decision, because the IOC has recently seemed fully committed to equalizing the Olympic Program for men and women. To this end, it has sponsored conferences on women and sport, at which all aspects of women's sports participation have been discussed. More recent societal questions have arisen, however. When South Africa banned blacks from its Olympic teams, the IOC took action, banning the South African Olympic Committee, effectively kicking South Africa out of the Olympics until that ban was lifted and apartheid became only a memory. Many nations, notably the Muslim nations, and until the recent Afghan war, especially Afghanistan, have had prohibitions against women in sport, in part because the standard athletic uniforms are often far too revealing for the religious strictures mandated in those nations. A prohibition against women in sport is as wrong as apartheid was in South African sports. The IOC has been mostly silent on this issue, but women's groups are mobilizing against these restrictions, and the problem may become more prominent in the near future.

As of the 2008 Games, three predominantly Islamic countries—Saudi Arabia, Brunei, and Qatar—had never had a woman compete on any of their Olympic teams, but the IOC exerted enough pressure that all three had women on their 2012 teams in London with Brunei and Qatar actually having a woman be their country's flag bearer during the opening ceremonies.

As of 2014, all of the 204 IOC member nations have had women compete on their Olympic teams.

In addition to bringing more women into the Olympic Program, the IOC has other problems with gigantism at the Olympic Games. Mainly, there are multiple sports that some want to be in the Olympics. In addition to the Olympic Sport Federations, whose sports are on the Olympic Program, the IOC recognizes 34 other International Sporting Federations, among them dance sport (ballroom dancing), sumo wrestling, water skiing, bowling, and netball. All of them have individuals who want these to be included in the Olympic Games. Further, in 2014, Sport Accord (formerly the General Association of International Sports Federations [GAISF]) recognized 92 sporting federations (and 17 other federations ancillary to sport). About two dozen members of Sport Accord are not even recognized by the IOC, but all would like to be. If recognized, it is certain that those in these sports will try to get their sport on the Olympic Program. Along those lines, the IOC was successful in removing both softball and baseball from the Olympic Program beginning in 2012. They will be replaced though by golf and rugby sevens in 2016. An attempt to remove wrestling from the 2020 program was met with strong opposition and that sport will continue.

At the December 1999 IOC Session in Lausanne, at which multiple changes to the *Olympic Charter* and other rules were made, one was made to the Olympic Program. The IOC mandated a maximum of 280 events in future Olympic Games, even though the Sydney Olympic Program for 2000 had 300 events, there were 301 events at Athens in 2004, and there were 302 in Beijing in 2008. Although both softball and baseball were removed in 2012 and only 32 sports were held versus the 34 in Beijing, the number of events in London remained at 302. With at least 14 IFs applying for admission to the Olympic Program, many close observers of the Olympic Movement feel this rule has no chance of ever being implemented at the level of 280 events.

The IOC also has an unwritten rule limiting the number of athletes at the Olympic Games to 10,000. There were 10,310 in Atlanta in 1996, 10,647 at Sydney, 10,560 at Athens in 2004, and 10,906 at Beijing in 2008. London in 2012 had a few less with 10,519 (5,864 men, 4,855 women). (The IOC has somewhat "solved" this problem by stating that the limit is now 10,500, although it did not hold to this limit in 2012.) So if it adds more events, or more sports, the IOC will need to decrease the number of athletes per event and sport. But there is another problem. The IOC is fully committed to having all member nations compete in the Olympics. In fact, the IOC 2000 Commission passed another change to the *Olympic Charter*, stating basically that all NOCs are expected to compete in the Olympic Games—in effect, an anti-boycott clause. So if there will be fewer athletes permitted per event, but all member

NOCs are expected to compete, there may be less room for elite athletes in the Olympic Games. But the IOC does not want this either. Each year the IOC opens up the Olympic Program to true professionals in more sports, and there are currently very few federations that limit who may compete in the Olympic Games in their sport. The IOC does limit participation, however, in an effort to keep down the number of competitors. In swimming, only two athletes per nation may compete in any individual event, and in both swimming and athletics, nations are limited to one male and one female competitor, if they do not have athletes who meet the minimum qualification standards. The problem of encouraging participation but allowing athletes who do not meet minimum qualification standards occasionally results in scenarios such as the 2000 Sydney Olympics 50 meter swimming event when Eric Moussambani of Equatorial Guinea who had only a few months of swimming experience in a small hotel pool was allowed to compete. Moussambani splashed home in 1:52.72 seconds, 50 seconds slower than the next-to-last competitor, and slower than the world record in the 200 meter freestyle.

None of these are easy problems for the Olympic Program, and it is not certain how they will be resolved. In an ideal world, all the best athletes from all the nations would compete in all the world's sports. But that would probably allow 20,000 athletes to compete and push gigantism up another notch and significantly increase the costs of the Olympic Games. Paying for these huge Games would be difficult, and the payment would likely be earned only by "selling the Olympic soul to the devil," or the television networks and other corporations.

Further, the world situation has made gigantism even more of an evil, because security costs have skyrocketed in response to terrorism, and they will likely rise more than linearly with an increasing number of athletes. The 1972 Olympic Games was the first so afflicted when Arab terrorists raided the Olympic Village, kidnapping the entire Israeli team and eventually murdering 11 of the team members.[26] After the World Trade Center attacks in September 2001, security at the 2004 Olympic Games was greatly increased, as fear was exacerbated by the proximity of Greece to the Middle East and its unique geography, surrounded by mountains and sea, which made protecting the border especially difficult. Prior to 1972, security was a relatively minor afterthought for Organizing Committees, but it is now foremost in their minds, and after the construction of new venues, it is probably the most expensive line item on their budgets.

Budgets have escalated in response to the growing size of the Olympic Games and security costs. In 2004, the bottom line for the Athens Olympic Games was quoted in the press as over $11 billion, a figure dwarfing all previous Olympics, but this did not even include major infrastructure projects done to improve the city for the Olympic Games. The previous "record holder" was Barcelona in 1992, with a quoted cost of $7 billion, although the 1964 Tokyo Olympics, costing about $2 billion, probably rivaled Athens as the most expensive Olympics ever, when adjusted for inflation. But the Athens record cost was far surpassed by Beijing in 2008, with a quoted cost of $40 billion. When adjusted for inflation, and on a cost per athlete basis in real dollars, the 1964 Olympic Games was by far the most expensive until Beijing. The Tokyo Olympics, after adjustment for inflation, cost $1.8 million per athlete in 2008 dollars. But Beijing more than doubled that, spending $3.7 million per athlete in 2008. This is for a sporting event and a number of rather large parties. In fact, the Beijing opening ceremony, though admittedly spectacular, was rumored to cost $300 million, or $28,000 per athlete. That was just for a big party. In contrast, the London Games were held for a total of $14.6 billion or $1.3 million per athlete—still an exorbitant amount.

The $11 billion spent for the Athens Games had to be raised among the smallest population of any Olympic nation since the Helsinki Olympics of 1952, when the budget was probably nearer $10 million, giving the Olympic Movement's thousand-fold absolute increase in costs in just over 50 years. And this in a country that within six years after the Olympics (2010) would all but declare bankruptcy as a nation. Much of the cost of modern Olympic Games is allocated to the construction of huge athletic venues, which often become white elephants to the host city after the Olympics are over, requiring millions of dollars yearly for upkeep but generating precious little income in the future. Even Sydney, in sports-mad Australia, has found the cost of maintaining the Olympic venues to be a problem. Amid the Greek financial crisis of 2010, articles have appeared blaming some of it on the Olympic Games, though economists think this unlikely. But it has been noted that more than half the Athens venues are barely used or empty, including the baseball and softball stadia; the whitewater canoe course; and arenas built for sports such as hockey (field), table tennis, and judo, which are simply never played in Greece.[27] Although the facilities constructed for the Sochi Winter Games were first rate, it remains to be seen whether or not they, too, will become expensive white elephants.

One has to wonder if these costs are worth it. Even Coubertin raised this issue almost 100 years ago: "It would be very unfortunate, if the often exaggerated expenses incurred for the most recent Olympiads, a sizeable part of which represented the construction of permanent buildings, which were moreover unnecessary—temporary structures would fully suffice, and the only consequence is to then encourage use of these permanent buildings by increasing the number of occasions to draw in the crowds—it would be very unfortunate if these expenses were to deter [small] countries from putting themselves forward to host the Olympic Games in the future."[28]

Further, the entire question of Olympic finance is a very difficult one. What counts as an Olympic cost and what does not? In 1996, Atlanta significantly upgraded Hartsfield International Airport, which badly needed improvement. The renovation was done in response to the Olympics coming to Atlanta. But was it an Olympic cost to upgrade the city's airport? The same argument applies to Athens, which built an entirely new airport, multiple access roads around the city, and a new train line to and from the port city of Piraeus, all badly needed and all of which was infrastructure that probably would not have been developed for decades had the Olympics not been coming to Greece. Is this an Olympic cost? If these infrastructure costs are added to Olympic bottom lines, then the costs would be far higher than those quoted above. But is this a bad thing or a good thing? The host cities obtain much-needed civic improvements and can excuse these costs as necessary to hold the Olympic Games. The question is asked often but answered only poorly, if at all.

One also must wonder if these costs are justified to the host nation, even if they increase taxes to its citizens and further increase national debts. It is known that the citizens of Montreal and Québec continued to pay taxes related to the financing of the 1976 Olympic Games long afterward, with the mortgages not paid off until 2006. Many city politicos, at least those who are pro-Olympic, argue that the Olympic Games are worth the cost by allowing them to place their city on an international stage unlike any other, burning brilliantly in the media sun for two full weeks (but rising and setting for months prior to and after the Olympic Games). Are the citizens of Athens, now facing years of draconian budget cuts and tax increases, happy that their nation spent so much to host the 2004 Olympic Games?

There is probably no other way for a city to obtain so much publicity, usually positive, for itself, and present itself in a better way to the world. Tokyo used the 1964 Olympic Games to signal to the world that it had recovered from the horrors of World War II. Munich tried a similar tack in 1972, though the Black September terrorist movement challenged that idea. Seoul in 1988 proved to the world that Korea's burgeoning Pacific Rim economy had made it a first-world nation. Atlanta, only a sleepy southern American city in the 19th and early 20th centuries, best known for being ravaged during the American Civil War, used the 1996 Olympic Games to proclaim itself a major international city. Barcelona is also considered a positive example, having used the Olympics to renew buildings and infrastructure, while also promoting itself successfully as a holiday destination.

Has all this worked? Have the positive exposures the cities received outweighed the huge debts incurred? Since 1984, most Organizing Committees, through accounting legerdemain, have made it look like the Olympic Games have actually made money. A few certainly have, notably Los Angeles in 1984, probably Sydney in 2000, and possibly Atlanta in 1996. But adding in the infrastructure the cities have built, the Olympic Games must be considered only a huge loss leader for the host cities. Has the loss leader brought the positive publicity, increased tourism, and additional business investment that the host cities and nations have sought? Most economic studies would suggest that it has not and that the Olympic Games still remain a huge financial drain on the citizens of the host nation. But there is no way to put a dollar amount on the publicity brought to the host city and the host nation by the positive aspects of the Olympic Games, by aligning their city with the Olympic rings, and becoming an "Olympic City." No generally acceptable answer exists, although politicians and economists continue to debate.[29]

Many other problems are currently plaguing the IOC. Drug use in sports has become even more rampant in the past decade, but the problem goes back to at least the 1950s. The IOC set up a medical working group in 1961 and a Medical Commission in 1966, which was specifically charged with investigating the use of drugs in sport. Testing for drugs first occurred at the 1968 Olympic Games in Mexico City. But testing has not deterred many athletes from using performance-enhancing drugs (PED), and several scandals related to drug use in sports have occurred.

It is certain that in the 1970s and 1980s, many of the athletes from East Germany (the German Democratic Republic) were supplied with PED by their coaches and trainers. This was never proven during their competitive era, and no GDR athlete ever tested positive for drugs at the Olympic Games. But after the fall of the Berlin Wall, official East German documents of the secret police, the Stasi, documented rampant and organized drug use by the sporting authorities. No sanctions against their athletes were ever imposed by the IOC.

In 1983, at the Pan-American Games in Caracas, Venezuela, the organizers had installed a new drug-testing lab that was much more sensitive and able to detect drug use at much lower levels. On the threshold of the Games, several athletes were found to be positive for PEDs. Further, when the results started leaking out to the athletes, numerous athletes withdrew and returned home from Venezuela to avoid the drug-testing procedure.

At the 1988 Olympic Games, Ben Johnson won the 100 meter dash, defeating his rival, Carl Lewis, as he had at the 1987 World Championships. But Johnson tested positive for anabolic steroids shortly after the race; his title and gold medal were withdrawn, and Lewis was eventually declared the champion. This created a furor in the press at the Seoul Olympics and eventually led to the Canadian government setting up the Dubin Investigation to look into the systematic use of drugs among Canadian athletes. During that investigation, Johnson and his doctor, Dr. Jamie Astaphan, admitted to the use of PED for several years.

In the early 1990s, several track performances by female Chinese athletes shattered world records at their national championships. The records were literally off the bell curve and caused at least one Olympic distance-running medalist, Lynn Jennings, to sit down and cry when she heard of the times the Chinese women were running. It was revealed that the Chinese were being coached by former East German coaches, and it was strongly suspected that these off-the-chart records were the result of doping. Within a few years of those performances, over a dozen Chinese women runners and swimmers tested positive for drug use.

In 1998, the Tour de France was rocked by revelations of drug use among professional cyclists (who were by then eligible to compete in the Olympic Games, beginning in 1996). This was not unexpected, given the history of drug use in professional cycling, but it received major play in the media—both written and spoken—and it again cast international professional sport in a very bad light. The scandal focused on the Festina team, which eventually withdrew from the Tour. One of the Festina trainers, Willy Voet, eventually wrote a book, *Massacre à la Chaîne: Révélations sur 30 ans de tricheries*, which described the systematic use of drugs in cycling.

In 2004, a drug scandal emerged involving an American drug and food supplement laboratory near the Bay Area of California, Bay Area Laboratory Co-Operative (BALCO). The head of BALCO was Victor Conte, Jr. Many American professional athletes, including baseball stars Barry Bonds and Jason Giambi, and 2000 Olympic star Marion Jones, were found to have worked with Conte and BALCO. The U.S. government began an investigation, which included grand jury testimony. Unfortunately, much of the grand jury testimony was leaked to the media (which is illegal); it implicated several athletes (notably Giambi and Bonds) as having used PED. In a televised interview, Conte also accused Jones of using human growth hormone. Although she initially denied that, Jones was later found to have tested positive several times, and in October 2007, she admitted to lying to U.S. federal agents about her steroid use prior to the 2000 Olympic Games, for which she later served six months in prison and performed 200 hours of community service.

The IOC has responded to these many scandals by forming the World Anti-Doping Agency (WADA). Announced in 1999, WADA was led from 1999 to 2008 by prominent Canadian IOC member Dick Pound. In early 1999, the IOC held a conference on the problem of doping in sport, which included setting up the structure of WADA. The IOC passed several rules to help, including adding an anti-doping statement to the Olympic Oath and *Olympic Charter*, and, perhaps most important, requiring that Olympic Sport

Federations and National Olympic Committees follow the rules of WADA and the IOC on doping in sport. WADA has set up a uniform set of regulations, termed the World Anti-Doping Code, that describes in great detail the measures that sport federations and international Games should take against doping and the penalties to be involved. WADA has also taken over responsibility for publishing the "Prohibited List of Drugs in Sport."

In addition to WADA, another international entity helps combat drugs in sports, the Court of Arbitration for Sport (CAS). The CAS was formed in the early 1980s and is based in Lausanne, Switzerland, to adjudicate any dispute related to sport and law. However, in the late 1990s, the IOC increased its importance by requiring Olympic athletes to allow any disputes during the Olympic Games to be settled by the CAS, rather than going to the judicial system. Thus, appeals for doping positives are usually heard by a panel of arbitrators chosen by the CAS.

The media response to drug use at the Olympics has been interesting. Much of the media have adopted a very politically correct response to this, especially in the United States, and rarely examine all the issues involved in a critical manner. The issue is far more complex than one would assume when reading about it in U.S. newspapers. Notably, the IOC is usually condemned as allowing and almost promoting drug use in sport, because so many Olympic athletes have been caught testing positive for drugs. But this argument fails to consider that the IOC was the first sports organization to test for drug use in sports (in 1968), the first sports organization to set up a Medical Commission to examine the issues of doping (in 1966), the first to institute random, out-of-competition tests to catch drug cheaters, and has penalties for doping that are far more stringent than those of most professional sports federations. In comparison, the four American professional sports (baseball, football, basketball, and ice hockey) test their athletes far less frequently than Olympic athletes are tested, they test for far fewer drugs, and their penalties are relative slaps on the wrist compared to those issued by the IOC and WADA.[30]

Despite knowing that extensive drug testing will be conducted before, during, and after the Games, the use of illegal performance-enhancing drugs still continues. There were 15 athletes who participated in London in 2012 who were disqualified for illegal drug use, including three who had won Olympic medals. Eight other athletes tested positive in Sochi.

The Olympic Movement was rocked by its greatest scandal ever in late 1998 and early 1999, one that threatened its very existence. In November 1998, a Salt Lake City television station revealed that the Salt Lake City Bid Committee had paid the tuition for the daughter of an IOC member. This was not an isolated event. The ensuing scandal eventually saw 10 members of the

IOC resign, and it spread beyond the Salt Lake City Bid Committee, with bid and organizing committees in Atlanta, Nagano, and Sydney being implicated. Further, the Toronto Bid Committee for the 1996 Olympics had released a report in 1991 that told of IOC members requesting and being given gifts in exchange for votes to become the Olympic host city.

The Olympic bribery scandal forced the IOC to confront its problems. It was investigated on several fronts, and several reports were issued about the scandal. The IOC formed a committee, headed by IOC Vice President Dick Pound, which released a report on the scandal in March 1999. Salt Lake City requested and received a similar report from its board of ethics. The U.S. Olympic Committee formed a commission, headed by former U.S. Senator George Mitchell, and its report was released in early March 1999. The U.S. Federal Bureau of Investigation also investigated the Olympic Movement and the IOC.

In response to these reports, the IOC formed two important new commissions: the IOC Ethics Commission and the IOC 2000 Commission. The Ethics Commission set up guidelines for conduct by IOC members and bid committees. The IOC 2000 Commission made 50 recommendations to the IOC, several based on the earlier reports, and in December 1999, at the IOC Session, the IOC enacted all 50 recommendations in an effort to overcome the effects of the scandal.

It is sad that the public, especially the American public, via the media, often hears about the Olympic Movement only during these times of controversy, for there is much good in the Olympic Movement, and the IOC attempts to accomplish many admirable things. The Olympic Movement is first and foremost a movement of internationalism, and the IOC wants to be known as a peace organization. To that end, it has recently reinstituted the Olympic truce, reminiscent of the truce of ancient Greece, with the Olympic truce receiving the imprimatur of the United Nations. During the 1990s, the IOC began a closer alliance with the United Nations, specifically the United Nations Educational, Scientific and Cultural Organization, and in 2008 the IOC was admitted to the United Nations as an observer. Together, these two organizations promoted the passage of a modern version of the Olympic truce, calling for the cessation of international hostilities during the celebration of the Olympic Games and Olympic Winter Games. Regrettably, this did not occur during the 2002 Olympic Winter Games, nor during the 2004 Olympic Games, with invasions of Afghanistan and Iraq by U.S.-led coalitions occurring concurrently with the sporting events.

Finally, the IOC has lately become more concerned with the environment. It now promotes and virtually demands acceptance of the concept of "green" Olympic Games. This concept really began with the Lillehammer Winter

Olympics of 1994. The Lillehammer Organizing Committee designed all of its sports stadia and settings with the intention of doing minimal harm to the environment. Later that summer, at the Centennial Olympic Congress, the topic of environmental concerns at the Olympic Games was discussed. The IOC has seized upon this idea as a good one and is now requiring that future candidate cities give primary consideration to this concept.[31] The *Olympic Charter* has been changed to reflect this emphasis, with Rule 2.13 stating: "[The IOC's role is] to encourage and support a responsible concern for environmental issues, to promote sustainable development in sport and to require that the Olympic Games are held accordingly."[32] The IOC has also stated that environmental issues will be reviewed when considering any sport for inclusion on the Olympic Program.

Thus, there are many good things that the IOC does under the umbrella of the Olympic Movement, even if many are not seen by the public. The IOC has been the recipient of a great deal of money since the early 1980s, and it is trying to use this money to accomplish what it considers necessary to promote international sport as a means to a more peaceful world. This would seem positive on the whole. Yet a few critics of the IOC have recently complained that it tries to do too much. They have insisted that the IOC should return to its primary mission—to hold international sporting events in the form of the Olympic Games and the Olympic Winter Games, and at a reasonable cost. It would seem difficult to criticize an organization for trying to do too many good things, although people who continually criticize the IOC add even that to their myriad polemics.

Thus we have come full circle, from a small, simple religious festival in ancient Greece to a huge festival seen on television by billions of people, which American sportscaster Jim McKay has labeled, "the largest peacetime gathering of humanity in the history of the world."[33] To the athletes, the Olympic Games are the supreme test of their abilities. To the athletes, the Olympic Games are special, witnessed by the statement of the late Al Oerter, an Olympic legend and four-time discus gold medalist: "There is no job, no amount of power, no money to approach the Olympic experience."[34] To the spectators, the atmosphere during the three-week period during the games can be an unbelievable thrill as the volunteers of the home nation go out of their way to welcome the visitors, and the comradery among people from many nations is a marvelous experience.

Though "just" a big sporting event, even the politicians have realized that the Olympics are more than that. Former California governor Jerry Brown once commented, "These are just games and people should see them for fun; there shouldn't be any ulterior motives to the Olympics. They're just games, frivolous things. They're not really necessary. But don't forget some of the least necessary things in life are the most important. Art, religion, friendship, leisure time, games—they make life worth living."[35]

Besides Coubertin, there were others who realized, almost from the start of the Olympic Movement, the good that the Olympic idea could accomplish. At the closing banquet after the 1908 Olympic Games, the Reverend Robert Stuart de Courcy Laffan, who was honorary secretary of the 1908 Olympic Games, noted, "The Olympic Movement was one with great ideals—the perfect physical development of a new humanity, the spreading all over the world of the spirit of sport, which was the spirit of the truest chivalry, and the drawing together of all the nations of the earth in the bonds of peace and mutual amity. They were at the beginning of one of those great world movements which was going to develop long after all present had passed away."[36]

The Olympic Movement itself encompasses much more than the Olympic Games. Via its philosophy of Olympism, it attempts to bring together people of all nationalities in peaceful competition, creating an air of internationalism rarely seen in today's divisive world. This has perhaps been best summed up by the emotional speech of Lord Killanin, outgoing IOC president, at the closing ceremonies of the 1980 Lake Placid Winter Olympics. Referring specifically to the planned U.S.-driven boycott of the Moscow Olympics, Killanin stated, "Ladies and gentlemen, I feel these Games have proved that we do have something to contribute to the mutual understanding of the world, what we have in common and not what our differences are. If we can all come together it will be for a better world and we shall avoid the holocaust which may well be upon us if we are not careful."[37]

NOTES

1. From which the modern word *stadium* is derived.

2. See David C. Young, *The Olympic Myth of Greek Amateur Athletes* (Chicago: Ares, 1984).

3. Background books on the Ancient Olympic Games are myriad. Please refer to the bibliography for a complete listing for further reference.

4. The most complete early description of the various attempts to revive the Olympic Games, though now somewhat dated, was given in Karl Lennartz, *Kenntnisse und Vorstellungen von Olympia und den Olympischen Spielen in der Zeit von 393–1896* (Schorndorf: Verlag Karl Hofmann, 1974). A more recent work focusing a bit more on the Greek efforts is Konstantinos Georgiadis, *Olympic Revival: The Revival of the Olympic Games in Modern Times* (Athens: Ektodike Athenon, 2003).

5. For information specifically about Coubertin's efforts to resuscitate the Olympic Games, see John J. MacAloon, *This Great Symbol: Pierre de Coubertin and the Origins of the Modern Olympic Games* (Chicago: University of Chicago Press, 1981); and David C. Young, *The Modern Olympics: A Struggle for Revival* (Baltimore: Johns

Hopkins University Press, 1996). Their approaches are different, with MacAloon emphasizing Coubertin's contributions, while Young discusses the efforts of Panagiotis Soutsos, a Greek poet of the mid-19th century, and William Penny Brookes, but they complement each other in subject matter.

6. By far the best and most complete description of Coubertin's works is the encyclopedic, three-volume set, Norbert Müller, ed., *Pierre de Coubertin: Textes Choisis* (Zürich/Hildesheim/New York: Weidmann, 1986). Now in DVD format.

7. There are many books on the 1896 Olympic Games, but the series by Mallon on the 1896–1920 Olympic Games (Jefferson, N.C.: McFarland, 1997–1999) provides background for the 1896, 1900, and 1904 Olympic Games. For 1900, see also André Drevon, *Les Jeux Olympiques Oublié* (Paris: CNRS Editions, 2000).

8. The best short analysis of the 1906 Olympic Games and their status as Olympic Games is the monograph by Karl Lennartz, "The 2nd International Olympic Games in Athens 1906," published in a special commemorative edition of the *Journal of Olympic History* 10 (December 2001–January 2002): 10–26.

9. Complete descriptions of all the controversies at the 1908 Olympics Games are given in Bill Mallon and Ian Buchanan, *The 1908 Olympic Games: Results for all Competitors in All Events, with Commentary* (Jefferson, N.C.: McFarland, 2000). The section describing the controversies and protests is found on pages 313–406 of that book.

10. For a comprehensive reference, see Miguelde Moragas Spà, Nancy K. Rivenburgh, and James F. Larson, *Television in the Olympics* (London: John Libbey, 1995).

11. See either Allen Guttmann, *The Olympics: A History of the Modern Games* (Urbana and Chicago: University of Illinois Press, 1992) or Alfred E. Senn, *Power, Politics, and the Olympic Games: A History of the Power Brokers, Events, and Controversies that Shaped the Games* (Champaign, Ill.: Human Kinetics, 1999).

12. Speech to the sports youth of all nations at Olympia, Greece, 17 April 1927; quoted in *The International Pierre de Coubertin Committee*, 15 (Lausanne: International Pierre de Coubertin, 1983).

13. Richard W. Pound, *Five Rings Over Korea: The Secret Negotiations Behind the 1988 Olympic Games in Seoul* (Boston: Little, Brown, 1994).

14. "Fundamental Principles" No. 4, *Olympic Charter* (Lausanne: International Olympic Committee, 4 July 2003), 9. Please note that the new edition of the *Olympic Charter*, as of 1 September 2004, does not contain quite this same phrase.

15. "Fundamental Principles" No. 6, *Olympic Charter* (Lausanne: International Olympic Committee, 1 September 2004), 9.

16. "Fundamental Principles" No. 1, *Olympic Charter* (Lausanne: International Olympic Committee, 1 September 2004), 9.

17. "Fundamental Principles" No. 2, *Olympic Charter* (Lausanne: International Olympic Committee, 4 July 2003), 9.

18. Conrado Durántez Corral, *Pierre de Coubertin: The Olympic Humanist* (Lausanne: International Olympic Committee and International Pierre de Coubertin Committee, 1994), 27.

19. Ibid., 29.

20. Ibid.

21. Ibid., 36.

22. A very solid analysis of the IOC's ventures into commercialism and the problems engendered there in is Robert K. Barney, Stephen R. Wenn, and Scott G. Martyn, *Selling the Five Rings: The International Olympic Committee and the Rise of Commercialism* (Salt Lake City: University of Utah Press, 2002).

23. Ibid., 33.

24. See Young, *Olympic Myth of Greek Amateur Athletes*.

25. *USA Today* (March 1995).

26. Further details of the massacre of the Israelis at the 1972 Olympics can be found in Serge Groussard, *The Blood of Israel: The Massacre of the Israeli Athletes: The Olympics 1972* (New York: Morrow, 1975); Simon Reeve, *One Day in September: The Full Story of the 1972 Munich Olympics Massacre and the Israeli Revenge Operation "Wrath of God"* (New York: Arcade, 2000); and Richard D. Mandell, *A Munich Diary: The Olympics of 1972* (Chapel Hill: University of North Carolina Press, 1991).

27. Christopher Rhoads, "The Newest Wonder of the World: The Ruins of Modern Greece," *Wall Street Journal*, 17 June 2010.

28. Pierre de Coubertin, *Olympic Review* (April 1911): 59–62.

29. The topic of the economics of the Olympic Games is a difficult one, but the first book-length analysis of the problem was Holger Preuss, *Economics of the Olympic Games: Hosting the Games 1972–2000* (Petersham, NSW, Australia: Walla Walla Press, 2000).

30. The fullest description of the problems of drug use in sport and also addressing some of the controversies can be found in Wayne Wilson and Edward Derse, *Doping in Elite Sport: The Politics of Drugs in the Olympic Movement* (Champaign, Ill.: Human Kinetics, 2000).

31. There is even now a Sport and Environment Commission.

32. "Fundamental Principles" Rule 2.13, *Olympic Charter* (Lausanne: International Olympic Committee, 1 September 2004), 12.

33. Bill Mallon, *The Olympics: A Bibliography* (New York: Garland, 1984), ix.

34. Ibid., v.

35. *Los Angeles Times*, July 1982.

36. Originally quoted in *The Times* (London), 2 November 1908, 17; see also Bill Mallon and Ian Buchanan, *The 1908 Olympic Game: Results for All Competitors in All Events, with Commentary* (Jefferson, N.C.: McFarland, 2000), 17.

37. Lord Killanin, *My Olympic Years* (London: Secker & Wartburg, 1983), 187.

AAMODT, KJETIL ANDRÉ (NOR–ASK). B. 2 September 1971, Oslo, Norway. Kjetil André Aamodt's record of eight **Olympic medals** (four gold, two silver, two bronze) in **Alpine skiing** is unmatched at the **Olympic Winter Games**, and his four gold medals are matched only by **Janica Kostelić** (CRO). Aamodt, five feet, nine inches (176 cm) tall, 187 lb (85 kg), competed in five Olympics (1992, 1994, 1998, 2002, and 2006) and was entered in a total of 20 events (the **downhill** and **super G** five times each, the **giant slalom** four times, **combined** and **slalom** three times each). He also won 12 medals at the World Championships, including five golds, three consecutively in the combined (1997–2001). He won 21 races in the World Cup (one downhill, one slalom, five super G, six giant slalom, eight combined), was overall World Cup champion in 1994, and also won nine seasonal World Cup **disciplines** titles.

ACROBATICS. Acrobatics has never been contested at the **Olympic Games**, even as a **demonstration sport**. The sport has been contested internationally since 1973 and was formerly governed by the International Federation of Sports Acrobatics (IFSA), which was previously recognized by the **International Olympic Committee**. In 1998, the IFSA dissolved itself and merged with the Fédération Internationale de Gymnastique.

AERIALS. Aerials for both men and **women** is one of the events contested in **freestyle skiing**. It was first held as a medal sport at Lillehammer in the 1994 **Olympic Winter Games** and has been contested in each of the five subsequent Winter Games. The only multiple medalists have been Li Nina of **China** (silver 2006 and 2010), Alisa Camplin of **Australia** (gold 2002, bronze 2006), and Lydia Ierodiaconou-Lassila of Australia (gold 2010, bronze 2014) in women's aerials and Aleksey Grishin (bronze 2002, gold 2010) and Dmitry Dashchinsky (bronze 1998, silver 2006), both of **Belarus**, in men's aerials.

AERONAUTICS. Aeronautics is governed internationally by the Fédération Aéronautique Internationale, which also calls itself the World Air Sports Federation. The federation was created in 1905 and is recognized by the **Interna-**

tional Olympic Committee. There were 105 affiliated nations as of 2014: 85 active members, 10 associate members, six temporary members, and four affiliate members. In addition, there were eight members listed as "suspended" members and one prospective member. At the 1936 **Olympic Games,** a gold medal for Merit for Aeronautics was presented to Hermann Schreiber (SUI), and a **gliding** exhibition was held at the 1936 Olympics in Berlin.

AFGHANISTAN (AFG). The Central Asian nation of Afghanistan (officially known as the Islamic Republic of Afghanistan) first competed at the 1936 Olympics in Berlin, the same year in which its **National Olympic Committee** (NOC) was recognized by the **International Olympic Committee** (IOC). Since then, the central Asian country was not represented at the **Olympic Games** of 1952, 1976, 1984, 1992, and 2000. Afghanistan's NOC was suspended by the IOC in 1999, and it was not eligible to compete at Sydney because the NOC did not follow the *Olympic Charter*, most notably by prohibiting **women** in sport under the ruling Taliban. After the Afghan War of 2001–2002, Afghanistan formed a new NOC and competed in 2004 at Athens, 2008 in Beijing, and 2012 in London. Afghanistan has never competed at the **Olympic Winter Games.**

In 13 Summer Games, Afghanistan has entered 101 athletes (98 men, three women) in seven sports: **athletics** (10 men, two women), **boxing** (five men), **football** (11 men), **hockey** (33 men), **judo** (one man, one woman), **taekwondo** (three men), and **wrestling** (35 men). Through the 20th century, the most successful Afghani at the Olympic Games was Sayid M. Yusuf, who won a gold medal in 1928 as a member of the **Indian field hockey** team. But in 2008 at Beijing, Rohullah Nikpai won a bronze medal in men's **flyweight** taekwondo, the first medal won by an Afghani athlete representing Afghanistan. Nikpai moved up to **featherweight** in 2012 and won his second Olympic bronze medal. Other notable performances by Afghani athletes include the 1936 men's field hockey team, which finished tied for fifth of 11 teams, Nesar Ahmad Bahawi who won two bouts and finished tied for fifth of 16 entrants in **welterweight** taekwondo in 2012, and Mohammad Ebrahimi who won two bouts and finished fifth of 21 entrants in 1964 featherweight **freestyle** wrestling.

AINSLIE, CHARLES BENEDICT "BEN" (GBR–SAI). B. 5 February 1977, Macclesfield, Cheshire East, **England.** The son of a noted **sailor,** Ben Ainslie is one of the top Olympic sailors. At six feet tall (183 cm) and 198 lb (90 kg), he has won four consecutive titles in one-person **dinghy,** from 2000 to 2012. After winning a silver medal in the 1996 Laser class, he upgraded to gold in Sydney, while in Athens, Beijing, and London, he collected gold in the Finn class. His five medals and four gold medals are both tied for the best accomplishments in Olympic sailing. In addition to his **Olympic medal** collection, he has won six world titles in the Finn, two in the Laser, and one in the Laser Radial. In European Championships, he won nine titles: four in Finn, four in Laser, and one in Laser Radial class. Ainslie was rated International Sailing Federation sailor of the year four times and was made Commander of the Order of the British Empire in 2008, following his third Olympic title. In 2013, he was titled a Knight Bachelor and is now properly addressed as Sir Ben Ainslie.

AIR PISTOL. Air pistol **shooting** at a distance of 10 meters for both men and **women** is one of the events contested in **Olympic Games** shooting competition. It has been held at each Summer Games since 1988. Wang Yifu of **China** has won four medals in men's competition (gold 1992, 2004; silver 1996, 2000). **Serbian** Jasna Šekarić won four medals in women's competition (gold for **Yugoslavia** 1988, silver in 1992 as an **independent Olympic athlete**, and silver again in 2000 and 2004 for **Serbia** and **Montenegro**).

AIR RIFLE. Air rifle **shooting** at a distance of 10 meters for both men and **women** is one of the events contested in **Olympic Games** shooting competition. It has been held at each Summer Games since 1984. Kateřina Kůrková-Emmons of the **Czech Republic** (bronze 2004, gold 2008) and Lyubov Galkina of **Russia** (silver medals in 2004 and 2008) are the only women to win multiple medals in this event. Zhu Qinan of **China** (gold 2004, silver 2008), Artyom Khadzhibekov of Russia (gold 1996, silver 2000), and Hans Riederer of **Germany** (bronze in 1988 representing **West Germany** and 1992 representing united Germany) are the only men to win multiple medals in this event.

ALBANIA (ALB). Albania's **National Olympic Committee** was founded in 1958 and recognized by the **International Olympic Committee** in 1959, but Albania did not compete at the Olympics until 1972. It then did not compete again at the Olympics for 20 years (although it is unclear whether the absences were due to **boycotts**) and returned in each of the next Summer Games from 1992 to 2012. The southeastern European nation of Albania (officially known as the Republic of Albania) has not won any medals and has competed at the **Olympic Winter Games** three times, having been represented by **Alpine skier** Erjon Tola in 2006, 2010, and 2014. He was joined by Suela Mëhilli in 2014 who competed in two **women**'s Alpine skiing events. Albania's best Winter Olympics result was Tola's 35th place of 82 entrants in the 2006 **giant slalom**.

In seven Summer Games Albania has competed in seven sports with 39 entrants (27 men, 12 women). They have participated in **athletics** (three men, four women), **cycling** (one man), **judo** (one man, one woman), **shooting** (five men, four women), **swimming** (three men, two women), **weightlifting** (11 men, one woman), and **wrestling** (three men). Their best performances were in shooting and weightlifting.

In 1972, Ismail Rama finished 22nd of 101 entrants in the **small-bore rifle** prone position event and is the only Albanian Olympian to finish in the top 25 percent of his class. Two other Albanian athletes in 2000 (Djana Mata, women's sporting pistol, tied for 11th of 42 competitors, and Ilirjan Suli, fifth of 17 in the **middleweight** weightlifting event) finished in the top third.

Suli's fifth-place finish is the highest for an Albanian Olympian and was nearly matched by Romela Begaj who was sixth of 12 entrants in the 2008 women's **lightweight** weightlifting.

Albania has had fairly good weightlifters, and a few of its lifters have emigrated to **Greece** and competed for that nation at the Olympics, notably **Pyrros Dimas**, who was born in Albania but won gold medals for Greece in weightlifting in 1996, 2000, and 2004 and a bronze medal in 2008.

ALEKSEYEV, VASILIY IVANOVICH (URS–WLT). B. 7 January 1942, Pokrovo-Shishkino, Ryazan Oblast, **Russia**, USSR. D. 25 November 2011, Munich, Bayern, **Germany**. Unbeaten from 1970 to mid-1978, Vasiliy Alekseyev is the greatest **super-heavyweight weightlifter** in history. His feat of winning eight successive gold medals at the **Olympic Games** and World Championships (1970–1977) equaled the record of Americans John Davis and **Tommy Kono**. Alekseyev won the gold medal in the unlimited weight class at the 1972 and 1976 Olympics. Although injured, he competed in 1980 at Moscow, but did not finish. The six-feet, one inch (185 cm), 353 lb (160 kg) Alekseyev also won eight European titles and set 79 world records. He was finally defeated at the 1978 World Championships when suffering from a damaged hip tendon.

ALGERIA (ALG). Algeria formed a **National Olympic Committee** in 1963 that was recognized by the **International Olympic Committee** in 1964 and first competed officially at the 1964 **Olympic Games**. The North African nation, officially known as the People's Democratic Republic of Algeria, has since competed at all Olympic Games save 1976, which they **boycotted** along with most of the other African countries. Algeria also competed at the **Olympic Winter Games** in 1992, 2006, and 2010. In 12 Summer Games, they have entered 314 athletes (267 men, 47 **women**) in 19 sports with most of the individual athletes competing in **athletics** (66 men, nine women), **boxing** (48 men), and **judo** (20 men, eight women). Algeria has also competed in men's **football** in 1980; men's **handball** in 1980, 1984, 1988, and 1996;

men's **volleyball** in 1992, and women's volleyball in 2008 and 2012. In three Winter Games, they have had three men and two women compete in **Alpine skiing** and two men in **cross-country skiing**, although none of their performances were exceptional, with Nacera Boukamoum's finish of 42nd of 69 in the women's **giant slalom** in 1992 being their best result.

Through 2014, Algerians have won 15 **Olympic medals** (five gold, two silver, eight bronze). Seven of their medals came in track and field athletics (four gold, one silver, two bronze), six in boxing (one gold, five bronze), and two in judo (one silver, one bronze). Boxer Hocine Soltani won two medals—a bronze in 1992 and a gold in 1996—and after becoming a professional boxer was found dead in 2004, presumably murdered in 2002. Algeria's other gold medalists were all won by 1,500 meter runners Hassiba Boulmerka (women's, 1992), Noureddine Morceli (men's, 1996), Nouria Mérah-Benida (women's, 2000), and Taoufik Makhloufi (men's 2012).

Prior to Algeria's independence in July 1962, several Algerian athletes competed for **France** at the Olympics. The first were four **gymnasts** from Oran, who took part in the 1900 Olympic Games, and they had the distinction of being the first African Olympians. Two Olympic **marathon** winners, Muhammad Boughera El Ouafi (1928) and Alain Mimoun (1956), were both Algerians representing France.

ALI, MUHAMMAD (né CASSIUS MARCELLUS CLAY) (USA–BOX). B. 17 January 1942, Louisville, Kentucky, **United States**. Muhammad Ali first gained international prominence as Cassius Clay by winning the **light-heavyweight** (176 lb [80 kg]) **boxing** gold medal at the 1960 Rome Olympics at six feet, two inches (187 cm) tall. As a professional boxer in February 1964, weighing 210 lb (95 kg) and one inch taller (191 cm), he upset Charles "Sonny" Liston to win the world **heavyweight** championship. Shortly after the fight, he embraced the Muslim faith and took the name Muhammad Ali. No fighter defeated him for the rest of the 1960s, but Ali was defeated by the United States draft board when he refused induction into military service based on a conscientious objection, and he was subsequently stripped of his heavyweight title. Eventually, Ali won his battle against the draft board in the Supreme Court, but the best years of his career had been lost. He returned to fighting in 1970 and the next year lost a much ballyhooed fight against another former Olympic champion, **Joe Frazier**. They fought two other times and after their final epic battle, "The Thrilla in Manila," his redoubtable opponent, Frazier, said of him, "Lawdy, lawdy, he's a great champion. I hit him with punches that'd bring down the walls of a city and he took them." In 1974, Ali regained the heavyweight championship against **George Foreman**, also an Olympic champion, and, after losing to former Olympian Leon Spinks in 1978, Ali became the only man to hold the title three times by defeating Spinks in a rematch. Ali's career professional record was 56 wins (37 by **knockout**) and five losses. Sadly, he later suffered from a relatively advanced case of Parkinson's disease, probably from many years of taking punches. In 1996, one of the highlights of the **Olympic Games** in Atlanta was when Ali was chosen to be the last torch bearer for the opening ceremony and ran up the stairs to light the **Olympic flame** in the cauldron. The unannounced surprise of seeing him run with the torch, although physically shaking from the effects of Parkinson's disease, brought chills to many of the spectators. In 2012, Ali made an appearance at the opening ceremony of the London Olympic Games.

ALL-AROUND. In the sport of **athletics**, the **decathlon** event for men and **heptathlon** for **women** recognize all-around performance, although the phrase "all-around" is not used formally for those events.

In the sport of **gymnastics**, the best all-around individual and team performances for both men and women are rewarded with medals. Men's individual all-around has been recognized in every **Olympic Games** since 1900. Alberto Braglia of **Italy** (silver 1906, gold 1908, 1912) and **Sawao Kato** of **Japan** (gold 1968, 1972, silver 1976) are the only three-time men's individual all-around medalists. Women's individual all-around has been recognized since 1952. **Larysa Latynina** of the **Soviet Union** (gold 1956, 1960, silver 1964) is the only three-time women's individual all-around medalist. Men's team all-around has been recognized in each Olympic Games since 1904. Japan has won the most medals in the team category with 12: six gold, three silver, and three bronze. Although a women's individual all-around champion has only been recognized since 1952, a women's team all-around champion has been rewarded since 1928. From 1952 through 1980, the Soviet Union won this title in every Olympic Games, and after their **boycott** in 1984, returned to win it once more in 1988. When the former Soviet republics competed as the Unified Team in 1992, they again won this title.

ALPINE SKIING. Alpine ski racing is a newer form of ski racing, as **Nordic**, or **cross-country**, competitions were held in the Scandinavian countries for many years before Alpine racing was developed. The first known Alpine skiing race was in 1911 at Montana, **Switzerland**, when the British organized a **downhill** race for a challenge cup given by Lord Roberts of Kandahar. The first **slalom**-style race was held in 1922 at Mürren, Switzerland.

Alpine skiing was first placed on the **Olympic Program** in 1936 at Garmisch-Partenkirchen. The only event that year was a **combined** competition of both downhill and slalom. In 1948, this was held again along with separate downhill and slalom races. In 1952, the **giant slalom** was added as an event, and in 1988, the **super G** became a fourth separate event. Alpine combination, originally a point-scored mix of downhill and slalom, returned to the **Olympic Winter Games** in 1988, after not being contested between 1952 and 1984. It has since been switched to being decided on time rather than points.

Events for both sexes were held in 1936 and have been at all Olympics since. Men and **women** contest Alpine skiing separately, but interestingly, the program for men and women has been identical at all Olympics. The sport is governed by the Fédération Internationale de Ski, which was founded in 1924 and had 118 member nations as of June 2014.

The greatest alpine skiers among the men have been **Toni Sailer** of **Austria** and **Jean-Claude Killy** of **France**, both of whom won all three gold medals available in 1956 and 1968, respectively, and **Kjetil André Aamodt** of **Norway**, who won a record eight medals, including four gold medals, in the sport. Two women, **Croatia**'s **Janica Kostelić** and **Sweden**'s **Anja Pärson**, both have six **Olympic medals**, a record for women, with Kostelić equaling Aamodt with four golds. In 2014, **Bode Miller** (USA) won his sixth medal, although it was a bronze medal in the super G in which he and Jan Hudec (CAN) tied to the hundredth of a second for third place. Through 2014, four skiers had each won five medals: **Alberto Tomba** of **Italy**, **Vreni Schneider** of Switzerland, **Katja Seizinger** of **Germany**, and Lasse Kjus of Norway. At Salt Lake City in 2002, Kostelić won three gold medals (in five events) and became the first Alpine skier to win four medals at a single Winter Olympics. Austria, Switzerland, and France have been the top nations in Olympic Alpine skiing, with Italy and the **United States** not far behind. Through 2014, there have been 2,735 participants (1,739 men and 996 women) from 101 countries who have competed in Alpine skiing in the 19 Winter Games in which it has been contested. *See also* MITTERMAIER, ROSEMARIE; VON FÜRSTEN-BERG-VON HOHENLOHE-LANGENBURG, HUBERTUS RUDOLPH; WENZEL, HANNELORE.

ALPINISM. Alpinism is governed internationally by the Union Internationale des Associations d'Alpinisme, also known as the International Mountaineering and Climbing Federation. It was created in 1932 in Chamonix, **France**, and is recognized by the **International Olympic Committee**, with 80 affiliated member nations in 50 countries as of 2014. Baron **Pierre de Coubertin** had plans for medals to be awarded for alpinism at the **Olympic Games** in his original Olympic Rules from the 1894 **Olympic Congress**. It is mentioned in the original program for the first Olympic Games, and eventually medals for Merit for Alpinism were presented at the 1924, 1932, and 1936 Olympic Games to a total of 24 men and one woman from six nations.

AMERICAN FOOTBALL. *See* FOOTBALL, AMERICAN.

AMERICAN SAMOA (ASA). The **United States** unincorporated territory islands of American Samoa located in the South Pacific has competed at each Summer **Olympic Games** from 1988 to 2012 and also the 1994 **Olympic Winter Games.** At the Winter Games, they entered the two-man **bobsledding** and finished 39th of 43 teams. They have had 23 competitors (19 men, four **women**) in eight sports in the Summer Games: **archery** (one man), **athletics** (five men, one woman), **boxing** (two men), **judo** (one man, one woman), **sailing** (two men), **swimming** (two men, two women), **weightlifting** (five men), and **wrestling** (two men). Alesana Sione was one of the few Olympians to compete in two different sports 12 years apart. He was a wrestler in 1988 and a weightlifter in 2000 but had minimal success in both endeavors.

In 1992, Maselino Masoe stopped his first two opponents in **light-middleweight** boxing before losing a unanimous decision in the quarter-final round to finish equal fifth of 30 in his class, the top finish to date from this small island nation. In 1988, Gary Fanelli was 51st of 118 competitors in the **marathon**. In 2000, Lisa Misipeka was 14th of 28 entrants in the women's **hammer throw**. American Samoans have done exceptionally well in American professional football and professional wrestling as well as in **sumo** wrestling and the **rugby** league. Unfortunately, none of these activities are contested in the Olympic Games.

AMMANN, SIMON (SUI–SKJ). B. 25 June 1981, Grabs, Sankt-Gallen, **Switzerland.** After **Matti Nykänen** of **Finland**, Simon Ammann is only the second **ski jumper** to have won four Olympic titles. Uniquely, he won both individual events (**normal hill, large hill**) at both the 2002 and 2010 **Olympic Winter Games.** His first two titles came as a complete surprise, as the five-foot, seven-inch (171 cm), 121 lb (55 kg) Ammann had never won a serious international competition prior to his Olympic victories. After a less successful period, Ammann dominated in 2010, winning the season's World Cup in addition to his Olympic titles. He also won two world titles, taking the large hill competition at the 2007 World Championships as well as the 2010 ski flying title. In World Cup competition since 1997, Ammann has won 21 events through June 2014. In 2014, he was the Swiss flag bearer during the opening ceremony at Sochi and competed in his fifth Olympic Winter Games.

AN, VIKTOR (né AN HYEON-SU) (KOR/RUS–STK). B. 23 November 1985, Seoul, **Korea.** Viktor An (sometimes spelled Ahn) is a Korean **short track speed skater** who after the 2014 Sochi **Winter Games** was tied with **Apolo Anton Ohno** for the most **Olympic medals** in the sport with eight.

An leads all short track speed skaters with six Olympic gold medals. He first competed for Korea in 2002 at the age of 16 and finished fourth in the 1,000 meter and 13th in the 1,500 meter races. In 2006, he won three gold medals and one bronze medal in four events. He then suffered some injuries and had some disputes with Korean skating officials and moved to **Russia**. The five-foot, seven-inch (170 cm), 143 lb (65 kg) An did not compete in the Olympics in 2010, but in 2014 he was one of the stars of that year's Games as he won three more gold and one bronze medal in four races. He has also won 34 medals (20 gold, 10 silver, four bronze) at the World Championships, six others (two gold) at the World Team Championships, five gold medals at the European Championships, and five other gold medals at the Asian Games.

AN HYEON-SU. *See* AN, VIKTOR.

ANCIENT OLYMPIC GAMES. The Ancient Olympic Games were one of the four great Panhellenic sporting festivals of ancient **Greece**, along with the **Isthmian, Nemean,** and **Pythian Games.** The Olympic Games were considered to be the greatest of the Panhellenic contests. The first recorded Olympics are known to have been held in 776 B.C., although it is probable that they began several centuries earlier. The Games lasted until A.D. 393, when they were banned by imperial decree of the Roman Emperor Theodosius I. The Ancient Olympic Games were held in Olympia, which was near the city-state of Elis on the Greek Peloponnesus. (They were *not* held on or near Mount Olympus, as is often incorrectly written.) The Ancient Olympic Games were held quadrennially, and winners at the Ancient Olympic Games received crowns of wild olive leaves.

The origins of the Ancient Olympic Games are uncertain, but several traditional explanations exist. One connects the Games to Pelops, after whom the Peloponnesus was named. Pelops was a Phrygian who made his way to the peninsula that would later take his name. There he defeated Oenomaus, king of Pisa, in a **chariot race,** which Oenomaus had ordered as a race in which Pelops could win the hand of his daughter, Hippodameia. Oenomaus was thrown from his chariot and killed, and Pelops was worshiped as a hero. He took over the kingdom, and the Games were supposedly held at his tomb and in his honor. Later beliefs, popularized by **Pindar,** state that the Games originated to honor Hercules, and he founded them after his victory over Augeas. Hercules declared the Games to be in honor of his father, Zeus.

Originally, the Ancient Olympic Games consisted of only a single footrace, one length of the Ancient Olympic stadium of about 192 meters, and now termed the *stadion* **race.** Champions are recorded in this event from 776 B.C. (**Coroebus of Elis**) until A.D. 269. A second race of two laps of the stadium, termed the *diaulos*, was added in 724 B.C., followed in 720 B.C. by the *dolikhos*, which was a long-distance race of about 20 to 25 laps of the stadium. **Wrestling** champions are recorded from 708 B.C., while **boxing** was added to the list of victors in 688 B.C. The **pentathlon**, an **all-around** championship of five events, was added at the Olympics of 708 B.C. The **pankration**, which was a brutal combination of wrestling and boxing, was known to have been contested at the Ancient Olympics from 648 B.C.

A number of horse races and chariot races were also contested at the Olympic Games. There were events at Olympia for boys, who were defined as being older than 12 but less than 18 years old. **Competitions for heralds** and lyre playing were also held at the Ancient Olympics.

Athletes from the Peloponnesus dominated the earliest Olympics, winning the first 13 *stadion* events, but Greeks from other city-states later produced many Olympic champions. Elis produced the most known Ancient Olympic champions, with 110 recorded victories, followed by Sparta, with 76 known victories. In the later years of the Ancient Olympics, athletes from the Roman Empire began to compete at Olympia, winning many titles. The Ancient Olympic Games reached their zenith in the Golden Age of Greece, dimming once the Roman Empire took over the celebrations. *See also APENE*; *KALPE*; *KELES*; LEONIDAS OF RHODES; MILON OF KROTON; RACE IN ARMOR; *SYNORIS*; *TETHRIPPON*; THEAGENES OF THASOS.

ANDERSEN, HJALMAR JOHAN (NOR–SSK). B. 12 March 1923, Rødoy, Nordland, **Norway**. D. 27 March 2013, Oslo, Norway. After failing to complete the 10,000 meter race at the 1948 St. Moritz **Olympic Winter Games** due to the altitude and warm slushy conditions, Hjalmar Andersen was the winner of three **speed skating** gold medals in Oslo at the 1952 Winter Games (1,500 meters, 5,000 meters, 10,000 meters). His winning margin in the 5,000 meters was an astounding 11 seconds, and he also won the 10,000 meters by a substantial margin. Andersen retired after the 1952 Games, but returned to competition in 1954 to win his fourth Norwegian title, having earlier won the World, European, and Norwegian **all-around** titles in 1950–1952. He entered two races at Cortina d'Ampezzo in the 1956 Winter Games and was 11th in 5,000 meters and sixth in the 10,000 meters. During his career, he set one world record at 5,000 meters and three at 10,000 meters. His grandson, Fredrik van der Horst, competed in two speed skating events for Norway at the 2010 Winter Games in Vancouver and finished in fourth place in the team **pursuit**.

ANDERSON, PAUL EDWARD (USA–WLT). B. 17 October 1932, Toccoa, Georgia, **United States**. D. 15 August 1994, Vidalia, Georgia, United States.

After winning the world **heavyweight weightlifting** title by a record margin in 1955, Paul Anderson won the Olympic gold medal in Melbourne the following year and in the process set new **Olympic Games** records for the **clean and jerk** lift and total lift. He actually was tied for the total lift with **Argentinean** Humberto Selvetti but was awarded the gold medal because his body weight of 303 lb (137.4 kg) at five feet, 10 inches (178 cm) was less than that of Selvetti who weighed 316 lb (143.3 kg). Anderson was quite possibly the strongest man who ever lived and set hundreds of records as a powerlifter, including a bench **press** of 625 lb (284 kg), a squat with 1,200 lb (545 kg), a dead-lift of 820 lb (373 kg), and three repetitions in the squat with 900 lb (409 kg). After the Olympic Games, Anderson went professional and gave strength exhibitions. In one exhibition in 1957, he lifted on his back a table weighing 6,270 lb (2,844 kg), the greatest weight ever lifted by a human. From 1958 to 1960, he was a professional **wrestler** and in 1960 appeared in four professional **boxing** bouts. A devout Christian, he built the Paul Anderson Youth Home in 1961 in Vidalia, Georgia, a "Christian residential home for troubled young men," and spent the rest of his life helping wayward boys. Although he died in 1994, the Home was still in operation in 2014.

ANDERSSON, AGNETA MONICA (SWE–CAN). B. 25 April 1961, Karlskoga, Örebro, **Sweden**. With seven **Olympic medals**, including three gold medals, Sweden's Agneta Andersson trails only **Birgit Fischer-Schmidt** of **East Germany** and Katalin Kovács of **Hungary** among female **canoeists** at the Olympics. The five-foot, eight-inch (172 cm), 150 lb (68 kg) Andersson began her Olympic career in 1980 and finished fifth in the K-1 and sixth in the K-2. Four years later, she did much better, winning gold in both the K-1 and K-2 events and silver in the K-4. She competed at the 1988 Olympics, but failed to medal. In 1992, she won silver in K-2 and bronze in K-4, while in 1996 she ended her career with gold in K-2 and bronze in the K-4 event. Andersson was less successful at the World Championships in terms of titles, claiming only the 1993 K-2 gold, but she won 11 medals at the Worlds in an international career that began in 1979.

ANDORRA (AND). At the end of 1967, an Andorran committee, which had been set up to form a **National Olympic Committee**, approached the **International Olympic Committee** (IOC) with a view to obtain recognition in time to send a team of **Alpine skiers** to the 1968 **Olympic Winter Games** in Grenoble. A few Andorrans had also represented **Spain** at the Olympic Winter Games prior to 1968. As the draft constitution submitted did not comply with the Olympic rules on many points, the application was rejected, and it was not until 1975 that the IOC approved a revised set of rules. This enabled

Andorra, a small mountainous landlocked European nation (181 square miles [468 sq km]) between Spain and **France**, to take part in the 1976 Olympic Winter Games in Innsbruck, and since it has competed in every Olympics, both Winter and Summer, although it has never had more than eight competitors at any Olympics, in 1992 at Barcelona and 1996 at Atlanta.

Andorra, officially known as the Principality of Andorra, in 10 Summer Games has had a total of 29 Olympians (20 men, nine **women**) competing in **athletics** (two men, four women), **boxing** (one man), **canoeing** (one woman), **cycling** (three men), **judo** (three men), **sailing** (two men, one woman), **shooting** (six men), and **swimming** (three men, three women) and 28 Winter Olympians (21 men, seven women) competing in Alpine skiing (19 men, six women), **biathlon** (one woman), **cross-country skiing** (one man), and **snowboarding** (one man).

The country has not yet won a medal at the Olympics, its best finish being in the 1988 men's cycling **road race** when Emili Pérez placed ninth, although he finished in the same group as the bronze medalist, 24 seconds behind the gold medalist. Other notable results by Andorran Olympians include Emili's brother, Xavier Pérez, finishing 31st of 154 entrants in the 1992 cycling road race, Daniel García finishing tied for ninth of 36 in 2012 men's **half-lightweight** judo, Gerard Escoda finishing 32nd of 119 in 1992 men's **slalom** Alpine skiing, and Escoda at 36th and Nahum Orobitg in 38th place of 131 contestants in the 1992 men's **giant slalom**. Vicky Grau is Andorra's top female Olympic athlete by virtue of her results in slalom competition in 1998 (19th of 57) and 2002 (24th of 68).

Marathon runner Toni Bernardó competed in five Olympic Games for Andorra with his best result in 2000 (49th of 100 entrants). Shooter Joan Tomas first competed for Andorra in **trapshooting** in 1980 at the age of 25, and 36 years later competed in his fifth Olympic tournament at the age of 61 after being the flag-bearer in the opening ceremony of 2012. The Andorran capital city of Andorra la Vella was an unsuccessful bidder to host the 2010 Olympic Winter Games.

ANDRIANOV, NIKOLAY YEFIMOVICH (URS–GYM). B. 14 October 1952, Vladimir, **Russia**, USSR. D. 21 March 2011, Vladimir, Russian Federation. Nikolay Andrianov was the most successful Olympic male **gymnast** of all time. Between 1972 and 1980, he won seven gold medals (six individual, one team), five silvers, and three bronzes, for a total of 15 medals, at the time an Olympic record for men in any sport. At the World Championships, he won gold on the **rings** in 1974, the **all-around** and rings in 1978, and the team event in 1979. At five feet, five inches (166 cm), 132 lb (60 kg), he also won seven silver medals at the World Championships.

Andrianov's international career started at the 1971 European Championships, where he was a late substitute; he won six medals that year, including a bronze in the all-around. In individual European Championships, he eventually won eight gold, six silver, and two bronze medals, including five gold in 1975. He was married to Lyubov Burda, a two-time gold medalist for the Soviet Union in gymnastics. In 1980, he was given the honor of reciting the **Olympic Oath** on behalf of the athletes during the opening ceremony of the Moscow **Olympic Games**.

ANGOLA (ANG). Angola's first application for Olympic recognition was rejected at the 1975 **International Olympic Committee** session in **Lausanne**, but after the formation of a **National Olympic Committee** in 1979, recognition was granted in 1980. After first competing at the Olympics that year, the Southern Africa nation of Angola (then officially known as the People's Republic of Angola) **boycotted** the 1984 Games. Since 1988, it has competed at each subsequent **Olympic Games**, but has not yet competed at the **Olympic Winter Games**. In 1992, the country became known officially as the Republic of Angola.

In the eight Summer Games in which it has participated, Angola has had 148 entrants (82 men, 66 **women**). They have competed in eight individual sports: **athletics** (11 men, four women), **beach volleyball** (two men), **boxing** (seven men), **canoeing** (two men), **judo** (10 men, one woman), **sailing** (three men), **shooting** (two men), and **swimming** (11 men, seven women) and two team sports: men's and women's **basketball** (34 men, 12 women) and women's **handball** (42 women). The top Angolan Olympic performance occurred in 2000 when João N'Tyamba finished 17th of 100 entrants in the men's **marathon**. He has competed in six Olympic Games at distances ranging from 800 meters to the marathon. In 1988, **lightweight** *judoka* Lotuala N'Dombassy finished in a two-way tie for ninth position out of 41 entrants. The men's basketball team has qualified for five Olympic tournaments (1992–2008) and are undoubtedly the best African basketball team in recent years. Their best Olympic Games result was in 1992 when they finished 10th of 12 teams and was the opponent of the **United States "Dream Team"** in the opening game of the tournament for the two teams. The Angola women's handball team has also been the top African team in that sport and represented their country in each of five consecutive Olympics from 1996 to 2012 with a best result of 10th of 12 teams in 2012.

ANTIGUA AND BARBUDA (ANT). Antigua and Barbuda formed a **National Olympic Committee** in 1965 with the objective of participating in the 1966 British **Commonwealth Games** that year. After being refused recognition in 1975 because its statutes did not conform to **International Olympic Committee** requirements, recognition was granted in 1976, and Antigua and Barbuda competed at the 1976 **Olympic Games.** It has participated at all subsequent Summer Games except for 1980, but has not yet competed at the **Olympic Winter Games.**

In nine Summer Games, the Caribbean island nation has had 63 entrants (47 men, 16 **women**) in six sports: **athletics** (25 men, 11 women), **boxing** (two men), **canoeing** (two men, one woman, two brothers and their sister), **cycling** (10 men), **sailing** (six men, two women), and **swimming** (two men, two women). Antigua and Barbuda has not yet won a medal at the Olympics, the top performances coming in athletics and include Lester Benjamin, 15th of 31 in the 1984 **long jump**, James Browne, 17th of 41 in the 1988 long jump, and Brendan Christian who reached the semifinal **round** of the 200 meter **sprint** in both 2008 and 2012 and missed qualifying for the final round in 2008 by 0.04 seconds.

ANTILLES (WEST INDIES) (ANL). *See* WEST INDIES FEDERATION.

APENE. The *apene* race was a **chariot race** at the **Ancient Olympics** in which two mules pulled the chariot. The first known winner was Thersias of Thessaly, in 500 B.C. The event was discontinued after 444 B.C. *See also* KALPE; KELES; SYNORIS; TETHRIPPON.

AQUATICS. The **International Olympic Committee** recognizes a sport called aquatics, which consists of five **disciplines: swimming, diving, open water swimming, synchronized swimming**, and **water polo.** Most people usually consider these to be separate sports, and they are listed here as such. Aquatics is governed by the Fédération Internationale de Natation, which was formed in 1908 and as of 2014 has 203 members.

ARCHERY. Archery is one of the oldest known sports. Use of the bow and arrow for hunting can be traced back to the Aurignacians, a race of people that existed 15,000 years ago. By the 14th century, archers were found to be valuable as soldiers, and the English kings made archery practice mandatory for their soldiers. Archery as a sport became popular in the 16th and 17th centuries. In 1676, the first organized group, the Royal Company of Archers, was formed in **England** for the purpose of advancing the sport. This was followed in 1781 by the Royal Toxophilite Society. The first British championships were conducted in 1844.

Archery is governed worldwide by the Fédération Internationale de Tir à l'Arc (FITA) (also now known as the International Archery Federation), which was founded in 1931 in **Poland**, with seven founding members: **France, Czechoslovakia, Sweden,** Poland, the **United States, Hungary,** and **Italy.** Through June 2014, 156 nations were members of FITA. Archery was first held as a sport in the 1900 Paris Olympics and again in 1904, 1908, and 1920, but then left the **Olympic Program.** In those years, it was possible for an athlete to compete in multiple events and win several medals. The top **Olympic medal** winner is **Hubert Van Innis** of **Belgium,** who competed in the 1900 and 1920 Olympics, winning 10 medals, six of them gold. **Kim Su-Nyeong** of **Korea** leads all **women** archers with four gold medals and six total.

When the sport was returned to the Olympics in 1972, there was only one event for men and one for women. In 1988, team events for men and women were added to the program. Also, in 1988 the individual formats were changed. Previously (1972–1984), men and women shot a double FITA **Round** (288 arrows at various distances). Now, qualifying is contested over 72 arrows, and the archers and teams then engage in single-elimination matches until a champion is crowned. The sport is currently dominated by Korea, especially among the women who have won 15 of 24 individual Olympic medals since 1984 with seven of eight gold medals. They have also won the women's team gold medal every year it has been contested since it was added to the Olympic program in 1988. In 15 summer Olympic competitions, there have been 1,028 athletes (571 men, 457 women) from 92 nations who have participated in Olympic archery.

ARGENTINA (ARG). Argentina first competed officially at the 1924 Olympics in Paris. Prior to that, at least three Argentine athletes had competed at the Olympics: Eduardo Camet as a **fencer** in 1900; Henri Torromé in 1908 in **figure skating**; and a **boxer,** Ángel Rodríguez, in 1920. Since 1924, Argentina has competed at every **Olympic Games** except 1980, which they **boycotted.** In 23 Summer Games, Argentina has entered 1,564 athletes (1,336 men, 228 **women**) and participated in 31 sports plus the **art competitions.** The only sports that were contested in five or more Olympic Games in which Argentina has not taken part are **badminton, baseball, rhythmic gymnastics,** and **tug-of-war.** The most popular summer sports for Argentina have been **athletics** (104 men, 29 women), boxing (118 men), **football** (109 men, 15 women), **hockey** (103 men, 60 women), **rowing** (140 men, 13 women), and **sailing** (96 men, 12 women).

Argentine athletes have won 70 **Olympic medals** (18 gold, 24 silver, 28 bronze). Officially known as the Argentine Republic and located on the southeastern coast of South America, Argentina has won more Olympic gold medals than any other South American country except for **Brazil**. Carlos

Espínola and Lucha Aymar have each won the most medals of any Argentine. Espínola won four in sailing from 1996 to 2008, with two silvers in **wind-surfing** and two bronzes in **multihull** Tornado class. Aymar won four medals (two silver, two bronze) in women's hockey from 2000 to 2012, and five of her teammates (Magdalena Aicega, Maripi Hernández, Mechi Margalot, Paola Vukojicic, Sole García) won three medals each during that time. Argentina's biggest Olympic victory occurred when they (led by Emanuel "Manu" Ginóbili, Andrés Nocioni, Carlos Delfino, Luis Scola, and Fabricio Oberto) won the basketball competition in 2004, defeating the **United States** team in the semifinal **round** and **Italy** in the final round.

Argentina has competed at the **Olympic Winter Games** of 1928, 1948, 1952, and all Winter Games since 1960 but has yet to win a medal in the Winter Games. In 18 Winter Games Argentina has entered 136 athletes (106 men, 30 women) and participated in eight sports with most of their athletes in four sports: **Alpine skiing** (51 men, 25 women), **biathlon** (15 men, three women), **bobsledding** (19 men), and **cross-country skiing** (16 men, one woman). They have also entered three men and one woman in **luge**, two men in **freestyle skiing**, and one man in each of **skeleton** and **snowboarding**. Luis Argel competed in both biathlon and cross-country skiing, and Justo del Carril competed in both Alpine skiing and bobsledding.

The Argentinean capital city of Buenos Aires made four unsuccessful bids to host the Summer Olympic Games in 1936, 1956, 1968, and 2004, but they will be the host of the III Summer Youth Olympic Games in 2018.

ARLEDGE, ROONE PINCKNEY, JR. (USA). B. 8 July 1931, Forest Hills, New York, **United States**. D. 5 December 2002, New York, New York, United States. Roone Arledge was a **television** producer who first popularized televising the **Olympic Games** to an American audience. After majoring in journalism at Columbia University, Arledge worked most of his career for American Broadcasting Company (ABC) Television, initially leading the sports division, but later also being named head of the news division. In 1961, he created and developed a sports anthology show, *ABC's Wide World of Sports*, which became hugely popular. He later produced telecasts of the Olympic Games of 1964, 1968, 1972, 1976, and 1984 and of the **Olympic Winter Games** of 1964, 1968, 1976, 1980, 1984, and 1988. His innovative style focused on bringing profiles of the athletes to the public, rather than simply showing the competitions. The profiles were titled "Up Close and Personal," coining the phrase for U.S. television audiences. Arledge also started the American television phenomenon of *Monday Night Football* in 1970. Arledge won numerous awards for his work, including 37 Emmy Awards, the Cannes Film Festival Grand Prize in 1965–1966, and three George Foster

Peabody Awards for promoting international understanding. In 1994, *Sports Illustrated* selected Arledge as the third most influential person in American sports in the past four decades.

ARMENIA (ARM). Armenia's first connection with the modern Olympics can be traced to the 1912 Olympics, when two Armenian **track and field** athletes represented **Turkey**. These two athletes, Mığır Mığıryan and Vahram Papazyan, comprised the entire Turkish team in 1912, but they had in fact been sent to Stockholm by the Armenian General Sports Union. Starting in 1918, Armenia enjoyed a brief period of independence and planned to take part in the 1920 Olympics, but its hopes were thwarted when the country was occupied by **Russian** forces in 1920. For many years, Russian **International Olympic Committee** (IOC) member Prince Urosov championed the cause of a group of émigrés known as the Young Armenian Emigrants Union, but he failed to gain Olympic recognition for them. In his Olympic memoirs, **Pierre de Coubertin** aptly wrote, "Armenia existed only as a hope and a memory in the hearts of its loyal subjects."

As part of the **Soviet Union**, Armenian athletes competed for the USSR Olympic team from 1952 to 1988, and in 1992 they were part of the Unified Team. The country eventually obtained independence, and a **National Olympic Committee** was established in 1990; IOC recognition was sought the following year. This was provisionally granted in 1992, and full IOC recognition was given in 1993, thereby enabling Armenia to compete as an independent nation at the Olympics. Armenia (officially the Republic of Armenia, a landlocked country on the border of southeastern Europe and western Asia) competed for the first time at the 1994 **Olympic Winter Games** in Lillehammer. At the Lillehammer opening ceremony, the Armenians wore replicas of the uniform that they had hoped to wear at the 1920 Olympics.

Armenia first competed at the Summer Olympics in 1996 and has since competed at all **Olympic Games**, Winter and Summer. In five Summer Games, Armenia has had 93 entrants (82 men, 11 **women**) and has competed in 13 sports: **athletics** (six men, four women), **boxing** (11 men), **canoeing** (one man), **cycling** (one man), **diving** (one man, one woman), **gymnastics** (two men), **judo** (four men), **shooting** (two men), **swimming** (two men, four women), **taekwondo** (one man), **tennis** (one man), **weightlifting** (22 men, two women), and **wrestling** (28 men).

Armenia has won 12 **Olympic medals**, one gold by Armen Nazaryan in 1996 **flyweight Greco-Roman wrestling**, two silver (Armen Mkrtchyan 1996 **light-flyweight freestyle** wrestling, Arsen Julfalakyan 2012 **middleweight** Greco-Roman wrestling), and nine bronze (one in boxing, three in wrestling, and five in weightlifting). Hrachik Javakhyan won his in **lightweight** boxing in 2008 with a **bye**, win by decision, win by **walkover**, and loss in the semifinal **round**. Two weightlifting bronze medals in 2008 went to similarly named athletes: lightweight Tigran G. Martirosyan and **light-heavyweight** Tigran V. Martirosyan. In 2012, Hripsime Khurshudyan became Armenia's first female medalist when she won the bronze medal in the women's **super-heavyweight** weightlifting class. Armenia's other bronze medalists were middleweight weightlifters Arsen Melikyan (2000) and Gevorg Davtyan (2008) and Greco-Roman wrestlers **featherweight** Roman Amoyan (2008), **heavyweight** Artur Aleksanyan (2012), and super-heavyweight Yury Patrikeyev (2008).

In six Winter Games, Armenia has had 28 entrants (18 men, 10 women) and has competed in five sports: **Alpine skiing** (four men, two women), **bobsledding** (four men), **cross-country skiing** (five men, four women), **figure skating** (four men, four women), and **freestyle skiing** (one man). Armenia's best performance at the Winter Games was in 2014 when Arman Serebrakyan finished 34th of 115 skiers in the **slalom** Alpine skiing event. Vanessa Rakedzhyan had the top effort for an Armenian female Olympic athlete with a 29th place of 68 entrants in the 2002 women's slalom. *See also* NOVIKOV, IGOR ALEKSANDROVICH.

ART COMPETITIONS (or CONTESTS). Art contests were held at the Olympics of 1912, 1920, 1924, 1928, 1932, 1936, and 1948. The winners of the competitions were awarded gold, silver, and bronze medals, similar to the winners of the athletic competitions. The events were inspired by **Pierre de Coubertin**, who wished to combine the competitions in sports with competitions in the arts. The art competitions were dropped from the **Olympic Program** because most of the artists were professionals, which the **International Olympic Committee** (IOC) opposed. Competitions were held in architectural designs; designs for town planning; sculpture–medals, sculpture–reliefs, and sculpture–any kind; applied graphics; drawings and watercolors; other graphic arts; paintings; dramatic works; epic works; literature–all kinds; lyrics; musical compositions for one instrument; musical compositions for orchestra of all kinds; musical compositions of songs for soloist or choir, with or without instrumental accompaniment; and music–all kinds. Two artists won three medals: Alex Walter Diggelmann of **Switzerland** (all in applied graphics) and Joseph Petersen of **Denmark** (one in epic works and two in literature–all kinds). **Jean Jacoby** of **Luxembourg** was the only artist to win two gold medals in the art competitions—one in drawings and watercolors and one in paintings. In 1912, Coubertin won a gold medal in the literature category. Coubertin's gold medal was for "Ode to Sport," which he entered under the dual pseudonym of Georg Hohrod and Martin Eschbach. Two arts medalists also won medals in sports at the **Olympic**

Games. Alfred Hajós of **Hungary** won two **swimming** gold medals in 1896 and a medal for designs for town planning in 1924, and **Walter Winans** won running deer **shooting** medals in 1908 and 1912 and also won an arts gold medal in sculpture in 1912. **Avery Brundage**, who would serve as the **IOC president** from 1952 to 1972, was an entrant in the 1932 and 1936 literature competition and received an honorable mention in 1932 for his work, *The Significance of Amateur Sport.* In seven summer Olympic Games, there were 1,792 individuals (1,599 men, 193 women) from 51 nations who participated in the Olympic art competitions.

ARTISTIC GYMNASTICS. *See* GYMNASTICS.

ARUBA (ARU). Aruba's **National Olympic Committee** was formed in 1985 and recognized by the **International Olympic Committee** in 1986. Aruba competed in the **Olympic Games** for the first time in 1988 at Seoul and has appeared in each Summer Games through 2012 but has not yet competed at the **Olympic Winter Games** and has not yet won a medal. The Caribbean island (considered as one of the four constituent countries that comprise the Kingdom of the **Netherlands**) has been represented by 26 different athletes—19 males and seven females—with the most in one Olympic Games being eight in 1988. Aruban athletes have competed in nine sports: **athletics** (four men, three **women**), **boxing** (two men), **cycling** (two men), **fencing** (one man), **judo** (four men), **sailing** (one man), **swimming** (three men, two women), **synchronized swimming** (two women), and **weightlifting** (two men). Their best performance is arguably the 53rd place of 110 entrants in the men's **marathon** in 1992 by Kim Reynierse, who finished in a creditable time of 2:25.31. Another commendable effort was that of Roswitha Lopez in the 1988 synchronized swimming solo event. She was one of only 18 swimmers to advance past the qualifying **round** in which 46 contestants took part, although she finished in 18th place in the final round. Prior to 1988, a few Aruban athletes competed with the **Netherlands Antilles** team, until the nation gained autonomous status from the other islands in 1986.

ASOCIACIÓN PANIBÉRICA DE ACADEMIAS OLÍMPICAS. The Pan-Iberic Association of Olympic Academies has as its mission to enhance the work of **National Olympic Academies** in Spanish and Portuguese language nations, in cooperation with the **International Olympic Academy**. Founded in Madrid in 1988 as the Asociación Iberoamericana de Academias Olímpicas, it was later renamed to include nations in Africa. The organization is recognized by the **International Olympic Committee** and currently (as of 2014) encompasses academies from 27 nations in Africa, Europe, and Latin America.

ASSOCIATION DES COMITÉS NATIONAUX OLYMPIQUES (ACNO). The ACNO was formed in 1968 by Giulio Onesti, then the president of the **Italian** Olympic Committee, as a method of uniting the various **National Olympic Committees** (NOCs). Originally called the Permanent General Assembly of National Olympic Committees, it allowed the NOCs a more unified voice to present their concerns to the **International Olympic Committee** (IOC). This union of NOCs greatly displeased **IOC President Avery Brundage**. The group was later renamed the Association of National Olympic Committees, but is better known by its French name. The ACNO is currently based in **Lausanne, Switzerland,** and its president, as of 2014, is Sheikh Ahmad Al-Farad Al-Sabah of **Kuwait.** Formation of the ACNO has been responsible for the foundation of various continental and regional associations of NOCs. *See also* EUROPEAN OLYMPIC COMMITTEES, THE; OCEANIA NATIONAL OLYMPIC COMMITTEES; OLYMPIC COUNCIL OF ASIA; ORGANIZACIÓN DEPORTIVA CENTROAMERICANA Y DEL CARIBE; PAN AMERICAN SPORTS ORGANIZATION.

ASSOCIATION DES COMITÉS NATIONAUX OLYMPIQUES D'EUROPE. *See* EUROPEAN OLYMPIC COMMITTEES, THE.

ASSOCIATION GÉNÉRALE DES FÉDÉRATIONS INTERNATIONALES DE SPORTS. *See* SPORTACCORD.

ASSOCIATION OF INTERNATIONAL OLYMPIC WINTER SPORTS FEDERATIONS (AIOWF). In 1982, led by **Marc Hodler** of **Switzerland** and the International Ski Federation, the Winter Sports Federations formed its own group, the Association of International Olympic Winter Sports Federations. The AIOWF deals with specific questions concerning winter sports in general and the **Olympic Winter Games** in particular. It is also responsible for choosing the delegations and appointments of the winter sports representatives to **International Olympic Committee (IOC) Commissions**. The group is based in Zürich, Switzerland. Hodler was the president until 2001, when he was replaced by René Fasel, who served until 2014 and was succeeded by Gian-Franco Kasper of Switzerland.

ASSOCIATION OF NATIONAL OLYMPIC COMMITTEES OF AFRICA (ANOCA). This group consists of the **National Olympic Committees** from the African nations and is also known as the Association des Comités Nationaux Olympiques d'Afrique (ACNOA), its French name. The association has its headquarters in Abuja, **Nigeria**. The president of ACNOA is General Lassena Palenfo of **Côte d'Ivoire**, and the secretary-general is Tomas Amos Ganda Sithole of **Zimbabwe** (as of June 2014).

ASSOCIATION OF SUMMER OLPYMPIC FEDERATIONS. On 20 May 1983, 21 **International Federations** governing sports on the program of the **Olympic Games** met in **Lausanne** and established the ASOIF. The ASOIF constitution defines its purpose as "to coordinate and defend the common interests of its members to ensure close cooperation between them, the members of the **Olympic Movement** and those of other organizations, with the aim of preserving the unity of the Olympic Movement while maintaining the authority, independence and autonomy of the member International Federations." The ASOIF is currently based in Lausanne, **Switzerland**, and its president, as of 2014, is Francesco Ricci Bitti of **Italy**, who is also the president of the International Tennis Federation.

ASSOCIATION OF THE IOC-RECOGNIZED INTERNATIONAL SPORTS FEDERATIONS (ARISF). The **International Olympic Committee** (IOC) recognizes a number of international sports federations whose sports are not yet on the **Olympic Program**. This recognition is important because it is a first step toward getting a sport admitted to the Program. As of 2014, the IOC has recognized the **International Federations** for the following sports (in addition to those on the Olympic Program): **aeronautics** (air sports), **American football**, automobile, **bandy, baseball** and **softball, billiards, bowling, bowls, bridge, chess, cricket, dance sport,** floorball, flying disc (Frisbee), **karate, korfball,** life-saving, **motorcycling,** mountaineering and climbing, **netball, orienteering, pelota basque, polo, powerboating, racquetball, roller** sports, ski mountaineering, sport climbing, **squash, sumo, surfing, tug-of-war, underwater sports, water skiing** and wakeboard, and **wushu.** These IOC-recognized International Sports Federations have grouped together to form the ARISF. It is headquartered in **Lausanne, Switzerland**, and currently has 35 member federations. The current (2014) president is Raffaele Chiulli of **Italy**, who is also president of the International Powerboating Federation. The statutes of the ARISF state that its aims are "to determine the consensus of the member federations on questions relating to the **Olympic Movement** . . . and to coordinate and defend the common interest of its members in [that] context."

ASTAKHOVA, POLINA GRIGORYEVNA (URS/UKR–GYM). B. 30 October 1936, Zaporizhzhia, **Ukraine**, USSR. D. 5 August 2005, Kyiv, Ukraine, USSR. Polina Astakhova won team gold medals at the 1956, 1960, and 1964 **Olympic Games**, a feat that she shares with **Larysa Latynina**, making them the only female **gymnasts** to be members of three gold medal–winning teams. Astakhova also won gold on the **uneven bars** and placed third in the individual **all-around** in both 1960 and 1964. The five-foot, five-inch (166 cm), 123 lb (56 kg) Polina added silver medals in both 1960 and 1964 in the **floor exercise**, and her final Olympic tally included 10 medals: five gold, two silver, and three bronze. At the world championships she was less successful, winning only two individual medals, but she was a member of the Soviet Union team that won the team title in both 1958 and 1962.

ATHLETES' COMMISSION. The Athletes' Commission was formed in 1981 as a response to the complaint at the 1981 **Olympic Congress** that Olympic athletes had very little say in the workings of the **International Olympic Committee** (IOC) and the **Olympic Movement**. It was felt that the IOC had too few former Olympic athletes among its members, and that those athletes were too far removed from their competitive days. The chairman of the Athletes' Commission from 1980 to 2000 was Peter Tallberg of **Finland**, an IOC member and a former yachtsman who competed in the **Olympic Games** in 1960, 1964, 1968, 1972, and 1980. In 2000, the chairman became Sergey Bubka of the **Ukraine**, the renowned **pole vaulter** and later an IOC member. **Sprinter** Frank Fredericks of **Namibia** followed as chairman, and as of 2014, the current chairperson is Claudia Bokel of **Germany**, a former silver medalist in **fencing**. The composition of the Athletes Commission is (1) eight summer sports athletes elected during the Games of the Olympiad (four at each edition of the Games); (2) four winter sports athletes elected during the **Olympic Winter Games** (two at each edition of the Games); and (3) five athletes appointed by the **IOC president** to ensure a fair balance in terms of gender, sport, and region. The 12 athletes elected during the Olympic Games and Olympic Winter Games serve an eight-year term and become IOC members during their term on the Athletes' Commission. The Athletes' Commission has been charged with three responsibilities: (1) discuss its views biannually with the **IOC Executive Board** and report to the IOC session, (2) delegate athlete representatives to other IOC Commissions, and (3) establish working groups to act as liaison to the **Organizing Committees of the Olympic Games**.

ATHLETICS. Athletics, or track and field, is the original Olympic sport. The first event contested in the **Ancient Olympics** was the *stadion*, a sprint of about 190 meters. Recorded victors in this event are known as far back as 776 B.C. Other athletics events in the Ancient Olympics included longer races; **races in armor**; and a **pentathlon** consisting of the *stadion*, **long jump**, **discus throw**, **javelin throw**, and **wrestling**.

Throughout recorded sports history, athletics has always been practiced. Many of the **attempts at revival** of the Olympics in the 19th century consisted mostly of athletics events. Since the revival of the Olympics in 1896, athletics has been the most publicized sport on the **Olympic Program**. Today, athletics is rivaled only by **football (soccer)** and **volleyball** as the sport practiced in the most countries in the world, based on number of nations within the **International Federation**. The sport is governed internationally by the International Association of Athletics Federations, which was formed in 1912 (as the International Amateur Athletic Federation and renamed in 2001) and had 212 member nations as of 2014—more members than the United Nations.

Athletics has been held at every Olympics. **Women**'s athletics began at the 1928 Olympics and has been contested continually since. The program has varied but has been fairly standard since 1932. The current program includes **sprint** races (100, 200, and 400 meters), middle-distance races (800 and 1,500 meters), distance races (5,000 meters, 10,000 meters, and **marathon** (26 miles, 385 yards [42.195 km]), **hurdle** races (110 meters for men, 100 meters for women, and 400 meters for both), **steeplechase** (3,000 meters for men and women), walking events (20 km for men and women, and 50 km for men), flat jumping events (long jump and **triple jump**), vertical jumping events (**high jump** and **pole vault**), throwing events (**shot put**, discus throw, **hammer throw**, and javelin throw), and **multievents** (**decathlon** for men and **heptathlon** for women). In 28 summer Olympic competitions, there have been 20,623 athletes (14,792 men, 5,831 women), far more than any other Olympic sport, from 223 nations who have participated in Olympic athletics. There have been only two nations (**Nauru** and **Bhutan**) who have not participated in Olympic athletics of the 225 nations who have competed in the Olympic Games.

Although women were first allowed to compete in only a few events, today they have a program with almost as many events as the men. The only current differences in the women's program are that they have only one walking event (20 km), and they compete in the heptathlon, as opposed to the decathlon for men (this may change in the future).

The **United States**' men have always been the top performers in the world in track and field athletics. **Finland** formerly dominated the distance events, which in recent years has been dominated by **Kenya** and **Ethiopia**. In the sprints, **Jamaica** has become the new leader, surpassing the United States. Among the women, the **Soviet Union** and the **German Democratic Republic** were the top powers after their admission to the Olympics and prior to their dissolution by the political events at the end of the 1980s. *See also* BEAMON, ROBERT; BIKILA, ABEBE; BLANKERS-KOEN, FRANCINA ELSJE; BOLT, USAIN ST. LEO; BORZOV, VALERIY PYLYPOVYCH; BRUND-

AGE, AVERY; BURGHLEY, LORD DAVID GEORGE BROWNLOW CECIL; COE, BARON SEBASTIAN NEWBOLD; CONNOLLY, JAMES BRENDAN BENNETT; COROEBUS OF ELIS; CUTHBERT, ELIZABETH ALYSE; DIDRIKSON, MILDRED ELLA; EWRY, RAYMOND CLARENCE; FLANAGAN, JOHN JOSEPH; GRIFFITH JOYNER, DELOREZ FLORENCE; HOLMES, KELLY; JOHNSON, MICHAEL DUANE; JOHNSON, RAFER LEWIS; KOLEHMAINEN, JOHAN PIETARI; KORZENIOWSKI, ROBERT MAREK; KRAENZLEIN, ALVIN CHRISTIAN; LEMMING, ERIC OTTO VALDEMAR; LEONIDAS OF RHODES; LEWIS, FREDERICK CARLTON; LOUIS, SPYRIDON; MATHIAS, ROBERT BRUCE; MORROW, BOBBY JOE; MOSES, EDWIN CORLEY; NURMI, PAAVO JOHANNES; O'BRIEN, WILLIAM PARRY, JR.; OERTER, ALFRED ADOLPH, JR.; OTTEY, MERLENE JOYCE; OWENS, JAMES CLEVELAND; PIETRI, DORANDO; PISTORIUS, OSCAR LEONARD CARL; RICHARDS, ROBERT EUGENE; RITOLA, VILJO EINO; ROSE, RALPH WALDO; RUDOLPH, WILMA GLODEAN; SANEYEV, VIKTOR DANILOVICH; SCHUHMANN, CARL; SHERIDAN, MARTIN JOSEPH; STRICKLAND DE LA HUNTY, SHIRLEY BARBARA; SZEWIŃSKA-KIRSZENSTEIN, IRENA; TARZAN AND THE OLYMPICS; THOMPSON, FRANCIS MORGAN; THORPE, JAMES FRANCIS; VIRÉN, LASSE ARTTURI; ZÁTOPEK, EMIL; ŽELEZNÝ, JAN.

ATTEMPTS AT REVIVAL. Prior to the 1896 Olympic Games in Athens, many efforts had been made to resurrect the **Ancient Olympic Games** and stage them with a program mainly containing contemporary events. These include **Robert Dover's Cotswold Olimpick Games**, the **Much Wenlock Olympian Games**, and the **Zappas Olympic Games** in Athens. Other attempts at Olympian-type festivals are known to have been held in Ramlösa, **Sweden** (near Helsingborg), in 1834 and 1836 under the initiative of Professor Gustav Johann Schartau of the University of Lund; in Montreal, Quebec, **Canada**, in the early 1830s and 1840s; in **England** by the **National Olympian Association** from 1866 to 1883, which was an offshoot of the Much Wenlock Olympian Games, as well as the Olympic Festivals of Liverpool (1862–1867); the Morpeth Olympic Games in Morpeth, England (1873–1958); and the Olympic Games at Lake Palić (1880–1914), a spa eight km east of Subotica, then in **Hungary** and now in the Vojvodina province of **Serbia**. In addition, various Highland and Caledonian Games were held in the 19th century, which brought together Celtic peoples in athletic competition. However, none of these events had the international flavor of **Pierre de Coubertin**'s revived Olympic Games.

Much of the impetus for revival in the 19th century was due to recent archaeological finds at ancient Olympia and other classical sites in **Greece**. These digs were initiated by Guillaume-Abel Blouet, a Frenchman, and were continued by the Germans, notably Ernst Curtius. Curtius began his digs in 1875, and reports on his finds were issued between 1890 and 1897. The German government published yearly reports between 1875 and 1881.

The idea of revival was also in the air for at least a century prior to Coubertin. The terms *Olympic* and *Olympian* were apparently used frequently even before that to refer to any athletic contest, for example, Shakespeare's phrases from the late 1500s: "such rewards as victors weare at the Olympian Games" (*Henry VI*, Act 2) and "Olympic wrestling" (*Troilus and Cressida*, Act 4). Milton used the phrase "As at the Olympian Games or Pythian fields" in *Paradise Lost* in 1667.

Professor John Lucas of Penn State University discovered a letter from T. B. Hollis written in 1788 to Josiah Willard, president of Harvard University, in which Hollis states: "Our documents carry mention of an eventual rebirth of the Olympic Games in America. The friends of this latter [idea] want and pretend to be capable of it: after having acted according to Greek Principles, they must practice Greek exercises."

In 1793, Johannes C. F. Guts-Muths discussed the Ancient Olympics in his *Gymnastik für Jugend*, and in the second edition in 1804, he was considering a revival. In 1813, the philologist and historian Bartold Georg Nicbuhr wrote of "a vast hall [in Rome], which, once properly decorated, could serve for the resumption of the Olympic Games."

Thus, Coubertin did not come to his Olympic idea without help. However, a great deal of credit is due him, as he was the only one who, apart from **William Penny Brookes**, really envisioned the possibility of a great international festival, bringing together the youth of all nations in peaceful competition. Even without Coubertin's vision, it is almost certain that the Olympic Games would have been revived. But it is not as certain that they would be anything like the Olympic Games we know today. Appendix XXII lists all known attempts at revival prior to 1896.

AUSTRALASIA (ANZ). In both the 1908 and 1912 **Olympic Games**, the two Oceanic nations of **Australia** and **New Zealand** entered a combined team and were known as Australasia. They competed in eight sports and had 53 athletes entered (51 men, two **women**) with several competing in more than one sport. Australasia competed in **athletics** (14 men), **boxing** (one man), **diving** (one man), **rowing** (10 men), **rugby** (15 men), **shooting** (one man), **swimming** (11 men, two women), and **tennis** (one man) and did quite well, earning 12 medals—three gold, four silver, and five bronze.

Gold medals were won by the 1908 men's rugby team, and in 1912 by the men's 4x200 swimming **relay** team and swimmer Fanny Durack in the women's 100 meter **freestyle**. Silver medals were won by **middleweight** boxer Reginald "Snowy" Baker and by swimmers Frank Beaurepaire (1908, men's 400 meter freestyle), Cecil Healy (1912, men's 100 meter freestyle), and Mina Wylie (1912, women's 100 meter freestyle). Baker was an extremely versatile athlete and competed in swimming and diving events in 1908 in addition to boxing. Outside of Olympic competition, he was also a famed **water polo** player, rower, **cricket** player, **wrestler**, and horse man.

Australasia's bronze medalists were Harry Kerr (1908, 3,500 meter walk), swimmers Frank Beaurepaire (1908, 1,500 meter freestyle) and Harold Hardwick (1912, 400 meter freestyle and 1,500 meter freestyle), and New Zealand tennis player Tony Wilding. Hardwick also was a member of the gold medal–winning relay team, and his three **Olympic medals** lead all Australasian athletes. Wilding was among the best tennis players of his era (ranked number one in 1911) and was a nine-time Wimbledon champion (four **singles**, four **doubles**, and one **mixed doubles**), Australian Open champion (singles twice, doubles once), and was a four-time member of the winning Davis Cup team. He was killed in combat in Europe during World War I. Since 1920, both Australia and New Zealand have entered separate teams in subsequent Olympic competition.

AUSTRALIA (AUS). Australia, whose **National Olympic Committee** was formed and recognized by the **International Olympic Committee** in 1895, has competed at every Summer **Olympic Games**, although in 1908 and 1912, it competed as **Australasia** in a combined team with **New Zealand**. In 26 Summer Games (exclusive of 1908 and 1912), Australia has entered 3,309 athletes (2,254 men, 1,055 **women**) and participated in 34 sports plus the **art competitions**, medaling in 24 of them. The only sports that were contested in five or more Olympic Games in which Australia has not taken part are **polo** and **tug-of-war**. The sports with the most entrants have been **athletics** (301 men, 167 women), **swimming** (192 men, 181 women), **rowing** (255 men, 75 women), **hockey** (138 men, 77 women), **cycling** (160 men, 35 women), and **basketball** (94 men, 47 women).

The Southern Hemisphere continent/country has won 475 medals (138 gold, 156 silver, 181 bronze) at the Summer Games. Australia (officially the Commonwealth of Australia) has been successful in many sports, but particularly so in swimming (183 medals, 57 gold) and athletics (73 medals, 20 gold). They have also earned 49 medals in cycling (14 gold) and 37 in rowing (10 gold).

Swimmer Ian Thorpe leads Australia's **Olympic medal** list, with nine (five gold, three silver, one bronze) medals. He won all his medals in just two Olympics, in 2000 and 2004. He was joined at the top of the list in 2012 by swimmer Leisel Jones, who won her ninth. From 2000 to 2012, she has three gold, five silver, and one bronze. They are followed by three female swimmers each with eight Olympic medals: **Dawn Fraser**, **Petria Thomas**, and **Susie O'Neill**. Swimmers Libby Lenton-Trickett and **Grant Hackett** each have seven. From 1948 to 1956, **Shirley Strickland de la Hunty** competed in 10 athletics events and won medals in seven of them—three gold, one silver, and three bronze. Australia has also been strong in women's basketball and has won medals in each of the last five Olympic tournaments (1996–2012) with Kristi Harrower and **Lauren Jackson** each winning four. Their men's basketball team (led by five-team Olympian Andrew Gaze) has participated in every Olympic tournament from 1972 to 2012, but their best effort was only fourth place, which they reached three times.

Australia has also competed at the **Olympic Winter Games**, in 1936 and continuously since 1952. In 19 Winter Games, they have entered 240 athletes (155 men, 85 women) and participated in 13 sports, all except **curling**, **military ski patrol**, and **ski jumping**. They did compete, however, in the **Nordic combined** in 1960, which includes ski jumping as part of the event. They have won 12 medals in the Winter Games (five gold, three silver, and four bronze). Australia Winter Olympians with two medals include Torah Bright (snowboarding 2010 gold, 2014 silver), Steven Bradbury (short track speed skating 1994 bronze, 2002 gold), and **freestyle skiers** Dale Begg-Smith (2006 gold, 2010 silver), Alisa Camplin (2002 gold, 2006 bronze), and Lydia Ierodiaconou-Lassila (2010 gold, 2014 bronze).

Australia has also hosted the Games of the XVIth **Olympiad** in 1956 in Melbourne, and more recently the sublime Games of the XXVIIth Olympiad in 2000 in Sydney, although they were unsuccessful bidders for the 1992 Games (Brisbane) and 1996 Games (Melbourne). *See also* CUTHBERT, ELIZABETH ALYSE; GOULD, SHANE ELIZABETH; PALUBINSKAS, EDWARD SEBASTIAN; PERKINS, KIEREN JOHN; ROSE, IAIN MURRAY.

AUSTRALIAN RULES FOOTBALL. *See* FOOTBALL, AUSTRALIAN RULES.

AUSTRIA (AUT). Austria competed at the first Olympics in 1896 and has missed only one Games since, those of 1920, when it was not invited because it had been an aggressor nation in World War I. In 27 Summer Games, Austria has entered 1,437 athletes (1,151 men, 286 **women**) and participated in 30 sports plus the **art competitions**. The only sports that were contested in five or more **Olympic Games** in which Austria has not taken part are the team sports of **baseball**, **basketball**, **polo**, and **volleyball**. Austria has entered the most participants in **athletics** (123 men, 56 women). They have also entered 105 contestants in the art competitions (99 men, six women). Other sports in which Austria has had its largest participation in are **cycling** (84 men, eight women), **fencing** (79 men, 14 women), **rowing** (91 men, seven women), and **swimming** (53 men, 36 women).

Triple Olympic medalists for Austria at the Summer Games are: Adolf Schmal (cycling 1896, gold, two bronze), Ellen Müller-Preis (fencing 1932 gold, 1936 bronze, 1948 bronze), Julius Lenhart (**gymnastics** 1904, two gold, one silver), Otto Scheff (swimming 1906 gold, bronze, 1908 bronze), and Otto Wahle (swimming 1900, two silver, 1904 bronze). Double Olympic medalists are: Edwin Grienauer (art competitions–sculpture, gold 1928, bronze 1948), Gregor Hradetzky (**kayak** 1936, two bronze), Max Raub and Herbert Wiedermann (kayak **pairs** 1952, 1956, two bronze), Karl Proisl (**canoeing** 1936, silver, bronze), Rupert Weinstabl (canoeing 1936, silver, bronze), Richard Verderber (fencing 1912, silver, bronze), Peter Seisenbacher (**judo** 1984 gold, 1988 gold), Josef Kloimstein and Alfred Sageder (rowing pairs 1956 bronze, 1960 silver), Hubert Raudaschl (**sailing**, 1968, 1980, both silver), Roman Hagara and Hans-Peter Steinacher (sailing 2000, 2004 both gold), Rudolf Dollinger (**shooting** 1972, 1976 both bronze), Wolfram Waibel, Jr. (shooting 1996, silver and bronze), Markus Rogan (swimming 2004, two silver), Karl Ruberl (swimming, 1900 silver, bronze), Hans Haas (**weightlifting** 1928 gold, 1932 silver), Josef Steinbach (weightlifting 1906 gold, silver), Nikolaus Hirschl (**wrestling** 1932 two bronze), and Rudolf Watzl (wrestling 1906, gold, bronze). Otto Herschmann was one of the few athletes to win Olympic medals in more than one sport. He won a silver medal in swimming in 1896 and a silver medal in fencing in 1912.

The Central European nation, officially known as the Republic of Austria, has also competed at every **Olympic Winter Games**, where it has often been the dominant nation in **Alpine skiing**. In 22 Winter Games, it has entered 859 athletes (663 men, 196 women) and has participated in all sports save the **military ski patrol** and **curling**. It is one of only three countries (with **Norway** and **Liechtenstein**) to have won more medals at the Winter Olympics than at the Olympic Games. Through 2014, Austrian athletes have won 218 medals (59 gold) at the Olympic Winter Games and 106 medals (25 gold) at the Summer Olympics. **Felix Gottwald** competed in five Olympic Games (1994–2010) and has won the most medals of any Austrian, with seven in the **Nordic combined**: three gold, one silver, and three bronze—all medals won from 2002 to 2010. Austrian Alpine skiers Hermann Maier, Benjamin Raich, Marlies Schild, and Stephan Eberharter each won four medals as did **ski jumpers** Thomas Morgenstern, Gregor Schlierenzauer, and Martin Höllwarth.

Austria has also twice hosted the Olympic Winter Games, in 1964 and 1976, both times at Innsbruck, and has made six additional unsuccessful bid attempts (1960, Innsbruck; 1964 Vienna; 2002 Graz; 2006 Klagenfurt; 2010 and 2014, Salzburg). *See also* KAMPER, ERICH; SAILER, ANTON ENGELBERT.

AUTOMOBILE RACING. Automobile racing has never been held at the **Olympic Games**, even as a **demonstration sport**. But in 1900 at Paris, auto racing was contested during the sporting events held in conjunction with the Exposition Universelle. As it is difficult to know which events were Olympic in that year, some historians list the auto racing events in their records. In 1908 at London, automobile racing was on the preliminary program, but the sport was not contested, and there have been no moves to include it in the Olympic Games since then. Internationally, automobile racing is governed by the Fédération Internationale de l'Automobile, which was founded in 1904 and currently (in 2014) has 235 affiliated members. Until recently, automobile racing was actually precluded by the *Olympic Charter*, in which Rule 47.4.2 stated, "Sports, **disciplines** or events in which performance depends essentially on mechanical propulsion are not acceptable"; in more recent versions of the *Charter*, this distinction has been removed.

AVEROF, GEORGIOS (GRE). B. 15 August 1815, Metsovo, **Greece**. D. 15 July 1899, Alexandria, **Egypt**. Georgios Averof was a Greek merchant, resident in Egypt, who acquired enormous wealth as a trader in Alexandria. Averof's donation of almost one million drachma for the excavation and rebuilding of the ancient Panathenaic stadium for the 1896 Games ensured that the first modern Olympics were staged in an appropriate setting. A dedicated patriot, he had already given several schools and a military academy to the nation, but as a man of a shy, retiring nature, he declined an invitation to be a guest at the **Olympic Games** that he had personally financed. His generosity was marked by the erection of a life-sized statue that was unveiled shortly before the Games opened. His nephew was a member of the **International Olympic Committee** from 1926 to 1930.

AZERBAIJAN (AZE). From 1952 to 1988, athletes from Azerbaijan formed part of the **Soviet Union**'s Olympic team, and at Barcelona in 1992, four Azerbaijani athletes were chosen for the Unified Team. After it gained independence and formed a **National Olympic Committee**, Azerbaijan was granted recognition by the **International Olympic Committee** in 1992. It first competed as an independent nation at the 1996 **Olympic Games** and the 1998 **Olympic Winter Games**. Officially known as the Republic of Azerbaijan, the eastern European/western Asian nation has since participated in all

Olympic and Olympic Winter Games and has sent 143 athletes (110 male, 33 female) to compete in 16 Summer Games sports: **athletics** (12 men, four **women**), **boxing** (21 men, one woman), **canoeing** (three men), **cycling** (one woman), **diving** (one man), **equestrian** (one man), **fencing** (one man, two women), **gymnastics** (one man), **judo** (12 men, three women), **rhythmic gymnastics** (nine women), **rowing** (one man, one woman), **shooting** (one man, two women), **swimming** (four men, three women), **taekwondo** (three men, one woman), **weightlifting** (11 men, two women), and **wrestling** (38 men, four women).

With 10 **Olympic medals** in 2012, Azerbaijani athletes increased their total medals won to 26 in the Summer Games with six gold, five silver, and 15 bronze. Gold medalists are Zemfira Meftəkhətddinova, 2000 women's **skeet** shooting; Namiq Abdullaev, 2000 men's **bantamweight freestyle** wrestling; Fərid Mənsurov, 2004 men's **welterweight Greco-Roman wrestling**; Elnur Məmmədli, 2008 men's **lightweight** judo; Şərif Şərifov, 2012 men's **light-heavyweight** freestyle wrestling, and Toğrul Əsgərov, 2012 men's lightweight freestyle wrestling. Azerbaijani dual medalists are Zemfira Meftəkhətddinova, women's skeet shooting (2000 gold, 2004 bronze) and wrestlers Mariya Stadnik women's **flyweight** freestyle (2008 bronze, 2012 silver), Namiq Abdullaev, men's 1996 flyweight silver and 2000 bantamweight gold; Rövşən Bayramov (2008 and 2012) men's **featherweight** Greco-Roman silver and Xetaq Qazyumov, men's **heavyweight** freestyle bronze (2008, 2012).

In five Winter Games, Azerbaijan has entered 13 athletes: three men and one woman in **Alpine skiing** and five men and four women in **figure skating**. The best performance by an athlete from Azerbaijan at the Winter Games was in 2014 when Alpine skier Patrick Brachner finished 53rd of 107 in the men's **giant slalom**. The best performance by an Azerbaijani woman in the Winter Games was by Yuliya Vorobyova who finished 16th of 28 in women's singles figure skating in 1998.

The capital city of Azerbaijan, Baku, entered a bid to host the 2016 and again for the 2020 Olympic Games, but did not advance to the final round of voting. *See also* RYSKAL, INNA VALERYEVNA.

B

BABASHOFF, SHIRLEY FRANCES (USA–SWI). B. 31 January 1957, Whittier, California, **United States**. Shirley Babashoff was the winner of a then-record nine **Olympic medals**, a total matched at the time among Olympic **women swimmers** only by **Kornelia Ender** and **Dawn Fraser**. Babashoff won two gold medals in the 4x100 meter **freestyle relay** (1972, 1976) and one gold medal in the 4x100 **medley** relay in 1972, to which she added two silver medals in 1972 and four silver medals in 1976. Babashoff, at five feet, 10 inches (178 cm) and 148 lbs (67 kg), was the world champion at 200 meters and 400 meters in 1975 and set many world records in individual and relay events between 1974 and 1976. Her performance at the 1976 Olympics, with one gold and four silvers, was considered somewhat disappointing, as she was favored in several events. At the time, she claimed she was beaten by East German females who were using illegal performance-enhancing drugs, claims that were later substantiated when files of the East German secret police, the Stasi, were reviewed after the fall of the Berlin Wall. Her brother, Jack, won a gold and silver medal at the 1976 Games for the United States in swimming.

BACH, THOMAS (GER–FEN/IOC). B. 29 December 1953, Würzburg, Bayern, **Federal Republic of Germany**. Thomas Bach became the **International Olympic Committee (IOC) president** when **Jacques Rogge**'s second term expired in 2013. A former Olympic champion in **foil fencing** (team gold in 1976), Bach entered the IOC in 1981 via the newly founded **Athletes' Commission** and then was co-opted to the IOC in 1991. He has since twice been named vice president of the IOC (2000–2004, 2006–2013). Possessing a law degree, Bach has been president of the appeals arbitration division of the **Court of Arbitration for Sport**. He is also a member of the German *Bundesversammlung*, a governmental body that elects the German president, for the liberal Free Democratic Party.

BACKSTROKE. The backstroke is one of the styles in **swimming** competition. Both 100 meter and 200 meter races for men and for **women** are contested, and the backstroke is one of the four swimming strokes that comprise the swimming **medley** events. Men's 100 meter backstroke has been held in each **Olympic Games** since 1908 (and a men's 100 yard backstroke event occurred in the 1904 Games). **Roland Matthes** of East Germany (gold 1968, 1972, bronze 1976) is the only three-time medalist in the 100 meter men's backstroke event. Although a 200 meter men's backstroke event was first held in 1900, it did not reappear on the Olympic schedule until 1964. Matthes is the only man to win two gold medals in the 200 meter backstroke, and **Aaron Peirsol** of the **United States** won three medals in this event (gold 2004, silver 2000, 2008) and won two more in the 100 meter backstroke, matching Matthes's total of five for the two backstroke events. A 100 meter women's backstroke event has been held since 1924, while the women's 200 meter backstroke first took place in 1968. Three women have each won two medals in the 100 meter event: **Krisztina Egerszegi** of **Hungary** (gold 1992, silver 1988), **Natalie Coughlin** of the United States (gold 2004, 2008), and Kristy Coventry of **Zimbabwe** (silver 2004, 2008). Egerszegi won the 200 meter gold medal three times (1988, 1992, and 1996), while Coventry won it twice (2004 and 2008).

BADMINTON. Badminton was invented in **India**. It was adopted by English soldiers there in the 19th century, who brought the game to **Great Britain** and eventually to many other countries. The game was originally called *poona*. The new sport took hold in **England** when it was exhibited there in 1873 at a party given by the Duke of Beaufort at his country estate, Badminton, in Gloucestershire.

Badminton was contested as a **demonstration sport** at the 1972 **Olympic Games** in Munich. After 1972, it did not appear at the Olympics until it showed up on the medal program at Barcelona, where it made its debut as a full medal sport in 1992. This was then an unusual mode of entry into the Olympics, as sports were usually added after several demonstration appearances. Men and **women** compete in **singles** and **doubles**, and there is also a **mixed doubles** event at the Olympics. Badminton is governed by the Badminton World Federation, originally known as the International Badminton Federation, which was formed in 1934 with 10 members: **Canada, Denmark**, England, **France, Ireland, Italy**, the **Netherlands, New Zealand, Scotland**, and **Wales**. It had 176 members as of 2014.

Badminton at the Olympics has been dominated by **China, Indonesia**, and **Korea**, which have won 74 of 91 available medals through 2012, and 28 of 29 gold medals. **Gao Ling** (CHN) is the only badminton player to have won four medals, with Kim Dong-Mun (KOR) and Gir Yeong-A (KOR) having each won three. Eight players have each won two gold medals, including Gao Ling and Kim Dong-Mun. Through 2012, there have been 721 participants (360 men and 361 women) from 66 countries who have competed in badminton in the six Olympic Games in which it was a full medal sport.

BAHAMAS, THE (BAH). As the Bahamas did not have a **National Olympic Committee** (NOC) at the time of the 1948 **Olympic Games**, its two leading yachtsmen, **Durward Knowles** and Sloan Farrington, chose to represent **Great Britain**, which was permitted under Olympic rules because the Bahamas was a British colony. In 1952, an NOC was established and recognized by the **International Olympic Committee**, and the Caribbean island nation, officially known as the Commonwealth of the Bahamas, competed at the Olympic Games under its own name for the first time that year. Since then, it has not been present only at the Moscow Games in 1980 but also has not yet competed in the Olympic Winter Games.

In 15 Summer Games, the Bahamas have entered 147 athletes (123 men, 24 **women**) in eight sports. They have participated in **athletics** (70 men, 20 women), **boxing** (six men), **cycling** (two men), **diving** (one woman), **sailing** (27 men), **swimming** (12 men, three women), **tennis** (four men), and **wrestling** (two men). Quite a few of their athletes have competed in multiple Olympic Games, with Durward Knowles leading with eight appearances (1948–1988)—the last seven for the Bahamas. Chandra Stump (1996–2012), Debbie Ferguson-McKenzie (1996–2012), Jackie Edwards (1992–2008), Laverne Eve (1988–2008), Mark Knowles (1992–2008), and Pauline David-Thompson (1984–2000) have each competed in five Games, and Chris Brown (2000–2012), Christine Amertil (2000–2012), Godfrey Kelly (1960–1972), Kenneth Albury (1952–1968), Percy Knowles (1960–1972), and Tom Robinson (1956–1968) each have four appearances.

Through 2014, Bahamian athletes have won 12 medals (five gold, two silver, five bronze), with all but two coming in athletics. The Bahamas has done exceptionally well in sprint relays, and the men's team won a gold medal in the 4x400 meters in 2012, a silver medal in the 4x400 meters in 2008, and a bronze medal in the 4x400 meters in 2000. The women's team won the gold medal in the 4x100 meters in 2000 and the silver medal four years previously. Pauline Davis-Thompson won the gold medal in the 200 meters in 2000, a second gold medal in the relay that year, and a silver medal in the 2004 relay. Debbie Ferguson-Mackenzie won a bronze medal in the 200 meters in 2004 to go with gold and silver medals in relays. Chris Brown is the third Bahamian to win three Olympic medals, winning one of each kind in relays in 2000, 2008, and 2012. Tonique Williams-Darling won a gold medal in the women's 400 meters in 2004. Sailor Durward Knowles won the gold medal in 1964 and a bronze in 1956 in the mixed two-person **keelboat** event.

BAHRAIN (BRN). The Bahrain **National Olympic Committee** was organized in 1978 and recognized by the **International Olympic Committee** in 1979. The Persian Gulf island nation, officially known as the Kingdom of Bahrain, has competed at all eight **Olympic Games** since 1984 but has never participated in the **Olympic Winter Games**. Bahrain has entered 59 athletes (46 men, 13 **women**) in seven sports: **athletics** (19 men, nine women), **cycling** (four men), **fencing** (four men), **modern pentathlon** (five men), **sailing** (five men), **shooting** (six men, one woman), and **swimming** (six men, three women). Three of the modern pentathlon contestants also entered individual fencing events.

In recent years, Bahrain has actively sought athletes from other nations to become Bahraini citizens, and several of them have performed exceptionally well for their newly adopted country. In 2012, Bahrain won its first medal when native **Ethiopian** Maryam Jamal finished third in the women's 1,500 meter run and won a bronze medal. Other notable performances by Bahraini Olympians include Jamal's fifth place finish in that event in 2008, native **Kenyan** Youssef Saad Kamel finishing fifth in the men's 800 meter run in 2008, and Shitaye Eshete, another native Ethiopian, finishing sixth in the women's 10,000 meter run in 2012. In 2008, **Moroccan**-born Rashid Ramzi won the men's 1,500 meter run but was later **disqualified** for **doping**.

BAILLET-LATOUR, COUNT HENRY DE (BEL–IOC). B. 1 March 1876, Antwerp, **Belgium**. D. 6 January 1942, Brussels, Belgium. Henry de Baillet-Latour (often misspelled Henri) was a Belgian aristocrat who proved himself to be an able sports administrator at an early age. Elected to the **International Olympic Committee** (IOC) in 1903 at the age of 27, he organized the **Olympic Congress** in Brussels two years later and, after playing a major role in securing the 1920 Games for Antwerp, he became president of the Belgian Olympic Committee in 1923, serving until 1942. He was named to the **IOC Executive Board** in 1921 and remained in that capacity until he took over as **IOC president** in 1925, following **Baron Pierre de Coubertin**'s resignation. During his presidency, the IOC was concerned with the problems of the definition of an *amateur* and the program of the **Olympic Games**. Baillet-Latour remained president until his death.

BALANCE BEAM. The balance beam is one of the exercises performed by female **gymnasts**. It has been included in the **Olympic Games** since 1952. Although seven **women** have won two medals each in balance beam competition, only **Nadia Comăneci** (ROU) has won two gold medals (1976, 1980) in this event.

BALCZÓ, ANDRÁS (HUN–MOP). B. 16 August 1938, Kondoros, Békes, **Hungary.** András Balczó was the winner of a record six individual and seven team titles in the **modern pentathlon** at the World Championships. After placing fourth at the 1960 Olympics in the individual event, he won team gold in 1960. In 1968 the five-foot, 11-inch (181 cm), 161 lb (73 kg) pentathlete again won team gold and added an individual silver medal. Then, in 1972, he won the individual title and a silver medal in the team event, for a total of five **Olympic medals** (three gold, two silver). Although the reigning world champion, Balczó did not compete in the 1964 Games, but his overall record is arguably the greatest of any modern pentathlete. (**Pavel Lednyov** has won seven Olympic medals in modern pentathlon but only two gold and neither of those in the individual event.) Balczó married Mónika Császár, a Hungarian **gymnast** who won a bronze medal at the 1972 **Olympic Games.**

BALLANGRUD, IVAR EUGEN (né ERIKSEN) (NOR–SSK). B. 7 March 1904, Lunner, Oppland, **Norway.** D. 1 June 1969, Trondheim, Sør-Trøndelag, Norway. Ivar Ballangrud's record of seven **Olympic medals** has only been matched by **Clas Thunberg** (FIN) and Sven Kramer (NED) among male **speed skaters.** In 1928, Ballangrud won the 5,000 meters and, in 1936, he was the winner at 500 meters, 5,000 meters, and 10,000 meters. He also won two silver medals (1932, 1936) and a bronze (1928). Ballangrud's record at the World Championships has never been approached; he won the 5,000 meters seven times and the 1,500 meters and 10,000 meters four times each, and was a four-time winner of the overall title (1926, 1932, 1936, and 1938). Ballangrud was **all-around** European Champion in 1929–1930, 1933, and 1936. He also set a total of five world records at 3,000 meters (one), 5,000 meters (three), and 10,000 meters (one).

BALLROOM DANCING. *See* DANCE SPORT.

BANDY. Bandy was contested as a **demonstration sport** at the 1952 **Olympic Winter Games.** It is an outdoor form of **ice hockey** played on a large rink with 11 players on each side, using a ball instead of a puck. The International Bandy Federation is a provisional member of **SportAccord**, and in 2003 it was given recognition by the **International Olympic Committee.** It was founded in 1955 and currently (as of 2014) has 29 affiliated nations.

BANGLADESH (BAN). The Bangladesh Olympic Association was formed in 1979 and recognized by the **International Olympic Committee** in 1980. The South Asian nation, officially known as the People's Republic of Bangladesh, did not compete in Moscow in 1980, but has been represented at all the **Olympic Games** since 1984. Bangladeshi athletes have never competed at the **Olympic Winter Games**. Through 2012, Bangladesh is the most populous nation (eighth largest in the world with more than 150 million people) that has not yet won an Olympic medal.

It has been represented by 32 Olympians (25 men, seven **women**) in five sports—**archery** (one man), **athletics** (12 men, three women), **gymnastics** (one man), **shooting** (three men, three women), and **swimming** (eight men, one woman)—with six Olympians in both 1988 and 1992. None of the entrants in archery or athletics advanced past the first round of competition. The best performances by Bangladesh Olympians all occurred in 2012. Rahman Md Mahfizur finished 39th of 58 contestants in the 50 meter **freestyle** swimming event. In shooting, Sharmin Ratna was 27th of 56 entrants in the women's **air rifle** 10 meter event. In gymnastics, Bangladesh was represented by American-born (of Bangladeshi parents), University of Michigan college student Quazi Syque Caesar, who finished his three exercises with respectable results: tied for 29th of 70 in **floor exercise**, 27th of 71 in **parallel bars**, and 50th of 70 in the **horizontal bar**.

BANTAMWEIGHT. Bantamweight is a **boxing** weight class with a maximum weight of approximately 119 pounds (54 kg). It has been contested in every summer **Olympic Games** in which boxing was held (1904, 1908, 1920–2012). **Cuban** Guillermo Rigondeaux (2000, 2004) is the only dual gold medal winner in this class. **Russian** Raimkul Malakhbekov won the bantamweight bronze medal in 1996 and the bantamweight silver medal in 2000 and is the only other bantamweight dual medalist. The term bantamweight is also used in the Olympic sports of men's (but not **women**'s) **weightlifting** and **wrestling**. Weight limits for the bantamweight class are slightly different in those two sports, but the class is still the second or third lightest weight class.

The bantamweight class in men's weightlifting has been contested at each Olympics since 1948. Halil Mutlu of **Turkey** was a bantamweight weightlifting dual gold medalist (2000, 2004) as was Chuck Vinci of the **United States** (1956, 1960). Imre Földi of **Hungary** won three medals (gold 1972, silver 1964, 1968) in bantamweight weightlifting. In wrestling, the bantamweight class was held in Olympic **Greco-Roman** style competition from 1924 to 2000 and in **freestyle** in 1904, 1908, and 1924–2000. Four bantamweight Greco-Roman wrestlers have each won two **Olympic medals**: Sheng Zetian of **China** (bronze 1992, 1996), Jakob Brendel of **Germany** (gold 1932, bronze 1936), Babis Kholidis of **Greece** (bronze 1984, 1988), and Ion Cernea of **Romania** (silver 1960, bronze 1964). Yojiro Uetake of **Japan** (1964, 1968) and Sergey Beloglazov of the **Soviet Union** (1980, 1988) are the only two dual gold medalists in Olympic bantamweight freestyle wrestling.

BARBADOS (BAR). The Barbados Olympic Association was formed in 1955, but Barbados did not compete in the Olympics as an independent country until 1964. However, in 1960 Barbados competed as part of the **West Indies Federation**. One of the Barbadan runners, James Wedderburn, ran with three **Jamaicans** as a member of the 4x400 meter **relay** team and helped win a bronze medal. The Caribbean island nation, whose official name is simply Barbados, has since competed at every **Olympic Games** except for 1980 which they **boycotted**. It has not yet competed at the **Olympic Winter Games**. In 11 Summer Games, it has entered 106 athletes (89 men, 17 **women**) and competed in 11 sports: **athletics** (38 men, 15 women), **boxing** (eight men), **cycling** (12 men), **judo** (four men), **sailing** (12 men), **shooting** (three men), and **swimming** (nine men, one woman). It also has had one woman compete in **synchronized swimming** and one man in each of **diving**, **gymnastics**, and **weightlifting**.

In 2000, Obadele Thompson won a bronze medal for Barbados in the 100 meter **sprint**, the only medal won by Barbados at the Olympics. He had previously finished fourth in the 200 meters in 1996 and was again fourth in that event in 2000. In 2004, he was seventh in the 100 meters. Among the other noteworthy Olympic performances for Barbados are the 1984 men's 4x400 meters relay sprint team, which finished sixth; Ryan Braithwaite, fifth in the men's 110 meter **hurdles** in 2012; Chemene Sinson, 11th of 50 in the women's solo event in the first Olympic Games synchronized swimming in 1984, Barry Forde, sixth of 19 in the men's 2004 sprint cycling, and Bradley Ally, ninth of 46 in the 200 meter individual **medley** swim in 2008 and 10th of 29 in the 400 meter individual medley at those same Games. Leah Martindale was fifth of 55 in the women's 50 meter **freestyle** swim and 12th of 48 in the 100 meters in 1996.

BASEBALL. Baseball is an American sport, the game having been developed in the early 19th century. Popular lore attributes its discovery to Abner Doubleday in Cooperstown, New York, but research indicates that it is highly unlikely he actually invented the game. Its exact origins are unclear, although it is probably based somewhat on the **British** games of **cricket** and rounders.

American baseball was contested at the Olympics as a **demonstration sport** in 1912, 1936, 1956, 1964, 1984, and 1988. In 1952, *pesäpallo* ("Finnish baseball") was demonstrated at the Helsinki Olympics. American baseball became a full medal sport at Barcelona in 1992. The Americans do not dominate the sport in international play, as the **Cubans** and several

Central American countries produce excellent teams, although the **United States** upset the Cubans and won the gold medal at Sydney in 2000. At the 2005 **International Olympic Committee** (IOC) Session, baseball, along with **softball**, was eliminated from the **Olympic Program**, a decision that was confirmed in 2006. The sport has lobbied to be added back to the program but faces a difficult battle. Internationally, baseball was governed by the International Baseball Federation, which was founded in 1938 and had 112 members as of 2010. In 2013, it merged with the International Softball Federation and formed the World Baseball Softball Confederation (WBSC) in an attempt to return the two sports to the **Olympic Games**. In 2014, the WBSC had 140 member nations.

There are several reasons for its exclusion. One is that Major League Baseball in the United States has been unable to set up a system similar to **ice hockey** and the National Hockey League, which allows all the best players to play, and the IOC wants this. Second, the sport is not very popular in Europe, which dominates the **Olympic Movement**. Third, the sport is seen as one played mainly in the United States, and the United States now has very little influence within the Olympic Movement. There are also concerns about **doping** use in Major League Baseball and limited reuse of Olympic baseball stadiums in most European nations.

In the five years in which baseball was an Olympic sport (1992–2008), there were 761 men from 16 countries who participated. Cuba was the gold medalist in 1992, 1996, and 2004 and was the silver medalist in 2000 and 2008. The United States won in 2000 and **Korea** in 2008. *See also* LAZO IGLESIAS, PEDRO LUIS.

BASKETBALL. Basketball is one of the few sports of which the precise origin is known. The game was invented in 1891 by James W. Naismith, an instructor at the International Young Men's Christian Association Training School in Springfield, Massachusetts, now Springfield College. The game was originally played with peach baskets, and an attendant on a ladder retrieved the ball after a made basket. Naismith formulated 13 rules of the game, of which 12 still form the basics of the modern game.

In 1936, men's basketball made its first appearance as a medal sport at the Olympics. In 1976, **women**'s basketball was added to the program. In St. Louis in 1904, a basketball tournament was held, but historians generally feel that it should not be considered part of the Olympic Games. The **United States** has dominated international basketball. It won all the Olympic titles until 1972, when it was upset by the **Soviet Union** in a very controversial game. The Soviet women were originally the top team on the female side, but the U.S. women have surpassed them, winning the gold medal in 1984,

1988, 1996, 2000, 2004, 2008, and 2012. In 18 summer **Olympic Games**, competitions there have been 3,232 athletes (2,390 men, 842 women) from 65 nations who have participated in Olympic basketball. Today, basketball has become one of the most popular sports in the world. College basketball is wildly popular in the United States, and the National Basketball Association (NBA) has engendered international interest. In addition, numerous international leagues have added to the growth of the sport. In 1992, for the first time, the United States was allowed to use professional players from the NBA. This NBA all-star team, dubbed "**The Dream Team**" by the world's media, is certainly the greatest basketball team ever assembled and it dominated the 1992 Olympic tournament. An NBA all-star team also represented the United States in 1996 and 2000, winning those gold medals as well, although the margin between the NBA and the rest of the world is shrinking, and in 2004, despite using NBA players, the U.S. men lost three games and only won a bronze medal. However, in 2008 and 2012, the U.S. team again won the gold medal, after instituting a program to restore the country to international prominence under the tutelage of Duke University coach Mike Krzyzewski. Basketball is governed worldwide by the Fédération Internationale de Basketball (FIBA), formerly known as the Fédération Internationale de Basketball Amateur. As a measure of its popularity, FIBA currently (2014) has 213 member nations.

Two women, **Lisa Leslie** and **Teresa Edwards**, have won four Olympic basketball gold medals, with Edwards adding a bronze, to make her the only Olympian with five basketball medals. **Australian** women Kristi Harrower and **Lauren Jackson** also have four medals, three silver and one bronze. Two men have also won four medals each: Soviets **Sergey Belov** and Gennady Volnov. *See also* JORDAN, MICHAEL JEFFREY; KURLAND, ROBERT ALBERT; PALUBINSKAS, EDWARD SEBASTIAN; SABONIS, ARVYDAS ROMAS; SCHMIDT, OSCAR DANIEL BEZERRA; SEMJONOVA, ULJANA LARIONOVNA; UNITED STATES MEN'S BASKETBALL TEAM—1960; UNITED STATES MEN'S BASKETBALL TEAM—1984; UNITED STATES WOMEN'S BASKETBALL; ZHENG, HAIXIA.

BASQUE COUNTRY. The region of the Pyrenees Mountains between **France** and **Spain** inhabited by people of Basque origin is sometimes referred to as Basque Country, although there is no separate sovereign state as such. The Basque sport of **pelota** (also known as jai-alai) was contested at the 1900 **Olympic Games** and has been held as a **demonstration sport** in 1924, 1968, and 1992. In addition, several Basque athletes have participated in other Olympic sports, including Maialen Chourraut Yurramendi, who won a bronze medal in the women's **kayak singles slalom** event, and Maider

Unda who won a bronze medal in women's **freestyle heavyweight wrestling** as representatives of Spain in 2012.

BASUTOLAND. *See* LESOTHO.

BASZANOWSKI, WALDEMAR ROMUALD (POL–WLT). B. 15 August 1935, Grudziądz, Kujawsko-Pomorskie, **Poland**. D. 29 April 2011, Warsaw, Mazowieckie, Poland. Never weighing more than 154 lb (70 kg) and just five feet, five inches (165 cm) tall, Waldemar Baszanowski was one of the greatest **weightlifters** ever, pound for pound. He won gold medals in both 1964 and 1968 at the Olympics in the **lightweight** class and was also World Champion in 1961 and 1965. He narrowly missed winning two more **Olympic medals** as he was fifth in 1960 and fourth in 1972. Baszanowski was a great technician who did very well in the quick lifts of **snatch** and **clean and jerk**. He was the first man to clean and jerk two and one-half times his body weight. He set 24 world records, capped by his greatest day, 26 June 1964, when he broke the world overall record three times in the same competition. From 1999 to 2008, he was the president of the European Weightlifting Federation.

BAUMGARTNER, BRUCE ROBERT (USA–WRE). B. 2 November 1960, Haledon, New Jersey, **United States**. Bruce Baumgartner is the greatest **heavyweight wrestler** ever produced in the United States. A **freestyler**, he competed four times at the **Olympic Games** (1984–1996) and won a medal at each Olympics, one of only six Olympic wrestlers to win medals at four Games. (The others are **Wilfried Dietrich, Germany; Aleksandr Karelin, Russia; Eino Leino, Finland;** Imre Polyak, **Hungary; Artur Taymazov, Uzbekistan.**)

Baumgartner won the **super-heavyweight** class freestyle gold medal in 1984 and 1992, won silver in 1988, and finished his career in Atlanta in 1996 with a bronze. When he competed in 1984, the super-heavyweight class had no weight restrictions, but since 1988, a maximum weight limit of 130 kg (287 lb) has been in effect. The six-foot, two-inch (188 cm) Baumgartner was World Champion in 1987, 1991, and 1995 and runner-up at the Worlds in 1989–1990 and 1994, winning nine World medals in all. He won the **Pan American Games** gold medal three times consecutively, in 1987, 1991, and 1995. His record in the World Cup was particularly impressive, with seven titles, in 1984–1986, 1989–1991, and 1994.

BEACH VOLLEYBALL. Beach **volleyball** became popular in the 1980s, played originally on the beaches of Southern California. It has been described in the media as "*Baywatch* with a medal ceremony." Unlike the indoor six-person game, beach volleyball is played usually by two-person teams, although events with four-person teams have been contested. The game is played on a sand-based surface. Beach volleyball was added to the **Olympic Program** in 1996 and a men's tournament and a **women**'s tournament has been contested in each subsequent Olympics. There have been a total of 321 participants (163 men, 158 women) from 36 nations in the five years of Olympic tournaments.

The first men's gold medal was won by the **United States** team of **Karch Kiraly**, often considered the greatest ever volleyballer, and his teammate, Kent Steffes. Two women have won three gold medals each: **Kerri Walsh** and **Misty May-Treanor** of the United States, who won the title in 2004, 2008, and 2012. Two **Brazilian** men—**Emanuel** (Emanuel Fernando Scheffler Rego) and **Ricardo** (Ricardo Alex Costa Santos)—have each won three medals—one gold, one silver, and one bronze. They were teammates in 2004, winning the gold, and in 2008 winning the bronze, but in 2000 Ricardo teamed with Zé Marco to win silver and in 2012 Emanuel teamed with Alison Cerutti to win silver.

BEAMON, ROBERT "BOB" (USA–ATH). B. 29 August 1946, Jamaica, New York, **United States**. With a single performance lasting no more than

Bob Beamon in-flight, which led to the greatest single track and field performance ever, when he obliterated the long jump world record at the 1968 Olympic Games. Courtesy of Erich Kamper

a few seconds, Bob Beamon achieved sporting immortality at Mexico City in October 1968. His **long jump** of 8.90 meters (29 feet two and a half inches) gave him the Olympic gold medal and a new world record by a massive margin. Rated by many as the greatest performance in track and field history, his record was thought to be unbeatable. But like all records, it was inevitably surpassed, and in 1991 the record fell to Mike Powell (USA). The six-foot, three-inch (191 cm), 154 lb (70 kg) Beamon never again approached the form he showed at the 1968 Olympics, and he turned professional in 1972. After first attending Adelphi University, Beamon graduated from the University of Texas at El Paso in 1970, where he also briefly played **basketball**. Beamon had little success as a professional trackster and spent most of his career in social work.

BECHUANALAND. *See* BOTSWANA.

BEERBAUM, LUDGER (FRG/GER–EQU). B. 25 August 1963, Detmold, Nordrhein-Westfalen, West Germany. Educated in the stable of **Olympic medalist** Paul Schockemöhle, Ludger Beerbaum has won all available **equestrian jumping** titles. The six-foot, three-inch (190 cm), 176 lb (80 kg) Beerbaum competed in six **Olympic Games** (1988–2008) and won three team jumping titles (1988, 1996, and 2000) and the individual title in 1992. The **German** team also placed first in Athens but was relegated to third when Beerbaum's result was scratched after his horse was discovered to have been given prohibited medicine. Beerbaum has earned two team world titles at the 1994 and 1998 World Equestrian Games and three team and two individual golds at European Championships. The 1993 World Cup Final also went to Beerbaum, who has won the Aachen Grand Prix three times. Markus Beerbaum, Ludger's brother, is also a noted show jumper, as is Markus's wife, **United States**–born Meredith Michaels.

BEHRENDT, JAN (GDR/GER–LUG). B. 29 November 1967, Ilmenau, Thüringen, East Germany; and **STEFAN KRAUßE (GDR/GER–LUG).** B. 17 September 1967, Ilmenau, Thüringen, East Germany. Jan Behrendt (five feet, seven inches [169 cm], 154 lb [70 kg]) and Stefan Krauße (six feet, one inch [186 cm], 198 lb [90 kg]) formed a redoubtable **doubles luge** team, competing first for the **German Democratic Republic** and from 1992 for **Germany**. At the Olympics, they won gold medals in 1992 and 1998, silver in 1988, and bronze in 1994. Behrendt and Krauße began to compete together internationally at the 1985 European Junior championships. Together, they won four World Championships (1989, 1991, 1993, and 1995) and were runners-up in 1996–1997. They were also World Cup champions in 1994–1996 and European champions in 1996. They announced their retirement after the 1998 **Olympic Winter Games.**

BELARUS (BLR). The **National Olympic Committee** of the Republic of Belarus (formerly Belorussia, or Byelorussia [White Russia]) was formed in 1991 after the breakup of the **Soviet Union.** Many Belarusan athletes competed from 1952 to 1988 for the Soviet Union, and Belarusan athletes were present at both Albertville and Barcelona in 1992 as members of the Unified Team. The Eastern European nation competed as an independent nation for the first time at the 1994 **Olympic Winter Games** in Lillehammer, with 33 athletes who won two medals. It first competed independently at the Summer **Olympic Games** in 1996. In five Summer Games, Belarus has entered 537 athletes (295 men, 242 **women**) and competed in 25 of the 34 sports that have been held during those five Games. They have not qualified for most of the team sports and have not taken part in **baseball, beach volleyball, handball, hockey, softball, volleyball,** and **water polo** as well as the individual sports of **taekwondo** and **triathlon.**

Belarusan athletes have won 12 gold medals and 76 medals overall. The most successful Olympians from Belarus each won four medals for their country. Female rower Yekaterina "Katya" Khodatovich-Karsten has competed in six Olympic Games. She won a bronze medal in the quadruple **sculls** in 1992 as a member of the Unified Team and in single sculls for Belarus (gold in 1996 and 2000, silver in 2004, and bronze in 2008). In 2012, at the age of 40, she was fifth in that event. Gymnast **Vitaly Shcherbo** won six gold medals for the Unified Team in 1992 and four bronze medals for Belarus in 1996. **Kayakers** Roman Petrushenko and Vadim Makhnyov also won four medals: bronze in **doubles** in 2004 and 2008, silver in doubles in 2012, and gold as members of the four-man team in 2008.

Fourteen other athletes have won multiple Olympic medals for Belarus: **heptathlete** Natasha Sazanovich (1996 silver, 2000 bronze); **discus thrower** Ellina Zvereva (1996 bronze, 2000 gold); **canoeist** brothers Aleksandr and Andrey Bogdanovich (2008 gold, 2012 silver); **rhythmic gymnasts** Anastasiya Ivankova, Kseniya Sankovich, and Alina Tumilovich (2008 bronze, 2012 silver), **rowers** Yuliya Bichik and Nataliya Gelakh (2004, 2008 bronze), **shooter** Igor Basinsky (1988 bronze for the Soviet Union and 1996 silver, 2000 bronze and silver for Belarus); shooter Sergey Martynov (2000 bronze, 2004 bronze, 2012 gold); swimmer Aleksandra Gerasimenya (2012 two silver); **tennis** player Viktoriya Azarenka (2012 bronze and gold), and weightlifter Andrey Rybakov (2004, 2008 both silver).

In six Winter Games, Belarus has entered 160 athletes (107 men, 53 women) and competed in 10 of the 15 sports contested during those years—

all but **bobsled, curling, luge, skeleton**, and **snowboarding**. They have won 15 medals: six gold, four silver, and five bronze. Multiple Winter Games medalists are Darya Domacheva (bronze in 2010 and three gold in 2014 in biathlon) and **freestyle skiers** Dmitry Dashchinsky (1998 bronze, 2006 silver) and Aleksey Grishin (2002 bronze, 2010 gold).

Belarus has never hosted an Olympic Games, but in 1980 during the Moscow Olympics several preliminary football matches were held in Minsk, the capital of Belarus. *See also* KORBUT, OLGA VALENTINOVNA.

BELGIAN CONGO. *See* CONGO, DEMOCRATIC REPUBLIC OF THE.

BELGIAN EAST AFRICA. *See* BURUNDI; RWANDA.

BELGIUM (BEL). Belgium has competed at every **Olympic Games** except 1896 and 1904. Belgium began competing at the **Olympic Winter Games** in 1924 and also competed in **figure skating** and **ice hockey** in 1920, but the country missed the 1960 and 1968 Olympic Winter Games. In 26 Summer Games, Belgium has entered 1,907 athletes (1,655 men, 252 **women**) and competed in 34 sports plus the **art competitions**. Their most popular sports have been **athletics** (217 men, 52 women), **cycling** (197 men, 11 women), **hockey** (136 men, 18 women), **rowing** (129 men, six women), **fencing** (113 men, 12 women), and **swimming** (64 men, 49 women).

Belgium has won 158 medals (42 gold, 56 silver, 60 bronze) in the Summer Games, including eight medals (two gold, one silver, five bronze) in the now defunct art contests. Six Belgian Olympians have won four or more **Olympic medals**, led by **archer Hubert Van Innis**, with 10 medals, including six golds, both records among Olympic archers. The other Olympic medalists for Belgium with four or more are archer Louis Van De Perck (1920 two gold, two silver), fencer Paul Anspach (1908 bronze, 1912 two gold, 1920 silver, 1924 silver), and **water polo** player Joseph Pletinckx (1908, 1920, 1924 silver, 1912 bronze). Gérard Blitz won medals in two sports: water polo (silver 1920, 1924, bronze 1936) and swimming (1920 bronze). Fernand de Montigny also won medals in two sports: fencing (1906 bronze, 1908 bronze, 1924 two silver) and field hockey (1920 bronze). He was also the architect who designed the 1920 Olympic Stadium in Antwerp. Victor Boin won medals in two different sports—water polo (silver 1908, bronze 1912) and fencing (bronze 1920)—as did Joseph De Combe (water polo silver 1924, bronze 1936, and swimming 1924 silver). But no Belgian has won more than three Olympic medals since World War II.

Belgium has competed in 20 Winter Games and has entered 124 athletes (104 men, 20 women) in eight sports: **Alpine skiing, freestyle skiing, snowboard-**

ing, **bobsledding**, **ice hockey**, **figure skating**, **speed skating**, and **short track speed skating** with the most—37 men and three women—in bobsledding. They have won five medals at the Winter Games: gold by Micheline Lannoy and Pierre Baugniet in 1948 **pairs** figure skating, silver by the 1948 four-man bobsledding team, bronze by the 1924 four-man bobsledding team, Robert Van Zeebroeck in 1928 figure skating, and Bart Veldkamp in 1998 speed skating.

Among Belgium's most noted Olympians is **Jacques Rogge**, who competed in **sailing** from 1968 to 1976 and served as **International Olympic Committee (IOC) president** from 2001 to 2013. One of the other IOC presidents, **Count Henry de Baillet-Latour**, was also a Belgian native. The Western European nation, officially known as the Kingdom of Belgium, hosted the Games of the VIIth **Olympiad** at Antwerp in 1920 and had three unsuccessful bids by Brussels in 1916, 1960, and 1964.

BELIZE (BIZ). As British Honduras, this country formed a **National Olympic Committee** in 1967 and made three Olympic appearances, in 1968, 1972, and 1976. As Belize, it has been represented at all the **Olympic Games** beginning in 1984, after **boycotting** the 1980 Olympic Games. This **Central American** nation has never competed at the **Olympic Winter Games** and has never won an **Olympic medal**. In 11 Summer Games, its 49 athletes (43 men, six **women**) have competed in seven Olympic sports: **athletics** (20 men, five women), **boxing** (one man), **cycling** (16 men, one woman), **judo** (one man), **shooting** (four men), **taekwondo** (one man), and **weightlifting** (one man) with one man competing in both athletics and cycling.

The best performance by a Belizean athlete was by Eugene Muslar, who finished 79th of 98 finishers and 118 starters, in the 1988 men's **marathon**. Other notable performances include Robert Hulse who was 63rd of 86 in mixed **small-bore rifle** prone shooting competition in 1968. (He was the only one of six shooters from Belize who did not finish last in their event.) Three Belizean runners (Jonathan Williams, men's 400 meter **hurdles**, 2008; Kenneth Medwood, men's 400 meter hurdles, 2012; and Kaina Martinez, women's 100 meters, 2012) each advanced to the second **round** in their competitions before being eliminated.

BELMONDO, STEFANIA (ITA–CCS). B. 13 January 1969, Vinadio, Cuneo, **Italy**. With 10 **Olympic medals**, the Italian **cross-country skier** Stefania Belmondo is tied with **Raisa Smetanina** (URS/EUN) and **Marit Bjørgen** (NOR) among female athletes at the **Olympic Winter Games** and trails only **Bjørn Dæhlie**, who won 12 Olympic medals in cross-country skiing. Belmondo first competed at the Winter Olympics in 1988. In 1992, she won three medals, including a gold medal in the 30 km race.

She won two medals at the 1994 Lillehammer Olympics, two more at Nagano in 1998, and in 2002 won three medals, including her second gold in the 15 km race, after which she retired. The 15 km gold medal was particularly dramatic, as Belmondo broke a pole with 4.5 km remaining and skied in with only one pole. Belmondo won the World Cup for cross-country skiing in 1999 and finished second in that competition three times (1991, 1992, 1997) and third three times (1993, 1998, 2002). She also won the Sprint World Cup in 1997 and was a five-time World Champion. Nicknamed "The Tiny Tornado" for her relatively small size of five feet, three inches (160 cm) and 100 lb (45 kg), Belmondo was renowned for her extensive training regimen, covering over 10,000 km per year on skis. In 2006, she was given the honor of lighting the **Olympic flame** at the opening ceremony of the Torino Olympic Winter Games.

BELOUSOVA, LYUDMILA YEVGENEVNA (later PROTOPOPOVA) (URS–FSK). B. 22 November 1935, Ulyanovsk, **Russia**, USSR; and **OLEG ALEKSEYEVICH PROTOPOPOV** (URS–FSK). B. 16 July 1932, St. Petersburg, Russia, USSR. The husband and wife team of Lyudmila Belousova (five feet, three inches [160 cm], 101 lb [46 kg]) and Oleg Protopopov (five feet, nine inches [175 cm], 157 lb [71 kg]) won the Olympic **pairs figure skating** title in 1964 and 1968 after finishing in ninth place in 1960. As the first **Russian** pair skaters to achieve international acclaim, they provided the stimulus that ultimately led to many successes by future generations of Soviet and Russian skaters. They began skating as a pair shortly before 1957 and were married that year. In addition to their two **Olympic gold medals**, they were World Champions four times (1965–1968). After losing their world title in 1969, Soviet authorities turned their sights on younger skaters and refused to allow them to compete at the 1972 **Olympic Winter Games**. Belousova and Protopopov then immigrated to **Switzerland** and turned professional, touring in many different ice shows.

BELOV, SERGEY ALEKSANDROVICH (URS–BAS). B. 23 January 1944, Nashchyokova, Tomsk Oblast, **Russia**, USSR. D. 3 October 2013, Perm, Perm Kray, Russia. Sergey Belov, at six feet, three inches (190 cm), 181 lb (82 kg), played guard for the Soviet national **basketball** team from 1967 until 1980. Although some sources erroneously list him as the brother of teammate Aleksandr Belov, that was not the case. Sergey won four Olympic medals: bronzes in 1968, 1976, and 1980 and a gold medal in 1972, a record for men he shares with Gennady Volnov. In addition, Belov played on teams that won the World Championships in 1967 and 1974 and European Championships in 1967, 1969, 1971, and 1979. In 1980, he was given the honor of lighting the **Olympic flame** during the opening ceremony of the Moscow Olympics. In 1992, he became the first international player elected to the Naismith Memorial Basketball Hall of Fame. He was married to Olympic basketball player Svetlana Zaboluyeva-Antipova, who won a gold medal in 1992 with the Unified Team and finished in fifth place in 1996 for Russia.

BENIN (BEN). Benin was originally part of French West Africa, but became independent from **France** under the name of Dahomey in 1960. Dahomey competed in the 1972 Olympics at Munich. The name was changed to Benin in 1975, officially the Republic of Benin. After missing the 1976 Games, Benin has competed at every Olympics since 1980. It has never competed in the **Olympic Winter Games** and has not yet won an **Olympic medal**.

In 10 Summer Olympic Games, Benin has had 48 entrants (41 men, seven **women**) and has participated in **athletics** (20 men, six women), **boxing** (12 men), **cycling** (two men), **judo** (two men), **swimming** (two men, one woman), **taekwondo** (two men), and **tennis** (one man). There have been no outstanding Olympic performances by an athlete from Benin. All but one of their boxers lost their first bout, and their only win was in 1980, when **featherweight** boxer Barthelemy Adoukonou received a first-round **bye**, won one match by **disqualification**, and then lost in the third **round** to place equal ninth of 35 boxers. In judo, taekwondo, and tennis, Beninese athletes were eliminated in the first round and their two cyclists did not finish the **road race**. In athletics, nearly all Benin's entrants were eliminated after their first **heat**, with only Issa Alassane-Ousséni in 1988 in the men's 100 meter **sprint** and Fabienne Féraez in 2004 in the women's 200 meter sprint reaching the second round of their event. Arguably the best Olympic performance for Benin occurred in swimming when Alois Dansou finished 60th of 83 entrants in the 50 meter **freestyle** in 2004 and was 62nd of 97 entrants in that event in 2008.

BERESFORD, JACK, JR. (GBR–ROW). B. 1 January 1899, Chiswick, Middlesex, **England**. D. 3 December 1977, Shiplake-on-Thames, Oxfordshire, England. With five medals, Jack Beresford was the most successful Olympic **rower** of the pre–World War II era. To his gold medals in the single **sculls** (1924), coxless fours (1932), and double sculls (1936), he added silver in the single sculls (1920) and the **eights** (1928). Beresford's remarkable career spanned five **Olympic Games**, and it was almost certainly only the cancellation of the 1940 Games that prevented his making a sixth Olympic appearance. He was awarded the **Olympic Diploma** of Merit in 1949. At Henley, he won the Diamond Sculls four times (1920 and 1924–1926), the Nickalls Challenge Cup in 1928 and 1929 (coxless **pairs** with Gordon Killick), and the Double Sculls Challenge Cup in 1939, with Dick Southwood. He also won the Wingfield Sculls for seven consecutive years from 1920. His father, Julius Beresford (né Wisniewski), won an Olympic silver medal in the coxed fours outriggers in 1912 as a member of the Thames Rowing Club. *See also* COXSWAIN.

BERG, LAURA KAY (USA–SOF). B. 6 January 1975, Santa Fe Springs, California, **United States**. Four **softball** players have won four **Olympic medals**, and four players have won three Olympic gold medals, but Laura Berg, at five feet, six inches (168 cm), 134 lb (61 kg), is the only softball player to belong to both groups, making her the most decorated softball Olympian. Softball, which was featured only four times on the **Olympic Program**, was dominated by the **United States** team, which won three gold medals (1996, 2000, and 2004) and one silver (2008). Berg played as a center fielder on all four teams. Berg also was on the victorious U.S. teams that became world champions in 1994, 1998, 2002, and 2006 and won three gold medals at the **Pan American Games** (1999, 2003, and 2007).

BERLIOUX, MONIQUE LIBOTTE (FRA–SWI). B. 22 December 1925, Metz, Moselle, **France**. Monique Berlioux was a French national swim champion, primarily in the **backstroke**, in the 1940s. During World War II, she worked for the French underground, often **swimming** across the River Seine with messages detailing **German** intelligence gathering. She competed at the 1948 **Olympic Games**, finishing sixth in a semifinal of the 100 meter backstroke. But her Olympic fame would come later. Berlioux was educated at the Sorbonne and then began a career in journalism. In the 1960s, she took a job at the **International Olympic Committee** (IOC) and shortly thereafter was made the media chief by **IOC President Avery Brundage**. In 1971, she was appointed director of the IOC, the first female to be so named. She worked under three IOC presidents, Brundage, **Lord Killanin**, and **Juan Antonio Samaranch**. But her relations with Samaranch were more difficult than with Brundage and Killanin, and in 1985, she "resigned" from her position as IOC director, a decision apparently made mutually after discussions with President Samaranch.

BERMUDA (BER). Bermuda first entered international competition in 1930, at the British Empire Games in **Canada**. Following this, a **National Olympic Committee** was formed in 1935, and **International Olympic Committee** recognition was granted in 1936. Bermuda, a British Overseas Territory in the North Atlantic Ocean, has competed at the **Olympic Games** since 1936, failing to appear only in 1980. It has competed at each **Olympic Winter Games** since 1992. Bermuda has sent 112 entrants (92 men, 20

women) to 17 Summer Games, participating in 10 sports: **athletics** (21 men, seven women), **boxing** (four men), **cycling** (four men), **diving** (two men, one woman), **equestrian** (two men, five women), **rowing** (one man), **sailing** (38 men, four women), **swimming** (18 men, two women), **tennis** (one man), and **triathlon** (one man, one woman).

Bermuda's athletes have won one **Olympic medal**, a bronze medal in heavyweight boxing in 1976 by Clarence Hill. Other notable Olympic performances by Bermudans include Frank Gosling, 10th in men's **springboard** diving in 1948; Nick Saunders, fifth place in 1988 men's **high jump**; Brian Wellman, fifth place in 1992 **triple jump** and sixth place in that event four years later; and in sailing, fourth place in 2000 two-person **keelboat** (Lee White and Peter Bromby), fifth place in three-person keelboat in 1964 (Conrad Soares, Kirk Cooper, Penny Simmons), and fifth place in **multihull** in 1984 (Alan Burland, Christopher Nash).

In seven Winter Games, Bermuda has sent only three different entrants, one for each Games, with one man competing in **cross-country skiing**, two men in **luge**, and one of the lugers also in **skeleton**. None of the three did exceptionally well. Patrick Singleton was 19th of 27 in the 2006 skeleton, Tucker Murphy was 88th of 95 in cross-country skiing 15 km in 2010 and 84th of 91 four years later, and Singleton finished 27th of 34 in the 1998 luge.

BHUTAN (BHU). Bhutan established a **National Olympic Committee** in February 1983. This was noted by the **International Olympic Committee** (IOC) **Executive Board** later that year, and provisional IOC recognition was granted in April 1984. The South Asian Himalayan nation of Bhutan took part in the 1984 Olympics, and since then it has been represented in its national sport of **archery** by a total of 18 Olympians (eight men, 10 **women**) at eight Olympics (1984–2012). Until 2012, Bhutan (officially the Kingdom of Bhutan) had not participated in any other sport at the **Olympic Games**, but in that year they had one woman compete in **shooting**. It has won no medals and has not yet competed at the **Olympic Winter Games**. Bhutan is one of only two nations (**Nauru** is the other) to take part in the Olympic Games that has not competed in the sport of **athletics** at the Summer Games. In 2004, Tashi Peljor (men) and Tshering Chhoden (women) both finished 32nd of 64 entrants in the individual archery events, the best finish yet by a Bhutanese Olympian.

BIATHLON. Attempts to introduce a winter multievent, patterned after the **modern pentathlon**, began in 1948, when the **winter pentathlon** was contested at the St. Moritz Olympics as a **demonstration sport**. It consisted of **cross-country** and **downhill skiing**, as well as **shooting**, **fencing**, and horse riding. Biathlon, which consists of cross-country skiing in which the runner stops at intervals to shoot a rifle at a target, was known in the 1920s but was not popular until the 1950s. The first World Championships were held in 1958 at Saalfelden, **Austria**. The sport was quickly placed on the **Olympic Program**, showing up at Squaw Valley in 1960. **Women**'s biathlon made its Olympic debut in 1992 as a full medal sport at Albertville. In 1924, a race known as **military ski patrol**, which was similar to a team biathlon event with team members skiing together, was a medal sport at the **Olympic Winter Games**.

Biathlon is currently governed by the International Biathlon Union, which has 59 member nations as of 2014. Beginning in 1948, biathlon was governed by the Union Internationale de Pentathlon Moderne et Biathlon, which oversaw both sports, but the organization split into two governing bodies in 1993.

Biathlon events consisted of a single men's race (20 km) and a men's **relay** (4x7.5 km) until 1980, when a second individual event (10 km **sprint**) was contested. The event is scored by time. In the longer individual race, a one-minute penalty is assessed for missing a bull's-eye, and a two-minute penalty is assessed for missing a target. In the shorter individual race and the relay, missing a target is penalized by requiring the biathlete to ski a 150 meter penalty loop. Women currently also compete in the Olympics in both a short (7.5 km) and a long (15 km) individual race and a relay race. In 2002, a new individual **pursuit** event for men (12.5 km) and women (10 km) was added, and in 2006 a **mass start** race for men (15 km) and women (12.5 km) was added to the Olympic Program. At the Sochi Olympics in 2014, there were five biathlon events for men and five for women and a new relay event with a mixed team of two men and two women competing.

In the 15 Winter Games in which biathlon has been contested, there have been 1,137 participants (765 men, 372 women) from 54 countries. **Germany** has been the most successful nation in Olympic biathlon, winning 45 medals, including 16 golds, followed by **Norway**, with 35 medals, including 15 golds. The most successful individual has been Norway's **Ole Einar Bjørndalen**, with 13 medals, including eight gold medals. **Uschi Disl** of Germany leads all women biathletes with nine medals, but only two gold. *See also* GROSS, RICCO; TIKHONOV, ALEKSANDR IVANOVICH; WILHELM, KATARINA.

BICYCLE POLO. First played in **Ireland** in 1891, bicycle polo's growing popularity led to a **demonstration** match between Ireland and **Germany** being included in the program at the 1908 **Olympic Games**. Although the sport has been included in the Asian Games, the chances of it becoming an Olympic sport are very remote, as its **International Federation** is currently unrecognized by the **International Olympic Committee** and is not a member of **SportAccord**.

BIJKERK, ANTHONY THEODOOR "TONY." B. 19 February 1931, Bandung, Dutch East Indies. Tony Bijkerk is an Olympic historian, researcher, and collector of Olympic memorabilia. During his youth, he was held captive during World War II at a Japanese detention camp in his native Bandung. He returned to the **Netherlands** following the war, attended the Naval Academy in Den Helder, and in 1953 became an officer in the Royal Netherlands Navy, where he served until 1966. He then became director for sports and recreation in the city of Leeuwarden. After retiring in 1990, he became more active with his interests of Olympic history and memorabilia collecting. In 1991, he was invited to become one of the founding members of the **International Society of Olympic Historians** (ISOH). In 1996, he became secretary-general of the ISOH and has held that position since. He was also editor of the ISOH's publication *Journal of Olympic History* from 1996 to 2002. With Ruud Paauw he published a book on Dutch participation in the **Olympic Games**. In 2004, he published *Olympisch Oranje*, the first book with complete results of all participants from one nation in the Olympic Games, and he has issued revised editions in 2008 and 2012. He was co-author with **Bill Mallon** of *The 1920 Olympic Games: Results for All Competitors in All Events*. In 2001, he received the **Olympic Order** from the **International Olympic Committee** and in 2007 was made an honorary member of the ISOH. Much of his vast memorabilia collection was sold to the Qatar Olympic and Sports Museum and can be seen there when that museum opens in 2015.

BIKILA, ABEBE (ETH–ATH). B. 7 August 1932, Jato, Amhara, **Ethiopia**. D. 25 October 1973, Addis Ababa, Ethiopia. Though his life came to a tragic early end, Abebe Bikila is usually considered the greatest marathoner ever. He was the first person to win the Olympic **marathon** consecutively, doing so in 1960 and 1964. His marathon career began only a few months before the Rome Olympics in 1960, when he won a trial race in the altitude of Addis Ababa. Between that race and a marathon he won in Seoul in October 1966, Bikila, at five feet, 10 inches (177 cm) and only 126 lb (57 kg), ran 15 marathons, winning 14, losing only the 1963 Boston Marathon, in which he finished fifth. He sustained an injury in 1967 and never fully recovered, which caused him to withdraw after starting the 1968 Olympic marathon in **Mexico** City. Late in 1969, Bikila was in a car accident, and the injuries he sustained rendered him a quadriplegic. After treatment at Stoke Mandeville Hospital, his condition improved to paraplegic, and he even competed as an **archer** in the 1969 Stoke Mandeville Games, the forerunner of the **Paralympic Games**. He lived only a few more years. His funeral in Addis Ababa was attended by thousands, who came to mourn their nation's first great, and still greatest, runner.

BILLIARDS. Billiards, and the many pool variants, have never been on the **Olympic Program**. But the World Confederation of Billiards Sports is currently recognized by the **International Olympic Committee**. Founded in 1992, the federation currently has 148 affiliated member nations.

BIONDI, MATTHEW NICHOLAS "MATT" (USA–SWI). B. 8 October 1965, Moraga, California, **United States**. Matt Biondi won 11 **swimming** medals at the 1984, 1988, and 1992 Olympics, matching the record then held by **Mark Spitz**. Biondi, six feet, seven inches (200 cm) tall and 209 lb (95 kg), was at his best at the 1988 Games, winning seven medals (five gold, one silver, one bronze), and, although essentially a **freestyle** swimmer, he won his silver medal in the 100 meter **butterfly** when he was upset by Anthony Nesty of **Suriname**. Biondi set seven individual world records and won six gold medals at the World Championships (1986, 1991). In 1986, he won seven medals at the World Championships and added four more in 1991.

BJØRGEN, MARIT (NOR–CCS). B. 21 March 1980, Trondheim, Sør-Trøndelag, **Norway**. **Cross-country skier** Marit Bjørgen was the top competitor at the 2010 Vancouver Games, with three gold medals, a silver, and a bronze, winning a medal in each of the five cross-country skiing events in which she competed. She grabbed the gold in the **sprint**, the 15 km **pursuit**, and the **relay**; won the silver in the 30 km **mass start**; and won the bronze in the 10 km. At earlier **Olympic Winter Games**, she had won two silver medals. In 2014, she won three more gold medals, bringing her **Olympic medal** total to 10. She is second only to countryman **Bjørn Dæhlie** in total Olympic cross-country medals and is tied with **Russian Raisa Smetanina** and **Italian Stefania Belmondo** for the most by a female cross-country skier. Bjørgen, at five feet, six inches (168 cm) tall and 141 lb (64 kg), is also a 12-time World Champion, winning her first gold in 2003 and three titles in 2005, four more in 2011, and four more in 2013. With 66 World Cup victories through mid-2014, Bjørgen is the winningest **woman** cross-country skier.

BJØRNDALEN, OLE EINAR (NOR–BIA). B. 27 January 1974, Drammen, Buskerud, **Norway**. Ole Einar Bjørndalen first competed at the **Olympic Winter Games** in 1994, but with only minimal success. In 1998 at Nagano, he won the 10 km **biathlon** event and won silver with the Norwegian

relay team. But prior to the 2001–2002 season, he gave no indication of what he would do at the Salt Lake City Olympics. Earlier in the season, he won two World Cup biathlon races, but at Salt Lake City, he won gold medals in all four biathlon events: 10 km, 20 km, **pursuit**, and relay. No biathlete before him had won more than two gold medals at a single Winter Olympics. In 2006, Bjørndalen won three more medals, but failed to win a race. In 2010, the five-foot, 10-inch (178 cm), 143 lb (65 kg) athlete added two more medals, including a gold in the relay. He added two more gold medals in 2014 and his total of 13 medals at the Winter Games is the most of any winter athlete regardless of sport. Following the 2014 Winter Games, he was elected to the **International Olympic Committee Athletes' Commission**.

Bjørndalen may have more medals in major competitions than any athlete in any sport. Through mid-2014, he has 39 World Championship medals, including 19 golds. He has won 94 World Cup biathlon races and one in **cross-country skiing**, and has been on the podium 170 times in the World Cup, three times in cross-country. His brother Dag was a silver medalist in the biathlon relay at the 1998 Winter Olympics. Ole Einar's wife, Nathalie Santer, competed in the biathlon in five Winter Olympics from 1992 to 2006 for **Italy** but never finished higher than seventh. Her sister Saskia Santer also competed in biathlon at the 2002 and 2006 Games for Italy, with a best result of 11th.

BLAIR, BONNIE KATHLEEN (later CRUIKSHANK) (USA–SSK). B. 18 March 1964, Cornwall-on-Hudson, New York, **United States**. With victories in the 500 meters in 1988, 1992, and 1994, Bonnie Blair is one of only two **women (Claudia Pechstein**, 5,000 meters 1994–2002 is the other) to have won an Olympic **speed skating** event at three successive Games. Bonnie also won the 1,000 meters in 1992 and 1994 after taking the bronze in 1988, and her total of five speed skating gold medals has only been bettered by the **Russian Lidiya Skoblikova**. The five-foot, five-inch (165 cm), 130 lb (59 kg) Blair won four World Championships: the World **Short-Track** Championships in 1986 and the World **Sprints** in 1989 (at which she set a long-standing world record of 159.435 points for the sprint **all-around**), 1994, and 1995. During her career, she set four world records in the 500 meters and five in the sprint all-around. She is the wife of Dave Cruikshank, also a speed skater who competed for the United States in the **Olympic Winter Games** of 1992, 1994, and 1998.

BLANKERS-KOEN, FRANCINA ELSJE "FANNY" (née KOEN) (NED–ATH). B. 26 April 1918, Baarn, Utrecht, **Netherlands**. D. 25 January 2004, Hoofddorp, Nord-Holland, Netherlands. Fanny Blankers-Koen was

Fanny Blankers-Koen, the Dutch mother and housewife who won four gold medals in track and field athletics at the 1948 Olympics. Courtesy of Erich Kamper

an outstanding **all-around** athlete who made her Olympic debut as a **high jumper** in 1936. World War II deprived her of the opportunity to make further Olympic appearances until 1948 when, at the age of 30 and as a mother of two, she was the star of the London Games. Blankers-Koen won the 100 meters, 200 meters, and 80 meter **hurdles** and ran the anchor leg on the winning **relay** team. She would likely have won more medals, but in 1948 she competed in only three individual track and field events, although she was at the time the world record holder in the high jump, **long jump**, and **pentathlon**. At five feet, nine inches (175 cm), and 139 lb (63 kg), she set world records at eight different events, won five European titles (1946–1950), and a statue was erected in her honor in her native Amsterdam. She married her coach, Jan Blankers, a 1928 Dutch Olympic **triple jumper**.

BLEIBTREY, ETHELDA MARGUERITE (later MACROBERT, then SCHLAFKE) (USA–SWI). B. 27 February 1902, Waterford, New York, **United States.** D. 6 May 1978, West Palm Beach, Florida, United States. Ethelda Bleibtrey was the first United States' female **swimmer** of international renown and the first female star of the Olympic pool. At the 1920 Games, she won a gold medal in each of the three swimming events for women—100 meters and 300 meters **freestyle** and **relay**—and would almost certainly have won a fourth had a **backstroke** event been included, as she was, at the time, a world record holder in this style. Bleibtrey set seven world records before turning professional in 1922, after which she became a swimming instructor.

BLONAY, BARON GODEFROY JEAN HENRI LOUIS DE (SUI). B. 25 July 1869, Wiederschöfal, **Switzerland**. D. 14 February 1937, Biskra, **Algeria**. Baron Godefroy de Blonay was appointed the first Swiss **International Olympic Committee** (IOC) member in 1899 and remained a member until his death in 1937. He was a founder of the Swiss Olympic Committee in 1912 and was its first president (1912–1915). During the latter part of World War I, he served as provisional **IOC president** (1916–1919) when **Pierre de Coubertin**, who had enlisted in the French army, felt that it would not be appropriate for a military man to serve as head of the IOC. After Coubertin was discharged from the military because of his age, Blonay relinquished his presidential duties, and Coubertin again took over the presidency. Blonay was a member of the IOC **Executive Board** from 1921 to 1937 and was president of the Executive Board from 1921 to 1925. He then was vice president of the IOC from 1925 until his death. Although Blonay was originally a close friend of Coubertin, severe tensions developed between them when Blonay attempted to obtain certain administrative functions for the Executive Board. A distinguished Egyptologist, Blonay lived in Paris for many years, but eventually settled in Switzerland, where he taught at the University of Neuchâtel.

BMX. Bicycle motocross (BMX) was added as an Olympic **cycling** event for both men and **women** in 2008. It is similar to motorcycle motocross (not an Olympic sport) in that it is contested over a serpentine dirt track with various jumps. Marius Strombergs of **Latvia** was gold medalist both years in the men's event, while the women's event had six different medalists with Anne-Caroline Chausson of **France** winning the gold in 2008 and Mariana Pajón of **Colombia** winning it in 2012.

BOARDERCROSS. Boardercross is an event in the **Olympic Winter Games** sport of **snowboarding** that was added to the **Olympic Program** in 2006 and has been contested in three Olympics. Several snowboarders race **downhill** simultaneously, with the fastest racers advancing to the next **round** of the competition. The only multiple Olympic medalists in this event are Seth Westcott of the **United States**, the winner of the men's gold medal in 2006 and 2010, and Dominique Maltais of **Canada**, who won the bronze medal in 2006 and the silver medal in 2014 in the **women**'s competition.

BOARDSAILING. *See* WINDSURFER.

BOBSLEDDING. Bobsledding (also known as bobsleigh) as a sport originated in **Switzerland** in 1888, when an Englishman, Wilson Smith, connected two sleighs with a board to travel from St. Moritz to Celerina. Bobsledding was first practiced on the Cresta Run at St. Moritz, but the run was not suitable for the faster bobsleds, so a separate bob run was constructed there in 1904, the world's first.

Bobsledding was on the program of the first **Olympic Winter Games** in 1924, with a single four-man event. In both 1924 and 1928, the event was for sleds with either four or five men. In 1932, the present men's program of two events began, one for two-man sleds and one for four-man sleds. In 2002 at Salt Lake City, **women** competed in Olympic bobsledding for the first time in a two-woman event. The Bobsledding Federation currently also governs the sliding sport of **skeleton**. Skeleton appeared on the **Olympic Program** at the Cresta Run in St. Moritz in both 1928 and 1948 and was put back on the Olympic Program beginning in 2002 at Salt Lake City.

Bobsledding has been contested at all Olympic Winter Games, except in 1960 at Squaw Valley. Because of the distance to travel to California, only nine countries indicated that they would enter bobsled teams. The Squaw Valley organizers thus decided not to build a bob run, and the sport was not held that year.

Bobsledding has been dominated by the Swiss, the **Italians**, and, until 1992, the **German Democratic Republic**. The most famous Olympic bobsled competitors, however, is that of the Caribbean island of Jamaica. In 1988, they entered both the two-man and four-man events. They finished a surprisingly good 30th of 41 entrants in the two-man race but in the four-man event overturned during the third race and the team walked the remainder of the track alongside their sled. The team became world famous and a Hollywood motion picture, *Cool Runnings*, was made about their exploits. Since 1988 and inspired by the Jamaicans, several other countries without snow (**Puerto Rico, United States Virgin Islands, Mexico, Trinidad and Tobago, Netherlands Antilles, American Samoa**, and **Brazil**) have competed in Olympic bobsleigh events.

The sport is governed by the Fédération Internationale de Bobsleigh et de Tobogganing, which was founded in 1923 and has 64 members as of 2014.

In the 21 Winter Games in which bobsled competition has been held, there have been 1,694 individual participants (1,584 men, 109 women) from 54 countries who have competed. Switzerland leads the bobsled medal list with 31 medals (including nine golds), the United States has 24 medals including seven golds, and **Germany** has 21 medals, including 10 golds. Including East and West Germany, Germany overall has won 40 medals, including 16 golds. Two German bobsledders, Kevin Kuske and **André Lange**, have each won four gold medals, while **Bogdan Musiol**, who competed for Germany and East Germany, has won the most medals, at seven. *See also* EAGAN, EDWARD PATRICK FRANCIS; GERMESHAUSEN, BERNHARD; HOPPE, WOLFGANG; LUGE; MONTI, EUGENIO; NEHMER, MEINHARD; OLYMPIC ANTIHEROES.

BOBSLEIGH. *See* BOBSLEDDING.

BODY BUILDING. Body building has never been on the **Olympic Program**, but the sport is governed by the International Federation of Body Building and Fitness (IFBB), which until 2003 had achieved provisional recognition by the **International Olympic Committee** (IOC). The title of the IFBB was International Federation of Body Builders until 2004. It is not currently recognized by the IOC. Founded in 1946, the IFBB has 182 affiliated member nations as of 2014.

BOHEMIA (BOH). Prior to becoming the largest section of **Czechoslovakia** in 1918, Bohemia, then part of the Austro–Hungarian Empire in Central Europe, appeared at the Olympics of 1900, 1906, 1908, and 1912. They entered 64 men and one **woman** and competed in the **art competitions** (one man) and eight sports: **athletics** (18 men), **cycling** (six men), **fencing** (16 men), **gymnastics** (three men), **rowing** (one man), **shooting** (one man), **tennis** (12 men and one woman), and **wrestling** (eight men). One man competed in gymnastics and also in the **marathon**. Another man combined wrestling and the **discus throw**.

Bohemian athletes have won six **Olympic medals**, one silver and five bronze. The silver medal was won by František Janda-Suk in the 1900 discus throw. Bronze medals were won by the men's **sabre** team in 1908 fencing competition and by sabre team member Vilém Goppold z Lobsdorfu, Sr., in the individual sabre event that year. In tennis in 1900, Hedwiga Rosenbaumová won bronze medals in the women's **singles** tournament and the **mixed doubles** with her British partner Archibald Warden. In 1906, Zdeněk Žemla won a bronze medal in men's singles and a second bronze medal in men's **doubles** with his brother Ladislav Žemla as his partner. In 1912, the Žemla brothers finished in fourth place in doubles and Ladislav was fourth in singles. The 1912 men's sabre team was also a fourth place finisher, and in 1906, **lightweight Greco-Roman wrestling** Karel Halík finished in a three-way tie for fourth place.

BOLIVIA (BOL). Bolivia formed a **National Olympic Committee** in 1932 and had a single **swimmer** and an additional entrant in the **art competitions** at the 1936 Olympics in Berlin, but the nation did not compete at the Summer Olympics again until 1964. It has since competed continuously, with the exception of the Moscow Games in 1980. Despite its appearance at 13 Summer Games, the South American nation of Bolivia, officially known as the Plurinational State of Bolivia, has been represented by only 64 Olympic athletes (50 men, 14 **women**) plus one male entrant in the art competition in 1932, with the largest contingent being 13 at Barcelona in 1992. Bolivia has entered athletes in **athletics** (11 men, eight women), **cycling** (five men), **fencing** (three men), **gymnastics** (one woman), **judo** (five men), **shooting** (13 men), swimming (six men, four women), **weightlifting** (two men, one woman), and one man in each of **boxing, canoeing, diving, equestrian, tennis,** and **wrestling**. Fernando Inchauste competed in canoeing in 1964 and 1968 and returned in 1972 to take part in shooting.

The most notable Olympic performances by Bolivian athletes include Juan Camacho, 38th of 107 in the men's 1984 **marathon** and 69th of 118 in the 1992 marathon. Roberto Nielsen-Reyes, tied for 22nd of 54 entrants in 1972 equestrian **jumping** and Claudia Balderrama, 33rd of 61 in the 2012 women's 20 k walk. Although Bolivian athletes have not yet won an Olympic medal, at the 2010 **Youth Olympic Games**, the Bolivian under-15 **football** team won the gold medal in that inaugural competition.

Bolivia has also competed five times (1956, 1980, 1984, 1988, 1992) at the **Olympic Winter Games**, sending a total of 13 male **Alpine skiers**. Its best performance at the Winter Games, and the only Bolivian athlete to finish in the top one-third in his event, occurred in 1984 when Scott Alan Sánchez finished 34th of 108 entrants in the **giant slalom**. Guillermo Avila finished 38th of 109 in the 1988 **slalom** and 50th of 119 four years later in that event.

BOLT, USAIN ST. LEO (JAM–ATH). B. 21 August 1986, Sherwood Content, Trelawny, **Jamaica**. Together with **Michael Phelps**, Usain Bolt was the star of the Beijing Games, in which he won three gold medals. His first victory came in the 100 meters, winning with ease in a world record time of 9.69, despite easing down in the final meters to celebrate. He added golds in the 200 meters, breaking **Michael Johnson**'s 1996 world record in the process, and the 4x100 meters **relay**, breaking another world record with his teammates. Bolt, having become the icon of track and field **athletics**, repeated this performance at the 2009 World Championships in Berlin, winning the same three events and recording world records in the 100 meters (9.58) and 200 meters (19.19). At six feet, five inches (196 cm) and 190 lb (86 kg), he is exceptionally large for a **sprinter**. In London at the 2012 Games, he duplicated his performance of four years earlier by again winning the three events and leading the relay team to a world record performance.

BORON, KATHRIN (later KÖPPEN) (GER–ROW). B. 4 November 1969, Eisenhüttenstadt, Brandenburg, **German Democratic Republic**. Kathrin Boron is one of the most successful female **rowers** of all time. Although four **Romanian** rowers have won more Olympic medals, Boron is unsurpassed at the World Championships. A large woman at six feet tall (184 cm) and 170 lb (77 kg), she won eight world titles between 1989 and 2001 in the double and quadruple **sculls**, adding five silver medals, the last one in 2007. Boron also attempted to compete in the **single** and placed fourth in the 1995 World Championships. Between 1992 and 2008, she won a medal at each **Olympic Games**, earning gold in the double sculls in 1992 and 2000 and gold in the quadruple sculls in 1996 and 2004, adding a bronze medal in that same boat in 2008.

BORZOV, VALERIY PYLYPOVYCH (URS/UKR–ATH). B. 20 October 1949, Sambir, Lviv, **Ukraine**, USSR. Valery Borzov first came to prominence in 1969, winning the European title in the 100 meters. The six-foot tall (183 cm), 176 lb (80 kg) sprinter repeated in 1971, also winning the 200 meters. This favored him for a medal at the 1972 **Olympic Games**. Two of his biggest rivals, Americans Hart and Robinson, were eliminated when they missed their quarter-final **heats** due to a misreading of the schedule. Borzov also nearly missed his quarter final, having dozed off and arriving on the track just in time to kneel down for the start. Borzov eventually won the final with relative ease. He then won the 200 meter race in a time of exactly 20 seconds and won a third **Olympic medal** as he ran the anchor leg for the **Soviet Union** in the 4x100 meter **relay** and finished second to the American team. Borzov again made the news at the 1976 Olympics, but not for athletic reasons. Ukrainian immigrants in **Canada** spread the rumor that Borzov would leave the Soviet team in Montreal and ask for political asylum. After this was widely reported in the media, Borzov received anonymous phone calls threatening he would be shot during the 100 meter final (in which Borzov eventually placed third). In 1977, Borzov won his seventh indoors European title indoor, a record that will likely never be equalled as the event is no longer held annually. With the 1980 Games in Moscow, Borzov tried for a third Olympics, but injuries prevented this, and he instead focused on a career in politics and sport administration. Married to quadruple Olympic **gymnastics** champion **Lyudmila Turishcheva**, Borzov became the first president of the Ukrainian **National Olympic Committee** in 1990 and was named an **International Olympic**

Committee member in 1994. In 1996, he also became president of the Ukrainian Track and Field Federation, a position he held through 2008. With the independence of Ukraine, Borzov was named the first minister of youth and sport, a position he held until 1997. From 1998 until 2006, he was a member of the Verkhovna Rada, the Ukrainian parliament.

Sprinter Valeriy Borzov, 1972 100 and 200 meter gold medalist. Courtesy of Volker Kluge

BOSNIA AND HERZEGOVINA (BIH, formerly BSH). Until 1992, Bosnia and Herzegovina was a republic in the nation of **Yugoslavia**. In that year, Bosnia and Herzegovina, along with several other Yugoslav republics, declared independence, but unfortunately the **Serbians** declared war on the republic. Still, Bosnia and Herzegovina quickly formed a **National Olympic Committee** and, on the eve of the 1992 Olympics, was granted provisional recognition by the **International Olympic Committee** and competed at Barcelona. Despite the civil war in the country, Bosnia and Herzegovina valiantly sent competitors to the 1994 **Olympic Winter Games** in Lillehammer. Officially known as the Federation of Bosnia and Herzegovina since 1995, the southeastern European nation has also competed at each **Olympic Games** and Olympic Winter Games since the Summer Games of 1992. The 14th Olympic Winter Games were held in Sarajevo in 1984 in what was then part of Yugoslavia, but Sarajevo is presently the capital city of Bosnia and Herzegovina. An additional bid by Sarajevo for the 2010 Winter Games was unsuccessful. With the conflicts in the Balkans, there have been nationalistic uprisings that may cause Bosnia and Herzegovina to split into two nations, although, as of 2014, this has not yet happened.

In six Summer Games, Bosnia and Herzegovina have entered 37 athletes (26 men, 11 **women**) and have participated in 10 sports: **athletics** (nine men, five women), **canoeing** (three men), **judo** (three men, one woman), **shooting** (two men, one woman), **swimming** (four men, three women), **table tennis** (two men), **tennis** (one woman), and one man in each of **taekwondo**, **weightlifting**, and **wrestling**. They have not yet won a medal. The most notable Olympic performances by Bosnians include a sixth place by Nedžad Fazlija in the 2000 men's **air rifle** event, eighth place by Mirjana Jovović-Horvat in the 1992 women's air rifle competition, Hamza Alić, 17th of 44 entrants in the 2008 men's **shot put**, and Elvir Krehmić, tied for 14th place of 35 contestants in the 2000 men's **high jump**.

In six Winter Games, the country has entered 28 competitors (20 men, eight women) who have taken part in five sports: **Alpine skiing** (five men, four women), **biathlon** (one man, two women), **bobsledding** (nine men), **cross-country skiing** (three men, two women), and **luge** (two men, one woman). One woman entered both biathlon and cross-country skiing events. The best performances by Bosnian Olympic Winter Games athletes were all in the Alpine skiing **slalom**: Žana Novaković, 26th of 88 entrants in the women's event in 2014; and in the men's event, Marko Schafferer, 30th of 93 in 2006; Marko Rudić, 36th of 101 in 2010; and Tahir Bisić, 29th of 77 in 2002. Although all four of the skiers were among the last to finish, they were all able to successfully negotiate their races while the majority of entrants in those slalom events did not complete the course.

BOTSWANA (BOT). Botswana formed a **National Olympic Committee** in 1978 and has competed at all nine **Olympic Games** since 1980. Formerly called Bechuanaland, the country never made an Olympic appearance under that name. The Southern African country, officially known as the Republic of Botswana, has not yet competed at the **Olympic Winter Games**. Through 2014, there have been 52 Batswana Olympians (50 men, two **women**), mostly in **athletics** (39 men, one woman), but they have also been represented in **boxing** (nine men), **sailing** (one man), and **swimming** (one man, one woman). Botswana won its first Olympic medal in 2012, a silver medal, when Nijel Amos finished second in the men's 800 meters run. Other notable performances include Glody Dube, who finished seventh in the final of the 2000 men's 800 meters; Amantle Montsho, eighth place in the women's 400 meters in 2008; eighth place also for the men's 4x400 meters 2004 **relay** team; Gable Garenamotse, ninth place in the men's **long jump** in 2008, and **bantamweight** boxer Khumiso Ikgopoleng, who won two bouts before being defeated in the quarter finals in 2008 and finishing tied for fifth place.

BOTTERILL, JENNIFER LORI (CAN–ICH). B. 1 May 1979, Ottawa, Ontario, **Canada**. The five-foot, nine-inch (175 cm), 157 lb (71 kg) daughter of Olympic speed skater Doreen McCannell and niece of speed skater Donna McCannell, Jennifer played in the first four Olympic **women**'s **ice hockey** tournaments and has won four **Olympic medals**, winning the gold in 2002 through 2010, while taking silver in 1998. Forward Botterill also featured on eight Canadian World Championship teams, taking gold in 1999–2001, 2004, and 2007, while playing runner-up in 2005, 2008, and 2009. Outside the national team, Botterill has played for Harvard University and in women's professional leagues with the Toronto Aeros of the National Women's Hockey League, and the Mississauga Chiefs of the Canadian Women's Hockey League. Her brother Jason played in the National Hockey League for six seasons between 1997 and 2004.

BOULES. *See* BOWLS.

BOWLING. Ten-pin bowling (as opposed to lawn bowling or **bowls**) was a **demonstration sport** in Seoul at the 1988 **Olympic Games**. Twelve men and 12 women from a total of 20 countries took part in a one-day competition. They bowled each of the other contestants of their gender in one-game matches. Each victory was worth 10 bonus points, which was added to their total pinfall. After the 11 matches, the top three players advanced to a stepladder final. The men's winners were Kwon Jong Yul, **Korea**, gold medal; Jack Lake Chin, **Singapore**, silver medal; and Tapani Peltola, **Finland**, bronze medal. The women's winners were Arianne Cerdena, **Philippines**, gold medal; Atsuko Asai, **Japan**, silver medal; and Annikki Maattola, Finland, bronze medal.

The sport's governing body, the Fédération Internationale de Quilleurs, was founded in 1952 with 11 members: **Austria, Belgium, Denmark**, Finland, **France, Luxembourg**, the **Netherlands, Sweden, Switzerland, West Germany**, and **Yugoslavia**. It is currently one of the **International Olympic Committee**–recognized **International Federations**, with 113 national members as of 2014.

BOWLS. Bowls has never been contested as a medal sport at the **Olympic Games**, but the Confédération Mondiale des Sports de Boules (CMSB) is currently one of the **International Olympic Committee**–recognized **International Federations**. There are 117 affiliated nations in the CMSB as of 2014. The similar sport of boccia is contested at the **Paralympics**.

BOXING. Boxing was contested at the **Ancient Olympic Games** and many other sporting festivals in ancient **Greece**. Boxing then was an even more brutal sport, as the combatants wore leather thongs on their hands. Originally the thongs were simple straps of leather, but later they were reinforced with sharp pieces of metal, and the glove was called a *cestus*. The first known Ancient Olympic boxing champion was Onomastos of Smyrna, who won in 688 B.C. The last known was Varasdates of **Armenia**, in A.D. 369, who is also the last known champion of the Ancient Olympic Games. Professional boxing has been around since the early 18th century, with a recognized list of professional champions dating from the late 1700s.

Boxing made its first Olympic appearance in 1904 at St. Louis. All the entrants were Americans, and the event doubled as the Amateur Athletic Union Championships for that year. Boxing was again contested at the 1908 Olympics in London, with all bouts taking place on just one day. As a result, several boxers fought three or four times on that one day. In 1912, boxing could not be on the **Olympic Program** because it required special permits in **Sweden** at that time. Since 1920, boxing has been on the program of every **Olympic Games.**

The **United States** was originally the premier nation in Olympic boxing. However, it has been surpassed in the past 30 years, first by the **Soviet Union** and more recently by **Cuba**. Three boxers have each won three Olympic gold medals: **László Papp** of **Hungary**, and **Teófilo Stevenson** and **Félix Savón** of Cuba. A number of Olympic boxers have gone on to become professional World Champions, notably Cassius Clay (**Muhammad Ali**), **George Foreman, Joe Frazier, Sugar Ray Leonard**, Floyd Patterson, Ingemar Johansson, Pascual Pérez, Floyd Mayweather, Jr., brothers Leon and Michael Spinks, Barry McGuigan, Riddick Bowe, Volodymyr Klychko, Oscar De La Hoya, and Lennox Lewis, although not all of them were Olympic champions.

In 24 summer Olympic competitions, there have been 5,051 athletes (5,015 men, 36 **women**) from 172 nations who have participated in Olympic boxing.

Olympic boxing has been contested in 12 weight classes, but in 2004 and 2008, only 11 classes were contested, and in 2012 only 10 classes for men. In 2012, three weight classes of women's boxing were added. Until 2000, matches were three **rounds** of three minutes each, but in 2000, 2004, and 2008, the duration was changed to four two-minute rounds. In 2012, the timing reverted to three three-minute rounds. Five judges score the match. Since 1992, scoring is done by a complicated system in which the judges register successful punches on a computer. If three of the five judges register a punch within one second, that scores one point for the boxer who lands the punch. Decisions are made only by the punches-landed point score. At the Olympics, all weight classes are conducted by single-elimination tournaments. There is currently no match for third place, with both losing semifinalists receiving bronze medals, although through 1948, the two losing semifinalists competed in an additional match for third place. There have been many controversial judging decisions at the Olympics, and because of the difficulty of judging the sport, the **International Olympic Committee** has told the Boxing Federation that it has to solve this problem to stay on the **Olympic Program**.

Boxing is the only Olympic sport that still does not allow professionals to compete. Amateur boxing is governed by the International Boxing Association, which was originally called the Association Internationale de Boxe Amateur (AIBA), although it still uses the acronym AIBA. It was founded in 1946 and currently (as of 2014) has 196 member nations. *See also* EAGAN, EDWARD PATRICK FRANCIS; KIRK, OLIVER LEONARD; LAGUTIN, BORIS NIKOLAYEVICH; MALLIN, HENRY WILLIAM; THEAGENES OF THASOS; VAL BARKER AWARD.

BOYARSKIKH, KLAVDIYA SERGEYEVNA (URS–CCS). B. 11 November 1939, Verkhnyaya Pyshma, Sverdlovsk, **Russia**, USSR. D. 12 December 2009, Yekaterinburg, Sverdlovsk, Russia. To three gold medals (five km, 10 km, and **relay**) at the 1964 Olympics, Klavdiya Boyarskikh added two further golds and a silver at the 1966 World Championships, to establish herself as the world's leading female **cross-country skier** of the 1960s. The five-foot, three-inch (159 cm), 132 lb (60 kg) skier also won three times at Holmenkollen, winning the 10 km in 1965–1966 and the five km in 1967.

BOYCOTTS AND POLITICS. The **Olympic Games** have rarely been able to escape the influence of politics since they became a major international event. The first significant intrusion of politics occurred in 1936 (*see* "Games of the XIth **Olympiad**" in "The Olympic Games and **Olympic Winter Games**" in the front matter), when several nations considered boycotting the Berlin Olympics to protest the policies of **Germany**'s Adolf Hitler, although previously, after World War I, the Central Powers (Germany, **Austria**, and **Bulgaria**) were not invited to the 1920 Olympics, and Germany was still excluded in 1924.

Minimal political intrusions occurred in 1948 and 1952. The major disruption in 1952 occurred at the opening ceremony, when a fairly large woman in a flowing white robe interrupted the proceedings, strode to the podium, and began to read a peace message, before being escorted away; obviously this was in an era of far less security. In 1956, a small boycott ensued because of the recent incursion of **Soviet** troops into **Hungary**, and an **Egyptian–Israeli** dispute over the Sinai Peninsula. (*See* "Games of the XVIth Olympiad" in "The Olympic Games and Olympic Winter Games" in the front matter.)

The Rome Olympics in 1960 were once again free of significant political conflicts. In 1964, a dispute arose concerning the eligibility of certain nations that had competed at the **Games of the New Emerging Forces** in 1963, as well as the first exclusion of **South Africa** because of racist policies in sports. (*See* "Games of the XVIIIth Olympiad" in "The Olympic Games and Olympic Winter Games" in the front matter.)

In 1968, the **Mexican** government faced numerous student protests over the presence of the Olympic Games in the Mexican capital, despite the poverty and hunger of many of its citizens. As the protest movement gathered momentum leading up to the Games, the Mexican army took charge on the night of 2 October. As 10,000 people demonstrated in the Square of the Three Cultures in Mexico City, the army surrounded the crowd and opened fire. More than 250 people were killed, and thousands were injured or imprisoned. (*See* "Games of the XIXth Olympiad" in "The Olympic Games and Olympic Winter Games" in the front matter.)

The worst intrusion of politics into the Olympics occurred in 1972, when Arab terrorists representing the Black September movement entered the **Olympic Village** and took 11 Israeli competitors and coaches hostage. The hostages were all eventually murdered. (*See* "Games of the XXth Olympiad" in "The Olympic Games and Olympic Winter Games" in the front matter.)

Shortly before the 1976 Olympics were due to start, they were marred by a boycott by 22 African countries, **Guyana**, and **Chinese Taipei** (then Taiwan). This was in protest against a recent tour of South Africa by the

New Zealand national **rugby** team. As South Africa was ostracized from international sporting competition, the African nations demanded that New Zealand not be allowed to compete at Montreal. However, as the **International Olympic Committee** (IOC) had no control of international rugby, New Zealand was properly allowed to start in the Olympics.

The Taiwan boycott occurred when the **Canadian** government did not allow the Taiwanese team to enter the country, as it did not recognize the island nation, in violation of its agreement as host country to admit all eligible nations in honoring the *Olympic Charter*. The Canadians eventually acquiesced and gave permission for Taiwan to compete, but refused to allow it to do so as the Republic of **China**, its official national name and the name by which it was then recognized by the IOC. Several other countries protested and threatened withdrawal, notably the **United States**. However, these protests were short-lived, and the IOC finally gave in to the Canadian government. Taiwan withdrew and did not compete. (*See* "Games of the XXIst Olympiad" in "The Olympic Games and Olympic Winter Games" in the front matter.)

The largest-scale Olympic boycott occurred in 1980. The Games were held in Moscow in July 1980. In December 1979, **Soviet** troops entered **Afghanistan**. The United States led a vocal protest and eventually boycotted the 1980 Olympic Games. It was joined by approximately 60 other nations that also boycotted. (*See* "Games of the XXIInd Olympiad" in "The Olympic Games and Olympic Winter Games" in the front matter; *see also* LIBERTY BELL CLASSIC.)

In 1984, the Soviet Union exacted its revenge on the United States when it boycotted the Los Angeles Olympic Games. This was officially because of concerns over security and the safety of its athletes, but there was little doubt about the reason, which was revenge for the 1980 U.S.-led boycott. The Soviet boycott was joined, quite naturally, by other members of the Soviet bloc, including Eastern Europe and **Cuba**. Only **Romania**, among Soviet bloc nations, defied the Soviet-led boycott. (*See* "Games of the XXIIIrd Olympiad" in "The Olympic Games and Olympic Winter Games" in the front matter; *see also* FRIENDSHIP GAMES.)

The IOC awarded the 1988 Olympics to Seoul. This was a highly controversial decision, as many prominent nations in the **Olympic Movement** did not have diplomatic relations with the Seoul government. The problem became more complicated in 1985, when North **Korea** demanded that it be allowed to cohost the Games with the **Republic of Korea**. Over the next three years, the IOC negotiated with North Korea and offered to allow it to stage several events. When the IOC would not concede further to the North's demands, North Korea announced that it would boycott the Seoul Olympics. By then, however, most of the Soviet bloc countries had agreed to compete in Seoul, making 1988 the first Summer Games competition in 12 years between the United States, the Soviet Union, and the **German Democratic Republic**. After North Korea's official boycott announcement, Cuba and **Ethiopia** also announced that they would boycott the Olympics. **Nicaragua**, **Albania**, and the **Seychelles** also did not attend the Olympics, although their reasons may not have been directly related to any boycott. (*See* "Games of the XXIVth Olympiad" in "The Olympic Games and Olympic Winter Games" in the front matter.)

In 1992, the Olympics were held in Barcelona. These Games were remarkably free of political protest and intrusions. They were the first Olympic Games since 1968 that saw no form of boycott, and there have been no Olympic boycotts since 1988. Albania either boycotted, or elected not to participate in, four different Olympic Games, consecutively from 1976 through 1988. Three nations boycotted three Olympic Games: Egypt (1956, 1976, 1980), Ethiopia (1976, 1984, 1988), and North Korea (1964, 1984, 1988).

The Winter Olympic Games have been relatively free of political intrusions, although prior to the Sochi Games in 2014, there was talk of possible boycotts. The Russian government had recently passed legislation prohibiting the promotion of nontraditional sexual relationships to minors, which was widely interpreted by the Western media as an anti-gay law and in some circles caused calls for boycotts, although they did not come to pass. There was also criticism of possible corruption regarding the construction of facilities for the Games as well as treatment of some of the construction employees.

In addition to boycotts of the Olympic Games, political problems have haunted the IOC since the end of World War II. This has mostly been in terms of the official recognition of certain nations. In many cases, the nations have not been on good political terms with other IOC members, and these IOC members have protested their official recognition.

In particular, the IOC has dealt with the problems of the "two" Germanys (Germany and the German Democratic Republic); the "two" Chinas (China and Chinese Taipei); the "two" Koreas (Democratic People's Republic of Korea and the Republic of Korea); and the recognition of South Africa despite its apartheid policies. Similar problems existed in the later 1960s and early 1970s concerning Rhodesia (*see also* **Zimbabwe**).

BRAZIL (BRA). The South American nation of Brazil (officially known as the Federative Republic of Brazil) has competed at every Olympics since 1920 except 1928 and has competed at every **Olympic Winter Games** since 1992. In 22 Summer Games, Brazil has entered 1,710 athletes (1,280 men, 430 **women**) and competed in 29 sports plus the **art competitions**. They have had the most entrants in **athletics** (157 men, 63 women), **swimming**

(113 men, 36 women), **rowing** (101 men, five women), and the team sports of **basketball** (101 men, 42 women), **football** (179 men, 43 women), and **volleyball** (84 men, 63 women).

Through 2014, Brazilian athletes have won 108 **Olympic medals**, 23 gold, 30 silver, 55 bronze, all at the Summer Games, the most medals for any South American country. Brazil's successes have come in a variety of sports. It has won medals in several different individual sports and has always had one of the top basketball, volleyball, and football teams. **Sailors** Torben Grael (six Games, 1984–2004, two gold, one silver, two bronze) and Robert Scheidt (five Games, 1996–2012, two gold, two silver, one bronze) have each won five Olympic medals, the most of any Brazilian. Swimmer Gustavo Borges has won four medals (1992–2004, two silver, two bronze) and swimmer Cesar Cielo Filho won three (2008 gold and bronze, 2012 bronze). Three medals have been won in **beach volleyball** by **Emanuel** (Emanuel Fernando Scheffler Rego) and **Ricardo** (Ricardo Alex Costa Santos), one gold, one silver, and one bronze. They were teammates in 2004, winning the gold, and 2008, winning the bronze, but in 2000 Ricardo teamed with Zé Marco to win silver and in 2012 Emanuel teamed with Alison Cerutti to win silver. In **equestrian** competition, Rodrigo Pessoa competed in six Games from 1992 to 2012 and won gold in 2004 and bronze in 1996 and 2000.

In team sports, Brazil has done well and has won five medals in men's volleyball and four in women's volleyball. Five volleyball players were each on three medal-winning teams. Hélia Rogério de Souza Pinto, better known as "Fofão," from 1992 to 2008 won one gold and two bronze and finished fourth twice as a member of the women's team. From 1984 to 2012, the men's team twice won gold, three times won silver and once finished fourth. Four of their players were each on three medal-winning teams: Gilberto Amauri "Giba" de Godoy Filho, Sérgio "Escadinha" Dutra dos Santos, Rodrigo "Rodrigão" Santana, and Dante Guimarães Santos do Amaral.

In basketball Brazilian teams have won three bronze medals in men's basketball and a silver and bronze in women's basketball. In football although Brazilian men have won the World Cup five times, they have yet to win an Olympic gold medal. They do have five medals (three silver, two bronze) and their women have two silver.

In seven Winter Games, Brazil has entered 21 athletes (22 men, 10 women) and competed in eight sports: **Alpine skiing** (eight men, three women), **bobsledding** (10 men, two women), and **cross-country skiing** (three men, two women), with token participation in **luge** (two men) and **biathlon**, **figure skating**, **freestyle skiing**, and **snowboarding**, with one woman in each of the latter four sports. Isabel Clark finished ninth of 23 entrants in the initial women's **boardercross** in 2006. **Mountainbike** cyclist Jaqueline Mourão competed in four Olympic Games over a span of six years from 2004 to 2010, cycling in the Summer Games in 2004 and 2008 and cross-country skiing in the Winter Games of 2006 and 2010. For good measure she added a third sport to her Olympic resume in 2014 when in addition to cross-country skiing she entered two biathlon events. Her best result was in her first Olympic Games when she finished 18th of 30 entrants in the women's mountainbike event. Brazil's top result in the Winter Games occurred in 2006 when Nikolai Hentsch was 30th of 82 entrants in the men's **giant slalom**. Their best result for a woman in the Winter Games was in 2014 when Maya Harrison finished 39th of 85 entrants in the women's slalom.

At the 2009 **Olympic Congress**, Rio de Janeiro was chosen to host the 2016 Olympic Games. This was Brazil's fifth bid attempt, having failed in 1936, 2004, and 2012 with Rio de Janeiro and 2000 with Brasilia as potential host city. *See also* SCHMIDT, OSCAR DANIEL BEZERRA.

BREASTSTROKE. The breaststroke is one of the four strokes in **swimming** competition. Both 100 meter and 200 meter breaststroke races for men and for **women** are contested, and the breaststroke is one of the four swimming strokes that comprise the swimming **medley** events. The men's 200 meter breaststroke event has been held in every Summer Games since 1908 and the 100 meter breaststroke event since 1968. A 440 yard breaststroke race was held in 1904 and a 400 meter race in both 1912 and 1920. The women's breaststroke began in Olympic competition in 1924 with a 200 meter race and a 100 meter race was added in 1968. Kosuke Kitajima of **Japan** won the men's 100 meter breaststroke in 2004 and 2008 and is the only dual gold medalist in that event. Kitajima also won the 200 meter breaststroke in those two years. His countryman Yoshiyuki Tsuruta won the 200 meter breaststroke in 1928 and 1932. Leisel Jones of **Australia** won three medals in the women's 100 meter breaststroke (gold 2008, silver 2000, bronze 2004) and added two more (silver 2004, 2008) in the 200 meter event. Rebecca Soni of the **United States** is the only dual gold medalist (2008, 2012) in the women's 200 meter breaststroke. Halyna Prozumenshchykova-Stepanova of the **Soviet Union** also won a total of five medals in women's Olympic breaststroke events (100 meters silver 1968, 1972; 200 meters gold 1964; bronze 1968, 1972).

BRIDGE. Bridge has never been contested at the Olympics, but the World Bridge Federation (WBF) was recognized by the **International Olympic Committee** in 2000. Founded in 1958, the WBF currently (as of 2014) has 123 national member federations.

BRITISH GUIANA. *See* GUYANA.

BRITISH HONDURAS. *See* BELIZE.

BRITISH VIRGIN ISLANDS (IVB). The British Virgin Islands formed a **National Olympic Committee** in 1980 that was recognized by the **International Olympic Committee** in 1982. The Caribbean island territory, a British overseas territory that is officially known simply as the Virgin Islands, has competed at every Olympic Summer Games since 1984 with 23 entrants (22 men, one **woman**) taking part in either **athletics** (14 men, one woman) or **sailing** (eight men). No athlete from this island has won an **Olympic medal**. Strangely, the first Olympic participation for British Virgin Islands was in 1984 at Sarajevo in the **Olympic Winter Games**, when Errol Fraser, a New Yorker who had dual citizenship, competed in **speed skating**. In 2014, Peter Crook entered the **halfpipe** event at the Sochi Winter Olympics. Neither of the two Winter Olympians did well though. The best Summer Olympic performance by a Virgin Islander was in the 1996 sailing mixed one-person **dinghy** when Robert Hirst finished 25th of 56 entrants. In 1988 Matthew Arneborg finished 29th of 45 contestants in the mixed **windsurfer** sailing competition. Their best result in athletics occurred in 2008 when Tahesia Harrigan-Scott finished third of eight in the first round of the women's 100 meter dash but was fifth in the second **round** and did not advance further.

BROAD JUMP. *See* LONG JUMP.

BRONZE MEDAL. *See* OLYMPIC MEDALS.

BROOKES, WILLIAM PENNY (GBR). B. 13 August 1809, Much Wenlock, **England**. D. 10 December 1895, Much Wenlock, England. William Penny Brookes was the founder of the **Much Wenlock Olympian Games**, an early influence on the thinking of **Pierre de Coubertin** about the revival of the Olympics. Brookes was a doctor who was educated at various schools in Shropshire and began his study of medicine at Guy's and St. Thomas's Hospitals in London in about 1827. He finished his studies in Paris and Padua, returning to Much Wenlock in 1831 to carry on the general practice of medicine that his father had started. He founded the **National Olympian Association** in 1865, the forerunner of the British Olympic Association. He was active in public affairs, serving as justice of the peace and commissioner for roads for the borough of Wenlock, and in 1841 formed the Wenlock Agricultural Reading Society. Brookes eventually became a licentiate of the Society of Apothecaries and, in 1881, a fellow of the Royal College of Surgeons.

Brookes was an invited dignitary to Coubertin's Sorbonne Congress of 1894, which founded the Modern **Olympic Games**, but he was unable to attend because of illness. He and Coubertin corresponded frequently, and Brookes had Coubertin visit the Much Wenlock Olympian Games in October 1890. In 1881, Brookes was the first person to propose that international Olympian Games be staged again, in Athens.

BRUNDAGE, AVERY (USA–IOC). B. 28 September 1887, Detroit, Michigan, **United States**. D. 8 May 1975, Garmisch-Partenkirchen, Federal Republic of Germany. Avery Brundage was an American who served as **International Olympic Committee (IOC) president** from 1952 to 1972, the longest term ever aside from **Pierre de Coubertin**, and equal to that of **Juan Antonio Samaranch**. A participant in the **Olympic Games** track and field events in 1912, Brundage was the first IOC president, and one of only three to date (also **Jacques Rogge**, **Belgian** sailor in 1968, 1972, and 1976, and **Thomas Bach**, gold medal fencer for West **Germany** in 1976), to have actually competed in the Olympics. At six feet tall (183 cm) and 201 lb (91 kg), Brundage was a formidable athlete and finished 22nd of 41 entrants in the **discus throw**, had a creditable result of sixth in the **pentathlon**, but withdrew from the **decathlon** after completing eight of the 10 events while competing against the great **Jim Thorpe**.

After retiring from track and field competition, he became an accomplished **American handball** player, and in 1932 and 1936 Brundage was an entrant in the Olympic **art competition** in literature, receiving an honorable mention in 1932. He enjoyed the financial freedom to devote his time to the administrative side of sport, having made a fortune in the construction business. Brundage served seven terms as president of the Amateur Athletic Union, was president of the United States Olympic Committee for 25 years, and after becoming a member of the IOC in 1936, he was elected to the IOC **Executive Board** in 1937 and elected as IOC vice president in 1946, before becoming president six years later. His dedication to amateurism bordered on the fanatical and anachronistic, but he gradually lost his lifelong battle against the rising tide of commercialism in sport. Although never terribly popular and undoubtedly the most controversial IOC president ever, Brundage traveled constantly in the cause of **Olympism** and did much to widen the international scope of the **Olympic Movement**.

BRUNEI (BRU). The Brunei **National Olympic Council** was formed in 1984 and recognized by the **International Olympic Committee** in that year. After sending an official as an observer to both Seoul (1988) and Barcelona (1992), the Southeast Asian oil-rich nation of Brunei, officially known as the Nation of Brunei, the Abode of Peace, and sometimes also referred to as Brunei Darussalam, first competed at the 1996 **Olympic Games**, where it was represented by a single competitor in the **skeet shooting** event. To date, Brunei has been represented by six different Olympic athletes (five men and one **woman**): one in 1996, two in 2000, one in 2004, and three in 2012, four (three men, one woman) in **athletics**, with one male shooter and one male **swimmer**. Brunei did not compete at the 2008 Olympics and has never been represented at the **Olympic Winter Games**. Jefri Bolkiah, Prince Abdul Hakeem, competed in skeet shooting in both 1996 and 2000 and placed tied for 49th of 54 competitors in 1996 and 45th of 49 in 2000. All of the other Bruneian athletes were eliminated in the first round of their events.

BUCHANAN, IAN (GBR). B. 28 January 1932, Sheffield, Yorkshire, **England**. D. 6 April 2008, Aylsham, Norfolk, England. Ian Buchanan was one of the founding members of the **International Society of Olympic Historians** (ISOH) and served as that organization's first president for two terms, from 1991 to 2000. He guided ISOH through its formative years and helped the group become internationally known and achieve official recognition by the **International Olympic Committee** (IOC). Buchanan was well known to the world of Olympic history, writing numerous books, including *British Olympians*, the definitive history of the British Olympic teams; *Quest for Gold: The Encyclopaedia of American Olympians* (with **Bill Mallon**), a similar study of the **United States** Olympic athletes; and the first three editions of this *Historical Dictionary of the Olympic Movement*. He also published a number of other works on sports history, notably *All-Time Greats of British and Irish Sports* (with Peter Matthews) in 1995 and *The Guinness International Who's Who of Sport* (with Peter Matthews and Bill Mallon). Buchanan's business career was as a reinsurance agent, primarily based in **Hong Kong**, although in retirement he settled back in his native England. For his work in Olympic history, he was made an honorary member of ISOH after he stepped down as president in 2000, and he was awarded the **Olympic Order** in Silver in 1997 by the IOC.

BUDO. Budo is a general term referring to the many different forms of **Japanese** martial arts. In 1964, the Japanese gave exhibitions of Japanese **archery** (*kyudo*), fencing (*kendo*), and wrestling (*sumo*) at the Tokyo Olympics, all of which are examples of *budo*.

BULGARIA (BUL). Five Bulgarian athletes went to Athens for the 1896 **Olympic Games**, but due to a misunderstanding over the use of the Gregorian and the Julian calendars, they arrived too late to compete. However, a **Swiss** competitor in 1896, Charles Champaud, worked in Sofia and is often listed as a Bulgarian national. It was not until 1923 that a **National Olympic**

Committee was formed, and **International Olympic Committee** recognition followed the next year. Bulgaria first competed at the Olympic Games in 1924, and it has since missed only the Olympic Games of 1932, 1948, and 1984, although it did have two entrants in the 1932 **art competitions**. Its first appearance in the **Olympic Winter Games** was in 1936, and it has competed at all celebrations since.

In 19 Summer Games, Bulgaria has entered 1,288 athletes (935 men, 353 **women**) and competed in 28 sports plus the art competitions. They have entered the most competitors in **athletics** (83 men, 94 women), **wrestling** (148 men, two women), **rowing** (61 men, 58 women), and **gymnastics** (58 men, 50 women).

Bulgaria, officially the Republic of Bulgaria, has had its greatest successes in strength sports, mainly **weightlifting** (36 medals) and wrestling (68 medals), and in the 1980s it was the premier nation in the world in weightlifting. Bulgarian athletes have won 214 Olympic medals in the Summer Games (52 gold, 85 silver, 78 bronze). A female **shooter**, Mariya Grozdeva, who competed in six Olympic Games from 1992 to 2012, has won the most Olympic medals for Bulgaria, with five in all, two gold and three bronze. **Kayaker** Vanya Gesheva has won four in 1980 and 1988 (one gold, two silver, one bronze). Gymnast Yordan Yovchev has competed in six Olympic Games from 1992 to 2012 and has won one silver and three bronze. Bulgarian Olympians with three medals are **canoeist** Nikolay Bukhalov (two gold, one bronze), rower Rumyana Dzhadzharova-Neykova (one gold, one silver, one bronze), shooter Tanyu Kiryakov (two gold, one bronze), and wrestlers Aleksandar Tomov (three silver) and Enyu Valchev (one gold, one silver, one bronze).

Bulgaria has competed in 19 Winter Games with a total of 180 participants (141 men, 39 women) in 11 sports with most of their competitors in **Alpine skiing** (35 men, two women), **cross-country skiing** (34 men, 11 women), and **biathlon** (19 men, 12 women). They have won six medals: one gold, two silver, three bronze. Evgeniya Radanova competed in five Winter Games (1994–2010) and has won two silver and one bronze in **short-track speed skating**. She also entered the **cycling** competition in the 2004 Summer Games. Ivan Lebenov won a bronze in cross-country skiing. In biathlon Ekaterina Dafovska won a gold and Irina Nikulchina won a bronze.

Sofia, Bulgaria, has unsuccessfully bid three times to host the Winter Games (1992, 1994, 2014).

BURGHLEY, LORD DAVID GEORGE BROWNLOW CECIL (later THE SIXTH MARQUESS OF EXETER) (GBR). B. 9 February 1905, Stamford, Lincolnshire, **England**. D. 22 October 1981, Stamford, Lincolnshire, England. Lord Burghley was the Olympic 400 meter **hurdles** champion in 1928 and later a distinguished sports administrator. He was a world record holder in the 440 yard hurdles, but his record lasted less than one day as it was bettered several hours later on the same day in a track meet in the **United States**. He also won a silver medal as a member of the **Great Britain** 4x400 meters **relay** team in 1932. In 1933, at the age of 28, he was elected a member of the **International Olympic Committee** (IOC), and three years later he became chairman of the British Olympic Association and president of the British Amateur Athletic Association. In 1946, Lord Burghley took over from **J. Sigfrid Edström** as president of the International Amateur Athletic Federation and was chairman of the Organizing Committee for the 1948 **Olympic Games**. He failed in a bid for the **IOC presidency** in 1952 and 1964, but served as vice president of the IOC from 1952 to 1966.

BURKINA FASO (BUR). Taka Gangua and Taki N'Dio competed in the **javelin throw** in 1924 for **France**, but were nationals of what was then called Upper Volta, a part of French West Africa. Upper Volta sent a single competitor, André Bicaba, to the 1972 Olympics, who competed in **athletics** and did not advance past the first round of the 100 meter **sprint**. Upper Volta also entered the 1976 **Olympic Games** but withdrew prior to competing in support of the African boycott. The landlocked West African country changed its official name to Burkina Faso in 1984, and as Burkina Faso, its first Olympic participation occurred in 1988 at Seoul.

It has competed at all Summer Olympics since 1988 and has had a total of 29 competitors (19 men, 10 **women**), including Bicaba in 1972. They have competed in **athletics** (nine men, six women), **boxing** (four men), **fencing** (one man), **judo** (two men, two women), and **swimming** (three men, two women). No athlete from this nation has won an **Olympic medal**, and the country has never been represented at the **Olympic Winter Games**. Among the best performances by a Burkinabé Olympian was in 1992 in athletics when Franck Zio was 24th of 50 entrants in the 1992 men's **long jump**. Four other athletes, Aïssata Soulama (women's 400 meter **hurdles**, 2008); Gérard Kobéané (men's 100 meter sprint, 2012); Harouna Pale (men's 200 meter sprint, 1988); and Idrissa Sanou (men's 100 meter sprint, 2004), each advanced past the first **round** but were eliminated in the second round. In swimming, Adama Ouedraogo finished 42nd of 58 contestants in the men's 50 meter **freestyle** event in 2012. Boxers Sounaila Sagnon (1988 **light-middleweight**) and Drissa Tou (2004 **flyweight**) each won their first bout, Sagnon by **knockout** and Tou by **walkover**, and each lost their second bout to finish in a tie for ninth place in their respective classes.

BURMA (BIR). *See* MYANMAR.

BURUNDI (BDI). In 1962, the former United Nations Trust Territory under **Belgian** administration known as Ruanda-Urundi or Belgian East Africa became the two independent nations of **Rwanda** and Burundi. It was not until 1990, however, that Burundi's **National Olympic Committee** was founded. It was given official recognition by the **International Olympic Committee** in September 1993. Burundi first competed at the 1996 **Olympic Games** and has competed in each subsequent Summer Games, but has not yet competed at the **Olympic Winter Games**. From 1996 to 2012, the southeastern African nation of Burundi (officially known as the Republic of Burundi) has competed in each of the Summer Olympics with a total of 20 athletes (13 men, seven **women**) in **athletics** (11 men, four women), **judo** (one woman), and **swimming** (two men, two women). Among the nations that have won Olympic gold medals, they are the nation that has entered the fewest total athletes. In 1996, Vénuste Niyangabo won the gold medal in the men's 5,000 meter race of track and field athletics. That same year, Aloÿs Nizigama finished fourth in the men's 10,000 meters. In 2000, Nizigama finished ninth in that event. Other Burundians with good performances include Diane Nukuri, who finished 31st of 118 entrants in the 2012 women's **marathon**, Francine Niyonsaba, who was sixth in the finals of the women's 800 meters in 2012, and Joachim Nshimirimana, who finished 32nd of 101 competitors in the 2004 men's marathon.

BUTTERFLY. The butterfly is one of the strokes in **swimming** competition. Both 100 meter and 200 meter races for men and for **women** are contested, and the butterfly is one of the four strokes that comprise the **medley** events. The men's 200 meter butterfly race has been held in every Summer Games since 1956 and the 100 meter butterfly since 1968. The women's butterfly began in Olympic competition in 1956 with a 100 meter race, and a 200 meter race was added in 1968. **Michael Phelps** of the **United States** (2004–2012) is a three-time winner of the 100 meter man's butterfly. Phelps also added three medals (gold 2004, 2008, silver 2012) in the 200 meter race. Three women—**Inge de Bruijn**, the **Netherlands** (gold 2000, bronze 2004), Andrea Pollack, East **Germany** (silver 1976, 1980), and Qian Hong, **China** (gold 1992, bronze 1988) have won two medals each in the 100 meter event. **Petria Thomas** (silver 1996, 2004; bronze 2000) and **Susie O'Neill** (gold 1996, silver 2000, bronze 1992), both of **Australia**, have each won three medals in the 200 meter event. Thomas also won the gold medal in the 2004 100 meter butterfly for a total of four in Olympic butterfly events.

BUTTON, RICHARD TOTTEN "DICK" (USA–FSK). B. 18 July 1929, Englewood, New Jersey, **United States**. Dick Button, at five feet, 10 inches tall (178 cm), was noted for bringing a new dimension of athleticism to **figure skating**. Between 1943 and 1952, he was only defeated twice, and his many victories included the **Olympic Winter Games** of 1948 and 1952. He was the world champion for five consecutive years (1948–1952), the United States champion for seven consecutive years (1946–1952); won the North American title in 1947, 1949, and 1951; and in 1948 became the only American to win the European championships. After that, the event was closed to non-Europeans. Thus, in 1948, he uniquely held the championships of the United States, North America, Europe, the Olympics, and the world. Known for his innovative, dynamic free-skating, Button was undefeated to the end of his career in 1952, after having finished second at the 1947 World Championships. A Harvard-educated lawyer, Button later became an award-winning television commentator and sports-event producer, with the American Broadcasting Company's popular series of the 1970s, *Superstars*, being his creation.

BYE. A bye occurs when the number of entrants in a tournament draw will not allow each one to contest a match in every **round** and the entrant receives a free pass into the next tournament round. In a tournament in which 48 athletes are entered, 32 of them will be matched in the first round, with the winners advancing to meet the remaining 16 contestants who receive a bye into the second round. Olympic sports that are structured as tournaments with head-to-head competition use byes.

C

CAMBODIA (CAM). Cambodia made its first Olympic appearance at the **Equestrian Olympic Games** of 1956 in Stockholm, although it did not compete at the Melbourne Olympics that year. It again participated in 1964 and 1972. Briefly known as Kampuchea, the country has retaken the name Cambodia, with its official name being the Kingdom of Cambodia. With its frequent changes in government, the status and even the existence of a **National Olympic Committee** has often been in doubt, but the latest body was recognized by the **International Olympic Committee** in 1994, and Cambodia has competed at each Summer Olympics since 1996. They have not yet participated in the **Olympic Winter Games**.

In eight **Olympic Games**, the Southeast Asian nation has entered 40 athletes (32 men, eight **women**) and competed in nine sports: **athletics** (seven men, four women), **boxing** (five men), **cycling** (six men), **equestrian** (two men), **judo** (one man), **sailing** (three men), **swimming** (seven men, three women), **taekwondo** (one woman), and **wrestling** (one man). It has yet to win an **Olympic medal**. In 1964, two Cambodian boxers placed equal ninth, with Khiru Soeun in **featherweight** and Touch Nol **light-welterweight**, each winning one match. But the top Cambodian Olympic performance was likely the 73rd place of 95 entrants in the 2008 men's **marathon** by Hem Bunting.

CAMEROON (CMR). In 1959, Cameroon approached the **International Olympic Committee** (IOC) for advice about the establishment of a **National Olympic Committee** (NOC). It took four years for plans to reach fruition, with the NOC being formed in 1963 and receiving IOC recognition in the same year. The Central African nation Cameroon (officially the Republic of Cameroon since 1984) made its Olympic debut in 1964 at Tokyo and has appeared at all Summer **Olympic Games** since. In 1976, it joined most of the other African nations in **boycotting** the games but did not withdraw from the Olympics until the second day, by which time Cameroon's four **cyclists** had competed in the 100 km team **time trial**. In 13 Summer Games, Cameroon has entered 205 athletes (156 men, 49 **women**) in 10 sports: **athletics** (22 men, 24 women), **boxing** (32 men), **cycling** (11 men), **football** (50 men, 17 women), **judo** (16 men, two women), **rowing** (one man), **swimming** (three men, one woman), **table tennis** (two women), **weightlifting** (seven men, two women), and **wrestling** (14 men, one woman).

Cameroon athletes have won five **Olympic medals**, two in boxing: a silver medal in the 1968 **welterweight** class by Joseph Bessala and a bronze medal in the 1984 **lightweight** class by Martin N'Dongo Ebanga. But the highlights of their Olympic performances have been the gold medal won at Sydney in 2000 by their men's football team and the gold medals won by Françoise Mbango Etone in the women's **triple jump** at Athens in 2004 and Beijing in 2008. Other notable efforts by Cameroonian athletes include Laure Ali, who finished seventh of 18 in women's **freestyle heavyweight** wrestling in 2012, and Vencelas Dabaya, who was fifth of 17 in 2004 lightweight weightlifting. He subsequently competed for **France** and won the silver medal in that class in 2008. In addition to their two medalists, three other Cameroon boxers (Jean-Pierre Mbereke-Baban, 1984 **light-welterweight**; Jean-Paul Nanga-Ntsah, 1984 **light-heavyweight**; Hassan Ndam Njikam, 2000 **middleweight**) reached the quarter-final round before losing and finishing equal fifth.

Cameroon has attended the **Olympic Winter Games** only in 2002 with just one athlete—**cross-country skier** Isaac Menyoli, who competed in the men's **sprint** and 10/10 km **pursuit**. In the sprint, he finished 65th, ahead of four other skiers and two others who were **disqualified**. In the pursuit, he was 80th of 83 in the first **heat** and did not qualify for the second heat.

CANADA (CAN). The North American country officially known simply as Canada first appeared at the 1904 **Olympic Games** in St. Louis. However, in 1900 four Canadian citizens competed in track and field **athletics**, titularly under **United States'** colors. Since 1900, Canada was not represented at only the 1980 Moscow Olympic Games, which they **boycotted**. In 26 Summer Games, Canada has entered 3,320 athletes (2,239 men, 1,081 **women**) and competed in 37 sports plus the **art competitions**—all 32 sports currently contested plus **baseball**, **golf**, **ice hockey**, **lacrosse**, and **softball**. They had the most participants in athletics (394 men, 183 women), **rowing** (287 men, 97 women), **swimming** (164 men, 157 women), and **sailing** (134 men, 18 women). Canada has won 281 **Olympic medals** (60 gold, 101 silver, 120 bronze) at the Summer Games. Rower Leslie Thompson-Willie (one gold, three silver, one bronze in seven Olympic Games from 1984 to 2012) and runner Phil Edwards (five bronze medals from 1928 to 1936) lead all Canadians with five medals each in the Summer Games. Adam Van Koeverden has four medals (one gold, two silver, one bronze) in men's **kayaking** from 2004 to 2012; Émilie Heymans has four in **diving** (two silver, two bronze from 2000 to 2012); swimmer Victor Davis won four from 1984 to 1988 (one gold, three silver), and runner Alex Wilson won four from 1928 to 1932 (one silver, three bronze). **Equestrian** competitor **Ian Millar** has participated in 10 Olympic Games (1972–2012), more than any other Olympic athlete.

Canada has appeared at every **Olympic Winter Games** since their inception in 1924, and, in addition, its ice hockey team competed in the 1920 hockey tournament, winning decisively. This began a trend that continued until the **Soviet Union** entered the Olympic ice hockey tournaments, starting in 1956. In 22 Winter Games, Canada has entered 1,279 athletes (869 men, 410 women) and competed in 15 sports, all but the **military ski patrol**, which was held only once and attracted just six nations.

Canada has won 170 medals at the Olympic Winter Games (62 gold, 56 silver, 52 bronze). Two female **speed skaters**—**Clara Hughes** and **Cindy Klassen**—lead Canada's medalists, with six each. Hughes won two bronze medals in **cycling** in 1996 and four (one gold, one silver, two bronze) in speed skating from 2002 to 2010. She returned to cycling in 2012 but did not medal that year. All of Klassen's medals (one gold, two silver, three bronze) were won in speed skating from 2002 to 2010. **Short-track speed skater** Marc Gagnon won five medals (three gold, two bronze) in his sport from 1994 to 2002, as did François-Louis Tremblay (two gold, two silver, one bronze, 2002–2010).

In ice hockey, **Jayna Hefford** and **Hayley Wickenheiser** each won five medals (silver in 1998, gold from 2002 to 2014). Wickenheiser also played softball in 2000 but did not medal. Caroline Ouellette was also a member of the four gold medal–winning **Canadian ice hockey teams** from 2002 to 2014. **Jennifer Botterill** and **Becky Kellar** both played on the 1998 silver medal–winning ice hockey team and the three subsequent gold medal teams and also won four medals. In short-track speed skating, Tania Vicent won four medals all in the women's 3,000 meter **relay** from 1998 to 2010, Éric Bédard won four medals (two gold, one silver, one bronze) from 1998 to 2006, and Charles Hamelin won three golds and one silver from 2006 to 2014. Canadian speed skaters with four Olympic medals are Gaeton Boucher (two gold, one silver, one bronze 1976–1988), Denny Morrison (one gold, two silver, one bronze, 2006–2014), and Kristina Groves (three silver, one bronze, 2002–2010).

Canada has also hosted the Games of the XXIst **Olympiad** at Montreal in 1976, the 15th Olympic Winter Games at Calgary in 1988, and the 21st Olympic Winter Games at Vancouver in 2010. They have also had 14 unsuccessful bid attempts with Montreal (1944, 1972) and Toronto (1996, 2008) bidding for the Summer Games and Banff (1972), Calgary (1964, 1968), Montreal (1932, 1936, 1944, 1956), Quebec (2002), and Vancouver-Garibaldi (1976, 1980) bidding for the Winter Games. *See also* COCKBURN, KAREN; MARTIN, KEVIN; POUND, RICHARD WILLIAM DUNCAN; WHITFIELD, SIMON ST. QUENTIN.

CANADIAN (CANOE). The sport of **canoeing** uses two types of boats. One is referred to as a **kayak** and uses a double-bladed paddle, while the other is termed a Canadian canoe and uses a single-bladed paddle. In the **Olympic Games** races are held for men in both kayak and Canadian canoes on both flatwater and slalom courses, while women compete only in kayak races. **Ivan Patzaichin** of **Romania** competed in men's Canadian-style canoeing in five Olympic Games from 1968 to 1984 and won four gold and three silver medals.

CANADIAN ICE HOCKEY TEAMS. **Canada** dominated men's **ice hockey** at the Olympics from 1920 through 1952, winning all the Olympic tournaments during that time except the 1936 **Olympic Winter Games**, when it was upset by a British team that contained a number of Canadians who held dual British citizenship. Canada was always represented by a club team during its ice hockey reign. The teams were as follows: 1920, Winnipeg Falcons; 1924, Toronto Granites (with the addition of two players from the Winnipeg Falcons and Montreal Victorias); 1928, Toronto Varsity Graduate Team; 1932, The Winnipegs (with the addition of two players from the Selkirk Fisherman); 1936, Port Arthur Bearcats (with the addition of several players from the Montreal Victorias); 1948, Royal Canadian Air Force Flyers; and 1952, Edmonton Mercurys. During this era of dominance, the Canadians posted a record of 35 wins, one loss, and three ties in Olympic competition. The loss was to **Great Britain**, 2–1, in 1936. The ties were in 1932 to the **United States** (2–2), in 1948 to **Czechoslovakia** (0–0), and in 1952 to the United States (3–3). In 1956, the **Soviet Union** entered the ice hockey tournament at the Olympic Winter Games and began its own period of dominance. Since women's ice hockey was added to the Winter Games in 1998, Canada won the silver medal in 1998 and the gold medal in the four subsequent Winter Games. In 2002, Canada saw both its men's ice hockey team win the gold medal at Salt Lake City, the first gold for the Canadian men in 50 years. In 2010 at Vancouver, Canadian pride swelled when both the men's and women's hockey teams won the gold medals. Both teams repeated their performance in 2014, giving the women's team four consecutive gold medals. *See also* SOVIET UNION (USSR) ICE HOCKEY TEAMS (1956–1992).

CANNE DE COMBAT. A French martial art, *canne de combat* is contested with a cane as the weapon. Related to the sport of **savate** ("French boxing"), *canne de combat* was held as a **demonstration sport** together with savate at the 1924 Olympics.

CANOEING AND KAYAKING. Canoeing began as a means of transportation. Competition in canoeing began in the mid-19th century. The Royal Canoe

Club of London was formed in 1866 and was the first organization interested in developing the sport. In 1871, the New York Canoe Club was founded.

In 1924, canoeing was on the **Olympic Program** as a **demonstration sport**. It became a full medal sport in 1936 with both canoe and kayak events. The program has varied a great deal over the years, with many events now discontinued and several new ones added. **Women** began Olympic canoeing in 1948, competing only in kayaks, which is still the case. Whitewater canoeing, or **slalom** canoeing, was held at the 1972 Olympics in Munich, returned to the Olympic Program in 1992 at Barcelona, and has been on the Olympic Program since. The two types of canoe events are often called flatwater and whitewater, or sprint and slalom. The two types of canoes used are the kayak, in which the paddler sits inside a covered shell, and the **Canadian**, in which the paddler kneels with the top of the canoe open. The events are usually designated by codes, such as K1-500. The code indicates the type of canoe (K = kayak, C = Canadian) and the number of canoeists (1, 2, or 4), followed by the distance (500 or 1,000 meters).

Canoeing is governed worldwide by the Fédération Internationale de Canoë, which was founded in 1924 and currently has 162 member nations. In 18 Summer Olympic competitions, there have been 3,010 athletes (2,365 men, 645 women) from 94 nations who have participated in Olympic canoeing and kayaking. The top medal winners in Olympic canoeing history have been **Sweden**'s **Gert Fredriksson** (eight medals, six gold) and **Romania**'s **Ivan Patzaichin** (seven medals, four gold). Among women, **Germany**'s **Birgit Fischer-Schmidt** (12 medals, eight gold), **Hungary**'s Katalin Kovács (eight medals, three gold), and **Sweden**'s **Agneta Andersson** (seven medals, three gold) have won the most canoeing medals. *See also* FERGUSON, IAN GORDON; WAGNER-AUGUSTIN, KATRIN.

CAPE VERDE (CPV). Cape Verde's **National Olympic Committee** was formed in 1989 and given official recognition by the **International Olympic Committee** in September 1993. The Atlantic Ocean island nation (officially named the Republic of Cabo Verde) made its Olympic debut in 1996 and has competed in each Summer Games, but it has not yet competed at the **Olympic Winter Games**. It has been represented by nine athletes (six men, three **women**) in its five Olympic appearances, competing in **athletics** (four men, two woman), **boxing** (one man), **judo** (one man), and **rhythmic gymnastics** (one woman). One of the top Olympic performances by a Cape Verdean was in 2008, when Nelson Cruz placed 48th of 95 competitors in the men's **marathon** with a respectable time of 2:23.47. Antonio Carlos Piña started and completed three marathons (1996, 2000, and 2004), with a best performance of 78th of 101 entrants in 2004 at the age of 38. Adysângela Moniz won her first bout in women's **heavyweight** judo in 2012 and finished in a tie for ninth place among the 20 entrants.

ČÁSLAVSKÁ, VĚRA (TCH–GYM). B. 3 May 1942, Prague, **Czechoslovakia**. Attractive, vivacious, and talented, Věra Čáslavská was the outstanding **gymnast** at the 1964 and 1968 Games. In Tokyo, the five-foot, three-inch (160 cm), 128 lb (58 kg) athlete won three gold medals and one silver, and in **Mexico** she won four golds (one shared) and two silvers. Having earlier won a silver medal, in 1960, Čáslavská's total of 11 Olympic medals, including seven golds, has only ever been bettered among female gymnasts by **Larysa Latynina** (URS). After winning her final gold medal in 1968, Věra married **Czech** Olympic silver medalist (1,500 meters in 1964) Josef Odložil in Mexico, but the couple later divorced. In 1989, she was appointed president of the Czech Olympic Committee, and in 1995 she was elected a member of the **International Olympic Committee** and served until 2001.

Věra Čáslavská (TCH), dominated women's gymnastics at the 1964 and 1968 Olympic Games. Courtesy of Erich Kamper

CAYMAN ISLANDS (CAY). The Cayman Islands **National Olympic Committee** was formed in 1973 and was recognized by the **International Olympic Committee** in 1976. The Cayman Islands, a British Overseas Territory, first competed at the 1976 **Olympic Games** and has been represented at every Olympics since then, except 1980. It has not yet won an **Olympic medal.** In 2010, Dow Travers competed in **Alpine skiing** for the Caribbean territory and finished 69th of 101 entrants in the **giant slalom,** in the nation's first **Olympic Winter Games** appearance. He competed again in 2014 at Sochi but was unable to finish in either of his two events. In nine Summer Games, the Cayman Islands has entered 35 athletes (30 men, five **women**) in four sports: **athletics** (four men, two women), **cycling** (12 men, one woman), **sailing** (11 men, one woman), and **swimming** (three men, one woman). The best performance by a Caymanian Olympian occurred in 2008, when Cydonie Mothersill placed eighth in the women's 200 meters in athletics. She had also reached the semifinals in that event in 2004. Other notable performances include Kareem Streete-Thompson finishing 13th of 53 entrants in the men's **long jump** in 2000, Perry Merren finishing 58th of 136 entrants in the men's cycling 196.8 km **road race** in 1988, and brothers Brett and Shaune Fraser finishing 15th and 16th of 60 entrants in the 2012 100 meters **freestyle** swimming event. Surprisingly, the Cayman Islands has not done well in sailing. They have entered 10 different sailing events and finished among the last few contestants in nine of them.

CENTRAL AFRICAN REPUBLIC (CAF). The present-day nation known as the Central African Republic was originally part of French Equatorial Africa and called Ubangi-Shari. After gaining independence from **France** in 1960, the nation adopted the official name of the Central African Republic. A **National Olympic Committee** (NOC) was formed in 1961 and, after lengthy negotiations over the suitability of the statutes of the NOC, the **International Olympic Committee** granted full recognition in 1965. Central Africa competed at the 1968 **Olympic Games,** but then missed the 1972, 1976, and 1980 Olympics. Since competing at the 1984 Olympic Games, Central Africa has competed at all subsequent Summer Olympics but has not yet competed at the **Olympic Winter Games** and has not yet won a medal at the Olympics. In nine Summer Games, the Central African Republic has entered 47 athletes (36 men, 11 **women**) in nine sports: **archery** (one woman), **athletics** (10 men, six women), **basketball** (12 men), **boxing** (five men), **cycling** (four men), **judo** (two men, two women), **swimming** (one man), **taekwondo** (two men, one woman), and **wrestling** (one woman).

The best Olympic performance by a Central African athlete occurred in 1988 when Adolphe Ambowodé placed 42nd of 118 entrants in the men's

marathon. In 2004, Ernest Ndissipou came in 44th of 101 runners in that event. Another notable performance was in 1988, when the men's basketball team qualified for the Olympic tournament and placed 10th of 12 teams. The team was led by Anicet Richard Lavodrama, who twice scored 30 points in one game in the 1988 Olympic tournament, was drafted by the Los Angeles Clippers of the National Basketball Association, and became the development and international relations manager for the Fédération Internationale de Basketball.

CENTRAL AMERICA. Central America is a region in the Western Hemisphere and, as such, has never had full recognition by the **International Olympic Committee** (IOC), nor has it ever competed at the **Olympic Games** as a region. But from 1918 to 1940, Pedro Jaime de Matheu was an IOC member of the Central American region. De Matheu was from **El Salvador**, which had become independent in 1839.

CEYLON (CEY). *See* SRI LANKA.

CHAD (CHA). Chad's **National Olympic Committee** was formed in 1963 and recognized by the **International Olympic Committee** in 1964. Chad, located in Central Africa, once part of French Equatorial Africa, but since gaining independence in 1960 (known officially as the Republic of Chad), it first competed at the **Olympic Games** in 1964. With the exception of the Olympics of 1976 and 1980, which it **boycotted**, Chad has taken part in every Summer Games since 1964. Chad has not yet competed at the **Olympic Winter Games** and has never won an **Olympic medal**. The first Chadian athlete to compete at the Olympics was **high jumper** Mahamat Idriss, who first represented **France** in 1960. In 10 Olympic appearances through 2012, Chad has been represented by 25 Olympians (21 men, four **women**) in three sports: **athletics** (18 men, three women), **boxing** (one man), and **judo** (two men, one woman).

The best Olympic performance by a Chadian was in the 1964 men's high jump, when Mahamat Idriss qualified for the final round and placed ninth of 28 entrants. In 1968, Idriss was 21st of 39 entrants, while teammate Ahmed Senoussi finished 12th. In judo in 1992, M'Bairo Abakar tied for 13th among 42 contestants in the **half-middleweight** class. In athletics, Chad had several runners who qualified in their first **heat** but were eliminated from competition following their second heat—Ahmed Issa (1964 men's 800 meters, 1968 men's 1,500 meters), Kaltouma Nadjina (2000 and 2004 women's 400 meters), and Saleh-Alah-Djaba (1972 men's 100 meters). In Chad's one venture into the boxing tournament, Noureddine Aman Hassan was stopped in the second round of his 1972 **light-heavyweight** bout by the eventual gold medalist and future world professional champion, Mate Parlov of **Yugoslavia**.

CHAND, DHYAN (IND–HOK). *See* DHYAN CHAND.

CHARIOT RACES. Several different chariot races were contested at the **Ancient Olympic Games**. These include the *apene*, the *synoris*, a foals' *synoris* race, the *tethrippon*, a foals' *tethrippon*, a chariot race for foals, a chariot race for 10 horses, and an event listed simply as chariot race. The last three were contested only in A.D. 65. *See also KALPE*; *KELES.*

CHARIOTS OF FIRE. This 1981 movie is perhaps the best-known cinematic depiction of the **Olympic Games**. Based on actual events, the story follows two **British** athletes, Harold Abrahams and Eric Liddell, who both managed to win a gold medal at the 1924 Olympics after overcoming various difficulties. As most historical movies tend to, *Chariots of Fire* used artistic license to change events and persons, to the annoyance of some Olympic historians. The most notable departure from reality concerns one of the film's pivotal moments, when Liddell, boarding a ship to leave for France, learns he cannot contest his favored 100 meters as the **heats** are scheduled for a Sunday, and as a devout Christian, Liddell never competed on Sundays. Although this was indeed the reason Liddell did not compete in the event, he knew this well in advance, rather than just before leaving for France.

The movie was a critical and financial success and earned seven Academy Award nominations, of which it won four: Best Picture, Original Music Score, Writing Original Screenplay, and Costume Design. The film's title track was also notable, with Vangelis's "Chariots of Fire" theme composition reaching the number one position on the U.S. singles chart.

CHARPENTIER, ROBERT (FRA–CYC). B. 4 April 1916, Maule, Yvelines, **France**. D. 29 October 1966, Issy-les-Moulineaux, Hauts-de-Seine, France. Robert Charpentier was the winner of the individual **road race** at the 1936 **Olympic Games**, where he also won gold medals in the team road race event and the 4,000 meter team **pursuit**. Charpentier got started in **cycling** when he was an apprentice to a butcher and made his deliveries on his bicycle. He was runner-up at the 1935 amateur World Championship road race. World War II prevented him from having any success after the 1936 Olympics as a professional.

CHASTAIN, BRANDI DENISE (USA–FTB). B. 21 July 1968, San Jose, California, **United States**. Although she had a long and distinguished career,

Brandi Chastain is best remembered for one moment in the 1999 World Cup final. After scoring the winning penalty goal in the shootout against **China**, she took off her jersey in celebration, an unorthodox move in **women**'s **football** that was widely publicized in the United States and abroad. Apart from the title in 1999, the five-foot, seven-inch (171 cm), 128 lb (58 kg) Chastain also played on the winning team at the 1991 World Cup and at the 1996 and 2004 Olympics, and was one of the losing finalists in the 2000 Olympics. In all, Chastain played 192 international matches for the United States between 1988 and 2004. She continued to play at a competitive level through 2010, despite having passed age 40.

CHESS. Chess has never been on the **Olympic Program**, even as a **demonstration sport**. However, in 1999, the **International Olympic Committee** recognized the world governing body of chess, the Fédération Internationale des Échecs (FIDE). Interestingly, FIDE was formed in 1924 after a failed attempt to have chess held at the Paris Olympics, and a competition, now known as the Chess Olympiad, was then held for the first time. In 2014, FIDE had 182 members.

CHILE (CHI). The southwestern South American nation of Chile is one of the most unusually shaped countries. It stretches for more than 4,300 km (2,670 miles) from north to south but is only 350 km (217 miles) at its widest point from east to west. Chile's initial Olympic appearance was in 1912. Since that time, however, it has missed only the **Olympic Games** of 1932 and 1980. Officially known as the Republic of Chile, its **National Olympic Committee** was formed in 1934 and was recognized by the **International Olympic Committee** in the same year. In 21 Summer Games, Chile has entered 448 athletes (408 men, 40 **women**) and competed in 24 sports, with the most entrants in **athletics** (84 men, 17 women), **football** (53 men), **cycling** (42 men, two women), **boxing** (35 men), **basketball** (31 men), and **shooting** (30 men, one woman).

Chilean athletes have won 13 **Olympic medals**, two gold (both in 2004), seven silver, and four bronze. Tennis player Fernando González has won three Olympic medals, one of each color, the most of any Chilean Olympian. In 2004, Chile won gold in men's **singles** and **doubles tennis**, with González partnering Nicolás Massú in doubles, and Massú also winning the singles. In **equestrian jumping** events, Óscar Cristi won two silver medals in 1952. The 2000 men's football team won the bronze medal. Other Chilean Olympians who won medals are Marlene Ahrens (silver, 1956 women's **javelin throw**), Manuel Plaza (silver, 1928 men's **marathon**), **skeet** shooter Alfonso de Irruarízaga (1988 silver), boxers **bantamweight** Claudio Barrientos (1956 bronze), **middleweight** Ramón Tapia (1956 silver), and **light-heavyweight** Carlos Lucas (1956 bronze).

Chile first competed at the **Olympic Winter Games** of 1948 and has competed at most subsequent Winter Olympics, missing only those of 1972 and 1980. In 16 Winter Games, Chile has entered 50 athletes (41 men, nine women) and competed in four sports: **Alpine skiing** (38 men, five women), **biathlon** (two men, two women), **cross-country skiing** (one man), and **freestyle skiing** (two women). The best results at the Winter Games for Chile include freestyle skiers Stephanie Joffroy (16th of 28 in 2014 women's **skicross**) and Dominique Ohaco (13th of 22 in 2014 women's slopestyle) and Alpine skiers Thomas Grob and his brother Rainer Grob (11th and 13th of 38 in 1998 men's **combined**), Juan Pablo Santiagos (25th of 109 in 1988 men's **slalom**, 23rd of 56 in 1988 men's combined), and the 1984 Chilean men's slalom team that finished 19th (Andres Figueroa), 20th (Dieter Linneberg), 21st (Hans Kossmann), and 23rd (Miguel Purcell) of 101 entrants.

CHINA, PEOPLE'S REPUBLIC OF (CHN). Although the current **National Olympic Committee** was recognized by the **International Olympic Committee** (IOC) in 1979, the first Chinese Olympic Committee was formed in 1910 and recognized in 1922. China competed at the **Olympic Games** of 1932, 1936, and 1948. In September 1949, Chinese Communists assumed control of the government, and many of the former rulers escaped to the island province of Taiwan, including many former members of the Chinese Olympic Committee (possibly as many as 19 of 26). Due to visa problems, only one athlete from the Chinese mainland could compete at the 1952 Olympic Games in Helsinki. Thus began a 40-year political problem for the IOC: the question of the "two Chinas."

In May 1954, at the 50th **IOC Session** in Athens, the IOC voted 23–21 to recognize both the "Olympic Committee of the Chinese Republic" in Beijing (then Peking) (in 1957 changed to the "Olympic Committee of the People's Democratic Republic of China") and the "Chinese Olympic Committee" in Taipei.

Both Chinas were invited to the 1956 Olympics in Melbourne. Beijing accepted the invitation on 20 November, which led Taipei to reject the invitation. However, Taipei changed its decision and elected to compete, which caused Beijing to withdraw in protest. At Melbourne, no athletes from mainland China competed, while 21 athletes from the island nation competed under the banner of the Republic of China. The Beijing committee withdrew from the IOC on 19 August 1958 in protest against the IOC's continued recognition of Taiwan.

A request to be recognized again was submitted in 1975. The IOC requested the All-China Sports Federation to send its rules for inspection, a standard procedure. The All-China Sports Federation took two years to comply, but its application was eventually approved on 25 November 1979.

In the interim, the IOC sent a three-member contingent, led by **New Zealander** Lance Cross, to inspect sporting facilities in China. Cross reported to the IOC at its 81st Session in Montevideo in April 1979. The IOC made the following recommendations at this Session: "In the Olympic spirit, and in accordance with the *Olympic Charter*, the IOC resolves: 1) to recognize the Chinese Olympic Committee located in Peking (Beijing), and 2) to maintain recognition of the Chinese Olympic Committee located in Taipei. All matters pertaining to names, anthems, flags and constitutions will be the subject of studies and agreements which will have to be completed as soon as possible." The full Session approved this motion, 36–30. The IOC **Executive Board** modified this slightly, changing item 2 to read "to maintain recognition of the Olympic Committee located in Taipei."

China returned to the Olympic fold in 1980 at Lake Placid. It did not compete in 1980 at Moscow, joining the **United States**–led **boycott**, but China has competed at all other Olympic Games and **Olympic Winter Games** since 1984.

In 12 Summer Games, China has entered 2,081 athletes (1,019 men, 1,062 **women**) and competed in 34 sports plus the **art competitions**. It is one of very few nations (**Bhutan** and **Saint Kitts and Nevis** are others) to have had more women than men compete in the Olympic Games and in both the Summer Games and Winter Games. **North Korea** also had more women than men at the Winter Games but not in the Summer Games or in total. China has had the most participants in **athletics** (134 men, 156 women), **swimming** (69 men, 92 women), **basketball** (78 men, 57 women), **shooting** (66 men, 43 women), and **rowing** (47 men, 58 women). Chinese athletes have won 473 **Olympic medals** at the Summer Games (201 gold, 144 silver, 128 bronze), all since 1984. They have won medals in 30 of the 34 Summer sports in which they have participated, failing to do so only in **baseball**, **equestrian**, **triathlon**, and **water polo**. Chinese athletes excel in **gymnastics**, **table tennis**, **diving**, and swimming.

In the Summer Games, six Chinese athletes have each won six medals, seven others have each won five medals, and 17 have won four medals. **Li Ning** was China's first star Olympian. He won six medals (three gold, two silver, one bronze) in gymnastics in 1984. He was followed in the gymnastics arena by Li Xiaoshuang, who won six (two gold, three silver, one bronze) in 1992 and 1996. Zou Kai is the third Chinese gymnast with six medals. His total of five gold medals is the most of any Chinese athlete, while eight others have each won four gold medals. In the 21st century, women's diving has been dominated by the Chinese. **Guo Jingjing** has four gold and two silver medals, three of which she won in synchronized **springboard** diving with her partner Wu Minxia, who also has a total of six medals: four gold, one silver, one bronze. The other Chinese athlete with six Olympic medals is pistol shooter Wang Yifu, who won two gold, three silver, and one bronze from 1984 to 2004 in six Games.

China has totally dominated the sport of table tennis at the Olympics, winning 24 of 28 gold medals and 47 of 88 total medals. In that sport, 10 players have won four or more medals and nine of them are Chinese. **Wang Nan** and Wang Hao (no relation) have each won five. China has also done exceptionally well in **badminton**, with 16 gold medals and 38 total medals. **Gao Ling** is the only athlete with four Olympic medals in badminton.

One of the best known Chinese athletes in the world competed in three Olympic Games, but not all of his teammates shared his skill level, and basketball star Yao Ming's Olympic teams never finished better than eighth place. The Chinese women's basketball team has done better with silver and bronze medals in seven appearances led by the six-foot, eight-inch (204 cm) 254 lb (115 kg) **Zheng Haixia.**

In 10 Winter Games, China has entered 311 athletes (127 men, 184 women) and competed in 11 sports, all except **Nordic combined** and the sliding sports of **bobsledding, luge**, and **skeleton**. Their largest contingents have been in **speed skating** (34 men, 39 women), **ice hockey** (45 women), and **cross-country skiing** (19 men, 23 women). They have won 53 medals (12 gold, 22 silver, 19 bronze) in five sports, with the most, by far (30) in **short-track speed skating**.

Short-track speed skater **Wang Meng** is the only Chinese athlete to win six medals at the Winter Games. She won four gold, one silver, and one bronze in 2006 and 2010. Three other short-trackers, Li Jiajun and the reduplicated name pair each named **Yang Yang**, have also each won five medals. Wang Meng is the only one with four gold medals. No one has won just four medals, but six others have won three each, including the figure skating **pairs** couple of Shen Xue and her husband, Zhao Hongbo.

China hosted the Games of the XXIXth **Olympiad** in Beijing in 2008, and Beijing is one of six cities bidding to host the 2022 Winter Games. Beijing was unsuccessful in a bid for the Summer Games in 2000, and Harbin was unsuccessful in a bid for the 2010 Winter Games. *See also* FU MINGXIA; HONG KONG, CHINA; MACAU; XIONG NI; ZHANG YINING.

CHINESE TAIPEI (aka TAIWAN, FORMOSA, REPUBLIC OF CHINA) (TPE). The Chinese Taipei **National Olympic Committee** (NOC) was first formed in 1949 by members of the mainland Chinese Committee who had fled to the island. The **International Olympic Committee**'s (IOC) official policy at this time was that the mainland Chinese Olympic Committee had simply changed its address and was now located on the island of Taiwan. For many years thereafter, the country was embroiled in a dispute with mainland **China** over recognition by the IOC.

In October 1959, the IOC **Executive Board** recommended that the Olympic Committee in Taiwan be recognized as the "Olympic Committee of the Republic of China," but it also insisted that, at the 1960 Olympic opening ceremony, this team should march behind a banner reading "Formosa." The banner eventually read "Taiwan/Formosa," but the placard bearer also posted a sign of his own, reading "Under Protest."

The greatest controversy over the participation of the athletes from Chinese Taipei occurred in 1976 at Montreal. In 1970, **Canada** had given political recognition to mainland China. Only a few weeks before the Montreal Olympics, Canada's government announced that it would not allow Chinese Taipei athletes to compete under the name of the "Republic of China." This was in complete violation of the *Olympic Charter* and the contract Montreal had signed as host of the **Olympic Games**, in which it agreed to allow all eligible athletes to enter the nation with the use of the **Olympic identity card.** The **United States** government protested vociferously, even threatening a **boycott**. Eventually, however, the U.S. athletes competed, although Chinese Taipei refused to compete under any name other than the Republic of China. On 11 July, only six days before the start of the Olympics, the IOC Executive Board gave in and proposed to the full IOC that the island nation should compete at Montreal as Taiwan. The IOC approved this recommendation, 58–2, with six abstentions, but Chinese Taipei/Taiwan/Republic of China withdrew in protest and did not compete at the 1976 Olympics.

After it competed for several years under the banner "China" or "Republic of China," the IOC eventually banned the country from competing under this name. The current NOC was recognized in its present form on 26 November 1979, and on 23 March 1981 it signed an agreement with the IOC in which the NOC agreed to change its name to the Chinese Taipei Olympic Committee and compete under a new flag and emblem.

Taiwan/Chinese Taipei first competed at the Olympic Games in 1956 and since then has taken part in every Olympics except 1976 and 1980. It has competed in 12 Olympic Games under various names: the Republic of China (1956), Taiwan/Formosa (1960), Taiwan (1964–1972), and Chinese Taipei (1984–2010).

In 13 Summer Games, Taiwan has entered 486 athletes (314 men, 172 **women**) and competed in 23 sports, with the largest contingents in **athletics** (36 men, 25 women), **baseball** (57 men), **swimming** (23 men, 26 women), **weightlifting** (30 men, eight women), **judo** (25 men, 12 women), and **soft-**

ball (34 women). The nation has won 21 **Olympic medals** (two gold, seven silver, 12 bronze), including its first two gold medals in 2004. Three athletes from the island nation have each won two medals, and two have won gold medals. But by far the best-known athletes from Chinese Taipei have been two competitors in track and field athletics, who did not win gold. Yang Chuan-Kwang, better known as "C. K. Yang," was the runner-up in the **decathlon** in 1960 and also competed in 1956 and 1964. He was a student at the University of California in Los Angeles, along with American decathlete **Rafer Johnson**. In 1960, their Olympic decathlon battle achieved much publicity, and Johnson defeated Yang for the gold by a narrow margin. Chi Cheng won a bronze in the 1968 women's 80 meter **hurdles**, and was the top woman **sprinter** in the world in 1969–1970. She was quite a versatile athlete and in three Olympic Games from 1960 to 1968 competed in the **long jump**, 100 meters, 4x100 meters **relay**, and **pentathlon** in addition to the hurdles.

Chen Jing won two medals in **table tennis** women's **singles** (silver in 1996, bronze in 2000). She had previously represented mainland **China** in 1988 and had won a gold and silver medal in those Olympics. Huang Chih-Hsiung won a bronze medal in men's **flyweight taekwondo** in 2000 and a silver in the **featherweight** class in 2004. Flyweight Chu Mu-Yen won gold in 2004 and bronze in 2008 in taekwondo. Taiwan's other gold medal also came in taekwondo when Chen Shih-Hsien won the women's flyweight title in 2004.

Taiwan's other Olympic medals have been won by the 2004 men's **archery** team (silver) and the 2004 women's archery team (bronze), the 1992 baseball team (silver) which comprised 11 players who had previously won the Little League World Series, and in taekwondo with featherweights Sung Yu-Chi (men's 2008 bronze) and Tseng Li-Chen (women's 2012 bronze) and flyweight Chi Shu-Ju (women's 2000 bronze). Taiwan's athletes also won six medals in weightlifting, with five of them won by women. Featherweight Tsai Wen-Yee (1984 bronze) is the only Taiwanese male to win an Olympic weightlifting medal. Flyweight Chen Wei-Ling (2008 bronze), featherweights Li Feng-Ying (2000 silver) and Hsu Shu-Ching (2012 silver), **middleweight** Lu Ying-Chi (2008 bronze), and **heavyweight** Kuo Yi-Hang (2000 bronze) are the Taiwanese female weightlifters with Olympic medals.

The nation has competed at nine **Olympic Winter Games**, as Taiwan 1972–1976 and as Chinese Taipei 1984–2010. In 11 Winter Games, Taiwan has entered 44 athletes (40 men, four women) and competed in eight sports: **Alpine skiing** (nine men), **biathlon** (two men), **bobsledding** (16 men), **cross-country skiing** (five men), **figure skating** (one man, one woman), **luge** (eight men, three women), **speed skating** (one man), and **short-track speed skating** (one man). They have not won any medals. In their first venture into Alpine skiing in 1972 the four members of the men's **slalom** team skied carefully and negotiated all the gates successfully. They were the last four skiers who completed the course and were placed 34th, 35th, 36th, and 37th of 72 entrants. Their times ranged from 15 to 30 seconds slower than the skier in 33rd place, yet they finished ahead of the 35 skiers who failed to complete the course. In 1988, the Taiwan two-man bobsled team of Chen Chin-San and Lee Chen-Tan finished 15th of 41 entrants for the country's best performance at the Winter Games.

CHUKARIN, VIKTOR IVANOVICH (URS/UKR–GYM). B. 9 November 1921, Mariupol, **Ukraine**. D. 26 August 1984, Lvov, Ukraine, USSR. A former World War II prisoner of war, Viktor Chukarin was 30 years old when the Soviet Union first competed at the **Olympic Games** in 1952. Despite his age, he dominated the **gymnastics** competition in Helsinki, winning the **all-around** title in addition to taking gold in the team event and two gold and two silver medals on the individual apparatus events. In 1956, Chukarin successfully defended his all-around title and added two more golds, a silver, and a bronze, bringing his tally of **Olympic medals** to a then-record total of 11. Chukarin was Soviet all-around champion in 1949–1951, 1953, and 1955. He was also World All-Around Champion in 1954. After retiring, he became head of gymnastics at the Lvov Institute of Physical Culture.

Viktor Chukarin of the Soviet Union, winner of the all-around men's gymnastics title in 1952 and 1956. Courtesy of Erich Kamper

CITIUS, ALTIUS, FORTIUS. *See* OLYMPIC MOTTO.

CLAUDIUS, LESLIE WALTER (IND–HOK). B. 25 March 1927, Bilaspur, Madhya Pradesh, **India**. D. 20 December 2012, Calcutta, West Bengal, India. Leslie Claudius shares with **Udham Singh** of India, Teun de Nooijer of the **Netherlands**, and Lucha Aymar of **Argentina (women**'s **hockey)** the distinction of being one of only four players to win four **Olympic medals** for field hockey. To his gold medals in 1948, 1952, and 1956, he added silver in 1960 when he captained the team. The diminutive Claudius, at five feet, four inches (162 cm), 117 lb (53 kg), was the first player ever to earn 100 caps, and he competed for India, in addition to the Olympics, on the team's European tour of 1949, **Malaysian** tour of 1952, **Australian** and **New Zealand** tours of 1955, and at the 3rd Asian Games in 1958. After the 1960 Olympics, he continued to compete domestically, retiring after the 1965 season. In 1971, he became the sixth Indian hockey player to be given the prestigious Padam-shree civil award by the Indian government.

CLAY, CASSIUS MARCELLUS (USA–BOX). *See* ALI, MUHAMMAD.

CLEAN AND JERK. The clean and jerk is one of the two lifts in Olympic **weightlifting** competition. (Prior to 1976, a third lift, the **press**, was also required.) The weight lifted in this method is added to the weight lifted in the **snatch** lift, and the total of the two lifts determines the winner. It is a two-part lift. In the first part, the weight is lifted from the ground to a position chest-high. From there the weight is lifted overhead. In 2004, Hossein Reza Zadeh of **Iran** set the Olympic **super-heavyweight** class record with a clean and jerk lift of 262.5 kg (578.7 lb).

CLOSING CEREMONY. *See* OLYMPIC CEREMONIES.

COCHELEA-COGEANU, VERONICA (ROU–ROW). B. 15 November 1965, Voineşti, Iaşi, **Romania**. Among **women**, only her countrywoman, **Elisabeta Lipă-Oleniuc**, has won more Olympic **rowing** medals than the six won by Veronica Cochelea-Cogeanu, although Romanians **Georgeta Damian-Andrunache** and Doina Ignat also have six. Lipă-Oleniuc and Cochelea-Cogeanu combined for five medals: 1988 **doubles sculls** silver medal, 1988 quadruple sculls bronze medal, 1992 double sculls silver medal, and 1996 and 2000 coxed **eights** gold medals. Cochelea-Cogeanu, at five feet, nine inches (175 cm), 172 lb (78 kg), also won a silver medal with the quad in 1992. She was less successful at the World Championships, winning only one gold, that in the 1993 eight. Her 1988 Olympic appearance was as Miss Cogeanu, but she competed as Veronica Cochelea after marrying.

COCKBURN, KAREN (-TURGEON) (CAN–TMP). B. 2 October 1980, Toronto, Ontario, **Canada**. Karen Cockburn, at five feet, three inches (161 cm), 121 lb (55 kg), has competed in all four Olympic Games **trampoline** competitions and has won three medals: bronze in 2000, silver in 2004 and 2008, and finished fourth in 2012. She has won more **Olympic medals** in the sport than anyone else—male or female. She won the individual gold medal at the 2003 World Championships and the synchronized trampoline event at the 2007 World Championships. She also has three silver and three bronze medals at the World Championships and a gold medal at the 2007 **Pan American Games**. After giving birth to a daughter in September 2013, she returned to the sport and hopes to compete in the 2015 Pan American Games in her hometown of Toronto. In 2007, she married Mathieu Turgeon, also an Olympic trampoliner, who won a bronze medal in 2000.

COE, BARON SEBASTIAN NEWBOLD, KBE (GBR–ATH). B. 29 September 1956, Chiswick, London, **England**. Sir Sebastian Coe is considered by many track experts to be the greatest 800 meter runner in history. His world record (1:41.73) for the distance, set in 1981, remained unbeaten for 16 years. The five-foot, nine-inch (175 cm), 119 lb (54 kg) Coe never won an Olympic title at this distance and had to settle for a silver medal in 1980 and 1984, but he won a gold medal in the 1,500 meters at both Games. His controversial omission from the 1988 British Olympic team denied him the opportunity of further honors. A prolific record breaker, he set nine outdoor and three indoor world records. After retirement, Coe continued to serve the sport as an administrator, and in 1992 was elected a member of the British Parliament, which he served through 1997. In 2000, Coe was created a life peer as Baron Coe of Ranmore, and in 2006 he was appointed a Knight Commander of the Order of the British Empire. He was the chairman of the **Organizing Committee** for the 2012 London **Olympic Games**.

COLOMBIA (COL). Colombia, located on the northwestern coast of South America, first competed at the 1932 **Olympic Games**, represented by a lone athlete, **marathon** runner Jorgé Perry Villate. The country first formed a **National Olympic Committee** (NOC) only in 1936, and this NOC was recognized by the **International Olympic Committee** in 1939. Colombia, officially known as the Republic of Colombia, has since competed at every Olympics except in 1952. In 19 Summer Games, Colombia has entered 523 athletes (409 men, 114 **women**) and competed in 21 sports plus the **art competitions** with the most participants in **cycling** (97 men, seven women), **athletics** (52 men, 37 women), **football** (70 men, 17 women), **boxing** (42 men), and **weightlifting** (30 men, 10 women).

Colombian athletes won 12 **Olympic medals** through 2010 and added eight more in 2012. The medal total of 20 consists of two gold, seven silver, and 11 bronze. They won their first gold medal in 2000, by María Isabel Urrutia in women's **heavyweight** weightlifting and their second one in 2012 by Mariana Pajón in the women's **BMX** cycling event. **Shooter** Helmut Bellingrodt won a silver medal in 1972 and matched that with another silver in 1984. Jackeline Rentería, with two bronze medals in women's **lightweight wrestling** in 2008 and 2012, is Colombia's only other dual medalist. Francis Henriquez de Zubiría was Colombia's first Olympic medalist when he won a silver as a member of the Racing Club of Paris **tug-of-war** team in 1900. Colombia's other Olympic medalists are: athletics, Ximena Restrepo (1992 bronze, 400 meters) and Catherine Ibargüen (2012 silver, **triple jump**); boxing, Jorge Julio (1988 bronze, **bantamweight**), Clemente Rojas (1972, bronze, **featherweight**), Alfonso Pérez (1972 bronze, lightweight); cycling, Rigoberto Urán (2012, silver, road race), Carlos Oquendo (2012, bronze, BMX), María Lusia Calle (2004, bronze, women's points race); **judo**, Yuri Alvear (2012, bronze women's **middleweight**); **taekwondo**, Oscar Muñoz (2012, bronze, **flyweight**); weightlifting, Óscar Figueroa (2012, silver, featherweight), Diego Fernando Salazar (2008, silver, featherweight), Mabel Mosquera (2004, bronze, women's featherweight).

Colombia competed at the **Olympic Winter Games** for the first time in 2010 but did not return in 2014. Colombia's sole winter athlete was **United States**–born Cynthia Denzler, who competed in the women's **slalom** and **giant slalom** and finished 51st of 88 in the slalom but did not finish the giant slalom.

COMĂNECI, NADIA ELENA (ROU–GYM). B. 12 November 1961, Onesti, Bacau, **Romania**. Nadia Comăneci was the first **gymnast** in Olympic history to be awarded a perfect score of 10.0. She achieved this landmark as a five-foot, four-inch (162 cm), 99 lb (45 kg) 14-year-old in 1976, first on the **uneven bars**. The judges awarded her maximum marks a further six times during the Games. In the 1976 and 1980 Games, Comăneci won a total of nine Olympic medals (five gold, three silver, one bronze). Following the 1980 Games, natural physical development began to impede her performance, and after a victory at the 1981 World Student Games, she retired. In 1989, she defected from Romania and settled in North America, and later married American Olympic gymnastic medalist Bart Conner.

Gymnast Nadia Comăneci, darling of the 1976 Olympic Games. Courtesy of Volker Kluge

COMBINED. In Olympic **Alpine skiing**, a combined event has been held for both men and **women**. It was first held in 1936 and 1948 and then resumed in 1988 and has been held at each subsequent Olympic Winter Games. It consists of a **downhill** race and a **slalom** race with the total time of both races determining the winner. Ivica Kostelić of **Croatia** has won three silver medals in the men's combined in 2006, 2010, and 2014. His sister **Janica Kostelić** won the women's combined in 2002 and 2006 and along with Maria Hofl-Riesch of **Germany** (gold medalist in 2010 and 2014) are the only multiple gold medalists in the women's combined race. There is also a **Nordic combined** competition, which combines **ski jumping** and **cross-country skiing**, but it is treated as a separate sport by the International Olympic Committee.

COMITÉ INTERNATIONAL PIERRE DE COUBERTIN. *See* INTERNATIONAL PIERRE DE COUBERTIN COMMITTEE.

COMMISSION FOR THE OLYMPIC MOVEMENT. The Commission for the **Olympic Movement** was formed in 1982, but its forerunner was the Tripartite Commission, which existed from 1975 to 1981. The Tripartite Commission was formed in response to complaints from the **National Olympic Committees** (NOCs) and **International Federations** (IFs), who felt that they had little say in the Olympic Movement and no process through which to voice their opinions officially. The Tripartite Commission consisted of members of the **International Olympic Committee** (IOC), the NOCs, and the IFs. The Commission for the Olympic Movement had a similar composition. The chairman of this commission was always the **IOC president,** originally **Lord Killanin** (Tripartite Commission), and beginning in 1980, **Juan Antonio Samaranch**. The Olympic Movement Commission was disbanded in 2001. It has essentially been superseded by the **Olympic Games Study Commission** and the **Olympic Program Commission**.

COMMISSIONS OF THE IOC. The **International Olympic Committee** (IOC) has created a number of commissions that deal with specific issues related to the **Olympic Movement**. These tend to come and go and can be difficult to track accurately. The currently recognized commissions (as of mid-2014) are as follows: **Athletes' Commission**; Audit Commission; Commission for Culture and Olympic Education; **Coordination Commission** for the Games of the XXXIe **Olympiad**—Rio de Janeiro 2016; Coordination Commission for the XXIII Olympic Winter Games—Pyeongchang 2018; Coordination Commission for the Games of the XXXIIe Olympiad—Tokyo 2020; Coordination Commission for the 2nd Winter Youth Olympic Games—Lillehammer 2016; Coordination Commission for the 3rd Summer Youth Olympic Games—Buenos Aires 2018; Entourage Commission; **Ethics Commission**; Evaluation Commission for the 3rd Winter Youth Olympic Games–2020; Evaluation Commission for the XXIV Olympic Winter Games–2022; **Finance Commission; International Relations Commission; Juridical Commission; Marketing Commission; Medical Commission; Nominations Commission; Olympic Philately, Numismatic, and Memorabilia Commission; Olympic Program Commission**; Olympic Solidarity Commission; **Press Commission; Radio and Television Commission; Sport and Environment Commission; Sport and Law Commission; Sport for All Commission**; Television Rights and New Media Commission; and the **Women and Sport Commission**. Several of the IOC Commissions have subcommissions, notably the following within the Medical Commission: Subcommission on **Doping** and Biochemistry of Sport, Subcommission on Biomechanics and Physiology of Sport, Subcommission on Sports Medicine and Coordination with the **National Olympic Committees**, and Subcommission on Out of Competition Testing. In addition, the IOC also recognizes several working groups that often have the status of a commission, at least briefly. Currently, these include the Remuneration Working Group and the Council of the **Olympic Order**. The IOC also forms ad hoc commissions to study certain problems, such as a Disciplinary Commission, which was formed to look into certain doping allegations.

COMMONWEALTH GAMES. As one of the best-known **regional international games**, the Commonwealth Games bring together countries from the (former) British Empire. The first edition was held as the British Empire Games in 1930; the 2010 celebration in Delhi hosted over 4,000 athletes from 72 nations and all continents. The games are staged by the Commonwealth Games Federation, which is an **International Olympic Committee**–recognized organization. In 2014, the Games were held in Glasgow, **Scotland**, from 23 July to 3 August.

COMMONWEALTH OF INDEPENDENT STATES (CIS). In 1992, former republics of the Union of Soviet Socialist Republics (**Soviet Union**) competed at the **Olympic Games** in Barcelona and the **Olympic Winter Games** in Albertville. By then, the former republics had formed the Commonwealth of Independent States. Because of the short time after the breakup of the Soviet Union, it was agreed that the former republics would compete as one team, which was called the Unified Team, or L'Équipe Unifiée, which loosely represented the Commonwealth of Independent States.

At Albertville, the Unified Team was a loose confederation of five former Soviet republics: **Russia, Belarus** (formerly Byelorussia), the **Ukraine, Kazakhstan**, and **Uzbekistan**. At Barcelona, the Unified Team had representatives from all the former Soviet republics, save for the Baltic states of **Estonia, Latvia**, and **Lithuania**, which competed independently. The Unified Team at Barcelona also included athletes from **Georgia**, which had not joined the Commonwealth of Independent States. In 1994, the republics began to compete independently. In their one Summer Games, the Commonwealth of Independent States entered 475 athletes (310 men, 165 **women**) and competed in 27 of the 29 sports contested that year—all except **baseball** and **football**. Their largest contingents were in **athletics** (50 men, 49 women), **rowing** (30 men, 17 women), **swimming** (18 men, 11 women), **handball** (12 men, 13 women), and **basketball** (12 men, 12 women).

The Commonwealth of Independent States won a total of 112 medals (45 gold, 38 silver, 29 bronze), one of the largest totals for any country in one Summer Games. The **gymnastics** team won 18, with medals in every one of the 14 events, and was led by **Vitaly Shcherbo,** who won six medals—all gold—and

Hryhoriy Misiutin, who won five medals (one gold, four silver). Tetiana Hutsu won four medals—two gold, one silver, one bronze. Swimmer **Aleksandr Popov** also won four medals—two gold, two silver. In **wrestling**, the Commonwealth of Independent States won medals in 16 of the 20 classes contested.

In team sports, the Unified Team women won the basketball tournament, while the men finished fourth; in handball, the men's team won the gold medal and the women's team the bronze; the women's **volleyball** team won silver and the men's **water polo** team won bronze. In individual sports that also had team events, the women's **archery** team won bronze; in athletics the women's 4x100 **relay** team won the silver and the women's 4x400 relay team won gold; in **fencing**, the men's **épée** team won bronze and the men's **sabre** team won silver; in gymnastics, both the men's and women's **all-around** teams won gold; the **modern pentathlon** team won silver; in rowing, the women's quadruple **sculls** team won bronze; in swimming, the Commonwealth of Independent States won gold in the men's 4x200 **freestyle** relay, silver in the men's 4x100 freestyle relay and 4x100 **medley** relay, and bronze in the women's 4x100 medley relay.

In their one Winter Games the Commonwealth of Independent States entered 129 athletes (86 men, 43 women) and competed in all 12 sports that were contested that year. They won 23 medals (nine gold, six silver, eight bronze) in six different sports and were second to **Germany**'s 26 in the overall medal count. **Cross-country skiers Lyubov Yegorova** (three gold, two silver) and **Yelena Välbe** (one gold, four bronze) each won five medals to lead all Commonwealth of Independent States winter athletes. **Biathletes** Yelena Belova (two bronze) and Anfitsa Retsova (gold, bronze) each won two medals in their sport. Other gold medal winners for the Commonwealth of Independent States were the men's **ice hockey** team, Yevgeny Redkin in the men's 20 k biathlon and **figure skaters** Viktor Petrenko in men's singles, Nataliya Mishkutyonok and **Artur Dmitriyev** in **pairs**, and Marina Klimova and Sergey Ponomarenko in **ice dancing**. *See also* KARELIN, ALEKSANDR ALEKSANDROVICH; LAVROV, ANDREY IVANOVICH; LAZUTINA, LARISA YEVGENYEVNA; SAUTIN, DMITRY IVANOVICH; SMETANINA, RAISA PETROVNA.

COMOROS ISLANDS (COM). The Comoros Islands **National Olympic Committee** was founded in 1979, but was not recognized by the **International Olympic Committee** until September 1993. The Indian Ocean island nation, officially known as the Union of the Comoros, first competed at the **Olympic Games** in 1996 but has not yet appeared at the **Olympic Winter Games**. The Comoros Islands has competed at each Summer Olympic Games from 1996 to 2012, represented by 12 different athletes (seven men, five

women) in three sports: **athletics** (five men, four women), **swimming** (one man, one woman), and **weightlifting** (one man).

No Comoran athlete has won an **Olympic medal**, nor have any advanced out of the **heats** in athletics or swimming. Feta Ahamada won a qualifying heat in the women's 100 meter **sprint** in 2012 but finished seventh in the next heat. Hadhari Djhaffar competed in three Olympic Games from 1996 to 2004 in athletics sprint races but did not advance past the first heat in any of them.

COMPETITION FOR HERALDS. This event was held at the **Ancient Olympic Games** from at least 396 B.C. to A.D. 261. The last four known championships were won by Valerius Eclectus of Sinope.

COMPETITION FOR TRUMPETERS. The competition for trumpeters was held from at least 396 B.C. to A.D. 217 at the **Ancient Olympic Games**. The event was won consecutively from 328 through 292 B.C. by Herodoros of Megara.

CONGO, DEMOCRATIC REPUBLIC OF THE (COD). This nation was formerly known as the Belgian Congo, but changed its name to the Democratic Republic of the Congo upon gaining independence in June 1960. In October 1971, the name was changed to Zaire, but in May 1997, the nation took back the name the Democratic Republic of the Congo. As the latter, Zaire was represented by five **cyclists** at the **Mexico** City Olympics in 1968. The nation's second Olympic appearance was 16 years later in Los Angeles, as Zaire, where it was represented by three track and field athletes—two men and a **woman**—and six **boxers**. Zaire also competed in 1988, 1992, and 1996. The country never competed in the Olympics as the Belgian Congo, and it competed as the Democratic Republic of the Congo again from 2000 through 2012. It has never competed at the **Olympic Winter Games**. No athlete from this variantly named nation has yet won an **Olympic medal**. It is also often referred to as Congo (Kinshasa) to differentiate it from the **Republic of the Congo**, which is then called Congo (Brazzaville).

The Central African nation under its various names has entered 65 athletes (46 men, 19 women) in nine Summer Games in seven sports. They have competed in **athletics** (11 men, seven women), **basketball** (12 women), boxing (14 men), cycling (10 men), **judo** (eight men), **swimming** (one man), and **table tennis** (two men). The country's best performance occurred in 1996, when Willy Kalombo placed 16th in the men's **marathon**, from 124 starters. He also finished 50th of 110 entrants four years previously. Runner Gary Kikaya qualified for the semifinal round of the 400 meters in both 2004 and 2008. Three Congolese boxers have placed equal ninth. **Welterweight**

Kitenge Kitengwa in 1984 received a **bye**, won one bout, and was defeated in his next bout. **Middleweight** Serge Kabongo had similar results in 1988. **Super-heavyweight** Meji Mwanba also finished equal ninth in 2012, although he lost his only bout as there were only 16 entrants in his weight class. The 1996 women's basketball team featured future Women's National Basketball Association player Mwadi Mabika and was funded by National Basketball Association star Dikembe Mutombo. It placed 12th and last, but just qualifying for the field of 12 teams in the Olympic Games was a significant accomplishment.

CONGO, REPUBLIC OF THE (CGO). Since making its Olympic debut in 1964, the Central African nation of the Congo has competed at every **Olympic Games** except 1968 and 1976. It has never competed at the **Olympic Winter Games**. It was known as the People's Republic of the Congo from 1970 to 1991, but since then it is officially known as the Republic of the Congo. It is also often referred to as Congo (Brazzaville) to differentiate it from the **Democratic Republic of the Congo**, which is then called Congo (Kinshasa).

In 11 Summer Games, the Congo has entered 66 athletes (39 men, 27 **women**) in seven sports: **athletics** (24 men, eight women), **boxing** (three men), **fencing** (one man), **handball** (14 women), **judo** (five men, one woman), **swimming** (four men, two women), and **table tennis** (two men, two women). Although they have yet to win an **Olympic medal**, notable Olympic results for Congolese athletes include Henri Elende, whose 1964 men's **high jump** qualified for the final round and was 20th of 28 contestants; the 1972 men's 4x100 meters **relay sprint** team reached the semifinal **round**; five other athletes reached the quarter-final round in 100 and 200 meters sprints; Emmanuel M'Pioh finished 52nd of 74 entrants in the men's **marathon** in 1980; Rony Bakale finished 43rd of 58 in the 2012 men's 50 meter **freestyle** swim, and Bienvenu Mbida tied for 14th place out of 34 entrants in men's **half-lightweight** judo in 1984. The women's handball team qualified for the 1980 Olympic tournament but finished sixth of six teams. **Light-heavyweight** boxer Anaclet Wamba lost his first bout in the 1980 Olympic tournament, but as a professional boxer he held the World Boxing Council's World's Cruiserweight Championship from 1991 to 1995 and retired with a professional record of 46 wins, two losses, and one draw.

CONNOLLY, JAMES BRENDAN BENNETT (USA–ATH). B. 28 November 1868, South Boston, Massachusetts, **United States**. D. 20 January 1957, Brookline, Massachusetts, United States. James Connolly was the first champion at the modern **Olympic Games** and the first known Olympic champion since Varasdates in the fourth-century A.D. Connolly achieved this distinction by winning the hop, step, and jump (now known as the **triple jump**) on 6 April 1896. He also tied for second place in the **high jump** and placed third in the broad jump (now called **long jump**) in Athens. In 1900, the five-foot, nine-inch (175 cm), 159 lb (72 kg) Connolly narrowly failed to retain his hop, step, and jump title and finished second. Connolly did not take part in the 1904 Games and made his final Olympic appearance in 1906, when he failed to record a valid jump in either of the horizontal jumps. Unable to obtain a leave of absence from Harvard University to travel to **Greece** for the first modern Games, he quit college, but his place in Olympic history no doubt provided ample compensation. James Connolly later became well known as a writer of seafaring novels.

COOK ISLANDS (COK). The Cook Islands Sports and Olympic Association was first organized and recognized by the **International Olympic Committee** in 1986. The Cook Islands, a dependency of **New Zealand** in the South Pacific, first competed at the 1988 Olympics in Seoul and has since competed at each Summer **Olympic Games**. The nation has not yet competed at the **Olympic Winter Games** and has not won an **Olympic medal**. It was represented by 24 Olympians through 2012, in six sports: **athletics** (six men, three **women**), **boxing** (three men), **canoeing** (one man, one woman), **sailing** (two women), **swimming** (two men, one woman), and **weightlifting** (four men, one woman). In 1988, Cook Islander Richard Pittman placed equal ninth in **featherweight** boxing, although he only won one match. In 2004, Sam Nunuke Pera placed 14th in **heavyweight** weightlifting, from 22 competitors. His son, Sam Pera Junior, placed 12th in the **super-heavyweight** class in 2008, but from only 14 starters. In the swimming competition in 2012 Celeste Brown finished 55th of 75 entrants in the women's 50 meter **freestyle** and Zac Payne was 41st of 58 competitors in the men's 50 meter freestyle.

COORDINATION COMMISSIONS FOR THE OLYMPIC GAMES. In 1985, the **International Olympic Committee** (IOC) formed the Study and Evaluation Commission for the Preparation of the **Olympic Games**. The name was changed to the Coordination Commission for the Olympic Games in 1986. The Coordination Commission consists of several subcommissions at any one time, as each Olympic Games in the planning stage has a subcommission of the Coordination Commission. For instance, there are currently (as of 2014) subcommissions for the Games of the XXXIe **Olympiad**—Rio de Janeiro 2016; for the Games of the XXXIIe Olympiad—Tokyo 2020; for the 2nd **Youth Olympic Winter Games**—Lillehammer 2016; and for the 3rd **Youth Olympic Games**—Buenos Aires 2018. Each subcommission has a separate chairman, with the members representing various entities: media, athletes, environment, as well as IOC members. The subcommissions work closely with their associated **Organizing Committee of the Olympic Games** (OCOG) to help plan and organize the Olympic Games and act as liaisons among the IOC, the OCOG, the **International Federations**, and the **National Olympic Committees**. The current (as of 2014) chairs of the Coordination Commissions are as follows: Rio de Janeiro 2016, Nawal El Moutawkel; Pyeongchang 2018, Gunilla Lindberg; Tokyo 2020, John Coates; 2016 Youth Winter Olympics, Angela Ruggiero; and 2018 Youth Olympics, Frank Fredericks.

COROEBUS OF ELIS (GRE–ATH). Fl. 800–750 B.C. Coroebus was a cook in the city-state of Elis in ancient **Greece**. His Olympic fame rests on the fact that he is the first recorded champion in Olympic history, as in 776 B.C. he won the *stadion* race. His feat was inscribed on his tomb.

COSTA RICA (CRC). Costa Rica's **National Olympic Committee** was formed and recognized in 1936 and they first competed in the **Olympic Games** that year. Their next appearance was in 1964 and they have entered each Summer Games since then. They first participated in the **Olympic Winter Games** of 1980 and have competed at a total of six Olympic Winter Games: 1980, 1984, 1988, 1992, 2002, and 2006. In 14 Summer Games, the **Central American** country, officially known as the Republic of Costa Rica, has entered 143 athletes (119 men, 24 **women**) and competed in 15 sports: **archery** (three men, one woman), **athletics** (14 men, six women), **boxing** (three men), **canoeing** (four men, one woman), **cycling** (12 men, one woman), **diving** (one woman), **fencing** (two men), **football** (44 men), **judo** (12 men), **shooting** (10 men, two women), **swimming** (seven men, 11 women), **taekwondo** (two men), **tennis** (one man), **triathlon** (one man, one woman), and **weightlifting** (four men).

Costa Rica's four **Olympic medals** have all been won by a pair of sisters, Silvia and Claudia Poll Ahrens. Silvia won a silver medal in the 200 meter **freestyle** swimming in 1988, and her younger sister Claudia won the gold medal in that event in 1996 and added two bronze medals in 2000 in the 200 and 400 meter freestyle. Other notable Olympic achievements by Costa Ricans include: the 2004 men's football team qualifying for the Olympic tournament and finishing eighth of 16 teams; José Luis Molina finishing 24th of 124 entrants in the 1996 men's **marathon** and 39th of 100 in the 2000 marathon; José Andrés Brenes, sixth of 43 entrants in the initial Olympic **mountainbike cross-country** race in 1996; Kristopher Moitland tied for sixth of 16 entrants in 2008 **heavyweight** taekwondo competition; and in swimming, in addition to their medals, Sylvia Poll finished in the top 10 in three other races and her sister Claudia did likewise. María París was the first Costa Rican swimmer with a top-10 result when she finished in seventh place in the 1980 100 meter **butterfly** race.

Costa Rica has competed at six Olympic Winter Games: 1980, 1984, 1988, 1992, 2002, and 2006. They entered six men in **Alpine skiing** and a seventh in the **biathlon**. Alpine skier Arturo Kinch also competed in **cross-country skiing** in four of his five Olympic Winter Games appearances. Costa Rica's best performance in a Winter Games event occurred in the men's **slalom** in 1984 when Eduardo Kopper finished ahead of just two other skiers who completed the race. Because there were 54 skiers who failed to finish, Kopper placed in the top one-half at 45th of 101 entrants. Julián Muñoz had a similar result in the 1988 slalom, finishing the race and placing 51st of 109 contestants, even though he had the fourth slowest time of those skiers who completed the course.

COSTA SANTOS, RICARDO ALEX (BRA-BVO). *See* RICARDO.

COSTAS, ROBERT QUINLAN "BOB" (USA). B. 22 March 1952, Queens, New York, United States. Bob Costas has succeeded **Jim McKay** as the voice of the Olympics on American **television**. Costas works for National Broadcasting Company (NBC) Television, which has televised all **Olympic Games** to the American public since 1988 and all **Olympic Winter Games** since 2002. He has been the main studio host for five Olympic Games or Olympic Winter Games, backing up Bryant Gumbel in 1988.

Costas began his career in broadcasting after majoring in communications at Syracuse University, known for its broadcasting curriculum. At only 22 years old, he was selected to broadcast basketball for the Spirits of St. Louis in the now defunct American Basketball Association. He then joined Columbia Broadcasting System Sports, covering regional football and basketball games. In 1980, he joined NBC and has since handled lead broadcast duties for baseball, basketball, and football. He has branched out from sports and for a time hosted *Later with Bob Costas*, a general interview show that aired after midnight on NBC. Costas has won numerous awards for his work, being named Sportscaster of the Year several times and winning nearly 20 Emmy Awards.

CÔTE D'IVOIRE (CIV). Prior to its independence in 1960, the country now known as Côte d'Ivoire was a part of French West Africa and was known as the Ivory Coast. Côte d'Ivoire formed a **National Olympic Committee** in 1962, which was recognized by the **International Olympic Committee** in 1963. It has competed in the **Olympic Games** since 1964, missing only the

1980 Games, and was one of the few African nations that did not join the 1976 **boycott**. The country has not yet appeared at the **Olympic Winter Games**.

In 12 Summer Games the West African nation, whose official name is République du Côte d'Ivoire, entered 116 athletes (81 men, 35 **women**) in 11 sports: **archery** (one man), **athletics** (33 men, 12 women), **boxing** (seven men), **canoeing** (12 men), **football** (16 men), **handball** (14 women), **judo** (six men, four women), **swimming** (two men, two women), **taekwondo** (one man, two women), **tennis** (two men), and **wrestling** (one man, one woman). Côte d'Ivoire can claim one **Olympic medal**, a silver won by Gabriel Tiacoh in the 400 meters (track and field athletics) in 1984. Other notable Olympic accomplishments by Ivoirian athletes include Murielle Ahoure finishing sixth in the women's 200 meter **sprint** and seventh in the 100 meter sprint, both in 2012; Gaoussou Koné tied for sixth in the men's 100 meters in 1964; the men's 4x100 **relay** team finishing eighth in 1992 finals and reaching the semifinals of that event in 1968, 1976, 1984, 1996, and 2000; the men's 4x400 relay team being semifinalists in 1988; brothers Claude and Clement N'Goran winning their first men's **doubles** tennis match and finishing tied for ninth place in 1996; **light-middleweight** boxer Gnohere Sery winning his first two bouts and reaching the quarter finals in 1988; canoeist N'Gama reaching the semifinals in **kayak doubles** in 1968 and **singles** in 1972; N'Guessan Sebastien Konan finishing tied for fifth in **welterweight** taekwondo in 2000; and the men's football team qualifying for the Olympic tournament and finishing sixth of 16 teams in 2008.

COTSWOLD OLIMPICK GAMES. *See* ROBERT DOVER'S GAMES.

COUBERTIN, BARON PIERRE DE (né PIERRE FRÉDY) (FRA). B. 1 January 1863, Paris, **France**. D. 2 September 1937, Geneva, **Switzerland**. Pierre de Coubertin was the founder of the **Olympic Movement**. His inspirational idea to revive the ancient Greek festivals grew out of his general interest in physical education and, at the early age of 24, he began a campaign to restructure educational methods in France along the lines of the British public school system, of which he was a great admirer. His idea of reviving the **Olympic Games** grew more from his interest in sociology, history, and education than from any particular enthusiasm for competitive sports, but it was these sports that would provide his lasting monument. In view of his aesthetic inclinations, it must have been a source of satisfaction that he won the prize for literature in the **art contests** in 1912. His entry, "Ode to Sport," was submitted under a pseudonym.

Taking over as president of the **International Olympic Committee** (IOC) from **Demetrios Vikelas** in 1896, Coubertin faced many problems in the turbulent early years of the Olympic Movement, and its current strength is a tribute to his dedication and diplomacy in the difficult pioneering days. From 1896 to 1924, he attended every celebration of the Games, except those of 1904 and 1906, but at the Paris Games of 1924, he resigned the **IOC presidency** at the age of 61 on the grounds that he was too old to continue in office. Surprisingly, his interest in Olympic matters seems to have declined rapidly, but he recorded a message that was replayed at the opening ceremony of the 1936 Olympic Games in Berlin. The following year, Coubertin collapsed and died from a heart attack while walking in Lagrange Park in Geneva and, although he is buried in Geneva, his heart is preserved in a marble stele at ancient Olympia on the grounds of the **International Olympic Academy**. Many other aspects of Coubertin's involvement with the Olympic Movement are covered in the separate entries on various subjects in this volume.

COUGHLIN HALL, NATALIE ANNE (USA–SWI). B. 23 August 1982, Vallejo, California, **United States**. Natalie Coughlin burst onto the international **swim** scene at the 2001 World Championships, winning a gold medal in the 100 meter **backstroke** and a bronze in the 50 meter backstroke. In 2002 at the Pan-Pacifics, she was more dominant, winning six medals (four gold), with three individual championships in the 100 meter **freestyle**, 100 meter **butterfly**, and 100 meter backstroke. Although somewhat overshadowed by the media attention given **Michael Phelps**, the five-foot, eight-inch (173 cm), 139 lb (63 kg) Coughlin was the top female swimmer at the 2004 **Olympic Games**, winning five medals, including two gold. Individually, she won the 100 meter backstroke and finished third in the 100 freestyle. She won her second gold medal in the 800 meter freestyle **relay** and added two silvers as a member of the U.S. teams in the other relays. In 2008, Coughlin added six more **Olympic medals**, which included defense of her 100 backstroke gold, and in 2012 she was a member of the bronze medal–winning 4x100 freestyle relay team. In three Olympic Games she entered 12 events and medaled in each one. Her 12 Olympic medals (three gold, four silver, five bronze) rank her first among female Olympic swimmers, tied with her countrywomen **Jenny Thompson** and **Dara Torres**. At the 2001–2007 World Championships, Coughlin won 15 medals, including five golds. At the 2002 and 2006 Pan-Pacifics, she won 12 medals, including eight golds.

COURT OF ARBITRATION FOR SPORT (CAS). Since the end of the 20th century and continuing in the new millennium, sport, like many other facets of society, has been beset by many legal challenges. Many of these deal with drug use in sport, or **doping**. When athletes are accused of doping, they usually challenge the legality of the testing system, ensuring a long, and often expensive, legal battle. The **International Olympic Committee** (IOC) has attempted to solve some of these legal problems by forming the CAS, based in **Lausanne, Switzerland**. The CAS was formed in 1983 by the IOC, but was restructured in 1994 as an independent body, after a legal decision noted that the IOC and the CAS were very closely aligned.

At major international sporting events, athletes must now sign an agreement that any legal problems that may ensue from their participation, including a doping **disqualification**, will be adjudicated by submitting the problem for arbitration to the CAS. Of minor importance in the first few years of its existence, the CAS has now assumed a prominent role at major international sporting events. Many of the **International Federations** and other sport governing bodies have agreed to give the CAS binding authority to rule on disputes involving sports law.

When a dispute arises, the parties may choose one arbitrator from CAS's pool of 150 internationally recognized arbitration experts, or each party may choose one arbitrator, with the CAS choosing a third arbitrator to serve as the president of the panel for that dispute. Costs of the arbitration process are paid by the loser in the dispute, as is common in European courts of law. During the **Olympic Games** a panel of CAS arbitrators is available for emergency decisions to be adjudicated within 24 hours.

COVENTRY, KIRSTY LEIGH (ZIM–SWI). B. 16 September 1983, Harare, **Zimbabwe**. Kirsty Coventry is Zimbabwe's top Olympian, having won seven of the country's eight **Olympic medals** to date. Although she competed in four events in Sydney in 2000, she did no better than 12th. One of the world's top **backstroke** and **medley swimmers**, she won three medals in the 2004 Olympics, including a gold in the 200 meter backstroke. She retained that title in 2008 and has added four silver and one bronze medals to her tally. Coventry, at five feet, eight inches (173 cm) and 132 lb (60 kg), has also won three long course world titles, winning the 100 and 200 meter backstroke in 2005 and her specialty event, the 200 meter backstroke, in 2009. At the 2008 short course World Championships, she triumphed in four events. She was the flag bearer for Zimbabwe in the 2012 opening ceremony and competed in three events but did not add to her medal collection.

COXED. *See* COXSWAIN.

COXLESS. *See* COXSWAIN.

COXSWAIN. A coxswain is a member of a **rowing** crew who sits facing the other crew members and is responsible for steering the boat and calling out a stroke cadence. The coxswain generally is typically a lightweight person, although rowing rules require a minimum weight, and if a coxswain is underweight, dead weight must be added to compensate. Olympic rowing has included men's races for **pairs** with coxswain, and both men's and **women**'s races for coxed fours and coxed **eights**, although in recent years only the eights races have included coxswains. Races without coxswains are dubbed coxless; those with coxswains are referred to as coxed.

A young French boy (middle) pulled from the crowd to serve as a coxswain for the Dutch team in the pairs with cox during the 1900 Olympics. He has never been identified; however, he is considered the youngest Olympic competitor, somewhere between seven and 11 years old. Courtesy of Erich Kamper

CRETE (CRT). The Mediterranean island of Crete, now part of **Greece**, was briefly (1898–1913) a semi-independent republic, following the Greco–**Turkish** War of 1897. Although there was no official national team at the time, eight male Cretan athletes competed in the **Intercalated Olympic Games** of 1906, and they may be considered representatives of this short-lived nation. None of the competitors made a serious impact: Epaminonas Anezakis finished 29th of 30 entrants in the standing **long jump** and also competed in the **discus throw** and **javelin throw** events without success. Seven athletes entered the **marathon** but none completed the course. Marathoner Nikolaos Malintretos also entered the **shooting** competition and finished 35th of 46 entrants.

CRICKET. Cricket was contested only at the 1900 Olympics, when a British squad beat a French team, which was mostly made up of British residents of **France**. The International Cricket Council (ICC) is currently (as of 2014) recognized by the **International Olympic Committee**, but there is almost no chance it will return to the **Olympic Program**. The ICC has 105 national member federations as of 2014: 10 full members (those that play test cricket), 38 associate members, and 57 affiliated members.

CROATIA (CRO). Until the **Yugoslavian** civil war of 1991, Croatia had never competed at the Olympics as an independent nation. However, prior to 1991, many top Yugoslavian athletes were from Croatia, including several of the top Yugoslavian **basketball** players. The Southeastern European nation, officially known as the Republic of Croatia, made its Olympic debut at the 1992 **Olympic Winter Games** in Albertville and has since competed at every Summer and Winter Olympics. Croatia has sent 335 athletes (250 men, 85 **women**) to take part in 21 sports in six Summer Games. The largest contingents have been for team sports, with **handball** (41 men, 14 women), basketball (29 men, 12 women), and **water polo** (36 men) having the most athletes. **Swimming** (22 men, 11 women), **athletics** (20 men, 10 women), and **rowing** (30 men) are the individual sports with the most entrants.

Croatians have won 23 **Olympic medals** (six gold, seven silver, 10 bronze) in the Summer Games. **Tennis** player Goran Ivanišević won the first two for Croatia (both bronze) in the men's **singles** and **doubles** (with partner Goran Prpić) in 1992. The men's basketball team won the silver medal in 1992, losing only to the **United States "Dream Team."** In 1996, the men's handball team won Croatia's first gold medal, and the men's water polo team won their second silver medal. **Bulgarian** native Nikolay Peshalov won a gold medal for Croatia in the 2000 men's **featherweight weightlifting** and also a bronze medal as a **lightweight** four years later. Croatia's coxed **eights** rowing team won a bronze medal in 2000. In 2004 the men's handball team repeated as gold medalists and were joined as medalists by swimmer Duje Draganja, 50 meters **freestyle** silver, brothers Nikša and Siniša Skelin, men's coxless **pairs** silver, and tennis players Mario Ančić and Ivan Ljubičić, men's doubles bronze. In 2008, Croatian women won Olympic medals for the first time in the Summer Games as Blanka Vlašić won a silver in the **high jump**, Snježana Pejčić won a bronze in the **air rifle shooting**, and in **taekwondo welterweight** Sandra Šarić and featherweight Martina Zubčić also won bronze medals. **Gymnast** Filip Ude won a silver medal in the men's **pommelled horse**. Three Croatian teams won medals in 2012: the men's water polo team won a gold medal, the men's quadruple **sculls** won silver in rowing, and the men's handball team won a bronze medal. In addition, individual athletes Giovanni Cernogoraz won the gold in men's **trap** shooting, Sandra Perković won the gold in women's **discus throw**, and Lucija Zaninović won the bronze in women's **flyweight** taekwondo.

At the Olympic Winter Games, Croatia has entered 51 athletes (35 men, 16 women) in seven Winter Games in seven sports and has won 11 medals. Jakov Fak won the bronze medal in the 2010 men's 10 k **sprint biathlon**, but the Croatian with the most Olympic medals and gold medals is **Alpine skier Janica Kostelić**, who won six medals, including four golds, from 1998 to 2006. She won three gold medals and a silver medal in 2002, and in 2006 she added a gold and silver as well as a fourth-place finish. She has won more Olympic gold medals than any other Alpine skier and is tied with **Kjetil André Aamodt** (NOR) for the most won in Alpine skiing competition by a man or a woman. Her six total medals in this sport is tied with **Anja Pärson** (SWE) for the most by a woman and is two behind Aamodt's total. Ivica Kostelić, Janica's brother, is also a formidable skier and has won four silver medals from 2006 to 2014.

CROQUET. Croquet was contested at the 1900 Olympics in Paris, with three events and 10 French participants including a brother and sister and their two cousins. Seven men and three **women**, among the first women to compete in the modern **Olympic Games**, took part. Gaston Aumoitte, a native of French Indo-China, won two of the three contests. In 1904, **roque**, an American variant of croquet, was on the **Olympic Program** as well. The name "roque" is derived by dropping the first and last letters from the name of its parent game of croquet. Neither sport has been held at the Olympics since 1904, and they are not currently recognized by the **International Olympic Committee** nor are they even members of **SportAccord**.

CROSS-COUNTRY. A men's cross-country race was held in the 1912, 1920, and 1924 **Olympic Games' athletics** competition. Runners began the race on a track at the Olympic Stadium and then continued the race outside the stadium, running through hilly, wooded terrain with total distances varying in the three Games from 8,000 to 12,000 meters. Medals were awarded both to the winning individuals and to the team with the three best individual scores. **Paavo Nurmi** of **Finland** won the race in both 1920 and 1924, and the Finnish team won the gold medal in both those years and the silver medal in 1912. A cross-country race is also held in **equestrian** competition. It is one part of the **three-day event**, which has been held in the Olympic Games from 1912 to 1960 for men only and for men and women as a mixed entry event since 1964. In the sport of **cycling, mountainbike** racing is also deemed cross-country since its course is laid out through woods and rough terrain.

CROSS-COUNTRY SKIING. Cross-country skiing has been practiced in the Scandinavian countries since the 18th century, and competitions are known from the early 19th century. The sport has been on the **Olympic Program** since the Chamonix games of 1924. It has been dominated, not surprisingly, by the Scandinavian countries and the **Soviet Union** and **Russia**.

Until the 1970s, all cross-country racers competed in the same style, alternating legs and arms with the stride being pushed straight backward, remaining in the ski track. In the 1970s, a new style was developed by American Bill Koch, making a skating-like motion with one of the skis. This technique was adopted to use two legs and turned out to be much faster. The Fédération Internationale de Ski was pushed to ban this style by the North Europeans, but it was decided instead to allow two styles. However, races are now designated as either "classical" or "**freestyle**," with skating being allowed in freestyle races.

Originally, all cross-country races were held in a **time trial** fashion, with skiers starting in intervals. However, after revision of the program in the early 21st century, only one such race is left on the Olympic Program, the 15 km for men and the 10 km for **women**. The other individual events are the **sprint**, in which four to six skiers race for approximately 1,500 meters; the **skiathlon**, in which half of the race is skied in classical style and half in freestyle; and the mass-start **marathon**, which is held over 50 km for men and 30 km for women. In addition, two team competitions are staged: the relay and the team sprint.

Norwegian **Bjørn Dæhlie** leads all Olympic cross-country skiers with 12 medals, eight gold. Female skiers **Marit Bjørgen** of **Norway** (six gold), **Raisa Smetanina** of the Soviet Union (four gold), and **Stefania Belmondo** of **Italy** (two gold) each have 10 medals. **Lyubov Yegorova** of Russia has nine total medals with six gold. Through 2014, there have been 2,402 participants (1,685 men and 717 women) from 81 countries who have competed in cross-country skiing in the 22 **Olympic Winter Games** in which it was contested. *See also* BOYARSKIKH, KLAVDIYA SERGEYEVNA; DI CENTA, MANUELA; GRØTTUMSBRÅTEN, JOHAN HAGBART PEDERSEN; HAKULINEN, VEIKKO JOHANNES; HÄMÄLÄINEN-KIRVESNIEMI, MARJA-LIISA; HAUG, THORLEIF; JERNBERG, EDY SIXTEN; KULAKOVA, GALINA ALEKSEYEVNA; LAZUTINA, LARISA YEVGENYEVNA; MÄNTYRANTA, EERO ANTERO; SVAN, GUNDE ANDERS; ULVANG, VEGARD; VÄLBE, YELENA VALERYEVNA; WILHELM, KATARINA; ZIMYATOV, NIKOLAY SEMYONOVICH.

CUBA (CUB). In 1900, the **fencer** Ramón Fonst competed at the **Olympic Games** and actually won the first gold medal for this Caribbean island country. Fonst also competed in the 1904 Olympics along with a few other Cuban athletes, and as of 2014 he is the all-time Cuban record-holder with five medals. In 1924, Cuba was represented by nine competitors, while in 1928, the country had one competitor. In 1948, Cuba sent a full team to the London Olympic Games, and its participation was continuous until it elected to **boycott** the 1984 Olympic Games in Los Angeles. In support of the North **Korean** government, Cuba also elected not to compete in 1988 in Seoul. Cuba returned to the Olympics in 1992. Cuban athletes have not yet competed in the **Olympic Winter Games** and are the country with the most participants in the Summer Games which has not taken part in the Winter Games.

In 20 Summer Games, Cuba has entered 1,207 athletes (921 men, 286 **women**) and competed in 28 sports plus the **art competitions**. It has had the most participants in **athletics** (125 men, 93 women), **boxing** (86 men), **rowing** (74 men, seven women), and **wrestling** (78 men, one woman). It has also participated in most of the team sports, with 73 men in **baseball**, 15 women in **softball**, 44 men and 30 women in **basketball**, 26 men in **football**, 27 men in **handball**, 16 men in **hockey**, 47 men and 49 women in **volleyball**, and 36 men in **water polo**.

Officially known as the Republic of Cuba, the country has been successful in several sports, winning 202 **Olympic medals** (61 gold, 65 silver, 66 bronze) through 2014, but by far its greatest success has been in boxing, with 67 medals including 34 gold. Since the mid-1970s, Cuba has probably had the best amateur boxers in the world. It is also the dominant nation internationally in baseball and won the gold medal in 1992, 1996, and 2004, with silvers in 2000 and 2008—the only five years in which it was an Olympic sport. Cuba has won Olympic medals in 15 of the 28 sports in which it has participated with 39 in athletics, 35 in **judo**, 19 in wrestling, and 10 in fencing.

Among Cuban athletes, fencer Ramón Fonst has won the most medals, five, including four gold medals all earned in 1900 and 1904. **Pedro Luis**

Lazo was a pitcher on four of Cuba's medal-winning baseball teams from 1996 to 2008. Other Cuban baseball team members with three medals (two gold, one silver) are Omar Ajete, Orestes Kindelán, Omar Linares, Antonio Pacheco, Eduardo Paret, Antonio Scull, and Luis Ulacia. Ariel Pestano and Norge Luis Vera each has two silver and one gold medal.

From 1992 to 2004 *judoka* Driulys González won four medals, a gold, silver, and two bronze in women's judo. Amarilys Savón won three bronze in women's judo from 1992 to 2004. In fencing, Elvis Gregory has two bronze and one silver in individual and team **foil** from 1992 to 1996. **Greco-Roman** wrestler Juan Luis Marén won a bronze and two silver medals from 1992 to 2000.

The Cuban women's volleyball team won three gold medals from 1992 to 2000. In 2004, they won the bronze medal. Regla Bell, Marlenis Costa, Mireya Luis, and Regla Torres were all members of the three gold medal–winning teams, and Ana Ivis Fernández and Yumilka Ruíz each won two gold and one bronze medals. In athletics, Alberto Juantorena won gold in both the 400 and 800 meters in 1976, only the second athlete ever to win both those events in the same year. **High jumper** Javier Sotomayor won gold in 1992 and silver in 2000. He is best known as the first man (and as of 2014, the only man) to jump eight feet (2.44 cm), and his record of 2.45 cm set in 1993 was still the record in 2014. But the best-known Cuban Olympians have been **heavyweight** boxers **Félix Savón** and **Teófilo Stevenson**, who each won three gold medals consecutively.

Havana, Cuba, the capital city, has unsuccessfully bid to host the 1936, 2008, and 2012 Summer Games.

CULTURAL COMMISSION. The Cultural Commission of the **International Olympic Committee** (IOC) was created in 1969, with Polish IOC member Włodzimierz Reczek serving as the first chairman of the commission. The Cultural Commission consisted of six IOC members, two representatives of the **International Federations** and **National Olympic Committees**, one athlete representative, and several independent members. Based on recommendations of the **IOC 2000 Commission** and approved at the 110th **IOC Session** in December 1999, the Cultural Commission and the Education/**International Olympic Academy** Commissions were merged into a single **Culture and Olympic Education Commission**. In 2000, the IOC also created a new Department of Culture and Education.

CULTURE AND OLYMPIC EDUCATION COMMISSION. The Commission for the **International Olympic Academy** (IOA) and Olympic Education was first formed in 1967, with Danish **International Olympic**

Committee (IOC) member Ivar Emil Vind as the first chairman. This Commission oversaw the IOA in Olympia, **Greece**, and had as its mission following the activities of the IOA, contributing to the success of the IOA, receiving the periodical reports of IOA Sessions, and keeping the IOC informed of the progress of the IOA. This Commission also helped promote Olympic education by spreading the message of **Olympism**. In addition to IOC members, the IOA/Education Commission had representatives from the **National Olympic Committees, International Federations**, and former Olympic athletes, as well as several academic scholars, usually sports historians or sociologists. The original name of this commission was the Commission for the International Olympic Academy, but the name was enlarged in 1993, reflecting the increased emphasis on Olympic education.

Upon the recommendations of the **IOC 2000 Commission**, the Commission for the International Olympic Academy and Olympic Education was merged with the **Cultural Commission** in early 2000. The current charge for this Commission is to develop links between sport and culture in all its forms, encourage cultural exchange, and promote the diversity of cultures. It helps organize special events and, with the National Olympic Committees, develops Olympic education programs. Its mission is described by the IOC thus: "The Commission for Culture and Olympic Education advises the IOC on the promotion of culture and Olympic education and supports the IOC programmes and activities related to the education of youth through sport." As of 2014, the chairman of this commission is IOC member Lambis Nikolau from Greece.

CURAÇAO. *See* NETHERLANDS ANTILLES.

CURLING. Curling is thought to have been invented in medieval **Scotland** in the 16th century. It was a **demonstration sport** at the 1932, 1988, and 1992 **Olympic Winter Games**. In 1924, it also appeared on the **Olympic Program**, and recent evidence indicates that curling was a full medal sport that year. Previously, it had been considered a demonstration sport. In addition, in 1936 and 1964, **German** curling (*Eisstockschießen*) was contested as a demonstration sport. Curling returned to the Olympic Winter Program as a full medal sport at the 1998 Olympic Winter Games in Nagano and has been held at all Winter Olympics since. The sport is governed by the World Curling Federation, which was founded in 1966 and has 53 member federations as of 2014, including some such as **Brazil, Israel**, and **Mongolia** that are not usually thought of as curling nations. **Canada** has won the most Olympic medals in this sport, with five gold, two silver, and three bronze. Since 1998, Canada has won three gold and two silver medals in men's curling and two gold, one silver, and two bronze in **women**'s curling, although the composition of their teams has varied from year to year. The **Swedish** women's team, Olympic winners in 2006 and 2010, comprised of **Anette Norberg**, her sister Catherine Lindahl, Eva Lund, and Anna Svärd-Le Moine, is the only team with the same four players with more than one gold medal. Through 2014, there have been 348 participants (188 men and 160 women) from 16 countries who have competed in curling in the seven Winter Games in which it was contested as a full-medal sport. *See also* MARTIN, KEVIN.

CUTHBERT, ELIZABETH ALYSE "BETTY" (AUS–ATH). B. 20 April 1938, Merrylands, Sydney, New South Wales, **Australia**. Betty Cuthbert won two gold medals in the individual track **sprints** and a third gold in the **relay** at the 1956 Olympics. The five-foot, seven-inch (169 cm), 126 lb (57 kg) 18-year-old Australian was instantly acclaimed as a national heroine by the Australian crowd. Injury spoiled her chances at the 1960 Games, but she came back to win the 400 meters in 1964 and claim her fourth Olympic gold medal. She is the only Olympian, male or female, to have won gold medals in the 100, 200, and 400 meter events. Including relays, Cuthbert set 18 world records. Sadly for such a fine athlete, she now suffers from multiple sclerosis, although at the opening ceremony in 2000 in Sydney, she carried the Olympic Torch into the stadium while in a wheelchair.

CYCLING. Bicycles were first developed in the late 18th century and have since been used as a form of transportation. Originally the front wheel was much larger than the rear wheel, and the rider was elevated a great deal, making cycles difficult to control and very dangerous. In 1885, J. K. Starley of England devised the more modern bike, with a chain and gearing to allow the wheels to be of equal size. Although bike races had been held on the old "penny farthings," the new bikes stimulated the growth of bicycle racing as a sport.

From 1880 to 1900, cycling became immensely popular both in Europe and the **United States**. The sport was primarily a professional one at that time. It continues its grip on the European continent to this day, but bike racing ceased to be a popular sport in the United States at about the time of the Great Depression. Only the American Olympic victories at Los Angeles in 1984 and the more recent exploits of Greg LeMond and Lance Armstrong have stimulated interest in bicycle racing in the United States.

Cycling is one of only five sports that has been on the program of every **Olympic Games**. The program has varied, but now consists of an individual pack-style **road race**, individual **time trial** road race, track races, **cross-country mountainbiking**, and **BMX** racing. In 1984, **women** were admitted to Olympic cycling with a single road race. In 1988, women's track events were also added. For 2012, the track cycling program was changed significantly. The popular individual **pursuit** race has been eliminated, as have the **Madison** race and points race. In an attempt to equalize the programs for men and women, they each competed in five track races: the **sprint**, team sprint, team pursuit, **keirin**, and **omnium**. The omnium is an **all-around** type of event, in which all the riders compete in five races: a 200 meter flying start time trial, a 5 km scratch race, a 3 km individual pursuit, a 15 km points race, and a 1 km time trial. Scoring is on a points-for-place basis. In 28 summer Olympic competitions, there have been 5,518 athletes (4,916 men, 602 women) from 140 nations who have participated in Olympic cycling.

Mountainbiking has recently become a very popular sport, and in 1993 the **International Olympic Committee** approved cross-country mountainbiking as an Olympic event, which appeared on the **Olympic Program** for the first time at the 1996 Atlanta Olympics. In 2008, BMX racing for men and women was also added to the Olympic Program.

The Europeans have dominated Olympic cycling, notably the **French**, British, **Italians**, and **Germans**. However, the East Europeans have also won many medals, especially on the track, though mostly prior to the fall of the **Soviet** bloc. **Chris Hoy** of **Great Britain** with seven cycling medals (six gold) and **Bradley Wiggins**, also of Great Britain, with seven medals (four gold) lead all Olympic cyclists in total medals won.

Cycling is governed by the Union Cycliste Internationale, which was founded in 1900 and has 179 members as of 2014. *See also* CHARPENTIER, ROBERT; HUGHES, CLARA; HURLEY, MARCUS LATIMER; LUDING-ROTHENBURGER, CHRISTA; MASSON, PAUL MICHEL PIERRE ADRIEN; MORELON, DANIEL YVES; SALUMÄE, ERIKA AKSELEVNA; ZIJLAARD-VAN MOORSEL, LEONTINE MARTHA HENRICA PETRONELLA.

CYPRUS (CYP). The Cyprus **National Olympic Committee** was formed in 1974 and recognized by the **International Olympic Committee** in 1978. Since making its official Olympic debut at the **Olympic Winter Games** of 1980 in Lake Placid, it has sent competitors to every Summer and Winter Olympics since. However, several athletes of Cypriot nationality competed in 1896, representing **Greece**, and this continued to occur through 1976.

In nine Summer Games from 1980 to 2012, this Eastern Mediterranean island nation, officially known as the Republic of Cyprus, has entered 97 athletes (68 men, 29 **women**) in 11 sports: **archery** (one man, one woman), **athletics** (20 men, 13 women), **cycling** (two men, one woman), **judo** (10 men), **rhythmic gymnastics** (three women), **sailing** (14 men, one woman),

shooting (nine men, three women), **swimming** (eight men, seven women), **tennis** (one man), **weightlifting** (one man), and **wrestling** (two men).

Cyprus won its first **Olympic medal** in 2012 when Pavlos Kontides won a silver medal in men's one-person **dinghy** sailing competition after finishing a respectable 13th of 43 in 2008 in that event. Most of Cyprus's other Olympic notable accomplishments have occurred in one event, **skeet** shooting, as follows: 2000 men, Antonis Andreou, eighth; 2000 women, Sofia Miaouli, ninth; 2004 men, Giorgos Akhilleos, eighth; 2008 men, Antonis Nikolaidis, fourth and Giorgos Akhilleos, fifth; and 2008 women, Antri Eleftheriou, seventh. In swimming in 1992, Stavros Mikhailidis finished 20th of 75 entrants in the men's 50 meter **freestyle** race; in sailing, Andreas Kariolou was 13th of 34 in the 2004 men's **windsurfer** and 13th of 35 four years later; *judoka* Kostas Papakostas tied for 10th in the 1980 men's **middleweight** competition; and in athletics, Kyriakos Ioannou qualified for the finals in the 2012 **high jump** and finished 13th and five others reached the semifinal round of their events. World-class Cypriot tennis player Marcos Baghdatis (sometimes transliterated from the Greek as Markos Pagdatis) won his first two matches in 2012 before being defeated by the eventual gold medalist, Andy Murray, in the round of 16. Baghdatis, a four-time Association of Tennis Professionals tournament winner who has reached the finals of the **Australian** Open and semifinals at Wimbledon in his career, was the flag-bearer for Cyprus in the 2012 opening ceremony.

Cyprus has competed in each Olympic Winter Games from 1980 to 2014 and has sent 14 skiers, 11 men and three women, to compete in **Alpine skiing** events. Although some of the **slalom** contestants have carefully successfully completed their races, they were among the last to finish but were placed ahead of those skiers who failed to finish the race. The best Winter Games results for Cypriot skiers were Lina Aristodimou, 21st of 45 in the women's slalom in 1984 and Karolina Fotiadou in 1988, 26th of 57 in the women's slalom and 27th of 64 in the **giant slalom.**

CZECH REPUBLIC (CZE). Formerly a part of **Czechoslovakia**, the Czech Republic has been represented at the Olympics by many athletes. However, it did not compete officially at the Olympics as an independent nation until its appearance at Lillehammer for the 1994 **Olympic Winter Games**. The Czech Republic has since competed at each subsequent Summer and Winter Games.

In five Summer Games the Czech Republic has entered 429 athletes (256 men, 173 **women**) and competed in 27 sports with the most entrants in **athletics** (48 men, 41 women), **canoeing** (39 men, 10 women), **cycling** (26 men, nine women), **shooting** (24 men, nine women), and **rowing** (24 men, six women).

As an independent nation, the Czech Republic has won 44 Summer **Olympic medals** (14 gold, 15 silver, 15 bronze). Kateřina Kůrková-Emmons has won three medals in shooting, one of each color from 2004 to 2012. Czech athletes with two Summer Olympic medals each are **javelin thrower Jan Železný** (two gold 1996–2000, also silver and gold for Czechoslovakia 1988–1992); **decathlete** Roman Šebrle (silver, gold 2000–2004); female javelin thrower Barbora Špotáková (two gold 2008–2012); canoeists Martin Doktor (two gold 1996), Štěpánka Hilgertová (two gold 1996–2000), Ondřej Štěpánek (bronze, silver 2004–2008), and Jaroslav Volf (bronze, silver 2004–2008); rower Ondřej Synek (two silver 2008–2012); and **tennis** player Jana Novotná (1996 silver and bronze, also 1988 silver for Czechoslovakia). The country's other gold medalists in summer sports are **mountainbiker** Jaroslav Kulhavý (2012), modern pentathlete David Svoboda (2012), **trapshooter** David Kostelecký (2008), and rower Miroslava "Mirka" Knapková (2012).

In six Winter Games, the Czech Republic has entered 267 athletes (202 men, 65 women) and competed in 14 sports—all except **curling**. They had 91 men in **ice hockey**, 32 entrants in **cross-country skiing** (15 men, 17 women), and 27 in **biathlon** (12 men, 15 women). They have won 24 medals (seven gold, nine silver, eight bronze) in the Winter Games. Kateřina Neumannová has won the most medals of any Czech Republic athlete, with six (one gold, four silver, one bronze) in cross-country skiing between 1992 and 2006. Neumannová also competed in cycling at the 1996 Summer Olympics. Martina Sáblíková won five in **speed skating** (three gold, one silver, one bronze) from 2006 to 2014. Ondřej Moravec won three medals in biathlon (two silver, one bronze), all in 2014. Lukáš Bauer won three (one silver, two bronze) in cross-country skiing from 1998 to 2014. The men's ice hockey team won gold in 1998 and bronze in 2006, and seven players were on both teams and each earned two medals. The other gold medals were won by men's **aerials** skier Aleš Valenta (2002) and **snowboarder** Eva Samková in 2014 women's **boardercross**.

Prague has unsuccessfully bid to host the 2016 Summer Games. It also bid unsuccessfully for the Summer Games in 1924 when the city was part of Czechoslovakia.

CZECHOSLOVAKIA (TCH). Czechoslovakia was a nation in Central Europe from October 1918 until 1 January 1993. During its 74-year history, the nation had several official names, among them the Czechoslovak Republic and Czechoslovak Socialist Republic. Athletes from what later became Czechoslovakia first competed at the 1900 Olympics, representing **Bohemia**. In 1920, Czechoslovakia sent its first true Olympic team to Antwerp. From 1920 to 1992, the only **Olympic Games** not attended by Czechoslovakia, including the **Olympic Winter Games**, was the 1984 Los Angeles Olympics. Czechoslovakia split peacefully into the **Czech Republic** and **Slovakia** on 1 January 1993.

In 16 Summer Games, Czechoslovakia entered 1,619 athletes (1,328 men, 291 **women**) and competed in 29 sports plus the **art competitions**. It had the largest contingents in **athletics** (178 men, 37 women), **rowing** (148 men, 24 women), **gymnastics** (71 men, 59 women), **canoeing** (98 men, 22 women), and **basketball** (70 men, 33 women). Czechoslovakia excelled in many sports at the Olympics and won 146 medals (49 gold, 50 silver, 47 bronze), winning medals in 20 of 30 summer sports. The country's most noteworthy athletes were distance runner **Emil Zátopek** and female gymnast **Věra Čáslavská**. She won 11 medals (seven gold, four silver) from 1960 to 1968, and only **Larysa Latynina** has won more gymnastics gold and total medals. Zátopek, known for the pained expression on his face while he ran, won five medals (four gold, one silver) from 1948 to 1956 and is the only runner ever to win the 5,000 meters, 10,000 meters, and **marathon** at the same Olympic Games. Gymnast Ladislav Vácha is the only other Czechoslovakian to win five Olympic medals at the Summer Games. Eva Bosáková-Věchtová, from 1952 to 1960, won four medals (one gold, two silver, one bronze) for Czechoslovakia in gymnastics. **Discus thrower** Ludvík Daněk, who had the misfortune to be competing at the same time as **Al Oerter**, won three medals, one of each color, and did not win the gold until 1972 when Oerter had retired. Other Czechoslovakian Olympians with three medals in summer sports are canoeist Jan Brzák-Felix (two gold, one silver 1936–1952) and gymnasts Emanuel Löffler (two silver, one bronze 1928), Robert Pražák (three silver 1924), and Bedřich Šupčík (one of each color 1924–1928). Czechoslovakia also had 36 other athletes who each won two Olympic medals at the Summer Games.

In 16 Winter Games, Czechoslovakia entered 480 athletes (403 men, 77 women) and competed in 11 sports. Its main sport was **ice hockey**, with 181 men entered from 1924 to 1992 and four silver and three bronze medals won. Czechoslovakia has also entered 55 men and 24 women in **cross-country skiing**, 41 men in **ski jumping**, and 37 men in **Nordic combined**. They have won 25 medals at the Winter Games—two gold, eight silver, and 15 bronze. Ice hockey player Jiří Holík won four medals (two silver, two bronze) as a left winger from 1964 to 1976. His teammates Oldřich Machač, František Pospíšil, Josef Černý, and Vladimír Dzurilla each won three medals as did cross-country skier "Květa" Jeriová (two bronze, one silver) from 1980 to 1984. Fifteen other Czechoslovakian ice hockey players each won two medals, and ski jumpers Pavel Ploc (one silver, one bronze 1984–1988) and Jiří Raška (one gold, one silver 1968–1972) did also. In 1972, **figure skater** Ondrej Nepela in men's singles competition won Czechoslovakia's only other Winter Games gold medal.

Prague bid unsuccessfully for the right to host the Summer Games in 1924. *See also* ŽELEZNÝ, JAN.

D

DÆHLIE, BJØRN ERLEND (NOR–CCS). B. 19 June 1967, Elverum, Hedmark, **Norway**. With 12 medals, including eight golds, Bjørn Dæhlie is the most successful male Nordic skier in Olympic history and is now considered the greatest **cross-country skier** of all time. In 1992, he won the **combined pursuit** and the 50 km classical and was a member of the winning **relay** team; in 1994, he was the winner of the 10 km classical and the combined pursuit. To these gold medals he added silver in the 30 km in 1992 and 1994 and a third silver in the relay in 1994. In 1998 at Nagano, the six-foot tall (184 cm), 168 lb (76kg) Dæhlie won four more medals: three golds in the 10 km, 50 km, and the relay, and a silver in the pursuit race. His 12 medals (eight gold) were absolute records for the **Olympic Winter Games** in any sport until surpassed by biathlete **Ole Einar Bjørndalen**, who won his 13th medal in 2014. Dæhlic has won a further nine titles at the World Championships and 17 World medals, and was World Cup champion for cross-country in 1992–1993 and 1995–1997.

DAHOMEY. *See* BENIN.

DAMIAN-ANDRUNACHE, GEORGETA (ROU–ROW). B. 14 April 1976, Dracsani, Botoşani, **Romania**. Georgeta Damian-Andrunache is one of only three **rowers** to have won five Olympic gold medals, together with **Stephen Redgrave** and **Elisabeta Lipă-Oleniuc**. Remarkably, Damian-Andrunache won her titles in just three Olympics, in 2000, 2004, and 2008. In each of these Games, she won the coxed **pairs** event, making her one of 10 Olympic rowers to win the same event three times in a row. At the Sydney and Athens Games, she was part of the victorious Romanian **eights** crew, which also featured Lipă-Oleniuc. In 2008, Damian-Andrunache, who is married to Olympic rower Valeriu Andrunache, added a bronze medal in the eights event. She also competed in 2012 but did not medal. Besides her five Olympic titles, the five-foot, 10-inch (178 cm), 165 lb (75 kg) rower won five World titles between 1997 and 2003, three in the eights and two in the coxless pairs.

DANCE SPORT. The International DanceSport Federation, which governs ballroom-type dancing competitions, was founded in 1957 and currently has 90 affiliated member nations. In 2011, it was renamed the World Dance-Sport Federation. It was given **International Olympic Committee** recognition in 1997.

DANIELS, CHARLES MELDRUM (USA–SWI). B. 24 March 1885, Dayton, Ohio, **United States**. D. 9 August 1973, Carmel Valley Village, California, United States. Charlie Daniels's three Olympic gold medals for **swimming** in 1904 and one in 1906 were won against rather limited opposition, but he proved his true worth in 1908 by winning the 100 meter **freestyle** against a truly international field. Despite the increased number of swimming events on the **Olympic Program**, Daniels's total of four individual gold medals in swimming was not beaten until 1996, when **Hungary**'s **Krisztina Egerszegi** won her fifth individual gold medal, and that record has since been shattered by **Michael Phelps**, who won 11 individual gold medals from 2004 to 2012. The six-foot tall (183 cm), 154 lb (70 kg) Daniels set seven world records over various distances between 1907 and 1911, but his most significant legacy to the sport was his development of the American crawl stroke. He was a fine **all-around** sportsman, excelling at **golf** and **squash** and also at **bridge**.

DAVYDOVA, ANASTASIYA SEMYONOVNA (RUS–SYN). B. 2 February 1983, Moscow. **Russia**, USSR. Together with her namesake, **Anastasiya Yermakova**, Davydova is the most successful Olympic **synchronized swimmer**. The five-foot, seven-inch (170 cm), 119 lb (54 kg) Davydova earned four of her five gold medals together with the similarly sized Yermakova, winning the **duet** competition at the 2004 and 2008 Games, while also joining the victorious Russian team on both occasions and adding a fifth in the team competition in 2012. The duo has also excelled in World Championships, winning five team golds and four duet golds between 2001 and 2007, adding a duet silver in 2001.

DEAN, CHRISTOPHER COLIN (GBR–FSK). *See* TORVILL AND DEAN.

DE BRUIJN, INGE (NED–SWI). B. 24 August 1973, Barendrecht, Zuid-Holland, **Netherlands**. Inge de Bruijn competed at the 1991 World **Swimming** Championships and helped the Netherlands win a bronze medal in the 400 meter **freestyle relay**. She then competed at the 1992 Olympics, with minimal success, and her career went into eclipse for several years. But she resurfaced in 1999, winning the 50 meter freestyle and the 100 meter **butterfly** at the European Championships and the 50 meter freestyle at the World Championships. She was named 1999 European Swimmer of the Year, though this was but a prelude to 2000. At the Sydney **Olympic Games**, de Bruijn won three individual gold medals—50 free, 100 free, and 100 fly—and won a silver medal as a member of the 4x100 freestyle relay team. She continued to compete after Sydney and in 2001 won the 100 free and the 50 fly at the Worlds, and the 50 and 100 free at the Europeans. She was named World Swimmer of the Year in both 2000 and 2001. At the 2003 World Championships, the five-foot, nine-inch (174 cm), 121 lb (55 kg) de Bruijn won her third consecutive world title in the 50 free and also won the 50 butterfly. Although she was 31 years old in 2004, considered ancient for a world-class swimmer, Inge de Bruijn again won the 50 meter freestyle at the Athens Olympics along with a silver medal in the 100 meter freestyle, a bronze medal in the 100 meter butterfly, and a second bronze as a member of the 4x100 meter freestyle relay team, for a total of eight Olympic swimming medals in her career. Her brother Matthijs was a member of the Dutch Olympic **water polo** team in 2000.

DECATHLON. The decathlon is a men's track and field event in which the winner has been proclaimed as the "world's greatest athlete." It has been held at the Olympic Games since 1912. It consists of 10 events contested over two days (although in 1912, three days were used). The events are 100 meter run, **long jump, shot put, high jump,** 400 meters, 110 meters **hurdles, discus throw, pole vault, javelin throw,** and 1,500 meter run. A points table is used to evaluate the athlete's performance against a standard for each event, with the decathlon winner the man who accumulates the highest points total. The first winner was **Jim Thorpe**, but he was later considered not to have been an amateur athlete and he was **disqualified**. The only multiple decathlon gold medalists have been American **Bob Mathias** (1948, 1952) and **Great Britain**'s **Daley Thompson** (1980, 1984). Other notable decathletes include Americans Glenn Morris, Milt Campbell, **Rafer Johnson**, Bill Toomey, Bruce Jenner, Dan O'Brien, Bryan Clay, Soviet Vasily Kuznetsov, Taiwan native C. K. Yang, Cuban Leonel Suárez, Finn Akilles Järvinen, Czech Roman Šebrle, and West German Hans-Joachim Walde. In 1912, competing against Jim Thorpe in this event was **Avery Brundage**, who later became **International Olympic Committee (IOC) president**.

DÉCUGIS, MAXIME OMER MATHIEU "MAX" (FRA–TEN). B. 24 September 1882, Paris, **France**. D. 6 September 1978, Biot, Alpes-Maritimes, France. Max Décugis was the winner of a record six **Olympic medals** (four gold, one silver, one bronze) for lawn **tennis** between 1900 and 1920.

His victories included the **mixed doubles** in 1906, when he was partnered by his wife, Marie. Although the Olympic tournaments during that era attracted many of the world's top players, Décugis's greatest non-Olympic achievement was to win the Wimbledon doubles with his countryman André Gobert in 1911, when they defeated the previously unbeaten holders, Tony Wilding (NZL) and Major Josiah Ritchie (GBR). Décugis was also an eight-time French **singles** champion (1903–1904, 1907–1909, and 1912–1914), although the event was then limited to French players only.

DEMONSTRATION SPORTS. Numerous sports have been contested at the **Olympic Games** and **Olympic Winter Games** as demonstration sports. These have usually been sports that were being considered for the **Olympic Program** or a sport indigenous to the country hosting the Olympic Games. In 1992, the **International Olympic Committee** announced that demonstration sports would no longer officially be contested at the Olympic Games, although an exhibition of **wushu** was given at the 2008 Beijing Olympics. *See also* BADMINTON; BANDY; BASKETBALL; BICYCLE POLO; BOWLING; *BUDO*; *CANNE DE COMBAT*; CANOEING AND KAYAKING; CURLING; DOGSLED RACING; FOOTBALL, AMERICAN; FOOTBALL, AUSTRALIAN RULES; FREESTYLE SKIING; GLIDING; GLÍMA; GOTLAND SPORTS; *JEU DE PAUME*; JUDO; KAATSEN; *KENDO*; KORFBALL; *KYUDO*; LACROSSE; MILITARY SKI PATROL; PELOTA BASQUE; *PESÄPALLO*; ROLLER HOCKEY; SAVATE; SHORT-TRACK SPEED SKATING; SKIJÖRING; SPEED SKATING; SPEED SKIING; *SUMO*; TAEKWONDO; TENNIS; WATER SKIING; WINTER PENTATHLON.

DENMARK (DEN). Denmark's connection with the **Olympic Movement** began in 1894, when Frederik Bajer, a member of the Danish Parliament, was an honorary member of the International Congress in Paris at which the **Olympic Games** were revived. After Denmark had participated in the 1896 Olympics, the first Danish **International Olympic Committee** member, Niels Holbeck, was co-opted in 1899, but it was not until 1905 that a Danish **National Olympic Committee** was formed. Denmark, a Northern European nation officially known as the Kingdom of Denmark, has competed at every Summer Olympic Games except 1904, but its attendance at the **Olympic Winter Games** has been less consistent. Since making its winter debut in 1948, Denmark has missed the Winter Olympics of 1956 and 1972–1984.

In 27 Summer Games, Denmark has entered 1,792 athletes (1,489 men, 303 **women**) and competed in 28 sports plus the **art competitions**, with the most participants in **rowing** (179 men, 28 women), **cycling** (167 men, seven women), **athletics** (125 men, 27 women), **gymnastics** (132 men, one woman), **sailing** (111 men, 20 women), **football** (105 men, 15 women), **handball** (67 men, 45 women), and **swimming** (41 men, 62 women).

Danish athletes have won 193 **Olympic medals** (46 gold, 74 silver, 73 bronze) in the Summer Games. Two **shooters** from the early 20th century won the most Olympic medals for Denmark, five: Lars Jørgen Madsen (two gold, two silver, one bronze, 1900–1924) and Niels Larsen (one gold, one silver, three bronze 1912–1924). This mark was tied in 2012 by rower Eskild Ebbesen, who was a member of the **lightweight** coxless fours team from 1996 to 2012, which won three gold and two bronze medals. But Denmark's greatest Olympian has likely been sailor **Paul Elvstrøm**, who won four gold medals, winning the monotype class consecutively from 1948 to 1960. **Greco-Roman heavyweight wrestler** Søren Jensen won four medals (two gold, two bronze) from 1906 to 1912, including one gold in 1906 in the so-called **all-around** competition in which he defeated the winners of the lightweight and **middleweight** weight classes. Shooter Anders Peter Nielsen also won four medals (one gold, three silver) from 1900 to 1924.

Thirteen Danish athletes have won three Olympic medals each in summer sports. In 1896, Viggo Jensen competed in seven events in four different sports. He won gold and silver medals in **weightlifting**, a bronze in free rifle shooting, was fourth in gymnastics rope climbing, fourth in the athletics **shot put**, sixth in military rifle shooting and did not place in the **discus throw**. He later competed in five different free rifle shooting events in 1900 with a best result of fourth place. Another versatile athlete in 1896 was Holger Nielsen. He won silver and bronze medals in shooting, a bronze medal in **fencing**, and also competed in the discus throw. Writer Josef Petersen is one of only two persons to win three medals in the art competitions. He won his in 1924, 1932, and 1948. From 1906 to 1912, the Danish football team won a gold and two silver medals—Charles Buchwald and Oscar Nielsen were both members of all three teams. Other three-time Danish Olympic medalists are cyclists Henry Hansen (two gold, one silver 1928–1932) and Willy Falck Hansen, no relation (1924–1924, one medal of each color), Niels Fredborg (1964–1976, one medal of each color), swimmer Karen Margrethe Harup (1948, one gold, two silver), rower Thomas Ebert (two gold, one bronze 2000–2008), **kayaker** Erik Hansen (one gold, two bronze 1960–1972), and sailors Jesper Bank (two gold, one bronze, 1984–2000) and Ole Berntsen (1948–1964, one of each color).

In 13 Winter Games, Denmark has entered 58 athletes (31 men, 27 women) and competed in eight sports, with most of the competitors in **curling** (11 men, 18 women), **Alpine skiing** (six men, three women), and **cross-country skiing** (six men, three women). Denmark has won one medal in the Olympic Winter Games, a silver in women's curling in 1998. Other notable results for Danish Winter Olympians include ninth place in men's singles **figure skating** in 1998 by Michael Tyllesen; ninth place by **speed skater** Kurt Stille in the 1964 men's 10,000 meters and 12th in the 5,000 meters that year; fifth by the 2010 women's curling team; and 28th of 63 by Tine Kongsholm in the 1998 women's slalom.

DePIETRO, JOSEPH NICHOLAS "JOE" (USA–WLT). B. 10 June 1914, Paterson, New Jersey, United States. D. 19 March 1999, Fair Lawn, New Jersey, United States. At just four feet, seven inches tall (140 cm), **weightlifter** Joe DePietro is probably the shortest male athlete to win an Olympic gold medal. He was also one of the strongest, as he won the 1948 **bantamweight** (56 kg, 123 lb) gold medal, setting a world record in the process. His arms were so short he could barely lift the bar over his head, but he won the 1947 World Championships, was third in the 1949 World Championships, won the 1951 **Pan American Games** title, and was a nine-time United States and North American champion.

DHYAN CHAND (IND–HOK). B. 28 August 1905, Allahabad, Uttar Pradesh, **India**. D. 3 December 1979, Delhi, India. Dhyan Chand won three gold medals as a center-forward and is considered the greatest **field hockey** player ever, although he was only five feet, seven inches (169 cm) tall. He learned the game from British army officers and had his first international competition in 1926 on a tour of Australia and New Zealand. He led India to gold medals in 1928, 1932, and 1936. In 1947–1948, Dhyan Chand was still the star of the Indian team but declined selection to the 1948 team, which prevented him from being the only hockey player to have won four gold medals. His younger brother Roop Singh played on the 1932 and 1936 Olympic teams, and his son Ashok Kumar won an Olympic bronze medal in 1972. He was honored in his native India by the issuance of a commemorative postage stamp, and he is the only Indian hockey player to be given the top civil award, the Padma Bhushan. In 1995, a statue of Dhyan Chand was erected in front of the National Stadium in Delhi, and in 2002, the stadium was renamed the Major Dhyan Chand National Stadium. The Indian Olympic Association named him the Player of the Century.

DI CENTA, MANUELA (ITA–CCS). B. 31 January 1963, Paluzza, Udine, **Italy**. In her first three Olympic appearances, Manuela Di Centa failed to win a single individual medal, but at Lillehammer in 1994 the five-foot, five-inch (164 cm), 121 lb (55 kg) athlete uniquely won a medal in all five Nordic skiing events. To her gold medals in the 15 km and 30 km, she added silver in the five km and **combined pursuit** and a bronze in the **relay**. Di Centa also claimed relay medals at the 1992 and 1998 **Olympic Winter Games**, giving her seven Olympic medals in all, a total surpassed by only 10 other **women**. In late 1999, Di Centa was named one of the new athlete members to the **International Olympic Committee**. On 23 May 2003, Di Centa achieved another athletic feat when she became the first Italian woman to reach the summit of Mount Everest. Her brother Giorgio Di Centa is also an Olympic **cross-country skiing** champion, with a silver medal in 2002 and two gold medals in 2006.

***DIAULOS* RACE.** The *diaulos* race was one of the major running events of the **Ancient Olympic Games**. It consisted of a race of two laps of the stadium or about 385 meters. Champions are known from 724 B.C. (Hypenos of Pisa) through A.D. 153 (Demetrios of Chios). The greatest champions of the *diaulos* were **Leonidas of Rhodes** (four titles, 164–152 B.C.), Chionis of Sparta (three titles, 664–656 B.C.), Hermogenes of Xanthos (three titles, A.D. 81–89), and Astylos of Kroton and Syracuse (three titles, 488–480 B.C.). An athlete from Argos also won the event four times, but his name is not known. *See also DOLIKHOS* RACE; *STADION* RACE.

DIBIASI, KLAUS (ITA–DIV). B. 6 October 1947, Solbad Hall, **Austria**. After winning a silver medal in the **platform diving** at the 1964 Olympics, Klaus Dibiasi, at five feet, 11 inches (180 cm) tall, 163 lb (74 kg), went on to win the gold on the platform at the next three Games (1968, 1972, 1976) and remains the only Olympic diver to have won three successive gold medals in the same event. A silver in the 1964 **springboard** gave him what was then a record total of five **Olympic medals** in diving. He also won the world platform title (1973, 1975), the European platform (1966, 1974), and the European springboard championship (1974). Dibiasi also won gold on both springboard and platform at the 1970 World University Games. Dibiasi was born in Austria of Italian parents, who returned to **Italy** when he was a child. He was coached by his father, Carlo, a former Italian champion and a 1936 Olympian.

DIDRIKSON, MILDRED ELLA "BABE" (née DIDRIKSEN, later ZAHARIAS) (USA–ATH). B. 26 June 1911, Port Arthur, Texas, **United States**. D. 27 September 1956, Galveston, Texas, United States. Babe Didrikson is considered by many authorities to be the greatest **all-around** sports**woman** in history. At the 1932 Olympics, she won gold medals in the 80 meter **hurdles** and the **javelin throw** and a silver in the **high jump**. She set new world records in each of these three disparate events. Didrikson was an All-American **basket-**

Babe Didrikson, considered the best all-around woman athlete ever, winning the javelin throw at the 1932 Olympics. Courtesy of Erich Kamper

ball player and held the world record for throwing a **baseball**, but she excelled as a **golfer** after giving up track and field **athletics**. She won the United States Women's Amateur title in 1946; the British Ladies' Amateur in 1947; and the U.S. Open in 1948, 1950, and 1954, her third victory being by a record margin of 12 strokes and occurring after surgery for colon cancer. A five-foot, seven-inch (169 cm), 126 lb (57 kg) athlete, she won 41 Ladies Professional Golf Association (LPGA) tournaments during her career, led the LPGA money list in 1950 and 1951, and is a member of the World Golf Hall of Fame.

DIEM, CARL (GER). B. 24 June 1882, Würzburg, **Germany**. D. 17 December 1962, Cologne, **Federal Republic of Germany**. Carl Diem is one of the cofounders of the **International Olympic Academy** and one of the most important writers and historians of the **Olympic Movement**, authoring dozens of books and articles on **Olympism** and the Olympic Movement. He studied at the University of Berlin, after which, from 1917 to 1933, he was secretary-general of the German Committee for Physical Education. He was secretary-general of the **Organizing Committee** of the 1936 Olympic Games and conceived the idea of the Olympic torch relay (*see also* **Olympic flame**). From 1938 to 1944, at **Pierre de Coubertin**'s request, he served as director of the International Olympic Institute in Berlin. After World War II, Diem was a sports consultant to the West German government. A sports university was founded in his honor, the Carl-Diem Sporthöchschule in Cologne (Köln), Germany.

DIETRICH, WILFRIED (FRG–WRE). B. 14 October 1933, Schifferstadt, **Germany**. D. 3 June 1992, Durbanville, **South Africa**. Wilfried Dietrich was arguably the greatest Olympic **wrestler** in history. An electrical welder by trade

Wilfried Dietrich performing a suplex move on 400-pound Chris Taylor at the Munich Games in 1972. Courtesy of Volker Kluge

and nicknamed the "crane of Schifferstadt," he was one of only seven wrestlers to compete in five different **Olympic Games** and is the only Olympic wrestler to win five medals. His most notable accomplishment was in lifting 400-pound **Chris Taylor** in a suplex move and pinning him in their first round **Greco-Roman** match in 1972. From 1956 to 1972, Wilfried Dietrich wrestled in seven Olympic tournaments (four **freestyle** and three Greco-Roman) and won five medals (one gold, two silver, two bronze), a record for an Olympic wrestler. All his medals were in the unlimited class and unusually included a gold in the freestyle and a silver in the Greco-Roman style in 1960. The six-foot tall (184 cm), 260 lb (118 kg) Dietrich was the World Champion in 1961 and was unbeaten in the unlimited freestyle from 1955 to 1962. At the World Championships, he also won two silver and two bronze medals between 1957 and 1969.

DIMAS, PYRROS (né PIRRO DHIMA) (GRE–WLT). B. 13 October 1971, Himarë, Vlorë, **Albania**. Although born in Albania, Pyrros Dimas always competed internationally for **Greece**. Though the weight classes changed several times in the 1990s, Dimas, at five feet, eight inches (173 cm) tall, was World Champion between 80 and 85 kg in 1993, 1995, and 1998. To those titles he added three consecutive Olympic gold medals in 1992, 1996, and 2000, one of only four **weightlifters** to have accomplished that feat. In 2004, he won a bronze medal at Athens, equaling the achievements of **Norbert Schemansky** (USA), Nikolay Peshalov (BUL/CRO), and Ronny Weller (GDR/GER) in winning Olympic weightlifting medals at four consecutive Olympics. Dimas also won one European Championship in 1995, and as a **light-heavyweight**, he set 11 world records. His sister Odyssea Dimas was also a national champion weightlifter.

DINGHY. A dinghy is a small one- or two-person boat used in Olympic **sailing** competition. Various classes have been contested—Finn, 470, and Laser are some. Olympic dinghy events have been held for men only, **women** only, and mixed, in which either men or women can compete. **Ben Ainslie** of **Great Britain** has competed in five **Olympic Games** from 1996 to 2012 and has won four gold medals and one silver medal in various dinghy sailing events. **Paul Elvstrøm** of **Denmark** also won four gold medals in dinghy sailing. He competed in the eight Olympic Games from 1948 to 1988.

D'INZEO, PIERO. (ITA–EQU). B. 4 March 1923, Rome, **Italy**. D. 13 February 2014, Rome, Italy; and **RAIMONDO D'INZEO**. B. 2 February 1925, Poggio Mirteto, Rieti, Italy. D. 15 November 2013, Rome, Italy. Piero and Raimondo D'Inzeo were Italian brothers who both competed in the

equestrian events at eight **Olympic Games** (1948–1976), a record bettered only by Canadian equestrian **Ian Millar**, who competed at 10 Olympics and **Austrian yachtsman** Hubert Raudauschl and **Latvian shooter** Afanasijs Kuzmins, who each competed in nine. The D'Inzeo brothers each won six Olympic medals (Raimondo, one gold, two silver, three bronze; Piero, two silver, four bronze), with their best collective performance occurring in 1960, when they took the first two places in the individual show **jumping**. (Raimondo won the event.) Raimondo was also the World Individual Champion in 1956 and 1960, while Piero won that title in 1959. Both brothers were similar in height (five feet, nine inches [176 cm], although Raimondo was slightly heavier (159 lb [72kg] to Piero's 141 lb [75kg]), and they both followed their father in making their career in the Italian cavalry.

DISCIPLINES. The **International Olympic Committee** (IOC) recognizes three levels of competition: sports, disciplines, and events. Sports are well known and relatively self-explanatory. Events are any competition at which final results occur and medals are awarded at the **Olympic Games**. Disciplines are considered a subcategory of sports. Rule 46.2 defines a discipline, which is essentially a branch of a sport. The standards of admission to the **Olympic Program** are the same for a discipline as they are for a sport. Most sports, such as track and field **athletics** or **shooting**, do not have disciplines, but consider all events part of one sport. There are seven summer Olympic sports that recognize disciplines: **aquatics**—**diving, swimming, open water swimming, synchronized swimming**, and **water polo** (most people outside the IOC consider these separate sports); **canoeing and kayaking**—**sprint** (flatwater) and **slalom** (whitewater); **cycling**—track, road, **mountainbiking**, and **BMX** racing; **equestrian**—**three-day event, dressage, jumping**; **gymnastics**—artistic, **rhythmic**, and **trampoline**; **volleyball**—indoor volleyball and **beach volleyball**; and **wrestling**—**freestyle** and **Greco-Roman**. There are three Winter Olympic sports that recognize disciplines: **bobsledding**—bobsled and **skeleton**; skating—**figure skating, speed skating**, and **short-track speed skating**; and skiing—**Alpine skiing, cross-country skiing, freestyle skiing, Nordic combined, ski jumping**, and **snowboarding**.

DISCUS THROW. The discus throw is one of the field events in **athletics**. It was one of the events in the **Ancient Olympic Games** and has been included in every modern Olympic Games in men's competition and since 1928 in **women**'s competition. It is also one of the 10 events that comprise the men's **decathlon**, but not one of the seven events in the women's **heptathlon**. The modern discus is a flat lenticular disc weighing two kg (4.4 lb) for men's competition and half that weight for women's competition. **Al Oerter** of the **United States** won the men's event four times from 1956 to 1968. Nina Romashkova-Ponomaryova (gold 1952, 1960; bronze 1956) of the **Soviet Union** and Lia Manoliu (gold 1968, bronze 1960, 1964) of **Romania** each won three medals in the women's discus throw.

DISL, URSULA "USCHI" (GER–BIA). B. 15 November 1970, Bad Tölz, Bayern, **Federal Republic of Germany**. Uschi Disl was the most successful **women**'s biathlete at the **Olympic Games** in terms of total medals. She had a very long career, starting **biathlon** in 1986, first competing internationally in 1990, and finishing fifth and eighth that year at the two World Championship events. Women's biathlon became an Olympic sport in 1992. In that year, Disl won her first **Olympic medal** (silver). Disl won nine Olympic medals, including gold in the **relay** events of 1998 and 2002, but did not win an individual Olympic gold medal, winning three silvers and three bronzes in individual events, with her last medal in the 2006 Games. At the World Championships, she won 19 medals, including eight golds, between 1991 and 2005. The five-foot, four-inch (163 cm), 126 lb (57 kg) Disl recorded 40 wins in World Cup events, but never ranked first in the World Cup standings for a full season. She also recorded three wins at Holmenkollen.

DISQUALIFICATION. A disqualification can occur in most Olympic sports. It is the result of a competitor breaking the rules, intentionally or unintentionally. It can occur in **athletics** or **swimming** races if the competitor starts ahead of the starter's signal. It also occurs in athletics **relay** events if the baton is dropped. A competitor that runs or swims out of his or her lane is also disqualified. In combat sports, a participant that fails to heed a referee's warning can be disqualified upon a subsequent rules infraction. In winter sports such as **slalom** skiing, failure to negotiate a gate successfully is also grounds for disqualification. In some team sports such as **football**, if a player is disqualified, his team must play short-handed, while in other team sports such as **basketball**, a player disqualified may be replaced with a substitute. In recent years, competitors found guilty of **doping** violations are disqualified, and this disqualification can occur after the event is completed.

DITYATIN, ALEKSANDR NIKOLAYEVICH (URS/RUS–GYM). B. 7 August 1957, Leningrad, **Russia**, USSR. Aleksandr Dityatin's first appearance at the **Olympic Games** was in 1976 where he won two silver medals. By winning a medal in all eight **gymnastics** events at Moscow in 1980, Aleksandr Dityatin established a record that has been equaled only by **Michael Phelps** in both 2004 and 2008. Dityatin's three gold medals were won in the team and individual **all-around** and on the **rings**, to which he added four silver medals and one bronze medal. His finest performance was in the **horse vault**, when he received the first perfect score (10) ever awarded to a male gymnast at the Olympics. The five-foot, 10-inch (178 cm), 154 lb (70 kg) Dityatin's total of 10 Olympic medals in gymnastics has been surpassed by only six other men. Dityatin was equally dominant at the World Championships, winning 12 medals (seven gold, two silver, three bronze). His best year was 1979, when he was all-around champion and won gold medals on the rings and the horse vault.

DIVING. Diving is not considered a separate sport by the organizing body of world **aquatics**, the Fédération Internationale de Natation Amateur (FINA). FINA contests five **disciplines** of aquatic competition: **swimming**, diving, **open water swimming**, **synchronized swimming**, and **water polo**. FINA was formed in 1908 and currently has 203 affiliated nations.

Diving contests are known to have been held in the 19th century, although the sport is relatively modern. It was held at the 1904 Olympics in St. Louis, and its appearance on the **Olympic Program** has been continuous since 1904. Diving has been contested in two basic events at the Olympics—three meter **springboard** and 10 meter **platform**—with both men and **women** contesting both events. Four new diving events were added to the Olympic Program for 2000, the first change to the diving program since 1924. These were two-person synchronized diving competitions for men and women on both platform and springboard. In 26 Summer Olympic competitions, there have been 1,393 athletes (796 men, 597 women) from 80 nations who have participated in Olympic diving.

The **United States** dominated the sport of diving until the 1990s, perhaps more than any sport has been dominated in the Olympics. In the late 1980s, the **Chinese** entered diving competition and posed the first serious threat to this dominance. While U.S. **Greg Louganis**, considered the greatest diver ever, was still competing, the Chinese men posted few victories, but Chinese men and women have been formidable since 1990. **Dmitry Sautin** of **Russia** leads all Olympic divers with eight medals, although only two were gold. Six divers have each won four gold medals—the Chinese women divers **Guo Jingjing**, Wu Minxia, **Fu Mingxia**, Chen Ruolin and the American **Pat McCormick**. Louganis is the only man with four gold medals. *See also* DIBIASI, KLAUS; ENGEL-GULBIN-KRÄMER, INGRID; XIONG NI.

DJIBOUTI (DJI). The Djibouti **National Olympic Committee** was founded in 1983, and recognition by the **International Olympic Committee** in 1984 enabled it to make its Olympic debut at the Los Angeles Games that year.

Since then, it has competed at every Summer Olympics, save for 2004, but has not yet participated in the **Olympic Winter Games**. In 2004, the Eastern African nation of Djibouti, officially known as the Republic of Djibouti, entered athletes in track and field **athletics** and **tennis**, but none of them competed for unknown reasons. Their appearances have been highlighted by their excellent **marathon** runners, one of whom, Ahmed Salah, competed in four **Olympic Games**, won a bronze medal in 1988 at Seoul, and finished a respectable 20th, 30th, and 42nd in his three other appearances. Other Djibouti men's marathoners of note include Djama Robleh (eight in 1984), Omar Abdillahi Charmarke (32nd in 1984), and Omar Moussa (49th in 1988). In 2012, Mumin Gala reached the final round of the 5,000 meters and finished 13th. A total of 22 Djiboutians (18 men, four **women**) have competed in athletics (13 men, three women), **judo** (two men), **sailing** (two men), **swimming** (one man), and **table tennis** (one woman).

DMITRIYEV, ARTUR VALERYEVICH (EUN/RUS–FSK). B. 21 January 1968, Bila Tserkva, Kyiv, **Ukraine**, USSR. Artur Dmitriyev began his **pairs figure skating** career with Nataliya Mishkutyenok; after placing third in 1990, they were World Champions in 1991–1992 and won the Olympic gold medal in 1992. At the 1994 Lillehammer Olympics, they placed second behind Sergey Grinkov and Ekaterina Gordeeva, who had been gold medalists in 1988, but Dmitriyev and Mishkutyenok recovered to win the 1994 World Championships. Dmitriyev then began competing with Oksana Kazakova, and together they won the gold medal at Nagano in 1998, after placing third at the 1997 World Championships. Dmitriyev, six feet tall (183 cm), 181 lb (82 kg), competed for the **Soviet Union** early in his career, for the Unified Team at Albertville in 1992, and later for **Russia**.

DOCHERTY, BEVAN JOHN (NZL–TRI). B. 29 March 1977, Taupo, Waikato, **New Zealand**. Bevan Docherty is one of only two men to win more than one medal in Olympic **triathlon**. The six-foot tall (185 cm), 157 lb (71 kg) Docherty won the silver medal in 2004 and the bronze in 2008. In 2012 he finished 12th. He won the gold medal at the 2004 Triathlon World Championships, the bronze medal four years later, and the silver medal at the 2006 **Commonwealth Games**. He was also third at the Ironman 70.3 (half the distance of the Ironman event) in 2012 and the winner of the 2013 New Zealand Ironman triathlon. His sister Fiona Docherty is a world-class triathlete who now specializes in the **marathon**.

DOGSLED RACING. A dogsled race with seven dogs per team was held at the 1932 **Olympic Winter Games** as a **demonstration sport**. The race was run over 40.5 km (25.1 miles), lasting two days. Twelve sled dog teams from **Canada** and the **United States** took part, with Émile St. Goddard of Canada winning the event.

DOHERTY, REGINALD FRANK "REGGIE" (GBR–TEN). B. 14 October 1872, Wimbledon, Surrey, **England**. D. 29 December 1910, Kensington, London, England. Reggie Doherty and his younger brother Laurie dominated world **tennis** at the turn of the 20th century. As a **doubles** pairing, they were virtually unbeatable, winning the Wimbledon title eight times, the **United States** title twice, and all five of their Davis Cup rubbers. Together they won the 1900 Olympic doubles title, and in 1908 Reggie won a second gold medal in doubles when he was partnered by George Hillyard. Reggie also won a bronze in men's **singles** in 1900 and gold in the **mixed doubles** with Charlotte Cooper. Doherty confirmed his status as the world's leading player of the era by winning the Wimbledon singles title four years in succession (1897–1900).

***DOLIKHOS* RACE.** The *dolikhos* race was the long-distance running race of the **Ancient Olympic Games**, consisting of a running event of 20 to 25 laps (4,000–5,000 meters). Champions are known from 720 B.C. (Akanthos of Sparta) through A.D. 221. The last known champion, Graos of Bithynia, is the only runner known to have won the race three times at Olympia. *See also DIAULOS* RACE; *STADION* RACE.

DOMINICA (DMA). Founded in 1987, the Dominican **National Olympic Committee** was recognized by the **International Olympic Committee** in 1993, and the country made its Olympic debut in 1996 at the Atlanta Olympics. Dominica (pronounced DOM-i-NEE-ka), a Caribbean island nation, officially known as the Commonwealth of Dominica, has since competed at the next four Summer Games, represented by 14 entrants in **athletics** (six men, five **women**) and **swimming** (two men, one woman). The best performance by a Dominican Olympian occurred in 1996, when Jérôme Romain qualified for the final **round** in the **triple jump**, finishing 12th of 43 entrants, but failed to make a fair jump in the final. Also in 1996 Dawn Williams reached the second round of the women's 800 meter run. In 2008, 200 meter **sprinter** Chris Lloyd, in his second Olympics, failed to qualify for the second round of competition by 0.01 seconds.

Dominica made its first appearance in the **Olympic Winter Games** in 2014 with two representatives in Sochi but not without controversy. Gary Di Silvestri, a 47-year-old resident of Montana in the **United States** and his 48-year-old wife, Angelica Morrone Di Silvestri, both were entered in **cross-country skiing** and marched in the opening ceremony. Neither was born or resided on the island but had purchased Dominican citizenship for an amount said to be in excess of $175,000. Gary dropped out of the 15 k classic event before he even reached the first checkpoint, while his wife, claiming injury, did not even start in her scheduled 10 k event. Subsequently, questions arose as to whether their entry was in accordance with the Olympic spirit, and eligibility rules may be changed for future Games.

DOMINICAN REPUBLIC (DOM). The Caribbean nation of the Dominican Republic shares the island of Hispaniola with the country of **Haiti** and occupies the eastern part of the island. The first Dominican Republic **National Olympic Committee** (NOC) was established in 1946 as a prerequisite to allow the Dominican Republic to participate in the **Central American** and Caribbean Games to be held that year. In 1953, the Olympic Sports Commission took control of participation in Olympic and Regional Games, and in 1962 the NOC was reestablished in its present form. This body was recognized by the **International Olympic Committee** in 1962. Albert Torres was the first Dominican athlete to make an Olympic appearance, competing in the 1964 100 meter dash. The Dominican Republic has competed at 12 **Olympic Games** since, never failing to appear since its debut. It has not yet competed in the **Olympic Winter Games**.

The Dominican Republic has entered 188 athletes (143 men, 45 **women**) and has participated in 16 sports with most of their athletes competing in **athletics** (27 men, eight women), **baseball** (20 men), **boxing** (45 men), **judo** (14 men, four women), **volleyball** (21 women), and **weightlifting** (13 men, three women). They have won six **Olympic medals**: a bronze by Pedro Nolasco in 1984 **bantamweight** boxing, gold in men's 400 meter **hurdles** by Félix Sánchez in 2004 and again in 2012, a gold by Félix Díaz in 2008 **lightwelterweight** boxing, a silver by Yulis Mercedes in 2008 **flyweight taekwondo,** and a silver medal in 2012 in the 400 meters run by Luguelín Santos. Other noteworthy results for Dominican Olympians include fifth place by Yudelquis Contreras in 2008 women's **featherweight** weightlifting; a fifth place tie by the 2012 women's volleyball team; six athletes in three sports reaching the quarter-finals of their respective tournaments and finishing tied for fifth place—flyweight boxers Laureano Ramírez (1984), Meluin de Leon (1988), Héctor Avila (1992), featherweight boxer Victoriano Damián Sosa (1992), women's **singles table tennis** player Nieves Wu (2008) and Yulis Mercedes in men's flyweight taekwondo (2004)—and sixth place by **gymnast** Yamilet Peña in the women's **horse vault** in 2012.

DOPING. Doping is the use of drugs to enhance performance in sport and is considered illegal by the **International Olympic Committee** (IOC) and the

International Federations (IFs). The IOC rules against doping are contained in the World Anti-Doping Code as administered by the **World Anti-Doping Agency** (WADA). Rule 43 of the *Olympic Charter* mandates that the World Anti-Doping Code governs the entire **Olympic Movement**. Basically, the IOC has a proscribed list of medications that are considered to be illegal for use by athletes taking part in its competitions. After each **Olympic Games**, all medalists, and certain other randomly selected athletes, must submit a urine sample, which is then tested for these drugs. If any of the proscribed drugs are present in the athlete's urine in sufficient quantities, he or she may be **disqualified** from competition, pending further urine studies and, usually, legal hearings. In recent years, when these penalties have been handed out, they have virtually always been contested by the athletes and their lawyers.

It is considered unlikely that previous IOC methods of testing for illegal drugs were sufficient to prevent athletes from using them. This is because athletes, coaches, and their doctors were able to learn enough about the drugs to know how long they had to be withdrawn from the athlete before a competition. This would enable the athlete to pass frequent drug tests despite being a habitual user of the drugs. This is now being circumvented by IFs, **National Olympic Committees**, and **National Governing Bodies** performing random, out-of-competition tests of athletes at all times of the year.

Doping is not new. In the Ancient Olympics, trainers gave athletes various concoctions that they felt would improve their performance. The first physician to be considered a specialist in sports medicine was Galen, who prescribed as follows: "The rear hooves of an Abyssinian ass, ground up, boiled in oil, and flavored with rose hips and rose petals, was the prescription favored to improve performance." The word *doping* comes from the 19th century, when the Dutch term *dop* was used to describe a South African drink, an extract of cola nuts to which were added xanthines (found in caffeine) and alcohol. The drink was intended to improve endurance.

Numerous doping scandals have occurred in sports. The most famous was at the 1988 Seoul Olympics, when the original 100 meter champion, Ben Johnson, tested positive for stanozolol, an anabolic steroid, and was disqualified. At the 1960 Rome Olympics, **Danish cyclist** Knut Enemark Jensen collapsed and died during the cycling road race. He was later found to have been given amphetamines (Ronital) and nicotinyl tartrate (a nicotine-type of stimulant). In the 1967 Tour de France, the great **British** cyclist Tommy Simpson collapsed and died while ascending Mont Ventoux. He was found to have been heavily dosed with stimulants. In 1998, a major doping scandal enveloped the Tour de France, and many of the professional cyclists and their team trainers, notably the Festina team, were subject to legal action by the **French** authorities.

The deaths of Jensen and Simpson alerted the sporting authorities to the dangers inherent in drug use in sports. At the 1968 **Olympic Winter Games**, the IOC tested for drugs for the first time. The first athlete to be disqualified in the Olympics for drug use was **Sweden**'s Hans-Gunnar Liljenvall at the 1968 **Olympic Games**. Liljenvall was a **modern pentathlete** who had helped his team win a bronze medal. Prior to the **shooting** event, he drank a few beers to help steady his nerves. This was commonplace among modern pentathletes in those days, but it cost him, and his teammates, a bronze medal.

In the 1970s and 1980s, the athletes of the **German Democratic Republic** were suspected of doping violations that were never detected (*see also* **Shirley Babashoff**). No German Democratic Republic athlete ever failed a doping test at the Olympics. After the fall of the Berlin Wall and the reunification of the two Germanys, former German athletes and coaches revealed that much of the success of the great German Democratic Republic athletic machine was due to the systematic use of illegal drugs. In the 1990s, the Chinese women swimmers and runners were suspected of using similar practices to make great strides in their sports. Adding to this suspicion was the fact that several of the former German Democratic Republic coaches were then coaching in **China**.

In the 1990s in the **United States**, a number of drug accusations centered on the enterprise Bay Area Laboratory Co-operative (BALCO), based in the Bay Area of California. BALCO is led by a former musician, Victor Conte, who has impugned many well-known American athletes, including baseball players Barry Bonds and Jason Giambi and Olympic athletes Marion Jones and Tim Montgomery, as users of performance-enhancing medications provided by BALCO.

In 1999, the IOC was instrumental in pushing the fight against drugs to a new level by forming the WADA. Headed at its inception by Canadian IOC member **Dick Pound**, WADA's task is to oversee and monitor the use of drugs in international sport and find better methods of prevention and detection, as well as educating athletes about the danger and impropriety of drug use in sports. The issue of drug use in sports is complicated, and many commentators question whether this stringent testing is always in sports' and the athletes' best interests. It is not politically correct to be on this side of the argument, as politicians, sports administrators, and the media have come down strongly against drugs. But there are a number of issues that should at least be presented.

The list of prohibited substances is quite long, numbering well over 100. In medical trials of drugs, the gold standard is termed a randomized, controlled, prospective, double-blind trial (RCT), in which the drug is compared to a placebo. Proof of improvement in athletic performance via RCTs, what is termed

Level I evidence-based medicine, is certainly lacking for most of the drugs on the prohibited list. The drugs that have been best studied, anabolic steroids, have had varying results when subjected to true RCTs, and even then, few of the gold standard–type studies have been done. Proponents of strict drug testing will demur, stating that it is "obvious" that these drugs enhance performance, and this can be seen by looking at the improved performances. But that reasoning neglects the strength of the placebo effect and that its psychological effects may mimic the physiologic effects of performance-enhancing drugs. Further, because of the opprobrium that now surrounds many of these substances, even performing an RCT may border on being unethical and be difficult to get through an Institutional Review Board. In fact, the WADA regulations now recommend that prohibited drugs not be given to athletes for medical studies. Thus, the political correctness of drug testing and the WADA regulations prevent the authorities from being able to conclusively prove that they are testing for substances that enhance athletic performance.

Other opponents of drug testing decry the invasion of the athletes' right to privacy. Currently, world-class athletes in Olympic sports can be tested at any time of the year, at any time of the day. They are required to inform sports administrators of their whereabouts at all times. Failure to do so constitutes a "positive test in absentia." In some countries, there are moral and religious objections to providing urine or blood samples, but the athlete must still do so or be considered in violation.

Furthermore, some authors have written that the current status of drug testing denies athletes due process, their right to be considered innocent until proven guilty. In fact, currently, if a positive drug test occurs, the athlete is considered guilty, and the onus is on the athlete to then prove his or her innocence. Though this may be acceptable in some nations, in the United States it is not, and U.S. athletes have fought the results many times using this argument. In addition, the publicity that ensues effectively convicts the athlete in the press, even if he or she is later exonerated. Paraphrasing the words of U.S. Secretary of Labor Ray Donovan in the early 1980s, after he was found innocent of charges made against him, "Where do [the athletes] go to get their reputation back?"

Finally, some argue that the fight against doping artificially draws a line against certain performance-enhancing techniques, while allowing others. Certainly, world-class athletes do many things in training and in their lives that are designed to make them better athletes. Not all of these are actually good for their health. Although running and aerobic exercise enhance one's health, nobody would argue that running 150 miles per week is good for one's general health. In fact, modern athletic training is designed to push the body to the brink of breakdown, but never pass that line.

As an example of nondrug methods that enhance performance, consider the use of altitude sleep chambers. Many distance runners and professional cyclists sleep in these chambers, which lower the oxygen content and mimic training at altitude, usually increasing the blood count, or hematocrit. This is legal. But it is not legal to take erythropoietin, a drug that stimulates red blood cell production and increases one's hematocrit. Both methods have the same result, but arbitrarily, one is legal, the other is not.

Still, even when viewing the arguments of those who oppose drug testing, it must be remembered that these world-class athletes are often role models to children and adolescents. More and more studies have shown that drug use has infiltrated high schools and even lower levels of school, where preadolescent athletes use the drugs, emulating their athletic idols, in an attempt to enhance their own athletic abilities. No one considers this a positive result of using drugs in sports.

Concerning drug use in sports, one approach that is usually used by the media is to simply say the Olympics are the "dirtiest" of all sporting events, because more Olympic athletes are caught for doping than athletes in most of the professional sports. But what this argument fails to consider is that the IOC was the first sports organization in the world to test for drugs in sport (1968); it was the first to institute random, out-of-competition testing; and it still imposes the strictest penalties for anyone caught using drugs. By comparison, in four American professional sports (**baseball, football, basketball, ice hockey**), drug testing procedures are far less frequent, they test for fewer drugs, and their penalties are relative slaps on the wrist compared to the IOC and WADA penalties. The National Football League began testing in 1982, but not for anabolic steroids until 1987. The National Basketball Association issued an antidoping policy in 1983, but the Major League Baseball organization did not issue an antidoping policy until 2003.

As an example, under the IOC and WADA rules, Olympic athletes, or athletes considered at a national level of competitiveness by the IFs, are subject to random, out-of-competition testing at any time of the year, on a 24/7/365 basis. The penalty for a positive doping test is a two-year suspension and a lifetime ban ensues after a second positive test. In Major League Baseball, until January 2005, the athletes were subject to one announced test at a specified time each year. The penalty for a positive test was probation and counseling, but not expulsion from the sport. The bans increased, but a lifetime ban did not occur until the athlete tested positive at least four times. There is one rather famous case in which an athlete was in legal trouble for drug use at least seven times and continued to play Major League Baseball. (In January 2005, Major League Baseball passed stricter doping regulations, but still far short of those enacted by the IOC and IFs.) In the National Football League, a first positive test results only in a four-game suspension, hardly punitive compared to the IOC penalties.

At the dawn of a new century, there are many more problems on the horizon. With the recent scientific analysis of the human genome, gene therapy and genetic manipulation of the human body are close to becoming a reality. Some of the gene therapies that are being studied concern building muscle to help people overcome diseases such as muscular dystrophy, multiple sclerosis, cerebral palsy, and other neuromuscular illnesses. But the gene therapies that would build muscle in these patients would likely also build supermuscular humans, who may well be tempted to try the therapies as methods to enhance athletic performance. These therapies do not exist yet, but already this nightmare scenario is envisioned and being discussed by the doping authorities.

The controversy concerning drug use in sport is not going away. It will continue to be argued at the highest levels of sports administration, in the media, by the athletes, by the lawyers, and by the scientists. As is so often the case, the scientists and physicians, who should properly be at the forefront in this argument, will probably take up the rear in this fight, shunted aside by lawyers, politicians, the media, and sports administrators. The final word is far from being written. *See also* BAHRAIN; COMMISSIONS OF THE IOC; COURT OF ARBITRATION FOR SPORT; IOC 2000 COMMISSION; JOHNSON, MICHAEL DUANE; KULAKOVA, GALINA ALEKSEYEVNA; MÄNTYRANTA, EERO ANTERO; MEDICAL COMMISSION; OLYMPIC OATH; OLYMPIC PROGRAM; OTTO, KRISTIN; PECHSTEIN, CLAUDIA; ROGGE, COUNT CHEVALIER DR. JACQUES.

DOUBLE TRAP. In double trap **shooting** two targets are thrown simultaneously and the shooter must hit both for a successful turn. Double trap is one of the events in Olympic shooting competition. It was added to the **Olympic Program** in 1996 and has been contested for men at each subsequent Summer Games. **Women**'s double trap shooting was held in 1996, 2000, and 2004 but not since then. Kim Rhode of the **United States** won the women's double trap gold medal in 1996 and 2004 and the bronze medal in 2000. After the double trap for women was discontinued, she won medals in **skeet** shooting in 2008 and 2012 and became the first American shooter to medal in five consecutive **Olympic Games**. Russell Mark of **Australia** was the only double medalist in the men's double trap competition. He won the gold medal in 1996 and silver in 2000.

DOUBLES. In some Olympic sports such as **badminton**, **canoeing**, **luge**, **table tennis**, and **tennis**, events are held for individual competitors and for teams of two competitors called doubles. In some other sports, such as **rowing** and **figure skating**, competition involving teams of two is referred to as **pairs**. **Synchronized swimming** has events for two swimmers called **duets**.

DOWNHILL. Downhill is one of the events in **Alpine skiing**. It has a minimum of turns compared to the **slalom** style races and consequently produces the fastest skiing. It has been included in the program of the **Olympic Winter Games** since 1948 for both men and **women**. No man has won the gold medal more than once, and five skiers have each won two medals in the men's downhill—Bernhard Russi of **Switzerland** (gold 1972, silver 1976), Lasse Kjus of **Norway** (silver 1998, 2002), Peter Müller of Switzerland (silver 1984, 1988), and Franck Piccard (silver 1992, bronze 1988) and Guy Périllat (silver 1968, bronze 1960) of **France**. Katje Seizinger of **Germany** (1994, 1998) is the only woman to win two gold medals in the downhill, while six other female skiers have won two medals each. The 2014 women's race produced a tie for first place with both skiers, Tina Maze of **Slovenia** and Dominique Gisin of Switzerland, having the exact time to the nearest one one-hundredth of a second.

DREAM TEAM, THE—1992 USA BASKETBALL. "The Dream Team" was the name given to the **basketball** team that represented the **United States** at the 1992 **Olympic Games**. For the first time, all basketball professionals were declared eligible to compete at the Olympics, including members of the National Basketball Association (NBA), the major U.S. professional league. This allowed the United States to field a team of professional all-stars, which was certainly the greatest basketball team ever assembled. In winning all eight games in the Olympic tournament, the team outscored their opponents 938–538, an average margin of 43 points per game. The team gained incredible attention from the media and fans, both in the United States and **Spain**, as well as throughout the world, and easily won the gold medal. The team members were Charles Barkley, Larry Bird, Clyde Drexler, Patrick Ewing, Earvin "Magic" Johnson, **Michael Jordan**, Christian Laettner, Karl Malone, Chris Mullin, Scottie Pippen, David Robinson, and John Stockton. Subsequent U.S. teams in 1996 and 2000, also made up of NBA players, have been labeled Dream Team II and Dream Team III, but the 1992 team is considered to be by far the most outstanding.

DRESDEN FOUR, THE—GDR COXLESS FOUR ROWING TEAM (1968–1972). Also known as the Einheit Dresden Four, this coxless four **rowing** team won Olympic gold medals in 1968 and 1972 and was never beaten in international competition. Representing the **German Democratic Repub-**

lic, they were World Champions in 1966 and 1970 and European Champions in 1967 and 1971. The team members were Frank Forberger, Dieter Grahn, Frank Rühle, and Dieter Schubert.

DRESSAGE. Dressage is one of the events contested in **equestrianism**. A horseback rider demonstrates his or her skills in training the horse through the performance of "tests," a prescribed series of movements ridden within a standard arena. Dressage was included in the **Olympic Games** from 1912 to 1948 in competition for men. Since 1952, the Olympic dressage event has been open to both men and **women**, with women winning the gold medal in 10 of 11 Olympics from 1972 to 2012. **Anky van Grunsven** of the **Netherlands**, who won this event three times from 2000 to 2008 and was the silver medalist in 1996, is the only three-time gold medalist. Isabel Werth of **Germany** also won four dressage **Olympic medals** (gold 1996, silver 1992, 2000, 2008). Dressage is also one of the three **disciplines** included in the equestrian **three-day event**.

DUET. Although in some sports two-person team events are known as **doubles** or **pairs**, in **synchronized swimming** one of the three Olympic events is known as **women**'s duet. Teams of two women perform a synchronized routine of elaborate moves in the water accompanied by music. It became a part of the **Olympic Program** in 1984 and has been contested in each subsequent Games save 1996. Teams from **Russia** have won Olympic gold medals in women's duet synchronized swimming four times—2000 to 2012. In the seven years in which this sport has been contested in the **Olympic Games**, **Japan** has won six medals, although none were gold.

DUTCH EAST INDIES. *See* INDONESIA.

DUTCH GUIANA. *See* SURINAME.

E

EAGAN, EDWARD PATRICK FRANCIS "EDDIE" (USA–BOX/BOB).
B. 26 April 1898, Denver, Colorado, **United States.** D. 14 June 1967, New York, New York, United States. Eddie Eagan was the Olympic **light-heavyweight boxing** champion in 1920 and a member of the winning four-man **bobsled** crew in 1932. He is the only person to have won an Olympic gold medal at both the **Olympic Games** and **Olympic Winter Games.** While a Rhodes scholar at Oxford University, Eagan made a second appearance at the Summer Games in 1924, where he was eliminated in the first round of the **heavyweight** boxing class. Eagan obtained a B.A. from Oxford in 1928 and in 1932 was admitted to the bar. He practiced law until the outbreak of World War II, when he rejoined the armed forces. Colonel Eagan served with distinction throughout the period of hostilities and was awarded ribbons for combat in all three theaters of operations. After the war, he was chairman of the New York State Athletic Commission from 1945 to 1951. In 2014, his dual gold medal feat was nearly matched by Lauryn Williams (USA), a gold medalist in the **women**'s 4x100 track **relay** in 2012 and a silver medalist in the two-woman bobsled in 2014. Her bobsled team finished only one-tenth of a second behind the gold medalists.

EAST GERMANY. *See* GERMAN DEMOCRATIC REPUBLIC.

EAST TIMOR. *See* TIMOR LESTE.

EBERSOL, DUNCAN "DICK" (USA). B. 28 July 1947, Torrington, Connecticut, **United States.** Dick Ebersol has succeeded **Roone Arledge** as the producer of Olympic **television** in the United States. Ebersol earned his college degree from Yale in 1971 and then began working under Arledge at American Broadcasting Company (ABC) Sports. He was the first person to be an Olympic researcher, producing reams of Olympic minutiae to be used by the ABC sportscasters during the Olympic broadcasts. In 1974, Ebersol was hired away from ABC and joined the National Broadcasting Company (NBC). There he first worked in programming and developed the still-running late night hit *Saturday Night Live* with Lorne Michaels. In 1989,

Ebersol became head of the NBC Sports Division. His primary influence on the Olympics has actually been in finance. In 1996, working in concert with **Dick Pound**, Ebersol negotiated a long-term contract between NBC and the **International Olympic Committee**, which brought NBC the broadcast rights to the 2000, 2004, and 2008 **Olympic Games** and the 2002 and 2006 **Olympic Winter Games**. The contract guaranteed income to the **Organizing Committees** of future Olympic Games and put the **Olympic Movement** on a much stronger financial footing. The long-term contracts have been extended, and NBC has garnered broadcast rights through 2032 to the Olympic Games for American television.

ECUADOR (ECU). Ecuador is located in northwestern South America and its official name is the Republic of Ecuador. The country sent three track and field competitors to the 1924 **Olympic Games**—Alberto Jurado González, Alberto Jarrín, and Belisario Villacís—prior to the Ecuadorian **National Olympic Committee** being formed in 1925. A gap of 44 years then occurred before it returned to the Olympics at **Mexico** City, and it has competed continuously since. It has never appeared at the **Olympic Winter Games**. In 13 Summer Games, Ecuador has entered 139 athletes (106 men, 33 **women**) and participated in 17 sports: **athletics** (26 men, 12 women), **boxing** (19 men), **cycling** (15 men), **diving** (two men), **equestrian** (one man, one woman), **gymnastics** (three men), **judo** (six men, five women), **shooting** (four men, four women), **swimming** (13 men, four women), **tennis** (three men), **weightlifting** (eight men, three women), and **wrestling** (four men, one woman). In addition in recent years Ecuador has also had single male representatives in **canoeing** and **sailing** and single female entrants in **table tennis, taekwondo,** and **triathlon**.

Ecuador's most accomplished Olympic athlete is **race walker** Jefferson Pérez. He competed in five Olympic Games from 1992 to 2008 and won the country's only two **Olympic medals**, a gold in the 20 km race in 1996 and a silver in the same event, a full 12 years later in 2008. He also finished fourth in that event twice—in 2000 and 2004 and was 12th of 54 entrants in the 2004 50 km race walk. Other notable performances by Ecuadorian Olympians include fourth place in the 200 meter **butterfly** swimming race in 1972 by Jorge Delgado, Jr., and seventh place in 1976 in the same event; fifth place in women's **lightweight** weightlifting by Alexandra Escobar in 2008 and seventh place in that event four years earlier; a fifth place tie by **middleweight** boxer Carlos Góngora in 2012; and seventh place by Alex Quiñónez in the 200 meter **sprint** in 2012 track and field competition. Ecuador also had several good results in both the men's **marathon** race (Silvio Guerra, 14th of 124 in 1996; Rolando Vera, 43rd of 110 in 1992 and 22nd of 124 in 1996; and Miguel Almachi, 50th of 105 in 2012) and women's marathon race (Martha Tenorio, 25th of 53 in 2000; and Sandra Ruales, 36th of 82 in 2004 and 35th of 81 in 2008).

EDSTRÖM, JOHANNES SIGFRID (SWE). B. 21 November 1870, Morlanda, Orust, Bohuslän, **Sweden**. D. 18 March 1964, Stockholm, Sweden. As **International Olympic Committee (IOC) president** as well as the International Amateur Athletic Federation (IAAF), Sigfrid Edström was a man of immense influence in sports. Born in Sweden and educated partly there and partly in the **United States** and **Switzerland** (1891–1893), he was one of the organizers of the 1912 **Olympic Games** in Stockholm. During those Olympic Games, he took the initiative of founding the IAAF, for which he served as the first president, remaining in that office from 1913 until 1946. Edström founded the International Chamber of Commerce in 1918 (president, 1939–1945) and the Federation of Swedish Industries in 1910 (chairman, 1928–1929), and was chairman of the Swedish Employers' Confederation from 1931 to 1942. His main business career was as managing director (1903–1933) and chairman of the board (1934–1949) for Allmänna Svenska Elektriska Aktiebolaget, a world leader in the high-tension current industry.

Edström was elected an IOC member in 1921 and became a member of the IOC **Executive Board** when it was created in the same year. He chaired the **Olympic Congresses** in 1921 and 1925 and was appointed vice president of the IOC in 1937. Following the death of IOC President **Henry de Baillet-Latour** in 1942, Edström, as a neutral, was well placed to keep the **Olympic Movement** alive during the war years as de facto president. In 1946, in the first postwar IOC session in **Lausanne**, he was elected president by acclamation. On his retirement in 1952, at the age of 81, he was given the title of honorary president of the IOC. In 1947, he was awarded the **Olympic Cup** for his contributions to the Olympic Movement.

EDWARDS, TERESA (USA–BAS). B. 19 July 1964, Cairo, Georgia, **United States**. One of the greatest female guards to ever play **basketball**, Teresa Edwards played at the University of Georgia, where she was a consensus All-American in 1984 and 1985. Her record is unmatched by **women** in international competition. She won gold medals at the 1984, 1988, 1996, and 2000 Olympics, and a bronze medal at the 1992 Olympics; her five **Olympic medals** and four golds are Olympic basketball records, although the four golds were equaled by **Lisa Leslie** in 2008. The five-foot, nine-inch (175 cm), 150 lb (68 kg) Edwards was also the playmaking leader of championship teams at the 1986 and 1990 World Championships, the 1986 and 1990 **Goodwill Games**, and the 1987 **Pan American Games**. In 1991, she played on the U.S. team that won a bronze at the Pan American Games, and she was the USA Basketball Player of the Year in both 1987 and 1991. She played professional basketball with Atlanta and Philadelphia in the women's American Basketball League from 1996 to 1998, with Minnesota in the Women's National Basketball Association (WNBA) and later coached in the WNBA. In 1996 she was given the honor of reciting the **Olympic Oath** on behalf of the athletes during the opening ceremony of the Atlanta **Olympic Games**.

EGERSZEGI, KRISZTINA (HUN–SWI). B. 16 August 1974, Budapest, **Hungary**. Krisztina Egerszegi established herself as one of the greatest **backstrokers** in **swimming** history. She won a gold and a silver in the two backstroke events at the 1988 **Olympic Games** when only 14 years old. In 1992, she returned to win three individual gold medals—in the 100 meter backstroke, the 200 meter backstroke, and the 400 meter individual **medley**. In 1996, at Atlanta, Egerszegi won her third consecutive gold medal in the 200 backstroke, making her only the second swimmer, after **Dawn Fraser** in the 100 meter **freestyle**, to win the same event at three straight Olympics. She was the first Olympic swimmer to have won five individual gold medals, a record later shattered by **Michael Phelps**'s 11 medals. At the European Championships, the five-foot, eight-inch (175 cm), 126 lb (67 kg) Egerszegi won three silver medals in 1989 and three gold medals in 1991 and 1993. At the 1991 World Championships, she won both backstroke events. She set two world records during her career, one each in the 100 meter and 200 meter backstroke. Egerszegi was inducted into the International Swimming Hall of Fame in 2001.

EGYPT (EGY). Egypt is located at the northeast corner of Africa and southwest corner of Asia and is officially known today as the Arab Republic of Egypt. The country first competed at the 1896 **Olympic Games** and afterward missed the Olympics of 1900 and 1904. It was not present at the 1908 Olympics, but after forming a **National Olympic Committee** (NOC) in 1910, it was more formally represented at the 1912 Stockholm Olympics. Since then, it has been absent only from the Olympics of 1932, 1956 (missing Melbourne, but not Stockholm), and 1980. Egypt's absence from the 1932 Olympics was the result of political turmoil that had resulted in its NOC being disbanded in 1929, but it was reestablished in time for a large team (53 athletes) to be sent to the Berlin Olympics in 1936. From 1960 through 1968, Egypt competed as the **United Arab Republic,** joining in a union in 1960 with **Syria,** although all but three of the 74 United Arab Republic athletes were Egyptian. Egypt also **boycotted** the Olympic Games of 1956, 1976 (withdrawing after the Games started and participating in a few events), and

1980, making it one of three nations to have boycotted three Olympics, along with **Ethiopia** and the **Democratic People's Republic of Korea**.

In 19 Summer Games, Egypt has entered 907 athletes (829 men, 78 **women**) and competed in 28 sports plus the **art competitions**. They have had the most entrants in **football** (125 men), **wrestling** (67 men, two women), **basketball** (62 men), **fencing** (54 men, eight women), **weightlifting** (57 men, five women), and **boxing** (59 men).

Egypt's greatest Olympic successes have been in the strength sports of weightlifting and wrestling, and it has won 24 **Olympic medals** (seven gold, eight silver, nine bronze). Three Egyptian Olympians have each won two medals: Farid Simaika in **diving** (1928 **springboard** bronze, **platform** silver), Ibrahim Hassanien Shams in weightlifting (1936 **featherweight** bronze, 1948 **lightweight** gold), and Karim Gaber in **Greco-Roman wrestling** (2004 **heavyweight** gold, 2012 **light-heavyweight** silver).

Egypt's Olympic boxing medals were all won in 2004 in the three heaviest weight classes: Ahmed Ismail (light-heavyweight bronze), Mohamed El-Sayed (heavyweight bronze), and Mohamed Aly (**super-heavyweight** silver). Aly should not be confused with the American Cassius Clay who fought professionally as **Muhammad Ali**. Other Egyptian Olympic medalists include **fencer** Alaaeldin Abouelkassem (2012 individual **foil** silver); *judokas* Mohamed Ali Rashwan (1984 open class silver) and Hesham Misbah (2008 **middleweight** bronze); **taekwondoka** Tamer Salah (2004 **flyweight** bronze); weightlifters Saleh Soliman (1936 featherweight silver), Mahmoud Fayad (1948 featherweight gold), Anwar Mousbah (1936 lightweight gold), Attia Mohammed Hamouda (1948 lightweight silver), Khadr El-Touni (1936 middleweight gold), Sayed Nosseir (1928 light-heavyweight gold), and Ibrahim Wasif (1936 light-heavyweight bronze); and Greco-Roman wrestlers Mahmoud Hassan (1948 **bantamweight** silver), Abdel Ahmed Al-Rashid (1952 featherweight bronze), Ibrahim Moustafa (1928 light-heavyweight gold), and Ibrahim Orabi (1948 light-heavyweight bronze).

Egypt has competed at the **Olympic Winter Games** only in 1984 at Sarajevo with only one participant. Jamil El-Reedy competed in **Alpine skiing** and finished 60th of 61 in the men's **downhill** with a time of 3:13.86, more than one minute slower than the 59th best racer. El-Reedy also was 46th of 101 in the **slalom** and did not finish the **giant slalom**.

Alexandria, Egypt, was unsuccessful in bids to host the 1916 and 1936 Summer Games and Cairo failed in its bid for the 2008 Games.

EHRIG-SCHÖNE-MITSCHERLICH, ANDREA (GDR–SSK). B. 1 December 1960, Dresden, Sachsen, **German Democratic Republic**. Andrea Ehrig won seven Olympic **speed skating** medals (one gold, five silver, one bronze). After starting with a silver in 1976 in the 3,000 meters, she failed to win a medal in 1980, and won her only gold in 1984 at her favorite distance of 3,000 meters. She also won silver in 1984 at 1,000 and 1,500 meters and ended her Olympic career in 1988 with silvers in the 3,000 and 5,000 meters and a bronze in the 1,500 meters. Primarily a distance skater, Ehrig set world records over the three distances at which she won **Olympic medals**. Her first Olympic appearance, when only 15 years old, was under her maiden name of Mitscherlich. The five-foot, five-inch (165 cm), 128 lb (58 kg) skater later competed under her married name of Schöne, and following her second marriage in 1985 to fellow Olympic speed skater Andreas Ehrig, she made her final Olympic appearance under that name.

EIGHTS. Eights are a type of boat used in **rowing** competition. It is designed for eight oarsmen, each with one oar, four rowing on each side of the boat. A **coxswain** is used for steering and to help coordinate the rowers' strokes. Eights races for men have been included in each **Olympic Games** rowing competition since 1900 except the **Intercalated Olympic Games** of 1906. The **United States** has won the men's Olympic eights race 12 times including eight consecutive times from 1920 to 1956. The United States has also won two silver medals and two bronze medals in men's eights races. **Women**'s eights races have been held in the Olympic Games since 1976 and **Romania**, the United States, and East Germany have each won three gold medals, with **Canada** winning once. Romania has also won three silver medals and two bronze medals in this event. Elena Georgescu of Romania was a member of their eights team in five consecutive Olympics (1992–2008) and won three gold, one silver, and one bronze medal in those five years.

EL SALVADOR (ESA). El Salvador's **National Olympic Committee** was formed in 1949, but it was not recognized by the **International Olympic Committee** until 1962. Six years then passed before the **Central American** nation, officially known as the Republic of El Salvador, competed at the **Olympic Games** in 1968 in **Mexico** City with 60 athletes, more than the total (58) of the nine subsequent Games in which El Salvador participated. (They were absent from the Olympics of 1976 and 1980.) They have not to date (as of 2014) won any Olympic medals and have not yet competed at the **Olympic Winter Games**. In 10 Summer Games, El Salvador has entered 118 athletes (93 men, 25 **women**) in 13 sports: **archery** (two men), **athletics** (19 men, eight women), **boxing** (two men), **cycling** (six men, two women), **football** (18 men), **judo** (six men), **rowing** (one man, one woman), **sailing** (three men), **shooting** (11 men, three women), **swimming** (19 men, nine women), **tennis** (one man), **weightlifting** (four men, one woman), and **wrestling** (one man, one woman). In addition, they had one male entrant in the **art competitions** of 1932.

The best Olympic performance by a Salvadorean was a fifth-place finish by Maureen Kaila Vergara in cycling in the 1996 women's points race. Other commendable results by El Salvador athletes include Luisa Maida, eighth place in 2008 women's sporting pistol; Patricia Rivas, 20th of 44 entrants in 2004 women's **air rifle** shooting; Emerson Hernández, 26th of 63 in the 2012 men's 50 km walk; Evelyn García, 26th of 66 in the 2012 women's **road race** cycling; Juan Vargas, tied for ninth in 1984 **lightweight** judo; Donald Martínez, winner of his first two bouts in 1988 **light-flyweight** boxing and tied for ninth place; tennis player Rafael Arévalo who won his first **singles** match in 2008 before being defeated by **Roger Federer**; and Ingrid Medrano, who won her first bout in women's **flyweight** wrestling in 2008 and finished in ninth place.

ELLICE ISLANDS. *See* TUVALU.

ELVSTRØM, PAUL BERT (DEN–SAI). B. 25 February 1928, Maglegård, Gentofte, Hovedstaden, **Denmark**. Paul Elvstrøm competed as a **sailor** in

Paul Elvstrøm, the Danish winner of four consecutive individual sailing gold medals from 1948 to 1960. Courtesy of Erich Kamper

eight **Olympic Games** over a 40-year period from 1948 to 1988. Although eight other competitors have had lengthy Olympic careers of eight or more appearances, none could match Elvstrøm's record of successes. He won the Firefly class in 1948 and the Finn class in 1952, 1956, and 1960 and was the first competitor in any sport to win individual gold medals at four successive Games. After being a reserve on the Danish team in 1964, the six-foot tall (182 cm), 187 lb (85 cm) Elvstrøm then competed in 1968 and 1972, without winning a medal, although he finished in fourth place in 1968. He also competed in 1984 and 1988, when his daughter Trine crewed for him and helped him again finish fourth in 1984.

EMANUEL (né EMANUEL FERNANDO SCHEFFLER REGO) (BRA–BVO). B. 15 April 1973, Curitiba, Paraná, **Brazil**. Like many Brazilian athletes, Emanuel is known in the sporting world only by his first name. He is one of only four people (two men, two women) to win three **Olympic medals** in **beach volleyball**. He made his first appearance at the **Olympic Games** in 1996 when he teamed with Zé Marco, but they only reached the third **round** of the tournament. In 2000, Emanuel and José Loiola were teammates but again lost in the round of 16 (third round). **Ricardo** (Ricardo Alex Costa Santos), who had won the silver medal in 2000 with Zé Marco, became Emanuel's partner in 2004, and the pair won the gold medal that year and the bronze medal in 2008. In 2012, the six-foot, two-inch (190 cm), 176 lb (80 kg) Emanuel again changed partners and won the bronze medal with Alison Cerutti. In addition to his Olympic triumphs, Emanuel won gold medals at the World Championships in 1999, 2003, and 2011 and at the 2007 and 2011 **Pan American Games**. His wife, Leila (de Gomes de Barros), is also a two-time bronze medalist in Olympic beach volleyball.

ENDER, KORNELIA (later MATTHES, then GRUMMT) (GDR–SWI). B. 25 October 1958, Plauen im Vogtland, Sachsen, **German Democratic Republic**. Kornelia Ender won a total of eight **Olympic medals** in **swimming**, including four gold medals in 1976 in the 100 and 200 meter **freestyle**, the 100 meter **butterfly**, and the 400 meter **medley relay**. The five-foot, eight-inch (172 cm), 130 lb (59 kg) swimmer also won four silver medals: in 1972, the 200 meter individual medley and the 4x100 meter medley relay, and in 1972 and 1976, the 4x100 meters freestyle relay. The most prolific record breaker of her era, she set 23 world records (1973–1976) in currently recognized events, and her total of 10 medals (eight gold, two silver) at the World Championships is also a record. She first married Olympic swimmer **Roland Matthes** and then Olympic **decathlete** Steffen Grummt.

ENDO, YUKIO (JPN–GYM). B. 18 January 1937, Akita, **Japan**. D. 25 March 2009, Tokyo, Japan. **Yukio Endo** won seven **Olympic medals**, including five gold medals in **gymnastics**. He helped Japan to the **all-around** team championship in 1960, 1964, and 1968. In 1964, the diminutive (five-foot, three-inch [161 cm], 128 lb [58 kg]) Endo was the individual all-around champion and added a gold medal on the **parallel bars**. His other two individual medals were silver in the 1964 **floor exercise** and the 1968 **horse vault**. Endo won only one individual title at the World Championships, the 1962 floor exercise title. In 1962, he won seven medals at the Worlds, following that with three more in 1966. In both years, he won golds with the Japanese team.

ENGEL-GULBIN-KRÄMER, INGRID (GDR–DIV). B. 29 July 1943, Dresden, Sachsen, **Germany**. Ingrid Krämer won gold in both **platform** and **springboard diving** in 1960, making her the first non-American **woman** to achieve this feat. After repeating this double at the 1963 European Championships, Engel-Krämer was a strong favorite to retain both titles in 1964, but she was successful only in the springboard, narrowly losing her platform crown. At her third **Olympic Games** in **Mexico** in 1968, the five-foot, two-inch (158 cm), 123 lb (56 kg) diver competed only in the springboard, where she finished fifth. She participated under three different names at the Olympics. She appeared under her maiden name of Krämer in 1960, then in 1964 she used the name of her first husband (Engel), and in 1968 she used that of her second husband (Gulbin).

ENGLAND. England is one of the constituent nations of the United Kingdom of **Great Britain** and Northern Ireland, along with **Scotland**, **Wales**, and Northern Ireland. However, England has only twice been represented at the **Olympic Games** by its own teams. In 1908, separate national teams were entered in the **hockey** tournament by England, **Ireland** (then part of Great Britain), Scotland, and Wales, with England winning the gold medal. In 1912, separate national teams were entered in the **cycling road race** by England, Ireland, and Scotland, with England winning the silver medal. All other English appearances at the Olympic Games have been as part of Great Britain's teams. Of note, however, England could theoretically form its own **National Olympic Committee**, as it has affiliations with more than the five requisite **International Olympic Committee**–recognized **International Federations** (IFs). England is an independent member of the following eight IFs: **badminton**, **basketball**, **boxing**, **curling**, **football**, hockey, **table tennis**, and **volleyball**.

ÉPÉE. An épée is one of the three weapons used in **fencing** competition. Men's individual épée contests have been conducted at every modern **Olympic Games** since 1900. Men's team épée contests have been held at each Games since 1906. **Women**'s individual épée events have been held at the Olympic Games since 1996 and women's team épée events since 1996, although they were not held in 2008. Ramon Fonst of **Cuba** won the first two Olympic épée titles in 1900 and 1904 and is the only man to win the tournament twice. Győző Kulcsár of **Hungary** (gold 1968, bronze 1972, 1976), Philippe Riboud of **France** (silver 1988, bronze 1980, 1984), **Edoardo Mangiarotti** of **Italy** (gold 1952, bronze 1948, 1956), and Pavel Kolobkov of **Russia** (gold 2000, silver 1992 for the Unified Team, bronze 2004) are the only fencers to win three medals in men's individual épée. When Mangiarotti won the gold medal in 1952, his brother Dario won the silver medal. In men's épée team competition, France has won nine gold medals, three silver medals, and five bronze medals to lead all nations. Italy has eight gold medals, three silver medals, and three bronze medals. Timea Nagy of Hungary was the women's Olympic épée champion in 2000 and 2004. **Laura Flessel-Colovic** of France won in 1996, was third in 2000, and second in 2004 and is the only three-time medalist in this event. Russia won the women's team épée tournament in 2000 and 2004 and was third in 1996. *See also* FOIL, SABRE.

EQUATORIAL GUINEA (GEQ). Equatorial Guinea's **National Olympic Committee** was formed in 1980 and recognized by the **International Olympic Committee** in 1984, which enabled the nation to make its Olympic debut at the Los Angeles Games that year. Since then, it has been represented at every **Olympic Games** but only had athletes in the track and field events until 2000 at Sydney, when two **swimmers** (one male and one female) and two track and field athletes represented the nation at the Olympics. In Beijing a male *judoka* competed for the nation. Through 2012, the West African nation of Equatorial Guinea, officially known as the Republic of Equatorial Guinea and once known as Spanish Guinea, has been represented by 26 Olympians, 18 men and eight **women**. The nation has not competed at the **Olympic Winter Games**. Gustavo Envela has been the most persistent Equatoguinean Olympian, appearing in four Olympic Games and seven different events (100, 200, and 400 meters sprints and the 4x100 relay) from 1984 to 1996 but never advanced past the opening **heat**. Equatorial Guinea has had one of the worst performances of any nation in the Olympic Games, with none of their entrants advancing past the first round. Their two swimmers in 2000, Eric Moussabani and Paula Barila Bolopa, turned in the slowest times, by far, in Olympic history in their events and became notorious for their performances. *See also* OLYMPIC ANTIHEROES.

EQUESTRIAN EVENTS. Equestrian events have been on the **Olympic Program** since 1900, when events were held at the **Olympic Games** in Paris. However, they were not held again until 1912 in Stockholm. Since that year, the sport has always been on the Olympic Program. Through 1948, Olympic equestrian was limited to military officers only. This was changed in 1952, and the sport became mixed at the Olympics, although the **three-day event** was only opened to both genders in 1956. In that year, the equestrian events were not held along with the other sports during the **Summer Games** because the site of the Games, Melbourne, **Australia**, had severe quarantine laws for animals. This led the **International Olympic Committee** to hold the equestrian events in Stockholm, **Sweden**, from 10–17 June while the remainder of the Summer Games took place during the Australian spring from 22 November to 8 December. In 2008, at the Beijing Olympics, the equestrian events were held on the **Chinese** island of **Hong Kong** because it had an established horse racing industry and had facilities available as well as strict quarantine measures that were likely to result in fewer problems with equine disease than in other parts of China.

Three equestrian **disciplines** are contested, with an individual and team event in each, making six events on the Olympic Program. These are **jumping** (or show jumping, or Grand Prix de Nations as a team event), **dressage**, and the three-day event. Jumping consists of jumping over a series of obstacles without touching the fences. Dressage is a sort of ballet on horseback, in which the rider has the horse perform certain intricate maneuvers of stepping. The scoring is done by judges who evaluate how well the horse executes the moves. The three-day event (sometimes known as eventing) combines the above two disciplines and adds a third competition of riding a **cross-country** course. Scoring is by a series of tables evaluating each day's performance. It now actually occurs over four days at the Olympics, as two days are devoted to the dressage. In 24 Summer Olympic competitions, there have been 2,234 athletes (1,815 men, 419 **women**) from 71 nations who have participated in Olympic equestrianism.

Equestrian sports are governed by the Fédération Équestre Internationale, which was formed in 1921 and has 125 member nations. The top nations at the Olympics in equestrian events have been **Germany**, Sweden, the **United States**, and **France**.

Anky van Grunsven (NED) has won nine medals in equestrianism, although only three golds. **Isabell Werth** (GER) and **Reiner Klimke** (FRG/GER) each have eight medals. Klimke has won the most gold medals, six, while Werth and **Hans Günter Winkler** (FRG/GER) have both won five golds, Winkler winning seven medals in all. *See also* BEERBAUM, LUDGER; D'INZEO, PIERO and RAIMONDO D'INZEO; MILLAR, IAN;

*Princess Ann, an equestrian competitor at the 1976
Montreal Olympic Games. Courtesy of Erich Kamper*

**NECKERMANN, JOSEF CARL PETER; SAINT CYR, HENRI JULIUS
REVERONY; UPHOFF, NICOLE.**

ERITREA (ERI). The **International Olympic Committee** granted provisional recognition to the **National Olympic Committee** for Eritrea in 1998, and full recognition followed in 1999. Eritrea, located in northeastern Africa and officially known as the State of Eritrea, was the northernmost province of **Ethiopia** until it became independent in May 1993. Prior to Eritrean independence, several of its athletes competed for Ethiopia at the **Olympic Games**. Eritrea first competed at the Olympics in 2000 at Sydney, represented by two men and one **woman** runners in track and field **athletics**.

For a country with a population of only six million, Eritrea has done exceptionally well in Olympic athletics distance events. In 2004, Zersenay Tadesse won a bronze medal for Eritrea in the men's 10,000 meter run and was seventh in the 5,000 meters. He finished fifth in the 10,000 meters in

2008 and sixth in 2012. His brother Kidane finished 10th in the 5,000 meter run in 2008 and 12th in the 10,000 meter run that same year. In 2012, Teklemariam Medhin finished seventh in the 10,000 meters and Yared Asmarom was eighth in the **marathon** in 2008 and 19th in 2012. Meb Keflezighi, the **United States** marathon silver medalist in 2004, is a native of Eritrea. Through 2012, Eritrean athletes (16 men and three women) have competed primarily in track and field athletics distance events at the Olympics, but in 2012, there was also one Eritrean entry in **cycling**. Eritrea has not yet participated in the **Olympic Winter Games**.

ESTONIA (EST). Three Estonian athletes were members of the **Russian** team at the 1912 **Olympic Games**, and as a separate nation, Estonia competed at the Olympic Games continuously from 1920 to 1936. From 1952 to 1988, Estonia was a republic of the **Soviet Union** and thus did not compete as an independent nation, but many Estonian athletes competed for the Soviet Union. When the Soviet Union dissolved in 1991, Estonia declared and was granted its independence and is now officially known as the Republic of Estonia. The northern Europe nation on the Baltic Sea returned to the Olympic fold by competing in 1992 in both Albertville and Barcelona and has competed at every Olympic Games and **Olympic Winter Games** since. Estonia has never hosted an Olympic Games, but in 1980 all of the **sailing** events of the Moscow Olympics were actually held in the Gulf of **Finland** off Tallinn, the capital of Estonia.

In 11 Summer Games, Estonia has entered 234 athletes (201 men, 33 **women**) and competed in 22 sports, with most of their participants in **athletics** (51 men, 12 women), **wrestling** (27 men), **rowing** (19 men), **swimming** (14 men, five women), **cycling** (15 men, three women), **sailing** (14 men, three women), and **weightlifting** (17 men). Estonia has won 33 medals at the Summer Games (nine gold, nine silver, 15 bronze) with 21 of them from 1920 to 1936. Eight athletes have each won two medals. **Discus thrower** Gerd Kanter won gold in 2008 and bronze in 2012; *judoka* Indrek Pertel won bronze in men's **heavyweight** in 2000 and 2004; rower Jüri Jaanson won silver in 2004 single **sculls** and silver in 2008 in double sculls; heavyweight weightlifter Arnold Luhaäär won silver in 1928 and bronze in 1936; and weightlifter Alfred Neuland won gold in 1920 in the **lightweight** class and silver in 1924 in the **middleweight** class. Three wrestlers also won two medals each: Voldemar Väli (1928 **Greco-Roman featherweight** gold, 1936 Greco-Roman lightweight bronze); **light-heavyweight** August Neo (1936 Greco-Roman bronze, 1936 **freestyle** silver), and heavyweight Kristan Palusalu, one of only two men to win gold medals in both Greco-Roman and freestyle wrestling in the same year.

Estonia's other gold medalists are Erki Nool (2000 **decathlon**), cyclist **Erika Salumäe** (1992 women's sprint); **bantamweight** wrestler Eduard Pütsep (1924 Greco-Roman), and lightweight wrestler Osvald Käpp (1928 freestyle).

At the 1924 Olympic Winter Games, Estonia was represented at the opening ceremony, but no athletes competed. Its athletes first competed at the Olympic Winter Games of 1928 and also competed in 1932 and 1936. In nine Winter Games, Estonia has entered 94 athletes (62 men, 32 women) and competed in eight sports, with most of the participants in **cross-country skiing** (22 men, 11 women) and **biathlon** (15 men, 11 women). They have won seven medals, all in cross-country skiing, with two Estonian skiers, Andrus Veerpalu and Kristina Šmigun-Vähi, each winning three. Veerpalu competed in six Winter Games from 1992 to 2010 and won gold in the men's 15 k in 2002 and 2006 and silver in the 50 k in 2002. Šmigun-Vähi competed in five Winter Games from 1994 to 2010 and won gold in the women's 10 k in 2006, gold in the 2006 **skiathlon**, and silver in the 10 k in 2010. Estonia's other Winter Games medal, a bronze, was won by Jaak Mae in the 2002 15 k.

ETHICS COMMISSION. The Ethics Commission was formed in 1999 in response to the **Olympic bribery scandal**. The Ethics Commission's primary focus was to address the responsibilities of the **International Olympic Committee** (IOC), to oversee the selection process of host cities, and to investigate any allegations of breaches of conduct by IOC members or Olympic candidate or host cities. The Ethics Commission currently (as of 2014) consists of nine members, chaired in 2014 by Youssoupha Ndiaye of **Senegal**. In the summer of 1999, the Ethics Commission produced an IOC Code of Ethics. The IOC website (www.olympic.org) notes that the Ethics Commission has three functions:

1. It draws up and continuously updates the ethical principles, including in particular the Code of Ethics as well as specific implementing provisions based on the values and principles enshrined in the *Olympic Charter*. It takes care that these texts are disseminated to the relevant stakeholders.
2. It conducts investigations into breaches of ethics submitted to it by the **IOC president** and, where necessary, makes recommendations for measures or sanctions to the IOC **Executive Board** and/or the IOC Session; these recommendations remain confidential until the IOC Executive Board makes a decision. All decisions taken are published in the section of the Ethics Commission on www.olympic.org.
3. It has a mission of preventing breaches of ethical principles and of advising the whole **Olympic Movement** in order to assist with the

application of the ethical principles and rules. In all cases, this advice remains confidential.

ETHIOPIA (ETH). Ethiopia, located in northeastern Africa, made its first Olympic appearance in 1956. It has since missed the 1976, 1984, and 1988 Olympics, all due to political **boycotts**, making Ethiopia one of only three nations—with **Egypt** and the **Democratic People's Republic of Korea**—to have boycotted three **Olympic Games**. In 12 Summer Games, Ethiopia has entered 206 athletes (162 men, 44 **women**) and competed in four sports: **athletics** (109 men, 43 women), **boxing** (24 men), **cycling** (28 men), and **swimming** (one man, one woman).

Ethiopia, officially known as the Federal Democratic Republic of Ethiopia, has won 45 **Olympic medals**, 21 gold, seven silver, 17 bronze, all in athletics. The top Ethiopian athletes have been distance runners. Heading this list is **Abebe Bikila**, Olympic **marathon** champion in 1960 and 1964, who is generally considered the greatest marathoner of all time. Mamo Wolde followed Bikila and won the 1968 marathon as well as a silver medal in the 1968 10,000 meters and a bronze medal in the 1972 marathon. Miruts Yifter was also a triple medalist, with bronze in 1972 10,000 meters and gold in 1980 5,000 and 10,000 meters. Had Ethiopia not boycotted the Games in 1976, 1984, and 1988, he most likely would have won more medals. Haile Gebrselassie won the 10,000 meters in 1996 and 2000. Kenenisa Bekele continued the Ethiopian tradition in 2004 by winning the 10,000 meters and finishing second in the 5,000 meters. In 2008, he won gold in each of those events, and in 2012, he finished fourth in the 10,000 meters. Sileshi Sihini was second in the 10,000 meters in both 2004 and 2008.

In women's athletics, Tirunesh Dibaba, from 2004 to 2012, has won five medals (three gold, two bronze) in women's 5,000 meter and 10,000 meter running events. Derartu Tulu competed in the 10,000 meters in four consecutive Games (1992–2004) and won gold in 1992 and 2000, bronze in 2004, and was fourth in 1996. Gete Wami won bronze in 1996 in 10,000 meters, bronze in 5,000 meters in 2000, and silver in 10,000 meters in 2000. Meseret Defar won medals in the 5,000 meters in three consecutive Games: gold in 2004 and 2012 and bronze in 2008.

In other sports, Ethiopian **light-flyweight** boxer Chanyalew Haile reached the quarter-finals in 1972 after stopping his first two opponents. In cycling, the 1956 men's **road race** team finished ninth of 20.

Ethiopia also competed at the 2006 and 2010 **Olympic Winter Games**, both times represented solely by **cross-country skier** Robel Teklemariam. He entered the men's 15 k event and finished 83rd of 99 in 2006 and 93rd of 95 in 2010. *See also* ERITREA.

EUROPEAN OLYMPIC COMMITTEES, THE (EOC). The **National Olympic Committees** from Europe formed this group to further their interests with the **International Olympic Committee**. The EOC is headquartered in Rome, **Italy**. The president, as of 2014, is Patrick Hickey of **Ireland**, and there are 49 current member federations. The group's name was changed to the European Olympic Committees in November 1994 at its meeting in Atlanta. Prior to that time it was known as the Association des Comités Nationaux Olympiques d'Europe.

EVANS, JANET BETH (USA–SWI). B. 28 August 1971, Fullerton, California, **United States**. Janet Evans is considered to be the greatest female long distance **swimmer** of all time. She entered the 1988 Olympics as the world record holder in the 400 meters, 800 meters, and 1,500 meters and improved her own world record in winning the 400 meters, in addition to taking gold medals in the 800 meters and the 400 meter individual **medley**. At her second Olympic appearance in 1992, Evans successfully defended her 800 meters title but suffered her first defeat in the 400 meters since 1986 when she placed second to Dagmar Hase (GER). The five-foot, six-inch (167 cm), 119 lb (54 kg) Evans won a host of medals at the World Championships (gold in the 400 and 800 in 1991), the **Goodwill Games**, and other major championships, including 12 U.S. titles each in the 400 and 800 **freestyles**, and brought a new dimension to long distance swimming for women. She was voted World Swimmer of the Year in 1987, 1989, and 1990. Evans finished her career at the 1996 **Olympic Games** where, by then past her prime, she finished sixth in the 800 meter freestyle. All of her world records lasted for a very long time: the 400 until 2006, the 800 until 2008, and the 1,500 until 2007.

EVENTING. *See* THREE-DAY EVENT.

EWRY, RAYMOND CLARENCE "RAY" (USA–ATH). B. 14 October 1873, Lafayette, Indiana, **United States**. D. 29 September 1937, Queens, New York, United States. Ray Ewry was a victim of polio as a child, but remedial leg-strengthening exercises resulted in his becoming the greatest exponent of the now defunct standing jumps. The six-foot, one-inch (185 cm), 174 lbs (79 kg) Ewry was unbeaten in 10 Olympic competitions, winning the standing **high jump** and standing **long jump** four times each (1900, 1904, 1906, 1908) and the standing **triple jump** twice (1900, 1904). His 10 individual gold medals remained an Olympic record for any sport, until broken by **Michael Phelps** in 2008. Ewry retired shortly after the 1908 Games, having won 15 Amateur Athletic Union titles and setting world records in each of his three specialty events.

EXECUTIVE BOARD OF THE IOC. Founded in 1921, it was known as the Executive Committee until 1955. The Executive Board of the **International Olympic Committee** (IOC) manages the affairs of the IOC. It functions by making its recommendations to the **IOC Sessions**. These recommendations are rarely overturned; thus the Executive Board effectively runs the IOC. It consists of the **IOC president**, four vice presidents, and beginning in 2000, 10 additional members, for a total of 15 members. Prior to 2000, the Executive Board consisted of 11 members—the president, four vice presidents, and six other members—but the size of the board was increased based on the recommendations of the **IOC 2000 Commission**. The Commission also mandated that future Executive Boards should have representative members from the various classes of IOC members: independent members, **National Olympic Committee** members, **International Federation** members, and athletes. Executive Board members are elected by the IOC Sessions. The vice presidents and board members are elected for four-year periods.

EXTRA-LIGHTWEIGHT. Extra-lightweight is the lightest weight class in **judo** competition for both men and **women**. Olympic competition for men in this category began in 1980 with a weight limit of 60 kg (132.25 lb) and for women in 1992 with a weight limit of 48 kg (106 lb). **Tadahiro Nomura** won three gold medals in the men's event (1992–2000). **Ryoko Tamura-Tani** of **Japan** (gold 2000, 2004; silver 1992, 1996; bronze 2008) has won five medals in the six years this class has been held in women's competition.

F

FALKLAND ISLANDS. The Falkland Islands (also known as Islas Malvinas) are an archipelago in the South Atlantic that is a British Overseas Territory and as such is not recognized by the **International Olympic Committee** (IOC). It does have a **National Olympic Committee**, but it is unlikely that it will achieve IOC recognition in the future, as the nation has affiliation with only one **International Federation**, that for badminton. The Falkland Islands has competed at the Island Games as well as each **Commonwealth Games** from 1982 to 2014.

FAROE ISLANDS. The Faroe Islands, located in the North Atlantic, does have a **National Olympic Committee** (NOC), the Faroese Confederation of Sports and Olympic Committee. It is possible that such a committee may achieve **International Olympic Committee** (IOC) recognition in the future, as the nation has affiliations with eight **International Federations: aquatics (swimming, diving, water polo), archery, badminton, football, handball, judo, table tennis,** and **volleyball**. The Faroe Islands is a constituent country of **Denmark** and as such may not be recognized by the IOC because it does not currently have independent nation status, although it first applied to the IOC in 1984 and met its requirements in 1987, prior to the more recent rule changes for dependent nations. The Danish NOC supports its inclusion. The Faroe Islands is recognized by the **International Paralympic Committee**, and its athletes have competed at each edition of the Summer Paralympics since 1984. The nation has also competed at the Island Games since their inception in 1985.

FEATHERWEIGHT. Featherweight is a weight class in **boxing, taekwondo, weightlifting,** and **wrestling**. In men's boxing and wrestling, it is the fourth lightest after **light-flyweight, flyweight,** and **bantamweight**. In **women**'s boxing and wrestling, the featherweight class does not exist. Philip Waruinge of **Kenya** (1968 bronze, 1972 silver) is the only featherweight boxer with more than one **Olympic medal**.

Imre Polyak of **Hungary** won four medals (gold 1964, silver 1952, 1956, 1960) in featherweight **Greco-Roman** style wrestling, and John Smith of the **United States** won two gold medals in **freestyle** featherweight wrestling (1988, 1992).

In taekwondo (which has Olympic competition in fewer weight classes), it is the second lightest class after flyweight. **Hadi Saei of Iran** (gold 2004, bronze 2000) and Servet Tazegul of **Turkey** (gold 2012, bronze 2008) are the only multiple Olympic medalists in men's featherweight taekwondo, while no female has won more than one medal in women's featherweight taekwondo.

In weightlifting, it is the third lightest class for men after flyweight and bantamweight, and in women's weightlifting it is the second lightest class as they do not have a bantamweight classification. The great **Naim Süleymanoğlu** of Turkey won the men's featherweight weightlifting Olympic gold medal three times from 1988 to 1996, while no woman has won more than one medal in women's featherweight weightlifting competition.

FEDERAL REPUBLIC OF GERMANY (FRG) (WEST GERMANY). After World War II, the western-central European nation of **Germany** split into two nations. The Federal Republic of Germany (FRG) (known as West Germany in many nations, but in Germany as the Bundesrepublik Deutschland [BRD]) was formed in Bonn on 23 May 1949 from the former **United States, British**, and **French** zones of occupation. The **German Democratic Republic** (GDR, East Germany) was formed on 7 October 1949 from the former Soviet zone of occupation. From 1952 to 1968, the problem of the "two Germanys" was a major political issue for the **International Olympic Committee** (IOC). The FRG **National Olympic Committee** (NOC) was formed on 24 September 1949 and requested IOC recognition immediately, which came when the IOC **Executive Board** gave provisional recognition on 29 August 1950, with full recognition following in May 1951 at the 46th **IOC Session** in Vienna. The German Democratic Republic formed an NOC on 22 April 1951 and also asked for recognition. In 1952, a German team was entered at Oslo and Helsinki. Although called a combined German team, it was only represented by athletes from the Federal Republic of Germany.

At the 51st IOC Session in Paris in 1955, the IOC granted recognition to the German Democratic Republic NOC by a vote of 27–7. However, the proviso to this recognition was that both Germanys would compete at the Olympics with a combined team, and they did so in 1956, 1960, and 1964, competing under one flag.

On 6 October 1965, at the 64th IOC Session in Madrid, the IOC gave the German Democratic Republic the right to enter a separate team at the 1968 **Olympic Games**. However, the IOC ruled that both Germanys had to compete with the same uniforms, using the same flag adorned with the Olympic symbol, and using the same anthem, the choral theme from

Beethoven's Ninth Symphony, and that the German Democratic Republic would compete as East Germany, a name it did not recognize. At the 68th IOC Session at **Mexico** City in 1968, the IOC voted 44–4 that, beginning in 1972, both the Federal Republic of Germany and the German Democratic Republic could compete separately at the Olympic Games, wearing their own uniforms, using their own flags and anthems, and with the correct names of their nations. This decision was no doubt influenced by the fact that the 1972 Olympics were to be held in München, West Germany. On 3 October 1990, the German Democratic Republic and the Federal Republic of Germany dissolved their separate governments to once again form a single united German state, and in 1992 a unified German team competed at Albertville and Barcelona.

During its relatively brief existence, the Federal Republic of Germany was a powerful nation in many sports, winning 204 medals (56 gold, 67 silver, 81 bronze) from 1968 to 1988 in the Summer Games and 39 medals (11 gold, 15 silver, 13 bronze) in the **Olympic Winter Games**.

In five Summer Games, West Germany entered 1,371 athletes (1,027 men, 344 **women**) and competed in 27 sports with the most participants in **athletics** (159 men, 81 women), **rowing** (107 men, 37 women), **swimming** (65 men, 51 women), **hockey** (53 men, 26 women), **canoeing** (53 men, 15 women), **cycling** (60 men, six women), and **fencing** (46 men, 18 women). Its top Olympians in summer sports were **Reiner Klimke** (EQU), with seven medals (five gold, two bronze) and **Michael Groß** (SWI), with six medals (three gold, two silver, one bronze). Four other athletes each won four medals: fencers Matthias Behr (one gold, three silver) and Alexander Pusch (two gold, two silver), **sprinter** Annegret Richter (two gold, two silver) and **equestrian Josef Neckermann** (one gold, two silver, one bronze). Twelve other West German athletes won three medals each.

In six Winter Games, West Germany entered 336 athletes (264 men, 72 women) and competed in 10 sports: **Alpine skiing** (28 men, 24 women), **biathlon** (18 men), **bobsled** (42 men), **cross-country skiing** (25 men, 10 women), **figure skating** (16 men, 20 women), **ice hockey** (78 men), **luge** (23 men, 10 women), **Nordic combined** (12 men), **ski jumping** (15 men), and **speed skating** (13 men, eight women). At the Winter Olympics, Peter Angerer won five medals (one gold, two silver, two bronze) in biathlon. Wolfgang Zimmerer won four in bobsled (one gold, one silver, two bronze). Three medals each went to Alpine skiers **Rosi Mittermaier** (two gold, one silver) and Christa Kinshofer-Güthlein (two silver, one bronze) and bobsledder Peter Utzschneider (one gold, two bronze). *See also* BEER-BAUM, LUDGER; DIETRICH, WILFRIED; HACKL, GEORG; UPHOFF, NICOLE; WINKLER, HANS GÜNTER.

FEDERATED STATES OF MICRONESIA (FSM). After becoming a member of the United Nations in 1991, the Federated States of Micronesia formed a **National Olympic Committee** in 1995. The **International Olympic Committee** recognized Micronesia in 1997. In four Summer Games, the country has entered 14 athletes (eight men, six **women**) and competed in four sports but has yet to come close to winning an **Olympic medal**. Micronesia first competed at the 2000 **Olympic Games** in Sydney, represented by five athletes: two in **athletics** (one man, one woman), two in **swimming** (one man, one woman), and one man in **weightlifting**. It competed in those three sports in each of the next three Summer Games and in 2012 also had one man enter in **wrestling**. The Western Pacific island country located just north of the equator has not yet appeared at the **Olympic Winter Games**. The five-foot, one-inch (155 cm) Micronesian Manuel Minginfel, who bills himself as "The Strongest Man in the Pacific," has competed in weightlifting in all four Olympic Games in addition to being the flagbearer in each at the opening ceremony. In 2000, he competed in the **bantamweight** class but failed to finish. From 2004 to 2012, in the **featherweight** class, he finished 10th of 20 entrants (2004), 11th of 17 (2008), and 10th of 15 (2012). In the 50 meter freestyle swimming event in 2012, Kerson Hadley won his initial **heat**, but his time was not good enough to qualify for the next **round** and he placed 40th of the 58 entrants.

FEDERER, ROGER (SUI–TEN). B. 8 August 1981, Basel, **Switzerland**. Roger Federer is arguably the greatest male **tennis** player of all time and will definitely be inducted into the International Tennis Hall of Fame once he has retired from active play. He became a professional player in 1998, but it was not until 2003 that he won his first Grand Slam **singles** championship. Since then, he has been nearly unbeatable in Grand Slam tournaments, with a total of 17 singles championships from 2003 to 2014. Along with those championships, he was also a losing Grand Slam finalist eight times. He won the **Australian** Open four times, Wimbledon seven times, the **United States** Open five times, and the French Open once. Probably Federer's most remarkable achievement was reaching the semifinal round in 23 consecutive Grand Slam events from 2003 to 2010. No other player in history is even close to that feat. In that time, he reached 10 consecutive Grand Slam finals and 18 of 19 finals from 2005 to 2010. The six-foot, one-inch (185 cm), 176 lb (80 kg) right-hander has a complete game—excellent serve, excellent forehand, excellent backhand, and has a likeable disposition that has made him quite popular among his opponents as well. He has competed in four **Olympic Games**—2000, 2004, 2008, and 2012—and has stated that he would like to play in 2016 before he retires from the sport. He finished fourth in the

2000 singles event, losing to Tommy Haas in the semifinals and Arnaud Di Pasquale in the bronze medal match. In 2004, he lost in the second round in both singles and **doubles**. In 2008, he lost in the quarter-finals of the men's singles, but he and partner Stanislaus Wawrinka won the doubles gold medal. In 2012, he reached the finals but lost in London, at the Wimbledon courts, to British native Andy Murray and had to settle for the silver medal. In 2009, Federer married his long-time girlfriend Mirka Vavrinec, a former professional tennis player whom he met at the 2000 Olympic Games and who has served as Roger's business manager. The couple became parents of twin girls in 2009 and twin boys in 2014.

FENCING. Fencing began as a form of combat and is known to have been practiced well before the birth of Christ. As a sport, fencing began in either the 14th or 15th century, and both **Italy** and **Germany** lay claim to the origins of the sport. In 1570, Henri Saint-Didier of **France** gave names to fencing's major movements, and most of that nomenclature is still used.

Until the 17th century, fencing weapons were large and unwieldy, like combat weapons. However, the combat sword evolved into the **épée** and, somewhat, into the **sabre**. The **foil** was originally a practice weapon for combat and became popular as a sporting weapon in the late 19th century.

The foil is a light, quadrangular, tapering blade with which only hits made with the blade point on the opponent's torso count. The épée, developed from the dueling weapons of European noblemen, is the same length as the foil, but is heavier and has a larger hand guard. Hits must also be made with the tip of the blade, but can be scored over the opponent's entire body. The sabre owes its origins to the Middle Eastern scimitar and the 18th-century cavalry sabre. Hits may be scored with the tip of the blade, with its front edge, or with the last one-third of its back edge. The target area is from the bend of the hips up, including the head and arms.

Fencing was first contested at the 1896 Olympics and is one of only five sports to have been contested at every **Olympic Games**. At the 1896 and 1900 Olympic Games, it was the only sport at which professionals, specifically fencing masters or teachers, were allowed to compete. **Women**'s fencing first appeared in the Olympics in 1924. Today, men compete in the Olympics with three types of swords—the foil, the épée, and the sabre—in both team and individual events, six events in all. Women competed only in foil at the Olympics until 1996, when women's épée was added, and women's sabre was added in 2000. In 28 Summer Olympic competitions, there have been 3,997 athletes (3,180 men, 817 women) from 99 nations who have participated in Olympic fencing.

Electronic scoring has been used for the foil and épée for decades now, while electronic scoring for the sabre made its Olympic debut at Barcelona in 1992.

Fencing is governed worldwide by the Fédération Internationale d'Éscrime, which was formed in 1913 and had 150 affiliated member nations as of 2014. Fencing has been dominated at the Olympics by France and Italy in the foil and épée, and by **Hungary** in the sabre. Italian **Edoardo Mangiarotti** has won the most Olympic fencing medals, 13 (six gold). **Aladár Gerevich** (HUN) has won 10 medals, including a record seven golds. *See also* BACH, THOMAS; FLESSEL-COLOVIC, LAURA ÉLODIE; KÁRPÁTI, RUDOLF; KOVÁCS, PÁL ÁDÁM; NADI, NEDO; SÁGI UJLAKY REJTŐ, ILDIKÓ; VEZZALI, MARIA VALENTINA.

FERGUSON, IAN GORDON (NZL–CAN). B. 20 July 1952, Taumarunui, Manawatu-Wanganui, **New Zealand**. After an undistinguished Olympic debut in 1980, Ian Ferguson retired from **canoeing** and went into business. After a two-year hiatus, the five-foot, 10-inch (179 cm), 187 lb (85 kg) Ferguson came back in 1983 and won a silver medal at the 500 meters at the World Championships. Then in 1984, at the age of 32, he won three gold medals at the Los Angeles Olympics in the K1-500, K2-500, and the K4 event. Paul McDonald joined Ferguson in the last two events, and at the 1988 Olympics they retained the Olympic K2-500 title as well as winning a silver in the K2-1,000. Ferguson's four canoeing gold medals trail only **Gert Fredriksson** among men at the Olympics. Ferguson's son Steven competed in **swimming** in the 2000 Olympics then switched to his father's sport of canoeing and participated in the 2004, 2008, and 2012 Games with a best finish of fifth place in K2-1000 in 2008.

FIELD HOCKEY. *See* HOCKEY (FIELD).

FIGURE SKATING. Figure skating began in the mid- to late-19th century almost concurrently in Europe and North America, but two Americans are responsible for major developments in its history. In 1850, Edward Bushnell of Philadelphia revolutionized skating technology when he refined the use of steel-bladed skates. This allowed the creation of fancy twists and turns on the ice. Another American, Jackson Haines, a ballet master, visited Vienna in the 1860s and added the elements of music and dance to figure skating. Originally, free skating was subordinate to school figures, or the tracing of pretty patterns on the ice.

International figure skating competitions were held in Europe in the 1880s, and the International Skating Union (ISU) was formed in 1892, the first true international governing body of any winter sport (now with 84 members, but representing only 60 nations). Originally men and **women** competed together, with the first world championship being held in what was then and is now St. Petersburg, **Russia** (formerly Leningrad) in 1896. The first women's championship was held in 1906.

Figure skating is the oldest sport on the **Olympic Winter Games** program. It was contested at the London Summer Olympics of 1908 and again in 1920 at the Summer Games in Antwerp. Events for men, women, and **pairs** were contested through 1972. In 1976, **ice dancing**, long a popular event, was added to the program as a fourth event; it had been held as a **demonstration event** in 1968. In 2014, a team competition was added. In 24 Olympic competitions (two summer, 22 winter), there have been 1,572 athletes (747 men, 825 women) from 55 nations who have participated in figure skating.

Scoring has evolved during the century also, as the former predominance of compulsory figures in the scoring gave way in the early 1970s. A short program of free skating was added, primarily to equalize results among skaters who were excellent at compulsories but less so at free skating with those who were poor compulsory skaters but top-notch free skaters. Examples in that era were Beatrix "Trixi" Schuba (AUT), who was an excellent skater in compulsories, but was a relatively poor free skater, and Janet Lynn (USA), who was a superb free skater but was usually beaten by Schuba because of her lesser skill in the compulsories. This gave impetus to the movement to decrease the importance of compulsory figures. At the end of the 1980s, the ISU ruled that compulsory figures would no longer be held at international competitions. They were last contested at the 1990 World Championships and have not been a part of the Olympic figure skating program since 1988.

After a controversial judging decision in the pairs at Salt Lake City in 2002, the ISU overhauled the scoring system again, replacing the time-honored system of 6.0 maximum points and positions decided by majority placements with a system that awards points to successful execution of various elements, with no theoretical limit on the number of points that may be scored.

Since World War II, figure skating has been dominated in the men's and women's **singles** by the **United States**, which has won seven men's gold medals and seven women's gold medals. In pairs and ice dancing, by far the dominant nation has been the **Soviet Union** and its former republics. Since 1964, the Soviet Union (or its former republics) has won every pairs and dance gold medal available except the 1984 ice dancing gold medal, which went to **Great Britain**'s Jayne Torvill and Christopher Dean; the 2002 ice dancing gold medal, won by **France**'s Marina Anissina and Gwendal Peizerat; and both 2010 mixed golds, won by the **Chinese** pair Shen Xue and Zhao Hongbo and the **Canadian** ice dance couple Tessa Virtue and Scott

Moir. In 2014, Meryl Davis and Charlie White won the first gold medal in ice dancing for the United States, but Russia won both the pairs and the new team event. **Gillis Grafström** of **Sweden** (three gold, one silver 1920–1932) and Yevgeny Plyushchenko of Russia (two gold, two silver 2002–2014) are the only skaters to win four medals in figure skating. **Sonja Henie** of **Norway** (1928–1936) and **Irina Rodnina** of the Soviet Union (1972–1980) are the only other skaters with three gold medals in figure skating. *See also* BELOUSOVA, LYUDMILA YEVGENEVNA and OLEG ALEKSEYEVICH PROTOPOPOV; BUTTON, RICHARD TOTTEN; DMITRIYEV, ARTUR VALERYEVICH; TORVILL AND DEAN; WITT, KATARINA.

Carol Heiss (left), gold medalist in 1960 women's figure skating, with her future husband, Hayes Alan Jenkins (right), winner of the 1956 men's figure skating gold medal. Courtesy of Erich Kamper

FIJI (FIJ). Fiji formed a **National Olympic Committee** in 1949 and first competed at the **Olympic Games** in 1956. It has since competed at all the Olympics with the exception of 1964 and 1980. In 13 Summer Games, the South Pacific island nation, officially known as the Republic of Fiji, has entered 79 athletes (59 men, 20 **women**) and participated in nine sports: **archery** (one man), **athletics** (25 men, six women), **boxing** (four men), **cycling** (one woman), **judo** (six men, four women), **sailing** (13 men, one woman), **shooting** (one man), **swimming** (six men, five women), and **weightlifting** (three men, three women).

Fiji has won no **Olympic medals**. Its best Olympic performance to date occurred in 1992, when Fijian Anthony Philp finished 10th of 43 sailors in **windsurfing**. He was the flag-bearer in the opening ceremony in 2000 and again placed 10th in the same class but of only 36 sailors that year. Philp competed in five Olympic Games from 1984 to 2000. His father, Colin, competed for Fiji in three Olympic Games from 1984 to 1992, and Philp's two brothers, David (1992) and Colin, Jr. (1988), also competed in Olympic sailing for Fiji. Other notable performances by Fijian Olympians include Josateki Basalusalu placing equal ninth of 36 *judoka* in the **middleweight** class in 1988; cyclist Kathlyn Ragg, 32nd of 45 entrants in the 1984 women's **road race**; swimmers Carl Probert, 40th of 83 entrants in the 2004 men's 50 meter **freestyle**, 36th of 73 in the 2000 100 meter freestyle, and Caroline Pickering, 35th of 74 in the 2000 women's 50 meter freestyle; Leslie Copeland, 13th of 44 entrants in the 2012 men's **javelin throw**; and Glenn Kable, 13th of 35 entrants in 2008 men's **trap** shooting.

Fiji competed at the **Olympic Winter Games** in both 1988 and 1994, its sole representative on each occasion being a Nordic skier, Rusiate Rogoyawa, and again in 2002, represented by **Alpine skier** Laurence Thoms. Their best result was by Thoms in the **giant slalom** when he finished the course ahead of two other skiers and was placed 55th of the 78 entrants, including 21 skiers who failed to complete the course.

FINANCE COMMISSION. The Finance Commission is one of the most important commissions because the **Olympic Movement**, like all organizations, depends on well-run finances to remain solvent. The Finance Commission was formed in 1967, at a time when the **International Olympic Committee** (IOC) was almost bankrupt. The original chairman was Lord Luke (Second Baron Luke of Pavenham) of **Great Britain**. Currently, the Finance Commission is chaired by Ng Ser Miang of **Singapore**. One of the previous chairmen was **Marc Hodler** (from Switzerland), who in late 1998 spoke to the media after the IOC Session and discussed the problems in the bidding process that led to the **Olympic bribery scandal** of 1999. With the exception of a financial advisor, all members of the Finance Commission are IOC members. On its website, the IOC lists the following as the mandates of the Finance Commission:

> 1) To ensure that the accounting records of the IOC and its subsidiaries are maintained according to International Financial Reporting Standards (IFRS) for the IOC and all its subsidiaries; 2) To ensure that the IOC and its subsidiaries have an efficient and transparent budgeting and financial control process and that the Financial Policies and Procedures approved by the **IOC Executive Board** are respected; and 3) To make recommendations to the IOC Executive Board on the strategy to be followed for its financial investments and then to monitor on a monthly basis through the Treasury and Financial Investment Committee that such strategy is followed or updated based on changing conditions in the financial markets.

FINLAND (FIN). Finland, located in northern Europe, first competed at the 1906 **Intercalated Olympic Games** in Athens and also appeared two years later at the 1908 London **Olympic Games**. Its first **Olympic Winter Games** appearance was in 1924 at Chamonix, although it had two skaters entered in the **figure skating** events in 1920. Since then, Finland's participation has been continuous, never missing an Olympic Games or an Olympic Winter Games.

In 25 Summer Games, Finland has entered 1,594 athletes (1,393 men, 201 **women**) and competed in 26 sports plus the **art competitions**. The sports with the largest participation have been **athletics** (400 men, 80 women), **wrestling** (167 men), **sailing** (118 men, 14 women), **shooting** (116 men, 11 women), and **gymnastics** (95 men, 15 women). Finland (officially the Republic of Finland) has won 311 **Olympic medals** in summer sports (106 gold, 86 silver, 119 bronze) in 13 different sports plus the art competitions, although only 14 of the medals were won by women.

Finland's greatest successes have been achieved in the distance running events in the Summer Games. In those events, led by **Hannes Kolehmainen**, **Paavo Nurmi**, and **Lasse Virén**, Finland has been the preeminent nation, until the recent advent of the African distance runners. Prior to World War II, Finland was also the dominant nation in wrestling. Paavo Nurmi has been the greatest Finnish Olympian, with 12 medals—nine gold and three silver—from 1912 to 1928. He is the only runner to win gold medals at 1,500, 3,000, 5,000, 10,000 meters and cross-country. **Ville Ritola**, a contemporary of Nurmi's in the 1920s, won eight medals—five gold and three silver—in 1924 and 1928 in similar distance races. Hannes Kolehmainen from 1912 to 1924 won four gold medals and one silver medal in races ranging from the cross-country to the **marathon**. Lasse Virén (four gold, 1972–1976) and Volmari Iso-Hollo (two gold, one silver, one bronze, 1932–1936) were two other Finnish distance runners with four medals each. Elmer Niklander, a weight thrower, also won four medals from 1908 to 1924 in the **shot put** and **discus throw** (one gold, two silver, one bronze).

Several Finnish gymnasts also earned four or more medals. Heikki Savolainen competed from 1928 to 1952 and won nine medals—two gold, one silver, and six bronze. He was given the honor of taking the athletes' oath at the Helsinki opening ceremony and Kolehmainen lit the **Olympic flame** there. Although there are 36 athletes who have won six or more gold medals, Savolainen is one of only five Olympians to win that many bronze medals. Paavo Aaltonen (three gold, two bronze, 1948–1952), Veikko Huhtanen (1948, three gold, one silver, one bronze), and Einari Teräsvirta (1932–1948, one gold, three bronze) were the other gymnasts with four or more medals. In one of the rare three-way ties for first place Savolainen, Aaltonen, and Huhtanen all received gold medals for the 1948 **pommelled horse** event. Magnus Wegelius won one silver and three bronze medals for shooting in 1920 and 1924. In 1908, he was a member of the 26-man Finnish gymnastics **all-around** team and won a bronze in that weird event. Two other Finnish summer Olympians won four medals: **freestyle** wrestler **Eino Leino** won a medal in four consecutive years from 1920 to 1932 (gold, silver, two bronze) and shooter Nestor Toivonen (1912–1920, silver, three bronze).

In the Winter Games, Finland has excelled at Nordic skiing and, in the early Games, at **speed skating**. In 22 Winter Games, Finland has entered 723 athletes (572 men, 151 women) and competed in 12 sports. They have won 161 medals (42 gold, 62 silver, 57 bronze) at the Olympic Winter Games and have medaled in each of the 12 sports in which they have participated. Twenty-two athletes have each won four or more medals for Finland in winter sports led by speed skater **Clas Thunberg** and **cross-country skiers Marja-Liisa Hämäläinen-Kirvesniemi**, **Eero Mäntyranta**, and **Veikko Hakulinen** who each have seven. Cross-country skiers Mika Myllylä and Harri Kirvesniemi each have six. **Ski jumper Matti Nykänen**, with five medals (four gold, one silver), has the most of any Olympian in that event. In **Nordic combined**, **Samppa Lajunen** has five medals. No other athlete in that sport has more gold medals than Lajunen's three and only **Felix Gottwald** of **Austria** has more total medals. Finland has also done well in men's **ice hockey** and has won two silver and four bronze medals from 1988 to 2014. Five hockey players, led by National Hockey League star and Finnish team captain Teemu Selänne, each have four medals.

Finland hosted the Games of the XVth **Olympiad** in Helsinki in 1952. They were previously awarded the 1940 Games, which were canceled due to World War II and bid unsuccessfully for the 1936 and 1944 Games. Finland has also had five unsuccessful bids to host the Olympic Winter Games (Lahti, 1964, 1968, 1972; Tampere, 1976; and Helsinki, 2006).

FINWEIGHT. Finweight is the lightest weight class in **taekwondo** competition for both men (54 kg, 119 lb limit) and **women** (46 kg, 101.4 lb limit). It was only contested in 1988 and 1992 when taekwondo was a **demonstration sport**. Juan Moreno of the **United States** finished second both years in the men's class. Monica Torres of **Mexico** was third both years in women's competition. No other Olympic sport uses the finweight weight class nomenclature.

FISCHER-SCHMIDT, BIRGIT (née FISCHER) (GDR/GER–CAN). B. 25 February 1962, Brandenburg, **German Democratic Republic**. Birgit Fischer-Schmidt is considered the greatest **woman canoeist** of all time. Her total of 28 gold medals (1977–1997) at the World Championships has never been matched, and her 12 (eight gold) **Olympic medals** are also a record for all canoeists—men or women. Representing the German Democratic Republic (East Germany), she won the Olympic K1 title in 1980 (as Miss Fischer) and the K2 and K4 in 1988. After a three-year break from competition, during which she gave birth to her second child, she won the K1 in 1992 as a member of the unified **German** team. She won her fifth Olympic gold medal in 1996, as a member of the German K4 team, again competing under her maiden name. At Sydney in 2000, Fischer won gold medals in both the K2 and K4 events, while in Athens in 2004, she won her eighth gold in the K4. In addition to her eight Olympic gold medals, Fischer-Schmidt also won silver medals in the 1988 K1, the 1992 K4, and the 1996 and 2004 K2. The only Olympic race in which she did not medal was the 1996 K1, where she finished fourth. The five-foot, eight-inch (172 cm), 152 lb (69 kg) Fischer is from a canoeing family: her brother Frank was a quadruple world champion, while her ex-husband, Jörg, was a world champion and Olympic silver medalist. Her sister-in-law is Sarina Hülsenbeck, a double Olympic **swimming** champion from 1980. Hülsenbeck's daughter, Fischer's niece, also won a gold medal in canoeing at the Beijing Games in 2008.

FLANAGAN, JOHN JOSEPH (USA/IRL–ATH). B. 28 January 1868, Moortown, Kilbreedy, County Limerick, **Ireland**. D. 4 June 1938, Kilmallack, County Limerick, Ireland. John Flanagan's three successive victories in the **hammer throw** (1900, 1904, 1908) remained an Olympic record for any track and field event until **Al Oerter** won his fourth consecutive gold medal in the **discus throw** in 1968. The five-foot, 10-inch (178 cm), 194 lb (88 kg) Flanagan would almost certainly have won four Olympic titles had the hammer been included in the program at the 1896 Games. Between 1896 and 1909, he improved the world best for the hammer no less than 18 times, setting his first record when he won the British title in 1896, shortly before he immigrated to the **United States**. He competed for the United States at all three of his **Olympic Games**, although he was likely an Irish (British) citizen in 1900. He also was a silver medalist in 1904 in the now obsolete 56-lb weight throw, competed in the discus throw in 1900, 1904, and 1908, finishing fourth in that event in 1904, and was a member of the fifth place U.S. **tug-of-war** team in 1908.

FLESSEL-COLOVIC, LAURA ÉLODIE (FRA–FEN). B. 6 November 1971, Pointe-a-Pitre, Guadeloupe, **France**. Laura Flessel-Colovic has been the top women's **épée fencer** at the **Olympic Games**. This discipline is relatively new for **women**, first appearing on the **Olympic Program** in 1996. But since that time, Flessel-Colovic, known as "The Wasp," has won five **Olympic medals**, including gold in both the individual and team events in 1996. She added an individual bronze in 2000 and an individual silver and team bronze in 2004. She also competed in the Olympic Games in 2008 and 2012 but did not medal in those years. Born on the island of Guadeloupe, she began fencing at age seven. Seeking stronger competition, she immigrated to France in 1990, and in her first year of competition there became French junior champion. In addition to her Olympic successes, Flessel-Colovic, at five-feet, seven-inches (171 cm), 121 lb (55 kg), was individual **épée** World Champion in 1998 and 1999; was on the World Champion épée team in 1998, 2005, and 2008; and was World Cup seasonal champion in 2002 and 2003.

FLOOR EXERCISE. The floor exercise is one of the **gymnastics** events and is held in both men and **women**'s competition. The gymnast performs various acrobatic routines on a 1,200 cm (39 feet) square spring floor mat. The women's floor exercise is done to music accompaniment and may be up to 90 seconds long, while the men's is not performed to music and has a limit of 70 seconds. The event was first held for men at the **Olympic Games** in 1932 and has been contested at each subsequent Olympics. **Nikolay Andrianov** of the **Soviet Union** won the event twice (1972, 1976), was the runner-up in 1980, and is the only three-time men's medalist. Zou Kai of **China** also won the event twice, in 2008 and 2012. The floor exercise has been included in women's Olympic gymnastics since 1952. Among the women, **Larysa Latynina** of the Soviet Union (gold 1956, 1960, 1964) is the only three-time medalist.

FLYWEIGHT. Flyweight is one of the lightest weights in most sports, although some sports also have a **light-flyweight** class. In the **Olympic Games**, it has been contested in **boxing** in 1904 and in each Olympics since 1920. It was the lightest weight class in the boxing tournament with a weight limit of approximately 51 kg (112 lb) until 1968 when a light-flyweight class was instituted. No man has won the flyweight boxing gold medal more than once. Artur Olech of **Poland** (silver 1964, 1968), Leo Rwabwogo of **Uganda** (silver 1972, bronze 1968), and Bolat Zhumadilov of **Kazakhstan** (silver 1996, 2000) have each won two medals in this class. In 2012, when **women**'s boxing was added to the Olympic program, a flyweight class for women was included.

Taekwondo has a flyweight class for both men and women as its lowest weight and has included competition at this weight in all four Olympic Games that the sport has been contested. Chu-Mu Yen of **Chinese Taipei** (gold 2004, bronze 2008) is the only man to win more than one Olympic medal at this weight. Wu Jingyu of **China** was the gold medalist in both 2008 and 2012 and is the only woman to win multiple medals in the taekwondo flyweight class.

The sport of **weightlifting** is yet another Olympic sport with a flyweight class. The men's class was held in each Olympics from 1972 to 1996, and a women's class was held from 2000 to 2012. No man or woman has won more than one medal at this weight.

The fourth Olympic sport that employs a flyweight class is **wrestling**. In 1904, both men's **freestyle** flyweight and light-flyweight competitions were held. From 1948 to 1996, both freestyle and **Greco-Roman** flyweight wrestling were contested in the Olympics. From 1972 to 1996, a light-flyweight class was also held. Petar Kirov of **Bulgaria** (1968, 1972) and Jon Rønningen of **Norway** (1988, 1992) are the only dual gold medalists in Olympic flyweight Greco-Roman wrestling. Šaban Trstena of **Yugoslavia** (gold 1984, silver 1988), Yuji Takada of **Japan** (gold 1976, bronze 1984), and Valentin Yordanov of Bulgaria (gold 1996, bronze 1992) are the only multiple medalist in flyweight freestyle wrestling. A women's flyweight freestyle wrestling class has been held from 2004 to 2012, and Carol Hunyh of **Canada** (gold 2008, bronze 2012), Chiharo Icho of Japan (silver 2004, 2008), and Iryna Merleni-Mykulchyn of the **Ukraine** (gold 2004, bronze 2008) have each medaled twice at this weight.

FOIL. A foil is one of the three weapons used in **fencing** competition. Men's individual foil contests have been conducted at every modern **Olympic Games** since 1896. Men's team foil contests were held in 1904 and at each Games since 1920. **Women**'s individual foil events have been held at the Olympic Games since 1924 and women's team foil events since 1960, although they were not held in 2004. Christian D'Oriola of **France** (1952, 1956) and **Nedo Nadi** of **Italy** (1912, 1920) are the only two-time men's Olympic foil individual gold medalists. D'Oriola, who also won the silver medal in 1948, Giulio Gaudini of Italy (gold 1936, bronze 1928, 1932), and Aleksandr Romankov of the **Soviet Union** (silver 1976, bronze 1980, 1988) are the only three-time Olympic foil individual medalists. In men's team foil competition, Italy and France have each won seven gold medals. Italy has also won five silver medals and one bronze medal. France has also won four silver medals and four bronze medals. The 1976 men's team gold medalists included **Thomas Bach**, the future president of the **International Olympic Committee** (IOC), the only **IOC president** to have been an Olympic gold medalist. In women's individual foil competition, **Valentina Vezzali** of Italy has competed in five Olympic Games (1996–2012) and has won five individual medals (gold 2000, 2004, 2008, silver 1996, bronze 2012) and four team medals (gold 1996, 2000, 2012, bronze 2008). In women's team competition, Italy and the Soviet Union have each won four gold medals. Italy and **Hungary** have each won seven total medals. *See also* ÉPÉE, SABRE.

FOOTBALL, AMERICAN. American football was a **demonstration sport** at the 1932 Olympics. It is not a recognized sport by the **International Olympic Committee** and will not become a part of the **Olympic Program** at any time in the near future.

FOOTBALL, ASSOCIATION (SOCCER). Football (soccer) is the world's most popular sport, played in more countries than any other sport. The World Cup of football, the quadrennial competition played in the even year between Olympics (last in 2014 in **Brazil**), is considered by some to be the most watched single sporting event on the planet, possibly surpassing even the **Olympic Games**. The sport is governed internationally by the Fédération Internationale de Football Association, which was formed in 1904 and had 208 members as of 2014. The origins of football are vague. The Greeks played a game that loosely resembled its modern counterpart, as did the Romans. By the 14th century, it was so popular in **England** that King Edward II issued a proclamation on 13 April 1314 forbidding the game, "forasmuch as there is great noise in the city caused by hustling over large balls from which many evils might arise which God forbid; we commend and forbid, on behalf of the King, on pain of imprisonment, such game to be used in the city of the future." In 1349, Edward III objected to the game because it interfered with the practice of **archery**, necessary for the military strength of the country. Banning the game had little effect, however, as similar edicts had to be issued in 1389 (Richard II), 1401 (Henry IV), 1436 (Henry VIII), 1457 (James II), and again in 1491.

Gradually, despite attempts to ban it, football spread throughout the world, becoming popular almost everywhere, with the **United States** being a notable exception. Football was first contested at the 1900 **Olympic Games**. The sport has been played at every Olympics since, with the exception of 1932 in Los Angeles. In 26 Olympic tournaments, there have been 5,762 (5,160 men, 602 **women**) participants from 90 countries.

The World Cup began in 1930 and brings together the world's top professional players. Olympic eligibility has always been problematic. After World War II, Eastern European countries stated that they had no true professionals, although their players were state supported. Thus they often entered similar teams in both the World Cup and the Olympics, and the Eastern Europeans were dominant in Olympic football from the 1950s until the fall of communism in the early 1990s. Recently, however, eligibility rules have changed, and other countries may be allowed to use some of their professional players who have competed in the World Cup. The problem is not yet fully resolved. Currently (in 2014), professional players may compete at the Olympics providing they are not more than 23 years old, although each team is allowed three exceptions to the age rule. There is some sentiment among **International Olympic Committee** officials to change this and allow all professionals to compete.

Football for women is now becoming more popular, with the first women's World Cup being contested in 1991. Women's football appeared on the **Olympic Program** for the first time in 1996. The United States has dominated women's Olympic football, winning four gold and one silver medal in the five tournaments, with **Christie Pearce-Rampone** of the United States the only person (male or female) to win four medals (three gold, one silver) in Olympic football. *See also* CHASTAIN, BRANDI DENISE; HAMM, MARIEL MARGARET; URUGUAY FOOTBALL TEAMS (1924 AND 1928).

FOOTBALL, AUSTRALIAN RULES (AUSSIE RULES). Australian rules football was a **demonstration sport** at the 1956 Olympics in Melbourne. It is not a recognized sport by the **International Olympic Committee**, is basically played only in **Australia**, and is unlikely to ever appear on the **Olympic Program**.

FOREMAN, GEORGE (USA–BOX). B. 10 January 1949 (some sources list 22 January 1948), Marshall, Texas, **United States**. The six-foot, three-inch (191 cm) George Foreman won the 1968 Olympic **heavyweight boxing** championship at a weight of 218 lb (99 kg). The 1968 Games was one in which several U.S. black athletes **boycotted**, citing various reasons for not competing, but some black athletes who did compete, such as Tommie Smith and John Carlos, staged a mild protest during their medal awards ceremony. In contrast, Foreman, after winning his Olympic title, paraded around the ring waving a small U.S. flag to the delight of many American viewers.

After the Olympics, Foreman quickly turned professional and began knocking out fighters left and right with his powerful punching ability. In 1973, he fought **Joe Frazier** for the heavyweight title, winning easily. Foreman defended the title twice but, on 30 October 1974 in **Zaire, Muhammad Ali** stopped him in eight rounds in a bout that Ali called "The Rumble in the Jungle." Foreman was never a championship factor again in his "first" career, and he retired after a 1977 loss to Jimmy Young. However, 10 years later, in 1987, Foreman, by then weighing close to 300 pounds, began a comeback. Throughout 1990, he was undefeated. In April 1991, he fought for the heavyweight title again and lost a 12-round decision to former Olympian Evander Holyfield. In 1994, however, George defeated Michael Moorer to claim the World Boxing Association and International Boxing Federation world heavyweight championships at the age of 46. Foreman lost those titles in 1995 when he refused to fight certain opponents, as mandated by those governing bodies, and retired. When he began his comeback in the mid-1980s, he also became a popular commercial spokesman for an electronically heated grill dubbed the "George Foreman Lean Mean Fat-Reducing Grilling Machine." He reportedly has earned much more from the sales of the machine than he did in his entire professional boxing career. In 1999, he was paid $137 million for the rights to use his name in lieu of his previous contractual arrangement for a percentage of the sales.

FORMOSA. *See* CHINESE TAIPEI.

FRANCE (FRA). The western European nation of France, officially the French Republic, can be said to be the home of the Modern **Olympic Games**, being the home of **Pierre de Coubertin**, their founder. Not unexpectedly, it has competed at every celebration of the Olympic Games and at every **Olympic Winter Games** along with **Great Britain** and **Italy**. In addition to appearing at all the Olympic Games, France has hosted five Olympic Games, second only to the **United States**. These were the Games of the IInd **Olympiad** in Paris in 1900, the Games of the VIIIth Olympiad in Paris in 1924, the First Olympic Winter Games in Chamonix in 1924, the 10th Olympic Winter Games in Grenoble in 1968, and the 16th Olympic Winter Games in Albertville in 1992. France has also bid unsuccessfully for the 1920 and 1968 Summer Games (Lyon), the 2004 Summer Games (Lille), and the 1992, 2008, and 2012 Summer Games (Paris) and the 2018 Winter Games (Annecy).

In 28 Summer Games, France has entered 5,093 athletes (4,247 men, 846 **women**) and competed in 41 sports plus the **art competitions**. They did not compete in **aeronautics, baseball,** *jeu de paume,* **lacrosse, pelota, racquets, roque,** and **softball.** They have had the most entrants in **athletics** (640 men,

179 women), **fencing** (394 men, 54 women), **rowing** (341 men, 27 women), **cycling** (329 men, 29 women), **gymnastics** (268 men, 81 women), and **swimming** (216 men, 119 women). French athletes have won 726 **Olympic medals** (222 gold, 234 silver, 270 bronze) at the Summer Games in 31 different sports plus the art competitions. France's greatest athletic successes have been in the sports of cycling and fencing, at which it has often been the dominant nation. Fencers Phillippe Catiau and Roger Ducret have each won eight medals (three gold, four silver, one bronze), which is the most of any French athlete at the Summer Games. Shooter Léon Moreaux has seven and seven others have six each. Five of them are fencers with the other two being **tennis** player **Max Décugis** and shooter Maurice LeCoq. Eight more have five medals and 16 others have four each. Among the French Olympians with four medals is **Algerian**-born Alain Mimoun, winner of the 1956 **marathon**.

In 22 Winter Games, France has entered 823 athletes (621 men, 202 women) and competed in all 16 sports—one of only two countries to do so (Italy being the other)—with the most entrants in **Alpine skiing** (90 men, 75 women), **ice hockey** (110 men), **cross-country skiing** (80 men, 22 women), and **bobsledding** (94 men). They have won 109 medals at the Winter Games (31 gold, 31 silver, 47 bronze) and have medaled in 11 sports. Their top medalist in winter sports is Martin Fourcade, who earned four medals in the **biathlon** in 2010 and 2014. Ten others have three each including their most famous winter sports athlete, Alpine skier **Jean-Claude Killy**, who won three gold medals in 1968 and is the only French athlete with three gold medals in the Winter Games. *See also* BERLIOUX, MONIQUE LIBOTTE; CHARPENTIER, ROBERT; FLESSEL-COLOVIC, LAURA ÉLODIE; MASSON, PAUL MICHEL PIERRE ADRIEN; MORELON, DANIEL YVES; PARISI, ANGELO.

FRASER, DAWN LORRAINE (AUS–SWI). B. 4 September 1937, Balmain, Sydney, New South Wales, **Australia**. Arguably the greatest female **sprint swimmer** ever, Dawn Fraser was the first **woman** swimmer to win eight **Olympic medals**, a record since surpassed by several swimmers. She won four gold and four silver medals at the **Olympic Games** of 1956, 1960, and 1964, including three successive golds in the 100 meter freestyle, a record for any Olympic swimming event equaled only by **Krisztina Egerszegi** (HUN) in the 200 **backstroke** in 1988–1996. The five-foot, eight-inch (172 cm), 148 lb (67 kg) Fraser was denied the opportunity of adding to her medal total when she received a lengthy suspension following misbehavior at the 1964 Games. Dawn Fraser set 27 individual and 12 relay world records. During her career, she won 30 Australian championships (23 individual and 7 team), and at the British Empire and **Commonwealth Games**, she won eight medals (six gold and two silver). She represented Balmain in the New South Wales Parliament from 1988 to 1991.

FRAZIER, JOSEPH WILLIAM "SMOKIN' JOE" (USA–BOX). B. 12 January 1944, Beaufort, South Carolina, **United States**. D. 7 November 2011, Philadelphia, Pennsylvania, United States. The six-foot tall (183 cm) Joe Frazier won a gold medal as a **heavyweight boxer** at the 1964 **Olympic Games** at a weight of 196 lb (89 kg). He first won the professional heavyweight World Championship in 1970 by stopping Jimmy Ellis in five rounds. He successfully defended the title four times before being knocked out by former Olympian **George Foreman**. Frazier also fought three tremendous battles with another ex-Olympic champion, **Muhammad Ali**. The first, in 1971, was the fight of the century, a battle of undefeated heavyweight champions, and Frazier won by a decision in 15 rounds. Frazier was on the losing end in the next two fights, but all three were great spectacles. After losing his heavyweight title, he continued to fight for a few years before retiring in the mid-1970s. Despite the acclaim accorded Muhammad Ali, which somewhat diminished Frazier's appeal, his opponent knew of his greatness, describing him as follows: "Fighting Joe Frazier is the closest thing to death that I know of. Of all the men I fought in boxing, including Sonny Liston and George Foreman, the roughest and toughest was Joe Frazier. If God ever calls me to a Holy War, I want Joe Frazier fighting beside me."

FREDRIKSSON, GERT FRIDOLF (SWE–CAN). B. 21 November 1919, Nyköping, Södermanland, **Sweden**. D. 5 July 2006, Nyköping, Södermanland,

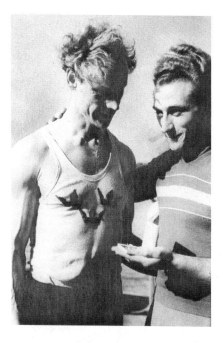

Gert Fredriksson of Sweden (left), considered the greatest male canoeist in Olympic history. Courtesy of Erich Kamper

Sweden. With eight medals (six gold, one silver, one bronze) won between 1948 and 1960, Gert Fredriksson is the most successful male **canoeist** in Olympic history. He was at his best in the K1 1,000 meters, winning a gold medal at three successive Games (1948–1956) and a bronze in 1960, and in the K1 10,000 meters, in which he won two gold medals (1948, 1956) and a silver (1952). He also won a gold medal in the K2 1,000 in 1960. The five-foot, nine-inch (176 cm), 159 lb (72 kg) athlete is one of only 25 Olympians to have won gold medals at four or more consecutive **Olympic Games**. At the World Championships, he won four individual titles and a further three in the **relay**. In 1956, Fredriksson was awarded the Mohammed Taher Trophy by the **International Olympic Committee**. *See also* Appendix V, "Awards of the International Olympic Committee."

FRÉDY, PIERRE. *See* COUBERTIN, BARON PIERRE DE.

FREE PISTOL. Free pistol (officially known as 50 meter pistol) **shooting** at a distance of 50 meters is one of the events contested in **Olympic Games** shooting competition. It was first contested for men in 1900 and then in 1906, 1912, and 1920. In 1908, the distance was 50 yards. From 1936 to 1964, it was held for men only, but from 1968 to 1980, it was open to both men and **women**. Since 1984, it has again been contested for men only, while women shooters have different events. Jin Jong-O of **Korea** (2008, 2012) is the only repeat gold medalist in Olympic free pistol shooting. He was also a silver medalist in 2004 and is one of only three three-time medalists in this event.

FREESTYLE. Freestyle is a term used in **swimming, wrestling**, and **skiing**. In swimming, the swimmer in a freestyle event may use any stroke but usually the front crawl is used as that is the fastest. Distances for Olympic freestyle swimming races range from 50 meters to 800 meters for women and 50 meters to 1,500 meters for men. Freestyle relays for both men and women are also contested, and in the **medley** races, freestyle is the last of four strokes used.

In Olympic wrestling, two **disciplines** are contested for men—**Greco-Roman** and freestyle—while **women** are limited to freestyle. In freestyle wrestling, holds below the waist are permitted, while in Greco-Roman wrestling they are not.

A third Olympic competition described as freestyle is freestyle skiing. It is considered a separate sport from **Alpine skiing** and **cross-country skiing** and involves acrobatic maneuvers. It was first added to the Olympic program in 1988, and in 2014 it had five disciplines—**moguls, aerials, halfpipe**, slope-style, and **skicross**.

FREESTYLE SKIING. Freestyle skiing was held at the 1988 **Olympic Winter Games** as a **demonstration sport**. In 1992, **moguls** was contested as a full-medal sport in Albertville, with **aerials** and ballet contested as demonstration events. In Lillehammer in 1994, both moguls and aerials were full-medal events. The moguls event consists of a timed race down a short course made up entirely of small hills or bumps, called *moguls*. The skier receives a point score for style, which is added to a point score for the time, to derive an overall score. Aerials is a jumping event in which skiers take off from an elevated platform after a short run and then execute intricate **gymnastics**-like maneuvers in the air. The contest is decided by point scores awarded by judges. The third event of freestyle skiing is ballet, but that event has not yet appeared on the **Olympic Program**, although it was demonstrated in 1988 and 1992. In 2010 at Vancouver, a third Olympic event was contested in freestyle skiing, **skicross**. The event is an analogue of snowboard cross, contested by two to four skiers racing down a specially prepared course in a single elimination tournament. Although the event is similar to an **Alpine skiing** event, it was included as part of the freestyle skiing program. In 2014, two more events were added to the Winter Olympics freestyle competition—**halfpipe** and slopestyle. Halfpipe is similar to the snowboarding halfpipe competition except that contestants use skis rather than snowboards.

Slopestyle is similar to **downhill** skiing except that the skiers perform several aerial maneuvers while descending the hill. Freestyle is considered a **discipline** of the sport of skiing by the **International Olympic Committee** and, as such, is governed by the Fédération Internationale de Ski. In seven Winter Games, 627 athletes (359 men, 268 women) from 41 nations have taken part in freestyle skiing. **Kari Traa** of **Norway** is the only freestyle skier to win as many as three Olympic medals in the events. Competing in moguls, she won bronze in 1998, gold in 2002, and silver in 2006.

FRENCH EQUATORIAL AFRICA. *See* CENTRAL AFRICAN REPUBLIC; CHAD; GABON.

FRENCH GUINEA. *See* GUINEA.

FRENCH POLYNESIA. French Polynesia is an overseas territory of **France**. Nearly 75 percent of the population lives on the largest and best-known island, Tahiti. The nation of French Polynesia is an archipelago of 130 islands and coral atolls in the South Pacific, only 25 of which are inhabited. Independently as Tahiti, it has affiliations with 13 **International Federations: aquatics (swimming, diving, water polo), archery, athletics, basketball, boxing, football, judo, sailing, table tennis, taekwondo,**

triathlon, volleyball, and **weightlifting**. **International Olympic Committee** recognition for either Tahiti or French Polynesia is a slim possibility in the near future, as the nation does have a **National Olympic Committee** and participates in the South Pacific Mini-Games.

FRENCH SUDAN. *See* MALI.

FRENCH WEST AFRICA. *See* BENIN; BURKINA FASO; CÔTE D'IVOIRE; GUINEA; MALI; MAURITANIA; NIGER; SENEGAL.

FRIENDSHIP GAMES. Shortly after the **Soviet Union** decided to **boycott** the 1984 Los Angeles **Olympic Games** and other Eastern bloc nations had followed suit, it declared it would stage alternative competitions. These Friendship Games were held in nine boycotting nations (**Bulgaria, Cuba, Czechoslovakia**, East Germany, **Hungary, Mongolia**, North Korea, **Poland**, and the Soviet Union) between June and September 1984, although most were held in the Soviet Union in August, shortly after the conclusion of the Olympic Games. Apart from the host nations, other boycotting nations that competed were **Afghanistan, Angola, Ethiopia**, South Yemen, and **Vietnam**. However, other nations were also welcome, and even some medalists from the **United States** and West Germany entered. But competition was dominated by the Soviet Union, which won 282 medals, including 126 golds. Several world records were broken, notably in **weightlifting** (30), but also **swimming** (five) and track and field (one). *See also* GERMAN DEMOCRATIC REPUBLIC; KOREA, DEMOCRATIC PEOPLE'S REPUBLIC OF; LIBERTY BELL CLASSIC.

FU MINGXIA (CHN–DIV). B. 16 August 1978, Wuhan, Hubei, **China**. China's Fu Mingxia was the top female **diver** of the 1990s. She has been at her best on the **platform**, winning the gold **Olympic medal** in that event in 1992 and 1996, and she was World Champion in 1991 and 1994. In 1996, Fu won both the **springboard** and platform at the Olympics, duplicating the feats of Vicky Draves (USA 1948), **Pat McCormick** (USA 1952, 1956), and **Ingrid Engel-Gulbin-Krämer** (GDR 1960), who also won both events at the same Olympics. The diminutive five-foot, three-inch (160 cm), 106 lb (48 kg) Fu retired briefly after the 1996 Olympics, but returned to compete in the 2000 Olympics, defending her springboard gold medal and winning a silver medal in the new synchronized springboard event.

G

GABON (GAB). Gabon is located on the west coast of Central Africa and was originally a part of French Equatorial Africa until its independence in 1960 when it became officially the Gabonese Republic. The new nation formed a **National Olympic Committee** in 1965, but did not compete at the Olympics until 1972, and has participated in nine **Olympic Games**, in 1972, 1984, and each subsequent Summer Games. It has never had an athlete compete at the **Olympic Winter Games**. There have been 45 Gabonese Olympic athletes (37 men, eight **women**) and they have competed in five sports: **athletics** (six men, five women), **boxing** (12 men), **football** (15 men), **judo** (two men, three women), and **taekwondo** (two men). Gabon's first **Olympic medal** was won by Anthony Obame who won the silver medal in the taekwondo **heavyweight** class in 2012. Gabonese *judoka* Mélanie Engoang competed in four Olympics and had a best finish of equal ninth of 20 entrants in the 1996 **middleweight** class. The men's football team was 12th of 16 teams in 2012, a notable achievement because just qualifying to compete in the Olympic tournament is an estimable feat. **Featherweight** boxer Serge Bouemba received a **bye** and then won his next bout to finish equal ninth of 48 contestants in 1988. Two Gabonese **sprinters** (Antoine Boussombo, men's 100 meters and also 200 meters, 2000 and Ruddy Zang-Milama, 100 meters in both 2008 and 2012) each qualified for the second **round** before being eliminated from further competition.

GAMBIA, THE (GAM). The Gambia's **National Olympic Committee** was formed in 1972 and recognized by the **International Olympic Committee** in 1976. The West African nation, the smallest country on the African continent, officially known as the Republic of the Gambia, has competed at each Summer **Olympic Games** since 1984, but has never competed at the **Olympic Winter Games**. It has yet to win an Olympic medal. There have been 29 Gambian athletes (22 men, seven **women**) who have competed at the Olympic Games—one man in **boxing**, three men in **wrestling**, and the others (18 men, seven women) in **athletics**. The country's best-known athlete has been 400 meter runner Dawda Jallow, who competed in four Olympic Games from 1984 to 1996, made the 1988 quarter-finals in that event, and carried its flag at the opening ceremony in 1988, 1992, and 1996. Other Gambian Olympic successes include Adama Damballey, who won his first bout in **welterweight freestyle** wrestling before being eliminated, and **sprinters** Amie N'Dow (1984 women's 200 meters), Jaysuma Saidy Ndure (2004 men's 100 and 200 meters), Saruba Colley (2012 women's 100 meters), and Su Wai'bou Sanneh (2012 men's 100 meters) who each qualified in their first **round** but lost in the second round.

GAMES OF THE NEW EMERGING FORCES (GANEFO). These were very controversial **Regional International Games**. In the summer of 1962, Jakarta hosted the Asian Games, but it refused to issue visas to athletes from Taiwan and **Israel**. For this, the **International Olympic Committee** (IOC) suspended the **Indonesian National Olympic Committee** (NOC). Unfortunately for the IOC, similar actions had recently been taken by **France** and the **United States**, which refused to issue visas to East German athletes competing in those countries. Those nations were not suspended. In response to the IOC actions, Indonesian President Sukarno proposed the Games of the New Emerging Forces in early 1963 to "promote the development of sports in new emerging nations so as to cement friendly relations among them." The original conference on these Games occurred in April 1963, with the following nations present: **Cambodia, China, Democratic People's Republic of Korea, Guinea, Indonesia, Iraq, Mali**, North **Vietnam, Pakistan**, the **Soviet Union**, and the **United Arab Republic**. Sukarno denounced the IOC in his opening speech and also noted, "Let us frankly declare that sport has something to do with politics. And Indonesia now proposes to mix sport with politics." GANEFO was an obvious attempt to compete against the **Olympic Games**. GANEFO I was held in November 1963 in Jakarta, Indonesia, with 50 nations present. The problem was that China, North Korea, and North Vietnam were present, none of which were recognized by several of the **International Federations** organizing the sports at GANEFO, notably the International Amateur Athletic Federation (athletics) and the Fédération Internationale de Natation (swimming). Indonesian athletes also competed, quite naturally, since they hosted the Games. In response, the IOC banned the athletes who competed at GANEFO, most notably those from Indonesia and North Korea, from participating at the 1964 Tokyo Olympics. (China and North Vietnam could not compete at Tokyo, as they did not have recognized NOCs.) Indonesia and North Korea responded by demanding that their athletes be reinstated or their entire teams would **boycott** the Tokyo Olympics. The athletes were not reinstated, and the two nations did not compete at Tokyo, although this happened after North Korean athletes were already in **Japan**. One athlete, North Korean runner Sin Kim-Dan, was sorely missed, as she was the world record holder in the 800 meters for **women** and would have been favored at Tokyo.

Sukarno was ousted from power in 1965, and the IOC rescinded its suspension of Indonesia's NOC. GANEFO II went on, however, in Phnom Penh, **Cambodia**, in 1966, and again North Korea competed. For this, North Korea was also suspended from the 1968 Olympic Games at **Mexico** City. By then, however, the idea of the Games of the New Emerging Forces had lost favor. They were not held again.

GAMES OF THE OLYMPIAD. *See* OLYMPIAD.

GAO LING (CHN–BDM). B. 14 March 1979, Wuhan, Hubei, **China**. Gao Ling is one of the world's best **badminton doubles** players. She has won more medals in Olympic badminton competition than any other player—male or female. The five-foot, six-inch (169 cm), 134 lb (61 kg) Gao won the gold medal in **mixed doubles** in 2000 and 2004 with partner Zhang Jun, a bronze in **women**'s doubles in 2000 with Qin Yuyuan, and a silver in women's doubles in 2004 with Huang Sui. In her homeland in Beijing in 2008, she entered the mixed doubles with a new partner, Zheng Bo, but they were upset in their first round match. Gao has also won four gold medals in doubles events at the World Championships from 2001 to 2006, a gold medal at the 2006 World Cup, five gold medals at the Uber Cup (also known as the World Team Championships for Women), and three more gold medals at the Sudirman Cup (a mixed team championship event).

GAY GAMES. In 1980, former **United States** Olympic **decathlete** Tom Waddell conceived the Gay Games. He saw them as a way to make homosexuality acceptable in the sports community, but also to make sports acceptable in the homosexual community. He planned to hold the first Gay **Olympic Games** in 1982, but the use of the word "Olympic" was heavily opposed by both the **International Olympic Committee** and the U.S. Olympic Committee, eventually forcing Waddell to drop it. Now simply called the Gay Games, the 1982 San Francisco event was a great success. The games have since been held every four years in New Orleans (United States, 1986), Vancouver (Canada, 1990), New York (1994), Amsterdam (Netherlands, 1998), Sydney (Australia, 2002), Chicago (United States, 2006), and Köln (Germany, 2010). The most recent games were held in Cleveland (United States) from 9–16 August 2014.

Many of the sports held at the Gay Games are the same as those at the **Olympic Games**, but non-Olympic sports are also contested, such as **billiards**, **body building**, **dance sport**, inline skating, martial arts, powerlifting, and sports climbing. Although there are no separate Winter Gay Games, **ice hockey** and **figure skating** are held as well. In some cases, sports events at the Gay Games deviate from international rules, for example, allowing same-sex **pairs** in figure skating and dance sport.

Like the Olympic Games, the Gay Games do not select participants based on sexual orientation. In fact, any athlete willing to participate may compete, unless not allowed by the **International Federation** of the sport involved. The last few Gay Games have attracted over 10,000 competitors, thus being similar in number of athletes to the Olympic Games. The Gay Games are organized by the Federation of Gay Games, which is headed by one male and one female copresident. As of 2014, the male is Kurt Dahl (USA) and the female position was vacant.

GEESINK, ANTONIUS JOHANNES "ANTON" (NED–JUD). B. 6 April 1934, Utrecht, **Netherlands**. D. 27 August 2010, Utrecht, Netherlands. With the introduction of **judo** to the **Olympic Program** in 1964, Anton Geesink provided one of the surprises of the Games by winning the **open class**. He had, however, earlier destroyed the myth of **Japanese** invincibility by becoming the first non-Japanese *judoka* to win a world title, in 1961. Between 1953 and 1967, the six-foot, five-inch (196 cm), 265 lb (120kg) Geesink won 13 European titles in the open and unlimited classes. In 1987, he became a member of the **International Olympic Committee** and served until his death.

GENDER VERIFICATION. Men and **women** compete in most Olympic events separately. The exceptions are few, but they have competed against each other in certain **shooting** events, **equestrian events**, and **sailing** and also compete concurrently in **figure skating** (**pairs** and **ice dancing**). They have also competed concurrently in **mixed doubles** in **tennis** and **badminton**, and did so in a few discontinued sports (**croquet** and **motorboating**).

The two sexes compete separately in most events because of the physical advantage claimed by men. Men posing as women would have a significant competitive advantage over natural women. At the 1936 **Olympic Games**, Dora Ratjen of **Germany** finished fourth in the women's **high jump**, but was later found (1938) to have been a man raised as a girl. There were several other similar examples in the 1930s, notably **Czechoslovakia**'s Ždenka Koubková, who competed in track and field events internationally, but never competed at the Olympics. The 1932 women's 100 meter Olympic champion was Stanisława Walasiewicz of **Poland**. After her death in 1980, an autopsy revealed she had mixed sexual characteristics.

In the 1960s, concern about this problem of men posing as women to gain a competitive advantage led to the introduction of gender verification, at the time called *sex testing*. At that time, several of the women track and field athletes were suspected of being genetically male. Sex testing began at the 1966 European Athletics Championships and was first used at the Olympics in 1968. At the 1966 European Athletics Championships, Ewa Kłobukowska of Poland was disqualified from further international competition. Kłobukowska had won a gold and bronze medal at the 1964 **Olympic Games**. Because of the obvious emotional and psychological trauma engendered by such an announcement, all subsequent sex testing results have not been released publicly.

From 1968 to 1988, all women wishing to compete in the Olympics were required to undergo sex testing. (With one exception, Princess Anne of **Great Britain**, who competed in the 1976 Olympics in the equestrian events.) Testing was initially done by obtaining a buccal smear, or a scraping of the cells of the inner wall of the mouth. The cells were examined for the presence of a Barr body, which occurs almost exclusively in females. (Females are genetically labeled as XX, while men are labeled as XY, those being the classifications of the respective sex chromosomes. The second X chromosome possessed by women contains a structure called the Barr body.)

Though some men did attempt to breach the rules and compete as women, the entire subject of mixed sexual characteristics is a highly complex and emotional one. A number of people with mixed sexual identity may have elected to compete as women for psychological reasons. In addition, doctors typically label babies with indeterminate genitalia as women. And in certain cases of mixed sex classification, some people who would be considered women lack a Barr body and would thus have been disqualified. Because of these problems, the test was later changed and the buccal smear was no longer used. Women were then cleared for international competition by doctors after simply undergoing a physical examination. In the late 1980s, this method was replaced by a polymerase chain reaction evaluation, looking for the Y-linked SRY gene (sex-determining region Y), and this method was used at both the 1992 and 1996 Olympics.

But problems still existed. It has been noted that the tests fail to exclude all potential impostors, are discriminatory against women with disorders of sexual development, and can be psychologically devastating for a female athlete failing such a test. Thus, during the 1996 **International Olympic Committee** (IOC) World Conference on Women and Health, the IOC passed a resolution "to discontinue the current process of gender verification during the Olympic Games." The IOC **Athletes' Commission** recommended to the IOC **Executive Board** in January 1999 that gender identification should be eliminated, and this decision was ratified by the IOC Executive Board in June 1999.

However, the IOC **Medical Commission** addressed the issue of sex reassignment in 2003–2004. Its recommendations were approved by the IOC Executive Board in May 2004. The conclusions of this study were that

1. Individuals undergoing sex reassignment of male to female before puberty should be regarded as girls and women (female);
2. Individuals undergoing sex reassignment of female to male before puberty should be regarded as boys and men (male);
3. Individuals undergoing sex reassignment from male to female after puberty (and vice versa) should be eligible for participation in female or male competitions, respectively, under the following conditions: a) surgical anatomical changes have been completed, including external genitalia changes and gonadectomy; b) legal recognition of the assigned sex has been conferred by the appropriate official authorities; c) hormonal therapy appropriate for the assigned sex has been administered in a verifiable manner and for a sufficient length of time to minimize gender-related advantages in sport competitions; d) eligibility should begin no sooner than two years after gonadectomy; and
4. Evaluation will occur on a confidential case-by-case basis.

The problem of gender in international sport again became prominent at the 2009 World Athletics Championships, when the women's 800 meter event was won by **South African** Castor Semenya. Questions were raised about the athlete's gender, and after the championship, it was revealed that Athletics South Africa had performed gender verification tests on Semenya prior to the meet and had not released the results.

GENERAL ASSOCIATION OF INTERNATIONAL SPORTS FEDERATIONS (GAISF). *See* SPORTACCORD.

GEORGIA (GEO). For most residents of the **United States** the place name "Georgia" denotes a state in the southeastern part of the country, but for most of the rest of the world, the place name Georgia denotes a country on the Europe–Asia border that was once part of the **Soviet Union**. Many of those Georgian athletes competed in the **Olympic Games** and **Olympic Winter Games** from 1952 to 1988 for the Soviet Union. Its top sports were **judo** and **wrestling** and, in fact, Georgian *judoka* won more medals for the Soviet Union than any other republic, including **Russia**. The most famous Georgian Olympic athletes under Soviet rule were wrestlers David Gobedzhishvili and Levan Tediashvili and track and field athletes **Viktor Saneyev** and Robert Shavlakadze. Georgian athletes were also present at

Barcelona in 1992 as members of the Unified Team. Georgia's first Olympic appearance as an independent nation occurred in 1994 at Lillehammer, where it was represented by five athletes who competed in **luge, Alpine skiing**, and **ski jumping**. Georgia has since competed at all Olympic Games and Olympic Winter Games.

In five Summer Games, Georgia has entered 124 athletes (101 men, 23 **women**) and participated in 18 sports, with more than half of their athletes competing in judo (25 men) and wrestling (39 men). They also had four men and six women in athletics, 10 men in **boxing**, and nine men in **weightlifting**. Officially known as the Republic of Georgia and located in both Europe and Asia, they have won 25 **Olympic medals** (six gold, five silver, 14 bronze), all at the Summer Olympics. Three athletes have each won two medals for Georgia since independence: Giorgi Asanidze in **light-heavyweight** weightlifting (2000 bronze, 2004 gold), Eldar Kurtanidze in **freestyle** wrestling (1996 light-heavyweight bronze, 2000 **heavyweight** bronze), and Giorgi Gogshelidze, men's heavyweight freestyle wrestling (both bronze, 2008, 2012).

In men's judo, Georgia has won six Olympic medals: Lasha Shavdatuashvili (gold 2012 **half-lightweight**), Zurab Zviadauri (gold 2004 **middleweight**), Irakli Tsirekidze (gold 2008 middleweight), Nestor Khergiani (silver 2004 **extra-lightweight**), Georgios Vazagkasvili (bronze 2000 half-lightweight), and Soso Liparteliani (bronze 1996 **half-middleweight**).

Georgian wrestlers have won 15 medals. In freestyle wrestling, in addition to the four won by Kurtanidze and Gogshelidze, Georgian winners have been Vladimer Khinchegashvili (silver **featherweight** 2012), Otar Tushishvili (bronze **welterweight** 2008), Revaz Mindorashvili (gold light-heavyweight 2008), Dato Marsagishvili (bronze heavyweight 2012), and Davit Modzmanashvili (silver **super-heavyweight** 2012). In **Greco-Roman** style wrestling, Georgia has won six Olympic medals. Winners were lightweights Akaki Chachua (bronze 2000) and Revaz Lashki (silver 2012), welterweight Manuchar Tskhadaia (bronze 2012), middleweight Manuchar Kvirkvelia (gold 2008), light-heavyweight Mukhran Vakhtangadze (bronze 2000), and heavyweight Ramaz Nozadze (silver 2004). Georgia's other Olympic medalists include heavyweight boxer Vladimir Chanturia (2000 bronze) and Nino Salukvadze, women's **air pistol** (2008, bronze; she also won gold and silver medals in **shooting** in 1988 as a representative of the Soviet Union).

In six Winter Games, Georgia has entered 15 athletes (11 men, four women) and competed in Alpine skiing, **figure skating**, luge, and ski jumping. Their best performances were by Alpine skiers Iason Abramashvili who finished 22nd of 115 competitors in the 2014 men's **slalom** and 29th of 82 in the 2006 **giant slalom** and Zurab Dzhidzhisvili who was 14th of 38 in the 1998 men's **combined**. Figure skater Elena Gedevanishvili finished 10th in

2006 and 14th in 2010 in the women's singles. Georgia's saddest Olympic moment occurred on 12 February 2010 when luger Nodar Kumaritashvili was fatally injured when he crashed on his final training run.

Borjomi, Georgia, bid unsuccessfully to host the 2014 Olympic Winter Games.

GEORGIADIS, KONSTANTINOS "KOSTAS." B. 2 October 1959, Athens, Greece. Kostas Georgiadis received a doctorate in sports science from the Johannes Gutenberg Universität of Mainz, Germany. In 1992, he became dean of the **International Olympic Academy** and is now an honorary dean. He is also a professor at the University of the Peloponnese and was its vice rector from 2010 to 2014. Currently, he is dean of the Faculty of Human Movement and Quality of Life Sciences, University of Peloponnese and director of the Master's degree Programme Olympic Studies, Olympic Education, Organisation and Management of Olympic Events. In 2006, he was honored as emeritus professor of the Capital Institute of Physical Education in Beijing, China. He has published books on the **Olympic Truce**, the Revival of the Olympic Games, and the history of the International Olympic Academy. Since 2000, he has been a member of the **International Olympic Committee**'s (IOC) Commission for Culture and Olympic Education. He was also a member of the **IOC Coordination Commission** for the First **Youth Olympic Games** in Singapore in 2010 and the Executive Board of the Athens 2004 **Organizing Committee for the Olympic Games.** He joined the **International Society of Olympic Historians** in 1992 and is a lifetime member. Since 1992, he has been a member of its Executive Committee and was honored by them in 2007 with the Vikelas Plaque for contributions to Olympic research.

GEREVICH, ALADÁR (HUN–FEN). B. 16 May 1910, Jászbéreny, Jász-Nagykun-Szolnok, Austria-**Hungary**. D. 14 May 1991, Budapest, Hungary. Aladár Gerevich was one of the greatest Olympic **fencers**. His six successive gold medals in the **sabre** team event at every Games from 1932 to 1960 stand as a record for any Olympic sport. In the sabre, he also won individual gold in 1948, silver in 1952, and bronze in 1936, and a further bronze in the **foil** team event in 1952. The five-foot, nine-inch (177 cm), 172 lb (78 kg) Gerevich confirmed his reputation as the world's greatest sabreur with three individual titles at the World Championships (1935, 1951, 1955). His wife (Erna Bogen-Bogáti), son (Pál Gerevich), and father-in-law (Albert Bógathy) were also Olympic medalists.

GERMAN DEMOCRATIC REPUBLIC (GDR). The German Democratic Republic (frequently referred to as East Germany) was formed on 7 October 1949 after the division of **Germany** into two countries after World War II.

The problem of the "Two Germanies" perplexed the **International Olympic Committee** (IOC) for two decades. From 1952 until 1964, the two nations purportedly competed at the Olympics as a single combined team. However, it should be noted that in 1952, a combined German team was planned and envisioned by the IOC, but the German Democratic Republic refused to start in an all-German team, and no East German athletes competed on the 1952 "combined" team. In 1968 at **Mexico** City and Grenoble, the two Germanys competed as separate teams, but under the same banner and using the same anthem and flag. The German Democratic Republic, however, was forced to use the name East Germany in 1968, a name that it detested. At the IOC Session in 1968, full recognition was given to the German Democratic Republic, and it was allowed to compete at the Olympics, beginning in 1972, using its correct name, with its own anthem, emblems, and uniforms.

Between 1956 and 1988, the German Democratic Republic developed into a true Olympic powerhouse. Beginning with the 1968 Olympics, it was one of the three most powerful sporting nations in the world, with the **United States** and the **Soviet Union**. The German Democratic Republic, competing as an independent nation, won 519 **Olympic medals**, 409 at the **Olympic Games** (153 gold, 129 silver, 127 bronze) and 110 at the **Olympic Winter Games** (39 gold, 36 silver, 35 bronze). Although the German Democratic Republic only competed in 11 Olympics, their total of 519 medals is 10th best among all nations. The sporting leviathan was fully state supported, with the help of a highly advanced sports medicine program, and the athletes were treated royally in their country. After the reunification of Germany, it was revealed that the German Democratic Republic's sports medical program had helped develop many of its athletes by the use of drugs.

In five Summer Games, East Germany entered 1,129 athletes (761 men, 368 **women**) and competed in 21 sports with most of their participants in **athletics** (127 men, 110 women), **rowing** (101 men, 62 women), **swimming** (45 men, 76 women), **canoeing** (53 men, 17 women), and **handball** (40 men, 20 women). Several of their athletes turned in outstanding performances, with swimmers **Kornelia Ender** (four gold, four silver 1972–1976) and husband **Roland Matthes** (four gold, two silver, two bronze 1968–1976) each earning eight medals. **Gymnast** Karin Janz won seven medals (two gold, three silver, two bronze, 1968–1972). Swimmer **Kristin Otto** won six gold medals, all in 1988. Andrea Pollack also won six medals in swimming (three gold, three silver 1976–1980). **Sprinter** Renate Stecher won six medals (three gold, two silver, one bronze 1972–1976) as did canoeist Rüdiger Helm (three gold, three bronze 1976–1980). Ines Diers won five (two gold, two silver, one bronze) in swimming in 1980. Gymnasts Roland Bruckner (one gold, one silver, three bronze, 1976–1980) and Erika Zuchold (four silver, one bronze, 1968–1972) each won five medals. In addition, 11 other representatives of the German Democratic Republic won four medals each in summer sports, including **Birgit Fischer-Schmidt** who won four medals (three gold, one silver) for the German Democratic Republic in 1980 and 1988 in canoeing and then won eight more (five gold, three silver) as a representative of united Germany from 1992 to 2004. Twenty-four others won three medals each, including Roswitha Krause who won a swimming silver medal in 1968 and then two more as a member of the handball team in 1976 and 1980.

In six Winter Games, East Germany entered 232 athletes (164 men, 68 women) and competed in 10 sports: **Alpine skiing** (one man), **biathlon** (22 men), **bobsledding** (21 men), **cross-country skiing** (16 men, 21 women), **figure skating** (16 men, 18 women), **ice hockey** (18 men), **luge** (25 men, 12 women), **Nordic combined** (14 men), **ski jumping** (20 men), and **speed skating** (11 men, 17 women). Their top medalists were speed skaters **Karin Kania-Busch-Enke** with eight medals (three gold, four silver, one bronze) and **Andrea Ehrig-Schöne-Mitscherlich** with seven medals (one gold, five silver, one bronze). The German Democratic Republic bobsled teams won 13 medals from 1976 to 1988 and **Bogdan Musiol** won six medals (one gold, four silver, one bronze) as a member of those teams. He added another silver in 1992 as a representative of united Germany. Four other German Democratic Republic bobsledders each won four medals and Frank Ulrich won four in biathlon. *See also* BEHRENDT, JAN; DOPING; ENGEL-GULBIN-KRÄMER, INGRID; GERMESHAUSEN, BERNHARD; HOPPE, WOLFGANG; KLUGE, VOLKER; LUDING-ROTHENBURGER, CHRISTA; NEHMER, MEINHARD; WALTER-MARTIN, STEFFI; WITT, KATARINA.

GERMAN FEDERAL REPUBLIC (FRG). *See* FEDERAL REPUBLIC OF GERMANY.

GERMANY (GER). Prior to World War II, the western-central European nation of Germany appeared at all Olympics (Winter and Summer) except the 1920 and 1924 Games, to which as an aggressor nation in World War I, it was not invited. Because of its actions in World War II, and because no true German state existed at the time, Germany was again not allowed to compete in 1948. After World War II, Germany split into two nations. The **Federal Republic of Germany** (FRG; West Germany) was proclaimed in Bonn on 23 May 1949, formed from the former **United States, British**, and **French** zones of occupation. The occupying powers restored civil status on 21 September 1949. The **German Democratic Republic** (GDR; East Germany) was formed on 7 October 1949 from the former **Soviet** zone of occupation. In addition, the province of the **Saar** formed an independent country, which lasted until 1956. The Saar competed independently in 1952, its only Olympic appearance.

From 1952 to 1968, the issue of the "two Germanies" was a major political problem for the **International Olympic Committee** (IOC). The FRG **National Olympic Committee** (NOC) was formed on 24 September 1949 and requested IOC recognition immediately. On 29 August 1950, the IOC **Executive Board** gave provisional recognition to the FRG Olympic Committee. Full recognition was granted in May 1951 at the 46th **IOC Session** in Vienna. The GDR formed an NOC on 22 April 1951 and also asked for recognition. In 1952, a German team was entered at Oslo and Helsinki. Although titularly a combined German team, it was made up entirely of athletes from the FRG.

At the 51st IOC Session in Paris in 1955, the GDR was granted recognition by the IOC by a vote of 27–7. However, the proviso to this recognition was that both Germanys would compete at the Olympics with a combined team. **IOC President Avery Brundage** boasted, "We have obtained in the field of sports what politicians have failed to achieve so far."

In 1956, 1960, and 1964, a combined East and West German team competed under one flag. On 6 October 1965, at the 64th IOC Session in Madrid, the IOC gave the GDR the right to enter a separate team at the 1968 Olympic Games. However, the decision mandated that both Germanies compete with the same uniforms, using the same flag adorned with the Olympic symbol, and using the same anthem, the choral theme from Beethoven's Ninth Symphony. In addition, the GDR agreed to compete as East Germany, a name it did not recognize.

At the 68th IOC Session at **Mexico** City in 1968, the IOC voted 44–4 that, beginning in 1972, both the FRG and the GDR could compete separately at the Olympic Games, wearing their own uniforms and using their own flag and anthem, with the correct names of their nations.

On 3 October 1990, the GDR and the FRG dissolved their separate governments and once again formed a single united German state with the official name of the Federal Republic of Germany. Competing in Albertville and Barcelona in 1992 was a single team representing a unified Germany.

Germany, united or separately, has always been one of the most powerful nations at the Olympics. It has hosted the Games of the XIth **Olympiad** in Berlin in 1936; the Fourth Olympic Winter Games in Garmisch-Partenkirchen, also in 1936; and the Games of the XXth Olympiad in Munich (then in West Germany) in 1972. In addition, the 1916 Olympic Games were originally planned for Berlin, and the 1940 Olympic Winter Games were rescheduled for Garmisch-Partenkirchen after Sapporo and then St. Moritz withdrew as hosts. Germany also has had several unsuccessful bids for the Summer Games—1908 Berlin; 1936 Cologne, Frankfurt and Nuremberg; 2000 Berlin; 2012 Leipzig—and Winter Games—1960 Garmisch-Partenkirchen, 1992 Bertchesgaden, and 2018 Munich.

In 19 Summer Games, Germany has entered 3,707 athletes (2,777 men, 930 **women**) and competed in 37 sports plus the **art competitions**, with the most entrants in **athletics** (490 men, 225 women), **rowing** (298 men, 78 women), **swimming** (150 men, 110 women), **hockey** (146 men, 55 women), art competitions (184 men, seven women), **cycling** (152 men, 23 women), and **gymnastics** (117 men, 45 women). They have won 728 medals in the Summer Games (213 gold, 248 silver, 267 bronze) and have won them in 31 different sports plus the art competitions.

Twelve athletes have won five or more medals while competing for Germany in Summer sports, led by swimmer **Franziska van Almsick** with 10 medals, though none were gold (four silver, six bronze). **Kayaker Birgit Fischer-Schmidt** (five gold, three silver) and **equestrian Isabell Werth** (also five gold, three silver) each won eight. Fischer-Schmidt also competed for the GDR in 1980 and 1988 and won three other gold and one bronze, giving her a total of 12 medals, more than anyone else in her sport, male or female. She and Werth also lead Germany in gold medals with five each.

In 14 Winter Games, Germany has entered 891 athletes (615 men, 276 women) and competed in 15 sports—all but the **military ski patrol**. They had the most participants in **ice hockey** (160 men, 41 women), **bobsledding** (95 men, 12 women), **cross-country skiing** (61 men, 28 women), **speed skating** (44 men, 34 women), **figure skating** (34 men, 42 women), and **Alpine skiing** (33 men, 39 women). They have won 228 medals in Winter sports (86 gold, 84 silver, 58 bronze). Biathlete **Uschi Disl** (two gold, four silver, three bronze) and speed skater **Claudia Pechstein** (five gold, two silver, two bronze) lead with nine medals each. Pechstein's five gold medals are more than any other German Winter Olympian. *See also* BACH, THOMAS; BEERBAUM, LUDGER; BEHRENDT, JAN; BORON, KATHRIN; DIEM, CARL; GROSS, RICCO; HOPPE, WOLFGANG; KLUGE, VOLKER; LANGE, ANDRÉ; LENNARTZ, KARL; NIEMANN-STIRNEMANN, GUNDA; SCHUHMANN, CARL; SEIZINGER, KATJA; WAGNER-AUGUSTIN, KATRIN; WILHELM, KATARINA; WITT, KATARINA.

GERMESHAUSEN, BERNHARD (GDR–BOB). B. 28 August 1951, Heilbad Heiligenstadt, Thüringen, **German Democratic Republic**. Bernhard Germeshausen won the two-man **bobsled** in 1976 with his compatriot **Meinhard Nehmer**, and they were both members of the winning four-man crew in 1976 and 1980. The three gold **Olympic medals** they each won stood as the Olympic record for bobsledding until 2010, when Germans **André Lange** and Kevin Kuske won their fourth gold medals. The six-foot tall (185 cm), 203 lb (92 kg) Germeshausen also won silver in the two-man event at the 1980 Olympics (partnering Hans-Jürgen Gerhardt), and he was the winner at the World Championships in the two-man in 1981 (with Gerhardt) and in the four-man in 1977 and 1981. He also won four-man World Championships medals in 1979 (silver) and 1978 (bronze).

GHANA (GHA). The West African nation of Ghana, officially known as the Republic of Ghana, first appeared at the Olympics in 1952 under its colonial name, Gold Coast. It did not attend the 1956 Olympics, but competed from 1960 through 1972. After **boycotting** the 1976 and 1980 Olympics, Ghana has attended the **Olympic Games** from 1984 through 2012. In 13 Summer Games, Ghana has entered 231 athletes (206 men, 25 **women**) and competed in six sports: **athletics** (66 men, 21 women), **boxing** (49 men), **football** (88 men), **judo** (one man), **table tennis** (two men, three women), and **weightlifting** (one woman).

Ghanian athletes have won four medals at the Olympic Games. **Light-wel-terweight** boxer Ike Quartey won Ghana's first **Olympic medal**, a silver, in 1960. In 1964 light-welterweight Eddie Blay won a bronze, and in 1972 **mid-dleweight** Prince Amartey won Ghana's third medal, also a bronze. Ghana's men's football team qualified for the Olympic tournament six times—1964, 1968, 1972, 1992, 1996, and 2004. Their 1992 team won a bronze medal. Other notable Olympic results for Ghanian athletes include three top-10 results in the men's **long jump**—fourth place in 1972 by Joshua Owusu, sixth place by Ignisious Gaisah in 2004, and seventh place by Michael Ahey in 1964; Alice Annum finished sixth in the women's 100 meter **sprint** in 1972 and seventh in the 200 meters that same year; Margaret Simpson finished ninth in the 2004 **heptathlon**; and Robert Kotei finished 10th in the 1960 men's **high jump**. In addition to their three medals in boxing, four other boxers reached the quarter-final round before losing and finished tied for fifth place—middleweight Joe Darkey and **light-middleweight** Eddie Davies in 1964 and **flyweights** Joseph Destimo in 1968 and Alfred Kotey in 1988.

In 2010, Kwame Nkrumah-Acheampong, known as "The Snow Leopard," competed in **Alpine skiing** at Vancouver, the only appearance by a Ghanian athlete at the **Olympic Winter Games**. He competed in the men's **slalom** and finished 47th of 101 entrants. He carefully skied down the hill and negotiated all the gates successfully, something that 53 other skiers could not accomplish. His time of 2:22.60 was 20 seconds faster than one other skier who completed the course but more than 40 seconds slower than the gold medalist.

GIANT SLALOM. The giant slalom is one of the events in **Alpine skiing**. The race is similar to the **slalom** but the gates are fewer and wider turns are needed to negotiate them. It has been included in the **Olympic Games** since 1952 for both men and **women**. **Alberto Tomba** (1988, 1992) and Deborah

Compagnoni (1994, 1998), both of **Italy**, are the only man and woman to win two gold medals in this race. Five other men and four other women have each won two medals in Olympic giant slalom races.

GIBRALTAR. Gibraltar is a British Overseas Territory located on the tip of the Iberian peninsula adjacent to **Spain** in southeastern Europe. The application of the Gibraltarian **National Olympic Committee** for **International Olympic Committee** (IOC) recognition was on the agenda for discussion at the San Francisco **IOC Session** in 1960 and on numerous subsequent occasions. Each time Gibraltar's application was denied, and it became increasingly apparent that Spain was making territorial claims on the British colony and actively opposing Gibraltar's recognition. Although the *Olympic Charter* prohibits any political interference, the Spanish Ministry of Foreign Affairs chose to blatantly ignore these provisions and issued a directive on 5 September 1985 banning Gibraltarians from competing in championships held on Spanish soil, even though Gibraltar was a member of several **International Federations** (IFs). After 40 years, Gibraltar remains excluded from the **Olympic Movement** and has never been permitted to compete at the Olympics. Yet, as of June 2010, Gibraltar was a member of 18 IFs and has competed in the **Commonwealth Games** each year since 1958.

GILBERT ISLANDS. *See* KIRIBATI.

GILBERT AND ELLICE ISLANDS. *See* KIRIBATI; TUVALU.

GLIDING. A gliding exhibition was held at the 1936 **Olympic Games** in Berlin. The sport is not recognized by the **International Olympic Committee** (IOC) or by **SportAccord**, although **aeronautics** is an IOC-recognized federation.

GLÍMA. The **Icelandic** form of **wrestling**, called glíma, was held at the **Olympic Games** twice as a **demonstration sport**. In both 1908 and 1912, the top Icelandic wrestlers competed at the Olympics, but it helped little in popularizing their sport, which is still competed in mostly by Icelanders.

GOLD COAST. *See* GHANA.

GOLD MEDAL. *See* OLYMPIC MEDALS.

GOLF. Golf was on the program of the 1900 and 1904 **Olympic Games**. In 1900, men and **women** competed in separate individual events. In 1904, a men's individual match-play event and a team stroke-play event were contested. Golf was on the Olympic schedule in both 1908 and 1920, but was not contested in either year. A total of 98 participants (88 men, 10 women) from five nations competed in the two Olympic golf tournaments. Representatives of the **United States** won 10 of the 13 medals, with Americans Chandler Egan winning a gold and a silver medal and Burt McKinnie and Frank Newton each winning a silver and a bronze medal.

The International Golf Federation (formerly the World Amateur Golf Council; the name changed in 2003) is recognized by the **International Olympic Committee** (IOC), headed by the executive directors of the U.S. Golf Association and the Royal and Ancient Golf Club of St. Andrews (**Scotland**). In the new millennium, golf began a push to again be included as an Olympic sport. It was approved for addition to the **Olympic Program** at a meeting of the IOC **Executive Board** in 2001, but the proposal was tabled, and in a vote by the **IOC Session** in July 2005, golf was not approved. However, in October 2009, at the 13th **Olympic Congress** in Copenhagen, **Denmark**, golf (and **rugby** sevens) was reinstated to the Olympic Program. Individual events for men and women will be held at the 2016 Olympic Games in Rio de Janeiro.

GOODWILL GAMES. The Goodwill Games were held for the first time in 1986 in Moscow. They were the brainchild of Ted Turner of Atlanta, Georgia, the head of Turner Broadcasting and the Cable News Network. Turner was upset about the **boycotts** of the Olympics in both 1980 and 1984 and saw the need to hold a "peaceful" sporting festival outside of the **Olympic Movement**. The games were held in 1990 in Seattle, Washington; in 1994 in St. Petersburg, **Russia** (the former Leningrad and Petrograd); and in 1998 in New York City. In 2000, the First Winter Goodwill Games were contested in Lake Placid, New York. The 2001 Goodwill Games were held in Brisbane, **Australia**, but with the breakup of the **Soviet Union**, the need for a Goodwill Games was far from clear. A sixth edition was scheduled for Phoenix, Arizona, in 2005 and second Winter Games were scheduled for Calgary, Alberta, **Canada**, but those games were canceled. In addition, all of the Goodwill Games hemorrhaged money, and they were discontinued after 2001.

GOROKHOVSKAYA, MARIYA KONDRATYEVNA (URS/UKR– GYM). B. 17 October 1921, Evpatoriya, Krym, **Ukraine**, USSR. D. 7 July 2001, Tel-Aviv, **Israel**. Mariya Gorokhovskaya's Olympic fame rests on one Olympics, the 1952 Helsinki Games. As a member of the **Soviet Union**'s **gymnastics** team, she won seven medals, which remains the record for the most medals at one **Olympic Games** by a **woman**. Although she was the first Olympian to win seven medals at one Games, that mark has been equaled by seven men and bettered by two men, **Aleksandr Dityatin** and **Michael Phelps**, both with eight (Phelps twice, in 2004 and 2008). In 1952, Gorokohovskaya won gold medals in the individual and team **all-around**, silver medals on all four apparatuses, and a silver medal in the team portable apparatus event. She never won an individual championship at the World Championships, and her competitive career predated the European Championships.

GOTLAND SPORTS. At the 1912 Olympics in Stockholm, a **demonstration** of three sports (or games) from the Swedish island of Gotland was given. The three events were *pärkspel* (a ball game in which the ball is hit with bare hands), *stångstörtning* (essentially the Swedish form of the Scottish caber toss), and *varpa* (a throwing game not dissimilar to horseshoe throwing).

GOTTWALD, FELIX (AUT–NCO). B. 13 January 1976, Zell am See, Salzburg, **Austria**. With **Samppa Lajunen** (FIN) and Ulrich Wehling (GDR), Felix Gottwald is one of only three **Nordic combined** athletes to have won three Olympic titles. After competing without winning a medal in 1994 and 1998, Gottwald won bronze medals in each of the three **combined** events at the 2002 Games. Four years later, he again won three medals, now winning the **sprint** and team events, while finishing a close second in the individual competition. At the 2010 Games, the five-foot, 10-inch (179 cm), 150 lb (68 kg) Gottwald helped the Austrian team to a second consecutive title. In World Championships, Austria's 2003 team victory gave Gottwald his only gold, although he won two silver and five bronzes between 1997 and 2005. Gottwald also won the Nordic Combined World Cup in 2001 and has won a total of 21 World Cup races throughout his career.

GOULD, SHANE ELIZABETH (AUS–SWI). B. 23 November 1956, Sydney, New South Wales, **Australia**. Shane Gould was a **swimmer** of phenomenal talent who became the first woman to hold the world **freestyle** record at every distance from 100 meters to 1,500 meters. She achieved this remarkable feat in December 1971, just three weeks after her 15th birthday. At the **Olympic Games** the following year, she won the 200 and 400 meter freestyles and 200 meter individual **medley**, each in a new world record time, and, in addition to her three gold medals, she took the silver in the 800 meters and the bronze in the 100 meter freestyle. In 1973, still only 16 years old, the five-foot, seven-inch (171 cm), 130 lb (59 kg) swimmer retired, but during her brief career she had become one of the legends of the sport. In the new millennium she returned to competitive swimming at the masters (40+ years) level and continued to break Australian and world records in this category.

GRAFSTRÖM, GILLIS EMANUEL (SWE–FSK). B. 7 June 1893, Stockholm, **Sweden**. D. 14 April 1938, Potsdam, **Germany**. Gillis Grafström was the supreme **figure skater** in the years following World War I. He won a record three **Olympic Winter Games** gold medals (1920, 1924, 1928) and in 1932 earned a silver medal in Lake Placid. His lifetime total of four medals in Olympic figure skating has not been surpassed and was only equaled by Yevgeny Plyushchenko in 2014. He was also a three-time World Champion (1922, 1924, 1929). A noted amateur painter and sculptor, he skated more for aesthetic pleasure than for the competitive challenge. Grafström was a professional architect who worked mainly in Germany and spent little time in his native Sweden. He was inducted into the World Figure Skating Hall of Fame in 1976.

GREAT BRITAIN (GBR). The British Isles are a group of islands located off the northwestern coast of continental Europe. The nomenclature of the British Isles can be quite confusing. The nation that is a member of the United Nations is properly referred to as the United Kingdom of Great Britain and Northern Ireland. That nation consists of four countries: **England**, **Wales**, **Scotland**, and Northern Ireland. When that nation is a competitor in the **Olympic Games**, its name has been traditionally shortened to Great Britain, although properly speaking Great Britain refers to only the island that contains England, Wales, and Scotland. A second nation within the British Isles is that of **Ireland**. It is located on a second island, known as Ireland, which contains the Nation of Ireland, also a member of the United Nations and an Olympic competitor, and the part of the United Kingdom known as Northern Ireland. Three smaller islands within the British Isles— the Isle of Man, Guernsey, and Jersey—are Crown dependencies and are not part of the United Kingdom.

Great Britain, **France**, and **Italy** are the only nations that have never missed the Olympic Games. They competed at the 1906 **Intercalated Olympic Games** in Athens, the 1908 **figure skating** events in London, the 1920 figure skating events in Antwerp, and the 1956 **Equestrian** Olympics in Stockholm. Through 1920, Great Britain competed as a combined team with Ireland, which was not yet an independent nation, and its 1904 participation is in fact due only to three Irish athletes. Great Britain has won 766 **Olympic medals**, 225 of them gold, all but 22 of them (nine gold) at the Summer Olympics. Great Britain has hosted the Olympic Games three times: the Games of the IVth **Olympiad** in London in 1908, the Games of the XIVth Olympiad in London in 1948, and the Games of the XXXth Olympiad in London in 2012. London was also selected to host the 1944 Summer Games, which were subsequently canceled due to World War II. Birmingham, England, bid unsuccessfully to host the 1992 Summer Games, and Manchester, England, was unsuccessful in bids for the 1996 and 2000 Games.

In 28 Summer Games, Great Britain has entered 5,441 athletes (4,139 men, 1,301 **women**) and competed in 42 sports plus the **art competitions**. They have not competed in **aeronautics, baseball, croquet, ice hockey** (as a summer sport), **pelota, roque,** and **softball**. They have won 811 medals (245 gold, 290 silver, 276 bronze) in summer sports and won medals in 34 different sports.

Henry Taylor, a **swimmer** from 1906 to 1920, leads the British Olympic medal list with eight, followed by **cyclists Chris Hoy** and **Bradley Wiggins** with seven and **rower Stephen Redgrave** and John Jarvis, swimmer and **water polo** player with six. Hoy leads British Olympians with six gold medals followed by Redgrave with five. Among other noteworthy British Olympians are **sailor Ben Ainslie** (four gold, one silver medal from 1996–2012), middle distance runner **Sebastian Coe** (two gold, two silver, 1980–1984), and **tennis** player **Reggie Doherty** (three gold, one bronze, 1900–1908).

In 22 **Olympic Winter Games**, Great Britain has entered 642 athletes (465 men, 177 women) and competed in 15 sports—all except **military ski patrol**. They have won 26 medals (10 gold, four silver, 12 bronze) in seven sports. Twelve mountaineers were also recipients of the special award for **alpinism** in 1924. The **ice dancing** pair of **Torvill and Dean** have each won two medals (gold 1984, bronze 1994) as well as figure skater Jeannette Altwegg (bronze 1948, gold 1952). *See also* BERESFORD, JACK, JR.; BROOKES, WILLIAM PENNY; BUCHANAN, IAN; BURGHLEY, LORD DAVID GEORGE BROWNLOW CECIL; HOLMES, KELLY; JENNINGS, ANDREW; MALLIN, HENRY WILLIAM; PARISI, ANGELO; PINSENT, MATTHEW CLIVE; RADMILOVIC, PAOLO FRANCESCO; THOMPSON, FRANCIS MORGAN; WINANS, WALTER.

GRECO-ROMAN WRESTLING. Greco-Roman wrestling is a style of **wrestling** in which holds below the waist are not permitted. As in other forms of wrestling, the object is a pin in which both of the opponent's shoulders are held to the mat. Modern-day matches are contested over three two-minute periods. Points are awarded for various maneuvers, and should a pin not occur, the wrestler with the most points is the victor. Men's Greco-Roman wrestling has been included in the modern **Olympic Games** in nearly every Games since 1896. There was no wrestling in the 1900 Olympic Games, and the 1904 Games had only freestyle wrestling. **Women**'s Olympic wrestling does not include the Greco-Roman style. **Aleksandr Karelin** of **Russia** won three gold medals in Greco-Roman wrestling in the **super-heavyweight**

class representing the **Soviet Union** in 1988, the Unified Team in 1992, and Russia in 1996. He won the silver medal in 2000 when he was upset by American Rulon Gardner. **Carl Westergren** of **Sweden** was also a three-time Greco-Roman gold medalist, winning the **middleweight** class in 1920, the **light-heavyweight** class in 1924, and **heavyweight** in 1932. Søren Jensen of **Denmark** was also a four-time Greco-Roman medalist, with gold medals in 1906 in the heavyweight and **all-around** classes and bronze medals in 1908 and 1912 in the heavyweight class. Imre Polyák of **Hungary** won the silver medal in the **featherweight** class in 1952, 1956, and 1960 and the gold medal in 1964. The 1912 Greco-Roman light-heavyweight (then called middleweight B) final produced an interesting result. After each man won five bouts to reach the final, Ivar Böhling of **Finland** and Anders Ahlgren of Sweden wrestled for nine hours in the final match before the referee **disqualified** both contestants. Both were only awarded silver medals and there was no gold medalist that year.

GREECE (GRE). Greece, located in southern Europe and officially named the Hellenic Republic, is the home of the Olympics, the **Ancient Olympic Games** having been held there from at least 776 B.C. through A.D. 393. The modern **Olympic Games** were revived and first held in Athens in 1896. Prior to 1896, several **attempts at revival** of the Olympics were contested in Greece, notably the **Zappas Olympics** of 1859, 1870, 1875, and 1889. Since 1896, Greek participation has been continuous at all Games of the **Olympiad**. In honor of being the ancestral home of the Olympics, at the opening ceremony the Greek athletes always march first into the stadium. Greece has also competed at the **Olympic Winter Games**, first appearing in 1936 and since then missing only the 1960 Squaw Valley Olympics. Greece hosted the Games of the Ist Olympiad in Athens in 1896, the **Intercalated Olympic Games** of 1906, and the Games of the XXVIIIth Olympiad in 2004. Greece also unsuccessfully bid to host the 1944 and 1996 Summer Games in Athens.

In 28 Summer Games, Greece has entered 1,593 athletes (1,258 men, 335 **women**) and competed in 35 sports plus the **art competitions**. The largest contingents have been in **athletics** (290 men, 69 women), **rowing** (153 men, six women), **shooting** (109 men, six women), **water polo** (87 men, 19 women), **swimming** (67 men, 28 women), and **wrestling** (88 men, five women). Greek athletes have won 147 medals in the Summer Games (39 gold, 56 silver, 52 bronze) in 18 different sports plus the art competitions, with 81 of those in 1896 and 1906 and 16 medals (six gold) in 2004.

Pyrros Dimas leads the Greek medalists, with four medals (three gold, one bronze) in **weightlifting**. He is the only Greek to win three gold medals, although he is an ethnic **Albanian**, but both Kostas Tsiklitiras (standing **long**

jump and standing **high jump**) and Nikolaos Georgantas (**discus** and stone throws) each won four medals (one gold, two silver, one bronze) in athletics in the early years of the modern Olympics. Shooters Georgios Orfanidis and Ioannis Frangudis and **fencer** Ioannis Georgiadis each won three medals between 1896 and 1906. Weightlifter **Akakios Kakiasvili** is the only other athlete to win two gold medals for Greece. One of Greece's more illustrious gold medalists was Crown Prince Konstantinos, who won the three-man **keelboat sailing** race in 1960. He was also the country's flag bearer in the opening ceremony that year.

In 18 Winter Games, Greece has entered 66 athletes (53 men, 13 women) and competed in eight sports, with most of their entrants in **Alpine skiing** (26 men, five women) and **cross-country skiing** (15 men, four women) and a few entering more than one sport. They have not won any medals in the Winter Games, and their best results have been Thanasis Tsakiris, 37th of 70 in 1994 in the men's 20 k biathlon, just one place behind all-time great champion **Ole Einar Bjørndalen** (NOR); Lefteris Fafalis, 29th of 80 in the men's cross-country **sprint** in 2006; and in Alpine skiing Vasilios Dimitriadis, 23rd of 93 in the 2006 men's **slalom**. *See also* AVEROF, GEORGIOS; COROEBUS OF ELIS; GEORGIADIS, KONSTANTINOS; INTERNATIONAL OLYMPIC ACADEMY; KETSEAS, IOANNIS; LEONIDAS OF RHODES; LOUIS, SPYRIDON; MILON OF KROTON; PINDAR; THEAGENES OF THASOS; VIKELAS, DEMETRIOS; ZAPPAS, EVANGELOS.

GREENLAND. Greenland, the world's largest island, is located in the North Atlantic and is an autonomous country within the Kingdom of **Denmark**. Traditionally, Greenland's Olympic affairs have been overseen by Denmark, but in 1996 it started to make efforts to establish its own Olympic identity. So far, Greenland has not been successful, although at the 1998 **Olympic Winter Games** three Greenlandic Nordic skiers competed as part of the Danish team. In the 2014 Sochi Games, Martin Møller, Greenland's Athlete of the Year in 2013, represented Denmark in **cross-country skiing** and competed in four events with a best finish of 45th of 64 entrants in the 50 km race. Greenland has competed independently at the Arctic Winter Games since their inception in 1970 and hosted them in Nuuk in 2002.

GRENADA (GRN). The Grenada Olympic Association was founded in 1982, and after provisional **International Olympic Committee** recognition was granted that year, full recognition was accorded in 1984. This enabled Grenada to make its Olympic debut at the 1984 **Olympic Games**, and it has competed at each of the Olympics since. It has not yet competed at the **Olympic Winter Games**. In eight Summer Games, 40 Grenadian athletes (27 men, 13 **women**) have competed in four sports at the Olympics: **athletics** (16 men, 11 women), **boxing** (eight men), **swimming** (three men, one woman), and **taekwondo** (one woman).

Their best performance has been that of 400 meter runner Kirani James, who won the gold medal at London in 2012—the Caribbean island nation's first **Olympic medal**. Other notable results include fourth place by Alleyne Francique in 2004 men's 400 meters; Randy Lewis, 15th in 2008 **triple jump** and 28th of 47 four years earlier; Patricia Sylvester, 21st of 42 entrants in 2008 women's **long jump**; Jacintha Bartholomew, 17th of 23 in 1984 long jump; and **welterweight** boxer Bernard Wilson, who won his first bout and finished tied for ninth in 1984. In addition five other runners qualified for the quarter-final **round** in their events.

GRIFFITH JOYNER, DELOREZ FLORENCE (USA–ATH). B. 21 December 1959, Los Angeles, California, **United States**. D. 21 September 1998, Mission Viejo, California, United States. Florence Griffith Joyner was a superb **sprinter** who completely dominated the **women**'s track and field season in 1988. After setting a world record for 100 meters at the 1988 U.S. Olympic trials, she won three gold and one silver medal at the Seoul Games. Victories in the 100 meters and 200 meters, in which she twice broke the world record, were followed by a third gold in the sprint **relay** and a silver in the 4x400 meters relay. The five-foot, six-inch (170 cm), 126 lb (57 kg) runner had previously won a silver medal in the 200 meters in 1984. The flamboyant outfits she wore on the track made her a darling of the media, who gave her the name "Flo-Jo" after her marriage in 1987 to the 1984 Olympic **triple jump** gold medalist, Al Joyner. She tragically died very young (at the age of 38) from an epileptic seizure. As of 2014, her world records for the 100 and 200 meters remain intact.

GRISHIN, YEVGENY ROMANOVICH (URS–SSK). B. 23 March 1931, Tula, **Russia**, USSR. D. 9 July 2005, Moscow, Russian Federation. Yevgeny Grishin was the winner of gold medals for **speed skating** in the 500 meters and 1,500 meters at both the 1956 and 1960 **Olympic Winter Games**. He set world records at both distances, but was at his best at 500 meters, winning six world titles and achieving the distinction of being the first skater to break the 40-second barrier. In 1964, he also won a silver medal in the 500 meters and four years later nearly won that race again as he finished fourth, just one-tenth of a second behind the two silver medalists who tied for second place. The five-foot, eight-inch (174 cm), 172 lb (78 kg) Grishin was European **All-Around** champion in 1956. In his era, there were no **sprint** world championships, and he never won a World All-Around title, as he could not skate distances well enough for that title. He did win the 500 meters at the World All-Around (1954, 1957, 1960–1963), as well as the European Championships (1954–1957, 1961–1962). Grishin set seven world records—four over 500 meters, one at 1,000 meters, and two at 1,500 meters. He became a coach with the national speed skating squad after he retired from competition.

GROß, MICHAEL (FRG–SWI). B. 17 June 1964, Frankfurt am Main, **Federal Republic of Germany.** Michael Groß won six **Olympic medals** (three gold), mostly in the **butterfly** and **sprint freestyle swimming** events. The six-foot, seven-inch (201 cm), 194 lb (88 kg) swimmer was known as "The Albatross" because of his enormous arm span of over seven feet (2.14 meters). At the World Championships, he won a then-record 13 medals (five gold, five silver, three bronze), and he also won a record 18 medals at four European Championships (13 gold, four silver, one bronze). During his career, Groß set 10 world records in individual events. His top Olympics performance was in 1984, when he won the 200 meter freestyle and the 100 meter butterfly and took silver at the 200 meter butterfly and in anchoring the 4x200 meter freestyle **relay**. In 1988, he won the 200 meter butterfly and won a bronze in the 4x200 freestyle relay.

GROß, RICCO (GER–BIA). B. 22 August 1970, Schlema im Erzgebirge, Sachsen, **German Democratic Republic.** Ricco Groß ranks as one of most successful **biathletes** of all time. His total of eight **Olympic medals** (four gold, three silver, one bronze) is tied for third best among all competitors. During his career, which stretches from his first World Cup race in 1990 until his farewell in 2007, in addition to his eight Olympic medals, he won 20 World Championship medals (including nine titles) and 33 World Cup wins (of which nine were individual). Groß regretted never winning an individual Olympic gold, winning all of his four titles with the German **relay** team, thereby equaling **Aleksandr Tikhonov**'s record. The five-foot, 10-inch (179 cm), 165 lb (75 kg) Groß won silver in 1992 and 1994 in the 10 km sprint and also in the 2002 relay. He won his Olympic bronze medal in the 2002 12.5 km **pursuit** event. He also won four individual World Championships, including the pursuit title in front of his home crowd in Oberhof in 2004. During his active career, Groß was a so-called sport soldier in the German army. After his retirement, he became a color commentator for biathlon events on German **television**.

GRØTTUMSBRÅTEN, JOHAN HAGBART PEDERSEN (NOR–CCS/ NCO). B. 24 February 1899, Sørkedalen, Oslo, **Norway.** D. 21 January 1983, Vestre Aker, Oslo, Norway. Together with fellow Norwegian **Thorleif Haug,**

Johan Grøttumsbråten dominated the Nordic skiing events at the early **Olympic Winter Games**. In 1924, he won silver at 18 km and bronze in the 50 km and the **Nordic combined** event, and then in 1928 he won the 18 km and the Nordic combined. The five-foot, 10-inch (180 cm) Grøttumsbråten won his third gold and sixth medal overall in 1932, when he successfully defended his title in the Nordic combined event. Grøttumsbråten was a five-time champion in Nordic combined at Holmenkollen, in 1923, 1926, 1928–1929, and 1931.

GRUNSVEN, THEODORA ELISABETH GERARDA VAN "ANKY" (NED–EQU). B. 2 January 1968, Erp, Noord-Brabant, **Netherlands**. Anky van Grunsven is the only **equestrian** Olympian to have won nine medals and the only rider to win an individual event three times in a row. She did so in the individual **dressage**, which she won in 2000 (on Bonfire), 2004, and 2008 (on Salinero). In addition, the five-foot, seven-inch (172 cm), 123 lb (56 kg) rider placed second in that event in 1996 and has won four silver team medals (in 1992, 1996, 2000, and 2008) and one bronze team medal in 2012. Van Grunsven has also excelled in other competitions, winning the individual gold in the World Equestrian Games of 1994 and 2006 and the dressage World Cup nine times (1995, 1996, 1997, 1999, 2000, 2004, 2005, 2006, and 2008).

GUAM (GUM). The Western Pacific island of Guam, officially an unincorporated territory of the **United States**, formed a **National Olympic Committee** in 1976, but it was not recognized by the **International Olympic Committee** until 1986. Guam's initial Olympic appearance was at the 1988 **Olympic Winter Games** with **biathlete** Judd Bankert who finished 71st of 72 entrants in the 10 km **sprint**, but it has not taken part in the Olympic Winter Games since then. Guam has participated in each **Olympic Games** since 1988. In eight Summer Games, they have entered 62 athletes (42 men, 20 **women**) and taken part in 10 sports: **athletics** (eight men, nine women), **cycling** (six men, one woman), **judo** (five men, one woman), **sailing** (three men, two women), **swimming** (10 men, five women), **weightlifting** (three men, one woman), **wrestling** (four men, one woman), and one man in each of **archery**, **boxing**, and **canoeing**.

Guamanian athletes have never approached a medal. One of the most notable athletes for Guam is Ricardo Blas, Jr. The son of 1988 Guam Olympic *judoka*, Ricardo Blas, Sr., Blas Jr. is the heaviest Olympian in history, weighing in at 218 kg (481 lb) in 2012. He competed in men's **heavyweight** judo in 2008 and 2012, winning one bout in 2012 and finishing tied for ninth place. One of Guam's best Olympic performances was in 1992 when Jen Allred finished 36th of 47 entrants in the women's **marathon** race. In

1992, **Egyptian**-born Atef Hussain finished tied for 13th of 28 entrants in men's heavyweight judo, and that year Erin Lum also tied for 13th of 21 entrants in women's **middleweight** judo. The 1992 Guamian men's 4x100 meter **freestyle** swimming **relay** team was 13th of 18 teams.

GUATEMALA (GUA). The **Central American** nation of Guatemala, officially known as the Republic of Guatemala, first competed in the 1932 Olympics with one **woman**, Antonia Matos, in the **art competitions**. In sports, Guatemala first competed at the 1952 **Olympic Games** and then did not appear again until 1968, but has not missed an Olympic Games since.

In 17 Summer Games, from 1952 to 2012, Guatemala has entered 221 athletes (193 men, 28 women) and has participated in 18 sports. It had the most competitors in **football** (49 men), **athletics** (30 men, nine women), **shooting** (25 men), **cycling** (23 men, one woman), **swimming** (15 men, five women), **wrestling** (14 men), and **weightlifting** (nine men, one woman). Guatemala's first and only **Olympic medal** was won in 2012 in the men's 20 km **race walk** when Erick Barrondo finished second and won the silver medal.

Other notable Olympic results for Guatemala include fourth place by Oswaldo Méndez in 1980 **equestrian jumping** and fourth place by Heidy Juárez in 2004 women's **welterweight taekwondo**; a fifth place tie by the 1968 men's football team; a fifth place tie by **light-flyweight boxer** Carlos Motta in 1984; fifth place ties also by taekwondo competitors Eudy Carías (2004 women's **flyweight**), Gabriel Sagastume (2004 men's **featherweight**), and Elizabeth Zamora (2012 women's flyweight); sixth place by Edgardo Zachrisson in 1976 **skeet** shooting; seventh place by Joseph Burge in 1972 featherweight **freestyle** wrestling; eighth place by 1996 shooters Attila Solti (running target, 10 m) and Sergio Sánchez (**free pistol**, 50 m); ninth place of 49 entrants by **sailor** Juan Ignacio Maegli (2012 one-person **dinghy**); Kevin Cordón, tied for ninth of 40 competitors in 2012 men's **singles badminton**; Doroteo Flores, 22nd of 66 in 1952 **marathon**; and **gymnast** Luisa Portocarrero, tied for 13th of 92 **balance beam** and 18th of 92 in women's **all-around** in 1992.

Guatemala appeared at its only **Olympic Winter Games** in 1988 at Calgary, with six competitors—three men and one woman in **Alpine skiing** and two men in **cross-country skiing**. Flamma Smith finished a respectable 27th of 57 in the women's **slalom**, ahead of one other woman who finished the race and 29 others who did not. She was the 29th and last finisher in the **giant slalom** but placed ahead of 35 others who were unable to finish. Smith also entered the **super G** but did not finish. In the men's Alpine ski races, Carlos Andrés Bruderer had the best result, 39th of 109 in the slalom. His brother Christian had a best of 50th of 94 in the Super G. The third Guatemalan men's skier was Alfredo Rego, whose best was 54th of 109 in the slalom. Brothers Dag and Ricardo Burgos entered the cross-country competition but finished 80th and 81st of 90 entrants in the 15 km race and 80th and 83rd of 90 skiers in the 30 km race.

GUINEA (GUI). Guinea formed a **National Olympic Committee** in 1964, which was recognized by the **International Olympic Committee** in 1965. Since making its Olympic debut in 1968, the West African nation of Guinea (once part of French West Africa and known as French Guinea and now officially the Republic of Guinea) has competed at each subsequent **Olympic Games**, missing only 1972 and 1976. It has never competed at the **Olympic Winter Games**, nor has any Guinean athlete won an **Olympic medal**. In 10 Summer Olympics, Guinea has entered 55 athletes (44 men, 11 **women**) in seven sports: **athletics** (11 men, five women), **boxing** (six men), **football** (15 men), **judo** (seven men, two women), **swimming** (three men, three women), **taekwondo** (one woman), and **wrestling** (two men). Most Guinean athletes have gone out in preliminary **rounds**, but in 1980 Mamadou Diallo finished 13th in **half-lightweight** judo, and in 1996, Joseph Loua made it to the second round of the men's 200 meter **sprint**.

GUINEA-BISSAU (GBS). The **National Olympic Committee** of Guinea-Bissau was given official recognition by the **International Olympic Committee** (IOC) in June 1995 at the 104th **IOC Session** in Budapest. The nation made its Olympic debut at the 1996 **Olympic Games** in Atlanta and has competed in each subsequent Summer Games. The West African nation of Guinea-Bissau (known as Portuguese Guinea prior to its independence in 1973 and officially known as the Republic of Guinea-Bissau) has not yet competed at the **Olympic Winter Games**. Guinea-Bissau has had 12 Olympians through 2012, eight track and field athletes (five men including two with identical names and three **women**) and four **wrestlers** (two men, two women). Prior to 2012, no Bissau-Guinean Olympian had advanced past preliminary **rounds**, but in 2012, Holder da Silva qualified in the 100 meter **sprint** initial round but did not continue after the second round. In wrestling, Augusto Midana won his first match in the **middleweight** competition and finished in seventh place overall of the 19 entrants. He improved on his performance of four years earlier when he finished 17th of 21 contestants in that event.

GUO JINGJING (CHN–DIV). B. 15 October 1981, Baoding, Hebei, **China**. Guo Jingjing is one of only six **divers** to have won four Olympic gold medals (the others are Wu Minxia, **Fu Mingxia**, and Chen Ruolin of China, and **Greg Louganis** and **Pat McCormick** of the **United States**) and is the female diver with the most **Olympic medals** (trailing only **Dmitry Sautin**). Guo has won her medals only on the **springboard** (three meters), while some of the others have also won medals from the **platform** (10 meters). After winning two silver medals in the 2000 Games, together with Fu Mingxia in the synchronized springboard, Guo doubled in the springboard and synchronized springboard at both the 2004 and 2008 Olympics, teaming up with Wu Minxia for the synchronized events on both occasions. At the World Championships, the five-foot, four-inch (163 cm), 108 lb (49 kg) diver has displayed a similar superiority. Between 2001 and 2009, she won five consecutive titles in both springboard events.

GUYANA (GUY). The South American nation of Guyana, located on the northern coast of the continent, has competed at nearly every **Olympic Games** since 1948, missing only 1976, when it joined the African **boycott** that year. It competed from 1948 to 1964 as British Guiana, appearing first as Guyana in 1968. Officially known as the Co-operative Republic of Guyana, it has never competed at the **Olympic Winter Games**. In 16 Summer Games, the country has entered 70 athletes (60 men, 10 **women**) but participated in only six sports: **athletics** (22 men, nine women), **boxing** (18 men), **cycling** (nine men), **judo** (one man), **swimming** (two men, one woman), and **weightlifting** (eight men).

Only one Guyanese has won an **Olympic medal**, a bronze medal in **bantamweight** boxing by Michael Anthony in 1980. Native British Guianan Phil Edwards won five bronze medals in athletics from 1928 to 1936, but competed for **Canada** because British Guiana did not yet have a **National Olympic Committee**. Edwards was the first person of African descent to graduate from McGill Medical School, and he became an authority on tropical diseases. Other notable results by Guyanese athletes in the Olympic Games include Martin Dias, eighth in bantamweight weightlifting in 1964; Mark Mason, 15th in the 1992 **long jump**; Aliann Pompey, 400 meter runner, quarter-finalist in 2000 and semifinalist in 2004, 2008, and 2012; James Gilkes, semifinalist in both 100 and 200 meter **sprints** in 1980; **light-welterweight** boxer Adrian Carew-Dodson, who won his first two bouts in 1992 and finished tied for ninth; and boxers Fitzroy Brown (1980 **featherweight**) and brothers Gordon Carew (1984 **lightweight**) and Dillon Carew (1992 light-welterweight), who each won one bout and finished tied for ninth.

GYARMATI, DEZSŐ (HUN–WAP). B. 23 October 1927, Miskolc, Borsod-Abaúj-Zemplén, **Hungary**. D. 18 August 2013, Budapest, Hungary. Dezső

Dezsö Gyarmati of Hungary won three gold medals and five medals in water polo between 1948 and 1964. Courtesy of Erich Kamper

Gyarmati is considered the greatest of all Olympic **water polo** players. His feat of winning medals at five successive **Olympic Games** (gold in 1952, 1956, 1964; silver in 1948; bronze in 1960) has never been matched. The six-foot, one-inch (186 cm), 183 lb (83 kg) Gyarmati also led Hungary to European Championships in 1954 and 1962. A national hero, he coached the Hungarian team that won the Olympic title in 1976 and later became a member of Parliament. Gyarmati married the 1952 Olympic 200 meter **breaststroke swimming** champion, Eva Székely. Their daughter, Andrea, was an Olympic silver medalist in the 100 meter **backstroke** in 1972, and she later married Mihály Hesz, a 1968 Olympic **canoeing** champion.

GYMNASTICS. Gymnastics is an ancient sport, having been practiced in various forms in ancient **Greece** and Rome. However, gymnastics competitions are relatively modern. The modern development of gymnastics began in the mid-19th century in Europe. Gymnastics societies were formed in **Germany** (Turnvereins) and **Bohemia**, part of the Austro-Hungarian empire (Sokols). Similar societies were formed in **France** and **Switzerland** and then spread generally throughout Europe. The sport is governed worldwide by the Fédération Internationale de Gymnastique (FIG), which was founded in 1881 and currently has 141 member federations. Originally called the European Federation of Gymnastics, it was renamed the FIG in 1921.

Modern competitive gymnastics has developed from two systems: the German Turnverein system, emphasizing apparatus work of a formal nature and stressing muscular development, and the Swedish system of free exercises, concerned with developing rhythmic movements.

Gymnastics has been contested at every **Olympic Games**. In 28 Games, there have been 4,005 athletes (2,577 men, 1,428 **women**) from 88 nations who have competed in Olympic artistic gymnastics. The program has varied widely, but since World War II it has been fairly constant. Men compete in teams on six apparatuses: still **rings, floor exercise, horizontal bar, parallel bars, pommelled horse**, and **horse vault**. The top competitors in the team event are eligible for the individual **all-around** event (maximum of three per nation). This is conducted again on all six apparatuses. The top performers in each apparatus are then advanced to the individual apparatus finals, now with a maximum of two performers from any nation per event.

Women's competition is similar, except that they compete in only four events: **uneven bars**, floor exercise, horse vault, and **balance beam**. In 1984, **rhythmic gymnastics** for women was added to the **Olympic Program**. **Trampoline** events for men and women were added to the gymnastics program at Sydney in 2000. With these new **disciplines** of gymnastics being contested at the Olympics, the traditional form is sometimes known as artistic gymnastics, to distinguish it from the other disciplines.

At the Olympics, the **Soviet Union** and its successor republics have been dominant in the women's events. **Romania** has also had superb female gymnasts, notably the remarkable **Nadia Comăneci**. Men's gymnastics has been divided almost evenly since World War II between the **Japanese** and Soviet Union. The **Chinese** men and women are also now of top caliber. Because gymnasts may compete in several events, 13 Olympic gymnasts have won 10 or more Olympic medals, led by **Larysa Latynina** (18), **Nikolay Andrianov** (15), and **Boris Shakhlin** (13) of the Soviet Union and **Takashi Ono** (13) of Japan. Latynina leads Olympic gymnasts with nine gold medals, while among men, **Sawao Kato** of Japan has won the most gold medals, eight. *See* *also* ASTAKHOVA, POLINA GRIGORYEVNA; ČÁSLAVSKÁ, VĚRA; CHUKARIN, VIKTOR IVANOVICH; DITYATIN, ALEKSANDR NIKOLAYEVICH; ENDO, YUKIO; GOROKHOVSKAYA, MARIYA KONDRATYEVNA; KELETI, ÁGNES; KIM, NELLYA VLADIMIROVNA; KORBUT, OLGA VALENTINOVNA; LI NING; NEMOV, ALEKSEY YURYEVICH; RETTON, MARY LOU; SCHUHMANN, CARL; SHAKHLIN, BORIS ANFIYANOVICH; SHCHERBO, VITALY VENEDIKTOVICH; TURISHCHEVA, LYUDMILA IVANOVNA.

H

HACKETT, GRANT GEORGE (AUS–SWI). B. 9 May 1980, Southport, Queensland, **Australia**. Grant Hackett succeeded his countryman **Kieren Perkins** as the top distance **swimmer** in the world, and his overall record rivals that of Perkins and **Vladimir Salnikov** as the greatest distance **free-styler** ever. Hackett was undefeated at his best distance, 1,500 meters, from 1997 until the 2007 Worlds, winning the gold **Olympic medal** in that event in both 2000 and 2004 and the silver medal in 2008. His record at major meets is remarkable, winning the 1,500 at the **Commonwealth Games** in 1997 and 2002; the 1,500 at the World Championships in 1998, 2001, and 2003; and at the Pan-Pacific Meet, the 400, 800, and 1,500 in 1997, the 1,500 in 1999, and the 800 and 1,500 in 2002. He also frequently won medals at international meets on the 4x200 meter freestyle **relay** team for Australia, including Olympic gold in 2000, silver in 2004, and bronze in 2008. In 2004, the six-foot, five-inch (198 cm), 212 lb (96 kg) Hackett was also a silver medalist in the 400 freestyle. Hackett set one world record at the 1,500 meters long course, 14:34.56, in winning the 2001 World Championship in Fukuoka, **Japan**, and two in short course 1,500 meters.

HACKL, GEORG (FRG/GER–LUG). B. 9 September 1966, Berchtesgaden, Bayern, **Federal Republic of Germany**. Georg Hackl was the first **luger** to have won gold medals at three consecutive **Olympic Winter Games** in **singles**. After a silver medal in 1988 at Calgary, Hackl became the first man to defend the Olympic luge singles title, winning in both 1992 and 1994. In 1998, Hackl won the Olympic singles luge for the third consecutive time; in Salt Lake City in 2002, he earned an individual silver medal. In addition to his Olympic successes, Hackl was a 10-time World Champion, with three wins in singles and seven wins in mixed team. The five-foot, seven-inch (172 cm), 174 lb (79 kg) luger was also a seven time runner-up in singles at the World Championships. Hackl was European Champion in singles in 1988 and 1990 and was a two-time season champion in World Cup in 1988–1989 and 1989–1990.

HAITI (HAI). Haiti formed a **National Olympic Committee** in 1956, which was recognized by the **International Olympic Committee** in the same year.

A Caribbean nation that occupies a portion of the island of Hispaniola along with the **Dominican Republic**, known officially as the Republic of Haiti, it has a curious, intermittent Olympic history. Two **fencers** and a **rugby** player from Haiti took part in the 1900 **Olympic Games** in Paris. The country's next appearances were in 1924, 1928, and 1932, followed by a long gap before its return to the Olympic fold in 1960. Haiti did not attend the 1964 or 1968 Olympics but appeared in 1972 and 1976 and each Olympics since 1984, but has never entered the **Olympic Winter Games**. In 15 Summer Games, Haiti has entered 66 athletes (52 men, 14 **women**) in 10 sports: **athletics** (26 men, nine women), **boxing** (five men), **fencing** (two men, two women), **judo** (nine men, two women), **shooting** (five men), **tennis** (one man, one woman), and one man in each of **rugby, swimming, taekwondo**, and **weightlifting**. It also had one man entered in the **art competitions** of 1932.

The first known black athlete in the modern Olympics, Haitian-born Constanin Henriquez played on the gold medal–winning rugby team in 1900 that consisted primarily of French players. Silvio Cator won the silver medal in the 1928 **long jump**. In 1924, a Haitian team won a bronze medal in free rifle shooting. Other notable Olympic performances by Haitian athletes include Ludovic Agustin finishing fifth, Ludovic Valborge, tied for sixth, Destin Destine, tied for 10th; and Astrel Rolland, 13th of 73 entrants in the 1924 individual free rifle prone shooting; Dieudonné Lamothe, 20th of 118 in the 1988 men's **marathon**; Dudley Dorival, seventh in 2000 110 meter **hurdles**; and Samyr Laine, 11th in 2012 **triple jump**. Dorival reached the semifinal **round** in 2004 in the 110 meter hurdles, and Nadine Faustin-Parker was a semifinalist in women's 100 meter hurdles that same year. In 1976, due primarily to the **boycott** by African nations after the competition began, **lightweight** boxer Yves Jeudy finished in a tie for fifth place without winning a bout. He had two **byes** and a **walkover** and reached the quarter-finals before actually boxing. After losing his first bout in the quarter-finals, he placed tied for fifth. **Welterweight** Wesly Felix that year also received a bye and walkover and lost his first bout to finish tied for ninth in his class.

At the other end of the spectrum was Olmeus Charles. While the 12 other runners in the first **heat** of the 1976 10,000 meter event tried their best to qualify for the final, Charles was content to simply finish the race and jogged the entire 10,000 meters. His time of 42:00.11 was more than eight minutes slower than the next to last runner and more than 13 minutes slower than the seven leaders who qualified for the final. He circled the track by himself for the final six laps before finishing. It was reported that Charles was a member of Haitian dictator "Papa Doc" Duvalier's personal guard who was rewarded for his service with a free trip to **Canada** for the Olympics but was also told that he must finish the race or face a severe penalty.

HAKULINEN, VEIKKO JOHANNES (FIN–CCS). B. 4 January 1925, Kurkijoki, **Finland**. D. 24 October 2003, Valekakoski, Finland. Veikko Hakulinen won seven medals (three gold, three silver, one bronze) in **cross-country skiing** at four **Olympic Winter Games**. His first gold came in the 1952 50 km event, the second in the 1956 30 km, and the last in the 1960 cross-country **relay**. At 35 years, 51 days old, he was the oldest male gold medalist in cross-country skiing at the Olympics. Hakulinen competed at the Olympics for a fourth time in 1964 in the **biathlon**, having previously won a world team silver at his new sport in 1963. He was also cross-country skiing World Champion in 1954 and 1958 over 15 km and in the relay in 1954. Hakulinen won four titles at Holmenkollen: the 50 km in 1953 and 1955, the 18 km in 1953, and the 15 km in 1957. The outstanding Nordic skier of his generation, the five-foot, eight-inch (173 cm), 146 lb (66 kg) Hakulinen continued competing well into his 60s, by which time he had also become proficient at ski **orienteering**.

HALF-HEAVYWEIGHT. The weight class "half-heavyweight" is only used in **judo** competition and is the weight class between **middleweight** and **heavyweight** that in other sports is termed "**light-heavyweight**." It has been contested in each **Olympic Games** judo competition since 1972 for men and since 1992 for **women**. The only woman with multiple medals in this class is **Japan**'s Yoko Tanabe, who won the silver medal in both 1992 and 1996. There have been six men who have won two medals each in the half-heavyweight class: Robert Van de Walle of **Belgium** (gold 1989, bronze 1988), Aurélio Miguel of **Brazil** (gold 1988, bronze 1996), Stéphane Traineau of **France** (bronze 1996, 2000), David Starbrook of **Great Britain** (silver 1972, bronze 1976), Naidangiin Tüvshinbayar of **Mongolia** (gold 2008, silver 2012), and Henk Grol of the **Netherlands** (bronze medal 2008, 2012).

HALF-LIGHTWEIGHT. The weight class "half-lightweight" is only used in **judo** competition and is the weight class between **extra-lightweight** and **lightweight** that in other sports is termed "**bantamweight**" or "**featherweight**." It has been contested in each **Olympic Games** judo competition since 1980 for men and since 1992 for **women**. Masato Uchishiba of **Japan** won the gold medal in this class in both 2004 and 2008. There have been four multiple medalists in men's half-lightweight competition: Israel Hernández (bronze 1992, 1996) and Yordanis Arencibia (bronze 2004, 2008) of **Cuba**, Udo Quellmalz of **Germany** (gold 1996, bronze 1992), and Janusz Pawłowski of **Poland** (silver 1988, bronze 1980). Xian Dong-Mei of **China** was the winner of the women's half-lightweight class in both 2004 and 2008. Three other women won two medals each in this class: Legna

Verdecia of Cuba (gold 2000, bronze 1998), An Kum-Ae of North **Korea** (gold 2012, silver 2008), and Noriko Sugawara-Narazaki of Japan (silver 2000, bronze 1998).

HALF-MIDDLEWEIGHT. The weight class "half-middleweight" is only used in **judo** competition and is the weight class between **lightweight** and **middleweight** that in other sports is termed "**welterweight**." It has been contested in each Olympic Games judo competition since 1972 for men and since 1992 for **women**. There have been five men who have each won two medals in this weight class: Frank Wieneke of West Germany (gold 1984, silver 1988), Ole Bischof of **Germany** (gold 2008, silver 2012), Jo In-Cheol of **Korea** (silver 2000, bronze 1996), Kim Jae-Beom of Korea (gold 2012, silver 2008), and Roman Hontiuk of the **Ukraine** (silver 2004, bronze 2008). Ayumi Tanamoto of **Japan** is the only woman who has won two gold medals in this weight class, although there have been three other women with two medals at this weight: Gella Vandecaveye of **Belgium** (silver 1996, bronze 2000), Jeong Seong-Suk of Korea (bronze 1996, 2000), and Urška Žolnir of **Slovenia** (gold 2012, bronze 2004).

HALFPIPE. A halfpipe (originally a hollowed out bottom half of a huge diameter pipe) is a structure in which the contestant can demonstrate various stunts and flips while traversing the structure from one side to the other on a skateboard or snowboard. Since 1998, halfpipe has been an event in both men's and **women**'s Olympic **snowboarding**. **Shaun White** of the **United States** won gold medals in men's halfpipe in both 2006 and 2010 and was fourth in 2014. In women's halfpipe, Kelly Clark of the United States won the gold medal in 2002, finished fourth in 2006, and won the bronze medal in 2010 and 2014.

HALL, LARS GÖRAN IVAR (SWE–MOP). B. 30 April 1927, Karlskrona, Blekinge, **Sweden**. D. 26 April 1991, Täby, Stockholm, Sweden. After winning the **modern pentathlon** World Championships in 1950 and 1951, Lars Hall won individual gold medals at the 1952 and 1956 **Olympic Games**. He was the first modern pentathlete in history to win two Olympic titles, and in 1952, he became the first nonmilitary winner of the event. Hall also won an Olympic team silver in 1952 and was a member of the winning team at the World Championships four times (1949–1951 and 1953).

HALMAY, IMRICH ZOLTÁN VON (HUN–SWI). B. 18 June 1881, Vyskoká pri Morave, Bratislava, Kingdom of **Hungary**. D. 20 May 1956, Budapest, Hungary. Zoltán von Halmay was the first great **swimmer** from continental Europe, winning nine **Olympic medals** in nine events entered (three gold, five silver, one bronze) between 1900 and 1908 at distances ranging from 50 yards to 4,000 meters. His gold medals were for the 50 and 100 yard **freestyle** in 1904 and the 4x250 meter **relay** in 1906. His 1904 50 yard freestyle victory came in a second race after the judges declared a dead **heat** in the first race between Halmay and J. Scott Leary of the **United States**. The six-foot, one-inch (187 cm), 183 lb (83 kg) Halmay won silver in 1900 in the 200 and 4,000 meter freestyle, in 1906 in the 100 meter freestyle, and in 1908 in the 100 meter freestyle and 4x200 meter freestyle relay. He also won a bronze in 1900 in the 1,000 meter freestyle. Halmay swam mostly with his arms, without any leg movements, but in 1905 he set what is considered the inaugural record for 100 meters. The record remained unbeaten for more than four years, a remarkable length of time during a period of rapid development in the sport.

HÄMÄLÄINEN-KIRVESNIEMI, MARJA-LIISA (née HÄMÄLÄINEN) (FIN–CCS). B. 10 September 1955, Simpele, Finnish South Karelia, **Finland**. After competing without distinction in the 1976 and 1980 **Olympic Winter Games**, Marja-Liisa Hämäläinen achieved unprecedented success at the 1984 Games. With victories in the five km, 10 km, and 20 km, she became the first woman to win three individual gold medals for Nordic skiing at one Games. A five-foot, nine-inch (176 cm), 143 lb (65 kg) skier, she also won a bronze medal in the **relay** and won a second relay bronze in 1988, but illness prevented her from adding to her medal tally at her fifth Olympics in 1992. At the 1994 Olympic Winter Games, she finished her Olympic career with bronze medals in the five km and 30 km races, giving her a total of seven **Olympic medals**. After her triple victory in 1984, she married Harri Kirvesniemi, himself an Olympic Nordic skiing bronze medalist. Hämäläinen-Kirvesniemi is one of only five women (Anna Orlova [LAT], Gerda Weissensteiner [ITA], Emese Nemeth-Hunyady [HUN/AUT], **Claudia Pechstein** [GER]) to compete in six Olympic Winter Games. She won one individual World title, the 1989 10 km, and skied on two relay World Champion teams in 1978 and 1989.

HAMM, MARIEL MARGARET "MIA" (later CORRY, then GARCIAPARRA) (USA–FTB). B. 17 March 1972, Selma, Alabama, **United States**. One of the best female **football** players in the world, Mia Hamm is possibly the best-known American player, male or female. In her career, she played in an amazing 275 matches for the U.S. national team, scoring no fewer than 158 goals. At five-foot, four-inches (165 cm), 123 lb (56 kg), she played in three **Olympic Games**, winning the inaugural **women**'s football title in 1996, being runner-up in 2000, and winning again in her final tournament in Athens in 2004. Hamm also played in four World Cups, winning the first Women's Cup in 1991 as well as the 1999 edition, while finishing third in 1995 and 2003. She was named Fédération Internationale de Football Association Female Player of the Year in 2001 and 2002. Hamm was cofounder of the Women's United Soccer Association, the first women's pro-league in the world, in which she played for the Washington Freedom. It folded in 2003, but its successor, Women's Professional Soccer, features a silhouette of Hamm in its logo, indicating her significance for the women's game.

HAMMER THROW. The hammer throw is one of the field events in **athletics**. It has been part of the men's Olympic competition since 1900, although it was not contested at the 1906 **Intercalated Olympic Games**. It has only been a **women**'s Olympic event since 2000. The "hammer" is actually a round weight attached to a chain and weighs 16 lb (about 7.3 kg) for men's competition and four kg (8.8 lb) in women's competition. **John Flanagan** of the **United States** won the event the first three times it was held at the **Olympic Games**—in 1900, 1904, and 1908. Other three-time Olympic hammer throw medalists are Matt McGrath of the United States (gold 1912, silver 1908, 1924), Gyula Zsivótzky of **Hungary** (gold 1968, silver 1960, 1964), and Yury Siedykh of the **Soviet Union** (gold 1976, 1980, silver 1988). Siedykh could have been a four-time medalist had his country not **boycotted** the 1984 Games. In the women's hammer throw, Olga Kuzenkova of **Russia** won the gold **Olympic medal** in 2004 and silver medal in 2000, and Yipsi Moreno of **Cuba** won silver medals in 2004 and 2008.

HANDBALL (AMERICAN). American handball is a sport played primarily in the **United States**. There are three versions: one-wall, three-wall, and four-wall. **Singles** or **doubles** are the usual forms. Players alternate hitting a small rubber ball against a wall and must retrieve it before it bounces twice. It has never been contested at the **Olympic Games** even as a **demonstration** sport and very likely never will be as it is not played in that many nations. The World Handball Council administers the sport internationally, and in 2014 it had nine member nations and 12 associate member nations. *See also* BRUNDAGE, AVERY.

HANDBALL (TEAM HANDBALL). Handball is a team sport that combines aspects of **basketball**, **football (soccer)**, and **water polo**. It is played on a **basketball**-sized court by teams of seven players, who attempt to score goals by throwing a ball slightly smaller than a **volleyball** into a goal on the ground that is about the size of a **lacrosse** goal.

The game was invented in **Germany** in the early 20th century and became very popular in Europe. At the 1936 **Olympic Games**, the Germans added it to the program, but it was contested outdoors on a large field with 11 men to a side. It was not on the **Olympic Program** again until 1972, when it was added to the Olympics at Munich. This time the sport was contested as described above, with seven men to a side and held indoors. In 1976, **women**'s handball became an Olympic sport. In 12 Summer Games, there have been 2,479 participants (1,550 men, 929 women) from 46 nations in Olympic handball.

Handball is immensely popular in Europe, surpassed by only football (soccer), **cycling**, **athletics** (track and field), and, perhaps recently, basketball and volleyball. The same popularity has not extended to other areas of the world, notably the **United States**; thus the sport has been dominated by the Europeans. The sport is governed worldwide by the International Handball Federation, which was founded in July 1946 and currently has 190 members. Two handball players have won four Olympic medals: **Oh Seong-Ok** (KOR) and **Andrey Lavrov** (URS/EUN/RUS). Twenty-two other Olympians have each won three medals, but only Lavrov has won three gold medals.

HAUG, THORLEIF (NOR–CCS/NCO). B. 29 September 1894, Lier, Buskerud, **Norway**. D. 12 December 1934, Lier, Buskerud, Norway. Thorleif Haug was the winner of all three Nordic skiing events (18 km, 50 km **cross-country**, and **Nordic combined**) at the 1st **Olympic Winter Games** in 1924, and the 29-year-old Norwegian was considered the star of the Games. Although his feat has been equaled on many occasions, no cross-country skier has yet succeeded in winning more than three gold medals at one Games. In 1924, he was also awarded the bronze medal in the **ski jump**, but 50 years later it was discovered that the scores had been incorrectly calculated and that Anders Haugen (USA) had finished third, with Haug in fourth place. Haug's daughter later presented her father's bronze medal to the rightful owner. Haug won nine titles at Holmenkollen, a record six in the 50 km (1918–1921, 1923–1924) and three in Nordic combined.

HEAT. In several racing type sports such as **athletics**, **cycling**, **rowing**, and **swimming**, when there are more entrants than can be accommodated in one race at the same time (as is usually the case), the field is divided into smaller groups. Races are then contested in heats, with the leaders advancing to the next round of competition. In some sports, such as cycling and rowing, the losers are given a second chance in a *repêchage* race.

HEAVYWEIGHT. Heavyweight is a weight class used in Olympic **boxing**, **judo**, **taekwondo**, **weightlifting**, and **wrestling**. Initially it referred to an unlimited weight class, but in some sports the unlimited class has been superseded by a **super-heavyweight** class. In boxing, from 1904 through 1980, heavyweight was the unlimited class, but a super-heavyweight class was added in 1984 and heavyweight is now the second heaviest class and has a weight limit of 201 lb (91 kg). **Women**'s Olympic boxing does not include a heavyweight class. **Teófilo Stevenson** and **Félix Savón** both of **Cuba** are the only three-time gold **Olympic medalists** in the heavyweight category, although when Stevenson won, it was the unlimited category while Savon competed in the 91 kg maximum weight class.

In judo, a heavyweight (unlimited weight) class has been contested in each Olympic Games in which judo was held. Men's competition began in 1964 and women's in 1992. David Douillet of **France** has won three medals in this class (gold in 1996, 2000, bronze in 1992). Hitoshi Saito of **Japan** also won two gold medals (1984, 1988) in heavyweight competition. In women's Olympic heavyweight judo, six women have each won two medals, but none has won more than one gold medal.

In the four Olympic Games in which taekwondo has been held, each one has had competition for men and for women in heavyweight (unlimited) weight classes. Chen Zhong of **China** won the gold medal in both 2000 and 2004 in women's heavyweight taekwondo, while Alexandros Nikolaidis of **Greece** (silver in 2004, 2008) and Pascal Gentil of France (bronze in 2000, 2004) are the only multiple medalist in men's heavyweight taekwondo.

In Olympic weightlifting, the heavyweight class was the unlimited class until 1968. In 1972, the unlimited class was termed "super-heavyweight." John Davis of the **United States** (1948, 1952) and Leonid Zhabotynskiy of the **Soviet Union** (1964, 1968) both won two gold medals in the heavyweight class, although at the time it was also the unlimited class. Women's weightlifting was added to the Olympic program in 2000 and the heavyweight class was the second heaviest as a super-heavyweight class also was included. Nataliya Zabolotnaya of **Russia** (silver 2004, 2012) is the only dual medalist in women's Olympic weightlifting.

Olympic wrestling also has a heavyweight category in both **freestyle** and **Greco-Roman disciplines**. Heavyweight was also the unlimited category through 1968, but in 1972 a super-heavyweight class was added. The super-heavyweight was an unlimited weight class through 1984, but since then a maximum weight limit has been imposed. In 1984, this limit was 130 kg (280 lb), but in recent years it has been lowered and is different for freestyle and Greco-Roman style. **Wilfried Dietrich** of **Germany** and West Germany won five Olympic medals in heavyweight (unlimited) wrestling—silver in 1956 and 1960 and bronze in 1964 in Greco-Roman style and gold in 1960 and bronze in 1968 in freestyle. Stanka Zlateva of **Bulgaria** won two silver medals (2008, 2012) in women's Olympic heavyweight wrestling.

HEFFORD, JAYNA (CAN–ICH). B. 14 May 1977, Trenton, Ontario, **Canada**. Forward Jayna Hefford is one of only two Canadian players to have competed in all five Olympic **ice hockey** tournaments to date (as of 2014). Together with **Hayley Wickenheiser**, Hefford has won four gold **Olympic medals** (2002, 2006, 2010, 2014) and one silver (1998). Her most important contribution was made in 2002, when in the last seconds of the second period, she scored what turned out to be the game-winning goal. The five-foot, four-inch (163 cm), 139 lb (63 kg) Hefford has consistently been the leading scorer for her club team, the Brampton Thunder of the National Women's Hockey League and Canadian Women's Hockey League. She has also been on 11 Canadian teams that won medals at the World Championships, winning seven titles (1997, 1999–2001, 2004, 2007, 2012) and four silver medals (2005, 2008, 2009, 2011).

HEIDEN, ERIC ARTHUR (USA–SSK). B. 14 June 1958, Madison, Wisconsin, **United States**. Eric Heiden is arguably the greatest **speed skater** of all time. In 1980, he was given the honor of reciting the **Olympic Oath** on behalf of the athletes during the opening ceremony of the Lake Placid **Olympic Winter Games**, which he then went on to completely dominate in speed skating, winning the gold medal at all five distances. He set new Olympic records in every event, adding a world record in the 10,000 meters. At the World Championships following the 1980 Olympics, he suffered his first defeat since 1977, after which he retired. Heiden was World Champion in the **all-around** in 1977–1979, in the **sprint** all-around in 1977–1980, and in the junior all-around in 1977–1978. The six-foot, one-inch (185 cm), 185 lb (84 kg) Heiden then turned to **cycling** and, after coming close to making the U.S. Olympic team in a second sport, he had a brief career as a professional cyclist, once winning the U.S. professional championship and competing in one Tour de France. His sister Beth was also an outstanding speed skater and cyclist, winning World Championships in both sports and a bronze medal at the 1980 Winter Games in the 3,000 meters. Eric Heiden later attended medical school and now practices as an orthopedic surgeon near Salt Lake City, Utah, specializing in sports medicine.

HENIE, SONJA (later TOPPING, GARDINER, and ONSTAD) (NOR–FSK). B. 8 April 1912, Kristania (Oslo), **Norway**. D. 12 October 1969, in flight, Paris, **France**–Oslo, Norway. Sonja Henie was a triple gold **Olympic**

medalist (1928, 1932, 1936), who did more to popularize **figure skating** than any other individual. After winning 10 world and three Olympic titles, she turned professional in 1936 and soon amassed a fortune. Her flair for showmanship ensured the success of the 12 feature films she made in Hollywood and accelerated the public awareness of ice skating as a sport. The diminutive Henie (five-feet, one-inch tall [155 cm], 99 lb [45 kg]) toured the world with spectacular ice reviews, achieving great popularity, particularly in the **United States**. She was initially idolized in her native Norway, but had some image problems after World War II, when she was perceived to have been a Nazi sympathizer who failed to support war relief efforts in Norway. Henie later suffered from leukemia and died during a flight from Paris to Oslo, on a trip to visit a medical specialist.

HEPTATHLON. The heptathlon is a **women**'s version of the **decathlon**. It is an **athletics** event that consists of seven different events that determines the best **all-around** female athlete. The seven events are 100 meter **hurdles**, 200 meter **sprint**, 800 meter run, **high jump, long jump, shot put**, and **javelin throw**. It was added to the **Olympic Program** in 1984 and has been held at each subsequent Olympic Games. Jackie Joyner-Kersee of the **United States** won the event in 1988 and 1992 after finishing second in 1984. From 1960 to 1980, a women's **pentathlon** was held, with 80 meter hurdles, 200 meter sprint, high jump, long jump, and shot put.

HIGH JUMP. The high jump, in which athletes use a running start and attempt to clear a bar raised several feet from the ground, has been held in each modern **Olympic Games** since 1896. From 1896 to 1924, the event was solely for men but since 1928 a **women**'s high jump has also been contested. From 1900 through 1912, a separate standing high jump (without a running start) was also held for men. No man has won the running high jump more than once, although **Ray Ewry** of the **United States** dominated the standing high jump with four wins in the five years it was contested. Prior to 1968, high jumpers attempted to clear the bar by hurdling it with their body facing the bar or hurdling it sideways. In 1968, American gold medalist Dick Fosbury pioneered a new style in which he turned prior to reaching the bar and leaped with his back facing the bar. This approach, which was dubbed the "Fosbury Flop," became the standard method, and virtually all high jumpers since use this method. Patrick Sjöberg of **Sweden** has won three medals in the running high jump (silver 1984, 1992, bronze 1988). Iolanda Balaş of **Romania** (1960, 1964) is the only multiple gold medalist in the women's high jump. Sara Simeoni of **Italy** (gold 1980, silver 1976, 1984) is the only three-time medalist in the women's event.

HILDGARTNER, PAUL (ITA–LUG). B. 8 June 1952, Chienes, Bolzano-Bozen, **Italy.** One of 11 lugers to win at least three **Olympic medals** and two gold medals, Paul Hildgartner uniquely won his gold medals 12 years apart. In 1972, Hildgartner joined Walter Plaikner to win the Olympic **doubles luge** gold medal. He then turned to **singles** luge, earning a silver medal in 1980 and winning the Olympic title in 1984 at Sarajevo. At five-foot, 10-inches (178 cm), 174 lb (79 kg), he competed in five **Olympic Winter Games** from 1972 to 1988. Hildgartner was also World Champion in singles in 1978 and in doubles in 1971 (with Plaikner). He was a four-time European Champion, twice in singles (1978, 1984) and twice in doubles (1971, 1974). Hildgartner was the singles World Cup leader in both 1981 and 1983.

HOCKEY (FIELD). Hockey is the oldest known ball and stick game. Records exist of it having been played in **Persia** in 2000 B.C. It became so popular by the Middle Ages that it was banned in **England** for a time because it interfered with the practice of **archery**, which was the basis for national defense.

The modern game of hockey, however, was developed in England in the late 19th century. It spread throughout the British Empire, and most of the dominant nations in the early years of the sport were members of that empire, including **India, Pakistan, Australia, New Zealand**, and the United Kingdom. India's dominance in this team sport at the Olympics is matched only by the **United States'** dominance in **basketball, Hungary**'s dominance in **water polo**, and **Canadian** and **Soviet** dominance in **ice hockey**. Between 1928 and 1956, India won six gold medals and 30 consecutive games. Although in principle the game of field hockey is quite similar to ice hockey, ironically none of the nations that excel in ice hockey also excel in field hockey.

Hockey appeared on the **Olympic Program** in 1908 and 1920. In 1928, it was held at Amsterdam and has been an Olympic sport since. In 1980, hockey for **women** was first introduced as an Olympic sport. In 22 Summer Games, there have been 3,594 participants (2,714 men, 880 women) from 41 nations in Olympic field hockey. The sport is governed internationally by the Fédération Internationale de Hockey, which was formed in 1924 and had 126 member nations in mid-2014. Although 49 Olympians have won three or more hockey medals, only **Udham Singh** (IND), **Leslie Claudius** (IND), Teun de Nooijer (NED), and Lucha Aymar (ARG) have won four. Eight Olympians have won three gold medals, among them Udham Singh and Leslie Claudius and five other Indian players: **Dhyan Chand**, Balbir Singh Sr., Ranganan-than Francis, Randhir Singh Gentle, and Richard Allen. Australian Rechelle Hawkes is the only non-Indian hockey Olympian to win three gold medals. *See also* INDIA FIELD HOCKEY TEAMS (1928–1964).

HODLER, MARC (SUI–IOC). B. 26 October 1918, Bern, **Switzerland**. D. 18 October 2006, Bern, Switzerland. Marc Hodler was a long-time **International Olympic Committee** (IOC) member, serving from 1963 until his death. He was a member of the IOC **Executive Board** twice (1985–1992, 1998–2001) and served as one of the IOC's vice presidents from 1993 until 1996. Hodler was also the president of the Fédération Internationale de Ski between 1951 and 1998. In that position, he strove to abolish the Olympic amateurism regulations, which notably affected **Alpine skiing**. But Hodler is better known for making the **Olympic bribery scandal** public in 1997, eventually causing reforms in the host city selection procedure. Hodler, who was himself on the Swiss skiing team in the 1930s, was also a team leader of the Swiss skiing team, vice president of the Swiss **National Olympic Committee** (1940–1951), and organizer of the Alpine events at the 1948 St. Moritz Games. He was also a good **bridge** player and a member of the Swiss national team in that sport.

HOLMES, KELLY (GBR–ATH). B. 19 April 1970, Pembury, Kent, **England**. Kelly Holmes's career as a middle-distance runner is a testament to her perseverance. Frequently hampered by injuries, she starred as a runner while an English schoolgirl but joined the army at age 18, where she played on the **volleyball** and **judo** teams, and she did not break through to world class until 1993. The five-foot, four-inch (163 cm), 121 lb (65 kg) Holmes won the **Commonwealth Games** 1,500 meters in 1994 and 2002, finished fourth in the 800 meters in Atlanta in 1996, and won a bronze medal in the 800 meters in Sydney in 2000, which were her major international achievements until the 2004 **Olympic Games**. At Athens, she became only the third female runner to win the 800 and 1,500 meters at the same Olympics, despite not being favored in either event. At the end of 2004, Lady Kelly Holmes was made a Dame for her efforts.

HONDURAS (HON). The **Central American** nation of Honduras, officially known as the Republic of Honduras, first competed at the **Olympic Games** of 1968. It did not enter in 1972 and **boycotted** in 1980 but has appeared at every other Summer Games since. In 10 Summer Games, Honduras has entered 113 athletes (96 men, 17 **women**) and participated in 12 sports: **athletics** (19 men, four women), **boxing** (four men), **football** (52 men), **judo** (four men, two women), **swimming** (12 men, eight women), **weightlifting** (two men), and one man in **rowing, taekwondo,** and **wrestling** and one woman in **fencing, shooting,** and **table tennis**.

No Honduran athlete has won an **Olympic medal.** The best performance by Honduras in the Olympic Games occurred in 2012 when their football team finished seventh. The 2000 football team finished 10th. The top Honduran Olympic athlete in an individual event has likely been walker Santiago Fonseca, who competed in the 20 km walk in 1976, 1988, and 1992, placing 27th, 31st, and 40th, respectively. Other notable results include Hipólito López, 41st and Luis Raudales, 49th of 67 entrants in the 1976 **marathon**; Leonardo Carcamo, tied for 13th of 34 entrants in 1996 **extra-lightweight** judo; Dora Maldonado, tied for 13th of 23 entrants in 1996 women's extra-lightweight judo; Sharon Fajardo, 51st of 90 in 2008 50 meter **freestyle** swimming; and Jorge Flores, 28th of 36 in the 1992 **decathlon**.

In 1992, Honduras competed at Albertville in its only appearance at the **Olympic Winter Games**, represented by Jenny Palacios-Stillo in **cross-country skiing**. She was last in two of three events but placed 50th of 53 competitors in the 15 k race.

HONG KONG, CHINA (HKG). Hong Kong, located in Asia on the south coast of **China**, first competed at the 1952 **Olympic Games** and has since missed only the 1980 Moscow Olympics. In 15 Summer Games, Hong Kong has entered 292 athletes (209 men, 83 **women**) and participated in 19 sports with substantial representation in most of them: **archery** (six men, four women), **athletics** (16 men, eight women), **badminton** (eight men, nine women), **boxing** (two men), **canoeing** (11 men, two women), **cycling** (19 men, three women), **diving** (six men), **equestrian** (two men, one woman), **fencing** (22 men, six women), **gymnastics** (one man, one woman), **hockey** (17 men), **judo** (10 men, three women), **rowing** (10 men, three women), **sailing** (23 men, five women), **shooting** (18 men, two women), **swimming** (26 men, 24 women), **table tennis** (11 men, 12 women), **triathlon** (one man, one woman), and **weightlifting** (one woman). One female athlete competed in both canoeing and rowing and another competed in both swimming and rowing.

Despite their long Olympic history, prior to 1996, no Hong Konger had ever finished in the top 10. In Atlanta, Lee Lai-Shan won Hong Kong's first **Olympic medal**, a gold in **windsurfing**, with Ko Lai Chak and Li Ching adding a silver medal in men's **doubles** table tennis in 2004. In 2012, Lee Wai Sze won the bronze medal in the women's **keirin** cycling race. Other notable results for Hong Kong Olympians include fourth place for the men's table tennis team in 2012 and fourth for gold medalist Lee Lai-Shan in windsurfing in 2004 and sixth place in 2000. In table tennis, athletes from Hong Kong have done well, with 23 reaching the quarter-final round of their tournaments and finishing tied for fifth place. In badminton women's **singles** in 2004, Wang Chen reached the quarter-finals as did Yip Puy Yin in 2012, and both finished in fifth place ties. King Yin Chan finished sixth in men's windsurfing in 2008. In 1988 Hung Chung Yam was 12th of 136 entrants in the men's cycling **road race**. Other creditable finishes in that event were recorded by Chow Kwong Man (36th of 132 in 1964), Wong Kam Po (37th of 144 in 2012), Leung Hung Tak (50th of 136 in 1988), and Chow Tai Ming (55th of 136 in 1988).

Hong Kong first competed at the **Olympic Winter Games** in 2002, represented by two female **short-track speed skaters**, and has competed in the three subsequent Winter Games. In four Winter Games, Hong Kong has entered three women and one man, all in short-track speed skating, but without exceptional results. Their best performance was by Han Yue Shuang, who finished 18th of 29 skaters in the women's 1,000 meter event in 2006.

On 1 July 1997, China regained sovereignty over Hong Kong, which is now officially a "Special Administrative Region of the People's Republic of China," but it was agreed that the territory would retain a separate Olympic identity as Hong Kong, China.

At the Beijing Olympics in 2008, Hong Kong was the site of the equestrian competition.

HONORARY IOC MEMBERS. The matter of honorary **International Olympic Committee** (IOC) membership was first raised in 1948. Following a proposal by Lord Arthur Porritt (New Zealand), it was agreed that those IOC members who had passed the age limit of 70 would be eligible to become honorary members and would be entitled to attend future **IOC Sessions**. They would be permitted to take part in the discussions, but would not be accorded a vote. The first honorary member to be appointed was the 86-year-old Riccardo Aldão (Argentina). The age at which **IOC members** may advance to honorary membership has varied. Currently, an IOC member may become an honorary member at the age of 70, if he or she has served on the IOC for 10 years and is nominated by the IOC **Executive Board**. Honorary members may attend the **Olympic Games**, **Olympic Congresses**, and IOC Sessions, but they no longer retain voting rights.

HOP, STEP, AND JUMP. *See* TRIPLE JUMP.

HOPLITE RACE. *See* RACE IN ARMOR.

HOPPE, WOLFGANG (GDR/GER–BOB). B. 14 November 1957, Apolda, Thüringen, **German Democratic Republic**. Wolfgang Hoppe started his sports career in track and field **athletics** and won the German Democratic Republic junior **decathlon** championship in 1976. He later turned his talents to **bobsledding** and became the world's top driver in the 1980s. In the two-man event, Hoppe won Olympic gold in 1984 and a silver in 1988 and was three times the World Champion. He was equally accomplished in the four-man event, winning an Olympic gold in 1984 and a silver in 1988 and 1992, and ending his Olympic career with a four-man bronze in 1994. Hoppe won 14 medals at the World Championships, including six gold medals, and at the European Championships he won the two-man title in 1986–1987 and the four-man event in 1987. The five-foot, 11-inch (181 cm), 196 lb (89 kg) Hoppe also won four seasonal World Cup titles.

HORIZONTAL BAR. The horizontal bar is one of the exercises performed by male **gymnasts**. The apparatus consists of a single cylindrical bar 278 cm (9.1 feet) above the floor supported by a metal frame. The bar is 2.8 cm (1.1 in) in diameter and 240 cm (7.9 ft) long. The exercise was included in the first modern **Olympic Games** in 1896, in 1904, and in every Olympic Games since 1924. **Takashi Ono** of **Japan** (1956, 1960) and Mitsuo Tsukahara of Japan (1972, 1976) are the only multiple gold medalists in this event.

HORSE VAULT. The horse vault is the briefest event that takes place at the **Olympic Games**. It is one of the **gymnastics** events and is held in both men's and **women's** competition. The gymnast runs down a 25 meter padded runway, jumps off a small springboard, and hurdles him- or herself over a padded table known as a horse (roughly four feet wide [1.2 meters] by three feet long [0.9 meter] with a height of slightly more than four feet), while executing acrobat spins and landing on both feet at the other side of the horse. Two separate runs are made during competition, with each lasting less than five seconds from start to finish. The event was first held for men at the Olympic Games in 1896. It was then held in 1904 and since 1924 has been contested at each Games. It has been included in women's Olympic gymnastics since 1952. The 1896 men's winner, **Carl Schuhmann** of Germany, also competed that year in **athletics, weightlifting,** and **wrestling** and in addition to four gold medals in gymnastics also won a gold medal in wrestling. **Nikolay Andrianov** (gold 1976, 1980, bronze 1972) of the **Soviet Union** is the only three-time medalist in the men's horse vault. **China's** Lou Yun (1984, 1988) and **Spain's** Gervasio Deferr (2000, 2004) each also won two gold medals in this event. Among the women, **Larysa Latynina** of the Soviet Union (gold 1956, bronze 1960, silver 1964) is the only three-time medalist, and **Věra Čáslavská** of **Czechoslovakia** is the only woman to win gold medals twice in this event.

HOY, CHRISTOPHER ANDREW "CHRIS" (GBR–CYC). B. 23 March 1976, Edinburgh, **Scotland**. One of the chief exponents of the British track **cycling** program, Chris Hoy led the very successful British cycling team in

Beijing in 2008, winning three gold medals. After anchoring the British team **sprint** squad to the title, the six-foot (185 cm), 205 lb (93 kg) Hoy dominated the match sprint and **keirin** competitions to win three gold medals, the best track cycling performance at a single Olympics since **Marcus Hurley** in 1904. The following year, he was recognized for his accomplishments by being named "knight bachelor." In 2012, Sir Christopher again won the keirin and team sprint to bring his total of Olympic cycling medals to a record seven. Until just a few years earlier, Hoy had specialized in the 1,000 meter time trial, an event he had won at the 2004 Athens Games. When that event was discontinued for Beijing, Hoy was forced to change to other track sprinting events. His switch proved very successful, as he has uniquely won world and Olympic titles in all four sprinting **disciplines**. He won his first **Olympic medal**, silver, in the 2000 team sprint. His medal total in World Championships was 25 (11 gold) when he retired from cycling on 18 April 2013. In 2012, the Sir Chris Hoy **Velodrome** was constructed in Edinburgh for the 2014 **Commonwealth Games**.

HUGHES, CLARA (CAN–CYC/SSK). B. 27 September 1972; Winnipeg, Manitoba, **Canada**. Of the five athletes (**Eddie Eagan** [USA–BOX/BOB], Jacob Tullin Thams [NOR–SAI/SKJ], **Christa Luding-Rothenburger** [GER–SSK/CYC], Lauryn Williams [USA–ATH/BOB]) to have won medals in both the **Olympic Games** and **Olympic Winter Games**, Clara Hughes is the only one to have won multiple medals in both seasons. Originally a **speed skater**, she was scouted as a talented **cyclist**. At the Atlanta Games in 1996, the five-foot, eight-inch (175 cm), 159 lb (72 kg) Hughes won bronze medals in both the **road race** and the individual **time trial**. She returned to speed skating in 2000 and won her third Olympic bronze medal in the 2002 5,000 meters competition. Four years later, she went on to win that event in a final-lap effort, adding to a silver medal in the team **pursuit**. She closed out her Winter Olympic career in front of a home crowd in Vancouver, with another medal in the 5,000 meters—her fourth Olympic bronze. In 2012, she returned to cycling and finished in the individual time trial at the London Games. In cycling, Hughes has also won a silver medal at the World Championships, eight **Pan American Games** golds, and a **Commonwealth Games** title.

HUNGARY (HUN). The central European nation of Hungary was one of the countries that attended the first **Olympic Games** in 1896 in Athens, although it was then part of the Austro-Hungarian empire. A **National Olympic Committee** was formed in Hungary in 1895 by Dr. Ferenc Kémény, one of the founding members of the **International Olympic Committee**. Hungary has missed only two Olympics, but has appeared at all celebrations of the

Olympic Winter Games. Hungary was not invited to the 1920 Olympics in Antwerp, having been an aggressor nation in World War I, and it chose not to attend the 1984 Los Angeles Olympics. Interestingly, in 2012, Hungary, which had been known officially as the Republic of Hungary since 1989, adopted a new constitution, which effective 1 January 2012, changed its official name to simply Hungary.

In 26 Summer Games, Hungary has entered 2,494 athletes (1,951 men, 543 **women**) and competed in 31 sports plus the **art competitions**. They have had the most entrants in **athletics** (290 men, 90 women), **swimming** (140 men, 77 women), **fencing** (149 men, 38 women), **wrestling** (64 men, one woman), **gymnastics** (94 men, 69 women), **handball** (87 men, 64 women), **water polo** (116 men, 27 women), **rowing** (116 men, 19 women), and **canoeing** (106 men, 26 women).

Hungary has won 490 **Olympic medals** in the Summer Games (170 gold, 151 silver, 169 bronze) in 18 different sports plus the art competitions. The nation has been very successful in a variety of sports, but by far its greatest honors have been earned in fencing (84 medals, 35 gold). In one fencing discipline, the **sabre**, it has been the dominant nation, and between 1908 and 1960, Hungary won nine of 11 team titles and 10 of 11 individual titles in this event.

Two Hungarian Olympians have won 10 medals: **Ágnes Keleti** (five gold, three silver, two bronze) in gymnastics (1952–1956) and **Aladár Gerevich** in fencing (1932–1960). Gerevich won seven gold medals (one silver, two bronze), while two Hungarians **Pál Kovács** and **Rudolf Kárpáti** have each won six gold medals, all in fencing. Swimmer **Zoltán von Halmay** won nine medals (three gold, five silver, one bronze) from 1900 to 1908. Katalin Kovács won medals (three gold, five silver) in eight of nine **kayak** races that she entered from 2000 to 2012 and finished fourth in the other race. Another Hungarian Olympian with eight medals is Margit Korondi, who won two gold, two silver, and four bronze in gymnastics in 1952 and 1956. Three athletes with seven medals each who represented Hungary in the Summer Games are the aforementioned fencer Pál Kovács, who won a bronze in addition to his six gold medals from 1936 to 1960; female fencer **Ildikó Sági Ujlaky Rejtő**, two gold, three silver, two bronze; and **Krisztina Egerszegi**, who won five gold, one silver, and one bronze from 1988 to 1996. Ildikó had the further distinction of winning medals under three different names—she was Miss Rejtő in 1960, Mrs. Ujlakiné Rejtő in 1964 and 1968, and as Mrs. Ságiné Ujlakiné Rejtő in 1972 and 1976. In **boxing**, **László Papp** was the first man to win three Olympic gold medals.

Hungary has also been very successful in men's water polo. In 21 tournaments from 1912 to 2012, they have won 15 medals (nine gold, three silver, three bronze), finished fourth once, fifth four times, and sixth once. From 1948 to 1964, they were led by **Dezső Gyarmati** who earned three gold, one silver, and one bronze and who has more Olympic medals in the sport than anyone else.

In 22 **Olympic Winter Games**, Hungary has entered 206 athletes (139 men, 67 women) and competed in 10 sports. They had the most participants in **figure skating** (19 men, 20 women), **ice hockey** (38 men), **Alpine skiing** (19 men, 16 women), **cross-country skiing** (17 men, nine women), and **biathlon** (12 men, 10 women). They have won six medals at the Winter Games—all in figure skating and five in **pairs**. Emília Rotter and László Szollás won bronze in 1932 and 1936 and the brother and sister pair of Marianna Nagy and her brother László won bronze in 1952 and 1956. Andrea Kékesy and Ede Király were silver medalists in 1948. Hungary's other Winter Games medal was won by the **ice dancing** couple Krisztina Regőczy and András Sallay in 1980.

The Hungarian capital city of Budapest has been unsuccessful in five bids to be the host city of the Summer Games—1916, 1920, 1936, 1944, 1960. *See also* BALCZÓ ANDRÁS; KÁRPÁTI, GYÖRGY; WEISSMULLER, JOHNNY.

HURDLES. One of the oldest forms of **athletics** competition is the hurdles. Several wooden barriers are placed on a running track and the runners have to jump over them on their way to the finish line. Olympic races for men are run at 110 meters and 400 meters, with the shorter race having higher hurdles (42 inches [107 cm]) and the longer race with lower hurdles (36 inches [91 cm]). **Women**'s Olympic hurdles races are at distances of 100 meters (80 meters from 1932 to 1968) and 400 meters with slightly lower hurdles. The men's 110 meter hurdles has been contested at every **Olympic Games** since 1896, and a **United States** runner has won 20 of the 28 races. Lee Calhoun (1956, 1960) and Roger Kingdom (1984, 1988) are the only two multiple gold medalists in this event. In the men's 400 meter hurdles, contested most years since 1900, Glenn Davis (1956, 1960), **Edwin Moses** (1976, 1984), and Angelo Taylor (2000, 2008), all of the United States, and Felix Sanchez of **Cuba** (2004, 2012) have each won the event twice, and Moses also won a bronze medal in 1988. **Shirley Strickland de la Hunty** of **Australia** won the women's 80 meter hurdles twice (1952, 1956) and was the bronze medalist in 1948. Deon Hemmings of **Jamaica** is the only woman to win multiple medals (gold 1996, silver 2000) in the 400 meter hurdles.

HURLEY, MARCUS LATIMER (USA–CYC). B. 22 December 1883, New Rochelle, New York, **United States**. D. 28 March 1941, New York, New York, United States. With four gold medals in the 1904 Olympic **cy-**

cling events (quarter-mile, third-mile, half-mile, and one mile races) and a bronze in the two-mile race, Marcus Hurley tied a record for individual golds at one Games, which stood until **Eric Heiden**'s domination of the 1980 **speed skating** events. The five-foot, 11-inch (181 cm) Hurley was the greatest American amateur cyclist of his era. He won the U.S. amateur sprint championship from 1901 until 1904 and was world amateur sprint champion in 1904. Hurley was also an excellent **basketball** player at Columbia University, captaining that team in 1908 and earning All-American honors from 1905 to 1908. He also captained the New York AC basketball team, which won the Metropolitan championship in 1905. Hurley was later enshrined in the College Basketball Hall of Fame.

I

ICE DANCING. Ice dancing is one of the events in Olympic **figure skating**. In was first included in the Grenoble **Olympic Winter Games** of 1968 as a **demonstration sport** and was then known as "rhythmic skating." It became an **Olympic medal** sport in 1976 at Innsbruck. The event differs from **pairs** figure skating in that requirements for lifts and spins are different and throws and jumps are disallowed. Originally couples were supposed to be in a dance hold throughout the program, but this restriction has been relaxed somewhat. In 11 Winter Games, there have been 312 participants from 35 countries in Olympic ice dancing. The **Soviet Union** and its successors, the Unified Team and **Russia**, have dominated the sport and won seven gold, six silver, and five bronze medals. The husband and wife team of Marina Klimova and Sergey Ponomarenko have won three medals—bronze in 1984, silver in 1988, and gold in 1992—to lead all competitors in the sport. They won their first two medals representing the Soviet Union and the third for the Unified Team. *See also* TORVILL AND DEAN.

ICE HOCKEY. Ice hockey is a Canadian sport that began in the early 19th century. Around 1860, a flat rubber disc known as a puck was substituted for a ball, and in 1879, two McGill University students, W. F. Robertson and R. F. Smith, devised the first rules, combining **field hockey** and **rugby** regulations. Originally the game was played nine to a side. The sport became the Canadian national sport, with leagues everywhere. (It did not officially become the national sport until 1994. Previously, **lacrosse** held that honor and since 1994 is still Canada's official national summer sport.) In 1894, Lord Stanley of Preston, governor general of **Canada**, donated the Stanley Cup that was first won in 1894 by a team representing the Montreal Amateur Athletic Association.

Ice hockey was contested at the 1920 Summer Olympics at Antwerp, held in early April. These were also the first World Championships and were played by seven-man sides, the only time seven-man teams played in the Olympics. In 1924, the Olympics began using the current standard of six players per team on the ice at a time—five skaters and one goaltender.

Ice hockey has been held at every **Olympic Winter Games**. In 23 Olympic tournaments (one at the Summer Games, 22 at the Winter Games), there have been 3,885 athletes (3,387 men, 498 women) from 34 nations who have played Olympic ice hockey. Canada dominated early Olympic ice hockey tournaments, as might be expected. In 1956, the **Soviet Union** first entered the Olympic Winter Games and won the ice hockey tournament quite handily. It was the preeminent country until its political division in the early 1990s, its dominance interrupted only by major upset victories by the **United States** in 1960 and 1980.

Professionalism has always been a consideration in Olympic ice hockey. Canada dominated the early years of Olympic hockey, despite not being able to use its pros. When the Soviet Union entered in 1956 and assumed that dominance, Canada was quite upset, claiming that the Soviet ice hockey players were amateurs in name only, which was likely correct. Canada then **boycotted** the Olympic ice hockey tournament, not sending a team in 1972 or 1976. Finally, in the late 1980s, some professionals were allowed to compete in Olympic ice hockey, and in 1998, all players from the National Hockey League (NHL) became eligible. In fact, the NHL shuts down for slightly over two weeks in midseason to allow its players to compete at the Olympics.

Women's ice hockey appeared on the **Olympic Program** for the first time in 1998 at Nagano. The sport is governed by the International Ice Hockey Federation, which was founded in 1908 and had 73 affiliated nations as of June 2014. **Jayna Hefford** and **Hayley Wickenheiser**, both of Canada, have each won five **Olympic medals** (four gold, one silver) from 1998 to 2014. Their teammate Caroline Ouellette played from 2002 to 2014 and won four

The 1980 USA Ice Hockey team, also known as "The Miracle on Ice Team," defeated the Soviet Union and captured the gold medal. Courtesy of Erich Kamper

gold medals. Thirteen other athletes (eight men, five women) have won four Olympic medals in ice hockey, with 42 winning three medals through 2014. *See also* BOTTERILL, JENNIFER LORI; CANADIAN ICE HOCKEY TEAMS; KELLAR, REBECCA D.; SOVIET UNION ICE HOCKEY TEAMS (1956–1992); TRETYAK, VLADISLAV ALEKSANDROVICH.

ICE SKATING. *See* FIGURE SKATING; ICE HOCKEY; SPEED SKATING.

ICELAND (ISL). The North Atlantic European island nation of Iceland sent one athlete to the 1908 **Olympic Games**, Johannes Jósefsson, a wrestler, although he marched with the Danish team at the opening ceremony. The country also sent two athletes to the 1912 Olympics, but did not appear again until 1936. Since that time, it has never failed to be present at an Olympic Games. Since 1944, the country has been officially known as the Republic of Iceland. In 20 Summer Games, Iceland has entered 220 athletes (184 men, 36 **women**) and competed in 11 sports: **athletics** (52 men, 10 women), **badminton** (two men, two women), **gymnastics** (one man), **handball** (71 men), **judo** (nine men), **sailing** (four men), **shooting** (three men), **swimming** (26 men, 24 women), **water polo** (eight men), **weightlifting** (five men), **wrestling** (two men), plus the **art competitions**. In 1908 and 1912, Icelandic athletes also took part in a **demonstration** of **glíma**, a form of wrestling popular in Iceland but virtually nowhere else.

Iceland has won four medals in the Olympic Games, a silver in the **triple jump** by Vilhjálmur Einarsson in 1956, a bronze in **half-heavyweight** judo by Bjarni Friðriksson in 1984, a bronze by Vala Flosadóttir in women's **pole vault** in 2000, and a silver by the men's handball team in 2008. It could be argued that Icelanders have also won a gold medal. In 1920, **Canada** won a gold medal in ice hockey at Antwerp, represented by the club team, the Winnipeg Falcons. Of the eight Canadians on that team, seven were of Icelandic origin and had dual citizenship.

Other notable results for Iceland in the Summer Games include their very first Olympic Games when their only athlete, Jóhannes Jósefsson, finished fourth in the **middleweight** class in **Greco-Roman wrestling**. In 2000, swimmer Örn Arnarson was fourth in the 200 meter **backstroke**. The Iceland men's handball team, in addition to their silver medal in 2008, also had a fourth place result in 1992, fifth place in 2012, and sixth place in 1984. Iceland athletes have also had three fifth place finishes in athletics: Vilhjálmur Einarsson in the 1960 triple jump, Siggi Einarsson in the 1992 **javelin throw**, and Þórey Edda Elísdóttir in the 2004 women's pole vault. In 1984, Einar Vilhjálmsson was sixth in the javelin throw. In gymnastics, Rúnar Alexandersson was seventh in the **pommelled horse** event in 2004. Guðrún Arnardóttir was also seventh in the 2000 women's 400 meter **hurdles**. **Middle-heavyweight** weightlifter Guðmundur Sigurðsson finished in eighth place in 1976.

Iceland has competed at all the **Olympic Winter Games** since 1948, except for 1972. In 17 Winter Games, Iceland has entered 75 athletes (61 men, 14 women) and competed in three sports: **Alpine skiing** (39 men, 14 women), **cross-country skiing** (19 men), and **ski jumping** (three men). One would think that a country called Iceland would excel at winter sports, but this is not the case. They have not won a medal at the Winter Games. Their best results have been in the **slalom**, where nine of their athletes finished between 16th and 25th place. Steinunn Sæmundsdóttir was 16th of 42 in the women's slalom in 1976. Daníel Hilmarsson was 24th of 109 in the 1988 men's slalom.

INDEPENDENT OLYMPIC ATHLETES (IOA). At Sydney in 2000, the **International Olympic Committee** (IOC) allowed athletes from the disputed nation of East Timor to compete under the designation of independent Olympic athletes. This was despite the fact that the nation did not yet have a **National Olympic Committee** (NOC) recognized by the IOC. East Timor was represented in 2000 by four athletes, three men and one **woman**, who competed in **athletics**, **boxing**, and **weightlifting**. Boxer Victor Ramos lost his first bout in the **lightweight** class and finished tied for 17th. **Bantam-weight** weightlifter Manuel Araujo finished 20th of 22, and Calisto da Costa was 71st of 100 in the men's **marathon**. Aguida Fatima Amaral was 43rd of 53 in the women's marathon.

In 2012, one athlete from **South Sudan** and three from Curaçao competed as IOAs. Guor Marial of South Sudan competed in the men's marathon and finished a creditable 47th of 105 entrants. Liemarvin Bonevacia of Curaçao reached the semifinals of the 400 meter run before being eliminated. *Judoka* Reginald de Windt received a **bye** in his first round **half-middleweight** match but lost the next and finished tied for 17th. **Sailor** Philipine van Aanholt finished 36th of 41 entrants in the women's one person **dinghy**.

On 4 December 2012, the IOC suspended the NOC of Curaçao on the basis of corruption, government interference, and not following guidelines of the IOC.

At the 2014 **Olympic Winter Games**, Shiva Keshavan of **India** was allowed to compete in the **luge** as an IOA due to India's suspension. This was his fifth Olympics as he had previously competed for India from 1998 to 2010 and had a best finish of 25th in 2006. In 2014, he finished 37th of 39. *See also* INDEPENDENT OLYMPIC PARTICIPANTS.

INDEPENDENT OLYMPIC PARTICIPANTS (IOP). In 1992 at the Barcelona Summer Games, 58 athletes (39 men and 19 **women**) from **Yu-**

goslavia were allowed to compete as independent Olympic participants. The United Nations Security Council Resolution No. 757 had placed a ban on Yugoslav teams competing internationally because of the war in **Bosnia and Herzegovina**. However, the **International Olympic Committee** made arrangements allowing individual athletes to compete, provided they did not officially represent Yugoslavia. Three of them won medals—all in **shooting**. Jasna Šekarić won a silver medal in women's **air pistol**. She had previously won the gold medal in that event and also a bronze medal in the women's sporting pistol in 1988 as a representative of Yugoslavia and she would compete for **Serbia and Montenegro** from 1996 to 2004 and win two more silver medals. In 2008 and 2012, she represented **Serbia** and competed in her sixth and seventh Olympic Games. Aranka Binder was the second IOP to win a medal. She won a bronze medal in women's **air rifle** and later competed for Serbia and Montenegro in 1996 and 2000. The third IOP with a medal was Stevan Pletikosić. He won the bronze medal in the men's **small-bore rifle** prone competition. From 1996 to 2004, he competed for Serbia and Montenegro and in 2008 represented Serbia.

Other notable results for IOPs in 1992 include Dragan Perić, seventh in the men's **shot put**; Dragutin Topić, tied for eighth in the men's **high jump**; Goran Maksimović, fifth in men's air rifle; Nemanja Mirosavljev, ninth in men's small-bore rifle, three positions; Jasna Šekarić, sixth in women's sporting pistol; the team of Ilija Lupulesku and Slobodan Grujić, tied for fifth in men's **table tennis doubles**; and **Greco-Roman wrestlers** Senad Rizvanović (eighth, **flyweight**), Goran Kasum (sixth, **middleweight**), Miloš Govedarica (ninth, **heavyweight**), and Milan Radaković (10th, **super-heavyweight**). *See also* INDEPENDENT OLYMPIC ATHLETES.

INDIA (IND). The South Asian country of India (officially the Republic of India), sometimes referred to as a subcontinent, the seventh largest country by area and second largest (behind **China**) in population, made its first Olympic appearance in 1900, when Norman Pritchard, a British resident of Calcutta, competed in the **sprints** at Paris, representing the London Athletic Club and **Great Britain**. (Some Olympic historians consider him to have competed for Great Britain in 1900.) India's next Olympic appearance occurred in 1920, although its **National Olympic Committee** was not formed until 1927. India has competed at all the **Olympic Games** since 1920.

In 23 Summer Games, India has entered 791 athletes (682 men, 109 **women**) and competed in 21 sports plus the **art competitions**. The largest contingents have been in **hockey** (217 men, 14 women), **athletics** (107 men, 42 women), and **wrestling** (71 men, one woman). They have won 26 **Olympic medals** (nine gold, six silver, 11 bronze). In 1928, India entered its first hockey team and won the gold medal. This was the first of six consecutive gold medals won by India in men's field hockey. Eleven of India's 26 medals in the Olympics have been won by its field hockey team, with eight of its nine golds being won in that sport. The other gold was won by Abhinav Bindra in men's **air rifle shooting** in 2008.

All the top medal winners for India have been male hockey players. Although 11 hockey Olympians have won at least three hockey medals, only **Udham Singh** and **Leslie Claudius** have won four. The other Indian hockey Olympians who have won three gold medals includes: Harbinder Singh, V. J. Peter, Prithipal Singh, **Dhyan Chand**, Balbir Singh, Sr., Shankar Laxman, Ranganathan Francis, Randhir Singh Gentle, and Richard Allen. There were 21 other Indian hockey players with two medals each. The only other multiple medalists for India are the aforementioned Norman Pritchard, who competed in five athletics events in 1900 and won silver in the 200 meters and 200 meters **hurdles,** and **welterweight freestyle** wrestler Sushil Kumar, who won bronze in 2008 and silver in 2012.

Indian medalists in sports besides hockey are Saina Nehwal (2012 women's **badminton singles**, bronze); **middleweight** boxer Vijender Singh (2008 bronze), **flyweight** women's boxer Mary Kom (2012 bronze), shooters Vijay Kumar (2012 silver), Gagan Narang (2012 bronze), and Radjavardhan Rathore (2004 silver); **weightlifter** Karnam Malleswari (women's **light-heavyweight**, 2000); freestyle wrestlers Khashaba Jhadav (1952 **bantamweight**) and Yogeshwar Dutt (2012 **lightweight**); and **tennis** player Leander Paes (1996 men's singles). Paes as a professional player is known as one of the world's best **doubles** players, and his Olympic singles victory is somewhat surprising.

India has competed at the 1964–1968, 1988–1992, and 1998–2014 **Olympic Winter Games.** In nine Winter Games, India has entered 14 athletes (12 men, two women) and competed in three sports: **Alpine skiing** (eight men, two women), **cross-country skiing** (three men), and **luge** (one man). India's best performances at the Winter Games include five-time Olympian Shiva Keshevan's 25th of 36 in 2006 luge; Shailaja Kumar's 28th of 57 in 1988 women's **slalom**, and Kishor Rathna Rai's 49th of 109 in 1988 men's slalom.

Additionally, in 1924 seven Indian sherpas were among the 21 men from several nations awarded a special Olympic medal for **alpinism** for their 1922 attempt at climbing Mount Everest. *See also* INDIA FIELD HOCKEY TEAMS (1928–1964).

INDIA FIELD HOCKEY TEAMS (1928–1964). India dominated Olympic men's **field hockey** from its first appearance in 1928 through 1964. During that time, India won 30 consecutive games (1928–1960), the streak being broken, 1–0, in the 1960 finals by **Pakistan**. India won the gold medal in seven of the eight Olympics between 1928 and 1964, losing only in 1960 to Pakistan, but still taking a silver medal. India continued to be one of the top nations in Olympic hockey through the 1970s, winning a bronze medal in 1968 and 1972 and another gold medal in 1980. Since that time, India's best finish has been fifth in 1984. Indian hockey reached an all-time low when it failed to qualify for the 2008 Games, the first time this had happened since the country's debut in 1928. In 2012, although they qualified for the tournament, they lost all six matches and finished 12th and last. Overall, India has an Olympic hockey record of 76 wins, 31 losses, and 13 ties. It has outscored its opponents 423 goals to 151 goals. India's **women** competed in Olympic hockey only in 1980, but with less success, finishing fourth of six teams.

INDONESIA (INA). The Southeast Asian archipelago of Indonesia, officially known as the Republic of Indonesia, is the world's fourth most populous country behind **China, India**, and the **United States** and was at one time a Dutch colony known as the Dutch East Indies. Indonesia formed a **National Olympic Committee** in 1946, but did not compete at the Olympics until 1952. It missed the 1964 **Olympic Games** when it withdrew after several of its athletes were banned for their participation in the 1963 **Games of the New Emerging Forces**. Indonesia also **boycotted** the 1980 Olympics. The country has never competed at the **Olympic Winter Games**.

In 14 Summer Games, Indonesia has entered 257 athletes (177 men, 80 **women**) and competed in 20 sports, with the most participants in its national sport of **badminton** (32 men, 26 women), at which it is one of the dominant countries in the world. Other sports with large contingents included **weightlifting** (28 men, six women), **athletics** (21 men, six women), **swimming** (15 men, four women), **boxing** (18 men), and **archery** (five men, 11 women).

Indonesia has won 27 **Olympic medals** (six gold, 10 silver, 11 bronze), 18 of them in badminton (six of each color), eight in weightlifting (three silver, five bronze), and one in archery (silver in 1988 women's team). Four Indonesian athletes have each won two Olympic medals: Raema Lisa Rumbewas in women's weightlifting (2000 **flyweight**, 2004 **featherweight**, both silver); Eko Irawan in men's weightlifting (2008 **bantamweight**, 2012 featherweight, both bronze); Triyatno in men's weightlifting (2008 featherweight bronze, 2012 **lightweight** silver); and Susi Susanti in badminton women's singles (gold 1992, bronze 1996). Susi's husband, Alan Budikusuma, also won a gold medal in men's badminton singles in 1992—one of the few times in Olympic history that a husband and wife both won gold medals in the same year. Indonesia's Olympic gold medals were all earned in badminton. Other winners were, in men's singles Taufik Hidayat (2004) and in men's **doubles** the teams of Rexy Mainaky and Ricky Subagja (1996), Candra Wijaya and Tony Gunawan (2000), and Markis Kido and Hendra Setjawan (2008). In some cultures within Indonesia, people are mononymous and thus "Triyatno" is the only name used by the medal-winning weightlifter.

INTERCALATED OLYMPIC GAMES. The dictionary definition of the verb *intercalated* is "to insert between existing elements or layers." The **Olympic Games** of 1906 were inserted between the regularly scheduled Games of 1904 and 1908 and are usually referred to as the Intercalated Olympic Games. They were held in Athens, Greece, from 22 April through 2 May 1906. Twenty-one nations attended, with 841 athletes competing (835 men and six women) in 13 sports. Today, the **International Olympic Committee** and some historians do not consider the 1906 Intercalated Olympic Games to be "true" Olympic Games. By doing so, they neglect the Games that may have helped save the **Olympic Movement**. After the debacles of 1900 and 1904, the Olympics were in desperate straits. The Greeks had wanted to host more Olympics, and they proposed holding "interim" Olympics, every four years in the even year between the Olympics. The first of these was scheduled in 1906. The Greeks later scheduled interim Olympics for 1910 and 1914, but political and economic events in Greece prevented those from being held. The Games of 1906 were not of the caliber of many Olympics of later years, but they were the best Olympics to that date. Since then, no other Intercalated Olympic Games have been held, but in 1994, the Olympic Winter Games schedule was changed and those Games are no longer held the same year as the Summer Games but in the intercalated years between the Summer Games.

INTERNATIONAL FAIR PLAY COMMITTEE (COMITÉ INTER-NATIONALE POUR LE FAIR PLAY) (CIFP). The International Fair Play Committee was founded in 1963 to promote the principles of fair play. Former **tennis** champion Jean Borotra of **France** (one of the famed "Four Musketeers of tennis"—Jacques Brugnon, Henri Cochet, René LaCoste were the others) was instrumental in its creation and was the organization's president from 1963 to 1988. He was succeeded by Willi Daume of **Germany** (1988–1996), Louis Guirandou N'Diaye of **Côte d'Ivoire** (1997–1999), and Dr. Jenö Kamuti of **Hungary** (2000–). Each year, the CIFP awards International Fair Play Prizes after receiving nominations from various groups. The athletes may be neophytes or Olympic champions and are chosen for their commitment to fair play. The CIFP notes that they award prizes for three achievements: (1) an act of fair play that cost or could have cost the victory to a contender who sacrificed or compromised his or her chances of winning by complying not only with the written rules of the sport, but also with the "unwritten" ones; (2) a general attitude of sportsmanship throughout a sports career, marked by an outstanding and constant spirit of fair play; and (3) an activity aimed at promoting fair play: organization of national or local campaigns, lectures, books, articles, reports, or comments in the media.

INTERNATIONAL FEDERATIONS (IF). International Federations are nongovernmental organizations that administer sports on an international level. The IFs' role is to establish and enforce the rules governing the practice of their sport, promote development of their sport internationally, and assume responsibility for the technical control of their sport at the **Olympic Games**. Currently, the **Olympic Program** is reviewed after each **Olympiad**, and the **International Olympic Committee** (IOC) makes the decision about which sports will or will not be on the program. There are two categories of IFs affiliated with the IOC. One is the International Olympic Federations, which govern sports currently on the Olympic Program. In 2014, there were 28 that are members of the **Association of Summer Olympic International Federations** and seven that are members of the **Association of International Olympic Winter Sports Federations**. A second category is IOC-Recognized International Federations, of which there are currently 35 and which are members of the **Association of the IOC-Recognized International Sports Federation**. These federations are not yet on the Olympic Program, but IOC recognition is a necessary first step to that end.

INTERNATIONAL OLYMPIC ACADEMY (IOA). The idea of an International Olympic Academy was first conceived in the 1930s by **Ioannis Ketseas**, an **International Olympic Committee** (IOC) member in **Greece**, and **Carl Diem**. The idea never died, but it took many years of informal discussions before the foundation of an academy, to be located at Olympia, Greece, was unanimously approved by the IOC during a session in Rome in 1949. Of the 80 invitations sent to **National Olympic Committees** for the first preliminary session, only four replies were received, and all of these were in the negative. Ketseas, who was now working closely with Diem, a German professor with a passionate interest in Olympic matters, persisted with his goal, and with the assistance of Olympic and archaeological bodies from Germany and Greece, the IOA eventually came into being and has subsequently prospered. The first session was held from 16–23 June 1961.

A plot of some 150 acres of land bordering the Ancient Olympic stadium was acquired by the IOA and buildings were erected. The complex, which now provides accommodations, an extensive library, and several sports facilities, is a popular center for students of the **Olympic Movement**. The IOA holds an annual session each summer, during which students of the Olympic Movement gather for several days to hear speeches and discussions on Olympic subjects. In addition, many other international symposia are held at the IOA each year. The idea of Olympic academies has spread, and there are more than 70 National Olympic Academies, helping to spread the message of **Olympism** and the Olympic Movement. *See also* GEORGIADES, KONSTANTINOS.

INTERNATIONAL OLYMPIC COMMITTEE (IOC). The International Olympic Committee is the international governing organization of the **Olympic Movement** and the **Olympic Games**. It is a nongovernmental, nonprofit organization of unlimited duration, in the form of an association with the status of a legal person, recognized by decree of the Swiss Federal Council of 17 September 1981. The IOC was founded by **Pierre de Coubertin** in 1894, at the **Olympic Congress** that reestablished the Olympic Games. The IOC is currently based in **Lausanne, Switzerland**, and has been since Coubertin moved there during World War I. The mission of the IOC is to lead the Olympic Movement in accordance with the *Olympic Charter*.

The IOC consists of members who are chosen and co-opted for membership. IOC member nations may have one member on the IOC, although not all do. However, until recently any nation that had hosted the Olympic Games or **Olympic Winter Games** was entitled to a second member on the IOC. IOC members are not considered to be members from their respective nations. Rather, they are considered to be IOC ambassadors to, or in, their respective nations. The **IOC 2000 Commission** helped change the structure of the IOC in late 1999. There are now four classes of IOC members: independent members, co-opted as they have always been; athlete members, who have competed in the most recent Olympic Games; **International Federation** (IF) president members; and **National Olympic Committee** (NOC) president members. The eventual size of the IOC was also restricted to 115 members: 70 independent members, 15 athlete members, 15 IF president members, and 15 NOC president members. Previously, IOC members were elected for life, but the new changes to the *Olympic Charter* call for reelection every eight years, with athlete members restricted to one term.

The IOC is led by the **IOC president**, four vice presidents, and an **Executive Board**. The president is elected initially for a term of eight years, but now may only be reelected for one further term of four years. Prior to 1999, presidents could be reelected with no term limits, but this was changed based on the recommendations of the IOC 2000 Commission. Vice presidents and Executive Board members are elected for a term of four years. They may not be reelected to the same position for consecutive terms, although they may return to that position on the Executive Board after a period of four more years.

IOC Sessions consist of meetings of the entire membership and are required to be held at least once a year. The IOC Session is considered to be the supreme organ of the IOC, but may delegate its powers to the Executive Board. The Executive Board meets more frequently and works by making recommendations to the IOC sessions, which is then responsible for enacting or denying its recommendations. Day-to-day decisions are delegated to the IOC president.

The *Olympic Charter* is the document that specifies the principles, rules, and bylaws of the IOC. Only IOC Sessions have the power to modify and interpret the *Olympic Charter*. *See also* BACH, THOMAS; BAILLET-LATOUR, COUNT HENRY DE; BLONAY, BARON GODEFROY JEAN HENRY LOUIS DE; BRUNDAGE, AVERY; EDSTRÖM, JOHANNES SIGFRID; KILLANIN, LORD; ROGGE, COUNT CHEVALIER DR. JACQUES; SAMARANCH (TORRELO), JUAN ANTONIO; VIKELAS, DEMETRIOS; and Appendix I for a list of IOC presidents; Appendix IV for a list of all IOC members.

INTERNATIONAL PARALYMPIC COMMITTEE (IPC). *See* PARALYMPIC GAMES.

INTERNATIONAL PIERRE DE COUBERTIN COMMITTEE. The International Pierre de Coubertin Committee was founded in 1976. It is committed to the dissemination and study of **Pierre de Coubertin**'s works and his humanitarianism. The first president of the International Pierre de Coubertin Committee was Dr. Paul Martin (Switzerland), followed in 1977 by Geoffroy de Navacelle (France), Coubertin's grand-nephew, and later by Conrado Durántez Corral (Spain). The current president is Dr. Norbert Müller (Germany), with Durántez and de Navacelle considered presidents of honor. There was previously an independent **International Olympic Committee** Commission, the Pierre de Coubertin Commission, although several executives served on both boards, but it has been disbanded.

INTERNATIONAL RELATIONS COMMISSION. The International Relations Commission was formed in 2002 with a mandate to facilitate and promote relations between the **Olympic Movement**, particularly the **International Olympic Committee** (IOC) and the **National Olympic Committees**, and governments and public authorities. It prepares position papers on specific political issues related to sport and advises the **IOC president** and the **Executive Board** accordingly. The Commission is composed of 23 IOC members, with the current chairman being Mario Pescante of **Italy**.

INTERNATIONAL SOCIETY OF OLYMPIC HISTORIANS (ISOH). The International Society of Olympic Historians was founded in 1991 to promote and study the history of the **Olympic Movement** and the **Olympic Games**. The immediate worldwide response from Olympic historians provided a clear indication of the need for such an organization, which in mid-2014 has nearly 450 members from more than 50 nations. The group's *Journal of Olympic History*, edited by **Volker Kluge**, is published three times per year (its website is www.isoh.org). The first president was **Ian Buchanan (Great Britain)**, who served two terms (1991–2000). Buchanan was followed as president by **Bill Mallon (United States)**, who served through 2004. The officers elected in 2004, and reelected in 2008, were president, **Karl Lennartz (Germany)**; vice president, **David Wallechinsky** (United States); secretary-general, **Tony Bijkerk (Netherlands)**; and treasurer, John Grasso (United States). In 2012, Wallechinsky became president, Christian Wacker (Germany/**Qatar**), vice president, and Bijkerk and Grasso were reelected as secretary-general and treasurer. Executive Committee members

International Society of Olympic Historians at Lausanne. From left, Francis Gabet, Director of the IOC Olympic Museum; Dr. Christian Wacker, ISOH Vice-President; Volker Kluge, Editor of the ISOH Journal of Olympic History; Dr. Bill Mallon, founder of the ISOH; Thomas Bach, President of the IOC; David Wallechinsky, President of the ISOH; Tony Bijkerk, Secretary-General of the ISOH; John Grasso, Treasurer of the ISOH. Courtesy of Volker Kluge

elected in 2012 were Philip Barker (Great Britain), former Olympic basketball player Leif Yttergren (**Sweden**), **Kostas Georgiadis** (**Greece**), and Volker Kluge (Germany). IOC member **Richard Pound** (Canada) serves on the ISOH Executive Committee as liaison with the IOC. In November 2004, the IOC **Executive Board** gave official recognition to ISOH.

The ISOH presents an annual scholarship (designated as the Ian Buchanan Memorial Scholarship since 2009) to a graduate student for Olympic studies and also presents annual awards to authors for the best book and article about the Olympic Movement as well as awards for lifetime contribution toward Olympic history.

INTERNATIONAL UNIVERSITY SPORTS FEDERATION (FISU). *See* UNIVERSIADE.

INTERNATIONAL WORLD GAMES ASSOCIATION (IWGA). *See* WORLD GAMES.

IOC 2000 COMMISSION. The IOC 2000 Commission was formed in response to the **Olympic bribery scandal**. The purpose of the IOC 2000 Commission was to study the structure of the **International Olympic Committee** (IOC) and the candidate city bidding process and make recommendations to update these entities to prevent many of the problems that were occurring. The IOC 2000 Commission was made up of 82 members, less than half of them IOC members, and with an **Executive Board** of 26 members, of whom 13 were IOC members. The commission produced an intermediary report in June 1999, and its final report was released in November 1999. The IOC 2000 Commission made 50 recommendations to the IOC in its final report, with recommendations made by each of the working groups. At the IOC Session in December 1999, the IOC approved all 50 of the recommendations, which has led to a major rewriting of the *Olympic Charter*. Following is a summary of the recommendations:

1. Members: The maximum IOC membership should be 115, with 15 active athletes (defined as having taken part in the **Olympic Games** or **Olympic Winter Games** within four years of their membership), 15 **International Federations** (IFs) presidents, 15 presidents of **National Olympic Committees** (NOCs) or Continental Associations, and 70 members elected on an individual basis.
2. Procedure for Selecting Candidates and Electing Members: Proposed forming a Nomination Committee. Each of the above classes of IOC members may propose candidate members. The Nomination Commit-

tee consists of seven members, including at least one athlete, elected for a four-year period; three members elected by the IOC; three by the IOC **Ethics Commission**; and one by the **Athletes Commission**. The Nomination Committee will evaluate prospective members, who will be voted upon by the full IOC Session.

3. Nationality: One member per nation for members chosen on an individual basis; one member per nation among the athletes; one member per nation among NOC presidents; no restrictions on nationality among IF presidents.

4. Terms of Office: Term limit of eight years, renewable, with reelection to follow the same procedure as election.

5. Age Limit: 70 years of age for all members and all functions. However, current members will be "grandfathered" to follow the limit of 80, which existed prior to this vote.

6. Rights and Responsibilities of Members: When a vote concerns a country of a member, the member may not take part in the vote.

7. Honorary Members: Awarded to members of 10 years' standing and for exceptional services.

8. Executive Board: Increase number of members to 15, with four vice presidents. Four-year term limits on the board.

9. President: Elected for an eight-year term; may be reelected one time for a four-year second term of office.

10. Current Members: Current members will be "grandfathered" in place for eight years, at which time they will be subject to reelection, as will all new members.

11. Transition Period: During the transition period, to conclude 1 January 2001, the number of IOC members may be greater than the recommended 115 (currently set at 130).

12. Entry into Force: The new rules will come into force on 1 January 2000, with an implementation period of one year allowed.

13. Program and Participation: 13.1. The obligation of each NOC to participate in the Games of the **Olympiad** will be added to the *Olympic Charter*—somewhat of an "anti**boycott**" clause. All NOCs will be allowed to enter six athletes in the Games of the Olympiad, even if they do not meet the minimum qualification standards. 13.2. Sports Program: A maximum of 280 events is recommended for future Games of the Olympiad. Events included in World Championships programs do not necessarily need to be included in the Olympic Games. Significant discussion followed this vote, as there will be 300 events at Sydney in 2000 and 14 sports are currently applying for admission to the **Olympic Program**. President **Juan Antonio Samaranch** suggested that the

IOC Sports Commission study this proposal and make recommendations to the next IOC Session.

14. Finance: The IOC will transfer knowledge concerning licensing programs to future Organizing Committees of the Olympic Games (OCOGs). The IOC will also provide guidelines and recommendations concerning ticketing and pricing to the OCOGs.

15. Paralympics: The Paralympics must be held in the same city as the Olympics, following the Games. The IOC will formalize its relationship with the **International Paralympic Committee**.

16. Management of the Olympic Games: The IOC established an operational structure to transfer knowledge and expertise from one edition of Olympic Games and Olympic Winter Games to the next.

17. Athletes (1): Defined an active Olympic athlete as one who is still competing or has participated in the most recent edition of the Olympic Games.

18. Athletes (2): Athletes should be represented at all levels of the Olympic Movement.

19. Athletes (3): The Athletes Commission should be represented on the IOC Executive Board, and recommends the same for IFs, NOCs, and **National Governing Bodies** (NGBs).

20. Athletes (4): OCOGs must include an athlete on their boards.

21. Athletes (5): The IOC Athletes Commission must be allocated a budget for its operation.

22. Athletes (6): During the closing ceremony of the Olympic Games and Olympic Winter Games, the elected athletes will be recognized by their peers and the **Olympic family**.

23. Role of **Olympic Solidarity**: Olympic Solidarity should act as the coordinator of development programs for all members of the Olympic Movement.

24. Decentralized Programs: Olympic Solidarity must provide support to Continental/Regional Games under IOC patronage and will also help develop Regional and Subregional Sports Training Centers.

25. Humanitarian Projects: These will be pursued and reinforced if they relate to members of the Olympic Movement and the development and practice of sport.

26. Information Transfer: Olympic Solidarity will ensure that all NOCs have access to the technology necessary for information transfer between sectors of the Olympic Movement.

27. Education: Proposed that NOCs include a session in all Olympic Solidarity–funded programs to educate the participants concerning the Olympic Movement.

28. Regional Information Centers: Proposed that Olympic Solidarity set up Regional and Subregional Sports Information Centers to help disseminate information on the Olympic Movement and sports administration.

29. Evaluation/Accountability: Better coordination between the IOC departments and an improved auditing procedure of Olympic Solidarity to be implemented.

30. Education and Culture (1): Merge the **Cultural Commission** and IOA/Education Commissions into a single Commission on Education and Culture. Create a new department of Education and Culture within the IOC. Hire additional professional staff for the **Olympic Studies Centre** at the **Olympic Museum**.

31. Education and Culture (2): Several recommendations to spread the message of **Olympism** to appropriate regional structures, including publishing the *Olympic Review* and the **Official Reports** of the Olympic Games on the Internet.

32. Education and Culture (3): Creation of a traveling exhibit of the Olympic Movement and Olympic History to be set up in host cities, with a clause added to the host city contract.

33. Education and Culture (4): Greater recognition of the IOC on the educational importance of the Olympic flame relay and participation by the IOC Executive Board in the flame-lighting ceremonies at Olympia.

34. **Doping** (1): The Athletes' Oath will be amended to include a statement concerning drug-free sport.

35. Doping (2): Implementation by the **World Anti-Doping Agency** (WADA) of an athletic passport concerning the athlete's health, allowing doping controls to be carried out and to monitor the participant's health.

36. Doping (3): The IOC will conduct out-of-competition drug tests beginning at the time of accreditation of athletes at the Olympic Games and Olympic Winter Games.

37. Doping (4): In the event of an appeal against sanctions, the "B" sample should be tested by a different laboratory than the one that tested the "A" sample.

38. Doping (5): Sports not conforming to the Olympic Movement Anti-Doping Code and that do not perform out-of-competition drug testing will be dropped from the Olympic Program. IOC-recognized sports not conforming to this code will lose their recognition.

39. Relations with Governments and Nongovernmental Organizations (NGOs) (1): The IOC will provide more assistance to the NOCs to develop closer relationships with their respective local governments.

40. Relations with Governments and NGOs (2): The passage of the United Nations' **Olympic Truce** could be supplemented by similar declarations from world leaders and other NGOs to support the Olympic Truce.

41. Relations with Governments and NGOs (3): The Olympic Truce will be given greater prominence. Six months prior to the Olympic Games or Olympic Winter Games, the IOC president will contact the protagonist nations in major internal and international conflicts and ask them to observe the Olympic Truce for the duration of the Games. During the opening ceremony, the IOC president will refer to the Olympic Truce and will note that it is a first step toward lasting peace.

42. Internal Communications: Internal communications within the Olympic Movement must be open, substantive, two-way, and timely.

43. External Communications: An IOC spokesperson will be appointed to support the IOC president and other IOC executives. The Communications Department of the IOC will develop a proactive approach to media relations. IOC Sessions will be open to the media on closed-circuit television.

44. Transparency (1): The flow of IOC funds for each Olympiad will be disclosed beginning with the current Olympiad, via independent, external auditors.

45. Transparency (2): The IOC will disclose the allocation of funds to each NOC and IF, and each entity of the Olympic Movement will submit to the IOC an accounting of its expenditure of funds provided by the IOC.

46. Transparency (3): The IOC will seek a more transparent disclosure of fund distribution to be phased in over future Olympiads.

47. Transparency (4): Each bid city must disclose the source of funding for bid expenditures, which will be audited at the conclusion of the bid process.

48. Transparency (5): The IOC will encourage NOCs and IFs to disclose their sources and uses of funds.

49. Role of the NOCs in the Bid Process: The NOC should be involved in any Olympic candidature as a full partner with the bid committee and should take responsibility for the Olympic bid to the IOC.

50. New Candidature Procedure: A new bid acceptance phase will be instituted, with a series of recommendations as follows:

    50.1. Strict minimum technical requirements applied to the selection of a bid city.

    50.2. In the new bid acceptance process, representatives of the IOC, IFs, NOCs, athletes, and external experts examine the proposed bids and recommend to the IOC Executive Board which cities should be accepted as candidate cities.

50.3. The IOC will enter into a contractual agreement with the NOC and the Bid Committee.

50.4. The IOC will issue candidate city manuals and prepare candidature files.

50.5. An Evaluation Commission will be formed to visit each of the candidate cities.

50.6. Selection of final candidate cities, if necessary. The Executive Board may reduce the number of candidates by selecting a limited number of cities.

50.7. It is not considered necessary for IOC members to visit the candidate cities nor for the representatives or candidate cities, or third parties acting on their behalf ("agents"), to visit IOC members.

In the end, all 50 recommendations of the IOC 2000 Commission were approved, most unanimously. The main points of contention were the age limit, which had eight dissenting votes, and Recommendation 50.7, which eliminated IOC members' visits to candidate cities, but even those passed with over 90 percent of the vote.

IOC EXECUTIVE BOARD. *See* EXECUTIVE BOARD OF THE IOC.

IOC MEMBERS. The **International Olympic Committee** (IOC) consists of individual members whose role is to spread the message of **Olympism** and the tenets of the **Olympic Movement**. IOC members are considered by the IOC to be ambassadors, not from their nations to the IOC, but from the IOC to their nations. They are co-opted into these positions by the **IOC Session**. In practice, until 2000 the **IOC president** usually proposed members for cooptation, and they were virtually rubber stamped by the IOC Session. Until the 1980s, there was only one category of membership, as members were co-opted for life. In the 1980s, an age limit was instituted, which has varied from 70 to 80, but is currently essentially at 70, at which age **IOC members** are required to step down. A second category was then established for these former members, called **honorary IOC members**. In the 1990s, IOC President **Juan Antonio Samaranch** expanded the concept of IOC membership and established three further categories of membership: (1) **National Olympic Committee** (NOC) presidents, (2) **International Federation** (IF) presidents, and (3) athlete members. NOC and IF presidents only remain IOC members while they continue to hold that role within their own organizations. Athlete members are nominated by the **Athletes Commission** after each **Olympic**

Games and **Olympic Winter Games**, and continue in that role on the IOC for eight years. In the late 1990s, Samaranch established a sixth category of IOC membership, honor members. These were five internationally recognized persons, chosen for their prominence but who otherwise had little to do with the Olympic Movement. Four of these five honor members have either died or resigned, leaving former **United States** Secretary of State Henry Kissinger as the only remaining honor member in 2010. Former IOC President **Jacques Rogge** did not appoint any honor members, and current (as of 2014) President **Thomas Bach** has not either.

After the **Olympic bribery scandal** and the work of the **IOC 2000 Commission**, the methods of becoming and continuing in IOC membership were changed. The IOC membership was limited to 115 members, with the following maxima: (1) 70 individual members, (2) 15 athlete members, (3) 15 NOC presidents, and (4) 15 IF presidents. Further, a Nominating Committee was established that proposes potential members to the IOC Session for final vote. Further, individual members were no longer to be elected for life, but would serve for eight years, after which time they could be reelected. To date, no IOC member has failed to be reelected.

Historically, most nations had only one IOC member, while some larger nations, or those nations that had hosted an Olympic Games or Olympic Winter Games, were permitted to have two. In the early years of the IOC, this restriction did not hold, and some European nations had three or four IOC members. The IOC 2000 Commission capped this at one individual member per nation, although current IOC members were grandfathered in, allowing many nations to retain two members. Athlete members, NOC president members, and IF president members do not count in this category, and there are no restrictions on their national representation. In fact, as of 2014, there are five Swiss IOC members. There are also four each from **Great Britain**, **Russia**, and the United States. IOC membership is dominated by Europeans, and as of 2014, there are 105 IOC members (39 former athletes who had competed in the Olympics) from 75 different nations, with 44 of them from European nations, 22 from Asia, 20 from the Americas, 14 from Africa, and five from Oceania. There are also 33 honorary members and one honor member, Henry Kissinger. Count Jacques Rogge is also included as the honorary president. *See also* WOMEN AT THE OLYMPICS; and Appendix IV for a list of all IOC members.

IOC PARTNERS. The **International Olympic Committee** (IOC) works with several organizations, which it considers partners, in assistance projects for human development via sport and physical activity. The IOC notes on its website: "It is a matter of using sport as a means for a positive change.

Although these projects are specific and merely symbolic, the Olympic Movement's contribution is intended to complement the efforts of the governments and inter- and non-governmental organizations to meet the challenges of our society. The IOC's commitment in this area is based on the need to place sport, which has become a real social force within society, at the service of human development." The IOC lists its partners as the United Nations Educational, Scientific and Cultural Organization, the World Health Organisation, the Office of the United Nations High Commissioner for Refugees, the United Nations Development Programme, the United Nations Office for Drug Control and Crime Prevention, the Office of the High Commissioner for Human Rights, the Food and Agriculture Organization, the United Nations Environment Programme, and the International Labour Organization (ILO). In 2009, its relationship with the United Nations (UN) was formalized when the UN granted the IOC observer status. *See also* OLYMPIC PARTNERS, THE (TOP).

IOC PRESIDENTS. The **International Olympic Committee** (IOC) is led by a president who is elected by the **IOC Session** and is responsible for the day-to-day operations of the IOC. Until the 1950s, the IOC president was effectively elected for life. But in the 1950s, the IOC established the policy that the president is elected for an initial eight-year term and can be reelected indefinitely for four-year terms after that. In 1999, this rule was changed to limit the IOC president to two terms, or a maximum of 12 years in office.

Over the course of its history since 1894, the IOC has been led by nine presidents, or perhaps 10, depending on one's interpretation. The original president was **Demetrios Vikelas** of **Greece**, who was elected at the 1894 Sorbonne IOC Congress, at the suggestion of **Pierre de Coubertin**, who felt that the IOC president should be from the first host country of the **Olympic Games**. Coubertin succeeded Vikelas in 1896 and served as IOC president until 1924, when he was succeeded by **Belgium**'s **Count Henry de Baillet-Latour**. But from December 1915 to February 1917, Coubertin served in the French military. He asked **Switzerland**'s **Baron Godefroy de Blonay** to serve as interim IOC president, as he did not feel that a military person should be the acting IOC president. Some historians do not consider Blonay to have been a true president of the IOC. Ballet-Latour served until his death in 1942, and the position was technically vacant until 1946. But **Sweden**'s **J. Sigfrid Edström**, the IOC vice president at that time, performed the duties during the interregnum, and he was elected IOC president in 1946, serving until 1952, when he was succeeded by **Avery Brundage** of the **United States**. Brundage served until 1972, at the time the second longest term as IOC president, and he was followed by **Ireland**'s Michael Morris, **Lord Killanin**. Lord Killanin was president until 1980, when **Spain's Juan Antonio Samaranch** was elected IOC president. Samaranch's term lasted until 2001, a slightly longer term than Brundage, when he was succeeded by the Belgian orthopedic surgeon and former Olympian **Jacques Rogge**. In 2013, **Thomas Bach** of **Germany**, a former Olympic gold medalist in **fencing**, succeeded Rogge. *See also* Appendix I, Presidents of the International Olympic Committee.

IOC SESSION. The main decision-making body of the **International Olympic Committee** (IOC) is the annual IOC Session. Currently, sessions are held once a year, although special sessions may be called by the **IOC president**. Every other year, one session is held immediately before either the **Olympic Games** or the **Olympic Winter Games**, at the site of those Games. Formerly, when the Olympic Games and Olympic Winter Games were held in the same year, two sessions were held in the Olympic year, one at the site of the Olympic Games and one at the site of the Olympic Winter Games, and immediately preceding those events. The session is a plenary meeting of the IOC and is considered its main rules-making body. In reality, the session is usually presented with a list of decisions made by the IOC **Executive Board**, which are almost universally approved; thus the Executive Board really has the authoritative power. The session also votes on the approval of prospective IOC members, but the choices of the IOC president are usually approved without dissension. The session also has the power to modify the *Olympic Charter*. The IOC Session in Sochi, **Russia**, prior to the 2014 Winter Games was the 126th IOC Session.

IRAN (IRI, formerly IRN). Although Iran was represented in 1900 by a **fencer**, Prince Freydoun Malkom, it was only in 1947 that it formed a **National Olympic Committee**. Iran was granted **International Olympic Committee** recognition in the same year. Since 1979, the western Asian country has been known officially as the Islamic Republic of Iran, and its three-letter abbreviation was changed from IRN to IRI. Apart from **boycotting** the Olympics of 1980 and 1984, Iran has competed at every **Olympic Games** since it made its Olympic debut as a team in 1948.

In 16 Summer Games, Iran has entered 463 athletes (441 men, 22 **women**) and competed in 21 sports. It had the most entrants in **wrestling** (131 men), **weightlifting** (52 men), **boxing** (49 men), and **football** (45 men). Nearly all of Iran's success has been in the strength or combative sports of weightlifting, wrestling, and **taekwondo**. It has won 60 **Olympic medals** (15 gold, 20 silver, 25 bronze) with 38 medals won in wrestling, 16 in weightlifting, five in taekwondo, and one in **athletics (discus throw)**. Three Iranian Olympians have each won three medals: *taekwondoka* **Hadi Saei** (two gold, one bronze 2000–2008), weightlifter Mohammad Nassiri (one gold, one silver, one bronze, 1968–1976), and **freestyle** wrestler Gholam Reza Takhti (one gold, two silver, 1952–1964). **Super-heavyweight** weightlifter Hossein Reza Zadeh is the only other Iranian Olympian besides Saei to win two gold medals (2000, 2004).

Other dual medalists for Iran are freestyle wrestlers Amir Reza Khadem Azgadhi (1992, 1996, both bronze) and his brother Rasoul Khadem Azgadhi (1992, 1996, bronze, gold), Asgari Mohammadian (1988, 1992, both silver), and **bantamweight** weightlifter Mahmoud Namdjou (1948–1956, silver, bronze). Iran's other gold medalists are **Greco-Roman** wrestlers Omid Norouzi (2012 **lightweight**), Ghasem Rezei (2012 **heavyweight**), Hamid Sourian (2012 **featherweight**); freestyle wrestlers Emam Ali Habibi (1956 lightweight), Abdullah Movahed (1968 lightweight), and Ali Reza Dabir (2000 featherweight); and weightlifters Behdad Salimi (2012 super-heavyweight) and Hossein Tavakoli (2000 heavyweight).

Although the sport with the third-most entrants in the Olympics for Iran is boxing, they have not come close to a medal and have had only three boxers reach the quarter-final round. One of their boxers, though, was famous for another achievement—Emanoul "Mike" Aghasi bantamweight/featherweight boxer, who lost his first bout in 1948 and 1952, is the father of 1996 gold medalist **tennis** player Andre Agassi and the father-in-law of Andre's wife, Steffi Graf, who won gold, silver, and bronze in 1988–1992 Olympic tennis.

Iran has competed at the **Olympic Winter Games** of 1956, 1964–1976, and 1998–2014. In those 10 Winter Games, Iran has entered 24 athletes (21 men, three women) and competed in two sports—**Alpine skiing** (18 men, two women) and **cross-country skiing** (three men, one woman). It has not won a medal in the Winter Games, and the best result has been 30th and 31st of 115 entrants in 2014 **slalom** by Mohammad Kiyadarbandsari and Hossein Saveh Shemsaki.

IRAQ (IRQ). The western Asian nation of Iraq, officially known as the Republic of Iraq, formed its **National Olympic Committee** (NOC) in 1948 and made its first Olympic appearance in that year. It then did not compete until the Rome Olympics of 1960. The nation missed the 1972 and 1976 **Olympic Games** but has competed continuously since, including the 1984 Olympic Games. Iraq has never competed at the **Olympic Winter Games**.

In 13 Summer Games, Iraq has entered 174 athletes (168 men, six **women**) and participated in 14 sports: **archery** (one woman), **athletics** (28 men, three women), **basketball** (10 men), **boxing** (18 men), **cycling** (three men), **football** (58 men), **judo** (one man), **rowing** (two men), **shooting** (one man, one woman), **swimming** (three men, one woman), **table tennis** (one man), **taekwondo** (one man), **weightlifting** (24 men), and **wrestling** (19 men). Ali Salman in 1948 took part in both athletics (100 meter, 200 meter) and basketball.

Only one Iraqi athlete has won an **Olympic medal**, a bronze by Abdul Wahid Aziz in **lightweight** weightlifting in 1960. Perhaps the greatest performance by Iraqi Olympic athletes occurred at the 2004 Olympic Games. Shortly after their country was invaded and fought a war, resulting in the ouster of President Saddam Hussein, Iraq qualified a football team for Athens. The team was known to have suffered torture in recent years at the orders of Uday Hussein, president of the Iraqi NOC and son of Saddam, whenever they did not perform well, which caused the NOC to be briefly suspended by the **International Olympic Committee**. But at Athens, the Iraqi football team went to the semifinals and narrowly lost out on a medal, finishing fourth. Other commendable performances by Iraqi Olympians include a tie for fifth place finish (losing quarter-finalists) by the 1980 men's football team and also by light-welterweight boxer Farouk Chancoun that same year. Sixth place results were achieved by **middleweight** weightlifter Mohammed Yaseen Mohammed in 1980 and by wrestler Ghazi Salah in the 1988 **Greco-Roman bantamweight** competition. In 1980, **freestyle** wrestlers lightweight Ali Hussain Faris and bantamweight Karim Salman Muhsin each finished seventh in their events, and in 2004, Raid Rasheed finished in a tie for seventh place in welterweight taekwondo. In weightlifting, bantamweight Ali Hussain Hussain was eighth in 1960 and **light-heavyweight** Shakir Salman in 1960 and **heavyweight** Nazar Kadir in 1992 came in ninth.

One of the less memorable results for Iraqi Olympians occurred in 1948 when they entered the basketball competition. In that year, it was open to all countries, unlike later years when the tournament was limited and nations had to qualify prior to the Games in order to participate in the tournament. Iraq played six games and lost by scores of 102–30, 100–18, 98–20, 120–20, 125–25, and 77–28.

IRELAND (IRL). Ireland formed a **National Olympic Committee** in 1922, shortly after it became independent of **Great Britain** in December 1921. Ireland first competed as a separate state in the 1924 **Olympic Games** at Paris. Prior to that time, however, many Irish athletes had competed, mostly for Great Britain. In addition, many of the great American weight-throwers were recent Irish emigrants. Ireland also entered separate teams in 1908 **field hockey** and the 1912 **cycling road race**, although both were technically second teams representing Great Britain. Since 1924, the Western Europe island nation of Ireland, commonly known (although not officially) as the Republic of Ireland, has competed at every Olympic Games except those of 1936.

In 20 Summer Games, Ireland has entered 716 athletes (585 men, 131 **women**) and competed in 23 sports plus the **art competitions**. The largest contingents were in **athletics** (127 men, 49 women), **boxing** (101 men, one woman), **equestrianism** (46 men, 22 women), **sailing** (50 men, seven women), cycling (43 men, three women), and **rowing** (44 men, two women).

Ireland has won 31 **Olympic medals**—nine gold, nine silver, and 13 bronze, with three of the medals coming in the art competitions (Oliver St. John Gogarty, 1924 literature, bronze; Jack Yeats, 1924 painting, silver; Letitia Hamilton, 1948 painting, bronze). Yeats was the brother of Nobel Prize–winning poet William Butler Yeats. Three athletes have won multiple medals for Ireland, with **swimmer** Michelle Smith winning four medals (three gold, one bronze) all in 1996, Pat O'Callaghan winning the **hammer throw** gold medal in both 1928 and 1932, and **light-flyweight** boxer Paddy Barnes winning bronze medals in 2008 and 2012. Ireland's other gold medalists are 1,500 meter runner Ron Delany (1956), 400 meter **hurdler** Bob Tisdall (1932), **welterweight** boxer Michael Carruth (1992), and women's **lightweight** boxer Katie Taylor (2012).

Their other Olympic medalists include John Treacy (1984 **marathon**, silver); Sonia O'Sullivan (2000, women's 5,000 meter run, silver); Cian O'Connor (2012 **equestrian jumping**, bronze), and sailors David Wilkins and Jamie Wilkinson (1980 two-man **dinghy**, silver). Irish boxers who won silver medals are **bantamweights** John McNally (1952), Wayne McCullough (1992), and John Joe Nevin (2012); welterweight Fred Tiedt (1956); and **light-heavyweight** Kenny Egan (2008). Irish boxers who won bronze medals are **flyweights** Johnny Caldwell (1956), Hugh Russell (1980), and Michael Conlan (2012); bantamweight Freddie Gilroy (1956); lightweights Tony Byrne (1956) and Jim McCourt (1964); and **middleweight** Darren Sutherland (2008).

Ireland has competed at the **Olympic Winter Games** in 1992 and 1998–2014. In six Winter Games, Ireland has entered 27 athletes (22 men, five women) and competed in five sports: **Alpine skiing** (four men, three women), **bobsledding** (nine men, two women), **cross-country skiing** (four men), **skeleton** (four men), and **snowboarding** (one man). Their best result was by Clifton Hugh Lancelot de Verdon Wrottesley, Sixth Baron Wrottesley, who finished fourth in the 2002 skeleton event. Seamus O'Connor finished a respectable 15th of 39 in the 2014 **halfpipe**.

Dublin, Ireland, bid unsuccessfully to host the 1936 Summer Games. *See also* FLANAGAN, JOHN JOSEPH; KILLANIN, LORD OF DUBLIN AND SPIDDAL; SHERIDAN, MARTIN JOSEPH.

ISRAEL (ISR). The formation of the State of Israel as an independent Jewish state occurred on 15 May 1948. Israel dates its **National Olympic**

Committee (NOC) to 1933, but that was a **Palestine** organization and not truly a precursor of the current NOC. The original Palestine Olympic Committee was recognized by the **International Olympic Committee** (IOC) in 1934 and was to represent Jews, Muslims, and Christians from the Palestine region. However, the rules of the original Palestine NOC stated, "Palestine is the National Home of the Jews, and so the Palestine NOC represents the Jewish National Home." Given that manifesto, the Palestine NOC refused to compete at the 1936 **Olympic Games** in Berlin, in protest against Adolf Hitler's policies. After World War II, the 1948 London Organizing Committee originally invited the Palestine NOC, but later withdrew the invitation. The problem of the status of the Palestine Olympic Committee was solved in 1951 when the Israel Olympic Committee was formed.

The western Asian nation, officially known as the State of Israel, competed at its first Olympics in 1952 at Helsinki, the same year in which its NOC was formally recognized by the IOC. Israel has missed only the 1980 Moscow Olympics since 1952. It made its first **Olympic Winter Games** appearance in 1994 at Lillehammer and also participated in 1998 at Nagano. The zenith of Israel participation was in 1992, when two Israeli *judoka* won the nation's first **Olympic medals**. The nadir occurred at Munich on 5 September 1972, when Arab terrorists savagely and cowardly murdered 11 Israeli athletes and officials (David Marc Berger, Zeev Friedman, Yossef Gutfreund, Eliezer Halfin, Yossef Romano, Amitzur Shapira, Kehat Shorr, Mark Slavin, Andrei Spitzer, Yacov Springer, and Moshe Weinberg).

In 15 Summer Games, Israel has entered 306 athletes (226 men, 80 **women**) and competed in 21 sports, with the most participants in **athletics** (33 men, 15 women), **swimming** (32 men, 10 women), **football** (32 men), **sailing** (22 men, nine women), and **shooting** (25 men, one woman). Through 2012, Israel has won seven Olympic medals (one gold, one silver, five bronze)—three in judo, three in sailing, and one in **canoeing**. Israel's top Olympian has been sailor Gal Fridman, who has won two medals, a bronze in 1996 men's **windsurfing**, and Israel's only gold in 2004, also in windsurfing. Israel's other Olympic medalists are canoeist Michael Kolganov (2000 bronze men's **kayak singles** 500 meters), sailor Shahar Zubari (2008 bronze men's windsurfing), and *judoka*s Shay Oren-Smadja (1992 bronze men's **lightweight**), Arik Ze'evi (2004 bronze men's **half-heavyweight**), and Yael Arad (1992 silver women's **half-middleweight**).

Other notable results for Israeli Olympians include fourth places in 1988 by sailors Eldad Amir and Yoel Sela in two person **heavyweight dinghy**; in 2000 by Anat Fabrikant and Shani Kedmi in women's two person dinghy; in 2008 by Nike Kornecki and Vered Buskila also in women's two person dinghy; in canoeing in 2000 by Michael Kolganov in kayak singles 1,000 meters; and in **Greco-Roman wrestling** in 2000 by **super-heavyweight** Yuriy Yevseychyk. Fifth place was achieved by Konstatin Matasevich in the 2000 **high jump**, by **featherweight weightlifter** Eduward Weitz in 1976, and by middleweight Greco-Roman wrestler Gotcha Tsitsiashvili in 1996. Fifth place ties (losing quarter-finalists) were earned by the **tennis doubles** team of Andy Ram and Jonathan Erhlich twice in 2004 and 2012; by featherweight **boxer** Ya'acov Shmuel in 1988; and by *judoka*s Yael Arad (1996 women's half-middleweight), Arik Ze'evi (2000 men's half-heavyweight), and Gal Yekutiel (2008 men's **extra-lightweight**). In addition, the men's football team in 1968 and 1976 also finished tied for fifth.

In six Winter Games, Israel has entered 13 athletes (eight men, five women) and competed in three sports: **Alpine skiing** (one man), **figure skating** (six men, four women), and **short-track speed skating** (one man, one woman). They have not won a medal at the Winter Olympics, and their best performance was in **ice dancing** by the pair of Galit Chait and Sergey Sakhnovsky who finished sixth in 2002 and eighth in 2006. *See also* OLYMPIC DEATHS.

ISTHMIAN GAMES. The Isthmian Games were ancient sporting festivals that were held biennially. With the **Olympic Games**, **Nemean Games**, and **Pythian Games**, they were one of the four great sporting festivals of ancient **Greece**. The Isthmian Games were contested at the sanctuary of Poseidon at the Isthmus of Corinth. They are first known to have been held in 582 B.C. and lasted through the fourth century A.D. Their origin is attributed to Sisyphus, king of Corinth. Champions at the Isthmian Games originally received crowns of dry wild celery, which was later changed to a crown of pine during Roman times. One report suggests that the Isthmian Games were highly commercialized. *See also* ANCIENT OLYMPIC GAMES.

ITALY (ITA). The South Central European nation of Italy, officially known as the Italian Republic, has never missed an **Olympic Games** or an **Olympic Winter Games** along with **Great Britain** and **France**. Although it is usually considered not to have competed in 1896, research in the 1990s discovered that an Italian **shooter** named Rivabella did compete in 1896. In 2009, Olympic historians discovered that Olympic **cyclist** Frank Bizzoni was still an Italian citizen when he competed in 1904. He was formerly thought to have been a **United States** athlete, but his appearance gives Italy a competitor at all Olympic Games. Italy did not form a **National Olympic Committee** until 1908, and it was not until 1915 that this committee was recognized by the **International Olympic Committee**.

In 28 Summer Games, Italy has entered 3,816 athletes (3,107 men, 709 **women**) and competed in 34 sports plus the **art competitions**. They have had the most entrants in **athletics** (410 men, 132 women), **rowing** (347 men, 15 women), cycling (253 men, 20 women), swimming (151 men, 86 women), **gymnastics** (147 men, 78 women), **fencing** (182 men, 42 women), and **football** (223 men).

They have won 577 medals (211 gold, 177 silver, 189 bronze) in Summer sports and won medals in 24 different sports plus the art competitions. Italy has had success in many different sports, but has often been the dominant country in cycling and fencing. Their top five medalists were all fencers. **Edoardo Mangiarotti** from 1936 to 1960 has won the most medals of any Italian Olympian, 13 (six gold, five silver, two bronze). **Valentina Vezzali** is next among Italian Olympians, with nine medals and five gold medals. She has won more total medals and more gold medals than any other woman fencer. Giulio Gaudini from 1928 to 1936 also won nine medals (three gold, four silver, two bronze), Giovanna Trillini has eight (four gold, one silver, three bronze) from 1992 to 2008, and Gustavo Marsi has seven (two gold, five silver) from 1928 to 1936. Fencer **Nedo Nadi** from 1912 to 1920 also won six gold medals. In other sports the **D'Inzeo** brothers, **Piero and Raimondo** each won six medals in **equestrianism** from 1956 to 1972. **Diver Klaus Dibiasi** was one of the greatest in his field, and he won three gold and two silver medals from 1964 to 1976. **Race walker** Ugo Frigerio won four medals (three gold, one bronze) at distances ranging from 3,000 meters to 50 km from 1920 to 1932.

In 22 Winter Games, Italy has entered 938 athletes (698 men, 240 women) and is one of only two nations (**France** is the other) that has competed in all 16 sports. The most entrants have been in **Alpine skiing** (101 men, 65 women), **ice hockey** (134 men, 20 women), **cross-country skiing** (102 men, 31 women), and **bobsledding** (125 men, six women). Twelve athletes have each won at least four medals in Winter sports, with cross-country skier **Stefania Belmondo**'s 10 (two gold, three silver, five bronze, 1992–2002) the most for any individual. **Manuela Di Centa** has seven (two gold, two silver, three bronze) in cross-country skiing from 1992 to 1998. **Luger Armin Zöggeler** has won more medals, six (two gold, one silver, three bronze) from 1994 to 2014, than anyone in his specialty. **Eugenio Monti**'s six bobsled medals (two of each color, 1956–1968) is second best in his sport. **Alberto Tomba**'s three gold and two silver medals from 1988 to 1994 places him among the leaders in Alpine skiing.

Italy hosted the Games of the XVIIth **Olympiad** at Rome in 1960, the 7th Olympic Winter Games at Cortina d'Ampezzo in 1956, and the 20th Olympic Winter Games in Torino (Turin) in 2006. Rome was also awarded the 1908 Olympic Games but had to forfeit that honor due to financial reasons. Cortina d'Ampezzo was also awarded the 1944 Winter Games, which were later canceled due to World War II. In addition, Milan (1908, 2000) and Rome (1924, 1936, 1944, 2004, 2020) also had unsuccessful bids for the Summer Games, and Cortina d'Ampezzo (1952, 1988, 1992), Aosta (1998), and Tarvisio (2002) had unsuccessful bids for the Winter Games. *See also* HILDGART-NER, PAUL; PIETRI, DORANDO; SAN MARINO; VATICAN CITY.

IVORY COAST (CIV). *See* CÔTE D'IVOIRE.

J

JACKSON, LAUREN ELIZABETH (AUS–BAS). B. 11 May 1981, Albury, New South Wales, **Australia**. Lauren Jackson is Australia's greatest female **basketball** player. She led her team to medals in four consecutive **Olympic Games** from 2000 to 2012—silver the first three times and bronze in 2012. They were defeated by the gold-medal winning **United States** team each time, and in 2012 met them in the semifinal round. The team's center, at six feet, five inches (196 cm), 187 lb (85 kg), she has been her team's leading scorer and in 32 games in the Olympic tournaments has scored 575 points for an 18.0 average. She was a member of the gold medal–winning Australia team at the World Championships in 2006 and also at the **Commonwealth Games** that same year. She played professional basketball in the Women's National Basketball Association with the Seattle Storm from 2001 to 2012, averaged 18.9 points per game in 317 games, and won league championships in 2004 and 2010. She has also played professional basketball in Australia, **Korea**, **Russia**, **Spain**, and **China**. In 2012, she was the flag bearer for Australia at the opening ceremony.

JACOBY, JEAN LUCIEN NICOLAS (LUX–ART). B. 26 March 1891, **Luxembourg**, Luxembourg. D. 9 September 1936, Mulhouse, Haut-Rhin, **France**. As the only person to have won two gold medals in the Olympic **art competitions**, Jean Jacoby can be considered the most successful Olympic artist. He won his first medal in 1924, when his three sport studies earned him a gold medal in the painting category. Four years later, his work *Rugby* was given first prize in the drawings and watercolors competition. In both 1932 and 1936, Jacoby sent in several works and received honorable mentions, but did not win any further medals. In 1936, his daughter Maria also competed in the art competition painting category. Jacoby, who had worked as an art teacher and church painter, frequently used sports as the theme of his work. Sixteen years after his death, a series of Luxembourg postage stamps issued for the 1952 Olympics featured several of Jacoby's drawings, including one of his son René.

JAGER, THOMAS MICHAEL "TOM" (USA–SWI). B. 6 October 1964, East St. Louis, Illinois, **United States**. Tom Jager won seven Olympic **swimming** medals, including five golds. All of his golds were for **relays**. His individual medals were a silver in the 1988 50 meter **freestyle** and bronze in the 1992 50 meter freestyle. The six-foot, two-inch (190 cm), 181 lb (82 kg) swimmer competed in seven Olympic events and medaled in each of them. Jager was a pure **sprinter**, specializing in the 50 free, at which he set six world records. He won the first two world championships at that event, in 1986 and 1991. His other major international titles were in the 50 free at the 1989 and 1991 Pan-Pacific Championships. His great sprint rivals were **Matt Biondi** (USA), who beat him at the Olympics in 1988, and **Aleksandr Popov** (RUS), who won the 50 freestyle in 1992 and 1996. Jager later became a college swim coach.

JAI-ALAI. *See* PELOTA BASQUE.

JAMAICA (JAM). The Caribbean island nation of Jamaica has sent athletes to all the **Olympic Games** since 1948. In 1960, athletes from Jamaica, **Barbados**, and **Trinidad and Tobago** combined to form the **West Indies Federation** team. That team won two medals, one of which was won by George Kerr, a Jamaican, in the 800 meters, while the other was a bronze in the 4x400 meter **relay**. Three members of that team were Jamaican, and one was from Barbados.

In 16 Summer Games, Jamaica has entered 320 athletes (207 men, 113 **women**) and competed in 13 sports. The vast majority of Jamaican Olympians have participated in **athletics** (141 men, 103 women). Jamaica has also entered in **boxing** (21 men), **cycling** (17 men), **sailing** (12 men), **swimming** (seven men and five women), **weightlifting** (four men), **table tennis** (three men), **shooting** (one man and one woman), **taekwondo** (one man), and one woman in each of **badminton, diving, equestrianism**, and **triathlon**.

Jamaica has won 67 Olympic medals through 2014, 66 of them in athletics, led by its outstanding **sprinters**. The other medal was a bronze in cycling, won by David Weller in the 1,000 meter **time trial** in 1980. In 2008 and again in 2012, Jamaican sprinters absolutely dominated track and field athletics, led by **Usain Bolt**, who won three gold medals—the 100 meters and 200 meters, and anchored the winning 4x100 meter relay in each year and setting world records in all three events in 2008. **Merlene Ottey-Page** won nine medals (three silver, six bronze) in sprint events from 1980 to 2000 and has won more Olympic medals in athletics than any other woman. After a dispute with Jamaican officials, she competed for **Slovenia** in 2004 at the age of 44 and narrowly missed qualifying for the 2008 games at age 48.

Other Jamaicans with multiple Olympic medals in athletics are: seven medals—Veronica Campbell-Brown (three gold, two silver, two bronze); four medals—Arthur Wint (two gold, two silver, 1948–1952), Herb McKenley (one gold, three silver, 1948–1952), Don Quarrie (one gold, two silver, one bronze, 1972–1984), Shelly-Ann Fraser-Pryce (two gold, two silver, 2008–2012); three medals—Juliet Cuthbert (two silver, one bronze, 1984–1996), Greg Haughton (one silver, two bronze, 1996–2000), Deon Hemmings (one gold, two silver, 1992–2000), Beverly McDonald (one gold, one silver, one bronze, 1996–2004), Tanya Lawrence (one gold, two silver, 2000–2004), Sherone Simpson (one gold, two silver, 2004–2012), Novlene Williams-Mills (three bronze, 2004–2012), Kerron Stewart (two silver, one bronze, 2008–2012), Shericka Williams (one silver, two bronze, 2008–2012), Yohan Blake (one gold, two silver, 2012); two medals—George Rhoden (two gold, 1952), Lennox Miller (one silver, one bronze, 1968–1972), Winthrop Graham (two silver, 1988–1992), Michael McDonald (one silver, one bronze, 1996–2000), Danny McFarlane (two silver, 2000–2008), Lorraine Graham (two silver, 2000), Sandie Richards (one silver, one bronze, 1988–2004), Michelle Burger (one silver, one bronze, 2000–2004), Nesta Carter (two gold, 2008–2012), Michael Frater (two gold, 2008–2012), Shereefa Lloyd (two bronze, 2008–2012), and Rosemarie Whyte (two bronze, 2008–2012).

In 1988, Jamaica competed at its first **Olympic Winter Games**, represented by the now famous Jamaican **Bobsled** Team. A movie, *Cool Runnings*, was later made about the team. Jamaica has since competed at all Olympic Winter Games, save 2006. In seven Winter Games, Jamaica has entered 11 men and competed in two sports—bobsled (10 men) and **freestyle skiing** (one man). Jamaica's best finish at the Winter Games occurred in 2010 when Errol Kerr finished ninth in **skicross**.

In Jamaica's first venture in bobsledding in 1988, Dudley Stokes and Michael White finished 30th of 41 in two-man bobsled, while the four-man team with Stokes, White, Devon Harris, and Dudley's brother Chris Stokes crashed in the third of four **heats** and failed to complete the event. They returned in 1992 and Devon Harris and Ricky McIntosh were 35th and Dudley and Chris Stokes were 36th of 46 in the two-man bobsled. In the 1992 four-man event, White, McIntosh, and the Stokes brothers were 25th of 31. In 1994, Jamaica had its finest result as they finished 14th of 30 in the four-man competition with Dudley and Chris Stokes, Winston Watts, and Wayne Thomas. In the 1994, two-man run Dudley Stokes and Wayne Thomas were 24th of 43 after their first three runs but were disqualified for having an overweight sled. In 1998, Jamaica was 21st of 31 in four-man and 29th of 38 in two-man. In 2002, they ran into funding problems and only entered the two-man race, where they finished 28th of 37, although they registered the fastest starts of the competition. Funding issues prevented Jamaica from entering in either 2006 or 2010, but in 2014 at Sochi they again entered a two-man sled with the now 46-year-old Winston Watts and a 30-year-old Marvin Dixon finishing 29th of 30.

JAPAN (JPN). Japan first competed at the 1912 **Olympic Games**, its delegation and Olympic Committee led by Dr. Jigoro Kano, the founder of **judo**. Japan has since missed competing only at the Games of 1948, when as an aggressor nation in World War II, it was not invited, and 1980, when it chose to **boycott** the Moscow Olympics.

In 21 Summer Games, Japan has entered 3,036 athletes (2,133 men, 903 **women**) and competed in 34 sports plus the **art competitions**. They have had the largest contingents in the sports of **athletics** (323 men, 115 women), **swimming** (182 men, 135 women), **wrestling** (169 men, five women), **football** (121 men, 47 women), **volleyball** (69 men, 94 women), **rowing** (142 men, nine women), **gymnastics** (74 men, 56 women), and **cycling** (82 men, 18 women).

They have won exactly 400 **Olympic medals** (130 gold, 126 silver, 144 bronze) in the Summer Games as of 2014, with medals won in 23 different sports plus the art competitions. Japan was the dominant country in men's gymnastics from 1956 until the mid-1980s. In addition, at times it has been the top country in swimming and one of the top in wrestling and **weightlifting**.

Fifteen Japanese Olympians have each won five or more medals in the Summer Games, with 10 of them being male gymnasts. They have been led by **Takashi Ono** with 13 (five gold, four silver, four bronze, 1952–1964), **Sawao Kato** with 12 (eight gold, three silver, one bronze, 1968–1976), and Akinori Nakayama with 10 (six gold, two silver, two bronze, 1968–1972). Eizo Kenmotsu and Mitsuo Tsukahara each have nine. Swimmer Kosuke Kitajima won seven from 2000 to 2012 (four gold, one silver, two bronze) and also has two fourth place finishes. The tiny female *judoka* **Ryoko Tamura-Tani**, just four feet, nine inches tall (146 cm), has won five medals (two gold, two silver, one bronze) in the **extra-lightweight** class from 1996 to 2008. This is more Olympic medals in judo than any other participant, male or female. In women's wrestling, both **lightweight** Saori Yoshida and **middleweight** Kaori Icho have each won three gold medals from 2004 to 2012.

At the **Olympic Winter Games**, Japan first competed in 1928 and has since missed only 1948, when it was not invited. In 20 Winter Games, Japan has entered 800 athletes (548 men, 252 women) and competed in all 15 sports that have been held since 1928. They have won 45 medals (10 gold, 17 silver, 18 bronze) at the Winter Games in eight different sports with most of them coming in **speed skating** (15) and **ski jumping** (11). Five Japanese athletes have each won three medals at the Winter Games: ski jumpers Kazoyushi Funaki (1998), Masahiko Harada (1994–1998), and Noriaki Kasai (1994–2014); **Nordic combined** skier Takanori Kono (1992–1994); and speed skater Hiroyasu Shimizu (1998–2002). None of them has won more than two gold medals. One of Japan's greatest triumphs at the Winter Games occurred in Sapporo in 1972 when as the host nation they won gold, silver, and bronze on the **normal hill** in ski jumping—their only medals of that Games and their first medals in the sport.

Japan hosted the Games of the XVIIIth **Olympiad** in Tokyo in 1964, the 11th Olympic Winter Games in Sapporo in 1972, and the 18th Olympic Winter Games in Nagano in 1998. Prior to the outbreak of hostilities, Japan was also scheduled to host both editions of the 1940 Olympics; the Olympic Winter Games were scheduled for Sapporo and the Games of the XIIth Olympiad were scheduled for Tokyo. In 2013, at the 125th IOC Congress in Buenos Aires, **Argentina**, Tokyo was named the host city of the 2020 Games of the XXXIInd Olympiad. Japan has also had several unsuccessful bids to host the Summer Games—Tokyo (1960, 2016), Nagoya (1988), Osaka (2008)—and Winter Games—Sapporo (1968, 1984). *See also* ENDO, YUKIO; MIYAKE, YOSHINOBU; NOMURA, TADAHIRO; WATANABE, OSAMU.

JAVELIN THROW. The javelin throw is one of the field events in **athletics**. A spear of approximately eight feet in length is thrown after the thrower has a running start. The javelin throw is one of the oldest Olympic events as it was contested in the **Ancient Olympic Games** and has been contested in every modern **Olympic Games** since 1908 for men and since 1932 for **women**. It is also included as part of the men's **decathlon** and women's **heptathlon**. **Jan Železný** of the **Czech Republic** has won the Olympic men's javelin throw three times (1992–2000) and finished second in 1988. Barbora Špotáková of the Czech Republic won the women's event in 2008 and 2012, and Ruth Fuchs of East Germany won in 1972 and 1976.

JENNINGS, ANDREW (GBR). B. 1943, **Scotland**. While covering a wide range of subjects, investigative reporter Andrew Jennings is well known as one of the greatest critics of the **International Olympic Committee**. He has published three books on the **Olympic Movement**: *The Lords of the Rings* (1992, also known as *Dishonest Games*), *The New Lords of the Rings: Olympic Corruption and How to Buy Gold Medals* (1996), and *The Great Olympic Swindle* (2000). In the first two books, written in a "tabloid style," he discusses a great number of bigger and smaller scandals, but primarily focuses on two aspects, Samaranch and the IOC. **IOC President Juan Antonio Samaranch** is labeled as a fascist due to his involvement in Spanish politics during the Franco era, and Jennings labels Samaranch's own tenure as a dictatorship of sorts. The IOC is described as an organization of corrupt men who take bribes, gifts, and even sexual favors in exchange for a vote for a host city. The **Olympic bribery scandal** that came to light in the late 1990s showed that Jennings's allegations in this matter were often correct. Jennings was unimpressed by the changes implemented by the IOC in the aftermath of the scandal, and in his most recent Olympic book he describes them as a deliberate smoke screen. Although he has not published any books on the Olympics since then, Jennings remains a vocal critic of the IOC in written media, for example, accusing Samaranch and the IOC of "selling" the 2008 Games to **China**.

JEON I-GYEONG (aka CHUN LEE-KYUNG) (KOR–STK). B. 6 January 1976, Gyeongsangbuk, **Korea**. Jeon I-Gyeong was the first **short-track speed skater** to win five **Olympic medals**. She competed in the 500 meters in 1992 but did not medal. In 1994 and 1998, she won the 1,000 meters at both Olympics and skated on the winning **relay** team both times, to earn her four gold medals. To that she added a bronze in the 500 meters in 1998. The five-foot, four-inch (163 cm), 119 lb (54 kg) Jeon was also a three-time **all-around** World Champion in 1995–1997, and in all, won 29 World Championship medals, including 13 golds. In 2002, she was elected to the Athletes' Committee of the **International Olympic Committee**.

JERNBERG, EDY SIXTEN (SWE–CCS). B. 6 February 1929, Lima, Malung-Sälen, Dalarna, **Sweden**. D. 14 July 2012, Mora, Dalarna, Sweden. Sixten Jernberg is one of the most successful male Olympic Nordic skiers, who set records that have only recently been broken by **Bjørn Dæhlie** (NOR). Between 1956 and 1964, Jernberg won four golds, three silvers, and two bronzes, for a record total at the time of nine **Olympic Winter Games** medals. He competed in 12 Olympic events and finished either fourth or fifth in the other three races. Not a particularly big man, at five feet, nine inches tall (177 cm), 159 lb (72 kg), he added three gold and two bronze medals at the 1954, 1958, and 1962 World Championships, including four medals in the 50 km. Between 1952 and 1964, he took part in 363 ski races, winning 134. In his prime years of 1954–1960, Jernberg won 86 of 161 races, including two wins at the Vasaloppet **Marathon**, as well as the Holmenkollen 15 km in 1954. Initially a blacksmith and then a lumberjack, his daily work provided the essential stamina for the rigors of long-distance **cross-country skiing**. In 1965, the **International Olympic Committee** awarded him the Mohammed Taher Trophy.

JEU DE PAUME **(COURT TENNIS OR REAL TENNIS OR ROYAL TENNIS).** *Jeu de paume*, or game of the hand, the original version of **tennis**, has been contested in the Olympics only in 1908, when the gold medal was won by American Jay Gould II, the grandson of the 19th-century railroad magnate Jay Gould. Only 11 men from the **United States** and **Great Britain** took part. The silver medal was won by Eustace Miles of Great Britain and the bronze went to Neville Lytton of Great Britain. The sport is variously also called court tennis (British), real tennis (American), and royal tennis (**Australian**).

JOHANSSON, IVAR VALENTIN (SWE–WRE). B. 31 January 1903, Norrköping, Östergötland, **Sweden**. D. 4 August 1979, Norrköping, Östergötland, Sweden. Ivar Johansson is one of only three men along with Kalle Antilla (FIN) and Kristjan Palusalu (EST) to have won gold **Olympic medals** in both styles of **wrestling** and also one of eight wrestlers (including two **women**) to have won a total of three Olympic gold medals. In 1932, he won the **freestyle middleweight** and the **Greco-Roman welterweight** titles, and in 1936, he won the Greco-Roman middleweight. Johansson won nine European Championships between 1931 and 1939, six at Greco-Roman and three at freestyle. He was a 22-time Swedish champion, winning 13 at Greco-Roman and nine at freestyle. He won his last Swedish title in 1943, at the age of 40.

JOHNSON, MICHAEL DUANE (USA–ATH). B. 13 September 1967, Dallas, Texas, **United States**. Michael Johnson, six feet (183 cm), 170 lb (77 kg), is acknowledged as the greatest long **sprinter** in the history of track and field, specializing in the 200 and 400 meters. Johnson made his Olympic debut in 1992, but was ill at the time, and his only medal, a gold, was in the 4x400 meter **relay**. At Atlanta in 1996, he won both the 200 and 400 meters, the first man to accomplish that feat at the Olympics, with his 200 meter victory achieved in the stunning world record time of 19.32 seconds. Johnson's Olympic career ended at Sydney, where he defended his 400 meter title and added a third gold in the 4x400 relay, giving him five gold medals in all. Subsequently, two of the members of that relay were found guilty of **doping** (although not Johnson), and the U.S. team was **disqualified** and the gold medals returned. At the World Championships, Johnson was even more dominant, winning the 200 meters in 1991 and 1995 and the 400 meters in 1993, 1995, 1997, and 1999. He added the 400 meter world record in August 1999, when he ran 43.18 in Seville, **Spain**. With his upright style and short, rapid strides, he was an unmistakable figure on the track and is universally recognized as the greatest one-lap runner ever.

JOHNSON, RAFER LEWIS (USA–ATH). B. 18 August 1935, Hillsboro, Texas, **United States**. One of the all-time great decathletes, Rafer Johnson won the silver medal in 1956 behind Milt Campbell, who had won the silver four years earlier. Johnson had also qualified to compete in the 1956 **long jump**, but an injury while competing in the **decathlon** caused him to withdraw from the long jump. In 1960, Johnson staged a memorable battle with his University of California, Los Angeles (UCLA) teammate C. K. Yang, who was representing Taiwan, and Johnson narrowly defeated Yang to win the gold medal. Johnson was also the 1955 **Pan American Games** decathlon winner. At UCLA, the six-foot, two-inch (190 cm), 201 lb (91 kg) Johnson was also a member of the **basketball** team under famed coach John Wooden and was drafted by the National Football League (NFL) but declined to play professional football. After retiring from athletics following his gold medal–winning performance in 1960, Johnson served briefly in the Peace Corps, acted in several films and television shows, and worked as a sportscaster.

One of the most memorable moments in his life occurred when he was campaigning for Robert F. Kennedy and was on stage with him when Kennedy was assassinated by Sirhan B. Sirhan. Johnson, along with football

Rafer Johnson, 1960 decathlon champion.
Courtesy of Volker Kluge

player Roosevelt Grier, helped to capture Sirhan immediately after Kennedy was shot. Johnson became quite active in the **Special Olympics** and founded the California Special Olympics. In 1984, Rafer was given the honor of lighting the **Olympic flame** during the opening ceremony in Los Angeles. His brother Jimmy Johnson played in the NFL for 16 years and has been elected to the Pro Football Hall of Fame. Rafer's daughter Jennifer Johnson-Jordan competed for the United States in **beach volleyball** in the 2000 Olympics, losing in the quarter-final **round**.

JORDAN (JOR). Jordan formed a **National Olympic Committee** in 1957, which was recognized by the **International Olympic Committee** in 1963. However, it was not until 1980 that Jordan's athletes competed on Olympian fields, and since that time they have participated at every **Olympic Games**. The western Asia nation of Jordan, officially known as the Hashemite Kingdom of Jordan, has not yet appeared at the **Olympic Winter Games**. In 2004, Ibrahim Kamal finished fourth in **heavyweight taekwondo**, the best ever finish by a Jordanian Olympian. In 1988 and 1992, Jordanian *taekwondokas* won three bronze medals when the sport was a **demonstration sport**. In 2012, Methkal Abu Drais finished 56th of 105 entrants in the **marathon**. That same year **light-heavyweight boxer** Ihab Darwish won one bout and finished equal ninth of 26 entrants. The 2000 Summer Games saw HRH Princess Haya Bint Al-Hussein compete in the mixed **equestrian jumping** event. In 2006, she became the president of the International Equestrian Federation (Fédération Équestre Internationale). In nine Summer Games, Jordan's 55 Olympians (37 men, 18 **women**) have competed in 10 sports: **archery** (one woman), **athletics** (nine men, five women), boxing (three men), equestrian (one man, one woman), **fencing** (two men), **shooting** (13 men), **swimming** (four men, five women), table **tennis** (four women), taekwondo (three men, two women), and **wrestling** (two men).

JORDAN, MICHAEL JEFFREY (USA–BAS). B. 17 February 1963, Brooklyn, New York, **United States**. Michael Jordan is considered by many experts to be the greatest **basketball** player of all time, although they will get an argument about that from fans of Wilt Chamberlain and Bill Russell. Jordan played collegiately at the University of North Carolina, where he helped it win a National Collegiate Athletic Association championship in 1983. In 1984, Jordan led the United States team to a gold **Olympic medal**. Turning to professional basketball after his junior year in college, he became one of the greatest scorers in the National Basketball Association (NBA), leading the league in scoring in 11 years and ending his career as the third highest scorer of all time behind Kareem Abdul-Jabbar and Karl Malone. In

Michael Jordan of the United States, arguably the greatest basketball player ever and winner of two Olympic gold medals in 1984 and 1992. Courtesy of Erich Kamper

1991, the six-foot, six-inch (198 cm), 198 lb (90 kg) Jordan finally achieved his greatest thrill, leading the Chicago Bulls to an NBA Championship and completing his Triple Crown of titles. Jordan eventually led the Bulls to six NBA titles (1991–1993, 1996–1998). In 1992, Jordan also played on the **Dream Team** that won the basketball gold medal at Barcelona. Jordan did not play in the NBA in 1994 and for most of the 1995 season, while he attempted a career in professional **baseball**, playing in the minor leagues. Since his retirement from the NBA after the 1998 season, Jordan has become an NBA owner, first of the Washington Wizards, and briefly returned to playing for that team for two years as well, but with less success than in his younger days. He has since become an owner of the Charlotte Bobcats (who were renamed Charlotte Hornets for the 2014–2015 season). *See also* UNITED STATES MEN'S BASKETBALL TEAM—1984.

JUDO. The founder of judo, Dr. Jigoro Kano, was a longtime member of the **International Olympic Committee**. Judo is a form of **wrestling** that was developed by Dr. Kano from the ancient **Japanese** schools of *yawara* and *jujitsu*. He founded his first *dojo* (judo school) in 1882, the *Kodokan*. The contestants are called *judoka* and are classified into grades consisting of pupils (*Kyu*) and degrees *(Dan)*. There are five classes of *Kyu*, advancing to first *Kyu*, and wearing a brown belt. Thereafter, the *judoka* achieve a *Dan*, beginning with first *Dan* (black belt) and advancing theoretically to 12th *Dan* (white belt). Fighting ability and technical knowledge advance a *judoka* to fifth *Dan*, after which advancement depends on service to the sport. Leading international *judoka* are usually fourth or fifth *Dan*. The 11th and 12th *Dan* have never been awarded.

Judo made its first Olympic appearance in 1964 but was not included on the program of the 1968 **Olympic Games**. Judo returned to the Olympic fold in 1972, and the 1992 Olympics included judo events for **women** for the first time. In 12 Summer Games, there have been 2,462 participants (1,797 men, 665 women) from 167 nations in Olympic judo.

The sport, not surprisingly, has been dominated by the Japanese, followed by the **Soviet Union**, with the **Koreans** also winning many medals. The sport is governed internationally by the International Judo Federation, which was formed in July 1951 and had 201 members as of June 2014.

The top Olympic judo medalists have been the diminutive female (four-foot, nine-inch [146 cm]) **Ryoko Tamura-Tani** (JPN), with five (two gold), and **Cuba**'s Driulys González (female) and **Angelo Parisi** (male), who represented both **France** and **Great Britain**, with four medals but only one gold each. **Tadahiro Nomura** of Japan is the only man to win three Olympic gold medals in judo, while 10 *judoka* have each won two gold medals. *See also* GEESINK, ANTONIUS JOHANNES; RUSKA, WILLEM.

JUDOKA. See JUDO.

JUMPING (EQUESTRIAN). Jumping, also known as show jumping or Grand Prix jumping, is one of the events in Olympic **equestrian** competition. Horses and riders must negotiate a series of obstacles (fences and water hazards) while completing a specified course. Penalties are assessed for failure to successfully clear an obstacle. The winner is determined by a combination of quickest time and fewest penalties. Jumping has been included in the **Olympic Program** from 1912 to 1952 in men's competition and from 1956 to 2012 in mixed competition, allowing **women** to compete in the same event with men. Mixed jumping was also held in 1900, although there is no record of women actually competing in that event. Pierre Jonquères d'Oriola of **France** is the only two-time Olympic equestrian jumping gold medalist. He won the men's event in 1952 and the mixed event in 1964.

JURIDICAL COMMISSION. Originally called the Legal Commission, the Juridical Commission was formed in 1974 with **Marc Hodler** as the original chairman. The current chairman is John Coates of **Australia**. There are five other members, all **International Olympic Committee** (IOC) members and all either lawyers in their day jobs or legally trained. Its charge by the IOC is listed as follows: (1) providing legal opinions to the **IOC president**, the IOC **Executive Board**, and the **IOC Session**, upon their request, on issues relating to the exercise of their respective competences; (2) providing preliminary opinions concerning draft amendments to the *Olympic Charter*; (3) considering actions or defenses concerning the IOC; (4) carrying out studies of a legal nature on issues that may affect the interests of the IOC; and (5) performing any other tasks of a legal nature entrusted to it by the IOC president, the IOC Executive Board, or the IOC Session.

K

KAATSEN. In this Dutch sport, predominantly played in the northern province of Friesland, the ball is handled by players with the bare hand. The sport is similar to games such as **pelota basque,** *jeu de paume*, and **American handball**. It was held as a **demonstration sport** at the 1928 **Olympic Games**.

KAHANAMOKU, DUKE PAOA KAHINO MAKOE HULIKOHOA (USA–SWI/WAP). B. 24 August 1890, Honolulu, Hawai'i, **United States**. D. 22 January 1968, Honolulu, Hawai'i, United States. Duke Kahanamoku was the world's best **swimmer** in the early part of the 20th century. He made his first appearance at the 1912 **Olympic Games** and won a gold medal in

Duke Kahanamoku, one of the first great Olympic swimmers. Courtesy of Volker Kluge

299

the 100 meter **freestyle** and a silver medal as a member of the 4x200 freestyle **relay** team. He returned to the Olympics in 1920, won gold in both of those events, and played on the United States **water polo** team that finished in sixth place. In 1924, he was defeated by **Johnny Weissmuller** and settled for a silver medal in the 100 meter freestyle. Third place in the event went to Duke's brother Sam Kahanamoku.

Only a few days after his initial gold medal in 1912, he competed at a meet in Hamburg, **Germany**, and set a world record for the 100 meter freestyle at 1:01.6 minutes. He held the record for 10 years and lowered it twice. The record was finally broken by the future Olympic champion Johnny Weissmuller. Like Weissmuller, Duke Kahanamoku starred in films during the 1920s and 1930s. He also gave exhibitions and popularized the Hawaiian sport of **surfing**. In 1925, while living in Newport Beach, California, Kahanamoku saved eight fishermen whose boat had capsized. Using his surfboard, he made several trips to bring them safely to shore.

KAKIASVILI, AKAKIOS (né KAKHI KAKHIASHVILI) (GRE/EUN– WLT). B. 13 July 1969, Tskhinvali, Shida Kartli, **Georgia**, USSR. Akakios Kakiasvili was born in Soviet **Georgia** and first competed at the **Olympic Games** in 1992, representing the Unified Team and earning a gold medal in the **middle-heavyweight** (90 kg) class and equaling the Olympic record in the process. The five-foot, nine-inch (176 cm) Kakiasvili then immigrated to **Greece**, for which he has competed internationally since 1995. Representing Greece, he was World Champion in 1995, 1998, and 1999 and won further gold **Olympic medals** in both 1996 with a world record lift and 2000 with an Olympic record lift, one of only four **weightlifters** to win three gold medals. Kakiasvili was also European Champion in 1992, 1993, 1995, and 1996 and has won seven medals at the European Championships. He competed in 2004 at Athens, but failed to complete a successful lift in the **clean and jerk** and did not officially finish.

KALPE. The *kalpe*, or race for mares, was a truly curious event contested in the **Ancient Olympic Games**. It is not known how many laps of the hippodrome were contested, but on the last lap, the rider dismounted and ran alongside the mare to the finish. The race was first contested in 496 B.C. and was dropped in 444 B.C. Only one winner is known, Pataikos of Dymai, in 496 B.C. *See also APENE*; CHARIOT RACE; *KELES*; *TETHRIPPON.*

KAMPER, ERICH. B. 22 June 1914, Mitterndorf, Mürztal, **Austria**. D. 9 November 1995, Graz, Austria. Erich Kamper was one of the first Olympic historians. He was a sports journalist and from 1947 to 1979 was the head of the sports department of the *Neue Zeit* (New Times) newspaper of Graz. He was a founding member of the Association of Track and Field Statisticians. His first book on the **Olympic Games** was published in 1964 and was titled *Lexikon der Olympischen Winterspiele* (Encyclopedia of the Winter Olympics). He followed that with the *Enzyklopädie der Olympischen Spiele* (Encyclopedia of the Olympic Games) in 1972. He then wrote a "Who's Who" of Olympic athletes—*Lexikon der 12,000 Olympioniken* (Encyclopedia of 12,000 Olympians) in 1975—and eight years later published an expanded edition—the *Lexikon der 14,000 Olympioniken* (Encyclopedia of 14,000 Olympians). He also wrote *Olympische Heroen* (Olympic Heroes) with Herbert Soucek in 1991 and *Who's Who der Olympischen Spiele 1896–1992* (Golden Book of the Olympic Games). The latter book was written with **Bill Mallon**. Kamper was named honorary president when the **International Society of Olympic Historians** was founded in 1991 and received the **Olympic Order** from the **International Olympic Committee** in 1987.

Erich Kamper, one of the first Olympic historians. Courtesy of Erich Kamper and Bill Mallon

KAMPUCHEA. *See* CAMBODIA.

KANIA-BUSCH-ENKE, KARIN (GDR–SSK). B. 20 June 1961, Dresden, **German Democratic Republic.** Initially a leading **figure skater,** Karin Kania later became a champion **speed skater** and is one of the very few athletes to have reached world class in both **disciplines.** As she felt that chances for improvement on her ninth place in the 1977 European Figure Skating Championships were limited, she turned to speed skating, with considerable success. In three **Olympic Winter Games,** she entered 10 events, setting world records in two of them and Olympic records in three others, won eight medals, and finished fourth in the other two races. Her total of eight medals (three gold, four silver, one bronze) between 1980 and 1988 was an Olympic record for speed skating until bettered by **Claudia Pechstein** in 2006 with nine, and Karin's record at the World Championships was even more impressive. She won the **sprint** title a record six times (1980–1981, 1983–1984, 1986–1987), and her five victories in the **all-around** event (1982, 1984, 1986–1988) were also a record for the championships. (She missed the 1985 championships because of pregnancy.) During her career, the five-foot, 10-inch (180 cm), 159 lb (72 kg) Kania set 10 world records, with at least one at every distance, as well as records for the **all-around,** the small all-around, and the sprint.

KARATE. Karate is a martial art developed in the 19th century in the Ryukyu Islands (Okinawa) and has never been on the **Olympic Program,** although the World Karate Federation (WKF) is recognized by the **International Olympic Committee.** Founded in 1992, the WKF had 188 affiliated member nations as of 2014. It was considered for inclusion on the **Olympic Program,** but was not selected at the 2009 Olympic Congress nor at the 125th **IOC Session** in Buenos Aires, **Argentina.**

KARELIN, ALEKSANDR ALEKSANDROVICH (URS/EUN/RUS– WRE). B. 19 September 1967, Novosibirsk, **Russia,** USSR. Aleksandr Karelin is one of only six men to have won three gold **Olympic medals** in **wrestling.** The others are **Ivar Johansson** (SWE), **Aleksandr Medved** (URS/UKR), Buvaisa Saytiyev (EUN/RUS/URS), **Artur Taymazov** (UZB) and **Carl Westergren** (SWE). Two women, Saori Yoshida and Kaori Icho, both of **Japan,** also have won three Olympic wrestling gold medals. Known for his strength, Karelin won his first gold medal in 1988 in the **super-heavyweight Greco-Roman** event, competing for the **Soviet Union.** He defended that title in 1992, competing for the Unified Team, and in 1996, competing for Russia. He was also World Champion in the class nine times—1989–1991,

1993–1995, and 1998–1999—being undefeated in international competition between 1988 and 1996. Karelin's 12 World and Olympic championships are an all-time best. The six-foot, three-inch (193 cm) Karelin competed at Sydney in 2000, attempting to win his fourth consecutive Olympic gold medal, for which he was the heavy favorite. In perhaps the biggest upset of the **Olympic Games**, he lost 1–0 in the final to the unheralded American Rulon Gardner. Karelin retired after the Sydney Olympics.

KÁRPÁTI, GYÖRGY (HUN–WAP). B. 23 June 1935, Budapest, **Hungary**. Considered the fastest **water poloist** in the world in his prime, György Kárpáti, five feet, five inches (167 cm), 157 lb (71 kg), played outside forward and used his speed to great effect. When only 17 years old, he won his first gold **Olympic medal** in 1952, following it with another gold in 1956, a bronze in 1960, and a third gold in 1964. Kárpáti was a member of the Hungarian water polo team that won the European Championships in 1954 and 1962.

KÁRPÁTI, RUDOLF (HUN–FEN). B. 17 July 1920, Budapest, **Hungary**. D. 1 February 1999, Budapest, Hungary. Rudolf Kárpáti was a member of the noted Hungarian **fencing** teams that dominated **sabre** competition for more than three decades. In team sabre, the five-foot, 10-inch (179 cm), 141 lb (64 kg) fencer won gold **Olympic medals** at four successive **Olympic Games** (1948–1960) and was a member of the winning team at five World Championships (1953–1955, 1957–1958). Individually, Kárpáti was twice Olympic sabre champion (1956 and 1960) and twice World sabre champion (1954 and 1959). After his retirement, he became president of the Hungarian Fencing Federation and an administrator with the Fédération Internationale d'Éscrime. He was also a talented musician and was the leader of the People's Army Central Artistic Ensemble.

KATO, SAWAO (JPN–GYM). B. 11 October 1946, Gosen, Niigata Prefecture, **Japan**. Sawao Kato was the winner of a men's record eight gold medals for **gymnastics** and won a total of 12 medals with three silver and one bronze also. He was a member of the winning **all-around** team in 1968, 1972, and 1976 and also took the individual title on the first two occasions, but had to settle for a silver medal in 1976. The five-foot, four-inch (163 cm), 130 lb (59 kg) Kato's other gold medals were for the individual **floor exercise** (1968) and the individual **parallel bars** (1972, 1976). He also won silver for **horizontal bar** and **pommelled horse** in 1972 and bronze for **rings** in 1968. His brother Takeshi Kato won a gold and bronze medal in gymnastics in 1968.

KAYAK. A kayak is a small narrow boat propelled by a double-bladed paddle. Kayak races were added to the **Olympic Games** as part of the **canoeing** program in 1936 and have been held in each subsequent Olympics. Race distances have varied from 200 meters to 10,000 meters with competition on flatwater courses for **singles, doubles,** and fours for men. **Women**'s Olympic flatwater kayak events have been held since 1948. **Birgit Fischer-Schmidt** of East Germany and later unified **Germany** has won 12 **Olympic medals** (eight gold, four silver) in women's kayaking from 1980 to 2004—far more than any other woman. **Gert Fredriksson** of **Sweden** from 1948 to 1960 won eight Olympic medals (six gold, one silver, one bronze) to lead all male kayakers.

In 1972, an Olympic whitewater kayak **slalom** event was also held for both men and women. It was not held again until the 1992 Games but has since been held in each subsequent Games. In this competition, an artificial whitewater is used with swirling rapids. Competitors must negotiate between 18 and 25 sets of gates and for some of them must paddle upstream. Pierpaolo Ferrazzi of **Italy** (gold 1992, bronze 2000) and Fabien Lefevre of **France** (silver 2008, bronze 2004) are the only multiple Olympic medalists in men's kayak whitewater slalom. Štěpánka Hilgertová of the **Czech Republic** (gold 1996, 2000), Elena Kaliská of **Slovakia** (gold 2004, 2008), and Dana Chladek of the **United States** (silver 1996, bronze 1992) are the only multiple medalists in women's kayak whitewater slalom.

KAYAKING. *See* CANOEING AND KAYAKING.

KAZAKHSTAN (formerly KAZAKSTAN) (KAZ, formerly KZK). Kazakhstan's **National Olympic Committee** was recognized by the **International Olympic Committee** in 1992, shortly after the breakup of the **Soviet Union**. Many Kazakh athletes competed from 1952 to 1988 for the Soviet Union, and Kazakh athletes were present at Barcelona and Albertville in 1992 as members of the Unified Team. The Central Asian nation of Kazakhstan, officially known as the Republic of Kazakhstan, first competed at the Olympics as an independent nation in 1994 at Lillehammer, where its great **cross-country skier** Vladimir Smirnov won three medals—one gold and two silvers. Kazakhstan made its summer debut at the 1996 **Olympic Games** in Atlanta.

In five Summer Games, Kazakhstan has entered 433 athletes (264 men, 169 **women**) and competed in 24 sports, with the largest contingents in **athletics** (26 men, 37 women), **water polo** (27 men, 20 women), **wrestling** (40 men, six women), **boxing** (33 men, two women), **judo** (22 men, 12 women), and **swimming** (24 men, seven women).

Kazakhstani athletes have won 52 medals (16 gold, 17 silver, 19 bronze) at the Summer Games. They have medaled in nine sports, with 41 of the 52 medals coming in boxing, **weightlifting**, and wrestling. Five athletes have each won two medals—boxers **flyweight** Bomat Zhumadilov (1996, 2000, both silver) and **light-middleweight** Yermakhan Ibraimov (1996 bronze, 2000 gold); **cyclist** Aleksandr Vinokurov (individual **road race** 2000 silver, 2012 gold); **shooter** Sergey Belyayev (1996 two silver in small-bore rifle); and **middle-heavyweight** weightlifter Ilya Ilyin (2008, 2012, both gold).

Kazakhstan's other gold medalists in the Summer Games are Olga Shishigina (2000 women's 100 meter **hurdles**); Olga Rypakova (2012 women's **triple jump**); Alex Parygin (1996 individual **modern pentathlon**); Yuri Melnichenko (1996 **bantamweight Greco-Roman** wrestling); 2012 women's weightlifters **featherweight** Zulfiya Chinshanlo, **middleweight** Maiya Maneza, and **heavyweight** Svetlana Podobedova; and boxers featherweight Bekzat Sattarkhanov (2000), **welterweights** Bakhtiyar Artiyev (2004), Bakhyt Sarsekbayev (2008) and Serik Sapyev (2012), and **light-heavyweight** Vasily Zhirov (1996).

In six **Olympic Winter Games**, Kazakhstan has entered 192 athletes (124 men, 68 women) and competed in 11 sports, with most of their competitors in **ice hockey** (37 men, 19 women), cross-country skiing (24 men, 15 women), **speed skating** (16 men, six women), and **biathlon** (11 men, 11 women). They have won seven medals in Winter sports (one gold, three silver, three bronze). Cross-country skier Vladimir Smirnov has won the most medals for Kazakhstan, four (one gold, two silver, one bronze), and actually won seven in all, three (two silver, one bronze) in 1988 for the Soviet Union. Kazakhstan's other Winter Games medalists are biathlete Yelena Khrustayova (2010 silver), **figure skater** Denis Ten (2014 bronze), and speed skater Lyudmila Prokoshova (1998 bronze).

Almaty, Kazakhstan, the country's largest city and formerly known as Alma Ata, bid unsuccessfully to host the 2014 Olympic Winter Games and is one of the cities still in the running to host the 2022 Winter Games.

KEELBOAT. A keelboat is a type of **sailing** boat used in Olympic sailing competition. It is among the larger sailboats and usually has a crew of two or three. Star, Soling, and Yngling are three of the classes of keelboats that have been used for Olympic events. Torben Grael of **Brazil** with five **Olympic medals** (two gold, one silver, two bronze) from 1984 to 2004 in keelboat sailing has the most of any Olympic sailor in this class of boat.

KEIRIN. One of the newer events in the sport of **cycling** is the keirin, one of the most exciting events because of the speeds. The event is a 2,000 meter paced event, in which the riders ride behind a motorized derny, which increases the potential speeds. The derny paces the riders for about 1,500 meters and then pulls off the track, at which time the cyclists begin a furious **sprint** to the finish. Keirin racing has traditionally been raced in **Japan**, where it has been a professional sport for over 20 years, and in which pari-mutuel betting on the riders is permitted. It was first held for men in the **Olympic Games** of 2000 and has been contested in each of the subsequent Games through 2012. **Chris Hoy** of **Great Britain**, gold medalist in 2008 and 2012, is the only multiple medalist in this event. It became a **women**'s Olympic event in 2012 with Vicki Pendleton of Great Britain the gold medalist.

KELES. In the **Ancient Olympic** sport of *keles*, or horse race, the horse with a rider covered six full laps of the hippodrome. The first known champion was in 648 B.C. (Krauxidas of Krannon), with champions known through A.D. 193 (Theopropos of Rhodes). Hieron, Tyrant of Syracuse, is the only known two-time champion, in 476 and 472 B.C. *See also APENE*; CHARIOT RACE; *KALPE*; *SYNORIS*; *TETHRIPPON*.

KELETI, ÁGNES (née KLEIN, later SÁRKÁNY, then BIRO) (HUN– GYM). B. 9 January 1921, Budapest, **Hungary**. Ágnes Keleti is the greatest **gymnast** produced by Hungary, but her life and career have been intertwined with the politics of her country and her religion. She first became interested in gymnastics shortly before World War II, but her career was interrupted by the war, during which her father was removed to Auschwitz, where he was killed by the Nazis. Ágnes Keleti and the rest of her family survived by finding refuge in a "Swedish House" administered by Raoul Wallenberg. After the war, Keleti returned to gymnastics and won her first Hungarian championship in 1946. In 1947, she made her first international impact when she dominated the Central European Gymnastics Championships. She initially earned her living as a fur worker, but she was also an accomplished musician, playing the cello professionally.

After serving as an alternate in 1948, Keleti competed in the 1952 and 1956 **Olympic Games**, at which she won 10 medals (five gold, three silver, two bronze). At the 1954 World Gymnastics Championships, she won on the **uneven bars**, her only individual world title, and also was on the winning Hungarian team in the team portable apparatus event. Her greatest gymnastics effort was at the 1956 Melbourne **Olympic Games**, when she won six medals, including four gold. But politics again interceded in her career. In late October, **Israel** invaded **Egypt**'s Sinai Peninsula, and then shortly before the 1956 Olympics, on 4 November 1956, Soviet tanks entered Budapest to quell an uprising there. The two events led to a small **boycott** of the Olympics.

Although Hungary competed, many of its athletes defected, and Keleti was among them. She stayed in **Australia** and then settled in Israel.

KELLAR, REBECCA D. "BECKY" (CAN–ICH). B. 1 January 1975, Hagersville, Ontario, **Canada**. One of five Canadian women to play in four or more Olympic **ice hockey** tournaments, the five-foot, six-inch (170 cm), 157 lb (71 kg) Becky Kellar has won three gold medals (2002, 2006, 2010) and a silver (1998). She played in various women's leagues in the **United States** and Canada, often recognized as one of the top defenders. She played for the Canadian team at seven World Championships, winning four times against the United States (1999–2001, 2004), but losing the other three finals.

KELLY, JOHN BRENDEN "JACK," SR. (USA–ROW). B. 4 October 1889, Philadelphia, Pennsylvania, **United States**. D. 20 June 1960, Philadelphia, Pennsylvania, United States. Jack Kelly is the greatest **sculler** the United States has ever produced. He joined the Vesper Boat Club in 1909. Between 1909 and his competitive retirement after the 1924 **Olympic Games**, the six-foot, two-inch (187 cm) Kelly won every sculling title available to him, including the World Championship in both **singles** and **doubles**, the 1920 Olympics in singles and doubles, the 1924 Olympic doubles, and many national titles in both boats. Kelly never won the Diamond Sculls at the Henley Regatta because he was denied entry as the Vesper Boat Club and its members were banned for, in the view of the British **rowing** officials, earlier professional activities. Kelly fathered two very famous children: John Kelly, Jr., another Olympic rower who was later United States Olympic Committee president, and the late Grace Kelly, the American movie star who became Princess Grace of **Monaco** and whose son, Prince Albert, has competed in five **Olympic Winter Games** in **bobsledding**.

KENDO. The **Japanese** form of **fencing**, called *kendo*, was one of the three traditional Japanese sports demonstrated at the 1964 **Olympic Games** (along with *kyudo* and *sumo*). The matches were not competitive in nature and did not yield a final ranking.

KENYA (KEN). The Kenyan **National Olympic Committee** was founded in 1955 and recognized by the **International Olympic Committee** in the same year. The country made its Olympic debut in 1956, and since then it has been absent only from the Olympics of 1976 and 1980, both of which it **boycotted**. In 13 Summer Games, Kenya has entered 452 athletes (363 men, 89 **women**) and competed in 14 sports, with the vast majority of them participating in **athletics** (196 men, 63 women), **hockey** (69 men), and **boxing** (49 men, one woman).

The East African nation, officially known as the Republic of Kenya, has won 86 **Olympic medals**—25 gold, 32 silver, 29 bronze. Kenya has won seven medals in boxing, but all of its other medals were earned by its excellent runners in races ranging in distance from 400 meters to the **marathon**. Kenya has especially dominated the men's 3,000 meter **steeplechase**. They have won gold medals in that event each year from 1984 to 2012 and also won in 1964 and 1968. Since 1968, they have also won seven silver medals and four bronze medals, and in both 1992 and 2004 won all three medals. Kenya's most outstanding runner was Kipchoge Keino, who in 1968 won the 1,500 meter run and was second in the 5,000 meters. In 1972, he was second in the 1,500 meters and won the 3,000 meter steeplechase. He set Olympic records in both of his gold medal–winning efforts.

Fourteen other Kenyan runners each won two medals: Julius Sang (1972, gold, bronze), Wilson Kiprugut (1964 bronze, 1968 silver), Bernard Lagat (2000 bronze, 2004 silver), Eliud Kipchoge (2004 bronze, 2008 silver), Paul Bitok (1992, 1996, both silver), Naftali Temu (1968 gold, bronze), Paul Tergat (1996, 2000, both silver), Eric Wainaina (1996 bronze, 2000 silver), Ezekiel Kemboi (2004, 2012, both gold), Brimin Kipruto (2004 silver, 2008 gold), Charles Asati (1968 silver, 1972 gold), Munyoro Nyamau (1968 silver, 1972 gold), Vivian Cheruiyot (2012 silver, bronze), and Catherine Ndereba (2004, 2008, both silver). **Featherweight** boxer Philip Waruinge also is a Kenyan dual Olympic medalist. He won a bronze medal in 1968 and silver in 1972. **Welterweight** Robert Wangila won a gold medal in 1988—the only gold medal for Kenya not won in athletics. The following year he became a professional boxer and had a professional record of 22–4 when he died following a bout in Las Vegas, Nevada, in 1994.

Kenya first competed at the **Olympic Winter Games** in 1998, when its sole representative, Philip Boit, competed in **cross-country skiing**. Boit is the nephew of former Kenyan middle-distance Olympian Mike Boit. Philip competed again at the 2002 and 2006 Winter Olympics and is still the only Kenyan to compete in the Winter Games. His best result was 64th of 71 entrants in the 2002 men's **sprint**.

KETSEAS, IOANNIS (GRE). B. 16 September 1887, Athens, **Greece**. D. 6 April 1965, Athens, Greece. Ioannis Ketseas was the cofounder of the **International Olympic Academy** (IOA), with **Carl Diem**. His lifelong interest in sports led to his becoming president of the Hellenic AAU (SEGAS) in 1929 and president of the Greek Federation of Lawn **Tennis** in 1939 (he competed at the 1906 **Intercalated Olympic Games** in tennis where he reached the quarter-finals in **doubles**). From 1946 to his death, he was an **International Olympic Committee** member in Greece. He was general director of the National Bank of Greece from 1906 to 1928, and he also served the Greek government as minister of foreign affairs from 1921 to 1922. He and Diem founded the IOA officially in 1961, although they had promulgated the idea for almost 30 years. Ketseas served as the first chairman of the Ephoria of the IOA, its ruling council, from 1961 to 1965.

KILLANIN, LORD OF DUBLIN AND SPIDDAL; SIR MICHAEL MORRIS (IRL). B. 30 July 1914, London, **England**. D. 25 April 1999, Dublin, **Ireland**. Lord Killanin was elected president of the Olympic Council of Ireland in 1950. He became an **International Olympic Committee** (IOC) member two years later. In 1967, he was elected to the IOC **Executive Board**. In 1968, he ascended to third vice president of the IOC, and in 1970 he was named first vice president. Lord Killanin was elected IOC **president** in 1972 and held that office until his retirement in 1980, when he was awarded the **Olympic Order** in Gold. He was also elected honorary president for life of the IOC. A noted journalist, author, and film producer, Lord Killanin served as a director of many leading Irish companies.

KILLY, JEAN-CLAUDE (FRA–ASK). B. 30 August 1943, Saint-Cloud, Hauts-de-Seine, **France**. At his Olympic debut in 1964, Jean-Claude Killy placed fifth in the **giant slalom**, but four years later he matched **Toni Sailer**'s 1956 record by winning Olympic gold in all three **Alpine skiing** events. Unlike Sailer, who won his events by substantial margins, all of Killy's victories were narrow ones, and he only won the **slalom** after the controversial **disqualification** of the **Austrian** Karl Schranz. Killy, five feet, 10 inches (178 cm) and 165 lb (75 kg), was also World Champion in the Alpine **combination** (1966, 1968) and **downhill** (1966) and was a convincing winner of the first two World Cup competitions (1967, 1968). Following his retirement at the end of the 1968 season, he amassed a fortune from endorsements and also became involved in motor racing, films, and professional ski racing. Killy was co-president of the **Organizing Committee** for the 1992 **Olympic Winter Games** in Albertville. He then became president of the Amaury Sport Organization, which controls the Tour de France, the Paris-Dakar auto rally, and *L'Équipe*, the French sporting daily newspaper. To date, Killy is the only person to have both won an Olympic gold medal and been awarded the **Olympic Order** in Gold. In addition, in 1995 Killy was elected a member of the **International Olympic Committee.**

KIM, NELLYA VLADIMIROVNA "NELLI" (URS/TJK–GYM). B. 29 July 1957, Shurab, Sughd, **Tajikistan**, USSR. Nelli Kim was born of a **Korean** father and a **Russian** mother. Blessed with strikingly good looks, she was the darling of the media, who also recognized her exceptional talent as a **gymnast**. She debuted at the World Championships in 1974 as a 17-year-old, finishing third on the **balance beam**.

At the 1976 Montreal **Olympic Games**, Kim won three gold medals, but she is best remembered for scoring a perfect 10.0 in the vault and **floor exercise**. Only four feet, 11 inches (152 cm) tall and 104 lb (47 kg), she also won a silver medal in the individual **all-around**. At the 1980 Olympics, she helped the Soviet Union retain the team championship and shared first place in the floor exercise. Kim was also impressive at the World Championships, at which she won 11 medals and five titles between 1974 and 1979. From 1977 to 1979, she was married to international gymnast Vladimir Akhasov. In 1981, she married Olympic gold medal cyclist Valery Movchan.

KIM SU-NYEONG (KOR–ARC). B. 5 April 1971, Chungcheonbuk Province, **Korea**. In only a few short years, Kim Su-Nyeong established herself as the greatest female **archer** of the modern era. In 1988, Kim won an individual and a team gold medal in archery at the Olympics. Nicknamed "Viper," she was the **women**'s individual and team world champion in both 1989 and 1991. Through 1990, she held every women's world record at all distances and overall as well. At the Barcelona Olympics, the five-foot, four-inch (175 cm), 128 lb (58 kg) archer again helped Korea to the team gold, but finished second in the individual event. Kim also competed at Sydney in 2000, winning a bronze medal in the individual event and helping Korea win another team gold medal. Kim won individual and team World Championships in both 1989 and 1991.

KIRALY, CHARLES FREDERICK "KARCH" (USA–VOL/BVO). B. 3 November 1960, Jackson, Michigan, **United States**. Karch Kiraly is regarded by many as the greatest **volleyballer** ever. In 1986, the Fédération Internationale de Volleyball declared him the top player in the world, the first time that distinction had been given. He won gold medals at the 1984 and 1988 Olympics, 1985 World Cup, 1986 World Championships, 1987 **Pan American Games**, and in **beach volleyball** at the 1996 Olympics. The six-foot, two-inch (190 cm), 190 lb (86 kg) Kiraly played at the University of California at Los Angeles, where he led the team to three National Collegiate Athletic Association (NCAA) championships and was twice named most valuable player of the NCAA Tournament. Playing professionally in **Italy**, he helped Il Messaggero win the 1991 World Club Championship. Later, as a star at beach volleyball, he was the leading professional money winner at that sport from 1991 to 1994, and when that sport debuted at the 1996 **Olympic Games**, Kiraly won the gold medal, partnered by Kent Steffes.

KIRIBATI (KIR). Kiribati (pronounced "Kiribass") is an archipelago nation in the South Pacific Ocean, formerly known as the Gilbert Islands, and was part of the Gilbert and Ellice Islands. The islands were a British colony from 1892, but achieved independence in 1979 as two states: Kiribati (Gilbert Islands) and **Tuvalu** (Ellice Islands). It formed a **National Olympic Committee** in 2002 and held its inaugural meeting in November that year. Kiribati was recognized by the **International Olympic Committee** at the 115th **IOC Session** in Prague on 3 July 2003. In three Summer Games, Kiribati has entered seven athletes (five men, two **women**) and competed in just two sports. At Athens in 2004, Kiribati was represented by three athletes: one female and one male in **athletics** and one male **weightlifter**. In 2008, a male weightlifter and a male 100 meter **sprinter** represented the island. Four years later, the Kiribati Olympic team consisted of three competitors— a male and a female sprinter and a male weightlifter, David Katoatau, who competed in his second **Olympic Games**. The best Kiribatian result was a 13th place (of 21 entrants) in the men's 85 kg weightlifting competition of 2004, by the then 16-year-old Meamea Thomas, who tragically was killed as a pedestrian by a drunk driver in 2013 at the age of 26. The country has not yet competed at the **Olympic Winter Games**.

KIRK, OLIVER LEONARD (USA–BOX). B. 20 April 1884, Beatrice, Nebraska, **United States**. D. 14 March 1960; Farmington, Missouri, United States. Oliver Kirk is the only **boxer** to win two gold medals in separate weight classes at the same Olympics, a feat he accomplished at the 1904 St. Louis **Olympic Games** and that will surely never again be equaled since modern rules prohibit boxers from entering more than one weight class in one Olympic tournament. Kirk first won the **bantamweight** division, knocking out George Finnegan, the only other competitor. Finnegan had earlier won the **flyweight** championship by **knockout**. Kirk was not entered in the **featherweight** class, but after only two boxers entered, the crowd wanted to see him fight the winner, Frank Haller. Kirk, from the Business Men's Gym in St. Louis, did so; he won by decision and was awarded the gold medal. Kirk later fought as a professional boxer throughout the midwestern United States from 1906 to 1915 with an undistinguished record of two wins, five losses, and six no decision bouts.

KLASSEN, CYNTHIA NICOLE "CINDY" (CAN–SSK). B. 12 August 1979, Winnipeg, Manitoba, **Canada**. In 2006, Cindy Klassen became only the fourth **speed skater** to win five medals in the same Olympics, after **Clas Thunberg** (FIN) (1924), Roald Larsen (NOR) (1924), and **Eric Heiden** (USA) (1980). Klassen did so by winning the 1,500 meters, finishing second in the 1,000 meters and the team **pursuit**, and coming in third in the 3,000 and 5,000 meters. Klassen, who had tried out for the 1998 Canadian Olympic **ice hockey** team, had already earned an Olympic bronze at the 2002 Games, in the 3,000 meters. Klassen's best performance was at the 2006 World All-round Championships, where she won her second title (after 2003) by setting two world records and two second-best times ever recorded. The five-foot, eight-inch (173 cm), 157 lb (71 kg) Klassen, who also won two titles and nine medals at World Single Distance Championships, also competed in the 2010 Vancouver Games after a long absence due to injuries, but could not reach her 2006 level.

KLIMKE, REINER (FRG/GER–EQU). B. 14 January 1936, Münster, Nordrhein-Westfalen, **Germany**. D. 17 August 1999, Münster, Nordrhein-Westfalen, Germany. Reiner Klimke's six gold and two bronze medals in **dressage** events stand as the Olympic record for any man in the **equestrian disciplines**, and he is the most successful dressage rider of all time. Although he began his career in dressage, he switched to eventing and in 1959 helped the Federal Republic of Germany win the European team three-day title. At six feet tall (184 cm), 146 lb (66 kg), he also competed at the 1960 Olympics in the **three-day event** before he returned to dressage. He was a five-time gold medalist with the German and West German Olympic dressage teams (1964, 1968, 1976, 1984, 1988) and won three other Olympic medals in individual dressage (bronze in 1968 and 1976 and gold in 1984). At the World Championships, Klimke was almost as successful, winning the individual title in 1974 and 1982 and helping West Germany to the team dressage World Championship in 1966, 1974, 1982, and 1986. At the European Championships, Klimke earned seven team and three individual gold medals (1967, 1973, and 1985). He won his Olympic individual gold in 1984 and his world individual gold in 1982 with his favorite horse, Ahlerich. In 1988, Ahlerich, by then 17 years old, also helped Klimke to his team gold medal at Seoul. Klimke's career was as a lawyer and a notary. His daughter Ingrid competed in the **Olympic Games** from 2000 to 2012 and won gold medals as a member of the German three-day event team in 2008 and 2012 aboard her horse Abraxxas.

KLUGE, VOLKER. B. 14 October 1944, Altenburg, **Germany**. Volker Kluge is a sportswriter and publicist. For more than 50 years beginning in the mid-1960s, he was the sports editor of several newspapers. He was the sports editor of the largest daily newspaper of the **German Democratic Republic** (GDR), press officer of the **National Olympic Committee** of the GDR from 1982 to 1990, press chief of the 90th **International Olympic Committee Session**, and personal member of the **National Olympic Committee** for Germany from 1990 to 1993. He is the author of more than 50 books, documentaries, and DVDs primarily on the **Olympic Movement** and Olympic history. His main work is a five volume history of the **Olympic Games**—four on the Summer Games titled *Olympische Sommerspiele—Die Chronik* and one on the **Olympic Winter Games**, *Olympische Winterspiele—Die Chronik.* He has also written sports histories of the German Democratic Republic—*Das Sportbuch DDR* and *Lexikon Sportler in der DDR*—and a biography of **heavyweight** champion **boxer** Max Schmeling—*Max Schmeling. Eine Biographie in 15 Runden.* Volker was one of the founding members of the **International Society of Olympic Historians** (ISOH) in 1991 and has been a member of its Executive Committee since 2008, the same year in which he was honored with the ISOH Lifetime Award. Since 2012, he has been the editor of the ISOH publication *Journal of Olympic History.*

KNOCKOUT. In the sport of **boxing**, if a contestant is knocked to the canvas, he or she is allowed 10 seconds in which to arise and continue boxing. Should he or she fail to do so, the opponent wins the bout by "knockout." If a contestant appears to be hurt and unable to successfully defend him- or herself, the referee may stop the bout and award the victory to the opponent. The term for this in professional boxing is "technical knockout" but in amateur boxing, as contested at the **Olympic Games**, the phrase is "**referee stops contest.**"

KNOWLES, DURWARD RANDOLPH (BAH–SAI). B. 2 November 1917, Nassau, New Providence, **Bahamas**. Durward Knowles's first appearance at the **Olympic Games** was in 1948. As his native Bahamas did not yet have a **National Olympic Committee** (NOC), he and his sailing partner Sloan Farrington represented **Great Britain** because the Bahamas at that time was a British colony. The pair finished fourth in the Star class two-man **keelboat**. In 1952, the Bahamas established an NOC and Knowles was able to compete for his native land. He and Farrington finished in fifth place that year. In 1956, they won a bronze medal. In 1960, they came in sixth.

In 1964, Knowles took on a new sailing partner, Cecil Cooke. That year they were victorious and Knowles won his second medal and first gold medal at the age of 46. He continued sailing and in 1968 competed in his sixth Olympic Games, this time with his step-brother Percy Knowles, who had previously sailed in the 1960 and 1964 Olympics on different-type boats.

The pair finished in fifth place. Durward was not finished sailing and entered again in 1972. This time, with Montague Higgs as his partner, they finished in 13th place of the 21 boats in the event. In 1988, Knowles decided to enter once more, and at the age of 70, with a 33-year-old sailing mate, Steven Kelly, Knowles competed in his eighth Olympic Games but finished in 19th place of the 21 teams. At the time, Knowles was one of only four men to compete in eight Olympic Games, but since then, **Ian Millar** has set the record with 10 appearances, two other athletes have made nine appearances, and two more have made eight.

On 24 July 1996, Sir Durward Knowles was conferred the honor of knighthood by Her Majesty the Queen.

KOLEHMAINEN, JOHAN PIETARI "HANNES" (FIN–ATH). B. 9 December 1889, Kuopio, Pohjois-Savo, **Finland**. D. 11 January 1966, Helsinki, Finland. Hannes Kolehmainen was the first of the great Finnish distance runners. At the 1912 **Olympic Games**, he won the 5,000 meters with a new world record, the 10,000 meters, and the individual **cross-country** race, in which he also won a silver medal in the team event. Kolehmainen also set a world record for 3,000 meters in a **heat** of the team event. The cancellation of the 1916 Games undoubtedly prevented him from winning further Olympic honors, but he returned in 1920 and won the gold medal in the **marathon**. He is the only person to win the Olympic 5,000 meters, 10,000 meters, marathon, and cross-country races. The five-foot, six-inch (168 cm), 128 lb (58 kg) Kolehmainen set eight world records or bests, at distances varying from 3,000 meters to the marathon. His three brothers, Willie, Kalle, and Tatu, were also accomplished distance runners, and Tatu competed in the 1912 and 1920 Olympic marathon, finishing 10th in 1920. In 1952, at the opening ceremony, Hannes lit the **Olympic flame** after receiving the torch from **Paavo Nurmi**, who had brought it into the Olympic stadium in Helsinki.

KONO, TAMIO "TOMMY" (USA–WLT). B. 27 June 1930, Sacramento, California, **United States**. Between 1953 and 1959, Tommy Kono was undefeated as a **weightlifter** in world and Olympic competition, adding six straight world titles to his two gold **Olympic medals** in the 1952 **lightweight** class and 1956 **light-heavyweight** class, and a silver in 1960 as a **middleweight**. In 1952, he set an Olympic record, and in 1956, he set a world record in his two gold medal victories. He also won three straight gold medals in the **Pan American Games**—in 1955, 1959, and 1963. Only five feet, five inches tall (167 cm), his weight varied from 148 to 179 lbs (67–81 kg). Kono is the only man to ever set world records in four distinct classes, and he won 11 Amateur Athletic Union (AAU) championships in three different weight classes. Kono was a very rare weightlifter who also competed successfully as a **body builder**, winning the AAU Mr. Universe title in 1954, 1955, and 1957. A Japanese American, he spent part of his teenage years at an internment camp in Tule Lake, California.

KORBUT, OLGA VALENTINOVNA (URS/BLR–GYM). B. 16 May 1955, Grodno, **Belarus**, USSR. **Olga Korbut** burst onto the world's **gymnastics** scene at the 1972 **Olympic Games** in Munich, amazing experts with her flexibility and daring moves. A fall on the **uneven bars** dropped her to seventh overall in the **all-around** individual. However, she won three gold medals: two individual in the apparatus finals (**balance beam** and **floor exercise**) and one with the **Soviet Union** all-around team along with a silver medal in uneven bars. Korbut never defeated her teammate in all-around **Lyudmila Turishcheva**, but the tiny (four-foot, 11-inch [152 cm], 86 lb [39 kg]) Korbut was the darling of the fans and the media for her courage in trying new moves and her willing smile. She later won the 1973 World University Games all-around title and was second at the 1973 Europeans and 1974 World Championships in all-around. She competed at the 1976 Olympics, winning a gold medal in the team event and a silver on the balance beam. Korbut retired from competition in 1977 and has now settled in Atlanta, Georgia (**United States**).

KOREA, DEMOCRATIC PEOPLE'S REPUBLIC OF (NORTH KOREA) (PRK). The Democratic People's Republic of Korea (DPRK; often referred to as North Korea) proclaimed its establishment on 9 September 1948. DPRK applied to the **International Olympic Committee** (IOC) for recognition in June 1956 and received provisional IOC recognition in 1957, on the understanding that it would only be allowed to compete at Rome in 1960 as a combined team with the **Republic of Korea** (South Korea).

Originally, the IOC policy was for both Koreas to form a combined team, similar to **Germany** in 1956–1964. DPRK agreed to this, but South Korea said it was impossible. DPRK received full IOC recognition for its **National Olympic Committee** in March 1962. DPRK then competed at the Innsbruck **Olympic Winter Games** in 1964, but with a flag that did not conform to the IOC decision made at the 1963 session in Baden-Baden.

DPRK was supposed to make its debut at the Olympic Games in 1964 in Tokyo but withdrew. This was because, in November 1963, DPRK had competed at the **Games of the New Emerging Forces** (GANEFO). These were highly controversial (*see also* "The Games of the XVIIIth **Olympiad**" in "The Olympic Games and Olympic Winter Games" in the front matter) and were not recognized by the IOC because GANEFO organizers refused admission to **Israel** and Taiwan. All athletes competing in **shooting**, **swimming**, and **athletics** at GANEFO were banned by their international federations from competing at Tokyo in 1964. This included several athletes from DPRK, including its greatest athlete, 800 meter world-record–holding runner Dan Sin-Kim. When these athletes were not allowed to compete, DPRK withdrew in protest.

GANEFO II was held from 25 November to 6 December 1966, and DPRK again competed at these games. Because of this, the track and field athletes from DPRK who had competed at GANEFO II were subsequently barred from the 1968 **Mexico** City Olympics, and the nation withdrew again, choosing not to send any athletes.

The 1968 withdrawal was also partly motivated by anger over a recent IOC decision. At the 68th **IOC Session** in Mexico City shortly before the Olympics, the IOC decided that, after 1 November 1968, the nation would be referred to as the Democratic People's Republic of Korea, but that at Mexico City, the nation would compete under its geographic name of North Korea. Precisely similar decisions were made with respect to East Germany and Taiwan, who were forced by the IOC to compete at Mexico City under names they did not recognize, rather than their proper names (**German Democratic Republic** and Republic of **China**, respectively).

DPRK made its first Olympic appearance at the Olympic Winter Games in Innsbruck in 1964. The nation has also competed at the Winter Games of 1972, 1984, 1988, 1992, 1998, 2006, and 2010. It has competed at nearly all Olympic Games since 1972, skipping the 1984 Los Angeles Olympics and the 1988 Seoul Olympics.

DPRK withdrew from the 1984 Olympics in obvious sympathy with the Soviet Union's **boycott** of the Los Angeles Olympics. It withdrew from the 1988 Olympics in protest against the hosting of the Games by the rival government of the Republic of (South) Korea. Long political discussions were held from 1985 to 1988 between representatives of the National Olympic Committees of the two countries. These dealt with demands by the North Koreans to cohost the 1988 Olympics or at least host several of the events. The Korean Olympic Organizing Committee and the IOC were never able to satisfy the demands of the North Koreans, and talks eventually broke off, resulting in the North Korean boycott (*see also* "The Games of the XXIVth **Olympiad**" in "The Olympic Games and Olympic Winter Games" in the front matter).

At the 2000 opening ceremony in Sydney, a historic event occurred when the teams from the Democratic People's Republic of Korea and the Republic of Korea marched into the stadium together, led by one flagbearer from each nation at the head of the combined contingent. This "athletic peace" was brokered by the IOC and occurred at a time when the two Koreas were also beginning to have some political exchanges for the first time in decades. The flagbearer for DPRK at Sydney was the official Pak Jang-Chul, while the Republic of Korea was led by **basketball** player Chung Eun-Song. This occurred again at the 2004 Athens opening ceremony, when **volleyballer** Ku Min-Jung carried the flag for Korea and the official Kim Song-Ho carried the DPRK flag. But the dual entrance did not occur in either 2008 or 2012.

In nine Summer Games, North Korea has entered 325 athletes (172 men, 153 **women**) and competed in 16 sports: **archery** (one man, 13 women), athletics (15 men, 10 women), **boxing** (20 men, one woman), **cycling** (three women), **diving** (four men, 12 women), **football** (15 men, 31 women), **gymnastics** (17 men, 22 women), **judo** (15 men, 11 women), **rhythmic gymnastics** (two women), **rowing** (six men), shooting (23 men, seven women), **synchronized swimming** (six women), **table tennis** (nine men, 13 women), volleyball (11 women), **weightlifting** (27 men, nine women), and **wrestling** (20 men, two women). They have won 47 medals (14 gold, 12 silver, 21 bronze) with medals coming in weightlifting (13, four gold), wrestling (10, three gold), boxing and judo (each eight, two gold), table tennis (three, no gold), gymnastics (two gold), shooting (two, one gold), and women's volleyball (one bronze).

Female *judoka* Kye Sun-Hui has won three medals for North Korea (gold in 1996 **extra-lightweight**, bronze in 2000 **half-lightweight**, silver in 2004 lightweight), and An Kum-Ae has won two in the women's judo half-lightweight class (2008 silver, 2012 gold). Other North Korean athletes with two Summer Games medals are **light-flyweight** boxer Li Byong-Uk (silver 1976, bronze 1980); table tennis player Li Bun-Hui (bronze in both 1992 women's singles and **doubles**); men's **light-flyweight freestyle** wrestler Kim Il-Ong (gold in both 1992 and 1996), and weightlifters Kim Myong-Nam (men's 1992 middleweight bronze, 1996 lightweight silver) and Ri Song-Hui (women's **lightweight** 2000, 2004 both silver).

Other North Korean gold medalists are **flyweight** boxer Choi Chol-Sul (1992) and **bantamweight** boxer Gu Yong-Jo (1976); gymnasts Pae Gil-Su (1992 men's **pommelled horse**) and Hong Un-Jong (2008 women's **horse vault**); shooter Li Ho-Jun (1972 men's **small-bore rifle**, prone); men's flyweight freestyle wrestler Li Hak-Son (1992); 2012 male weightlifters bantamweight Om Yun-Chol and **featherweight** Kim Un-Guk, and female weightlifters middleweight Pak Hyon-Suk (2008) and **light-heavyweight** Rim Jong-Sim (2012).

In eight Olympic Winter Games, North Korea has entered 62 athletes (25 men, 37 women) and competed in five sports: **Alpine skiing** (one man, one woman), **cross-country skiing** (four men, four women), **figure skating** (seven men, six women), **speed skating** (10 men, 19 women), and **short-track speed skating** (10 men, 19 women). They have won two medals in the Winter Games. Han Pil-Hwa won a silver medal in women's 3,000 meters speed skating in 1964, and Hwang Ok-Sil won a bronze medal in the 1992 women's 500 meters short-track event.

KOREA, REPUBLIC OF (SOUTH KOREA) (KOR). The Republic of Korea, as we know it today, was formally created on 15 August 1948, after the end of World War II. Korea, located in East Asia, first officially competed at the 1948 **Olympic Games** in London. However, in both 1932 and 1936, during the occupation of the country by the **Japanese** (1910–1945), several Korean athletes competed at the Olympic Games wearing the colors of Japan including the winner of the men's **marathon** race Son Gi-Jeon, who appeared under the Japanese name of Kitei Son. Korea has competed at all Olympics since 1948 with the exception of 1980, when it **boycotted** the Moscow Olympics. Korea also made its first **Olympic Winter Games** appearance in 1948 and has since missed only the Winter Games of 1952.

In 16 Summer Games, Korea has entered 2,003 athletes (1,320 men, 683 **women**) and competed in 31 sports, with the largest contingents in **athletics** (102 men, 52 women), **wrestling** (117 men, three women), **shooting** (66 men, 46 women), and the team sports of **volleyball** (72 men, 87 women), **hockey** (63 men, 84 women), **handball** (63 men, 76 women), **football** (131 men), and **basketball** (56 men, 47 women). They have won 243 medals in the Summer Games (81 gold, 82 silver, 80 bronze) with medals won in 19 different sports.

Korea has done well in combative sports, winning 109 of its 243 medals in **boxing**, wrestling, **judo**, and **taekwondo**. The women have also medaled in volleyball, basketball, handball, hockey, **table tennis**, and **archery**. Korean women have dominated the sport of archery, winning the team gold medal each year from 1988 to 2012 and winning 16 medals (seven gold) in individual competition from 1984 to 2012. Archer **Kim Su-Nyeong** has won the most medals among Korean Olympians, six, with four gold, one silver, and one bronze from 1988 to 2000, although she did not compete in 1996. Pistol shooter Jin Jong-O won five medals (three gold, two silver) from 2004 to 2012. Four other Korean athletes have won four medals each at the Summer Games: swimmer Park Tae-Hwan (one gold, three silver, 2004–2012); table tennis player Yu Nam-Gyu (one gold, three bronze, 1988–1996); **Oh Seong-Ok** (one gold, two silver, one bronze, women's handball, 1992–2008), and Park Seong-Hyun (three gold, one silver, women's archery, 2004–2008). Sixteen other Korean Olympians have each won three medals at the Summer Games.

In 17 **Olympic Winter Games**, Korea has entered 259 athletes (164 men, 95 women) and competed in 13 sports, with 44 men and 38 women in **speed skating** and 23 men and 21 women in **short-track speed skating**. Korea has won 53 medals (26 gold, 17 silver, 10 bronze) in winter sports, with 42 of them (21 gold) coming in short-track speed skating. Three short-track speed skaters have each won five medals: one man, Lee Ho-Seok (one gold, four silver, 2006–2014) and two women, **Jeon I-Gyeong** (four gold, one bronze, 1994–1998) and Park Seung-Hui (two gold, three bronze, 2010–2014). Choi Eun-Gyeong won four in women's short-track (two gold, two silver, 2002–2006). Korean-born An Hyeon-Su won four medals in short-track (three gold, one bronze in 2006) and then, after a dispute with Korean officials, moved to **Russia** where, competing as **Viktor An**, he won four more medals in 2014 to lead all short-track skaters. Seven other Korean skaters have each won three medals in short-track speed skating, with Jin Seon-Yu (2006) and Kim Gi-Hun (1992–1994) each winning three gold medals. In other winter sports, Lee Seung-Hun won three medals (one gold, two silver) in regular speed skating from 2010 to 2014. Figure skater Yu-Na Kim won the gold medal in 2010 and silver medal in 2014 in women's **singles figure skating**.

Korea ably hosted the Games of the XXIVth **Olympiad** in Seoul in 1988 and Pyeongchang, Korea, will be the host of the 2018 Winter Games after bidding unsuccessfully for the Winter Games of 2010 and 2014. *See also* KOREA, DEMOCRATIC PEOPLE'S REPUBLIC OF; KOREA WOMEN'S ARCHERY TEAMS (1988–2012).

KOREA WOMEN'S ARCHERY TEAMS (1988–2012). Olympic **archery** added a **women**'s team event in 1988. Teams of three women compete in a series of **rounds**, each round eliminating several teams until a final round is reached. In the seven **Olympic Games** that this event has been contested, **Korea** has won each year. **Kim Su-Nyeong** was a member of three teams—in 1988, 1992, and 2000. Although archery returned to the Olympic program in 1972, Korea did not enter a team until 1984. Since then, in the women's individual archery event, a Korean woman has won the gold medal in seven of the eight Olympics from 1984 to 2012. They also won five silver medals and four bronze medals in that time. In 1988 and again in 2000, Korean women won gold, silver, and bronze.

KORFBALL. Korfball is a sport that was invented in the early 20th century by Nico Broykheusen, a Dutch schoolteacher. It has elements of **netball** and **basketball** and is played by teams of eight players—either all female or four female and four male. It was contested as a **demonstration sport** at the Olympics of 1920 and 1928. The International Korfball Federation (IKF) is recognized by the **International Olympic Committee**. Founded in 1933, the IKF has 62 affiliated member nations as of June 2014.

KORZENIOWSKI, ROBERT MAREK (POL–ATH). B. 30 July 1968, Lubaczów, Podkarpackie, **Poland**. Robert Korzeniowski is the most successful **race walker** at the Olympics, with four titles. In 1996, 2000, and 2004, he won the 50 kilometers event, making him the only person to have won an **Olympic Games** race walking event more than twice. He also became the first person to win both the 20 and 50 km competitions, doing so at the same Olympics, in 2000. Primarily a 50 km specialist, Korzeniowski won that event three times at the World Championships (1997, 2001, and 2003) and twice at the European Championships (1998 and 2002). At five feet, six inches (168 cm), 132 lb (60 kg), he had less success at the 20 km distance, not finishing the race in 1992 in Barcelona, and finishing eighth in 1996 in Atlanta before winning it in 2000. Korzeniowski retired after the 2004 Olympics, in which his sister Sylwia also competed as a race walker, though with less success than her brother.

KOSOVO. Kosovo was a semiautonomous province in southern **Serbia** and was a part of the former **Yugoslavia**, then of **Serbia and Montenegro**. It was the site of a brutal war in the early 1990s, as Serbian President Slobodan Milošević invaded the region and threatened ethnic cleansing, as he had done in **Bosnia and Herzegovina**. Kosovo's legal status is in dispute as of 2014. Technically, it is still under the control of a United Nations (UN) peacekeeping force, as it has been since 1999. In 2005, the UN began discussions about whether Kosovo should remain a part of Serbia or become a separate nation. After several referenda, Kosovo declared its independence on 17 February 2008; however, the international community does not fully recognize this. Serbia, in particular, does not recognize it, considering Kosovo a UN-governed entity within Serbia, the Autonomous Province of Kosovo and Metohija. It is also not yet recognized by the UN as an independent nation. Kosovo has formed a **National Olympic Committee**, which has affiliations with the **International Federations** (IFs) for **table tennis** and **weightlifting**, and its **archery** group is provisionally recognized by the IF. The Olympic Committee of Kosovo has not yet been recognized by the **International Olympic Committee** however, pending resolution of its international status as a nation and recognition by the UN and because it needs to have more sports groups affiliated with the IFs. Kosovo-born Majlinda Kelmendi competed in the 2012 London **Olympic Games** as a representative of **Albania** in the women's **half-lightweight judo** competition and finished tied for ninth place.

KOSS, JOHANN OLAV (NOR–SSK). B. 29 October 1968, Drammen, Buskerud, **Norway**. Johann Olav Koss was the winner of the 1,500 meters, 5,000 meters, and 10,000 meters **speed skating** events at the 1994 **Olympic**

Winter Games, setting an Olympic record in each event and a world record in the 10,000 meters. The six-foot, two-inch (189 cm), 170 lb (77 kg) Koss had previously won Olympic gold in the 1,500 meters and silver in the 10,000 meters in 1992. In 1994, he donated his first gold medal cash bonus to Olympic Aid for Sarajevo and retired shortly after the Lillehammer Games to pursue a career in medicine. He later became leader of an **International Olympic Committee** (IOC)–recognized charitable organization, **Right to Play**. Koss was world **all-around** champion in 1990, 1991, and 1994 and was also World Cup champion at the distance events in 1991. During his career, he set 10 world records, five at 5,000 meters, two at 10,000 meters, and one each at 1,500 meters, 3,000 meters, and in the all-around. Koss served as an athlete member of the IOC from 1999 to 2001.

KOSTELIĆ, JANICA (CRO–ASK). B. 5 January 1982, Zagreb, **Croatia, Yugoslavia**. When only 16 years old, Janica Kostelić competed at the 1998 **Olympic Winter Games**, with a best finish of eighth place in the **Alpine combined**. Her skiing improved dramatically as she grew older, and in 2000–2001, she won the overall World Cup title, which stamped her as a favorite going into the Salt Lake City Winter Olympics. She then became the first athlete to be featured on a Croatian postage stamp. Although much was expected of her in 2002, she exceeded expectations at Salt Lake City by winning three gold medals and adding a silver for her fourth medal. Her golds were in the **slalom, giant slalom**, and Alpine **combined**, and she finished second in the **super G**. Kostelić was the first Alpine skier, male or female, to win four medals at one Olympics and the first woman to win three gold medals at the same Olympic Winter Games. The five-foot, eight-inch (175 cm), 168 lb (76 kg) Kostelić won two medals at Torino in 2006, including defending her title in Alpine combined, giving her a career total of four gold medals and six **Olympic medals**. She won the overall World Cup title in 2000–2001, 2002–2003, and 2003–2006; won 10 World Cup seasonal titles in all; and was a five-time world champion. Her brother Ivica Kostelić is also a four-time Olympic silver medalist in Alpine skiing.

KOVÁCS, PÁL ÁDÁM (HUN–FEN). B. 17 July 1912, Debrecen, Hadjú-Bihar, Austria-**Hungary**. D. 8 July 1995, Budapest, Hungary. Pál Kovács began his sports career as a promising **hurdler**, but he later turned to **fencing** and was a member of the winning Hungarian **sabre** team at five successive Olympics (1936–1960). In the individual sabre, he was Olympic champion in 1953 after winning a bronze in 1948. Kovács, at five feet, 10 inches (179 cm), 176 lb (80 kg), was also world sabre champion in 1937 and 1953. In 1980, he became vice president of the Fédération Internationale d'Éscrime. His two sons, Attila and Tamás, both fenced in the **Olympic Games**, and Tamás won two bronze medals in team sabre competition in 1968 and 1972.

KRAENZLEIN, ALVIN CHRISTIAN "AL" (USA–ATH). B. 12 December 1876, Milwaukee, Wisconsin, **United States**. D. 6 January 1928, Wilkes Barre, Pennsylvania, United States. At the 1900 Games, Alvin Kraenzlein won the 60 meters, the 110 and 200 meter **hurdles**, and the **long jump**, and his four individual gold medals remain the unmatched record for a track and field athlete at one Games. A six-foot tall (183 cm), 165 lb (75 kg) athlete, his pioneering technique of straight-leg hurdling brought him two world hurdle records in addition to his five world records in the long jump. Although a qualified dentist, Kraenzlein never practiced, preferring to become a track coach, notably of the **German** and **Cuban** national teams and at the University of Michigan.

KRAUßE, STEFAN. *See* BEHRENDT, JAN.

KULAKOVA, GALINA ALEKSEYEVNA (URS–CCS). B. 29 April 1942, Logachi, Udmurtskaya, **Russia**, USSR. Galina Kulakova was the greatest **cross-country skier** of the 1970s, setting records for Olympic medals that would stand until the program was expanded for **women** in the late 1980s. Her finest Olympics were in 1972 at Sapporo, when she won both individual events for women—five km and 10 km—and helped the **Soviet Union** to a **relay** gold medal. She repeated this triple at the 1974 World Championships. Only five feet, two inches (160 cm), 126 lb (57 kg), she won eight **Olympic medals**—four gold, two silver, two bronze—at four Olympics in 1968 through 1980. She earned five golds at the World Championships, with a five km individual and relay gold in 1970 added to her feats of 1974. Her career was marred somewhat by a **doping** positive for ephedrine at the 1976 Olympics. In an unusual ruling, the **International Olympic Committee** gave her a warning but no suspension and allowed her to enter the remaining races.

KURLAND, ROBERT ALBERT "BOB" (USA–BAS). B. 23 December 1924, St. Louis, Missouri, **United States**. D. 29 September 2013, Sanibel Island, Florida, United States. Bob "Foothills" Kurland was the first dominating seven-footer (2.14 meters) to play college **basketball**; so dominant, in fact, that he caused the rules-makers to outlaw goaltending (touching the ball while it is directly above the opponents' basket), because he could block almost every shot from going into the basket. In 1945 and 1946, he led his Oklahoma A&M team to the National Collegiate Athletic Association championship and then went on to play for six years with the Phillips 66ers, being named Amateur Athletic Union All-America every year he played. While playing with Phillips, the 220 lb (100 kg) Kurland became the first man to play on two Olympic championship teams (1948 and 1952). He was inducted into the Naismith Memorial Basketball Hall of Fame in 1961.

KUWAIT (KUW). Kuwait's **National Olympic Committee** was formed in 1957 and recognized by the **International Olympic Committee** in 1966. The Western Asian nation, located on the Arabian peninsula and officially named the State of Kuwait, has competed continuously at the **Olympic Games** since 1968. It has never competed at the **Olympic Winter Games**. In 12 Summer Games, Kuwait has entered 192 athletes (189 men, three **women**) and competed in 13 sports: **athletics** (31 men, one woman), **boxing** (three men), **diving** (six men), **fencing** (22 men), **football** (50 men), **handball** (25 men), **judo** (19 men), **shooting** (nine men, one woman), **swimming** (19 men, one woman), **table tennis** (two men), and one man in **rowing**, **taekwondo**, and **weightlifting**.

Kuwaiti athletes have won two **Olympic medals**, a bronze for Fehaid al-Deehani in 2000 in **double trap** shooting and a second bronze in 2012 in single **trap** shooting. He has competed in five Olympic Games from 1992 to 2012 and has also finished fourth in double trap in 2012 and eighth in 2004. The 1980 Kuwaiti football team tied for fifth among the 16 teams in 1980. Other notable Olympic performances for Kuwait include Khaled Al-Mudhaf placing fourth place in 2000 trap shooting and sixth place in that event in 2004, **skeet** shooter Abdullah Al-Rashidi tied for seventh in 2008 and tied for eighth in 2004, Fehaid Al-Deehani, eighth in double trap in 2004, Fahad Al-Farhan, ninth in 1980 **lightweight** judo, and Fahed Salem tied for ninth in 1976 **half-heavyweight** judo.

KYRGYZSTAN (KGZ). Kyrgyzstan's **National Olympic Committee** was recognized by the **International Olympic Committee** in 1992 shortly after the breakup of the **Soviet Union**. Several Kyrgyz athletes competed from 1952 to 1988 for the Soviet Union, and Kyrgyz athletes were present at Barcelona in 1992 as members of the Unified Team. The first Olympic appearance as an independent nation of this Central Asian nation, officially named the Kyrgyz Republic, occurred in 1994 at Lillehammer, where they were represented by **biathlete** Yevgeniya Roppel. They have since competed at every **Olympic Games** and every **Olympic Winter Games** through 2014.

In five Summer Games, Kyrgyzstan has entered 110 athletes (85 men, 25 **women**) and competed in 13 sports: **athletics** (11 men, eight women), **boxing** (nine men), **canoeing** (two men), **cycling** (one man), **fencing** (two men), **judo** (seven men, three women), **modern pentathlon** (two men, one woman), **sailing** (one man), **shooting** (four men), **swimming** (21 men, 12 women), **taekwondo** (one man), **weightlifting** (four men), and **wrestling** (20 men, one woman). Kyrgyzstani athletes have won three medals: **extra-light-weight** Aydin Smagulov won a bronze in judo in 2000 and in **Greco-Roman wrestling** in 2008, Kanat Begaliyev won silver in the **welterweight** class, and Ruslan Tumenbayev won a bronze in the **lightweight** class. Other notable Olympic results for Kyrgyzstan athletes include, in wrestling: fifth place for Aleksandr Kovalevsky (1996 freestyle **super-heavyweight**) and Gennady Chkhaidze (2004 Greco-Roman **heavyweight**), and a fifth place tie for Bazar Bazarguruyev (2008 freestyle lightweight), sixth place for Konstantin Aleksandrov (1996 **freestyle** heavyweight), and seventh place for Magomed Musayev (2012 freestyle heavyweight). In athletics, runner Irina Bogacheva finished 21st of 88 entrants in the 1996 women's **marathon** and 14th of 53 in 2000. Shooter Yury Lomov tied for 11th of 52 in the 1996 **small-bore rifle** prone event, and teammate Yury Melentyev tied for 12th of 50 that year in **air pistol** competition.

At the Winter Games, Kyrgyzstan has entered all six since 1994, although with only one or two athletes each year and a total of seven participants (five men, two women). They have competed in **Alpine skiing**, **biathlon**, **cross-country skiing**, and **ski jumping**. Their best results were Aleksandr Tropnikov in the 1998 men's 20 k biathlon when he finished 36th of 72 entrants and Yevgeny Timofeyev in the 2012 men's **slalom** (41st of 115).

KYUDO. The **Japanese** version of **archery**, called *kyudo*, was one of the three traditional Japanese sports demonstrated at the 1964 Olympics (along with *kendo* and *sumo*). No competition results from this display are known.

L

LACROSSE. Lacrosse, the official national summer sport of **Canada**, was twice on the **Olympic Program** as a full medal sport, in 1904 and 1908, with the gold medal won by Canada each time. In those two Summer Games, there were 60 men from Canada, the **United States**, and **Great Britain** who took part in Olympic lacrosse. It has also been contested as a **demonstration sport** at the Olympics in 1928, 1932, and 1948. In 2008, the federations for men's and women's lacrosse merged to form the Federation of International Lacrosse (FIL). As of 2014, the FIL has 29 member nations (including the Iroquois Nation [aka Haudenosaunee]), as well as 21 associate member nations, but the sport is unlikely to return to the **Olympic Games** in the near future.

LAGUTIN, BORIS NIKOLAYEVICH (URS/RUS–BOX). B. 24 June 1938, Moscow, **Russia**, USSR. Boris Lagutin began his **boxing** career in 1955. He won his first international title in 1961, the European Championship, after winning a bronze medal in the **light-middleweight** class at the Rome Olympics in 1960. In 1964 and 1968, the five-foot, eight-inch (172 cm) Lagutin won the gold medal in the light-middleweight class, making him the third Olympic boxer to win three **Olympic medals** (after **László Papp** [HUN] in 1948–1956 and Zbigniew Pietrzykowski [POL] in 1956–1964) and only the third to defend his Olympic title in the same class, after Papp and **Great Britain**'s **Harry Mallin** (1920–1924). Lagutin was also European Champion in 1961 and 1963.

LAJUNEN, SAMPPA KALEVI (FIN–NCO). B. 23 April 1979, Turku, Varsinais-Suomi, **Finland**. Samppa Lajunen is the only man to have won three **Nordic combined** gold medals at the same **Olympic Games**. At the 2002 Games, the first time three Nordic combined competitions were scheduled, Lajunen crossed the line first in the individual, team, and **sprint** events. Four years earlier, the five-foot, nine-inch (177 cm), 143 lb (65 kg) Lajunen had won silver medals in the individual and team events, bringing his **Olympic medal** tally to a record five (since surpassed only by **Felix Gottwald**). Lajunen was slightly less dominant at the World Nordic Skiing Championships, winning eight medals between 1997 and 2003, his only title being in the 1999 team competition. Lajunen also won the Nordic Combined World Cup twice (1997 and 2000), earning a total of 20 World Cup wins.

LANGE, ANDRÉ (GER–BOB). B. 28 June 1973, Ilmenau, Thüringen, **Germany.** André Lange is the most dominant **bobsledder** of the 21st century so far. At the **Olympic Winter Games**, he has won four titles, winning the four-man event in 2002, both events in 2006, and the two-man competition in 2010, while placing second in the four-man competition. At World Championships between 2000 and 2009, Lange has earned 17 medals, including eight titles in the two-man (2003, 2007, 2008) and four-man (2000, 2003, 2004, 2005, 2008) events. The six-foot, two-inch (188 cm), 220 lb (100 kg) Lange has also won eight European titles and 36 World Cup races, as well as five seasonal World Cups. After the Vancouver Olympics, where Lange was the flagbearer of the German team at the opening ceremony, Lange announced his retirement from the sport. One of Lange's regular runners was Kevin Kuske, who shares the record for most Olympic bobsled titles with Lange.

LAOS (LAO). Laos formed a **National Olympic Committee** in 1975 and saw it recognized by the **International Olympic Committee** in 1979. Laos's first Olympic appearance was in 1980 at Moscow, where it had 19 entrants. The country has since competed in each Summer Games from 1988 through 2012. It has not yet competed at the **Olympic Winter Games**. In eight summer **Olympic Games**, the Southeast Asian country of Laos, officially known as the Lao People's Democratic Republic, has had a total of 43 competitors (36 men, seven **women**) in **archery** (one man), **athletics** (16 men, six women), **boxing** (nine men), **shooting** (six men), and **swimming** (four men, one woman). Laotian competitors have not yet come close to winning a medal—all nine boxers lost their first bout, their archer and six shooters finished last or next to last, all of their runners and their relay team finished last or next to last in their initial **heat**, and their swimmers finished in the bottom 10 percent, with Sikhounxay Ounkhamphanyayong's finish of 70th of 77 entrants in the 2000 men's 50 meter freestyle being the best performance among Laotian swimmers. Arguably the greatest Olympic performance by a Laotian athlete was by women's **marathon** runner Sirivanh Ketavong, who twice completed the marathon (1996, 2000). In 1996, her 64th place result was ahead of that of 21 women who did not finish the distance and one who did. In 2000, Ketavong was the 45th and last to complete the race but was ahead of eight others who did not finish.

LARGE HILL. In **ski jumping**, the large hill is the larger of two hills used in the sport. It was initially 80 meters and since 1968 has been 90 meters. The method used for hill measurement has been changed in recent years, although the heights of the hills have not. Men's ski jumping from the large hill has been a sport in every **Olympic Winter Games** since 1968. **Matti Nykänen** of **Finland** (1984, 1988) and **Simon Ammann** of **Switzerland** (2002, 2010) are the only multiple gold medalists in this event. Adam Małysz of **Poland** (silver 2002, 2010) and Jens Weißflog of East **Germany** (silver 1984, gold 1994 for united Germany) also won two medals at the large hill. Since 1988, a large hill team competition is held in which the combined results of four skiers from a country determine the winner. Germany has won the team event three times, with **Austria** and Finland victors twice each.

LATVIA (LAT). Prior to its annexation by the **Soviet Union** in 1940, Latvia competed at the **Olympic Games** of 1924, 1928, 1932, and 1936, winning three medals. It also competed at the **Olympic Winter Games** of 1924, 1928, and 1936. From 1952 to 1988, many Latvians competed for the Soviet Union. After the Soviet revolution of 1991, Latvia declared and was granted its independence, and its **National Olympic Committee** was recognized by the **International Olympic Committee** in 1991. A northern Europe country located on the Baltic Sea, Latvia returned to the Olympic fold in 1992, competing at both Albertville and Barcelona, and has competed at all Olympic Games, Summer and Winter, since.

In 10 Summer Games, Latvia has entered 239 athletes (179 men, 60 **women**) and competed in 19 sports plus the **art competitions**. They had the most participants in **athletics** (52 men, 30 women), **cycling** (32 men, one woman), **basketball** (seven men, 12 women), and **wrestling** (15 men, one woman). Latvia has won 19 medals at the Summer Games (three gold, 11 silver, five bronze). In 2000, **gymnast** Igors Vihrovs competing in the men's **floor exercise** won the country's first gold **Olympic medal**. Latvia's two other gold medals were both won by Māris Štrombergs in 2008 and 2012 in the men's cycling **BMX** race. **Canoeist** Ivans Klementjevs won two silver medals for Latvia in men's **Canadian singles** 1,000 meters in 1992 and 1996. He had competed for the Soviet Union in 1988 and had won the gold medal that year. **Super-heavyweight weightlifter** Viktors Ščerbatihs was also a dual medalist for Latvia as he won silver in 2004 and bronze in 2008. Latvia's other Olympic silver medalists in the Summer Games are wrestler Edvīns Bietags (1936 **Greco-Roman light-heavyweight**), shooter Afanasijs Kuzmins (1992 men's **rapid-fire pistol**), gymnast Jevgēņijs Saproņenko (2004 men's **horse vault**), **modern pentathlete** Jeļena Rubļevska (1992 women's individual), **race walkers** Jānis Dāliņš (1932 50 k) and Aigars Fadejevs (2000 50 k), and **javelin throwers** Vadims Vasiļevskis (2004) and Ainārs Kovals (2008). Latvia's other bronze medalists are the 2012 men's **beach volleyball** team of Mārtiņš Pļaviņš and Jānis Šmēdiņš, race walker Adalberts Bubenko (1936 50 k), cyclist Dainis Ozols (1992 men's individual **road race**), and *judoka* Vsevolods Zeļonijs (2,000 men's **lightweight**).

In 10 Winter Games, Latvia has entered 194 athletes (162 men, 32 women) and competed in 12 sports—all but **curling, ski jumping**, and **snowboarding**. They have won seven medals—four silver and three bronze. Brothers Andris and Juris Šics have each won three medals in **luge** (2010 silver, 2014 two bronze), Martins Dukurs won two silvers in **skeleton** (2010, 2014), Mārtiņš Rubenis won bronze in 2006 luge singles and was a member of the 2014 **relay** team that also won bronze, and the 2014 four-man **bobsled** team also won silver. *See also* SEMJONOVA, ULJANA LARIONOVNA.

LATYNINA, LARYSA SEMYONOVNA (née DIRIY) (URS/UKR– GYM). B. 27 December 1934, Kherson, **Ukraine**, USSR. Larysa Latynina was a Soviet **gymnast** whose total of 18 **Olympic medals** is an absolute

Gymnast Larysa Latynina, winner of more Olympic medals than any other female athlete. Courtesy of Volker Kluge

Olympic record. She has won more Olympic medals and more gold medals than any other female athlete and is second only to **Michael Phelps**, with 22, for total medals and third behind Phelps and **Ray Ewry** for gold medals. Between 1956 and 1964, she won nine gold, five silver, and four bronze medals, with individual gold being won in the **floor exercise** (1956, 1960, 1964), the **horse vault** (1956), and the individual **all-around** (1956, 1960). She participated in only one Olympic event without medaling: the 1956 horse vault, in which she tied for fourth place. Only five feet, three inches (161 cm), 115 lb (52 kg), Latynina dominated other major championships to a similar extent, and at the Olympic, World, and European Championships, she won 24 gold, 15 silver, and five bronze, for a total of 44 medals. This phenomenal record was achieved even though her career was interrupted when she gave birth to two children.

LAUSANNE, SWITZERLAND. Lausanne, **Switzerland**, bills itself as the Olympic city, serving as the headquarters of the **International Olympic Committee** (IOC). The city is located in southwestern Switzerland, on the banks of Lake Geneva (Lac Léman, in French). Lausanne is the capital of the French-speaking canton of Vaud and has a population of approximately 600,000. It rivals Geneva as the intellectual and cultural center of French Switzerland, with several European writers having lived there, including Voltaire, Rousseau, Charles Dickens, Victor Hugo, Shelley, and Lord Byron. It is home to the Federal Court of Justice and is known as a center for international fairs and conferences. Lausanne was the site of the 1922–1923 peace conference at the end of World War I, at which the Treaty of Lausanne was created, between the Allies and the Ottoman empire. In 1932, representatives from Britain, **Belgium**, **Italy**, and **France** met in Lausanne and agreed that the Great Depression made the continued payment of **German** war reparations impossible, and the Lausanne Protocol of 1932 ended those payments.

During World War I, **Pierre de Coubertin** felt that the IOC should be based in a neutral country and chose Switzerland, which he had frequently visited. He moved to Lausanne in 1915, and on 10 April 1915, in the Lausanne town hall, signed an agreement to transfer the base of operations of the IOC to Lausanne, despite objections from other **IOC members**. But because of the war, the move officially occurred only in 1922, when the IOC headquarters was moved to Coubertin's home, Mon Repos. The IOC moved its headquarters to Château de Vidy in 1968, an older building on the banks of Lake Geneva that has since been enlarged several times to house the significantly expanded administrative staff of the IOC. The IOC has organized two **Olympic Congresses** (1913, 1922) in Lausanne, as well as a record 12 **IOC Sessions**.

In addition, the **Olympic Museum** is based in Lausanne, in the Ouchy section, about four miles (seven km) from the IOC headquarters, on a hill overlooking Lake Geneva (Lac Léman). Because of the presence of the IOC, several **International Federations** and the **Court of Arbitration for Sport** have established their headquarters in Lausanne as well.

LAVROV, ANDREY IVANOVICH (URS/EUN/RUS–HAN). B. 26 March 1962, Krasnodar, Krasnodar Kray, **Russia**, USSR. Andrey Lavrov is the only man to win four medals in Olympic **handball** and the only one with three gold medals as well. A six-foot, five-inch (197 cm), 207 lb (94 kg) goalkeeper, Lavrov played in five Olympic handball tournaments from 1988 to 2004. He won the gold medal in 1988 with the **Soviet Union** team and in 1992 with the **Commonwealth of Independent States** team. In 1996, playing for Russia, his third team in three Olympics, the team failed to medal and finished fifth, but in 2000, they won the gold medal and in 2004 the bronze medal. In 2000, he had the honor of being the flagbearer for Russia during the opening ceremony. He was also twice a member of the gold medal–winning team at the World Championships (1993, 1997) and twice a member of the silver medal–winning team at that event (1990, USSR; 1999, Russia).

LAWN TENNIS. *See* TENNIS.

LAZO IGLESIAS, PEDRO LUIS (CUB-BSB). B. 15 April 1973, Pinar del Rio, **Cuba**. Pedro Luis Lazo is one of the best **baseball** pitchers in the 21st century. Unfortunately, he has not had a chance to demonstrate his ability in Major League Baseball. He was a member of the Cuban Olympic baseball team from 1996 to 2008 and won four medals—two gold and two silver. He has won more Olympic baseball medals than anyone else. The six-foot, three-inch (192 cm), 236 lb (107 kg) Lazo has been primarily used as a relief pitcher in international play, although he is used mainly as a starter in the Cuban National League. As a relief pitcher, he helped Cuba win four **Olympic medals**. He appeared in 17 games in the Olympic tournaments and was the winning pitcher in four, losing pitcher in one, and was also credited with three saves. Cuba won 14 of the 17 games he appeared in. As a member of the Cuban National team, he won four gold and two silver medals at the Baseball World Cup from 1998 to 2009, three gold and one silver at the Intercontinental Cup from 1995 to 2006, three gold medals at the **Pan American Games** from 1995 to 2007, and two gold medals at the **Central American and Caribbean Games** in 1998 and 2006.

LAZUTINA, LARISA YEVGENYEVNA (née PTITSYNA) (EUN/RUS–CCS). B. 1 July 1965, Kondopoga, Respublika Kareliya, **Russia**, USSR.

Larisa Lazutina followed in the ski steps of **Galina Kulakova, Yelena Välbe,** and **Raisa Smetanina** as the greatest Russian female **cross-country skier.** The five-foot, five-inch (167 cm), 126 lb (57 kg) Lazutina won 11 championships at the Olympics and World Championships, trailing only the 16 won by Välbe. These include six relay titles: Olympics in 1992, 1994, and 1998, and Worlds in 1993, 1995, and 1997. In 1998 at Nagano, she put on her greatest performance, winning medals in all five events open to **women**, with three gold (five km, **pursuit, relay**), a silver in the 15 km, and a bronze in the 30 km. Her individual World Championships were earned in the 1993 and 1995 five km, the 1995 15 km, and the 1995 pursuit. Lazutina also took part in the 2002 Olympics and would have won two gold medals in the 15 k and 30 k and a silver medal in the pursuit, but she was **disqualified** after a positive drug test. The ensuing two-year ban ended her competitive career. She later worked as an adviser on sports matters to the Russian president.

LEBANON (LIB). After the establishment of a **National Olympic Committee** in 1947, Lebanon was awarded **International Olympic Committee** recognition in 1948, and it made its Olympic debut that year. Since then, the west Asian nation, officially known as the Lebanese Republic, has competed at every Summer **Olympic Games** except 1956, when it **boycotted** in protest against the **Israeli** occupation of the Sinai peninsula.

In 16 Summer Games, Lebanon has entered 140 athletes (123 men, 17 **women**) and competed in 13 sports: **athletics** (13 men, five women), **boxing** (eight men), **cycling** (eight men), **fencing** (17 men, one woman), **judo** (14 men, one woman), **rowing** (one man), **sailing** (three men), **shooting** (19 men, one woman), **swimming** (11 men, six women), **table tennis** (two women), **taekwondo** (one woman), **weightlifting** (nine men), and **wrestling** (20 men).

Lebanese athletes have won four **Olympic medals**, a silver medal by weightlifter Mohamed Kheir Tarabulsi in the 1972 **middleweight** class, and three medals in **Greco-Roman wrestling**—Zakaria Chihab (1952 **bantamweight** silver), Khalil Taha (1952 **welterweight** bronze), and Hassan Bechara (1980 **super-heavyweight** bronze).

Other notable Olympic results for Lebanon include fifth place in 1952 middleweight weightlifting by Moustafa Laham and in Greco-Roman wrestling, fourth place by **lightweight** Cherif Damage in 1948, sixth place tie by **featherweight** Sahi Taha in 1948 and by **light-heavyweight** Michel Skaff in 1952, and seventh place by middleweight Yacob Romanos in 1960. Several other Lebanese Olympians finished in ties for ninth place—*judokas* Sihad Keyrouz (1980 **extra-lightweight**), Fadi Sakali (1992 **half-middleweight**), and Rudy Hachache (2008 **heavyweight**); Greco-Roman wrestler Michel Nakouzi (1960 bantamweight); and Andrea Paoli in women's featherweight taekwondo in 2012.

Lebanese **Alpine skiers** have competed at nearly every **Olympic Winter Games** since 1948, only missing the Winter Olympics of 1994 and 1998. In 16 Winter Games, Lebanon has entered 31 athletes (28 men, three women) and competed in three sports. George Gereidi is one of the few athletes to compete in both Alpine skiing and **cross-country skiing** in the same year (1956) but did not fare well in either endeavor. In 1980, Farida Rahmeh finished 19th of 47 in the women's **slalom**. Her time of 2:28.48 was nearly 30 seconds slower than the 18th place contestant and over one minute slower than the gold medalist, but she did finish the race, which was better than more than half the other entrants. Elias Majdalani in the 1988 men's **super G** race finished 32nd of 94 entrants, 57 of whom finished the race.

LEDNYOV, PAVEL SERAFIMOVICH (URS/UKR–MOP). B. 25 March 1943, Gorky, **Russia**, USSR. D. 23 November, 2010, Moscow, Russian Federation. Although Pavel Lednyov never won the Olympic individual **modern pentathlon** title, he won a record seven Olympic medals in the sport. In the team event, he took gold in 1972 and 1980 and silver in 1976, and in the individual event he won silver in 1976 and bronze in 1968, 1972, and 1980. In contrast to his Olympic record, the six-foot tall (184 cm), 176 lb (80 kg) Lednyov was the individual winner at the World Championships four times (1973, 1974, 1975, 1978) and was twice a member of the winning team at the World Championships (1973, 1974).

LEE, WILLIS AUGUSTUS, JR. (USA–SHO). B. 11 May 1888, Natlee, Kentucky, **United States**. D. 25 August 1945, Portland, Maine, United States. Willis Lee is the only man to win five gold medals for **shooting** at one Games. He achieved this feat in 1920, when he also won a silver and a bronze, and all seven medals were won in team events as he competed in the remarkable total of 15 shooting events. A U.S. Naval Academy graduate, the five-foot, 10-inch (179 cm) Lee enjoyed a highly successful naval career and commanded the U.S. Pacific fleet during World War II, eventually rising to the rank of vice admiral. Lee was a member of champion navy rifle teams in 1908, 1909, 1913, 1919, and 1930. He was a distant relative of American Confederate General Robert E. Lee.

LEINO, EINO AUKUSTI (FIN–WRE). B. 7 April 1891, Kuopio, Pohjois-Savo, **Finland**. D. 30 November 1986, Tampere, Pirkanmaa, Finland. Eino Leino had a very unusual **wrestling** career. He won medals in **freestyle** at four consecutive **Olympic Games**, making him one of only six wrestlers to win medals at four Games (the others being **Bruce Baumgartner** [USA], **Wilfried Dietrich** [FRG/GER], **Aleksandr Karelin** [URS/EUN/RUS], **Artur**

Taymazov [UZB] and Imre Polyák [HUN]). In 1920, Leino won the gold medal in the **middleweight** division, his only Olympic title. The five-foot, eight-inch (174 cm) wrestler followed this with a **welterweight** silver in 1924, a **lightweight** bronze in 1928, and a welterweight bronze in 1932. Leino never competed at the European or World Championships, as these were not yet organized. From 1920 he lived in the **United States**, competing mostly there, and winning Amateur Athletic Union Championships in 1920 and 1923.

LEMMING, ERIC OTTO VALDEMAR (SWE–ATH). B. 22 February 1880, Göteborg, Västra Götaland, **Sweden.** D. 5 June 1930, Göteborg, Västra Götaland, Sweden. Eric Lemming was the first of the great modern **javelin throwers.** He was Olympic javelin champion in 1906, 1908, and 1912, winning both the orthodox and **freestyle** events in 1908. He would almost certainly have been the champion in 1900 had the javelin been on the program, but in the absence of his specialty event, he competed in six other field events, placing fourth in the **pole vault** and the **hammer throw.** In 1906, the six-foot, two-inch (190 cm), 194 lb (88 kg) athlete also won bronze medals in the **shot put, pentathlon,** and **tug-of-war** and competed in five other events: standing **long jump, triple jump,** stone throw, **discus throw,** and Greek style discus throw. As a 19-year-old, Lemming set a world javelin best of 49.32 meters (161 feet, 10 inches) in 1899 and made 13 further improvements to the record, culminating with a mark of 62.32 meters (204 feet, five inches) in 1912, which was later accepted as the first official International Amateur Athletic Foundation record.

LENNARTZ, KARL. B. 19 March 1940, Aachen, Germany. D. 2 May 2014, Bad Oeynhausen, Germany. Karl Lennartz received his doctorate in historical geography from the University of Bonn and was a professor at universities in Bonn and Cologne. From 1980 until his retirement in 2005, he was at the German Sports University in Cologne (Deutschen Sporthochschule Köln) and was also the director of the Carl and Liselott Diem Archive there. He also served as a visiting professor at the University of the Peloponnese in Greece and the Sports University of Beijing. An Olympic historian, he was a prolific writer and the author of more than 40 books and hundreds of articles on the **Olympic Games.** Among the books are a four-volume series on Germany's participation in the Olympic Games from 1896 to 1908 and a five-volume series cowritten with Jürgen Buschmann on Olympic **football.** (Other of his works are listed in the bibliography in this volume.) In 1997, he was awarded the **Olympic Order** in Silver by the **International Olympic Committee** (IOC) and was a member of the IOC Commission for Culture and Olympic Education from 2002 until his death.

He was one of the early members of the **International Society of Olympic Historians** (ISOH), its president from 2004 to 2012, and also the coeditor of the ISOH publication, the *Journal of Olympic History*. He also was a founding member of the International Society of the History of Physical Education and Sport. In addition, he was a **marathon** runner, with a personal best set in 1985 at the age of 45 of 2:42.2. He also ran ultra-marathons and recorded a time of 8:33:00 hours in a 100 km race. He trained marathon runners in Sankt Augustin, Germany, and both his daughter and son are also ultra-marathoners. He was politically active in Sankt Augustin and was a council member and vice mayor as well as chairman of the Sankt Augustin sports federation. During the latter years of his life, he had heart problems and had a pacemaker installed. He died following heart surgery.

LEONARD, RAY CHARLES "SUGAR RAY" (USA–BOX). B. 17 May 1956, Wilmington, North Carolina, **United States**. Boxer Sugar Ray Leonard

Sugar Ray Leonard, one of the most popular boxers ever, shortly after winning a boxing gold medal in 1976. Courtesy of Erich Kamper

won a gold medal at the 1976 **Olympic Games** in Montreal rather easily. He won all six of his **light-welterweight** Olympic bouts by three-**round** decisions, and with five judges scoring each round of each bout, Leonard only lost three rounds of the 90 rounds scored. A year after the Olympics, Leonard became one of the top professional **welterweight boxers**. In 1979, the five-foot, 10-inch (178 cm) Leonard won his first world title by defeating Wilfred Benitez for the World Boxing Council version of the welterweight championship. Leonard eventually won world titles in five weight classes, from welterweight to **light-heavyweight**. One of the fastest boxers ever, his skills were virtually unmatched, and he deserves comparison as a fighter to his namesake, Sugar Ray Robinson. His popularity also enabled him to command ring fees that made him one of the wealthiest athletes of his time.

LEONIDAS OF RHODES (GRE–ATH). Fl. 180–130 B.C. Leonidas of Rhodes was the greatest runner and sprinter of the **Ancient Olympic Games**. He won 12 Olympic titles, the most by any athlete, ancient or modern. In 164, 160, 156, and 152 B.C., he was proclaimed *triastes* or Olympic champion in three events, the *stadion*, *diaulos*, and **race in armor** (hoplite).

LESLIE, LISA DESHAWN (later LOCKWOOD) (USA–BAS). B. 7 July 1972, Gardena, California, **United States**. In 2008, **Lisa Leslie** became only the second **basketball** player ever to win four gold **Olympic medals**, after **Teresa Edwards** of the United States. Leslie won hers from 1996 to 2008. A six-foot, five-inch (1.96 meters), 170 lb (77 kg) center, she was the first player to dunk in the **Women's** National Basketball Association (WNBA), the U.S. women's pro basketball league founded in 1997. Playing for the Los Angeles Sparks her entire professional career, Leslie won the WNBA title in 2001 and 2002. She earned three Most Valuable Player Awards (2001, 2004, and 2006) and was selected for eight All-Star teams. When she retired from the league in 2009, she was the all-time leader in points and rebounds.

LESOTHO (LES). The landlocked South African nation of Lesotho, completely surrounded by the **Republic of South Africa** and formerly known as Basutoland, formed a **National Olympic Committee** in 1971, which was recognized by the **International Olympic Committee** in 1972. Lesotho, officially known as the Kingdom of Lesotho, made its Olympic debut that year and has since competed at every **Olympic Games** except 1976, when it joined the African **boycott**. Lesotho has never competed at the **Olympic Winter Games** and has never won an **Olympic medal**. In 10 Summer Games, Lesotho has entered 45 athletes (35 men, 10 **women**) and competed in four sports: **athletics** (26 men, seven women), **boxing** (eight men), **swimming** (one woman), and **taekwondo** (one man, two women).

Lesotho's best Olympic Games performances have all occurred in the men's **marathon** race. Thabiso Moqhali finished 16th of 100 entrants in 2000 and 33rd of 110 contestants in 1992. Thabisio Ralekhetla was 29th of 124 in 1996, and Vincent Rakhabele was 36th of 74 in 1980 and 61st of 107 in 1984. Frans Ntaole was 40th in 1984. Other notable Olympic results for Basothos include **middleweight** boxer Sello Mojela winning his first bout in 1988 and finishing tied for ninth place and a similar result for **welterweight** Mokete Mokhosi in 2000 taekwondo.

LEWIS, FREDERICK CARLTON "CARL" (USA–ATH). B. 1 July 1961, Birmingham, Alabama, **United States**. Carl Lewis is considered by many to be the greatest track and field athlete of all time, and with nine Olympic gold medals, 11 **Olympic medals**, and seven golds at the World Championships, this is a justifiable claim. His Olympic gold medals were won in 1984 (100 meters, 200 meters, 4x100 meters **relay**, **long jump**), 1988 (100 meters, long jump), 1992 (4x100 meters relay, long jump), and 1996 (long jump). His four victories in 1984 matched the record set by **Jesse Owens** at the 1936 Games. Lewis's lone silver medal came in the 1988 200 meters. The six-foot, two-inch (188 cm), 176 lb (80 kg) Lewis twice set individual world records at 100 meters (1988, 1991), and in the relays he was a member of teams that posted world records at 4x100 meters six times and 4x200 meters three times. In 1996, at Atlanta, Lewis ended his Olympic career by equaling the record of winning the same individual Olympic event four times consecutively (held by **Al Oerter** [USA] and **Paul Elvstrøm** [DEN]), with Lewis's feat occurring in the long jump. His sister Carol was also a formidable athlete who twice competed for the United States in the Olympics in the long jump but did not medal.

LI NING (CHN–GYM). B. 8 September 1963, Liuzhou, Guangxi Zhuang, **China**. The first Olympic star from China, **gymnast** Li Ning won six **Olympic medals** at the 1984 Olympics, with gold medals in the **rings**, **pommelled horse**, and **floor exercise**. In addition, he won silver in the team **all-around** and the **horse vault** and a bronze in the individual all-around. The five-foot, four-inch (164 cm), 128 lb (58 kg) Li also won 11 World Championship medals, including world titles in the rings (1985) and the team all-around (1983). Retiring after the 1988 **Olympic Games**, Li founded Li Ning Company Ltd., a sports shoe and apparel manufacturer, which has since become one of the leading brands in China. During the opening ceremony of the 2008 Olympics, Li was the last torchbearer and was allowed to light the **Olympic flame**, being lifted into the air with cables.

LIBERIA (LBR). The West African nation of Liberia, officially known as the Republic of Liberia, first competed at the Olympics in Melbourne in 1956. It has since missed the **Olympic Games** of 1968, 1976, 1980, and 1992. It has not competed at the **Olympic Winter Games** and has not won an **Olympic medal**. It has had 40 entrants (33 men, seven **women**) but has participated in only two sports: **athletics** (29 men, seven women) and **boxing** (four men) in the 11 Olympics in which it has competed.

In 2012, Liberia had an entrant in **judo** but shortly prior to his first match it was discovered that he had been a practitioner of **karate** and was unfamiliar with the rules of the sport of judo and consequently he was not allowed to participate. Liberia's most successful Olympian is Jangy Addy who competed in the **decathlon** in 2008 and 2012 and finished 20th of 40 entrants in 2008. Four Liberian runners also advanced to the second round and one, Sayon Cooper, missed advancing to the semifinal round of the 100 meter **sprint** in 2000 by just 0.01 seconds. Boxer Sammy Stewart, who after a **bye** in the opening round and a victory by decision in the second round of competition, reached the third **round** of the 1988 **light-flyweight** competition, ranking equal ninth.

LIBERTY BELL CLASSIC. Also known as the "**Boycott** Olympics," the Liberty Bell Classic was a track and field competition held in Philadelphia in July 1980. Athletes from 29 countries that boycotted the 1980 **Olympic Games** participated, notably **Canada**, **China**, **Kenya**, the **United States**, and West **Germany**. In all but one event (men's 110 meter **hurdles**), the Olympic champions outperformed the winners of the Liberty Bell Classic, although marks in different competitions are difficult to compare for some events. *See also* FRIENDSHIP GAMES; GOODWILL GAMES.

LIBYA (LBA). The North African nation of Libya formed a **National Olympic Committee** in 1962, and although it was recognized by the **International Olympic Committee** in 1963, it did not take part in the 1964 **Olympic Games**. Libya's first appearance was in 1968. After a second appearance in 1980, the country has attended all Olympic Games since 1988. In nine Summer Games, Libya has entered 61 athletes (54 men, seven **women**) in eight sports: **athletics** (15 men, three women), **cycling** (11 men), **judo** (five men), **swimming** (four men, four women), **table tennis** (one man), **taekwondo** (two men), **volleyball** (nine men), and **weightlifting** (seven men). Libya, officially known as the State of Libya, has not competed at the **Olympic Winter Games** and has not won an **Olympic medal**.

Ezedin Salem Tlish finished in a tie for seventh place in the 2004 men's **flyweight** taekwondo event of 16 entrants, even though he lost his only bout. But in the peculiar scoring unique to this sport, he was placed seventh because he lost to the eventual champion. Consequently, he has the best finish of any Libyan Olympian. Other notable results by Libya in the Olympic Games include **middleweight** weightlifter Mohamed Eshtiwi, 15th of 25 in 2004; **marathon** runner Ali Mabrouk El-Zaidi, 39th of 101 in 2004, and marathon runners Issa Chetoui, 44th of 74, and Enemri Najem Al-Marghani, 49th of 74, in 1980.

LIECHTENSTEIN (LIE). The Central European Alpine country of Liechtenstein made its first Olympic appearances at the Games of 1936, both Winter and Summer. Since that time, it has only missed the 1952 Oslo Winter Olympics, the 1956 Melbourne Olympics, and the 1980 Moscow Olympics. Liechtenstein, officially known as the Principality of Liechtenstein, has the rare distinction of having won medals at the **Olympic Winter Games** but not at the Games of the **Olympiad**. This is because of the country's outstanding **Alpine skiers**, especially those from two families, the Frommelts and the Wenzels, who together won eight of Liechtenstein's nine **Olympic medals**.

Liechtenstein, with a population of only 37,000, holds the distinction of having the largest number of Olympic athletes per capita as well as the largest number of Olympic medals per capita.

In 16 Summer Games, Liechtenstein has entered 51 athletes (42 men, nine **women**) in four main sports: **athletics** (13 men, four women), **cycling** (seven men, one woman), **judo** (nine men, two women), and **shooting** (11 men). They have also had one male entrant in **equestrian** and **gymnastics**, and one female entrant in **swimming** and **tennis**. They have not come close to a medal in the Summer Games, and their best performances have been in judo where **middleweight** Magnus Buchel in 1984 and **lightweight** Johannes Wohlwend in 1988 finished in a seventh place tie. In 1984, Wohlwend tied for ninth place. In cycling, Yvonne Elkuch was 17th of 53 entrants in the women's individual **road race** in 1988 and Alois Lampert was 30th of 111 entrants in the men's individual road race in 1952 and Ewald Hasler was 43rd in that same race. In 1988, Peter Hermann was 54th of 136 entrants in the road race.

The Winter Games, however, have been a different story. In 18 Winter Games, Liechtenstein has entered 80 athletes (67 men, 13 women) in four sports: Alpine skiing (39 men, 12 women), **bobsledding** (six men), **cross-country skiing** (11 men, one woman), and **luge** (11 men). They have won nine medals (two gold, two silver, five bronze), all in Alpine skiing. Liechtensteiners who have won medals are **Hanni Wenzel** (bronze 1976 women's **slalom**, silver 1980 **downhill**, gold 1980 in both slalom and **giant slalom**), her brother Andi Wenzel (1980 silver, 1984 bronze both in giant slalom), Willi Frommelt (1976 men's slalom bronze) and his brother Paul Frommelt (1988 men's slalom bronze), and Ursula Konzett (1984 women's slalom bronze).

LIGHT-FLYWEIGHT. Light-flyweight is the lightest weight class contested in Olympic **boxing**. It has a weight limit 106 lb (48 kg) and was added to the Olympic program in 1968. Zou Shiming of **China** has won three medals at this weight—gold in 2008 and 2012 and bronze in 2004.

Light-flyweight is also a weight class in Olympic **wrestling**. From 1972 to 1996, it was the lightest class in both **Greco-Roman** and **freestyle** wrestling. Kim Il-Ong of North **Korea** won the gold medal in both 1992 and 1996 in freestyle competition. Vincenzo Maenza of **Italy** won gold in 1984 and 1988 and silver in 1992 in this class in Greco-Roman style.

LIGHT-HEAVYWEIGHT. Light-heavyweight was the second heaviest weight class in Olympic **boxing** from 1920 until 1980. Since 1984, it is the third heaviest weight class. There have been some exceptional boxers who have won Olympic light-heavyweight championships. **Cassius Clay** (later known as **Muhammad Ali**) was the gold medalist in 1960. Leon Spinks, later a victor over Ali for the world's professional **heavyweight** championship, was the 1976 Olympic titlist. **Eddie Eagan**, the first Olympic light-heavyweight titlist in 1920 is also the only Olympian to win gold medals in both Summer and Winter Games. No man has won more than one gold medal in this class, but Sverre Sørsdal of **Norway** (1920 silver, 1924 bronze) and Polish boxers Zbigniew Pietrzykowki (1960 silver, 1964 bronze) and Janusz Gortat (1972, 1976 both bronze) each won two light-heavyweight medals. Gortat's son, Marcin, has been a professional **basketball** player in the National Basketball Association.

Light-heavyweight is also a category in **weightlifting**, although that sport has three heavier weight classes. **Pyrros Dimas** of **Greece** (1992–2004) has three gold and one silver medals as a light-heavyweight weightlifter. **Women**'s weightlifting also has had a light-heavyweight class since it was added to the Olympic program in 2000. Liu Chunhong of **China** has won two gold medals (2004, 2008) in this class.

Olympic **wrestling** is the third sport that employs a light-heavyweight weight class. For most of the years in which wrestling has been on the Olympic program, there has been a light-heavyweight class, which has been either the second or third heaviest weight class in both **Greco-Roman** and **freestyle disciplines**. Makharbek Khadartsev, who competed for the **Soviet Union**, the Unified Team, and **Russia**, has two gold medals and a silver medal in this class in freestyle wrestling. Onni Pellinen of **Finland** and Karl-Erik Nilsson of **Sweden** each won three medals in light-heavyweight Greco-Roman wrestling.

LIGHT-MIDDLEWEIGHT. Light-middleweight is an Olympic **boxing** weight class with a limit of 156 lb (71 kg). It was added to the **Olympic Pro-**

gram in 1952 and was contested in each subsequent Olympic Games until 2000. **László Papp** of **Hungary** won two gold medals at this weight (1952, 1956). **Boris Lagutin** of the **Soviet Union** also was a dual light-middleweight gold medalist (1964, 1968) and in addition won the bronze in 1960. Neither **wrestling, weightlifting,** or **taekwondo,** the three other Olympic sports with weight classifications, have ever used a "light-middleweight" classification.

LIGHTWEIGHT. Lightweight is a weight class in **boxing, weightlifting,** and **wrestling.** It is also used in certain events in **rowing.** In men's boxing and wrestling, it is the fifth lightest after **light-flyweight, flyweight, bantamweight,** and **featherweight.** In **women**'s boxing it is one of only three classes contested—flyweight, lightweight, and middleweight. Mario Kindelán of **Cuba** (2000, 2004) is the only dual gold medalist in the lightweight class in Olympic boxing. Józef Grudzień of **Poland** (gold 1964, silver 1968) and Dick McTaggart of **Great Britain** (gold 1956, bronze 1960) are the only other dual medalists in this class. Several Olympic lightweight champions became well-known professional boxers, including Americans Howard Davis, Jr. (1976), Pernell Whitaker (1984), and Oscar de la Hoya (1992).

Emil Väre of **Finland** won two gold medals (1912, 1920), in lightweight **Greco-Roman** style wrestling and Arsen Fazdeyev of the **Soviet Union** and Unified Team won two gold medals in lightweight wrestling (1988, 1992). In women's lightweight wrestling, Saori Yoshida of **Japan** was the gold medalist in the first three years that it was contested (2004–2012).

In weightlifting, it is the fourth lightest class for men after flyweight, bantamweight, and featherweight, and in women's weightlifting, it is the third lightest class as they do not have a bantamweight classification. Waldemar Basenowski of **Poland** (1964, 1968) is the only dual gold medalist in men's lightweight weightlifting and Chen Yanqing of **China** (2004, 2008) the only one in women's lightweight weightlifting.

The sport of rowing since 1996 has held men's and women's lightweight double **sculls** and men's lightweight coxless fours. According to the International Rowing Federation, this weight category was introduced "to encourage more universality in the sport especially among nations with less statuesque people." This has not held true in the **Olympic Games,** and the winners in lightweight Olympic rowing have been from nations that normally do well in all rowing events such as **Romania, Denmark,** and Poland.

LIGHT-WELTERWEIGHT. Light-welterweight is an Olympic **boxing** weight class with a limit of 140 lb (63.5 kg). It was added to the **Olympic Program** in 1952 and has been contested in each subsequent **Olympic Games** through 2012. Jerzy Kulej of **Poland** (1964, 1968) and Hector Vinent of **Cuba**

(1992, 1996) are the only two men with multiple gold medals at this weight. **Sugar Ray Leonard** of the **United States**, the 1976 gold medalist, is probably the best known of the Olympic light-welterweight champions. Neither **wrestling, weightlifting**, or **taekwondo**, the three other Olympic sports with weight classifications, have ever used a light-welterweight classification.

LIPĂ-OLENIUC, ELISABETA (née OLENIUC) (ROU–ROW). B. 26 October 1964, Siret, Suceava, **Romania**. Elisabeta Lipă-Oleniuc is the only **rower** (male or female) to have won eight **Olympic medals**, and the first **woman** rower to have won five gold medals. In 1984, as Miss Oleniuc, she won the **double sculls** (with Marioara Popescu), and after her marriage she took the silver medal in this event in 1988 and 1992 (with **Veronica Cochelea-Cogeanu**). She also won a second gold in the single sculls in 1992 and a bronze in the quadruple sculls in 1988. Her Olympic career continued with golds in the Romanian eight in 1996, 2000, and 2004. Remarkably, the six-foot tall (183 cm) 176 lb (80 kg) Lipă-Oleniuc won only a single world title, in the 1989 single sculls. She did win nine silver medals at the World Championships, including eight in the double sculls, between 1983 and 2003.

LITHUANIA (LTU, formerly LIT). Prior to its annexation by the **Soviet Union** in 1940, the north European nation of Lithuania, located on the Baltic Sea, competed at the **Olympic Games** of 1924 and 1928, but failed to win any medals. Lithuania also competed at the 1928 **Olympic Winter Games**. From 1952 to 1988, many Lithuanians competed for the USSR. After the Soviet revolution of 1991, Lithuania declared and was granted its independence, and its **National Olympic Committee** was recognized by the **International Olympic Committee** in 1991. Lithuania returned to the Olympic fold in 1992, competing at both Albertville and Barcelona. The nation, officially named the Republic of Lithuania, has competed at every Olympics since then.

In eight Summer Games, Lithuania has entered 258 athletes (188 men, 70 **women**) and competed in 18 sports, with most of their participants entered in **athletics** (31 men, 32 women), **basketball** (47 men), **cycling** (20 men, 14 women), **swimming** (18 men, six women), **rowing** (10 men, five women), **boxing** (13 men), and **football** (11 men). Lithuania has won 21 medals in the Summer Games (six gold, five silver, 10 bronze). Three of these Olympic titles have been won in the men's **discus throw**, with Romas Ubartas winning a gold in 1992 and Virgilijus Alekna winning that event in 2000 and 2004 and winning a bronze in 2008.

The Lithuanian men's basketball team has also excelled, winning bronze medals in 1992, 1996, and 2000 and finishing fourth in 2004 and 2008. Gintaras Einikis was on all three medal-winning teams. In the 2000 semifinals against the **United States**, Lithuania narrowly missed upsetting the United States as Lithuanian guard Šarūnas Jasikevičius missed a three-point field goal attempt a few seconds before the end of the game and the United States hung on to win by two points, 85–83. Several Lithuanian players from those teams played in the National Basketball Association, including Jasikevičius, Darius Songaila, **Arvydas Sabonis**, and Šarūnas Marčiulionis. One of Lithuania's other gold medals was won by Laura Asadauskaitė-Zadneprovskienė in the 2012 women's **modern pentathlon**. Her husband, Andrejus Zadneprovskis, also won two medals in that event, silver in 2004 and bronze in 2008. Lithuania's other two gold medals were won by Daina Gudzinevičiūtė in 2000 women's **trap shooting** and by swimmer Rūta Meilutytė in the 2012 women's 100 meter **breaststroke**. Lithuanian athletes have also won **Olympic medals** in boxing, **canoeing**, cycling, rowing, **sailing**, and **wrestling**.

In eight Winter Games, Lithuania has entered 26 athletes (17 men, nine women) and competed in six sports: **Alpine skiing** (three men, one woman), **biathlon** (four men, two women), **cross-country skiing** (seven men, four women), **figure skating** (two men, two women), **speed skating** (one man), and **short-track speed skating** (one woman), with one woman competing in both biathlon and cross-country skiing. Lithuania has yet to win a medal at the Winter Games, and its best performance was in **ice dancing** where the pair of Povilas Vanagas and Margarita Drobiazko improved each year from 1992 to 2002 when they finished fifth of 24 couples. Other notable Winter Games results for Lithuanian athletes include cross-country skiers Vida Vencienė (11th of 53 in 1992 women's 15 k) and Ričardas Panavas (30th of 97 in 1998 10 k); biathletes Gintaras Jasinskas (19th of 94 in 1992 20 k) and Diana Rasimovičiūtė (18th of 83 in 2006 women's **sprint**); and Alpine skier Vitalijus Rumiancevas (44th of 93 in 2006 men's **slalom).**

LOCHTE, RYAN STEVEN (USA–SWI). B. 3 August 1984, Canandaigua, New York, **United States**. Only one man (**Michael Phelps**) has won more Olympic swimming medals than Ryan Lochte.

From 2004 to 2012, Lochte won 11 **Olympic medals** (five gold, three silver, three bronze) and has medaled in 11 of the 12 events he has entered, with a fourth place in the 2012 200 meter **freestyle** the only one in which he failed to medal. In 2004, he was a member of the gold medal-winning U.S. 4x200 meter freestyle **relay** team, and he won a silver medal in the 200 meter individual **medley** event. In 2008, he set a world record in winning the 200 meter **backstroke** and won a second gold medal in the 4x200 meter freestyle relay, also in world-record time. The six-foot, two-inch (188 cm), 196 lb (89 kg) Lochte added two bronze medals in the 200 meter and 400 meter individual medley events. In 2012, he won gold in the 4x200 meter freestyle relay and

400 meter individual medley; silver in the 4x100 meter freestyle relay and 200 meter individual medley; and bronze in the 200 meter backstroke.

While he was doing all this, he took a back seat to the accomplishments of his teammate, Phelps, who was winning an unprecedented total of 22 medals, 18 of which were gold.

LONG JUMP. The long jump is an **athletics** event once known as the broad jump. The athlete takes a running start and then leaps from a fixed point. It has been included in the men's **Olympic Program** since the 1896 **Olympic Games** and in the **women**'s program since 1928. One of the most incredible performances in athletics history occurred in the long jump event. On 18 October 1968 at the **Mexico** City Olympic Games, **Bob Beamon** of the **United States** jumped 8.90 meters (29 feet, 2.5 inches), breaking the world record by 55 cm (21.75 inches). **Carl Lewis** of the United States won the Olympic long jump four times from 1984 to 1996. From 1900 to 1912, a standing long jump was also contested and won by **Ray Ewry** of the United States four times.

LOPEZ, STEVEN (USA–TKW). B. 9 November 1978, New York, New York, **United States**. Along with **Hadi Saei** (IRI) and Hwang Gyeong-Seon (KOR), Steven Lopez is one of three Olympians to win three medals in **taekwondo**. The six-foot, three-inch (191 cm) Lopez won his first title in the **featherweight** (68 kg) class in Sydney, then moved up to the **welterweight** (80 kg) class for his second gold in 2004. On the 2008 U.S. Olympic team, Lopez was accompanied by his siblings, Mark and Diana. All three of them medaled, with Steven taking bronze (80 kg), Mark, silver (68 kg), and Diana, bronze (57 kg). Besides his Olympic medals, Lopez has won a record five world titles, one in the **lightweight** division (2001) and four consecutive ones in the welterweight division (2003, 2005, 2007, and 2009).

LOUGANIS, GREGORY EFTHIMIOS "GREG" (USA–DIV). B. 29 January 1960, San Diego, California, **United States**. Greg Louganis is considered the greatest **diver** of all time. After winning Olympic silver on the **platform** in 1976, he missed the 1980 **Olympic Games** because of the **boycott**, when he would have been favored to win both diving events. But Louganis returned to win the **springboard**-platform double in both 1984 and 1988. His 1988 springboard gold was the stuff of high drama, when he struck his head on the board during qualifying. He required stitches to continue competing, but managed to qualify and won the gold medal the next day. The five-foot nine-inch (175 cm), 161 lb (73 kg) Louganis also took both titles at the World Championships of 1982 and 1986, having earlier won the platform in 1978. Of **Samoan** and **Greek** descent, he studied classical dance for many years, and this training provided the basis for the elegance and artistry of his performances. Louganis's superiority over his contemporaries was considerable, and he held many records for the highest marks ever achieved in competition. After his career ended, it was revealed that he had been HIV positive at the time of the 1988 Olympics when he sustained his head wound during qualifying.

LOUIS, SPYRIDON "SPYROS" (GRE–ATH). B. 12 January 1873, Marousi, Athina, Attiki, **Greece**. D. 26 March 1940, Marousi, Athina, Attiki, Greece. As the winner of the first Olympic **marathon** at Athens in 1896, Spyridon Louis's place in sporting history was ensured. Having placed only

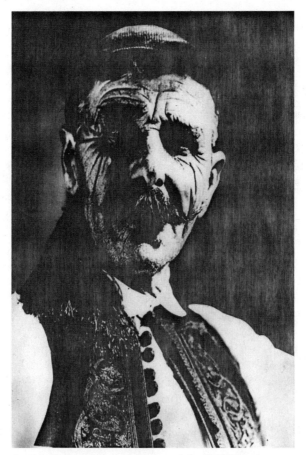

Spyridon Louis of Greece, winner of the first Olympic marathon. Courtesy of Erich Kamper

fifth in one of the Greek trial races, he was not favored to win the Olympic title, but his unexpected triumph gave Greece its only victory in a track and field **athletics** event at the 1896 **Olympics Games**, and he was accorded the status of a national hero. Despite the acclaim, Louis returned to his village of Marousi, where he worked as a shepherd and mineral water seller, and he never raced again. He later became a rural police officer, but lost his job when he was imprisoned on charges of falsifying military documents in 1926. He spent more than a year in jail before his trial on 28 June 1927, when he was acquitted. He remained an Olympic legend and was a guest of the **Organizing Committee** at the 1936 Games in Berlin. Over a century after Louis's victory, the main stadium for the 2004 Games was built in Marousi, now a suburb of Athens, and was named after the town's Olympic hero.

LUDING-ROTHENBURGER, CHRISTA (née ROTHENBURGER) (GDR–SSK/CYC). B. 4 December 1959, Weißwasser, Sachsen, **German Democratic Republic**. Christa Luding-Rothenburger is the only Olympian to have won Summer and Winter **Olympic medals** in the same year—a feat that will not happen again given the current timing of the Games. She achieved this in 1988, when she won the 1,000 meters **speed skating** event in Calgary and placed second in the track **cycling** match **sprint** event in Seoul. In addition to her 1988 medals, she has won three more medals in 500 meters speed skating, having a complete collection of gold (1984), silver (1988), and bronze (1992) medals. The five-foot, five-inch (164 cm), 132 lb (60 kg) athlete was a World Champion at both sports, winning the speed skating sprint title in 1985 and 1988 and the cycling sprint championship in 1986. Although many athletes have demonstrated proficiency in both cycling and speed skating, few have competed at the top level in both sports at the same time. The only other **woman** to have won Olympic medals in both sports is **Clara Hughes**.

LUGE. Tobogganing is one of the oldest winter sports. Descriptions of it in the 16th century are found in literature. As a racing sport, it can be traced to the mid-19th century, when British tourists started sledding on the snow-bound roads of the Alps. The original form of the sport was the **skeleton** sleds that were used on the Cresta Run at St. Moritz. The sport of skeleton was contested twice in the Olympics, in 1928 and 1948, both times when the **Olympic Winter Games** were held at St. Moritz.

Luge spread to **Switzerland** in the 1890s as a variant of the skeleton race. The first recorded competitions took place in 1890 at the Innsbruck-based Academic Alpine Club. An International Tobogganing Association was formed in 1913, and the first European Championships were held in 1914 at Reichenfeld, **Austria**.

At the **International Olympic Committee** meeting in Athens in 1954, luge tobogganing was recognized as an official Olympic sport, replacing skeleton, for which only one suitable track existed at the time (in St. Moritz). The first world luge championships were contested in Oslo in 1955, and an International Federation, the Fédération Internationale de Luge de Course (FIL), was formed in 1957. As of 2014, the FIL has 53 member nations, including several where snow and ice is a rarity such as **Bermuda, Brazil, Puerto Rico, Tonga, Venezuela**, and the **United States Virgin Islands**.

In 1959, luge was approved for the 1964 Winter Olympics in Innsbruck. Since that time, luge has been contested at all Olympic Winter Games, with **singles** events for men and **women** and a **doubles** event, which is technically open to women, but in practice is only contested by men. In 2014, a three-person team **relay** event featuring men's singles, men's doubles, and women's singles was added to the competition. In 14 Winter Games, there have been 772 participants (544 men, 228 women) from 49 nations that have participated in luge at the Olympic Games. **Armin Zöggeler** of **Italy** has won the most medals in luge—six (two gold, one silver, three bronze from 1994 to 2014). **Georg Hackl** and Felix Loch, both of **Germany**, have each won three gold medals.

The sport is dominated by German-speaking athletes from Germany, Austria, and Italy (South Tyrol), who have together won 111 of the 129 medals awarded in the sport. Sadly, luge has also seen two **Olympic deaths**: Kazimierz Kay-Skrzypecki (1964) and Nodar Kumaritashvili (2010) were killed during training sessions. *See also* BEHRENDT, JAN; BOBSLEDDING; HILDGARTNER, PAUL; WALTER-MARTIN, STEFFI.

LUXEMBOURG (LUX). The Western Europe nation of Luxembourg, officially known as the Grand Duchy of Luxembourg, was formerly considered to have first competed at the 1912 **Olympic Games**, the same year in which it formed its National Olympic Committee. However, in the 1980s, French athletics' historian Alain Bouillé discovered that Michel Théato, the winner of the 1900 **marathon**, was from Luxembourg, not **France**, as previously believed. Luxembourg has competed at a total of 22 celebrations of the **Olympiad** since 1912, missing only the 1932 Los Angeles Games. Through 1960, Luxembourg had a fair-sized contingent at the Summer Games, with as many as 52 entrants in one Games, but since then, they have only entered a few each year with no more than 13 in any one Games.

In 24 Summer Games, Luxembourg has entered 363 athletes (330 men, 33 **women**) and competed in 18 sports plus the **art competitions**. They have had the most participants in **football** (60 men), **gymnastics** (53 men, three women), **athletics** (43 men, five women), **cycling** (40 men, one woman),

swimming (18 men, nine women), and **boxing** (26 men). Luxembourgers have only won three Olympic medals (two gold, one silver) in summer sporting events. The aforementioned Michel Théato won the marathon in 1900, Josy Barthel won the 1,500 meter run in 1952, and Jos Alzin was the **heavyweight weightlifting** silver medalist in 1920. Luxembourg has also won three Olympic medals in the now-defunct art competitions. Illustrator **Jean Jacoby** is the only artist to have won two Olympic art titles, in 1924 and 1928. Sculptor Frantz Heldenstein won a silver medal in 1924.

Although Luxembourg has only won a few medals at the Summer Games, they have had more than their share of results in the top 10 in quite a few sports. These include in athletics: a sixth place finish by the men's 4x100 track relay in 1920; 10th by Josy Bartel in the 1,500 meter run in 1948; ninth by Charel Sowa in the 50 kilometer walk in 1964 and 10th in that event in 1972; and seventh by Danièle Kaber in the 1988 women's marathon. Heavyweight Ernest Toussaint (1936) was a losing quarter-finalist in boxing and finished tied for fifth. **Canoeist** Joé Treinen was sixth in the C1-1,000 in 1936. In cycling, the men's **road race** team was eighth in 1924, 10th in 1928, and seventh in 1952; Kim Kirchen was sixth in 2004 and Andy Schleck was fourth in 2008 in the men's individual road race. In **fencing**, Emile Gretsch was eighth in the men's individual **épée** in 1948 and as a member of the Luxembourg épée team were losing quarter-finalists that finished tied for fifth that year. In 1952, Leon Buck was fourth in the individual épée and a member of the fourth place Luxembourg épée team. The épée team again tied for fifth in 1960. In **judo**, Marie Muller was a losing quarter-finalist in the women's **half-lightweight** class in 2012 and finished tied for fifth. In swimming, Laury Koster was sixth in the 1924 women's 200 meter **breaststroke**. Nic Schleiter was fifth in 1936 **light-heavyweight** weightlifting, and Nancy Arendt-Kemp finished 10th in the inaugural women's **triathlon** in 2000.

Luxembourg has also sporadically competed at the **Olympic Winter Games**, attending in 1928, 1936, 1988–1998, 2006, and 2014. In those eight Winter Games, Luxembourg has entered 12 athletes (11 men, one woman) and competed in four sports: **Alpine skiing** (two men), **bobsledding** (eight men), **cross-country skiing** (one man), and **figure skating** (one man, one woman). Native **Austrian** Marc Girardelli won two silver medals for Luxembourg in 1992—one in **super G** and one in **giant slalom**.

M

MACAU. Macau, located in Southeast Asia, was formerly Portuguese, but is now a Special Administrative Region of the People's Republic of **China** (similar to **Hong Kong**), which has a **National Olympic Committee** (NOC) that is affiliated with numerous **International Federations**. However, it is not recognized by the **International Olympic Committee** because of the current *Olympic Charter*, which requires NOCs to be from an independent state recognized by the international community. Although other NOCs, like that of Hong Kong, do not meet these requirements either, it is unlikely Macau will be represented at future Olympics. Of note, Macau has competed at each **Paralympic Games** from 1988 to 2012, although no Macanese athlete has yet won a medal.

MACEDONIA, FORMER YUGOSLAV REPUBLIC OF (FYROM) (MKD, formerly MCD). This former **Yugoslav** republic declared its independence from Yugoslavia on 8 September 1991. The Olympic Committee of the Former Yugoslav Republic of Macedonia was formed in 1992 and recognized by the **International Olympic Committee** (IOC) in 1993. The republic first competed at the **Olympic Games** as an independent nation in 1996 and at the **Olympic Winter Games** in 1998. It has been represented at every Olympic Games since then.

In five Summer Games, Macedonia has entered 32 athletes (21 men, 11 **women**) in five sports: **athletics** (three men, four women), **canoeing** (three men, one woman), **shooting** (two men, one woman), **swimming** (six men, five women), and **wrestling** (seven men). At the 2000 Olympics, Macedonia won its first **Olympic medal** as an independent nation, a bronze won by Mogamed Ibragimov in **light-heavyweight freestyle** wrestling. All the other notable Summer Olympic results for Macedonian athletes also occurred in freestyle wrestling. They include **bantamweight** Šaban Trstena, 1996 fifth place; **lightweight** Murad Ramazanov, 2008 seventh place; **middleweight** Nasir Gadžihanov, 2000 seventh place; **welterweight** Valerij Verhušin, 1996 10th place; and **light-flyweight** Vlatko Sokolov, 1996 11th place.

Macedonia has also participated in five Winter Games with six men and four women competing in **Alpine skiing** and **cross-country skiing**. They have not yet medaled, and their best Winter Games results occurred in Alpine skiing where Antonio Ristevski finished 29th of 117 entrants in 2014 **slalom** and Jana Nikolovska was 33rd of 56 in the 1998 women's **giant slalom**.

The name of the nation, since its independence from Yugoslavia, is very controversial. **Greece**, **Bulgaria**, **Serbia**, and **Albania** all lay claim to regions of (historical) Macedonia and to the name. The European Community recognizes Macedonia's independence, but only under the name Former Yugoslav Republic of Macedonia, which is also used by the IOC. In late 2004, the **United States** controversially recognized Macedonia under the name Republic of Macedonia, which is the country's official name.

From 1924 to 1988, a few Yugoslav Olympians were from Macedonia. The best-represented sport at the Olympics among Macedonians has been wrestling. Both Šaban Trstena and Šaban Šejdi from Skopje won two wrestling medals at the Olympics between 1980 and 1988. Two Macedonians also competed in the 1992 Olympics, as **independent Olympic participants**. In the **Ancient Olympic Games**, it is known that Macedonians, who then were part of ancient Greece, won nine championships, including four in the *stadion* (**sprint**) event. Two of these were consecutive, won by Antigonos in 292–288 B.C. The greatest Olympic champion of ancient Macedonia was Philip II, the father of Alexander the Great, who won three Olympic titles.

MADAGASCAR (MAD). Known as the Malagasy Republic from 1958 to 1975, the Indian Ocean island country now known as Madagascar formed a **National Olympic Committee** in 1964, which was recognized by the **International Olympic Committee** that year. Madagascar, officially the Republic of Madagascar, made its Olympic debut in the same year and has since missed only the Games of 1976 and 1988. In 11 Summer Games, Madagascar has entered 72 athletes (49 men, 23 **women**) and competed in eight sports: **athletics** (23 men, 11 women), **boxing** (10 men), **cycling** (one man), **judo** (10 men, one woman), **swimming** (four men, seven women), **tennis** (two women), **weightlifting** (one man, one woman), and **wrestling** (one woman).

No Madagascan athlete has yet won an **Olympic medal**. Its top athlete has been the **sprinter** Jean-Louis Ravelomanantsoa, who finished eighth in the 100 meters in 1968, the country's best finish ever. Other notable results for Madagascar at the Olympic Games include Justin Andriamanantena, ninth in 1972 **half-middleweight** judo; Sylvain Rybary, tied for 13th of 29 in 1980 **half-lightweight** judo; Toussaint Rabenala, 14th of 47 in 1992 **triple jump**; Jules Randrianarivelo, 25th of 74 in the 1980 **marathon**; Clarisse Rasoarizay, 43rd of 82 in 2004 women's marathon, and swimmer Tojohanitra Andriamanjatoarimanana (one of the longest named Olympians), 60th of 90 in the 2008 women's 50 meter **freestyle**. In addition, boxers Paul Rasamimanana (1980 **welterweight**), Anicet Rasoaniavo (1996 **light-flyweight**), and Heritovo Rakotomanga (1992 **featherweight**) each won their first bout and finished tied for ninth. In track and field, the 2000 Madagascar women's 4x100 **relay** team reached the semifinal round as did Jean-Louis Ravelomanantsoa (1972 100 meter) and Nicole Ramalalanirina (1996 100 meter **hurdles**).

Madagascar has appeared at only one **Olympic Winter Games** (2006), represented by Mathieu Razanakolona, a Canadian of Madagascan origin who finished a commendable 39th of 82 entrants in the **giant slalom** but failed to finish the **slalom**.

MADISON. The Madison is a type of **cycling** race in which teams of two riders compete. One rider on the team races until he decides to tag his partner who then continues the race. The race had its origins in the 19th century when legislation was passed restricting six-day bicycle races, a popular event of the era held at Madison Square Garden in New York City. A rider was limited to no more than 12 hours of racing per day, so to circumvent the law and enable six-day races to continue, teams of two riders would race. The Madison was an Olympic men's cycling event of 60 km in 2000 and 50 km in 2004 and 2008 but was replaced by the **omnium** in 2012. **Australia** was the winning team in both 2000 and 2004.

MALAGASY REPUBLIC. *See* MADAGASCAR.

MALAWI (MAW). Founded in 1968, Malawi's **National Olympic Committee** was initially granted only provisional recognition by the **International Olympic Committee**, and full recognition did not follow until 1971. Malawi first competed at the 1972 **Olympic Games**, but was absent in 1976 and 1980. Since 1984, it has been present at each Olympics. Malawi, officially the Republic of Malawi, located in southeastern Africa and known as Nyasaland prior to its independence in 1964, has never competed at the **Olympic Winter Games** and has never won an **Olympic medal**. In nine Summer Games, Malawi has entered 54 athletes (44 men, 10 **women**) and has competed in **athletics** (21 men, seven women), **boxing** (15 men), **cycling** (six men), and **swimming** (two men, three women). 1984, Peter Ayesu, a **flyweight** boxer, won two matches and lost one, to finish equal fifth of 32 competitors, the best finish ever by a Malawian Olympian. Other notable Olympic performances include **marathoner** Mike Tebulo, who was 44th of 105 entrants in 2012, and **light-welterweight** boxer Lyton Mphande, who won two bouts and lost one in 1988 and finished equal ninth of 45 entrants.

MALAYA (MAL). Malaya, on the Malay peninsula in Southeast Asia, formed a **National Olympic Committee** in 1953, which was recognized by the **International Olympic Committee** the following year. It made its debut at the 1956 **Olympic Games** and competed again in Rome in 1960. It did not enter the **Olympic Winter Games** during its brief existence. In those two years, Malaya sent 40 athletes (39 men, one **woman**) to the Olympic Games, competing in **athletics** (nine men, one woman), **hockey** (17 men), **shooting** (five men), **swimming** (three men), and **weightlifting** (five men). The country expanded to form **Malaysia** in 1963 after merging with **North Borneo** (Sabah), Sarawak, and **Singapore** and has since competed under that name. The top performance of a Malayan Olympian was in 1956 weightlifting, when Tan Kim Bee came in sixth of 15 entrants in the men's **middle-heavyweight** division. Chung Kum Weng was 11th of 28 entrants in the men's **featherweight** division in 1960.

MALAYSIA (MAS). In 1963, **Malaya**, **North Borneo** (Sabah), Sarawak, and **Singapore** joined to form the Federation of Malaysia. Three of these states had previously competed at the Olympics, but they would march under one banner at the 1964 Tokyo Games. Singapore separated from Malaysia in 1965, and since then Singapore has competed on its own again. Malaysian athletes have since competed at all Games of the **Olympiad** except in 1980 but have never competed in the **Olympic Winter Games**.

In 12 Summer Games, Malaysia has entered 282 athletes (236 men, 46 **women**) and competed in 19 sports, with the most athletes in **hockey** (91 men), **athletics** (30 men, eight women), **swimming** (14 men, 14 women), **badminton** (19 men, six women), and **cycling** (22 men, one woman). The Southeast Asian country won its first **Olympic medal**, a bronze in men's badminton, its national sport, in 1992, and has won six Olympic medals—three silvers and three bronzes, five in badminton. Badminton player Lee Chong Wei, men's **singles** silver medalist in 2008 and 2012, is the only multiple medal winner. Other medalists are Adul Sidek Mohamed (1996 bronze badminton singles), his brothers Jalani Haji "Alan" Sidek Mohamed and Ajib Sidek Mohamed, 1992 badminton **doubles** bronze, and the pair of Cheah Soon Kit and Yap Kim Hock, 1996 badminton doubles silver medalists. In 2012, Pandelela Pamg was the flagbearer at the opening ceremony and the winner of a bronze medal in women's **platform diving**. She also competed in both synchronized **springboard** and synchronized platform diving, but the Malaysian team did not do well in those two events.

Other notable Olympic results for Malaysia include fourth place in men's badminton doubles in 1996 (Soo Beng Kiang and Tam Kim Her), in 2000 (Choong Tan Fook and Lee Wan Wah), and 2012 (Koo Kien Keat and Tan

Boon Heong). Several other Malaysian badminton players were losing quarter-finalists and finished tied for fifth place: in men's singles—Adul Sidek Mohamed (1992), Wong Choong Hann (2000); women's singles— Wong Mew Choo (2008); and men's doubles—Choong Tan Fook and Lee Wan Wah (2004) and Koo Kien Keat and Tan Boon Heong (2008). In other sports, Malaysia finished sixth (of 12) in men's team **archery** in 2008, Mohamad Khairul Anuar was sixth of 64 in the men's individual archery event in 2012 and Cheng Chu Sian was eighth of 64 in 2008; Josiah Ng (2004) and Mohd Azizulhasni Awang (2012) were sixth in the men's **keirin** cycling; Awang also was eighth in the men's cycling sprint in both 2008 and 2012. In women's **taekwondo**, **featherweight** Elaine Teo and **heavyweight** Che Chew Chan each finished tied for seventh in 2008. **Bantamweight weightlifter** Amirul Ibrahim was eighth in 2008, and the men's hockey team finished eighth in both 1972 and 1976.

The city of Kuala Lumpur placed a bid to host the 2008 Summer Games but did not advance to the final round of voting.

MALDIVES (MDV). The Maldives **National Olympic Committee** was founded and recognized by the **International Olympic Committee** in 1985. The Indian Ocean island nation of the Maldives, officially the Republic of the Maldives, first competed at the 1988 **Olympic Games** and since then at all subsequent Summer Games. The nation has not yet competed at the **Olympic Winter Games** and has never won an **Olympic medal**. The Maldives have had 29 competitors (20 men, nine **women**) and have entered **swimming** (six men, three women), **badminton** (one man), and **athletics** (13 men, six women). Only Azneem Ahmed (2012 100 meters) has got past the first **round** in athletics, but he was eliminated in the next round. Hussein Haleem finished 86th of 110 entrants in the 1992 men's **marathon**. Their best result in swimming occurred in 2008 when Maldivian Rouya Hussein finished 72nd of 90 contestants in the women's 50 meter **freestyle**.

MALI (MLI). Prior to its independence in 1960, Mali was part of French West Africa and was known as French Sudan. In 1962, Mali formed a **National Olympic Committee**, which was recognized by the **International Olympic Committee** in 1963. In 1964, Mali made its first appearance at the Olympics and has since missed only the 1976 **Olympic Games**, joining the African **boycott**. The West African nation has entered 70 athletes (48 men, 22 **women**) in seven sports during the 12 Summer Games in which it has competed. It has had entrants in **athletics** (11 men, eight women), **basketball** (12 women), **boxing** (four men), **football** (16 men), **judo** (12 men), **swimming** (four men, two women), and **taekwondo** (one man). Mali has never won an

Olympic medal and has not participated in the **Olympic Winter Games**. Its best Olympic performance was in 2004, when the Malian men's football team reached the quarter-finals, in which it was eliminated by **Italy**. In 2012, Daba Modibo Keita reached the bronze medal match in the men's **heavyweight** taekwondo event but was unable to compete due to injury and finished tied for fifth among the 16 contestants. In 2008, the women's basketball team, led by Women's National Basketball Association player Hamchétou Maïga-Ba, qualified for the Olympic tournament but finished in 12th and last place. Other notable achievements by Malian Olympians include three-time Olympic **discus thrower** Namakoro Niaré who reached the finals of the men's discus event in 1972 and finished 13th. Sprinter Ousmane Diarra entered both the 100 meter and 200 meter races in 1988, 1992, and 1996 and reached the quarter-final **round** three times. Kadiatou Camara reached the quarter-finals of the women's 200 meter **sprint** in 1992 and missed advancing to the semi-finals by just 0.02 seconds.

MALLIN, HENRY WILLIAM "HARRY" (GBR–BOX). B. 1 June 1892, Shoreditch, London, **England**. D. 8 November 1969, Lewisham, London, England. With victories in the **middleweight** division at the 1920 and 1924 **Olympic Games**, Harry Mallin became the first man to successfully defend an Olympic **boxing** title. Even in those days, the competence and partiality of the judges posed problems, and the five-foot, 10-inch (180 cm) Mallin only won his second gold medal after the decision giving the quarter-final bout to French hometown hero Roger Brousse had been overturned as Mallin's claim of being bitten by Brousse on the chest and shoulder was substantiated. Mallin's record was incomparable; he was unbeaten in more than 300 bouts and won five British amateur titles. His brother Fred was also a formidable boxer who finished fourth in the 1928 Olympic middleweight class.

MALLON, WILLIAM JAMES "BILL." B. 2 February 1952, Paterson, New Jersey, United States. Bill Mallon is one of the leading Olympic historians. A graduate of Duke University, he played professional **golf** on the Professional Golf Association tour from 1975 to 1978 and was twice a winner of the New England Open. He then returned to Duke University to study medicine. He worked as an orthopedic surgeon in Durham, North Carolina, specializing in elbow and shoulder surgery while pursuing his hobby of Olympic history. In 1992, he formed the **International Society of Olympic Historians**.

He has written more than 20 books, mostly on the **Olympic Games**, including detailed books on each of the early Modern Olympic Games from 1896 to 1920 and the first five editions of this *Historical Dictionary of the*

Olympic Movement. He also created a vast database of Olympic Games results and athletes and served as a consultant to the **International Olympic Committee** (IOC). In 2001, he was awarded the **Olympic Order** in silver by the IOC for his work. Although he retired from active medical practice in December 2013 and relocated to New Hampshire, he was still the president of the American Shoulder and Elbow Surgeons in 2014 and continues to pursue his Olympic historian activities.

MALTA (MLT). The Mediterranean island nation of Malta first competed at the **Olympic Games** in 1928. It has participated rather sporadically since then, missing the Olympic Games of 1932, 1952, 1956, 1964, and 1976. Officially known as the Republic of Malta, it competed at the **Olympic Winter Games** for the first time in 2014 with one **Alpine skier**, Elise Pellegrin, who finished 65th of 89 entrants in the **women's** **giant slalom** and 42nd of 85 in the **slalom**. In 15 Summer Games, Malta has had 77 entrants (63 men, 14 women) and participated in nine sports: **archery** (one man, one woman), **athletics** (seven men, seven women), **cycling** (10 men), **judo** (two men, two women), **sailing** (eight men), **shooting** (eight women), **swimming** (six men, four women), **water polo** (18 men), and **wrestling** (three men).

Malta's top Olympic moment occurred in 1928 when its water polo team won one match, defeating **Luxembourg** 3–1, before losing to **France** in the second **round**. This placed it equal fifth of a starting field of 14 teams. Other notable Olympic performances by Maltese athletes include William Chetcuti in men's **double trap** shooting. He finished ninth in 2004, eighth in 2008, and ninth in 2012. Larry Vella tied for 11th of 34 entrants in 1980 mixed **trap** shooting. Peter Bonelli was ninth in the men's **windsurfer** sailing event in 1984. In wrestling, Jesmond Giordemaina won his first bout and reached the third round of the 1984 **flyweight freestyle** class before exiting the tournament. In 1960, cyclist Paul Camilleri finished 41st of 142 entrants in the men's **road race**.

MANCHUKUO. From 1932 to 1945, **Japan** controlled a portion of Manchuria, located in northeast **China**. They created a nation called Manchukuo that historians refer to as a "puppet state." Manchukuo attempted to enter the 1932 **Olympic Games**, but their top athlete, Liu Changchun, refused to compete for them and instead became the first athlete to represent China in the Olympics. In 1936, Manchukuo again attempted to enter the Olympics but were rebuffed by the **International Olympic Committee**, which did not allow participation by an unrecognized state. Had the 1940 Olympics been held as planned in Tokyo, it is possible that Manchukuo would have been able to participate.

MANGIAROTTI, EDOARDO (ITA–FEN). B. 7 April 1919, Renate Veduggio, Milan, **Italy**. D. 25 May 2012, Milan, Italy. Edoardo Mangiarotti was the winner of a record 13 **Olympic medals** (six gold, five silver, two bronze) for **fencing** from 1936 to 1960. He was most successful in the **épée** team event, winning four gold medals (1936, 1952, 1956, 1960) and a silver (1948). His other gold medals were won in the épée individual (1952) and the **foil** team (1960). In 14 Olympic events, he failed to medal in only one. At the World Championships, he won two individual épée titles and was a member of 13 winning teams in the épée and foil. Mangiarotti later became secretary-general of the Fédération Internationale d'Éscrime. His brother Dario was also a member of the Italian medal-winning Olympic épée teams in 1948 and 1952.

The Mangiarotti family had several other contestants in Olympic fencing. Edoardo's father, Giuseppe, competed in the 1908 Games and finished fourth with the Italian épée team. Edoardo's brother Dario competed in 1948 and 1952 and won a gold and two silver medals. The third generation of the family, Edoardo's daughter Carola, competed in 1976 and 1980 with a fifth place result in **women**'s team foil competition both years.

MÄNTYRANTA, EERO ANTERO (FIN–CCS). B. 20 November 1937, Lamkojärvi, Pello, Lapland, **Finland**. D. 30 December 2013, Oulu, Pohjois-Pohjanmaa, Finland. Eero Mäntyranta competed at four **Olympic Winter Games** (1960–1972), winning **cross-country skiing** medals at three of them. A member of the Finnish 4x10 km **relay** team from 1960 to 1968, he won a gold in 1960, a silver in 1964, and a bronze in 1968. At his peak in 1964, Mäntyranta won both the 15 km and the 30 km and added a silver and a bronze in these two events in 1968, bringing his total medal haul to seven. The five-foot, six-inch (170 cm), 143 lb (65 kg) skier was also World Champion at 30 km in 1962 and 1966. By the time of his fourth Olympic appearance in 1972, he was past his prime and was selected only for the 30 km, in which he finished 19th. He career ended soon afterward when it became known that he had had a **doping** positive at the Finnish trials. However, Mäntyranta's family has been extensively studied by medical experts since the late 1980s, because he has hereditary polycythemia vera due to a mutation in the erythropoietin receptor gene, which was identified following a DNA study done on over 200 members of his family. This confluence of genetics increased Mäntyranta's oxygen-carrying capacity and may have helped his ascent to the highest levels of endurance sport. Eero's nephew Pertti Teurajärvi competed in the 1976 and 1980 Winter Games, earning a gold and a bronze medal with the Finnish cross-country relay team.

MARATHON. The marathon is the longest running event conducted in the track and field **athletics** program at the **Olympic Games**. The marathon standard distance is 42,195 meters (26 miles, 385 yards), although in the early years of the Olympics, it varied from 25 miles to just under 27 miles. The standard distance was first used at the 1908 Olympic Games in London, when the race started near the gardens of Windsor Castle so that the queen's children could watch the start. The distance from Windsor Castle to the finish line at the White City Stadium was 42,195 meters. This was adopted as the standard in the 1920s.

The marathon is one of just a few sports events to have been invented especially for the Olympic Games. Michel Bréal, a friend of **Pierre de Coubertin**, suggested it to him, based on the ancient legend of a messenger running from the Battle of Marathon to announce the Greek victory (before dying, in some versions of the legend). The 1896 race hence started in the town of Marathon, as would those of 1906 and 2008.

Two marathoners have won the Olympic race twice: **Abebe Bikila** (ETH) in 1960 and 1964 and Waldemar Cierpinski (GDR) in 1976 and 1980. Although it was not always so, the men's marathon now is usually the last event on the last day of the Olympics. **Women** began competing in an Olympic marathon in 1984. In 28 Summer Games, there have been 1,560 athletes from 160 nations who have taken part in the men's marathon race. In the eight Games in which the women's marathon has been contested, there have been 460 women from 106 nations who have competed in the race. No woman has won the marathon more than once, but four women, Rosa Mota (POR), Yuki Arimori (JPN), Valentina Yegorova (EUN/RUS), and Catherine Ndereba (KEN), have each won two medals.

MARKETING COMMISSION. The Marketing Commission was formerly called the New Sources of Financing Commission and was formed in 1983. The most notable chairman of this commission was **Richard Pound**, the **Canadian International Olympic Committee** (IOC) member who has become well known for his negotiating skills with television networks and prospective sponsors of the **Olympic Movement**. Pound and this commission were responsible in 1984–1985 for forming The Olympic Programme, which recruits a small number of major corporations to be supporting sponsors of the Olympic Movement for each **Olympiad**. The current commission has 20 IOC members and is headed by Tsunekazu Takeda of **Japan**. The IOC lists the mandate for this commission as (1) to review and study possible sources of financing and revenue for the IOC and the Olympic Movement, while ensuring that control of sport rests with sports authorities; (2) to make recommendations to the IOC **Executive Board** regarding marketing and related programs; (3) to monitor the implementation of the IOC's marketing and related programs and report thereon to the IOC Executive Board; and (4) to seek means of maximizing the potential benefits to the Olympic Movement available through association with marketing partners.

MARSHALL ISLANDS (MHL). The Marshall Islands was elected as the 203rd **National Olympic Committee** at the 118th **International Olympic Committee (IOC) Session** in Torino on 9 February 2006. Its cause was initially taken up in 1993 by Paul Wallwork, formerly the **IOC member** to **Samoa**, but the IOC's original response was that, because citizens of the Marshall Islands carry **United States** passports, the United States could, in effect, send a second team to the Olympics. This unusual reply completely overlooked the fact that other territories (e.g., **Guam, Puerto Rico, British Virgin Islands, Netherlands Antilles**, and **American Samoa**) were in a similar situation but had already been accorded membership in the IOC.

The Marshall Islands, located in the northern Pacific Ocean and officially known as the Republic of the Marshall Islands, finally competed in Beijing in 2008 with five Marshallese athletes competing in **athletics** (one man, one **woman**), **swimming** (one man, one woman), and **taekwondo** (one man) of which **freestyle** swimmer Julianne Kirchner arguably did the best, despite being eliminated in the qualification round of the 50 meter freestyle and finishing 75th of 90 entrants. The Marshall Islands sent a team of four athletes to the 2012 Games—two men and two women, one each in athletics and swimming. Ann-Marie Hepler finished 50th of 75 entrants in the women's 50 meter freestyle. Haley Nemra entered the women's 800 meter run for the second consecutive Olympics and did not advance past the first **heat** either time. They have yet to compete at the **Olympic Winter Games**.

MARTIN, KEVIN (CAN–CUR). B. 31 July 1966, Killam, Alberta, **Canada**. Although Kevin Martin's **Olympic medal** record is equaled among men by Norwegian Torger Nergård, Martin is arguably the best-known male Olympic **curler**. After appearing at the 1992 Olympics, where curling was a **demonstration sport**, Martin returned to the **Olympic Winter Games** in 2002. In the final, he lost the gold to **Norway** in a last-rock decision. After forming a new team in 2007, the six-foot tall (185 cm), 205 lb (93 kg) curler, known as "the Old Bear," won his first international title at the 2008 World Championships (he placed second in 1991 and 2009) and followed up with the Olympic gold in front of a home crowd at Vancouver. Martin has also claimed a record-tying four wins at what is often considered the most difficult tournament to win: the Tim Horton's Brier, or the Canadian Championships.

MASS START. The phrase mass start is used for some **biathlon** events. In some biathlon races, the contestants begin the race separately and their elapsed time determines the winner. In a mass start race, all competitors begin at the same time and are on the course together. The race is limited to 30 entrants to minimize congestion. A 15 km mass start race for men was added to the **Olympic Program** in 2006 along with a 12.5 km mass star race for **women**. Martin Fourcade of **France** (silver medal in 2010 and 2014) is the only multiple **Olympic medalist** in this race. No woman has won more than one medal in the three Olympic mass start races as of 2014.

MASSON, PAUL MICHEL PIERRE ADRIEN (FRA–CYC). B. 11 October 1876, Mostaganem, **Algeria**. D. 30 November 1944. At the first modern **Olympic Games** in 1896, Paul Masson won three **cycling** events: the match **sprint**, the one-lap **time trial**, and the 10,000 meter track event. The three cycling golds at one Games have been bettered among men only by **Marcus Hurley** (USA) in 1904 and equaled only by **Robert Charpentier** (FRA) in 1936 and **Chris Hoy** in 2008. Masson had no significant international record prior to the 1896 Olympics. After the Olympics, he turned professional, adopting the name Paul Nossam (Masson spelled backward). His only significant performance as Paul Nossam was third in the world professional sprint championship in 1897. Paul Masson was not related to the namesake of the famous wine company.

MATHIAS, ROBERT BRUCE "BOB" (USA–ATH). B. 17 November 1930, Tulare, California, **United States**. D. 2 September 2006, Fresno, California, United States. Bob Mathias was the first of only two men to win successive Olympic **decathlon** titles. He won his first gold medal in 1948 when, as a 17-year-old, he became the youngest-ever winner of an Olympic track and field event. Mathias set his third world record while defending his title in 1952, but the following year the six-foot, two-inch (190 cm), 203 lb (92 kg) athlete forfeited his amateur status by starring in a film about his life, *The Bob Mathias Story*, in which he played himself and featured Ward Bond as his coach. Although a professional, as a marine officer he was eligible to compete in the 1956 Inter-Services Championships, where he won his 11th and final decathlon competition to maintain his unbeaten record in the event. A politician later in life, Mathias was first elected as a Republican congressman for California in 1966. He served four terms in the House of Representatives before losing out in the Democratic landslide of 1974. In 1973, he introduced legislation to amend the U.S. *Olympic Charter* that effectively created a Bill of Rights for amateur athletes. *See also* JOHNSON, RAFER LEWIS; THOMPSON, FRANCIS MORGAN.

Bob Mathias, two-time Olympic decathlon champion.
Courtesy of Volker Kluge

MATTHES, ROLAND (GDR–SWI). B. 17 November 1950, in Pößneck, Thüringen, **German Democratic Republic**. With victories in the 100 meter and 200 meter **backstrokes** at both the 1968 and 1972 **Olympic Games**, Roland Matthes, six feet, two inches (189 cm), 163 lb (74 kg), is one of the most successful male backstroke **swimmers** at the Olympics. He also won two silver medals and one bronze medal in the **relays** and added his eighth Olympic medal (a bronze) in the 1976 100 meter backstroke. Matthes set 16 world backstroke records (eight at each distance), but was also a world-class performer in other events, winning silver medals at the European Championships in the freestyle and **butterfly** and setting three European butterfly records. He was briefly married to Olympic swimmer **Kornelia Ender**.

MAURITANIA (MTN). Prior to gaining independence in 1960, Mauritania was a part of French West Africa located in the northwestern part of the continent. In 1962, Mauritania formed a provisional **National Olympic Committee**, but in 1977 a more formal body was constituted. After the **International Olympic Committee** granted provisional recognition in 1979, full recognition followed in 1980. Mauritania first competed at the **Olympic Games** in 1984 and has been present at each of the subsequent Olympics, although from 2000 to 2012 only one male and one female athlete have been entered in each Games—both competing in **athletics**. A total of 21 athletes have represented Mauritania in Olympic competition in athletics (12 men, four **women**) and **wrestling** (five men). Officially known as the Islamic Republic of Mauritania, the country has never competed at the **Olympic Winter Games**. All Mauritanian athletes have been eliminated in the preliminary rounds of competition and have yet to win an **Olympic medal**. Their best performance was that of **freestyle heavyweight** wrestler Babacar Sar, who won his first two bouts, both by fall, before losing his next two. That same year, **Greco-Roman** style heavyweight wrestler Oumar Samba Sy won his first bout before being eliminated from the tournament.

MAURITIUS (MRI). The Indian Ocean nation of Mauritius, located off the southeast African coast, formed a **National Olympic Committee** in 1971, but did not compete at the Olympics until 1984 in Los Angeles. Mauritius has not missed a single edition of the **Olympic Games** since, but has never competed at the **Olympic Winter Games**.

In eight Summer Games, Mauritius has entered 80 athletes (50 men, 30 **women**) and competed in 13 sports: **archery** (one man, one woman), **athletics** (19 men, six women), **badminton** (three men, six women), **beach volleyball** (two women), **boxing** (11 men), **cycling** (one woman), **judo** (two men, three women), **sailing** (one woman), **swimming** (six men, eight women), **table tennis** (three men), **triathlon** (one woman), **weightlifting** (four men, one woman), and **wrestling** (one man).

Officially known as the Republic of Mauritius, the island nation won its first medal at the 2008 Olympics, when Mauritian boxer Bruno Julie made it to the semifinals of the **bantamweight** division and earned a bronze. Other notable results for Mauritius athletes include a sixth place finish for Stéphane Buckland in the 200 meter **sprint** in 2004. He also reached the semifinal **round** in that event in 2000 and 2008. Christine Legentil tied for seventh place in the 2012 women's **half-lightweight** judo event. Jonathan Chimier was 10th in the 2004 **long jump**. Boxer Richarno Colin won his first bout in both 2008 and 2012 in the **light-welterweight** class and finished tied for ninth place each year. **Featherweight** Josian Lebon also won his first bout in 1996 and was tied for ninth. In judo, Antonio Felicite tied for ninth in the 1996 **half-heavyweight** class as did **middleweight** Jean-Claude Raphaël in 2000.

MAY, MISTY ERIE (later TREANOR) (USA–BVO). B. 30 July 1977, Costa Mesa, California, **United States**. The daughter of Robert "Butch" May, a 1968 **volleyball** Olympian, Misty May competed in four Olympics in **beach volleyball**, winning gold medals in 2004, 2008, and 2012, while partnering **Kerri Walsh**. The five-foot, eight-inch (175 cm), 159 lb (72 kg) May has also won more professional beach tournaments than any female player, with 112 through 2014. May played collegiate volleyball (indoor) at California State University, Long Beach, earning first-team All-American honors and being named National Collegiate Athletic Association Player of the Year in 1998. After college, she immediately began playing beach volleyball, partnering Holly McPeak at the 2000 **Olympic Games**, placing fifth. In 2001, May teamed up with Walsh, and they formed the most dominant female beach volleyball pair ever, winning three gold medals and 112 consecutive matches, a streak broken shortly after the 2008 Olympics. May's cousin is **tennis** professional Taylor Dent, who finished fourth in the Olympic men's **singles** in 2004. Misty May is married to former major league **baseball** player Matt Treanor.

MBAYE, KÉBA (SEN–IOC). B. 6 April 1924, Kaolack, **Senegal**. D. 12 January 2007, Dakar, Senegal. For some 20 years, Kéba Mbaye was one of the more influential **International Olympic Committee** (IOC) members, probably serving on more commissions than any nonpresidential **IOC member** except **Dick Pound**. Mbaye's background is as a lawyer, allowing him to serve as a vice president of the International Court of Justice and as honorary chief justice of the Supreme Court of Senegal. He served as chairman of the **Court of Arbitration for Sport** from 1983 until his death. First elected to the IOC in 1973, he served on the IOC **Executive Board** (1984–1988 and 1993–1998) and as an IOC vice president (1988–1992 and 1998–2002). He became an **honorary IOC member** in 2002. He served as chairman of the following **IOC Commissions**: Apartheid and Olympism (1989–1992), Information on the Olympic Movement in the Baltic States (1990–1991), **Sport and Law** (1995–2002), **Juridical** (1993–2002), Study of the Centennial Olympic Congress, Congress of Unity (1994–1996), **Ethics** (1999–2007), and **Nominations** (2000–2002).

McCORMICK, PATRICIA JOAN "PAT" (née KELLER) (USA–DIV). B. 12 May 1930, Seal Beach, California, United States. With victories in both the **springboard** and **platform** at the 1952 and 1956 **Olympic Games**, Pat McCormick became the first **diver** in history to win four gold **Olympic medals**. Her second double victory at Melbourne came only five months after the birth of her son. McCormick, only five feet, three inches (162 cm) tall, 128 lb (58 kg) won 17 Amateur Athletic Union (AAU) titles at the out-door championships, at all three levels—one meter and three meter spring-board and the 10 meter platform—and nine indoor AAU championships. Her husband, John McCormick, was the AAU champion at both spring-board and platform, and her daughter Kelly was on the U.S. diving team at the 1983 **Pan American Games**. Kelly also competed for the United States at the 1984 and 1988 Olympics, winning a silver in 1984 and a bronze in 1988, both on the springboard.

McKAY, JAMES KENNETH "JIM" (né JAMES KENNETH MCMA-NUS). B. 24 September 1921, Philadelphia, Pennsylvania, United States. D. 7 June 2008, Monkton, Maryland, United States. In the United States, Jim McKay achieved fame as the "Voice of the Olympics." He was host or cohost on the U.S. **television** network that broadcast the Olympics an unprec-edented seven times: six times for American Broadcasting Company (ABC) Sports (1976 and 1984 for the **Olympic Games** and the **Olympic Winter Games** consecutively from 1976 through 1988) and once for the Columbia Broadcasting System (CBS) in 1960. McKay was not the main studio host in 1972 at Munich, but it was there that he achieved his greatest fame as an Olympics host. He was called on to broadcast the news reports of the horrific **Israeli** hostage massacre and was on the air in the United States for over 15 consecutive hours. He was the one who eventually told the viewers, in his own poignant words, "They're all gone." He was awarded an Emmy for that broadcast, one of 10 Emmys he won, nine for sportscaster of the year and one for lifetime achievement.

MEAGHER, MARY TERSTEGGE (USA–SWI). B. 27 October 1964, Louisville, Kentucky, **United States**. Mary T. Meagher is the greatest female **butterfly swimmer** ever, and for her feats, she earned the nickname "Ma-dame Butterfly." She won three gold medals at the 1984 **Olympic Games**, in both butterfly events, and on the 4x100 meter **medley relay**. In 1988, by then past her prime, she earned a bronze in the 200 meter butterfly and a silver with the medley relay. The five-foot, seven-inch (172 cm), 141 lb (64 kg) Meagher would likely have won both butterfly events in 1980 had the United States not **boycotted** the Moscow Olympics. She was World Champion in 1982 over 100 meters and in 1986 over 200 meters. She set two world but-terfly records over 100 meters and five over 200 meters, beginning in 1979. Her performance at the 1981 U.S. Nationals remains her greatest effort: she set world records of 57.93 for 100 meters and 2:05.96 for 200 meters, both of which held until the late 1990s.

MEDICAL CODE. The *Olympic Movement Medical Code*, first published by the **International Olympic Committee** (IOC) **Medical Commission** in 1995, is designed "to ensure that sport is practiced without danger to the health of the athletes and with respect for fair play and sports ethics." The latest version of the document, dated 1 October 2009, is intended for use by the IOC, the **International Federations**, and the **National Olympic Committees**; it describes the relationship between athletes and medical personnel and health-related rules during competition and training.

MEDICAL COMMISSION. The Medical Commission is the oldest permanent **International Olympic Committee** (IOC) commission, having been officially formed in 1967, but actually started as a working group in 1961. The current chairman is Ugur Erdener, a Turkish **IOC member**. The longest serving chairman was the **Belgian** IOC member Prince Alexandre de Merode, now deceased. The commission has several consultant members, along with members from the **National Olympic Committees**, **International Federations**, and **Organizing Committees of the Olympic Games**. The Medical Commission's primary responsibilities are the fight against **doping** and writing and rewriting the medical bylaws to the *Olympic Charter*. This Commission has also dealt with the question of determining female identity, originally called sex testing, but now known by the politically correct term **gender identification**. The IOC notes that the Medical Commission is charged with (1) protection of the health of athletes, (2) respect for both medical and sport ethics, and (3) equality for all competing athletes. It also describes the work of the Medical Commission as having included (1) establishing the **Olympic Movement** Anti-Doping Code, which is applicable to all constituents of the Olympic Movement; (2) the IOC World Congress on Sport Sciences, the main forum for all the scientists working close to the athlete, held every two years; and (3) the IOC Olympic Prize on Sport Sciences, which is awarded to researchers who have excelled in the field of science applied to human movement, physical activity, and sports. Finally, the Medical Commission is responsible for the *Medical Code*, which was first published in 1995. Some of its work on doping control has now been ceded to the **World Anti-Doping Agency**.

MEDLEY. In swimming competition some races are called medley races in which the contestants demonstrate their ability to swim four different strokes. In the individual medley race, the swimmers first use the **butterfly** stroke, then the **backstroke**, then the **breaststroke**, and finish the race with a **freestyle** stroke, which may not be any of the previous three strokes and is generally the front crawl. In team medley **relay** competition, the race is begun with the backstroke followed by breaststroke, butterfly, and freestyle. In team competition, a different swimmer is used for each stroke. In Olympic swimming, a 400 meter individual medley race for men and a separate one for **women** has been contested since 1964. Each swimmer must use each stroke for 100 meters before changing to the next stroke. Tomas Darnyi of **Hungary** (1988, 1992), Tom Dolan of the **United States** (1996, 2000), and **Michael Phelps** of the United States (2004, 2008) have each won the men's race twice. Six other swimmers have also won two medals in this event. Yana Klochkova of the **Ukraine** (2000, 2004) is the only woman to win this event twice. The 200 meter individual medley for men and for women was first held at the **Olympic Games** in 1968. It was contested again in 1972 but not in 1976 or 1980. Since then, it has been a part of every **Olympic Program**. Phelps has won the 200 meter individual medley three times—in 2004, 2008, and 2012. Klochkova again (2000, 2004) is the only woman to win this twice. A 4x100 medley relay has been held for men and women since 1960. The United States has won the men's race in every Olympics with the exception of 1980 when they did not compete in the Olympic Games. They have also won the women's medley relay nine times, with East **Germany** (three times) and **Australia** (twice) the other winners.

MEDVED, ALEKSANDR VASILYEVICH (URS/UKR–WRE). B. 16 September 1937, Bila Tserkva, Kyiv, **Ukraine**, USSR. With victories in the freestyle **light-heavyweight** (1964), **heavyweight** (1968), and **super-heavyweight** (1972) divisions, Aleksandr Medved was the first **wrestler** to win gold medals at three successive **Olympic Games**. He also won seven world titles. Medved's record was the more remarkable because his physique (six feet, two inches [190 cm] 225–242 lbs [102–110 kg]) seldom matched that of his opponents, and on his way to the Olympic super-heavyweight title in 1972, he overcame the giant 400 lb (182 kg) American bronze medalist **Chris Taylor**, who enjoyed a weight advantage of well over 100 pounds (45 kg). Medved's World Championships were in light-heavyweight (1962, 1963, and 1966) and super-heavyweight (1967, 1969, 1970, and 1971). Medved was the European champion in 1966, 1968, and 1972, competing less often at that meet. Medved is one of very few people to be the flagbearer in the opening ceremony for more than one nation. In 1972, as one of the athletes on the **Soviet Union** team, he was awarded that honor. After the breakup of the Soviet Union, he became a coach of the Belorussian team and was the flagbearer for **Belarus** in 2004. In 1980, he received an additional honor and was chosen to recite the Officials' Oath during the 1980 opening ceremony in Moscow.

MEXICO (MEX). Mexican athletes first competed at the 1900 **Olympic Games** when three **polo** players played at Paris in a mixed North American team. Mexico did not compete again at the Olympics until 1924, but it has competed since without fail. In 22 Summer Games, Mexico has entered 1,426 athletes (1,153 men, 273 **women**) and competed in 30 sports plus the **art competitions**. Mexico's most popular sports have been **athletics** (171 men, 45 women), **football** (147 men, 17 women), **swimming** (76 men, 51 women), **boxing** (88 men), and **cycling** (73 men, four women).

It has won 61 **Olympic medals** (13 gold, 21 silver, 27 bronze), all at the Games of the **Olympiad**. Its most successful competitor was **diver** Joaquín Capilla who won bronze, silver, and gold medals from 1948 to 1956 in **platform diving** and a bronze in 1956 **springboard** diving. **Equestrian** Humberto Mariles won two golds and a bronze at the 1948 Olympics. Five other Mexican athletes have each won two Olympic medals: diver Paola Espinosa (2008 bronze, 2012 silver, women's synchronized platform); **heavyweight** *taekwondoka* María Espinoza (2008 gold, 2012 bronze); **race walker** Raúl González (1984 20 k silver, 50 k gold); and equestrians Joaquín Pérez (1980 individual and team **jumping**, both bronze) and Rubén Uriza (1948 individual jumping silver, team jumping gold).

Other gold medals were won by the 2012 men's football team, race walkers Daniel Bautista (1976 20 k) and Ernesto Canto (1984 20 k), **flyweight** boxer Ricardo Delgado (1968), **featherweight** boxer Antonio Roldán (1968), Alberto Valdés, Sr., with the 1948 men's equestrian jumping team, swimmer Felipe Muñoz (1968 200 meter **breaststroke**), flyweight *taekwondoka* Guillermo Pérez (2008), and **weightlifter** Soraya Jiménez (2000 women's **lightweight**).

Mexico sent five **bobsled** competitors to the 1928 **Olympic Winter Games** and in 1932 entered another bobsled team, but it did not compete. Mexico's other Winter Olympic appearances were in 1984, 1988, 1992, 1994, 2002, 2010, and 2014. In those eight Winter Games, Mexico has entered 32 athletes (27 men, five women) and competed in five sports: **Alpine skiing** (10 men, three women), bobsledding (14 men), **cross-country skiing** (one man), **figure skating** (one man, two women), and **skeleton** (one man). Mexico has not won any medals in the Winter Games. In 1988, four brothers named Tamés (Jorge, José, Luis Adrián, Roberto) entered the bobsled in two two-man teams and finished 36th and 37th of the 41 teams. The legendary **Hubertus von Fürstenburg-von Hohenlohe** competed in five Winter Olympics for Mexico from 1984 to 2014 when he became one of the oldest Winter Olympians at age 55. His best result was 26th of 101 in the **slalom** in 1984. Mexico's best Winter Games performances also include the 1928 bobsled team, 11th of 23 entrants.

Mexico, officially known as the United Mexican States, hosted the Games of the XIXth Olympiad at Mexico City in 1968 after unsuccessfully bidding for the Games of 1956 and 1960.

MEYER, DEBORAH ELIZABETH "DEBBIE" (later REYES) (USA–SWI). B. 14 August 1952, Annapolis, Maryland, **United States**. With victories in the 200 meter, 400 meter, and 800 meter **freestyle** in 1968, the five-foot, six-inch (170 cm), 115 lb (52 kg) Debbie Meyer became the first **woman swimmer** to win three individual gold medals at one **Olympic Games**. She won each event by a large margin and achieved her unique Olympic treble despite a severely upset stomach in **Mexico** City. Between 1967 and 1970, Meyer set 15 world records; she retired before her abilities had been fully extended.

MIDDLE-HEAVYWEIGHT. In the sport of **weightlifting**, a middle-heavy-weight class is one of the men's weight classes and has been included in the **Olympic Games** since 1952. Arkady Vorobyov of the **Soviet Union** (1956, 1960) and Ilya Ilyin of **Kazakhstan** (2008, 2012) are the only two multiple gold medalists in this class.

MIDDLEWEIGHT. Middleweight is a weight class in **boxing, weightlift-ing**, and **wrestling**. In men's boxing, it is the fourth heaviest after **super-heavyweight, heavyweight**, and **light-heavyweight**. In **women**'s boxing, it is the heaviest class. **Harry Mallin** of **Great Britain** (1920, 1924) and Ariel Hernandez of **Cuba** (1992, 1996) are the only dual gold medalists in Olym-pic men's boxing. Among the Olympic boxers in this weight class who went on to fame as professionals are Americans Floyd Patterson, Michael Spinks, Marvin Johnson, and Virgil Hill and Chris Finnegan of Great Britain.

In wrestling, there were three heavier and three lighter classes in men's Olympic wrestling in 2012, but middleweight is the second heaviest of four weight classes for women. Lothar Metz of **Germany** and East Germany won three Olympic medals in the **Greco-Roman** middleweight class (gold 1968, silver 1960, bronze 1964), while Väinö Kokkinen of **Finland** (1928, 1932) and Axel Grönberg of **Sweden** (1948, 1952) are the only dual gold medalists. Buvaisar Sayteyev of **Russia** is the only dual gold medalist in Olympic men's middleweight **freestyle** competition. Kaori Icho of **Japan** won the women's middleweight event all three years (2004–2012) it was contested.

In weightlifting, middleweight is just that—in 2012 there were three lighter and three heavier classes in both men's and women's competition. In men's middleweight weightlifting, both Carlo Galimberti of **Italy** (gold 1924, silver 1928, 1932) and Pete George of the **United States** (gold 1952, silver 1948,

1956) have each won three **Olympic medals** in this class, and no middle-weight weightlifter has won more than one gold medal. No woman has won more than one medal in women's Olympic middleweight weightlifting.

MILITARY SKI PATROL. A military ski patrol event was held at the **Olympic Winter Games** in 1928, 1936, and 1948 as a **demonstration sport**. The event was also contested at the 1924 Olympic Winter Games in Chamonix and, until recently, had always been considered a demonstration event. But more recent evidence makes it clear that this was a full medal event in 1924 and not a demonstration. Six nations (**Switzerland, Finland, France, Czechoslovakia, Italy**, and **Poland**) each with four-man teams were represented in the 1924 Olympic event. Military ski patrol is an event similar to team **biathlon**, in which all the team members ski together over a course, stopping periodically to shoot at targets. The event is still held at World Military Skiing Championships, but no **International Federation** exists for the sport.

MILLAR, IAN (CAN–EQU). B. 6 January 1947, Halifax, Nova Scotia, **Canada**. Ian Millar first participated in the **Olympic Games** in 1972 at the age of 25. In the most remarkable string of participation of any Olympian, he has taken part in each Olympic Games in **equestrian jumping** competition from 1972 through 2012 with the exception of 1980 when his Canadian team **boycotted** the Games. His attendance in 10 Olympic Games is unmatched by any other Olympian. His perseverance was rewarded in 2008 when in his ninth Games he won a silver medal as a representative of the Canadian jumping team. The team had previously finished fourth in 1984 and 1988, fifth in 1976, and sixth in 1972. The best performance in the individual jumping event for the six-foot tall (185 cm), 168 lb (76 kg) rider occurred in 2012 when he finished tied for ninth at the age of 65. In **Pan American Games** competition, he has won three gold medals (individual in 1987 and 1999; team in 1987), four silver, and two bronze, with one of the bronze medals in 1979 for individual jumping. In 1986, he was made a Member of the Order of Canada.

MILLER, SAMUEL BODE (USA–ASK). B. 12 October 1977, Easton, New Hampshire, **United States**. Bode Miller has competed in five **Olympic Winter Games** from 1998 to 2014 and has won more medals in **Alpine skiing** than anyone except **Kjetil André Aamodt** of **Norway**. Miller's total of six medals (one gold, three silver, two bronze) is the most by a skier representing the United States, two more than Julia Mancuso and four more than any male American skier. In his first Winter Games in 1998, the six-foot, two-inch (188 cm), 201 lb (91 kg) Miller did not finish either of the two races in which he was entered. In 2002, he won silver medals in the **giant slalom** and the **combined** and became just the second American male Alpine skier to win two medals at one Winter Games. (Tommy Moe in 1994 was the first.) The Torino Games in 2006 was a disappointment for Miller as he entered five events and was only able to finish two of them, although he did place fifth in one and tied for sixth in the other. The Vancouver Games in 2010 was Miller's greatest success. He won a gold, silver, and bronze there—the first American male Alpine skier to win three medals at one Winter Games and one of only six American males to win three or more medals at one Winter Games regardless of sport. In 2014, he won his sixth medal, albeit by the narrowest of margins. In a sport measured in hundredths of seconds, he tied for third place with a time of 1:18.67, the identical time that Jan Hudec of **Canada** recorded. Otmar Streidinger of **Austria** finished only two hundredths of a second behind them and had to settle for fifth place. At the World Championships, Miller has won four gold medals and one silver medal.

MILON OF KROTON (GRE–WRE). Fl. 540–508 B.C. The son of the well-known athlete Diotimos, Milon of Kroton was the greatest **wrestler** of ancient **Greece** and the **Ancient Olympic Games**. He was champion six times at the **Olympic Games** (540 B.C. in boys' wrestling and 532–516 B.C. in wrestling), seven times at the **Pythian Games**, ten times at the **Isthmian Games**, and nine times at the **Nemean Games**. In four **Olympiad**s, he was *periodonikes*, meaning he won all of the four major festival titles. The base of his statue at ancient Olympia reads, "he had never been brought to his knees." Milon's strength was supposedly developed when he was a young boy and began carrying a wild heifer on his shoulders. As the heifer grew, Milon continued to carry it for exercise, and his strength became legendary, but it eventually killed him. One day in a forest, he saw a tree that had been cut open with wedges in it. He decided to pull open the trunk with his massive hands, but when he did this, the wedges flew out, and the trunk trapped his hands. He was caught in the tree, and wild beasts tore him to pieces that night.

MITCHELL REPORT. *See* OLYMPIC BRIBERY SCANDAL.

MITTERMAIER, ROSEMARIE "ROSI" (later NEUREUTHER) (FRG–ASK). B. 5 August 1950, Reit im Winkl, Bayern, **Germany**. Rosi Mittermaier had a long career in international **Alpine skiing**, winning 10 individual World Cup races between 1969 and 1976. In 1976, she was the world champion in Alpine **combined** and led the overall World Cup, although she did not lead in any of the individual **disciplines**. Only five feet, two inches (159 cm) tall and 121 lb (55 kg), Mittermaier's greatest fame came at the 1976 **Olympic Winter Games**, when she won the **slalom** and **downhill**. With the **giant slalom** still to come, she had a chance to equal the feats of **Toni Sailer** and **Jean-Claude Killy** by winning all three available Alpine ski events. However, in the giant slalom, she finished second, losing out by 12 one hundredths of a second to **Canada**'s Kathy Kreiner. Mittermaier later married Christian Neureuther, another German Olympic skier. Their son Felix followed in his parents' footsteps, competing in Olympic Alpine skiing at the 2006, 2010, and 2014 Games, but his best finish was only eighth. Rosi's sister Heidi also competed in the 1964 Winter Games.

MIXED DOUBLES. Mixed doubles events in both **badminton** and **tennis** consist of two-player teams of one man and one **woman**. Surprisingly, the sport of **table tennis** has not yet had a mixed doubles event. Mixed doubles was included in the Olympic tennis program in 1900, 1906, 1912, 1920, and 1924. It was not included when tennis returned as an Olympic sport in 1988 but was added in 2012. In 1900, several of the teams consisted of players from different countries, but since 1906, all mixed doubles teams have had both partners from the same country. The 1906 gold medalists were the **French** team of **Max Décugis** and his wife, Marie. In 1920, he teamed with Suzanne Lenglen to win the mixed doubles for a second time. Mixed doubles were added to the badminton program in 1996 and have been won by teams from **China** in three of the five years it has been contested. The Chinese team of Zhang Jun and his partner **Gao Ling** won in both 2000 and 2004. They are the only multiple medalists in badminton mixed doubles.

MIYAKE, YOSHINOBU (JPN–WLT). B. 24 November 1939, Murata, Miyagi, **Japan**. Yoshinobu Miyake was Japan's greatest **weightlifter**. He finished second in the 1960 Olympic **bantamweight** class, but won gold medals at the 1964 and 1968 **Olympic Games** as a **featherweight**. He nearly won his fourth medal in 1972 but finished fourth in the featherweight class, lifting just five pounds less than the bronze medalist. Barely five feet tall (154 cm), Miyake also won World Championships in 1962–1963 and 1965–1966. He set 25 world records, including 10 consecutive records in the **snatch** and nine consecutive total records in the 60 kg (featherweight) class. Miyake later became the coach of the Japanese national team. His brother Yoshiyuki was also a weightlifter who won the bronze medal in the 1968 Olympic featherweight class and World Championships in 1969 and 1971. Yoshiyuki's daughter (Yoshinobu's niece) Hiromi is also a weightlifter, competing in the 2004 and 2008 Games and winning the **flyweight** silver medal in 2012.

MODERN PENTATHLON. Modern pentathlon was invented by the founder of the **Olympic Games,** the Baron **Pierre de Coubertin.** It is better labeled the "military pentathlon," as it supposedly mimics the skills needed by a 19th-century soldier. He must first ride a horse and then fight off an enemy with a sword. He must then swim a river to escape, then fight off more enemies with a pistol, and finally effect the final escape by running a **cross-country** course.

Coubertin was able to get the sport on the **Olympic Program** in 1912. The order of the events has varied, but the current order is as in the soldier's trial: riding, **fencing, swimming, shooting,** and cross-country running. The riding is a cross-country **steeplechase** course. The fencing is a series of one-touch bouts done with **épée** swords. The shooting is done with an **air pistol** from 10 meters (through 2008), but was formerly performed with a **rapid fire pistol.** The swim is now a 200 meter **freestyle** (formerly 300 meters), and the run is a 3,000 meter cross-country event (formerly 4,000 meters). The final event is now arranged so that the runners leave the start in the order of their positions after four events. Further, the starts are arranged so that the time intervals correspond to the number of points separating the competitors. Thus, the finishing order in the run now corresponds exactly to the finishing order of the entire pentathlon, adding to the drama of the event. Beginning at the 1995 World Championships and the 1996 Olympics, the modern pentathlon was changed so that all the events are now contested in one day.

Modern pentathlon was originally dominated by the **Swedes.** After World War II, the **Hungarians** and the **Soviets** became the top countries. Scoring was originally on a points-for-place system, with the lowest score winning, but the competition is now scored using tables for each of the five events.

Modern pentathlon is governed by the Union Internationale de Pentathlon Moderne, which was founded in 1948 and currently (as of 2014) has 114 members. Originally, **biathlon** and modern pentathlon were governed together, by the Union Internationale de Pentathlon Moderne et Biathlon, but the federation split into two separate groups in 1993, with the International Biathlon Union governing that sport. A modern pentathlon event for **women** debuted on the Olympic Program at Sydney in 2000, although a British girl had attempted to compete in the inaugural event in 1912. In 23 Summer Games, there have been 822 athletes (726 men, 96 women) from 56 nations who have competed in the Olympic Games modern pentathlon. **Pavel Lednyov** of the Soviet Union won seven Olympic medals (two gold, two silver, three bronze) in the sport from 1968 to 1980. **András Balczó** of Hungary is the only competitor to win three gold medals. From 1960 to 1972, he won three gold and two silver medals. In the first Olympic modern pentathlon competition, the fifth place finisher was Lieutenant George S. Patton, who later became a world-famous general of the U.S. army during World War II.

Probably the most obscure sport on the Olympic Program, there have frequently been suggestions to remove it from the program. Although the sport remains for the time being, since 1992 the team event has been discontinued, the number of participants has decreased, and the number of competition days has been reduced. In 2008, it was announced that the sport would combine the cross-country running and shooting phases into one competition, similar to a dry land biathlon, and in 2010 it was announced that the air pistols would be replaced by laser pistols. The 2012 event was held with these changes. *See also* HALL, LARS GÖRAN IVAR; NOVIKOV, IGOR ALEKSANDROVICH.

MOGULS. Moguls are a series of bumps on a skiing trail. The sport of mogul skiing developed where skiers perform acrobatic maneuvers over a **downhill** ski course containing moguls and are judged on their skill in performing them in addition to their speed in negotiating the course. It was added to the **Olympic Program** in 1992 for both men and **women** after being a **demonstration sport** in 1988 and is one of the events in **freestyle skiing**. Alexandre Biladeau of **Canada** (2010, 2014) is the only multiple gold medalist in men's moguls and Edgar Grospiron of **France** (gold 1992, bronze 1994), Janne Lahtela of **Finland** (gold 2002, silver 1998), and Dale Begg-Smith of **Australia** (gold 2006, silver 2010) are the only other multiple medalists in this event. No woman has won this event more than once, and **Kari Traa** of **Norway** (gold 2002, silver 2006, bronze 1998) is the only three-time medalist. In 2014, Justine Dufour-Lapointe of Canada won the gold medal and her sister Chloe won the silver medal.

MOLDOVA (MDA). The Eastern European nation of Moldova was formerly the Moldovian Soviet Socialist Republic, which achieved independence after the **Soviet** breakup of 1991. Its **National Olympic Committee** was formed shortly thereafter and was recognized by the **International Olympic Committee** in 1993. Although it is the smallest of the former Soviet Republics, a few Moldavan athletes competed from 1952 to 1988 for the Soviet Union, and Moldavan athletes were present at Barcelona in 1992 as members of the Unified Team. Moldova, officially known as the Republic of Moldova, first competed at the Olympics as an independent nation in 1994 at Lillehammer, represented by one male and one female **biathlete**. It competed at the **Olympic Games** in Atlanta in 1996 and has attended all editions since.

In five Summer Games, Moldova has entered 101 athletes (79 men, 22 **women**) and competed in 10 sports: **archery** (one man, two women),

athletics (15 men, 12 women), **boxing** (five men), **canoeing** (four men), **cycling** (seven men), **judo** (seven men, one woman), **shooting** (two men, one woman), **swimming** (16 men, four women), **weightlifting** (11 men, one woman), and **wrestling** (11 men, two women). Ludmila Cristea competed in both women's judo in 2000 (at the age of 14) and women's wrestling in 2008. Moldovan athletes have won seven **Olympic medals**—two silvers and five bronze. The nation's most successful Olympians are canoeists Nikolae Juravschi and Victor Reneischi, who together won two gold medals competing for the USSR in 1988 and one silver as Moldovans (1996 **Canadian doubles**, 500 meter). Other Moldovan medalists are boxers Vitalie Gruşac (**welterweight** bronze 2000) and Vaeceslav Gojan (**bantamweight** bronze 2008); shooter Oleg Moldovan (running target, 10 meters, silver 2000); weightlifters Cristina Iovu (women's **featherweight** bronze 2012) and Anatolii Cîrîcu (men's **middle-heavyweight** bronze 2012); and wrestler Sergei Mureico (**Greco-Roman super-heavyweight** bronze 1996). Other notable results for Moldova at the Summer Games include fourth place by Alexandru Bratan in 2004 **heavyweight** weightlifting and sixth in that event in 2000; fifth place by Vadim Vacarciuc in **light-heavyweight** weightlifting in 1996 and again in 2000 in the middle-heavyweight class; fifth place by Juravschi and Reneischi in the 1996 Canadian **doubles** 1,000 meter race; and a fifth place tie by Victor Bivol in 2004 lightweight judo.

In six **Olympic Winter Games**, Moldova has entered 15 athletes (11 men, four women): three men in **Alpine skiing**, four men and four women in **biathlon**, four men and two women in **cross-country skiing**, and two men in **luge**. The two female cross-country skiers also competed in biathlon as did two men. The country's best results in Olympic winter sports were achieved by Natalia Levcencova, who finished eighth (of 82 entrants) in the women's 15 k biathlon in 2006 and Christophe Roux who was 28th of 101 contestants in men's **slalom** in 2010.

MONACO (MON). The southwest European micronation of Monaco (population around 30,000), officially known as the Principality of Monaco, competed at the 1920 **Olympic Games** and has since missed only the Games of 1932, 1956, and 1980.

In 20 Summer Games, Monaco has entered 67 competitors (65 men, two **women**) and participated in the **art competitions** (four men) and 13 sports: **athletics** (six men), **fencing** (four men), **gymnastics** (two men), **judo** (four men), **rowing** (six men), **sailing** (11 men), **shooting** (19 men, one woman), **swimming** (five men, one woman), **weightlifting** (two men), and one man in **archery**, **cycling**, **taekwondo**, and **triathlon**. One man competed in both athletics and sailing and another in both the art competitions and shooting.

No Monégasque athlete has won an **Olympic medal** in a sporting event, but in 1924 Julien Médecin won a bronze medal in the architecture portion of the now-defunct art contests. Notable performances by Monaco in Olympic sports include Yann Siccardi (tied for ninth of 37 entrants in 2012 **extra-lightweight** judo), Michel Porasso (12th of 25 in 1920 individual gymnastics **all-around**), Edmond Médécin (15th of 19 in 1920 **pentathlon** and 21st of 29 in 1920 **long jump**), Gaston Médécin (17th of 30 in 1924 pentathlon, 20th of 36 in 1924 **decathlon**, 22nd of 34 in 1924 long jump), René Battaglia (16th of 24 in 1964 **light-heavyweight** weightlifting), and Joe Barral (31st of 101 in 1972 **small-bore rifle** prone shooting). A special mention should be made of the persistence of Monaco shooters. Fabienne Diato-Pasetti competed in six Olympic Games (1988–2008) in women's **air rifle**, Herman Schulz and Roger Abel each entered four Olympics from 1924 to 1952, and Pierre Masson competed in four Games from 1936 to 1960.

Since first competing at the **Olympic Winter Games** in 1984, Monaco has been represented at each of the subsequent Winter Olympics. The country has been represented in the **bobsledding** events by Albert Grimaldi, prince of Monaco, an **International Olympic Committee** member and the son of Prince Rainier and Princess Grace. He competed in five Winter Games from 1988 to 2002 in both two-man and four-man events and had a best finish of 25th of 41 in 1988 two-man competition. In eight Winter Games, Monaco has entered 16 athletes, including one woman, and has competed in **Alpine skiing** and bobsledding. Their best result in bobsled occurred in 2006 in the two-man event when they finished in 12th place of 29 entries. Alexandra Coletti, Monaco's lone female Winter Olympian, competed in three Winter Games from 2006 to 2014 with several respectable performances (19th of 34 in 2010 **combined**, 24th of 44 in 2010 **downhill**, 25th of 53 in 2010 **super G**, 33rd of 64 in 2006 **slalom**).

MONGOLIA (MGL). The east central Asian country of Mongolia, formerly referred to as Outer Mongolia, has competed at the **Olympic Games** since 1964, its only absence being the 1984 Los Angeles Olympics, which it **boycotted**.

In 12 Summer Games, Mongolia has entered 226 athletes (177 men, 49 **women**) and competed in 10 sports: **archery** (four men, 10 women), **athletics** (six men, six women), **boxing** (39 men), **cycling** (13 men), **gymnastics** (one man, five women), **judo** (36 men, 12 women), **shooting** (nine men, five women), **swimming** (three men, three women), **weightlifting** (nine men, one woman), and their most popular sport, **wrestling** (57 men, seven women).

Until the 2008 Olympics, Mongolia had won the most **Olympic medals** (15) without winning an Olympic title. But that drought was ended when

Mongolians Naidangiin Tüvshinbayar (judo) and Enkhbatyn Badar-Uugan (boxing) both won gold medals, leaving the **Philippines** the new owner of this doubtful Olympic record. Mongolia now has a total of 24 Olympic medals (two gold, nine silver, 13 bronze). *Judoka* Naidangiin Tüvshinbayar added a silver medal in 2012 and is the only Mongolian athlete with two Olympic medals. Mongolia's first Olympic medals were won in **freestyle** wrestling in 1968 when **flyweight** Chimedbazaryn Damdinsharav, **lightweight** Danzandarjaagiin Sereeter, and **welterweight** Tömöriin Artag each won bronze and **middleweight** Jigjidiin Mönkhbat won silver. Mongolia has won a total of nine medals (four silver, five bronze) in wrestling, seven in judo (one gold, two silver, four bronze), six in boxing (one gold, two silver, three bronze), and two in shooting (one silver, one bronze).

Mongolia's first Olympic appearance at the Winter Olympics was in 1964, and it has since missed only the 1976 **Olympic Winter Games**. In 13 Winter Games, Mongolia has entered 39 athletes (33 men, six women) and competed in four sports: **biathlon** (four men), **cross-country skiing** (20 men, five women), **short-track speed skating** (four men), and regular **speed skating** (seven men, one woman). Two men in 1964 competed in both biathlon and cross-country skiing. Mongolia has not had any outstanding performances in the Winter Olympics. Their best short-track skater, Batchuluuny Bat-Orgil, was 24th of 29 in the 1994 500 meters. Their best biathlete, Bayanjavyn Damdinjav, was 38th of 60 in the 1968 20 k race. Their best cross-country skier, Ziitsagaany Ganbat, was 62nd of 90 in the 1988 15 k race. Their best speed skater, Tsedenjavyn Lkhamjav, was 20th of 28 in the 1964 3,000 meter race.

MONTENEGRO (MNE). Montenegrin athletes competed for **Yugoslavia** and, later, **Serbia and Montenegro**. In that capacity, they have won medals in most team sports: **basketball**, **football**, **handball**, **volleyball**, and **water polo**. The southeastern Europe country seceded from **Serbia** in late 2006 and was elected into the **International Olympic Committee** the following year. It has since competed in the 2008 and 2012 Summer **Olympic Games** and the 2010 and 2014 **Olympic Winter Games**. In two Summer Games, Montenegro entered 41 athletes (24 men, 17 **women**) and participated in eight sports: **athletics** (two men, two women), **boxing** (two men), handball (14 women), water polo (17 men), and one man in **judo**, **sailing**, and **shooting** and one woman in **swimming**.

The 2012 women's handball team won Montenegro's first **Olympic medal**—a silver one. Both the 2008 and 2012 Montenegrin men's water polo teams finished in fourth place. The best results for an athlete in an individual sport were obtained by Srđan Mrvaljević who finished tied for ninth in the **half-middleweight** class in judo competition in both 2008 and 2012. Milivoj

Dukić was 30th of 49 in the men's one person **dinghy** sailing event in 2012, and Goran Stojiljković was 62nd of 95 in the 2008 men's **marathon**.

In two Winter Games, Montenegro has entered two men and one woman in **Alpine skiing**. All three skiers have done reasonably well. In 2010, Bojan Kosić was 40th of 101 in the men's **slalom** and 61st of 101 in the **giant slalom**. In 2014, Ivana Bulatović was 44th of 88 in the women's slalom and Tarik Hadžić was 38th of 115 in the men's slalom and 62nd of 107 in the giant slalom.

MONTI, EUGENIO (ITA–BOB). B. 28 January 1928, Dobbiaco, Bolzano-Bozen, **Italy**. D. 1 December 2003, Belluno, Italy. Eugenio Monti is considered the greatest **bobsled** driver in history. After winning two Olympic silver medals in 1956, he was deprived of the opportunity to gain further honors in 1960 because the bobsled was not included in the program at Squaw Valley. At his second Olympics in 1964, the five-foot, seven-inch (172 cm), 161 lb (73 kg) Monti won two bronze medals and, in 1968, took the gold medals in both events and became the first bobsledder to win six **Olympic medals**. The bobsled events at the 1968 **Olympic Winter Games** also carried the status of the World Championships, and including his Olympic victories, Monti won the world title in the two-man event eight times and was the world four-man champion three times. He retired after the 1968 Olympics and became the Italian team manager. In addition to his championships, he is known for his sportsmanship at the 1964 Innsbruck Winter Olympics. Trailing the British team of Anthony Nash and Robin Dixon going into the final run, he lent them a bolt off his own sled when their sled failed. Nash and Dixon won the gold medal, but for this magnanimous action, Monti was awarded the **International Fair Play** Award. At the victory ceremony, Nash and Dixon pulled Monti up to the top step of the podium to share in their victory.

MORELON, DANIEL YVES (FRA–CYC). B. 24 July 1944, Bourg-en-Bresse, Ain, **France**. Between 1966 and 1975, Daniel Morelon won a record nine world amateur **sprint** titles and three gold **Olympic medals**. He won the Olympic match sprint in 1968 and 1972, becoming the first of only two men (Jens Fiedler of Germany was the other) to claim a repeat victory in the event. In 1968, partnered by Pierre Trentin, he also won the **tandem** match sprint. Together they had also won the world title in 1966. The five-foot, 11-inch (181 cm), 174 lb (79 kg) Morelon was also a bronze medalist in 1964 and silver medalist in 1976 in the sprint. He won a total of 14 French titles and set a world indoor record for 500 meters in 1976. He was almost exclusively a track sprinter and only turned professional briefly, after having become the French sprint **cycling** coach.

*Daniel Morelon compiled the finest Olympic record
of any track cyclist ever, mostly in the match sprint.
Courtesy of Erich Kamper*

MOROCCO (MAR). After gaining independence from **France**, the north-west African nation of Morocco, officially known as the Kingdom of Morocco, first competed in the 1960 **Olympic Games**. It has since missed only the 1980 Games. It joined the 1976 African **boycott**, but some of its athletes had already competed by then.

In 13 Summer Games, Morocco has entered 402 athletes (360 men, 42 **women**) and competed in 20 sports, with most of the participants taking part in **athletics** (88 men, 29 women), **football** (108 men), **boxing** (56 men, one woman), **wrestling** (25 men), and **judo** (19 men, one woman). Moroccan athletes have won 22 **Olympic medals** (six gold, five silver, 11 bronze), 19 in track and field athletics and three bronze in boxing. With two gold medals in the 1,500 and 5,000 meters in 2004 and a silver medal in the 1,500 in 2000, middle distance runner Hicham El Guerrouj is the country's top Olympian. Morocco's first Olympic medalist was Rhadi Ben Abdesselam who won a silver medal in the 1960 **marathon** finishing second behind the great **Abebe Bikila** of **Ethiopia**. The country's next medal, their first gold medal, was won by a woman. Nawal El-Moutawakel won the women's 400 meter **hurdles** in 1984. In 1998, she became a member of the **International Olympic Committee**. In 1984, Said Aouita won the first of his two Olympic medals—gold in the 5,000 meters. Four years later, he was the bronze medalist in the 800 meters. Hasna Benhassi is Morocco's only other dual Olympic medalist. She won silver in the 2004 800 meters and bronze in that event in 2008.

Morocco's other Olympic medalists in athletics are Braham Boutayeb (1988, gold, 10,000 meters); Khalid Skah (1992, gold, 10,000 meters); Rachid El-Basir (1992, silver, 1,500 meters); Khalid Boulami (1996, bronze, 5,000 meters); Salah Hissou (1996, bronze, 10,000 meters); Nezha Bidouane (2000, bronze women's 400 meter hurdles); Ali Ezzine (2000, bronze, 3,000 meter **steeplechase**); Brahim Lahlafi (2000, bronze, 5,000 meters); Jaouad Gharib (2008, silver, marathon); and Abdelaati Iguider (2012, bronze, 1,500 meters). Moroccan boxers with Olympic medals are **featherweight** Abdel Hak Achik (1988) his brother **bantamweight** Mohamed Achik (1992) and featherweight Tahar Tamsamani (2000).

Morocco has sent athletes to the **Olympic Winter Games** in 1968, 1984, 1988, 1992, 2010, and 2014. In those six Winter Games, Morocco has entered 24 athletes (21 men, three women) and competed in two sports—**Alpine skiing** (18 men, three women) and **cross-country skiing** (three men). Their best result was in 1984 when Ahmad Ouchit was 38th of 101 in the men's **slalom**. In 2014, Adam Lamhamedi finished a respectable 47th of 107 in the men's **giant slalom** race.

MORROW, BOBBY JOE (USA–ATH). B. 15 October 1935, Harlingen, Texas, **United States**. Bobby Joe Morrow was the winner of gold medals in the 100 meters, 200 meters, and the 4x100 meter **relay** at the 1956 **Olympic Games**. In winning the 200 meters, he became the first man to set an official world record for this distance at the Olympic Games. The six-foot, one-inch (186 cm), 165 lb (75 kg) athlete also equaled the world record for 100 meters three times during the Olympic year, equaled the world 100 yards record in 1957, and was a member of six world record-breaking teams in the **sprint relays** (4x100 and 4x200, or the Imperial equivalents). Morrow won four Amateur Athletic Union titles between 1955 and 1958, but he failed to make the 1960 U.S. Olympic team.

MOSES, EDWIN CORLEY (USA–ATH). B. 31 August 1955, Dayton, Ohio, **United States**. Edwin Moses dominated the 400 meter **hurdles** as few athletes have ever dominated an event. He won the gold **Olympic medal** in

1976 and 1984, and only the American **boycott** of the Moscow Olympics in 1980 prevented him from winning a certain third gold medal. In 1988, the six-foot, one-inch (186 cm), 159 lb (72 kg) Moses competed again, but he was past his prime and only won a bronze medal. Moses set the first of his four world records in the event in the 1976 Olympic final, and at one stage of his career, he won 122 successive races, including the first World Championships in 1983. Moses took the **Olympic Oath** on behalf of the competitors at the opening ceremony of the 1984 **Olympic Games**. He was also briefly a member of the U.S. World Cup **bobsled** team in 1990–1991, although he never competed in the **Olympic Winter Games** in that event.

MOTORBOATING. Motorboating was contested at the **Olympic Games** only in 1908. The competitions could hardly be called successful, with only one competitor finishing in each of the three events. In that one Olympic competition, 12 men and one **woman** from **Great Britain** and one man from **France** took part. Until recently, the *Olympic Charter* precluded sports depending on mechanical propulsion from appearing on the **Olympic Program**, preventing a return of motorboating, or powerboating, to the Olympic fold. Although this clause has now been removed, environmental considerations are part of the evaluation criteria of new sports, making a return unlikely. The Union Internationale Motonautique (UIM) does have **International Olympic Committee** recognition. Founded in 1922, the UIM currently (as of 2014) has 56 members.

MOTORCYCLING. At the 1900 Exhibition, two motorcycling events were held that are considered Olympic by some historians. One was a race from Paris to Toulouse and back, while the other was a reliability competition, with prizes awarded to the manufacturers of the motorcycles. No motorcycling events have been held since, and it is highly unlikely that motorcycling will be on the **Olympic Program** at any time in the foreseeable future. Although the *Olympic Charter* no longer forbids motorized sports from appearing on the Olympic Program, potential Olympic sports are also evaluated on the basis of environmental impact, which would negatively influence a choice for motorcycling. The **International Olympic Committee** recognized the Fédération Internationale de Motocyclisme (FIM) during the Sydney 2000 Games. Founded in 1904, the FIM currently (as of 2014) has 110 members.

MOUNTAINBIKE. A mountainbike is a type of bicycle designed for off-road **cycling**. A **cross-country** mountainbike race over rugged terrain of approximately 20 miles (35 km) was added to the Olympic cycling program in 1996, and a men's and **women**'s race has been contested in each **Olympic**

Games since. Julien Absalon of **France** (2004, 2008) is the only multiple gold medalist in the men's race. Paola Pezzo of **Italy** won the women's race twice (1996, 2000), while Sabine Spitz of **Germany** is the only three-time medalist (gold 2008, silver 2012, bronze 2004) in the women's event.

MOZAMBIQUE (MOZ). Since making its Olympic debut in 1980, the southeast African nation of Mozambique has competed at each of the subsequent **Olympic Games**. Officially named the Republic of Mozambique, it has not yet competed at the **Olympic Winter Games**.

In nine Summer Games, Mozambique has entered 47 athletes (35 men, 12 **women**) but participated in only four sports: **athletics** (17 men, six women), **boxing** (four men), **judo** (two men), and **swimming** (12 men, six women).

The only Mozambican **Olympic medal** winner has been the female middle-distance running phenomenon Maria Mutola, who won a bronze in the women's 800 meters in 1996 and succeeded to the gold medal in that event in 2000. She competed in six Olympic Games from 1988, at age 15, to 2008, at age 35 and in the 800 meters was fourth in 2004 and fifth in 1992 and 2008. She was also ninth in the 1,500 meters in 1992. Other notable Olympic results for Mozambique include **bantamweight** boxer Albert Machaze, who won his first bout in 1988 and finished tied for ninth, and swimmers Chakyl Camal, 38th of 58 in 2012 in the 50 meter **freestyle**, and Jessica Vieira, 45th of 74 in 2012 in the women's 50 meter freestyle.

MUCH WENLOCK OLYMPIAN GAMES. The Much Wenlock Olympian Games were one of the various **attempts at revival** of the **Ancient Olympic Games** that preceded **Pierre de Coubertin**'s successful attempt. Much Wenlock is a small town in Shropshire, **England**, 12 miles south of Shrewsbury and 40 miles west of Birmingham. On 22 October 1850, these Games were held for the first time. They were the brainchild of British sports enthusiast **William Penny Brookes** (1809–1895).

The Games were only national in nature, and the events were those of a British medieval country fair, enriched by modern athletic sports **disciplines**. The original events in 1850 consisted of **cricket**, 14-per-side **football**, **high** and **long jumping**, quoits, a hopping race, and a running race. However, several athletic events were added in the next few editions. In 1855, a popular event was the blindfolded wheelbarrow race, and in 1858 a pig race was contested in which the pig "led its pursuers over hedge and ditch right into the town where it took ground in the cellar of Mr. Blakeway's house; and where it was captured by a man called William Hill." The most popular event was tilting-at-the-ring, which was first held in 1858. The competitors, compulsorily dressed in medieval costume, rode down a straight course and used their lances to spear a small ring, suspended from a bar over the course.

The Much Wenlock Olympian Games, altogether 45 in number up to 1895, achieved their high point in the 1860s and 1870s. In those years, representatives of the **German Gymnastic** Society (which was based in London) competed regularly. In 1859, Brookes contacted the Greeks and donated a £10 prize to the **Zappas Olympic Games**. The winner of the long footrace at the 1859 Zappas Olympics, Petros Velissariou, was made an honorary member of the Much Wenlock Olympian Society.

In 1860, 1861, 1862, and 1864, Brookes also organized the Shropshire Olympian Games on a regional level in, respectively, Much Wenlock, Wellington, Much Wenlock, and Shrewsbury. These were followed by the Games organized by the National Olympic Association: 1866 (London), 1867 (Birmingham), 1868 (Wellington), 1874 (Much Wenlock), 1877 (Shrewsbury), and 1883 (Hadley).

The Much Wenlock Olympian Games were held more sporadically after Brookes's death in 1895, but they are actually still held today, sponsored by the Much Wenlock Olympian Society, which celebrated the 100th Much Wenlock Olympian Games in 1986. The Much Wenlock Olympian Games are important in the history of Olympic revivals because of their influence on **Pierre de Coubertin**. Coubertin knew of Brookes's efforts and visited the Much Wenlock Olympian Games as a guest of honor in October 1890. In 1891, he donated a gold medal that was given to the winner of tilting-at-the-ring. However, as early as 1881, William Penny Brookes was the first person to propose that an International Olympic Festival be staged in Athens.

In 2014, the Much Wenlock Olympian Games were held from 5–21 July and the program contained these events: **archery**, **athletics**, **badminton**, **bowls**, clay pigeon **shooting**, **equestrian**, **fencing**, 5-per-side football, **gliding**, **golf**, **field hockey**, junior **biathlon** (running and swimming), kwik cricket, long distance walk, **marathon** and half-marathon, **netball**, seven-mile **road race**, **tennis**, **triathlon**, and **volleyball**. Many of the events use modified arenas, and youth participation is highly encouraged. The long distance walk, for example, is not a race but a physical challenge to complete a 50-mile walk in 24 hours.

MULTIEVENTS (BIATHLON, DECATHLON, HEPTATHLON, PENTATHLON, TRIATHLON). Since the late 19th century, there have always been multievents contested in track and field **athletics** in an attempt to determine the greatest **all-around** athlete. The first of these to be held at the Olympics was the all-around event, which was contested at the 1904 **Olympic**

Games. In 1906, a **pentathlon** event similar to the ancient pentathlon was contested at Athens. In 1912, men began competing in the five-event pentathlon and the 10-event **decathlon**. The pentathlon was abandoned after 1924, but the decathlon remains on the program. It is considered the truest test of all-around athletic ability. A portion of the track and field athletics program, it consists of 10 events conducted over two days: day one, 100 meters, **long jump**, **shot put**, **high jump**, and 400 meters; day two, 110 meter **hurdles**, **discus throw**, **pole vault**, **javelin throw**, and 1,500 meters. The winner of the Olympic decathlon is usually given the title "World's Greatest Athlete." Two decathletes have won the Olympic decathlon twice: **Bob Mathias** (USA) in 1948 and 1952 and **Daley Thompson** (GBR) in 1980 and 1984.

Women first began competing in athletics multievents in 1964, with the addition of a pentathlon to the program, consisting of the 200 meters, high jump, long jump, shot put, and originally the 80 meter hurdles. The 200 meters was later replaced by the 800 meters, and the hurdle event was lengthened to 100 meters. In 1984, the women's multievent was changed to a seven-event **heptathlon** over two days, consisting of the following events: day one, 100 meter hurdles, high jump, shot put, and 200 meters; day two, long jump, javelin throw, and 800 meters. Following the addition of women's pole vault, the International Association of Athletics Federations has recognized the women's decathlon, but there are no current plans to replace the heptathlon. The best-known female heptathlete has been Jackie Joyner-Kersee (USA), who won the silver medal in 1984 and the gold medal in 1988 and 1992 and was the first woman to better 7,000 points. *See also* BIATHLON; MODERN PENTATHLON; NORDIC COMBINED; TRIATHLON.

MULTIHULL. Multihull is a type of sailboat that was used in Olympic **sailing** competition from 1976 to 2008. The primary model used was a catamaran known as the Tornado. It was a two-person boat and the event was open to crews of both men and **women**. In the nine **Olympic Games** in which multihull sailing was contested, it was won by **Spain**, **Austria**, and **France** twice each. **Australia**, which never won the gold medal, won silver medals three times and bronze twice to lead all nations with five total medals.

MUSIOL, BOGDAN (GDR/GER–BOB). B. 25 July 1957, Świętochłowice, Śląskie, **Poland**. A former **shot putter**, Bogdan Musiol was the winner of an Olympic gold medal with the **German Democratic Republic** four-man **bobsled** team in 1980, when he also won a bronze medal in the two-man team. The six-foot tall (183 cm), 190 lb (86 kg) Musiol went on to win silver medals in 1984 and 1988 at both the two-man and four-man races, and in 1992, he won his silver medal in the two-man race. His seven **Olympic medals** are more than any other bobsledder. In his unusually long bobsledding career (he also competed in the 1994 **Olympic Winter Games**), Musiol won three world titles. In 1978, he was part of the victorious four-man crew, and he was the brakeman for **Wolfgang Hoppe** in 1989 (two-man) and 1991 (four-man), the same pilot he raced with in the 1988 and 1992 Games.

MYANMAR (MYA). After gaining independence as Burma in 1948, the Southeast Asian country made its Olympic debut at the London Games that same year. It has competed at all Olympic Games since then, with the exception of the 1976 Games. The country changed its name to Myanmar in May 1989, with the official name being the Republic of the Union of Myanmar, and has used that name at the Olympics since the 1992 Games. Myanmar has never attended the **Olympic Winter Games**. In 16 Summer Games, Myanmar/Burma has entered 79 athletes (63 men, 16 **women**) and participated in 11 sports: **archery** (one man, two women), **athletics** (12 men, six women), **boxing** (17 men), **canoeing** (one man), **football** (13 men), **judo** (two women), **rowing** (one woman), **sailing** (three men), **shooting** (four men), **swimming** (two men, one woman), and **weightlifting** (10 men, four women).

Myanmar has yet to win a medal but came close in 2000, when Win Kay Thi finished fourth in the women's 48 kg (**flyweight**) weightlifting class. Many of the country's other top results also were in weightlifting, with fifth place results by Gyi Aung Maung (1972 men's flyweight) and Win Swe Swe (women's 2000 **featherweight**), sixth place by Khin Moe Nwe (women's 2000 **lightweight**), seventh place by Tun Maung Kywe (1960 men's featherweight), and eighth place by Nil Tun Maung (1956 lightweight). There have also been five Burmese boxers who won their first bout, with 1964 featherweight Tin Tun and 1960 **bantamweight** Thein Myint each winning their first two bouts and finishing tied for fifth place. A weightlifter from what is now Myanmar, U Zaw Weik, competed for **India** in the 1936 **Olympic Games**. In 1972, the Burma football team qualified for the Olympic tournament and finished in a tie for ninth place of the 16 teams. **Marathon** runners Thin Sumbwegam (35th of 68 in 1964 and 18th of 75 in 1968) and Myitung Naw (26th of 46 in 1956, 27th of 69 in 1960) also had commendable results.

N

NABER, JOHN PHILLIPS (USA–SWI). B. 20 January 1956, Evanston, Illinois, **United States**. At the 1976 Games, John Naber won four **swimming** gold medals, each in world record time, and his records in the 100 and 200 meter **backstroke** remained unbeaten for seven years. He also won gold in the 4x100 meter **freestyle relay** and the **medley** relay and won a silver in the 200 meter freestyle. Perhaps the greatest of these performances was in the 200 meter backstroke, when the six-foot, five-inch (198 cm), 194 lb (88 kg) Naber became the first man to break two minutes for the distance. After winning three gold medals at the 1977 **Pan American Games**, he retired from international competition.

NADI, NEDO (ITA–FEN). B. 9 June 1894, Livorno, **Italy**. D. 29 January 1940, Portofino, Genova, Italy. Nedo Nadi was the most versatile **fencer** in

Nedo Nadi of Italy, winner of five gold medals in fencing at the 1920 Olympic Games. Courtesy of Erich Kamper

history, who uniquely won an Olympic title with each of the three weapons at the same Games. In 1912, the six-foot, two-inch (188 cm) Nadi won the individual **foil** title and then, in 1920, he produced one of the greatest of all Olympic performances. He won the individual foil and **sabre** titles and led the Italians to victory in all three team events. His brother Aldo also won a gold medal in each of the three team events. After the 1920 Olympics, Nedo Nadi taught as a professional in South America, but upon his return to Italy, he was reinstated as an amateur and served as president of the Italian Fencing Federation.

NAMIBIA (NAM). Namibia's **National Olympic Committee** was recognized by the **International Olympic Committee** (IOC) at its summer session in 1991. The country, officially known as the Republic of Namibia but once known as German South-West Africa and located in that part of the continent, has competed at each **Olympic Games** since 1992. In that year, Namibian **sprinter** Frank Fredericks won silver medals in both the 100 and 200 meter races. He repeated in those events in 1996 and has earned all four of Namibia's **Olympic medals**. In 2004, he became the nation's first **IOC member**. Namibia has not yet competed at the **Olympic Winter Games**. In six Summer Games, Namibia has entered 34 athletes (26 men, eight **women**) and has participated in **athletics** (eight men, five women), **boxing** (10 men), **cycling** (four men), **gymnastics** (one woman), **shooting** (one man, one woman), **swimming** (one man, one woman), and **wrestling** (two men). In addition to Fredericks's successes, Namibians have done well in other events: **marathon**er Helalia Johannes finished 12th of 118 entrants in the 2012 women's marathon, with teammate Beata Naigambo in 38th place that year. Naigambo had been 28th of 81 entrants in the previous Olympic marathon. Stephen Louw was 13th of 38 in the 2008 men's **long jump**. Also in 2008, Erik Hoffmann was 21st of 143 entrants in the 245.4 km cycling **road race**, and after more than six hours of racing was less than two and one-half minutes behind the winner. In 1996, Friedhelm Sack had a notable performance in shooting when he finished in eighth place of 50 contestants in the men's **air pistol** 10 meters event.

NATIONAL GOVERNING BODIES (NGB). Each sport on the **Olympic Program** is governed by an **International Federation** (IF). Each nation competing at the **Olympic Games** must have a properly formed **National Olympic Committee** (NOC). In each nation, the various sports have NGBs, which are responsible for the administration of that sport in that nation. The NGBs are invariably members of both their own NOC and the respective IF. As an example, the governing body of track and field **athletics** in the **United**

States is the USA Track and Field, which is a member of the U.S. Olympic Committee and the International Amateur Athletic Federation.

NATIONAL OLYMPIAN ASSOCIATIONS. *See* WORLD OLYMPIANS ASSOCIATION.

NATIONAL OLYMPIC ACADEMIES. *See* INTERNATIONAL OLYMPIC ACADEMY.

NATIONAL OLYMPIC COMMITTEES (NOC). NOCs are the bodies responsible for the **Olympic Movement** in their respective countries. The *Olympic Charter* states that their mission "is to develop, promote and protect the Olympic Movement in their respective countries, in accordance with the *Olympic Charter*."

The *Olympic Charter* also stipulates that *country* means "an independent State recognized by the international community." This rule presently prevents **Greenland** (a dependency of **Denmark**) and **Kosovo** (not globally recognized) from having NOCs. This rule only came into force in the mid-1990s, and several nonindependent nations formed NOCs and were recognized by the **International Olympic Committee** (IOC) before that time. For example, in the early 20th century, the **Bohemian** NOC was recognized, despite forming part of the Austro-Hungarian empire. More recently, the IOC recognized NOCs from various overseas dependencies and territories, such as **Puerto Rico**, which is a Commonwealth of the **United States**. For the most part, however, NOCs represent independent nations. They are recognized by the IOC at the **IOC Sessions**. There are currently (as of 2014) 204 National Olympic Committees recognized by the IOC.

NOCs are very important to the athletes competing in the **Olympic Games**. Specifically, athletes may not enter the Olympic Games independently or as individual competitors, but may only represent an NOC, and they must be entered by their NOC. In addition, NOCs often provide financial assistance for training and allow athletes to compete internationally.

NOCs are supposed to be autonomous and resist political pressures and influences of any kind, but in the past, that principle has been recognized more in word than deed. Notably, prior to the fall of the **Soviet** bloc, all the Eastern European Communist nations had NOCs that basically were puppets of their governments. And in 1980, the U.S. Olympic Committee was coerced into **boycotting** the Moscow Olympics (against its wishes) by the U.S. president and government to protest the Soviet invasion of **Afghanistan**. More recently, the **Iraqi** NOC was headed by Uday Hussein, the son of dictator Saddam Hussein.

NAURU (NRU). Nauru's **National Olympic Committee** (NOC) was recognized by the **International Olympic Committee** at the 1994 **Olympic Congress** after having been given provisional recognition earlier in 1994. Nauru first competed in the **Olympic Games** in 1996, and has since competed in the four subsequent Summer Games with a total of six different men and two **women**. Itte Detenamo competed for Nauru in the 2004, 2008, and 2012 Games and his cousin Quincy Detenamo represented Nauru in 1996. The South Pacific island's first six representatives competed in **weightlifting**, but in 2012, they had a man compete in **judo**. Their top competitor, Yukio Peter, placed eighth of 17 entrants in the 2004 men's **lightweight** weightlifting event. Nauru and **Bhutan** are the only two nations that have never competed in **athletics**, the most popular Olympic sport. The tiny nation, officially known as the Republic of Nauru, is the least-populated sovereign state (with the exception of **Vatican City**) with an estimated population of 9,378 in 2011. Its best-known Olympian is Marcus Stephen. He represented Western Samoa at the 1992 Games due to the absence of a Nauruan NOC, which he later helped found. In 1996 and again in 2000, he represented Nauru in weightlifting and had a best result of 11th of 21 entrants in the **featherweight** class. In 2007, he was elected president of the tiny island nation and served through November 2011. Nauru has not competed at the **Olympic Winter Games**.

NECKERMANN, JOSEF CARL PETER (FRG–EQU). B. 5 June 1912, Würzburg, Bayern, **Germany**. D. 13 January 1992, Dreieich, Hessen, Germany. Josef Neckermann was an extremely wealthy man, who earned his money from his mail order and department store businesses. His wealth allowed him and his family to pursue their passion for **equestrian** sports. The six-foot tall (183 cm), 143 lb (65 kg) Neckermann competed in **dressage** at four **Olympic Games** (1960–1972) and won a medal on each occasion. To his gold medals in the team event in 1964 and 1968, he added two silver and two bronze medals. His daughter Eva-Maria Pracht won a team bronze representing **Canada** in 1988, and her daughter Martina also represented Canada at the 1992 Olympics.

NEHMER, MEINHARD (GDR–BOB). B. 13 January 1941, Bobolin, Zachodniopomorskie, **Poland**. Meinhard Nehmer only took up **bobsledding** after retiring from athletics, in which he was a nationally ranked **javelin thrower**. Although well past the age of 30, the six-foot tall (183 cm), 209 lb (95 kg) athlete formed a formidable partnership with **Bernhard Germeshausen**, and they won the 1976 Olympic two-man race and were both members of the winning four-man crew in 1976 and 1980. Nehmer also won a bronze

Olympic medal in the two-man race in 1980 with **Bogdan Musiol**, and he was coach of the **United States** bobsled team for the 1992 **Olympic Games**.

NEMEAN GAMES. The Nemean Games were one of the four great Panhellenic sporting festivals, along with the **Olympic Games**, **Isthmian Games**, and **Pythian Games**. They were held biennially, with the first known Nemean Games being contested in 573 B.C. The Nemean Games were held in honor of Zeus. They were held in July in the Nemean sanctuary in Argolis. The sanctuary was near the site of the Peloponnesus where Hercules killed and skinned the Nemean lion, the first of his famed 12 labors. Winners in the Nemean Games were crowned with a wreath of fresh wild celery. *See also* ANCIENT OLYMPIC GAMES.

NEMOV, ALEKSEY YURYEVICH (RUS–GYM). B. 28 May 1976, Barashevo, Ulyanovsk, **Russia**, USSR. Aleksey Nemov has won 12 Olympic medals in **gymnastics**, the most of any gymnast since the breakup of the Soviet juggernaut gymnastic teams of the 1960s and 1970s. He starred at the 1996 and 2000 **Olympic Games**, unusually winning two gold, one silver, and three bronze medals both times. The five-foot, eight-inch (174 cm), 165 lb (75 kg) gymnast won three individual Olympic gold medals: in 1996 for the **horse vault** and in 2000 for **all-around** and the **horizontal bar**. Nemov also competed in 2004, but because he was well past his prime, his top performance was a fifth on the horizontal bar, his best event. Nemov won 11 medals at the World Championships between 1993 and 2002, including five individual gold medals. He also won eight medals at the European Championships, including four gold medals, three in individual events.

NEPAL (NEP). The Nepalese **National Olympic Committee** was founded in 1962 and recognized by the **International Olympic Committee** in the following year. Nepal first competed at the **Olympic Games** in 1964; since then it has missed only the 1968 Olympics. In 12 Summer Games, Nepal has entered 70 athletes (50 men, 20 **women**) and has competed in seven sports: **athletics** (21 men, seven women), **boxing** (14 men), **judo** (two men, one woman), **shooting** (one man, six woman), **swimming** (four men, five women), **taekwondo** (one man, one woman), and **weightlifting** (seven men).

Nepal has yet to win an Olympic sports medal, but at least one Sherpa, Tejbir Bura, was part of the British expedition that was awarded an Olympic gold medal in 1924 for its **Alpinism** efforts. In 1988, Bidhan Lama also won third place in the taekwondo **demonstration sport**, the best sporting performance by a Nepalese at the Olympic Games. Among Nepal's best Olympic results are men's **marathon** runner Baikuntha Manandhar, who was 50th of 67 entrants in 1976, 37th of 74 in 1980, 46th of 107 in 1984, and 54th of 118 in 1988; Arjun Pandit, 63rd of 107 in 1984; Arjun Kumar Basner, 45th of 95 in the 2008 men's marathon; Jagadish Pradhan, 14th of 20 entrants in the 1984 **bantamweight** weightlifting; and boxers Bishnu Bahadur Singh (1988 **flyweight**) and Om Prasad Pun (1964 **light-welterweight**) who each won one bout before being eliminated from the tournament.

This south Asian Himalayan country, officially known as the Federal Democratic Republic of Nepal, first competed at the **Olympic Winter Games** in 2002 at Salt Lake City and has reappeared in each of the following three Winter Games. **Cross-country skier** Jay Khadka entered the men's **sprint** and men's **pursuit** in 2002, and Dachhiri Sherpa entered the men's 15 k race in 2006, 2010, and 2014. Sherpa's finish of 86th of 92 entrants in 2014 was their best result.

NETBALL. Netball has never been contested at the **Olympic Games**, even as a **demonstration sport**. However, its governing body, the International Netball Federation, is recognized by the **International Olympic Committee**. Founded in 1960, it currently (as of 2014) has 51 full member and 22 associate member nations. It is not very likely that netball will be held at the Olympics, as it is primarily played by **women**.

NETHERLANDS, THE (NED, formerly HOL). The Netherlands, located in north central Europe and often erroneously referred to as Holland, is a constituent country of the Kingdom of the Netherlands. Its first Olympics activity was in 1900 when they sent 35 athletes to the Paris Olympics. After missing the 1904 St. Louis Olympics, the Netherlands has never missed another **Olympic Games**, although in 1956 it competed only at the **Equestrian** Games in Stockholm, **boycotting** the 1956 Olympic Games in protest against the **Soviet** invasion of **Hungary**.

In 25 Summer Games, the Netherlands has entered 2,582 athletes (1,897 men, 685 **women**) and competed in 32 sports plus the **art competitions**. They have had the most entrants in **rowing** (244 men, 79 women), **athletics** (164 men, 95 women), **hockey** (173 men, 79 women), **swimming** (103 men, 136 women), **cycling** (194 men, 27 women), and **water polo** (121 men, 23 women). It has won 277 medals at the Summer Games (80 gold, 88 silver, 109 bronze) and has won them in 21 different sports plus the art competitions. The most medals at the Summer Games for the Netherlands belongs to equestrian **Anky van Grunsven**. She has competed in seven Olympic Games from 1988 to 2012 and won her ninth medal at the London Games.

She has won three gold, five silver, and one bronze, all in individual and team **dressage**. Her total of nine medals in equestrianism leads all other competitors in that sport, male or female. Swimmer **Inge de Bruijn** has won eight medals (four gold, two silver, two bronze) in 2000 and 2004. Pieter van den Hoogenband also won seven medals in swimming at those two Olympic Games. Cyclist **Leontien Zijlaard-van Moorsel** won six medals with four gold in 2000 and 2004 and has won more total medals and more gold medals than any other female cyclist. **Fanny Blankers-Koen** won four gold medals in women's athletics in 1948 and is one of four Dutch athletes with four gold medals in summer sports. She is the only one to win them in just one year. The Netherlands has always had strong teams in field hockey and have won nine medals in men's hockey and seven in women's hockey. They have also finished fourth four times in men's hockey. Teun de Nooijer has played on their team from 1996 to 2012 and has won four medals. He is one of only four men's hockey players with four Olympic medals. Women's hockey was only added in 1980, and the Dutch women have medaled in seven of the eight tournaments in which they participated. One other Dutch athlete in summer sports worthy of mention is the **heavyweight** *judoka* **Anton Geesink**. In one of the most surprising upsets in Olympic history, he won the very first **judo** tournament in 1964. The fact that it was held in Tokyo and he defeated the best **Japanese** entrant added to the upset. He later served as a member of the International Olympic Committee.

The Netherlands first appeared at the **Olympic Winter Games** in 1928, then missed the 1932 Lake Placid Games, but has appeared continuously since. In the Summer Games, the Netherlands has had a variety of successes in various sports, but has never dominated any sport. In the Winter Olympics, however, the Netherlands has always been one of the very top nations in **speed skating**.

In 20 Winter Games, the Netherlands has entered 214 athletes (127 men, 87 women) and competed in eight sports, with most of their entrants (73 men, 53 women) in speed skating. They have won 110 medals (37 gold, 38 silver, 35 bronze) in winter sports with nearly all of them (105) coming in speed skating. There have been eight Dutch speed skaters who have each earned four or more Olympic medals. Irene Wust, with four gold, three silver, and one bronze from 2006 to 2014, leads them. Sven Kramer during those same years has won seven medals (three gold, two silver, two bronze).

The Netherlands hosted the Games of the IXth **Olympiad** in Amsterdam in 1928, and Amsterdam also made unsuccessful bids for the Games of 1916, 1920, 1924, 1952, and 1992. *See also* BIJKERK, ANTHONY THEODOOR; RUSKA, WILLEM; SCHENK, ADRIE.

NETHERLANDS ANTILLES (AHO). Curaçao, the chief island of the Netherlands Antilles, formed a **National Olympic Committee** (NOC) in 1931 with a view to participating in the 1932 Los Angeles Olympics. Although it was recognized by the **International Olympic Committee** (IOC) in 1931, representation at the 1932 Olympics did not materialize, and there was little Olympic activity in the nation for many years. IOC recognition was reconfirmed in 1950 as the Netherlands Antilles, and the nation first competed at the Olympics in 1952, represented by a football team that finished tied for ninth place among the 25 teams in the tournament solely by virtue of receiving a **bye** in the opening round. The nation did not travel to Melbourne in 1956 and **boycotted** the 1980 Olympics, but has otherwise competed at every **Olympic Games** since 1952.

The Netherlands Antilles was an autonomous Caribbean country within the Kingdom of the **Netherlands** until 2010 and consisted of the islands of **Aruba**, Bonaire, Curaçao, Sint Maarten, Saba, and Sint Eustatius. Aruba became an independent country in 1986 and on 10 October 2010, the Kingdom of the Netherlands dissolved the Netherlands Antilles. The island of Curaçao attempted to create an NOC, but it had not yet been recognized by the IOC and consequently three athletes from Curaçao competed as **independent Olympic athletes** at the 2012 Olympic Games.

During its existence, the Netherlands Antilles competed in 13 Summer Games, entered 52 athletes (42 men, 10 **women**), and participated in 11 sports: **athletics** (eight men, three women), **equestrian** (one man), **fencing** (one man, two women), **football** (11 men), **judo** (three men), **sailing** (four men, one woman), **shooting** (three men, one woman), **swimming** (four men, one woman), **synchronized swimming** (two women), **triathlon** (one man), and **weightlifting** (seven men). Beto Adriana competed in both weightlifting (1960) and shooting (1972).

The country has won one **Olympic medal**, a silver by Jan Boersma in **windsurfing** in 1988. Twenty years later, Churandy Martina appeared to have won a second silver medal in the men's 200 meters behind **Usain Bolt**, but lost it after a late **disqualification**. That year the luckless Martina also competed in the 100 meter dash and finished in fourth place, 0.02 seconds behind the bronze medalist. Other notable Olympic results for Antillean athletes include 1988 swimmer Hilton Woods finishing 16th in both the 50 meter and 100 meter **freestyle** races with 71 entrants in the 50 meter race and 77 in the 100 meter race; **bantamweight** weightlifter Hector Curiel finishing 11th of 22 in 1960; **middle-heavyweight** weightlifter Jose Flores finishing 13th of 20 in 1960; and rider Eddy Stibbe finishing 13th of 38 in the 2000 three-day equestrian event.

The Netherlands Antilles made its **Olympic Winter Games** debut in 1988 at Calgary, competing in the two-man **bobsledding** where they finished 29th of the 41 entrants—a commendable accomplishment for a non-northern country. Bobsledder Bart Carpentier Alting also competed in the **luge** and finished 36th of 38. In 1992, they again competed in two-man bobsledding and were 37th of 46.

NEW HEBRIDES. *See* VANUATU.

NEW ZEALAND (NZL). The southwestern Pacific Ocean island country of New Zealand was first represented at the 1908 **Olympic Games**. In that year, it formed a combined team with **Australia** as **Australasia**. One New Zealand competitor, Harry Kerr, a **race walker**, won a bronze medal in the 3,500 meter walk. In 1912, three New Zealanders competed with Australasia, with Malcolm Champion winning a **swimming** gold with the **freestyle relay** team. Finally, in 1920 at Antwerp, New Zealand took part in the Olympic Games as a separate nation, and it has never missed an Olympic Games since. New Zealand competed at its first **Olympic Winter Games** in 1952 at Oslo. It missed the Winter Games of 1956 and 1964, but has competed at all the others since then.

In 23 Summer Games, New Zealand has entered 1,112 athletes (760 men, 352 **women**) and competed in 30 sports, with the largest contingents in **hockey** (109 men, 72 women), **rowing** (128 men, 120 women), **athletics** (89 men, 43 women), **cycling** (86 men, 24 women), **swimming** (50 men, 51 women), and **sailing** (77 men, 19 women). They have won 99 medals in the Summer Games—42 gold, 18 silver, 39 bronze, with medals coming in 12 different sports. New Zealand has had its greatest success in track and field, with several of its middle-distance runners being Olympic champions. Its top Olympian, however, is Mark Todd, who won six medals (two gold, one silver, three bronze) in **equestrian** competition from 1984 to 2012. **Canoeists Ian Ferguson** (four gold, one silver, 1976–1992) and Paul McDonald (three gold, one silver, one bronze, 1984–1992) have each won five medals. Blyth Tait won four medals (one gold, one silver, two bronze) in equestrian events from 1992 to 2004.

Peter Snell is probably the best known of New Zealand's Olympians. He won three gold medals in 1960 and 1964 in the 800 and 1,500 meter track races. He later earned a doctorate in exercise physiology from Washington State University in the **United States** and in 2009 was created Knight of the New Zealand Order of Merit and is now known as Sir Peter Snell. Other New Zealanders with three Olympic medals are **windsurfer** Barbara Kendall (one medal of each color, 1992–2008), swimmer Danyon Loader (two gold, one silver, 1992–1996), equestrian Andrew Nicholson (one silver, two bronze, 1984–2012), and rower Simon Dickie (two gold, one bronze, 1968–1976). New Zealand also has 22 other Olympians who each won two medals, with 10 of the 22 winning them in rowing and five others in cycling.

In 15 Winter Games, New Zealand has entered 90 athletes (55 men, 35 women) and competed in 11 sports, with **Alpine skiing** being the most popular (24 men, 15 women). In 1992, Annelise Coberger won New Zealand's sole Winter **Olympic medal**, a silver medal in the women's **slalom**, the first Winter medal for a Southern Hemisphere country. *See also* DOCHERTY, BEVAN JOHN.

NEWFOUNDLAND (NFL). Before being incorporated as part of **Canada** in 1949, the North Atlantic island of Newfoundland enjoyed a similar autonomous status as Canada, and as such was entitled to send athletes to the **Olympic Games**. A **National Olympic Committee** was even established in the 1920s, but due to financial troubles, a Newfoundland delegation to the Olympics never materialized. However, in 1904, one Newfoundland citizen, Bob Fowler (who lived in Boston), competed in the Olympic **marathon** and was one of 18 who did not finish the race that 32 runners started. Fowler later became a **United States** citizen and was part of the official American delegation for the 1906 Olympics, but could still be considered this former nation's representative in 1904. Other Newfoundlanders have usually represented Canada, even before the union of 1949.

NICARAGUA (NCA). Although the **International Olympic Committee** recognized its **National Olympic Committee** in 1959, Nicaragua, a **Central American** nation officially known as the Republic of Nicaragua, did not compete at the 1960 or 1964 Olympics, and it was not until 1968 that it first competed at the **Olympic Games**. Apart from **boycotting** the 1988 Olympics in Seoul, Nicaragua's Summer Olympic participation has been continuous since 1968. The country has never competed in the **Olympic Winter Games**.

In 11 Summer Games, Nicaragua has entered 91 athletes (76 men, 15 **women**) and competed in 10 sports: **athletics** (17 men, seven women), **baseball** (20 men), **boxing** (14 men), **cycling** (four men, one woman), **judo** (four men), **shooting** (two men, one woman), **swimming** (six men, four women), **taekwondo** (one man), **weightlifting** (seven men, two women), and **wrestling** (one man).

Nicaragua has yet to win an **Olympic medal**, and its best Olympic performance occurred in 1996, fittingly in the country's national sport, baseball.

The Nicaraguan team made the semifinals and eventually placed fourth. There have been few other noteworthy Olympic results for Nicaraguans. Weightlifter Alvaro Marenco finished 11th in the **flyweight** class in 1992, but there were only 17 entrants in that class. Likewise, Karla Moreno was also 11th in women's flyweight weightlifting in 2008 but again among only 14 competitors. Boxers Mario Romero (1992 **welterweight**) and Osmar Bravo (2012 **light-heavyweight**) each won their first bout and finished tied for ninth place in their class. *Judokas* Ricky Dixon (**half-middleweight**) and Arnulfo Betancourt (**heavyweight**) each finished tied for 13th in their class in 1996. Swimmer Walter Soza was 20th of 39 in the 1996 men's 200 meter individual **medley**. Nicaragua's most famous athlete, World Champion boxer Alexis Argüello, never competed in the Olympics but was his country's flagbearer at the opening ceremony of the Beijing Olympic Games in 2008.

NIEMANN-STIRNEMANN, GUNDA (née KLEEMANN) (GER–SSK). B. 7 September 1966, Sondershausen, Thüringen, **Germany**. Gunda Niemann-Stirnemann has won eight **Olympic medals**, including three golds at the **Olympic Winter Games** of 1992, 1994, and 1998, equaling the marks of fellow German **Karin Kania-Enke**. Primarily a distance **speed skater**, Gunda's golds were for the 3,000 meters in 1992 and 1998 and the 5,000 meters in 1992. She won silver in 1992 in the 1,500 meters, in 1994 in the 5,000 meters, and in 1998 in both the 1,500 and 5,000 meters. She also won bronze in the 1994 1,500 meters. At the World **All-Around** championships, the five-foot, six-inch (170 cm), 143 lb (65 kg) Niemann-Stirnemann won eight championships: 1991–1993 and 1995–1999, breaking Kania-Enke's record of five titles. She also won eight European Championships (1989–1992, 1993–1996, 2001) and 11 distance world titles (1996–2001, in 1,500 meters, 3,000 meters, and 5,000 meters). She won a record 98 World Cup races and claimed seasonal 18 World Cups, in the 1,500 meters and 3,000/5,000 meters. Finally, Gunda Niemann-Stirnemann broke 18 world records throughout her career, including seven each in the 3,000 and 5,000 meters.

NIGER (NIG). Niger (not to be confused with **Nigeria**) is a landlocked West African nation north of Nigeria and officially known as the Republic of Niger. Prior to its independence in 1960, it was part of French West Africa. After recognition by the **International Olympic Committee** early in 1964, Niger made its Olympic debut in Tokyo later that year, represented by one **boxer**. Niger did not take part in the 1976 or 1980 **Olympic Games**, but has competed at all the other Olympics since 1964. It has never competed at the **Olympic Winter Games**. In 11 Summer Games, Niger has entered 36 athletes (28 men, eight **women**) and participated in five sports: **athletics** (11 men, five women), boxing (11 men), **judo** (two men), **rowing** (one man), and **swimming** (three men, three women).

Issaka Dabore is the only Nigerien athlete to win an Olympic medal, which he won in 1972 when he finished third in **light-welterweight** boxing. Other commendable results by Niger Olympians include Dabore's effort in the **welterweight** class in 1964 when he won two bouts and finished tied for fifth place, and in 1968 as a light-welterweight when he won one bout and was tied for ninth place; 1988 men's **marathoners** Abdou Manzo (47th of 118 entrants) and Inni Aboubacar (59th of 118); and *judoka* Zakari Gourouza (2012 **extra-lightweight**) and **bantamweight** boxers Mayaki Seydou (1972) and Moumouni Siuley (1988) who each won their first bout before eliminated from the tournament.

NIGERIA (NGR). Nigeria is a West African nation officially known as the Federal Republic of Nigeria. A Nigerian **National Olympic Committee** was formed in 1951 and recognized by the **International Olympic Committee** in the same year. Nigeria first competed in the **Olympic Games** in 1952. It has since missed only the 1976 Games, owing to the African **boycott**. Nigeria has not yet competed at the **Olympic Winter Games**.

In 15 Summer Games, Nigeria has entered 513 athletes (353 men, 160 **women**) and competed in 14 sports: **athletics** (117 men, 71 women), **badminton** (one man, two women), **basketball** (12 men, 12 women), **boxing** (65 men, one woman), **canoeing** (one man), **football** (96 men, 34 women), **handball** (16 women), **judo** (five men, three women), **swimming** (four men, three women), **table tennis** (10 men, nine women), **taekwondo** (three men, one woman), **tennis** (four men), **weightlifting** (15 men, six women), and **wrestling** (20 men, two women).

Nigerians have won 23 **Olympic medals** (three gold, eight silver, 12 bronze) in athletics (two gold, three silver, eight bronze), boxing (three silver, three bronze), football (one gold, one silver), taekwondo (one bronze), and weightlifting (one silver). Two of their gold medals were won in 1996, when **long jumper** Chioma Ajunwa and the Super Eagles (the Nigerian football team) became Olympic Champions. Their third gold medal was won by the 2000 men's 4x400 relay team in athletics. Four years later, that team also won the bronze medal and so did the men's 4x100 relay team. In 2008, the football team won the silver medal after losing the final match to **Argentina**, 1–0.

In boxing, silver medals were won by **featherweight** Peter Konyegwachie (1984), **heavyweight** David Izonritei (1992), and **super-heavyweight** Richard Igbeneghu (1992), and bronze medals went to **light-middleweight** Nojim Maiyegun (1964), **light-heavyweight** Isaac Ikhouria, and super-heavyweight Duncan Dalnajeneso Danagogo Dokiwari (1996). Chika Chukwumerije won a bronze in men's heavyweight taekwondo in 2008. Ruth Ogbeifo won a silver in women's heavyweight weightlifting in 2000. Most of Nigeria's Olympic medals have been won in athletics—doing especially well in **relays**.

The men's 4x100 relay team won silver in 1992 and bronze in 2004; the 4x400 relay team won bronze in 1984 and 2004 in addition to the gold in 2000; the women's 4x100 relay team won bronze in 1992 and 2008; and their 4x400 relay team won silver in 1996. In 2008, Blessing Okagbare won bronze in the women's **high jump**; Glory Alozie won silver in the 2000 100 meter **hurdles**; Falilat Ogunkoya won bronze in the 1996 400 meters; and Mary Onyali-Omagbemi won bronze in the 1996 200 meters. Dual medalists were Enefiok Udo-Obong, with a gold and bronze in relays, Ogunkoya with a relay silver, and Onyali-Omagbemi with a bronze in a relay in addition to their bronzes in solo events.

NIUE. Niue is a small island nation in the South Pacific with a population of about 1,400. It is classified as a self-governing state in free association with **New Zealand**. Although not a member of the United Nations (UN), it is recognized by the UN and is a member of some UN specialized agencies. Niue does not yet have a **National Olympic Committee**, although it does have a Niue Island Sports **Commonwealth Games** Association and has competed in the Commonwealth Games since 2002.

NOMINATIONS COMMISSION. The Nominations Commission was formed at the 110th **International Olympic Commission (IOC) Session** in 1999 to institute a procedure for electing and reelecting **IOC members**. The commission's charge is to prepare a report on each prospective IOC candidate and present it to the IOC **Executive Board**. Based on these reports, the board presents candidates to the IOC Session, which votes on inclusion of new members.

The Nominations Commission is composed of seven members, three chosen by the IOC **Ethics Commission**, three by the IOC Session, and one by the IOC **Athletes' Commission**. The members serve a four-year term and may be reelected. The current chairman is HRH the Princess Royal of **Great Britain**.

NOMURA, TADAHIRO (JPN–JUD). B. 10 December 1974; Koryo, Nara, **Japan**. Tadahiro Nomura is the only *judoka* to have won three Olympic titles. He even won them consecutively, claiming the **extra-lightweight** (up to 60 kg) title in 1996, 2000, and 2004. This feat is even more remarkable considering that Nomura only managed to win a single World Championship (in 1997), partially due to the tough qualifying contests in Japan. Only five feet, four inches (164 cm) tall, he was also eliminated in national competition for the 2008 Games. His **judo** skills run in the family; his father coached 1984 Olympic champion Shinji Hosokawa, and Tadahiro's uncle, Toyokazu Nomura, was himself an Olympic judo champion in 1972.

NORBERG, ANETTE CHARLOTTE (SWE–CUR). B. 12 November 1966, Härnösand, **Sweden**. Active in the sport since the early 1980s, Anette Norberg is the only **curler** to have skipped two teams to Olympic gold. Her rink claimed the title in 2006 and 2010. Norberg had earlier participated in the **demonstration** competitions of 1988 (as an alternate) and 1992 (fifth). The five-foot, eight-inch (174 cm), 154 lb (70 kg) Norberg has also won nine World Championship medals, including titles in 2005, 2006, and 2011, and has been European Champion seven times. Remarkably, after winning the 2006 Olympic gold, Norberg's rink was invited to partake in a video clip of the Swedish metal band HammerFall.

NORDIC COMBINED. Nordic combined consists of a **cross-country ski** race and **ski jumping**. It was considered the most important Nordic skiing event by the Scandinavians and has been held at the **Olympic Winter Games** since the start in 1924, with participation limited to men. In 22 Games, 605 men from 31 countries have participated. **Norway** has been most successful in this sport, winning 13 of the 34 titles through 2014. Three Olympians have each won three gold medals in Nordic combined: **Felix Gottwald** (AUT), **Samppa Lajunen** (FIN), and Ulrich Wehling (GDR). Gottwald competed in five Winter Games from 1994 to 2010 and won three gold, one silver, and three bronze medals. Lajunen entered five events in 1998 and 2002 and medaled in each one, with three gold and two silver. Wehling won the title three times in a row (1972–1980), at a time when just one combined event was held.

From 1924 to 1984, only one event was held. It consisted of ski jumping from the **normal hill** followed by a cross-country ski race of 18 km from 1924 to 1952. In 1956, the race was shortened to 15 km and remained that distance through 2006. In 1988, a team competition was added with three man teams. In 2002, a **sprint** event was added with a single jump from the **large hill** followed by a 7.5 km cross-country ski race. In 2010 and 2014, the two individual events both featured 15 km cross-country skiing, preceded by a ski jump from either the large hill or the normal hill. In the team event, first introduced in 1988, each member takes a jump from the large hill, followed by a 4x5 km relay. In each cross-country race, the ski jumping leader starts first, with the other competitors starting behind him, with the delay determined by the difference in ski jumping points. *See also* GRØTTUMSBRÅTEN, JOHAN HAGBART PEDERSEN; HAUG, THORLEIF.

NORDIC GAMES. The **Olympic Winter Games** formally began in 1924 at Chamonix, France, although they were originally known as the Semaine internationale des sports d'hiver (International Winter Sports Week). Prior to that time, winter sports events had been held during the Summer Games of 1908 (**figure skating**) and 1920 (figure skating and **ice hockey**). But there was an earlier international winter sports festival, the Nordic Games, which began in 1901. Suggested by **Sweden**'s Professor E. Johan Widmark, the initiative to hold Nordic Games was taken in 1899, the first being arranged in 1901. After this inaugural event in Stockholm, Sweden, Nordic Games were held in 1905, 1909, 1913, 1917, 1922, and 1926, always during February, mostly in Stockholm. They began, and were perpetuated, largely through the work of the influential Swedish sports administrator Viktor Gustaf Balck. The Nordic Games were not without political problems, nor were they originally planned as precursors to the Olympic Winter Games, as is often stated. In fact, despite Balck's influential status on the **International Olympic Committee** (IOC), he and other Swedish and Norwegian sporting leaders opposed early suggestions to start Olympic Winter Games. The Olympic Winter Games themselves began only after several heated IOC debates about their merits. The Nordic Games ended after 1926, partly because of the growth of the Olympic Winter Games, partly because of Balck's death and the loss of his leadership, and partly because of the growth of the Fédération Internationale de Ski.

NORDIC SKIING. *See* BIATHLON; CROSS-COUNTRY SKIING; NORDIC COMBINED; SKI JUMPING.

NORELIUS, MARTHA MARIA (later MCALLISTER, WRIGHT, BROWN) (USA–SWI). B. 22 January 1909, Stockholm, **Sweden**. D. 25 September 1955, St. Louis, Missouri, **United States**. Martha Norelius was America's first great female **swimmer**. She was originally coached by her father, Charles Norelius, who swam for Sweden at the 1906 Olympics. She was the top U.S. swimmer from 1924 to 1929, with her fame resting primarily on her Olympic accomplishments. In 1924 at Paris, she won the 400 meter **freestyle** event, and in 1928 she defended that championship, winning the final with a world record of 5:42.8. She is the only **woman** to have defended the 400 meter event at the Olympics. At the 1928 **Olympic Games**, Norelius won her third gold medal when she swam on the 4x100 meter freestyle **relay** team.

Norelius won 11 individual Amateur Athletic Union (AAU) titles between 1925 and 1929, and between 1925 and 1928 she set 19 world records and 30 American records. In 1929, Norelius was suspended by the AAU for giving an exhibition in the same pool as some professionals. She therefore decided to turn professional herself and won the $10,000 Wrigley **Marathon** in Toronto.

While there, she met Joe Wright, one of **Canada**'s greatest **rowers**. Wright had won an Olympic silver medal for Canada in the 1928 double **sculls** and also played professional Canadian football with the Toronto Argonauts of the Canadian Football League. Norelius and Wright were subsequently married on 15 March 1930.

NORMAL HILL. In **ski jumping**, the normal hill is the smaller of two hills used in the sport. It was traditionally measured at 70 meters, while the **large hill** was initially 80 meters and since 1968 has been 90 meters. The method used for hill measurement has been changed in recent years, although the heights of the hills have not. Ski jumping from the normal hill for men has been a sport in every **Olympic Winter Games** since 1924. Birger Ruud won the gold medal in 1932 and 1936 and the silver medal in 1948 and is the only three-time **Olympic medalist** on the normal hill. **Simon Ammann** of **Switzerland** is the only other dual gold medalist. **Women**'s normal hill ski jumping was added to the **Olympic Program** in 2014, and Carina Vogt of **Germany** was the initial winner.

NORTH BORNEO (NBO). Borneo is one of the world's largest islands, bordering the South **China** Sea. The northern section of the island was formerly an independent Crown colony of **Great Britain** called North Borneo. North Borneo competed at the **Olympic Games** one time only, at Melbourne in 1956, when it sent two **triple jumpers**, Gabuh bin Piging and Sium bin Diau, but neither of the two North Bornean athletes advanced past the qualifying round. The northern part of the island is now divided into two states of **Malaysia**: Sabah and Sarawak, and the independent sultanate of **Brunei**. The southern part of the island is ruled by **Indonesia** and is known as Kalimantan.

NORTH KOREA. *See* KOREA, DEMOCRATIC PEOPLE'S REPUBLIC OF.

NORTH YEMEN. *See* YEMEN ARAB REPUBLIC.

NORTHERN RHODESIA. *See* ZAMBIA.

NORWAY (NOR). Norway, a northern European nation located on the Scandinavian peninsula and officially known as the Kingdom of Norway, competed at the Olympics of 1900 and has since missed only the 1980 **Olympic Games**, which it **boycotted**.

In 26 Summer Games, Norway has entered 1,371 athletes (1,132 men, 239 **women**) and competed in 25 sports plus the **art competitions**. It has had the most participants in **athletics** (172 men, 28 women), **sailing** (180 men, 16 women), **gymnastics** (112 men, 14 women), **rowing** (116 men, seven women), **shooting** (111 men, eight women), and **football** (66 men, 44 women). Norway has won 154 medals (59 gold, 51 silver, 44 bronze) at the Summer Games and won them in 18 different sports plus the art competitions. Norway has had 12 athletes who have won four or more medals at the Summer Games, with nine of them participated in shooting, from 1900 to 1924. Otto Olsen leads all Norwegian Summer Games medalists with nine (four gold, three silver, one bronze in 1920 and 1924). Einar Liberg won eight from 1908 to 1924 (four gold, two silver, one bronze). Ole Lilloe-Olsen has the most gold medals, five, of any Norwegian Olympian in summer sports. **Kayaker** Knut Holmann (1988–2000) won six medals—three gold, two silver, one bronze—and has the most of any Norwegian in summer sports outside of shooting.

Norway has competed at every **Olympic Winter Games**. Until 1984, Norway could claim to be the top nation at the Olympic Winter Games in terms of medals and gold medals won. In that year, however, the **Soviet Union** surpassed it in both categories. With the demise of the Soviet Union, Norway again tops the list of most medals won by a single country at the Olympic Winter Games, with 329 (118 gold, 111 silver, 100 bronze). It also has the most gold medals, the most silver medals, and the most bronze medals. Norway shares with **Liechtenstein** and **Austria** the unusual distinction of having won more medals in the Winter Games than in the Summer Olympics. Prior to the Sochi Games in 2014, Norwegian **cross-country skier Bjørn Dæhlie** had won the most medals, 12, but in Sochi, his countryman, **biathlete Ole Einar Bjørndalen** set the current record for any Winter Olympian when he won his 13th medal.

In 22 Winter Games, Norway has entered 820 athletes (657 men, 163 women) and competed in 15 sports—all but the **military ski patrol**, which was only held in 1924 and in which only six nations took part. Although Norway is first in the Winter Games medal count, they are only 10th in the number of Winter Games participants. They have had 158 entrants in cross-country skiing (112 men, 46 women), 148 men in **ice hockey**, and 104 men and 16 women in **speed skating**. Three of the five athletes with the most medals at the Winter Games are Norwegian—Ole Einar Bjørndalen, Bjørn Dæhlie, and **Marit Bjørgen**. Ole Einar Bjørndalen is a biathlete who in six Winter Games from 1994 to 2014 has won 13 medals (eight gold, four silver, one bronze). He has won more total medals and more gold medals than any other athlete in the Winter Games. Bjørn Dæhlie is a cross-country skier who has won 12 medals (eight gold, four silver) in just three Games from 1992 to 1998. His total of eight gold medals in winter sports has been matched only by Ole Einar Bjørndalen. Marit Bjørgen is a cross-country skier who has won

10 medals (six gold, three silver, one bronze), which is the most by a female athlete and has been matched only by **Stefania Belmondo** (ITA) and **Raisa Smetanina** (URS/EUN). Marit's total of six gold medals is the most by a woman and has been matched by **Lyubov Yegorova** (EUN/URS) and **Lidiya Skoblikova** (URS). One other of Norway's most famous Winter Games athletes is figure skater **Sonja Henie**, who first competed in Olympic figure skating at the age of 11 in Chamonix in 1924 and then won the gold medal in the next three Olympic Winter Games.

Norway has twice hosted the Olympic Winter Games, in 1952 in Oslo and in 1994 in Lillehammer, and Oslo was one of the finalists in the bidding for the 2022 Olympic Winter Games but on 1 October 2014 withdrew its bid because of the prohibitive cost of holding the Games. Norway also had several unsuccessful bids for the Winter Games—Oslo (1932, 1944, 1968) and Lillehammer (1992). *See also* AAMODT, KJETIL ANDRÉ; ANDERSEN, HJALMAR JOHAN; BALLANGRUD, IVAR EUGEN; GRØTTUMSBRÅTEN, JOHAN HAGBART PEDERSEN; HAUG, THORLEIF; KOSS, JOHANN OLAV; TRAA, KARI; ULVANG, VEGARD.

NOVIKOV, IGOR ALEKSANDROVICH (URS/ARM–MOP). B. 19 October 1929, Drezna, Moscow Oblast, **Russia**, USSR. D. 30 August 2007, St. Petersburg, Russian Federation. Igor Novikov was one of the most consistent performers in the **modern pentathlon**. At the 1952–1964 Olympics, he finished fourth, fourth, fifth, and second in the individual event. In the team event, the six-foot tall (183 cm), 165 lb (75 kg) Novikov won two gold medals (1956 and 1964) and a silver (1960). He was heavily favored to win the individual gold medal in 1960, based on his string of world titles (1957–1959, and later in 1961), but he finished fifth because of difficulty in the riding sequence. Strong at all five **disciplines**, Novikov set a world pentathlon best for the **fencing** section when he won the 1957 World Championship. Novikov became a coach and held several administrative positions in sports. Most notably, he was president of the Union Internationale de Pentathlon Moderne from 1988 to 1992.

NURMI, PAAVO JOHANNES (FIN–ATH). B. 13 June 1897, Turku, Varsinais-Suomi, **Finland**. D. 2 October 1973, Helsinki, Uusimaa, Finland. Paavo Nurmi was an Olympic legend whose dedication to a rigorous training schedule and mastery of pace judgment brought a new dimension to distance running. Between 1920 and 1928, he won nine Olympic gold medals (seven individual; two team) and three individual silver medals. No other competitor in **athletics** has ever won more medals. The five-foot, eight-inch (174 cm), 143 lb (65 kg) runner medaled in each one of the 12 Olympic events he entered. His medals were in a wide range of events: 1,500 meters, 3,000 meters

Paavo Nurmi of Finland leads his countryman, Ville Ritola, at the 1924 Olympic Games. Together, they won nine gold medals in distance running. Courtesy of Erich Kamper

(team), 5,000 meters, 10,000 meters, **steeplechase**, and cross-country. In 1932, Nurmi was banned for alleged professionalism and missed the chance to add the 1932 **marathon**, for which he was the favorite, to his list of Olympic successes. Although subsequently reinstated as an amateur for domestic races, he continued to be excluded from international competition, a decision that left him embittered for the rest of his life. However, Nurmi returned to the Olympic arena in 1952 when he carried the torch at the opening ceremony in Helsinki. The incomparable "Flying Finn" set 22 official and 13 unofficial world records, and statues (done by Waino Aaltonen in 1925) honoring his feats stand in his hometown of Turku, outside the Olympic stadium in Helsinki, and in the park of the **Olympic Museum** in **Lausanne**.

NYASALAND. *See* MALAWI.

NYKÄNEN, MATTI ENSIO (FIN–SKJ). B. 17 July 1963, Jyväskylä, Keski-Suomi, **Finland**. Matti Nykänen was the winner of a record four gold **Olympic medals** for **ski jumping**. Although his record for gold medals was tied by **Simon Ammann** in 2010, Nykänen still holds the record for most total medals with five. At the 1984 **Olympic Winter Games**, the five-foot, nine-inch (177 cm), 119 lb (54 kg) Nykänen won on the **large hill** and placed second on the **normal hill** before winning both events in 1988, when he won a further gold medal in the newly introduced team event. He was also the World Champion on the large hill in 1982 and won four World Cup titles between 1983 and 1988. A controversial and often ill-tempered individual, Nykänen earned considerable respect for his sporting talents but little for his general behavior. He is regularly written about in the pages of Finnish tabloids for his exploits, which have included a pop singing career, a cooking show on television, a stint as a stripper, alcohol abuse, several marriages and divorces, and arrests and convictions for assault and battery.

O

O'BRIEN, WILLIAM PARRY, JR. (USA–ATH). B. 28 January 1932, Santa Monica, California, **United States**. D. 21 April 2007, Santa Clarita, California, United States. Parry O'Brien was one of only three men to win the Olympic **shot put** championship twice and one of only two men to win three **Olympic medals** in the event. Although his records have now been surpassed, Parry O'Brien is, by the standards of his contemporaries, the greatest shot putter of all time. At the University of Southern California, which he attended via a football scholarship, he won the National Collegiate Athletic Association shot put championship in 1952 and 1953. He won a total of 17

Parry O'Brien, 1952, 1956 shot put gold medalist. Courtesy of Volker Kluge

Amateur Athletic Union (AAU) titles, and between July 1952 and June 1956, he had a winning streak of 116 consecutive victories. He won the Olympic gold medal in 1952 and 1956, both times with Olympic record throws, won a silver medal in 1960, again bettering the Olympic record, and placed fourth at the Tokyo Olympics in 1964.

The six-foot, two-inch (190 cm), 245 lb (111 kg) O'Brien broke the world record 17 times, although only 10 of these were ratified, and he was the first man to beat the 18-meter, 60-foot, and 19-meter barriers. O'Brien set his last world record in 1959 and had a career best in 1966, two years after his final Olympic appearance. O'Brien was also **Pan American Games** champion in 1955 and 1959. In the **discus throw**, he also won two medals at the Pan American Games—silver in 1955 and bronze in 1959. He also won the 1955 AAU discus championship.

Apart from his multiple victories and records, Parry O'Brien made a significant contribution to the sport by pioneering a new style in which he faced the back of the shot put circle and spun 180 degrees as he released the shot. He died from a heart attack while competing in a master's level **swimming** event.

O'NEILL, SUSAN "SUSIE" (AUS–SWI). B. 2 August 1973, Mackay, Queensland, **Australia**. Susie O'Neill's record approaches that of **Dawn Fraser** among Australian distaff **swimmers**. O'Neill competed at the 1992, 1996, and 2000 **Olympic Games**, winning eight medals, including individual gold medals in the 200 **butterfly** in 1996 and the 200 freestyle in 2000. Her top career performance may have been at the 1999 World Championships, when she won the 200 fly, breaking the 19-year-old world record that had been set by **Mary T. Meagher**. The five-foot, seven-inch (171 cm), 139 lb (63 kg) O'Neill was remarkably consistent. Between 1990 and 2000, she never failed to win a medal at an international competition. She won 10 gold medals at the **Commonwealth Games**, the most for any Australian in any sport. O'Neill was named Australian Female Athlete of the Year in 1996 and 1998, and in 1997 was given the Order of Australia. Shortly after the Sydney Olympics, O'Neill was elected by her peers as an athlete member of the **International Olympic Committee**. She resigned from this membership in January 2005, citing family commitments.

OCEANIA NATIONAL OLYMPIC COMMITTEES (ONOC). The ONOC, headquartered in **Fiji**, is a confederation of 17 **National Olympic Committees** from Oceania and is one of the recognized organizations of the **International Olympic Committee**. It was created on 25 September 1981 to promote the **Olympic Movement** and its ideals in Oceania and to encourage and assist in the promotion and development of Olympic sports in Oceania.

The presidents of ONOC have been Harold Austad (NZL) (1981–1983), Sir Lance Cross (NZL) (1983–1989), IOC member Kevan Gosper of **Australia** (1989–2009), and Robin E. Mitchell (FIJ) (2009–present).

OERTER, ALFRED ADOLPH "AL," JR. (USA–ATH). B. 19 September 1936, Astoria, New York, **United States**. D. 1 October 2007, Fort Myers, Florida, United States. Al Oerter, a **discus thrower**, was the first track and field **athlete** to win four successive Olympic titles, a feat since equaled by **Carl Lewis** in the **long jump**. Oerter won the gold medal in the discus in 1956, 1960, 1964, and 1968, setting a new Olympic record on each occasion,

Al Oerter of the United States, considered the finest discus thrower ever, won the gold medal at four consecutive Olympic Games from 1956 to 1968. Courtesy of Erich Kamper

although he was never the favorite to win the event. His third victory in 1964 was remarkable for the fact that he overcame the handicap of neck and rib injuries to set a career best. The six-foot, three-inch (192 cm), 276 lb (125 kg) Oerter also won the **Pan American Games** title in 1959 and set four world records, the first of which, in 1962, gave him the distinction of being the first man to record a legal throw of over 200 feet (60.96 meters). In 1979, Oerter came out of retirement with the goal of earning a fifth gold medal. He threw well in 1980, finishing fourth at the U.S. Olympic trials, but his chances were lost earlier than that by the 1980 U.S. **boycott**. Later that year, he threw a lifetime best of 227 feet, 11 inches. In 1984, at the age of 47, he again attempted to qualify for the Olympic team, but during the Olympic trials, he tore a calf muscle and was unable to qualify. For much of his athletic career, he worked as a computer manager for Grumman Aircraft on Long Island, New York. In retirement, he became an abstract painter and founded Art of the Olympians, a program to help athletes promote their artistic work.

OFFICIAL REPORTS. At the end of every **Olympic Games** and **Olympic Winter Games**, the **Organizing Committee** of the Games is required to compile a comprehensive report of the organization, planning, finances, and results of the Games. The *Olympic Charter* now requires that the Official Report be published in at least French and English. It is now common for the report to be published in French, English, and the language of the host nation, and often in Spanish and German as well. Some of the reports are compiled as one book, with parallel texts in differing languages, but the more recent ones, which are larger, tend to be published as separate editions by language. There have only been a few instances in which an Official Report was not issued. In 1900, the report consisted of the report of the Physical Culture section of the *Exposition Universalle*. In 1904, there were two reports, neither of which would be considered comprehensive by today's standards. For the 1924 Winter Games, only declared Olympic retroactively, no separate report was issued, but the report of the 1924 Paris Olympic Games included details of the Chamonix events. There were reports issued by the scheduled host cities for the 1916 Olympic Games and the 1940 Olympic Games and Olympic Winter Games. No reports were ever issued for the scheduled 1944 Olympics.

OH SEONG-OK (KOR–HAN). B. 10 October 1972. Oh Seong-Ok is one of only two people (the other being **Andrey Lavrov** [URS/EUN/RUS]) to win four medals in Olympic **handball**, and she and Lavrov are the only two to play in five Olympic handball tournaments. She is also the only **Korean** woman to appear in five Olympic Games and one of three Korean athletes to do so. She played from 1992 to 2008 and won the gold medal in 1992, silver in 1996, was fourth in 2000, won silver in 2004, and won bronze in 2008. The five-foot, seven-inch (171 cm), 141 lb (64 kg) Oh scored 128 goals in 32 games in Olympic competition, averaging four goals per game.

OHNO, APOLO ANTON (USA–STK). B. 22 May 1982; Seattle, Washington, **United States**. **Japanese** American short-tracker Apolo Anton Ohno has won eight Olympic medals, the highest total in the sport but tied by **Viktor An** in 2014. In Salt Lake City, the five-foot, eight-inch (173 cm), 150 lb (68 kg) Ohno won a silver medal (1,000 meters) and a gold in the 1,500 meters, following a controversial defeat of **Korean** opponent Kim Dong-Seong. Ohno won a second title in the 2006 500 meters, while adding bronzes in the 1,000 meters and the **relay**. In Vancouver, he added three more medals to his totals, winning silver in the 1,500 meters and bronze in the relay and 1,000 meters. In World Championships, Ohno has won nine titles, including one **all-around** title and one team title, both in 2008. In 2014, he took up the sport of **triathlon**, completed his first one in June, and in October completed the Ironman Triathlon in Hawaii in the respectable time of 9:52:27.

OLYMPIAD. An Olympiad is a measure of time, designating a period of four consecutive years. Until the most recent edition of the *Olympic Charter*, the definition of an Olympiad has been that it begins with the opening of one edition of the Games of the Olympiad and ends with the opening of the following edition. However, in the current edition of the *Olympic Charter*, as of 9 September 2013, the rule has been changed, and an Olympiad is now defined as a period of four consecutive calendar years, beginning on the first of January of the first year and ending on 31 December of the fourth year. Unfortunately, the current rule does not actually define the "first year of . . ." or "the fourth year of . . . ," but based on a later rule, an Olympiad now appears to begin on 1 January of the year in which the Games of the Olympiad are held. The term comes from the Greeks, who used the term *Olympiad* to measure the time between Olympic Games. Olympiad may be the term associated with the Olympics that is most often misused by the public, the media, and broadcasters. Specifically, the **Olympic Games** are not an "Olympiad." They are correctly termed the "Games of the Olympiad."

OLYMPIC ANTHEM. An Olympic anthem, also called the Olympic hymn, was composed for the 1896 **Olympic Games** by Greek composer Spyros Samaras (1863–1917), with words added by his colleague Kostis Palamas. The Olympic anthem was first played at the 1896 Olympic opening ceremony, performed by nine bands and a chorus. It was used again in 1906. Thereafter, a variety of musical offerings provided the background to the opening ceremony until 1960. In 1954, the **International Olympic Committee** (IOC) launched a worldwide competition for a new version of an Olympic anthem. From the 392 scores submitted, the first prize went to Michael Spisak for his ultramodern atonal work, with lyrics extracted from **Pindar**'s odes. It was never terribly popular, and Spisak's demands for excessive royalties resulted in it not being chosen as the official Olympic anthem. The IOC chose to return to the Samaras/Palamas composition as the official Olympic anthem.

The Samaras/Palamas anthem was played and sung at the 55th **IOC Session** in 1958 in Tokyo. It was such an impressive demonstration that **IOC member** Prince Axel (Denmark) suggested that it should be adopted as the official anthem. This was unanimously approved, although two years of legal work then took place dealing with the heirs of Samaras and Palamas.

The Olympic anthem was first used as such at the opening ceremony in Rome two years later, and since then it has become an established part of the Olympic ceremonies. The *Olympic Charter* calls it the Olympic anthem, although it is often referred to as the Olympic hymn. In English, the lyrics to the Olympic anthem are as follows:

> Immortal spirit of antiquity,
> Father of the true, beautiful and good,
> Descend, appear, shed over is thy light
> Upon this ground and under this sky
> Which has first witnessed thy unperishable fame
>
> Give life and animation to those noble games!
> Throw wreaths of fadeless flowers to the victors
> In the race and in the strife!
> Create in our breasts, hearts of steel!
>
> In thy light, plains, mountains and seas
> Shine in a roseate hue and form a vast temple
> To which all nations throng to adore thee,
> Oh immortal spirit of antiquity!

OLYMPIC ANTIHEROES. Although most athletes remembered for their Olympic exploits are winners, or at least contenders, sometimes the antiheroes become more famous than the medalists. An early example of this is **Dorando Pietri**, who was **disqualified** after winning the 1908 Olympic **marathon** for being aided by officials after he collapsed in the final lap of the track. More recent, and better known, is Eddie "the Eagle" Edwards, a British **ski jumper** who competed in the 1988 **Olympic Winter Games**. With thick glasses, a nonathletic posture, and just two years of experience, Edwards attracted more media attention than winner **Matti Nykänen**. He finished dead last in both his events, by a wide margin. (At the **normal hill**, Edwards finished in 58th place with two jumps of 55 meters each; the jumper in 57th place, Bernat Sola of Spain, jumped 71 meters and 68.5 meters; the winner, Nykänen, jumped 89.5 each time. Edwards's point total for the two jumps was 69.2, Sola's was 140.4, and Nykänen's was 229.1.)

However, not everybody was happy with competitors like Edwards; some officials felt they distracted attention from the top competitors, while some athletes who had failed to qualify for their Olympic team found Edwards's presence offensive. During the 1990s, the **International Olympic Committee** and the **International Federations** gradually adopted stricter qualification criteria for the Olympics, decreasing the chance of someone like Edwards getting to compete. But as the Olympic ideals desire all countries to take part in the Games, in some sports, athletes may compete who have not met qualification criteria.

One such athlete was Eric "The Eel" Moussambani of **Equatorial Guinea**. At the Sydney Olympics, he made newsreels all over the world by his performance in the **swimming** pool. With both opponents in his 100 meter **freestyle heat** disqualified after a false start, Moussambani was the sole swimmer in his race. Having only a few months of swimming experience in a small hotel pool, Moussambani splashed home in 1:52.72, 50 seconds slower than the next-to-last competitor, and slower than the world record in the 200 meter freestyle. Yet the **Australian** crowds loudly cheered him on. Ironically, since his heat was the first to be contested, he actually was in first place in the overall competition following the completion of his swim.

Not all Olympic antiheroes place last. A famous example is the **Jamaican bobsled** team that competed in the 1988 Olympics. The team was initially widely ridiculed, coming from a nation without any history in winter sports. But it achieved a credible 30th place in the two-man event (with 41 entries), and in the 1994 event reached 14th place in the four-man competition. The team's extraordinary story was made into a successful comedy movie by Disney, titled *Cool Runnings*.

In 1998, a similar situation occurred when **Kenyan** Philip Boit became the first black African **cross-country skier** to compete in the Olympics. When he finished the 10 km events, in 92nd and last place, he was greeted at the line by the winner, **Bjørn Dæhlie**. But critics noted that Boit had been heavily sponsored by sporting goods company Nike, accusing the company of deliberately creating an antihero for publicity reasons.

OLYMPIC BRIBERY SCANDAL. On 24 November 1998, the Salt Lake City (Utah) television station, KTVX, reported that the Salt Lake Olympic **Organizing Committee** for the **Olympic Winter Games** of 2002 (SLOC) had been paying for Sonia Essomba to attend American University in Washington. Sonia Essomba was the daughter of René Essomba, the late **International Olympic Committee** (IOC) member (1978–1998) from **Cameroon**.

The payments, it would be revealed, were part of a larger scheme set up by the SLOC to award scholarships to the family members and friends of **IOC members** in an effort to win their votes to become the host city. Within a few days after the revelation of the Essomba "scholarship," the media reported that, beginning in 1991, shortly after Salt Lake City had lost the 1998 Winter Olympic bid to Nagano, 13 individuals had received scholarship assistance worth almost $400,000 from the Salt Lake Bid Committee or SLOC. Of these 13 individuals, at least six were close relatives of IOC members.

Shortly thereafter, at the close of the IOC **Executive Board** on 12 December 1998, Swiss IOC member **Marc Hodler** spoke openly to the press, stating that at least 5 to 7 percent of IOC members had taken or solicited bribes by bid cities. Within a few days, all manner of revelations were published by the media, which descended like sharks in a feeding frenzy. Shortly before Hodler's interview, upon the recommendation of the **Juridical Commission**, President **Juan Antonio Samaranch** had already formed an ad hoc commission to look into the allegations and accusations made against the host cities and bid cities. **Canada's Dick Pound** was named to head the inquiry, usually called the Pound Commission.

At the beginning of 1999, investigating the IOC and the bid city process seemed to be all the rage. In addition to the Pound Commission, the SLOC formed its own Board of Ethics to investigate its own practices. The **United States** Olympic Committee (USOC) also formed an investigative panel, headed by the former U.S. senator from Maine, George Mitchell. Concurrently, the Federal Bureau of Investigation began its own inquiry into the SLOC to determine if any federal laws were violated relating to bribery and the Foreign Corrupt Practices Act. Of note, only the Pound Commission actually interviewed the IOC members under investigation, allowing them a chance to answer the charges before them.

New announcements from Salt Lake City appeared in the press almost daily in January 1999. On 7 January, the Associated Press reported that IOC member Jean-Claude Ganga of the **Republic of the Congo** had earned a $60,000 profit on a land deal arranged by a member of the SLOC. On 8 January 1999, the president and chief executive officer of the SLOC, G. Frank Joklik, resigned, as did his senior vice president, Dave Johnson. At his press conference, Joklik described some of the transgressions of the bid committee and the SLOC:

> Therefore, I have today obtained the resignation of David Johnson, who was a vice president of the bid committee, and has been acting as senior vice president of the organizing committee until today. I have recommended the appointment of a new Chief Operating Officer. The other two principal members of the Bid Committee, Tom Welch, who was CEO, and Craig Peterson, who was the Chief

Administrative Officer, are no longer employees of the corporation. . . . Finally, to ensure that the Games go immediately forward, I must take steps of my own. Although I had no knowledge of these improper payments during my tenure as the volunteer Chairman of the Board of Trustees of the Bid Committee, in order to assure the people of Salt Lake City, the State of Utah, and the world that the Organizing Committee is distinct from the Bid Committee and is off to a fresh start, I have tendered my resignation today.

Tom Welch was the main impetus behind the Salt Lake City bid to host the 2002 Winter Olympics. Though no longer in an administrative position with the SLOC, he was on their payroll as a consultant when the scandal hit. Joklik stated that Welch's consulting agreement was terminated as of his announcement. Over the next few months, Welch was a marked man, and a reclusive one, who made no public statements but spoke only through his lawyers.

On 15 January 1999, Samaranch called for an extraordinary **IOC Session** to be held in **Lausanne, Switzerland**, on 17–18 March, but he also stated that he would not resign, despite frequent calls in the media for him to do so. On 19 January, Finnish IOC member Pirjo Häggmann resigned. She was one of the first two female members of the IOC, having served since 1981. Her "crime" was that her ex-husband had worked for the Salt Lake City bid committee and had also worked for the Toronto Bid Committee when that city bid to host the 1996 Olympics. The second IOC member to resign was the **Libyan** Bashir Mohamed Attarabulsi, who did so on 22 January. It was revealed that his son had attended an English language center at Brigham Young University in Salt Lake City, with tuition paid by the SLOC, and the son was provided with $700 per month by the organizing committee. The Sydney bid for the 2000 Olympics, to this time, had been relatively unscathed. But on the same day that Attarabulsi resigned, John Coates, who had headed the Sydney bid, admitted that he had made last-minute offers of $70,000 to two African IOC officials, but said the action was legitimate.

On 23 January, the IOC Executive Board met in Lausanne to discuss the preliminary findings of the Pound Commission and make some early decisions. At the end of the meeting, Samaranch announced that the IOC had made mistakes, that it was responsible, and that this must never happen again. Six IOC members were suspended, pending the final Pound Report, with a vote to be taken on their possible expulsion at the special IOC Session in March.

The six IOC members suspended (and eventually expelled) were Lamine Keita of **Mali**, Agustin Arroyo of **Ecuador**, Charles Mukora of **Kenya**, Zein El-Abdin Mohamed Ahmed Abdel Gadir of the **Sudan**, Sergio Santander Fantini of **Chile**, and the aforementioned Jean-Claude Ganga. A third member resigned voluntarily, David Sibandze of **Swaziland**, while investigations continued into the status of other members.

On 8 February 1999, the Board of Ethics of the Salt Lake Organizing Committee for the Olympic Winter Games of 2002 report was released. It described a litany of indiscretions by the bid committee and the SLOC. These included payment of hundreds of thousands of dollars to IOC members and their families, usually in the form of "scholarship assistance." As an example, the revelations that began the scandal, the payments to Sonia Essomba, were noted to total $108,350. The Board of Ethics report also revealed direct monetary payments to IOC members, often in the form of sports assistance programs for their **National Olympic Committees**. The Board of Ethics did not stop with the above, and it noted that, "Many witnesses before the Board of Ethics described Mr. [Jean-Claude] Ganga as the IOC member who most took advantage of the Bid Committee's and the community's generosity." The report then gave details of a litany of indiscretions concerning Ganga and the Salt Lake City Bid Committee.

On 1 March 1999, the Mitchell Commission released its report. The Mitchell Report was more encompassing, dealing with several arms of the **Olympic Movement**. It looked at the bidding process, the IOC structure, and the USOC itself. Its 50 pages of documentation ended with seven pages of conclusions and recommendations, aimed at revamping both the structure of the IOC and the bid city selection process.

The IOC Extraordinary Session was planned for 17–18 March. Before this meeting, the Executive Board met again, and the final Pound Commission report was released. The Pound Report began with a short description of the conclusions of the Board of Ethics Report and the Mitchell Report. It then made its final recommendations near the beginning of the document, although these recommendations were supported by almost 50 pages of documentation describing the transgressions of certain IOC members. The report recommended expelling six IOC members: Agustin Arroyo, Zein El-Abdin Mohamed Ahmed Abdel Gadir, Jean-Claude Ganga, Lamine Keita, and Sergio Santander Fantini, and Paul Wallwork of **Samoa**. Charles Mukora, whose expulsion had been recommended earlier, had since resigned. Nine other IOC members had been investigated, but were given only warnings with no recommendations for expulsion.

After describing its recommendations about the IOC members, the Pound Report made several conclusions. It noted that the IOC must take action to correct the problems within its membership and must implement reforms to be certain these problems could never occur again. The Commission also noted that the IOC should have done more to prevent the problems concerning Salt Lake City's candidacy. The Pound Report then recommended changes in the host city selection process, limitations on travel by IOC members to bid cities, and creation of an IOC **Ethics Commission**.

The IOC met in full session a few days later. It voted to expel the members as recommended by the Pound Report, meaning that fully 10 members of the IOC lost their positions as a result of the scandal. But more important, the IOC voted to form two new commissions to help reform the structure of the IOC and the Olympic Movement and to ensure that such problems would never happen again.

The two commissions were the Ethics Commission and the **IOC 2000 Commission**. The IOC 2000 Commission was charged with reforming the entire structure of the Olympic Movement into the next millennium to help prevent such ethical breaches in the future. It was made up of 82 members, with less than half of them IOC members, and with an Executive Board of 26 members, of whom 13 were IOC members. The commission produced an intermediary report in June 1999, and its final report was released in November 1999, although early leaks of information were available. Altogether, the IOC 2000 Commission studied more than 100 possible ideas for reform of the Olympic Movement and eventually made 50 separate recommendations to the IOC.

The Ethics Commission's primary focus was to address the responsibilities of the IOC, oversee the selection process of host cities, and set guidelines for future conduct by members of the Olympic Movement. The Ethics Commission produced an IOC Code of Ethics in the spring of 1999, which addressed many of the concerns voiced by the public and in the media about the recent actions of several IOC members and the Organizing Committees.

During 1999, the U.S. Congress also began hearings into the conduct of the IOC. The House Commerce Subcommittee on Oversight and Investigation also requested an investigation into the Atlanta bid for the 1996 Olympic Games. This was assigned to the Atlanta law firm of King & Spaulding and was headed by former U.S. Attorney General Griffin B. Bell. Its final document, termed the Bell Report, was released on 15 September 1999.

The IOC met in Extraordinary Session in Lausanne on 11–12 December to vote on the recommendations made by the IOC 2000 Commission. At this historic session, the IOC voted to enact all the recommendations made by the commission. The most important changes implemented were (1) an age limit of 70 for IOC members; (2) term limits of eight years for most IOC members; (3) creation of four categories of IOC members: (a) athletes, (b) National Olympic Committee (NOC) presidents, (c) **International Federation** presidents, and (d) individual members; (4) eliminate visits by IOC members to the bid cities; (5) a complete change in the process of selecting host cities; (6) opening IOC sessions to the media via closed-circuit television; and (7) much more transparency in the financial transactions of the IOC, the bid cities, and the **Organizing Committees of the Olympic**

Games. In the end, all 50 recommendations of the IOC 2000 Commission were approved, most unanimously.

After the implementation of the numerous IOC reforms, IOC President Juan Antonio Samaranch testified in the U.S. House of Representatives before the House Commerce Subcommittee on Oversight and Investigations on 15 December 1999. It was a somewhat contentious appearance, as the members of the subcommittee were underwhelmed by the IOC's reform process. Representative Joe Barton (Republican–Texas) asked Samaranch to resign on the spot. However, Samaranch was supported by former senators Howard Baker and George Mitchell, who had been involved in the reform process, as noted above. Both stated that the IOC was cleaning house, and Mitchell noted that the IOC had even gone beyond the recommendations made by his commission.

Why did the Olympic scandal occur, and why did these problems seemingly hit all at once? As has been well documented elsewhere, the IOC was once in dire financial straits, and it was only in the 1980s that it began to achieve financial independence. But all this happened quickly, too quickly for the IOC to adjust. And it is unlikely that the problems described here began only with the Salt Lake City bid. There were similar allegations going back to the mid-1980s. During his testimony before the U.S. House of Representatives on 14 October 1999, IOC Director-General François Carrard said: "Unfortunately, while the Games evolved, our organizational structure did not keep up with the pace of change. In effect, we did not realize we were going through a growth crisis. The result of an old-fashioned structure managing modern Games was not corruption, but a situation in which some of the less responsible members—a small minority—showed poor judgment and abused the system. Our problems were caused by weak people, structures, and procedures."

Were the new reforms undertaken by the IOC at its December 1999 session adequate to address the problems? The media were critical of these reforms and skeptical that they would truly solve the problems. Some of the criticisms were valid, but as George Mitchell noted, in many ways the IOC either enacted all of the commission's recommendations, or in some cases, went even farther.

OLYMPIC BROADCAST SERVICES (OBS). In 2001, the **International Olympic Committee** (IOC) set up a separate organization to ensure high-quality broadcasts of the **Olympic Games**, called Olympic Broadcast Services. Its main duties include the operation of the International Broadcast Centre in the Olympic host city, the operation of broadcast installations at the venues, and, most important, to deliver the **television** footage to the national broadcasters who televise the Olympics. OBS worked at the 2008 and 2010 Olympics as a joint venture with the Organizing Committee of the Olympic Games for local support, called Beijing Olympic Broadcasting in 2008 and Olympic Broadcasting Services Vancouver in 2010. In London in 2012 and Sochi 2014, OBS did not have such an arrangement. Hosted in Madrid, **Spain**, the chairman of OBS was IOC honorary member Hein Verbruggen (**Netherlands**). He was replaced on 4 April 2014 by **Richard Pound**.

OLYMPIC CEREMONIES. A number of ceremonies accompany the **Olympic Games**, notably the opening ceremony, the closing ceremony, and the victory, medals, and **Olympic Diplomas** ceremonies. These ceremonies are conducted according to strict protocols defined in Rule 55 of the *Olympic Charter* (opening and closing ceremonies) and Rule 56 of the *Olympic Charter* (victory, medals, and diplomas ceremonies).

The opening ceremony has a number of recurring features, which are interspersed with an artistic program. This program is usually designed to have some symbolic nature, representing both the **Olympic Movement** and the national features of the host country. The formal part of the opening begins with the head of state of the host country (normally) entering the stadium, accompanied by the **International Olympic Committee (IOC) president** and the president of the **Organizing Committee of the Games**. After the national anthem of the host nation is played, the parade of nations follows. The athletes of all participating countries enter the stadium, marching in alphabetical order, using the alphabetical designation of the language of the host country. However, **Greece** always enters the stadium first, as the founding nation of the **Ancient Olympic Games**, and the last nation to enter is always the host country. (In 2004, the Greek flag entered first, while the Greek team came in last.) Each nation is led by a flagbearer carrying the flag of the nation or the **National Olympic Committee**.

The president of the Organizing Committee then speaks for no more than three minutes. The IOC president then speaks briefly and ends by inviting the head of state of the host country to open the Olympic Games. He or she gives no speech, but opens the Games by stating, "I declare open the Games of . . . [name of city] celebrating the . . . **Olympiad** of the Modern Era [or the . . . **Olympic Winter Games**]."

The **Olympic flag** is then carried into the stadium and raised while the **Olympic anthem** is played. The flagbearers then form a semicircle around the main rostrum, and a competitor and an official of the host country take the **Olympic Oath** on behalf of all competitors and officials. The ceremony ends with the conclusion of the Olympic torch relay. The torch is brought into the stadium, usually by former Olympians from the host nation. The **Olympic**

flame is lit by the final runner—whose name is kept secret until the last minute—followed by a symbolic release of pigeons, signifying peace.

The closing ceremony ends the Olympic Games. The flagbearers of each nation first march into the stadium, followed by the athletes of all nations. The athletes march in no specific order and typically intermingle, signifying the friendships developed during the Olympic Games. This change to the closing ceremony was suggested by John Ian Wing, a young British boy of Chinese origin, to the organizers of the 1956 Olympic Games in Melbourne.

The president of the IOC and the Organizing Committee mount the rostrum in the center of the stadium. Three flags are then raised in the following order: the Greek flag on the right flagpole, the flag of the host country on the center flagpole, and the flag of the host country of the next Olympic Games (or Olympic Winter Games) on the left flagpole. All are raised to the playing of their respective national anthems.

The mayor of the host city then hands the official Olympic flag to the IOC president, who in turn hands it to the mayor of the host city of the next Olympic Games. The president of the Organizing Committee gives a brief speech. The IOC president then speaks briefly and ends the Olympic Games by stating, "I declare the Games of the . . . Olympiad [or the . . . Olympic Winter Games] closed and, in accordance with tradition, I call upon the youth of the world to assemble four years from now at . . . [next host city] to celebrate with us there the Games of the . . . Olympiad [or the . . . Olympic Winter Games]." A fanfare then sounds, the Olympic flame is extinguished, and while the Olympic anthem is played, the Olympic flag is lowered from the flagpole.

The victory, medals, and diplomas ceremonies consist of the awarding of these respective items. The medals are to be presented by the IOC president or an IOC member designated by the president. (In reality, the IOC president now awards only a very few medals.) The three place winners mount the victory platform (known as the podium), the winner (gold medalist) on the highest step, the second place finisher (silver medalist) to his or her right on a slightly lower step, and the third place finisher (bronze medalist) to the winner's left on an even lower step. Their names are announced, and the medals are awarded to them. The national flags of the three medal winners are raised, the national flag of the winner on the central flagpole. While the flags are raised, the national anthem of the champion is played, usually in a shortened version. This ceremony was adopted in 1932; previously all medals were handed out at the end of the Games, usually by the head of state of the host nation.

At the Sochi Winter Games in 2014, at some venues a brief awards ceremony was held and the victors were presented with flowers instead of medals. On a subsequent day, another awards ceremony was held in the main Olympic park (accessible to more spectators) and the medals were then presented to the winners.

OLYMPIC CHARTER. The *Olympic Charter* is, effectively, the constitution of the **International Olympic Committee** (IOC) and the **Olympic Movement**. It sets out, basically in outline form, the principles, rules, and bylaws that govern the workings of both the IOC and the Olympic Movement and stipulates the conditions for the celebration of the **Olympic Games**. The *Olympic Charter* was first adopted in 1908, based on a handwritten set of rules created by **Pierre de Coubertin** shortly after the formation of the IOC. The 1908 list of rules was not called the *Olympic Charter*, but rather *Comité International Olympique: Annuaire* (in French only). Since that time, the International Olympic Committee's governing rules have been published under several different names, including *Olympic Rules*, *Protocol*, *Olympic Statutes*, and *Rules*, being first published officially as the *Olympic Charter* only in 1978.

Though the *Olympic Charter* is often held to be inviolate, it is, in fact, fairly easily modified and has been changed many times since its inception, with the most recent modification (as of mid-2014) occurring on 9 September 2013. Modifications, or amendments, can be made according to Rule 18 governing the Sessions, which states, "The Session . . . is the IOC's supreme organ." Rule 18.2 provides that among the powers of the Session are "to adopt or amend the *Olympic Charter*."

The *Olympic Charter* underwent major changes at the end of 1999, based on recommendations made by the **IOC 2000 Commission** in response to the **Olympic bribery scandal**. The changes were sweeping and made significant structural alterations to the Olympic Movement, many of which are discussed in various entries in this dictionary. Details of these recommendations can be found in the entry for IOC 2000 COMMISSION.

OLYMPIC CODE. *See* OLYMPIC CREED.

OLYMPIC COINS. Olympic coins are often minted by the host country of the **Olympic Games** (or **Olympic Winter Games**) as a means of raising revenue to finance the Games. This practice follows that of nations that produce **Olympic stamps**. However, Olympic stamps date back to the first modern Olympic Games in 1896, whereas Olympic coins were first minted by the host nation in 1952, when **Finland** minted a single 500 markka Finnish coin to raise revenue for the Helsinki Olympics. The next issuance of Olympic coins, and the first for an Olympic Winter Games, occurred in 1964 for Innsbruck, when **Austria** struck a commemorative 50 schilling coin for the event. In 1964, **Japan** produced two coins, 100¥ and 1,000¥. In 1972, Munich produced the first large-scale series of Olympic coins, with six coins of differing designs, although all were for 10 DM. In 1976, Montreal put the Olympic coin practice into overdrive with a series of 28 silver coins and the first gold Olympic coins, valued at $100 (Canadian). Since Tokyo and Innsbruck in 1964, every **Organizing Committee**, with the exception of Grenoble in 1968, has earned revenue from the sale of Olympic coins in its home nation. The most prolific nation to date has been **Australia** for the 2000 Sydney Games, with 59 coins in its series.

In addition, many other nations also now produce Olympic-related coins, often honoring some of their Olympic heroes. Between 1992 and 1996, in honor of the 1996 centennial of the modern Olympic Games, the **International Olympic Committee** oversaw the production of an international commemorative coin program. The series was struck as follows: 1992, Royal Canadian Mint; 1993, Royal Australian Mint; 1994, Monnaie de Paris; 1995, Münze Österrech; and 1996, Banknote Printing Works, the Bank of **Greece**. There have also been several books produced concerning Olympic coins. The first notable one was *Coins of the Modern Olympic Games* by Michele Menard (self-published in 1991), which dealt only with coins produced by host nations, listed as Volume 1. Volume 2 was to deal with coins produced by nonhost nations, but it never appeared. In 1994, Victor Gadoury also self-published the book *Olympic Medals and Coins, 510 BC–1994*. This book covered medals and coins and had information on coins of the **Ancient Olympic Games** and coins produced since 1952 by both host nations and nonhost nations. *See also* OLYMPIC PHILATELY, NUMISMATIC, AND MEMORABILIA COMMISSION.

OLYMPIC CONGRESSES. Olympic Congresses are gatherings of all the various bodies and individuals involved in the **Olympic Movement**. The *Olympic Charter* now states that they are to be held, in principle, every eight years at a place and date determined by the **International Olympic Committee** (IOC). It should be noted that this has not always been the case. Baron **Pierre de Coubertin** intended Olympic Congresses to be held from "time to time" to discuss the Olympic Movement. However, a gap of 43 years occurred between the 9th Olympic Congress and the 10th Olympic Congress in 1973. The Olympic Congress has no official power to make rules concerning the **Olympic Games** or to modify the *Olympic Charter*, but only acts as a consultant to the Olympic Movement. The 13th Olympic Congress was held in Copenhagen, **Denmark**, from 3–5 October 2009. Plans for the 14th Olympic Congress, to be held in 2017, were made at the 126th IOC Session in February 2014 in Sochi.

OLYMPIC COUNCIL OF ASIA (OCA). The OCA is a confederation of the **National Olympic Committees** from Asia, which was formed in November 1982. The OCA is in overall charge of sports in Asia, coordinates the activities of Asian countries in sports at the regional and international levels, and conducts the Asian Games and Asian Winter Games every four years. It is headquartered in **Kuwait** and, since 1991, its president is Sheikh Ahmad Al-Fahad Al-Sabah of Kuwait. There are currently 45 affiliated nations, including **Macau**, which is not recognized by the **International Olympic Committee**.

OLYMPIC CREED. "The most important thing in the **Olympic Games** is not to win but to take part, just as the most important thing in life is not the triumph, but the struggle. The essential thing is not to have conquered but to have fought well." This is the current form of the Olympic Creed (also called the Olympic Code, the Olympic Credo, an alternative **Olympic motto**, or the Olympic Competition motto) as it appears on the scoreboard at the opening ceremony of the Olympic Games, although many permutations of this basic message have been seen. The exact origin of this phrase is not clear, but it is possible that **Pierre de Coubertin** adopted it after hearing Ethelbert Talbot, the bishop of Central Pennsylvania, speak at St. Paul's Cathedral on 19 July 1908 during the London Olympics. The service was given for the Olympic athletes, who were all invited.

Talbot was in London for the fifth Conference of Anglican Bishops. During the conference, many of the visiting bishops spoke in various churches. Talbot actually did not say anything close to the above words during his speech, stating instead, "The only safety after all lies in the lesson of the real Olympia—that the Games themselves are better than the race and the prize. St. Paul tells us how insignificant is the prize. Our prize is not corruptible, but incorruptible, and though only one may wear the laurel wreath, all may share the equal joy of the contest."

However, Coubertin heard Talbot speak and, at a banquet at the Grafton Galleries on 24 July 1908, he echoed Bishop Talbot's words as follows, "L'important dans ces Olympiades, c'est moins d'y gagner que d'y prendre part" (The important thing at these **Olympiads** is not so much to win as to take part). He then went on to say that these very words were the foundation of a clear and sound philosophy: "L'important dans la vie ce n'est point le triomphe mais le combat. L'essentiel ce n'est pas d'avoir vaincu mais de s'être bien battu" (The important thing in life is not the triumph but the struggle. The essential thing is not to have won but to have fought well).

More recent research by David C. Young indicates that Coubertin probably had this thought in mind prior to hearing the speech of the bishop of

Central Pennsylvania. Young attributes the phrase to Ovid's *Metamorphoses*, which Coubertin had read in school. A sentence in that work reads, "Nec tam turpe fuit vinci quam contendisse decorum est," which can be translated as It was not so shameful to be beaten as it is honorable to have contended. Coubertin's knowledge of this statement is supported by a speech he gave in November 1894 to the Parnassus Literary Society in Athens, in which he said, "Le déshonneur ne consisterait pas ici à être battu: il consisterait à ne pas se battre." This is literally translated as The dishonor here would consist not of being beaten, it would consist of not contending.

In connection with the Olympic Games in Stockholm (1912) and Antwerp (1920), Coubertin again spoke of the words of the bishop of Central Pennsylvania, but this did not attract any notice. At the Olympic Games in 1924 and 1928, no reference was made to Bishop Talbot's sermon in St. Paul's Cathedral. However, at the Olympic Games in Los Angeles (1932), the message appeared during the opening ceremony on the great scoreboard of the Los Angeles Memorial Coliseum. It was finally established at the 1936 Olympic Games in Berlin when, at the opening ceremony, Coubertin's voice was heard over the loudspeaker, in a recording, delivering his message,

> Important aux Jeux Olympiques, ce n'est pas tant d'y gagner que d'y avoir pris part; car l'essentiel dans la vie, ce n'est pas tant de conquérir que d'avoir bien lutté (Important in the Olympic Games is not winning but taking part; for the essential thing in life is not conquering but fighting well).

OLYMPIC CUP. The Olympic Cup was instituted by Baron **Pierre de Coubertin** in 1906. It is awarded to an institution or association with a general reputation for merit and integrity that has been active and efficient in the service of sport and has contributed substantially to the development of the **Olympic Movement**. The Olympic Cup is one of the two awards currently given by the **International Olympic Committee** outside the Olympic Games. *See also* OLYMPIC ORDER; Appendix V for a list of recipients of the Olympic Cup.

OLYMPIC DEATHS. Unfortunately, a number of athletes and officials have died, or been killed, during the **Olympic Games** and **Olympic Winter Games**. Through 2014, this has occurred with seven athletes and one official during competition or training runs. In addition, in 1972, 11 **Israeli** athletes and coaches were savagely murdered during a terrorist attack by the Black September group. There have been other deaths associated with the Olympics, including a few spectators or family members who have died. Most recently, these include the father of Ron Karnaugh, 1992 **United States swim-**

mer, who sustained a heart attack during the opening ceremony and later died; and Thérèse Rochette, the mother of Joanie Rochette, 2010 **Canadian figure skater**, who died from a heart attack just after arriving in Vancouver to watch her daughter skate in the Winter Olympics.

The first athlete to die in Olympic competition was **Portuguese marathoner** Fernando Lazaro, who collapsed during the 1912 Olympic marathon and died the next morning. In the 1936 Berlin Games, **featherweight boxer** Nicolae Berechet of **Romania** lost by decision in the first **round** of the boxing tournament. He died three days later of what was termed "blood poisoning," although it has been suggested that the blows he took in the bout may have contributed to his death. A gap of 24 years then occurred until the Rome Olympic Games. During the team **time trial, cyclist** Knud Enemark Jensen from **Denmark** collapsed and could not be revived. His death was attributed to a combination of heat stroke and Ronicol, a stimulant, traces of which were found in his blood. This was actually one of the factors that later led to the **International Olympic Committee** testing for drug use by athletes.

Since then, five deaths have occurred at the Winter Olympics. In 1964, two athletes died in Innsbruck during training for the Winter Olympic competition. These were Ross Milne, an **Australian** skier, who crashed and struck a tree training for the **downhill** ski race; and Kazimierz Kay-Skrzypecki, a British lugeist who was a Polish émigré, who died during a **luge** training run. In 1988 at Calgary, Jörg Oberhammer, the **Austrian** ski team doctor, was killed when he was struck by a ski grooming machine that was preparing the courses prior to the second run of the **giant slalom**. Four years later, in Albertville, Nikolay Bochatay, competing in the **speed skiing demonstration sport**, died during a training run when he crashed into a ski grooming machine. Finally, on the morning of the 2010 Vancouver opening ceremony, **Georgian** lugeist Nomar Komaritashvili flew off the luge track during a training run, crashing into a steel stanchion, and was killed instantly.

The greatest Olympic tragedy occurred on 5 September 1972 at the Munich Olympics, when Black September terrorists invaded the **Olympic Village** and entered the Israeli team rooms. They took hostage 11 Israeli athletes and coaches. Some were killed in their village rooms, while most died later that evening during a shootout at the Fürstenfeldbruck Airport, outside of Munich. The murdered Israelis were Mark Slavin (**wrestler**); Eliezer Halfin (wrestler); David Mark Berger (**weightlifter**); Ze'ev Friedman (weightlifter); Yossef Romano (weightlifter); Andre Spitzer (**fencing coach**); Moshe Weinberg (wrestling coach); Amitzur Shapira (**track** coach); Yossef Gutfreund (wrestling referee); Yakov Springer (weightlifting judge); and Kehat Shorr (**shooting** coach).

OLYMPIC DIPLOMAS. Diplomas are given to the first eight finishers of all events at an **Olympic Games** or **Olympic Winter Games**. It is not well known that the first three finishers receive these diplomas in addition to their medals. In team events, the members of the first eight teams also all receive diplomas.

OLYMPIC DISTANCE. The **triathlon** involves **swimming, cycling,** and running in consecutive competition. Triathlons are held using various distances. One of the more celebrated triathlons is billed as the Ironman Triathlon, which consists of 2.4-mile (3.9 km) swimming, 112-mile (180 km) cycling, and a full **marathon** run of 26 miles, 385 yards (42.195 km). When the triathlon was added to the **Olympic Program** in 2000, a shorter version labeled the "Olympic distance," was used. It consists of 1,500 meter (1,600 yards) swimming, 40 km (24.9 miles) cycling, and a 10 km (6.2 mile) run. **Simon Whitfield** of **Canada** (gold 2000, silver 2008) and **Bevan Docherty** of **New Zealand** (silver 2004, bronze 2008) have each won two medals in the men's event, while no female athlete has won more than one medal in the four years the triathlon has been contested at the **Olympic Games**.

OLYMPIC FAMILY. This term is used by the **International Olympic Committee** (IOC) to describe people considered to have certain privileges during the **Olympic Games** and **Olympic Winter Games**. The Olympic family consists of athletes, officials, media representatives, sponsors and their guests, and invited guests from the IOC, **National Olympic Committees, International Federations,** and **Organizing Committees of the Olympic Games**. At the Olympic Games and Olympic Winter Games, members of the Olympic family are given access to preferred lodging, private transportation, and privileged seating at the Olympic sporting events. These privileges and access are prioritized, with **IOC members** given the highest consideration.

OLYMPIC FILMS. Numerous Olympic films and movies have been produced. The **Organizing Committee** of each **Olympic Games** now produces its own official Olympic film celebrating "its" Olympics. This began in 1932, but is usually considered to have started with the 1936 Olympic Games in Berlin, when German film producer Leni Riefenstahl, at the behest of Adolf Hitler, produced the most famous and haunting of all Olympic films, *Olympia*. Prior to that, the filmed record of the Olympics came from cinema newsreels. Other well-known official Olympic films have been *Tokyo Olympiad*, celebrating the 1964 Olympic Games in Tokyo, and *Visions of Eight*, celebrating the 1972 Olympic Games in Munich.

In addition to official Olympic films, many independent producers have created Olympic movies. The American **television** network that broadcasts the Olympics now usually produces a cinematic summary of the Olympics, and the coverage is often available to be bought and viewed on DVD.

The most famous, and controversial, official Olympic film has been that of the 1936 Berlin Olympics. Although widely considered to be a tour de force in terms of its artistry, Riefenstahl has been castigated because of her close association with Hitler, and the film is sometimes considered a propaganda film produced to glorify the Third Reich, similar to one of her earlier works on the Nuremburg Rallies, *Triumph of the Will.*

The best-known privately produced, nondocumentary film on the Olympics was *Chariots of Fire* (produced by David Puttnam and directed by Hugh Hudson), which focused on the 1924 Olympic Games and two British runners, Eric Liddell and Harold Abrahams. *Chariots of Fire* won the Academy Award for Best Picture in 1981.

The most prominent producer of Olympic films has been the late American Jonah J. "Bud" Greenspan, who was initially assisted by his wife, Cappy Greenspan, in their film company, Cappy Productions. Greenspan has produced a remarkable series of Olympic movies called "The Olympiad Series." In addition, he has been the producer of many of the official Olympic films. The following are the Official Olympic films:

SUMMER

1932   *Los Angeles 1932.* Produced by the COJO Los Angeles 1932.

1936   *Olympia—Part I: Festival of the People; Part II: Festival of Beauty.* Produced and directed by Leni Riefenstahl.

1948   *The Glory of Sports.* Produced by the COJO London 1948. Directed by Castleton Knight.

1952   *Helsinki 1952.* Produced by the COJO Helsinki 1952. Directed by Chris Marker.

1956   *Melbourne 1956.* Produced by the COJO Melbourne 1956. Directed by René Lucot.

1960   *The Grand Olympics.* Produced by the COJO Rome 1960. Directed by Romolo Marcellini. (Also released in Italian as *La Grande Olimpiade.*)

1964   *Tokyo Olympiad.* Produced by Suketaru Taguchi. Directed by Kon Ichikawa.

1968   *The Olympics in Mexico.* Produced by Federico Amerigo. Directed by Alberto Isaac.

1972   *Visions of Eight*. Produced by David L. Wolper. Directed by Milos Forman, Kon Ichikawa, Claude Lelouch, Yury Ozerov, Arthur Penn, Michael Pfleghar, John Schlesinger, and Mai Zetterling.

1976   *Montreal 1976—Games of the XXIst Olympiad*. Produced by the COJO Montreal 1976. Directed by Jean-Claude Labrecque, Jean Beaudin, Marcel Carrière, and Georges Dufaux.

1980   *Olimpijskij Prazdnik*. Produced by the COJO Moscow 1980. Directed by Yury Ozerov.

1984   *The 1984 Summer Olympics. 16 Days of Glory*. Produced and Directed by Bud Greenspan and Cappy Productions.

1988   *Seoul 1988: Games of the XXIV Olympiad*. Produced by the National Film Production Center. Directed by Lee Kwang-Soo.

1992   **Marathon**. Produced by Ibergroup SA, a consolidated company formed from three Spanish film production companies: Group Films, Iberoamericana Films Internacional, and Lola Films. Directed by Carlos Saura.

1996   *Atlanta's Olympic Glory*. Produced and directed by Bud Greenspan and Cappy Productions.

2000   *Sydney 2000 Olympics: Gold from Down Under*. Produced and directed by Bud Greenspan and Cappy Productions.

2004   *Athens 2004: Stories of Olympic Glory*. Produced and directed by Bud Greenspan and Cappy Productions.

2008   *The Everlasting Flame: Beijing 2008*. Directed by Gu Jun and produced by Central Newsreel and Documentary Film Studio.

2012   *First: The Official Film of the London 2012 Games*. Directed and produced by Caroline Rowland.

WINTER

1936   *Jugend der Welt*. Produced by the Institut für den Wissenschaftlichen Film.

1948   *Olympic Games in White*. Produced by the COJO St. Moritz 1948. Directed by Torgny Wickman.

1952   Title not listed in the Official Report. Produced by Norsk Film A/S.

1956   *White Vertigo*. Produced by the COJO Cortina d'Ampezzo 1956. Directed by Giorgio Ferroni.

1960   *Flame in the Snow: An Official Film of the VIII Olympic Winter Games*. Produced by Marvin Becker Films in cooperation with the COJO Squaw Valley 1960.

1964   *Innsbruck 1964*. Produced by the COJO Innsbruck 1964.

1968   *Grenoble 1968—Treize Jours en **France**.* Produced by Georges Derocles. Directed by Claude Lelouch and François Reichenbach.

1972   *Sapporo Winter Olympics—1972.* Produced by the COJO Sapporo 1972.

1976   *White Rock—Innsbruck 1976.* Produced by the COJO Innsbruck 1976.

1980   Per the 1980 Olympic Winter Official Report (p. 123), "No 'official film' rights were granted by the Organizing Committee, and no 'official film' was produced by the Organizing Committee. A videotape copy of ABC's coverage of the Games was delivered to the IOC in compliance with the IOC's Rule 48 (1974 version) to document the Games."

1984   *A Turning Point—the Official Film of the XIV Winter Games.* Produced by the COJO Sarajevo 1984.

1988   *Calgary '88. 16 Days of Glory.* Produced and directed by Bud Greenspan and Cappy Productions.

1992   *One Light One World.* Produced by Jalbert Productions.

1994   *Lillehammer '94: 16 Days of Glory.* Produced and directed by Bud Greenspan and Cappy Productions.

1998   *Nagano '98 Olympics: Stories of Honor and Glory.* Produced and directed by Bud Greenspan and Cappy Productions.

2002   *Salt Lake 2002: Stories of Olympic Glory.* Produced and directed by Bud Greenspan and Cappy Productions.

2006   *Torino 2006: Stories of Olympic Glory.* Produced and directed by Bud Greenspan and Cappy Productions.

2010   *All Together Now—Vancouver 2010.* Directed by Fx Goby and Matthieu Landeur. Produced by Nexus Productions/Christine Ponzevera.

2014   *Rings of the World.* Directed by Sergei Miroshnichenko.

OLYMPIC FINANCE. Olympic finance is a complex topic, which has been the subject of many articles and one fairly definitive book in two editions. Interested readers should refer to the authoritative work by Holger Preuß, *The Economics of Staging the Olympics: A Comparison of the Games 1972–2008* (the most recent edition is Cheltenham: Edward Elgar Publishing, 2006).

Originally, the **International Olympic Committee** (IOC) was financed by Baron **Pierre de Coubertin,** who used his family fortune to support the organization that he had built, although it almost bankrupted him. The only income that the IOC had initially was dues paid by the members, which amounted to 300 Swiss francs per year after World War II, which was only rescinded in 1975. After World War II, the host cities were also requested to support the IOC with contributions of varying amounts, noted to be 100,000 Swiss francs in the 1950s. The IOC has been criticized because many of its members are wealthy, and several of them have been members of nobility or royalty. But Coubertin designed it this way on purpose. With little money supporting the IOC, he realized that he needed wealthy members so they could afford to travel to the **Olympic Games** and to **IOC Sessions**, and so they could support the IOC themselves, if necessary.

In the 1950s, the Olympic Games and the IOC found a new source of financing for their projects: **television**. The first televised broadcast of the Olympic Games occurred in 1936 at Berlin, but there were only a few people with television sets, and nobody outside a 10-mile radius from Berlin received the signal. In 1948 in London, the British Broadcasting Corporation paid the IOC about $3,000 for television rights. In 1952 at Helsinki and 1956 at Melbourne, television was available for local broadcasts, but technical limitations prevented the signal from being sent worldwide. It was not until 1960 that the Olympic Games were first broadcast to a worldwide audience.

Avery Brundage was the **IOC president** in the late 1950s, and he was concerned that television money would bring great problems to the IOC. It was in 1958 that the IOC first amended the *Olympic Charter* to mention television, with Rule 49 in the 1958 version of the *Charter* reading as follows: "The direct, or what is commonly called Live Television Rights, to report the Games, shall be sold by the **Organizing Committee**, subject to the approval of the International Olympic Committee, and the proceeds from this sale shall be distributed according to its instructions."

But neither Squaw Valley nor Rome would even discuss handing over television rights to the IOC for 1960. Their attitude was that the IOC had made this rule after they had been selected to host the Olympics, and that it did not apply to them retroactively. Rome eventually gave the IOC 5 percent of the money it collected from television rights, which totaled almost $1.2 million (U.S.). Over the next few Olympics, the income from televising the Olympics began to escalate. And in 1965, Brundage's prediction came true when the **International Federation** (IFs) demanded a one-third share of the television money. The **National Olympic Committee** (NOCs) followed suit shortly thereafter.

The IOC **Executive Board** addressed the situation at its meeting in Rome in 1966. **Marc Hodler**, Swiss **IOC member** who was chairman of the **Finance Commission**, came up with a scheme to divide the money, which was eventually accepted. Despite the increased money that the IOC was receiving from television, it was in dire financial straits by the early 1970s. Brundage ran the IOC much as Coubertin had, bearing the brunt of the costs from his own fortune, although he never lost his wealth in the process. But in the years

1968–1971, the IOC ran a deficit in its capital account of U.S. $1.5 million. IOC President **Lord Killanin** later commented, "I recall that when I took office in 1972 the IOC was working on borrowed money. After Moscow (1980), the IOC became a financially sound organization, but earlier I entered my caveat and reservations on that."

In 1971, the IOC amended the *Olympic Charter* further by establishing the fact that television moneys were the property of the IOC, and that the IOC would decide on the amounts distributed to the IFs, NOCs, and OCOGs. In the 1970s, the television rights fees expanded dramatically. Note the following total rights fees earned from 1968 to 1980:

1968	Mexico City	$9,750,000
1972	Munich	$17,792,000
1976	Montreal	$34,922,200
1980	Moscow	$100,200,784

With the increased television money, the IFs and NOCs increased their demands for a greater percentage. Further, not all IFs considered themselves equals. The International Association of Athletics Federations (IAAF), which governs track and field **athletics**, has long considered itself the most important IF and that track and field is the showcase sport of the Olympic Games. The IAAF demanded a larger proportion of money than the other IFs and threatened to break away from the Olympic Games and conduct separate world championships if its demands were not met—there were none until 1983.

At the same time, the Olympic Games themselves were becoming more and more expensive. The tragedy at Munich, in which 11 **Israeli** athletes and coaches were murdered by terrorists, brought a new dimension to Organizing Committee (OCOG) costs: vastly increased security expenses. And as the Games got bigger and bigger, the cost per athlete also escalated. Further, the host cities began to see the Olympics as a way to pay for civic improvements to the city, using some of the money generated to pay for infrastructure needed by the city, above and beyond the Olympics.

The OCOG budgets have escalated in response to the growing size of the Olympic Games and the security costs. In 2004, the bottom line for the Athens Olympic Games was quoted in the press as over U.S. $11 billion, a figure dwarfing all previous Olympics. The previous "record holder" was Barcelona in 1992, with a quoted cost of U.S. $7 billion, although the 1964 Tokyo Olympics, costing about U.S. $2 billion, probably rivaled Athens as the most expensive Olympics ever, when corrected for inflation. But even Athens looked like a cheapskate when Beijing spent upward of U.S. $40 billion for the 2008 Olympic Games.

The Athens U.S. $11 billion had to be raised among the smallest population of any Olympic nation since the Helsinki Olympics of 1952, when the budget was probably nearer U.S. $10 million (in 2008 dollars), giving the **Olympic Movement** a thousand-fold absolute increase in costs in just over 50 years. Much of the cost has been allocated to the construction of new athletic venues, which often become white elephants to the host city after the Olympics are over, requiring millions of dollars yearly for upkeep but generating precious little income. Many of the Athens venues now sit fallow. Even Sydney, in sports-mad **Australia**, found the cost of maintaining the Olympic venues to be a problem, with over $35 million Australian dollars allocated per year for upkeep of the facilities alone.

Over 100 years ago, even Coubertin asked if these costs were worth it:

It would be very unfortunate, if the often exaggerated expenses incurred for the most recent **Olympiads**, a sizeable part of which represented the construction of permanent buildings, which were moreover unnecessary—temporary structures would fully suffice, and the only consequence is to then encourage use of these permanent buildings by increasing the number of occasions to draw in the crowds—it would be very unfortunate if these expenses were to deter [small] countries from putting themselves forward to host the Olympic Games in the future.

With these increasing costs beginning in the 1970s, the Olympic Games have rarely been profitable. In 1976 at Montreal, the OCOG ran up debt estimated by some at $1 billion (Canadian) and left the citizens of Quebec with a tax debt that they finished paying only in 2006. Faced with these escalating costs, very few cities want to host the Olympic Games. In 1980, **Juan Antonio Samaranch** succeeded to the presidency of the IOC. He noted that "the financing of the IOC is a matter of some urgency." Samaranch set it as one of his goals to make the IOC financially solvent. Despite the increased television revenues, the leaching of money by the IFs and NOCs kept the IOC in a difficult financial situation, to say nothing of the host cities. And the IOC was fully dependent on television money, notably from the **United States** networks, which paid the greatest rights fees. At the IOC Session in Berlin in 1985, Samaranch expressed the hope that the IOC "would no longer be totally dependent on the revenues from the sale of television rights."

In 1978, former **Canadian** Olympic **swimmer Dick Pound** was co-opted as a member of the IOC. Pound was a tax lawyer who brought immediate financial expertise to the IOC, and Samaranch was quick to take advantage of it. In the 1980s, Pound was placed in charge of negotiating television rights and of a new IOC commission, the New Sources of Financing Commission.

Samaranch charged Pound with making the IOC financially independent, loosening the grip held by American television.

At almost the same time, the Los Angeles Olympic Organizing Committee (LAOOC) chose a former college **water polo** player named **Peter Ueberroth** as its president. Ueberroth, a self-made businessman who had started one of the largest travel agencies in Southern California, approached the problem of financing the 1984 Olympic Games in a way not done before by organizing committees. He looked at the economic history of the Olympic Games by studying the previous **Official Reports** and immediately noted two things. One was that the greatest cost for all OCOGs was the building of new stadia and sports facilities. Second, he noted that the OCOGs had sold Olympic sponsorship, but had done so indiscriminately, to almost any bidder. In 1976 at Montreal, there were 168 sponsors, with more than 200 in 1980 at Moscow, and fully 380 at Lake Placid in 1980.

Ueberroth was fortunate in that he was organizing the Games in a city that had already held the Olympics, in 1932. Further, Los Angeles had numerous major sports facilities. Ueberroth was able to hold the Olympic Games in 1984 by building only a **cycling velodrome** and a **swimming** stadium, and he had both of them paid for by sponsors. For the main Olympic stadium, he was able to use the Los Angeles Coliseum, the site of the 1932 Olympics.

Ueberroth's financial acumen was brought to bear on the second problem of Olympic sponsorship. He protected the Olympic emblems, making them highly desired entities for sponsors. He sought not more sponsors, but fewer. His reasoning was that he would vastly increase the rights fees for each sponsor, but he would guarantee the sponsors use of the Olympic emblems and also guarantee them exclusivity within their own category of sales. For instance, there would be one soft drink company sponsoring the Olympics, not several, but that company would pay dearly.

And it worked. In the end, the LAOOC realized a profit of about U.S. $220 million. The profit brought howls of protests from numerous sources, as Ueberroth had often pleaded poverty to bring in and save more money, and the extra money gave his critics additional ammunition. Eventually the profits were used to support the U.S. Olympic Committee (USOC) and sports programs in Los Angeles.

Dick Pound saw all this happen and realized that Ueberroth's approach was a new paradigm that was ideal for the IOC and the Organizing Committees. The IOC had what nobody else had—the Olympic symbol, the **Olympic flag**, and the Olympic rings—and it could control the rights to these emblems. The IOC could produce large amounts of revenue by granting exclusive rights to the emblems. But like Ueberroth and the LAOOC, the IOC would limit the number of these sponsorships, making them highly valuable and sought after. Enter The Olympic Programme, later renamed **The Olympic Partners** (TOP).

TOP began in 1984 as a means of developing worldwide sponsorship of the Olympic Movement. Previously, a corporation could only sponsor the various OCOGs, the IFs, or the NOCs. It was difficult for them to be guaranteed worldwide rights to the Olympic emblems.

Each TOP program lasts for four years. It is an exclusive group, as for each Olympiad only nine to 12 worldwide sponsors are selected. Further, each sponsor is guaranteed exclusivity within its own category. Thus, Coca-Cola has always been the only soft drink associated with Olympic sponsorship under TOP. But the sponsors pay a very large rights fee, following the concept that Ueberroth brought to the Olympic Movement, now paying close to $100 million per quadrennium, but bringing in more than $900 million to the IOC for the 2009–2012 Olympiad, or TOP VII.

The IOC actually keeps only 10 percent of TOP income to finance itself. TOP money is distributed 50 percent to the Organizing Committees and 50 percent to the **Olympic family**. The Olympic family money is currently (as of 2014) distributed as follows: 20 percent to the NOCs, 10 percent to the IOC, and 20 percent to the USOC. No TOP money is allocated to the IFs, but they receive money from television rights fees distributed by the IOC.

Note that the USOC receives fully 20 percent of TOP monies, although it was only 12 percent for TOP I. This is an unusual arrangement and has engendered great controversy within the Olympic Movement. The USOC demanded this money from the IOC because most of the TOP sponsors were primarily based in the United States. It was the USOC's reasoning that by bringing these sponsors into TOP, this was sponsorship money that had formerly been available to the USOC exclusively. It felt it should be reimbursed above and beyond the other NOCs and threatened not to participate in TOP if this demand was not met. Negotiations to change this are a major concern among many IOC members, who feel that the USOC receives an unfair proportion, and this has led to much ill will and resentment against the United States from other members of the Olympic Movement.

TOP has been very successful, achieving Samaranch's goals. At the 93rd IOC Session in Puerto Rico in 1989, Dick Pound confirmed that "The Olympic Movement no longer depends solely on the revenues from American television." Mission accomplished. But the money brought problems. First, it was no longer true that no city wanted to host the Olympics. Cities were lining up to be selected. For the 1992 Olympics, there were six candidate cities, but this number increased over the next few years: for 1996, six; for 2000, eight; and for 2004, 11. With the increased number of cities bidding, it became more difficult for cities to get noticed, and the **Olympic bribery**

scandal, which was exposed in late 1998 and early 1999, was surely a result of this and of the fact that the Olympic Games were now awash in cash.

With the increased revenue from TOP, there has been a concomitant increase in the rights fees paid by the television networks. In fact, Dick Pound produced still another new method of bringing in revenue or at least guaranteeing its availability. The U.S. television network National Broadcasting Company (NBC) was chosen to broadcast the 1996 Olympic Games. Shortly before those Olympics, Pound and NBC President **Dick Ebersol** announced that the IOC and NBC had signed a contract in which NBC would televise the next five Olympic Games: 2000 Sydney, 2002 Salt Lake City, 2004 Athens, 2006 Torino, and 2008 Beijing. In 2011, NBC signed a contract with the IOC to televise the 2014, 2016, 2018, and 2020 Games for the price of U.S. $4.38 billion.

The early announcement came as a shock, especially to the competing networks, but it was a win-win situation for both NBC and the IOC. NBC could count on hosting the Games long term and make plans accordingly, possibly saving itself money by not having to reinvent the wheel with a new production organization for each Olympiad. The IOC could count on revenue for its own coffers and for the members of the Olympic Movement. And the OCOGs could plan their expenditures more precisely, knowing in advance how much television money they were to receive, both from television and from TOP. Further, since some of this money would be paid in advance, both the IOC and the OCOGs could generate further revenue from interest earned. This policy has since continued, with networks bidding for the Olympic Games in groups of several games on an international basis, and has also continued somewhat in TOP, with a few companies signing on for more than one Olympiad in advance.

The television money greatly escalated. The worldwide rights fees for the 1984–2008 Olympics went up, in U.S. dollars, as follows:

1984	Los Angeles	$286,914,000
1988	Seoul	$402,593,652
1992	Barcelona	$635,430,000
1996	Atlanta	$902,087,500
2000	Sydney	$1,328,500,000
2004	Athens	$1,498,300,000
2008	Beijing	$1,900,000,000

The rights fees for the Olympic Winter Games have also increased commensurately. With all this increased television revenue, the other parts of the Olympic Movement have increased their calls for greater percentages to be given to them. Currently, Olympic television rights fees are distributed by the IOC as follows:

Organizing Committees	49.0%
Olympic Family	51.0%
IOC	14.0%
International Federations	14.0%
Olympic Solidarity	14.0%
USOC	9.0%

Nothing is allocated to the NOCs directly, except for the USOC, which has again demanded an exception, but the money allocated to Olympic Solidarity eventually finds its way to the NOCs, although it is distributed by Olympic Solidarity to the neediest NOCs, and not evenly.

Not all IFs are considered equal when it comes to distribution of funds realized from television. The IOC recognizes four categories of IFs, Categories A–D, with Category A receiving the most money and Category D the least. The categories and IFs within them and the current distribution of funds (Summer IFs only) are as follows:

Category A	20.0%	Track and Field Athletics
Category B	7.8%	Basketball, Football (Soccer), Gymnastics, Swimming, Volleyball
Category C	3.1%	Cycling, Equestrian, Handball, Hockey (Field)
Category D	1.6%	Rowing, Tennis, Archery, Badminton, Baseball, Boxing, Canoeing, Fencing, Judo, Modern Pentathlon, Sailing, Shooting, Softball, Table Tennis, Weightlifting, Wrestling

Other problems related to Olympic finance still exist, and they are far from solved. In addition to the bribery problems, the IOC must now address the problem of rampant commercialism at the Games, which turned downtown Atlanta in 1996 into an almost circus-like marketplace. After Atlanta, the IOC took steps to curtail commercialization at future Olympic Games, and Sydney was a major improvement. But to some degree, commercialization is necessary to support the increased costs of the Olympics. *Business Life* noted in 1996, "There is little doubt that the prudent development of marketing and sponsorship has saved the Games. . . . Without such corporate support, it would be extremely difficult for a modern city to host the Games."

The IOC is also concerned about companies that attempt to use the Olympic image for their own promotion, without actually supporting the Olympic Movement financially. The use of the Olympic rings and Olympic symbols is expressly forbidden without permission from the IOC, NOCs, or the Organizing Committees. But many companies attempt to circumvent the huge costs of sponsorship in what the IOC terms "ambush marketing."

The Internet has also brought many new problems. Should real-time video be allowed on the Internet, which usurps the exclusive rights of television networks to video presentation? In December 2000, the IOC hosted an international conference on new media to address many questions and policies related to the Internet. It has since formed a new IOC commission to look into these problems.

So we have come full circle. From an Olympic Movement completely financed by the deep pockets and personal fortune of a French baron, the IOC has seen the depths of corporate near bankruptcy in the 1970s followed by a flow of almost unimagined riches. Like all sudden wealth, problems have come with the acquisition of money. These problems are ongoing, but the IOC has begun to address many of them through its response to the Olympic bribery scandal of 1999. But there are surely more issues to come.

OLYMPIC FLAG. The Olympic flag has a plain white background with no border. In the center is the Olympic symbol, which consists of five interconnected rings. They form two rows, of three rings above and two below. The rings of the upper row are, from left to right, blue, black, and red. The rings of the lower row are yellow and green. The rings are thought to symbolize the five continents: Europe, Asia, Africa, **Australia**, and America. The colors of the rings are thought to have been chosen because at least one of these colors can be found in the flag of every nation.

The origin of the flag's design is in some dispute. It is thought to be Baron **Pierre de Coubertin** who designed the symbol to honor and represent the 1914 **Olympic Congress** in Paris. Some sources state that Coubertin saw the rings at Delphi in 1913, but classics scholars believe this is highly unlikely and that they are of his own, modern invention. The idea of a flag was raised by the **International Olympic Committee** (IOC) in 1910, and a special committee worked to plan it. Several suggestions were made, notably by Theodore Cook (Great Britain) and Clarence von Rosen (Sweden), but little progress was made until Coubertin came up with his design. He commented in the August 1913 edition of *Revue Olympique*, "These five rings represent the five parts of the world from this point on won over to **Olympism** and given to accepting fruitful rivalry. Furthermore, the six colors [including the white background] thus combined reproduce the colors of all the nations, with no exception." The flag was first flown at Chatsby Stadium in Alexandria, **Egypt**, for the Pan-Egyptian Games on 5 April 1914. It was presented to the IOC by Coubertin at the Olympic Congress in 1914 at the Sorbonne in Paris, where it was officially approved on 15 June 1914. The flag was also flown in 1915 at the San Francisco Exhibition and at the 1919 **IOC Session** in **Lausanne**, before it made its debut at the Olympic Games in 1920 at Antwerp, **Belgium**. The "primary" Olympic flag was thus known as "the Antwerp flag" and was the main Olympic flag flown at the stadium at all Olympic Games through 1984. In 1984, Seoul presented a new Olympic flag to the IOC, made of fine **Korean** silk, which was first flown at the 1988 Olympics. A second "primary" Olympic flag is used for the **Olympic Winter Games**, which was donated in 1952 by the host city of Oslo, **Norway**.

The Olympic flag is raised at the opening ceremony and flies over the main stadium throughout the **Olympic Games**. It is lowered at the closing ceremony. The mayor of the Olympic host city then presents the Olympic flag to the mayor of the next Olympic host city. The flag is to be kept in the town hall of the host city until the next Olympic Games. *See also* OLYMPIC CEREMONIES.

OLYMPIC FLAME, OLYMPIC TORCH, AND TORCH RELAY. The Olympic flame is a symbol reminiscent of the **Ancient Olympic Games**, in which a sacred flame burned at the altar of Zeus throughout the Games. The flame was first used at the modern Olympics in Amsterdam in 1928 and was lit again throughout the 1932 Los Angeles Olympics, but this marked the last time the flame was kindled at the site of the Games.

In 1936, **Carl Diem**, chairman of the **Organizing Committee** for the Berlin Olympics, proposed the idea of lighting the flame at ancient Olympia and transporting it to Berlin via a torch relay. This was done and has been repeated at every Olympics since.

The flame for the Olympic Games is lit in the Altis of the Ancient Olympic stadium at ancient Olympia, on the Greek Peloponnesus. The flame is lit during a ceremony by women dressed in robes similar to those worn by the ancient Greeks. It is lit naturally by the rays of the sun at Olympia, reflected off a curved mirror, and the high priestess then presents the torch to the first relay runner.

The flame for the **Olympic Winter Games** has not always been lit in Olympia. In 1952 and 1960, the flame for the Olympic Winter Games was lit at the hearth of Sondre Nordheim, the father of modern skiing, at his ancient home in Morgedal, **Norway**. In 1956, it was lit at the Temple of Jupiter in Rome for the Games in Cortina d'Ampezzo, **Italy**. Since 1964, the flame for the Olympic Winter Games has also been lit in ancient Olympia. In 1994, a second, unofficial flame was lit in Morgedal for the Lillehammer Olympics, which greatly upset the Greeks, who claim proprietary rights to the Olympic flame.

OLYMPIC GAMES. The Olympic Games refer to the sporting festival held in the summer months, often referred to as the Summer Olympics or Summer Games. The proper name of the sporting celebration is the Games of the . . .th **Olympiad**. The Games of the . . .th Olympiad are always held during the first year of the Olympiad that they celebrate. The Olympic Games are entrusted to a single host city, which is now elected seven years in advance of the scheduled Olympic Games.

OLYMPIC GAMES KNOWLEDGE SERVICES (OGKS). For each **Olympic Games**, an **Organizing Committee** (OCOG) is formed to manage the affairs and organize the forthcoming Games. In the late 1990s, it became apparent to the **International Olympic Committee** (IOC) that each of these OCOGs was forced to reinvent the wheel and essentially start from scratch. Knowledge, documents, and other material accumulated by each OCOG were rarely being passed along to the next OCOG. In response to this obvious lack of coordination of the OCOGs, in February 2002 the IOC formed the Olympic Games Knowledge Services as the exclusive knowledge management services company of the IOC. The role of OGKS is to pass information and know-how from one OCOG to the next and assist the OCOGs in beginning their organization of the next Olympic Games.

OLYMPIC GAMES STUDY COMMISSION. The Olympic Games Study Commission was formed in 2002 to study all aspects of the **Olympic Games**, primarily looking at ways to reduce the size, cost, and complexity of the Games. The commission prepared a report focusing on five areas of the organization of the Games: (1) Games format, (2) venues and facilities, (3) Games management, (4) number of accredited persons, and (5) service levels. The commission was chaired by **International Olympic Committee (IOC) member Richard Pound** from Canada and presented its report to the 115th **IOC Session** in Prague. After the report was presented, the commission was dissolved by **IOC President Jacques Rogge**.

OLYMPIC HYMN. *See* OLYMPIC ANTHEM.

OLYMPIC IDENTITY CARD. The Olympic identity card is an important political document. It is given to all members of the **Olympic family**, that is, athletes, officials, **International Olympic Committee (IOC) members** and delegates, **National Olympic Committee** members and delegates, and **International Federation** members and delegates. Its importance is that it establishes the identity of the holder and, with an appropriate national passport, is supposed to allow free passage into the country in which the host Olympic city is situated. Thus the card serves as, and supplants, a travel visa. Host cities are required to agree to recognize the right of all members of the **Olympic family** to enter the country of the host city, based on a valid passport and the Olympic identity card, and not require a visa.

OLYMPIC LITERATURE. The literature surrounding the Olympic Games is voluminous. The **International Olympic Committee** now publishes various magazines, journals, press releases, and books. Each **National Olympic Committee** and **International Federation** may also publish literature about the Olympic Games and often does so. The **Organizing Committees** publish a great deal of official information in addition to press releases and packets.

Private authors have also developed an enormous amount of Olympic literature. Books on the Olympics are now produced prior to and after each Olympic Games, in most of the major languages of the world. With the advent of advanced technology, some are now being produced on CD-ROMs to be read on computers.

No current up-to-date bibliography of Olympic literature exists. The two most complete and most recent are currently almost 30 years old: *The Olympics: A Bibliography*, compiled by **Bill Mallon** (New York: Garland Press, 1983) and *Bibliography: Geschichte der Leibesübungen, Band 5, Olympische Spiele*, 2nd ed., compiled by **Karl Lennartz** (Bonn: Verlag Karl Hofmann, 1983).

However, because of computer technology and Internet capabilities, it is unlikely that a full-scale book-type bibliography will be produced again. Probably the most complete and up-to-date Olympic bibliography can be found by searching the SPORTDiscus site, which is the sport bibliography of the Canadian literary resource Sport Information Resource Centre and is updated quarterly (the URL for this site is www.sirc.ca/products/, although it does require a subscription to use the database). *See also OLYMPIC MESSAGE; OLYMPIC REVIEW.*

OLYMPIC MASCOTS. In 1968, the Grenoble **Organizing Committee** produced the first Olympic mascot, although it was considered unofficial. For those **Olympic Winter Games**, the mascot was a small man on skis, which was given no name originally, but became known as "Schuß." Later that year, the **Mexico** City Organizing Committee had a small red Jaguar as its Olympic mascot, again with no known name. In 1972, there was no mascot for the Sapporo Winter Olympics, but Munich had a stuffed toy in the form of a dachshund, named Waldi, as its mascot. Since those Olympics, every **Organizing Committee** has had a mascot, or several, which are now used for marketing and publicizing the coming Olympics. The mascots selected for the Sochi Games in 2014 were chosen in a unique way. A nationwide design contest was held in **Russia**, from 1 September to 5 December 2010 resulting in 24,000 designs being submitted for the contest. A short list of 11 designs were announced in December 2010 and were presented to the public on 7 February 2011. A live national television broadcast included a nationwide text message voting, where Russians voted for their favorite mascot. The various mascots are listed in the following tables.

Olympic Games Mascots

Year	Host City	Mascot(s)	Name(s)	Notes
1968	Mexico City	Red jaguar		
1972	Munich	Dachshund	Waldi	A popular dog breed in Bavaria.
1976	Montréal	Beaver	Amik	Amik is Algonquin for beaver.
1980	Moscow	Bear	Misha	The full name was Mikhail Potapych Troptygin.
1984	Los Angeles	Eagle	Sam	In the form of a bald eagle, the American national bird.
1988	Seoul	Tigers	Hodori, Hosuni	Male and female tiger cubs.
1992	Barcelona	Dog	Cob	A cubist Catalan sheepdog.
1996	Atlanta	Computer designed mascot	Izzy	The original name was "Whatizit."
2000	Sydney	Platypus, Echidna, Kookaburra	Sid, Millie, Olly	
2004	Athens	Cartoon depictions of Olympia gods	Phèvos, Athenà	Phèvos was the Olympian god of light and music, known as Apollo. Athenà was the goddess of wisdom and the patron of the city of Athens.
2008	Beijing	Five trolls, in Chinese, "Fuwa."	Beibei, Jinjing, Yingying, Nini, Huanhuan	Beibei = blue, Jingjing = black, Yingying = yellow, Nini = green, Huanhuan = red, Originally called the "Five Friendlies."

Year	Host City	Mascot(s)	Name(s)	Notes
2012	London	Computer-generated morphs	Wenlock, Mandeville	Named for Much Wenlock, site of an attempt at resurrection of the Olympics in the 19th century, and Stoke Mandeville, site of the forerunner of the Paralympics.

Olympic Winter Games Mascots

Year	Host City	Mascot(s)	Name(s)	Notes
1968	Grenoble, small man on skis	Schuss	Unofficial mascot, originally with no name.	
1972	Sapporo	none		
1976	Innsbruck	Snowman	Name never announced	
1980	Lake Placid	Raccoon	Roni	Named for the Adirondack Mountain Range.
1984	Sarajevo	Wolf	Vučko	Symbol of humans befriending animals.
1988	Calgary	Polar bears	Howdy and Hidy	Howdy = male, Hidy = female.
1992	Albertville	Half-man, half-star symbol	Magique	
1994	Lillehammer	Historical children characters	Kristin, Håkon	Based on Kristin (née 1181), the daughter of King Sverre, and Håkon, king of Norway from 1217 to 1263, who as an infant was rescued from enemies by two medieval Birkebeiner warriors.
1998	Nagano	Snowlets	Suki Nokki	These replaced Snowple, a white ermine, Lekki, and Tsukki, characteristic of the Japanese Alps. They resembled snowflake-like young owls (owlets).

Year	Host City	Mascot(s)	Name(s)	Notes
2002	Salt Lake City	Snowshoe hare, Coyote, American black bear	Powder, Copper, Coal	Three cartoon depictions of animals that have appeared as major characters in the myths and legends of Native Americans. The three mascots also represented the Olympic motto "Citius, Altius, Fortius": swifter, higher, stronger. Each mascot character wore a charm around its neck fashioned after the original Anasazi or Fremont-style petroglyph to remind the mascots of their heritage.
2006	Torino	Stylized cartoon characters	Neve, Gliz	Neve (the female) had a snowball for a head, and an orange body; Gliz (the male) had an ice cube for a head, and a blue body.
2010	Vancouver	Snowboarding sea-bear, Shy and gentle Sasquatch, Animal guardian spirit, Vancouver Island marmot	Miga, Quatchi, Sumi, Mukmuk	Quatchi and Miga represented the Winter Olympics. Sumi represented the Paralympic Games. Mukmuk was the sidekick, considered an honorary member of the mascot team.
2014	Sochi	Polar bear, Leopard, Hare	Bely Mishka, Snow Leopard, Zaika	Designed by Silvia Petrova (bear), Vadim Pak (leopard), Oleg Serdechney (hare). First mascots chosen by popular vote.

OLYMPIC MEDALS. Olympic Medals are given as awards for finishing in the first three places in the events of the **Olympic Games**. The champion receives a gold medal, the runner-up a silver medal, and the third place finisher a bronze medal. At the 1896 Olympics, the winner received only a silver medal and the runner-up a bronze medal.

The medals must be at least 60 mm in diameter and 3 mm thick. They are designed by the **Organizing Committee of the Olympic Games**, upon approval by the **International Olympic Committee (IOC) Executive Board**. The "gold" medal is actually silver gilt, which must be gilded with at least six grams of pure gold. It was only in 1908 and 1912 that the gold medalists received medals of pure gold. The metal for the first and second place medals must be silver of at least 925/1000 grade.

Since 1932, Olympic medals have been given to the medalists at ceremonies at the conclusion of their events. The medals are draped around the athletes' necks, hung from a ribbon or other decorative necklace. This custom did not begin until 1960 in Rome. Prior to that time, the medals were handed to the athletes in specially designed boxes. Until 1932, medals were awarded as a part of the closing ceremony.

OLYMPIC MESSAGE. The *Olympic Message* was a publication of the **International Olympic Committee**. It was first published in May 1982 and was published three or four times per year. Its publication was discontinued after the December 1994 issue (Volume 40). The *Olympic Message* was different from the *Olympic Review* in that each issue usually studied in detail a single theme of the **Olympic Movement**.

OLYMPIC MOTTO. The official Olympic motto is "*Citius, Altius, Fortius*," a Latin phrase meaning "swifter, higher, stronger." The Olympic motto was adopted by Baron **Pierre de Coubertin** for the **International Olympic Committee** after hearing of its use by Reverend Father Henri Martin Didon of Paris, a Dominican friar and teacher. Didon, headmaster of Arcueil College, used the phrase while describing the athletic accomplishments of his students at that school. He had previously been at the school Albert Le Grand, where the Latin words were carved in stone above the main entrance. Coubertin used the motto in the very first issue of *Revue Olympique. See also* OLYMPIC CREED.

OLYMPIC MOVEMENT. "Olympic Movement" is a phrase often used by the **International Olympic Committee** (IOC) and practitioners and administrators of international sport. However, it is not well defined. The *Olympic Charter* states simply that, "The Olympic Movement, led by the IOC, stems from modern **Olympism**." The IOC has, however, defined the phrase more fully in some of its press releases. It has stated that the Olympic Movement encompasses the IOC, the **International Federations**, and the **National**

Olympic Committees, and that the IOC is the supreme authority of the Olympic Movement. In addition, the IOC has stated its purpose and its fundamental principles as "to contribute to building a peaceful and better world by educating youth through sport practiced without discrimination of any kind and in the Olympic spirit, which requires mutual understanding with a spirit of friendship, solidarity, and fair play. The activity of the Olympic Movement is permanent and universal. It reaches its peak with the bringing together of the athletes of the world at the great sport festival, the **Olympic Games**."

OLYMPIC MUSEUM. An Olympic Museum had been a dream of the **International Olympic Committee** (IOC) for many years. In 1915, **Pierre de Coubertin** announced his intention to set up an Olympic Museum in **Lausanne** to store the archives of the IOC and to become a public information center on the **Olympic Movement**. **IOC President Juan Antonio Samaranch** made the dream a reality. He began his plans for an Olympic Museum in 1981, shortly after his election as IOC president, when the IOC bought a building at 18 avenue Ruchonnet in Lausanne and established a provisional museum. In 1984, the IOC acquired two plots of land in the Ouchy section of Lausanne, overlooking Lake Geneva (Lac Léman). Construction on the permanent Olympic Museum began on this land in 1988. On 23 June 1993, the Olympic Museum was inaugurated on the 99th anniversary of the creation of the IOC. The Olympic Museum is intended to be the universal depository of the written, visual, and graphic memory of the **Olympic Games**. Samaranch stated that "the Olympic Museum will be a global source of information on the impact of the Olympic tradition on art, culture, the economy and world peace. The focal point of the meaning of the Olympic Games and their role in modern society, the Olympic Museum will be both a witness and a center for reflection."

The collection of the Olympic Museum features many pieces of sports equipment and clothing used by famous Olympians, as well as medals, torches, flags, collectibles, pieces of art, and so forth, all pertaining to the Olympic Games. In 2012–2013, the museum underwent a substantial renovation and was reopened in December 2013.

There are other Olympic museums in other parts of the world, although not operated by the IOC. Lake Placid, New York, has a museum (officially known as the 1932 and 1980 Lake Placid Winter Olympic Museum) commemorating the two Olympic Games that were held in that small town. Cologne, **Germany**, has an extensive museum, the German Sports and Olympics Museum, on the banks of the Rhine River. In 2007, the city of Barcelona, **Spain**, opened the Joan Antoni Samaranch Olympic and Sports Museum. **Qatar** has recently begun work on a 9,000 square meter Qatar Olympic and Sports Museum that has its planned opening in Doha in 2015.

OLYMPIC OATH. The Olympic Oath is a pledge to uphold the spirit of sportsmanship and is taken at the opening ceremony by representatives of the host country on behalf of all competitors and officials. In the July 1906 edition of the *Revue Olympique*, **Pierre de Coubertin** referred to the urgent need to introduce into the few but very important **Olympic ceremonies** an athletes' oath of fairness and impartiality. The protocol was first introduced at Antwerp in 1920, when the noted Belgian **fencer** Victor Boin performed the ceremony. A similar ceremony was conducted at the first **Olympic Winter Games** at Chamonix in 1924, when all competitors took the oath collectively, although they were led by **France**'s Camille Mandrillon. The first **woman** to take the oath was the Italian skier Giuliana Chenal-Minuzzo, at the 1956 Olympic Winter Games in Cortina d'Ampezzo. The first woman to take the oath at the **Olympic Games** was **German** track and field athlete Heidi Schüller, at the 1972 Olympic Games in Munich.

Boin initially recited the following words: "We swear that we will take part in the Olympic Games in a spirit of chivalry, for the honor of our country and for the glory of sport." This oath was modified slightly in 1961, when the term *swear* was replaced by *promise*, and the phrase "the honor of our country" was replaced by "the honor of our teams," in an obvious attempt to eliminate nationalism from the Games.

In 1999, the **IOC 2000 Commission** recommended a change to the Olympic Oath, which was enacted by the **IOC Session**. This change added a statement to the oath in which the Olympic athletes would renounce the use of drugs in sport. The current edition of the ***Olympic Charter*** establishes the following text for the Athletes' Oath: "In the name of all the competitors I promise that we shall take part in these Olympic Games, respecting and abiding by the rules which govern them, committing ourselves to a sport without **doping** and without drugs, in the true spirit of sportsmanship, for the glory of sport and the honor of our teams." Since 1972, the judges have also sworn an oath, the text of which, in conformity with the current *Olympic Charter*, is as follows: "In the name of all the judges and officials, I promise that we shall officiate in these Olympic Games with complete impartiality, respecting and abiding by the rules which govern them, in the true spirit of sportsmanship." *See also* OLYMPIC CEREMONIES; *OLYMPIC REVIEW*; Appendix VII.

OLYMPIC ORDER. The Olympic Order is the supreme individual honor accorded by the **International Olympic Committee**. It was created in 1974 and is to be awarded to "any person who has illustrated the Olympic Ideal through his/her action, has achieved remarkable merit in the sporting world, or has rendered outstanding services to the Olympic cause, either through his/her own personal achievement(s) or his/her contribution to the development of sport." Originally, the Olympic Order was separated into three categories: gold, silver, and bronze. Currently, there are only gold and silver categories. *See also* Appendix V for a list of recipients of the Olympic Order in Gold.

OLYMPIC PARTNERS, THE (TOP). Formerly known as The Olympic Programme, The Olympic Partners is a fund-raising program administered by the **International Olympic Committee** (IOC), which began in the early 1980s. It is used to generate revenue for the IOC and has been very successful. TOP works by soliciting only a few sponsors, no more than 12 at a time to date (as of 2014), guaranteeing them exclusive marketing rights to the Olympic symbol within their market niche, and providing that guarantee for a complete **Olympiad**. Each TOP edition thus lasts for four years. To date, there have been TOP I through TOP VII, with TOP VIII currently active, running from 2013 through 2016. Because of the exclusivity of the program, the IOC has been able to command large amounts of revenue from the sponsors, which has guaranteed the success of TOP. During the TOP VII program (2009–2012), the IOC earned U.S. $950 million, which accounts for some 16 percent of the IOC's total marketing revenue. The 10 current TOP partners are Atos Origin, Coca-Cola, Dow, General Electric, McDonald's, Omega, Panasonic, Procter & Gamble, Samsung, and Visa.

OLYMPIC PHILATELY, NUMISMATIC, AND MEMORABILIA COMMISSION. Olympic stamps helped fund the 1896 Olympics, and thousands of stamps, coins, and other Olympic memorabilia are now sold for every Games. On 14 June 1993, the Olympic Philately, Numismatic, and Memorabilia Commission was formed by combining three associations that were recognized by the **International Olympic Committee** (IOC): the Fédération International de Philately Olympique, the Fédération Internationale de Numismatic Olympique, and the Association of Collectors of Olympic Memorabilia. Former **IOC President Juan Antonio Samaranch**, an avid stamp collector, chaired this commission until his death in 2010; he was succeeded by Gerhard Heiberg (Norway). In 2014, the chairman was Wu Ching-Kuo of **Chinese Taipei**. The commission sponsors an annual Olympic Collectors World Fair and an Olympic stamp show, Olymphilex. *See also* OLYMPIC COINS.

OLYMPIC PROGRAM. Rule 45 of the *Olympic Charter* covers the "Programme of the Olympic Games." This rule does not specify many details, declaring that (45.1) the program is reviewed by the **International Olympic Committee** (IOC) for each edition of the Games; (45.2) the program can be divided into sports, **disciplines**, and events; (45.3) the **IOC Session** decides whether to include a sport, although only World Anti-Doping Code–compliant sports may be elected; and (45.4) the IOC **Executive Board** can decide to include disciplines or events.

The *Olympic Charter* does not specifically define the term *sport*, and Olympic sports are defined only as being governed by the **International Federations** (IFs) referred to in the bylaws to Rule 45. These bylaws define, for both the Summer and the Winter Olympics, a set of "core sports." For the Summer Games, the *Charter* lists 26 IFs, of which at least 25 must be selected by the IOC Session to be held at the next Olympics. Additional sports may be added to the program, with a maximum of 28. The core list for the Winter Olympics includes seven IFs, all of which must be selected. Additional sports may be picked for the Winter Games as well, with no maximum set.

A few of these Olympic sports are actually viewed by many as several different sports, such as aquatics and skating. In IOC terminology, such sports are subdivided into disciplines, defined as "a branch of a sport comprising one or several events." Eleven of the Olympic sports are subdivided into disciplines:

- **Aquatics**: **diving, open water swimming, swimming, synchronized swimming**, and **water polo**
- **Athletics**: track, field, road, and combined
- **Bobsledding**: bobsleigh and **skeleton**
- **Canoeing and kayaking**: **sprint** and **slalom**
- **Cycling**: track, road, **mountainbiking**, and **BMX**
- **Equestrianism**: dressage, eventing, and **jumping**
- **Gymnastics**: artistic gymnastics, **rhythmic gymnastics**, and **trampolining**
- **Skating**: **figure skating, short-track speed skating**, and **speed skating**
- **Skiing**: **Alpine skiing, cross-country skiing, freestyle skiing, Nordic combined, ski jumping**, and **snowboarding**
- **Volleyball**: volleyball and **beach volleyball**
- **Wrestling**: **freestyle** and **Greco-Roman**

Finally, Rule 45 defines an *event*, which is "a competition in a sport or in one of its disciplines, resulting in a ranking and giving rise to the award of medals and diplomas."

Past versions of the *Olympic Charter* defined rules for the inclusion of sports, disciplines, and events. For example, motorized sports were not admissible, and events had to have been included in at least two World Championships. Presently, no such rules exist. Instead, the IOC Program Commission analyzes the Olympic sports after every Olympics, based on a set of evaluation criteria composed in 2004. These 33 criteria are grouped in seven areas:

history and tradition, universality, popularity, image and environment, athlete health, IF development, and cost. These evaluation reports are used by the IOC Session to vote on addition of new sports, and by the IOC Executive Board to decide on new disciplines and events. Present Olympic sports are also evaluated using the same criteria, to review their suitability.

According to the *Charter*, new sports should be included no later than the session at which the host city is elected, and new events no later than three years before the Games. In practice, these rules are often violated, using Bylaw 45.1.5, which allows the IOC to bypass the aforementioned deadlines with approval of the IF, the **Organizing Committee of the Olympic Games** (OCOG), and the IOC Executive Board. This shortcut for new sports and events has been used several times, such as for the inclusion of skeleton for the 2002 Winter Olympics, which was approved only in October 1999.

The influence of the IOC on the Olympic Program has changed considerably since 1896. The 1894 Sorbonne Congress had devised a list of Olympic sports and events, but this was not fully followed by the Athens organizers; for example, the sport of ice skating was impossible to organize in 19th-century **Greece**. In following editions, the number of sports and events fluctuated wildly, with determination of the program virtually at the discretion of the OCOGs, with some input from the IFs, if they even existed at all. Several of the IFs were only formed in response to problems governing their sports at the Olympics, notably the track and field athletics federation, the International Amateur Athletic Federation.

But the IOC knew that the idea of having no organization or design behind the program was not acceptable. The 7th **Olympic Congress** was held in **Lausanne** 2–7 June 1921. Its subject was, "The Modification of the Olympic Program and Conditions of Participation." It was the first major attempt by the IOC to formalize the Olympic Program, but it would not be the last. However, the Congress did not fully achieve its aims, because the IFs would not relinquish their control over the program of their sports. Norbert Müller notes in *One Hundred Years of Olympic Congresses 1894–1994*, "The Congress could not bring about a more concise Program of competition. The federations present referred to their right to determine the Program of competition themselves. The IOC had to realize that it had underestimated the self-confidence of the federations and the result[ant] resistance against cancellations."

Still, one of the demands passed by the IOC was that Olympic sports had to have an IF. This led to the formation of several IFs, such as for (field) **hockey**, which had been banned from the 1924 Games because of the lack of an IF. Over the years, the influence of the IOC on the Olympic Program gradually increased to the current level, while the roles of the IFs and the OCOGs have become marginal.

In addition to the question of admitting new sports and events, the Olympic Program Commission must address the problem of "gigantism" of the Olympic Games. The size of the Olympic Games has increased dramatically since 1896. In Athens, 43 events were contested, with just 176 athletes competing. In the first post–World War II Games at London, 59 nations sent 4,372 competitors to the Olympics, competing in 149 events. And at the most recent Summer Games in London, 302 gold medals were contested by 10,519 athletes from 205 countries. With this increase in size comes commensurate increase in cost. The cost increases at more than a linear rate relative to the athletes, because of the increased security, the increased complexity of the competitions and venues, and the growing number of spectators and media. With these increased costs, ways must be found to pay for the Olympic Games, and some of these options, notably increasing marketing and commercialization, are not really palatable to the Olympic Movement.

The main option would seem to be to limit the number of events. For example, one may wonder if there needs to be 17 swimming events for men and for **women** or if **boxing** needs 10 different weight classes. The IOC has tried to follow this path, initially suggesting a cap on the number of Olympic events at 280, later at 300. But neither of these goals was achieved, as it turned out to be difficult to replace events. In fact, if Olympic events are removed at all, they are usually replaced by another event in that same sport. The Program Commission has also advocated the removal of sports (e.g., **modern pentathlon**) and disciplines (e.g. Greco-Roman wrestling), but these did not meet with approval of the IOC Session in 2005. At the session in **Singapore**, **baseball** and **softball** became the first sports since skeleton (abolished after the 1948 Winter Games) to be removed from the Olympic Program. However, in 2009 the IOC Session recommended two new sports to be added for the 2016 Games, **golf** and **rugby**, thereby increasing the number of events again.

Since reducing the number of events on the Olympic Program has not worked out, the IOC has now set its sights on limiting the number of competitors and officials. The bylaw of Rule 45 of the *Olympic Charter* states that "In the absence of a decision to the contrary taken by the IOC Executive Board and written into the Host City Contract, the number of athletes competing in the Games of the **Olympiad** shall be limited to ten thousand five hundred (10,500) and the numbers of officials to five thousand (5,000)." The target number of 10,500 is fairly ambitious, as this number has been surpassed at the four most recent Olympics (2000, 2004, 2008, and 2012). However, the number of athletes is restricted more and more. Each of the sports on the Olympic Program is allotted a maximum number of athletes—the exact number is determined in cooperation with the IF—and for several sports, especially those recently added, this number is fairly low. For example, only 32 trampolining competitors (16 men, 16 women) were allowed to compete in 2008 and 2012. In addition, the number of sports in which any country can enter a competitor, regardless of meeting qualifying limits, has been reduced to two. This has not strictly been adhered to, as for example in speed skating in Sochi, where the Netherlands won gold, silver, and bronze in several events. Only in athletics and swimming can any nation enter competitors, and even then this is restricted to one man and one woman (unless qualifying norms are met). In other sports, wild card spots are available to ensure an international field, but the number of spots is limited.

It remains to be seen if the IOC can retain the current size of the Olympics without removing sports. The Olympic Program features several sports that are relatively obscure (e.g., modern pentathlon, **archery**) or that fail to attract the best athletes in the world (e.g., **football**, boxing), while many sports, often more popular internationally, are lining up for a place at the Olympics. One thing seems certain: the Olympic Program will be different at every Olympics.

OLYMPIC PROGRAM COMMISSION. The Olympic Program Commission reviews and analyzes the **Olympic Program**, reviewing sports, **disciplines**, and events for each sport at the Games of the **Olympiad** and the **Olympic Winter Games**. It also develops recommendations on the principles and structure of the **Olympic Program**, most recently published in the form of 39 criteria in 2012. These criteria are grouped in seven areas: general, governance, history and tradition, universality, popularity, athletes, development of the **International Federation** (IF) and finance. The Commission makes recommendations to the **International Olympic Committee** (IOC) **Executive Board** and presents reports to the **IOC Session**. The Commission is composed of **IOC members** and representatives from the **National Olympic Committees** and the IFs. The current (as of 2014) chairman is Franco Carraro from Italy.

OLYMPIC PROGRAMME, THE. *See* OLYMPIC PARTNERS, THE.

OLYMPIC REVIEW. The *Olympic Review* is the official journal of the **International Olympic Committee**. It has been published under various titles relatively continuously since 1894. Originally published by **Pierre de Coubertin**, its first title was *Bulletin du Comité International des Jeux Olympiques.* From 1901 to 1914, it first took its current name in French, *Revue Olympique.* From 1938 to 1944, it was published in Berlin with the German title *Olympische Rundschau*, although French and English editions were also available. Other titles used during its publishing history include *Bulletin* *du Comité International Olympique, Bulletin Officiel du Comité International Olympique, Pages de critique et d'histoire,* and *Lettre d'information/Newsletter/Carta información.* It is now published monthly in English, French, German, and Spanish. Since 1970, the official title has remained *Olympic Review, Revue Olympique, Olympische Rundschau,* and *Revista Olimpica. See also OLYMPIC MESSAGE.*

OLYMPIC RINGS. *See* OLYMPIC FLAG.

OLYMPIC SOLIDARITY. Olympic Solidarity is a program through which the **International Olympic Committee** (IOC) helps the sporting development of underprivileged nations. Certain IOC fundraising is distributed via Olympic Solidarity to the **National Olympic Committees** (NOCs) that the IOC recognizes to be in the greatest need. This has taken the form of coaching assistance, technical assistance, and funds to help athletes travel to the **Olympic Games** and other international sporting events. The goal of Olympic Solidarity is stated in the *Olympic Charter* thus: "The aim of Olympic Solidarity is to organise assistance to NOCs, in particular those which have the greatest need of it."

Olympic Solidarity began in 1961 as the International Olympic Aid Committee at the suggestion of Jean, Count de Beaumont of France. In 1968, this committee became a **Commission of the IOC**, while retaining the same name. In 1971, Adriaan van Karnebeek of the Netherlands took the initiative for further developments by setting up an Olympic Solidarity Commission through the Permanent General Assembly of National Olympic Committees (*see also* ASSOCIATION DES COMITÉS NATIONAUX OLYMPIQUES). In 1972, the two groups merged to become what is now known as Olympic Solidarity. It was originally headquartered in Rome, but in 1979, at the 81st **IOC Session**, Olympic Solidarity was moved to its present headquarters in **Lausanne**. In 1982, Anselmo López became its first full-time director, a position he held through 1995. He remains the honorary director, with the post of director being held since 1995 by Pere Miró. The chairman of the Olympic Solidarity Commission is IOC member Cheikh Ahmad Al-Fahad Al-Sabah of **Kuwait.**

OLYMPIC SOLIDARITY COMMISSION. *See* OLYMPIC SOLIDARITY.

OLYMPIC STAMPS. Olympic stamps have been issued since the first modern Olympic Games in Athens in 1896. The Greek government issued a series of 12 different stamps as a means to help finance the Ist **Olympic Games** of the modern era. This has since become a common method used by **Organiz-**

ing **Committees** to raise money. The 1896 Olympic stamps are considered the first stamps in the world to feature a sports theme. No stamps were issued for the 1900 or 1904 Olympic Games or for the Olympic Games of 1908 or 1912. But **Greece** issued a series of 14 stamps for the 1906 **Intercalated Olympic Games**. In 1920, **Belgium** issued a series of three stamps to assist in financing the Games. Since 1920, every host nation has produced a series of Olympic stamps. In 1924, **Uruguay** produced three stamps to commemorate its **football** team's gold medal and repeated this in 1928: both the football gold medal and the commemorative stamps. These were the first stamps issued by a nonhost nation related to the Olympic Games. **Czechoslovakia** also produced a series of three stamps in honor of hosting the 8th **Olympic Congress** in Prague in 1925, and in 1928, **Portugal** issued a series of Olympic stamps in honor of the 1928 Olympic Games. Since the 1920s, it has become common for many nonhost countries to produce Olympic stamps. The **International Olympic Committee** (IOC) has recognized this and formed the **Olympic Philately, Numismatic, and Olympic Memorabilia Commission**. The Commission was led until his death by former **IOC President Juan Antonio Samaranch**, who was an avid stamp collector. The hobby of collecting Olympic stamps has become widespread, and an organization has been formed devoted to it: the Fédération Internationale Philately Olympique, which has 31 national chapters as of 2014. *See also* OLYMPIC COINS.

OLYMPIC STUDIES CENTRE. The Olympic Studies Centre is located in a separate building adjacent to the **Olympic Museum** in **Lausanne, Switzerland**. It was created by the **International Olympic Committee** (IOC) to preserve and disseminate information about the **Olympic Movement** and to coordinate and promote research. The Centre contains a large library, which is open to the public, as well as the IOC Historical Archives, parts of which may be examined by scholars with prior, written approval. The Olympic Studies Centre also conducts conferences and symposia to spread the message of **Olympism**. There are also more than 30 locations throughout the world primarily in educational institutions that have Olympic Studies Centers that are not administered by the IOC.

OLYMPIC SYMBOL. *See* OLYMPIC FLAG.

OLYMPIC TORCH AND TORCH RELAY. *See* OLYMPIC FLAME.

OLYMPIC TRUCE. It is often stated that in ancient **Greece**, a sacred Olympic truce, or *ekecheiria*, existed that provided for all wars to cease during the **Olympic Games**. In addition, all persons traveling to or from the Olympic

Games were guaranteed free passage to Olympia, in the city-state of Elis, even if passing through lands or city-states that were at war. It is quite certain that the Olympic truce never existed fully in this form, and recent research by classical scholars indicates that this is an oversimplification of the facts. It has been noted that the Olympic truce "never stopped a war, nor indeed were the Eleans so foolishly utopian as to imagine they could achieve that" (Finley and Pleket, *The Olympic Games*, 98 [London: Chatto & Windus, 1976]). Apparently, the Olympic law only forbade open warfare against the Eleans, and the truce was specifically meant only to not disrupt the Olympic Games, allowing safe passage for all athletes, artists, and spectators traveling to and from Olympia.

In 1992, the **International Olympic Committee** (IOC) took steps to reinstitute this important part of Olympic lore by creating the Olympic Truce Project. Contact was made by **IOC President Juan Antonio Samaranch** with all of the **National Olympic Committees**, many nongovernmental organizations, and the United Nations General Assembly, in which he proposed an Olympic truce to take place during the period of and surrounding the Olympic Games. This was eventually approved by the United Nations General Assembly in Resolution A/Res/48/11 on 25 October 1993 at its 36th Plenary Meeting. It has been renewed by the United Nations every two years, one year before each edition of the Olympic Games or **Olympic Winter Games**. The most recent Resolution on the Olympic Truce was approved on 17 October 2011 by the 66th Session of the United Nations General Assembly, beginning with the start of the Games of the XXX **Olympiad**, on 27 July, and ending with the close of the XIV **Paralympic Games**, on 9 September.

In July 2000, the IOC established an International Olympic Truce Foundation (IOTF), headquartered in **Lausanne, Switzerland**, with a symbolic office in Olympia and a Foundation Board chaired by IOC President **Jacques Rogge**. It has listed its objectives as (1) to promote the Olympic ideals to serve peace, friendship, and understanding in the world, and in particular, to promote the ancient Greek tradition of the Olympic truce; and (2) to initiate conflict prevention and resolution through sport, culture, and the Olympic ideals, by cooperating with all inter- and nongovernmental organizations specializing in this field, by developing educational and research programs and by launching communications campaigns to promote the Olympic truce. The IOTF has established the International Olympic Truce Centre, headquartered in Athens, with a liaison office in Lausanne and a symbolic office in Olympia. It is responsible for the implementation of projects related to the worldwide promotion of a culture of peace through sport and the Olympic ideal.

OLYMPIC VILLAGE. At the 1924 Paris Olympics, many of the Olympic competitors were first housed in a purpose-built village, the Olympic Village. This has since become standard, and **Organizing Committees of the Olympic Games** (OCOGs) are required to build one according to *Olympic Charter* Rule 38. In recent years, with the spread of the **Olympic Games** over very large areas, many OCOGs have provided several Olympic Villages, particularly at **Olympic Winter Games**. Recently, the host cities to the Olympic Games have used the Olympic Villages to provide low-cost housing to their citizens after the Olympics are over.

OLYMPIC WINTER GAMES. The Olympic Winter Games are held every four years. Originally they were held in the same year as the Games of the **Olympiad**, but in 1994 this was changed and they are now contested every four years, but during the second calendar year following the beginning of the Olympiad. This ruling was made at the 91st **International Olympic Committee (IOC) Session** in 1986 in **Lausanne**, by a vote of 78–2, specifically to take advantage of the better use of advertising and television dollars to fund the **Olympic Movement**.

OLYMPISM. Olympism is a philosophy that is felt to be the cornerstone of the **Olympic Movement**. It is not easily defined and probably means different things to different people. The **International Olympic Committee** defines *Olympism* in the *Olympic Charter* as follows:

> Olympism is a philosophy of life, exalting and combining in a balanced whole the qualities of body, will and mind. Blending sport with culture and education, Olympism seeks to create a way of life based on the joy found in effort, the educational value of good example, and respect for universal fundamental ethical principles. The goal of Olympism is to place everywhere sport at the service of the harmonious development of man, with a view to encouraging the establishment of a peaceful society concerned with the preservation of human dignity.

Dr. John Powell, an eminent lecturer and author on Olympic ideals, has proposed another definition, which in 1986 was adopted by the Executive Committee of the Canadian Olympic Association: "Olympism is a harmony of ideas and ideals that affirm the value of Olympic sport in promoting and developing sound physical and moral qualities in individuals, and in contributing to a better and more peaceful world by enabling representatives of nations to meet in an atmosphere of mutual respect and international amity."

OMAN (OMA). Oman, officially known as the Sultanate of Oman, formed a **National Olympic Committee** in 1982, which the **International Olympic Committee** recognized in the same year. Oman, located on the southeast coast of the Arabian peninsula in southwest Asia, made its Olympic debut in

1984 at Los Angeles, where it was represented in **shooting**, track and field **athletics**, and **sailing**. It has also competed in every **Olympic Games** since then, but has never competed at the **Olympic Winter Games**. In eight Summer Games, it has entered 39 athletes (37 men, two **women**) in six sports: athletics (18 men, two women), **boxing** (two men), **cycling** (one man), sailing (one man), shooting (12 men), and **swimming** (three men). The best Olympic finish for an Omani athlete was in 1988, when Mohamed Al-Malky finished eighth in the 400 meters in track and field athletics. Oman's only other results where competitors finished in the top 50 percent of their class occurred in 1988 men's **air rifle** shooting, where Abdul Latif Al-Bulushi was tied for 17th of 46 shooters, and in 2000 when Hilal Al-Rasheedi came in tied for 25th among 53 entrants in men's **small-bore rifle** prone position shooting.

OMNIUM. The omnium is an **all-around** type of **cycling** event in which all riders compete in six events, with a point-for-place system. In case of a tie on points, the **time trial** is used as a tie breaker. The six races are: flying lap: an individual time trial over 250 meters (820.2 feet) with a "flying start"; points race: a 30 km (18.6 mile) points race, with scoring for intermediate **sprints** as well as for lapping the pack; elimination race: a "miss-and-out" elimination race, with the last rider in every sprint (each two laps) eliminated; individual **pursuit**: a four km (2.5 miles) individual pursuit, with placing based on time; scratch race: a 15 km (9.3 miles) scratch race, with all riders competing at once and first across the line winning; time trial: a one km (0.6 mile) time trial, with two riders (starting opposite the track) riding at once. Distances in the **women**'s event were 20 km (12.4 miles) in the points race, three km (1.9 miles) individual pursuit, 10 km (6.2 miles) scratch race, and a 500 meter (1,640.4 feet) time trial. It was held for the first time in the **Olympic Games** in 2012 with both men's and women's contests. Lasse Norman Hansen of **Denmark** was the men's winner and Laura Trott of **Great Britain** was the women's winner. It replaced the points race, individual pursuit, and **Madison** on the **Olympic Program**.

ONO, TAKASHI (JPN–GYM). B. 26 July 1931, Noshiro, Akita Prefecture, **Japan**. Takashi Ono was the first Japanese to win an individual Olympic gold medal for **gymnastics**. He won in the **horizontal bar** in 1956 and 1960, shared first place in the **horse vault** in 1960, and won team gold in 1960 and 1964. To his five gold medals he added four silver and four bronze, highlighted by silvers in the **all-around** in both 1956 and 1960. His total of 13 **Olympic medals** is the third highest by a gymnast, behind **Larysa Latynina** and **Nikolay Andrianov**, and is tied with **Boris Shakhlin**. At the World

Championships, the diminutive Ono (five-foot, two-inch [160 cm], 128 lb [58 kg]) won four silver medals and a bronze in 1958 and won the World Championships on the horizontal bar in 1962. He was chosen to recite the **Olympic Oath** for athletes at the 1964 **Olympic Games** in Tokyo. At these Games, his wife, Kiyoko Ono, also competed as a gymnast, winning bronze in the team competition. She later served as a representative in the Japanese House of Councillors from 1986 to 2007.

OPEN CLASS. The open class was contested in Olympic **judo** in just five competitions from 1964 to 1984. It was open to entrants regardless of weight. In the initial event in 1964, a major upset occurred when Dutchman **Anton Geesink** defeated Akio Kaminaga of **Japan**. Kaminaga, in an earlier round of the competition, had won a bout in just four seconds for an Olympic record.

OPEN WATER SWIMMING. In the 2008 Olympic Games, a distance **swimming** event of 10 km was added to both the men's and **women**'s programs. Rather than contest it in an indoor pool, as with all other Olympic swimming competitions, it was held outdoors and was referred to as an "open water" swim. Oussama Mellouli of **Tunisia** won the event in 2012 and also won the (indoor) 1,500 meters gold in 2008 and bronze in 2012. Thomas Lurz of **Germany** was the men's silver medalist in 2012 and bronze medalist in 2008, while in the women's event there were no multiple medalists, although Kerri Ann Payne nearly was one as she won the silver medal in 2008 and finished fourth in 2012 just four-tenths of a second behind the bronze medalist after nearly two hours of swimming.

OPENING CEREMONY. *See* OLYMPIC CEREMONIES.

ORGANIZACIÓN DEPORTIVA CENTROAMERICANA Y DEL CARIBE (ODECABE). The ODECABE is a confederation of **National Olympic Committees** (NOCs) of the **Central American** and Caribbean region. It is the oldest association of NOCs, having been founded on 4 July 1924 as the Central American and Caribbean Sports Association. It contests the Central American and Caribbean Games, which are the oldest **Regional International Games**, having first been held in 1926. The organization, with 31 affiliated NOCs, is headquartered in San Juan, **Puerto Rico**, and its president in 2014 is Héctor Cardona of Puerto Rico.

ORGANIZACIÓN DEPORTIVA PANAMERICANA. *See* PAN AMERICAN SPORTS ORGANIZATION.

ORGANIZACIÓN DEPORTIVA SUDAMERICANA (ODESUR). All of the South American **National Olympic Committees** are members of the **Pan American Sports Organization**. But that group is somewhat dominated by the North American nations of the **United States** and **Canada**, so in 1976, the president of the **Bolivian** Olympic Committee, José Gamarra Zorrilla, began the process of forming an organization devoted to promoting the interests of the South American National Olympic Committees. ODESUR was formed on 26 March 1976 and also began contesting one of the **Regional International Games**, the South American Games, in 1978. The 15 NOCs that comprise ODESUR are **Argentina, Aruba,** Bolivia, **Brazil, Chile, Colombia, Ecuador, Guyana, Netherlands Antilles, Panama, Paraguay, Peru, Suriname, Uruguay,** and **Venezuela**. The current (as of 2014) president is Carlos Arthur Nuzman of Brazil.

ORGANIZING COMMITTEES OF THE OLYMPIC GAMES. The organization of each **Olympic Games** or **Olympic Winter Games** is entrusted by the **International Olympic Committee** to an Organizing Committee, which is then in charge of producing the Games. The committees are formed exclusively for the purpose of putting on the Olympics, and as such, dissolve shortly after the Olympics are held. The French name is Comité d'Organisation des Jeux Olympiques.

ORIENTEERING. Orienteering has never been contested at the **Olympic Games**, even as a **demonstration sport**. However, the International Orienteering Federation (IOF) has been recognized by the **International Olympic Committee** since 1977. The IOF was founded in 1961 and currently has 78 affiliated member nations.

OSBURN, CARL TOWNSEND (USA–SHO). B. 5 May 1884, Jacksontown, Ohio, **United States**. D. 28 December 1966, St. Helena, California, United States. Carl Osburn was the most successful Olympic marksman in history. At the **Olympic Games** of 1912, 1920, and 1924, he won five gold, four silver, and two bronze medals, for a record total of 11. The five-foot, 10-inch (180 cm) shooter won three of his five gold medals in 1920. Osburn was a career naval officer who graduated from Annapolis in 1906 and rose to the rank of commander. Besides his Olympic **shooting** success, Osburn competed internationally for the United States at the World Championships of 1921, 1922, 1923, and 1924 and at the Pan American Matches of 1913.

OTTEY, MERLENE JOYCE (briefly PAGE) (JAM/ SLO–ATH). B. 10 May 1960, Cold Spring, Hanover, **Jamaica**. Merlene Ottey is one of only eight **women** to compete in at least seven **Olympic Games**, and her nine medals, won in **athletics** (track and field), is the best mark for women in that sport. A **sprinter** who competed in the 100 meter, 200 meter, and the 4x100 **relay**, she has competed at the Olympics of 1980, 1984, 1988, 1992, 1996, 2000, and 2004, changing her allegiance to **Slovenia** in 2004 after a dispute with Jamaican officials. A five-foot, eight-inch (175 cm), 137 lb (62 kg) sprinter, she has never won an Olympic gold medal, but came very close several times, winning three silver and six bronze medals. At the World Championships, she has won 10 medals, including the gold medal over 200 meters in both 1993 and 1995. She won gold medals at the **Commonwealth Games** in the 100 meters in 1990 and the 200 meters in 1982 and 1990. Ottey won a silver medal in 2000 as a member of the Jamaican 4x100 relay team, when she was over 40 years old, making her the oldest female athletics medalist at the Olympic Games. She continued to run and at the age of 48, narrowly missed (by 0.028 seconds) qualifying for her eighth Olympics. In 2012, at the age of 52, she competed in the 4x100 relay for Slovenia at the European Athletics Championships.

OTTO, KRISTIN (GDR–SWI). B. 7 February 1966, Leipzig, **German Democratic Republic**. Kristin Otto's six gold medals at one Games (1988) are a **women**'s record for any sport. In Seoul, Otto uniquely won gold medals in three different strokes—**freestyle, backstroke**, and **butterfly**—setting new Olympic records in these three events, and her overall performance at the 1988 Games ranks as one of history's greatest sporting achievements. Only one woman has won more Olympic **swimming** titles, but **Jenny Thompson** needed three appearances to collect her eight titles. At the World Championships (1982, 1986), Otto won seven gold medals. A tall athlete, at six feet (185 cm), 154 lb (70 kg), she set two individual world records and contributed to four relay world records in her career. As happened to many East German swimmers, Otto was accused of **doping** use, but she has always denied knowingly taking performance-enhancing drugs. Since her retirement, she has worked as a sports presenter and commentator on German **television**.

OUTER MONGOLIA. *See* MONGOLIA.

OWENS, JAMES CLEVELAND "JESSE" (USA–ATH). B. 12 September 1913, Oakville, Alabama, **United States**. D. 31 March 1980, Tucson, Arizona, United States. Jesse Owens, at five feet, 10 inches (178 cm), 157 lb (71 kg), is an Olympic legend whose four gold medals at the 1936 Games (100 meters, 200 meters, 4x100 meters **relay**, and **long jump**) did much to undermine Adolf

Hitler's myth of Aryan superiority. His place in sporting history had already been assured when he set six world records in one day (25 May 1935), and his long jump record of 26 feet 8.25 inches (8.13 meters), also set that day, remained a world best for more than 25 years. At the end of the 1936 season, Owens turned professional, and in his later years he traveled extensively as a speaker promoting the cause of **Olympism** and related philosophies.

P

PAIRS. Although competition for two-person teams occurs in several Olympic sports, the phrase **doubles (tennis)** or **duet (synchronized swimming)** or two-man **(bobsled)** is used. **Figure skating** and **rowing** are the only Olympic sports to use the designation "pairs." In rowing, pairs are contested both with and without **coxswain**. Pairs figure skating with one male and one female skater has been contested in every **Olympic Games** in which figure skating was included—the two Summer Games of 1908 and 1920 and all **Olympic Winter Games** from 1924 to 2014. The **Soviet Union** won the event in seven consecutive years from 1964 to 1988. After the breakup of the USSR, the Unified Team won in 1992 and **Russia** has won in 1994, 1998, 2006, and 2014 and tied for first in 2002. In several years, the Soviet Union, the Unified Team, and Russia also won silver medals in this event. **Irina Rodnina** of the Soviet Union is the only skater to win three gold medals (1972–1980) in pairs figure skating.

PAKISTAN (PAK). The South Asian nation of Pakistan, officially known as the Islamic Republic of Pakistan, first competed at the **Olympic Games** in 1948. It has attended all subsequent Summer Games, except the 1980 Moscow Olympics. In 16 Summer Games, Pakistan has entered 354 athletes (346 men, eight **women**) and participated in 11 sports: **athletics** (63 men, five women), **boxing** (39 men), **cycling** (11 men), **hockey** (165 men), **rowing** (three men), **sailing** (eight men), **shooting** (11 men), **swimming** (13 men, three women), **table tennis** (one man), **weightlifting** (eight men), and **wrestling** (25 men).

Pakistan owes almost its entire Olympic success to one sport, hockey, earning eight of its 10 Olympic medals in that sport. It won a medal in hockey at every celebration from 1956 through 1976, but has failed to medal since 1992. Pakistan's most celebrated Olympic victory occurred in 1960, when they won the hockey gold medal, defeating **India** in the final and ending India's 32-year Olympic winning streak. Pakistan won the gold again in both 1968 and 1984, the silver in 1956, 1964, and 1972, and the bronze in 1976 and 1992. Pakistan's other two Olympic medalists were **welterweight** wrestler Muhammad Bashir, bronze medalist in 1960 freestyle competition, and **middleweight** boxer Syed Hussain Shah, bronze medalist in 1988. Other notable Olympic results for Pakistan include fourth place by their hockey team in 1948, 1952, and 2000, fifth place in 1988 and 2004, and sixth place in 1996. In other sports, Muhammad Akhtar was sixth in **featherweight freestyle** wrestling in 1960 and Abdul Majeed was seventh in **light-heavyweight** freestyle wrestling in 1984; Muhammad Manzoor was 11th in 1976 **bantamweight** weightlifting; Farjad Saif won three of seven matches in 1988 men's **singles** table tennis and finished tied for 25th of 64 entrants; Khurram Inam tied for 23rd of 49 in 2000 men's **skeet** shooting; Siraj Din tied for fifth in the 1976 middleweight boxing; and **hammer thrower** Muhammad Iqbal was 11th in 1956 and 12th in 1960.

The nation debuted at the **Olympic Winter Games** in Vancouver 2010, with a single Pakistani entrant in **Alpine skiing**, Muhammad Abbas. He competed in the **giant slalom** and placed 79th of 101 entrants, carefully completing the course successfully in both **heats** for a total time of 3:20.58, nearly 45 seconds slower than the gold medalist but ahead of two other skiers who also finished and 20 others who failed to complete the course. In 2014, Pakistani Muhammad Karim entered the giant slalom with similar results to those of Abbas. Karim was 71st of 107 entrants, ahead of one competitor who finished the course and 35 others who did not.

PALAU (PLW). The Palau **National Olympic Committee** was granted provisional recognition by the **International Olympic Committee** in 1998, and full recognition followed in 1999. Palau made its Olympic debut in 2000 at Sydney, represented by five athletes. The Pacific island nation, known officially as the Republic of Palau, also attended the next three **Olympic Games**. In four Summer Games, Palau entered 18 athletes (nine men, nine **women**) in **athletics** (four men, three women), **judo** (one woman), **swimming** (one man, four women), **weightlifting** (one man, one woman), and **wrestling** (three men). The best result by a Paluan was a 51st place of 75 entrants in the women's 50 meter **freestyle** swimming event in 2012 by Keesha Keane. None of their other 17 competitors have had a noteworthy result. Palau has not yet competed in the **Olympic Winter Games**.

PALESTINE (PLE). A Palestine **National Olympic Committee** (NOC) existed prior to World War II, formed in 1933. Palestine was ruled under a British mandate from 1921 through 1948. During those years, it had a NOC that was recognized by the **International Olympic Committee** (IOC), although it never competed at the **Olympic Games**. The Palestine Olympic Committee was titularly intended to represent Jews, Muslims, and Christians from the region of Palestine, but the rules of the original Palestine NOC stated that they "represent the Jewish National Home." Thus, that Olympic Committee was more a precursor of the **Israeli** Olympic Committee than of the current Palestine Olympic Committee.

Palestine, officially known as the State of Palestine, located in Western Asia between the Mediterranean Sea and the Jordan River, currently has no exact geographic boundaries, but its NOC was given provisional recognition by the IOC at its annual meeting in Monte Carlo in September 1993. This occurred shortly after the historic agreement signed between the Palestine Liberation Organization and the State of Israel in that same month. Palestine first competed at the Olympic Games in 1996, when it was represented by a single athlete, who finished next to last in his **heat** of the 10,000 meters. Palestine has competed in each of the next four Summer Games but has not yet entered the **Olympic Winter Games**. In five Summer Games, Palestine has had 15 entrants (nine men, six **women**): **athletics** (five men, three women), **swimming** (three men, three women), and **judo** (one man). None of its participants has reached the final stage of competition. The best performance by a Palestinian Olympian occurred in 2012 when Sabine Hazboun finished 52nd of 75 entrants in the women's 50 meter **freestyle** swimming event.

PALUBINSKAS, EDWARD SEBASTIAN "EDDIE" (AUS–BAS). B. 17 September 1950, Canberra, Australian Capital Territory, **Australia**. **Basketball** player Eddie Palubinskas attended Ricks Junior College and Louisiana State University, graduating in 1974. The six-foot, two-inch guard was selected by the Atlanta Hawks in the 1974 National Basketball Association (NBA) draft but did not play in the NBA. He was on the 1972 and 1976 Australian Olympic basketball teams, and, although he was unable to lead them to better than an eighth place result in 1976 and ninth place in 1972, he had some of the best individual performances in the history of the Olympic basketball tournaments. He averaged 25.6 points per game in the two tournaments, the second highest Olympic career average for players who have competed in more than one **Olympic Games**. In seven games in 1976, he averaged 31.3 points per game, never scoring less than 26 points, and on 21 July 1976 he set the Olympic record with 48 points in one game (broken in 1988 by **Oscar Schmidt**). Palubinskas was also an outstanding free throw shooter, and his free throw percentage of 0.917 in 1976, making 55 of 60, ranks among the best Olympic performances. He became a free throw coach and has made an instructional video on the subject. In 1978, he became the head coach of the team **handball** team of **Bahrain**. In 1981, he earned a master's degree from Brigham Young University. He has worked as an artist and is the president of Universal Sports Art and Graphics, a company that specializes in painting large wall and floor murals for sports facilities. His basketball coaching includes a stint as assistant coach with the Los Angeles Lakers of the NBA in 2000–2001. In 1996, he opened the Palubinskas Basketball Academy to teach shooting fundamentals.

PAN AMERICAN GAMES. The Pan American Games began in 1951 and are a quadrennial multisport competition for athletes from Western Hemisphere countries. They have been held every four years since then without fail in the year prior to the Summer **Olympic Games** and the 2015 Pan American Games, scheduled for Toronto, Ontario, **Canada**, will be the 17th Games. They are administered by the **Pan American Sports Organization** and are open to athletes from any of its 41 member nations. In 2011, more than 6,000 athletes took part in the Games held in Guadalajara, **Mexico**, and several neighboring Mexican cities. Most of the sports that are contested in the Olympic Games are also held during the Pan American Games along with several other non-Olympic sports such as **pelota basque**, ten-pin **bowling**, **karate**, **racquetball**, **roller skating**, and **squash**. The **United States** has dominated competition and through 2011 has won more than 4,000 medals, while the runner-up nation, **Cuba**, has won slightly less than 2,000 total medals.

PAN AMERICAN SPORTS ORGANIZATION. The Pan American Sports Organization is a confederation of **National Olympic Committees** (NOCs) in the Americas. It was founded on 8 August 1948; in 1955, the current structure was put in place, and the current name of the group was adopted. The official languages of the group are English and Spanish, and its name is listed as both the Pan American Sports Organization and the Organización Deportiva Panamericana. The group's goals, as listed in its charter, are "to strengthen and tighten the bonds of friendship and solidarity among the peoples of America; to further the development and growth of the Olympic Ideal; to cooperate with the NOCs of the Americas; to ensure the periodic celebration of the **Pan American Games**; and to coordinate the Olympic and Pan American Solidarity Programs." The organization is headquartered in **Mexico** City, and the current president is Mario Vázquez Raña, one of Mexico's **International Olympic Committee members**. As of 2014, there are 41 member nations.

PANAMA (PAN). The **Central American** nation of Panama was represented at the **Olympic Games** in 1928, 1948, and 1952 by a single athlete. It has sent larger contingents since 1960, although the country did not attend the 1980 Moscow Olympics. It has never competed in the **Olympic Winter Games**.

In 16 Summer Games, Panama has entered 79 athletes (64 men, 15 **women**) and competed in 11 sports: **athletics** (nine men, seven women), basketball (12 men), **boxing** four men), **canoeing** (one man), **fencing** (two women), **judo** (three men, one woman), **shooting** (one man, one woman), **swimming** (10 men, three women), **taekwondo** (one woman), **weightlifting** (12 men), and **wrestling** (12 men).

Officially known as the Republic of Panama, the country has won three **Olympic medals**. Two of these were won by its lone competitor in 1948, Lloyd LaBeach, who won bronze in both the 100 meter and 200 meters athletics events. In 2008, Panamanian **long jumper** Irving Saladino earned the country's first Olympic gold medal. Other notable accomplishments by Panamanian Olympians include fifth place by Guy Abrahams in the 1976 100 meter dash and by Bayano Kamani in the 2004 400 meter **hurdles**, seventh place by José Díaz in 1984 **flyweight** weightlifting, and a seventh place tie by Carolena Carstens in 2012 women's flyweight taekwondo. In Panama's only venture in Olympic basketball in 1968, they were led by Davis Peralta who set an Olympic record (later broken) by averaging 23.8 points per game for the nine-game tournament, while the team finished 12th of the 16 entrants.

PANKRATION. The pankration was a violent sport contested at the **Ancient Olympics**, with virtually no holds barred, in which kicking played an important part. It was a very popular sport with the fans and was actually less brutal than **boxing**, because the pankratiasts wore no gloves, which inflict so much harm on boxers. Plato described it as "a contest combining incomplete wrestling with incomplete boxing." The first recorded champion was Lygdamis of Syracuse in 648 B.C., and champions are recorded through Aurelius Phoibammon of **Egypt** in A.D. 221. Five separate athletes won at least three championships at Olympia in the pankration. A boys' pankration was held from 200 B.C. through A.D. 117. One of the most famous pankration champions, Arrikion of Figaleia, was killed while successfully defending his title in this sport. He was awarded the title posthumously when his opponent was disqualified. *See also* THEAGENES OF THASOS.

PAPP, LÁSZLÓ (HUN–BOX). B. 25 March 1926, Budapest, **Hungary**. D. 16 October 2003, Budapest, Hungary. After winning the Olympic **middleweight boxing** title in 1948, László Papp won the **light-middleweight** crown in 1952 and 1956, the first boxer to win three Olympic gold medals. Possibly his finest victory in the Olympic ring was in the 1956 final, when he defeated José Torres (USA), a future world professional champion. A five-foot, five-inch (165 cm), skillful, hard-punching southpaw, Papp was the first fighter from the **Soviet** bloc to turn professional, and he won the European middleweight title in 1962. However, in 1965 the Hungarian authorities withdrew their permission for him to fight professionally, and the chance of a world title bout was denied him. He retired with an undefeated professional record of 27 wins (15 by **knockout**) and two draws.

PAPUA NEW GUINEA (PNG, formerly NGU). The South Pacific island nation of Papua New Guinea, officially known as the Independent State of Papua New Guinea, has competed at every **Olympic Games**, with the exception of 1980, since it made its debut in 1976. In nine Summer Games, Papua New Guinea has entered 56 athletes (43 men, 13 **women**) and competed in eight sports: **athletics** (20 men, eight women), **boxing** (12 men), **judo** (one man), **sailing** (one man), **shooting** (two men), **swimming** (two men, three women), **taekwondo** (one woman), and **weightlifting** (five men, one woman).

In 2004, Dika Toua posted the best Olympic performance by a Papua New Guinean. A **featherweight** weightlifter, she placed sixth, but in a field of only eight competitors. More impressive was the performance of **butterfly** swimmer Ryan Pini, who came in eighth in the final of the 100 meters in Beijing, with 64 other swimmers competing. He also was 18th of 59 in the 100 meter butterfly in 2004 and 20th of 44 in the 100 meter **backstroke** in 2004. Other notable achievements by Papua New Guinean Olympians include Henry Kungsi winning his first bout in 1992 **lightweight** boxing and finishing tied for ninth; **marathoner** Tau John Tokwepota, 66th of 107 in 1984; swimmer Anna-Liza Mopio-Jane finishing 42nd of 90 in 2008 50 meter women's **freestyle**; and **light-heavyweight** weightlifter Steven Kari, 15th of 23 in 2012. In 1976, boxers Zoffa Yarawi and Tumat Sogolik both finished tied for ninth but only as a result of receiving **byes** as they each lost their first bout. No athletes from Papua New Guinea have competed in the **Olympic Winter Games**.

PARAGUAY (PAR). Paraguay, located in central South America and known officially as the Republic of Paraguay, has competed at every **Olympic Games** since its debut in 1968, with the exception of 1980, which it **boycotted**. In 11 Summer Games, it has entered 97 athletes (83 men, 14 **women**) and taken part in 11 sports: **athletics** (15 men, three women), **boxing** (four men), **fencing** (seven men), **football** (33 men), **judo** (four men), **rowing** (one man, two women), **sailing** (one man, one woman), **shooting** (seven men, one woman), **swimming** (eight men, four women), **table tennis** (one man), and **tennis** (two men, three women).

Although 17 Paraguayan athletes have each won **Olympic medals** (all members of the 2004 football team), the country has won only one medal at the Olympic Games. In 2004, its football team was defeated by **Argentina** in the final, earning a silver medal. The 1992 Paraguayan Olympic team finished sixth of 16 teams. The best Olympic performances in individual sports by Paraguayans include **flyweight** boxer Oppe Pinto finishing tied for ninth in 1984 after winning one bout and receiving a **bye**; tennis player Rossana de los Ríos also was tied for ninth in 2000 after she won her first two matches, although her second win was by **walkover**; Vicente Céspedes was tied for 14th in 1988 **half-lightweight** competition; and **discus thrower** Ramón Jiménez-Gaona, who competed in three Olympic Games and was the country's flagbearer in the opening ceremony all three times, twice finished in 16th place (1988, 1992). Paraguay competed at the **Olympic Winter Games** for the first time in 2014 with one participant. Julia Marino finished 17th of 22 entrants in the inaugural women's slopestyle **freestyle skiing** event.

PARALLEL BARS. The parallel bars is one of the exercises performed by male **gymnasts**. The apparatus consists of two wooden bars 200 cm (6.6 feet) above the floor supported by a metal frame. The bars are 4 cm (1.6 inch) wide and 350 cm (11.5 feet) long. The exercise was included in the first modern **Olympic Games** in 1896, in 1904, and in every Olympic Games since 1924. Li Xiaopeng of **China** won the gold medal in this event in 2000 and 2008 and the bronze medal in 2004. The only other dual gold medalist is **Sawao Kato** of **Japan** (1972, 1976).

PARALLEL GIANT SLALOM. The parallel **giant slalom** is a **snowboarding** event that was first contested in 2002 and has been run in each subsequent **Olympic Winter Games**. Two snowboarders race a giant slalom course head-to-head with the winner advancing to the next round of competition. Philipp Schoch of **Switzerland** won this event in both 2002 and 2006. In the latter year, he defeated his brother, Simon, in the final round. A **women's** parallel giant slalom has also been held from 2002 to 2014 with no repeat medalists. In 2014, a second similar event, the parallel **slalom**, was also held.

PARALYMPIC GAMES. The Paralympic Games are an international sporting event specifically for athletes with disabilities. Rule changes mandated by the **IOC 2000 Commission** have made it mandatory that the Paralympics be held just after the **Olympic Games** in the same city. The Paralympic Games are organized by the International Paralympic Committee (IPC), which is recognized by the **International Olympic Committee** (IOC). The Paralympics trace their beginnings to shortly after World War II and the Stoke Mandeville Games. The Stoke Mandeville Hospital in **England** is a well-known spinal cord injury research and treatment center. The hospital began sponsoring a series of Games in 1948, called the Stoke Mandeville Games. The Games were originally for athletes with paralysis and were started by Dr. Ludwig Guttman.

The Paralympics first began in 1960 at Rome and have expanded on the Stoke Mandeville concept to include many other disabilities, including amputees and blind athletes. The IPC has its headquarters in Bonn, **Germany**. In addition to the IPC, the IOC recognizes several other organizations for athletes with disabilities: the Cerebral Palsy International Sports and Recreation Association, the International Blind Sports Federation, the International Sports Federation for Persons with an Intellectual Disability, the International Sports Organization of the Disabled, the Comité International des Sports des Sourds (for deaf athletes), and the forerunner of them all, the International Stoke Mandeville Wheelchair Sports Federation. The Stoke Mandeville Wheelchair Games continue to be held annually in Buckinghamshire, England.

Although the first two Paralympic Games were held in the same cities as the Olympics, between 1968 and 1984 the Paralympics were held in different cities: 1968, Tel Aviv, **Israel** (not **Mexico** City); 1972, Heidelberg, West **Germany** (not Munich); 1976, Toronto, **Canada** (not Montreal); 1980, Arnhem, **Netherlands** (not Moscow); 1984, Stoke Mandeville, **Great Britain**, and New York, **United States** (not Los Angeles).

The Paralympics have been expanded to include a winter version, conducted since 1976. Like the Summer Paralympics, they are now held in the same city as the **Olympic Winter Games**, but were previously held elsewhere: 1976, Ornskoldsvik, **Sweden** (not Innsbruck); 1980, Geilo, **Norway** (not Lake Placid); 1984, Innsbruck, **Austria** (not Sarajevo); 1988, Innsbruck, Austria (not Calgary). *See also* PISTORIUS, OSCAR LEONARD CARL; SPECIAL OLYMPICS.

PARISI, ANGELO (GBR/FRA–JUD). B. 3 January 1953, Arpino, Frosinone, **Italy**. With four **Olympic medals** (one gold, two silver, one bronze), Angelo Parisi is one of the most successful *judokas* in Olympic history. Italian born, he won a bronze in the **judo open class** in 1972 representing **Great Britain**, and then represented **France** in 1980 and 1984, following his marriage to a Frenchwoman. In 1980, Parisi won the unlimited class title and placed second in the open class; in 1984, he won his fourth medal, a silver in the unlimited class. Parisi never managed to win at the World Championships, but reached 12 European Championship finals, winning six. The six-foot tall (185 cm) Parisi weighed around 242 lb (110 kg) for most of his matches.

PÄRSON, ANJA SOFIA TESS (SWE–ASK). B. 25 April 1981, Umeå, Västerbotten, **Sweden**. One of the dominant female **Alpine skiers** of the first decade of the 21st century, Anja Pärson has won six **Olympic medals**, tying **Janica Kostelić** for the most medals won by a female Alpine skier. In World

Championships, the five-foot, six-inch (170 cm), 179 lb (81 kg) skier has won 13 medals, making a combined total of 19, a record for women. Among her Olympic medals is a single gold medal, won in the 2006 **slalom**; one silver (**giant slalom**, 2002); and four bronze medals. In World Championships, she won seven titles between 2001 and 2007, at least one in each of the five Alpine events. In addition, Pärson won the overall World Cup in 2004 and 2005, as well as five event World Cups and 42 World Cup races.

PATZAICHIN, IVAN (ROU–CAN). B. 26 November 1949, Mila 23, Tulcea, **Romania**. **Ivan Patzaichin** won 13 **canoeing** titles at the **Olympic Games** and World Championships, equaling the record for men set by **Gert Fredriksson** (SWE) and Rüdiger Helm (GDR). His Olympic record included seven medals, of which four were gold and three silver. Patzaichin, at five feet, nine inches (176 cm), 174 lb (79 kg), competed at five Olympic Games, from 1968 through 1984, representing the Dinamo Bucharest club for Romania. His Olympic titles were the C2-1,000 in 1968, the C1-1,000 in 1972, the C2-1,000 in 1980, and the C2-1,000 in 1984. His World Championships were the C2-500 in 1979; C2-1,000 in 1970, 1973, and 1981; the C1-1,000 in 1977; and the C1-10 k in 1978.

PEARCE-RAMPONE, CHRISTIE PATRICIA (USA–FTB). B. 24 June 1975, Point Pleasant, New Jersey, **United States**. Christie Pearce-Rampone has won more medals in Olympic **football** than anyone else, male or female. She has been a member of the U.S. team from 2000 to 2012 and won a silver medal in 2000 and gold medals in the next three **Olympic Games**. At five feet, six inches (168 cm), 141 lbs (64 kg), she plays defense. In the Women's World Cup with the U.S. team she won gold in 1999, bronze in 2003 and 2007, and silver in 2011. She has 294 caps (appearances for the national team) as of mid-June 2014, one of the highest totals of all time. She gave birth to her first child on 29 September 2005 and her second on 6 March 2010.

PECHSTEIN, CLAUDIA (GER–SSK). B. 22 February 1972, Berlin, **Germany**. **Claudia Pechstein** has won more Olympic **speed skating** medals than anyone else, male or female. And she has done this despite a two-year ban by the International Skating Union for alleged **doping**. She made her first appearance at the **Olympic Winter Games** in 1992 and has appeared in six Games, missing the 2010 Games as a result of her suspension. She has won nine medals—five gold, two silver, and two bronze—winning the 5,000 meters three times, the 3,000 meters once, and the team **pursuit** once. In 2014, at the age of 41, she narrowly missed winning her 10th medal as she finished fourth in the 3,000 meters and fifth in the 5,000 meters. She has won 39 medals (six gold, 20 silver, 13 bronze) at the World Championships from 1996 to 2013 and 11 medals (three gold, six silver, two bronze) at the European Championships. In 2012, she attempted to qualify for the London Olympics in **cycling** but failed to do so.

PEIRSOL, AARON WELLS (USA–SWI). B. 23 July 1983, Irvine, California, **United States**. The most dominant **backstroke swimmer** since **Roland Matthes**, Aaron Peirsol was undefeated in the 100 meter event between 2002 and 2009. During that time, he won three World Championships and two Olympic titles. The six-foot, three-inch (191 cm), 201 lb (91 kg) swimmer was also rarely defeated in the double distance, winning the 2004 Olympic gold and world titles in 2003, 2005, and 2009. His **Olympic medal** collection further sports two **medley relay** golds (from Athens and Beijing) and two 200 meter backstroke silvers (from Sydney and Beijing), while Peirsol also swam on the winning medley relay teams at the 2003, 2005, and 2009 World Championships. He has also set the world record in both backstroke distances several times and has won six titles at the short course (25 meter pool) World Championships (2002, 2004) and six golds at the Pan Pacific Championships (2002, 2006).

PELOTA BASQUE. Pelota is a generic name for various hand-and-ball or racquet-and-ball games, derived from the ancient French racquet sport *jeu de paume*. The best-known version of the sport is probably *chistera* (also *xistera* or *cesta punta*), which uses baskets to handle the ball. In the **United States**, it is better known as the betting sport jai-alai. Pelota basque, predominantly played in the **Basque** regions and contiguous provinces of **France** and **Spain**, has been an Olympic **demonstration sport** three times, in 1924, 1968, and 1992. In addition, at the unusual **Olympic Games** of 1900, a version of pelota can be considered to have been an Olympic sport. The Federación Internacional de Pelota Vasca was founded in 1929 and is recognized by the **International Olympic Committee**, with 27 affiliated national members as of 2014. *See also* KAATSEN.

PENTATHLON. At the **Ancient Olympics**, the five events of the pentathlon were jumping, a *stadion* **race** (sprint of about 190 meters), the **discus throw**, the **javelin throw**, and **wrestling**. The origin of the event is attributed to Jason (of Argonaut fame). According to mythology, Jason was to award the prizes at an ancient games, and his friend Peleus was second in all the contests. Jason combined the events out of a desire to honor his friend and thus created the pentathlon.

It is unclear how the winner of the pentathlon was decided. The precise order of the events is also unclear. It is only known with certainty that the last event was wrestling. If any athlete won any three events, he was immediately declared the winner, and the ancient term *triakter* is often applied, meaning the winner of three events. However, classics and Olympics scholars do not agree on how the victor was determined in other circumstances. In 1906, at the **Intercalated Olympic Games**, a pentathlon was held consisting of the same five events as the ancient pentathlon.

From 1912 to 1924, in addition to the 10-event **decathlon**, there was also a five-event pentathlon contested for men as part of the athletics competition. It consisted of the **long jump**, javelin throw, discus throw, 200 meter sprint, and 1,500 meter run. The famed Native American **Jim Thorpe** won this event in 1912 and Eero Lehtonen of **Finland** won in both 1920 and 1924. A **women**'s pentathlon consisting of **shot put**, long jump, **high jump**, 80-meter **hurdles** (100 meters from 1972), and 200 meter run was held from 1964 to 1980, but in 1984 it was replaced by the seven-event **heptathlon**. No woman won the event more than once, and only Burglinde Pollak of East **Germany** (two bronze) was able to win more than one medal. *See also* MODERN PENTATHLON; MULTIEVENTS; WINTER PENTATHLON.

PEOPLE'S DEMOCRATIC REPUBLIC OF YEMEN. *See* YEMEN DEMOCRATIC REPUBLIC.

PEOPLE'S OLYMPIAD. The Spanish city of Barcelona had bid to host the 1936 Olympics but lost to Berlin. In an era of increasing tension between communism and fascism in Europe, the fact that the 1936 **Olympic Games** were hosted by Nazi **Germany** did not sit well with socialists and communists, particularly in **Spain**, where the Frente Popular (a coalition of a handful of left-wing parties) had gained power in January 1936. They soon declared that Spain would **boycott** the Berlin Olympics and would instead stage alternate Olympic Games. This Olimpiada Popular was to be held in Barcelona, between 19–26 July 1936, a few weeks before the Berlin Games. The organization was in the hands of the Sozialistische Arbeiter Sport Internationale (Socialist Workers' Sport International), which also organized the socialist **Workers' Olympiad**, and because of this, the 1936 People's Olympiad is occasionally listed as having been planned as the 3rd Workers' Olympiad.

Sixteen sports, including track and field **athletics** and **swimming**, but also non-Olympic sports like **pelota** and **chess**, were scheduled to be held. The Montjuïc stadium was to be used as the main venue; it would serve that same function in 1992, when the Olympics came to Barcelona. Some 6,000 athletes were said to have entered for competitions, with most delegations coming from Europe, but the **United States** also sent a contingent. It was not necessary to enter a national team, and there were entries from Jewish groups, German exiles, and French colonies.

On 17 July, General Francisco Franco and various other dissatisfied officers launched a coup from Spanish islands and North African enclaves. The insurgency quickly spread, and by 19 July—the scheduled date of the opening ceremony of the People's Olympiad—fights had broken out in the streets of Barcelona. Of course the Games were canceled. Most athletes evacuated to **France** soon afterward, although a few supposedly stayed behind to join the fight on the Republican side, with the International Brigades.

PERKINS, KIEREN JOHN (AUS–SWI). B. 14 August 1973, Brisbane, Queensland, **Australia**. Kieren Perkins is considered by many to be the best distance **freestyle swimmer** ever, rivaling **Vladimir Salnikov** (URS) and Perkins's countryman **Grant Hackett**. The six-foot, four-inch (194 cm), 198 lb (90 kg) Perkins burst onto the international scene in 1991, winning the 400, 800, and 1,500 meters at the Pan-Pacific meet, setting a world record of 7:47.85 in the 800 meter race. At the 1992 Australian Olympic trials, he won the 400 and 1,500 meters in world record times. Later that year, Perkins won the 1,500 meter Olympic gold medal in a world record 14:43.48. In the 400 meter race at the 1992 Olympics, he bettered his 400 meter world record by over a second, recording 3:45.16, but was touched out for the gold by the Unified Team's Yevgeny Sadovyi. Perkins's performance at the 1994 **Commonwealth Games** may be his finest ever, winning the 200 and 400 meters, swimming on the winning 800 meter freestyle relay, and breaking his own world record in the 1,500 meter race. In addition, his interval split during the 1,500 meter race broke his 800 meter world record. In 1996, Perkins defended his Olympic title in the 1,500 meters. After 1996, his performances dropped off, and he was surpassed in the distances by Hackett. It was not certain whether he would even make the 2000 Australian team, but he reached back, recalling past glories, and followed Hackett to the wall for a silver medal in the 1,500 meter freestyle. During his career, Perkins set three world records at 800 meters, three at 1,500 meters, and two at 400 meters.

PERSIA. *See* IRAN.

PERU (PER). Peru's initial involvement in the **Olympic Games** occurred in 1900 when Carlos de Candamo competed as a **fencer**. He was the son of the Peruvian ambassador to **France** and nephew of the future president of Peru, **Manuel** González de **Candamo** e **Iriarte**. De Candamo was active in several sports and played **tennis** in the forerunner of the French Open tournament and was a member of the 1892 French **rugby** champions, whose final match was reportedly refereed by Baron **Pierre de Coubertin**. In 1909, de Candamo became a member of the **International Olympic Committee**. Peru's next Olympic appearance was in 1936. The western South American nation, officially known as the Republic of Peru, has since missed only the 1952 Games in Helsinki.

In 19 Summer Games, Peru has entered 327 athletes (241 men, 86 **women**) and competed in 22 sports plus the **art competitions**, with the most participants in **athletics** (39 men, 10 women), **volleyball** (49 women), **shooting** (37 men, two women), **swimming** (22 men, 12 women), **basketball** (32 men), and **football** (31 men). Peru has won four **Olympic medals**, one gold and three silver, with three of the four in shooting events. It is one of just three nations that has won more than two Olympic medals but has not won a bronze medal.

Edwin Vásquez won Peru's first Olympic medal and, as of 2014, their only gold medal. He won the men's **free pistol** event in 1948. Francisco Boza was their second Olympic medalist. He also won his in shooting—a silver medal in 1984 **trap** shooting. Ironically, Edwin Vásquez was Peru's flagbearer that year in the opening ceremony. In 1988, the Peruvian women's volleyball team won a silver medal. And in 1992, Juan Jorge Giha, Jr., won a silver medal in **skeet** shooting.

Other noteworthy events for Peru in the Olympics include the fortunes of their basketball teams. In the first basketball tournament in 1936, Peru won its first two games and reached the quarter-final round. However, in the football tournament, Peru met **Austria** in the quarter-finals and defeated them in extra time in a very rough match in which several Peruvian spectators interfered with play. Austria filed a protest, which was upheld, and the game was to be replayed. Peru did not agree with the decision and removed its entire Olympic contingent, including the basketball team, which consequently forfeited its final two games and was placed seventh. Peru's 1948 basketball team was competitive (unlike some of the other teams in that year's tournament) and finished 10th of 23. Peru's third venture into Olympic basketball was in 1964. Their team featured four brothers, the Duartes—Enrique, Luis, Raúl, Ricardo—the only time that Olympic basketball had four siblings play on the same team. Although the team finished 15th of 16 teams, Ricardo Duarte set a single-game scoring record (later broken) with 44 points on 16 October 1964. His brother Raúl was one of the first international players to be drafted by the National Basketball Association, although he did not play in that league.

Peru's women's volleyball teams were among the best in the world for a period of time, and in addition to their silver medal in 1988, it finished fourth in 1968 and also in 1984. Peru also had two other fourth place finishes—swimmer Juan Carlos Bello in the 1968 200 meter individual and trap shooter Francisco Boza in 1988. In 1968, skeet shooter Pedro Gianella finished fifth. Three other athletes were losing quarter-finalists and finished tied for fifth—boxers Luis Minami (1968 **lightweight**) and Oscar Ludeña (1972 **heavyweight**) and Peter López in 2008 **featherweight taekwondo**. The 1936 men's football team (mentioned above) also was placed in a tie for fifth after they left the tournament following their quarter-final match. Shooters Guillermo Baldwin (1948 **small-bore rifle** prone) and Antonio Vita (1964 free pistol) also achieved sixth place results.

The Andes nation sent its first athletes to the **Olympic Winter Games** in Vancouver in 2010—**cross-country skier** Roberto Carcelén and the brother and sister pair of Manfred and Ornella Oettl in **Alpine skiing**. The three also competed in Sochi in 2014. Carcelén finished 94th of 95 in 2010 and 87th of 91 in 2014 in the men's 15 k race. Manfred entered the **slalom** and **giant slalom** in both 2010 and 2014, with a best result of 67th of 101 in the 2010 giant slalom. His sister Ornella also entered the slalom and giant slalom in both years, and her best result was 57th of 89 in the 2014 giant slalom.

PESÄPALLO. Also known as Finnish **baseball,** *pesäpallo* is a variant of normal baseball, created in the early 20th century in **Finland**. It is predominantly played there and was demonstrated with a single game at the 1952 **Olympic Games** in Helsinki. It was invented by Lauri "Tahko" Pihkala who had competed for Finland in **athletics** at the 1908 (**high jump** and **discus throw**) and 1912 (800 meters) Olympic Games.

PHELPS, MICHAEL FRED, II (USA–SWI). B. 30 June 1985, Baltimore, Maryland, **United States**. By most measures, Michael Phelps is the most successful Olympic athlete in history. With 18 **swimming** gold medals in 2004, 2008, and 2012, he has won more titles than any other Olympian. No one has won more **Olympic medals** than Phelps's total of 22. In addition, Phelps won eight gold medals at a single Olympics in 2008, breaking **Mark Spitz**'s 1972 record of seven after "failing" to do so in 2004, when Phelps had only won six golds and two bronzes, which nevertheless made him only the second person to win eight medals in a single Olympics (after **Aleksandr Dityatin** [URS]). In both Athens and Beijing, the six-foot, three-inch (193 cm), 196 lb (89 kg) Phelps competed in the same eight events: the 100 and 200 meter **butterfly**, the 200 and 400 meter **medley**, the 200 meter **freestyle**, and the three **relay** events. As a 15-year-old, Phelps entered only the 200 meter butterfly at the Sydney Olympics and finished fifth. He then medaled in 22 of his next 23

Olympic races from 2004 to 2012, with only a fourth place finish in the 400 meter individual medley in 2012, spoiling his perfect record.

Unsurprisingly, Phelps is also a record-breaking athlete outside of the Olympics. With a total of 26 titles in 2001 (1), 2003 (4), 2005 (5), 2007 (7), 2009 (5), and 2011 (4), he has won the most titles at the World Championships. During his career, Phelps has broken a world record 39 times as of July 2014, which is also a record. Although he announced his retirement following the 2012 Games, he made a comeback in 2014 and won the 100 meter butterfly at the Pan-Pacific Championships in **Australia** in August.

PHILIPPINES, THE (PHI). The Southeast Asian island nation of the Philippines first competed at the **Olympic Games** in 1924 and has since missed only the 1980 Moscow Olympics. It competed at the **Olympic Winter Games** of 1972, 1988, 1992, and 2014. The Philippines, officially known as the Republic of the Philippines, has won nine **Olympic medals** (two silver, seven bronze) in **boxing, swimming**, and track and field **athletics**, yet no Filipino has ever won a gold medal and the Philippines is currently (as of 2014) the nation with the most medals without an Olympic title. However, Arianne Cerdena won the women's **bowling** event in that **demonstration sport** at the 1988 Olympics.

In 20 Summer Games, the Philippines has entered 375 athletes (328 men, 47 **women**) and competed in 18 sports as well as the **art competitions**. Most of their competitors participated in boxing (64 men), **basketball** (63 men), swimming (46 men, 14 women), athletics (32 men, 19 women), and **shooting** (34 men, one woman).

The only Filipino Olympian with more than one Olympic medal is swimmer Teófilo Yldefonso, who won bronze medals in 1928 and 1932 in the 200 meter **backstroke** and finished in seventh place in 1936 in that event. His great-grandson Daniel Coakley competed for the Philippines in the 2008 Olympics 50 meter **freestyle** event. In 1932, Simeon Toribio won a bronze medal in the **high jump** and José Luis Villanueva won a bronze medal in **bantamweight** boxing. In 1936, Miguel White won a bronze in the 400 meter **hurdles**. Since then, the Philippines only Olympic medals have come in boxing. Anthony Villanueva, son of José Luis, won the country's first silver medal in 1964 in the **featherweight** class. The Philippines last three medals came in the **light-flyweight** class in consecutive Games: Leopoldo Serrantes won bronze in 1988, Roel Velasco won bronze in 1992, and his brother, Mansueto, won silver in 1996.

Other notable results for the Philippines in the Summer Games include Simeon Toribio finishing fourth in the 1928 high jump and shooter Martin Gison fourth in 1936 **small-bore rifle** prone. Fifth place behind bronze medalist Yldefonso in the 1932 200 meter backstroke went to teammate Jikirum Adjaluddin. In **weightlifting**, Rodrigo del Rosario was fifth in 1948 featherweight competition and fourth in that class in 1952, bantamweight Pedro Landero was sixth in 1952, and featherweight Alberto Nogar was eighth in 1960.

In boxing, in addition to their five medalists, several boxers were losing quarter-finalists who placed tied for fifth—bantamweight Oscar de Larrazabal (1936), **lightweight** José Padilla (1936), **welterweight** Simplicio de Castro (1936), lightweight Rodolfo Arpon (1964), bantamweight Rey Fortaleza (1976), lightweight Leopoldo Cantancio (1984), lightweight Ronald Chavez (1992), and **flyweight** Elias Recaldo (1996). In **taekwondo**, Toni Rivero was also a losing quarter-finalist in the 2004 women's welterweight class as was featherweight Jasmin Strachin in 2000. In **judo**, Thomas Ong finished seventh in the 1964 **open class**.

In basketball, one of the most popular sports in the Philippines, they competed in each tournament from 1936 to 1960 and in 1968 and 1972. The 1936 team finished fifth of 23 teams. It was led by their captain Ambrosio Padilla, who later became active in politics and served as a senator. The 1956 team was seventh of 15.

In four Winter Games, the Philippines has entered five men—three in **Alpine skiing** and one each in **figure skating** and **luge**. Their best result was obtained in 1992 when Alpine skier Michael Teruel finished a respectable 49th of 119 entrants in the men's **slalom**.

PIERRE DE COUBERTIN COMMISSION. The **Pierre de Coubertin Commission** was created in 1975 and worked to promulgate the teachings of Baron Pierre de Coubertin and his philosophy. It worked very closely with the **International Pierre de Coubertin Committee** in this regard, but is no longer recognized by the **International Olympic Committee**.

PIETRI, DORANDO (ITA–ATH). B. 16 October 1885, Correggio, Reggio Emilia, **Italy**. D. 7 February 1942, San Remo, Imperia, Italy. Dorando Pietri is the most famous loser in Olympic history. Entering the stadium at the end of the 1908 Olympic **marathon**, he had a comfortable lead over Johnny Hayes (USA), but then collapsed five times and had to be helped across the finishing line. This assistance from well-meaning officials resulted in his **disqualification**, but Pietri's fame in defeat far exceeded that of the winner. Queen Alexandra presented him with a large gold cup, an exact replica of the one awarded to the Olympic champion, and Irving Berlin wrote the popular song "Dorando" in his honor. Pietri turned professional shortly after the 1908 Olympics and enjoyed a successful career in America

After collapsing multiple times on the stadium track, Italy's Dorando Pietri is helped over the finish line at the 1908 Olympic marathon. He was later disqualified. Courtesy of Erich Kamper

and Europe. A relatively little-known fact about Pietri is that he had previously entered the 1906 Olympic marathon but was one of the 38 entrants who failed to complete the distance from Marathon, **Greece**, to Athens, as only 15 were able to do so. Pietri also competed with the three-man Italian team in the three-mile team event in London 10 days prior to the 1908 marathon. *See also* OLYMPIC ANTIHEROES.

PINDAR (GRE). Fl. ca. 520–440 B.C. Pindar was a Greek lyric poet, considered the greatest of the Greek choral lyricists. Few details remain of his life, but he was known to have been an aristocrat from Thebes who studied in Athens. Pindar is best known for his *epinicia*, which were odes celebrating athletic victories. Forty-four of these have survived, most celebrating victories in the **Olympic, Isthmian, Nemean,** and **Pythian Games**. The odes were usually commissioned by the victor or his family. *See also* ANCIENT OLYMPIC GAMES.

PING PONG. *See* TABLE TENNIS.

PINSENT, MATTHEW CLIVE (GBR–ROW). B. 10 October 1970, Holt, Norfolk, **England**. Matthew Pinsent graduated from St. Catherine's College at Oxford, where he captained the Oxford **Rowing** Club and led the Oxford **eight** to victories over Cambridge in the 1990 and 1991 Boat Race. Since that time, he has not failed to be at the top stage of international rowing, partnering **Stephen Redgrave** through much of his career, primarily in the coxless **pairs**, though later in the coxless fours. Beginning in 1991, Pinsent and Redgrave won a gold **Olympic medal** or a World Championships gold medal at every edition until Redgrave's retirement after the 2000 **Olympic Games**. Pinsent then began rowing with James Cracknell. Pinsent and Cracknell formed an unbeatable pair, winning the world title in 2001 and 2002 in coxless pairs and in 2001 in the coxed pairs. The six-foot, five-inch (196 cm), 238 lb (108 kg) Pinsent has won gold medals at the 1992, 1996, 2000, and 2004 Olympics: in the coxless pairs in 1992 and 1996 with Redgrave and coxless fours in 2000 and 2004 with Redgrave and Cracknell (Tim Foster in 2000 and Ed Goode in 2004 rounded out the four). His record of four Olympic rowing gold medals is surpassed only by Redgrave, **Elisabeta Lipă-Oleniuc**, and **Georgeta Damian-Andrunache**, all with five. Pinsent also claims 14 championships at the Henley Royal Regatta, all in the coxless pairs or fours, since 1990, only failing in 1992. Pinsent retired from competitive rowing after the 2004 season and was knighted shortly thereafter. *See also* COXSWAIN.

PISTORIUS, OSCAR LEONARD CARL (RSA–ATH). B. 22 November 1986, Pretoria, Gauteng, **South Africa**. Oscar Pistorius is unique among Olympic athletes. He is the only runner to compete without feet. He is a bilateral amputee whose legs were amputated below the knee when he was an infant. He uses artificial blades as replacements for his lower legs and has proven to be quite adept. So adept, in fact, that after competing in the **Paralympic Games** he attempted to qualify for the regular **Olympic Games**. Pistorius had a battle to reach the Olympic Games as the International Association of Athletics Federations (IAAF) did not want him to compete against able-bodied athletes, claiming that his blades gave him an unfair advantage. The organization passed a ruling in 2007 that in effect prohibited Pistorius from competing. After testing by a professor of biomechanics in 2007, the IAAF officially ruled Pistorius ineligible in January 2008. Pistorius took his case to the **Court of Arbitration for Sport** in **Lausanne**, which upheld his appeal and reversed the IAAF's decision.

He was able to meet the qualifying time in a race on 19 July 2011 when he was clocked in 45.07 seconds for the 400 meters, and he then represented South Africa at the 2012 London Games where he ran in the 400 meters and was a member of South Africa's 4x400 meter **relay** team. In the 400 meter race, he was second in the first **heat** with a time of 45.44 seconds and qualified for the next heat. In that heat, he could only manage a time of 46.54 and was eliminated from the competition. In the relay event, the South African team filed a protest after they were bumped by the **Kenyan** team during the first baton exchange. Although South Africa finished seventh of eight teams in that heat, they were allowed to advance to the final round as their protest was upheld. In the final, South Africa finished eighth of nine teams, with Pistorius running the anchor leg. Pistorius then carried the South African flag during the closing ceremony.

Following the 2012 Olympic Games, Pistorius took part in the Paralympic Games, also held in London, a few weeks after the end of the Olympic Games. There he was the flagbearer in the opening ceremony, won a silver medal in the 200 meters (after setting a Paralympic world record in a preliminary heat), won gold medals in the 400 meters and 4x100 relay, and finished fourth in the 100 meters.

Early in 2013, Pistorius's life took a tragic turn as he was accused of murdering his girlfriend. He admitting shooting her, but claimed he mistook her for an intruder. On 21 October 2014, he was found guilty of "culpable homicide" and was sentenced to five years in prison. In December, he was granted permission to appeal the verdict.

PLATFORM DIVING. Platform diving, in which athletes dive from a platform 10 meters above the water, has been an Olympic event for men since 1906 and for women since 1928. **Klaus Dibiasi** of **Italy** won the silver medal in 1964 and the gold medal in the next three **Olympic Games**. No other man has won the event more than twice nor won more than three total medals in platform diving. Four women have won the Olympic platform diving event twice—Dorothy Poynton-Hill of the **United States** (1932, 1936), **Pat Mc-Cormick** of the United States (1952, 1956), **Fu Mingxia** of **China** (1992, 1996), and Chen Ruolin of China (2008, 2012). Paula Jean Myers-Pope of the United States is the only woman to win three medals in Olympic platform diving (silver 1952, 1960, bronze 1956).

POLAND (POL). The Eastern European nation of Poland competed continuously at the **Olympic Games** from 1924 through 1980, and after **boycotting** Los Angeles in 1984, returned to the Olympic fold in 1988 at Seoul. Prior to 1924, several Poles probably competed for other countries. In 1908, Jerzy Gajdzik, his name Americanized to George Gaidzik, won a **diving** bronze medal for the **United States**, and in 1912 the Polish-born Julius Beresford (né Wisniewski) won a silver medal with the British **eight**-oared crew. The 1912 **Russian** Olympic team included eight Poles, and one Polish sculptor was entered in the first Olympic **art competitions**. Poland, officially known as the Republic of Poland, has also competed at all the **Olympic Winter Games** since 1924.

In 21 Summer Games, Poland has entered 2,324 athletes (1,788 men, 536 **women**) and competed in 29 sports plus the art competitions. They have had the most entrants in **athletics** (287 men, 149 women), **rowing** (156 men, 43 women), **fencing** (104 men, 37 women), **canoeing** (99 men, 33 women), **cycling** (112 men, 10 women), **wrestling** (106 men, three women), and **boxing** (104 men, one woman). Poland has won 279 Olympic medals in the Summer Games (67 gold, 84 silver, 128 bronze) in 19 different sports plus the art competitions. With four gold medals from 1996 to 2004, the most successful Pole is **race walker Robert Korzeniowski**, although **Irena Szewińska-Kirszenstein** has won seven medals (three golds, two silver, two bronze) from 1964 to 1976. Remarkably she has won medals in five different athletics events—100 meters (bronze 1968), 200 meters (silver 1964, gold 1968, bronze 1972), 400 meters (gold 1976), **long jump** (silver 1964), and 4x100 meters **relay** (gold 1964).

In 22 Winter Games, Poland has entered 511 athletes (404 men, 107 women) and competed in 15 sports—all except **curling**—with the most participants in **ice hockey** (154 men) and **cross-country skiing** (42 men, 27 women). They have won 20 medals in five Winter sports (six gold, seven silver, seven bronze). Cross-country skier Justyna Kowalczyk has won five medals (two gold, one silver, two bronze) from 2006 to 2014 in events ranging from the women's **sprint** to the 30 km race. **Ski jumper** Adam Małysz has won three silver and one bronze medal from 1998 to 2010.

Poland has made two unsuccessful bids to host the Winter Games—Zakopane, Poland, in 2006 and Krakow, which bid for the 2022 Games but then withdrew its bid. *See also* BASZANOWSKI, WALDEMAR ROMUALD.

POLE VAULT. The pole vault is an **athletics** event. The athlete, carrying a long pole, takes a running start and then places the end of the pole in the ground and uses it to propel him- or herself over a high bar. It has been included in the men's **Olympic Program** since the 1896 **Olympic Games** and in the women's program since 2000. **Bob Richards** of the **United States**, in 1952 and 1956, is the only man to win this event twice at the Olympic Games, and he also won a bronze medal in 1948, making him the only three-time medalist as well. Yelena Isinbayeva of **Russia** also won the women's pole vault twice (2004, 2008) and finished third once (2012). Arguably the greatest pole vaulter of all time, Sergey Bubka of the **Ukraine**, who broke the world record 35 times, only managed to win the Olympic gold medal once in three attempts.

POLITICS. *See* BOYCOTTS AND POLITICS.

POLO. Polo was contested at the **Olympic Games** in 1900, 1908, 1920, 1924, and 1936 but never managed to attract a large field of competing nations. In 1936, two of the five competing teams were so weak that they were not given the chance to compete for the gold and could at most earn a bronze medal. **Argentina** won the gold medal in 1924 and 1936 and **Great Britain** won in 1908 and 1920. The 1900 tournament consisted of club teams with players from various nations. In five Summer Games, there have been 87 men from nine nations who have taken part in Olympic polo competition. The Fédération Internationale de Polo (FIP) was founded in 1985 and is an **International Olympic Committee**–recognized federation, currently (as of 2014) with 59 full members, 14 corresponding members, and 10 contact national members. One of the FIP's main goals is to restore its Olympic status, but the sport's exclusivity makes that unlikely.

POMMELLED HORSE. The pommelled horse (also known as pommel horse or side horse) is one of the exercises performed by male **gymnasts**. It is a metal frame covered with foam rubber and leather with two handles (or pommels) on top. The apparatus is 115 cm (3.77 feet) high, 160 cm (5.2 feet) long, and just 35 cm (14 inches) wide. It is an ancient device that was developed for soldiers to practice mounting and dismounting horses. It was included in the first modern **Olympic Games** in 1896 and in every Olympic Games since 1924. The event is somewhat unusual in that there have been five occasions in which the gold medal was shared, including two three-way ties for first place. Zoltán Magyar of **Hungary** (1976, 1980), Miroslav Cerar of **Yugoslavia** (1964, 1968), and **Boris Shakhlin** of the **Soviet Union** (1956, 1960) each won two gold medals in this event, while Marius Urzică of **Romania** has won three total medals in the pommelled horse.

POPOV, ALEKSANDR VLADIMIROVICH (EUN/RUS–SWI). B. 16 November 1971, Lesnoy, Sverdlovsk, **Russia**, USSR. Known by a variety of nicknames ("Sasha," "The Russian Rocket," "Ice Man," and "Big Dog"), Aleksander Popov is arguably the greatest **sprint freestyle swimmer** ever. In both 1992 and 1996, Popov won gold medals in the 50 and 100 meter freestyle sprint events. He competed at the Sydney Olympics in 2000, but was touched out in the 100 meter by Pieter van den Hoogenband, winning a silver medal. The six-foot, six-inch (200 cm), 192 lb (87 kg) Popov also competed in 2004, without winning a medal, and retired shortly after the Athens **Olympic Games**. At the World Championships, he won the 50 meter freestyle in 1994 and 2003 and the 100 meter freestyle in 1994, 1998, and 2003. His comeback to world-class swimming after the Atlanta Olympics was the stuff of legends. During an altercation on a Moscow street with an Azeri watermelon vendor, he was stabbed in the abdomen. The knife grazed his lung and an artery to his kidney. He required emergency surgery and spent three months in rehabilitation. He returned in 1997 to defend his European titles in both the 50 and 100 meter freestyle events. Popov set one world record at both of the two sprint distances. In 1999, he was elected as an **International Olympic Committee (IOC) member**.

PORTUGAL (POR). The southwestern European nation of Portugal, officially known as the Portuguese Republic, has competed at the **Olympic Games** continuously since 1912. It has attended the **Olympic Winter Games** less frequently, attending in 1952, 1994, 1998, 2006, and 2010 with a sole competitor, and with five in 1988 and two in 2014.

In 23 Summer Games, Portugal has entered 661 athletes (561 men, 100 **women**) and competed in 27 sports plus the **art competitions**. They have had the most participants in **athletics** (117 men, 39 women), **sailing** (62 men, six women), **swimming** (48 men, 14 women), **fencing** (48 men, two women), **shooting** (45 men, four women), and **football** (48 men).

Portugal has won 23 **Olympic medals** (four gold, eight silver, 11 bronze), all at the Summer Games in nine different sports. Portuguese athletes have particularly excelled in the **marathon**, and three of the nation's four Olympic titles were won in that event. Best known of these is probably Carlos Lopes, who won the 1984 men's marathon at age 37. He had previously won a silver medal in the 1976 10,000 meter race. Rosa Mota won the women's marathon in 1988 after having won a bronze medal in that event in 1984. Fernanda Ribeiro was also a dual medalist for Portugal with a gold medal in 1996 and a bronze medal four years later both in the women's 10,000 meter run. **Equestrian** Luís Silva is Portugal's fourth dual Olympic medalist, with bronze medals in team **jumping** in 1936 and team **dressage** in 1948. Portugal's other gold medal was won by Nelson Évora in the 2008 **triple jump**.

The other Olympic medalists for Portugal include women's **triathlete** Vanessa Fernandes (2008 silver), **trap** shooter Armando Marques (1976 silver), *judoka* Nuno Delgado (2000 men's **half-middleweight** bronze), **cyclist** Sérgio Paulinho (2004 men's individual road race), the 1928 men's **épée** fencing team, the 1924 equestrian jumping team, and sailors Nuno Barreto and Hugo Rocha (1996 two-man **dinghy** bronze) and three medals in the two-man **keelboat** race—brothers Duarte Manuel Bello and Fernando Bello (1948 silver), Francisco de Andrade and Joaquim Fiúza (1952 bronze), and brothers Mário Quina and José Manuel Quina (1960 silver). In 2012, the Portuguese team of Fernando Pimenta and Emanuel Silva won a bronze medal in K2-1,000 canoeing. Portugal's other medals were in athletics: a silver medal by **Nigerian** native

Francis Obikwelu in the 2004 100 meter dash, a bronze by Rui Silva in 2004 in the 1,500 meter run, and a bronze by António Leitão in the 1984 5,000 meters.

In seven Winter Games, Portugal has entered 12 athletes (10 men, two women) and competed in five sports: **Alpine skiing** (three men, one woman), **bobsledding** (five men), one man in **cross-country skiing**, one man in **speed skating**, and one woman in **freestyle skiing**. They have not won any medals, and their best results were by Georges Mendes who finished 32nd of 61 in the 1994 men's **giant slalom** and by Camile Dias who finished 40th of 85 in the 2014 women's **slalom**.

PORTUGUESE GUINEA. *See* GUINEA-BISSAU.

PORTUGUESE TIMOR. *See* TIMOR LESTE.

POUND REPORT. *See* OLYMPIC BRIBERY SCANDAL.

POUND, RICHARD WILLIAM DUNCAN "DICK," Q.C. (CAN–SWI). B. 22 March 1942, St. Catharines, Ontario, **Canada**. **Dick Pound** was a **swimming** finalist (sixth in the 100 meter **freestyle**) at the 1960 **Olympic Games**, who became president of the Canadian Olympic Association in 1977 and a member of the **International Olympic Committee** (IOC) the following year. In 1987, he was appointed as vice president of the IOC, and throughout the 1980s and 1990s, he exerted considerable influence in the financial sphere, particularly in negotiations with sponsors, setting up The Olympic Programme (later **The Olympic Partners**), and in the sale of **television** rights. A Montreal-based lawyer specializing in tax law, Pound earned his undergraduate and law degrees at McGill University in Montreal. His legal skills provided invaluable support to President **Juan Antonio Samaranch** in the negotiations with the **Democratic People's Republic of Korea** over the 1988 Games.

Pound was one of the prime candidates to succeed Samaranch as **IOC president** in 2001, but failed in his bid to win the IOC presidency. He was chairman of the IOC **Finance Commission** from its inception until he resigned in 2001 after the election. He was also the chairman of the IOC commission that oversaw the **Olympic bribery scandal** in 1999 and was named the first chairman of the **World Anti-Doping Agency**, a post he resigned after a second term in 2007. From 2002 to 2004, Pound also chaired the **Olympic Games Study Commission**, which prepared a report on ways to streamline the costs of the Olympic Games and **Olympic Winter Games**. Dick Pound is likely the most influential **IOC member** who has never succeeded to the IOC presidency.

POWERBOATING. *See* MOTORBOATING.

PRESS. The press was formerly (until 1976) one of the three lifts in Olympic **weightlifting** competition. (Since the 1976 Games, only two lifts, the **snatch** and **clean and jerk**, are required.) The weight lifted in this method was added to the weight lifted in the snatch and clean and jerk lifts and the total of the three lifts determined the winner. In the press lift, the weight was lifted chest high and held there until upon a referee's signal the weight was lifted overhead without moving the legs. In 1972, **Vasily Alekseyev** of the **Soviet Union** set the Olympic record with a press lift of 235 kg (518.1 lb).

PRESS COMMISSION. The Press Commission was originally called the Press and Public Relations Commission, which was formed in 1967 and lasted until 1972. A separate Press Commission was formed in 1973. The current chairman is American Lawrence F. Probst, III. There are three other **International Olympic Committee** (IOC) members on the Commission, along with representatives of the world's sporting press. Prior to becoming **IOC presidents**, both **Lord Killanin** and **Juan Antonio Samaranch** served as chairmen of this Commission.

PROTOPOPOV, OLEG ALEKSEYEVICH (URS–FSK). *See* BE-LOUSOVA, LYUDMILA YEVGENEVNA.

PUERTO RICO (PUR). The Commonwealth of Puerto Rico is an unincorporated island territory of the **United States** located in the Caribbean Sea. It has its own **National Olympic Committee** and first competed at the 1948 Olympics in London and has not failed to compete at the **Olympic Games** since then, notably attending the 1980 Olympics (although they only sent a token team of three athletes—all boxers) even though they were **boycotted** by the United States.

In 17 Summer Games, Puerto Rico has entered 516 athletes (443 men, 73 **women**) and competed in 22 sports. The sports with the most participants are **athletics** (75 men, 16 women), **boxing** (88 men), **basketball** (70 men), **swimming** (35 men, 15 women), and **shooting** (38 men).

Puerto Rican athletes have won two silver and six bronze medals at the Olympic Games, all in boxing, until 2012, when Javier Culson won a bronze in the 400 meter **hurdles** and Jaime Espinal won silver in **light-heavyweight freestyle wrestling**. Puerto Rico's boxing silver medalist was **lightweight** Luis Ortíz (1984). Its bronze medalists were **light-flyweight** Orlando Maldonado (1976), **bantamweight** Juan Venegas (1948), **welter-**

weights Anibál Acevedo (1992) and Daniel Santos (1996), and **middle-weight** Arístides González (1984).

Other notable Olympic results for Puerto Ricans include fourth place in 1960 for **pole vaulter** Rolando Cruz, swimmer Carlos Berrocal in the 100 meter freestyle in 1976, and in 1984 for bantamweight freestyle wrestler Orlando Cáceres. Sixth place was won by gymnast Tommy Ramos in 2012 **rings**, by shooter Jaime Santiago in 1972 **small-bore rifle** prone, and bantamweight weightlifter Fernando Báez in 1968.

Quarter-final round losers in boxing (placed tied for fifth) were in 1976 welterweight Carlos Santos and **light-middleweight** Wilfredo Guzman, in 1980 **featherweight** Luis Pizarro and **light-welterweight** José Angel Molina, in 1984 light-flyweight Rafael Ramos and light-welterweight Jorge Maysonet, in 1988 light-middleweight Rey Rivera, in 1996 light-heavyweight Enrique Flores, in 2008 **flyweight** McWilliams Arroyo, and in 2012 flyweight Jeyvier Cintron and lightweight Felix Verdejo. Losing quarter-finalists in women's welterweight **taekwondo** were Ineabelle Díaz (2004) and Asunción Ocasio (2008).

Possibly the most memorable Olympic moment for Puerto Rico occurred in the opening game of the 2004 basketball tournament when they defeated the United States in the opening round, 92–73. The Puerto Rican team was led by Carlos Arroyo and included three other players who played in the National Basketball Association (NBA), although none were major stars. The United States team, on the other hand, was composed of all NBA players and included such stars as Tim Duncan, LeBron James, Allen Iverson, Dwyane Wade, Stephon Marbury, and Carmelo Anthony. This was only the third U.S. loss in Olympic basketball and was by the widest margin. Although the Puerto Rican team only finished in sixth place in 2004, they did finish in fourth place in 1964 when the United States, the USSR, and **Brazil** all had stronger teams.

Puerto Rico also competed at each **Olympic Winter Games** from 1984 to 1998. In those five Winter Games, Puerto Rico entered 17 athletes (16 men, one woman) and competed in five sports: **Alpine skiing** (six men, one woman), **biathlon** (one man), **bobsledding** (six men), **freestyle skiing** (two men), and **luge** (two men). One man competed in both Alpine and freestyle skiing. The best performance was by the Kevin Wilson in 1988 **slalom** skiing, who finished 43rd of 109 entrants, ahead of 11 others who completed the course and 55 others who did not. The 1994 two-man bobsled team finished 25th of 30 entrants.

San Juan, Puerto Rico, made an unsuccessful bid to host the 2004 Summer Games.

PURSUIT. Pursuit is a type of race in which one or more competitors chase after a leader. In **cycling**, the individual pursuit has two competitors start at opposite sides of the track in an attempt to overtake each other. This rarely happens in Olympic competition, and the winner of the race is the rider with the best time. In other sports such as **modern pentathlon, biathlon**, or **cross-country skiing**, a multipart competition is held, and the leaders after the initial part of the competition then start the concluding race ahead of the other contestants, who then start the race at timed intervals based on their results of the previous parts. The winner of the final race is then the event's winner.

PYTHIAN GAMES. The Pythian Games were one of the four great Panhellenic sporting festivals, along with the **Olympic Games, Isthmian Games**, and **Nemean Games**. They were held in honor of Apollo at Delphi. They were the only one of the four main Greek festivals that also featured musical contests. The Pythian Games were first recorded in 582 B.C. and continued until the fourth century A.D. They were held quadrennially, in the third year of each **Olympiad**. The victors at the Pythian Games were awarded a laurel crown. *See also* ANCIENT OLYMPIC GAMES.

QATAR (QAT). Qatar made its initial Olympic appearance in Los Angeles in 1984 with a team of eight track and field **athletes**, a **football** team, and four **shooters**. Qatar has appeared at every **Olympic Games** since. In eight Summer Games, Qatar has entered 108 athletes (104 men, four **women**) and competed in 10 sports: athletics (53 men, one woman), football (31 men), **sailing** (two men), **shooting** (seven men, one woman), **swimming** (four men, one woman), **table tennis** (one man, one woman), **weightlifting** (three men), and one man in each of **archery, fencing,** and **taekwondo**.

The Arabian peninsula nation, whose official name is the State of Qatar, won its first **Olympic medal** in 1992, when Mohamed Sulaiman finished third in the men's 1,500 meters in track and field athletics. In 2000, Said Asaad added another bronze medal, won in the **heavyweight** (105 kg) class weightlifting. In 2012, Qatar won two more bronze medals—Nasser Al-Attiya (in his fifth Olympic Games) won one in **skeet** shooting after finishing sixth in 2000 and fourth in 2004, and **high jumper** Mutaz Essa Barshim tied for third place with two other jumpers. Other notable Olympic results by Qatari Olympians include fourth place finishes by **super-heavyweight** weightlifter Jaber Salem in 2000 and **steeplechase** runner Musa Amer in 2004. Seventh place results were recorded by 400 meter runner Ibrahim Ismail in 1992 and Rashid Al-Athba in 2012 **double trap** shooting. Ismail was also eighth in the 400 meter in 1996. The 1992 Qatari football team finished eighth of 16 teams, and eighth place results in individual events were accomplished by **middle-weight** weightlifter Nader Sufyan Abbas in 2004 and three track and field athletes in 2008—Abubaker Ali Kamal (3,000 meter steeplechase), James Kwalia (5,000 meter), and Ahmad Hassan Abdullah (10,000 meter).

At recent Olympics, Qatar has fielded a number of athletes who have been "bought" from other nations, notably **Kenyan** runners and **Bulgarian** weightlifters. The aforementioned Said Asaad, for example, was born under the name Angel Popov, and Ahmad Hassan Abdullah, Musa Amer, and James Kwalia were born in Kenya. Qatar has never competed at the **Olympic Winter Games**.

Qatar's capital city, Doha, has bid unsuccessfully to host the 2016 and 2020 Summer Games, although it was successful in its bid to host the football World Cup in 2022.

R

RACE IN ARMOR. The race in armor was contested at the **Ancient Olympic Games** from 520 B.C. through at least A.D. 185. It was also known as the hoplite event, referring to Greek foot soldiers. The event was held over two laps of the stadium, or about 385 meters. **Leonidas of Rhodes** won four championships consecutively, from 164 to 152 B.C. *See also APENE; DIAULOS* RACE; *DOLIKHOS* RACE; *STADION* RACE.

RACE WALKING. Race walking is one of the more unusual events in the sport of **athletics**. A race walker's back toe cannot leave the ground until the heel of the front foot has touched. The second rule requires that the supporting leg must straighten from the point of contact with the ground and remain straightened until the body passes directly over it. The sport is difficult to officiate since the two main rules are only judged by the human eye. Race walking has been included in the **Olympic Games** since 1908. The early Olympic Games had relatively short distance walking contests (1,500 meters and 3,000 meters in 1906 and 3,500 meters in 1908). A 10 km walk was held in 1912, 1920, 1924, 1948, and 1952. No Olympic race walking took place in 1928. A 50 km walk was instituted in 1932 and held at each subsequent Olympic Games except 1976. In 1956, a 20 km walk was added and has been held at each games through 2012. **Women**'s race walking was added in 1992 for a 10 km distance. It remained at 10 km in 1996, but since 2000 has been a 20 km event. The best Olympic male race walker has been **Robert Korzeniowski** of **Poland** who won the 50 km race in 1996, 2000, and 2004 and the 20 km race in 2000. Volodomyr Holubnichiy of the **Soviet Union** won four medals in the 20 km race (gold 1960, 1968, silver 1972, bronze 1964). John Ljunggren of **Sweden** won three medals in the 50 km race (gold 1948, silver 1960, bronze 1956). He was also fourth in the 1956 20 km race. In women's Olympic race walking Olga Kanaskina of **Russia** (gold 2008, silver 2012) and Kjersti Tysse-Plätzer of **Norway** (silver 2000, 2008) are the only multiple medalists.

RACQUETBALL. Racquetball is decidedly different from **racquets** and is a very modern sport. It has not been contested at the **Olympic Games**, but the International Racquetball Federation is recognized by the **International**

Olympic Committee (IOC). It was founded in 1968 and currently has 103 affiliated member nations, including Catalonia and Saipan, both of which are not recognized separately by the IOC.

RACQUETS. Racquets (or rackets, in British English) has been contested as an Olympic sport only in 1908, when men's **singles** and **doubles** events were held in London. Seven men, all representing **Great Britain** took part. John Jacob Astor, V, of the famed Astor family, then a student in **England**, won a bronze medal in the Olympic singles competition and teamed with Vane Pennell to with the gold medal in **doubles**. Although its offshoot, **squash**, has become a popular sport worldwide, racquets remains obscure. It is mainly contested in the **United States** and Great Britain and lacks an international governing body. *See also* RACQUETBALL.

RADIO AND TELEVISION COMMISSION. The Radio and **Television** Commission has been known by various names. The first "media" commission was the Press and Public Relations Commission, which was formed in 1967 and lasted until 1972. At that time, two separate commissions, the **Press Commission** and the Television Commission, were created. A Radio Commission existed briefly in 1984. In 1985, this was merged with the Television Commission to form the Radio and Television Commission. The current (as of 2014) chairman of the Commission is Gerardo Werthein of **Argentina**. There are eight **International Olympic Committee (IOC) members** on the Commission, but the bulk of them are representatives of the television and radio networks worldwide, as well as representatives of the **Organizing Committees of the Olympic Games** who deal with the electronic media.

RADMILOVIC, PAOLO FRANCESCO "PAUL" (GBR–WAP/SWI). B. 5 March 1886, Cardiff, Glamorgan, **Wales**. D. 29 September 1968, Weston-super-Mare, North Somerset, **England**. Radmilovic had a Yugoslavian father and an Irish mother. Paul Radmilovic won **water polo** gold medals at three successive **Olympic Games** (1908, 1912, 1920) and also swam on the British 4x200 **freestyle relay** team that won the gold medal in 1908. Radmilovic competed in Olympic water polo again in 1924 and 1928. His career was marked by its extraordinary length and by the range of distances over which he excelled. The five-foot, 10-inch (180 cm), 168 lb (76 kg) athlete also had a fourth place finish in the 100 meter freestyle at the 1906 Olympics and a fourth place finish in water polo in 1928. He won his first national **swimming** title in 1901 and the last in 1929, and he won championships at distances from 100 yards to five miles. In 1967, he was the first Briton to be inducted into the International Swimming Hall of Fame.

RAPID-FIRE PISTOL. The rapid-fire pistol from 25 meters is one of the men's **shooting** events at the **Olympic Games**. It was held in 1924, 1932–1964, and 1984–2012. Ralf Schuhmann of **Germany** has won the event three times (1992, 1996, 2004) and was second in 1988 and 2008. His five medals lead all shooters in this event.

REAL TENNIS. *See JEU DE PAUME.*

REDGRAVE, STEPHEN GEOFFREY (GBR–ROW). B. 23 March 1962, Marlow, Buckinghamshire, **England**. With five gold **Olympic medals** and one bronze, Steve Redgrave is the most successful male Olympic oarsman of all time, only surpassed by female colleague **Elisabeta Lipă-Oleniuc** of **Romania**. After winning the coxed fours in 1984, he won the coxless **pairs** at the next three Games (1988, 1992, 1996) and added a bronze in the coxed pairs in 1988. At Sydney in 2000, he added his fifth gold medal in the coxless fours. Redgrave won gold medals at the World Championships in coxless pairs in 1991, 1993, 1994, and 1995 and in the coxless fours in 1997 and 1999. In 1986, the six-foot, three-inch (193 cm), 227 lb (103 kg) Redgrave became the first **rower** to win three gold medals at the **Commonwealth Games**. At Henley, he was also Diamond **Sculls** champion in both 1983 and 1985. In 1989, Redgrave was also a member of the crew who won the British four-man **bobsled** title, although he never competed in the **Olympic Winter Games**. He married Ann Callaway, a member of the British women's **eight** at the 1984 Olympics. In 2001, he became a knight bachelor and is now properly addressed as Sir Stephen.

REFEREE STOPS CONTEST (RSC). In **Olympic Games boxing**, if the referee decides that a boxer is not defending him- or herself well or has taken too much punishment, the referee will stop the bout and award the victory to the boxer's opponent. In professional boxing, this is referred to as a technical **knockout**, but in amateur boxing the result is recorded as "referee stops contest" or RSC.

REGIONAL INTERNATIONAL GAMES. In addition to the **Olympic Games**, numerous international sporting events are held throughout the world each year. Many of these are simply international championships in the various sports, such as the World **Gymnastics** Championships or the World **Athletics** Championships. But in addition, since the 1910s, the nations of the world have gathered together to compete in regional international multisport competitions. The **International Olympic Committee** has encouraged this because it follows some of the principles of **Olympism** and the **Olympic**

Movement, bringing together the various peoples of the world in peaceful sporting competition. In addition, as the Olympic Games continue to grow, the Regional International Games often now serve as qualifying events for the Games. Thus, they have become even more important. In addition, two of the Regional Games have had definite importance to the various political battles afflicting the Olympic Movement. These are the **Games of the New Emerging Forces** and the **Goodwill Games**. Also of note are the **World Games**, which function as the "Olympic Games for non-Olympic sports."

There are probably more than 100 Regional Games, but the most important of them are the African Games, Arab Games, Arctic Winter Games, Asian Games, Asian Winter Games, Baltic Sea Games, Black Sea Games, Bolivarian Games, **Central American** and Caribbean Games, Central American Games, Central Asian Games, **Commonwealth Games**, East Asian Games, Far East Championships, Games of the Small Countries of Europe, Games of the New Emerging Forces, Goodwill Games, Goodwill Winter Games, Indian Ocean Islands Games, Inter-Allied Games, Island Games, Jeux de la Francophonie, Mediterranean Games, Micronesian Games, **Nordic Games**, Pacific Ocean Games, **Pan American Games**, South American Games, South Asian Federation Games, South East Asian Games, South Pacific Games, South Pacific Mini Games, and the West Asian Games.

RELAY. A relay is a type of team race in which the first athlete traverses the course and then tags a teammate who then also traverses the course. The remaining team members do likewise. Most relay races are contested with teams of four athletes. The sports of **athletics, cross-country skiing**, and **swimming** have traditionally included relay events, but in recent years other sports such as **biathlon** and **luge** have also added them to the **Olympic Program**.

REPÊCHAGE. The French word *repêchage*, meaning fishing out or rescuing, is used in some sports to allow athletes who are unsuccessful in a **round** of competition to have a second chance. Most **rowing** events have a *repêchage* race for the rowers who failed to qualify in their **heat**. Winners of the *repêchage* race can then continue in the competition. Other sports such as **cycling** and **fencing** and the combat sports of **judo, taekwondo**, and **wrestling** often allow a competitor who has lost to a finalist in an earlier round to compete for a bronze medal by virtue of a *repêchage* round.

RETTON, MARY LOU (USA–GYM). B. 24 January 1968, Fairmont, West Virginia, **United States**. **Women**'s **gymnastics** became popular in the United States during the 1970s as the **televised** coverage was expanded to highlight the achievements of first **Olga Korbut** (URS) and then **Nadia Comăneci**

(ROU). Television networks found a sport that appealed to women viewers and devoted many hours to an activity that was previously of little interest in the United States. The country had not had much prior success in the sport, but all that changed when in 1984, tiny four-foot, nine-inch (145 cm), 93 lb (42 kg) Mary Lou Retton won the individual **all-around** gold medal and two silver and two bronze medals at the age of 16. She had been inspired to take up the sport by watching Nadia Comăneci in prior Olympics and was able to train under Comăneci's former coaches **Romanians** Béla and Márta Károlyi, after they came to the United States. After winning the **Olympic medals**, Mary Lou became a celebrity and was sought after for commercial endorsements. After winning the prestigious American Cup event for the third consecutive year in 1985, she retired from competition. Since then, the United States has won medals every year in women's gymnastics as first Phoebe Mills (1988), then Shannon Miller (1992, 1996), Elise Ray (2000), Carly Patterson (2004), Nastia Liukin (2008), and Gabby Douglas (2012) and others have continued the tradition that was begun by Mary Lou Retton.

REVIVAL OF THE OLYMPIC GAMES. *See* ATTEMPTS AT REVIVAL.

REVUE OLYMPIQUE. See *OLYMPIC REVIEW.*

RHODESIA (RHO). *See* ZIMBABWE.

RHYTHMIC GYMNASTICS. Rhythmic **gymnastics** is a discipline of gymnastics, together with artistic (regular) gymnastics and **trampolining**. It evolved from the mass gymnastics popular in Europe in the late 19th and early 20th centuries, combined with music and elements from dance. As a sport, it first emerged in the **Soviet Union**, where the first championships were held in 1948. The Fédération Internationale de Gymnastique recognized it as a discipline in 1961, with the first World Championships being held in 1963. The sport has five different apparatuses, or more correctly, attributes: rope, hoop, ball, ribbon, and, previously, clubs. There is also an **all-around** competition, in which the results of the four apparatuses are combined. In group competitions, teams consist of five members, with two events: five hoops and three ribbons plus two ropes. Only **women** are allowed to participate in rhythmic gymnastics internationally, although men do compete in some countries, notably **Japan**.

The sport was approved for the Olympics in 1980. However, in 1952 and 1956, a very similar event was part of the women's gymnastics program: the team event with portable apparatus. In that event, teams were allowed to pick an attribute of their choice, such as balls, hoops, or clubs.

When rhythmic gymnastics made its Olympic debut in Los Angeles in 1984, the competition suffered because of the Soviet **boycott**, as that country and its successor nations have dominated the sport since the beginning. This has also been the case at the Olympics, with **Russia** being the only country to have won more than one gold medal in the sport, and **Spain** and **Canada** the only nations outside the former USSR to have won a gold medal. Only two events are held at the **Olympic Games**, the individual all-around event (since 1984) and the group all-around event, held since 1996. Only three women, all Russian, have managed to win more than one gold medal: Nataliya Lavrova (2000–2004) and Yelena Posevina (2004–2008), both doubled in the group competition, and in 2012, Yevgeniya Kanayeva became the first to repeat as individual champion. In eight Summer Games, there have been 494 women from 48 countries who have participated in Olympic rhythmic gymnastics.

RICARDO (né RICARDO ALEX COSTA SANTOS) (BRA–BVO). B. 6 January 1975, Salvador, Bahia, **Brazil**. Ricardo, like many other Brazilian athletes, is known by just one name. He along with **Emanuel** (Emanuel Fernando Scheffler Rego) are the only two men to win three **Olympic medals** in **beach volleyball**. Ricardo won his first, a silver, in 2000 when he teamed with Zé Marco. In 2004, Ricardo changed partners, teamed with Emanuel, and won the gold medal. In 2008, the pair won the bronze medal. Ricardo returned to the Olympics in 2012 and, teaming with Pedro da Cunha, reached the quarter-final **round** before being eliminated. The six-foot, six-inch (200 cm), 225 lb (102 kg) Ricardo won a gold medal at the World Championships in 2003 and three silver medals (2001, 2011, 2013) and a gold medal at the 2007 **Pan American Games**.

RICHARDS, ROBERT EUGENE "BOB" (USA–ATH). B. 20 February 1926, Champaign, Illinois, **United States**. Bob Richards was one of the greatest **pole vaulters** in history, although he never held the world record in that event. At the age of 20, he became an ordained minister in the Church of the Brethren, a Christian sect of German origin and a historic peace church similar to the Mennonites and Quakers. Throughout his sporting career, he was dubbed the Reverend Bob Richards or the "Vaulting Vicar." At the University of Illinois, he tied for the National Collegiate Athletic Association pole vault championship, and during his athletic career, he won 17 Amateur Athletic Union pole vault titles and three **decathlon** titles. The five-foot, 10-inch (178 cm), 165 lb (75 kg) athlete was the second man to clear 15 feet in the pole vault and was a bronze medalist at the 1948 **Olympic Games**. He improved his performance and won the gold medal in 1952 and 1956, setting a new Olympic record each time. He won the pole vault gold medal at the **Pan**

American Games in 1951 and 1955 and in the latter year also won a silver medal in the Pan Am decathlon. In 1956, he also entered the Olympic decathlon but an injury forced him to withdraw prior to completing the event. Following the Olympic Games, he became a spokesman for Wheaties breakfast cereal and was the first athlete to be pictured on the front of a Wheaties box (although several others had previously appeared on other parts of the box). He then spent much of his life as a motivational speaker. His four sons also were accomplished pole vaulters, and in 1985, his son Brandon set a United States high school record that lasted for 14 years. In 1984, Richards ran for president of the United States on the U.S. Populist Party ticket. He also runs a ranch in north central Texas breeding miniature horses.

Pole vaulter Bob Richards, 1948 bronze medalist, 1952, 1956 gold medalist. Courtesy of Volker Kluge

RIGHT TO PLAY. Right to Play is a nongovernmental charity that has grown out of Olympic Aid, a program set up by the organizers of the 1994 Lillehammer Olympics to help people in war zones. The program gained worldwide coverage after speed skater **Johann Olav Koss** donated his bonuses for his three Olympic gold medals to Olympic Aid. Koss remained the chief athlete ambassador for Olympic Aid, which since then has focused on helping children. Renamed Right to Play in 2003, the organization's mission is to "improve the lives of children in some of the most disadvantaged areas of the world by using the power of sport and play for development, health and peace." It does so with the help of many athlete ambassadors, including Koss (who is also the chief executive officer of Right to Play International). According to its own statements, Right to Play currently helps about one million children in some 20 countries to regularly participate in sports.

RINGS. The rings is one of the exercises performed by male **gymnasts**. The apparatus consists of two rings that hang freely from a rigid metal frame. Each ring is supported by a strap, which in turn connects to a steel cable that is suspended from the metal frame. The gymnast, who grips one ring with each hand, must control the movement of the rings. It was included in the first modern **Olympic Games** in 1896, in 1904, and in every Olympic Games since 1924. Albert Azaryan of the **Soviet Union** (1956, 1960) and Akinori Nakayama of **Japan** (1968, 1972) are the only two gymnasts to win multiple gold medals in this event. Ten other gymnasts have earned two **Olympic medals** in rings competition.

RITOLA, VILJO EINO "VILLE" (FIN–ATH). B. 18 January 1896, in Peräseinäjoki, Seinäjoki, Etelä-Pohjanmaa, **Finland**. D. 24 April 1982, Helsinki, Uusimaa, Finland. Ville Ritola was an outstanding distance runner who rivaled his legendary countryman **Paavo Nurmi**. At the 1924 **Olympic Games**, the five-foot, eight-inch (175 cm), 146 lb (66 kg) Ritola won the **steeplechase** in his first attempt at the race and improved his own 10,000 meter world record to win that event. He also won two further gold medals, in the 3,000 meter team event and the team cross-country event. Ritola and Nurmi met on the track for the first time at these Olympics, with Nurmi claiming the honors by winning the 5,000 meters and defeating Ritola in the cross-country and 3,000 meters. At the 1928 Amsterdam Olympics, the match-up was in the 5,000 meters, with Ritola defeating Nurmi to win the gold medal. In nine Olympic Games events, Ritola medaled in eight of them. His total of eight Olympic medals has only been topped by five others in the sport of **athletics**. The 14th of 20 children, Ritola left home in 1913 to immigrate to the **United States** and eventually won 14 Amateur Athletic

Union titles, returning home in the Olympic years. He never competed in the Finnish national championships.

ROAD RACE. One of the events on the Olympic **cycling** program is the road race. Typically about 250 km (155.3 miles) long, the race is conducted on the streets of the host city with as many as 150 riders (144 from 63 nations in 2012). Depending on the course, the race lasts between five and six hours and about one-third of the entrants usually do not finish. The **women**'s race is shorter, usually about 125 to 140 km (75–87 miles), lasting between three and four hours with about 65 entrants. Aleksandr Vinokurov of **Kazakhstan**, winner of the 2012 race and silver medalist in 2000, is the only man to win more than one **Olympic medal** in this grueling event. A men's cycling road race has been held at every Olympic Games since 1896 except 1900, 1904, and 1908, although the distance in the early years was often considerably shorter (just 87 km [54 miles] in 1896) and was held as a **time trial** rather than a **mass start**. The women's Olympic cycling road race was added in 1984. Monique Knol of the **Netherlands** (gold 1988, bronze 1992) and Jeannie Longo-Ciprelli of **France** (gold 1996, silver 1992) are the only two multiple winners of the women's race.

ROBERT DOVER'S GAMES (COTSWOLD OLIMPICK GAMES). Robert Dover's Games, or Cotswold Olimpick Games, were probably first contested in 1612, during Whitsun (Pentecostal) Week, on the Cotswold Hills. The Games were started by Robert Dover, a local lawyer who lived in the Cotswold Hills. The Games were basically a medieval country fair type of festival, but they achieved great fame. They were held from about 1612 to 1642 and were immortalized in a collection of 30 laudatory poems, titled *Annalia Dubrensia* and published in 1636. Four of the poems were composed by great poets of the era: Ben Jonson, Michael Drayton, Thomas Heywood, and Sir William Davenant. It is slightly conjectural, but apparently even William Shakespeare knew of these Games, possibly mentioning them in *Sir John Falstaff and the Merry Wives of Windsor*: "Slender: '. . . How does your fallow greyhound, sir? I heard say he was outrun on Cotsall.'"

The Cotswold Olimpicks did not end after 1642, but were simply suspended during the Civil War in **England**. They were revived in the 1660s and were then held at unknown intervals for two centuries. They were revived in 1851, but were shortly thereafter suspended again. After another century, the Cotswold Olimpicks were revived in 1951, were briefly suspended, and then resumed in 1963, continuing to this day. In 2014, they were held on 30–31 May on Dover's Hill in Chipping Camden, England, and included such contests as shin-kicking, **tug-of-war**, and a fancy dress parade.

Though they were quite famous in their era and have been contested for many centuries, the only justification to call them "Olympick" Games rests on the fact that they adopted that name and had been brought into contact with the **Olympic, Pythian, Nemean,** and **Isthmian Games** via the *Annalia Dubrensia.* They had no significant influence on **Pierre de Coubertin** or others who attempted to revive the Olympic Games.

RODNINA, IRINA KONSTANTINOVA (later ZAYTSEV) (URS–FSK). B. 12 September 1949, Moscow, **Russia,** USSR. Irina Rodnina was the most successful **pairs** skater in history. Olympic victories in 1972 with Aleksey Ulanov and in 1976 and 1980 with Aleksandr Zaytsev gave her a record total of three gold medals, only equaled at the **Olympic Games** by **singles** skaters **Gillis Grafström** and **Sonja Henie.** Her record at the World Championships was even more impressive. The diminutive Rodnina, only four-feet, 11-inches tall (152 cm), 90 lb (41 kg), won the title for 10 successive years (1969–1978), the first four with Ulanov and the next six with Zaytsev. She married Zaytsev in 1973, and their successes in the latter part of their partnership were as husband and wife. Rodnina is now a **figure skating** coach. In 2014, she was given the honor of lighting the **Olympic flame** along with **Vladislav Tretyak** during the opening ceremony at the Sochi **Olympic Winter Games.**

ROGGE, COUNT CHEVALIER, JACQUES, DR. (BEL). B. 2 May 1942, Ghent, **Belgium.** On 16 July 2001, Jacques Rogge was elected to succeed **Juan Antonio Samaranch** and become the eighth **International Olympic Committee (IOC) president.** Rogge was an accomplished **sailor,** competing in three **Olympic Games** (1968, 1972, 1976), with his best finish in that sport being 14th in the Finn Monotype Class in 1972 at Munich. He also competed on one World Championship team in sailing and was 16 times the Belgian champion. In addition, he competed internationally for Belgium in **rugby,** at which he was selected 10 times for the national team. Rogge is the former chairman of the International Sailing Federation Medical Commission, serving in his capacity as an orthopedic surgeon and specializing in sports medicine. He was formerly chief of the Orthopaedic Surgery Department at Ghent Hospital, although he stopped practicing medicine after his election as IOC president. As a sports administrator, he became head of the Comité Olympique et Interfédéral Belge in 1989 and in 1990 became president of the **European Olympic Committees.** He was elected as an **IOC member** in 1991 and was appointed to the IOC **Executive Board** in 1998. Rogge, who was reelected as president for his final term in 2009, worked to further the fight against **doping,** streamline the **Olympic Program,** and also try to control some of the costs of both the Olympic Games and running the IOC itself. He was succeeded as IOC president by **Thomas Bach** in September 2013 and has been given the title of honorary IOC president.

ROLLER HOCKEY. In 1992, roller hockey was contested as a **demonstration sport** at the Barcelona Olympics, supposedly at the wish of **International Olympic Committee (IOC) President Juan Antonio Samaranch**, an avid roller hockey player in his youth. Roller hockey has never been contested at the Olympics at any other time. It is governed by the Fédération Internationale de Roller Sports, which also governs **roller skating**.

ROLLER SKATING. Roller skating has never been contested at the **Olympic Games**, although it is contested at many of the **Regional International Games**, including the **Pan American Games**. It is governed by the Fédération Internationale de Roller Sports (FIRS), which was founded in 1924, and is recognized by the **International Olympic Committee**. The FIRS currently (as of 2014) has 132 affiliated member nations. *See also* ROLLER HOCKEY.

ROMANIA (ROU, formerly ROM). Romania's first Olympic participant was future **International Olympic Committee (IOC) member** Gheorghe Plagino, who competed in the clay **trap shooting** event in 1900. The nation next competed at the 1924 **Olympic Games** and has since missed only the 1932 and 1948 Olympics. Romania defied pressure from its neighbors and valiantly was the only Warsaw Pact country to compete at the 1984 Olympics in Los Angeles.

In 21 Summer Games, Romania has entered 1,455 athletes (994 men, 461 **women**) and competed in 27 sports plus the **art competitions**, with the most entrants in **athletics** (68 men, 106 women), **rowing** (83 men, 89 women), **gymnastics** (63 men, 74 women), **canoeing** (81 men, 24 women), **fencing** (75 men, 29 women), and **wrestling** (98 men, two women). The Southeastern European nation of Romania has won 301 Olympic medals at the Summer Games (88 gold, 94 silver, 119 bronze) with medals won in 16 different sports. Romania is best known for its outstanding women gymnasts and has also produced several excellent rowers and canoeists. The most famous Romanian Olympian is certainly gymnast **Nadia Comăneci**, who in 1976 became the first person to earn a perfect 10.0 in Olympic competition and won a total of nine medals, five gold, three silver, and one bronze in 1976–1980. Other Romanian woman gymnasts who have excelled at the Olympic Games are Simona Amânar, Lavinia Miloşovici, Daniela Silivaş, Cătălina Ponor, Gina Gogean, and Ecaterina Szabo, each of whom has won at least five medals and is no more than five-feet, two-inches (157 cm) tall and 100 lb (45 kg).

Romania is also known for its stellar female rowers led by **Elisabeta Lipă-Oleniuc**, who leads all rowers, male or female, with eight Olympic medals. Other Romanian woman rowers with five or more medals each are **Veronica Cochelea-Cogeanu**, **Georgeta Damian-Andrunache**, Doina Ignat, Viorica Susanu, Elena Georgescu, and Constanța Pipotă-Burcică, each of whom (with the exception of **coxswain** Georgescu) exceeds five feet, nine inches and 150 lb (175 cm, 68 kg).

In other sports, Romanian canoeist **Ivan Patzaichin**, with seven medals (four gold, three silver), is second only to **Gert Fredriksson** among all Olympic canoeists. Vasile Dîba won four **kayaking** medals. The men's **handball** team won medals (one silver, three bronze) in four consecutive Olympics from 1972 to 1984. Lia Manoliu competed in six Olympics and won three medals (one gold, two bronze) in the women's **discus throw** from 1960 to 1968. Middle distance runner Gabriela Szabo won three medals, one of each color, in 1996 and 2000. Laura Cârlescu-Badea and Olga Orban-Szabo each won three medals in fencing. Other Romanian athletes with three Olympic medals include **weightlifter** Nicu Vlad, wrestler Ștefan Rusu and canoeists Toma Simionov, Aurel Vernescu and Leon Rotman.

Romania has competed at each **Olympic Winter Games** since their inception in 1924, missing only 1960. In 20 Winter Games, Romania has entered 281 athletes (227 men, 54 women) and competed in 13 sports, with most of the entrants in **bobsledding** (76 men, six women), **ice hockey** (52 men), **Alpine skiing** (29 men, nine women), **cross-country skiing** (21 men, 12 women), and **biathlon** (20 men, 11 women). Only a single bronze medal by bobsledders Nicolae Neagoe and Ion Panțuru in 1968 has been earned in the Winter Olympics by Romania. The country did have some other notable results at the Winter Games, including fourth place by the two-man bobsled team in 1932 and by the four-man bobsled team in 1968 and fifth place by the 1972 two-man team. Virgil Brenci was 20th of 72 in the 1972 men's **slalom**. In 2014, Alexandru Barbu was 21st of 115 in the men's slalom. In 2002, Zsolt Antal was 26th of 78 in the men's 30 km cross-country race. **Speed skater** Mihaela Dascălu competed from 1992 to 1998 and finished sixth in the women's 1,000 meters in 1992 and eighth in two other races in 1998. In **luge**, the team of Ioan Apostol and Liviu Cepoi was fourth in men's **doubles** in 1992 and sixth in 1994. In biathlon, Eva Tofalvi was 11th of 64 in the women's 15 k in 1998. Vilmoș Gheorghe was fifth in the 20 k biathlon in 1964.

ROQUE. In 1904, roque, an American variant of **croquet**, was on the **Olympic Program**. Four American men took part in the contest, with the 64-year-old Charles Jacobus, the organizer of the tournament, defeating the 59-year-old Smith Streeter to win the gold medal. The name roque is derived

by dropping the first and last letters from the name of its parent game of croquet. The sport has not been held at the Olympics since 1904. Both roque and
croquet are not currently recognized by the **International Olympic Committee**, nor are they even a member of **SportAccord**. Croquet was contested only
at the 1900 Olympics in Paris, with three events.

ROSE, IAIN MURRAY (AUS–SWI). B. 6 January 1939, Nairn, Highland,
Scotland. D. 15 April 2012, Sydney, New South Wales, **Australia**. **Swimmer** Murray Rose was a triple gold medalist at the 1956 **Olympic Games**;
he won the 400 and 1,500 meter **freestyle** and was a member of the world
record-breaking team in the 4x200 meter freestyle **relay**. After the Melbourne
Games, Rose enrolled at the University of Southern California, and at the

*Murray Rose of Australia, considered the dominant
Olympic distance swimmer from 1956 to 1964.
Courtesy of Erich Kamper*

1960 Olympics, he retained his 400 meter title, won silver in the 1,500 meter race, and won a bronze in the relay. His total of six Olympic medals (in six races) would surely have been greater except for the fact that he was not selected for the 1964 Games, as he refused to return from California for the Australian Championships, the qualifying meet. Earlier in the year, the six-foot tall (185 cm), 176 lb (80 kg) Rose had set world records for 880 yards and 1,500 meters and would certainly have been a medal contender in Tokyo. Rose continued to enjoy competitive swimming long after his Olympic career was over, and in 1981, he won the World Master's title in faster times than he had recorded at the 1956 Games.

ROSE, RALPH WALDO (USA–ATH). B. 17 March 1884, Healdsburg, California, **United States**. D. 16 October 1913, San Francisco, California, United States. In 1904, 19-year-old Ralph Rose, a six-foot, six-inch (198 cm), 235 lb (107 kg) giant, won six **Olympic medals**. His best performance in St. Louis was in the **shot put**; after trailing Wesley Coe in the early rounds, he came back to win the Olympic title with a new world record. Rose lost his world record to the Irishman Denis Horgan later in the season, and Coe made a further improvement in 1905, but Rose recaptured the record in 1907 and beat both Horgan and Coe at the 1908 Olympics. Rose also won the both-hands shot put gold medal in 1912, a silver in the 1904 **discus throw** (losing in a throw-off to **Martin Sheridan**) and 1912 shot put, and a bronze in the 1904 **hammer throw**.

By 1909, Rose's weight had risen to a massive (for the era) 286 lb (130 kg) and, in winning his third straight Amateur Athletic Union (AAU) title, he became the first man to break the 50-foot barrier. Rose eventually won four AAU shot titles, won the discus twice, and was the inaugural AAU **javelin throw** champion in 1909. Rose attended the University of Michigan and later studied law at Chicago. He was the U.S. flagbearer in 1908 at the opening ceremony and refused to dip the flag as he walked past the English king, leading to the American tradition that survives to this day. Rose was prevented from adding to his six Olympic medals when he died at the age of 28 from pneumonia.

ROUND. The word round is used in various Olympic sports to mean different things. In some sports such as **athletics**, if the number of entrants exceeds the capacity of the track (which is usual), a series of **heats** are held with the winners and those with the best times advancing to the next round of competition. In the sport of **boxing**, a round is the interval of the boxing contest. An Olympic boxing contest originally consisted of three rounds of three minutes each with a one-minute rest period. In 2000 and 2004, this was changed to four two-minute rounds with one-minute rest periods, but in 2008, it reverted back to three three-minute rounds.

ROWING. Rowing was first known as a means of transportation in the ancient cultures of **Egypt**, **Greece**, and Rome. Rowing as a sport probably began in **England** in the 17th and early 18th centuries. By the 19th century, rowing was popular in Europe and had been brought to America. Early races were usually contested by professionals, with heavy betting on races common. Competitive rowing precedes most of the other Olympic sports in its recorded modern history. Collegiate rowing competition began in the 19th century. The first Oxford–Cambridge race took place in 1828, and Yale and Harvard first rowed against each other in 1852. The sport was also the first to form an international governing body, in 1892.

Only in 1896 was rowing not contested in the Olympics. It was actually on the program that year, but rough seas forced cancellation of the events. There have been several events for men in both sweep events (single oar used by alternate oarsmen) and **sculling** events (two oars used by a single sculler or by two or more scullers). Through 1992, these included races for single, double, and quadruple sculls, and in sweep events, races for two and four oarsmen or **-women**, with and without **coxswain**, and the large boats with eight oarsmen or -women and a coxswain.

Women were admitted to the Olympic rowing program in 1976. They compete in a streamlined program, with only one sweep event for four oarswomen, but they also compete in single, double, and quad sculls and the eight-oar sweep event. The rowing program for the 1996 Olympics underwent a drastic change, with the introduction of **lightweight** events. The men's coxed **pairs** and coxed fours were discontinued, replaced by the lightweight double sculls and lightweight coxless fours. The women's coxless pairs was also discontinued, replaced by lightweight double sculls. In 27 Summer Games, there have been 7,356 athletes (6,021 men, 1,335 women) from 92 nations who have taken part in Olympic rowing events.

The **United States** was the dominant nation in Olympic rowing until about 1960. The **Soviet Union** quickly became a power in the sport, but during its existence, the **German Democratic Republic** in the 1970s and 1980s was by far the preeminent nation. The top list of Olympic rowers, however, mainly consists of British and **Romanian** competitors. Three have won five gold medals: **Elisabeta Lipă-Oleniuc** and **Georgeta Damian-Andrunache** of Romania and **Stephen Redgrave** of **Great Britain**.

The world governing body of rowing is the Fédération Internationale des Sociétés d'Aviron, which was formed in 1892 and has 142 member nations as of 2014. *See also* BERESFORD, JACK, JR.; BORON, KATHRIN;

COCHELEA-COGEANU, VERONICA; DRESDEN FOUR, THE—GDR COXLESS FOUR ROWING TEAM (1968–1972); KELLY, JOHN BREN-DEN, SR.; PINSENT, MATTHEW CLIVE.

RUANDA-URUNDI. *See* BURUNDI; RWANDA.

RUDOLPH, WILMA GLODEAN (later WARD, ELDRIDGE) (USA–ATH). B. 23 June 1940, St. Bethlehem, Tennessee, **United States**. D. 12 November 1994, Brentwood, Tennessee, United States. Although born with polio and contracting scarlet fever and double pneumonia at the age of four, Wilma Rudolph overcame all these handicaps to become one of the greatest **women** sprinters of all time. As a 16-year-old, she won a bronze medal in the **relay** at the 1956 **Olympic Games**, and four years later she was the heroine of the 1960 Games. After setting a world 200 meter record (22.9) at the 1960 U.S. Championships, she was a triple gold medalist at the Rome Olympics, winning the 100 meters, 200 meters, and relay races. A following wind de-prived her of a world record in the 100 meters, but the five-foot, 10-inch (180 cm), 130 lb (59 kg) athlete anchored the U.S. team to a world record in the **heats** of the relay. The following year, Rudolph equaled the world 100 meter record (11.3), and four days later she posted a new record of 11.2 in addition to leading the United States to another world relay record. Her brilliant career ended with her retirement in 1962, after which she devoted herself to coach-

Wilma Rudolph wins her fourth gold medal at the 1960 Rome Olympics, leading the United States team to victory in the 4x100 meter relay. Courtesy of Erich Kamper

ing and worked extensively with underprivileged children. She died fairly young, from a brain tumor at the age of 54.

RUGBY. Rugby (specifically rugby union) was contested at the **Olympic Games** in 1900, 1908, 1920, and 1924. Amazingly, the defending Olympic champion is the **United States**—not known for its outstanding rugby teams—which won the gold medals in both 1920 and 1924. In the four years in which rugby was an Olympic sport, a total of 155 men from seven countries took part. Five players from the United States were on both 1920 and 1924 gold medal–winning teams, and Dan Carroll, who represented **Australasia** in 1908 and the United States in 1920, also won two golds. Adolphe Bousquet of **France**, who was on both runner-up teams in 1920 and 1924, is the only other Olympic dual medalist in rugby.

The International Rugby Board governs the sport worldwide and is recognized by the **International Olympic Committee** (IOC). Founded in 1886, it currently (as of 2014) has 120 member nations. Rugby sevens, or seven-a-side rugby football, was approved for inclusion to the **Olympic Program** by the IOC **Executive Board** in 2001. This proposal was tabled by the **IOC Session** and dismissed at the 2005 IOC Session. It was again brought up in 2009, when the IOC approved it for inclusion in the 2016 Rio de Janeiro Games.

RUSKA, WILLEM "WIM" (NED–JUD). B. 29 August 1940, Amsterdam, Noord-Holland, **Netherlands**. Of just 11 *judokas* to have won more two or more Olympic titles, Wim Ruska is the only one to win two at the same Olympics. In 1972, he was the Olympic champion in the **judo heavyweight** and the **open class**. Since 1988, the latter event is no longer contested at the Olympics, making a repeat double impossible for other competitors. Ruska was also heavyweight World Champion in 1967 and 1971. To this he added seven European titles and 10 Dutch championships during his career. He was not particularly large for the heavyweight or open class (220 lb [110 kg]) at only six-feet, two-inches (189 cm), but was extremely muscular and cut a striking figure with his light blond hair. Ruska began his judo career at age 20 and traveled to **Japan** to train and learn from the Japanese masters. He retired after the 1972 **Olympic Games**.

RUSSIA (RUS). Prior to the Bolshevik Revolution, Russia, one of the few countries located in both Europe and Asia, competed at the Olympics of 1900, 1908, and 1912. Although at the first two celebrations its representation was only four and six athletes, respectively, in 1912, it sent a large team of 169 athletes. At those Olympics, Russia won one gold, four silver, and three bronze medals. After the Bolshevik Revolution, Russia became the largest republic of the **Soviet Union** (USSR). The Soviet Union did not compete in the Olympics from 1920 to 1948, but returned to the **Olympic Games** at Helsinki in 1952 and competed in the Olympics through 1988. With the political events of 1991, Russia again became eligible to compete as an individual nation and is now known officially as the Russian Federation. At Albertville and Barcelona, Russia joined with other former Soviet republics to compete as the Unified Team, representing the **Commonwealth of Independent States**. It returned to the Olympic fold after an absence of 82 years at Lillehammer in 1994 and has been present with a large contingent since.

In nine Summer Games, Russia has entered 1,637 athletes (945 men, 692 **women**) and competed in 32 sports plus the **art competitions**. They have had the most participants in **athletics** (190 men, 201 women), **swimming** (64 men, 49 women), **wrestling** (77 men, 10 women), **shooting** (60 men, 24 women), **fencing** (53 men, 23 women), **volleyball** (36 men, 35 women), and **cycling** (49 men, 21 women). They have won 405 medals in 27 different summer sports (134 gold, 126 silver, 145 bronze), with 397 of them coming in just five Games since they returned in 1996.

The best Russian performer has been **gymnast Aleksey Nemov**, who won 12 medals (four gold, two silver, six bronze) in 1996 and 2000. He is one of only four Olympic athletes to win six bronze medals in any summer sport. Svetlana Khorkina has won seven medals (two gold, four silver, one bronze) in women's gymnastics from 1996 to 2004. Russian **diver Dmitry Sautin** has won more Olympic medals in his sport than anyone else. Seven of his eight medals were won representing his native Russia, and he won an eighth as a member of the Unified Team in 1992. **Synchronized swimmer Anastasiya Davydova** has won the most gold medals of any Russian summer Olympian. Her five gold medals (won from 2004 to 2012) is also the most by any synchronized swimmer. Tatyana Lebdeva has won five medals for Russia from 2000 to 2008 in the women's **long jump** and **triple jump**. Two other Russians with five medals each in the Summer Games are diver Yuliya Pakhalina (one gold, three silver, one bronze) and swimmer **Aleksandr Popov** (two gold, three silver).

In six **Olympic Winter Games**, Russia has entered 616 athletes (382 men, 234 women) and competed in all 15 sports contested during their years participating. They have had the most entrants in **ice hockey** (94 men, 41 women), **cross-country skiing** (43 men, 26 women), and **figure skating** (32 men, 32 women). They have won 124 medals (49 gold, 40 silver, 35 bronze) in Winter sports with medals in 13 of the 15 sports in which they have taken part. They have won 33 medals in cross-country skiing, 26 in figure skating, and 24 in biathlon. Their top Winter athletes are cross-country skiers Yuliya

Chepalova (three gold, two silver, one bronze) and **Larisa Lazutina** (four gold, one silver, one bronze) and biathlete Albina Akhatova (one gold, one silver, three bronze). Seven other Russian Winter Olympians have each won four medals including **Korean**-born **short-track speed skater Viktor An**, who won four in 2014 competing for Russia to go with the four previous ones he won for his native country.

The 2014 Winter Games were designated as the Sochi, Russia, Games, although in actuality the Games took place in neighboring Adler, Russia, and in the mountains of Krasnaye Polyana. Russia also has had several unsuccessful bids for the Games since separating from the Soviet Union—St. Petersburg (2004 Summer Games), Moscow (2012 Summer Games), and Sochi (2002 Winter Games). *See also* DMITRIYEV, ARTUR VALERYEVICH; KARELIN, ALEKSANDR ALEKSANDROVICH; LAVROV, ANDREY IVANOVICH; VÄLBE, YELENA VALERYEVNA; YEGOROVA, LYUBOV IVANOVNA; YERMAKOVA, ANASTASIYA NIKOLAYEVNA.

RWANDA (RWA). In 1962, the former United Nations Trust Territory under **Belgian** administration known as Ruanda-Urundi or Belgian East Africa became the two independent nations of Rwanda and **Burundi**. The Central African nation of Rwanda (officially known as the Republic of Rwanda) first competed in the **Olympic Games** in 1984 and has since participated in every edition, although it has yet to make its first **Olympic Winter Games** appearance. Rwanda has been represented by a total of 32 athletes (21 men, 11 **women**) in four sports: track and field **athletics** (at every Games—14 men, nine women), **cycling** (1992 only—three men), **swimming** (since 2000—two women, three men), and **judo** (2012 only—one man). No Rwandan athlete has ever won an **Olympic medal**. The top Rwandan Olympic result was eighth place by Mathias Ntawulikura in the finals of the 1996 10,000 meter track race. He had finished third in his preliminary **heat** to qualify for the final. Dieudonné Disi competed in the 10,000 meter race in two Olympic Games and had commendable results of 17th of 24 in 2004 and 19th of 38 entrants in 2008. Two Rwandan **marathoners** also turned in good performances—Ildephonse Sehirwa in the 1992 men's marathon was 60th of 110 entries and Marcianne Mukamurenzi was 38th of 69 contestants in the 1988 women's marathon. In swimming, the best performance by a Rwandan swimmer occurred in 2012 when Alphonsine Agahozo finished 59th of 74 entrants in the women's 50 meter **freestyle**.

RYSKAL, INNA VALERYEVNA (URS/AZE–VOL). B. 15 June 1944, Baku, **Azerbaijan**, USSR. Inna Ryskal won four consecutive Olympic medals playing for the **Soviet Union volleyball** team from 1964 to 1976, making her the only female volleyball player with four **Olympic medals**. Until 2012, the five-foot, seven-inch (172 cm), 163 lb (74 kg) Ryskal was the only athlete (male or female) with four such medals, but in that year, Sergey Tetyukhin (RUS) and Samuele Papi (ITA) each won their fourth. In 1972 and 1976, she helped the Soviets to gold medals, and she won silver medals in 1964 and 1976. She also played on a World Championship team in 1970 and European Championship teams in 1963, 1967, and 1971.

S

SAAR. In 1952, the Saar Protectorate's separate **National Olympic Committee** was recognized by the **International Olympic Committee**, and the Saar competed at the Helsinki **Olympic Games**, represented by 36 athletes (31 men, five **women**) in nine sports: **athletics** (two men, four women), **boxing** (three men), **canoeing** (two men, one woman), **fencing** (five men), **gymnastics** (six men), **rowing** (seven men), **shooting** (two men), **swimming** (one man), and **wrestling** (three men) but won no medals. The Saar, located in the western part of **Germany**, was reunited with the **Federal Republic of Germany** in 1956. Its athletes were absorbed by the combined German teams, and the Saar Olympic Committee was dissolved on 20 September 1956. Its best finishes in 1952 include Toni Breder (their flagbearer in the opening ceremony), 19th of 27 entrants in men's **long jump**, gymnast Arthur Schmitt, who placed in the top half of the 185 entrants in both **horizontal bar** and **rings** exercises, and Therese Zenz, ninth in women's **kayak singles** canoeing. Zenz later went on to win three silver medals for West Germany in 1956 and 1960. Wrestlers Erich Schmidt and Norbert Kohler each reached the third round before being eliminated from the tournament. The Saar did not compete in the **Olympic Winter Games**.

SABONIS, ARVYDAS ROMAS (URS/LTU–BAS). B. 19 December 1964, Kaunas, **Lithuania**, USSR. Arvydas Sabonis, a seven-foot, three-inch (223 cm), 269 lb (122 kg) center, played for the **Soviet Union basketball** team in the 1982 and 1986 World Championships and won a gold medal in 1982 and a silver medal in 1986. In 1983, 1985, and 1989 at the European Championships, he won bronze, gold, and bronze with the Soviet Union team. His most impressive international appearance was at the 1988 **Olympic Games** where he teamed with fellow Lithuanians, Valdemaras Chomičius, Rimas Kurtinaitis, and Šarūnas Marčiulionis, and teammates from five other Soviet republics to defeat the **United States** and win the Olympic gold medal. After Lithuania received its independence, he won bronze medals with them in the 1992 and 1996 Olympic Games. In 1995, he won a silver medal as a member of the Lithuanian team in the European Championships. In three Olympic Games tournaments, he played in 23 games and averaged 18.2 points per game. He holds the Olympic career record for most defensive rebounds and total rebounds and is second in blocked shots.

Sabonis played professional basketball in Lithuania, the Soviet Union, and **Spain** from 1981 until 1995. He was selected by the Portland Trail Blazers in the 1986 National Basketball Association (NBA) draft, but did not join them until 1995 and played for them until 2003. By the time he played in the NBA though, his best years were behind him, and although he could no longer run and jump as well as he once could, still had an excellent shooting touch and was an accomplished passer. His NBA career totals for seven years are 470 regular season games and a 12.0-point and 7.3-rebound per game average. In 2003, he returned to Zalgiris and played two more seasons with them before retiring. In 2008, he was named one of the 35 greatest players in the 50 years of the Euroleague competition. He was inducted into the Naismith Memorial Basketball Hall of Fame in 2011.

SABRE. A sabre (sometimes spelled saber) is one of the three weapons used in **fencing** competition. Men's individual sabre contests have been conducted at every modern **Olympic Games** since 1896. Men's team sabre contests have been held at each Games since 1906. **Women**'s individual sabre events have been held at the Olympic Games since 2004, and women's team sabre events were only held in 2008. Five men have won the individual sabre competition twice: Ioannis Georgiadis of **Greece** (1896, 1906), Jeno Fuchs of **Hungary** (1908, 1912), **Rudolf Kárpáti** of Hungary (1956, 1960), Viktor Krovopuskov of the **Soviet Union** (1976, 1980), and Jean-François Lamour of **France** (1984, 1988). Lamour also won a bronze medal in 1992. He and **Aladár Gerevich** of Hungary (gold 1948, silver 1952, bronze 1936) are the only three-time medalists in this event. **Italy** and Hungary have been the two dominant nations in the men's sabre team competition. Hungary won the gold medal in seven consecutive Olympics from 1928 to 1960 and has a total of 10 gold, three silver, and three bronze medals. Italy has four gold, 11 silver, and five bronze. Mariel Zagunis of the **United States** has won two of the three women's Olympic sabre tournaments (2004, 2008), and Sada Jacobson of the United States was third in 2004 and second in 2008. The women's sabre team competition in 2008 was won by the **Ukraine**, with **China** second and the United States third. *See also* ÉPÉE, FOIL.

SAEI BONEHKOHAL, HADI (IRI–TKW). B. 10 June 1976, Ray, Tehran, **Iran**. Hadi Saei is one of just five *taekwondokas* to have won two titles in the young Olympic sport, and one of three (with **Steven Lopez** of the **United States** and Hwang Gyeong-Seon of **Korea**) to have earned an additional bronze medal. The five-foot, 11-inch (182 cm) Saei won his bronze medal at the sport's debut in 2000 in the 68 kg division, which he won four years later in Athens. He then moved up to the 80 kg class for the Beijing Games to win his second Olympic gold. This title also made him the most decorated Iranian athlete at the Olympics, along with two others. Besides his Olympic successes, Hadi Saei has won two World Championships, in 1999 and 2005, both in the non-Olympic 72 kg division. In 2003, Saei auctioned off his Olympic bronze medal to help victims of the earthquake that hit the Iranian city of Bam.

SÁGI UJLAKY REJTŐ, ILDIKÓ (HUN–FEN). B. 11 May 1937, Budapest, **Hungary.** **Fencer** Ildikó Rejtő Ujlaky Sági has the unusual distinction of winning Olympic medals under three different names: as Miss Rejtő in 1960, as Mrs. Ujlaky Rejtő in 1964 and 1968, and as Mrs. Sági Rejtő in 1972 and 1976. She shares this distinction with German **speed skater Andrea Ehrig-Schöne-Mitscherlich.** Ildikó won seven Olympic medals, including gold in the individual and team **foil** in 1964. At the World Championships, the five-foot, four-inch (164 cm), 123 lb (56 kg) fencer won four titles: individual foil in 1963 and team foil in 1962, 1967, and 1973.

SAILER, ANTON ENGELBERT "TONI" (AUT–ASK). B. 17 November 1935, Kitzbühel, Tirol, **Austria.** D. 24 August 2009, Innsbruck, Tirol, Austria. Toni Sailer, known as "The Blitz from Kitz" because of his hometown, was arguably the greatest **Alpine skier** in Olympic history. Although his feat of winning all three Alpine events at the 1956 **Olympic Winter Games** was matched by **Jean-Claude Killy** 12 years later, Sailer's overall performance was far more impressive. He won the **downhill** by 3.5 seconds, the **slalom** by 4.0 seconds, and the **giant slalom** by a remarkable 6.2 seconds, whereas Killy's margins of victory were far narrower. Sailer was also World Champion at the Alpine combination (1956, 1958) and the downhill and slalom (1958). His career at the international level lasted only four seasons before he retired to become a hotelier and an occasional film actor and singer. A national hero, he was appointed technical director of the Austrian Alpine skiing team in 1972.

SAILING. Sailing as a competitive sport was called yachting until recently. The **International Federation** changed the sport's competitive name in an attempt to limit the elitist connotation associated with the term *yachting*. The sport was called yachting at the Olympics through 1996, and sailing, in effect, made its Olympic debut in 2000 at Sydney.

Yachting actually began as a form of sailing, which has been practiced since antiquity as a means of transport. In the modern sense, yachting probably originated in the **Netherlands**, and the word seems to come from the Dutch *jacht* (meaning hunting), which was originally used for fast, light ships.

Sailing as a sport was brought to **England** by King Charles II in about 1660, after his exile to Holland. International yacht racing began in 1851, when a syndicate of members of the New York Yacht Club built a 101-foot schooner named *America*. The yacht was sailed to England, where it won a trophy called the Hundred Guineas Cup, in a race around the Isle of Wight under the auspices of the Royal Yacht Squadron. The trophy was renamed the America's Cup (after the yacht, not after the **United States**, as is commonly thought). Sailing is now governed worldwide by the International Sailing Federation, formerly the International Yacht Racing Union, which was formed in 1907 and currently has 140 nations.

Sailing was first contested at the 1900 **Olympic Games**. It made its next Olympic appearance in 1908 and has been on every **Olympic Program** since that year. Sailing has had a very varied program that is usually changed every few **Olympiads** as the popularity of various boats waxes and wanes. **Women** have always been allowed to compete in Olympic sailing with men, and the first woman to compete in the Olympics was a sailor, in 1900. In 1988, separate sailing events exclusively for women were introduced, and as of 2008, only three sailing events allowed mixed crews. In 2012, the sailing program included six events for men and four for women, with none for mixed crews. In 1984, the popular sport of boardsailing (also known as **windsurfing**) was also added to the Olympic Program, and a separate boardsailing event for women was placed on the program for the first time in 1992. The current Olympic sailing program has 10 events, each of which defines a type of boat. The exact class of boat used for the event may differ from one Olympics to the next. Sailing is contested at the Olympics in a series of fleet races, with points awarded for the placement in each race. In 2008, the so-called Medal Race was added to make the sport more suitable for television; these races featured only the top 10 boats and took only 30 minutes.

In 25 Summer Games, there have been 4,263 competitors (3,740 men, 523 women) from 118 nations who have taken part in Olympic sailing events. Robert Scheidt and Torben Grael of **Brazil** and **Ben Ainslie** of **Great Britain** have each won five medals, with Ainslie and **Paul Elvstrøm** of **Denmark** each winning four gold medals. *See also* KNOWLES, DURWARD RANDOLPH; ROGGE, COUNT CHEVALIER, JACQUES, DR.

SAINT CYR, HENRI JULIUS REVERONY (SWE–EQU). B. 15 March 1902, Stockholm, **Sweden**. D. 27 July 1979, Kristianstad, Skåne, Sweden. Henri Saint Cyr began his Olympic career in 1936 with the Swedish three-day **equestrian** team. In 1960, he ended his Olympic career, having appeared in five different Olympics with five different horses. He was the first rider to win two individual Olympic gold medals in **dressage**, in 1952 and 1956, and he led Sweden to team gold medals at both **Olympic Games**. In 1956, he took the Athletes' Oath at the opening ceremony on behalf of the competitors at the Olympic Equestrian Games in Stockholm.

SAINT KITTS AND NEVIS (SKN). Saint Kitts and Nevis was given official recognition by the **International Olympic Committee** in September 1993 and has competed at all **Olympic Games** since then. The Caribbean island nation, officially known as the Federation of Saint Kitts and Nevis, has not yet competed at the **Olympic Winter Games**. Through 2012, all 17 of Saint Kitts and Nevis's Olympians (eight men, nine **women**) have participated in **athletics**. They are one of very few countries to have had more female than male Olympians. Its star competitor has been **sprinter** Kim Collins, who entered all five Summer Games (although he scratched prior to his event in 2012) and reached three Olympic finals (100 meters in 2000, seventh place, and in 2004, sixth place; 200 meters in 2008, sixth place). Several other Kittitian sprinters (Antoine Adams, Valma Bass, Diane Francis, Virgil Hodge, and Tiandra Ponteen) advanced past the preliminary **round** but not past the second round.

SAINT LUCIA (LCA). The Caribbean island nation of Saint Lucia was given official recognition by the **International Olympic Committee** in September 1993, and the country first competed at the Atlanta **Olympic Games** in 1996. It has been represented at the next four Summer Games but has not yet competed in the **Olympic Winter Games**. In five Summer Games, Saint Lucia has had 17 different entrants (nine men, eight **women**) competing in **athletics** (seven men, four women), **sailing** (one man, one woman), and **swimming** (one man, three women). They have not yet won an **Olympic medal**, and the best Olympic performances by Lucian athletes include Erma-Gene Evans, who finished 30th of 54 entrants in the women's **javelin throw** competition in 2008, and Levern Spencer, in her second Olympics, who was 19th of 35 entrants in the women's **high jump** in 2012.

SAINT VINCENT AND THE GRENADINES (VIN). The Caribbean island nation of Saint Vincent and the Grenadines first competed in the Olympics in 1988 at Seoul, when it was represented by six track and field athletes, five male and one female. The nation has competed at all subsequent Games of the **Olympiad**, but has not yet competed at the **Olympic Winter Games**. It has not yet won any **Olympic medals**. There have been 25 athletes from Saint Vincent (18 men, seven **women**) who have competed in the **Olympic**

Games in either **athletics** (16 men, six women) or **swimming** (three men, one woman). In 2000, runner Pamenos Ballentyne placed 31st (in a field of 100) in the men's **marathon**, the best result for a competitor from Saint Vincent and the Grenadines. Other notable performances by Vincentian athletes include Tolga Akcalyi, 45th of 58 in the 2012 swimming 50 meter **freestyle**, and Eswort Coombs, who reached the semifinals of the 1996 400 meter **sprint**. One of the country's most noted athletes is former National Basketball Association star Adonal Foyle, but he did not compete in the Olympic Games.

SALNIKOV, VLADIMIR VALERYEVICH (URS–SWI). B. 21 May 1960, Leningrad, **Russia**, USSR. At the 1980 Games, swimmer Vladimir Salnikov won gold medals in the 400 meters, the 1,500 meters (with the first ever sub-15-minute time), and the 4x200 meter **freestyle relay**. He remained the world's greatest long distance **swimmer**, although the **Soviet Union**'s **boycott** of the 1984 Games denied him the opportunity of Olympic honors in that year. But he returned from near retirement to win a somewhat surprising victory in the 1,500 freestyle at the 1988 Seoul Olympics. The five-foot, 11-inch (181 cm) 163 lb (74 kg) Salnikov set six world records at 400 meters (1979–1983), four at 800 meters (1979–1986), and three at 1,500 meters (1980–1983), and at the World Championships, he won the 400 meters and 1,500 meters in both 1978 and 1982.

SALUMÄE, ERIKA AKSELEVNA (URS/EST–CYC). B. 11 June 1962, Pärnu, Pärnumaa, **Estonia**, USSR. Erika Salumäe came to sports late; she took up **cycling** in 1981 and made the Soviet national team in 1984. She won the 1987 and 1989 world **sprint** championship and in 1988 and 1992 was Olympic match sprint champion. Her victory in 1992 at the Olympics was poignant because it was the first victory for Estonia at the **Olympic Games** after its independence from the **Soviet Union**. The five-foot, four-inch (165 cm), 139 lb (63 kg) Salumäe also set several world records for the 200 meters (flying start) and 1,000 meter **time trial** from a standing start.

SAMARANCH (TORRELO), JUAN ANTONIO, MARQUIS DE SA-MARANCH (ESP). B. 17 July 1920, Barcelona, **Spain**. D. 21 April 2010, Barcelona, Spain. Juan Antonio Samaranch served as the seventh president of the **International Olympic Committee** (IOC). First appointed to the IOC in 1966, he became a vice president in 1974 before succeeding **Lord Killanin** as president in 1980. He was also appointed as Spanish ambassador to the **Soviet Union** in 1977. His period of office as president of the IOC was marked by the transformation of the **Olympic Movement** into a vast, businesslike organization, although not all the changes met with the approval of the traditionalists. Ably supported by a dedicated group of vice presidents, he brought the Olympic Movement into the modern era. Although not unique among **IOC presidents** in having to face situations that threatened the fabric of the Olympic Movement, his diplomatic skills were invaluable in such matters as containing the **boycotts** of the 1984 and 1988 Games. In 1991, he was ennobled by the king of **Spain** for his services to **Olympism**.

Samaranch's term was marred by the **Olympic bribery scandal** of 1998–1999, the events of which occurred during his term of office. In mid-1999, the IOC supported Samaranch by giving him an almost unanimous vote of confidence. Samaranch stepped down as president after the **IOC Session** in 2001 and was then given the **Olympic Order** in Gold by his successor, **Jacques Rogge**, and made honorary president for life. In 2009, Samaranch made an appeal to the **Olympic Congress** in an attempt to have the 2016 Olympic Games awarded to Madrid, in his home country Spain, but it was not successful. He died a few months later.

SAMOA (SAM). Formerly called Western Samoa, Samoa first competed at the **Olympic Games** of 1984 and has not been absent since. The South Pacific island nation, officially known as the Independent State of Samoa, has not yet competed at the **Olympic Winter Games**. In eight Summer Games, Samoa has entered 45 athletes (39 men, six **women**) and has competed in nine sports: **archery** (one man, one woman), **athletics** (six men, two women), **boxing** (17 men), **canoeing** (one man), **cycling** (one woman), **judo** (two men), **taekwondo** (one man, one woman), **weightlifting** (eight men, one woman), and **wrestling** (three men).

Ele Opeloge, a 2008 weightlifter, came close to being the first Samoan medalist when she missed the bronze medal in the women's **super-heavyweight** class by just one kilogram and finished in fourth place. Four years later in the same event, she finished in sixth place. Other notable results for Samoan Olympians include ninth place in 1992 for weightlifter Marcus Stephen in the **featherweight** class; **heavyweight** weightlifter Sione Sialaoa, 11th of 16 in 1984; and boxers Apelu Ioane (1984 **light-welterweight**), Paulo Tuvale (1984 **middleweight**), and Ulaipalota Tauatama (1988 featherweight) each winning one bout before losing their next one.

SAMOA, AMERICAN. *See* AMERICAN SAMOA.

SAN MARINO (SMR). The European microstate of San Marino (officially known as the Republic of San Marino) is entirely surrounded by **Italy** and is only 24 square miles (61 square km), with a population of just 30,000. With 89 entrants, San Marino has the highest ratio of Olympians to population, with nearly one out of every 300 Sammarinese citizens participating in the **Olympic Games**. It made its first appearance at the Olympic Games of 1960 and has competed at 13 Olympic Games, missing only 1964, and nine **Olympic Winter Games** since 1976, missing only 1980 and 1998. In 13 Summer Games, San Marino has entered 74 athletes (63 men, 11 **women**) and competed in 11 sports: **archery** (two men), **athletics** (eight men, three women), **cycling** (10 men), **gymnastics** (one man), **judo** (four men), **sailing** (three men), **shooting** (23 men, four women), **swimming** (seven men, four women), **tennis** (two men), **weightlifting** (two men), and **wrestling** (one man).

The shooters from this tiny country have delivered the best results, with the top performance by a Sammarinese being in 2012 when Alessandra Perilli was part of a three-way tie for second place in women's **trap** shooting but in the subsequent shoot off was last and placed fourth for the event. The country's previous best was in 1984, when Francesco Nanni was fifth in the **small-bore rifle** prone competition. Other notable results for San Marino Olympians included trap shooters Emanuela Felici, seventh in the women's event in both 2000 and 2004, and Francesco Amici, tied for seventh in the men's event in 2004. Mauricio Zonzini, San Marino's only gymnast, had a creditable performance in the **rings** and finished tied for 34th of the 71 entrants, although his results in the other gymnastic exercises were not nearly as good. Alberto Franchini competed in **extra-lightweight** judo in four Games from 1980 to 1992 and finished between 17th and 20th in each of his four appearances, and **middleweight** *judoka* Franch Casadei competed in three tournaments and finished between 13th and 19th.

In nine Winter Games, San Marino entered 14 men and one woman and participated in **Alpine skiing** (11 men, one woman), **bobsledding** (two men), and **cross-country skiing** (one man). Their best results were obtained by Alpine **slalom** skiers Francesco Cardelli (40th of 101 in 1984, 44th of 109 in 1988), Christian Bollini (43rd of 101 in 1984), and Nicola Ercolani (45th of 109 in 1988).

SANEYEV, VIKTOR DANILOVICH (URS/GEO–ATH). B. 3 October 1945, Sukumi, Apkhazeti, **Georgia**, USSR. Viktor Saneyev was the most outstanding **triple jumper** in Olympic history. He won an unprecedented total of four medals in his event, with three consecutive gold medals (1968–1976) and a silver medal in 1980. The **Soviet Union boycott** of 1984 deprived him of a chance to compete in five Olympic Games, although at the age of 38 in 1984 it is unlikely that he would have medaled. At the 1968 Games, the high altitude of **Mexico** City resulting in several remarkable jumping events. **Bob Beamon** (USA) set the world record in the **long jump** with a jump of nearly two feet longer than the previous record. In the triple jump, the world record was broken five times in the course of the competition. In the qualifying round, Giuseppe Gentile (ITA) broke the world record with a jump of 17.10 meters. On his first jump in the final round, he increased his record to 17.22 meters. Saneyev passed that on his third jump with 17.23 meters. Nelson Prudencio (BRA) topped that with 17.29 meters on his fifth jump, and the six-foot, two-inch (188cm), 172 lb (78 kg) Saneyev surpassed that on his sixth jump, with 17.39 meters, to win the gold medal. Although his record was broken by **Cuban** Pedro Pérez in 1971, Saneyev regained the record in a meet in the Soviet Union in 1972 and held it until 1975.

SÃO TOMÉ AND PRÍNCIPE (STP). São Tomé and Príncipe was given official recognition by the **International Olympic Committee** in September 1993, and the country first competed at the **Olympic Games** in Atlanta in 1996. The West African island nation, officially known as the Democratic Republic of São Tomé and Príncipe, has appeared with one male and one female track athlete at every edition it has attended from 1996 to 2012. In 2008, it also had one male enter the **canoeing** event, and in five Summer Games has had a total of six men and five **women** competing. Alcino Silva entered both the 500 meter and 1,000 meter **kayak** races. São Tomé and Príncipe has not yet competed in the **Olympic Winter Games**, and no São Toméan has advanced beyond the first round of competition. Fumilay da Fonseca completed the women's 20 km **race walk** in 2004. She was the 52nd and last competitor to cross the finish line, but finished ahead of five other entrants who failed to complete the distance.

SAUDI ARABIA (KSA, formerly SAU). Recognized by the **International Olympic Committee** in 1965, Saudi Arabia (officially the Kingdom of Saudi Arabia) has competed at every **Olympic Games** since 1972, with the exception of 1980. It has never competed in the **Olympic Winter Games**. The West Asian nation, which comprises most of the Arabian peninsula, entered its first two female competitors in 2012. In 10 Summer Games, Saudi Arabia has entered 142 athletes (140 men, two **women**) and competed in 12 sports: **archery** (five men), **athletics** (58 men, one woman), **cycling** (nine men), **equestrian** (seven men), **fencing** (eight men), **football** (30 men), **judo** (one man, one woman), **shooting** (nine men), **swimming** (four men), **table tennis** (two men), **taekwondo** (one man), and **weightlifting** (six men).

The first two Olympic medals won by Saudi Arabian athletes were at Sydney in 2000. Hadj Souan Somayli won a silver in the men's 400 meter **hurdles**, and Khaled Al-Eid won a bronze in equestrian individual show **jumping**. In 2012, another bronze medal was won in equestrianism for team jumping. Other notable results for Saudi Arabian athletes include fourth place by Khaled Al-Dosari in 2000 **heavyweight** taekwondo, fourth place by Kamal Bahamdan in 2012 individual equestrian jumping, and a ninth place tie by Eisa Majrashi in 2012 **extra-lightweight** judo. In 2008, Hussain Taher Al-Sabee finished 11th in the **long jump** for the best Saudi Arabian result in athletics.

SAUTIN, DMITRY IVANOVICH (EUN/RUS–DIV). B. 15 March 1974, Voronezh, **Russia**, USSR. With eight Olympic medals, Dmitry Sautin has won more **Olympic medals** than any other **diver**. Representing the Unified Team in 1992, he earned a bronze on the **springboard**. In 1996, he was the gold medalist on the **platform**, representing Russia. The addition of synchronized events in 2000 allowed Sautin to enter four diving events in Sydney, and he won medals in all four events, topped by a gold medal in the synchronized platform event. The five-foot, seven-inch (172 cm), 143 lb (65 kg) Sautin won his seventh Olympic medal, a bronze, in 2004 on the springboard. His eighth medal, silver, was won in 2008 on synchronized springboard. Sautin was also world champion on the springboard in 1998 and 2001, the platform in 1994 and 1998, and the synchronized springboard in 2003. In addition, he took six European titles on the springboard, three on the platform, and three synchronized titles.

SAVATE. Savate is a **French** form of kickboxing and is the only form of kickboxing in which the contestants wear shoes. The French word savate means "old shoe." The sport originated in the early 19th century, possibly among sailors in Marseilles. It is also known as French boxing, as opposed to the well-known sport of English boxing. It is strongly connected with the *canne de combat* (cane fighting), and these two sports were **demonstrated** together at the 1924 **Olympic Games** in Paris.

SAVÓN FABRÉ, FÉLIX (CUB–BOX). B. 22 September 1967, San Vicente, Guantánamo, **Cuba**. Félix Savón was likely the greatest **heavyweight boxer** of the later 1980s and early 1990s, amateur or professional. He began his international career by winning the 1986 World Championship in the heavyweight class and later won that title six times consecutively: 1986, 1989, 1991, 1993, 1995, and 1997. Cuba **boycotted** the 1988 **Olympic Games** in Seoul, which prevented Savón from winning a certain gold medal. But in 1992, 1996, and 2000, he easily won the gold **Olympic medal** in the heavyweight division. The six-foot, five-inch (198 cm) Savón also won **Pan American Games** gold medals in 1987, 1991, and 1995 and won the International Boxing Association World Challenge matches for his weight class in 1989–1990, 1992, and 1994. He never turned professional because of Cuba's insistence on keeping its athletes amateur only, but he would certainly have been a leading contender to become a professional heavyweight world champion. As an amateur, he defeated future professional heavyweight champions Michael Bentt, Ray Mercer, Shannon Briggs, Lamon Brewster, Ruslan Chagaev, and Sultan Ibragimov.

SCHEFFLER REGO, EMANUEL FERNANDO. *See* EMANUEL.

SCHEMANSKY, NORBERT "NORB" (USA–WLT). B. 30 May 1924, Detroit, Michigan, **United States**. Norb Schemansky was the first man in history to win four medals in Olympic **weightlifting**, a feat since equaled by three others. After placing second to John Davis in the **heavyweight** division at the 1947 World Championships, the five-foot, 11-inch (181 cm) Schemansky again finished as runner-up to Davis at the 1948 **Olympic Games**. Schemansky then won a gold medal at the 1952 Games and two bronzes in 1960 and 1964. When Schemansky won his fourth medal (1964), he had passed his 40th birthday and is the oldest man ever to win a medal in Olympic weightlifting.

SCHENK, ADRIE "ARD" (NED–SSK). B. 16 September 1944, Anna Paulowna, Noord-Holland, **Netherlands**. In his 1968 Olympic debut, Ard Schenk tied for second place in the 1,500 meter **speed skating**, but four years later he won three gold medals (1,500 meters, 5,000 meters, 10,000 meters). Each victory was by a wide margin, and he posted new Olympic records in the 5,000 meters and 10,000 meters. The six-foot, two-inch (190 cm), 198 lb (90 kg) Schenk emphasized his superiority over his rivals two weeks later, when he became one of only four men to win all four events at the World Championships. He set 18 world records at distances from 1,000 meters to 10,000 meters between 1966 and 1972, including four world records for the **all-around**. He was European champion in 1966, 1970, and 1972 and World Champion for three consecutive years (1970–1972). A professional speed skating circuit was set up around Schenk following his Olympic successes, but although Schenk won the pro European and world titles, the league was unsuccessful and folded in 1974. In that year, he also competed in the American television multisport competition *Superstars* and won the preliminary round with wins in the 100-yard dash, half-mile run, and bicycle race. Schenk later was a technical committee member for the International Skating Union and served as the Dutch *chef de mission* at three Winter Olympics.

SCHMIDT, OSCAR DANIEL BEZERRA "MÃO SANTO" (BRA–BAS). B. 16 February 1958, Natal, Rio Grande del Norte, **Brazil**. Although not as well known as some of the American **basketball** players, Oscar Schmidt has been the finest offensive performer at the **Olympic Games**. He competed for Brazil in five consecutive Olympic Games from 1980 to 1996; was the leading scorer at the 1988, 1992, and 1996 Olympics; and is the all-time leading scorer in Olympic history. He never won an Olympic medal, as Brazil's best finish from 1980 to 1996 was fifth (three times). His individual performance in 1988 was especially remarkable, averaging 42.3 points per game; only one other Olympic basketball player has averaged more than 30 points in an Olympic tournament (**Edward Palubinskas** of **Australia** in 1976). When considering the highest scoring individual games at the Olympics, Schmidt has seven of the top 10, and five of the top six, led by his 55-point explosion against **Spain** in 1988. Schmidt is a six-foot, eight-inch (202 cm), 235 lb (107 kg) forward who played little defense and was known for his outside shooting, with an almost unlimited range. His most outstanding performance came at the 1987 **Pan American Games** where he led his Brazilian team to an upset victory over the **United States**. Schmidt scored 46 points, 35 in the second half, as Brazil overcame a 16-point deficit to defeat the United States team in Indianapolis, Indiana. He never played in the National Basketball Association, but remained a legend in his home country, where he is known simply as Oscar. He was enshrined in the Naismith Memorial Basketball Hall of Fame in 2013.

SCHNEIDER, VERENA "VRENI" (SUI–ASK). B. 26 November 1964, Elm, Glarus, **Switzerland**. Vreni Schneider was the first female **Alpine skier** to win five **Olympic medals**, a total since surpassed by **Janica Kostelić** and **Anja Pärson**. Schneider won both the **slalom** and **giant slalom** at the 1992 **Olympic Winter Games**. In 1994 at Lillehammer, she won three more medals, repeating as champion in the slalom, while earning a silver in the Alpine **combined** and a bronze in the giant slalom. At the World Championships, the five-foot, six-inch (170 cm), 150 lb (68 kg) Schneider won the giant slalom in 1987 and 1989 and the slalom in 1991. She was overall World Cup champion in 1989, winning the following event championships: 1986, 1987, 1989, and 1991 giant slalom; and the 1989, 1990, 1992, and 1993 slalom. Among **women**, Schneider's 55 victories trail only **Austria**'s Annemarie Moser-Pröll in overall World Cup race wins.

SCHOLLANDER, DONALD ARTHUR "DON" (USA–SWI). B. 30 April 1946, Charlotte, North Carolina, **United States**. In 1964, Don Schollander became the first **swimmer** to win four gold medals at one **Olympic Games**. His victories were in the 100 and 400 meter **freestyles** and in both **relays**, and in all but the 100 meters he set a world record. He was unfortunate that the

200 meters was not on the program at the Tokyo Games, as he later went on to set nine world records at this, his best distance (1963–1968). He also posted three world records at 400 meters and shared in eight world records in the freestyle relays. At the 1968 Games, he was unable to defend his 100 and 400 meter Olympic titles, as he failed to make the U.S. team at these distances, but Schollander won his fifth gold in the 4x200 meter freestyle relay and took the silver in the 200 meter freestyle. In two Olympic Games, the five-foot, 10-inch (180 cm), 174 lb (79 kg) Schollander medaled in all eight events that he entered with seven gold and one silver.

American swimmer Don Schollander (right), is congratulated by Scotland's Robby McGregor (left), after winning the 100 meter freestyle, one of his four gold medals at the 1964 Olympics. Courtesy of Erich Kamper

SCHUHMANN, CARL (GER–ATH/GYM/WRE/WLT). B. 12 May 1869, Münster, Nordrhein-Westfalen, **Germany.** D. 24 March 1946, Charlottenburg, Berlin, Germany. Carl Schuhmann was a gymnast who participated in the 1896 **Olympic Games** in Athens. As with many of the other athletes, he was invited to enter several different sports competitions even though he had not practiced them beforehand. He competed in five of the six gymnastic events and won three gold medals—the **horse vault** and the team events for **parallel bars** and **horizontal bar**. Although only five feet, two inches tall (159 cm), 154 lb (70 kg), he won the **Greco-Roman** style unlimited weight class **wrestling** event in an upset and also competed in **weightlifting**, where he finished tied for fourth with a lift of 90 kg (198 lb), **athletics**, where he competed in the **long jump** (then known as the broad jump), the **shot put**, and finished fifth in the **triple jump** (then called the hop, step, and jump). Although he did not participate in any other Olympic competition, he remained an active participant and teacher of gymnastics and in 1936 took part in a gymnastics exhibition at the Berlin Games at the age of 67.

SCOTLAND (SCO). Scotland is located on the northern part of the island of **Great Britain** and is a member of the **United Kingdom** of Great Britain and Northern Ireland. Scottish athletes have nearly always competed as part of the team of Great Britain. However, Scotland was allowed to field separate teams in 1908 in **field hockey**, which finished third, and in the 1912 **cycling road race**. Scotland still has membership in several **International Federations**, including **football**, field hockey, and **curling**, but at the Olympics, only Great Britain is allowed to enter a team. Scotland has also hosted several Olympic events: in 1908, the 12 meter **yachting** competition was held on the River Clyde in Glasgow, and in 2012, preliminary football matches were held at Hampden Park in Glasgow.

On 18 September 2014, Scotland held a referendum for independence from the United Kingdom. The vote for independence was defeated and as a result they will not establish their own **National Olympic Committee** and send a Scottish team to the 2016 **Olympic Games** in Rio de Janeiro but continue to include their athletes as members of the Great Britain team.

SCULLS. Sculls is a type of **rowing** competition in which each rower propels two oars, one on each side of the boat. Olympic sculls events are contested for both men and **women** for single, double, and quadruple sculls. Vyacheslav Ivanov of the **Soviet Union** (1956–1964) and Pertti Karppinen of **Finland** (1976–1984) are both triple gold medalists in men's single sculls. In the early years (1904–1932), the **United States** dominated the men's double sculls, but since then, many other countries have won the event. Quadruple sculls was only added to the program in 1976, and **Germany** and **Italy** have each won four medals in the men's competition. Yekatarina Khodatovich-Karsten of **Belarus** is the only dual gold medalist in women's single sculls (1996–2000). She also won the silver medal in 2004 and the bronze medal in 2008. Germany has dominated the women's quadruple sculls, winning four of the seven times it has been held. They have also won the double sculls twice and were runners up twice in that event.

SEIZINGER, KATJA (GER–ASK). B. 10 May 1972, Datteln, Nordrhein Westfalen, West **Germany**. Katja Seizinger was the top female power skier of the 1990s, winning five medals at the Olympics, including three gold medals, matched at that time only by **Vreni Schneider** (SUI) among **women**. Seizinger won the **downhill** in 1994 and 1998, becoming the first person, man or woman, to defend the Olympic downhill title. She added a third gold in the Alpine **combined** in the 1998 **Olympic Winter Games**. Her other Olympic medals were bronze in the **super G** in 1992 and in the **giant slalom** in 1998. The five-foot, seven-inch (171 cm), 141 lb (64 kg) Seizinger was less successful in the World Championships, winning only the 1993 super G. However, she posted a remarkable record in the World Cup events, winning 36 times and reaching the podium 76 times. She was overall World Cup champion in 1996 and 1998 and won the following individual World Cup titles: super G (1993–1996 and 1998) and downhill (1992–1994 and 1998).

SEMJONOVA, ULJANA LARIONOVNA (URS/LAT–BAS). B. 9 March 1952, Medumi, Daugavpils novads, **Latvia**, USSR. Uljana Semjonova towered over her competition. Officially listed as six feet, 10 inches (210 cm), 282 lb (128 kg), she was probably closer to seven feet, two inches (218 cm). Regardless of the official measurement, she was head and shoulders above her teammates and opponents. During her competitive era, only Anne Donovan of the **United States** and **Zheng Haixia** of **China**—both six feet, eight inches (203 cm)—approached her size. But she was not just tall, she was also an effective player, shooting 65 percent from the free throw line and a record 72 percent from the field during her two gold **Olympic medal** performances in 1976 and 1980. She competed for 18 seasons in international competition, winning two Olympic gold medals, three World Championship gold medals, and 10 European Cup Championships and scoring more than 15,000 points in her career. Named the most popular athlete in Latvia 12 times from 1970 to 1985, in 1995 she received the highest honor of the Republic of Latvia the Commander of the Order of the Three Stars. A member of the TTT Daugawa and Riga Latvia club teams in the former USSR, she later played professionally for Tintoretto in **Spain** and Valenciennes Orchies in **France**. In 1993, she became the first international **woman** to be enshrined in the Naismith Memorial Basketball Hall of Fame, and when the Women's Basketball Hall of Fame opened in 1999, she was included in their first class.

SENEGAL (SEN). The West African nation of Senegal (officially the Republic of Senegal) first competed at the 1964 **Olympic Games** and has competed at every Olympics since, one of the few African nations not to join the 1976 **boycott**. In 13 Summer Games, Senegal has entered 215 athletes (175 men, 40 **women**) and participated in 13 sports: **athletics** (62 men, 15 women), **basketball** (29 men, 12 women), **boxing** (six men), **canoeing** (two men, one woman), **fencing** (three men, two women), **football** (17 men), **judo** (31 men, four women), **sailing** (one man), **shooting** (two men), **swimming** (three men, four women), **table tennis** (one man), **taekwondo** (one woman), and **wrestling** (18 men, one woman).

Amadou Dia Bâ won the nation's only medal to date, a silver in the 1988 400 meter **hurdles**. He also had finished fifth in that event in 1984. Prior to Dia Bâ's medal in 1988, it can be argued that Senegal had won a medal in 1960. In that year, Abdoulaye Seye won a bronze in the 200 meters while representing **France**. Seye was a Senegalese national, but the country was still part of a French territory (known as French West Africa), so he had to compete under the French flag. The first Senegalese national to compete in the Olympics was probably Cire Samba, who competed for France in the **javelin throw** in 1924. Other representatives of Senegal with noteworthy Olympic performances include fourth place in athletics by Amadou Gakou (1968, men's 400 meters) and the 1996 4x400 meters men's **relay** team. In **freestyle** wrestling, **super-heavyweight** Mamadou Sakho finished eighth in 1976 and improved to sixth in 1980 and fifth in 1984. Isabelle Sambou tied for fifth in 2012 women's **flyweight** freestyle wrestling. The men's football team was sixth in 2012, and sixth place results were also achieved by Mansour Dia in the 1972 men's **triple jump** and Ndiss Kaba Badji in the 2008 men's **long jump**. Dia also finished eighth in the 1968 triple jump.

Senegal competed at the **Olympic Winter Games** in 1984, 1992, 1994, 2006, and 2010, with three men competing in **Alpine skiing**. Lamine Gueye competed in eight events from 1984 to 1994 with a best finish of 45th of 55 in the 1992 **downhill**. Alphonse Gomis entered all five events in 1992 but only managed to finish one of them—74th of 131 in the **giant slalom**. Leyti Seck was Senegal's entrant in 2006 and 2010, and his best result was 55th of 63 in the 2006 men's **super G**. *See also* MBAYE, KÉBA.

SERBIA (SRB). The Southeastern European nation of Serbia is unique in there being 96 years between the nation's first and second Olympic appearances. Serbia first competed at the 1912 **Olympic Games**, when it sent two athletes to the Games, a **marathon** runner and a 100 meter **sprinter**. On 4 December 1918, Serbia became part of the country that was then called the Kingdom of Serbs, Croats, and Slovenes and would later become **Yugoslavia**. Serbian athletes competed under that banner through the 1992 **Olympic Winter Games**. Despite the breakup of Yugoslavia, the former states of Serbia and **Montenegro** continued to compete as Yugoslavia, although this name was later adjusted to **Serbia and Montenegro**.

This union dissolved with the secession of Montenegro in 2006, and Serbia (officially known as the Republic of Serbia) competed for the second time in Beijing in 2008, where it won three medals, and in the next three Games. Its most notable performance was achieved by Milorad Čavić, a **butterfly swimmer** who was only beaten by star athlete **Michael Phelps** in the last inches of the race.

It can be claimed that Serbia was also represented at the first Olympics in 1896. Momcsilló Tapavicza (Serbian: Momčilo Tapavica) placed third in the Olympic **tennis** tournament, sixth in the **weightlifting**, and tied for fourth in **wrestling**. He represented **Hungary**, as his native Vojvodina region was at that time part of the Austro-Hungarian empire. In three Summer Games (1912, 2008, 2012), Serbia has entered 159 athletes (115 men, 44 **women**) and competed in 16 sports. Most of their athletes competed in team sports: **football** (15 men), **handball** (15 men), **volleyball** (18 men, 16 women), and **water polo** (19 men). Serbia also competed in **athletics** (10 men, seven women), **boxing** (one man), **canoeing** (six men, six women), **cycling** (three men), **judo** (one man), **rowing** (six men, one woman), **shooting** (four men, six women), swimming (seven men, four women), **table tennis** (two men), **taekwondo** (one man, two women), tennis (four men, two women), and wrestling (three men).

Serbia has won one gold, two silver, and four bronze medals in the Summer Games. The gold medal was won by Milica Mandić in 2012 women's **heavyweight** taekwondo. Silver medals were won by Ivana Maksimović in women's **small-bore rifle** shooting in 2012 and by swimmer Milorad Čavić in the 2008 men's 100 meter butterfly. Bronze medalists include world-renowned tennis star Novak Đoković in 2008 men's **singles**. He also finished fourth in 2012. Andrija Zlatić won a bronze medal in men's **air pistol** shooting in 2012. The Serbian men's water polo team were bronze medalists in both 2008 and 2012.

In two Winter Games (2010, 2014), Serbia has entered 15 athletes (nine men, six women) and competed in five sports: **Alpine skiing** (one man, three women), **biathlon** (one man who also competed in **cross-country skiing**), **bobsledding** (five men), cross-country skiing (three men, two women), and

snowboarding (one woman). They did not win a medal, and their best performance was by Nevena Ignjatović in the 2014 women's **giant slalom** when she finished 28th of 89 entrants.

SERBIA AND MONTENEGRO (SCG). After the breakup of **Yugoslavia**, the former republics of **Serbia** and **Montenegro**, located in Southeastern Europe, continued to compete as Yugoslavia through 2002. But that name was not recognized by the international community, and it was changed to Serbia and Montenegro in 2003. Under these two names, Yugoslavia/Serbia and Montenegro, the country participated in all three **Olympic Games** between 1996 and 2004. Following the secession of Montenegro in 2006, Serbia and Montenegro have competed separately.

In three Summer Games, Serbia and Montenegro entered 193 athletes (167 men, 26 **women**) and competed in 19 sports, with most of their athletes competing in **athletics** (19 men, 12 women) and the team sports of **basketball** (26 men), **water polo** (23 men), **volleyball** (21 men), **football** (17 men), and **handball** (15 men). Nine medals were won by the country in this period—gold by the 2000 men's volleyball team and by **shooter** Aleksandra Ivošev in women's **small-bore rifle**, three positions. Silver medals were won by the 1996 men's basketball team, which featured Vlade Divac and several other National Basketball Association players, the 2004 men's water polo team, and shooter Jasna Šekarić in women's **air pistol** in 2000 and again in 2004. Bronze medals were won by the 1996 men's volleyball team, the 2000 men's water polo team, and by Aleksandra Ivošev in women's **air rifle** in 1996.

In three **Olympic Winter Games** from 1998 to 2006, Serbia and Montenegro entered 12 athletes (eight men, four women) and competed in five sports: **Alpine skiing** (two men, three women), **bobsledding** (four men), **cross-country skiing** (one man, one woman), and one man in **biathlon** and in **figure skating**. None of their Winter Games results was particularly noteworthy, but Marko Đorđević finished 26th of 77 in 2002 in the men's **slalom** and Mirjana Granzov was 27th of 57 in 1998 in the women's slalom. Although she was the last to complete the course, she finished ahead of 30 other skiers who failed to do so.

SEX TESTING. *See* GENDER VERIFICATION.

SEYCHELLES (SEY). A Seychellois, Henri Dauban de Silhouette, represented **Great Britain** in the **javelin throw** at the 1924 Olympic Games. The Indian Ocean island country of Seychelles (officially the Republic of Seychelles) has competed at eight **Olympic Games** since 1980. For reasons not precisely clear, the Seychelles did not compete in 1988 at Seoul; possibly it **boycotted** the Games. It has entered 58 athletes (44 men, 14 **women**) and participated in eight sports: **athletics** (17 men, eight women), **badminton** (one man, one woman), **boxing** (10 men), **canoeing** (one man), **judo** (two men), **sailing** (three men, one woman), **swimming** (seven men, three women), and **weightlifting** (three men, one woman).

Its best Olympic performance was in 1992, when **light-heavyweight** boxer Roland Raforme won two matches to finish equal fifth of 27 in his class, and in 1996 when another boxer, Rival Cadeau, equaled that finish in the **light-middleweight** class. Other good performances include Paul Nioze who was 22nd of 47 entrants in the 1992 men's **triple jump**, Lindy Agricole who was 29th of 54 in the 2008 women's javelin throw, and Allan Julie who was 20th of 42 entrants in the mixed one-person **dinghy** sailing event in 2004.

The Seychelles has never competed at the **Olympic Winter Games**.

SHAKHLIN, BORIS ANFIYANOVICH (URS/UKR–GYM). B. 27 January 1932, Ishim, Tyumen, **Russia**, USSR. D. 27 May 2008, Kyiv, **Ukraine**. Boris Shakhlin won six gold medals in individual **gymnastic** events, which remains an Olympic best for men, equaled only by **Nikolay Andrianov**. Between 1956 and 1964, Shakhlin won a total of 13 **Olympic medals** (seven gold, four silver, two bronze), with his strongest individual event being the **pommelled horse**, in which he won gold in 1956 and 1960. The five-foot, seven-inch (171 cm), 157 lb (71 kg) Shakhlin also won a total of 14 medals at the World Championships.

SHCHERBO, VITALY VENEDIKTOVICH (EUN/BLR–GYM). B. 13 January 1972, Minsk, Belorussian SSR, USSR. Vitaly Shcherbo was the most successful **gymnast** at the 1992 **Olympic Games**, when he won six gold medals, adding four individual apparatus championships to the individual and team **all-around** titles. Shcherbo's record at the World Championships was also excellent. He won the all-around in 1993, the **floor exercise** in 1994–1995, the **horizontal bar** in 1994, the **parallel bars** in 1993 and 1995, and the **horse vault** in 1993–1994. The five-foot, seven-inch (169 cm), 150 lb (68 kg) gymnast competed again at the Olympics in 1996. He won four medals, this time all bronze.

SHERIDAN, MARTIN JOSEPH (USA–ATH). B. 3 March 1881, Bohola, County Mayo, **Ireland**. D. 27 March 1918, New York, New York, **United States**. Martin Sheridan was the world's finest all-round athlete until the arrival of **Jim Thorpe** and the greatest **discus thrower** until **Al Oerter**. In addition to winning the discus throw at the 1904, 1906, and 1908 **Olympic Games**, Sheridan won the **shot put** in 1906 and the Greek-style discus in

1908. To these five gold medals he added three silver medals in 1906 in the stone throw and the standing jumps and a bronze medal in the standing **long jump** in 1908. Between 1904 and 1911, the six-foot, three-inch (190 cm), 194 lb (88 kg) Sheridan won 11 Amateur Athletic Union titles at a variety of events, including three in the **All-Around** Championship. He was at his best before world records were officially recognized, but from 1902 to 1911, he set no less than 15 new "World Bests" in the discus, although irregularities in the specification of the throwing circle would have precluded some of these performances from being officially recognized under more stringent modern conditions. Born in Ireland, Sheridan immigrated to the United States at the age of 16 and died during the 1918 pneumonia pandemic at the age of 37, while serving with the New York Police Department.

Martin Sheridan, considered the best discus thrower, prior to Al Oerter, and the top all-around track and field athlete in the world during the first decade of the 20th century. Courtesy of Erich Kamper

SHOOTING. Shooting originated as a means of survival, used in hunting game for food. In the 19th century, as the Industrial Revolution developed and hunting for food became less necessary for more people, shooting as a sport evolved. The sport was first popular in English-speaking countries, notably **England** and the **United States**, but also in **Ireland** and **South Africa**. The National Rifle Association was formed in 1871 and provided the impetus for the development of organized sport shooting in the United States. The world governing body is the International Shooting Sport Federation, formerly the Union Internationale de Tir (UIT), which was formed in 1907 and had 161 member nations in 2014.

Shooting has been contested at most of the **Olympic Games**. Baron **Pierre de Coubertin** was an avid pistol shot, so he saw to it that the sport was included on the program in 1896. There were also events in 1900, but none were contested in 1904 at St. Louis. In 1928 at Amsterdam, shooting events were also not included on the program. In 26 Summer Games, there have been 4,674 competitors (4,020 men, 654 **women**) from 148 nations who have participated in Olympic shooting.

The program has varied more than any other sport (with the possible exception of **sailing** or **yachting**). In 1908, 1912, 1920, and 1924, there were dozens of events, including numerous team events, and it was possible for shooters to win several medals at each Olympics. After the sport's hiatus in 1928, it returned to the Olympics in 1932 with only two events, one for pistols and one for rifles.

Women were first allowed to compete in Olympic shooting in 1968, and in that year **Mexico, Peru,** and **Poland** each entered one female contestant. In 1976, Margaret Murdock (USA) won a silver medal in the **small-bore rifle** (three positions) event. In 1984, the UIT introduced separate events for women. Since 1984, the women's shooting program has been expanded at each Olympics, and the number of mixed events has decreased. Beginning in 2000 at Sydney, men and women competed in fully separate shooting programs, with 10 events for men and seven for women. In 2008, this was trimmed to nine for men and six for women.

Shooting events at the Olympics have been held in several types of events: long-distance rifle, small-bore rifle, **air pistol** and rifle shooting, pistol shooting, **skeet** and **trap** shooting, and running target events. Team shooting events were discontinued after the 1924 Olympics.

The top medal winners in this sport all date from the period 1896–1924. Six marksmen have won five gold medals. **Carl Osburn** of the United States stands out among them as having won the most total medals (11), while **Willis Lee** of the United States uniquely won all his five golds at the same Games, in 1920. As shooting is one of the few sports in which people past the age of 50 can effectively compete, it is no surprise that the oldest Olympic participant as well as oldest medalist was a shooter. Oscar Swahn of **Sweden**, 72 years, 281 days when he competed in three events in 1920, won a silver medal in one and finished fourth in other. He was a gold medalist in 1912 at the age of 64 and is also the oldest Olympic gold medalist. *See also* SWAHN, ALFRED GOMER ALBERT; WINANS, WALTER.

SHORT-TRACK SPEED SKATING. In the **United States** and **Canada**, **speed skating** was not conducted in **time trial** fashion, but in small pack races. This format was used at the 1932 **Olympic Winter Games**, but never used again outdoors at the Olympics. However, races in indoor halls, frequently also used for **ice hockey** and **figure skating**, became increasingly popular in North America, and in 1967 the International Skating Union recognized short-track skating as a separate sport. Since 1981, World Championships have been held, and in 1988 the sport was **demonstrated** at the Winter Olympics in Calgary.

It became a full medal sport in 1992, with an individual event and a **relay** event for both men and **women**. This program has gradually been expanded to eight events. Both men and women contest 500 meters, 1,000 meters, and 1,500 meters individually, as well as a relay event (3,000 meters for women, 5,000 meters for men). In seven Winter Games, there have been 444 athletes (235 men, 209 women) from 35 countries who have participated in Olympic short-track speed skating.

Although Europeans have dominated traditional speed skating, North American and Asian countries have taken the bulk of Olympic medals in this sport. In particular, South **Korea** has excelled, having won 21 gold medals out of 48 events contested. The most decorated short-track skater is **Viktor An** (born An Hyeon-Su), with eight medals—six gold and two bronze. He first competed in 2002 for Korea but did not medal. In 2006, he won three gold and one bronze. After a dispute with Korean officials, he became a **Russian** citizen and in 2014 won three more gold and one bronze. **Apolo Anton Ohno** of the United States has also earned a total of eight medals in short-track speed skating, although he only won two gold medals. **Wang Meng** of **China** and **Jeon I-Gyeong** of Korea have each won four gold medals. *See also* YANG YANG.

SHOT PUT. The shot put is one of the field events in **athletics**. The shot is a round metal ball, 16 lb (7.26 kg) for men and 8.8 lb (4 kg) for women. The event simply consists of throwing the shot in a pushing motion, with the farthest throw being the winner. It has been part of the men's Olympic competition since 1896 and has been a **women**'s Olympic event since 1948. Three men have won the Olympic shot put gold medal twice: **Ralph Rose** of the **United States** (1904, 1908), **Parry O'Brien** of the United States (1952, 1956), and Tomasz Majewski of **Poland** (2008, 2012). O'Brien also won a silver medal in 1960 and Rose won a silver medal in 1912. They are the only three-time **Olympic medalists** in the men's shot put. Tamara Press of the Soviet Union (1960, 1964) and Valerie Adams-Vili of **New Zealand** (2008, 2012) are the only two women to win this event twice. **Soviet Union** shot putters Nadezhda Chizhova (gold 1972, silver 1976, bronze 1968) and Galina Zybina (gold 1952, silver 1956, bronze 1964) are the only three-time medalists in Olympic women's shot put.

SHOW JUMPING. *See* JUMPING.

SIAM. *See* THAILAND.

SIERRA LEONE (SLE). In 1960, a Sierra Leone athlete, Alifu Albert Massaquoi, represented **Liberia** in the Olympic **marathon**. He came in 62nd of 69 entrants with a time of 3:43:18, nearly 45 minutes slower than the runner before him, but he completed the distance unlike seven other entrants who failed to do so. Eight years later, he competed for Sierra Leone and finished 45th of 75 entrants with an improved time of 2:52:28 as Sierra Leone made its Olympic debut as an independent nation in 1968, after having been recognized by the **International Olympic Committee** in 1964. The West African nation, officially named the Republic of Sierra Leone, has since missed only the 1972 and 1976 **Olympic Games**, but has never competed at the **Olympic Winter Games**. In 10 Summer Games, it has had 58 entrants (47 men, 11 **women**) and competed in **athletics** (34 men, 11 women), **boxing** (nine men), **cycling** (one man), **swimming** (one man), and **weightlifting** (two men). Its best Olympic performance was in 1996, when Eunice Barber finished fifth in the women's **heptathlon**. That year she was also 19th of 47 entrants in the women's **long jump**. Other notable performances by Sierra Leonean athletes include Israel Cole, 1984 **light-middleweight** boxer who won two bouts and finished tied for fifth place of 34 entrants, and Tom Ganda, 27th of 50 in the 1992 men's **long jump**. In 1992, both Sansui Turay in the 100 meters **sprint** and Francis Dove-Erwin in the 200 meters sprint advanced to the quarter-final **round** before being eliminated. The Sierra Leone 4x100 meter relay team in both 1992 and 1996 also reached the quarter-finals.

SILVER MEDAL. *See* OLYMPIC MEDALS.

SINGAPORE (SIN). The Southeast Asian island nation of Singapore (officially named the Republic of Singapore) has competed independently at 12 **Olympic Games** since 1948, missing only 1964 and 1980. In 1964, Singaporean athletes also competed at the Olympic Games, but under the banner of **Malaysia** in a combined team with **Malaya** and **North Borneo**. Singapore left the Malaysian Federation in 1965. In 15 Summer Games, Singapore has entered 156 athletes (114 men, 42 **women**) and competed in 15 sports: **athletics** (11 men, seven women), **badminton** (five men, eight women), **basketball** (10 men), **boxing** (one man), **canoeing** (one woman), **fencing** (two men), **gymnastics** (one woman), **hockey** (17 men), **judo** (two men), **sailing** (18 men, five women), **shooting** (five men, three women), **swimming** (20 men, 10 women), **table tennis** (four men, six women), **water polo** (10 men), and **weightlifting** (nine men, one woman).

Singapore has won a total of four Olympic medals—two silver and two bronze. In 1960, Tan Howe-Liang "Tiger" Tan won Singapore's first Olympic medal, a silver in **lightweight** weightlifting. The country's second silver medal was won in 2008 by its female table tennis team, the members of which were all born in **China**. In 2012, that team won a bronze, and Feng Tian Wei won an individual bronze in **singles** competition, giving her a total of three medals as she was a member of both medal-winning teams.

Other notable Olympic results for Singapore include fourth place in table tennis women's singles for Jing Jun Hong (2000) and Li Jia Wei (2004, 2008); fifth place for swimmer Tao Li in the 2008 women's 100 meter **butterfly**; sixth place for **featherweight** weightlifter Chay Weng Yew in 1952; seventh place for Tan Ser Cher in 1956 featherweight weightlifting; and eighth place for **bantamweight** weightlifter Lon bin Mohamed Noor in 1952. In addition, badminton players Ronald Susilo (men's singles 2004) and the women's **doubles** team of Jiang Yanmei and Lee Yujia (2008) and women's singles table tennis players Zhang Xueling (2004), Feng Tian Wei (2008), and Wang Jue Gu (2012) along with the 2012 men's team of Gao Ning, Yang Zi, and Zhan Jian all were losing quarter-finalists and placed in a fifth place tie.

Singapore has not competed at the **Olympic Winter Games**.

SINGH, UDHAM KULAR (IND–HOK). B. 4 August 1928, Sansarpur, Jalandhar, Punjab, **India**. D. 23 March 2000, Sansarpur, Jalandhar, Punjab, India. Of the seven Indian players to win three Olympic gold medals for **hockey**, only Udham Singh and **Leslie Claudius** also won a silver medal. Singh won gold in 1952, 1956, and 1964 and a silver in 1960. Singh, at five feet, six inches (168 cm), 128 lb (58 kg), was a center-forward who was the leading scorer at the 1956 **Olympic Games**, with 14 goals.

SINGLES. In some Olympic sports such as **badminton, canoeing, luge, table tennis**, and **tennis**, competition is held for single participants called singles and for teams of two participants called **doubles**. Entrants often compete in both forms of the sport.

SKATING. *See* FIGURE SKATING; ICE HOCKEY; SHORT-TRACK SPEED SKATING; SPEED SKATING.

SKEET. Skeet is a form of **shooting** competition. It is similar to **trap** shooting in that a flying target is used. The difference is that in trap shooting, the targets are launched from a single "house" or machine, generally away from the shooter, while in skeet shooting, targets are launched from two "houses" in somewhat "sideways" paths that intersect in front of the shooter. Skeet shooting has been held in the **Olympic Games** since 1968. From 1968 to 1992, the event was open to both men and **women**, and in 1992, Zhang Shan of **China**, a woman, won the gold medal in a competition with 60 entrants, nearly all men. In 1996, Olympic skeet shooting was limited to men only, and since 2000, there have been separate Olympic skeet shooting contests for men and women. Vincent Hancock of the **United States** won gold medals in 2008 and 2012 and is the only person to win two gold medals in Olympic skeet shooting. In women's Olympic skeet shooting, there have been four multiple medalists but no repeat gold medalists.

SKELETON. Skeleton is a sledding sport founded on the famed Cresta Run at St. Moritz, **Switzerland**. In skeleton, the sliders lie prone on their sleds. As there was initially only one skeleton track in the world, the sport could only be held when the **Olympic Winter Games** were held in St. Moritz, in 1928 and 1948. After its second appearance, skeleton was replaced with **luge**, but the sport made a comeback in 2002, with events for both men and **women**. In six Winter Games, there have been 147 athletes (101 men, 46 **women**) from 28 countries who have participated in Olympic skeleton competition. As of 2014, no slider has won more than one gold medal in the sport, but America's Jack Heaton remarkably won two silver medals 20 years apart, in 1928 and 1948. Skeleton is governed by the Fédération Internationale de Bobsleigh et de Tobogganing, which is also the **International Federation** for **bobsledding**.

SKI JUMPING. Jumping off hills on skis was pioneered by Norwegian Sondre Norheim in the 19th century and had developed into a full sport by the 20th century. It has been contested in the **Olympic Winter Games** since the start in 1924. Originally dominated by participants from **Norway**, the top competitors now also hail from **Finland** and Central Europe.

Three men's events are contested at the Olympics, but since 2009, **women** also compete in World Championships, and in 2014, a women's event was finally added to the **Olympic Program**. In 22 Winter Games, there have been 876 athletes (846 men, 30 women) from 37 countries who have participated in Olympic ski jumping. **Matti Nykänen** of Finland won five medals (four gold, one silver) in 1984–1988 in the sport. **Simon Ammann** of **Switzerland** also won four gold medals from 1998 to 2014. Although he competed in five Winter Games, he won all of his medals in 2002 and 2010. In the inaugural Olympic women's ski jumping, held on the **normal hill**, Carina Vogt of **Germany** won the gold medal.

There are two types of hills used: a normal hill and a **large hill**. The exact size of the hills, most commonly measured by the distance of the calculation point (or K-point), has gradually increased. In 1924, the normal hill K-point was still at 71 meters; in 2014, it was at 95 meters, and the large hill was at 125 meters.

SKIATHLON. The skiathlon is a type of **cross-country skiing** event in which competitors race part of the distance using the classical style ski and then change skis to complete the race using **freestyle** skis. It was first included in the 2006 **Olympic Winter Games** for both men (30 km race) and **women** (15 km race) and has been held in the two subsequent Winter Games. Marcus Hellner of **Sweden** is the only man to win two medals in this event (2010 gold, 2014 silver). **Marit Bjørgen** of **Norway** won the women's event in both 2010 and 2014 and is the only woman with multiple medals in skiathlon.

SKICROSS. Skicross is a relatively new form of skiing competition in which four skiers compete simultaneously over a bumpy **downhill** course with the top two advancing to the next round of the event. It was added to the **freestyle skiing** program for both men and **women** in 2010 and also held in 2014. There have been no repeat medalists in either the men's or women's races.

SKIFF. A skiff is a type of **sailing** boat. One type of two-person skiff, known as a 49er (based on its hull length of 4.99 meters), has been used in Olympic sailing races since 2000. From 2000 to 2008, the race was open to both men and **women**, but in 2012, the race was limited to men. Only three Olympians have won more than one medal in skiff competition. The **Spanish** team of Xavier Fernández and Iker Martínez won the gold medal in 2004 and silver in

2008; Simon Hiscocks of **Great Britain** won the silver in 2000 with partner Ian Barker and the bronze in 2004 with partner Chris Draper.

SKIING. *See* ALPINE SKIING; BIATHLON; FREESTYLE SKIING; MILITARY SKI PATROL; SKIJÖRING; SNOWBOARDING; SPEED SKIING.

SKIJÖRING. Skijöring, originally called skid-körning, was held as a **demonstration sport** at the 1928 **Olympic Winter Games** in St. Moritz. In skijöring, skiers are towed behind horses, although other methods of propulsion are also used (motorcycles, dogs). It was considered a military competition in **Norway** and **Sweden** and was part of the **Nordic Games** in 1901, 1905, and 1909. It is today contested primarily in **Switzerland** and Sweden.

SKOBLIKOVA, LIDIYA PAVLOVNA (later POLOZKOVA) (URS–SSK). B. 8 March 1939, Zlatoust, Chelyabinsk, **Russia**, USSR. Lidiya Skoblikova holds the record with six Olympic gold medals for **speed skating**. She was a world class performer before speed skating for **women** was added to the **Olympic Program** in 1960 at the Squaw Valley Games. In 1960, Skoblikova won gold medals in the 1,500 meters, setting a new world record, and in the 3,000 meters. At the 1964 **Olympic Winter Games**, she became the first woman to win all four speed skating events at one Games, setting new Olympic records in the 500 meters, 1,000 meters, and 1,500 meters, and was only deprived of a fourth record by adverse ice conditions in the 3,000 meters. After these successes, her third Olympic appearance in 1968 was a disappointment; she finished 11th in the 1,500 meters. A teacher from Siberia, the five-foot, four-inch (163 cm), 130 lb (59 kg) Skoblikova set world records at 1,000 meters and 3,000 meters and was the world overall champion in 1963 and 1964, winning all four events in both years.

SLALOM. The slalom is one of the events in **Alpine skiing** and is the most technically demanding. The skier must ski between a series of two poles (called gates) on an exceptionally winding **downhill** course. Often more than half of the entrants fail to complete the race successfully by skiing outside of one of the gates. For example, in 2014, there were 115 men who attempted the slalom at the **Olympic Winter Games**, yet only 43 completed the course without missing a gate. Ironically, among the skiers who completed the course were several who were not among the best but skied slowly and carefully. The 43rd finisher, Yohan Gonçalves of **Timor Leste**, took 2:30.89, while the winner, Mario Matt of **Austria**, had a time of 1:41.84. The **slalom** for both men and **women** has been a part of the program in each Olympic

Winter Games since 1948. No man has won the slalom more than once, and **Alberto Tomba** of **Italy** won three medals in slalom competition (gold 1988, silver 1992, 1994). **Vreni Schneider** of **Switzerland** is the only woman to win the slalom twice (1988, 1994). Marlies Schild (silver 2010, 2014, bronze 2006) is the only three-time medalist in the women's Olympic slalom.

The sport of **canoeing** also has several whitewater slalom events in which **kayakers** and canoeists attempt to negotiate a course with swirling waters and multiple gates, including several upstream gates. Michal Martikán of **Slovakia** has won five medals (two gold, two silver, one bronze from 1996 to 2012) in **Canadian singles** slalom competition. The Hochschorner twins, Peter and Pavol, of Slovakia are four time medalists (three gold, one bronze, 2000–2012) in Canadian **doubles** slalom events. *See also* GIANT SLALOM; SUPER G.

SLEDDING. *See* BOBSLEDDING; LUGE; SKELETON.

SLOANE, WILLIAM MILLIGAN. B. 12 November 1850, Richmond, Ohio, **United States**. D. 11 September 1928, Princeton, New Jersey, United States. William Milligan Sloane was the pioneer of the **Olympic Movement** in America and a founding member of the **International Olympic Committee** (IOC). A close friend and supporter of **Pierre de Coubertin**, he was the driving force behind the establishment, maintenance, and development of the strong links between the Olympic Movement and the United States. A professor of history at Princeton University and a distinguished academician, he later held the Roosevelt chair at Berlin University, but gave up most of his appointments after becoming ill in 1921, although it was not until 1924 that he resigned from the IOC. His best-known academic work was his four-volume *Life of Napoleon Bonaparte.*

SLOVAKIA (SVK). Slovakia, which split from **Czechoslovakia** on 1 January 1993 along with the **Czech Republic**, competed in the **Olympic Games** as an independent nation for the first time at Lillehammer in 1994. Prior to the division, many Czechoslovakian athletes were actually from Slovakia. A Slovakian **National Olympic Committee** was actually first formed in June 1939, and it attempted to revive its activities after World War II in 1945. However, in June 1947, it was co-opted into the Czechoslovak Olympic Committee. The Slovakian Olympic Committee was re-created in October 1990 and was then formed officially on 19 December 1992, before the nation's split from the Czech Republic on 1 January 1993. It received provisional recognition from the **International Olympic Committee** (IOC) on 16 March 1993 and official recognition at the 101st **IOC Session** in **Monaco** in September

1993. Since 1994, the Central European nation of Slovakia, whose official name is the Slovak Republic, has competed at all Olympic Games and **Olympic Winter Games**.

In five Summer Games, Slovakia has entered 232 athletes (163 men, 69 **women**) and competed in 21 sports, with the most participants in **athletics** (32 men, 12 women), **canoeing** (33 men, seven women), **cycling** (17 men, three women), **football** (18 men), **tennis** (six men, nine women), and **water polo** (13 men). Slovakia has won 24 **Olympic medals** (seven gold, nine silver, eight bronze), and they have been earned in just five sports: canoeing, **shooting, judo, swimming**, and **wrestling**. Slovakians have particularly excelled in **slalom** canoeing, winning all seven Olympic gold medals in that sport. Three of these were claimed by the Hochschorner twins, Pavol and Peter, who won the C-2 slalom title three times in a row (2000, 2004, and 2008) and won the bronze medal in that event in 2012. Michal Martikán has won five medals in slalom canoeing, one in each Games from 1996 to 2012—two gold, two silver, and one bronze. Elena Kaliská has won two gold medals in women's slalom **kayak** singles (2004, 2008). Swimmer Martina Moravcová competed in five Summer Games from 1992 to 2008 and won two silver medals in 2000—the 200 meter **freestyle** and 100 meter **butterfly**. Other Slovakian Olympians with multiple medals are shooters Jozef Gönci (bronze medals 1996 **small-bore rifle** prone, 2004 **air rifle**) and Zuzana Štefečeková (silver medals 2008, 2012 women's **trap** shooting). The Slovakian men's kayak fours team also won two medals (2004 bronze, 2008 silver). Three of the four team members competed in both years and won two medals each— Erik Vlček and brothers Michal and Richard Riszdorfer.

In six Winter Games, Slovakia has entered 201 athletes (143 men, 58 women) and competed in 12 sports, with most of the participants in **ice hockey** (83 men, 19 women). They also entered 12 men and 12 women in **biathlon**, seven men and nine women in **Alpine skiing**, eight men and seven women in **cross-country skiing**, and 11 men and four women in **luge**. Slovakian athletes have won five medals at the Winter Games—two gold, two silver, and one bronze. Biathlete Anastasia Kuzmina has won three medals—gold in the **sprint** in 2010 and 2014 and silver in 2010 10 k **pursuit**. The other medals were won by Pavel Hurajt in the 2010 men's 15 k biathlon and by **snowboarder** Radoslav Židek in the 2006 men's **boardercross**.

The Slovakian city of Poprad made unsuccessful bids to host the 2002 and 2006 Winter Olympics.

SLOVENIA (SLO). Prior to 1992, Slovenia, located in south Central Europe, had never competed at the Olympics as a sovereign nation. However, many **Yugoslav** athletes were natives of Slovenia, notably gymnast Leon Štukelj (from Maribor) who won, between 1924 and 1936, more medals (six) and gold medals (three) than any other Yugoslav Olympian. Slovenia was also responsible for all of Yugoslavia's medals in the **Olympic Winter Games** between 1984 and 1988. Slovenia made its Olympic debut at both Albertville and Barcelona in 1992 after becoming an independent nation, officially known as the Republic of Slovenia, following the breakup of Yugoslavia. It has since competed at all editions of the **Olympic Games**.

In six Summer Games, Slovenia has entered 226 athletes (147 men, 79 **women**) and competed in 16 sports, with the most participants in **athletics** (26 men, 26 women), **swimming** (13 men, 16 women), **handball** (24 men), **canoeing** (18 men, three women), and **rowing** (21 men). They have won 19 medals at the Summer Games (four gold, six silver, nine bronze). With a complete set of medals in rowing (gold, silver, two bronze), Iztok Čop, who has competed at all six Games in which Slovenia has participated (1992–2012), stands out as the most decorated Slovenian athlete. Shooter Rajmond Debevec first competed for Yugoslavia in 1984 and has entered each Summer Games since, for a total of eight, with the last six as a representative of Slovenia. He won a gold medal in 2000 and bronze medals in 2008 and 2012, the latter at the age of 49. Urška Žolnir won bronze in 2004 and gold in 2012 in women's **half-middleweight judo**. Slovenian **hammer thrower** Primož Kozmus is also a dual medalist, as he won gold in 2008 and silver in 2012, and so is **sailor** Vasilij Žbogar (2004 bronze, 2008 silver one-person **dinghy**).

Other Summer Games medalists for Slovenia are Brigita Bukovec (1996 silver women's 100 meter **hurdles**), Jolanda Čeplak (2004 bronze women's 800 meters), Andraž Vehovar (1996 silver **kayak slalom singles**), Lucija Polavder (2008 bronze women's **heavyweight** judo), Denis Žvegelj (Iztok Čop's partner 1992 bronze men's coxless **pairs** rowing), Luka Špik (Iztok Čop's partner 2000 gold, 2004, silver, 2008 bronze men's double **sculls**), swimmer Sara Isakovič (2008 silver, women's 200 meter freestyle), and the men's coxless fours rowing team (1992 bronze).

In seven Winter Games, Slovenia has entered 158 athletes (112 men, 46 women) and competed in 11 sports all except **bobsledding, curling, short-track speed skating**, and regular **speed skating**. The sports with the most participants have been **Alpine skiing** (27 men, 19 women), **ski jumping** (20 men, four women), **biathlon** (15 men, seven women), and **ice hockey** (22 men). They have won 15 medals at the Winter Games—two gold, four silver, and nine bronze. Alpine skier Tina Maze has won four medals (two silver in 2010, two gold in 2014). Ski jumper Peter Prevc earned both a silver and bronze in 2014 as did **snowboarder** Žan Košir. *See also* OTTEY, MERLENE JOYCE.

SMALL-BORE RIFLE. The small-bore rifle is one of the **shooting** events at the Olympic Games. Several different contests have been held at distances varying from 25 meters to 100 yards. Events have been held for prone position, standing position, and kneeling. In 2012, small-bore rifle events for men and **women** were three positions at 50 meters and for men prone at 50 meters. Among the best Olympic shooters with the small-bore rifle have been Sergey Martynov of **Belarus**, Malcolm Cooper of **Australia**, and among the women, Renata Mauer-Różańska of **Poland**.

SMETANINA, RAISA PETROVNA (URS/EUN–CCS). B. 29 February 1952, Mokhcha, Komi, **Russia**, USSR. Over a long career that encompassed five Olympics, Raisa Smetanina compiled one of the greatest records of any female **cross-country skier**. Smetanina first came to international attention at the 1974 World Championships, where she helped the **Soviet Union**'s relay team to the championship. This led to her greatest Olympic performance, at Innsbruck in 1976. Only five feet, three inches tall (162 cm), 117 lb (53 kg), she competed in three events, medaling in all three, with a silver at five km and golds in the 10 km and **relay**. Smetanina competed at the **Olympic Winter Games** in 1976, 1980, 1984, 1988, and 1992, retiring after the Albertville Olympics. During that time, she won 10 **Olympic medals**, including four gold. Two of the gold medals were won in 1976, and she added another individual gold in 1980 in the five km. Smetanina's Olympic career ended after she helped the **Commonwealth of Independent States women**'s relay team to a gold medal at the 1992 Winter Olympics. Raisa Smetanina also won 13 medals at the World Championships. In addition to her international triumphs, she was 21 times champion of the Soviet Union and was named an emeritus master of sport of the USSR.

SNATCH. The snatch is one of the two lifts in Olympic **weightlifting** competition. (Prior to 1976 a third lift, the **press**, was also required.) In the snatch lift, the weight is lifted overhead in one continuous motion. The weight lifted in this method is added to the weight lifted in the **clean and jerk** lift, and the total of the two lifts determines the winner. In 2000, Hossein Reza Zadeh of **Iran** set the Olympic record with a snatch lift of 212.5 kg (468.5 lb).

SNOWBOARDING. Snowboarding is a sport combining elements of **surfing**, skateboarding, and **skiing**. The snowboarders slide down a snow-covered surface on a single board affixed onto their boots. The sport developed in the 1960s, with the first mass-produced snowboard being sold in 1966, termed the "Snurfer." In the late 1970s, snowboarding became more popular and snowboarders began to "invade" traditional snow resorts, often met by opposition from skiers who tried to exclude the snowboarders from "their" mountains. By the 1990s, almost all ski resorts allowed snowboarding, and the resorts have found the snowboarders to be an excellent source of new revenue.

Competition in snowboarding developed in the late 1970s and early 1980s. World Championships in the sport were first held in 1993 for both men and **women**. Six events are contested at the World Championships: **parallel giant slalom**, parallel slalom, **halfpipe, boardercross** or snowboard cross, and a **combined** competition. Parallel slalom and **giant slalom** are similar to **slalom** racing done in professional skiing, in which two skiers race down parallel race courses of identical design. The first snowboarder to finish the course advances to the next round. Halfpipe is an acrobatic event, conducted on a tube, termed the halfpipe, which is bounded by two steep parallel walls of ice. Boardercross is a very exciting, almost combative, event that is contested in rounds and **heats**, with each heat consisting of several snowboarders (four to eight). The snowboarders race pack-style down the same course, with the first finishers advancing to the next round. The event is fast, with lots of action, skills, and contact, and was added to the **Olympic Program** in 2006 at Torino.

Snowboarding was admitted to the Olympic Program for the 1998 **Olympic Winter Games** in Nagano. At the Olympics, men and women each compete in three events: parallel giant slalom, halfpipe, and snowboard cross. Another event, superpipe, which is similar to halfpipe, but with higher vertical walls, was considered for inclusion at the 2014 Olympic Winter Games but was not included. A parallel slalom and a slopestyle event were added in 2014 though. In five Winter Games, there have been 567 athletes (328 men, 239 women) from 35 nations who have participated in Olympic snowboard events.

Snowboarding is governed by the Fédération Internationale de Ski (FIS), according to the **International Olympic Committee** (IOC), although this has been controversial. When snowboarding sought recognition as an Olympic sport, it tried to do so under the aegis of its own federation, the International Snowboard Federation (ISF), which was not recognized by the IOC. The IOC agreed to allow snowboarding on the Olympic Program, but only if governed by the FIS as a discipline of skiing; the ISF, after losing that control, eventually ceased operations in 2002. The decision was not well accepted by the snowboarding community, and several top snowboarders skipped the first Olympic competition in protest. Kelly Clark of the **United States** in four Winter Games from 2002 to 2014 has won three medals in halfpipe (one gold, two bronze) and also has a fourth place finish. She leads all Olympic snowboarders in medal count. Thirteen other snowboarders have won two Olympic medals through 2014, with four winning two gold medals: **Shaun White** (USA), Seth Wescott (USA), Vic Wild (RUS), and Philipp Schoch (SUI).

SOCCER. *See* FOOTBALL, ASSOCIATION (SOCCER).

SOFTBALL. Softball began in the 1890s as a variant of **baseball**, usually played by **women**. It was originally called mushball, kittenball, or indoor baseball, but had acquired the name softball by the 1920s. In the **United States**, the sport became organized with the formation of the Amateur Softball Association in 1933. Several variants of the sport exist in the United States, including fast-pitch, modified fast-pitch, and slow-pitch. In 2009, the **International Olympic Committee** (IOC) decided to remove softball, as well as baseball, from the **Olympic Program**, although it noted that the sport could reapply for 2016, which it did but was rejected. The sport's international organization was formerly the International Softball Federation (ISF), which was formed in 1952 and had 127 member nations as of July 2010. After baseball and softball were removed from the Olympic Program, on the advice of the IOC, one organization was formed in the hopes of returning the two sports to the Olympic Games. In 2013, the ISF merged with the International Baseball Federation to form the World Baseball Softball Confederation, which as of mid-2014 had 140 members.

Softball (fast-pitch) made its debut as a full-medal sport for women at the 1996 Olympics in Atlanta. In four Olympic Games, there have been 367 women from 13 nations who have participated in softball.

It has been the only sport on the Olympic Program open only to women and not men, although two **disciplines** also fall into this category: **synchronized swimming** and **rhythmic gymnastics**. Softball has been contested only four times at the Olympics, being dominated by the United States. That team claimed the first three titles and was upset by **Japan** in the 2008 final. Four U.S. players competed on all three winning American teams, with outfielder **Laura Berg** also playing in Beijing. *See also* WICKENHEISER, HAYLEY MARIE.

SOLOMON ISLANDS (SOL). The Solomon Islands **National Olympic Committee** was recognized by the **International Olympic Committee** in 1983, and the country made its Olympic debut in 1984. The South Pacific nation has since competed at each subsequent Summer Games but has never competed at the **Olympic Winter Games**, and its athletes have yet to win a medal. Its 18 Olympic athletes (13 men, five **women**) have entered **athletics** (seven men, three women), **weightlifting** (three men, two women), and one man in **archery**, **boxing**, and **judo**. In 2012, Solomon Islander Tony

Lomo recorded the country's best Olympic performance as he won his first match in the **extra-lightweight** judo competition and finished tied for ninth of the 37 competitors.

SOMALIA (SOM). Somalia has competed at eight **Olympic Games**, those of 1972, 1984, 1988, and 1996 through 2012. It entered the 1992 Olympics but did not compete, probably because of the famine in the country. It has competed only in track and field, sending 16 male competitors and four **women**, just one each from 2000 through 2012. Somalia, an eastern African nation, officially known as the Federal Republic of Somalia, has not competed in the **Olympic Winter Games** and has not yet won an **Olympic medal**. Abdi Bile, a former World Champion in the 1,500 meters, recorded the best Somali performance when he placed sixth in that event in 1996. Ahmed Mohamed Ismail finished 47th of 107 entrants in the **marathon** in 1984. In 1988, Ibrahim Okash reached the semifinals of the 800 meters. Due to the unstable political situation in the country, many Somali athletes have fled the country and now compete for other nations. In 2008, more Somalis competed for other teams than for Somalia. One of Somalia's greatest athletes is Mohamad "Mo" Farah, who won two gold medals in track and field distance events for **Great Britain** in 2012.

SOUTH AFRICA (RSA, formerly SAF). With the exception of the **Intercalated Olympic Games** of 1906, South Africa's participation at the **Olympic Games** was continuous from 1904 through 1960. From 1964 to 1988, however, it was not allowed to compete at the Olympics. This was due to the country's policy of apartheid and, in particular, its use of the policy in choosing its athletic teams, which is forbidden by **International Olympic Committee** (IOC) policy. It is ironic that the first South African Olympians were two Tswana tribesmen, who ran in the 1904 **marathon**—Len Tau and Jan Mashiani—both black men.

The story of South Africa's banishment from the Olympics is one of the most complex issues the IOC has ever faced. South Africa did not always practice apartheid as a sporting policy. In the 1930s, there was frequent interracial competition, but in June 1956, a South African law was passed requiring an end to interracial sport. In 1958, **IOC member** Olav Ditlef-Simonsen of **Norway** informed **IOC President Avery Brundage** that his country would exclude an all-white South African team if his nation were awarded the Olympics. In 1959, the **Indians**, **Egyptians**, and **Soviets** pressed the IOC for South Africa's ouster from the Olympics, but the IOC was content with the promise that its 1960 Olympic team would be a multiracial one. It was not.

In 1962, South African Interior Minister Jan de Klerk commented publicly, "Government policy is that no mixed teams should take part in sports inside or outside the country." The IOC could scarcely ignore this message. At the 60th **IOC Session** in Moscow in 1962, the IOC voted to suspend the South African National Olympic Committee (SANOC) "if the policy of racial discrimination practiced by the government . . . does not change before our Session in Nairobi which takes place in October 1963." SANOC was eventually suspended at the 62nd IOC Session in Innsbruck in January 1964.

Further problems arose in December 1966 in Bamako, **Mali**, when 32 African nations formed the Supreme Council for Sport in Africa (SCSA). The SCSA's stated purpose was to coordinate and promote sport, but its true objective was to attack South Africa's apartheid policies in sport. At its founding conference, the SCSA resolved "to use every means to obtain the expulsion of South African sports organizations from the **Olympic Movement** and from **International Federations** should South Africa fail to comply fully with the IOC rules."

In mid-September 1967, an IOC commission visited South Africa to inspect the sporting facilities and see if the South Africa sporting groups were in violation of Olympic principles. The commission consisted of three IOC members: future IOC president **Lord Killanin (Ireland)**, Reginald Alexander (**Kenya**, a white man), and Sir Adetokunbo Ademola (**Nigeria**, a black man). They presented their report to the IOC on 30 January 1968, and it was felt to be generally positive. By a mail ballot, the IOC voted to restore recognition to SANOC, allowing a multiracial South African team to compete at the 1968 Olympics.

This prompted mass **boycott** demands from the African nations, which vehemently opposed this decision. The IOC **Executive Board** subsequently met in **Lausanne, Switzerland**, on 20 April 1968 and decided to poll the IOC members. By a postal ballot of 47–17 (with eight abstentions), the IOC reversed its course and withdrew its recognition of SANOC, preventing a huge boycott of the 1968 Olympics. In May 1970, at the 70th IOC Session in Amsterdam, the South African Olympic Committee was expelled from the IOC by a vote of 35–28, with three abstentions.

In 1976, the South African question again became prominent when several African nations boycotted in protest against a **New Zealand rugby** team's having played several games on tour in South Africa. Ironically, rugby had not been an Olympic sport since 1924, and the New Zealand rugby team was named the All-Blacks.

In 1990, South Africa began to take steps to eliminate apartheid. In April 1991, the IOC, anticipating apartheid's elimination, gave provisional recognition to the South African Olympic Committee. On 9 July 1991, the IOC granted full recognition to the SAOC and lifted its 21-year ban on its participation in the Olympics. In 1992, at Barcelona, South Africa competed on the Olympic stage for the first time in 32 years. The nation's return to the Olympics was celebrated fittingly when Elana Meyer, a white 10,000 meter runner, won a silver medal, the country's first medal since 1960, and celebrated it by running her victory lap hand-in-hand with the black winner, Derartu Tulu (ETH). South Africa (officially known as the Republic of South Africa since 1961) has competed in all Summer Olympics since Barcelona.

In 18 Summer Games, South Africa has entered 852 athletes (645 men, 207 **women**) and competed in 30 sports plus the **art competitions**. They have had their largest contingents in **athletics** (151 men, 33 women), **hockey** (52 men, 44 women), **swimming** (49 men, 33 women), **boxing** (69 men), and **cycling** (43 men, 10 women).

South Africa has won a total of 78 medals (23 gold, 27 silver, 28 bronze) in nine sports, of which 25 medals (seven gold) were won in the postapartheid era. Two South Africans have each won two Olympic titles: **tennis** player Charles Winslow (1912) and swimmer Penny Heyns (1996). Winslow won both men's **singles** and **doubles** and added a bronze medal in singles in 1920. He is one of only four South African Olympians with three medals. Penny Heyns is one of the others. She won both the 100 meter and 200 meter **breaststroke** in 1996 and won a bronze medal in 2000 in the 100 meter breaststroke. Swimmer Roland Schoeman won three medals, one of each color in 2004. He won bronze in the 50 meter **freestyle**, silver in the 100 meter freestyle, and was a member of the gold medal–winning 4x100 freestyle **relay** team. The fourth South African with three Olympic medals is Bevil Rudd. The grandson of Charles Rudd, one of the co-founders of the DeBeers diamond mining company, Bevil competed in athletics in 1920 and won the 400 meters, bronze in the 800 meters, and silver with the 4x400 meter relay team. Eleven other South African athletes have each won two medals at the Summer Games but none won more than one gold medal. One of the most notable South African Olympians is **Oscar Pistorius**, a runner who competes on artificial legs.

South Africa entered the 1960 **Olympic Winter Games** and the 1994–2010 Winter Games. In those six Winter Games, South Africa has entered 11 athletes (six men, five women) and competed in five sports: **figure skating** (two men, four women), **Alpine skiing** (two men), one man in **cross-country skiing** and **skeleton**, and one woman in **short-track speed skating**. They have not won any medals at the Winter Games, and their best performances were by Alex Heath who finished 26th of 65 in the men's **slalom** in 1998, 27th of 77 in 2002, and 27th of 82 in the **giant slalom** in 2006. At the country's first Winter Games in 1960, Marcelle "Cookie" Matthews became one of the youngest Olympians ever when she competed in the **pairs** figure skating at the age of 11. She and her 20-year-old partner, Gwyn Jones, finished 13th and last. Also on the South African figure skating team that year was 12-year-old Pat Eastwood, who finished 24th of 26 in women's singles.

South Africa bid for the 2004 Olympics to be held in Cape Town, but was eliminated in the third voting round. After the successful 2010 **Football** World Cup, it is planning to bid again.

SOUTH SUDAN. South Sudan became an independent nation in 2011, officially known as the Republic of South Sudan, after seceding from the Northeastern African nation of **Sudan** following a civil war. Although it had not established a **National Olympic Committee** with recognition by the **International Olympic Committee**, a South Sudanese athlete, Guor Marial, was allowed to compete in the 2012 **Olympic Games** as an **independent Olympic athlete**. He finished a respectable 47th of 105 entrants in the **marathon**.

SOUTH VIETNAM (VNM). Formally the Republic of Vietnam, South Vietnam first competed at the 1952 **Olympic Games** and, despite the ongoing war with North Vietnam, did not fail to attend until the nation was merged with North Vietnam in 1975. In six Olympic Games (no **Olympic Winter Games**), it sent 39 athletes (37 men, two **women**) to compete in seven sports: **athletics** (four men), **boxing** (one man), **cycling** (17 men), **fencing** (three men), **judo** (three men), **shooting** (four men), and **swimming** (five men, two women). The Southeast Asian nation's athletes failed to achieve impressive results, however, with the best performances by Lu'u Quan, who finished 47th of 111 entrants in the 1952 cycling **road race**, and Ho Min Thu, who was 43rd of 69 entrants in the mixed **free pistol** 50 meters shooting event. Since 1980, athletes from South Vietnam have competed for the unified Vietnamese team.

SOUTH YEMEN. *See* YEMEN DEMOCRATIC REPUBLIC.

SOUTH-WEST AFRICA. *See* NAMIBIA.

SOVIET UNION (URS). Although **Russia** competed from 1900 through 1912 at the Olympics, it did not return after World War I. After the Bolshevik Revolution, the Soviet Union (formally the Union of Soviet Socialist Republics, or USSR) did not attend the Olympics, although a few Soviet artists sent in works for the 1924 Olympic **art competitions**. In fact, the Soviet Union was absent from international sports, instead choosing to compete in separate socialist events, which also attracted participation from other nations.

After World War II, the USSR competed in the European Championships in track and field **athletics** in 1946, but it did not attend the **Olympic Games** until 1952 at Helsinki. It made its inaugural **Olympic Winter Games** appearance in 1956 at Cortina. It competed at every Olympics from 1956 to 1988, with the exception of the 1984 Los Angeles Olympics, which it **boycotted**, and in 1992 its constituent republics competed as the Unified Team. The Soviet Union was disbanded in late 1991 after the August Revolution. It no longer competes as a single nation at the Olympics, as its 15 former republics now compete as independent nations, but the central core of the former nation still competes at the Olympics as Russia.

In nine Summer Games, the Soviet Union entered 2,475 athletes (1,872 men, 603 **women**) and competed in all 27 sports that were contested in those years. They had the most entrants in athletics (363 men, 185 women), **rowing** (193 men, 68 women), **swimming** (122 men, 70 women), **wrestling** (129 men), **volleyball** (51 men, 56 women), **basketball** (75 men, 28 women), and **fencing** (78 men, 23 women). After returning to the Olympics, the Soviet Union was a dominant force in almost all Olympic sports. It was the second nation after the **United States** to win more than 1,000 **Olympic medals**. The Soviet Union won 1,010 medals at the Summer Games, second most of any nation. They had 395 gold, 319 silver, and 296 bronze and won medals in 24 different sports, failing to do so only in three sports that were introduced in 1988, their last year of competition. They won their most medals in athletics (193), **gymnastics** (182), and wrestling (116). They were also strong in team sports, especially men's basketball (nine medals in nine tournaments including two gold when they defeated the previously undefeated U.S. team) and women's basketball (three medals in three tournaments with two gold). They also medaled in all six men's and women's volleyball tournaments, with seven total gold medals. They won medals in seven of nine men's **water polo** tournaments. In women's **handball**, the USSR won medals in all three tournaments they entered and won medals in three of four men's handball tournaments. They also won medals in five of six men's **football** tournaments.

Eighteen USSR athletes each won at least six medals in the Summer Games. Of that total, 14 were gymnasts with three fencers and one **modern pentathlete**. Gymnast **Larysa Latynina** won 18 medals (nine gold, five silver, four bronze). This was the most Olympic medals won by any female athlete, summer or winter, regardless of sport. She had won more than anyone until 2012 when swimmer **Michael Phelps** surpassed her total. Only Phelps with 18 and track star **Ray Ewry** with 10 have more gold medals than Larysa, who still has the most gold medals of any female Olympian. Gymnasts **Nikolay Andrianov** (15 total medals), **Boris Shakhlin** (13), and **Viktor Chukarin** (11) each have seven gold medals. **Aleksandr Dityatin** and **Po-**

lina Astakhova each have 10 total medals. Some of the Soviet Union's other gymnasts have fewer medals but made more of an impact in the public eye. **Olga Korbut**, with four gold medals and six total medals in 1972 and 1976, was the first Olympic gymnast to receive extensive television coverage. Her teammates **Lyudmila Turishcheva** and **Nelli Kim** also received much publicity and helped make their sport more attractive to the public. In 1972 and 1976, **sprinter Valeriy Borzov** defeated the U.S. athletes at their specialty, the men's 100 and 200 meter dashes.

Wrestling is another sport that was dominated by Soviet Union athletes. They competed in each Olympic wrestling tournament except 1984 when they boycotted the Games and had 129 entrants who took home a total of 116 medals—62 gold, 31 silver, and 23 bronze in the nine Olympics from 1952 to 1988. Ninety percent of their wrestlers won a medal and nearly half of them won gold medals. The Soviet Union's total of 116 medals is second only to that of the United States, which earned 124 medals in 25 Olympic Games.

In nine Winter Games, the Soviet Union entered 473 athletes (362 men, 111 women) and competed in 10 sports: all except **freestyle skiing**, which was only introduced in 1988. They had the most entrants in **ice hockey** (106 men), **speed skating** (65 men, 32 women), **cross-country skiing** (37 men, 28 women), and **figure skating** (33 men, 28 women). They won 194 medals (78 gold, 57 silver, 59 bronze) and medaled in all 10 sports in which they participated. The men's ice hockey team was nearly unbeatable, winning the gold medal in seven of the nine tournaments in which they entered and winning a silver and bronze medal in the other two after being upset by the United States. **Raisa Smetanina** won nine medals in cross-country skiing (three gold, five silver, one bronze). **Galina Kulakova** won eight in that sport (four gold, two silver, two bronze). **Lidiya Skoblikova** won six gold medals in speed skating in 1960 and 1964, the most gold medals by a Soviet Winter Olympian. They also did especially well in figure skating, winning 12 medals (seven gold) in **pairs** and eight (three gold) in **ice dancing**.

The Soviet Union hosted the Games of the XXIInd **Olympiad** in Moscow in 1980 after Moscow bid unsuccessfully for the 1976 Games. *See also* ALEKSEYEV, VASILIY IVANOVICH; BELOUSOVA, LYUDMILA YEVGENEVNA; BELOV, SERGEY ALEKSANDROVICH; BOYAR-SKIKH, KLAVDIYA SERGEYEVNA; GOROKHOVSKAYA, MARIYA KONDRATYEVNA; GRISHIN, YEVGENY ROMANOVICH; KARE-LIN, ALEKSANDR ALEKSANDROVICH; LAGUTIN, BORIS NIKO-LAYEVICH; LAVROV, ANDREY IVANOVICH; LEDNYOV, PAVEL SE-RAFIMOVICH; MEDVED, ALEKSANDR VASILYEVICH; NOVIKOV, IGOR ALEKSANDROVICH; RODNINA, IRINA KONSTANTINOVA; RYSKAL, INNA VALERYEVNA; SABONIS, ARVYDAS ROMAS;

SALNIKOV, VLADIMIR VALERYEVICH; SALUMÄE, ERIKA AK-
SELEVNA; SANEYEV, VIKTOR DANILOVICH; SEMJONOVA, UL-
JANA LARIONOVNA; SHCHERBO, VITALY VENEDIKTOVICH; SO-
VIET UNION (USSR) ICE HOCKEY TEAMS (1956–1992); SOVIET
UNION (USSR) WOMEN'S BASKETBALL TEAMS (1976–1988); SO-
VIET UNION (USSR) WOMEN'S GYMNASTICS TEAMS (1952–1992);
TIKHONOV, ALEKSANDR IVANOVICH; TRETYAK, VLADISLAV
ALEKSANDROVICH; ZIMYATOV, NIKOLAY SEMYONOVICH.

SOVIET UNION (USSR) ICE HOCKEY TEAMS (1956–1992). The
Soviet Union first entered the **Olympic Winter Games** in 1956 and immediately established itself as a dominant force in most winter sports. However,
it was in **ice hockey** that it would be most dominant over the next 36 years.
From 1956 through 1992, the Soviet Union won all but two of the Olympic
gold medals in ice hockey (eight in all), losing only in 1960 and 1980 to the
"hometown" **United States** teams. Its last gold medal in 1992 was won as the
Unified Team, after the dissolution of the Soviet Union. During this time, Soviet and Unified ice hockey teams posted a record of 61 wins, six losses, and
two ties. None of the teams from the former Soviet Republics has been able
to match these results; **Russia**'s best performance was a silver medal in 1998.

**SOVIET UNION (USSR) WOMEN'S BASKETBALL TEAMS (1976–
1988).** For more than three decades, the **Soviet Union** had the best **women**'s
basketball team in the world. From the 1950s through the mid-1980s, they
compiled a record of 152–2 in major international competition. After losing
to the **United States** in the World Championships in 1957 and **Bulgaria** in
the 1958 European Championships, they proceeded to win all their games
for nearly three decades until defeated twice by the United States in 1986—
first at the **Goodwill Games** and then at the World Championships. After
finishing second to Bulgaria at the 1957 World Championships, the USSR
won in 1959, 1964, 1967, 1971, and 1975. They **boycotted** the 1979 World
Championships that were held in South **Korea** but won again in 1983. At the
European Championships, their record was even more impressive. From 1950
to 1991, they won the title in 21 of 22 years, losing only to Bulgaria in 1958.
In that time, the Soviet Union won 114 consecutive games.

Led by the extremely tall **Uljana Semjonova**, officially listed at six feet,
10 inches (210 cm) but probably closer to seven feet, two inches (218 cm),
throughout the 1970s and 1980s they were undefeated in international competition. They easily won the first two Olympic women's basketball tournaments
in 1976 and 1980. In 1976, they won all five games by an average margin of
101–69. In 1980, the margin was even greater, 111–63. When they returned

to the Olympic Games in 1988, Semjonova had retired. They had previously lost twice to the United States, and they settled for the bronze medal. In 1992, the Unified Team did win the gold medal, but since 1996, **Russia** has only been able to twice win bronze medals (2004, 2008) in women's basketball.

SOVIET UNION (USSR) WOMEN'S GYMNASTICS TEAMS (1952–1992). The **Soviet Union**'s **women**'s **gymnastics** teams produced a nonpareil record at the **Olympic Games**; they never lost. From 1952 to 1988, and as the Unified Team in 1992, the Soviet Union won every women's team **all-around** title in gymnastics (eight consecutive and nine titles), with the lone exception of 1984, when it did not compete because of the **boycott**. Since the breakup of the Soviet Union, no team from the former Soviet Union has won the title, although **Russia** finished runner-up on three occasions. Although the Soviet Union teams dominated the all-around competition, they did not win the majority of the individual apparatus events.

SPAIN (ESP). In 1900, Spain was represented by 14 athletes at the Paris Olympics. A Spanish **National Olympic Committee** was formed in 1905, at the urging of the Greeks, and 20 Spanish athletes competed at Athens in 1906. Spain next appeared on the Olympic stage in 1920 and has since missed only the 1936 Berlin **Olympic Games**, when the nation was involved in civil war. In addition, Spain **boycotted** Melbourne in 1956 because of the Hungarian Revolt, although Spanish riders did compete in the Olympic **Equestrian** Games at Stockholm in 1956.

In 21 Summer Games, Spain has entered 2,325 athletes (1,774 men, 551 **women**) and competed in 34 sports plus the **art competitions**. They have had the most participants in **athletics** (249 men, 88 women), **hockey** (142 men, 47 women), **football** (159 men), **swimming** (101 men, 66 women), **handball** (89 men, 39 women), **cycling** (110 men, 15 women), **sailing** (91 men, 24 women), **water polo** (103 men, 12 women), **basketball** (82 men, 28 women), and **rowing** (96 men, five women). Spain has won 131 **Olympic medals** (37 gold, 59 silver, 35 bronze) in 27 sports. **Canoeist** David Cal has won five medals (four silver, one bronze) from 2004 to 2012. Three other Spanish competitors have won four medals, with track **cyclist** Joan Llaneras also winning two gold and two silver medals. **Synchronized swimmer** Andrea Fuentes has won four medals from 2008 to 2012 (three silver, one bronze) and also has a fourth place finish in 2004. **Tennis** star Arantxa Sánchez Vicario won medals in both **singles** and **doubles** in 1992 and 1996 and has a silver and bronze in each event. Conchita Martínez won three women's doubles medals—two silver, one bronze—from 1996 to 2004. **Gymnast** Gervasio Deferr has three medals (two gold, one silver, from 2000 to 2008). From 1996 to 2008, Spain was three times a bronze medalist in men's handball, and Demetrio Lozano was a member of all three teams. **Kayaker** Herminio Menéndez won three medals in 1980 and 1984—two silver and one bronze. The only other Spanish athletes with two gold medals were **sailors** Theresa Zabell in 1992 and 1996 and Luis Doreste in 1984 and 1992. Spain's men's basketball team was runner-up in 1984, 2008, and 2012 to the **United States**. The 21st-century teams included quite a few National Basketball Association players such as the Gasol brothers, Pau and Marc, Ricky Rubio, Rudy Fernández, and José Calderón.

Spain's first winter appearance was in 1936 at Garmisch-Partenkirchen, and it has never failed to compete in the **Olympic Winter Games** since. In 19 Winter Games, Spain has entered 132 athletes (99 men, 33 women) and competed in 10 sports, with most of the participants in **Alpine skiing** (41 men, 18 women), **cross-country skiing** (18 men, three women), and **bobsledding** (13 men). They have only won two medals—gold in men's **slalom** in 1972 by Francisco Fernández Ochoa, and bronze in 1992 in the women's slalom by his sister Blanca Fernández Ochoa. Three other siblings, Juan Manuel (1976), Luis (1984, 1988), and Dolores (1984) also competed in Alpine skiing at the Winter Games. Francisco, known as "Paquito," had the honor of being Spain's flagbearer at the opening ceremony of the 1972 Winter Games, the 1972 Summer Games, and the 1976 and 1980 Winter Games. He is the only person to be his country's flagbearer in both Summer and Winter Games in the same year. His sister Blanca also had that honor at the 1984 and 1992 Winter Games.

Other notable results for Spain at the Winter Games include fourth place for Jordi Font in men's **boardercross** in 2006 and for Javier Fernandez in men's singles **figure skating** in 2014. Blanca Fernández Ochoa was fifth in 1988 in the slalom and sixth in 1984 in the **giant slalom**. Mariá Josá Rienda was also sixth in 2002 in the giant slalom. Lucas Eguibar was seventh in boardercross in 2014, and Francisco Fernández Ochoa was ninth in the 1976 slalom. Laura Orgue was 10th in women's 30 km cross-country in 2014.

In 1992, Barcelona hosted the Games of the XXVth **Olympiad**. These Olympics proved a huge boost for Spanish Olympic performances; prior to these Olympics, Spain had won 27 medals (six gold), but it won 22 medals in Barcelona and 83 more in subsequent Summer Games. Spain has also had eight unsuccessful bid attempts at hosting the Summer Olympics (Barcelona 1924, 1936), Madrid (1972, 2012, 2016, 2020), and Seville (2004, 2008) and four unsuccessful bid attempts for the Winter Games by Jaca (1998, 2002, 2010, 2014). *See also* ANDORRA; BASQUE COUNTRY; GIBRALTAR; SAMARANCH (TORRELO), JUAN ANTONIO, MARQUIS DE SAMARANCH.

SPANISH GUINEA. *See* EQUATORIAL GUINEA.

SPARTAKIAD. Dissatisfied with the lack of dedication to the communist cause of the socialist Sozialistische Arbeiter Sport Internationale (International Socialist Workers' Sport; *see also* **Workers' Olympiad**), on 23 July 1921, Nikolay Podvoysky founded the International Association of Red Sports and Gymnastics Associations, better known as the Sportintern or Red Sport International (RSI). Within a few years, it had attracted members from outside the **Soviet Union** and had been recognized by the Communist International (Comintern).

In 1928, it organized the first Spartakiad, intended as a proletarian alternative for the **Olympic Games** held in Amsterdam that same year. This name was a combination of **Olympiad** and Spartacus, the leader of a major slave rebellion in the first century B.C., who had become a heroic figure for communist and socialist organizations. Although most of the participants in the event were from the Soviet Union, there were delegations from 14 other nations: 12 from Europe, as well as **Algeria** and **Uruguay**.

In 1930, RSI decided to hold a second Spartakiad in Berlin, as a counter-manifestation to the socialist 2nd Workers' Olympiad that would be held in Vienna in 1931. But it was marred by organizational troubles. After suffering difficulties with venues and passport issues for the invited Soviet guests, a new law made political manifestations illegal (as these frequently amounted to violence). In the end, some sport competitions were held, although illegally, but they could hardly be called international. This also signaled the beginning of the end for the RSI, and it was eventually disbanded in 1937.

The Spartakiads did not die, however, and throughout the 1930s the word was tacked onto many different kinds of local and national sport manifestations throughout the Soviet Union. After the Soviet Union started competing in the Olympic Games in 1952, the Spartakiad became a national multisport festival held approximately every four years, often featuring international competitors from Eastern bloc nations. These Spartakiads were held 10 times between 1956 and 1991, with seven winter editions staged between 1962 and 1990.

SPECIAL OLYMPICS. The **International Olympic Committee** also recognizes Special Olympics International, an American group that organizes sporting events for people with intellectual disabilities. Originally, Special Olympics began as an American sports festival, but it has expanded and now includes international events as well, highlighted by the Special Olympic World Games, which are also held in both summer and winter versions. The Special Olympic World Games began in 1968 in Chicago, while the Special

Olympics World Winter Games began in 1977 in Steamboat Springs, Colorado. *See also* PARALYMPIC GAMES.

SPEED SKATING. Speed skating emerged on the canals of Holland as early as the 13th century. Competition has been held in the **Netherlands** since at least 1676. The sport spread throughout Europe, and national competitions were held in the 1870s. The first World Championships were contested in 1889, although the International Skating Union (ISU) held its first championships in 1893, one year after its formation.

Speed skating was contested at the 1924 **Olympic Winter Games** and has been on the **Olympic Program** since. **Women** first competed at the Olympics in 1932, when it was a **demonstration sport**. Women's speed skating as a full medal sport was planned for 1940, but did not actually begin until 1960. In 22 Winter Games, there have been 1,582 participants (1,054 men, 528 women) from 41 nations in Olympic speed skating. The sport is governed by the ISU, which also governs **figure skating**. The ISU was formed in 1892 and has 84 members (representing 64 nations) as of 2014.

Olympic speed skating has almost always been contested in the European system of skating **time trials** in two-man **pairs**. In 1932 at Lake Placid, the Americans convinced the ISU to hold the events in the North American style of pack racing. Several top Europeans **boycotted** the events as a result, and the Americans won all four gold medals. In 1992, the related sport of **short-track speed skating**, in which several racers compete at the same time, was added to the Olympic Program.

Speed skating has been dominated by the Dutch, the Norwegians, and the former **Soviet Union** and its republics. The Netherlands, with a total of 105 total medals (35 gold, 36 silver, 34 bronze), leads all nations. **Norway** has 80 (25 gold, 28 silver, 27 bronze). In addition, the women of the former **German Democratic Republic** were outstanding speed skaters. The **United States** has produced excellent sprinters, winning many medals and gold medals by both men and women. In addition, in 1980 **Eric Heiden** (USA) won all five available gold medals, a dominance in speed skating matched only by the USSR's **Lidiya Skoblikova**, who won all four women's events in 1964. As she also won two additional gold medals in 1960, Skoblikova is the most successful Olympic speed skater. **Claudia Pechstein** of **Germany** has won the most medals in speed skating, with nine (five gold), from 1992 to 2006. After not competing in 2010, she came back in 2014 at the age of 41 and narrowly missed adding to her medal collection as she finished fourth in the 3,000 meters and fifth in the 5,000 meters. *See also* ANDERSEN, HJALMAR JOHAN; BALLANGRUD, IVAR EUGEN; BLAIR, BONNIE KATHLEEN; EHRIG-SCHÖNE-MITSCHERLICH, ANDREA; GRISHIN, YEVGENY

ROMANOVICH; HUGHES, CLARA; KANIA-BUSCH-ENKE, KARIN; KLASSEN, CYNTHIA NICOLE; KOSS, JOHANN OLAV; LUDING-ROTHENBURGER, CHRISTA; NIEMANN-STIRNEMANN, GUNDA; SCHENK, ADRIE; THUNBERG, ARNOLD CLAS ROBERT.

SPEED SKIING. Speed skiing was a **demonstration sport** at the 1992 **Olympic Winter Games** in Albertville. The event was marred by the death of competitor Nicolas Bochatay, who crashed with a snow groomer while training.

SPITZ, MARK ANDREW (USA–SWI). B. 10 February 1950, Modesto, California, **USA.** Considered the greatest **swimmer** ever until the advent of **Michael Phelps**, Mark Spitz remains an Olympic legend who won seven gold medals (four individual, three **relay**) for swimming, each in a new world record time, at the 1972 Olympics. At the 1968 Games, he had won four medals (two gold, one silver, one bronze), and his overall total of 11 Olympic medals has only been surpassed by Phelps among male swimmers as has his nine gold medals. The six-foot tall (183 cm), 161 lb (73 kg) Spitz set 26 individual world records and six in the relays. He returned to competition in 1991 with the aim of making the 1992 Olympic team but, as he was over 40 years of age, it was a forlorn hope and an unfortunate end to a career of unrivaled achievements.

SPORTACCORD. In the early 1960s, many sports federations were unhappy that they had so little influence with the **International Olympic Committee** (IOC). Led by the Frenchman Roger Coulon, president of the Fédération Internationale des Luttes Amateurs (**wrestling**), the **International Federations** banded together in 1967 to form the General Assembly of International Federations, later the General **Association of International Sports Federations** (GAISF), or Association Générale des Fédérations Internationales de Sports. In 2003, the GAISF began holding a yearly convention of sports federations called SportAccord. The 7th SportAccord Conference in Denver, Colorado, in April 2009 voted to rebrand GAISF as SportAccord.

The headquarters of SportAccord is currently in Monte Carlo, and the president from 2004 to 2013 was Hein Verbruggen of the **Netherlands**. On 31 May 2013, Marius L. Vizer of **Austria** succeeded him. As of 2014, there are 92 sports member federations and 17 associate members. Many of these federations govern Olympic sports, several are IOC-recognized federations, and about two dozen are not directly affiliated with the IOC, and SportAccord gives them a small voice within the **Olympic Movement**. The aims of SportAccord are "to act as a forum for the exchange of ideas and for discussion on common problems in sport; to collect, collate, and circulate information; to provide members with secretarial and translating services, the organization of meetings, technical documentation and consultancy; to collect news bulletins, technical rules and regulations from members; to assemble and coordinate the dates of main international competitions; and to publish a half-yearly calendar." *See also* Appendix XXIII.

SPORT AND ENVIRONMENT COMMISSION. The Sport and Environment Commission was formed in 1995, after the 1994 Lillehammer **Olympic Winter Games**, in response to the Norwegian policy of conducting a "Green" Olympics, quite a feat at the Olympic Winter Games. But the **International Olympic Committee** (IOC) thought the Lillehammer policies toward the environment were important and formed the commission to help institute similar policies in international sport. The chairman is Albert II, Prince of **Monaco**. The commission has eight other IOC members and 21 other members who act as consultants on the environment. The commission succeeded in having the following section added to the *Olympic Charter*, Rule 2.13: "[The IOC's role is] to encourage and support a responsible concern for environmental issues, to promote sustainable development in sport and to require that the **Olympic Games** are held accordingly."

SPORT AND LAW COMMISSION. The Sport and Law Commission was formed in 1996, with Judge **Kéba Mbaye** as its first chairman. The current chairman is John Coates (Australia). It consists of four other **International Olympic Committee (IOC) members**, Anita DeFrantz (United States), Nicole Hoevertsz (Aruba), Denis Oswald (Switzerland), and **Richard Pound** (Canada) along with four others who act as legal consultants.

SPORT FOR ALL COMMISSION. The **International Olympic Committee** (IOC) formed a Sport for All Working Group in 1983, and in 1985 the IOC formed the Mass Sport Commission, which was renamed the Sport for All Commission in 1986. The concept of the availability of Sport for All was a basic tenet of Baron **Pierre de Coubertin**'s philosophy of **Olympism**. The concept attempts to provide sport as a human right for all individuals regardless of race, social class, and gender and encourages the practice of sport by people of all ages, genders, and social and economic conditions. The current chairman is Sam Ramsamy of **South Africa**. The commission consists of 11 other IOC members and 16 independent members. In 1987, the Sport for All Commission developed the concept of an Olympic Day Run, held on 23 June each year (the anniversary of the founding of the IOC at the 1894 Sorbonne Congress).

SPRINGBOARD. Olympic **diving** competition takes place from two different starting points—springboard and **platform**. The springboard is approximately five meters (16 feet) long and a half-meter (18 inches) wide and extends out over the water at a height of three meters (10 feet). Springboard diving has been an Olympic event for men since 1904 (with the exception of the **Intercalated Olympic Games** of 1906) and for **women** since 1920. **Xiong Ni** of **China** (1996, 2000) and **Greg Louganis** of the **United States** (1984, 1988) are the only multiple men's gold medalists. **Dmitry Sautin** of **Russia** is a three-time bronze medalist (1992 for the Unified Team, 2000, 2004 for Russia); Tan Liangde of China (1984–1992) is a three-time silver medalist, and Franco Cagnotto of **Italy** (silver 1972, 1976, bronze 1980) is a three-time medalist in Olympic springboard diving. The leader in women's Olympic springboard diving is **Guo Jingjing** of China who won the event in 2004 and 2008 after finishing second in 2000. Wu Minxia of China also won three medals in this event—silver in 2004, bronze in 2008, and gold in 2012. Four other women have won gold twice in Olympic springboard diving—**Pat McCormick** of the United States (1952, 1956), **Ingrid Engel-Gulbin- Krämer** of East **Germany** (1960, 1964), Gao Min of China (1988, 1992), and **Fu Mingxia** of China (1996, 2000).

SPRINT. A sprint is a race of short duration. In **athletics**, the 100 and 200 meter races are known as sprints. In **swimming**, the 50 and 100 meter races are called sprints. The term is also used in **cross-country skiing**, **Nordic combined**, and **cycling**.

SQUASH. Originally called squash rackets, after its parent sport **racquets**, this sport is different from both racquets and **racquetball**, but it has never been contested at the **Olympic Games**, even as a **demonstration sport**. However, the World Squash Federation is recognized by the **International Olympic Committee**, with 142 affiliated members as of 2014. It was one of the sports considered for Olympic status in 2016, but lost out to **golf** and **rugby**.

SRI LANKA (SRI). Sri Lanka has competed at all **Olympic Games** since its independence in 1948, except for the 1976 Games. Through 1968, it competed under the name of Ceylon, but that name was formally changed to Sri Lanka on 22 May 1972. Sri Lanka has yet to compete at the **Olympic Winter Games**. In 16 Summer Games, Ceylon/Sri Lanka has entered 87 athletes (66 men, 21 **women**) and competed in 10 sports: **athletics** (29 men, 12 women), **badminton** (two men, one woman), **boxing** (13 men), **cycling** (one man), **diving** (two men), **sailing** (three men), **shooting** (six men, three women), **swimming** (six men, five women), **weightlifting** (three men), and **wrestling** (one man).

The first Ceylonese national to compete at the Olympics was Carl Van Geyzel, who competed for Great Britain in the 1928 high jump. In 1948, Duncan White won a silver medal in the 400 meter **hurdles** in track and field athletics for Ceylon. The other medal for this nation was a silver in the women's 200 meters in 2000, won by Susanthika Jayasinghe. She originally received a bronze medal, but it was upgraded to a silver medal after the delayed **disqualification** of Marion Jones (USA). Jayasinghe also reached the semifinals of the 100 meters in 2000 and 200 meters in 2008. Other outstanding performances in the Olympic Games by Sri Lankans include boxers Albert Perera (1948 **bantamweight**) and Hatha Karunaratne (1968 **light-flyweight**) who each received a **bye**, won one bout and finished tied for fifth place; Pushpamali Ramanayake who competed in three Olympic Games from 1992 to 2004 and had a best result of 25th of 49 entrants in women's **air rifle** shooting in 1996; and Anuradha Cooray who finished 30th of 101 competitors in the 2004 men's **marathon** race.

STADION* RACE. The *stadion* race was the original event of the **Ancient Olympic Games**. It is a simple **sprint** of one length of the Ancient Olympic stadium of approximately 192 meters. From this event, our modern word for stadium is derived. The first known champion was **Coroebus of Elis** in 776 B.C. The last known champion of the *stadion* was Dionysios of Alexandria in A.D. 269. In the earliest Ancient Olympic Games, the *stadion* was the only event contested. **Leonidas of Rhodes** won four consecutive titles in this event from 164 to 152 B.C. Five other athletes are known to have won at least three titles. *See also DIAULOS* RACE; *DOLIKOS* RACE.

STEEPLECHASE. The steeplechase is an event in **athletics**. It is primarily a distance **hurdles** event with one of the hurdles being a water jump, in which the water portion is sufficiently long so that the athletes usually land in it after negotiating the hurdle in front of it. It became a part of the men's **Olympic Program** in 1900 at distances of both 2,500 and 4,000 meters. The distance was standardized at 3,000 meters in 1920 and has been contested at that distance in every Summer Olympic Games since. Volmari Iso-Hollo of **Finland** (1932, 1936) and Ezekiel Kemboi of **Kenya** (2004, 2012) are the only multiple gold medalists in the men's steeplechase. Iso-Hollo's victory in 1932 actually was over a distance of approximately 3,460 meters since the officials miscounted the laps and all runners actually ran an additional lap. Since 1984, a Kenyan has won every Olympic steeplechase. The event was added to the **women**'s Olympic Program in 2008, with **Russian** women winning the first gold medals.

STEVENSON LAURENCE, TEÓFILO (CUB–BOX). B. 29 March 1952, Puerto Padre, **Cuba**. D. 11 June 2012, Havana, Cuba. Téofilo Stevenson is one of only three men to win three gold **Olympic medals** for **boxing** (the others being **László Papp** and **Félix Savón**). On his way to winning the **heavyweight** title in 1972, 1976, and 1980, Stevenson had 12 scheduled bouts; one of his opponents withdrew, and he won nine of his 11 Olympic fights by a **knockout**. His devastating punching power resulted in all four of his bouts at the 1976 Games ending in a knockout. At his peak, he was undoubtedly the best heavyweight in the world, but he resisted many lucrative offers to fight professionally. Had he done so, there is little doubt that he would have been the world champion. And had Cuba not **boycotted** the 1984 Olympics, the six-foot, three-inch (190 cm), 209 lb (95 kg) Stevenson would have been the favorite to win his fourth gold medal. He was world amateur champion in 1974, 1978, and 1986.

STRICKLAND DE LA HUNTY, SHIRLEY BARBARA (née STRICK-LAND) (AUS–ATH). B. 18 July 1925, Northam, Western Australia, **Australia**. D. 11 February 2004, Perth, Western Australia, Australia. With seven **Olympic medals**, Shirley Strickland de la Hunty set a record for **women**'s track and field that was subsequently equaled by **Irena Szewińska-Kirszenstein** (POL) and Veronica Campbell-Brown (JAM), and bettered by **Merlene Ottey** (JAM/SLO). The Australian **sprinter/hurdler** won three gold medals in the 80 meter hurdles (1952, 1956) and the 4x100 meter **relay** (1956). Strickland de la Hunty also won one silver and three bronze medals in three Olympic appearances (1948–1956). She also competed in the 1950 British Empire Games (later known as the **Commonwealth Games**), winning silver medals in both the 100 and 200 meters. Strickland should have won eight Olympic medals. In the 1948 200 meters, the five-foot, seven-inch (172 cm), 126 lb (57 kg) runner was ranked fourth. However, a finish photo discovered later revealed that she had in fact crossed the line as the third runner and should have won the bronze.

SUDAN (SUD). A Northeastern African nation, officially known as the Republic of the Sudan, formed a **National Olympic Committee** in 1956, which was recognized by the **International Olympic Committee** in 1959. Since making its Olympic debut in 1960, Sudan has missed only the **Olympic Games** of 1964, 1976, and 1980. It has never competed at the **Olympic**

Winter Games. In 11 Summer Games, Sudan has entered 76 athletes (69 men, seven **women**) and has competed in eight sports: **athletics** (25 men, six women), **boxing** (17 men), **football** (14 men), **judo** (two men), **shooting** (three men), **swimming** (three men, one woman), **table tennis** (one man), and **weightlifting** (four men).

The country won its first **Olympic medal** at the Beijing Olympics, when Sudanese runner Ismail Ahmed Ismail placed second in the men's 800 meters. Although Sudan has competed in eight Olympic sports, all their other exceptional performances occurred in the sport of athletics. Yamilde Aldama was fifth in the 2004 women's **triple jump**, Abubaker Kaki Khamis seventh in the 2012 men's 800 meters, and eighth place finishes were recorded by Omer Khalifa (1984 1,500 meters) and Ismail Ahmed Ismail (2004 800 meters). Ahmed Musa Jouda was 10th in the 1984 10,000 meters, and Omer Khalifa was 12th in the 1988 800 meters. Six other Sudanese runners reached the semifinals in their races. Although Sudan qualified to compete in the 1972 men's football tournament, an accomplishment in itself, they finished in the last quarter of the competition, tied for 13th place of the 16 teams in the event. In judo, Hamid Fadul finished tied for 17th place among the 42 contestants in the men's **half-middleweight** class in 1992. *See also* SOUTH SUDAN.

SÜLEYMANOĞLU, NAIM (né NAIM SULEIMANOV, aka NAUM SHALAMANOV) (TUR–WLT). B. 23 January 1967, Ptichar, Kardzhali, **Bulgaria**. It is likely that Naim Süleymanoğlu is the strongest man who has ever lived, pound for pound. He set his first **weightlifting** world record at age 15, and at the 1984 European Championships he became the second man to lift three times his bodyweight overhead. Süleymanoğlu was also the first man to **snatch** two and one-half times his own bodyweight (27 April 1988). He was born in Bulgaria, but defected to **Turkey** at the 1986 World Cup finals. Born Naim Suleimanov and of Bulgarian Turkish descent, he was quite upset when the Bulgarians changed his name to Naum Shalamanov in 1985 to remove vestiges of its Turkish origins. Once in Turkey, he changed his name again to a more Turkish one, and at the 1988 **Olympic Games**, Süleymanoğlu was absolutely dominant. He was world champion at 60 kg (132 lb) in 1985, 1986, 1989, and 1991 and at 64 kg (141 lb) in 1993–1995. He did not compete in 1987 because of his defection. Süleymanoğlu also did not compete in 1990, retiring briefly before making a successful comeback. Nicknamed the "Pocket Hercules" because of his height (four feet, 11 inches [150 cm]), he defended his Olympic championship in 1992 in Barcelona and won again in 1996 at Atlanta. His 10 championships at the Olympics and World Championships are an all-time best, as are his three Olympic gold medals, although the latter have been matched by three more lifters: Halil Mutlu (TUR), **Akakios**

Kakiasvili (EUN/GRE), and **Pyrros Dimas** (GRE). Süleymanoğlu retired after Atlanta but returned to compete in Sydney, although he failed to make a successful lift at the 2000 Olympics.

SUMMER GAMES. *See* OLYMPIC GAMES.

SUMO. Sumo, the **Japanese** traditional form of **wrestling**, was contested as a **demonstration sport** at the 1964 Olympic Games in Tokyo, as part of the *budo* demonstration, along with *kendo* (**fencing**) and *kyudo* (**archery**). *Sumo* wrestling is governed internationally by the International Sumo Federation (IFS), which was founded in 1946 and is recognized by the **International Olympic Committee**. The IFS currently (as of 2014) has 84 affiliated members, including the **United States**' state of Hawaii.

SUPER G. The super G (short for super **giant slalom**) is one of the events in **Alpine skiing**. The race is similar to the giant slalom but the course is longer, although not as long as the downhill course. It has been included in the **Olympic Games** since 1988 for both men and **women**. **Kjetil André Aamodt** has won the men's race three times (1992, 2002, and 2006), won the bronze medal in 1994, and finished fifth in 1998. Three women each have two medals, although no woman won the gold medal more than once. Michaela Dorfmeister of **Austria** won the gold medal in 2006 and the silver in 1998; **Janica Kostelić** of **Croatia** won the silver medal in 2002 and 2006, and Alexandra Meissnitzer of Austria was the bronze medalist in both 1998 and 2006.

SUPER-HEAVYWEIGHT. Super-heavyweight is a weight category in **boxing**. It was added in 1984 and is the unlimited weight class formerly known simply as **heavyweight**. Although no man has won more than one gold medal in this class, Roberto Camarelle of **Italy** has won three medals—bronze in 2004, gold in 2008, and silver in 2012. This is quite an unusual feat since most boxers become professionals following Olympic success. Among the Olympic super-heavyweight medalists are Lennox Lewis (CAN), Riddick Bowe (USA), Volodymyr Klychko (UKR), and Francesco Damiani (ITA), all of whom became professional heavyweight champions.

Olympic **wrestling**, both **freestyle** and **Greco-Roman**, is another sport that uses a super-heavyweight class. It was added in 1972 and replaced heavyweight as the unlimited weight class. In 1988, a maximum weight was imposed for super-heavyweight, and it is no longer an unlimited weight class in Olympic wrestling. **Artur Taymazov** of **Uzbekistan** won the silver medal in 2000 and has won three consecutive gold medals, 2004–2012, in super-heavyweight freestyle competition. **Bruce Baumgartner** of the **United**

States also has four medals (gold 1984, 1992, silver 1988, bronze 1996) in this class. In super-heavyweight Greco-Roman wrestling **Aleksandr Karelin** won gold from 1988 to 1996 and silver in 2000. He represented the **Soviet Union** in 1988, the Unified Team in 1992, and **Russia** in 1996 and 2000.

Weightlifting is the third Olympic sport with a super-heavyweight category. As in boxing, it is an unlimited weight class and was added in 1972. **Vasily Alekseyev** of the Soviet Union (1972, 1976), Aleksandr Kurlovich of the Soviet Union and Unified Team (1988, 1992), and Hossein Reza Zadeh of **Iran** (2000, 2004) each won two gold medals in this class. When **women**'s weightlifting was added to the Olympic program in 2000, a super-heavyweight class was included. No woman has won more than one gold medal, but Agata Wrobel of **Poland** (silver 2000, bronze 2004) and Jang Mi-Ran of **Korea** (silver 2004, gold 2008) have each won two medals in this class.

SURFING. Surfing has never been on the **Olympic Program**, and it is unlikely that it will be, as surfing can only be contested at oceanside locations. However, the International Surfing Association was founded in 1976 and is recognized by the **International Olympic Committee**, with 85 affiliated members as of 2014, including Dubai, Hawaii, and Tahiti (all without a recognized **National Olympic Committee**). *See also* KAHANAMOKU, DUKE PAOA KAHINO MAKOE HULIKOHOA.

SURINAME (SUR). The South American country of Suriname (once known as Dutch Guiana and now officially the Republic of Suriname) has competed at 10 **Olympic Games** since its debut in 1968, missing only the 1980 Moscow Olympics but has not yet competed in the **Olympic Winter Games**. Through 2012, Suriname has entered 28 athletes (22 men, six **women**) and has taken part in five sports: **athletics** (nine men, three women), **badminton** (two men), **cycling** (one man), **judo** (three men), and **swimming** (seven men, three women). In 1960, Suriname sent one athlete to the Olympics, Wim Essajas, who was entered in the 800 meters but, after being told the **heats** were in the afternoon, slept through the heats, which were held that morning. One Surinamese athlete, Anthony Nesty, is responsible for both medals won at the Olympics by the South American country. A swimmer, Nesty won a gold medal in the 1988 100 meter **butterfly**, in a shocking upset over **Matt Biondi**, and a bronze medal in the same event in 1992. Nesty, who won in an Olympic record time, became the first black swimmer from any country to win a gold medal. Letitia Vreisde, a middle-distance runner, has participated in five Olympic Games from 1988 to 2004 but never got past the second **round** of either the women's 800 meters or 1,500 meters, although in both 1992 and 1996, she failed to qualify for the 800 meters final by less than one-tenth of a second. Several other Surinamese runners (Tommy Asinga, Eddy Monsels, Sammy Monsels, and Jurgen Themen) reached the second round of their events but did not advance further.

SVAN, GUNDE ANDERS (SWE–CCS). B. 12 January 1962, Vansbro, Dalarna, **Sweden**. Prior to the advent of **Norway's Bjørn Dæhlie** in the 1990s, Gunde Anders Svan was the most bemedaled international **cross-country skier** ever. Svan began his Olympic career in 1984, winning gold in the 15 km and **relay**, silver in the 50 km, and bronze in the 30 km. He returned to the Olympics to win gold in 1988 in the 50 km and in the relay, giving him six **Olympic medals** (four golds). Svan was World Cup champion five times—1984–1986 and 1988–1989—placing in the top three for eight consecutive years in 1983–1990. He won five individual World Championships: in 1989, the 15 km; in 1985 and 1991, the 30 km; and in 1985 and 1989, the 50 km. Overall the six-foot, two-inch (188 cm), 179 lb (81 kg) Svan won 372 of 615 races at the national and international levels from 1965 to 1991, won 30 World Cup races, and was Swedish national champion 16 times.

SWAHN, ALFRED GOMER ALBERT "ALF" (SWE–SHO). B. 20 August 1879, Uddevalla, Västra Götaland, **Sweden**. D. 16 March 1931, Stockholm, Sweden. Alf Swahn was the son of Oscar Swahn, who holds the record as the oldest medalist and gold medalist in Olympic history. Together, father and son competed in **shooting** for Sweden at the 1908, 1912, and 1920 **Olympic Games**. Alfred Swahn also competed again in 1924. Alfred won nine **Olympic medals**, including three golds, and is second only to **Carl Osburn** (USA), who won 11 shooting medals. Alf specialized in the running deer events and was certainly helped by the proliferation of shooting events on the **Olympic Program**, especially team events, in the era in which he competed. His Olympic medals were as follows: in 1908, running deer shooting (single-shot team; gold); in 1912, running deer shooting (single shot; gold), and running deer shooting (single-shot team; gold); in 1920, running deer shooting (single shot; silver), running deer shooting (double-shot team; silver), and **trap** shooting (team; bronze); in 1924, running deer shooting (single-shot team; silver), running deer shooting (double shot; bronze), and running deer shooting (double-shot team; bronze).

SWAZILAND (SWZ). The Southern African nation of Swaziland (officially the Kingdom of Swaziland) debuted at the 1972 **Olympic Games**, but did not attend the next two Games due to **boycotts**. Since 1984, it has been present at all editions, as well as at the 1992 **Olympic Winter Games**. In nine Summer Games, Swaziland has had a total of 41 entrants (34 men, seven

women) competing in **athletics** (18 men, four women), **boxing** (eight men), **shooting** (one man), **swimming** (four men, three women), **taekwondo** (one man), and **weightlifting** (two men). Although Swaziland has yet to win an **Olympic medal**, the country's best performances, by far, have occurred in the men's **marathon** run. Of the nine times Swaziland has entered the marathon, their runners have finished in the top half seven times, with one other runner finishing 51st of 100 entrants. The best Swazi marathoners have been Richard Mabuza, who was 17th of 74 entrants in 1972, and Sam Hlawe, who was 45th of 107 in 1984 and improved that to 44th of 118 in 1988. Their lone winter Olympian Keith Fraser finished 63rd of 131 entrants in the 1992 **giant slalom**, his best performance of the three **Alpine skiing** events he entered.

SWEDEN (SWE). With the exception of the 1904 St. Louis Olympics, the Northern European nation of Sweden (officially the Kingdom of Sweden) has competed at every **Olympic Games** and every **Olympic Winter Games**. It was one of the more successful competing nations at the Olympics until 1952, placing second in the medal rankings of 1912, 1920, and 1948. It is also one of the top countries at the Winter Games.

In 27 Summer Games, Sweden has entered 2,801 athletes (2,320 men, 481 **women**) and competed in 33 sports plus the **art competitions**. They have had the most entrants in **athletics** (463 men, 62 women), **swimming** (141 men, 114 women), **sailing** (219 men, 18 women), **shooting** (183 men, 12 women), **football** (119 men, 53 women), and **wrestling** (157 men, five women). It has won 498 medals in Summer sports (144 gold, 169 silver, 185 bronze) with medals in 24 different sports plus the art competitions. The most successful Swede at the Summer Olympics was shooter **Alf Swahn**, who won three medals of each color from 1908 to 1924. His father, Oscar Swahn, also won six medals from 1908 to 1920 and won his last medal, silver, in 1920 at the age of 72. He was the oldest competitor and oldest medalist at the Olympic Games in any sport. **Canoeist Gert Fredriksson** collected six gold, one silver, and one bronze medals between 1948 and 1960. He is the only Swedish Summer Olympian with six gold medals. Shooter Vilhelm Carlberg won eight medals (three gold, four silver, one bronze) from 1906 to 1924. **Kayaker Agneta Andersson** has the most medals won by a female Swedish Olympian with seven (three gold, two silver, two bronze from 1984 to 1996). **Eric Lemming** was a very versatile track and field athlete in the early 20th century. From 1900 to 1912, he won seven medals (four gold, three bronze) in the **javelin throw** (his specialty), **shot put**, ancient **pentathlon**, and **tug-of-war** and had fourth place finishes in the **high jump, pole vault, hammer throw**, stone throw, **discus throw**, and javelin throw with both hands. He also competed in **long jump, triple jump**, and standing long jump but did not medal.

In 22 Winter Games, Sweden has entered 902 athletes (679 men, 223 women) and competed in 14 sports: all except the **military ski patrol** and **skeleton**. They have had the most entrants in **ice hockey** (256 men, 61 women), **cross-country skiing** (103 men, 55 women), and **Alpine skiing** (43 men, 34 women). They have won 144 medals in Winter sports—50 gold, 40 silver, 54 bronze—and have medaled in 11 sports, with 74 of their medals coming in cross-country skiing.

Cross-country skier **Sixten Jernberg** won nine medals (four gold, three silver, two bronze) from 1956 to 1964. **Gunde Svan** also had four gold (and one silver, one bronze) in cross-country skiing in 1984 and 1988. Johan Olsen matched their total from 2006 to 2014 but only had two gold medals. Alpine skier **Anja Pärson** has six medals. Charlotte Kalla is the only other Swedish Winter sports athlete with five medals. The men's ice hockey team has won nine medals (two gold, three silver, four bronze) and has finished fourth six times and fifth six times. In five tournaments, the women's team has a silver and bronze medal and two fourth place results. In women's **curling**, Sweden has won four medals (two gold) in five tournaments, while the men have two medals and two fourth place finishes in six tournaments.

Stockholm, Sweden, hosted the Games of the Vth **Olympiad** in 1912. Stockholm also hosted the **Equestrian** Games of the XVIth Olympiad in 1956 when **Australia** was unable to hold the equestrian events in Melbourne because of the country's strict quarantine laws. Stockholm bid for the 2022 Winter Games but withdrew its bid two months later because of lack of political support. Sweden also bid to host the 2004 Summer Olympics (Stockholm) and the Winter Olympics of 1984 (Göteborg), 1988 (Falun), 1992 (Falun), 1994 (Östersund), 1998 (Östersund), and 2002 (Östersund), but these bids all failed. *See also* EDSTRÖM, JOHANNES SIGFRID; GRAFSTRÖM, GILLIS EMANUEL; HALL, LARS GÖRAN IVAR; JOHANSSON, IVAR VALENTIN; NORBERG, ANETTE CHARLOTTE; NORELIUS, MARTHA MARIA; SAINT CYR, HENRI JULIUS REVERONY; WESTERGREN, CARL OSCAR.

SWIMMING. Swimming is an ancient practice, because prehistoric people had to learn to swim in order to cross rivers and lakes. There are numerous references in Greek mythology to swimming, the most notable being that of Leander swimming the Hellespont (now the Dardenelle Straits) nightly to see his beloved Hero. Swimming as a sport probably was not practiced widely until the early 19th century. The National Swimming Society of **Great Britain** was formed in 1837 and began to conduct competitions. Most early swimmers used the **breaststroke** or a form of it. In the 1870s, British swimming instructor J. Arthur Trudgeon traveled to South America where he saw natives there using an alternate arm overhand stroke. He brought it back to

England as the famous trudgeon stroke, a crawl variant with a scissors kick. In the late 1880s, Englishman Frederick Cavill traveled to the South Seas, where he saw the natives there performing a crawl with a flutter kick. Cavill settled in **Australia**, where he taught the stroke, which became the famous Australian crawl.

Swimming has been held at every **Olympic Games**. The early events were usually only conducted in **freestyle** (crawl) or breaststroke. **Backstroke** was added later. In the 1940s, breaststrokers discovered they could go much faster by bringing both arms overhead together. This was banned in the breaststroke shortly thereafter, but then became the **butterfly** stroke, which is now the fourth stroke used in competitive swimming. **Women**'s swimming was first held at the 1912 Olympics. It has since been conducted at all the Olympics. In 28 Summer Games, there have been 8,183 participants (4,816 men, 3,367 women) from 193 nations who have competed in Olympic swimming.

The current program has events for men and women in freestyle, backstroke, breaststroke, butterfly, individual **medley**, and **relays**. Both men and women compete in freestyle over 50, 100, 200, and 400 meters. The long distance event for women is 800 meters and for men is 1,500 meters. Backstroke, breaststroke, and butterfly events are contested over both 100 and 200 meters. Individual medley is held at 200 and 400 meters. Men and women now compete in the same three relays: 4x100 meter freestyle relay, 4x100 meter medley relay, and 4x200 meter freestyle relay. Since 2008, two swimming events are also held outside the Olympic pool; both men and women compete in 10 km **open water** races. Both the **triathlon** and **modern pentathlon** also include a swimming competition as part of their events.

The **United States** has been by far the dominant nation in this sport at the Olympics. At various times, Australia, **Japan**, and previously the **German Democratic Republic** women have made inroads into that dominance. All of the top medal winners are American, however: **Michael Phelps** (18 gold, 22 total medals), **Natalie Coughlin**, **Dara Torres**, and **Jenny Thompson** with 12 medals each and **Mark Spitz**, **Matt Biondi**, and **Ryan Lochte** with 11 medals each. Phelps has won the most medals and most gold medals of any Olympian in any sport.

The governing body is the Fédération Internationale de Natation Amateur, which was formed in 1908 and had 203 member nations as of July 2014. *See also* BABASHOFF, SHIRLEY FRANCES; BERLIOUX, MONIQUE LIBOTTE; BLEIBTREY, ETHELDA MARGUERITE; COVENTRY, KIRSTY LEIGH; DANIELS, CHARLES MELDRUM; DE BRUIJN, INGE; EGERSZEGI, KRISZTINA; ENDER, KORNELIA; EVANS, JANET BETH; FRASER, DAWN LORRAINE; GOULD, SHANE ELIZABETH; GROSS, MICHAEL; HACKETT, GRANT GEORGE; HALMAY, IMRICH

ZOLTÁN VON; JAGER, THOMAS MICHAEL; KAHANAMOKU, DUKE PAOA KAHINO MAKOE HULIKOHOA; MATTHES, ROLAND; MEAGHER, MARY TERSTEGGE; MEYER, DEBORAH ELIZABETH; NABER, JOHN PHILLIPS; NORELIUS, MARTHA MARIA; O'NEILL, SUSAN; OTTO, KRISTIN; PEIRSOL, AARON WELLS; PERKINS, KIEREN JOHN; POPOV, ALEKSANDR VLADIMIROVICH; POUND, RICHARD WILLIAM DUNCAN; RADMILOVIC, PAOLO FRANCESCO; ROSE, IAIN MURRAY; SALNIKOV, VLADIMIR VALERYEVICH; SCHOLLANDER, DONALD ARTHUR; THOMAS, PETRIA ANN; VAN ALMSICK, FRANZISKA; WEISSMULLER, JOHNNY.

SWIMMING, UNDERWATER. *See* UNDERWATER SPORTS.

SWITZERLAND (SUI). The Central European country of Switzerland (officially known as the Swiss Confederation) first competed at the 1896 **Olympic Games**, when it was represented by Louis Zutter, a gymnast from Neuchâtel. Switzerland also competed at the first **Olympic Winter Games** in 1924 and was represented before that in 1920 at Antwerp in both the **figure skating** and **ice hockey** events. It has been represented at every Olympic Games and every Olympic Winter Games, one of only four countries to make this claim (**Great Britain, France**, and **Italy** are the others). It took part in the 1956 Summer Games **equestrian** competition in **Sweden** but did not have any athletes in 1956 in Melbourne. In 27 Summer Games, Switzerland has entered 1,805 athletes (1,546 men, 259 **women**) and taken part in 36 sports. The only Summer sports they did not take part in that were contested in more than three Olympic Games were **baseball, polo, rugby, softball, tug-of-war**, and **volleyball**. As with most countries, the sport with the most Swiss entrants was **athletics** (209 men, 55 women). Other popular Swiss sports have been **rowing** (166 men, four women), **cycling** (142 men, 21 women), **sailing** (103 men, seven women), and **shooting** (94 men, 13 women). They have won medals in 21 sports and through 2014 have a total of 202 in Summer Games (55 gold, 80 silver, 67 bronze). They have won at least one in every Olympic Games except for the 1908 Summer Games (when they only had one athlete) and 1964 Winter Games (a major disappointment as they entered 72 athletes in 10 sports).

From 1924 to 1936, Georges Mierz won eight medals in **gymnastics** (four gold, three silver, one bronze). His feat was matched by his teammate Eugen Mack, who also won eight medals in gymnastics from 1928 to 1936. He had two gold, four silver, and two bronze. In shooting, Konrad Stäheli won six medals from 1900 to 1906—four gold, one silver, and one bronze. His teammate during those years Louis Richardet also won six shooting medals but had five gold and one silver. Christine Stuckelberger, who competed in **dressage** in six Olympic Games over a period of 28 years from 1972 to 2000, won five medals—one gold, three silver, and one bronze. Gustav Fischer (three silver, two bronze) and Henri Chammartin (one gold, two silver, and two bronze) also each won five medals in dressage from 1952 to 1968.

Switzerland has really never been the dominant country in any sport. In the early Games, it had topnotch gymnasts. Until the **German Democratic Republic** became dominant, it was the top nation in **bobsledding** in the Winter Games. Most of its medals, however, have been won in **Alpine skiing**, where the Swiss have always belonged to the top nations. In 22 Winter Games, Switzerland is one of only three nations to have entered more than 1,000 athletes. It has entered 1,007 athletes (753 men, 254 women) and has competed in 15 of the 16 Winter Olympic sports, missing out only in **short-track speed skating**. They have won 138 medals (50 gold, 40 silver, 48 bronze) at the Winter Games. Their most decorated Winter Games' athletes are Alpine skier **Vreni Schneider**, winner of three gold, one silver, and one bronze from 1988 to 1994, and Fritz Feierabend, who won three silver and two bronze in bobsled competition from 1936 to 1952. Beat Hefti won four medals in bobsled from 2002 to 2014, with one silver and three bronze. **Ski jumper Simon Ammann** competed from 1998 to 2014 and won four gold medals, winning both **normal** and **large hill** events in both 2002 and 2010. In **cross-country skiing**, Dario Cologna has won three gold medals competing in 2010 and 2014. Hippolyte Kempf won three medals, one of each color, in the **Nordic combined** from 1988 to 1994.

St. Moritz, Switzerland, hosted the 2nd Olympic Winter Games in 1928 and the 5th Olympic Winter Games in 1948 and also was awarded the 1940 Winter Games that were not held due to World War II. Several Swiss towns have tried to host the Winter Games again (Davos and Engelberg in 1928; St. Moritz, 1936, 1960; Sion, 1976, 2002, 2006; Bern 2010) but never passed the bid stage. The city of **Lausanne**, home of the **International Olympic Committee** and site of the **Olympic Museum**, claims to be the "Olympic City" and has also unsuccessfully tried to host the Games on four occasions (1936, 1944, 1948, 1960). *See also* BLONAY, BARON GODEFROY JEAN HENRI LOUIS DE; FEDERER, ROGER; HODLER, MARC.

SYNCHRONIZED SWIMMING. Synchronized swimming is one of the few sports or **disciplines** that are contested only by **women** (**rhythmic gymnastics** and **softball** are the others). It is not considered a separate sport but rather a discipline of **swimming**, or technically **aquatics**, and as such is governed by the Fédération Internationale de Natation Amateur (FINA).

Synchronized swimming is a relatively new sport, with its origins dating to the beginning of the 20th century. Water show activities first received notice in the **United States** when Annette Kellerman (1886–1975), an **Australian** swimmer who toured the United States, performed her water **acrobatics** in a glass tank. Katherine Curtis was responsible for developing the sport in the United States after she began to experiment around 1915 with water figures who performed to musical accompaniment. Her students performed at the 1933–1934 Chicago "Century of Progress" Fair, where the announcer, former Olympic swimming gold medalist Norman Ross, coined the term "synchronized swimming."

American film star Esther Williams later popularized synchronized swimming when she performed water ballet in several American movies. The competitive aspect was developed about the same time when Frank Havlicek, a student of Curtis, drew up a set of rules. Synchronized swimming was recognized as a separate discipline of swimming by FINA in 1952. World Championships in synchronized swimming have been held since 1973, when FINA first established them. Synchronized swimmers compete at the World Championships in solo, **duet**, and team competition. Men are not allowed to compete at the international level, although they occasionally appear in national events.

At the Olympics, synchronized swimming was first held in 1984 with solo and duet events, and these events were also contested in 1988 and 1992. However, both events were discontinued in 1996 at Atlanta, replaced by an eight-person team event. Since 2000, the program has consisted of a duet and team event. In eight Summer Games, there have been 489 women from 46 countries who have participated in **Olympic Games** synchronized swimming.

Initially, the Olympic synchronized swimming events were dominated by the United States and **Canada** (winning all golds), but since 2000, all golds have been won by **Russian** swimmers. **Anastasiya Davydova** of Russia has won five gold medals, and her duet partner **Anastasiya Yermakova** has won four golds. **Japanese** swimmers Miya Tachibana and Miho Takeda have each also won five medals—four silver and one bronze.

SYNORIS. The *synoris* was a two-horse **chariot race** at the **Ancient Olympic Games**, lasting for eight circuits of the hippodrome (ca. 9,000 meters). Champions are known from 408 B.C. (Euagoras of Elis) through 60 B.C. (Menedernos of Elis). *See also APENE; KALPE; KELES; TETHRIPPON.*

SYRIA (SYR). The western Asian nation of Syria (officially the Syrian Arab Republic) sent one athlete to the 1948 **Olympic Games**. In 1960, the

United Arab Republic (UAR; **Egypt** and Syria) competed at Rome with 74 athletes. Syria was a member of the UAR at that time, but only three of the74 athletes were Syrian. Syria and Egypt split their political alliance in 1961, and Syria did not compete in the 1964 Olympic Games. It returned to the Olympic fold in 1968 and has since missed only 1976. It has yet to compete at an **Olympic Winter Games**. In 12 Summer Games, Syria has entered 129 athletes (118 men, 11 **women**) in 12 sports. The vast majority of their athletes (65 men, two women) were entered in the 1980 Moscow Olympic Games. Syria has competed in **athletics** (17 men, seven women), **boxing** (17 men), **cycling** (one man), **diving** (two men), **equestrian** (one man), **football** (15 men), **judo** (eight men), **shooting** (10 men, one woman), **swimming** (six men, two women), **triathlon** (one man), **weightlifting**, (eight men, one woman) and **wrestling** (32 men).

It has so far won three **Olympic medals**, the first in 1984 (Joseph Atiyeh, silver in **freestyle** wrestling), followed by Ghada Shouaa's gold in 1996 (women's **heptathlon**) and Naser El-Shami in 2004 (bronze, **heavyweight** boxing). Other notable performances by Syrian Olympians include Zouheir Shourbagi, 10th in 1948 **platform diving**, Samir El-Najjar, tied for seventh in 1980 men's **extra-lightweight** judo, Ahed Jougali, sixth in 2012 men's heavyweight weightlifting, and Talal Najjar, eighth in 1980 men's **super-heavyweight** weightlifting. Syria's best Olympic results were in the sport of wrestling. In 1980, Radwan Karout, a **Greco-Roman featherweight**, was seventh; Mohamed El-Oulabi, **middleweight**, was seventh in Greco-Roman and eighth in freestyle; and Abdel Nasser El-Oulabi, Greco-Roman **flyweight**, was eighth. In 1984, Mohamed Moutei Nakdali was sixth in the Greco-Roman **lightweight** class. In 1988, Greco-Roman **light-flyweight** Khaled El-Farej was fifth. In 1996, Ahmed Al-Aosta was eighth in light-weight freestyle class. For some reason, Syria has not competed in Olympic wrestling since 1996.

SZEWIŃSKA-KIRSZENSTEIN, IRENA (POL–ATH). B. 24 May 1946, Leningrad, **Russia**, USSR. With a total of seven **Olympic medals** in women's track and field, Irena Szewińska-Kirszenstein equaled the record of **Australian Shirley Strickland de la Hunty**, a record since broken only by **Jamaica's Merlene Ottey** and tied by Veronica Campbell-Brown (JAM). Irena won gold medals in the 4x100 meter **relay** (1964), the 200 meters (1968), and the 400 meters (1976), and she also won two silver and two bronze medals. Her Olympic career ended in 1980 when, in her fifth Games, she pulled up with a muscle strain in the semifinals of the 400 meters. The five-foot, nine-inch (176 cm), 132 lb (60 kg) Szewińska-Kirszenstein's tally of 13 world records includes her Olympic victories of 1968 (200 meters) and 1976 (400 meters), and at the European Championships she won 10 medals (five gold, one silver, and four bronze). Born to Polish parents in the Soviet city of Leningrad, she returned to **Poland** at an early age, and during an outstanding career, she set 38 Polish records. In 1967, she married her coach, Janusz Szewiński. In 1998, Irena Szewińska was co-opted as a member of the **International Olympic Committee.**

T

TABLE TENNIS. Table tennis was developed in the late 19th century, though its origins are not well documented. Several different sources for its invention are credited, but the modern game is said to have started with the introduction of the celluloid ball in around 1891. This development can be attributed to the Englishman James Gibb, a world-record–holding distance runner, who discovered the celluloid ball during a visit to America. This ensured the success of the game as a domestic pastime, initially known as Ping Pong, from which a competitive game emerged.

The sport is widely practiced throughout the world. However, it made an unusual entry into the **Olympic Program**. Table tennis made its Olympic debut as a full medal sport in 1988 at Seoul. It was never contested at the Olympics as a **demonstration sport**, which the **International Olympic Committee** then usually required of new sports. Men and **women** compete in four Olympic events, **singles** and **doubles** for men and women. In 2008, the doubles event was replaced by a three-player team event consisting of two singles and one doubles match. In seven Summer Games, there have been 666 participants (328 men, 338 women) from 98 countries in Olympic table tennis.

Since the late 1950s, the **Chinese** have been by far the dominant factor in table tennis and have won 24 of the 28 Olympic table tennis titles, with the remaining ones going to South **Korea** and **Sweden**. Chinese players have also won 15 silver and eight bronze medals. Three Chinese players have each won four titles, with **Wang Nan** being the only one to win an additional silver medal. Wang Hao of China also has five Olympic medals—two gold and three silver.

The Chinese dominance has in fact become a problem for the sport, with even many of the non-Chinese competitors having been born in China (and having changed allegiance for various reasons). The replacement of the doubles events by the team was intended to give other nations an opportunity to compete for the medals, although this has not happened, and China has won both men's and women's team events in 2008 and 2012.

The governing body of the sport is the International Table Tennis Federation, which was formed in 1926 and had 220 member nations as of 2014. *See also* ZHANG YINING.

TAEKWONDO. Taekwondo is a martial arts combat sport that originated in **Korea**. It is a fairly new sport, having been developed during the 1950s by the South Korean military. The Korean word *tae* means "to strike with the foot," the word *kwon* means "to strike with the hand," and the word *do* meaning "the way." Taekwondo first appeared on the Olympic stage in Korea as a **demonstration sport** at the 1988 Seoul **Olympic Games**. It reappeared as a demonstration in 1992, before being granted official status for the 2000 Games. The sport's **International Federation**, the World Taekwondo Federation, was recognized by the **International Olympic Committee** in 1973 and currently (as of 2014) has 206 members. In order to limit the number of total Olympic competitors, just four weight categories were contested per gender, whereas eight are held at World Championships. In four Summer Games, there have been 379 participants (193 men, 186 **women**) from 98 nations in Olympic taekwondo.

Hadi Saei of Iran (2000 bronze **featherweight**, 2004 gold featherweight, 2008 gold **welterweight**), **Steven Lopez** of the **United States** (2000 gold featherweight, 2004 gold welterweight, 2008 bronze welterweight), and Hwang Gyeong-Seon of Korea (women's welterweight 2004 bronze, 2008, 2012 gold) are the three athletes with the most medals in Olympic taekwondo.

TAHITI. *See* FRENCH POLYNESIA.

TAIWAN. *See* CHINESE TAIPEI.

TAJIKISTAN (TJK). As a former member of the **Soviet Union**, a few Tajikistani athletes competed from 1952 to 1988 for the Soviet Union. Tajikistani athletes were also present at Barcelona in 1992 as members of the Unified Team. The landlocked central Asian country of Tajikistan (officially known as the Republic of Tajikistan) made its Olympic debut as an independent nation in 1996 and has attended each Summer Games since.

Tajikistan has sent 38 athletes (28 men, 10 **women**) to the Summer Olympics and two men to the **Olympic Winter Games**. They have competed in 11 sports: **Alpine skiing** (two men), **archery** (two women), **athletics** (two men, three women), **boxing** (five men, one woman), **diving** (one man, one woman), **judo** (seven men), **shooting** (one man), **swimming** (two men, one woman), **taekwondo** (two men), **weightlifting** (one man), and **wrestling** (seven men, two women).

At the 2008 Beijing Games, the country won its first medals, with a silver medal in **light-heavyweight freestyle** wrestling for Yusuf Abdusalomov and a bronze in judo for Rasul Bokiyev in the **lightweight** class. In 2012, the Tajik lightweight boxer Mavzuna Choriyeva won a bronze medal in the inaugural women's Olympic boxing tournament.

Tajikistan first competed at the Olympic Winter Games in 2002 and has also had representation at each subsequent Winter Games. Andrey Drygin entered nine Alpine skiing events from 2002 to 2010, with a best result of 44th of 63 entrants in the **super G** of 2010. In 2014, Alisher Quadratov entered the **slalom** but did not complete the race. *See also* KIM, NELLYA VLADIMIROVNA.

TAMURA-TANI, RYOKO (JPN–JUD). B. 6 September 1975, Fukuoka Prefecture, **Japan**. One of history's most successful *judokas*, Ryoko Tamura-Tani is the only **judo** Olympian to have won five **Olympic medals**. After claiming a silver medal in Barcelona at age 16, the tiny Ryoko (just four feet, nine inches tall [146 cm], 109 lb [48 kg]) dominated the **extra-lightweight** division, winning World Championships in 1993, 1995, 1997, 1999, 2001, 2003, and 2007 (missing 2005 due to pregnancy). She suffered a shocking defeat in the 1996 Olympic final at the hands of Kye Sun-Hui (PRK), but claimed the gold in 2000 and 2004. Tamura was defeated in the semifinals in 2008, her first international defeat since 1996, and had to be satisfied with bronze. She has been married since 2003 to professional baseball player Yoshitomo Tani, who has also won two Olympic medals in that sport.

TANDEM. From 1906 to 1972, one of the **Olympic Games cycling** events was a 2,000 meter **sprint** race for tandem bicycles. Each bike held two riders, one behind the other, with two sets of handlebars and pedals. Teams from **France** won four of the 14 Olympic events. **Great Britain** teams won seven medals in this event—two gold, four silver, and one bronze.

TANGANYIKA. *See* TANZANIA.

TANZANIA (TAN). The southeastern African nation of Tanganyika sent three athletes to the 1964 **Olympic Games**. In late 1964, the former nations of Tanganyika and Zanzibar merged to form Tanzania. Tanzania (officially known as the United Republic of Tanzania) has competed at every Olympic Games since 1968, except in 1976. It has never competed at the **Olympic Winter Games**. In 12 Summer Games, Tanzania has entered 105 athletes (96 men, nine **women**) in only four sports, with the vast majority competing in **athletics** (49 men, eight women) and **boxing** (29 men). They also had 16 men in the 1980 **hockey** tournament, where they finished in sixth and last place and two men and one woman in **swimming**.

In 1980 at Moscow, Filbert Bayi won a silver medal in the **steeplechase**. In 1976, Bayi had been a cofavorite with **New Zealand**'s John Walker in the 1,500 meters, and the battle between the Tanzanian and the New Zealander was anticipated to be one of the great races in track history. It never occurred, as Tanzania joined the 1976 African **boycott** in protest against a New Zealand **rugby** team playing in **South Africa**. Tanzania's other Olympic medal also was won in 1980, when Suleiman Nyambui finished second in the 5,000 meters in track and field athletics.

Other notable Olympic Games result for Tanzania include, in athletics, Emmanuel Ndiemandoi, Gidamis Shahanga, and Leodigard Martin finished 14th, 15th, and 23rd of 74 entrants in the 1980 **marathon**, and Moses Luiga (800 meters, 1980), Zakariah Barie (5,000 meters, 1980, 1984), James Igohe (1,500 meters, 1984), and Samuel Mwera (800 meters, 2004) reached the semifinal **round** in their races. Barie was also 13th in the final of the 1984 10,000 meters. In 1984, marathoners Juma Ikangaa, Agapius Amo, and Gidamis Shahanga were sixth, 21st, and 22nd in their race of 107 entrants. Ikangaa also had a seventh place finish in the 1988 marathon and 34th in 1992. Andrew Sambu was 10th in the 1992 5,000 meter race, Marku Hhawu, 12th in the 1996 10,000 meter race, and Fabiano Joseph 10th in the 2004 10,000 meter race. In the 2008 10,000 meter race, three Tanzanian runners had good results—Fabiano Joseph, ninth, Dickson Mkami 14th, and Samwel Shauri 21st.

In boxing, Tanzania had several athletes reach the quarter-finals: **flyweight** Benjamin Mwangata and **lightweight** Rashi Ali Hadj Matumla in 1992, **super-heavyweight** Willie Isangura in 1984, and **bantamweight** Gerald Issaick, **light-welterweight** William Lyimo, and **light-middleweight** Leonidas Njunwa in 1980.

TARZAN AND THE OLYMPICS. Edgar Rice Burroughs's famous jungle character Tarzan has been featured in more than 50 films. Elmo Lincoln was the first to achieve fame in portraying Tarzan in films with his first appearance in 1918. The second actor chosen for Tarzan films was the **United States** Olympic champion **swimmer Johnny Weissmuller**. He made his feature film screen debut in 1932 in *Tarzan, the Ape Man*. This picture led to a series of a dozen Tarzan films produced throughout the 1930s and 1940s. Clarence Linden "Buster" Crabbe II became the next major Tarzan actor. Crabbe was also a former Olympic swimming champion and was signed by Paramount Studios to compete with MGM's Tarzan series featuring Weissmuller. Crabbe then left the Tarzan films and was featured in westerns as Billy the Kid and in science fiction films as Flash Gordon.

The 1928 Olympic **shot put** silver medalist Herman Brix was the next former Olympian to play Tarzan. He starred in a 1935 MGM film *The New*

Adventures of Tarzan. He had changed his name to Bruce Bennett when he became an actor, but capitalized on his Olympic success for this film and was billed under his real name. Brix had played college football at the University of Washington and appeared in the 1926 Rose Bowl. As Bruce Bennett, he appeared in more than 100 films and television series. He lived to the age of 100 and reportedly went skydiving at the age of 96.

Another Olympic champion who played Tarzan was the 1936 **decathlon** gold medalist Glenn Morris. He had a brief film career and only appeared in one Tarzan film, *Tarzan's Revenge* in 1938. He then briefly played professional football, enlisted in the U.S. Navy during World War II, and was wounded in combat.

The fifth Olympic champion with a Tarzan connection was Don Bragg. He was the 1960 **pole vault** gold medalist and was nicknamed "Tarzan," since one of his goals in life was to portray Tarzan in the movies. Reportedly after receiving the gold medal, he did the famous Tarzan yell from the podium. He twice was offered Tarzan film roles, but due to injury was unable to take advantage of the offers. He did get a chance to play Tarzan in a 1964 film called *Tarzan and the Jewels of Opar*, but the film was never released due to legal problems.

TAYLOR, CHRISTOPHER J. "CHRIS" (USA–WRE). B. 13 June 1950, Dowagiac, Michigan, **United States**. D. 30 June 1979, Story City, Iowa, United States. Chris Taylor would not be allowed to compete in the Olympic Games in the 21st century unless he went on a diet and lost more than 100 pounds. When he competed in the 1972 **Olympic Games' Greco-Roman** and **freestyle heavyweight wrestling** class, both classes were unlimited weight classes, and Taylor's 401 lb (182 kg) weight was acceptable on his six-foot, five-inch (196 cm) frame. In the Greco-Roman competition, Taylor was eliminated in the third round after being lifted off the ground in a suplex move and pinned by **Wilfried Dietrich** in his first round match. In the freestyle competition, Taylor won four of five matches and the bronze medal. In his one loss (to **Aleksandr Medved**), the referee felt sorry for Medved and penalized Taylor a point for stalling, although in fact it was Medved who should have received the penalty. The referee was later banned from international officiating. Despite his size, Taylor was a competent technical wrestler who twice won the National Collegiate Athletic Association championship while at Iowa State University. Taylor became a professional wrestler shortly after the Olympic Games, but he suffered from various health problems, and after wrestling about 250 matches from 1973 to 1977, he died at the age of 29.

TAYMAZOV, ARTUR BORISOVICH (UZB–WRE). B. 20 July 1979, Nogir, **Russia**, USSR. Artur Taymazov is one of just eight **wrestlers** to win four or more Olympic medals and is arguably the best **freestyle** wrestler in history. He has competed in the **super-heavyweight** freestyle class in each **Olympic Games** from 2000 to 2012. He was the runner-up in 2000 and silver medal winner, but in his next three Olympic tournaments was the champion and gold medalist. As a youth, he began competing in **weightlifting** along with his older brother Tymur. At the age of 11, Artur switched to wrestling when a wrestling club started in his hometown. Although born in Russia, Artur relocated to **Uzbekistan** when he realized he would not be able to make the Russian Olympic wrestling team. The six-foot, two-inch (190 cm), 265 lb (120 kg) wrestler competed for Uzbekistan in all four Olympic Games and is that country's most decorated Olympian. He is one of only four Uzbek Olympians to win a gold medal, and no other representative of that country has won more than one. At the World Championships, Taymazov won the super-heavyweight gold medal in 2003 and 2006, the silver medal in 2001 and 2010, and the bronze medal in 2007. His brother Tymur Taimazov is a world-class weightlifter who won the Olympic **heavyweight** I (100 kg) silver medal in 1992, competing for the Unified Team, and the gold medal in the heavyweight II (108 kg) class in 1996, representing the **Ukraine**.

TEAM HANDBALL. *See* HANDBALL (TEAM HANDBALL).

TELEVISION. Television is the method by which most of the world watches the **Olympic Games**. The rights fees paid by television networks are also critical to the continued success of the **Olympic Movement**, as they are the primary method of financing the Olympic Games and the activities of the **International Olympic Committee** (IOC). The Olympic Games were televised for the first time in 1936, but with only a few viewers in **Germany**. The next few **Olympiads** also saw Olympic Games telecast within the host country, but with no significant rights fees. Television first began worldwide broadcasts in 1960 at Rome, with most of Europe seeing the Games live, and the **United States** viewing them on tape delay. The rights fee paid by the U.S. host television network, Columbia Broadcasting System, was $395,000. By contrast, the National Broadcasting Company (NBC), which televised the 2004 Athens Olympic Games in the United States, paid $793 million for the rights to the Games. The rights fees for recent Games were as follows: 2000 Sydney, U.S. $715 million and worldwide $1.338 billion; 2002 Salt Lake City, U.S. $545 million and worldwide $738 million; 2004 Athens, U.S. $793 million and $1.498 worldwide billion; 2006 Torino, U.S. $613 million and worldwide $832 million; 2008 Beijing, U.S. $894 million and worldwide $1.715 billion; and 2010 Vancouver, U.S. $820 million and worldwide $1.187

billion. In 2011, NBC signed a $4.38 billion contract with the IOC for the rights to telecast the 2014, 2016, 2018, and 2020 Olympics.

Although only one country was able to watch the Olympic Games of 1936, 1948, and 1956 on television, 21 nations watched the 1960 Olympics on television, and that number increased to over 200 for the 2004 Olympics. It was estimated that the gross cumulative television audience for the 2000 Olympics was 36.1 billion people, and the average broadcast minute of the Beijing Games (2008) was viewed by 114.3 million people. *See also* RADIO AND TELEVISION COMMISSION; TV RIGHTS AND NEW MEDIA COMMISSION.

TENNIS. Tennis, originally lawn tennis, was designed and patented by Major Walter Wingfield, a British army officer, in 1873 using the name "sphairistike." However, tennis variants are much older than that. Court tennis, or royal tennis, real tennis, or *jeu de paume*, was known to have been played in the Middle Ages.

Tennis was contested at every **Olympic Games** from 1896 through 1924 as a regular medal sport, with **women**'s tennis added in 1900. The first tournament in 1896 was interesting in that in order to fill out the field, athletes were recruited from other sports to enter the tennis competition. Third place in tennis went to Momcsilló Tapavicza, a **Serbian wrestler** and **weightlifter**, and Teddy Flack, an **Australian** who won gold in the 800 and 1,500 meter runs. Track and field athletes Fritz Traun (GER) and George Stuart Robertson (GBR) also participated in tennis that year.

In 1908 and 1912, there were both indoor and outdoor tennis events. After 1924, the sport was discontinued at the Olympic Games, although it was on the schedule as a **demonstration sport** in 1968 and 1984. The reasons for dropping tennis as an Olympic sport probably were that the **International Olympic Committee** was upset that many of the top tennis players, though considered amateurs, infringed upon its strict definition of amateurism, and that the tennis establishment, especially in **Great Britain**, was concerned that the Olympic events might become more important than Wimbledon and did not want that to occur.

Tennis returned to the Olympics as a full medal sport in 1988, as it became possible for full-scale professionals to play in the Olympics, with no other restrictions. Initially not all top players attended the Olympic Games, as they considered it of less importance than, or found it interfering with, their preparation for the **United States** Open Grand Slam tournament, which is usually held around the same time. In recent years this has no longer been the case, and many tennis professionals regard the Olympic Games with the same respect they have for the four so-called major tennis tournaments—Australian, French,

U.S., and Wimbledon. The 2012 London Olympic tournament included all the top players, and the highlight (especially for the British fans) was the Scotsman Andy Murray winning the men's **singles** by defeating **Roger Federer** in the event held at the famed Wimbledon courts.

In 15 Summer Games, there have been 1,137 participants (698 men, 439 women) from 88 nations in Olympic tennis. **Max Décugis** of **France** has won six medals (four gold, one silver, and one bronze from 1900 to 1920). Sisters **Serena** and **Venus Williams** have also each won four gold medals—one each in singles and three as **doubles** partners.

There have recently been four Olympic events, singles and doubles for both men and **women**, while **mixed doubles** was held in London 2012 for the first time since 1924. The governing body of the sport is the International Tennis Federation, which was founded in 1913 and had 210 members in July 2010. *See also* DOHERTY, REGINALD FRANK.

TETHRIPPON. The *tethrippon* was a four-horse **chariot race** at the **Ancient Olympic Games** that was contested over 12 laps of the hippodrome (ca. 14,000 meters). Champions are known from 680 B.C. (Pagondas of Thebes) through A.D. 241 (Titus Domitius Prometheus of Athens). Euagoras of Sparta was the only three-time champion in this event (548–540 B.C.). *See also APENE; KALPE; KELES; SYNORIS.*

THAILAND (THA). The Southeast Asian nation of Thailand, officially known as the Kingdom of Thailand and formerly called Siam, has competed in the Olympics since 1952. Thailand has missed only the 1980 Moscow **Olympic Games**, which it **boycotted**. In 15 Summer Games, Thailand has entered 422 athletes (321 men, 101 **women**) and participated in 20 sports. The four main sports with Thai Olympic participation have been **athletics** (67 men, 35 women), **boxing** (62 men), **shooting** (48 men, 11 women), and **weightlifting** (15 men, 14 women). Thai athletes have won 24 Olympic medals: seven gold, six silver, and 11 bronze. Although their national sport of Thai boxing (known as Muay-Thai) is not an Olympic sport, "normal" boxing has been the top sport for Thai Olympians, who collected a total of 14 medals in the sport. In recent Games, female weightlifters from Thailand have also won seven medals—three gold, one silver, and three bronze. Thailand's other three Olympic medals have come in **taekwondo**—one silver and two bronze—all in the women's **flyweight** class.

Light-welterweight boxer Manus Boonjumnong (gold 2004, silver 2008) is the only Thai athlete with more than one Olympic medal. Other Thai boxers who won gold medals are flyweight Wijan Ponlid (2000) and Somjit Jongjohor (2008) and **featherweight** Somluck Kamsing (1996).

Thai weightlifters who won gold medals are **heavyweight** Pawina Thong-suk (2004) and featherweights Udomporn Polsak (2004) and Prapawadee Jaroenrattanatarakoon (2008).

Thailand has also competed in the **Olympic Winter Games** in 2002, 2006, and 2014. In 2002 and 2006, Prawat Nagvajara entered three **cross-country skiing** races and had a best finish of 66th of 71 entrants in 2002. In 2014, two Thai skiers entered **Alpine skiing**. Kanet Sucharitakul was 65th of 107 entrants in the men's **giant slalom** race in which 72 skiers completed the course. He also entered the **slalom** but failed to complete that race. Vanessa-Mae Vanakorn, a world-famous violinist, entered the women's giant slalom and was 67th and last but ahead of 22 skiers who did not complete the race.

Bangkok, Thailand, made an unsuccessful bid to host the 2008 Summer Games.

THEAGENES OF THASOS (GRE–BOX/WRE). Fl. 480–460 B.C. Theagenes is credited with more than 1,400 victories in various sporting festivals in ancient **Greece**. He won at Olympia in 480 B.C. in **boxing** and in 476 B.C. in the **pankration**. He and Kleitomachos of Thebes are the only two athletes to have won the boxing and pankration at Olympia. The Thasians erected a statue to Theagenes in the town. A former athlete who hated Theagenes attacked the statue one night, and it fell on him and killed him. The Thasians followed Draconian law and threw the statue into the sea. A great drought fell upon the island of Thasos and crops suffered, with many animals dying as a result. The oracle at Delphi told the people this could be corrected by bringing back to the country all its exiles. They did this, but the drought and famine continued. They then consulted the wise Pythia at Delphi, who told them, "You have forgotten your great Theagenes, whom you threw in the sand, where he now lies, though before he won a thousand prizes." Several Thasian fishermen hauled the statue back in their nets; it was re-erected in its former position and the drought ended. Later the Thasians sacrificed to Theagenes as a hero of healing. *See also* ANCIENT OLYMPIC GAMES.

THOMAS, PETRIA ANN (AUS–SWI). B. 25 August 1975, Lismore, New South Wales, **Australia**. Primarily a **butterfly swimmer**, Petria Thomas has overcome major shoulder injuries to become one of the top butterflyers ever. Thomas first competed at the **Olympic Games** in 1996, winning a silver medal in the 200 butterfly. At Sydney in 2000, she won three medals, bronze in the 200 butterfly and silvers in two relays. Her best Olympic performance was in Athens, when she won four medals, including three golds. She also won her first individual gold medal in the 100 butterfly, adding gold in the 400 free **relay** and the **medley** relay. In 10 Olympic races, the five-foot, eight-inch (173 cm), 141 lb (64 kg) swimmer medaled in eight and finished fourth in the other two. Thomas's best meet may have been the 2001 World Championships, when she won three gold medals, including both the 100 and 200 butterfly and the medley relay. In 2002, she became the first swimmer to win the same event at three consecutive **Commonwealth Games**, when she won the 200 butterfly in Manchester, **England**. Thomas has accomplished this despite having suffered numerous shoulder dislocations, which have required surgery on both shoulders.

THOMPSON, FRANCIS MORGAN "DALEY" (GBR–ATH). B. 30 July 1958, Notting Hill, London, **England**. Daley Thompson shares with **Bob Mathias** the distinction of successfully defending an Olympic **decathlon** title. Thompson won his gold **Olympic medals** in 1980 and 1984, setting his fourth and final world record at the Los Angeles Games. In 1988 in Seoul, he nearly became the first man to win three medals in the decathlon as he finished fourth. The six-foot (184 cm), 203 lb (92 kg) Thompson also competed in the 1976 Summer Games and is one of only four decathletes to have taken part in four **Olympic Games**. (Georg Werthner of **Austria** [1976–1988], Erki Nool of **Estonia** [1992–2004], and Roman Šebrle of the **Czech Republic** [2000–2012] are the others.) Thompson was also the World (1983), European (1982, 1986), and British Commonwealth (1978, 1982, 1986) champion. He set four world records in the decathlon.

THOMPSON, JENNIFER BETH "JENNY" (USA–SWI). B. 26 February 1973, Danvers, Massachusetts, **United States**. With 12 medals (eight golds), Jenny Thompson has won more **swimming** medals and gold medals than any **woman** in Olympic history. But all eight of her gold medals were for **relays**, and this immensely talented swimmer was frustrated in her attempt to win an individual Olympic gold medal. Her only individual medals were a silver in the 1992 100 meter **freestyle** and a bronze in the same event in 2000. Twenty-three times a national champion, she was more successful individually at the World Championships, winning the 100 meter freestyle and 100 **butterfly** at the 1998 World Championships. At the other major international event, the Pan-Pacifics, the five-foot, nine-inch (177 cm), 152 lb (69 kg) Thompson also won the 50 meter freestyle four times (1989, 1991, 1993, 1999), the 100 meter freestyle four times (1993–1999), and the 100 meter flystyle three times (1993, 1997–1999). Among all female Olympians, Thompson's eight gold medals are surpassed only by **Larysa Latynina**'s nine. Thompson seemingly retired after the 2000 Olympics and attended medical school at Columbia University, but she returned to competition and won two silver medals in relays at Athens in 2004.

THORPE, JAMES FRANCIS "JIM" (né **WA-THO-HUCK** [**Sac-and-Fox Indian name meaning "BRIGHT PATH"**]) (USA–ATH). B. 28 May 1888, Bellemont, Oklahoma, **United States**. D. 28 March 1953, Lomita, California, United States. Jim Thorpe is often described as the greatest all-around athlete in history. The accolade is well merited when judged by his superiority over his contemporaries. At the 1912 **Olympic Games**, he won the **pentathlon** and **decathlon** by huge margins, setting world records in both events. The following year, his name was struck from the roll of Olympic champions after it was revealed that he had earlier been paid for playing minor league **baseball**. The amount involved was a minuscule U.S. $15 per week, but it was not until 1982 that the **International Olympic Committee**

Jim Thorpe, the greatest all-around athlete of all time and winner of the pentathlon and decathlon at the 1912 Olympic Games. Courtesy of Erich Kamper

reversed its decision and, after an interval of 70 years, the medals were returned, posthumously, to the family of their rightful owner. Part French and Irish and part Sac-and-Fox Indian, Thorpe attended Carlisle Indian School, where he established an awesome reputation as a **football (American)** player, being voted All-American in 1911 and 1912.

The six-foot tall (183 cm), 190 lb (86 kg) Thorpe later played Major League Baseball for the New York Giants, Boston Braves, and Cincinnati Reds. He also played professional American football for the Canton Bulldogs and in 1920–1921 was named the president of the fledgling American Professional Football Association (APFA), the forerunner of today's National Football League (NFL), while also playing for Canton. The APFA presidency was primarily a nominal one and was instituted by the new league to attempt to capitalize on Thorpe's name. He was replaced after one year by Joseph Carr, a proper sports administrator, but continued to play professional football for most of the decade, including a two-year stint with the Oorang Indians, an all Native American NFL team.

THREE-DAY EVENT. The three-day event (also known as eventing or horse trials) consists of a rider and horse displaying their combined abilities in three **equestrian** contests—**dressage**, **cross-country** riding, and show **jumping**. It has been included in the **Olympic Games** program since 1912 and is occasionally contested over four days, with dressage being held on the first two days. From 1912 to 1960, the competition was limited to men, but since 1964, it has been a mixed event with both men and **women** taking part. As of 2012, no woman has won an Olympic gold medal in this event, although several have won silver or bronze medals. HRH Princess Anne of **Great Britain** was one of the contestants in this event in 1976. Mark Todd of **New Zealand** is the only repeat gold medalist (1984, 1988) in the Olympic three-day event. He also won a bronze medal in 2000 to become the only three-time medalist as well.

THUNBERG, ARNOLD CLAS ROBERT (FIN–SSK). B. 5 April 1893, Helsinki, Uusimaa, **Finland**. D. 28 April 1973, Helsinki, Uusimaa, Finland. Clas Thunberg's record of five Olympic gold medals for men's **speed skating** was equaled by **Eric Heiden** in 1980 but has never been bettered. In 1924, Thunberg won the 1,500 meters, the 5,000 meters, and the **combined** event, placed second in the 10,000 meters, and placed third in the 500 meters. Four years later, the five-foot, six-inch (167 cm), 148 lb (67 kg) skater won the 500 meters and successfully defended his 1,500 meters crown. Further Olympic honors seemed likely at the 1932 Games but, like many leading European skaters, Thunberg refused to compete at Lake Placid as a protest against the **mass start** style of racing. An unusual character, he made his World Championship debut in 1922 at the age of 28, and his final appearance was in 1935, at age 42. During this period, he missed three championships (1926, 1930, 1935) but still won 14 individual titles and was the overall champion five times. Thunberg set five world records, the last in 1931 at the age of 38. He later became a member of the Finnish parliament.

TIKHONOV, ALEKSANDR IVANOVICH (URS–BIA). B. 2 January 1947, Uyskoye, Chelyabinsk Oblast, **Russia**, USSR. During his Olympic **biathlon** career, which ran from 1968 to 1980, Aleksandr Tikhonov won five medals, of which four were gold. All of his gold medals, however, were won as a member of the winning **Soviet relay** teams, four times consecutively. Until 2014, he was the only athlete to have won a gold medal in the same event at four consecutive **Olympic Winter Games**, but in 2014, the Canadian **women's ice hockey** team won for the fourth consecutive time and team members **Hayley Wickenheiser**, **Jayna Hefford**, and Caroline Ouellette each matched Tikhonov's feat. To his team gold medals, the five-foot, eight-inch (173 cm), 146 lb (66 kg) Tikhonov added a silver medal in the 20 km in the 1968 individual event. He also finished fourth in that event in 1972 and fifth in 1976. At the World Championships, he won individual titles in 1969–1970 and 1973 in the 20 km and the 10 km in 1977. Tikhanov won a further six relay gold medals at the World Championships, giving him a total of 13 biathlon gold medals at the Olympic and World Championships.

TIME TRIAL. A time trial is a type of **cycling** event in which cyclists ride a fixed course individually and the rider with the shortest elapsed time is the champion. Time trial events have been held in the **Olympic Games** for individuals as well as teams. In team events, usually four riders to a team, the combined times for individual racers are added to determine the winning team. From 1928 to 2004, the men's Olympic cycling time trial was a 1,000 meter race. No man won this race more than once, and Niels Frebourg of **Denmark** won three medals in this event (gold 1972, silver 1968, bronze 1976). From 1996 to 2012, the men's Olympic individual time trial has been conducted over a race course of approximately 25 miles (40 km). Vyacheslav Yekimov of **Russia** won this race in both 2000 and 2004 and is the only multiple medalist. An Olympic cycling women's time trial has also been held over a road course (about 30 km [18 miles]) from 1996 to 2012, and Kristin Armstrong (2008, 2012) of the **United States** and **Leontien Zijlaard-van Moorsel** of the **Netherlands** (2000, 2004) have each won it twice.

TIMOR LESTE (TLS). Timor is an island in the Lesser Sunda Islands, a portion of the **Indonesian** archipelago, south of Sulawesi. The island was controlled by the Portuguese for 400 years and was known as Portuguese Timor, but in the 20th century, it was divided into a Portuguese half (East) and an Indonesian half (West). In 1975, Indonesia invaded East Timor and seized it, but a separatist movement developed almost immediately. On 30 August 1999, East Timor was allowed to vote in a referendum, and 79 percent of the population opted to secede from Indonesia. Rioting and violence ensued when Indonesia refused to allow this, and United Nations' forces entered East Timor on 12 September 1999. In early 2000, East Timor was granted provisional independence by Indonesia.

East Timor first competed at the **Olympic Games** in 2000 at Sydney, although not under that name. The **International Olympic Committee** (IOC) allowed athletes from East Timor to compete under the designation of **independent Olympic athletes** (IOA). Four athletes represented East Timor at Sydney: three men (one each in **athletics, boxing,** and **weightlifting**) and one woman in athletics. East Timor was recognized by the IOC at the 115th **IOC Session** in Prague on 3 July 2003. At Athens in 2004, East Timor, officially known as the Democratic Republic of Timor Leste, was represented by two athletes, one man and one woman in track and field athletics, while in Beijing in 2008, one female track and field athlete represented the nation. In London in 2012, again one East Timorese male and one female athlete entered. All competed in the **marathon** only, with one finisher, Aguida Fatima Amaral, placing 65th in 2004 of 66 women who completed the race ahead of 16 others who failed to last the distance. She had also competed in 2000 as an IOA and was 43rd of 45 finishers. In 2014, Timor Leste had its first **Olympic Winter Games** entrant, a native Frenchman with dual citizenship. Yohan Gonçalves completed both of his slalom runs and finished in 43rd place, last of all skiers who completed both runs but ahead of 34 others who were unable to negotiate both runs successfully.

TOGO (TOG). Togo debuted at the 1972 **Olympic Games**. It then missed the 1976 and 1980 editions because of **boycotts,** but has since attended all Games with a total of 36 participants (32 men, four **women**) in eight sports: **athletics** (15 men, three women), **boxing** (eight men), **canoeing** (one man), **cycling** (five men), **judo** (one man), **swimming** (one woman), **table tennis** (one man), and **tennis** (one man). The West African nation, officially known as the Togolese Republic, won its first **Olympic medal** in 2008, when Benjamin Boukpeti won a surprise bronze medal in the K-1 **kayak slalom** canoeing event. He also finished 10th of 22 entrants in that event in 2012. Togo's results in other events were unimpressive, although two of their **sprinters** and one of the Togolese sprint **relay** teams advanced to the second **round** but not further. Togo competed at the **Olympic Winter Games** in 2014 for the first time with two female entrants—Alessia Afi Dipol in **Alpine skiing** (55th of 90 entrants in **giant slalom**) and Mathilde Amivi Petitjean in **cross-country skiing** (68th of 75 entrants in the 10 k classic).

TOMBA, ALBERTO (ITA–ASK). B. 19 December 1966, San Lazzaro di Savena, Bologna, **Italy.** An **Alpine skiing** gold **Olympic medalist** in the **slalom** and **giant slalom** in 1988, Alberto Tomba successfully defended his giant slalom title in 1992, when he also took the silver medal in the slalom. At his third **Olympic Winter Games** in 1994, the five-foot, 11-inch (182 cm), 203 lb (92 kg) Tomba placed second in the slalom, giving him a total of five Olympic medals, which was a record at that time (since surpassed by **Janica Kostelić** and **Kjetil André Aamodt**). In his fourth Winter Games in 1998, he failed to complete the course in both slalom and giant slalom. Surprisingly, in view of his Olympic successes, he had a poor record at the World Championships, where he won a solitary bronze medal in 1987. In contrast, he enjoyed a superb record in the World Cup, winning the slalom in 1988, 1992, and 1994–1995; the giant slalom in 1988, 1991–1992, and 1995; and the overall title in 1995. A flamboyant, dashing character both on and off the slopes, he was the idol of the Italian sporting public, to whom he was known as "La Bomba."

TONGA (TGA). The South Pacific island nation of Tonga first competed at the 1984 **Olympic Games** and has attended all subsequent editions. It first competed at the **Olympic Winter Games** in 2014 when Bruno Banani entered the **luge** and finished 32nd of 39 contestants. In eight Summer Games, Tonga had had 31 entrants (28 men, three **women**) who competed in **athletics** (eight men, three women), **boxing** (13 men), **weightlifting** (four men), and one man in each of **archery**, **judo**, and **swimming**. Officially known as the Kingdom of Tonga, the country's one **Olympic medal** to date was won in 1996, when boxer Paea Wolfgramm finished second in the **super-heavyweight** class. Wolfgramm won three bouts but was defeated by 7–3 decision in the final by future professional world **heavyweight** champion Wladimir Klitschko of the **Ukraine.** Three other Tongan boxers won their first bout but lost their second one. Other notable Tonga Olympic Games performances include Ana Siulolo Liku, who was 28th of 47 in the women's **long jump** in 1996, Homelo Vi, who was 26th of 36 in the 1992 **decathlon**, and weightlifter Tevita Kofe Ngaulu, who was 13th of 21 entrants in the heavyweight class in 2000.

TOP (THE OLYMPIC PARTNERS). *See* OLYMPIC PARTNERS, THE.

TORRES, DARA GRACE (USA–SWI). B. 15 April 1967, Beverly Hills, California, **United States**. Dara Torres has had the longest successful career of any Olympic **swimmer**, one that has seen her win 12 **Olympic medals** (four gold, four silver, and four bronze). She is the only Olympian to win exactly four medals of each color and one of only three to win at least four of each color (**Larysa Latynina** [URS] and **Takashi Ono** [JPN] are the others). Torres began her career in 1984, winning a gold medal in the 4x100 meter **freestyle relay**. She added a silver and bronze in relays in 1988 and seemingly ended her swimming career with another gold in the 4x100 meter freestyle relay in 1992. Tall and strikingly attractive, Torres then began a career as a model, becoming the first athlete to appear in *Sports Illustrated*'s swimsuit issue. She also achieved notice as a commercial spokeswoman on an infomercial for a fitness training method. But in late 1998, she elected to return to competitive swimming. With seemingly little time to prepare, she returned to the Olympic pool at Sydney and won five medals, including two golds in relays. The six-foot (183 cm), 150 lb (68 kg) Torres won three individual bronze medals at Sydney, in the 50 meter freestyle, the 100 meter freestyle, and the 100 meter **butterfly**. Torres appeared to retire, but in 2008 she qualified for her fifth Olympics, becoming one of the oldest competitors in the sport at age 41. In the pool, she added three silver medals to her Olympic tally, placing second in the 50 meter freestyle and the 4x100 meter freestyle and **medley** relays. In 2012, she just missed out in qualifying for the U.S. Olympic team at age 45.

TORVILL, JAYNE. *See* TORVILL AND DEAN.

TORVILL AND DEAN (GBR–FSK). Jayne Torvill (later Christensen), B. 7 October 1957, Nottingham, **England**, and Christopher Colin Dean, B. 27 July 1958, Nottingham, England. The **ice dance** partnership of Jayne Torvill (five feet, two inches [160 cm], 106 lb [48 kg]) and Christopher Dean (five feet, 10 inches [180 cm], 161 lb [73 kg]) produced one of the legendary performances in Olympic history. Their interpretation of Ravel's "Bolero" at the 1984 **Olympic Winter Games** in Sarajevo drew the maximum score of 6.0 for artistic impression on all nine judges' scorecards. They were clear winners of the gold **Olympic medal** and set a new standard against which ice dancing was to be judged in the future. Only four weeks later, they repeated their own superlative Olympic performance to win their fourth consecutive world title. A successful and lucrative professional career followed, but after their Olympic eligibility had been restored, they took the bronze medal at the 1994 Olympic Winter Games, having earlier won the 1994 European title. Dean has twice been married to **figure skating** world champions, first to Isabelle Duchesnay, **French pairs** world champion (1991), and later to the 1990 world ladies' champion, Jill Trenary (USA).

TRAA, KARI (NOR–FRS). B. 28 January 1974, Voss, Hordaland, **Norway**. Kari Traa has won more medals in Winter Olympics **freestyle skiing** than anyone else—male or female. She specializes in **moguls** skiing and has won a gold, silver, and bronze in that event. She entered her first **Olympic Winter Games** in 1992 and finished 14th. After missing the 1994 Winter Games in her homeland due to a knee injury, she finished third in 1998, won the gold medal in 2002, and the silver medal in 2006. At the World Championships, she won four gold and three silver medals from 1999 to 2005 and has won 37 World Cup events. In 2002, the five-foot, six-inch (168 cm), 143 lb (65 kg) skier began her own sportswear company.

TRACK AND FIELD. *See* ATHLETICS.

TRAMPOLINING. After the Fédération Internationale de Trampoline managed to get its sport on the **Olympic Program** for the Sydney 2000 Games, the governing body became part of the Fédération Internationale de Gymnastique, which also governs acrobatic and rhythmic **gymnastics**. At the Olympics, only an individual event (one for men and one for **women**) is contested. In four Games, there have been a total of 73 athletes (38 men, 35 women) from 22 countries who have participated in Olympic trampolining. **Karen Cockburn** of **Canada** won a medal at each of the first three Olympics in which the sport was contested, earning two silvers and one bronze medal. Chinese female trampoliners He Wenna (2008 gold, 2012 bronze) and Huang Shanshan (2004 bronze, 2012 silver) have each won two medals. Among the men, Aleksandr Moskalenko (RUS) was the first champion in the sport to win more than one medal, adding a silver in 2004 to his gold medal in the 2000 Games. Lu Chunlong (2008 gold, 2012 bronze) and Dong Dong (2008 bronze, 2012 gold), both of **China**, also have won two Olympic medals.

TRAP. Trap **shooting** is a form of shooting competition in which a target is thrown into the air by a mechanical device and the shooter must hit the target to be successful. The original targets were live birds, but in modern-day competition, clay disks are used instead. Men's trap shooting has been included on the **Olympic Program** 14 times (1900, 1908, 1912, 1920, 1924, 1952–1964, and 1996–2012). From 1968 to 1992, the Olympic trap shooting contest was open to either men or **women**. Michael Diamond of the **United States** is the only two-time gold medalist (1996–2000), and Giovanni Pellielo of **Italy** (silver medal 2004, 2008, bronze 2000) is the only three-time medalist in men's

Olympic trap shooting. Luciano Giovannetti of Italy also won two gold medals in 1980 and 1984 when the event was also open to women. Women's trap shooting has been included in the Summer Olympics since 2000, with Zuzana Štefečeková of **Slovakia** (silver 2008, 2012) and Delphine Racinet-Reau of **France** (silver 2000, bronze 2012) the only dual medalists.

TRETYAK, VLADISLAV ALEKSANDROVICH (URS–ICH). B. 25 April 1952, Orudyevo, Moscow Oblast, **Russia**, USSR. Of the six men's **ice hockey** players to have won three gold **Olympic medals**, Vladislav Tretyak is the only one to have added a silver medal to his collection. Recognized as one of the greatest goalkeepers of all time, he won Olympic gold in 1972, 1976, and 1984 and silver in 1980, when the **United States** defeated the **Soviets** in a major upset. In an inexplicable move, Tretyak was replaced to begin the second period of the 1980 game with the United States, and the United States went on to win the game dubbed "the Miracle on Ice." The six-foot, one-inch (185 cm), 174 lb (79 kg) Tretyak was also on the winning team at nine World Championships, and his talents attracted the attention of many National Hockey League (NHL) clubs. The Montreal Canadiens drafted him, but the authorities in the USSR refused to let him play abroad, although he later coached the NHL Chicago Black Hawks' goaltenders. Tretyak enjoyed the distinction of being the first Soviet player in the Hockey Hall of Fame. In 2014, he was given the honor of lighting the **Olympic flame** along with **Irina Rodnina** during the opening ceremony at the Sochi **Olympic Winter Games**.

TRIATHLON. Triathlon is a relatively new sport that consists of **swimming**, **cycling**, and running. Its origins date to the 1970s, when the first major triathlon, the Ironman Race, was held in Hawaii. Triathlon is governed by the International Triathlon Union, which was recognized by the **International Olympic Committee** in 1989, currently (as of 2014) with 150 member nations. Triathlon first appeared on the **Olympic Program** at the 2000 **Olympic Games**, with two events, one for men and one for **women**. In four Olympic Games, there have been 297 athletes (145 men, 152 women) from 48 nations who have participated in triathlon.

The Olympic triathletes race over what was already known as the "**Olympic distance**": 1,500 meter swim, 40 km cycling, and 10 km running, which is the same for both men and women. Canadian **Simon Whitfield**, who has competed in four Olympic triathlons from 2000 to 2012, is the most successful Olympic triathlete, with one gold in 2000 and one silver medal in 2008. **Bevan Docherty** of **New Zealand** also has two triathlete medals, silver in 2004 and bronze in 2008. No female triathlete has more than one **Olympic medal**.

TRINIDAD AND TOBAGO (TRI). The Caribbean island nation of Trinidad and Tobago (officially the Republic of Trinidad and Tobago), located just north of South America, has competed continuously at the **Olympic Games** since its debut in 1948, competing only as Trinidad through 1956 and in 1964. In 1960, it had one **cyclist** and one track and field athlete competing in a combined team with **Jamaica** and **Barbados** under the name of the **West Indies Federation**, termed the Antilles by the Rome organizing committee. Though the West Indies Federation won two medals, no Trinidadian athlete was a medal winner in 1960. In 16 Summer Games (not including 1960), Trinidad has entered 153 athletes (123 men, 30 **women**) in 10 sports, with the vast majority of them competing in **athletics** (79 men, 23 women). Cycling (19 men), **swimming** (five men, five women), and **sailing** (six men) have been the next three most popular sports, and **boxing**, **shooting**, **weightlifting** (four men each), **taekwondo** (one man, one woman), **badminton** (one woman), and **table tennis** (one man) have also had entrants.

Trinidad and Tobago has won 18 Olympic medals (two gold, five silver, 11 bronze), 14 in track and field athletics, three in weightlifting, and one in swimming. Its first gold medal was won in 1976 when Hasely Crawford won the men's 100 meters in track and field athletics. Keshorn Walcott won the country's second gold medal in 2012 in the **javelin throw**. Ato Bolden has been the country's most decorated Olympian, with four medals (one silver, three bronze) in 1998 and 2002 in the 100 and 200 meter **sprints**. The men's 4x100 meters sprint **relay** team won the silver medal in 2008 and bronze in 2012. Keston Bledman, Marc Burns, Emmanuel Callender, and Richard Thompson comprised the team, with Aaron Armstrong an alternate in 2008. Thompson won a third medal, silver, in the 2008 men's 100 meter sprint. Lalonde Gordon also won two bronze medals in 2012, one for the 400 meters and the second as a member of the 4x400 meter relay team. Wendell Mottley was a dual medalist in 1964, winning a silver medal in the 400 meters and a bronze as a member of the 4x400 meter relay team. Edwin Roberts, also a member of that relay team, won a second bronze medal in the 200 meters that year and was fourth in the 200 meters in 1968.

Rodney Wilkes, Trinidad's first Olympic medalist, won a silver medal in 1948 and bronze in 1952 in men's **featherweight** weightlifting. He also finished in fourth place in that event in 1956. Weightlifter Lennox Kilgour won a bronze medal in the **middle-heavyweight** class in 1952 and was seventh in that event four years later. Swimmer George Bovell, bronze medalist in 2004 in the men's 200 meter individual **medley**, is Trinidad's only medalist in that sport. He also finished a creditable seventh in the 50 meter **freestyle** in 2012.

Trinidad and Tobago competed in the **Olympic Winter Games** for the first time in 1994 at Lillehammer and competed again in 1998 and 2002. After seeing the acclaim and popularity of the **Jamaican bobsled** team, Trinidad decided to enter a two-man team in the bobsled competition, and the team of Gregory Sun and Curtis Harry finished 37th in 1994 ahead of six other countries, including Jamaica. The team repeated in 1998 and was 32nd of 38 that year. In 2002, Sun teamed with Andrew McNeilly for the first two runs and Errol Aguilera for the last two, but the teams finished 37th and last.

TRIPLE JUMP. The triple jump, formerly known as the hop, step, and jump, is one of the field events in **athletics**. It has been contested for men at every modern **Olympic Games** but was only added to **women**'s Olympic competition in 1996. The jumper sprints down a runway and, in one continuous motion, takes off into the air on one foot, lands on the same foot, leaps forward landing on the other foot, and then leaps forward again landing on both feet. **Viktor Saneyev** of the **Soviet Union**, three-time gold medalist from 1968 to 1976, added a silver medal in 1980 and is the only person to win three gold medals and the only one to win four total medals in this event. Tatyana Lebedeva of **Russia** has won medals in this event in three of the five years (silver 2000, 2008, bronze 2004) it has been held for women, while Françoise Mbango of **Cameroon** is the only two-time gold medalist (2004, 2008) in the women's event.

TUG-OF-WAR. In 1900, 1904, 1906, 1908, 1912, and 1920, tug-of-war was contested as a part of the track and field **athletics** program. The sport has not returned to the Olympics since. Three British athletes—Frederick Humphreys, Edwin Mills, and James Shephard—won three tug-of-war medals, two of them gold. In six **Olympic Games**, there have been 160 men from 13 nations who have participated in tug-of-war. The sport is governed internationally by the Tug of War International Federation, which is provisionally recognized by the **International Olympic Committee**.

TUNISIA (TUN). The North African nation of Tunisia (officially the Tunisian Republic) has competed at the **Olympic Games** since 1960, missing only the 1980 Olympic Games, and **boycotting** the 1976 Games after a few of its athletes had already competed in **boxing, swimming**, and **handball**. It has never competed at the **Olympic Winter Games**. In 13 Summer Games, Tunisia has entered 382 athletes (334 men, 48 **women**) in 21 sports. Their largest contingents were in **football** (65 men), **volleyball** (61 men), handball (48 men), **athletics** (36 men, seven women), boxing (36 men, two women), **judo** (15 men, 12 women), and **wrestling** (18 men, three women). They have done rather well in being able to qualify for the Olympic Games in several team sports. They have competed in four men's football tournaments, with a best result of ninth place tie in 1988. In four men's handball tournaments, their best finish was eighth in 2012. Tunisia has taken part in men's volleyball in six Olympic Games but has not had much success in that sport. In 2012, Tunisia competed in the men's **basketball** tournament for the first time and finished 11th of 12 teams, finishing ahead of **China**, which had three former National Basketball Association players on its team.

Tunisians have won 10 **Olympic medals**, four of them by distance runner Mohamad Gammoudi in the 5,000 and 10,000 meter races (gold 1968, silver 1964, 1972, bronze 1968), three by distance swimmer Oussama Mellouli (gold 2008, 1,500 meter **freestyle**, gold 2012, 10 km **open water**, bronze 2012, 1,500 meter freestyle), two bronze in **light-welterweight** boxing (Habib Galhia, 1964 and Fathi Missaoui, 1996), and a silver medal in 2012 by **steeplechase** runner Habiba Al-Ghribi-Boudra, the only Tunisian woman to win an Olympic medal.

TURISHCHEVA, LYUDMILA IVANOVNA (later BORZOVA) (URS–GYM). B. 7 October 1952, Grozny, Chechnya, **Russia**, USSR. Lyudmila Turishcheva ranks with **Larysa Latynina** as one of the two greatest Soviet female **gymnasts** ever. But Turishcheva never won the fans' affections, which were often reserved during her career for her teammates **Olga Korbut** and **Nelli Kim**. The five-foot, two-inch (160 cm), 115 lb (52 kg) Turishcheva won nine Olympic medals in three Games from 1968 to 1976, four of them gold. She was **all-around** champion at the 1972 Olympics, 1970 and 1974 World Championships, 1971 and 1973 European Championships, and the first World Cup in 1975, when she uniquely won all five individual events. She later married Soviet **sprint** great **Valeriy Borzov** and became coach of the Soviet gymnastics teams.

TURKEY (TUR). Turkey, officially known as the Republic of Turkey and located in southeastern Europe and western Asia, is one of the few nations that is located on two continents. It was first represented at the **Olympic Games** of 1906, when an **Armenian** student at Robert College in Constantinople (now Istanbul) competed in the 800 and 1,500 meter track events. Several **Greek** competitors living in cities that belonged to the Ottoman empire (as Turkey was then known) also competed in these Games, but these can hardly be considered Turkish. It is often claimed that during a visit to Turkey in 1907, **Pierre de Coubertin** invited his guide Aleko Mulas to take part in the **gymnastic** events at the 1908 Olympics, but there is no evidence that Mulas competed or was even officially entered. There were two Turkish entrants at the 1912 Olympics (again both ethnic Armenians), and Turkey sent its first serious team in 1924, a 21-man squad entered in the Paris Olympics. Since then, it has missed only the Games of 1932 (although it did have an entrant in the **art competitions**) and 1980 in support of the **boycott**.

In 22 Summer Games, Turkey has entered 678 athletes (560 men, 118 **women**) and participated in 21 sports plus the art competitions. In 2012, it competed for the first time in **badminton**, women's **basketball**, gymnastics, and **volleyball**. A large portion of Turkey's athletes have participated in **wrestling** (174 men, one woman), with athletics being Turkey's second most entered sport (109 athletes—66 men, 43 women). **Football** (63 men), **boxing** (56 men), and **weightlifting** (36 men, six women) are the next most popular. Turkey has won 88 **Olympic medals** (39 gold, 25 silver, 24 bronze), all in the Summer Games. Turkish wrestlers account for an outstanding 58 of these, with 28 gold medals, 16 silver medals, and 14 bronze medals. Its most notable competitors, however, have been weightlifters: both Halil Mutlu and **Naim Süleymanoğlu** (acclaimed as the strongest weightlifter pound for pound of all time) won three gold medals in that sport. Wrestler Hamit Kaplan has also won three medals, one of each color, in **freestyle** wrestling from 1956 to 1964. Other multiple medalists for Turkey include **Ethiopian**-born track star Elvan Abeylegesse (2008 silver medalist in women's 5,000 and 10,000 meters) and Servet Tazegül (2008 bronze medalist and 2012 gold medalist in men's **featherweight taekwondo**). Turkish wrestlers with two Olympic medals are Mehmet Akif Pirim (gold 1992, bronze 1996), Mithat Bayrak (gold 1956, 1960), Hamza Yerlikaya (gold 1996, 2000), Ahmet Kireççi (bronze 1936, gold 1948), Husein Akbas (bronze 1956, silver 1964), Mustafa Dağıstanlı (gold 1956, 1960), İsmail Oğan (silver 1960, gold 1964), Hasan Güngör (gold 1960, silver 1964), and Ahmet Ayık (silver 1964, gold 1968).

Turkey first competed at the **Olympic Winter Games** in 1936 and has since missed only the Winter Games of 1952, 1972, and 1980. They have entered 63 athletes (58 men, five women) and competed in **Alpine skiing, cross-country skiing**, and **figure skating**. Turkey's best results in the Winter Games include Muzaffer Demirhan, 33rd of 75 in the 1956 men's **downhill**, Yakup Kadri Birinci, 27th of 101 in the 1984 men's **slalom**, Arif Alaftargil, 29th of 65 in the 1998 men's slalom, his brother Atakan Alaftargil, 32nd of 77 in the 2002 men's slalom, and Sabahattin Oğlago, 55th of 99 in the 2006 15 km cross-country race. Turkey's sole female cross-country skier, Kelime Aydın-Çetinkaya, has competed in four Winter Games (2002–2014) and entered 12 events. One of her best results was in the 2006 30 km race when she finished 49th of 61 entrants.

Turkey has attempted to host the Olympics several times, with Istanbul unsuccessfully bidding for the 2000, 2004, 2008, 2012, and 2020 Olympics.

TURKMENISTAN (TKM). As a former member of the **Soviet Union**, Turkmenistan's athletes competed from 1952 to 1988 on the former Soviet teams, and its athletes were present at Barcelona in 1992 as members of the Unified Team. Located on the Caspian Sea in Central Asia, Turkmenistan first competed independently at the 1996 **Olympic Games** and has entered each subsequent Summer Games, but it has not yet participated in the **Olympic Winter Games**. Turkmenistan has had 33 athletes (20 men, 13 **women**) who competed in **athletics** (five men, four women), **boxing** (four men), **judo** (one man, four women), **shooting** (one man, one woman), **swimming** (three men, three women), **table tennis** (one woman), **weightlifting** (four men), and **wrestling** (two men). Turkmenistan has yet to win its first **Olympic medal**. Its best Olympic performances include Viktoriya Brigadnaya, 13th of 27 in the 2000 women's **triple jump**, Igor Pirekeyev, seventh of 53 entrants in 2000 **small-bore rifle** prone 50 meters shooting, and four-time Olympic **featherweight** weightlifter Umurbek Bazabayew, sixth of 15 in 2012. He was also seventh of 20 in 2004.

TUVALU (TUV). Once known as the Ellis Islands and part of the British colony of Gilbert and Ellis Islands, Tuvalu became an independent nation in 1976. For many years afterward, the South Pacific island of Tuvalu was one of only two wholly independent nations of the world without an **International Olympic Committee** (IOC)–recognized **National Olympic Committee** (along with the **Vatican City**). This changed in July 2007, when the IOC gave recognition to Tuvalu at the **IOC Session** in **Guatemala** City. At Beijing in 2008, Tuvalu made its Olympic debut, represented by three athletes, two men and a **woman**, who competed in track and field **athletics** and **weightlifting**. Weightlifter Logona Esau placed 23rd in a field of 30 competitors in the men's **lightweight** class, while the two entrants in athletics did not advance past the initial **round** in the 100 meter dash. In 2012, the diminutive (four feet, seven inches [140 cm]) weightlifter Tuau Lapua Lapua competed for Tuvalu in the men's **featherweight** class and finished 12th of 15 competitors. That year, they again had two entrants (one male, one female) in the 100 meter dash who did not advance past the first round. Tuvalu's population in 2012 was 10,837, making it the third-least populous sovereign state in the world behind the Vatican City and **Nauru**.

TV RIGHTS AND NEW MEDIA COMMISSION. The TV and Internet Rights Commission was formed in 2002 in response to concern about streaming images of Olympic events being sent out over the Internet. It was renamed the TV Rights and New Media Commission. It is responsible for preparing and implementing the overall **International Olympic Committee** (IOC) strategy for future broadcast rights negotiations. It is composed of eight **IOC members** and is chaired by **IOC President Thomas Bach**.

U

UBANGI-SHARI. *See* CENTRAL AFRICAN REPUBLIC.

UEBERROTH, PETER VICTOR. B. 2 September 1937, Evanston, Illinois, **United States**. After the financial disaster of the 1976 Games and the **boycott** in 1980, there was no longer any great enthusiasm among cities to host the **Olympic Games**. Los Angeles was the only city to apply to stage the 1984 Games, and under Peter Ueberroth's able direction as president of the **Organizing Committee**, they proved a great success. Although the Games had no public funding, a successful drive for corporate sponsorship and the sale of television rights resulted in a surplus of over $220 million. This resulted in a worldwide revival of interest in hosting future editions of the Games. Although the European press initially vilified Ueberroth's methods, his marketing ideas have been adopted by the **International Olympic Committee** and subsequent organizing committees and are now considered de rigueur. Ueberroth later served as commissioner of Major League **Baseball** in the United States, but after he lost the support of the owners, he did not seek reelection for a second term. He also ran unsuccessfully for governor of California in 2004, losing to Arnold Schwarzenegger.

UGANDA (UGA). The East African country of Uganda, officially known as the Republic of Uganda, competed at the Olympics for the first time in 1956, although at the time it was a protectorate of the **United Kingdom** and did not become an independent nation until 1962. Its Olympic participation was continuous through 1972, the highlight that year being John Akii-Bua winning the first Ugandan gold medal with his world record performance in the 400 meter **hurdles**. In 1976, after the overthrow of Idi Amin and joining in the African **boycott**, Uganda did not participate at Montreal. It did compete, however, in both 1980 and 1984 and all subsequent Olympics but has never competed at the **Olympic Winter Games**.

In 14 Summer Games, Uganda has entered 162 athletes (140 men, 22 **women**) and competed in nine sports, although the vast majority of their entrants have been in **athletics** (52 men, 15 women) and **boxing** (57 men). They also entered 17 men in the 1972 **field hockey** tournament and had one woman compete in **archery**, one man in **badminton**, two men in **cycling**, five men and three women in **swimming**, one man and two women in **table tennis**, and five men and one woman in **weightlifting**.

Ugandan athletes have won seven **Olympic medals**, three in track and field athletics and four in boxing, with Akii-Bua being joined by Stephen Kiprotich, the 2012 **marathon** winner, as the country's second gold medalist. The country's first two Olympic medalists were boxers Eridadi Mukwanga and Leo Rwabogo in 1968. Mukwanga won four of five bouts on his way to the **bantamweight** silver medal, and Rwabogo won three bouts before losing in the semifinal round of the **flyweight** class and earning the bronze medal. He came back in 1972 and won the silver medal and is the only Ugandan Olympian to win two medals. In 1980, **welterweight** John Mugabi won a silver medal. He later had an outstanding professional boxing career, billed as John "The Beast" Mugabi, and was the world's **light-middleweight** champion. Uganda's other Olympic medalist is Davis Kamoga, the bronze medalist in the men's 400 meter run in 1996.

Other notable results by Uganda in the Olympic Games athletics competition include fourth place by Boniface Kiprop in the 10,000 meters in 2004 and by Moses Kipsiro in the 5,000 meters in 2008, seventh place by the men's 4x400 meters **relay** team in 1984, eighth place by Amos Omolo in the 1964 400 meter race, and ninth place by Benjamin Kiplagat in the 2008 3,000 meter **steeplechase**. In boxing, 10 Ugandan boxers reached the quarterfinals before losing and each finished tied for fifth place. Kiprop (in 2008) and Kipsiro (in 2012) both also finished 10th in the 10,000 meters.

UKRAINE (UKR). As a separate nation, Ukraine, located in Eastern Europe, had never competed at the Olympics until its debut in 1994 at Lillehammer at the **Olympic Winter Games** and in 1996 at the **Olympic Games** in Atlanta. This is due mostly to the fact that, until the Soviet revolution of 1991, Ukraine had only been truly independent in the 20th century for a brief period around the time of the Bolshevik Revolution (and was in a civil war for most of that time). Many Ukrainians competed for the **Soviet Union** at the Olympic Games, however. The Ukrainian SSR was second only to **Russia** among Soviet republics in terms of medals won.

Ukrainian athletes were present at Albertville and Barcelona in 1992 as members of the Unified Team. At Lillehammer, the Ukraine accounted for two **Olympic medals**, highlighted by the gold-medal–winning performance of Oksana Baiul in **women's figure skating**.

The Ukraine has never hosted an Olympic Games, but in 1980 several preliminary football matches were held in Kiev. Lviv, Ukraine, submitted a bid to host the 2022 Winter Games but has since withdrawn that bid.

In only five Summer Games, the Ukraine has entered 817 athletes (454 men, 363 women) and participated in 29 sports: all sports contested during this era except **baseball, beach volleyball, football, hockey,** and **softball.** They entered the most competitors in **athletics** (92 men, 106 women), **swimming** (33 men, 28 women), and **wrestling** (47 men, eight women). They have won medals in 19 of the 29 sports. Through 2014, the Ukraine has won 115 Olympic medals (33 gold, 27 silver, 55 bronze) in the Summer Games. Its star Olympian is swimmer Yana Klochkova, who won back-to-back victories in the two individual **medley** swimming events of 2000 and 2004 as well as a silver medal in the 800 meters **freestyle** event in 2000. **Canoeist** Inna Osypenko-Radomska won four medals for the Ukraine. She was winless in 2000 and then won bronze in 2004, gold in 2008, and two silver medals in 2012 in flatwater **kayak** events. **Gymnast** Liliya Podkopaieva won three medals in 1996—two gold and one silver. Olena Kostevych won three medals in **shooting**—gold in 2004 and two bronze medals in 2012. Ruslana Taran won three medals in **sailing**—silver in 2004 and bronze in 1996 and 2000.

Other Ukrainians with multiple Olympic medals are in **archery**: Olena Sadovnycha (silver 2000, bronze 1996) and Viktor Ruban (gold 2008, bronze 2004); in **boxing**: Vasyl Lomachenko (gold 2008, 2012); in canoeing Yuriy Cheban (gold 2012, bronze 2008); in **fencing**: Olha Kharlan (gold 2008, bronze 2012); in gymnastics: Rustam Sharipov (gold 1996, bronze 1996, gold 1992 as a member of the Unified Team), Oleksandr Svitlychiniy (silver 2000, bronze 1996), Oleksandr Beresh, (silver 2000, bronze 2000), Valeriy Honcharov (gold 2004, silver 2000), and Hryhoriy Misiutin (bronze 1996, gold, four silver 1992 with the Unified Team); in **judo**: Roman Hontiuk (silver 2004, bronze 2008); in **rhythmic gymnastics**: Hanna Bezsonova (bronze 2004, 2008); in sailing: Olena Pakholchyk (bronze 1996, 2000); and in wrestling: Elbrus Tedieiev (gold 2004, bronze 1996) and Iryna Meleni-Mykulchyn (gold 2004, bronze 2008).

Boxer Volodomyr Klychko (sometimes spelled Wladimir Klitschko) won the 1996 **super-heavyweight** gold medal and has since become the professional world's **heavyweight** champion with more heavyweight championship bouts than any other boxer except Joe Louis.

One of the most well-known Ukrainian athletes is **pole vaulter** Sergey Bubka, who competed in the Olympic Games for the Soviet Union in 1988 and won the gold medal. He also was a member of the Unified Team in 1992 and the Ukraine team in 2000. Since retiring from active participation, he has become president of the Ukraine **National Olympic Committee**, a member of Parliament in the Ukraine, and a member of the **International Olympic Committee**. In 2013, he was defeated in a bid for the presidency of the IOC by **Thomas Bach**. Sergey's son, also named Sergei, is a noted **tennis** player and a member of the Ukrainian Davis Cup team.

In six Winter Games, the Ukraine has entered 198 athletes (120 men, 78 women), has participated in 13 sports (all except **curling** and **skeleton**), and has won seven medals—two gold, one silver, and four bronze. The Ukraine's top Winter Olympian is Viktoria "Vita" Semerenko, who won gold and bronze medals in the **biathlon** at the 2014 Winter Games in Sochi. Her twin sister Valentyna "Valj" Semerenko was also a member of the gold-medal–winning biathlon **relay** team. One of the Ukraine's other medals at the Winter Games was a bronze medal in 2006 in **ice dancing** won by the team of Olena Hrushyna and Ruslan Honcharov. *See also* ASTAKHOVA, POLINA GRIGORYEVNA; BORZOV, VALERIY PYLYPOVYCH; CHUKARIN, VIKTOR IVANOVICH; GOROKHOVSKAYA, MARIYA KONDRATYEVNA; LATYNINA, LARYSA SEMYONOVNA; LEDNYOV, PAVEL SERAFIMOVICH; MEDVED, ALEKSANDR VASILYEVICH; SHAKHLIN, BORIS ANFIYANOVICH.

ULVANG, VEGARD (NOR–CCS). B. 10 October 1963, Kirkenes, Sør-Varanger, Finnmark, **Norway**. After achieving only modest success at the 1988 **Olympic Winter Games**, Vegard Ulvang dominated **cross-country skiing** at the 1992 Games. At Calgary in 1988, he won a bronze medal in the 30 km, but four years later at Albertville he won three golds (10 km, 30 km, and relay) and a silver (**combined pursuit**). In 1994, the five-foot, 10-inch (180 cm), 161 lb (73 kg) Ulvang was no longer a major contender for individual honors, but won his sixth **Olympic medal** with a silver in the **relay**. When he competed in 1994, he was injured and shortly before had suffered the trauma of his younger brother's being lost and dying while running in the woods in the autumn of 1993. Ulvang spent one summer training by skiing across **Greenland** and climbing Mount McKinley (Denali) in Alaska. In 1994, he was given the honor of reciting the **Olympic Oath** on behalf of the athletes during the opening ceremony of the Lillehammer Olympic Winter Games.

UNDERWATER SPORTS. Underwater sports, which includes various **disciplines** such as fin **swimming**, underwater hockey, and spearfishing, have never been contested as a separate sport at the **Olympic Games**, even as a **demonstration sport**. However, the Confédération Mondiale des Activités Subaquatiques is recognized by the **International Olympic Committee**. Founded in 1959, it currently has 134 affiliated members from 90 nations. In 1900 at Paris, the swimming program did include an underwater swimming event, and the 1904 Olympic swimming program included a plunge for distance event.

UNEVEN BARS. The uneven bars is one of the exercises performed by female **gymnasts**. It has been included in the **Olympic Games** since 1952. The apparatus is similar to the men's **parallel bars** except that one of the two bars is higher than the other. The upper bar is 250 cm (8.2 ft) high while the lower bar is 170 cm (5.6 ft) high. **Polina Astakhova** of the **Soviet Union** (1960, 1964) and Svetlana Khorkina of **Russia** (1996, 2000) are the only two-time gold medalists in this event, while **Larysa Latynina** of the Soviet Union is the only three-time medalist (silver 1956, 1960, bronze 1964).

UNIFIED TEAM (ÉQUIPE UNIFIÉ). *See* COMMONWEALTH OF INDEPENDENT STATES.

UNION OF SOVIET SOCIALIST REPUBLICS. *See* SOVIET UNION.

UNITED ARAB EMIRATES (UAE). The United Arab Emirates, located on the Arabian peninsula on the Persian Gulf in Asia, has competed at each **Olympic Games** since 1984. It is no surprise that the UAE, a desert nation, has never competed at the **Olympic Winter Games**. In eight Summer Games, the UAE has entered 67 athletes (63 men, four **women**) and participated in 10 sports: primarily **athletics** (16 men, one woman), **cycling** (nine men), **football** (18 men), **shooting** (five men), and **swimming** (12 men). They have also had token participation in five other sports—two men in **judo**, one man in **sailing**, and one woman in each of **equestrian**, **taekwondo**, and **weightlifting**.

In 2004, Ahmed Al-Maktoum won a gold medal in **double trap** shooting, the first Olympic medal for an Emirati and only medal as of 2014. In addition to his medal, he also finished fourth in the single **trap** event that year and was seventh in double trap in 2008. In 2000, Sheikh Saeed Al-Maktoum, a relative of Ahmed and son of the Dubai emir, finished tied for ninth in **skeet** shooting and in 2012 he was 13th. The UAE qualified for the Olympic football tournament in 2012, a significant accomplishment, although they finished 15th of the 16 teams.

UNITED ARAB REPUBLIC (UAR). From 1958 until 1961, the Middle Eastern nations of **Egypt** and **Syria** combined to form the United Arab Republic and in 1960 sent a delegation to the **Olympic Games** in Rome. After Syria seceded in 1961, the nation of Egypt continued being known officially as the United Arab Republic until 1971. The 1960 UAR Olympic team consisted of 75 men and no **women** and competed in 12 sports: **athletics** (two men), **boxing** (four men), **diving** (three men), **equestrianism** (three men), **fencing** (six men), **football** (18 men), **gymnastics** (six men), **rowing** (nine men), **shooting** (three men), **water polo** (10 men), **weightlifting** (seven men), and **wrestling** (four men). **Greco-Roman flyweight** wrestler Osman El-Sayed won a silver medal and **flyweight** boxer Abdel Moneim El-Gindy won a bronze medal. Other notable achievements by the UAR at the Rome Olympic Games include fourth place for the mixed **jumping** equestrian team, fourth place by **heavyweight** weightlifter Mohamed Mahmoud Ibrahim, sixth place by **featherweight** Hosni Mohamed Abbas, and fifth place ties (quarter-final losers) for boxers **lightweight** Salah Shokweir and **light-welterweight** Sayed Mahmoud El-Nahas. The UAR did not compete at the **Olympic Winter Games**.

UNITED KINGDOM. *See* GREAT BRITAIN.

UNITED STATES MEN'S BASKETBALL TEAM—1960. The **United States** 1960 Olympic **basketball** team was one of the greatest basketball teams ever assembled. It is almost certainly the greatest amateur team ever, and its lineup would match up well with almost any professional team ever. The team easily won the gold medal at Rome in 1960. They won all eight games and outscored their opponents 815–476, an average of more than 42 points per game. The team members were Jay Arnette, Walter Bellamy, Bob Boozer, Terry Dischinger, Burdette Haldorson, Darrall Imhoff, Allen Kelley, Lester Lane, Jerry Lucas, Oscar Robertson, Adrian Smith, and Jerry West. The starting lineup usually consisted of Robertson and West at guard, and as professionals, they would later be considered the two finest guards of their era.

UNITED STATES MEN'S BASKETBALL TEAM—1984. The **United States** 1984 Olympic **basketball** team rivaled the U.S. 1960 team as a great amateur unit. The team was coached by Bob Knight of Indiana University and was never challenged in winning the gold medal. It was led by **Michael Jordan** of the University of North Carolina, who would later be considered as possibly the greatest professional player ever. The team members were Steve Alford, Patrick Ewing, Vern Fleming, Michael Jordan, Joseph Kleine, Jon Koncak, Chris Mullin, Samuel Perkins, Alvin Robertson, Wayman Tisdale, Jeffrey Turner, and Leon Wood. Ewing, Jordan, and Mullin would also later play on the 1992 **Dream Team**.

UNITED STATES MEN'S BASKETBALL TEAM—1992. *See* DREAM TEAM, THE.

UNITED STATES OF AMERICA (USA). The United States has competed at every **Olympic Games** except the 1980 Moscow Games, which it **boycot-**

ted, and has never missed the **Olympic Winter Games**. In addition, it had skaters present in both 1908 and 1920 when those events were held with the summer celebration. In 27 Summer Games, it has entered 7,602 athletes (5,694 men, 1,908 **women**) and has participated in 43 of the 51 sports plus the **art competitions**. They did not take part in **aeronautics, alpinism, cricket, croquet, motorboating, pelota,** and **racquets**—all sports contested in only one or two Games. The United States has won medals in 39 of the 44 sports, failing to medal in **badminton, handball, rhythmic gymnastics, table tennis,** and **trampolining**.

It has been the dominant country in terms of medals won since the inception of the Games, with 2,425 medals won (990 gold, 765 silver, 670 bronze) in the Summer Games and 282 (96 gold, 102 silver, 84 bronze) in the Winter Games. However, in the era from 1952 to 1988, the **Soviet Union** won slightly more medals, and the **German Democratic Republic** threatened this dominance prior to its merger with West **Germany** in October 1990.

Unsurprisingly, many of the most successful Olympians have been from the United States, notably **Michael Phelps** (22 medals—18 gold, two silver, two bronze), **Ray Ewry** (10 gold medals), **Mark Spitz** (nine gold, one silver, one bronze), and **Carl Lewis** (nine gold, one silver). The United States has had 74 athletes in nine sports, each winning five or more medals, with 21 of them winning at least five gold medals. The United States has also dominated the **basketball** competition, with the men's team winning the gold medal in 14 of the 17 tournaments, a silver medal in 1972, and bronze medals in 1988 and 2004 and recording a winning streak of 63 games from 1936 until their controversial defeat by the Soviet Union in 1972. The U.S. women's team has also medaled in all nine tournaments, winning seven.

In 22 Winter Games, the United States has entered 1,697 athletes (1,174 men, 523 women) and competed in 15 sports, missing only the **military ski patrol** in 1924. They have medaled in all except **biathlon**, where their best result was sixth of 13 teams in the 1972 men's relay. Their most bemedaled Winter Olympians have been **Apolo Anton Ohno**, who has won eight medals (two gold, two silver, four bronze) in **short-track speed skating, Bode Miller,** who has won six medals in **Alpine skiing** (one gold, three silver, two bronze), and **speed skaters Eric Heiden, Bonnie Blair,** and Chad Hedrick. Heiden won five gold medals in five races in 1980, setting Olympic records in each one and a world record in the 10,000 meters. Blair won five gold medals from 1988 to 1994 and also won a bronze medal. Hedrick won five medals (one gold, two silver, two bronze) in 2006 and 2010. The most memorable Winter Olympic performance, however, was by the U.S. men's **ice hockey** team in 1980. They defeated the powerful Soviet Union team in the semifinal game in a game called "The Miracle on Ice" and went on to win the gold medal. They also upset the Soviet Union in ice hockey in 1960, but that game did not get the same amount of publicity as the 1980 game did. The 2010 ice hockey final between the U.S. and Canadian professional teams was also a memorably exciting game that was won by the host Canadian team in overtime in Vancouver. The U.S. women's ice hockey team has also done well, winning five medals in five tournaments, although they only won a gold medal in the first in 1998.

The United States has also been host to the **Olympic Games** more than any other country. Four times the Games of the **Olympiad** have been held in the United States: in 1904 in St. Louis, Missouri, in 1932 in Los Angeles, California, and in 1984 again in Los Angeles, and in 1996 in Atlanta, Georgia. The **Olympic Winter Games** have also been held in the United States four times: in 1932 in Lake Placid, New York, in 1960 in Squaw Valley, California, and in 1980 again in Lake Placid, and in 2002 in Salt Lake City, Utah. The United States was actually awarded the 1904 Games to be held in Chicago, but the sponsors deferred that right to St. Louis, which was the site of a World's Fair in 1904. The 1976 Winter Games were also awarded to Denver, which at the last minute declined the opportunity. In addition, the United States has also had 30 unsuccessful bids to host the Summer Games (far more than any other country) and 14 unsuccessful bids to host the Winter Games. The city of Detroit has had more unsuccessful bids than any other city with seven (1944, 1952, 1956, 1960, 1964, 1968, 1972). Los Angeles was also unsuccessful seven times (1924, 1928, 1948, 1952, 1956, 1976, 1980), although they were successful twice in 1932 and 1984. Surprisingly, New York City, which has many large sports facilities as well as plenty of hotels and extensive public transportation in its metropolitan area, has only bid once (2012) but was not successful. *See also* ALI, MUHAMMAD; ANDERSON, PAUL EDWARD; ARLEDGE, ROONE PINCKNEY, JR.; BABASHOFF, SHIRLEY FRANCES; BAUMGARTNER, BRUCE ROBERT; BEAMON, ROBERT; BERG, LAURA KAY; BIONDI, MATTHEW NICHOLAS; BLEIBTREY, ETHELDA MARGUERITE; BRUNDAGE, AVERY; BUTTON, RICHARD TOTTEN; CHASTAIN, BRANDI DENISE; CONNOLLY, JAMES BRENDAN BENNETT; COSTAS, ROBERT QUINLAN; COUGHLIN HALL, NATALIE ANNE; DANIELS, CHARLES MELDRUM; DEPIETRO, JOSEPH NICHOLAS; DIDRIKSON, MILDRED ELLA; DREAM TEAM, THE—1992 USA BASKETBALL; EAGAN, EDWARD PATRICK FRANCIS; EBERSOL, DUNCAN; EDWARDS, TERESA; EVANS, JANET BETH; FLANAGAN, JOHN JOSEPH; FOREMAN, GEORGE; FRAZIER, JOSEPH WILLIAM; GRIFFITH JOYNER, DELOREZ FLORENCE; HAMM, MARIEL MARGARET; HURLEY, MARCUS LATIMER; JAGER, THOMAS MICHAEL; JOHNSON, MICHAEL DUANE; JOHN-

SON, RAFER LEWIS; JORDAN, MICHAEL JEFFREY; KAHANAMOKU, DUKE PAOA KAHINO MAKOE HULIKOHOA; KELLY, JOHN BRENDEN, SR.; KIRALY, CHARLES FREDERICK; KIRK, OLIVER LEONARD; KONO, TAMIO; KRAENZLEIN, ALVIN CHRISTIAN; KURLAND, ROBERT ALBERT; LEE, WILLIS AUGUSTUS, JR.; LEONARD, RAY CHARLES; LESLIE, LISA DESHAWN; LOCHTE, RYAN STEVEN; LOPEZ, STEVEN; LOUGANIS, GREGORY EFTHIMIOS; MALLON, WILLIAM JAMES; MATHIAS, ROBERT BRUCE; MAY, MISTY ERIE; MCCORMICK, PATRICIA JOAN; MCKAY, JAMES KENNETH; MEAGHER, MARY TERSTEGGE; MEYER, DEBORAH ELIZABETH; MORROW, BOBBY JOE; MOSES, EDWIN CORLEY; NABER, JOHN PHILLIPS; NORELIUS, MARTHA MARIA; O'BRIEN, WILLIAM PARRY, JR.; OERTER, ALFRED ADOLPH, JR.; OSBURN, CARL TOWNSEND; OWENS, JAMES CLEVELAND; PEARCE-RAMPONE, CHRISTIE PATRICIA; PEIRSOL, AARON WELLS; RETTON, MARY LOU; RICHARDS, ROBERT EUGENE; ROSE, RALPH WALDO; RUDOLPH, WILMA GLODEAN; SCHEMANSKY, NORBERT; SCHOLLANDER, DONALD ARTHUR; SHERIDAN, MARTIN JOSEPH; SLOANE, WILLIAM MILLIGAN; TAYLOR, CHRISTOPHER J.; THOMPSON, JENNIFER BETH; THORPE, JAMES FRANCIS; TORRES, DARA GRACE; UEBERROTH, PETER VICTOR; UNITED STATES MEN'S BASKETBALL TEAM—1960; UNITED STATES MEN'S BASKETBALL TEAM—1984; UNITED STATES WOMEN'S BASKETBALL (1976–2012); UNITED STATES WOMEN'S FOOTBALL (SOCCER) (1996–2012); UNITED STATES WOMEN'S SOFTBALL (1996–2008); WALLECHINSKY, DAVID; WALSH, KERRI LEE; WEISSMULLER, JOHNNY; WHITE, SHAUN ROGER; WILLIAMS, SERENA JAMIKA; WILLIAMS, VENUS EBONY STARR; WINANS, WALTER.

UNITED STATES VIRGIN ISLANDS (ISV). Since making its Olympic debut in 1968, the **United States** Virgin Islands, officially known as the Virgin Islands of the United States, has only missed the **Olympic Games** of 1980, which it **boycotted**. In 11 Summer Games, it has entered 121 athletes (103 men, 18 women) in 10 sports: **athletics** (19 men, 10 women), **boxing** (eight men), **cycling** (one man, one woman), **equestrian** (three men, one woman), **fencing** (three men, one woman), **sailing** (33 men, two women), **shooting** (15 men), **swimming** (16 men, three women), **weightlifting** (one man), and **wrestling** (four men). Virgin Islander Peter Holmberg won a silver medal in 1988 Finn monotype sailing, the only medal won by an athlete from the U.S. Caribbean Island territory. He also finished 11th of 28 entrants in that class in 1984.

Other notable Olympic results for the Virgin Islands include Flora Hyacinth finishing ninth in the 1992 women's **long jump** and several Virgin Island track and field athletes (Tabarie Henry, LaVerne Jones, Allison Peter), reaching the semifinal **rounds** of their events. Five boxers finished tied for ninth place in their classes by virtue of either a win or **bye** in the first bout. In 1968, the Virgin Islands only weightlifter, Leston Sprauve, finished 12th of 17 in the **heavyweight** class.

Among the more dedicated of the Virgin Islands' Olympians was John Foster Sr. He competed in sailing events in five Olympic Games from 1972 to 1992, including three with his son, John, Jr., with a best result of 13th. Foster Sr., also took part in the 1988 **Olympic Winter Games** and finished in 38th place in the two-man **bobsledding** ahead of three teams that did not complete the race. Possibly the best-known Virgin Islander who took part in the Olympic Games is **basketball** player Tim Duncan, although he did not represent the Virgin Islands. He played for the U.S. team that won the bronze medal in 2004 and as of 2015 has played in the National Basketball Association for 18 years. His sister Tricia was a member of the 1988 Virgin Islands swimming team.

The Virgin Islands has competed at Olympic Winter Games from 1988 to 2002 and again in 2014. They sent 26 athletes (22 men, four women) and competed in **Alpine skiing** (one man, two women), bobsledding (20 men), and **luge** (one man, two women). In the 1988 women's **giant slalom**, Seba Johnson finished 28th and next to last but ahead of 35 other skiers who were unable to complete the course. John Campbell finished 62nd of 131 skiers in the 1992 giant slalom. His daughter Jasmine Campbell finished 56th of 89 skiers in the 2014 women's giant slalom. Anne Abernethy competed in the women's singles luge event in five Olympics from 1988 to 2002 and was 48 years old and known as "Grandma Luge" when she raced her last race in 2002. Her best result was in 1988 when she finished 16th of 24 competitors. The men's two-man and four man bobsleigh teams finished among the last few in each attempt but did have the satisfaction of finishing ahead of the U.S. team on more than one occasion.

UNITED STATES WOMEN'S BASKETBALL (1976–2012). In 1976, the **Soviet Union** won the gold medal in **women's basketball**, with the **United States** team finishing second. The USSR won again in 1980, although the United States did not compete because of the U.S.-led **boycott**. But from 1984 to 2012, the U.S. women's basketball team won the gold medal seven times—1984, 1988, 1996, 2000, 2004, 2008, and 2012—failing only in 1992, when they earned a bronze medal behind the Unified Team. The United States was led during this period by several star players who later played in the Women's National Basketball Association. **Teresa Edwards** is the only player, man or woman, to win five medals in Olympic basketball, with gold medals in 1984, 1988, 1996, and 2000, and a bronze in 1992. **Lisa Leslie** was also on four gold-medal–winning teams (1996 through 2008), while six others have won three gold medals: Sue Bird, Tamika Catchings, Katie Smith, Dawn Staley, Sheryl Swoopes, and Diana Taurasi. During this period of Olympic dominance, the U.S. women have won the World Championships in 1979, 1986, 1990, 1998, 2002, 2010, and 2014, losing only in 1983 (USSR), 1994 (**Brazil**), and 2006 (**Australia**).

UNITED STATES WOMEN'S FOOTBALL (SOCCER) (1996–2012). **Women**'s **football (soccer)** was added to the **Olympic Program** in 1996 at Atlanta. The **United States** women have been the dominant team at the Olympics and internationally. They won the first Olympic tournament in 1996. In 2000 at Sydney, the U.S. women lost in the final match to **Norway**, 3–2, earning a silver medal. In 2004, the U.S. defeated **Brazil** after extra time in the final match to win a second gold medal. They repeated in Beijing in 2008 and in London in 2012 and have won four of the five Olympic women's tournaments. The United States has also dominated at the Women's World Cup, winning that title in both 1991 and 1999, losing in the final game in 1995, and finishing third in 2003 and 2007. In 2011, they were runners-up to **Japan**, losing the final on penalty kicks. The 1999 World Cup victory was memorable, with the championship in the final game against **China** earned on penalty kicks. On the final kick, **Brandi Chastain** scored the winning goal and yanked off her jersey, exposing her sports bra, for the start of an exultant victory celebration. It became one of the best-known sports photographs of the year. The U.S. women's football team has been led by several players during this time, with **Mia Hamm** often considered the best women's player of the 1990s. Team members Shannon Boxx, Heather Mitts, and Heather O'Reilly each won three gold medals. Chastain, Joy Fawcett, Julie Foudy, Hamm, Kristine Lilly, Cindy Parlow, and Kate Sobrero-Markgraf each have three Olympic medals—two gold and one silver. **Christie Pearce-Rampone** was a member of the team from 2000 to 2012 and has won three gold medals and one silver medal to lead all Olympic football players (male or female) in the medal count.

UNITED STATES WOMEN'S SOFTBALL (1996–2008). **Softball** was admitted to the **Olympic Program** in 1996, and the **United States' women** won three of the four Olympic tournaments. In 1996 and 2004, the U.S. team was unchallenged, going undefeated at both tournaments. The 2004 team was particularly dominant, winning nine games and outscoring their opponents

51–1; **Australia** managed the only run in the final round loss, 5–1. The 2000 victory was a bit unusual. The team was highly favored, coming into the Olympics with an international winning streak of 110 games. But at Sydney, the United States lost three games in the round-robin tournament and barely qualified for the four-team playoff. Two of those losses were consecutive, which was the first time that had happened to the U.S. softball team since 1983. However, they then won three consecutive games in the medal round to win the gold medal, defeating Australia 1–0 in the final game. The U.S. team was again favored in the 2008 tournament, when it had already become clear the sport would be removed from the Olympics for 2012. The team won its first eight matches, before surprisingly succumbing to **Japan** in the final, despite having beaten that team twice before in the tournament. **Laura Berg** is the only woman to have played on all four Olympic teams, thus having earned three golds and a silver medal. Lisa Fernandez, Lori Harrigan, and Leah O'Brien-Amico have all earned three gold medals. The U.S. softball team also won all the World Championships contested from 1974 to 2010 (except when it was not competing in 1982) but was defeated by Japan in 2012.

UNIVERSIADE. Since 1924, "Student **Olympic Games**" have been held under a variety of names. Since 1959, they have taken the name Universiade (from combining university and **Olympiad**) and have been organized by the International University Sports Federation (FISU). The Fédération Internationale du Sport Universitaire (its original French name) was founded in 1949 and organizes the biannual Universiades and Winter Universiades, as well as World University Championships in various sports. The FISU is an **International Olympic Committee**–recognized organization.

UNKNOWN COUNTRY OF ORIGIN. In the 1912 Stockholm **Olympic Games**, there were two entrants in the **art competitions** architecture contest, Fritz Eccard and A. Laffen, whose country of origin has yet to be discovered by Olympic historians. They are the only two Olympians of the more than 125,000 participants for whom this is true.

UPHOFF, NICOLE (FRG/GER–EQU). B. 25 January 1967, Duisburg, Nordrhein-Westfalen, **Federal Republic of Germany**. A **dressage** rider, Nicole Uphoff won her first international event in 1987 aboard Rembrandt. This presaged her dominance of dressage for the coming years. In both 1988 and 1992, she won the individual dressage gold medal and helped **Germany** to the team title at the Olympics. The five-foot, eight-inch (173 cm), 132 lb (60 kg) Uphoff repeated her double victories at the 1989 Europeans and 1990

World Championships. She retired after the 1996 **Olympic Games**, and married German Olympic show **jumper** Otto Becker.

UPPER VOLTA. *See* BURKINA FASO.

URUGUAY (URU). Uruguay, located in southeastern South America, first competed at the 1924 **Olympic Games** in Paris and has competed at every Summer Games since, with the exception of the 1980 Games in Moscow, which they **boycotted**. It had only one competitor in a sporting event in 1932 (and had a second in the **art competitions**), but he did quite well; Guillermo Douglas won a silver medal in the **singles sculls rowing**. In 20 Summer Games, Uruguay has entered 352 athletes (327 men, 25 **women**) and participated in 18 sports plus the art competitions. They had the most competitors in **basketball** (60 men), **cycling** (49 men), **football** (39 men), **boxing** (33 men), and rowing (33 men). Uruguay has won 10 **Olympic medals**. Two of these were gold, the outstanding victories by the **Uruguayan football teams** in 1924 and 1928. The Uruguayan basketball team was also successful, winning the bronze medal in both 1952 and 1956 behind the basketball powerhouses of the **United States** and the **Soviet Union**. Most of Uruguay's Olympic success has come in rowing, where they won four medals. In 1948, Eduardo Risso won a silver medal in the men's singles sculls event, and the duo of William Jones and Juan Rodríguez won the bronze medal in the men's **doubles** sculls. Rodríguez won a second bronze medal in 1952 when he teamed with Miguel Seijas to again win the doubles sculls. Uruguay's fourth rowing medal was won by the aforementioned Douglas in 1932. In 2000, Milton Wynants won a silver medal in the men's cycling points race, and in 1968 **bantamweight** boxer Washington Rodríguez was the bronze medalist after he was defeated by the eventual champion Takao Sakurai of **Japan** in their semifinal bout.

Other notable results by Uruguayan Olympians include the men's basketball team finishing fifth of 23 teams in 1948 and sixth of 21 teams in 1936, the four-man cycling team finishing fourth in the 4,000 meters team **pursuit** in 1948, Leonel Rocca being tied for fifth place in the 1948 cycling men's **sprint**, Luis Serra also tied for fifth in the 1952 1,000 meters cycling **time trial**, Milton Wynants adding a seventh place in 1996 and ninth place in 2004 to his 2000 silver medal in the cycling points race, Alvaro Paseyro finishing tied for fifth in 2000 **half-middleweight** class **judo**, Félix Sienra finishing sixth in the one person **dinghy** sailing competition in 1948, Alejandro Foglia's eighth place in that event in 2012, and swimmer Ana María Norbis finishing eighth in both the 100 meter and 200 meter **breaststroke** in 1968.

Officially known as the Oriental Republic of Uruguay, the country competed in the Olympic Winter Games only once, in 1998, when Gabriel Hottegindre finished 24th of 65 entrants in the **Alpine skiing slalom** competition.

URUGUAY FOOTBALL TEAMS (1924 AND 1928). In both 1924 and 1928, **Uruguay** won the gold medal in the Olympic **football** tournament. This was considered a major upset in 1924, as Uruguay had never before even entered the Olympic football tournament. In fact, from 1928 through 2008, Uruguay did not compete in the Olympic football tournament but did make a third appearance in 2012, finishing ninth.

Although its sportive qualities were not in question, its amateur status is somewhat doubtful: the Uruguayan team of the 1920s toured Europe for months before and after both Olympics, for which the players were not allowed to receive any compensation according to the then-current rules.

In 1930, the Uruguayan team confirmed its status as the best team in the world when several of its Olympic players helped Uruguay to win the inaugural World Cup in football. The players who played on both the World Cup team and at least one of Uruguay's gold medal teams were Héctor Castro (1924, 1928 Olympic, 1930 World Cup), Pedro Cea (1928 Olympic, 1930 World Cup), José Nasazzi (1924, 1928 Olympic, 1930 World Cup), José Andrade (1924, 1928 Olympic, 1930 World Cup), Lorenzo Fernández (1928 Olympic, 1930 World Cup), Alvaro Gestido (1928 Olympic, 1930 World Cup), and Hector Scarone (1924, 1928 Olympic, 1930 World Cup). Uruguay even considers its Olympic titles of 1924 and 1928 to be world titles. Each team that has lifted the World Cup is allowed to wear a star on its shirt. Uruguay, which won the 1930 and 1950 World Cup, has four stars, also counting the 1924 and 1928 gold medals.

UZBEKISTAN (UZB). Many Uzbek athletes competed from 1952 to 1988 for the **Soviet Union**, and Uzbek athletes were present at Barcelona and Albertville in 1992 as members of the Unified Team. As an independent nation, Uzbekistan, located in central Asia and officially known as the Republic of Uzbekistan, has competed at each **Olympic Winter Games** since 1994 and each **Olympic Games** since 1996. In the Summer Games, they have entered 228 athletes (175 men, 53 **women**) and competed in 17 sports, with most of the entrants in **athletics** (26 men, 20 women), **wrestling** (29 men), **boxing** (28 men), **judo** (24 men, two women), **swimming** (19 men, seven women), **canoeing** (20 men, five women), and **weightlifting** (12 men, one woman). Uzbekistan athletes have won 20 medals in the Summer Games—five gold, five silver, and 10 bronze. Four medals were won by **super-heavyweight freestyle** wrestler **Artur Taymazov**, who won three golds and a silver between 2000 and 2012. **Greco-Roman** wrestler Aleksandr Dokturishivili won the gold medal in the middleweight class in 2004. Magamed Ibragimov, a freestyle **heavyweight**, won a silver medal in 2004, and Soslan Tigiyev won the **middleweight** freestyle silver medal in 2008. Uzbekistan has also done well in boxing with seven medals. **Light-welterweight** Mukhammad Kadyr Abdullayev won the gold medal in 2000. Bronze medals were won by Karim Tulyaganov, **light-middleweight** 1996; Sergey Mikhailov, **light-heavyweight**, 2000; Rustam Saidov, super-heavyweight, 2000; Bakhodirdzhon Sultanov, **bantamweight**, 2004; Utkirbek Khaydarov, light-heavyweight, 2004; and Abbos Atayev, middleweight, 2012. In judo, **extra-lightweight** Rishod Sobirov won bronze medals in 2008 and 2012, middleweight Armen Bagdasarov was the 1996 silver medalist, and heavyweight Abdullo Tangriyev won the silver medal in 2008. **Gymnast** Anton Fokin won a bronze medal for his performance on the **parallel bars** in 2008. In **trampolining**, Yekaterina Khilko won a bronze medal in the women's individual competition, also in 2008.

In six Olympic Winter Games, Uzbekistan has entered 21 athletes (11 men, 10 women) in the sports of **Alpine skiing**, **figure skating**, and **freestyle skiing**. Their only medalist was Lina Cheryazova, who won a gold medal in 1994 freestyle skiing **aerials**.

The city of Tashkent was unsuccessful in its bid to host the 2000 Summer Games.

VAL BARKER AWARD. The Val Barker Award is given at each **Olympic Games** to the **boxer** who is judged to be the best overall technical boxer. It is named in honor of Val Barker of **Great Britain**, a former president of the Association Internationale de Boxe Amateur, and was first awarded in 1936. Though typically it is given to one of the boxing gold medalists, three times it has been awarded to a nonchampion—in 1936 to **flyweight** bronze medalist Lou Lauria (USA); in 1968 to **featherweight** bronze medalist Philip Waruinge (KEN); and in 1988 to **light-middleweight** silver medalist Roy Jones, Jr. (USA).

VÄLBE, YELENA VALERYEVNA (née TRUBIZINA) (EUN/RUS–CCS). B. 20 April 1968, Magadan, Siberia, **Russia**, USSR. With 16 victories at the **Olympic Games** and World Championships, Yelena Välbe has won more major championships than any other female **cross-country skier**. She was World Cup champion in 1989 and 1991–1992 and was favored to win several medals at the 1992 **Olympic Winter Games**. The five-foot, four-inch (164 cm), 119 lb (54 kg) skier succeeded in earning a medal in every event, but in the four individual events, she won four bronze medals. She won three gold **Olympic medals** in the 1992, 1994, and 1998 **relay**. Her greatest performance was at the 1997 Worlds, when she won a gold medal in all five cross-country events for **women**. At the World Championships, she has won the following titles: 1989, 10 km and 30 km; 1991, 10 km and 15 km; 1993, 15 km and relay; 1995, 30 km and relay; and 1997, five km, 15 km, 30 km, **pursuit**, and relay.

VAN ALMSICK, FRANZISKA (GER–SWI). B. 5 April 1978, East Berlin, **German Democratic Republic**. With 10 medals, Franziska Van Almsick trails only Americans **Jenny Thompson** (12), **Dara Torres** (12), and **Natalie Coughlin** (11) among female Olympic **swimmers**, and she is one of only nine women to have won 10 or more **Olympic medals** in the Summer Games. Van Almsick first competed at the **Olympic Games** in 1992, when she was only 14. She won four medals, including a silver in the 200 meter **freestyle** and a bronze in the 100 meter freestyle. Favored in 1996 at her best distance, the 200 meter freestyle, she finished second again. The five-foot, 11-inch (181 cm), 146 lb (66 kg) Van Almsick also added two **relay** medals in 1996. In 2000, her only medal was a bronze in the 800 meter freestyle relay. At Athens in 2004, she won two more relay medals. Most of Van Almsick's Olympic success has been in relays, but she has not won an Olympic gold medal. Van Almsick was World Champion in the 200 meter freestyle in 1994 and in the 4x200 meter relay in 1998. Most of her success has come at the European Championships, in which she has won 17 gold medals, with five each in 1993, 1995, and 2002. She has set two world records in the 200 meter freestyle.

VAN INNIS, GERARD THEODOR HUBERT (BEL–ARC). B. 24 February 1866, Elewijt, Vlaams Brabant, **Belgium**. D. 25 November 1961, Zemst, Vlaams Brabant, Belgium. Hubert Van Innis must be considered the supreme Olympic **archer**, with his record 10 medals (six gold) at the **Olympic Games** of 1900 and 1920. He competed in 11 events, medaled in 10 of them, and was fourth in the other. Although the exceptional number of archery events at these Games clearly helped him toward his record medal total, this advantage was countered by his absence from the 1904 and 1908 Games and by the fact that archery events were not held at the 1906 or 1912 Games. After his successes in 1920, archery was never again an Olympic sport during his lifetime, but in 1933, at the age of 67, Van Innis won a team gold medal at the World Championships and in all probability would have won further **Olympic medals** had he been given the opportunity. Van Innis was an architect by profession.

VANUATU (VAN). The South Pacific island nation, Vanuatu, once known as the New Hebrides, formed a **National Olympic Committee** in 1987 and was recognized by the **International Olympic Committee** that year. Vanuatu made its Olympic debut in 1988 at Seoul and has competed in each subsequent Summer **Olympic Games**. Officially known as the Republic of Vanuatu, it has not yet competed at the **Olympic Winter Games**, and its athletes have not yet won a medal. In fact, none of its athletes has progressed beyond the first **round** of competition thus far. There have been 22 different athletes from Vanuatu (14 men, eight **women**) who have competed mostly in **athletics** (10 men, six women) or **table tennis** (one man, two women), with one man in each of **archery**, **boxing**, and **judo**. The best performance by a Ni-Vanuatu Olympian is that of 62-year-old archer Francois Latil, who scored better than three other archers in the qualifying round in 2000 and finished 61st of 64 entrants.

VATICAN CITY. The Vatican City, with an area of just 110 acres (44 hectares) and a population of around 840, with more than half being clergy, is the smallest independent state in the world. Not surprisingly, the Vatican does not have a **National Olympic Committee** and most likely never will. But in the early 21st century, Pope John Paul II established a Vatican sport department, and the Vatican does have a national **football (soccer)** team that has played several international matches.

VELODROME. A velodrome is an arena specially built for **cycling** competitions. It generally consists of a steeply banked oval track with two straight sections connected by 180-degree circular bends. The track length has ranged from 138 meters to 500 meters, with most modern ones at 250 meters (the current **Olympic Games'** minimum). Seating capacity at velodromes is rather small compared with arenas used for other indoor sports and is usually only around 5,000. In Olympic cycling, events such as the **sprint, Keirin, pursuit,** and **omnium** take place at the velodrome, while the **road race, time trials,** and **mountainbike cross-country** are held outdoors or at other venues.

VENEZUELA (VEN). Venezuela formed a **National Olympic Committee** in 1935 and achieved **International Olympic Committee** recognition in the same year. Although a Venezuelan took part in the **Olympic Games'** **art competition** of 1932, it was not until 1948 that Venezuelans competed in a sports event at the Olympics. Venezuela, located on the northern coast of South America and officially known as the Bolivarian Republic of Venezuela, has been represented at the Olympic Games without fail since then. It first competed in the **Olympic Winter Games** in 1998, when it was represented by a single **luger**, and also attended the 2002, 2006, and 2014 Winter Games. In 18 Summer Games, Venezuela has entered 491 athletes (388 men, 103 **women**). They have participated in 27 sports—all the sports that have been held in more than three Olympic Games from 1948 to 2012 with the exception of **badminton, baseball, handball, hockey, modern pentathlon, rhythmic gymnastics, trampolining,** and **water polo.**

Venezuela has won 12 **Olympic medals** (two gold, two silver, eight bronze): five in **boxing,** two in **taekwondo,** and one each in men's **athletics, fencing, shooting, swimming,** and **weightlifting.** The only Venezuelan Olympic champions are Francisco Rodríguez, who won the **light-flyweight** boxing title in 1968, and Rubén Limardo, who was the individual **épée** fencing champion in 2012. Venezuela's other medalists are jumper Asnoldo Devonish (1952 **triple jump** bronze), shooter Enrico Forcella (1960 **small-bore rifle** prone bronze); boxers Pedro José Gamarro (1976 **welterweight** silver),

José Piñango (1980 **bantamweight** silver), Marcelino Bolívar (1984 light-flyweight bronze), and Omar Catari (1984 **featherweight** bronze); swimmer Rafael Vidal (1984 200 meter **butterfly** bronze); weightlifter Israel José Rubio (2004 featherweight bronze); and taekwondo athletes Adriana Carmona (2004 **heavyweight** bronze) and Dalia Contreras (2008 **flyweight** bronze).

Other notable results by Venezuelan Olympians include a fourth place finish by swimmer Rafael Vidal in the 100 meter butterfly in 1984, fifth place finishes by the 1960 4x100 meters track **relay** team, swimmer Alberto Mestre in the 200 meter **freestyle** in 1984, and by weightlifters Julio César Luna (2004 **middle-heavyweight**) and Junior Sánchez (2012 lightweight).

In Olympic Winter Games competition, Venezuela has competed in the luge with three male and one female athletes, with a best finish of 31st of 50 entrants in 2002 by Chris Hoeger. Their one **Alpine skier**, Antonio José Pardo, entered the **giant slalom** in 2014 but did not successfully complete the course.

VEZZALI, MARIA VALENTINA (ITA–FEN). B. 14 February 1974, Jesi, Ancona, **Italy**. In Beijing in 2008, Valentina Vezzali became the first **woman** in Olympic history to win five gold medals in **fencing**. In London in 2012, she won her sixth gold medal. Between 1996 and 2012, she won the individual **foil** three times (2000, 2004, 2008), won silver in 1996, and bronze in 2012. The five-foot, four-inch (164 cm), 119 lb (54 kg) Vezzali also won three gold medals in the team competition (1996, 2000, 2012) and a bronze in 2008. Her total of nine Olympic fencing medals leads all female fencers and trails only Eduardo Mangiarotti of Italy with 13 and **Aladár Gerevich** of **Hungary** with 10.

Outside of the Olympics, Vezzali's record is no less impressive. She won 15 world titles in foil fencing (six individual, nine team) and 24 medals in total, as well as 13 European titles (five individual, eight team). Her extensive medal cabinet also features gold medals from the Mediterranean Games and **Universiades**. In 2013, she became a member of the Italian Chamber of Deputies, one of the two houses of the Italian parliament.

VIETNAM (VIE). Though **South Vietnam** had competed in the Olympics between 1952 and 1972, its northern neighbor had not. But after the conclusion of the Vietnam War, a new unified **National Olympic Committee** was formed on 20 December 1976, and it was recognized by the **International Olympic Committee** in time for the 1980 Olympics. Vietnam has since only missed the 1984 **Olympic Games**, which it **boycotted**. It has never competed at the **Olympic Winter Games**. In eight Summer Games, Vietnam has entered 90 athletes (50 men, 40 **women**) and has competed in 15 sports: **athlet-**

ics (10 men, 12 women), **badminton** (one man, one woman), **boxing** (two men), **canoeing** (one woman), **gymnastics** (one man, two women), **judo** (two women), **rowing** (four women), **shooting** (11 men, one woman), **swimming** (11 men, nine women), **taekwondo** (three men, five women), **weightlifting** (two men, two women), **wrestling** (six men, one woman), and one man in each of **cycling**, **fencing**, and **table tennis**.

Vietnam, located on the Indochina peninsula in Southeast Asia and officially named the Socialist Republic of Vietnam, won its first **Olympic medal** in 2000 at Sydney, when Trần Hiếu Ngân finished second in women's **featherweight** class taekwondo, and it added a second silver medal in 2008, earned by Vietnamese weightlifter Hoàng Anh Tuấn in the **bantamweight** class. Other notable Olympic results for Vietnamese athletes include Hoàng Xuân Vinh in 2012—fourth in men's **free pistol** shooting and ninth in **air pistol** shooting; Trần Lê Quốc Toàn, fourth place in 2012 men's bantamweight weightlifting; Nguyễn Thị Thiết, women's **middleweight** weightlifting, sixth in 2004 and fifth in 2008; and Nguyễn Quốc Huân, tied for fifth in 2004 men's **flyweight** taekwondo.

VIKELAS, DEMETRIOS (GRE). B. 6 June 1835, Syra, **Greece**. D. 7 July 1908, Athens, Greece (some sources have B. 15 February 1835, D. 20 July 1908). Demetrios Vikelas was the first **International Olympic Committee (IOC) president** (1894–1896). Vikelas was better known as a writer and for his interest in literature and the arts than for his sporting inclinations. But because he lived in Paris and was well acquainted with **Pierre de Coubertin**, he represented Greece and the Pan-Hellenic Gymnastic Club at the 1894 **Olympic Congress** in Paris. It was felt that the IOC president should come from the country hosting the next Games, and with Athens being awarded the 1896 Games, Vikelas was appointed president. Despite his lack of experience in sports administration, he proved an able and enthusiastic president before handing the office over to Coubertin at the successful conclusion of the 1896 Games.

VIRÉN, LASSE ARTTURI (FIN–ATH). B. 27 July 1949, in Myrskylä, Itä-Uusimaa, **Finland**. At Munich in 1972, Lasse Virén became, after **Emil Zátopek**, **Hannes Kolehmainen**, and Vladimir Kuts, only the fourth man to win the Olympic 5,000 and 10,000 meters at the same Games. Virén repeated this feat in 1976, a unique double-double. Despite falling early in the 1972 10,000 meters, his time was a new world record. Attempting to emulate Zátopek's 1952 triple, which included a **marathon** victory, Virén entered the 1976 marathon as well, finishing fifth. The five-foot, 10-inch (180 cm), 132 lb (60 kg) Virén also competed at the 1980 **Olympic Games**, finishing fifth in the

10,000 meters and failing to finish the marathon. Virén was less successful at other major meets, with his best efforts at the European Championships being a fourth in the 5,000 meters and third in the 10,000 meters in 1974.

VIRGIN ISLANDS, BRITISH. *See* BRITISH VIRGIN ISLANDS.

VIRGIN ISLANDS, UNITED STATES. *See* UNITED STATES VIRGIN ISLANDS.

VOLLEYBALL. Volleyball, like **basketball**, is a sport whose origin is known almost to the day. Oddly, both sports were invented at the same college and within a few years of one another. Volleyball was invented in 1895 by William G. Morgan, a student at Springfield College and a director of the YMCA at Holyoke, Massachusetts. The game was originally called "minionette."

Volleyball quickly spread around the world and became more popular in other countries than in the **United States**. The sport was introduced in the Olympics in 1964 by the **Japanese**, although it was never contested as a **demonstration sport** at the Olympics. In 13 Summer Games, there have been 2,287 participants (1,261 men, 1,026 **women**) from 45 nations in Olympic volleyball. No country has been truly dominant in volleyball, although the **Soviet Union** has won the most medals with 12. Originally the Japanese had the world's best women's players, while the United States had the best men's team in the world for most of the 1980s. In recent years, the **Cuban** women's team has dominated, and four Cuban women have earned three gold medals. Only **Inna Ryskal** of the Soviet Union has won more medals, with two golds and two silvers. In men's volleyball, Samuele Papi of **Italy** (two silver, two bronze from 1996 to 2012) and Sergey Tetyukhin of **Russia** (one gold, one silver, two bronze from 1996 to 2012) have each earned four medals.

Volleyball has now reached new heights of popularity, spurred on by **beach volleyball**, played by the ocean or on any sand-covered court by two-person teams of scantily-clad players. In 1993, the **International Olympic Committee** approved beach volleyball as an Olympic sport; it was contested at the 1996 Atlanta Olympics for the first time and has been included in each subsequent **Olympic Games**.

The international governing body of volleyball is the Fédération Internationale de Volleyball, which was formed in 1947 and had 220 member nations as of July 2014. *See also* KIRALY, CHARLES FREDERICK; MAY, MISTY ERIE; RYSKAL, INNA VALERYEVNA; WALSH, KERRI LEE.

VOLLEYBALL, BEACH. *See* BEACH VOLLEYBALL.

VON FÜRSTENBERG-VON HOHENLOHE-LANGENBURG, HU-BERTUS RUDOLPH (MEX–ASK). B. 2 February 1959, Mexico City, D.F., **Mexico**. Hubertus von Fürstenberg is one of the more interesting characters to have competed in the **Olympic Games**. Although born in Mexico, he was raised in Europe (**Spain, Austria**) and is currently (2014) a citizen and resident of **Liechtenstein**. He claims to be a descendant from a former **German** principality, and on occasion uses the title "Prince." He is employed as a photographer, businessman, and singer known as "Andy Himalaya" and sometimes as "Royal Disaster." In 1981, he founded the Mexican Ski Federation, was its president, and since 1984 has represented Mexico in the **Olympic Winter Games** as a participant in **Alpine skiing**. He skied in the 1984, 1988, 1992, and 1994 Games and then resumed his Olympic participation in 2010 and 2014. His best result was in his first Olympics in 1984, when he finished 26th of 101 entrants. In 2014, at the age of 55, he entered the **slalom** but failed to finish the race. As Mexico's sole athlete at the 1994, 2010, and 2014 Winter Games, he was also his country's flagbearer for the opening ceremony. In addition to his six Winter Olympic Games, he has also participated in 15 World Alpine Skiing Championships. Hohenlohe has stated that the only reason why he continues to participate is because it seems that the "exotic skiers" (those from countries without a tradition in winter sports) are disappearing, and that he wants to keep that tradition alive. His uncle Max Emanuel Maria Alexander Vicot Bruno de la Santisima Trinidad y Todos los Santos von Hohenlohe Langenburg, also known as Max, Prince von Hohenlohe, competed for Liechtenstein in the men's **downhill** at the 1956 Winter Games.

W

WAGNER-AUGUSTIN, KATRIN (GER–CAN). B. 13 October 1977, Brandenburg an der Havel, **German Democratic Republic**. Katrin Wagner has won four Olympic titles in **kayaking**, including three consecutive wins in the K4 (2000–2008). Her fourth title was won in the K2 in Sydney in 2000. The five-foot, 10-inch (179 cm), 154 lb (70 kg) Wagner also earned an individual bronze in the K1 in 2008 and a silver in the K4 in 2012. Wagner, who is married to fellow **canoeist** Lars Augustin, also won 10 world titles between 1997 and 2014, winning 28 medals in total. Her medal cabinet also contains 25 medals from European Championships, including 11 golds.

WALES. Wales is located on the island of **Great Britain** and is a country that is part of the nation of the **United Kingdom**. It was allowed to enter a separate team in 1908 **hockey**, finishing third, but in all other Olympics, and in all the other sports at the 1908 Olympics, Wales has competed as a member of the United Kingdom of Great Britain and Northern Ireland. A significant number of participants on Great Britain's Olympic teams have been Welsh. In 2012, 30 of the 530 members of the British team at the London Olympics were Welsh. Welsh Olympians have won more than 50 **Olympic medals**, with Cardiff-born **Paolo Radmilovic** the most decorated. He competed in six **Olympic Games** from 1906 to 1928 and won four gold medals—one in **swimming** and three in **water polo**. Cardiff, Wales was the site of several preliminary **football** matches during the 2012 London Olympics.

WALKOVER. A walkover occurs in Olympic **boxing** when a boxer's opponent does not show up to box at the scheduled time. This can be due to failure to make the weight, illness or injury, or political action (a country refusing to allow their fighter to meet a representative from another country for political reasons). The term walkover is occasionally used in other sports in which an event is uncontested. It originated in **athletics** when there was only one eligible contestant in a race who could then just "walk over" the course rather than run it. This happened in the final of the 400 meters in 1908. After an incident in which one of the American runners, John Carpenter, was disqualified for interfering with the British runner Wyndham Halswelle, the officials ordered the race to be rerun two days later. The other two runners, both American, refused to enter the rescheduled race, and Halswelle became the only runner in the final. To his credit, Halswelle did not in fact walk over the course but ran it in a respectable (for that era) 50 seconds.

WALLECHINSKY, DAVID (né WALLACE). B. 5 February 1948, Los Angeles, California, **United States**. David Wallechinsky is the son of the author and screenwriter Irving Wallace. In 1975, David wrote the *People's Almanac*, a book of history that told little-known interesting facts about its subjects. The book became a best seller and was followed by several sequels. One part of the book was devoted to lists, and *The Book of Lists*, another spinoff, also was quite popular. He first attended the **Olympic Games** in 1960 as a 12-year-old with his father and became quite interested in the Games. In 1983, he wrote the *Complete Book of the Olympics*, one of the most comprehensive histories that not only had the results but also many interesting sidelights about the people involved with the Games. That, too, became popular and he has continued to update it following each Olympic Games. In recent years, it has become two separate books, one devoted to the Summer Games and one to the Winter Games. In 1991, he was one of the founding members of the **International Society of Olympic Historians** and served as its treasurer from 1996 to 2004, its vice president from 2004 to 2012, and was elected its president in 2012. He has worked in both radio and television, and one of his biennial assignments is broadcasting the Olympic Games. A world traveler, he has been to more than 50 countries, including some such as Albania, North Korea, and the Central African Republic that most travelers seldom visit. One of his most recent books, released in 2012 (cowritten with his nephew Jaime Loucky), combined two of his interests and is titled *The Book of Olympic Lists.*

WALSH, KERRI LEE (later JENNINGS) (USA–VOL/BVO). B. 15 August 1978, Saratoga, California, **United States**. Kerri Walsh played **volleyball** at Stanford University, where she was a four-time first-team All-American. After college, the six-foot, three-inch (191 cm), 157 lb (71 kg) Walsh played on the U.S. national team in indoor volleyball, competing at the 2000 **Olympic Games** in that sport, finishing fourth as a team. After the 2000 Olympics, she turned to **beach volleyball** and teamed up with **Misty May**. Together they would form the most dominant female beach volleyball pair ever, winning gold medals in 2004, 2008, and 2012 and winning 112 consecutive matches, a streak broken shortly after the 2008 Olympics. She is married to Casey Jennings, who is also a professional beach volleyball player.

WALTER-MARTIN, STEFFI (née MARTIN) (GDR–LUG). B. 17 September 1962, Schlema im Erzgebirge, Sachsen, **German Democratic Republic**. Steffi Walter-Martin is the first **woman** to win two gold **Olympic medals** for **luge**, later equaled by compatriots Sylke Otto and Natalie Geisenberger. The five-foot, 10-inch (180 cm), 163 lb (74 kg) Walter-Martin took the title in 1984 and 1988 and on each occasion led the East Germans to a clean sweep of the medals. She was also the World Champion in 1983 and 1985 and won the World Cup in 1984.

WANG MENG (CHN–STK). B. 10 April 1985, Qitaihe, Heilongjiang, **China**. Wang Meng is one of only three **short-track speed skaters** to have won four gold **Olympic medals**, the others being Chun Lee-Kyung and **Viktor An** (who won six). The five-foot, five-inch (167 cm), 132 lb (60 kg) Wang is the only female to win four. She won three of her titles during the 2010 Vancouver Games, where she outperformed the competition in the 500 meters and 1,000 meters, while captaining the victorious Chinese **relay** team. Four years earlier, she had won a gold medal in the 500 meters, while adding a silver and a bronze in the two other individual events. Wang has also been successful at World Championships. In 2008, she claimed the overall title and won three distances. In other years, she has won four more distance titles.

WANG NAN (CHN–TTN). B. 23 October 1978, Fushun, Liaoning, **China**. Just three **table tennis** players have managed to win four gold **Olympic medals**: Deng Yaping, Wang Nan, and **Zhang Yining**. These three have dominated women's table tennis for successive periods, with Wang succeeding Deng, and Zhang replacing Wang at the top of the pantheon. Wang Nan was ranked number one in the world for almost four years between 1999 and 2002, and she won all the major titles in that period, including the **singles** and **doubles** title at the 2000 Olympics. At the next two Olympics, she won two more golds, in the doubles event (with Zhang) and the 2008 team event. In singles, the five-foot, five-inch (166 cm), 132 lb (60 kg) Wang was defeated in the 2004 quarter-finals and in the 2008 final, losing out to Zhang. At World Championships, Wang has won no less than 15 titles, three in singles, five in doubles, six in the team event, and one in **mixed doubles**. Wang ended her career after the Beijing Olympics, at which point she had already been enshrined in the International Table Tennis Federation Hall of Fame for several years.

WATANABE, OSAMU (JPN–WRE). B. 21 October 1940, Wassamu, Hokkaido, **Japan**. It is possible that Osamu Watanabe is the greatest **wrestler**

ever, pound for pound. He had a very short career, but he was never beaten. It is known that he won at least 187 consecutive matches prior to his victory in the 1964 **Olympic Games** at Tokyo, when he won the **featherweight freestyle** gold medal. In that tournament, the five-foot, two-inch (160 cm) Watanabe won all of his matches without sacrificing a single point. This followed Watanabe's victories in the 1962 and 1963 World Championships. He was not immensely strong, but very quick, and his technical skills were unmatched in his era.

WATER POLO. Water polo was developed in Europe and the **United States** as two separate sports. In the United States, it was termed softball water polo, as the ball was an unfilled bladder, and the sport was very rough, often degenerating into numerous fights. In 1897, Harold Reeder of New York formulated the first rules for that sport, which were intended to decrease the excessive roughness of the game. The European style of water polo predominated and today is the form of the game practiced universally. It is more scientific, faster, and less dangerous than the American game.

Water polo was played at the **Olympic Games** of both 1900 and 1904. It was not on the 1906 **Olympic Program**, but has been contested at all Games since. In 26 Summer Games, there have been 2,449 participants (2,169 men, 280 **women**) from 52 nations in Olympic water polo. **Great Britain** won four of the first five Olympic tournaments, but by far the greatest exponents of water polo have been the Hungarians. Between 1928 and 1980, **Hungary** never failed to medal in the sport at the Olympics, and the country has won 15 Olympic medals in total, including nine golds. Ten players have won three Olympic water polo titles: two British and eight Hungarian players. Among them is **Dezső Gyarmati**, who also won a silver and a bronze medal. His total of five Olympic water polo medals is the most of any Olympian.

Women's World Championships have been held in water polo since 1986, and women competed in water polo at the 2000 Olympic Games for the first time. The United States has medaled in each of the four tournaments (one gold, two silver, one bronze), and team members Heather Petri and Brenda Villa have each won four medals. Water polo, like **swimming** and **diving**, is governed by the Fédération Internationale de Natation Amateur, which was formed in 1908 and in 2014 had 204 affiliated nations. *See also* KAHANAMOKU, DUKE PAOA KAHINO MAKOE HULIKOHOA; KÁRPÁTI, GYÖRGY; RADMILOVIC, PAOLO FRANCESCO; WEISSMULLER, JOHNNY.

WATER SKIING. Water skiing was a **demonstration sport** at the 1972 Olympics. The sport is governed by the International Waterski and Wakeboard Federation, which was formed in 1955 and is recognized by the

International Olympic Committee. There are currently (as of 2014) 88 affiliated member nations. It was thought that water skiing might be added to the **Olympic Program** for the 2004 **Olympic Games** in Athens, but that was voted down by the **Executive Board** in December 2000.

WEIGHTLIFTING. Weightlifting in various forms has been popular for centuries. Strongmen of all types often performed at various fairs in the Middle Ages. In the 19th century, professional strongmen often toured with carnivals or vaudeville shows. However, weightlifting as a sport became organized only in the late 19th century. The governing body is the International Weightlifting Federation, which had 188 member nations in mid-2014. The first governing body of weightlifting was founded in 1905 as the Amateur Athleten Weltunion. The current federation was founded in 1920 as the Fédération Internationale Haltérophile and adopted its current name in 1972.

Weightlifting has been on the program of the **Olympic Games** except in 1900, 1908, and 1912. The program has varied little except for the addition of more weight classes in recent years and the addition of **women**'s competition in 2000. Originally there were no weight classes, only an open competition, and in 1920 and 1924, there were also one-handed lifts. Beginning in 1928, the three Olympic lifts were standardized as the military **press**, the **snatch**, and the **clean and jerk**. Because of difficulties judging the press, and because there was some concern that the lift was biomechanically dangerous to lifters' backs, it was eliminated from international competition after the 1972 Olympics. Today, lifters compete only in the snatch and the clean and jerk at the Olympics. Women made their Olympic debut in weightlifting at the 2000 Olympic Games in Sydney, with seven weight classes.

In 25 Summer Games, there have been 2,708 participants (2,428 men, 280 women) from 148 nations who competed in Olympic weightlifting. The sport was dominated by the **Soviet Union** after its entry into the Olympics in 1952. In the 1970s and 1980s, **Bulgaria** challenged that dominance, although a number of its lifters ran afoul of drug testing, notably in 1992. The **United States** was once a weightlifting power, but has won only one Olympic medal in men's weightlifting since 1968 (and none since 1976), with the exception of the 1984 Olympics, which were not attended by the East European nations. The United States did win two medals in women's weightlifting in 2000, the first year that women participated in the sport. In recent Games, **China** has emerged as a strong nation in the sport, and with 29 Olympic titles, it is currently second only to the Soviet Union, which earned 39. The four lifters who won three Olympic golds, however, are all from **Turkey** and **Greece**: Halil Mutlu and **Naim Süleymanoğlu** from Turkey and **Pyrros Dimas** and **Akakios Kakiasvili** from Greece.

Beginning in 1993, the weight classes in international weightlifting have been changed, with a completely new set of world records. This is to eliminate the possibility of earlier records having been set by drug users prior to stricter drug controls. Another restructuring of weight classes happened for the 2000 Olympics to allow for the women's events. *See also* ALEKSEYEV, VASILIY IVANOVICH; ANDERSON, PAUL EDWARD; BASZANOWSKI, WALDEMAR ROMUALD; DEPIETRO, JOSEPH NICHOLAS; KONO, TAMIO; MIYAKE, YOSHINOBU; SCHEMANSKY, NORBERT; SCHUHMANN, CARL.

WEISSMULLER, JOHNNY (né PETR JÁNÓS WEISZMÜLLER) (USA–SWI/WAP). B. 2 June 1904, Freidorf, Timisoara, Kingdom of **Hungary**, Austria-Hungary (now **Romania**). D. 20 January 1984, Acapulco, Guerrero, **Mexico. Swimmer** Johnny Weissmuller was the winner of the 100 meter **freestyle** in 1924 and 1928 and the 400 meter freestyle in 1928 and was a member of the winning 4x200 meter freestyle **relay** team in both years. He also won the bronze medal with the **United States** men's **water polo** team in 1924. He set 28 world records, and his margin of superiority over his contemporaries was such that some authorities still rate him ahead of **Mark Spitz** and **Michael Phelps** as the greatest swimmer of all time. Because of the limited number of events available to Weissmuller, his Olympic record cannot be fairly compared with that of Spitz or Phelps, but the longevity of his records is testament to his greatness. His 1927 world record for the 100 yard freestyle was unbeaten for 17 years, a remarkable length of time. Much of his success was due to his revolutionary high-riding stroke, flutter kick, and head-turning breathing. Invited for a screen test for the role of **Tarzan**, the six-foot, three-inch (191 cm), 190 lb (86 kg) Weissmuller was preferred to 150 other applicants and went on to become the most famous screen Tarzan of all, playing the role in 19 movies between 1934 and 1948. He also starred as Jungle Jim in an additional 13 films from 1948 to 1954 and a 26-episode television series in 1955–1956.

WELTERWEIGHT. Welterweight is a weight class for men in Olympic **boxing, taekwondo,** and **wrestling**. It is a medium-weight class with a limit of approximately 147 lb (67 kg). In Olympic boxing, welterweight competition was first held in 1904 and has been included in every Olympic Games since 1920. Oleg Saitov of **Russia** (1996, 2000) is the only multiple Olympic welterweight boxing gold medalist. He also won the bronze medal in 2004 and is also the only three-time Olympic welterweight medalist.

In taekwondo, welterweight for both men and **women** is one of only four weight classes included in Olympic competition. Taekwondo has only been an Olympic sport since 2000 and **Steven Lopez** of the **United States** (gold 2004, bronze 2008) and Mauro Sarmiento of **Italy** (silver 2008, bronze 2012) are the only two multiple men's welterweight medalists. Hwang Gyeong-Seon of **Korea** (gold 2008, 2012, bronze 2004) is the only women's multiple welterweight gold medalist as well as the only triple medalist.

Welterweight has also been a weight class in wrestling in both **freestyle** and **Greco-Roman** competition. It has been held since 1932 in Greco-Roman style and in 1904 and since 1924 in freestyle competition. Józef Tracz of **Poland** has won three Olympic medals in welterweight Greco-Roman wrestling (silver 1992, bronze 1988, 1996). Five wrestlers have each won two Olympic medals in freestyle wrestling, but none have won more than one gold medal. *See also* LIGHT-WELTERWEIGHT.

WENZEL, HANNELORE (later WEIRATHER) "HANNI" (LIE–ASK). B. 14 December 1956, Straubing, **Federal Republic of Germany**. With a total of four medals, Hanni Wenzel, at five feet, five inches (165 cm), 126 lb (57 kg), trails only **Janica Kostelić**, **Vreni Schneider**, **Anja Pärson**, and **Katja Seizinger** as the most successful of all **women** Olympic **Alpine skiers**. After winning a bronze medal in the **slalom** in 1976, Wenzel won gold in the slalom and giant slalom and a silver in the **giant slalom** in 1980. Born in West **Germany**, Wenzel moved to **Liechtenstein** as an infant and was granted citizenship after winning the slalom at the 1974 World Championships. Both her brother Andi and sister Petra were Olympic Alpine skiers. Hanni married Olympic skier Harti Weirather, and their daughter Tina has also become an Olympic skier.

WERTH, ISABELL REGINA (GER–EQU). B. 21 July 1969, Rheinberg, Nordrhein-Westfalen, **West Germany**. One of the most successful **equestrian dressage** riders in history, Isabell Werth won eight **Olympic medals**. With the dominant German team, she won four team gold medals (1992–2000, 2008) as well as the 1996 individual title. The remaining three medals are silver medals won in the individual dressage (1992, 2000, and 2008). Isabell Werth, at five feet, six inches (168 cm), 141 lb (64 kg), is also a six-time world champion (three times team, one time individual, two times GP Special) and a multiple European Champion. She won most of her medals with her horse Gigolo, which she rode between 1992 and 2000, while her 2008 Olympic medals were won with Satchmo.

WEST GERMANY. *See* FEDERAL REPUBLIC OF GERMANY.

WEST INDIES FEDERATION (WIF). A short-lived nation (existing between 3 January 1958 and 31 May 1962), the West Indies Federation consisted of 13 present-day Caribbean island nations and territories: Anguilla, **Antigua and Barbuda, Barbados, Cayman Islands, Dominica, Grenada, Jamaica,** Montserrat, **Saint Kitts and Nevis, Saint Lucia, Saint Vincent and the Grenadines, Trinidad and Tobago,** and Turks and Caicos Islands. This nation sent a team to the 1960 **Olympic Games** but not to the **Olympic Winter Games.** The Rome organizing committee called the "nation" the Antilles, a term that has unfortunately often been copied in many books. The West Indies team consisted of 12 men, one from Barbados, four from Trinidad, and seven from Jamaica, who competed in **athletics** (five men from Jamaica, one from Barbados, one from Trinidad), **cycling** (one man from Trinidad), **sailing** (two men from Trinidad), **shooting** (two men from Jamaica), and **weightlifting** (one man from Jamaica). The team won two bronze medals in athletics—one by Jamaican George Kerr in the 800 meters and one by the 4x400 meters **relay** team, which consisted of three Jamaicans (Kerr, Keith Gardner, and Mal Spence) and one Barbadian (Jim Wedderburn). Gardner also finished fifth in the finals of the 110 meters **hurdles** and Paul Foreman was 12th in the finals of the **long jump.**

WESTERGREN, CARL OSCAR (SWE–WRE). B. 13 October 1895, Malmö, Skåne, **Sweden.** D. 5 August 1958, Malmö, Skåne, Sweden. Prior to the 1990s, Carl Westergren was the most successful Olympic **wrestler** in the **Greco-Roman** style, and his Olympic records in that discipline have been equaled only by **Russia's Aleksandr Karelin.** A four-time Olympian, Westergren won gold in 1920 (**middleweight**), 1924 (**light-heavyweight**), and 1932 (**heavyweight**), but in 1928, when he was defending his light-heavyweight title, he was surprisingly defeated in the first round by Onni Pellinen of **Finland** and withdrew from the competition. His total of three Olympic Greco-Roman gold medals is a record shared with **Ivar Johansson** (SWE), **Aleksandr Medved** (URS), and Karelin. Westergren was a three-time European champion and was the world middleweight champion in 1922.

WESTERN SAMOA. *See* SAMOA.

WHITE, SHAUN ROGER (USA–SNB). B. 3 September 1986, San Diego, California, **United States.** Shaun White is one of four Olympic **snowboarders** to win two titles, with back-to-back golds in the **halfpipe** (2006, 2010). In the Winter **X Games,** he has won 18 medals, including 13 golds, in superpipe and slopestyle. White, at five feet, nine inches (175 cm) and 154 lb (70 kg), overcame a congenital heart disorder as a baby, and has also won five Summer X Games medals (two gold) in the vert skateboarding competition. Nicknamed the "Flying Tomato" because of his long red hair, he is the best-known snowboarder in the world, with self-invented tricks and his own video game.

WHITFIELD, SIMON ST. QUENTIN (CAN–TRI). B. 16 May 1975, Kingston, Ontario, **Canada**. Simon Whitfield is one of two men to have won more than one medal in **Olympic Games triathlon** competition. The five-foot, nine-inch (177 cm), 154 lb (70 kg) Whitfield won the inaugural Olympic triathlon in Sydney in 2000, despite a crash during the **cycling** portion, was 11th in 2004, and won the silver medal in 2008. In 2012, he was the flag-bearer for Canada in the opening ceremony and competed again in the event in 2012 but failed to finish the race after falling during the cycling portion, breaking his collarbone. He also won the gold medal at the **Commonwealth Games** in 2002 and the bronze medal at the 1999 **Pan American Games**.

WICKENHEISER, HAYLEY MARIE (CAN–ICH/SOF). B. 12 August 1978, Shaunavon, Saskatchewan, **Canada**. Along with **Jayna Hefford**, Hayley Wickenheiser is one of only two Canadian players to compete in all five Olympic **women**'s **ice hockey** tournaments. The pair has each won four gold medals (2002–2014) and a silver (1998). The five-foot, 10-inch (178 cm), 170 lb (77 kg) Wickenheiser has also competed in the Summer Olympics, placing eighth with the Canadian **softball** team in the Sydney Games. Wickenheiser starred at the 2002 and 2006 Olympics as the top scorer in 2002 and Most Valuable Player of both competitions. Apart from her Olympic accomplishments, Wickenheiser has won seven World Championship golds (and five silvers), and in 2003, playing for HC Salamat in the Finnish professional men's league, she became the first woman to score a goal in a men's professional league match. At the opening ceremony of the 2010 **Olympic Winter Games** in Vancouver, Wickenheiser recited the **Olympic Oath** for athletes.

WIGGINS, BRADLEY MARC (GBR–CYC). B. 28 April 1980, Ghent, Oost-Vlanderen, **Belgium**. Born the son of a track **cyclist**, Bradley Wiggins initially specialized in endurance track cycling events. He has won seven **Olympic medals** in the sport, a record he shares with **Chris Hoy**. Wiggins won three of these medals in the team **pursuit**, improving from bronze in 2000 to silver in 2004 and gold in 2008. Wiggins earned two more Olympic golds in the individual pursuit, winning that event in both Athens and Beijing. He won a bronze in the 2004 **Madison** competition. The six-foot, three-inch (191 cm), 170 lb (77 kg) Wiggins also collected a total of 10 World Championship medals, including six titles. He won three world titles in the 2008 event held in Manchester. After these successes, Wiggins changed his focus to the road. On 22 July 2012, he became the first British rider to win the Tour de France. Five days later he rang the Opening Bell to begin the opening ceremony at the London Olympics, and on 1 August he won his fourth Olympic gold medal and seventh overall in his individual **time trial**. On 10 December 2013, he was knighted for services to cycling and is now Sir Bradley Wiggins.

WILHELM, KATARINA "KATI" (GER–CCS/BIA). B. 2 August 1976, Schmalkalden, Thüringen. **German Democratic Republic**. After competing in **cross-country skiing** at the 1998 Winter Games, Kati Wilhelm came into contact with **biathlon** and switched sports. She came home from the next **Olympic Winter Games** with three medals, a total she expanded to seven in 2006 and 2010. The five-foot, eight-inch (173 cm), 132 lb (60 kg) Wilhelm has won three gold medals, in the **sprint** (2002), **pursuit** (2006), and **relay** (2002), as well as three silvers and a bronze medal. Wilhelm, known for her bright red hair and cap, also won the World Cup in 2006 and collected 13 World Championship medals, winning five titles between 2001 and 2009.

WILLIAMS, SERENA JAMIKA (USA–TEN). B. 26 September 1981, Saginaw, Michigan, **United States**. Serena Williams has become the dominant **women's tennis** player in the 21st century. Although she is four inches shorter than her older sister, at five feet, nine inches (175 cm), she is solidly built and has one of the most powerful serves in the history of women's tennis. She has amassed 34 major titles—19 **singles**, 13 **doubles** (all with her sister, **Venus Williams**), and two **mixed doubles**. She has been ranked as the number one women's tennis player on six different occasions, with the first one in 2002 and the last in 2013. In 2013, she became the oldest female tennis player to be ranked number one. She and Venus were Olympic doubles champions in 2000, 2008, and 2012, and Serena was the Olympic women's singles champion in 2012. In 2015, she was still the number one–ranked player and most likely will add several additional championships before she retires.

WILLIAMS, VENUS EBONY STARR (USA–TEN). B. 17 June 1980, Lynwood, California, **United States**. Venus Williams and her sister **Serena Williams** are the only female **tennis** players to have won four Olympic titles and the only ones to have done so after the sport's reintroduction at the 1988 Games. One of the dominant players in the **women's** game since 2000 when she won the **Olympic Games** women's **singles** gold medal, Venus Williams has won 22 major titles through 2014, including seven singles titles. Her sister Serena is also a top tennis player, having surpassed Venus as a singles player in terms of championships, but the two won the Olympic women's **doubles** in 2000, 2008, and 2012. They have also frequently been rivals, meeting each other in eight Grand Slam finals between 2001 and 2009, with Venus winning two of the encounters. Known for her powerful game, Venus Williams, one of the tallest women's tennis players at six feet, one inch (185 cm), has been ranked number one on the Women's Tennis Association list three times, for a total of 11 weeks.

WINANS, WALTER (USA–ART/SHO). B. 5 April 1852, St. Petersburg, **Russia**. D. 12 August 1920, Barking, London, **England**. Walter Winans is the only person to have won gold **Olympic medals** in both a regular sport and the Olympic **art competitions**. He was a noted rifle and pistol **shooter** and won the running target (double shot) event in 1908, as well as a silver medal in the 1912 running target team event. He entered five individual shooting events in 1908 and four in 1912 and also two team shooting events in 1912. Winans was also a well-known equestrian sculptor, and his "An American Trotter" was awarded first prize in the 1912 Olympic sculpture competition. At the 1908 **Olympic Games**, a question was raised about Winans's eligibility because he had never set foot in America, and he was required to swear his allegiance to the **United States** consul general in order to participate in the Olympics. Winans did eventually visit the United States, but not until he was 58 years old. Trotting, another of his interests, led to his death. While driving in a race in England, he suffered a heart attack, fell, and broke his skull, dying instantly.

WINDSURFER. A windsurfer is one of the newer forms of **sailing**. The device, which was created in the 1960s, adds a sail to a surfboard and is sometimes known as boardsailing. It became an event for men in the **Olympic Games** sailing competition in 1984. A mixed windsurfing event was held in the 1988 Olympic Games, and since 1992, separate Olympic windsurfing events for men and for **women** have been on the **Olympic Program**. No man has won the event more than once. Multiple men's medalists are Carlos Espínola of **Argentina** (silver 1996, 2000), Nikos Kaklamanakis of **Greece** (gold 1996, silver 2004), Gal Friedman of **Israel** (gold 2004, bronze 1996), Nick Dempsey of **Great Britain** (silver 2012, bronze 2004), Mike Gebhardt of the **United States** (silver 1992, bronze 1988), and Bruce Kendall of **New Zealand** (gold 1988, bronze 1984). Alessandra Sensini of **Italy** has won four medals in women's Olympic windsurfing competition (gold 2000, silver 2008, bronze 1996, 2004).

WINKLER, HANS GÜNTER (FRG–EQU). B. 24 July 1926, Barmen, Wuppertal, Nordrhein-Westfalen, **Germany**. Hans Günter Winkler has the finest record ever of any German **equestrian** show **jumper**, and his overall record internationally is rivaled only by **France**'s Pierre Jonquères d'Oriola and **Italy**'s **Raimondo D'Inzeo**. A five-foot, nine-inch (174 cm), 159 lb

(72kg) rider, Winkler won seven **Olympic medals** (five gold, one silver, one bronze), but only one in the individual event. Winkler won that individual medal, a gold, in 1956 in show jumping in Stockholm. He competed in six Olympic Games from 1956 to 1976 and led Germany to team golds in 1956, 1960, 1964, and 1972, a bronze in 1968, and a silver in 1976. Winkler's 1956 championship was his third consecutive internationally; in 1954 and 1955, he won the first two World Championships in show jumping. Most of his success came on the back of his horse Halla.

WINTER GAMES. *See* OLYMPIC WINTER GAMES.

WINTER OLYMPICS. *See* OLYMPIC WINTER GAMES.

WINTER PENTATHLON. In 1948 at St. Moritz, a winter **pentathlon** event was held as a **demonstration sport**. The events of the winter pentathlon were **cross-country skiing**, **shooting**, **downhill skiing**, **fencing**, and horse riding. The second-place finisher in the event, Wille Grut of **Sweden**, was a truly versatile athlete, who would win the Olympic gold medal in the **modern pentathlon** later that year.

WINTER X GAMES. *See* X GAMES.

WITT, KATARINA (GDR/GER–FSK). B. 3 December 1965, Staaken, Berlin, **German Democratic Republic**. As a gold medalist in 1984 and 1988, Katarina Witt became the first woman **figure skater** to retain an Olympic title since **Sonja Henie**. Witt was also a six-time European Champion (1983–1988) and four-time World Champion (1984–1985, 1987–1988), and after taking the Olympic and world titles in 1988, she turned professional. With the return to Olympic eligibility of certain professionals, Witt took part in the **Olympic Winter Games** for a third time in 1994, but some of the magic of the earlier days had gone, and she finished in seventh place. Witt became enormously wealthy because of her talent, but also because of her beauty (at five feet, five inches tall [165 cm], 121 lb [55 kg]), which attracted many commercial endorsements. She led the unsuccessful Munich bid to host the 2018 Winter Olympics.

WOMEN AND SPORT COMMISSION. In 1995, a Women and Sport Working Group was formed by the **International Olympic Committee** (IOC) to advise the **IOC president** on suitable policies to be developed in this field. The working group became a formal IOC Commission in 2004. The commission has a consultative purpose and meets once a year, forwarding its policies to the IOC **Executive Board**. It consists of members from the IOC, the **National Olympic Committees**, and the **International Federations**, as well as athletes' representatives and members from the **Paralympic** Movement. The current (as of 2014) chairperson is Lydia Nsekera of **Burundi**. *See also* WOMEN AT THE OLYMPICS.

WOMEN AT THE OLYMPICS. The first connection between women and the **Olympic Games** can be traced back to the 10th century B.C., when the Herean Games, a sporting and religious festival exclusively for women, were held at Olympia, although not as part of the **Ancient Olympic Games**. The Herean Games were held quadrennially in honor of Hera, the wife of Zeus. There was only one event, a footrace of about 160 meters, but it was divided into three age categories, allowing young girls to compete. The women were given crowns of olive, similar to the Olympic prizes, and they also received a portion of a heifer that was sacrificed to Hera.

The first recorded Ancient Olympic Games occurred in 776 B.C., although it is considered that their origins date to the 12th century B.C. Discrimination against women in sport is as old as these Games themselves, as women could not take part in the Ancient Olympic Games. In fact, with few exceptions, they were not even allowed as spectators. Strangely, young girls could watch, although the athletes were competing nude. Pausanias noted, "They do not prevent virgins from watching." Only one adult woman was allowed to witness the Games, that being the Priestess of Demeter Chamyne, who was awarded this honorary office every four years from the Eleans. The penalty for women watching the Olympic Games was severe. Any woman caught watching the Games, or even crossing the River Alpheios on the days the Olympics were held, would be put to death by being tossed from the cliffs of Mount Typaion.

The Olympic **boxing** crown in 404 B.C. was won by Eukles, who was the son of Akousilaos and the grandson of Diagoras, who won the Olympic boxing championships in 464 and 448 B.C. To this time, legend has it that women were put to death if they were discovered watching the events. However, Eukles's mother, Kallipateira, attended his matches, disguised as a trainer. When he won, she leaped over the barrier behind the trainer's station and exposed herself as a woman. The judges withheld the death penalty "out of respect for her father and her brothers and son" (Finley and Pleket, pp. 45–46). A rule was then enacted requiring all trainers to thereafter attend all Olympic contests naked, like the athletes.

In 396 B.C., the first female Olympic champion was crowned when Princess Kyniska of Sparta, the daughter of Sparta's King Archidamos, won the *tethrippon*, a four-horse **chariot race**. But it should be mentioned that in the Ancient Olympics, the winners of the chariot races were considered to be the owners of the chariots and horses, not the drivers.

No females officially competed in the first modern Olympics in 1896. There is fairly good evidence, however, that a woman ran the **marathon** course near the time of the Olympic race after she was not allowed to compete in the actual race. The Greek woman runner's name was Stamata Revithi, but this has only recently been discovered. For years, she has been known as Melpomene, a name chosen by the Greek media to honor the Greek muse of tragedy.

The 1900 Olympic Games were very odd, as they were held in conjunction with a large World's Fair, the Paris International Exposition. It is not precisely certain which events conducted at the fair should be considered "Olympic," and years later, many athletes did not even know that they had competed in the 1900 Olympic Games. But the Games of 1900 are important because they involved the first official female Olympic participants when a total of 23 competitors from **Bohemia** (1), **France** (12), **Great Britain** (1), **Italy** (1), **Switzerland** (1), and the **United States** (7) took part in **croquet, equestrian, golf, sailing,** and **tennis**. The first woman known to compete in the Olympics was a Swiss yachtswoman, Helen de Pourtalès, who crewed on her husband's yacht in the one- to two-ton class. By winning the tennis **singles** and **mixed doubles** on 11 July 1900, Charlotte Cooper of Great Britain became the first individual female champion at the modern Olympic Games. There was a women's golf competition, won by Margaret Abbott of the United States, although in later life Ms. Abbott did not even know she had competed at the Olympic Games. Women also competed in ballooning competition at the fair, although again, it is uncertain if this was an Olympic event. It is interesting to note that there was also a Feminist Congress held within the walls of the 1900 Paris Exposition.

Over the next few Olympics, women gradually were allowed to compete in a few Olympic sports. A detailed table of how women's sports have been added to the **Olympic Program** appears below. Briefly, in 1904 at St. Louis, there was a women's **archery** event. In 1908, women competed at London in **figure skating** and **motorboating**. A big step forward occurred in 1912, when women competed in **swimming** and **diving** at the Olympic Games, the first true "athletic" events at the Summer Olympics.

Through the 1924 Olympics, women were not allowed to compete in track and field **athletics**, the most well-publicized sport at the Olympic Games. In response, women formed their own organization, the Fédération Sportive Feminine Internationale, which sponsored the **Women's Olympics** in Paris in 1922 and the Second International Ladies' Games in Göteborg, **Sweden,** in 1926. Only after these events proved that women could turn in credible athletic performances did the International Amateur Athletic Federation agree to allow them to compete in the 1928 Games, albeit only in five events.

All went well except in the 800 meters, when Lina Radke, the **German** winner, left a field of exhausted runners sprawled in various stages of collapse behind her. The **International Olympic Committee** (IOC) then banned women from any events beyond 200 meters on the grounds that they were not physically equipped to run long distances. The ban remained in effect for 32 years, until the 1960 Olympics, when the 800 meters women's event was reinstated, with longer races to follow beginning in 1972.

Why was there so much resistance to allowing women to compete at the Olympic Games? Much of the problem can be traced to the founder of the modern Olympic Games, Baron **Pierre de Coubertin**. He did not want women to compete on Olympian fields, and his philosophy toward women and sports is the greatest stain on his remarkable achievement. Although Coubertin has been deified by some followers of the **Olympic Movement**, others have not treated him so kindly because of his views on women in sports. Jean-Marie Brohm wrote of him, "It is indeed confusion to declare Coubertin a great humanist when his written texts or his quoted remarks are clearly those of a blind reactionary for anyone who knows how to read them, [consisting of] elitism and sexism."

Coubertin wrote a great deal during his life, and his writings on women in sports, when read in the 21st century, do not reflect well on him. Note the following, "With regard to boys . . . sporting competition . . . is vital with all its consequences and all its risks. Feminized it becomes something monstrous." And, "I still . . . think that . . . feminine athletics . . . are bad and that these athletics should be excluded from the Olympic Program—that the **Olympiads** have been restored for the rare and solemn glorification of the [male adult]." Since 1928, women's presence in the Olympic stadium has increased almost at every Olympic Games, although they do not yet have an equal role with men. Since 1900, only in 1920, 1932, 1956, and 1972 was the women's program at the Olympics not enlarged in some way. It is instructive to look at some of the numbers regarding women's participation at the Olympics. In 1912, there were 15 sports open exclusively to men, three for women, and two mixed sports. Men could compete in 143 events, while women could only compete in 21, with 14 of those mixed events. At London in 2012, there were 302 events in 32 sports, with 32 sports open to women, and only 30 open to men. Of these 302 events, there were 162 events for men only, 132 for women only, and eight mixed events. Women now actually compete at the Olympics in two sports or disciplines not open to men: **rhythmic gymnastics** and **synchronized swimming**, and in 2012, women competed in all male sports, including **boxing** for the first time.

The **Olympic Winter Games** are even better for women, and near equality is upon women on the snow and ice. At Sochi in 2014, there were 98 events in seven sports and 15 disciplines with 50 events for men, 43 for women, and five mixed. Women and men have equal programs in **Alpine skiing**,

biathlon, cross-country skiing, curling, figure skating, **freestyle skiing, ice hockey, short-track speed skating, skeleton, snowboarding**, and **speed skating**. Women still lag slightly, with fewer events than men in **bobsledding** (one vs. two), **luge** (one vs. two), **ski jumping** (one vs. three), and **Nordic combined**, which is still an exclusively men's sport.

As noted, the list of sports, **disciplines**, and events in which women compete at the Olympic Games has increased at almost every Olympics. The following table lists the sports that have been added to the Olympic Program for women and the years in which they were added.

Year	Olympic Games	Olympic Winter Games
1900	Croquet, golf, tennis, sailing	—
1904	Archery	—
1908	Motorboating	Figure skating
1912	Diving, swimming	—
1924	Fencing	—
1928	Gymnastics, track and field	—
1936	—	Alpine skiing
1948	Canoeing and kayaking	—
1952	Equestrian events	Nordic skiing
1960	—	Speed skating
1964	Volleyball	Luge
1968	Shooting*	—
1976	Basketball, handball, rowing	—
1980	Hockey (Field)	—
1984	Cycling, shooting†	—
1988	table tennis, sailing§	—
1992	Badminton, judo	Biathlon, freestyle
1994	**	—
1996	Football (soccer), softball	**
1998	**	Curling, ice hockey
2000	Modern pentathlon, taekwondo Triathlon, weightlifting	**
2002	**	Bobsled, skeleton
2004	Wrestling (freestyle)	**
2006	**	—
2008	—	**
2010	**	—
2012	Boxing	**
2014	**	Ski jumping

*Women were admitted to shooting in 1968 in mixed events.
†Separate shooting events for women began in 1984.
§Separate sailing events for women began in 1988.
**Games were not held that year.

There are other roles women may play in the Olympic Movement. In 1956 at Cortina, Italian skier Giuliana Chenal Minuzzo was the first woman to take the Athletes' Oath on behalf of the competitors. At Mexico City in 1968, Enriqueta Basilio de Sotelo became the first woman to light the main Olympic torch in the stadium, although Sweden's Karin Lindberg had lit one of the torches in 1956 at the Equestrian Olympic Games. Heidi Schüller (FRG) was the first woman to take the Athletes' Oath, at the Summer Olympics in 1972 at Munich.

The IOC resisted female membership for a long time, and it was not until 1981 that the first women became **IOC members**. Two were elected in that year, Flor Isava-Fonseca (Venezuela) and Pirjo Vilmi-Häggman (Finland). Three women to date have served on the IOC **Executive Board**, which really has the power within the IOC. One is Anita DeFrantz of the United States, who was elected as a vice president in 1997 and in 2000 advanced to first vice president. DeFrantz was also an Olympic medalist, winning a bronze medal in rowing **eights** in 1976. The first female Executive Board member was Ms. Isava-Fonseca, serving from 1990 to 1994. They were joined in 2000 by Sweden's Gunilla Lindberg, in 2008 by **Morocco**'s Nawal El Moutawakel, and in 2012 by Germany's Claudia Bokel, who were elected to the Executive Board.

The IOC has publicly stated that it is committed to bringing more and more women into the highest levels of sports administration. In 1996, the IOC mandated that **National Olympic Committees, International Federations**, and other members of the Olympic Movement should reach a goal of 10 percent of women in administrative positions by the year 2000, with that percentage increasing to 20 percent by 2005. Through 2006, the full list of women elected to the IOC is as follows:

Dates of Service	Name (Nation/Type)
1981–1999	Pirjo Vilmi–Häggman (FIN)
1981–2002	Flor Isava-Fonseca (VEN)
1982–1993	Dame Mary Alison Glen Haig (GBR)
1984–	Her Royal Highness Princess Nora (LIE)
1986–	Anita Luceete DeFrantz (USA)
1988–	Princess Anne, Her Royal Highness the Princess Royal (GBR)
1990–2001	Carol Anne Letheren (CAN)
1995–2001	Věra Čáslavská (CZE)
1996–2001	Lu Shengrong (CHN)
1996–2006	Princess Doña Pilar de Borbon (ESP/FEI)
1996–	Gunilla Lindberg (SWE)
1998–	Irena Szewińska-Kirszenstein (POL)
1998–	Nawal El-Moutawakel Bennis (MAR)

Dates of Service	Name (Nation/Type)
1999–2000	Hassiba Boulmerka (ALG/Athlete)
1999–2004	Charmaine Crooks (CAN/Athlete)
1999–2010	Manuela Di Centa (ITA/Athlete)
2000–2005	Susan O'Neill (AUS/Athlete)
2001–	Els van Breda-Vriesman (NED/FIH)
2002–2003	Sandra Baldwin (USA/United States OC)
2002–2010	Pernilla Wiberg (SWE/Athlete)
2004–2012	Rania El-Wani (EGY/Athlete)
2006–	Beatrice Allen (GAM/Gambian OC)
2006–	Nicole Hoevertsz (ARU/Aruban OC)
2006–2014	Beckie Scott (CAN/Athlete)
2007–	HRH Haya Bint Al-Hussein (UAE/FEI)
2007–	Rita Subowo (INA/NOC)
2008–	Claudia Bokel (GER/Athlete)
2008–	Yumilka Ruíz (CUB/Athlete)
2009–	Lydia Nsekera (BDI)
2010–	Angela Ruggiero (USA/Athlete)
2010–	Yang Yang (A) (CHN/Athlete)
2010–	Marisol Casado Estupiñán (ESP)
2011–	Barbara Anne Kendall (NZL/Athlete)
2012–	Lingwei Li (CHN)
2012–	Aïcha Garad Ali (DJI)
2013–	Danka Bartekova (SVK/Athlete)
2013–	Kirsty Coventry (ZIM/Athlete)
2013–	Mikaela Cojuangco Jaworski (PHI)
2013–	Dagmawit Girmay Berhane (ETH)
2014–	Hayley Wickenheiser (CAN/Athlete)

WOMEN'S OLYMPIC GAMES. Angry that athletics for **women** were not being held at the Olympics, the Frenchwoman Alice Milliat founded the Fédération Sportive Féminine Internationale (FSFI) in 1921. The next year, she held the first Women's **Olympic Games** in Pershing Stadium, Vincennes, **France**, just outside of Paris, which attracted participants from five nations (**Czechoslovakia**, France, **Great Britain**, **Switzerland**, and the **United States**). During the 1922 Women's Olympic Games, 18 world records were bettered. The **International Olympic Committee** was not happy with the use of the word "Olympic," and the second edition, held in Göteborg, **Sweden**, in 1926 used the name 2nd International Ladies Games. It had 10 participating nations, and as in 1922, many world records were broken.

After the success of Milliat's organization, the International Amateur Athletic Federation (IAAF, now the International Association of Athletics Federations) was forced to take notice, after snubbing women's athletics for many years. The IAAF had altered its rules in July 1924 to draw up some to manage women's athletics, but was insistent at the time that no women's events should be contested at the Olympic Games. The IAAF held its 8th Congress from 5–8 August 1926, shortly before the 1926 Women's World Games began, and considered a report by a Special Committee on Women's Athletics. Addition of women's track and field to the program of the 1928 Olympics was passed by the Congress by a vote of 12–5, with **Australia, Finland, Hungary, Ireland,** and Great Britain opposing the motion, and it was decided that the FSFI would govern the women's sport, but under the aegis of the IAAF. At the 4th Congress of the FSFI, held in Göteborg from 27–29 August 1926, during the Ladies Games, the International Committee voted to accept the IAAF's offer to include women's **athletics** in the Olympics, with only Great Britain voting against, but also noted that the program should consist of 10 events.

Only five women's events were eventually contested in Amsterdam. This led to a **boycott** by the British Women's Athletic Association, which had been the strongest nation at the 1922 and 1926 Women's Olympics and had opposed the idea at the 1926 Congress. Also, Milliat and the FSFI were determined to continue with the Women's World Games (the new name of the event) and rival to the Olympic Games. To that end, sports other than track and field were included in the editions of 1930 (Praha), contested by 17 nations, and 1934 (London), with 19 nations competing. But by 1936, despite the FSFI having 30 member nations, the IAAF had gained near full control of women's athletics, the foundation of the Women's World Games, and the FSFI and the Women's World Games ceased to exist.

WORKERS' OLYMPIAD. As the concept of amateurism existed in part to banish manual laborers from competing against the those in the upper classes, it is not surprising that the rise of international socialism in the early 20th century also brought about dedicated sports clubs for workers. World War I thwarted the first attempt to organize workers' sports internationally, but the organization reformed in 1920. Although it originally lacked the word in its name, it was renamed the Socialist Workers' Sport International in 1926, better known by its German acronym SASI (Sozialistische Arbeiter Sport Internationale). The organization was frequently plagued by political squabbling, and the communists soon seceded from SASI, joining the Sportintern. The first major event held by SASI was a **gymnastics** festival organized in Prague in 1921 to celebrate the third anniversary of the nation of **Czechoslovakia**. Twelve countries sent competitors, and the event (confusingly known as the Spartakiáda) became a precursor of the Workers' Olympiad, which were to be held at six-year intervals.

The first edition was held in 1925 in Frankfurt am Main, **Germany,** with the winter competitions held in Schreiberhau (now Szklarska Poręba,

Poland). The second Olympiad was held in **Austria**, with the main event held in Wien (Vienna) and Mürzzuschlag staging the winter events. In 1936, SASI organized a distinct **People's Olympiad** in Barcelona, **Spain**, which could not be held because the Spanish Civil War broke out just days before the opening ceremony. Antwerp, **Belgium**, hosted the third edition of the Workers' Olympiad in 1937, with winter competitions taking place in Janské Lázně, Czechoslovakia. A fourth edition was planned for Helsinki, **Finland**, in 1943, but like the Olympic Games scheduled to be held there in 1940, these were canceled due to World War II. These Workers' Olympiads were well attended by both athletes and the public. The 1931 edition claimed 80,000 competitors, with mass running, **swimming**, and gymnastic events being held.

The movement was primarily European, although it also had affiliations in, for example, **Palestine** and the **United States**. The majority of members were from Germany, Austria, and Czechoslovakia, and SASI suffered major blows when their affiliates were forbidden by the right-wing governments of Germany (1933) and Austria (1934). SASI vanished during World War II, but was reborn as the International Workers' Sports Confederation (CSIT, Comité Sportif International du Travail) in 1946. But no new Workers' Olympiads were ever held, and by 1952 even the **Soviet Union** had started competing in the **Olympic Games**. The CSIT still exists (now known as the Confédération Sportive Internationale du Travailliste et Amateur) and has been recognized by the **International Olympic Committee** since 1986. It still aims to bring together the working population through sports, but is no longer as politically motivated as in the past.

WORLD ANTI-DOPING AGENCY (WADA). In February 1999, the **International Olympic Committee** (IOC) convened the World Conference on **Doping** in Sport. The conference proposed the formation of an organization to police doping violations, and in November 1999, the World Anti-Doping Agency was established in **Lausanne, Switzerland**. WADA was formed in response to the proliferation of doping, or drug use, in sports. Its express purpose is to oversee drug testing in sports, educate athletes against the use of drugs, and eventually eliminate doping. The first president of WADA was the **Canadian IOC member Dick Pound**, who served two terms through 2007 and was succeeded by former **Australian** minister of finance John Fahey. Sir Craig Reedie of **Scotland** became president on 1 January 2014. WADA is composed of a Foundation Board, an Executive Committee, a Board of Directors, and several working committees. The Foundation Board is the decision-making body of WADA, but it delegates management of the agency to the Executive Committee. WADA has published a uniform list of prohibited substances, the World Anti-Doping Code of anti-doping principles; has established and recognized specific drug-testing laboratories; and has been responsible for getting virtually all sports federations to be cognizant of the need to eliminate drugs in sport, and to that end, to test diligently for doping by athletes, both in and out of competition, by accepting the uniform code.

WORLD GAMES. The World Games can be considered "the **Olympic Games** for non-Olympics sports or events." They are organized by the International World Games Association, which cooperates with and is recognized by the **International Olympic Committee** (IOC). It requires its member **International Federations** to be recognized by the IOC and/or **SportAccord**.

The first World Games were held in 1981 in the **United States** in Santa Clara, California, and have since been held in London, **England** (1985); Karlsruhe, West **Germany** (1989); Den Haag, the **Netherlands** (1993); Lahti, **Finland** (1997); Akita, **Japan** (2001); Duisburg, **Germany** (2005); Kaohsiung, **Taiwan** (2009); and Cali, **Colombia** (2013).

At the 2013 edition, 32 sports were contested: acrobatic **gymnastics**, aerobic gymnastics, air sports, artistic **roller skating**, beach handball, **billiard** sports, boules (**bowls**) sports, **bowling**, canoe polo, **dance sport**, field **archery**, fin swimming, fistball, flying disc, jiu jitsu, **karate**, **korfball**, lifesaving, **orienteering**, powerlifting, **racquetball**, **rhythmic gymnastics**, roller inline **hockey**, **rugby** sevens, track **speed skating**, sport climbing, **squash**, *sumo*, **trampoline gymnastics**, **tug-of-war**, tumbling gymnastics, and **water skiing** and wakeboarding. In addition, five invitational sports were contested: canoe **marathon**, duathlon, **softball**, road speed skating, and **wushu**. There were 2,870 athletes from 98 nations who participated.

Sports that have "graduated" from the World Games to the Olympics are **badminton** (became Olympic in 1992), **taekwondo**, trampolining, and **triathlon** (all became Olympic in 2000). **Baseball** and softball were also contested at the World Games before being admitted to the Olympics, but did not feature at the Olympics in 2012 nor will they in 2016. Rugby sevens and **golf**, both (former) World Games sports, will be held at the 2016 Games in Rio de Janeiro.

WORLD OLYMPIANS ASSOCIATION (WOA). The World Olympians Association was established on 21 November 1995 during a meeting at the **Olympic Museum** in **Lausanne, Switzerland**, with 25 founding members present. The group is essentially an alumni association of former Olympic athletes. Its mission, as stated in the WOA constitution, is "to unite Olympians and promote **Olympism** by bringing the Olympians of the world together and encouraging their involvement in public service." Several nations have also formed National Olympian Associations.

WRESTLING. Wrestling is the most ancient known competitive sport. It was introduced into the **Ancient Olympic Games** in 708 B.C., shortly after the Games began in 776 B.C. Ancient Olympic champions are recorded from Eurybatos of Sparta (708 B.C.) through Aurelius Aelix of Phoenicia (A.D. 213). The most titled champions at Olympia were **Milon of Kroton**, who won five titles in wrestling (532–516 B.C.) and one in boys' wrestling (540 B.C.), and Hipposthenes of Sparta, who also won five wrestling titles (624–608 B.C.) and one boys' wrestling title (632 B.C.) at ancient Olympia.

Only in 1900 was wrestling not on the **Olympic Program**. Four main forms of amateur competitive wrestling are practiced in the world: **Greco-Roman** wrestling, **freestyle** wrestling, **judo** wrestling, and sambo wrestling (sometimes called "sombo," although it is an acronym for the Russian phrase "*samozashchita bez oruzhiya*," meaning self-defense without weapons). Judo is considered a separate sport at the Olympics. Sambo is a combination of freestyle and judo and is most popular in the Asian republics of the former **Soviet Union**, but it has not yet been contested in the Olympics. Currently, both freestyle and Greco-Roman wrestling are contested at the Olympics, and both have been held since 1920. Prior to that (except in 1908), only one form was used, usually Greco-Roman. Freestyle wrestling is similar to American collegiate style, or folkstyle wrestling. Holds are relatively unlimited, provided they are not dangerous, and can be applied to any part of the body. Greco-Roman wrestling limits holds to the upper body.

Women's freestyle wrestling was added to the Olympic Program in 2004 at Athens. In 27 Olympic Games, there have been 4,770 athletes (4,624 men, 146 women) from 129 nations who have participated in wrestling. The dominant country in wrestling has been the Soviet Union and its former republics, especially in Greco-Roman style. The **United States** is close to the Soviets in freestyle, however. Other nations that produce good wrestlers include **Iran**, **Turkey**, and **Japan**. **Wilfried Dietrich** of **Germany** has won five Olympic medals but only one gold medal. Eight wrestlers (including two women) have won three Olympic gold medals, with **Aleksandr Karelin** (URS/EUN/RUS) and **Artur Taymazov** (UZB) also winning silver medals.

The wrestling international federation is the Fédération Internationale de Luttes Associées, which was formed in 1912 and had 175 affiliated nations as of July 2014.

On 11 February 2013 the IOC announced that wrestling would be dropped from the list of 25 core sports for the 2020 Olympic Games program and would have to apply to be reinstated. Seven months later at their meeting in Buenos Aires, they changed their decision and added wrestling to the 2020 Olympic program. *See also* BAUMGARTNER, BRUCE ROBERT; JOHANSSON, IVAR VALENTIN; LEINO, EINO AUKUSTI;

MEDVED, ALEKSANDR VASILYEVICH; SCHUHMANN, CARL; TAY-
LOR, CHRISTOPHER J.; THEAGENES OF THASOS; WATANABE,
OSAMU; WESTERGREN, CARL OSCAR.

WUSHU. Wushu is a Chinese martial art. *Wu* in Chinese refers to the military
or warfare, while *shu* refers to the method of performing an activity. Wushu
has never been on the **Olympic Program**, but the International Wushu Federation, which currently (as of 2014) has 147 members, was recognized by
the **International Olympic Committee** (IOC) in 1999. Strangely, the IOC
allowed the Beijing **Organizing Committee** to hold a wushu tournament during the Olympics, although **demonstration sports** were abolished after 1992,
and no international sports events are normally allowed to be held in the host
city during the Olympics.

X GAMES. The X Games is a sports event featuring extreme sports that has been organized annually by the Entertainment and Sports Programming Network (ESPN). It began in 1995 and consists of various events in moto-cross, **mountain biking**, skateboarding, **BMX**, and various motor sports. A second version featuring winter sports, called the Winter X Games, began in 1997 and includes **snowboarding**, skiing, and snowmobiling. Primarily a **United States** series of events, attempts have been made in recent years for international competition, and X Games Asia and Winter X Games Europe have also been held. It does not seem likely that this type of competition will be added to the **Olympic Games** in the near future, although some of these type of events have been included in the **Olympic Winter Games freestyle skiing** program since the 1990s.

XIONG NI (CHN–DIV). B. 6 January 1974, Changsha, Hunan, **China**. With five **Olympic medals**, Xiong Ni trails only **Dmitry Sautin** among male Olympic **divers** and is tied with **Greg Louganis** and **Klaus Dibiasi** for second most medals. In 1988, Xiong won his first Olympic medal, a silver, behind Greg Louganis on the **platform**. In 1992, Xiong, at five feet, five inches (166 cm), 121 lb (55 kg), finished third in the Olympic platform event. Turning his emphasis to the **springboard**, he won the gold medal in 1996 and 2000, and in 2000 also added a gold medal in the new event of synchronized springboard diving, partnered by Xiao Hailiang. In 2000, Xiong and Xiao also won the World Cup and the Grand Prix Super Final in synchronized springboard. Xiong never won a world title, his best finish being second in the 1991 platform event.

Y

YACHTING. *See* SAILING.

YANG YANG (CHN–STK). **Short-track speed skating** competition in the early 1990s had the complication of two world-class female athletes with similar reduplicated names—both born in the same province in **China** within one year of each other and both of similar height and weight. To help differentiate the pair, the older was designated by writers as Yang Yang (A) (for August, the month of her birth) and the younger was Yang Yang (S) (for September). Yang Yang (A) was born 24 August 1976 in Tangyuan, Heilongjiang, China, and is listed at five feet, five inches (166 cm), 128 lb (58 kg). She competed in the **Olympic Winter Games** from 1998 to 2006 and won five medals (two gold, two silver, one bronze). When she won the 500 meter race in 2002, she became the first Chinese athlete to win a Winter Olympics gold medal.

Yang Yang (S) was born 14 September 1977 in Qitaihe, Heilongjiang, China, and is listed as being one cm shorter and two kg heavier. She competed in the Winter Olympics from 1994 to 2002 and also won five medals (four silver, one bronze). Two of her medals came in the 1998 and 2002 3,000 meters **relay**, in which one of her teammates was Yang Yang (A).

There has also been one other Chinese Olympian with the name Yang Yang, although there would be no confusion with the short-track speed skating pair. A six-foot tall (184 cm), 183 lb (83 kg) male, he was born in 1983 and was a catcher for the Chinese **baseball** team in the 2008 Olympic baseball tournament. A fourth person named Yang Yang was the winner of the 1988 Olympic **badminton** men's **singles** when badminton was played as a **demonstration sport**. He was born in 1963 and was a five-foot, nine-inch (1.76 cm) left-hander who won several other international major badminton championships.

YEGOROVA, LYUBOV IVANOVNA (EUN/RUS–CCS). B. 5 May 1966, Seversk, Tomsk, **Russia**, USSR. Lyubov Yegorova was the winner of a female record six gold medals for Nordic skiing. She won three golds in 1992 (15 km, **combined pursuit**, and **relay**) and a further three in 1994 (five km, combined pursuit, and relay). She also won two silver medals in 1992 (five km and 30 km) and one in 1994 (15 km). In two **Olympic Winter Games**, she entered a total of 10 events and won medals in nine of them with a fifth place result in the 30 km race in 1994 her only nonmedal event. At five feet, six inches (167 cm) and 128 lb (58 kg), she was the World Cup champion in 1992–1993 and took bronzes in 1990–1991 and 1991–1992. After an absence during which she became a mother, she returned with her fourth world title in Trondheim at the 1997 World Championships. But a few days after her victory, she was found to have used the illegal substance bromantan, and Yegorova was subsequently stripped of her title and banned from competition for two years. She returned to competition after these two years, but was unable to reach her previous level, although she managed a fifth place in the Salt Lake 10 km race.

YEMEN (YEM). The Republic of Yemen was formed on 22 May 1990 by combining the nations of the People's Democratic Republic of Yemen (South Yemen) and the **Yemen Arab Republic** (North Yemen). It was shortly thereafter recognized by the **International Olympic Committee**. Yemen, located in the southern portion of the Arabian peninsula in Asia, has since competed at the **Olympic Games** of 1992 and each subsequent Summer Games but has not yet appeared in the **Olympic Winter Games**. They have had 25 athletes (22 men, three **women**) competing in a total of six sports: **athletics** (10 men, three women), **gymnastics** (one man), **judo** (six men), **swimming** (two men), **taekwondo** (two men), and **wrestling** (one man). With few exceptions, Yemeni athletes have been eliminated in the first **round** of competition. In 1996, Mohamed Al-Saadi finished 101st of 124 entrants in the **marathon**, and in 2012, Tameem Al-Kubati won his first bout in the Taekwondo **flyweight** class and lost in the quarter-final round. In 2008, Nashwan Al-Harazi finished 81st of 98 entrants in the individual **all-around** gymnastics event.

YEMEN ARAB REPUBLIC (YAR). North Yemen, formally the Yemen Arab Republic and located on the Arabian peninsula in Western Asia, first competed in the 1984 **Olympic Games**, with two athletes, brothers Ali Saleh Al-Ghadi and Abdul Raab Al-Ghadi. Abdul ran in the 800 meters, while Ali competed in both the 5,000 and 10,000 meters. In 1988, there were eight male competitors—four in **athletics**, two in **judo**, and two in **wrestling**, none of whom managed to reach the next round of competition. The best performance was that of Mohamed Moslih in the judo **lightweight** class. He finished tied for 19th of the 41 entrants. After 1988, North Yemen athletes competed for the unified **Yemen**. *See also* YEMEN DEMOCRATIC REPUBLIC.

YEMEN DEMOCRATIC REPUBLIC (YMD). The Yemen Democratic Republic, popularly known as South Yemen but officially the People's Democratic Republic of Yemen, is located on the Arabian peninsula in

Western Asia and only competed at the 1988 **Olympic Games**, with five men—three track and field **athletes** and two **boxers**. Both boxers were stopped in the first **round** of their bouts. The three track and field runners (100 meters, 200 meters, and 5,000 meters) were each eliminated after their first **heat**. After 1988, South Yemen athletes competed for the unified **Yemen**. *See also* YEMEN ARAB REPUBLIC.

YERMAKOVA, ANASTASIYA NIKOLAYEVNA (RUS–SYN). B. 8 April 1983, Moscow, **Russia**, USSR. Together with her partner **Anastasiya Davydova**, Anastasiya Yermakova, at five feet, seven inches (169 cm), 121 lb (55 kg), is one of the most successful **synchronized swimmers** in history, leading the Russian dominance of the sport in the 21st century. The two won back-to-back gold medals in both the **duet** and team events at the 2004 and 2008 **Olympic Games**, making them the only synchronized swimmers to claim four gold medals. (Davydova added a fifth in the team event in 2012.) They have also excelled in World Championships, winning five team golds and four duet golds between 2001 and 2007, and adding a duet silver in 2001 and another silver for Yermakova in the solo event of 2003.

YOUTH OLYMPIC GAMES. The Youth Olympic Games is a new concept developed by the **International Olympic Committee** (IOC), and more specifically, the brainchild of **IOC President Jacques Rogge**. The first edition of these was held from 14–26 August 2010 in **Singapore**. Over 3,600 athletes from more than 200 nations took part. The Youth Olympic Games (YOG) are open to athletes between the ages of 14 and 18. The program is similar to Olympic sports, but with a shortened program and with fewer events and **disciplines**. The 2nd Youth Olympic Games were held in Nanjing, **China**, from 16–28 August 2014. The 3rd Youth Olympic Games are scheduled for Buenos Aires, **Argentina**, from 11–23 September 2018. A separate **Youth Olympic Winter Games** is also held, with the first celebration from 13–22 January 2012 in Innsbruck, **Austria**.

YOUTH OLYMPIC WINTER GAMES. Similar to the **Youth Olympic Games**, the Youth **Olympic Winter Games** is a new concept developed by the **International Olympic Committee** (IOC), and more specifically, as the brainchild of **IOC President Jacques Rogge**. The first Youth Olympic Winter Games was held in Innsbruck, **Austria**, from 13–22 January 2012. The Games are open to athletes aged 14 to 18. The program will be similar to that of the Olympic Winter Games, but with a smaller number of events. The 2nd Youth Olympic Winter Games are scheduled for Lillehammer, **Norway**, from 12–21 February 2016.

YUGOSLAVIA (YUG). Although its official name at the time was the Kingdom of Serbs, Croats, and Slovenes, the southeastern European nation of Yugoslavia first competed at the Olympics in 1920, although **Serbia** had already been represented by two athletes in 1912 at Stockholm. From 1920 to 1988, Yugoslavia appeared at every Summer **Olympic Games** celebration, although in 1932 it was represented by a lone track and field athlete. Yugoslavia was one of only two communist countries to not **boycott** the 1984 Los Angeles Games. It first appeared at the **Olympic Winter Games** at their inception in 1924 and returned every four years, with the exception of 1932 and 1960. In 1984, Yugoslavia hosted the Winter Games in Sarajevo, Bosnia. It subsequently was unsuccessful in its bid to host the 1992 and 1996 Summer Games in Belgrade.

In the early 1990s, a civil war caused the country to fall apart. **Croatia, Slovenia,** and **Bosnia and Herzegovina** competed independently from 1992 on. Due to a United Nations' resolution, athletes from the other republics were forced to compete in Barcelona as **independent Olympic participants** under the **Olympic flag.** In 1996, a team again appeared at the Olympics under the name Yugoslavia, but this was essentially the nation later known as **Serbia and Montenegro.** Macedonia, the remaining republic, appeared independently under the politically correct name the Former Yugoslav Republic of Macedonia.

At the Summer Olympics between 1920 and 1988, 1,035 Yugoslav athletes (895 men, 140 **women**) entered and Yugoslavians won 83 **Olympic medals** (26 gold, 29 silver, 28 bronze). In addition, they entered 235 athletes (206 men, 29 women) and won three silver medals and one bronze medal at the Winter Olympics. They entered virtually every Olympic sport contested during that era—25 summer sports and 10 winter sports—all Olympic sports that were held in more than three Olympic Games from 1920 to 1988 with the exception of **modern pentathlon** and **field hockey.**

Yugoslavian athletes excelled in team sports. In **basketball,** the women's team won the silver medal in 1988 and the bronze medal in 1980; the men's team won gold in 1980 in a major upset over the **Soviet Union,** silver in 1968, 1976, and 1988, and bronze in 1984. In men's **football,** Yugoslavia won gold in 1960, silver in 1948, 1952, and 1956, and bronze in 1984. In **handball,** the women's team won gold in 1984 and silver in 1980, and the men's team won gold in 1972 and 1984 and bronze in 1988. The men's **water polo** team won gold in 1968, 1984, and 1988 and silver in 1952, 1956, 1964, and 1980.

Even in primarily individual sports, Yugoslavia won many of its medals in team events. The 1928 **gymnastics** team won the bronze medal, with all five of their **rowing** medals from team events: 1952 men's coxless fours gold, 1980 double **sculls** silver and coxed **pairs** bronze, 1984 **doubles** sculls bronze, and 1988 coxless pairs bronze. In **canoeing**, Yugoslavia won a gold a silver medal in **Canadian**-style **doubles** in 1984. In 1988, the first year that **table tennis** was an official sport, Yugoslavian pairs won both men's and women's doubles. In strictly individual sports, Yugoslavia won two silver medals in **athletics** (1948 **hammer throw**, 1956 **marathon**), 11 medals in **boxing** (three gold, two silver, six bronze), two bronze medals in **judo**, two gold and one bronze in **shooting**, one gold and one silver in **swimming**, and 15 medals in **wrestling** (four gold, six silver, five bronze). In gymnastics, in addition to their team medal, individual gymnasts won five gold, two silver, and three bronze medals. And in canoeing Yugoslavian canoeists won three individual medals, one of each color.

Individual Yugoslav athletes with the most medals are led by Leon Štukelj, from present-day **Slovenia**, who won six medals in gymnastics from 1924 to 1936—three gold, one silver, and two bronze. Martija Ljubic, a canoeist, won four medals (two gold, one silver, one bronze) from 1976 to 1984. Gymnast Miroslav Cerar won three medals from 1964 to 1968—two gold in **pommelled horse** and a bronze in **horizontal bar**. Basketball players Andro Knego, Dražen Dalipagić, Krešimir Ćosić, and Rajko Žižić each won three medals. Ćosić and Dalipagić have both been inducted into the Naismith Basketball Hall of Fame.

The Yugoslavian Winter Olympians who had the most success at the Winter Games include Matjaž Debelak, who won a bronze medal in the **large hill ski jumping** event in 1988 and won a silver medal as a member of the second-place four-man team that year. In 1988, Mateja Svet won a silver medal in the women's **slalom Alpine skiing** event, and Jure Franko, the flagbearer at the opening ceremony in Sarajevo in 1984, won a silver medal that year in the men's **giant slalom**. *See also* KOSOVO.

Z

ZAIRE. *See* CONGO, DEMOCRATIC REPUBLIC OF THE.

ZAMBIA (ZAM). A landlocked country in Southern Africa formerly known as Northern Rhodesia, this nation took the name Republic of Zambia on 24 October 1964. Zambia has competed at each **Olympic Games** from 1968 to 2012 with the exception of 1976, which they **boycotted**. In addition, the country competed at Tokyo in 1964 as Northern Rhodesia. Zambia has never competed at the **Olympic Winter Games**. In 12 Summer Games (including 1964), the nation has had 140 entrants (128 men, 12 **women**) in eight sports: **athletics** (34 men, eight women), **badminton** (one man), **boxing** (43 men), **fencing** (one woman), **football** (32 men), **judo** (11 men), **swimming** (five men, three women), and **wrestling** (two men).

In 1984, Keith Mwila won a bronze medal in **light-flyweight** boxing, the first medal won by a Zambian athlete at the Olympics. The nation's second Olympic medal was won in 1996, when Samuel Matete finished second in the men's 400 meter **hurdles**. Zambia has twice competed in the men's Olympic football tournament and in 1988 reached the quarter-final **round** and finished tied for fifth place. Other notable Olympic results for Zambia include five boxers reaching the quarter-final round and being tied for fifth place. In 1980, **featherweight** Winifred Kabunda and **light-middleweight** Wilson Kaoma, in 1984, light-middleweight Christopher Kapopo and **middleweight** Moses Mwaba, and in 1988, **light-welterweight** Anthony Mwamba each were defeated in the quarter-final round with Kabunda, Mwaba, and Mwamba losing to the eventual gold medalist. In athletics, Samuel Matete, in addition to his silver medal in 1996, reached the semifinal round in the 400 meter hurdles in both 1992 and 2000. Four other Zambian runners also reached the semifinal round in their events: 1984 Davison Lishebo, 400 meters; 1996, Godfrey Siamusiye, 3,000 meter **steeplechase**; 2008, Rachel Nachula, women's 400 meters; and 2012, Gerald Phiri, men's 100 meters.

ZANZIBAR. *See* TANZANIA.

ZAPPAS, EVANGELOS. B. 1800, Labovë, Ottoman Empire. D. 19 June 1865, Broşteni, Ialomiţa, **Romania**. Evangelos Zappas was a wealthy landowner and businessman of Greek background, but he never set foot in Athens, where he would become famous for sponsoring an early effort at Olympic revival. He lived most of his life in Romania, settling there after fighting for **Greece** in the Greek War of Independence. In early 1856, Zappas proposed to the Greek government a permanent revival of the **Olympic Games** and offered to finance the project. The first of the **Zappas Olympic Games** was held in 1859. Zappas had earmarked funds for restoration of the ancient Panathenaic Stadium, but this was not done for the 1859 Games. After his death, his will provided ample money to support a permanent revival of the **Ancient Olympic Games** and for restoration of the stadium. Prior to the 1870 Zappas Olympics, the Panathenaic Stadium was restored, thanks to Zappas's largesse.

ZAPPAS OLYMPIC GAMES. Numerous attempts at revival of the Olympic Games occurred prior to the successful efforts of Baron **Pierre de Coubertin**. Perhaps the most significant of these were the Zappas Olympic Games. They are today usually called by this name, although in the 19th century the Greeks called them **Olympic Games** for **Greece**. The Zappas Olympic Games were conducted four times: in 1859, 1870, 1875, and 1889. They were held in Athens. The Games were the brain-child of Panagiotis Soutsos, but were sponsored by **Evangelos Zappas**, a wealthy Greek who then lived in **Romania**. In 1856, he wrote to King Otto and offered to fund the entire Olympic revival himself. In early November 1859, a series of three festivals was conducted. The first was a series of agri-industrial contests. One week later, **chariot races** were conducted for professionals and laymen (the word "amateur" in reference to sports had not yet been invented).

On 15 November 1859, the athletic Games were conducted at Plateia Loudovikou, a city square on the edge of town. There were **sprint** races, a 1,500 meter race, two **javelin throws** (one for distance, the other for accuracy), and two **discus throws** (one for distance and one for accuracy). The winner of the 1,500 meters was Petros Velissariou, who came from Smyrna, and won a first prize of 280 drachmas, the largest prize of the first Zappas Olympics, because **William Penny Brookes**'s Much Wenlock prize of £10 was included. In 1870, the Zappas Olympics were moved to the ancient Panathenaic Stadium in the center of Athens. The stadium had been restored at Zappas's expense, although he had died in 1865. These Games, held on 15 November 1870, were the most successful of the Zappas Olympics, with the newspapers calling them a resounding success. More than 30,000 spectators attended these Games.

The 1875 Zappas Olympics are considered by classics scholar David Young to have been a "disaster." In 1870, the winner of the 400 meters had been Evangelis Skordaras, a butcher, and the **wrestling** winner was Kardamylakes, a manual laborer. Several of Athens's elite then suggested that the Games be restricted only to athletes from the upper class and that the general public be banned. This early attempt at elitism and using the early British concepts of amateurism proved highly detrimental to the Zappas Olympics. Only 24 athletes took part in 1875, with a small crowd that left large sections of the stadium empty.

The 1889 Zappas Olympics took place in May in a small gym, rather than in the stadium, and were not well organized. In fact, they were scheduled, begun, canceled, and then conducted again a few days later. Again, only a few privileged, upper-class athletes competed, and the crowd was much smaller. In 1891 and 1893, Panhellenic Gymnastic Society Games were contested, which were not organized by the Zappas Committee. Interestingly, several Greek athletes who competed in 1893 also competed at the 1896 Olympics.

The Zappas Olympic Games rank with the **Much Wenlock Olympian Games** as the most significant attempts to revive the Ancient Olympic idea. They probably surpass the Much Wenlock Games because they were national sporting contests. Though he later denied any knowledge of them, Coubertin was keenly aware of the efforts of the Zappas Committee to hold Olympic Games, having been told of them by **Demetrios Vikelas**, who would later be the first **International Olympic Committee (IOC) president**.

The Games themselves were fairly successful in 1859, and especially in 1870, but were "ruined" by elitism, antiathleticism, bigotry, and attempts to impose an amateur-type code on the athletes. The Zappas Olympics never had the international flavor that Coubertin would instill in the modern Olympic Games. But they were the closest attempt yet to a true Olympic revival.

ZÁTOPEK, EMIL (TCH–ATH). B. 19 September 1922, Koprivnice, Moravia, **Czechoslovakia**. D. 21 November 2000, Prague, **Czech Republic**. Emil Zátopek was a supreme distance runner whose rugged training regimen was rewarded with unprecedented success. At the 1948 **Olympic Games**, he won the gold medal in the 10,000 meters and finished second in the 5,000 meters. Then at Helsinki in 1952, he produced one of the greatest performances in distance running history. He won the 5,000 meters, successfully defended his 10,000 meters title, and then took his third gold medal in his first-ever **marathon** race, to complete a "triple," which remains unique in Olympic history. Zátopek, at six feet, one inch (182 cm), 159 lb (72 kg), closed his Olympic career four years later when he placed sixth in the marathon in Melbourne. Between 1949 and 1954, he set 18 world records at every distance from 5,000 meters to 30,000 meters, a remarkable display of versatility at the very highest level. His wife, Dana (née Ingrová), was the Olympic gold medalist in the **javelin throw** in 1952 and silver medalist in 1960. The couple shared a birthday, both born on the same day and year.

Zátopek's was a remarkable life. Under the **Soviet** regime, his athletic feats earned him and his wife many perquisites not available to other Czech citizens. But despite that, after the Soviet tanks attacked Prague in 1968, he spoke out against the Soviet invasion, for which he paid dearly. For that he lost most of the favors bestowed upon him, and he spent much of the rest of his life as a trash collector, his status only restored after the fall of the Iron Curtain.

ŽELEZNÝ, JAN (CZE/TCH–ATH). B. 16 June 1966, Mladá Boleslav, Středočeský kraj, **Czech Republic**. Jan Železný, at six feet, one inch (185 cm), 190 lb (86 kg), is considered the greatest **javelin thrower** in track and field history. As of January 2015, he has the five longest throws of all time, including the world record of 98.48 meters (323.1 feet) set on 25 May 1996. At the 1988 **Olympic Games**, he narrowly missed winning the gold medal, settling for silver, but he won the gold medal at the 1992, 1996, and 2000 Olympic Games. He was also World Champion with the javelin in both 1993 and 1995. Although the javelin specifications have changed twice during his career, he set six world records with the various spears. In December 1999, Železný was elected a member of the **International Olympic Committee** as an athlete member, having previously been a member of the **Athletes' Commission**.

ZHANG YINING (CHN–TTN). B. 5 October 1981, Beijing, **China**. Zhang Yining was the most dominant female **table tennis** player of the first decade of the 21st century. Not only did she earn 10 world titles—**singles** (2005, 2009), **doubles** (2003, 2005, 2007), and team (2000, 2001, 2004, 2006, 2008)—she also won four Olympic titles, winning the singles and doubles in Athens 2004 and the singles and team competitions in front of a home crowd at Beijing in 2008. Underlining her dominance, Zhang, at five feet, six inches (168 cm), 119 lb (54 kg), is also a four-time winner of the World Cup and has won the Pro Tour Grand Finals on six occasions. She was ranked first on the International Table Tennis Federation World Ranking from January 2003 through November 2009, only dropping to second during two months in 2008. In 2008, she was given the honor of reciting the **Olympic Oath** on behalf of the athletes during the opening ceremony of the Beijing **Olympic Games**. She began a career break after her marriage in 2009 and retired in 2011 to attend college in the **United States** at the University of Wisconsin.

ZHENG HAIXIA (CHN-BAS). B. 10 March 1967, Tuocheng, Henan Province, **China**. There are very few female athletes who admit to weighing more than 250 pounds, but China's Zheng Haixia is one of them. With nicknames of "Baby Huey," "Big Girl," and "The Wall," she was the second heaviest Olympic **women's basketball** player at 254 lb (115 kg). But on her six-foot, eight-inch (204 cm) frame, with size 18 sneakers on her feet, that weight did not prohibit her from being one of the most effective players of all time. She was selected to the Chinese national team at the age of 15 and was on the bronze medal–winning team at the 1983 World Championships. In 1994, she was named the most valuable player of the World Championships as China won the silver medal. She appeared in four Olympic tournaments from 1984 to 1996 and won a bronze medal in her first one at the age of 17 years and 145 days—the youngest women's basketball **Olympic medalist** ever. Ironically, on that 1984 team, she was not even the tallest player on her own team—the six-foot, nine-inch (205 cm) Chen Yuefang held that distinction. In the Barcelona Olympics in 1992, Zheng helped lead China to the silver medal. She is one of only two women to twice score 31 or more points in an Olympic basketball game. In 1997, she became the first Chinese person (man or woman) to play professional basketball in the **United States** when she signed with the Los Angeles Sparks of the Women's National Basketball Association (WNBA). She played one additional year in the WNBA and retired after the 1998 season. She later became head coach of the Bayi team in the Chinese professional women's basketball league.

ZIJLAARD-VAN MOORSEL, LEONTINE MARTHA HENRICA PETRONELLA "LEONTIEN" (NED–CYC). B. 22 March 1970, Boekel, Noord-Brabant, **Netherlands**. **Cyclist** Leontien Zijlaard first competed at the **Olympic Games** in 1992, as Leontien van Moorsel, finishing eighth in individual **pursuit** and 23rd in the **road race**. This was somewhat disappointing, considering her record to that time at the World Championships. Van Moorsel was world road champion in 1991 and 1993 and won the individual pursuit in 1990. But she was tortured by other demons, suffering from anorexia and bulimia (eating disorders), and shortly thereafter lost 20 kg (44 lb) from a five-foot, six-inch (168 cm) frame not considered obese. Her cycling career suffered, but she returned to prominence in the late 1990s, winning the individual **time trial** World Championship in 1998 and 1999 and the World Pursuit title again in 2001–2003. At the Sydney Olympics in 2000, she had the most successful Olympics ever for a **woman** cyclist. She won the individual pursuit in world record time, won the road race and the individual time trial, and added a silver medal on the track in points race. Van Moorsel continued competing and, at Athens in 2004, won a gold medal in the individual time trial and a bronze medal in the individual pursuit, after a crash during the road race. She was also a two-time winner of the Tour de France Féminin (1992, 1993), and in 2003 set the World Hour Record with 46.06511 km.

ZIMBABWE (ZIM). Zimbabwe, a landlocked country in southern Africa, was formerly Rhodesia, a British colony that was self-governing from 1923, and as Rhodesia competed at three **Olympic Games**, in 1928, 1960, and 1964. In those three Summer Games, Rhodesia entered 44 athletes (35 men, nine **women**) and competed in **athletics** (five men), **boxing** (seven men), **diving** (one man, three women), **hockey** (15 men), **sailing** (four men), **shooting** (three men), and **swimming** (six women). The men's hockey team finished tied for 11th place of 15 teams in 1964. The best Olympic result by Rhodesian athletes occurred in 1960 when David Butler and Christopher Bevan finished fourth in the mixed two-person **heavyweight dinghy** sailing event. Boxers Abe Bekker, 1960 **featherweight**, and Cecil Bissett, 1928 **lightweight**, each reached the quarter-final round before losing and finished tied for fifth place.

On 11 November 1965, Rhodesian Prime Minister Ian D. Smith announced his nation's unilateral declaration of independence from **Great Britain**. Britain declared the act illegal and demanded that Rhodesia broaden voting rights to provide for eventual rule by the majority Africans. In May 1968, the United Nations (UN) Security Council condemned the white-dominated Rhodesian government, asking that Rhodesian passports not be accepted for international travel. Rhodesia did not compete at the 1968 Olympics, one reason being that the **International Olympic Committee** (IOC) did not recognize its independent status, another being that **Mexico** honored the UN Security Council ruling.

At the 71st **IOC Session** in **Luxembourg** in 1971, the IOC ruled that Rhodesian athletes could compete at the 1972 Olympics under the same conditions as in 1968, using British uniforms, the Union Jack as a flag, and with "God Save the Queen" as an anthem. Initially, this placated the African nations. However, shortly before the 1972 Munich Olympics, the African nations threatened a mass **boycott** if Rhodesia were allowed to compete. The petition stated that the Rhodesians had entered **Germany** not on British passports, as still required by the UN Security Council, but using the **Olympic identity card**. Two days before the 1972 opening ceremony, the IOC voted narrowly (36–31, with three abstentions) to withdraw the invitation to Rhodesia for the 1972 Olympics.

In 1975, the IOC sent a three-member contingent to Rhodesia to inspect the sporting facilities and groups. Led by Major Sylvio Magalhães de Padilha of **Brazil**, this commission of inquiry was not kind to Rhodesian sports, and the IOC expelled the Rhodesian Olympic Committee by a 41–26 vote.

After a civil war and eventual free elections, Rhodesia became officially the Republic of Zimbabwe on 18 April 1980. Zimbabwe first appeared at the Olympics in 1980 at Moscow, and the highlight of its appearance was the gold medal performance of its women's hockey team. Zimbabwe has competed at all subsequent Olympic Games. In nine Summer Games from 1980 to 2012, Zimbabwe entered 135 athletes (90 male, 45 female) in 14 events: **archery** (four men, one woman), athletics (32 men, eight women), boxing (seven men), **cycling** (seven men), diving (two men, four women), hockey (15 women), **judo** (four men, one woman), **rowing** (one man, four women), sailing (five men), shooting (12 men, one woman), swimming (eight men, eight women), **tennis** (five men, three women), **triathlon** (two men), and **weightlifting** (one man). It competed at the **Olympic Winter Games** for the first time in 2014 as Alpine skier Luke Stein finished 57th of 109 entrants in the **giant slalom** and entered but did not finish the **slalom**.

In 2004 and 2008, Zimbabwean swimmer **Kirsty Coventry** won seven medals—gold in the 200 meter **backstroke** in 2004 and 2008, silver in the 100 meter backstroke in 2004 and 2008, silver in both the 200 and 400 meter individual **medley** in 2008, and bronze in the 2004 200 meter individual medley, bringing her nation's medal total to eight. She also competed in the 2000 and 2012 Olympics but did not medal in either of those years, although she had a creditable sixth-place finish in both the 200 meter backstroke and 200 meter individual medley in 2012.

Other notable Olympic results by athletes from Zimbabwe include fourth-place finishes in 2008 by Brian Dzingai in the men's 200 meters and by Ngoni Makusha in the men's **long jump**; the team of Wayne Black and Kevin Ulyett reaching the quarter-finals in men's **doubles** tennis and finishing in a tie for fifth place; Ndaba Dube also a quarter-finalist and tie for fifth in 1984 **bantamweight** boxing; Lesley Smith finishing in seventh place in women's **springboard** diving in 1984; Zephaniah Ncube, 11th in the 10,000 meters in 1984; and **marathon** runners Cuthbert Nyasango (seventh in 2012), Tendai Chimusasa (ninth in 2000, 13th in 1996), Mike Fokoroni (11th in 2008), and Wirimai Juwaso (15th in 2012).

ZIMYATOV, NIKOLAY SEMYONOVICH (URS/RUS–CCS). B. 28 June 1955, Rumyantsevo, Moscow, **Russia**, USSR. Nikolay Zimyatov, at six feet (183 cm), 150 lb (68 kg), is the greatest **Soviet** or Russian male **cross-country skier**. His fame rests primarily on his performance at the 1980 Olympics in Lake Placid, when he won three gold medals in the 30 km and 50 km and on the Soviet **relay** team. He added two further Olympic medals in 1984, defending his 30 km title and helping the Soviets win a silver in the relay. At other championships, he was much less successful, winning only one World Championship, in the 1982 relay event. His best individual finish at a World Championship was second in the 30 km at Lahti in 1978.

ZÖGGELER, ARMIN (ITA–LUG). B. 4 January 1974, Merano, Bolzano-Bozen, **Italy.** Armin Zöggeler is the only man to win six Olympic **luge** medals. He won them in six consecutive **Olympic Winter Games.** Between 1994 and 2014, the five-foot, 11-inch (181 cm), 194 lb (88 kg) South Tyrolean has won two gold, a silver, and three bronze medals. His two titles were won in Salt Lake City (2002) and Torino (2006). Zöggeler has also been dominant in other international competition, winning 14 World Championship medals (including titles in 1995, 1999, 2001, 2003, 2005, and 2011), 10 World Cups (1998, 2000, 2001, 2004, 2006–2011), and three European titles (1994 [team], 2004, and 2008).

Appendix I:
Presidents of the International Olympic Committee

1894–1896	Demetrios Vikelas (Greece)
1896–1924*	Pierre Frédy, Baron de Coubertin (France)
1925–1942§	Count Henry de Baillet-Latour (Belgium)
1946–1952	J[ohannes] Sigfrid Edström (Sweden)
1952–1972	Avery Brundage (United States)
1972–1980	Sir Michael Morris, Lord Killanin of Dublin and Spiddal (Ireland)
1980–2001	Juan Antonio Samaranch Torello, Marqués de Samaranch (Spain)
2001–2013	Jacques Rogge (Belgium)
2013–	Thomas Bach (Germany)

*During World War I, between December 1915 and February 1917, Baron Godefroy de Blonay of Switzerland served as an interim president of the IOC. This was at the request of Baron de Coubertin, who felt that the IOC president should represent a country that was neutral during the war.
§The IOC presidency was technically vacant from 1942 to 1946; however, J. Sigfrid Edström served as de facto president during that time.

Appendix II: The Games of the Olympiads: Sites, Dates, Nations, Athletes

Year	Site	Dates	*Nations	Athletes	Men	Women
1896	Athens	6–15 Apr.	12	176	176	0
1900	Paris	14 May–28 Oct.	31	1,223	1,200	23
1904	St. Louis	1 July–23 Nov.	15	650	644	6
1906	Athens	22 Apr.–2 May	21	841	835	6
1908	London	27 Apr.–31Oct.	22	2,024	1,980	44
1912	Stockholm	5 May–27 July	28	2,377	2,324	53
1920	Antwerp	23 Apr.–12 Sept.	29	2,663	2,586	77
1924	Paris	4 May–27 July	44	3,067	2,932	135
1928	Amsterdam	17 May–12 Aug.	46	2,878	2,604	274
1932	Los Angeles	30 July–14 Aug.	37	1,333	1,207	126
1936	Berlin	1–16 Aug.	49	3,954	3,625	329
1948	London	29 July–14 Aug.	59	4,072	3,679	393
1952	Helsinki	19 July–3 Aug.	69	4,932	4,411	521
1956	Total		72	3,345	2,962	383
	Stockholm	10–17 June	29	158	145	13
	Melbourne	22 Nov.–8 Dec.	67	3,189	2,818	171
1960	Rome	25 Aug.–11 Sept.	83	5,350	4,738	612
1964	Tokyo	10–24 Oct.	93	5,137	4,457	680
1968	Mexico City	12–27 Oct.	112	5,557	4,774	783
1972	Munich	26 Aug.–11 Sept.	121	7,113	6,053	1,060
1976	Montreal	17 July–1 Aug.	92	6,073	4,812	1,261
1980	Moscow	19 July–3 Aug.	80	5,259	4,136	1,123
1984	Los Angeles	28 July12 Aug.	140	6,798	5,229	1,569
1988	Seoul	17 Sept.–2 Oct.	159	8,453	6,251	2,202
1992	Barcelona	25 July–9 Aug.	169	9,386	6,663	2,723
1996	Atlanta	19 July–4 Aug.	197	10,341	6,821	3,520
2000	Sydney	14 Sept.–1 Oct.	200	10,647	6,579	4,068
2004	Athens	13–29 Aug.	201	10,561	6,257	4,304
2008	Beijing	8–24 Aug.	204	10,901	6,290	4,611
2012	London	27 July-12 Aug.	205	10,519	5,864	4,655

*Statistics for the first few Games are not definitely known. Totals do not include entrants in the art competitions.

Appendix III: The Olympic Winter Games: Sites, Dates, Nations, Athletes

Year	Site	Dates	Nations	Athletes	Men	Women
1908	London*	28–29 Oct.	6	21	14	7
1920	Antwerp*	23–29 Apr.	10	86	74	12
1924	Chamonix	24 Jan.–5 Feb.	16	292	279	13
1928	St. Moritz	11–19 Feb.	25	461	433	28
1932	Lake Placid	4–15 Feb.	17	252	231	21
1936	Garmisch-partenkirchen	6–16 Feb.	28	668	588	80
1948	St. Moritz	30 Jan.–8 Feb.	28	668	591	77
1952	Oslo	14–25 Feb.	30	694	585	109
1956	Cortina d'Ampezzo	26 Jan.–5 Feb.	32	821	689	132
1960	Squaw Valley	18–28 Feb.	30	665	521	144
1964	Innsbruck	29 Jan.–9 Feb.	36	1,094	894	200
1968	Grenoble	6–18 Feb.	37	1,160	949	211
1972	Sapporo	3–13 Feb.	35	1,008	802	206
1976	Innsbruck	4–15 Feb.	37	1,129	898	231
1980	Lake Placid	13–24 Feb.	37	1,072	837	235
1984	Sarajevo	8–19 Feb.	49	1,273	996	277
1988	Calgary	13–28 Feb.	57	1,425	1,110	315
1992	Albertville	8–23 Feb.	64	1,801	1,313	488
1994	Lillehammer	12–27 Feb.	67	1,738	1,216	522
1998	Nagano	7–22 Feb.	72	2,180	1,391	789
2002	Salt Lake City	8–24 Feb.	77	2,399	1,513	886
2006	Torino	10–26 Feb.	79	2,494	1,539	955
2010	Vancouver	12–28 Feb	82	2,536	1,503	1,033
2014	Sochi	7–23 Feb.	89	2,748	1,643	1,105

*1908 and 1920 were not Winter Games but the winter sports of figure skating (1908, 1920) and ice hockey (1920), which were held during the Summer Games.

Appendix IV:
Members of the International Olympic Committee

Dates of Service	Member (Nation)
1894–1925	Pierre Frédy, Baron Pierre de Coubertin (FRA)
1894–1895	Ferdinando Lucchesi Palli (ITA)
1894–1897	Demetrios Vikelas (GRE)
1894–1898	Arthur Oliver Russell, Lord Ampthill (GBR)
1894–1898	Duke Riccardo d'Andria Carafa (ITA)
1894–1900	General Aleksey Butowsky (RUS)
1894–1901	Count Maxime de Bousies (BEL)
1894–1905	Leonard Albert Cuff (NZL)
1894–1906	Charles Herbert (GBR)
1894–1907	Dr. Ferenc Kémény (HUN)
1894–1907	José Benjamin Zubiaur (ARG)
1894–1913	Ernst Callot (FRA)
1894–1921	General Viktor Gustaf Balck (SWE)
1894–1924	Professor William Milligan Sloane (USA)
1894–1943	Dr. Jiří Guth-Jarkovský (BOH/TCH)
1896–1909	Karl August Willibald Gebhardt (GER)
1897–1919	Count Eugenio Brunetta d'Usseaux (ITA)
1897–1925	Count Alexandros Merkati (GRE)
1897–1927	Reverend Robert Stuart de Courcy Laffan (GBR)
1898–1924	Baron Frederik Willem Christiaan Hendrik van Tuyll van Serooskerken (NED)
1899–1902	Prince Gheorghe Bibesco (ROM)
1899–1903	Count Archambauld Talleyrand de Perigord (GER)
1899–1906	Niels Vilhelm Sophus Holbeck (DEN)
1899–1937	Baron Godefroy de Blonay (SUI)
1900–1903	Theodore Stanton (USA)
1900–1904	Caspar Whitney (USA)
1900–1908	Prince Sergey Beloselsky-Belotsersky (RUS)
1900–1911	Henri Hébrard de Villeneuve (FRA)
1900–1916	Count Nikolao Ribeaupierre (RUS)
1900–1948	Count Carl Clarence von Rosen (SWE)
1901–1903	Robert François Joseph Nicolas Ghislain Reyntiens (BEL)
1901–1905	Prince Eduard Max Vollrath Friedrich of Salm-Horstmar (GER)
1901–1908	Sir Charles Edward Howard Vincent (GBR)
1901–1931	Miguel de Beistegui (MEX)
1902–1921	Antonio de Mejorada del Campo, Marquis de Villamejor (ESP)

Dates of Service	Member (Nation)
1903–1908	James Hazen Hyde (USA)
1903–1914	Count Caesar Erdmann von Wartensleben Carow (GER)
1903–1942	Count Henry de Baillet-Latour (BEL)
1904–1920	Count Albert Bertier de Sauvigny (FRA)
1905–1907	Henrik August Angell (NOR)
1905–1909	Alexander, Prince von Solms Braunfels (AUT)
1905–1909	Count Egbert Hoyer von der Asseburg (GER)
1905–1913	William Henry Grenfell, Lord Desborough of Taplow (GBR)
1905–1922	Don Carlos F. de Candamo (PER)
1905–1932	Richard Coombes (AUS)
1906–1912	Dimitri Tzokov (BUL)
1906–1912	Duke Antonio de Lancastre (POR)
1906–1912	Torben Grut (DEN)
1907–1908	Thomas Thomassen Heftye (NOR)
1907–1910	Manuel de la Quintana (ARG)
1907–1938	Count Géza Andrassy (HUN)
1908–1909	Prince Scipione Borghese (ITA)
1908–1910	Prince Simon Trubetskoy (RUS)
1908–1919	Baron Reinhold Felix von Willebrand (FIN)
1908–1920	Allison Vincent Armour (USA)
1908–1927	Johan Tidemann Sverre (NOR)
1908–1930	Selim Sirri Bey Tarcan (TUR)
1908–1939	Count Albert Gautier Vignal (MON)
1908–1949	Gheorghe A. Plagino (ROM)
1909–1914	Attilio Brunialti (ITA)
1909–1914	Baron Karl von Wenningen-Ullner von Diepburg (GER)
1909–1915	Sir Theodore Andrea Cook (GBR)
1909–1938	Jigoro Kano (JPN)
1909–1946	Gyula von Muzsa (HUN)
1910–1919	Count Adalbert von Francken-Sierstorpff (GER)
1910–1929	Jean-Maurice Pescatore (LUX)
1910–1933	Prince Léon Durusov (RUS)
1910–1963	Angelos Khristos Bolanaki (EGY)
1911–1914	Abel Ballif (FRA)
1911–1914	Oscar N. Garcia (CHI)
1911–1917	Evert Jansen Wendell (USA)
1911–1919	Otto, Prince zu Windisch-Gritz (AUT)
1911–1919	Rudolf, Count Colloredo-Mansfield (AUT)
1911–1921	John Hanbury-Williams (CAN)
1912–1921	Fritz Hansen (DEN)
1912–1940	Count José Carlos Peñha Garcia (POR)
1912–1949	Svetomir V. Ðukić (SER/YUG)
1913–1915	Georges Aleksandrovich Duperron (RUS)
1913–1919	Count Adolf von Arnim-Muskau (GER)
1913–1920	Algernon St. Maur Somerset, Duke of Somerset (GBR)
1913–1929	Dimitri Stanciov (BUL)

Dates of Service	Member (Nation)
1913–1938	Baron Edouard-Émile de Laveleye (BEL)
1913–1938	Raul de Rio Branco (BRA)
1913–1944	Albert Glandaz (FRA)
1914–1919	Sydney Howard Farrar (RSA)
1914–1939	Carlo Montu (ITA)
1914–1950	Marquis Melchior de Polignac (FRA)
1918–1922	Bartow Sumter Weeks (USA)
1918–1929	Eduardo Dorn y de Alsua (ECU)
1918–1940	Pedro Jaime de Matheu (ESA/Central America)
1919–1922	Carlos Silva-Vildosola (CHI)
1919–1925	Arthur Marryatt (NZL)
1919–1929	Marquis Giorgio Guglielmi (ITA)
1919–1933	Count Justinien de Clary (FRA)
1920–1927	Sir Dorabji Jamsetji Tata (IND)
1920–1943	Henry Nourse (RSA)
1920–1946	Franjo Bučar (YUG)
1920–1948	Ernst Edvard Krogius (FIN)
1921–1923	Henrique Echevarrieta (ESP)
1921–1923	Nizzam Eddin Khon (IRI)
1921–1932	Marcelo T. de Alvear (ARG)
1921–1933	Reginald John Kentish (GBR)
1921–1936	Francisco Ghigliani (URU)
1921–1946	James George Bower Merrick (CAN)
1921–1952	Johannes Sigfrid Edström (SWE)
1921–1954	Baron Guell de Santiago (ESP)
1921–1957	Wang Chengting (CHN)
1922–1924	Prince Stefan Lubomirski (POL)
1922–1931	Ivar Nyhölm (DEN)
1922–1936	Charles Hitchcock Sherrill (USA)
1922–1948	William May Garland (USA)
1922–1951	John Joseph Keane (IRL)
1923–1924	José Carlos Rincon Gallardo, Marquis de Guadalupe (MEX)
1923–1927	Joseph Pentland Firth (NZL)
1923–1927	Prince Samad Khan Momtazos Saltaneh (IRI)
1923–1929	Gerald Oakley, Earl of Cadogan (GBR)
1923–1936	Porfirio Franca y Alvarez de la Campa (CUB)
1923–1939	Jorgé Matte Gormaz (CHI)
1923–1949	Ricardo Camillo Aldao (ARG)
1923–1957	Alfredo Benavides (PER)
1923–1961	Arnaldo Guinle (BRA)
1923–1962	José Ferreira Santos (BRA)
1924–1927	David Kinley (USA)
1924–1927	Fernando Alvarez, Duke d'Alba (ESP)
1924–1927	Jorgé Gomez de Parada (MEX)
1924–1928	Dr. Martin Haudek (AUT)
1924–1929	Oskar Ruperti (GER)

Dates of Service	Member (Nation)
1924–1930	Prince Kasimierz Lubomirski (POL)
1924–1933	Seichi Kishi (JPN)
1924–1938	Theodor Lewald (GER)
1924–1944	James Taylor (AUS)
1924–1957	Pieter Wilhelmus Scharroo (NED)
1925–1943	Baron Alphert Schimmelperminck van der Oye (NED)
1925–1953	Count Alberto Bonacossa (ITA)
1926–1930	Giorgios Averof (GRE)
1926–1947	Jānis Dikmanis (LAT)
1926–1956	Duke Adolf Friedrich von Mecklenburg-Schwerin (GER)
1927–1933	George Kemp, Lord Rochdale (GBR)
1927–1936	Ernest Lee Jahncke (USA)
1927–1950	Sir Thomas Fearnley (NOR)
1928–1930	Bernard Cyril Freyberg (NZL)
1928–1930	Marquis François Manuel de Pons (ESP)
1928–1932	Friederik Akel (EST)
1928–1932	Miguel Moises Saenz (MEX)
1928–1938	Theodor Schmidt (AUT)
1928–1939	Ignasz Matuszewski (POL)
1928–1939	Sir George McLaren Brown (CAN)
1929–1933	Don Alfredo Ewing (CHI)
1929–1944	Stepan G. Shaprachikov (BUL)
1929–1957	Clarence Napier Bruce, Lord Aberdare of Duffryn (GBR)
1929–1964	Karl Ferdinand Ritter von Halt (GER)
1930–1931	Augusto Turati (ITA)
1930–1932	Kremalettin Sami Pascha (TUR)
1930–1933	Nikolaos Politis (GRE)
1931–1933	Cecil J. Wray (NZL)
1931–1945	Stanisław Rouppert (POL)
1931–1952	Count Federico Suarez de Vallelano (ESP)
1932–1952	Horacio Bustos Moron (ARG)
1932–1958	Axel Kristian George, Prince of Denmark (DEN)
1932–1964	Count Paolo Thaon di Revel (ITA)
1932–1966	Guru Dutt Sondhi (IND)
1933–1936	Jotaro Sugimoura (JPN)
1933–1950	Sir Francis Noel Curtis Bennett (GBR)
1933–1951	Sir Harold Daniel Luxton (AUS)
1933–1952	Rechid Saffet Atabinen Bey (TUR)
1933–1981	David George Brownlow Cecil, Lord Burghley,6th Marquess of Exeter (GBR)
1934–1948	Count Michimasa Soyeshima (JPN)
1934–1966	François Piétri (FRA)
1934–1967	Lord Arthur Espie Porritt (NZL)
1934–1968	Mohamed Taher Pascha (TUR)
1934–1973	Segura Marte Rodolfo Gomez (MEX)
1936–1939	Prince Iesato Tokugawa (JPN)

Dates of Service	Member (Nation)
1936–1942	Joakhim Puhk (EST)
1936–1972	Avery Brundage (USA)
1936–1980	His Royal Highness Prince Franz-Josef II (LIE)
1936–1980	Jorgé B. Vargas (PHI)
1937–1939	Henri Guisan (SUI)
1937–1948	Frédéric René Coudert (USA)
1937–1956	Joaquin Serratosa Cibils (URU)
1938–1942	Walther von Reichenau (GER)
1938–1955	Antonio Prado (BRA)
1938–1967	Johan Wilhelm Rangell (FIN)
1938–1969	Miguel Angel de los Dolores Amado de Jesus Moenck y Peralta (CUB)
1939–1939	Albert Victor Lindbergh (RSA)
1939–1948	Miklós von Horthy (HUN)
1939–1949	Giorgio Vaccaro (ITA)
1939–1950	Matsuzo Nagai (JPN)
1939–1955	Kong Xiangxi (CHN)
1939–1957	Baron Gaston de Trannoy (BEL)
1939–1967	Shingoro Takaishi (JPN)
1946–1951	Sydney Charles Dowsett (RSA)
1946–1954	John Coleridge Patteson (CAN)
1946–1955	Rodolphe William Seeldrayers (BEL)
1946–1956	José Joaquim Fernandes Pontes (POR)
1946–1964	Charles Ferdinand Pahud de Mortanges (NED)
1946–1965	Ioannis Ketseas (GRE)
1946–1965	Josef Gruss (TCH)
1946–1966	Benedikt G. Waage (ISL)
1946–1968	Albert Roman Mayer (SUI)
1946–1970	Armand Émile Massard (FRA)
1946–1975	Hugh Richard Weir (AUS)
1946–1982	Reginald Honey (RSA)
1946–1998*	His Royal Highness Grand Duke Jean (LUX)
1947–1958	Shou Tungyi (CHN)
1947–1967	Sidney Dawes (CAN)
1947–1969	Manfred Mautner Ritter von Markhof (AUT)
1947–1992	Raja Bhalindra Singh of Patiala (IND)
1948–1952	Enrique O. Barbosa Baeza (CHI)
1948–1952	Miguel Ydigoras Fuentes (GUA)
1948–1959	Stanko Bloudek (YUG)
1948–1961	Ferenc Mező (HUN)
1948–1961	Jerzy Loth (POL)
1948–1965	Bo Daniel Ekelund (SWE)
1948–1967	Olaf Christian Ditlev-Simonsen (NOR)
1948–1968	John Jewett Garland (USA)
1948–1976	Erik von Frenckell (FIN)
1949–1950	Rainier Grimaldi III, Prince of Monaco (MON)
1949–1956	Ahmed E. H. Jaffer (PAK)

Dates of Service	Member (Nation)
1950–1951	James Brooks Bloodgood Parker (USA)
1950–1964	Pierre Grimaldi, Prince of Monaco (MON)
1950–1968	Ryotaro Azuma (JPN)
1951–1974	Lewis Luxton (AUS)
1951–1988	Ian St. John Lawson Johnston, Lord Luke of Pavenham (GBR)
1951–1988	Konstantin Andrianov (URS)
1951–1990	Count Jean Robert Maurice Bonin de la Bonninie de Beaumont (FRA)
1951–1992	Giorgio de Stefani (ITA)
1952–1959	Enrique Alberdi (ARG)
1952–1967	Augustin A. Sosa (PAN)
1952–1968	Julio B. Bustamente (VEN)
1952–1970	Gustaf Peder Wilhelmsson Dyrssen (SWE)
1952–1971	Aleksey Romanov (URS)
1952–1971	José de Jesús Clark de Flores (MEX)
1952–1980	Sir Michael Morris, Lord Killanin of Dublin and Spiddal (IRL)
1952–1984	Douglas Fergusson Roby (USA)
1952–1985	Pedro Ybarra y McMahon, The Second Marquis de Guell (ESP)
1952–1986	Julio Gerlein Comelin (COL)
1952–1987	Sheik Gabriel Gemayel (LIB)
1952–1987	Vladimir D. Stoychev (BUL)
1955–1960	Lee Ki-Poong (KOR)
1955–1980	Prince Gholam Reza Pahlavi (IRI)
1955–1984	Suat Erler (TUR)
1955–1985	Alejandro Rivera Bascur (CHI)
1955–1998	Alexandru Siperco (ROM)
1956–1991	Willi Daume (GER)
1957–1962	Saul Cristovão Ferreira Pires (POR)
1958–1964	His Royal Highness Prince Albert of Liege (BEL)
1958–1977	Ivar Emil Vind (DEN)
1958–1982	Eduardo Dibos de Lima (PER)
1959–1996	Syed Wajid Ali (PAK)
1960–1974	Mario Luis Jose Negri (ARG)
1960–1987	Boris Bakrač (YUG)
1960–1990	Reginald Stanley Alexander (KEN)
1960–1993	Ahmed El-Demerdash Touny (EGY)
1961–1997	Mohamed Ben Hadj Addelouahed Benjelloun (MAR)
1961–1996	Włodzimierz Reczek (POL)
1963–1974*	His Majesty King Konstantinos (GRE)
1963–1975	Alfredo Inciarte (URU)
1963–1985	Sir Adetokunbo Ademola (NGR)
1963–1989	Raúl Cordiero, Pereira de Castro (POR)
1963–2006	Marc Hodler (SUI)
1963–2011	João Marie Godefroid Faustin Havelange (BRA)
1964–1966	Lee Sang-Beck (KOR)
1964–1977	Jonkheer Herman Adriaan van Karnebeek (NED)
1964–1983	Arpád Csánadi (HUN)
1964–1983	Giulio Onesti (ITA)

Dates of Service	Member (Nation)
1964–1995	Sylvio Magalhães de Padilha (BRA)
1964–2002	Prince Alexandre de Merode (BEL)
1965–1969	Amadou Barry (SEN)
1965–1981	František Kroutil (TCH)
1965–1981	Pyrros Lappas (GRE)
1965–1996	Gunnar Lennart Vilhelm Ericsson (SWE)
1965–2010	Mohamed Mzali (TUN)
1966–1971	Georg von Opel (FRG)
1966–1971	His Royal Highness, Prince George Wilhelm von Hanover (IOA)
1966–1980	Heinz Schöbel (GDR)
1966–2001	Juan Antonio Samaranch Torrelo, Marquis de Samaranch (ESP)
1967–1977	Chang Key-Young (KOR)
1967–1981	Paavo Honkajuuri (FIN)
1967–1981	Prince Tsuneyoshi Takeda (JPN)
1967–1989	James Worrall (CAN)
1967–2000	Jan Staubo (NOR)
1968–1971	Henri René Rakotoke (MAD)
1968–1976	Hamengku Buwono, IX (INA)
1968–1981	José A. Bercasa (VEN)
1968–1982	Abdel Mohamed Halim (SUD)
1968–1999	Agustin Carlos Arroyo Yeroui (ECU)
1969–1976	Rudolf Nemetschke (AUT)
1969–1988	Sir Cecil Lancelot Stewart Cross (NZL)
1969–1989	Masaji Kiyokawa (JPN)
1969–1991	Raymond Gafner (SUI)
1969–1994	Virgilio E. de Léon (PAN)
1969–1999	Louis Guirandou-N'Diaye (CIV)
1970–1976	Sven Alfred Thofelt (SWE)
1970–1988	Henry Heng Hsu (TPE)
1970–1994	Maurice Herzog (FRA)
1971–1974	Prabhas Charusathiara (THA)
1971–1987	Ydnekatcheu Tessema (ETH)
1971–	Vitaly Smirnov (URS/RUS)
1972–1988	Berthold Beitz (GER)
1972–1994	Pedro Ramírez Vázquez (MEX)
1973–1993	Manuel Gonzalez Guerra (CUB)
1973–2000*	Ashwini Kumar (IND)
1973–2002	Kéba M'Baye (SEN)
1973–2000	Roy Anthony Bridge (JAM)
1974–1981	David Henry McKenzie (AUS)
1974–1986	Julian Kean Roosevelt (USA)
1974–1990	Dawee Chullasapya (THA)
1974–1991	Eduardo Hay (MEX)
1974–2001	Mohamed Zerguini (ALG)
1975–1977	Epaminondas Petralias (GRE)
1976–1993	Matts Wilhelm Carlgren (SWE)
1976–1994	Kevin Patrick O'Flanagan (IRL)

Dates of Service	Member (Nation)
1976–1995	José Dalmiro Vallarino Veracierto (URU)
1976–	Peter Julius Tallberg (FIN)
1977–1983	Kim Taik-Soo (KOR)
1977–1986	Cornelis Lambert "Kees" Kerdel (NED)
1977–1999	Roberto Guillermo Peper (ARG)
1977–1989	Dadang Suprayogi (INA)
1977–1990	German Rieckehoff (PUR)
1977–1999	Bashir Mohamed Attarabulsi (LBA)
1977–1999	Lamine Keita (MLI)
1977–2000	Philipp von Schöller (AUT)
1977–2002*	Niels Holst-Sørensen (DEN)
1977–2007*	Shagdarjav Magvan (MGL)
1977–2014*	Richard Kevan Gosper (AUS)
1978–1986	Nikolaos Nissiotis (GRE)
1978–1994	Kim Yu-Sun (PRK)
1978–1998	René Essomba (CMR)
1978–2004	Honorable Tan Seri Hamzah bin Haji Abu Samah (MAS)
1978–	Richard William Duncan Pound (CAN)
1981–1990	Sheik Fahad Al-Ahmad Al-Sabah (KUW)
1981–1992*	Günther Heinze (GDR/GER)
1981–1999	Pirjo Vilmi-Häggman (FIN)
1981–2002*	Flor Isava-Fonseca (VEN)
1981–2002*	Vladimir Cernušak (TCH/SVK)
1981–2005	Nikolaos Filaretos (GRE)
1981–2009*	He Zhenliang (CHN)
1982–1993*	Dame Mary Alison Glen Haig (GBR)
1982–2012*	Chiharu Igaya (JPN)
1982–	Franco Carraro (ITA)
1982–	Ivan Dibos (PER)
1982–2012*	Philip Walter Coles (AUS)
1983–1999	Zein El-Abdin Mohamed Ahmed Abdel Gadir (SUD)
1983–1999	His Royal Highness Prince Faisal Fahd Abdul Aziz (KSA)
1983–2007	Anani Matthia (TOG)
1983–	Pál Schmitt (HUN)
1983–2011	Roque Napoleon Muñoz Peña (DOM)
1984–1985	Park Chong-Kyu (KOR)
1984–1988	Turgut Atakol (TUR)
1984–1999	David Sikhulumi Sibandze (SWZ)
1984–	Her Royal Highness Princess Nora (LIE)
1985–1991	Robert Hanna Helmick (USA)
1985–1998	Carlos Ferrer Salat (ESP)
1985–	Albert Grimaldi, Prince of Monaco (MON)
1985–2013*	Francisco J. Elizalde (PHI)
1985–2006	Henry Edmund Olufemi Adefope (NGR)
1986–1999	Jean-Claude Ganga (CGO)
1986–2005	Kim Un-Yong (KOR)
1986–	Anita Luceete DeFrantz (USA)

Dates of Service	Member (Nation)
1986–	Lambis V. Nikolaou (GRE)
1987–1995	Slobodan Filipović (YUG)
1987–1999	Seuili Paul Wallwork (SAM)
1987–2005	Ivan Borissov Slavkov (BUL)
1987–2010	Antonius Johannes Geesink (NED)
1988–1992	Marat V. Gramov (URS/RUS)
1988–2003	Sinan Erdern (TUR)
1988–2005*	Tennant Edward "Tay" Wilson (NZL)
1988–2005*	Borislav Stanković (YUG)
1988–2005*	Fidel Mendoza Carrasquilla (COL)
1988–2007	Rampaul Ruhee (MRI)
1988–2011	Francis Were Nyangweso (UGA)
1988–	Princess Anne Windsor, Her Royal Highness the Princess Royal (GBR)
1988–	Willi Kaltschmitt Lujan (GUA)
1988–	Wu Ching-Kuo (TPE)
1989–2009*	Fernando F. Lima Bello (POR)
1989–2009*	Walther Tröger (GER)
1990–1996	Philippe Chatrier (FRA/ITU)
1990–1999	Charles Nderitu Mukora (KEN)
1990–2001	Carol Anne Letheren (CAN)
1990–2006	Antonio Rodriguez (ARG)
1990–	Nat Indrapana (THA)
1990–	Richard L. Carrion (PUR)
1990–2012*	Shun-Ichiro Okano (JPN)
1991–	Denis Oswald (SUI)
1991–2013**	Dr. Jacques Rogge (BEL)
1991–2012	Mario Vázquez Raña (MEX)
1991–	Thomas Bach (GER)
1992–1994	Olaf Poulsen (NOR)
1992–1999	Sergio Santander Fantini (CHI)
1992–1999	Primo Nebiolo (ITA/IAAF)
1992–	Sheik Ahmad Al-Fahad Al-Sabah (KUW)
1994–2004	Mohamed "Bob" Hasan (INA)
1994–	Alex Gilady (ISR)
1994–2013*	Alpha Ibrahim Diallo (GUI)
1994–2012*	Arne Ljungqvist (SWE)
1994–	Austin L. Sealy (BAR)
1994–	Craig Reedie (GBR)
1994–	Gerhard Heiberg (NOR)
1994–	James Leland Easton (USA)
1994–	Mario Pescante (ITA)
1994–	Robin Mitchell (FIJ)
1994–	Shamil Tarpichev (RUS)
1994–	Valery Borzov (UKR)
1995–1996	Yury Titov (RUS/FIG)
1995–2001	Věra Čáslavská (CZE)
1995–2012*	Antun Vrdoljak (CRO)

Dates of Service	Member (Nation)
1995–2014	Jean-Claude Killy (FRA)
1995–2009*	Mustapha Larfaoui (ALG/FINA)
1995–	Olegario Vázquez Raña (MEX)
1995–	Patrick Joseph Hickey (IRL)
1995–	René Fasel (SUI/IIHF)
1995–	Reynaldo González López (CUB)
1995–	Sam Ramsamy (RSA)
1995–	Toni Khoury (LIB)
1996–1998	George Killian (USA/FIBA)
1996–2001	Lu Shengrong (CHN)
1996–2003	Tomas Amos Ganda Sithole (ZIM)
1996–2006*	Hein Verbruggen (NED/UCI)
1996–2006*	Princess Doña Pilar de Borbon (ESP/FEI)
1996–	Gunilla Lindberg (SWE)
1996–	Guy Drut (FRA)
1996–	Julio Cesar Maglione (URU)
1996–	Lee Kun-Hee (KOR)
1996–	Ottavio Cinquanta (ITA/ISU)
1996–	Syed Shahid Ali (PAK)
1996–	Ung Chang (PRK)
1998–	HRH the Grand Duke of Luxembourg (LUX)
1998–2013*	His Royal Highness Prince of Orange (NED)
1998–	Irena Szewińska-Kirszenstein (POL)
1998–	Leopold Wallner (AUT)
1998–	Melitón Sánchez Rivas (PAN)
1998–	Mohammad Samih Moudallal (SYR)
1998–	Mounir Saleh Sabet (EGY)
1998–	Nawal El-Moutawakel Bennis (MAR)
1998–	Ser Miang Ng (SIN)
1999–2000	Hassiba Boulmerka (ALG/Athlete)
1999–2001	Johann Olav Koss (NOR/Athlete)
1999–2001	Vladimir Smirnov (KAZ/Athlete)
1999–2004	Roland Barr (GER/Athlete)
1999–2004	Charmaine Crooks (CAN/Athlete)
1999–2001, 2004–	Jan Železný (CZE/Athlete)
1999–	Sergey Bubka (UKR/Athlete)
1999–2008	Robert Ctvrtlik (USA/Athlete)
1999–2010*	Manuela Di Centa (ITA/Athlete)
1999–	Aleksandr Popov (RUS/Athlete)
1999–	Joseph S. Blatter (SUI/FIFA)
1999–2014*	Lamine Diack (SEN/IAAF)
2000–2002	Alfredo Goyeneche Moreno (ESP/Spain OC)
2000–2002	William J. Hybl (USA/United States OC)
2000–2003	Robert Steadward (CAN/IPC)
2000–2004	Manuel Estiarte Duocastella (ESP/Athlete)
2000–2004	Ruben Acosta Hernández (MEX/FIVB)
2000–2004	Seyed Mostafa Hashemi Taba (IRI/Iran OC)

Dates of Service	Member (Nation)
2000–2004	Paul Henderson (CAN/ISAF)
2000–2005	Susan O'Neill (AUS/Athlete)
2000–2007	Henri Serandour (FRA/France OC)
2000–2009*	Tamas Ajan (HUN/IWF)
2000–2004	Bruno Grandi (SUI/FIG)
2000–	Gian-Franco Kasper (SUI/AIWF)
2000–2010*	Kipchoge Keino (KEN/Kenya OC)
2000–2013*	Carlos Arthur Nuzman (BRA/Brazil OC)
2000–2012*	Lassana Palenfo (CIV/Côte d'Ivoire OC)
2000–	Yu Zaiqing (CHN/China OC)
2000–2003	Giovanni Agnelli (ITA/Honor)
2000–2005	Yoshiaki Tsutsumi (JPN/Honor)
2000–2006	Alain Danet (FRA/Honor)
2000–2008	Kurt Furgler (SUI/Honor)
2000–	Henry Alfred Kissinger (USA/Honor)
2001–	Tsun-Ting "Timothy" Fok (HKG)
2001–2014	Randhir Singh (IND)
2001–	John Dowling Coates (AUS/Australia OC)
2001–	Issa Hayatou (CMR)
2001–	Juan Antonio Samaranch Jr. (ESP)
2001–2009	Els van Breda-Vriesman (NED/FIH)
2002–2003	Sandra Baldwin (USA/United States OC)
2002–2004	Matthew Pinsent (GBR/Athlete)
2002–2005	Kikis N. Lazarides (CYP/Cyprus OC)
2002–2007	Park Yong-Sung (KOR/Korea OC)
2002–2008	Kai Holm (DEN)
2002–2008	Youssoupha Ndiaye (SEN)
2002–2010	Pernilla Wiberg (SWE/Athlete)
2002–	Patrick S. Chamunda (ZAM)
2002–2014	Nawaf Faisal Fahad Abdul Aziz (KSA/Saudi Arabia OC)
2002–	Tamim bin Hamad Al-Thani (QAT/Qatar OC)
2002–2004	François Narmon (BEL/Belgium OC)
2002–2006	Jari Kurri (FIN/Athlete)
2002–2006	Ådne Søndrål (NOR/Athlete)
2003–	Phil Craven (GBR/IPC)
2004–2012	Jan Železný (CZE/Athlete)
2004–2012	Hicham El Guerroj (MAR/Athlete)
2004–	Frank Fredericks (NAM/Athlete)
2004–2012	Rania El-Wani (EGY/Athlete)
2006–	Barbara Anne Kendall (NZL/Athlete)
2006–	Beatrice Allen (GAM/Gambian OC)
2006–	Nicole Hoevertsz (ARU/Aruban OC)
2006–	HRH Prince Tunku Imran (MAS/Malaysian OC)
2006–	Francesco Ricci Bitti (ITA/ITF)
2006–2014	Beckie Scott (CAN/Athlete)
2006–2014	Saku Koivu (FIN/Athlete)
2007–	HRH Haya Bint Al-Hussein (UAE/FEI)

Dates of Service	Member (Nation)
2007–	Rita Subowo (INA/NOC)
2007–	Patrick Baumann (SUI/FIBA)
2007–	Andrés Botero (COL/NOC)
2008–	Claudia Bokel (GER/Athlete)
2008–	Yumilka Ruíz (CUB/Athlete)
2008–	Mun Dae-Seong (KOR/Athlete)
2009–	HRH Prince Frederik (DEN)
2009–	Richard Peterkin (LCA)
2009–	Habu Gumel (NGR)
2009–	Habibi Abdul Nabi Macki (OMA)
2009–	Göran Petersson (SWE/ISAF)
2009–	Lydia Nsekera (BDI)
2010–	Angela Ruggiero (USA/Athlete)
2010–	Adam Pengilly (GBR/Athlete)
2010–	Yang Yang (A) (CHN/Athlete)
2010–	Barry Maister (NZL/NOC)
2010–	Pat McQuaid (IRL/ICU)
2010–	HRH Prince Faisal (JOR)
2010–	Marisol Casado Estupiñán (ESP)
2010–	Dagmawit Girmaye Berhane (ETH)
2011–	José Perurena (ESP)
2011–	Gerardo Werthein (ARG)
2011–	Barbara Kendall (NZL)
2012–	Lingwei Li (CHN)
2012–	Frank Fredericks (NAM)
2012–	Tsunekazu Takeda (JPN)
2012–	Baron Pierre-Olivier Beckers-Vieujant (BEL)
2012–	Aïcha Garad Ali (DJI)
2013–	Danka Bartekova (SVK)
2013–	James Tomkins (AUS)
2013–	Kirsty Coventry (ZIM)
2013–	Tony Estanguet (FRA)
2013–	Octavian Morariu (ROU)
2013–	Bernard Rajzman (BRA)
2013–	Mikaela Cojuangco Jaworski (PHI)
2013–	Alexander Zhukov (RUS)
2013–	Paul K. Tergat (KEN)
2013–	Lawrence F. Probst III (USA)
2013–	Dagmawit Girmay Berhane (ETH)
2013–	Camiel Eurlings (NED)
2013–	Stefan Holm (SWE)
2014–	Poul-Erik Høyer (SWE)
2014–	Hayley Wickenheiser (CAN)
2014–	Ole Einar Bjørndalen (NOR)

*Honorary member in 2014.
**Honorary president in 2014.

Appendix V:
Awards of the International Olympic Committee

The International Olympic Committee has given out several awards, apart from the medals and diplomas given to Olympic athletes. Currently, the IOC presents only two awards, the Olympic Order and the Olympic Cup. The IOC discontinued the following awards at the 75th IOC Session in Vienna in 1974: the Olympic Diploma of Merit (first awarded in 1905), the Sir Thomas Fearnley Cup (donated in 1950), the Mohammed Taher Trophy (donated in 1950), the Count Alberto Bonacossa Trophy (presented in 1954), the Tokyo Trophy (presented in 1964), and the Prix de la Reconnaissance Olympique (presented in 1972).

RECIPIENTS OF THE OLYMPIC ORDER

The Olympic Order is the supreme individual honor accorded by the International Olympic Committee. It was created in 1974 and is to be awarded to "any person who has illustrated the Olympic Ideal through his/her action, has achieved remarkable merit in the sporting world, or has rendered outstanding services to the Olympic cause, either through his/her own personal achievement(s) or his/her contribution to the development of sport." Originally, the Olympic Order was separated into three categories: gold, silver, and bronze. The bronze Olympic Order was discontinued in 1984, and currently there are only gold and silver categories. Only the recipients of the Olympic Order in Gold are listed below. Through mid-2010, there have been 1,049 recipients of the Olympic Order in Silver and 111 recipients of the Olympic Order in Bronze.

Gold (89)

Year	Person	Country
1975	Avery Brundage	USA
1980	Lord Killanin of Dublin and Spiddal	GBR
1981	Lord Burghley, Marquess of Exeter	GBR
	His Majesty, King Olaf of Norway	NOR

Year	Person	Country
	Amadou Mahtar M'Bow	SEN
	Pope John Paul II	VAT
1982	His Majesty, King Pertuan Agung of Malaysia	MAS
1983	Indira Gandhi	IND
1984	François Mitterrand	FRA
	Peter Victor Ueberroth	USA
	Branko Mikulić	YUG
1985	His Majesty, King Juan Carlos de Borbon	ESP
	Erich Honecker	GDR
	Nicolae Ceauçescu	ROU
1986	Li Wan	CHN
1987	Todor Zhivkov	BUL
	His Majesty, King Bhumibol Adulyadej	THA
	His Excellency, Kenan Evren	TUR
1988	Frank W. King	CAN
	Mario Vázquez Raña	MEX
	His Royal Highness, Prince Rainier III	MON
	His Royal Highness, Prince Bertil Bernadotte	SWE
1989	Chevalier Raoul Mollet	BEL
	His Imperial Majesty, Emperor Akihito	JPN
	His Excellency, Raphael Hernandez Colon	PUR
1990	Giulio Andreotti	ITA
1991	Count Jean de Beaumont	FRA
	Yoshiaki Tsutsumi	JPN
	Willi Daume	FRG
1992	Josep Miguel Abad	ESP
	Michel Barnier	FRA
	Javier Gomez-Navarro	ESP
	Jean-Claude Killy	FRA
	Pasqual Marragal	ESP
	Jordi Pujol	ESP
	Leopoldo Rodes	ESP
	Carlos Salinas de Gortari	MEX
	Narcis Serra	ESP
	Javier Solana	ESP
	Boris Yeltsin	RUS
1994	Joaquin Leguina	ESP
	Richard von Weizsäcker	GER
	Dr. Mauno Koivisto	FIN
	His Majesty, King Harald of Norway	NOR
	Gerhard Heiberg	NOR
	Her Majesty, Queen Sonja of Norway	NOR
1995	Arpád Goncz	HUN
	Robert Mugabe	ZIM
1996	Konstantino Stephanopoulo	GRE

Year	Person	Country
	Adolphus Drewery "A. D." Frazier	USA
	Andrew Young	USA
	William Porter Payne	USA
	Islam Karimov	UZB
1997	Blaise Compaore	BUR
	El-hadj Omar Bongo	GAB
	Nursultan Nazarbaev	KAZ
	Elias Hrawi	LIB
	Ernesto Zedillo Ponce de Léon	MEX
	Aleksander Kwasniewski	POL
	Suleyman Demirel	TUR
1998	Eishiro Saito	JPN
	Grand Duke Jean	LUX
1999	Eduardo Shevardnadze	GEO
	Helmut Kohl	GER
	Petru Lucinschi	MDA
	Yury Luzhkov	RUS
2000	Michael Knight	AUS
	David Richmond	AUS
	John Dowling Coates	AUS
	Adolf Ogi	SUI
2001	His Majesty, Sultan Qaboos bin Said	OMA
	Tong Goh Chok	SIN
	Vladimir Putin	RUS
	Juan Antonio Samaranch	ESP
	Abdoulaye Wade	SEN
2002	Kéba Mbaye	SEN
	Mitt Romney	USA
	Fraser Bullock	USA
	Jacques Chirac	FRA
2003	Emile Lahoud	LIB
2004	Johannes Rau	GER
	Abdellaziz Bouteflika	ALG
	Gianna Angelopoulos	GRE
	Martinos Simitsek	GRE
2005	Théodor Angelopoulos	GRE
2007	Kofi Annan	GHA
2008	Qi Liu	CHN
2009	Jack Poole	CAN
2010	John A. Furlong	CAN
2013	King Willem Alexander	NED
	Jacques Rogge	BEL
	King Philip VI	ESP
	Pope Francis	VAT

RECIPIENTS OF THE OLYMPIC CUP

The Olympic Cup was instituted by Baron Pierre de Coubertin in 1906. It is awarded to an institution or association with a general reputation for merit and integrity that has been active and efficient in the service of sport and has contributed substantially to the development of the Olympic Movement. It has been given to individuals four times (1927, 1942, 1947, and 1999).

Year	Recipient
1906	Touring Club de France
1907	Henley Royal Regatta
1908	Sveriges Centralförening för Idrottens Främjande
1909	Deutsche Turnerschaft
1910	Česka obec Sokolska
1911	Touring Club Italiano
1912	Union des Sociétés de Gymnastique de France
1913	Magyar Athletikai Club
1914	Amateur Athletic Union of America
1915	Rugby School, England
1916	Confrérie Saint-Michel de Gand
1917	Nederlandsche Voetbal Bond
1918	Equipes Sportives du Front Interallié
1919	Institut Olympique de Lausanne
1920	YMCA International, Springfield, Massachusetts, USA
1921	Dansk Idræts Forbund
1922	Amateur Athletic Union of Canada
1923	Associación Sportiva de Cataluña
1924	Finnish Gymnastic and Athletic Federation
1925	National Physical Education Committee of Uruguay
1926	Norges Skiforbund
1927	Colonel Robert M. Thomson (USA)
1928	Junta Nacional Mexicana
1929	Y.M.C.A. World's Committee
1930	Association Suisse de Football et d'Athlétisme
1931	National Playing Fields Association, Great Britain
1932	Deutsche Hochschule für Leibesübungen
1933	Société Fédérale Suisse de Gymnastique
1934	Opera Dopolavoro Roma
1935	National Recreation Association of the USA
1936	Union of Hellenic Gymnastics and Athletics Associations, Athens
1937	Österreichischer Eislauf Verband
1938	Königlich Akademie für Körpererziehung in Ungam
1939	"Kraft durch Freude"
1940	Svenska Gymnastik–och Idrottsföreningarnas Riksförbund
1941	Finnish Olympic Committee
1942	William May Garland (USA)

Year	Recipient
1943	Comité Olímpico Argentino
1944	City of Lausanne
1945	Norges Fri Idrettsførbund, Oslo
1946	Comité Olímpico Colornbiano
1947	J. Sigfrid Edström (SWE)—IOC president
1948	The Central Council of Physical Recreation, Great Britain
1949	Fluminense Football Club, Rio de Janeiro
1950	Comité Olympique Belge
	New Zealand Olympic and British Empire Games Association
1951	Académie des Sports, Paris
1952	City of Oslo
1953	City of Helsinki
1954	Ecole Fédérale de Gymnastique et de Sports, Macolin (SUI)
1955	Organizing Committee of the Central American and Caribbean Games, Mexico
	Organizing Committee of the Pan-American Games, Mexico
1956	Not awarded
1957	Federazione Sport Silenziosi d'Italia, Milano
1958	Not awarded
1959	Panathlon Italiano, Génève
1960	Centro Universitario Sportivo Italiano
1961	Helms Hall Foundation, Los Angeles
1962	IV Juegos Deportivos Bolivarianos, Barranquilla
1963	Australian British Empire and Commonwealth Games Association
1964	City of Tokyo
1965	Southern California Committee for the Olympic Games (USA)
1966	Comité International des Sports Silencieux, Liège (BEL)
1967	Juegos Deportivos Bolivarianos
1968	City of Mexico
1969	Polish Olympic Committee
1970	Organizing Committee of the Asian Games in Bangkok (THA)
1971	Organizing Committee of the Pan-American Games in Cali (COL)
1972	Turkish Olympic Committee
	City of Sapporo
1973	Population of Munich
1974	Bulgarian Olympic Committee
1975	Comitato Olímpico Nazionale Italiano (CONI)
1976	Czechoslovak Physical Culture and Sports Association
1977	Comité Olympique Ivoirien
1978	Comité Olympique Hellenic
1979	Organizing Committee of the 1978 World Rowing Championships in New Zealand
1980	Ginasio Clube Português
1981	Confédération Suisse
	International Olympic Academy
1982	Racing Club de France
1983	Puerto Rico Olympic Committee

Year	Recipient
1984	Organizing Committee of the 1st World Championships in Athletics at Helsinki
1985	Chinese Olympic Committee
1986	City of Stuttgart
1987	L'Équipe (French sporting daily newspaper)
1988	The People of Australia
1989	City of Calgary
	City of Seoul
	La Gazzetta dello Sport (Italian sporting daily newspaper)
1990	Panhellenic Athletic Club of Athens
1991	Japanese Olympic Committee
1992	Département de la Savoie (Région Rhône-Alpes)
	City of Barcelona
1993	Comité Olympique Monégasque
1994	Comité National Olympique et Sportif Français
	The Norwegian People
1995	Korean Olympic Committee
1996	City of Baden-Baden (GER)
1997	Not awarded
1998	People of Nagano
1999	Leon Štukelj (YUG/SLO)
2000	People of Sydney
2001	Kip Keino School Eldoret
2002	People of Salt Lake City
2003	Team Alinghi (2003 America's Cup Crew)
2004	People of Athens
2005	People of Singapore
2006	People of Torino
2007	1932 and 1980 Lake Placid Winter Olympic Museum
2008	The People of Beijing
2010	The People of Singapore
2011	South African Sports Confederation and Olympic Committee and the people of Durban
2012	The citizens of London

Appendix VI: Final Olympic Torchbearers (Within the Olympic Stadium)

GAMES OF THE OLYMPIADS

1936   Fritz Schilgen (GER)

1948   John Mark (GBR)

1952   Hannes Kolehmainen (lit main flame) (FIN)
        Paavo Nurmi (lit auxiliary flame) (FIN)

1956   Ron Clarke (AUS)

1960   Giancarlo Peris (ITA)

1964   Yoshinori Sakai (JPN)

1968   Enriqueta Basilio de Sotelo (MEX)

1972   Günter Zahn (FRG)

1976   Stéphane Prefontaine (lit flame concurrently) (CAN)
        Sandra Henderson (lit flame concurrently) (CAN)

1980   Sergey Belov (URS)

1984   Rafer Johnson (lit flame) (USA) Gina Hemphill (USA)

1988   Sohn Kee-Chung (KOR) Lim Chun-Ae (KOR)
        Chung Sun-Man (KOR) (lit flame)
        Kim Won-Tak (KOR) (lit flame)
        Sohn Mi-Chung (KOR) (lit flame)

1992   Antônio Rebollo (archer; lit flame) (ESP)
        Herminio Menéndez Rodriguez (ESP)
        Juan Antônio San Epifanio Ruiz (ESP)

1996   Muhammad Ali (lit flame) (USA)
        Janet Evans (USA)
        Paraskevi "Voula" Patoulidou (GRE)
        Evander Holyfield (USA) Al Oerter (USA)

2000   Catherine Freeman (lit flame) (AUS)
        Raelene Boyle (AUS)
        Betty Cuthbert (AUS)
        Shirley Strickland de la Hunty (AUS)
        Dawn Fraser (AUS)
        Shane Gould (AUS)
        Debbie Flintoff-King (AUS)

2004   Nikolaos Kaklamanakis (lit flame) (GRE)
        Dimitrios "Mimis" Domazos (GRE)
        Nikos Gallis (GRE)
        Akakios Kakiashvili (GRE)

Ioannis Melissanidis (GRE)
Paraskevi Patoulidou (GRE)
2008   Li Ning (CHN) (lit flame)
Sun Jinfang (CHN)
Chen Zhong (CHN)
Zhang Ju (CHN) Zhang Xugang (CHN)
Li Xiaoshuang (CHN) Gao Min (CHN)
Xu Haifeng (CHN)
2012   Callum Airlie (GBR)
Jordan Duckitt (GBR)
Desiree Henry (GBR)
Cameron MacRitchie (GBR)
Aidan Reynolds (GBR)
Adelle Tracey (GBR)
Katie Kirk (GBR)

OLYMPIC EQUESTRIAN GAMES

1956   Hans Wikne (lit flame) (SWE)
Karin Lindberg (SWE)
Henry Eriksson (SWE)

OLYMPIC WINTER GAMES

1952   Eigil Nansen (NOR)
1956   Guido Caroli (ITA)
1960   Kenneth Henry (USA)
1964   Joseph Rieder (AUT)
1968   Alain Calmat (FRA)
1972   Hideki Takada (JPN)
1976   Christl Haas (lit main flame) (AUT)
Josef Feistmantl (lit auxiliary flame) (AUT)
1980   Charles Morgan Kerr (USA)
1984   Sandra Dubravčić (YUG)
1988   Robyn Perry (CAN)
1992   Michel Platini (lit flame) (FRA)
François-Syrille Grange (lit flame) (FRA)
1994   Crown Prince Haakon Magnus (lit flame) (NOR)
Stein Gruben (ski jumper) (NOR)
Catherine Nottingnes (NOR)
1998   Midori Ito (lit flame) (JPN)
Hiromu Suzuki (JPN)
Takanori Kono (JPN)
Masaki Chiba (JPN)

	Chris Moon (NZL)
2002	The 1980 United States Ice Hockey Team (lit flame)
	Dick Button (USA)
	Dorothy Hamill (USA)
	Scott Hamilton (USA)
	Peggy Fleming (USA)
	Bill Johnson (USA)
	Phil Mahre (USA)
	Dan Jansen (USA)
	Bonnie Blair (USA)
	Jim Shea (USA)
	Jim Shea Jr. (USA)
	Picabo Street (USA)
	Cammi Granato (USA)
2006	Stefania Belmondo (ITA) (lit flame)
	Alberta Tomba (ITA)
	Maurilio De Zolt (ITA)
	Marco Albarello (ITA)
	Giorgio Vanzetta (ITA)
	Silvio Fauner (ITA) Piero Gros (ITA)
	Deborah Compagnoni (ITA)
2010	Wayne Gretzky (CAN) (lit flame and lit accessory flame in town)
	Steve Nash (CAN) (lit flame)
	Nancy Greene (CAN) (lit flame)
	Catriona Le May Doan (CAN) (was to have lit flame but there was a malfunction)
	Rick Hansen (CAN)
2014	Vladislav Tretyak (RUS)
	Irina Rodnina (RUS)

Appendix VII:
Speakers of the Olympic Oath

GAMES OF THE OLYMPIADS—ATHLETES

1920	Victor Boin (Water Polo/Fencing)
1924	Georges André (Athletics)
1928	Harry Dénis (Football)
1932	George Calnan (Fencing)
1936	Rudolf Ismayr (Weightlifting)
1948	Donald Finlay (Athletics)
1952	Heikki Savoläinen (Gymnastics)
1956	John Landy (Athletics)
1960	Adolfo Consolini (Athletics)
1964	Takashi Ono (Gymnastics)
1968	Pablo Garrido (Athletics)
1972	Heidi Schüller (Athletics)
1976	Pierre St. Jean (Weightlifting)
1980	Nikolay Andrianov (Gymnastics)
1984	Edwin Moses (Athletics)
1988	Huh Jae (Basketball) Son Mi-Na (Handball)
1992	Luis Doreste Blanco (Yachting)
1996	Teresa Edwards (Basketball)
2000	Rechelle Hawkes (Field Hockey)
2004	Zoi Dimoskhaki (Swimming)
2008	Zhang Yining (Table Tennis)
2012	Sarah Stevenson (Taekwondo)

OLYMPIC EQUESTRIAN GAMES—ATHLETE

1956	Henri Saint Cyr (Equestrian)

OLYMPIC WINTER GAMES—ATHLETES

1924	Camille Mandrillon (Nordic Skiing)
1928	Hans Eidenbenz (Nordic Skiing)
1932	Jack Shea (Speed Skating)
1936	Wilhelm Bögner (Alpine Skiing)
1948	Riccardo "Bibi" Torriani (Ice Hockey)

1952   Torbjørn Falkanger (Ski Jumping)
1956   Guilliana Chenal-Minuzzo (Alpine Skiing)
1960   Carol Heiss (Figure Skating)
1964   Paul Aste (Bobsledding)
1968   Leo Lacroix (Alpine Skiing)
1972   Keichi Suzuki (Speed Skating)
1976   Werner Delle Karth (Bobsledding)
1980   Eric Heiden (Speed Skating)
1984   Bojan Križaj (Alpine Skiing)
1988   Pierre Harvey (Nordic Skiing)
1992   Surya Bonaly (Figure Skating)
1994   Vegard Ulvang (Nordic Skiing)
1998   Kenji Ogiwara (Nordic Combined)
2002   Jim Shea Jr. (Skeleton)
2006   Giorgio Rocca (Alpine Skiing)
2010   Hayley Wickenheiser (Ice Hockey/Softball)
2014   Ruslan Zakharov (Short Track Speed Skating)

GAMES OF THE OLYMPIADS—OFFICIALS

1972   Heinz Pollay (Equestrian Official)
1976   Maurice Fauget (Track and Field Athletics Official)
1980   Aleksandr Medved (Wrestling Official)
1984   Sharon Weber (Gymnastics Official)
1988   Lee Hak-Rae (Judo Official)
1992   Eugeni Asensio (Water Polo Official)
1996   Hobie Billingsley (Diving Official)
2000   Peter Kerr (Water Polo Official)
2004   Lazaros Voradis (Basketball Official)
2008   Huang Liping (Gymnastics Official)
2012   Amrik "Mik" Basi (Boxing Official)

OLYMPIC WINTER GAMES—OFFICIALS

1972   Fumio Asaki (Ski Jumping Official)
1976   Willi Köstinger (Nordic Skiing Official)
1980   Terry McDermott (Speed Skating Official)
1984   Dragan Perović (Alpine Skiing Official)
1988   Suzanne Morrow-Francis (Figure Skating Official)
1992   Pierre Bornat (Alpine Skiing Official)
1994   Kari Karing (Nordic Skiing Official)
1998   Junko Hiromatsu (Figure Skating Official)
2002   Allen Church (Nordic Skiing Official)
2006   Fabio Bianchetti (Speed Skating Official)
2010   Michel Verrault (Short-track Speed Skating Official)
2014   Vyacheslav Vedenini (Cross-Country Skiing Official)

Appendix VIII:
Official Openings of the Olympic Games

GAMES OF THE OLYMPIADS

1896   King Giorgios I (Greece)
1900   None
1904   President David Rowland Francis (Louisiana Purchase Exposition/United States)
1906   King Giorgios I (Greece)
1908   King Edward VII (England)
1912   King Gustaf V (Sweden)
1920   King Albert I (Belgium)
1924   President Gaston Doumergue (France)
1928   His Royal Highness, Prince Hendrik (The Netherlands)
1932   Vice President Charles Curtis (United States)
1936   Reichsführer Adolf Hitler (Germany)
1948   King George VI (England)
1952   President Juho Kusti Paasikivi (Finland)
1956   His Royal Highness Philip, The Duke of Edinburgh (United Kingdom)
1960   President Giovanni Gronchi (Italy)
1964   Emperor Hirohito (Japan)
1968   President Dr. Gustavo Díaz Ordaz (Mexico)
1972   President Dr. Gustav Heinemann (Federal Republic of Germany)
1976   Queen Elizabeth II (England)
1980   President Leonid Ilyich Brezhnev (Soviet Union)
1984   President Ronald Wilson Reagan (United States)
1988   President Roh Tae-Woo (Korea)
1992   King Juan Carlos I (Spain)
1996   President William Jefferson Clinton (United States)
2000   Governor-General Sir William Patrick Deane (Australia)
2004   President Kostas Stephanopoulos (Greece)
2008   President Hu Jintao (China)
2012   Queen Elizabeth II (England)

OLYMPIC EQUESTRIAN GAMES

1956   King Gustaf VI Adolf (Sweden)

OLYMPIC WINTER GAMES

1924 Undersecretary for Physical Education Gaston Vidal (France)
1928 President Edmund Schulthess (Switzerland)
1932 Governor Franklin Delano Roosevelt (New York, United States)
1936 Reichsführer Adolf Hitler (Germany)
1948 President Enrico Celio (Switzerland)
1952 Her Royal Highness, Princess Ragnhild (Norway)
1956 President Giovanni Gronchi (Italy)
1960 Vice President Richard Milhous Nixon (United States)
1964 President Dr. Adolf Schärf (Austria)
1968 President General Charles de Gaulle (France)
1972 Emperor Hirohito (Japan)
1976 President Dr. Rudolf Kirchschläger (Austria)
1980 Vice President Walter Frederick Mondale (United States)
1984 President Mika Spiljak (Yugoslavia)
1988 Governor-General Jeanne Sauvé (Canada)
1992 President François Mitterrand (France)
1994 King Harald V (Norway)
1998 Emperor Akihito (Japan)
2002 President George Walker Bush (United States)
2006 President Carlos Azeglio Ciampi (Italy)
2010 Governor-General Michaëlle Jean (Canada)
2014 President Vladimir Putin (Russia)

Appendix IX:
Most Olympic Medals Won: Summer, Men

Medals	Athlete (Nation-Sport)
22	Michael Phelps (USA-SWI)
15	Nikolay Andrianov (URS-GYM)
13	Edoardo Mangiarotti (ITA-FEN)
13	Takashi Ono (JPN-GYM)
13	Boris Shakhlin (URS-GYM)
12	Sawao Kato (JPN-GYM)
12	Paavo Nurmi (FIN-ATH)
12	Aleksey Nemov (RUS-GYM)
11	Matthew Biondi (USA-SWI)
11	Viktor Chukarin (URS-GYM)
11	Carl Osburn (USA-SHO)
11	Mark Spitz (USA-SWI)
11	Ryan Lochte (USA-SWI)
10	Aleksandr Dityatin (URS-GYM)
10	Raymond Ewry (USA-ATH)
10	Aladár Gerevich (HUN-FEN)
10	Carl Lewis (USA-ATH)
10	Akinori Nakayama (JPN-GYM)
10	Vitaly Shcherbo (EUN/BLR-GYM)
10	Hubert Van Innis (BEL-ARC)
10	Gary Hall Jr. (USA-SWI)

Appendix X:
Most Olympic Medals Won: Summer, Women

Medals	Athlete (Nation-Sport)
18	Larisa Latynina (URS-GYM)
12	Birgit Fischer-Schmidt (GDR/GER-CAN)
12	Jennifer Thompson (USA-SWI)
12	Dara Torres (USA-SWI)
12	Natalie Coughlin (USA-SWI)
11	Věra Čáslavská (TCH-GYM)
10	Polina Astakhova (URS-GYM)
10	Ágnes Keleti (HUN-GYM)
10	Franziska Van Almsick (GER-SWI)
9	Nadia Comăneci (ROM-GYM)
9	Lyudmila Turishcheva (URS-GYM)
9	Merlene Ottey (JAM-ATH)
9	Anky van Grunsven (NED-EQU)
9	Leisel Jones (AUS-SWI)
9	Valentina Vezzali (ITA-FEN)
9	Shirley Babashoff (USA-SWI)
8	Kornelia Ender (GDR-SWI)
8	Dawn Fraser (AUS-SWI)
8	Sofiya Muratova (URS-GYM)
8	Susan O'Neill (AUS-SWI)
8	Margit Plachyné-Korondi (HUN-GYM)
8	Isabell Werth (GER-EQU)
8	Elisabeta Lipă-Oleniuc (ROU-ROW)
8	Inge de Bruijn (NED-SWI)
8	Giovanna Trillini (ITA-FEN)
8	Katalina Kovacs (HUN-CAN)
8	Petria Thomas (AUS-SWI)

Appendix XI:
Most Olympic Gold Medals Won: Summer, Men

Golds	Athlete (Nation-Sport)
18	Michael Phelps (USA-SWI)
10	Ray Ewry (USA-ATH)
9	Paavo Nurmi (FIN-ATH)
9	Mark Spitz (USA-SWI)
9	Carl Lewis (USA-ATH)
8	Sawao Kato (JPN-GYM)
8	Matt Biondi (USA-SWI)
7	Nikolay Andrianov (URS-GYM)
7	Boris Shakhlin (URS-GYM)
7	Viktor Chukarin (URS-GYM)
7	Aladár Gerevich (HUN-FEN)
7	Don Schollander (USA-SWI)
6	Usain Bolt (JAM-ATH)
6	Chris Hoy (GBR-CYC)
6	Edoardo Mangiarotti (ITA-FEN)
6	Hubert Van Innis (BEL-ARC)
6	Akinori Nakayama (JPN-GYM)
6	Vitaly Shcherbo (EUN-GYM)
6	Gert Fredriksson (SWE-CAN)
6	Reiner Klimke (FRG-EQU)
6	Pál Kovács (HUN-FEN)
6	Nedo Nadi (ITA-FEN)
6	Rudolf Kárpáti (HUN-FEN)

Appendix XII:
Most Olympic Gold Medals Won: Summer, Women

Golds	Athlete (Nation-Sport)
9	Larisa Latynina (URS-GYM)
8	Birgit Fischer-Schmidt (GER-CAN)
8	Jenny Thompson (USA-SWI)
7	Věra Čáslavská (TCH-GYM)
6	Kristin Otto (GDR-SWI)
6	Valentina Vezzali (ITA-FEN)
6	Amy Van Dyken (USA-SWI)
5	Anastasiya Davidova (RUS-SYN)
5	Ágnes Keleti (HUN-GYM)
5	Polina Astakhova (URS-GYM)
5	Nadia Comăneci (ROU-GYM)
5	Isabell Werth (GER-EQU)
5	Elisabeta Lipă-Oleniuc (ROU-ROW)
5	Krisztina Egerszegi (HUN-SWI)
5	Nelli Kim (URS-GYM)
5	Georgeta Damian-Andrunache (ROU-ROW)

Appendix XIII:
Most Olympic Medals Won: Winter, Men

Medals	Athlete (Nation-Sport)
13	Ole Einar Bjørndalen (NOR-BIA)
12	Bjørn Dæhlie (NOR-CCS)
9	Sixten Jernberg (SWE-CCS)
8	Ricco Groß (GER-BIA)
8	Kjetil André Aamodt (NOR-ASK)
8	Sven Fischer (GER-BIA)
8	Apolo Anton Ohno (USA-STK)
8	Viktor An (KOR/RUS-STK)
7	Clas Thunberg (FIN-SSK)
7	Ivar Ballangrud (NOR-SSK)
7	Veikko Hakulinen (FIN-CCS)
7	Eero Mäntyranta (FIN-CCS)
7	Felix Gottwald (AUT-NCO)
7	Bogdan Musiol (GDR-BOB)
7	Vladimir Smirnov II (KAZ-CCS)
7	Sven Kramer (NED-SSK)
6	Johan Olsson (SWE-CCS)
6	Bode Miller (USA-ASK)
6	Thomas Alsgaard (NOR-CCS)
6	Gunde Svan (SWE-CCS)
6	Vegard Ulvang (NOR-CCS)
6	Halvard Hanevold (NOR-BIA)
6	Johan Grøttumsbraaten (NOR-NCO)
6	Sergey Chepikov (RUS-BIA)
6	Wolfgang Hoppe (GDR-BOB)
6	Eugenio Monti (ITA-BOB)
6	Mika Myllylä (FIN-CCS)
6	Roald Larsen (NOR-SSK)
6	Rintje Ritsma (NED-SSK)
6	Harri Kirvesniemi (FIN-CCS)
6	Armin Zöggeler (ITA-LUG)

Appendix XIV:
Most Olympic Medals Won: Winter, Women

Medals	Athlete (Nation-Sport)
10	Raisa Smetanina (EUN-CCS)
10	Stefania Belmondo (ITA-CCS)
10	Marit Bjørgen (NOR-CCS)
9	Lyubov Yegorova (RUS-CCS)
9	Claudia Pechstein (GER-SSK)
9	Uschi Disl (GER-BIA)
8	Galina Kulakova (URS-CCS)
8	Karin Kania-Enke (GDR-SSK)
8	Gunda Niemann-Stirnemann-Kleemann (GER-SSK)
8	Irene Wüst (NED-SSK)
7	Larisa Lazutina (RUS-CCS)
7	Kati Wilhelm (GER-BIA)
7	Marja-Liisa Kirvesniemi-Hämäläinen (FIN-CCS)
7	Yelena Välbe (EUN-CCS)
7	Manuela Di Centa (ITA-CCS)
7	Andrea Ehrig-Schöne-Mitscherlich (GDR-SSK)
6	Lidiya Skoblikova (URS-SSK)
6	Bonnie Blair (USA-SSK)
6	Janica Kostelić (CRO-ASK)
6	Meng Wang (CHN-STK)
6	Yuliya Chepalova (RUS-CCS)
6	Kateřina Neumannová (CZE-CCS)
6	Cindy Klassen (CAN-SSK)
6	Anja Pärson (SWE-ASK)
6	Claudia Künzel-Nystad (GER-CCS)

Appendix XV:
Most Olympic Gold Medals Won: Winter, Men

Golds	Athlete (Nation-Sport)
8	Bjørn Dæhlie (NOR-CCS)
8	Ole Einar Bjørndalen (NOR-BIA)
6	Viktor An (KOR/RUS-STK)
5	Clas Thunberg (FIN-SSK)
5	Thomas Alsgaard (NOR-CCS)
5	Eric Heiden (USA-SSK)
4	Sixten Jernberg (SWE-CCS)
4	Ricco Groß (GER-BIA)
4	Kjetil André Aamodt (NOR-ASK)
4	Sven Fischer (GER-BIA)
4	Ivar Ballangrud (NOR-SSK)
4	Gunde Svan (SWE-CCS)
4	Yevgeny Grishin (URS-SSK)
4	Johann Olav Koss (NOR-SSK)
4	Matti Nykänen (FIN-SKJ)
4	Nikolay Zimyatov (URS-CCS)
4	Aleksandr Tikhonov (URS-BIA)
4	André Lange (GER-BOB)
4	Kevin Kuske (GER-BOB)
4	Simon Ammann (SUI-SKJ)
4	Thomas Wassberg (SWE-CCS)
4	Emil Hegle Svendsen (NOR-BIA)

Appendix XVI:
Most Olympic Gold Medals Won: Winter, Women

Golds	Athlete (Nation-Sport)
6	Lyubov Yegorova (RUS-CCS)
6	Lidiya Skoblikova (URS-SSK)
6	Marit Bjørgen (NOR-CCS)
5	Claudia Pechstein (GER-SSK)
5	Larisa Lazutina (RUS-CCS)
5	Bonnie Blair (USA-SSK)
4	Raisa Smetanina (EUN-CCS)
4	Galina Kulakova (URS-CCS)
4	Janica Kostelić (CRO-ASK)
4	Meng Wang (STK-CHN)
4	Chun Lee-Kyung (KOR-STK)
4	Irene Wüst (NED-SSK)
4	Caroline Ouellette (CAN-ICH)
4	Jayna Hefford (CAN-ICH)
4	Hayley Wickenheiser (CAN-ICH)
3	30 athletes tied

Appendix XVII:
Most Appearances: Summer, Men

Appearances	Athlete (Nation-Sport; Years)
10	Ian Millar (CAN-EQU; 1972–1976, 1984–2012)
9	Afanasijs Kuzmins (LAT/URS-SHO; 1976–1980, 1988–2012)
9	Hubert Raudaschl (AUT-SAI; 1964–1996)
8	Piero D'Inzeo (ITA-EQU; 1948–1976)
8	Raimondo D'Inzeo (ITA-EQU; 1948–1976)
8	Rajmond Debevec (SLO/YUG-SHO; 1984–2012)
8	Paul Elvstrøm (DEN-SAI; 1948–1960, 1968–1972, 1984–1988)
8	Durward Knowles (BAH/GBR-SAI; 1948–1972, 1988)
7	Francisco Boza (PER-SHO; 1980–2004)
7	Andrew Hoy (AUS-EQU; 1984–2004, 2012)
7	Frans Lafortune (BEL-SHO; 1952–1976)
7	Ivan Osiier (DEN-FEN; 1908–1932, 1948)
7	Jörgen Persson (SWE-TTN; 1988–2012)
7	J. Michael Plumb (USA-EQU; 1960–1976, 1984, 1992)
7	Zoran Primorac (YUG/CRO-TTN; 1988–2012)
7	Jean-Michel Saive (BEL-TTN; 1988–2012)
7	Ragnar Skanåker (SWE-SHO; 1972–1996)

Appendix XVIII:
Most Appearances: Summer, Women

Appearances	Athlete (Nation-Sport; Years)
8	Josefa Idem-Guerrini (FRG/ITA-CAN; 1984–2012)
7	Jeannie Longo-Ciprelli (FRA-CYC; 1984–2008)
7	Merlene Ottey (JAM/SLO-ATH; 1980–2004)
7	Kerstin Palm (SWE-FEN; 1964–1988)
7	Jasna Šekarić (IOP/SCG/SRB/YUG-SHO; 1988–2012)
7	Lesley Thompson (CAN-ROW; 1984–2000, 2008-2012)
7	Anky van Grunsven (NED-EQU; 1988–2012)
6	Oksana Chusovitina (EUN/UZB/GER-GYM; 1992–2012)
6	Fabienne Diato-Pasetti (MON-SHO; 1988–2008)
6	Birgit Fischer-Schmidt (GDR/GER-CAN; 1980, 1988–2004)
6	Christilot Hanson-Boylen (CAN-EQU; 1964–1976, 1984, 1992)
6	Štěpánka Hilgertová (CZE-CAN; 1992–2012)
6	Ekaterina Karsten (EUN/BLR-ROW; 1992–2012)
6	Agi Kasoumi (GRE-SHO; 1984–2004)
6	Kyra Kyrklund (FIN-EQU; 1980–1996, 2008)
6	Lia Manoliu (ROU-ATH; 1952–1972)
6	Nonka Matova (BUL-SHO; 1976–1980, 1988–2000)
6	Maria Mutola (MOZ-ATH; 1988–2008)
6	Sue Nattrass (CAN-SHO; 1976, 1988–1992, 2000–2008)
6	Elisabeta Lipă-Oleniuc (ROU-ROW; 1984–2004)
6	Nino Salukvadze (EUN/GEO/URS-SHO; 1988–2008)
6	Tessa Sanderson (GBR-ATH; 1976–1996)
6	Christine Stückelberger (SUI-EQU; 1972–1976, 1984–1988, 1996–2000)
6	Jan York-Romary (USA-FEN; 1948–1968)

Appendix XIX:
Most Appearances: Winter, Men

Appearances	Athlete (Nation-Sport; Years)
7	Albert Demchenko (EUN/RUS/URS-LUG; 1992–2014)
7	Noriaki Kasai (JPN-SKJ; 1992–2014)
6	Jochen Behle (FRG/GER-CCS; 1980–1998)
6	Ole Einar Bjørndalen (NOR-BIA; 1994–2014)
6	Ilmārs Bricis (LAT-BIA; 1992–2010)
6	Marco Büchel (LIE-ASK; 1992–2010)
6	Sergey Chepikov (EUN/RUS/URS-BIA/CCS; 1988–2006)
6	Colin Coates (AUS-SSK; 1968–1988)
6	Mike Dixon (GBR-BIA/CCS; 1984–2002)
6	Sergei Dolidovich (BLR-CCS; 1994–2014)
6	Alfred Eder (AUT-BIA; 1976–1994)
6	Carl-Erik Eriksson (SWE-BOB; 1964–1984)
6	Georg Hackl (FRG/GER-LUG; 1988–2006)
6	Raimo Helminen (FIN-ICH; 1984–2002)
6	Wilfried Huber (ITA-LUG; 1988–2006)
6	Harri Kirvesniemi (FIN-CCS; 1980–1998)
6	Markus Prock (AUT-LUG; 1984–2002)
6	Andrus Veerpalu (EST-CCS; 1992–2010)
6	Hubertus von Hohenlohe (MEX-ALP; 1984–1994, 2010–2014)
6	Armin Zöggeler (ITA-LUG; 1994–2014)

Appendix XX:
Most Appearances: Winter, Women

Appearances	Athlete (Nation-Sport; Years)
6	Emese Hunyady (AUT/HUN-SSK; 1984–2002)
6	Marja-Liisa Kirvesniemi-Hämäläinen (FIN-CCS; 1976–1994)
6	Anna Orlova (LAT-LUG; 1992–2010)
6	Claudia Pechstein (GER-SSK; 1992–2006, 2014)
6	Gerda Weissensteiner (ITA-BOB/LUG; 1988–2006)
5	Anne Abernathy (ISV-LUG; 1988–2002)
5	Stefania Belmondo (ITA-CCS; 1988–2002)
5	Manuela Di Centa (ITA-CCS; 1984–1998)
5	Uschi Disl (GER-BIA; 1992–2006)
5	Margarita Drobiazko (LTU-FSK; 1992–2006)
5	Susi Erdmann (GER-BOB/LUG; 1992–2006)
5	Martina Ertl-Renz (GER-ASK; 1992–2006)
5	Monika Gawenus-Holzner-Pflug (FRG-SSK; 1972–1988)
5	Edel Therese Høiseth (NOR-SSK; 1984–1998)
5	Mária Jasenčáková (TCH/SVK-LUG; 1980–1984, 1992–1998)
5	Martina Jašicová-Schwarzbacherová-Halinárová (SVK-BIA; 1994–2010)
5	Kateřina Neumannová (TCH/CZE-CCS; 1992–2006)
5	Tomomi Okazaki (JPN-SSK; 1994–2010)
5	Gabriella Paruzzi (ITA-CCS; 1992–2006)
5	Evgeniya Radanova (BUL-STK; 1994–2010)
5	María José Rienda (ESP-ASK; 1994–2010)
5	Nathalie Santer (ITA-BIA; 1992–2006)
5	Tae Satoya (JPN-FRS; 1994–2010)
5	Raisa Smetanina (EUN/URS-CCS; 1976–1992)
5	Kristina Šmigun-Vähi (EST-CCS; 1994–2010)
5	Sabina Valbusa (ITA-CCS; 1994–2010)
5	Yelena Volodina-Antonova (KAZ-CCS; 1994–2010)
5	Nataliya Yakushenko (EUN/UKR-LUG; 1992–1998, 2006–2010)

Appendix XXI:
List of All Positive Drug Tests at the Olympic Games

Listed after each athlete's name is his or her country, sport and event, finish before disqualification, and the name of the illegal drug detected.

1968 Mexico City (1)

Hans-Gunnar Liljenvall (SWE)—Modern pentathlete—3rd—Alcohol (depressant).

1972 Sapporo (1)

Alois Schröder (FRG)—Ice hockey—7th—Ephedrine (stimulant). (Note: The team doctor, Franz Schlickenrieder, was disqualified from serving in that capacity for life.)

1972 Munich (7)

Bakhaava Buida (MGL)—Judo, 63 kg class—2nd—drug unknown.
Miguel Coli (PUR)—Basketball—6th—Ephedrine (stimulant).
Richard DeMont (USA)—Swimming, 400 meter freestyle—1st—Ephedrine (stimulant).
Jamie Huelamo (ESP)—Cycling, individual road race—3rd—Coramine (stimulant).
Walter Legel (AUT)—Weightlifting, 67.5 kg class—15th—Amphetamines (stimulant).
Arjomand Mohamed Nasehi (IRI)—Weightlifting, 52 kg class—10th—Ephedrine (stimulant)
Aad van den Hoek (NED)—Cycling, 100 km team time trial, 3rd—Coramine (stimulant) (team disqualified).

1976 Innsbruck (2)

Galina Kulakova (URS)—Nordic skiing, 5 km—3rd—Ephedrine (stimulant). (Note: Kulakova also finished 3rd in the 10 km and 1st on the 4 3 5 km relay team at these Olympic Winter Games, but was allowed to keep those medals.)

František Pospíšil (TCH)—Ice hockey—2nd—Codeine (narcotic pain medication). (Note: The team doctor, Treffný, was disqualified from serving in that capacity for life.)

1976 Montreal (11)

Blagoi Blagoev (BUL)—Weightlifting, 82.5 kg class—2nd—Anabolic steroid.

Mark Cameron (USA)—Weightlifting, 110 kg class—5th—Anabolic steroid.

Paul Cerutti (MON)—Shooting, Trap shooting—43rd—Amphetamines.

Valentin Khristov (BUL)—Weightlifting, 110 kg class—1st—Anabolic steroid.

Dragomir Ciorislan (ROM)—Weightlifting, 75 kg class—5th—Fencanfamine (stimulant).

Phillip Grippaldi (USA)—Weightlifting, 90 kg class—4th—Anabolic steroid.

Zbigniew Kaczmarek (POL)—Weightlifting, 67.5 kg class—1st—Anabolic steroid.

Lorne Leibel (CAN)—Yachting, Tempest class—7th—Phenylpropanolamine (stimulant).

Ame Norback (SWE)—Weightlifting, 60 kg class—eliminated—Anabolic steroid.

Petr Pavlagek (TCH)—Weightlifting, 110 kg class—6th—Anabolic steroid.

Danuta Rosani-Gwardecka (POL)—Track and field athletics, Discus throw—14th in qualifying (DNQ)—Anabolic steroid.

1980 Lake Placid (0)

No positive drug tests.

1980 Moscow (0)

No positive drug tests.

1984 Sarajevo (1)

Purevjalyn Batsukh (MGL)—Nordic skiing, 15 km—69th/30 km—65th/ 4 3 10 k in relay/15th—Methandienone (anabolic steroid).

1984 Los Angeles (12)

Serafim Grammatikopoulos (GRE)—Weightlifting, Unlimited class—did not finish—Nandrolone (anabolic steroid).

Vesteinn Hafsteinsson (ISL)—Track and field athletics, Discus throw—14th in qualifying round—Nandrolone (anabolic steroid).

Thomas Johansson (SWE)—Wrestling, Unlimited Greco–Roman class—2nd—Methenolone (anabolic steroid).

Stefan Laggner (AUT)—Weightlifting, Unlimited class—4th—Nandrolone (anabolic steroid).

Göran Petterson (SWE)—Weightlifting, 110 kg class—6th—Nandrolone (anabolic steroid).

Eiji Shimomura (JPN)—Volleyball—7th—Testosterone (anabolic steroid).

Mikiyasu Tanaka (JPN)—Volleyball—7th—Ephedrine (stimulant). (Note: The trainer of the Japanese volleyball team was banned from the Olympics for life.)

Ahmed Tarbi (ALG)—Weightlifting, 56 kg class—9th—Nandrolone (anabolic steroid).

Mahmoud Tarha (LBA)—Weightlifting, 52 kg class—4th—Nandrolone (anabolic steroid).

Gian-Paolo Urlando (ITA)—Track and field athletics, Hammer throw—4th—Testosterone (anabolic steroid).

Martti Vainio (FIN)—Track and field athletics, 10,000 meters—2nd—Methenolone (anabolic steroid).

Anna Verouli (GRE)—Track and field athletics, Javelin throw—13th in qualifying round—Nandrolone (anabolic steroid).

1988 Calgary (1)

Jaroslav Morawiecki (POL)—Ice hockey—10th—Testosterone (anabolic steroid).

1988 Seoul (11)

Alidad (AFG)—Wrestling, 62 kg freestyle class—eliminated third round—Furosemide (Lasix) (diuretic, masking agent).

Kerrith Brown (GBR)—Judo, 71 kg—3rd—Furosemide (Lasix) (diuretic, masking agent).

Kálmán Csengeri (HUN)—Weightlifting, 75 kg class—4th—Stanozolol (anabolic steroid).

Angel Genchev (BUL)—Weightlifting, 67.5 kg class—1st—Furosemide (Lasix) (diuretic, masking agent).

Mitko Grablev (BUL)—Weightlifting, 56 kg class—1st—Furosemide (Lasix) (diuretic, masking agent).

Ben Johnson (CAN)—Track and field athletics, 100 meters—1st—Stanozolol (anabolic steroid).

Fernando Mariaca (ESP)—Weightlifting, 67.5 kg class—13th—Pemoline (stimulant).

Jorge Quezada (ESP)—Modern pentathlon—24th—Propranolol (beta antagonist/blocker).

Andor Szányi (HUN)—Weightlifting, 100 kg class—2nd—Stanozolol (anabolic steroid).

Alexander Watson (AUS)—Modern pentathlon—61st—Caffeine (stimulant).

Sergiusz Wolczaniecki (POL)—Weightlifting, 90 kg class—3rd—Stanozolol (anabolic steroid).

1992 Albertville (0)

No positive drug tests.

1992 Barcelona (5)

Madina Biktagirova (EUN)—Track and field athletics, Marathon—4th—Norephedrine (stimulant).

Bonnie Dasse (USA)—Track and field athletics, Shot put—14th in qualifying round—Clenbuterol (beta agonist).

Judson Logan (USA)—Track and field athletics, Hammer throw—4th—Clenbuterol (beta agonist).

Nijole Medvedeva (LTU)—Track and field athletics, Long jump—4th—Meziocarde (stimulant).

Wu Dan (CHN)—Volleyball—7th—Stimulant with a strychnine base.

1994 Lillehammer (0)

No positive drug tests.

1996 Atlanta (2)

Iva Prandzheva (BUL)—Athletics, long jump, 7th—triple jump, 4th—Methadienone (stimulant).

Nataliya Shekhodanova (RUS)—Athletics, 100 meter hurdles, 7th—Stanozolol (anabolic steroid).

Note: Two noncompetitors were disqualified, a coach and physician to the Lithuanian cycling team, as several of their athletes did test positive for Bromantan: Boris Vasilyev (LTU), coach of the Lithuanian cycling team and Vitaly Slionsarenko (LTU), physician to the Lithuanian cycling team. Both were expelled from the Olympics because of offenses involving performance-enhancing drugs. There were an additional six positive tests, but four of these were for the controversial drug Bromantan. The four athletes were originally disqualified, but on appeal, all were reinstated because the drug was new, it was not certain if it was an ergogenic aid, and it had not been announced in advance. A sixth positive test for phenylpropanolamine was announced, but the athlete was given only a warning, as that drug is commonly found in cold medications. The positive tests were as follows:

Zafar Gulyev (RUS)—Greco–Roman wrestling, 48 kg—3rd—Bromantan.

Andrey Korneyev (RUS)—Swimming, 200 meter breaststroke—3rd—Bromantan.

Marie McMahon (IRL)—Track and field athletics, 5,000 meters—14th/heat two/round one—Phenylpropanolamine (an OTC cold remedy).

Rita Ražmaite (LTU)—Cycling, match sprint—13th—Bromantan.

Estella Rodriguez Villanueva (CUB)—Judo, Unlimited class—1st—Furosemide (Lasix). (It is unclear why this decision was made.)

Marina Trandenkova (RUS)—Track and field athletics, 100 meters—5th—Bromantan.

1998 Nagano (0)

There were no drug disqualifications. However, in men's giant slalom snowboarding, the winner, Ross Rebagliati (CAN), was disqualified two days after winning the event, when he tested positive for marijuana use. He was reinstated as the gold medalist on 12 February after a ruling by the Court of Arbitration for Sport (CAS).

2000 Sydney (12)

Fritz Aanes (NOR)—Wrestling, 85 kg Greco-Roman—4th—Nandrolone (anabolic steroid).

Ashot Danielyan (ARM)—Weightlifting, Unlimited class—3rd—Stanozolol (anabolic steroid).

Izabela Dragneva (BUL)—Weightlifting, 48 kg class—1st—Furosemide (Lasix) (diuretic, masking agent).

Ivan Ivanov (BUL)—Weightlifting, 56 kg class—2nd—Furosemide (Lasix) (diuretic, masking agent).

Alexander Leipold (GER)—Wrestling, 76 kg freestyle—1st—Nandrolone (anabolic steroid).

Svetlana Pospelova (RUS)—Track and field athletics—400 meters—4th in heat of round one—Stanozolol (anabolic steroid).

Oyunbileg Puervbaatar (MGL)—Wrestling—58 kg freestyle—5th—Furosemide (Lasix) (diuretic, masking agent).

Andreea Raducan (ROM)—Gymnastics—Individual all-around—1st—Pseudoephedrine (stimulant).

Andris Reinholds (LAT)—Rowing—Single sculls—8th—Nandrolone (anabolic steroid).

Minchev Angelov Sevdalin (BUL)—Weightlifting—62 kg class—3rd—Furosemide (Lasix) (diuretic, masking agent).

Marion Jones (USA) won five medals and three gold medals in athletics (100, 200, 4 3 100) at the time of the 2000 Olympic Games. In 2007, she admitted to the systematic use of performance-enhancing drugs. Her medals were removed, and the U.S. medals in the 4 3 100 and 4 3 400 meter relays were also removed.

Antonio Pettigrew (USA) helped the United States win a gold medal in the 4 3400 meter relay in athletics. In 2008, he admitted to the use of performance-enhancing drugs and voluntarily returned his medals. The USA 4 3400 meter relay was disqualified.

2002 Salt Lake City (7)

Alain Baxter (GBR)—Alpine skiing slalom—3rd—Methamphetamine (stimulant).

Olga Danilova (RUS)—Cross-country skiing, 30 km—8th—Darbopoietin (Erythropoietin [EPO] analog).

Larisa Lazutina (RUS)—Cross-country skiing, 30 km—1st—Darbopoietin (Erythropoietin [EPO] analog).

Marc Mayer (AUT)—Cross-country skiing, 50 km, 24th—Pursuit, 50th—Sprint, 21st—Blood doping.

Johann Mühlegg (ESP)—Cross-country skiing, 50 km—1st—Darbopoietin (Erythropoietin [EPO] analog).

Vasily Pankov (BLR)—Ice hockey—4th—Nandrolone (anabolic steroid).

Achim Walcher (AUT)—Cross-country skiing, 30 km, 45th—Pursuit, 43rd—Blood doping.

2004 Athens (13 competitors—28 total athletes)

Adrian Annus (HUN)—Track and field athletics hammer throw, 1st—Tampering with urine sample and then refusing to submit to a second test.

Robert Fazekas (HUN)—Track and field athletics discus throw, 1st—Refusal to provide a urine sample.

Mabel Fonseca (PUR)—Wrestling, freestyle, 55 kg class—5th—Stanozolol (anabolic steroid).

Anton Galkin (RUS)—Track and field athletics 400 meters, 4th in semifinal—Stanozolol (anabolic steroid).

Ferenc Gyurkovics (HUN)—Weightlifting, 105 kg, 2nd—Oxandrolone (anabolic steroid).

Irina Korzhanenko (RUS)—Track and field athletics shot put, 1st—Stanozolol (anabolic steroid). Zoltán Kovács (HUN)—Weightlifting, 105 kg, DNF—Refusal to provide a urine sample.

Aleksey Lesnichiy (BLR)—Track and field athletics high jump, did not qualify, in Group B of qualifying—Clenbuterol (beta agonist).

Aye Khine Nan (MYA)—Weightlifting, 56 kg class, 4th—Anabolic steroid (not released).

Olena Olefirenko (UKR)—Rowing quadruple sculls, 3rd—Etamivan (stimulant).

Leonidas Sambanis (GRE)—Weightlifting, 62 kg class—3rd—Testosterone (anabolic steroid).

Thing Baijan Sanamacha Chanu (IND)—Weightlifting, 53 kg class—4th—Furosemide (Lasix) (diuretic, masking agent).

Olga Shchukina (UZB)—Track and field athletics shot put, 18th in Group A of qualifying—Clenbuterol (beta agonist).

Marion Jones (USA) competed in athletics (long jump, 4 3100 meters) at the 2004 Olympic Games, though with much less success than she had had in 2000. In 2007, she admitted to the systematic use of performance-enhancing drugs. Her placement in the long jump was removed, and the United States was disqualified from the 4 3100 meter relay.

Crystal Cox (USA) ran in the heats of the 4 3400 meter relay for the United States at the 2004 Olympic Games, and the team eventually won a gold medal. However, in 2010, Cox admitted to the use of performance-enhancing drugs from 2001 to 2004, and the U.S. 4 3 400 meter team was disqualified.

Two equestrian athletes were disqualified when their horses were found to have doping positives. These were Cian O'Connor (IRL), who rode Waterford Crystal in the show jumping events, and Ludger Beerbaum (GER), who rode Goldfever in the show jumping events. Both originally won gold medals, O'Connor in the individual show jumping and Beerbaum in the team show jumping. Although Beerbaum was disqualified, his German team scores still allowed them to earn a bronze medal in team show jumping.

In addition to the above, there were nine athletes disqualified for positive doping tests prior to the start of their competitions, and they were excluded from the Olympic Games and never competed, as follows:

Wafa Ammouri (MAR)—Weightlifting—Substance not released.

Andrew Brack (GRE)—Baseball—Stanozolol (anabolic steroid).

Viktor Chislean (MDA)—Weightlifting—Substance not released.

Zoltán Kecskes (HUN)—Weightlifting—Substance not released.

Albina Khomich (RUS)—Weightlifting—Anabolic steroid.

Pratime Kumari (IND)—Weightlifting—Substance not released.

David Munyasi (KEN)—Boxing—Caffeine (stimulant).

Derek Nicholson (GRE)—Baseball—Hydrochlorothiazide (HCTZ) (Diuretic, masking agent).

Sule Sahbaz (TUR)—Weightlifting—Substance not released.

Also, Maria Luisa Calle Williams (COL) was originally disqualified from the women's cycling points race (3rd place) for the use of Heptaminol, a stimulant. However, she appealed this and was reinstated by the Court of Arbitration for Sport.

Finally, Tyler Hamilton (USA), gold medalist in the men's cycling individual team trial, was later found to have an A-sample, which suggested he may have used blood doping. His B-sample was frozen, and when analysis was attempted, it was found to be not suitable for testing. Because both samples must be positive, he was not felt to be guilty of doping. The Russian Olympic Committee protested, as their rider Vyacheslav Yekimov would have moved up to the gold medal position. This protest was eventually disallowed by the Court of Arbitration for Sport, and Hamilton retained his gold medal.

2006 Torino (1 competitor/13 athletes)

Olga Pyleva (RUS)—Biathlon, 15 km—2nd—Carphedon (stimulant).

The following Austrian cross-country skiers and biathletes were found to have been involved in an elaborate, systematic blood doping scheme. They were disqualified, and all of their results were nullified: Roland Diethart (AUT/CCS); Johannes Eder (AUT/CCS), Wolfgang Perner (AUT/ BIA); Jürgen Pinter (AUT/ CCS); Wolfgang Rottmann (AUT/BIA); and Martin Tauber (AUT/CCS).

Also, the following cross-country skiers were found to have an excessive hematocrit level and were not allowed to start in certain events. After retesting, several of the following were allowed to start in other events. Alen Abramović (CRO); Sean Crooks (CAN); Sergey Dolidovich (BLR); Jean-Marc Gaillard (FRA); Pavel Korostelev (RUS); Aleksandr Lazutkin (BLR); Nataliya Matveyeva (RUS); Nikolay Pankratov (RUS); Kikkan Randall (USA); Evi Sachenbacher-Stehle (GER); Robel Teklemariam (ETH); and Leif Zimmerman (USA).

2008 Beijing (8 athletes, 7 horses, 2 disqualified prior to the opening ceremony)

Vanja Perišič (CRO)—Track and field athletics, 800 meters—2nd in heat—CERA (continuous erythropoietin receptor activator).

Rashid Ramzi (BRN)—Track and field athletics, 1,500 meters, 1st— CERA (continuous erythropoietin receptor activator).

Athanasia Tsoumeleka (GRE)—Track and field athletics, 20 km walk, 9th—CERA (continuous erythropoietin receptor activator).

Kim Jong-Su (PRK)—Shooting, Air Pistol, 3rd; Free Pistol, 2nd—Propranolol (beta antagonist/blocker).

Courtney King (USA)—Equestrian events, Dressage, 13th; Team Dressage—4th—Felbinac (Horse tested positive for substance).

Marco Kutscher (GER)—Equestrian events, Jumping, 39th qualifying; Team Jumping, 9th—Lactanase (Horse tested positive for substance).

Denis Lynch (IRL)—Equestrian events, Jumping—8th—Capsaicin (Horse tested positive for substance).

Thi Ngan Thuong Do (VIE)—Gymnastics, All-Around—59th—Furosemide (Lasix) (diuretic, masking agent).

Rodrigo Pessoa (BRA)—Equestrian events, Jumping, 27th; Team Jumping, 10th—Capsaicin (Horse tested positive for substance).

Davide Rebellin (ITA)—Cycling, Road race—2nd—CERA (continuous erythropoietin receptor activator).

Stefan Schumacher (GER)—Cycling, Individual time trial—13th; Road race, did not finish—CERA (continuous erythropoietin receptor activator).

Adam Seroczyński (POL)—Canoeing, K2-1,000—4th—Clenbuterol (beta agonist).

Bernardo Alves (BRA)—Equestrian events, Jumping, 3rd; Team Jumping, 10th—Capsaicin (Horse tested positive for substance).

Christian Ahlmann (GER)—Equestrian events, Jumping, 28th qualifying; Team Jumping, 5th—Capsaicin (Horse tested positive for substance).

Tony Andre Hansen (NOR)—Equestrian events, Jumping, 1st qualifying; Team Jumping, 3rd—Capsaicin (Horse tested positive for substance).

The following athletes tested positive very shortly after the 2008 Olympic Games ended, but were disqualified:

The following two athletes tested positive after arriving in Beijing and were not allowed to compete:

Anastasios "Tasos" Gousis (GRE)—Track and field athletics—Methyltrienolone (anabolic steroid).

María Isabel "Maribel" Moreno (ESP)—Cycling—Erythropoietin (EPO).

2010 Vancouver (2)

Kornelia Marek (POL)—Cross-country skiing, 10 km, 30 km, pursuit, team sprint, relay—Erythropoietin (EPO).

Svetlana Terentyeva (RUS)—Ice hockey—Tuaminoheptane. Reprimanded, but not disqualified, as the drug was only illegal in competition, not out of competition.

2012 London (15)

Ghfran Almouhamad (SYR)—Athletics—Methylhexanamine. IOC precompetition testing; disqualified.

Victoria Baranova (RUS)—Cycling—Testosterone. IOC pre-Games testing, disqualified.

Kissya Cataldo (BRA)—Rowing—EPO. IOC pre-Games testing, disqualified.

Nicholas Delpopolo (USA)—Judo—Cannabis. IOC postevent testing, disqualified.

Luiza Galiulina (UZB)—Gymnastics—Furosemide. IOC pre-Games testing, disqualified.

Hassan Hirt (FRA)—Athletics—EPO. IOC pre-Games testing, disqualified.

Amine Laâlou (MAR)—Athletics—Furosemide. IAAF postcompetition testing, disqualified.

Marina Marghiev (MDA)—Athletics—Furosemide. IOC pre-Games testing, disqualified.

Nadzeya Ostapchuk (BLR)—Athletics—Methenelone. IOC postevent testing, women's shot put gold medalist disqualified.

Diego Palomeque (COL)—Athletics—Exogenous testosterone. IOC precompetition testing, disqualified.

Darya Pischalnikova (RUS)—Athletics—Oxandrolone. Random pre-Games testing, women's discus throw silver medalist disqualified.

Hysen Pulaku (ALB)—Weightlifting—Stanozolol. IOC precompetition testing, disqualified.

Alex Schwazer (ITA)—Athletics—EPO. IOC pre-Games testing, disqualified.

Soslan Tigiev (UZB)—Wrestling—Methylhexanamine. Bronze medalist 74 kg freestyle, disqualified.

Tameka Williams (SKN)—Athletics—Blast Off Red. Did not fail test but confessed to using illegal stimulant, disqualified.

2014 Sochi (8)

Nicklas Bäckström (SWE)—Ice hockey—Pseudoephedrine. Silver medal awarded despite doping violation.

Johannes Dürr (AUT)—Cross-country skiing—Erythropoietin.

Ralfs Freibergs (LAT)—Ice hockey—Dehydro chloromethyl testosterone

William Frullani (ITA)—Bobsleigh—Methylhexanamine.

Marina Lisogor (UKR)—Cross-country skiing—Trimetazidine.

Vitalijs Pavlovs (LAT)—Ice hockey—Methylhexanamine.

Evi Sachenbacher-Stehle (GER)—Biathlon—Methylhexanamine.

Daniel Zalewski (POL)—Bobsleigh—Stimulant.

Appendix XXII:
Attempts at Olympic Revival Prior to 1896

1612   Robert Dover's Games, also known as the Cotswold Olimpick Games, are first contested in the Cotswold Hills in England, during Whitsun (Pentecostal) Week. The Games continue to 1642 and then are discontinued until the 1660s. They will be held intermittently from the 1660s to the 1850s. Resumed again a few decades later, they continue to be held sporadically. Rather than true sporting contests, the Games resemble more a medieval country fair.

1834   Ramlösa, Sweden (near Helsingborg). "Olympic Games" are organized under the initiative of Professor Gustav Johann Schartau of the University of Lund.

1836   Ramlösa, Sweden. The second, and last, Swedish attempt at revival occurs.

1830–
1840s   Olympic-type festivals are held in Montreal, Quebec, Canada.

1850   First Much Wenlock Olympian Games are held in Much Wenlock, a small town near Shrewsbury, Shropshire, England. Altogether, 45 are held consecutively, except in 1874, through 1895. They are later held sporadically and continued to the 1990s.

1859   First Zappas Olympic Games in Athens, Greece, are sponsored by the Greek philanthropist Evangelis Zappas.

1860   First Shropshire Olympic Games are organized in Much Wenlock, England, by the Shropshire Olympic Society.

1861   Second Shropshire Olympic Games are held in Wellington, Shropshire, England.

1862   Third Shropshire Olympic Games are held in Much Wenlock, Shropshire, England. First Grand Olympic Festival is held in Liverpool, England, sponsored by the Liverpool Olympian Society.

1863   Second Grand Olympic Festival is held in Liverpool, England, sponsored by the Liverpool Olympian Society.

1864   Fourth, and last, Shropshire Olympic Games are held in Much Wenlock, England. Third Grand Olympic Festival is held in Liverpool, England, sponsored by the Liverpool Olympian Society.

1866   First Olympic Games sponsored by England's National Olympian Association are held in London, England. Fourth Grand Olympic Festival is held in Llandudno, Wales, sponsored by the Liverpool Olympian Society.

1867   Second Olympic Games sponsored by the National Olympian Association are held in Birmingham, England. Fifth, and last, Grand Olympic Festival is held in Liverpool, England, sponsored by the Liverpool Olympian Society.

1868	Third Olympic Games sponsored by the National Olympian Association are held in Wellington, Shropshire, England.
1870	Second Zappas Olympic Games are held in Athens, Greece.
1873	First Morpeth Olympic Games are held in Morpeth, England. The Games are held almost annually until 1958.
1874	Fourth Olympic Games sponsored by the National Olympian Association are held in Much Wenlock, England.
1875	Third Zappas Olympic Games are held in Athens, Greece.
1877	Fifth Olympic Games sponsored by the National Olympian Association are held in Shrewsbury, England.
1880	First Olympic Games are held at Lake Palić, in Palić, a spa eight kilometers east of Subotica, then in Hungary and now in the Vojvodina province of Serbia. The Games are held sporadically from 1880 until 1914.
1883	Sixth, and last, Olympic Games sponsored by the National Olympian Association are held in Hadley, Shropshire, England.
1889	Fourth Zappas Olympic Games are held in Athens, Greece.
1891	First Panhellenic Gymnastic Society Games, modeled after the Zappas Olympics, are held in Athens.
1893	Second Panhellenic Gymnastic Society Games, modeled after the Zappas Olympics, are held in Athens.
April 1896	Games of the Ist Olympiad, celebrating the First Olympiad of the modern era, are held in Athens, Greece, signaling the final resurrection of the Olympic Games after 15 centuries.

Appendix XXIII:
International Federations—SportAccord

SportAccord is the umbrella organization for all international sports federations as well as organizers of multisports games and sport-related international associations. It has 109 members—92 full members (specific sports) and 17 associate members (other organizations).

FULL MEMBERS

Aikido	IAF	International Aikido Federation
Air Sports	FAI	Féderation Aeronautique Internationale
American Football	IFAF	International Federation of American Football
Aquatics	FINA	Fédération Internationale de Natation
Archery	WA	World Archery Federation
Athletics	IAAF	International Association of Athletics Federations
Automobile	FIA	Fédération Internationale de l'Automobile
Badminton	BWF	Badminton World Federation
Baseball & Softball	WBSC	World Baseball Softball Confederation
Basketball	FIBA	Fédération Internationale de Basketball
Basque Pelota	FIBV	Federacion Internacional de Pelota Vasca
Biathlon	IBU	International Biathlon Union
Billiards Sports	WCBS	World Confederation of Billiard Sports
Bobsleigh	FIBT	Fédération Internationale de Bobsleigh et de Tobogganing
Bodybuilding	IFBB	International Federation of Bodybuilding & Fitness
Boules Sport	CMSB	Confederation Mondiale des Sportes de Boules
Bowling	FIQ	Fédération Internationale des Quilleurs
Boxing	AIBA	Association Internationale de Boxe
Bridge	WBF	World Bridge Federation
Canoe	ICF	International Canoe Federation
Casting	ICSF	International Casting Sport Federation
Cheer	ICU	The International Cheer Union
Chess	FIDE	Fédération Internationale des Eschecs
Climbing & Mountaineering	UIAA	International Climbing and Mountaineering Federation
Cricket	ICC	International Cricket Council
Curling	WCF	World Curling Federation
Cycling	UCI	Union Cycliste Internationale
Dance Sport	WDSF	World DanceSport Federation

725

Darts	WDF	World Darts Federation
Dragon Boat	IDBF	International Dragon Boat Federation
Draughts	FMJD	Fédération Mondiale du Jeu de Dames
Equestrian Sports	FEI	Fédération Equestre Internationale
Fencing	FIE	Fédération Internationale d'Escrime
Fistball	IFA	International Fistball Association
Floorball	IFF	International Floorball Federation
Flying Disc	WFDF	World Flying Disc Federation
Football	FIFA	Fédération Internationale de Football Association
Go	IGF	International Go Federation
Golf	IGF	International Golf Federation
Gymnastics	FIG	Fédération Internationale de Gymnastique
Handball	IHF	International Handball Federation
Hockey	FIH	Fédération Internationale de Hockey
Ice Hockey	IIHF	International Ice Hockey Federation
Icestocksport	IFI	International Federation Icestocksport
Ju-Jitsu	JJIF	Ju-Jitsu International Federation
Judo	IJF	International Judo Federation
Karate	WKF	World Karate Federation
Kendo	FIK	International Kendo Federation
Kickboxing	WAKO	World Association of Kickboxing Organizations
Korfball	IKF	International Korfball Federation
Lacrosse	FILx	Federation of International Lacrosse
Life Saving	ILS	International Life Saving Federation
Luge	FIL	Fédération Internationale de Luge de Course
Minigolf	WMF	World Minigolfsport Federation
Modern Pentathlon	UIPM	Union Internationale de Pentathlon Moderne
Motorcycling	FIM	Fédération Internationale de Motocyclisme
Muaythai	IFMA	International Federation of Muaythai Amateur
Netball	INF	International Netball Federation
Orienteering	IOF	International Orienteering Federation
Polo	FIP	Federation of International Polo
Powerboating	UIM	Union Internationale Motonautique
Powerlifting	IPF	International Powerlifting Federation
Racquetball	IRF	International Racquetball Federation
Roller Sports	FIRS	Fédération Internationale de Roller Sports
Rowing	FISA	Fédération Internationale des Societes d'Aviron
Rugby	IRB	International Rugby Board
Sailing	ISAF	International Sailing Federation
Sambo	FIAS	Fédération Internationale de Sambo
Savate	FISav	Fédération Internationale de Savate
Sepaktakraw	ISTAF	International Sepaktakraw Federation
Shooting Sport	ISSF	International Shooting Sport Federation
Skating	ISU	International Skating Union
Ski Mountaineering	ISMF	International Ski Mountaineering Federation
Skiing	FIS	Fédération Internationale de Ski
Sleddog	IFSS	International Federation of Sleddog Sports

Soft Tennis	ISTF	International Soft Tennis Federation
Sport Climbing	IFSC	International Federation of Sport Climbing
Sports Fishing	CIPS	Confédération Internationale de la Pêche Sportive
Squash	WSF	World Squash Federation
Sumo	IFS	International Sumo Federation
Surfing	ISA	International Surfing Association
Table Tennis	ITTF	International Table Tennis Federation
Taekwondo	WTF	World Taekwondo Federation
Tennis	ITF	International Tennis Federation
Triathlon	ITU	International Triathlon Union
Tug of War	TWIF	Tug of War International Federation
Underwater Activities	CMAS	Confédération Mondiale des Activités Subaquatiques
Volleyball	FIVB	Fédération Internationale de Volleyball
Water Skiing	IWWF	International Water Ski and Wakeboard Federation
Weightlifting	IWF	International Weightlifting Federation
Wrestling	FILA	Fédération Internationale des Luttes Associées
Wushu	IWUF	International Wushu Federation

ASSOCIATE MEMBERS

Commonwealth Games	CGF	Commonwealth Games Federation
European Broadcasting	EBU/ UER	European Broadcasting Union
Masters Games	IMGA	International Masters Games Association
Mediterranean Games	CIJM	International Committee of the Mediterranean Games
Military Sport	CISM	Conseil Internationale du Sport Militaire
Mind Sports	IMSA	International Mind Sports Association
Panathlon	PI	Panathlon International
Paralympic	IPC	International Paralympic Committee
School Sports	ISF	International School Sport Federation
Special Olympics	SOI	Special Olympics, Inc.
Sports Chiropractic	FICS	Fédération Internationale de Chiropractique du Sport
Sports Facilities	IAKS	International Association for Sports and Leisure Facilities
Sports for the Deaf	CISS	International Committee of Sports for the Deaf
Sports Medicine	FIMS	International Federation of Sports Medicine
University Sports	FISU	Fédération Internationale du Sport Universitaire
Workers & Amateurs Sports	CISU	International Workers and Amateurs in Sports Confederation
The World Games	IWGA	International World Games Association

Appendix XXIV:
Olympic Summer Games Participants

Country	From	To	Participants	Sports	Gold	Silver	Bronze	Total
AFG Afghanistan	1936	2012	101	7			2	2
AHO Netherlands Antilles	1952	2008	52	11		1		1
ALB Albania	1972	2012	39	7				
ALG Algeria	1964	2012	314	19	5	2	8	15
AND Andorra	1976	2012	29	8				
ANG Angola	1980	2012	148	10				
ANT Antigua and Barbuda	1976	2012	63	6				
ANZ Australasia	1908	1912	53	8	3	4	5	12
ARG Argentina	1900	2012	1,564	32	18	24	28	70
ARM Armenia	1996	2012	93	13	1	2	9	12
ARU Aruba	1988	2012	26	9				
ASA American Samoa	1988	2012	23	8				
AUS Australia	1896	2012	3,310	35	138	156	181	475
AUT Austria	1896	2012	1,437	31	25	40	41	106
AZE Azerbaijan	1996	2012	143	16	6	5	15	26
BAH Bahamas	1952	2012	147	8	5	2	5	12
BAN Bangladesh	1984	2012	32	5				
BAR Barbados	1968	2012	106	11			1	1
BDI Burundi	1996	2012	20	3	1			1
BEL Belgium	1900	2012	1,907	35	42	56	60	158
BEN Benin	1972	2012	48	7				
BER Bermuda	1936	2012	112	10			1	1
BHU Bhutan	1984	2012	19	2				
BIH Bosnia and Herzegovina	1992	2012	37	10				
BIZ Belize	1968	2012	49	7				

	First	Last						
BLR Belarus	1996	2012	537	25	12	24	40	76
BOH Bohemia	1900	1912	66	9		1	5	6
BOL Bolivia	1936	2012	66	15		1		1
BOT Botswana	1980	2012	52	4				1
BRA Brazil	1900	2012	1,710	30	23	30	55	108
BRN Bahrain	1984	2012	59	7			1	1
BRU Brunei	1996	2012	6	3				
BUL Bulgaria	1924	2012	1,288	29	51	85	78	214
BUR Burkina Faso	1972	2012	29	5				
CAF Central African Republic	1968	2012	47	9				
CAM Cambodia	1964	2012	38	8				
CAN Canada	1900	2012	3,320	38	60	101	120	281
CAY Cayman Islands	1976	2012	35	4				
CGO Congo (Brazzaville)	1964	2012	66	7				
CHA Chad	1964	2012	25	3				
CHI Chile	1912	2012	448	24	2	7	4	13
CHN China	1932	2012	2,081	35	201	144	128	473
CIV Cote d'Ivoire	1964	2012	116	11		1		1
CMR Cameroon	1964	2012	207	10	3	1	1	5
COD Congo (Kinshasa)	1968	2012	65	7				
COK Cook Islands	1988	2012	24	6				
COL Colombia	1900	2012	523	22	2	6	11	19
COM Comoros	1996	2012	12	3				
CPV Cape Verde	1996	2012	9	4				
CRC Costa Rica	1936	2012	143	15	1	1	2	4
CRO Croatia	1992	2012	335	21	6	7	10	23

Country	From	To	Participants	Sports	Gold	Silver	Bronze	Total
CRT Crete	1906	1906	8	2				
CUB Cuba	1900	2012	1,207	29	71	65	66	202
CYP Cyprus	1980	2012	97	11		1		1
CZE Czech Republic	1996	2012	429	27	14	15	15	44
DEN Denmark	1896	2012	1,792	29	46	74	73	193
DJI Djibouti	1984	2012	22	5			1	1
DMA Dominica	1996	2012	14	2				
DOM Dominican Republic	1964	2012	188	16	3	2	1	6
ECU Ecuador	1924	2012	139	17	1	1		2
EGY Egypt	1906	2012	907	29	7	8	9	24
ERI Eritrea	2000	2012	20	2			1	1
ESA El Salvador	1932	2012	119	14				
ESP Spain	1900	2012	2,325	35	37	59	35	131
EST Estonia	1920	2012	234	22	9	9	15	33
ETH Ethiopia	1956	2012	206	4	21	7	17	45
EUN Unified Team	1992	1992	475	27	45	38	29	112
FIJ Fiji	1956	2012	79	9				
FIN Finland	1906	2012	1,594	27	106	86	119	311
FRA France	1896	2012	5,093	42	222	234	270	726
FRG West Germany	1968	1988	1,371	27	56	67	81	204
FSM Fed. States of Micronesia	2000	2012	14	4				
GAB Gabon	1972	2012	45	5		1		1
GAM Gambia	1984	2012	29	3				
GBR Great Britain	1896	2012	5,441	43	245	290	276	811
GBS Guinea Bissau	1996	2012	12	2				

GDR East Germany	1968	1988	1,129	21	153	129	127	409
GEO Georgia	1996	2012	124	18	6	5	14	25
GEQ Equatorial Guinea	1984	2012	26	3				
GER Germany	1896	2012	3,707	38	213	248	267	728
GHA Ghana	1952	2012	231	6		1	3	4
GRE Greece	1896	2012	1,593	36	39	56	52	147
GRN Grenada	1984	2012	40	4	1			1
GUA Guatemala	1932	2012	222	19		1		1
GUI Guinea	1968	2012	55	7				
GUM Guam	1988	2012	62	10				
GUY Guyana	1948	2012	70	6			1	1
HAI Haiti	1900	2012	67	11		1	1	2
HKG Hong Kong	1952	2012	292	19	1	1	1	3
HON Honduras	1968	2012	113	12				
HUN Hungary	1896	2012	2,494	32	170	151	169	490
INA Indonesia	1952	2012	257	20	6	10	11	27
IND India	1900	2012	791	22	9	6	11	26
IOA Individual Olympic Athletes	1992	2012	66	16		1	2	3
IRI Iran	1900	2012	463	21	15	20	25	60
IRL Ireland	1924	2012	716	24	9	9	13	31
IRQ Iraq	1948	2012	174	14			1	1
ISL Iceland	1908	2012	220	12		2	2	4
ISR Israel	1952	2012	306	21	1	1	5	7
ISV United States Virgin Islands	1968	2012	121	10		1		1
ITA Italy	1896	2012	3,816	35	211	177	189	577
IVB British Virgin Islands	1984	2012	23	2				

Country	From	To	Participants	Sports	Gold	Silver	Bronze	Total
JAM Jamaica	1948	2012	320	13	17	30	20	67
JOR Jordan	1980	2012	55	10				
JPN Japan	1912	2012	3,036	35	130	126	144	400
KAZ Kazakhstan	1996	2012	433	24	16	17	19	52
KEN Kenya	1956	2012	452	14	25	32	29	86
KGZ Kyrgyzstan	1996	2012	110	13		1	2	3
KIR Kiribati	2004	2012	7	2				
KOR South Korea	1948	2012	2,003	31	81	82	80	243
KSA Saudi Arabia	1972	2012	142	12		1	2	3
KUW Kuwait	1968	2012	192	13			2	2
LAO Laos	1980	2012	43	5				
LAT Latvia	1924	2012	239	20	3	11	5	19
LBA Libya	1968	2012	61	8				
LBR Liberia	1956	2012	40	2				
LCA Saint Lucia	1996	2012	17	3				
LES Lesotho	1972	2012	45	4				
LIB Lebanon	1948	2012	140	13		2	2	4
LIE Liechtenstein	1936	2012	51	8				
LTU Lithuania	1924	2012	258	18	6	5	10	21
LUX Luxembourg	1900	2012	363	19	4	2		6
MAD Madagascar	1964	2012	72	8				
MAL Malaya	1956	1960	40	5				
MAR Morocco	1960	2012	402	20	6	5	11	22
MAS Malaysia	1964	2012	282	19		3	3	6
MAW Malawi	1972	2012	54	4				

MDA	Moldova	1996	2012	101	10		2	5	7
MDV	Maldives	1988	2012	29	3				
MEX	Mexico	1900	2012	1,426	31	13	21	27	61
MGL	Mongolia	1964	2012	226	10	2	9	13	24
MHL	Marshall Islands	2008	2012	8	3				
MKD	Macedonia	1996	2012	32	5			1	1
MLI	Mali	1964	2012	70	7				
MLT	Malta	1928	2012	77	9				
MNE	Montenegro	2008	2012	41	8		1		1
MON	Monaco	1920	2012	67	14			1	1
MOZ	Mozambique	1980	2012	47	4	1		1	2
MRI	Mauritius	1984	2012	80	13			1	1
MTN	Mauritania	1984	2012	21	2				
MYA	Myanmar	1948	2012	79	11				
NAM	Namibia	1992	2012	34	7		4		4
NBO	North Borneo	1956	1956	2	1				
NCA	Nicaragua	1968	2012	91	10				
NED	Netherlands	1900	2012	2,582	33	80	88	109	277
NEP	Nepal	1964	2012	70	7				
NFL	Newfoundland	1904	1904	1	1				
NGR	Nigeria	1952	2012	513	14	3	8	12	23
NIG	Niger	1964	2012	36	5			1	1
NOR	Norway	1900	2012	1,371	26	59	51	44	154
NRU	Nauru	1996	2012	8	2				
NZL	New Zealand	1900	2012	1,112	30	42	18	39	99
OMA	Oman	1984	2012	39	6				

Country	From	To	Participants	Sports	Gold	Silver	Bronze	Total
PAK Pakistan	1948	2012	354	11	3	3	4	10
PAN Panama	1928	2012	79	11	1		2	3
PAR Paraguay	1968	2012	97	11		1		1
PER Peru	1900	2012	327	23	1	3		4
PHI Philippines	1924	2012	375	19		2	7	9
PLE Palestine	1996	2012	15	3				
PLW Palau	2000	2012	18	5				
PNG Papua New Guinea	1976	2012	56	8				
POL Poland	1912	2012	2,324	30	67	84	128	279
POR Portugal	1912	2012	661	28	4	8	11	23
PRK North Korea	1972	2012	325	16	14	12	21	47
PUR Puerto Rico	1948	2012	516	22		2	6	8
QAT Qatar	1984	2012	108	10			4	4
ROU Romania	1900	2012	1,455	28	88	94	119	301
RSA South Africa	1904	2012	852	31	23	27	28	78
RUS Russia	1900	2012	1,637	33	134	126	145	405
RWA Rwanda	1984	2012	32	4				
SAA Saar	1952	1952	36	9				
SAM Samoa	1984	2012	45	9				
SCG Serbia and Montenegro	1996	2004	193	19	2	4	3	9
SEN Senegal	1964	2012	215	13		1		1
SEY Seychelles	1980	2012	58	8				
SIN Singapore	1948	2012	156	15		2	2	4
SKN Saint Kitts and Nevis	1996	2012	17	1				
SLE Sierra Leone	1968	2012	58	5				

Code	Country							
SLO	Slovenia	1992	2012	226	16				19
SMR	San Marino	1960	2012	74	11				
SOL	Solomon Islands	1984	2012	18	5				
SOM	Somalia	1972	2012	20	1				
SRB	Serbia	1912	2012	159	16	1	2	4	7
SRI	Sri Lanka	1948	2012	87	10		2		2
STP	Sao Tome and Principe	1996	2012	11	2				
SUD	Sudan	1960	2012	76	8		1		1
SUI	Switzerland	1896	2012	1,805	36	55	80	67	202
SUR	Suriname	1968	2012	28	5	1		1	2
SVK	Slovakia	1996	2012	232	21	7	9	8	24
SWE	Sweden	1896	2012	2,801	34	144	169	185	498
SWZ	Swaziland	1972	2012	41	6				
SYR	Syria	1948	2012	129	12	1	1	1	3
TAN	Tanzania	1964	2012	105	4		2		2
TCH	Czechoslovakia	1920	1992	1,619	30	49	50	47	146
TGA	Tonga	1984	2012	31	6		1		1
THA	Thailand	1952	2012	422	20	7	6	11	24
TJK	Tajikistan	1996	2012	38	10		1		
TKM	Turkmenistan	1996	2012	33	8			2	3
TLS	Timor Leste	2004	2012	5	1				
TOG	Togo	1972	2012	36	8			1	1
TPE	Chinese Taipei	1956	2012	486	23	2	7	12	21
TTO	Trinidad and Tobago	1948	2012	153	10	2	5	11	18
TUN	Tunisia	1960	2012	382	21	3	3	4	10
TUR	Turkey	1906	2012	678	22	39	25	24	88

Country	From	To	Participants	Sports	Gold	Silver	Bronze	Total
TUV Tuvalu	2008	2012	5	2				1
UAE United Arab Emirates	1984	2012	67	10	1			1
UAR United Arab Republic	1960	1960	74	12		1	1	2
UGA Uganda	1956	2012	162	9	2	3	2	7
UKR Ukraine	1996	2012	817	29	33	27	55	115
Unknown	1912	1912	2	1				
URS Soviet Union	1952	1988	2,475	27	395	319	296	1010
URU Uruguay	1924	2012	352	19	2	2	6	10
USA United States	1896	2012	7,602	44	990	765	670	2425
UZB Uzbekistan	1996	2012	228	17	5	5	10	20
VAN Vanuatu	1988	2012	22	5				
VEN Venezuela	1932	2012	491	27	2	2	8	12
VIE Vietnam	1980	2012	90	15		2		2
VIN Saint Vincent	1988	2012	25	2				
VNM South Vietnam	1952	1972	39	7				
WIF West Indies Federation	1960	1960	13	5			2	2
YAR North Yemen	1984	1988	10	3				
YEM Yemen	1992	2012	25	6				
YMD South Yemen	1988	1988	5	2				
YUG Yugoslavia	1920	1988	1,035	25	26	29	28	83
ZAM Zambia	1964	2012	140	8		1	1	2
ZIM Zimbabwe	1928	2012	179	14	3	4	1	8
Totals	1896	2012	110,799	3,146	4,921	4,896	5,243	15,060

Appendix XXV:
Olympic Winter Games Participants

Country	From	To	Participants	Sports	Gold	Silver	Bronze	Total
AHO Neth. Antilles*	1988	1992	3	2				
ALB Albania	2006	2014	2	1				
ALG Algeria	1992	2010	7	2				
AND Andorra	1976	2014	28	4				
ARG Argentina	1928	2014	136	8				
ARM Armenia	1994	2014	28	5				
ASA American Samoa*	1994	1994	2	1				
AUS Australia	1924	2014	240	14	5	3	4	12
AUT Austria	1924	2014	859	14	59	78	81	218
AZE Azerbaijan	1998	2014	13	2				
BEL Belgium	1924	2014	124	8	1	1	3	5
BER Bermuda*	1992	2014	3	3				
BIH Bosnia& Herzegovina	1994	2014	28	5				
BLR Belarus	1994	2014	160	10	6	4	5	15
BOL Bolivia	1956	1992	13	1				
BRA Brazil	1992	2014	32	8				
BUL Bulgaria	1936	2014	180	11	1	2	3	6
CAN Canada	1924	2014	1,279	15	62	56	52	170
CAY Cayman Islands*	2010	2014	1	1				
CHI Chile	1948	2014	50	4				
CHN China	1980	2014	311	11	12	22	19	53
CMR Cameroon	2002	2002	1	1				
COL Colombia	2010	2010	1	1				
CRC Costa Rica*	1980	2006	7	3				
CRO Croatia	1992	2014	51	7	4	6	1	11

CYP Cyprus	1980	2014	14	1	7	9	8	24
CZE Czech Republic	1994	2014	267	14			1	1
DEN Denmark	1948	2014	58	8				
DMA Dominica*	2014	2014	1	1				
EGY Egypt	1984	1984	1	1				
ESP Spain	1936	2014	132	10	1		1	2
EST Estonia	1928	2014	94	8	4	2	1	7
ETH Ethiopia	2006	2010	1	1				
EUN Unified Team	1992	1992	129	12	9	6	8	23
FIJ Fiji*	1988	2002	2	2				
FIN Finland	1924	2014	723	12	42	62	57	161
FRA France	1924	2014	823	16	31	31	47	109
FRG West Germany	1968	1988	336	10	11	15	13	39
GBR Great Britain	1924	2014	642	16	10	4	12	26
GDR East Germany	1968	1988	232	10	39	36	35	110
GEO Georgia	1994	2014	15	4				
GER Germany	1928	2014	891	15	86	84	58	228
GHA Ghana*	2010	2010	1	1				
GRE Greece	1936	2014	66	8				
GUA Guatemala	1988	1988	6	2				
GUM Guam*	1988	1988	1	1				
HKG Hong Kong	2002	2014	4	1				
HON Honduras*	1992	1992	1	1				
HUN Hungary	1924	2014	206	10		2	4	6
IND India	1924	2014	21	4				
IOA Individ. Oly. Athletes	2014	2014	1	1				

Country	From	To	Participants	Sports	Gold	Silver	Bronze	Total
IRI Iran	1956	2014	24	2				
IRL Ireland	1992	2014	27	5				
ISL Iceland	1948	2014	75	3				
ISR Israel	1994	2014	13	3				
ISV U.S. Virgin Is.*	1988	2014	26	3				
ITA Italy	1924	2014	938	16	37	34	43	114
IVB British Virgin Is.*	1984	2014	2	2				
JAM Jamaica*	1988	2014	11	2				
JPN Japan	1928	2014	800	15	10	17	18	45
KAZ Kazakhstan	1994	2014	192	11	1	3	3	7
KEN Kenya	1998	2006	1	1				
KGZ Kyrgyzstan	1994	2014	7	4				
KOR South Korea	1948	2014	259	13	26	17	10	53
LAT Latvia	1924	2014	194	12		4	3	7
LIB Lebanon	1948	2014	31	3				
LIE Liechtenstein	1936	2014	80	4	2	2	5	9
LTU Lithuania	1928	2014	26	6				
LUX Luxembourg	1928	2014	12	4		2		2
MAD Madagascar	2006	2006	1	1				
MAR Morocco	1968	2014	24	2				
MDA Moldova	1994	2014	15	4				
MEX Mexico	1928	2014	32	5				
MGL Mongolia	1964	2014	39	4				
MKD Macedonia	1998	2014	10	2				
MLT Malta	2014	2014	1	1				

MNE Montenegro	2010	2014	3	1				
MON Monaco	1984	2014	16	2				
NED Netherlands	1928	2014	214	8	37	38	35	110
NEP Nepal	1924	2014	3	2				
NOR Norway	1924	2014	820	15	118	111	100	329
NZL New Zealand	1952	2014	90	11		1		1
PAK Pakistan	2010	2014	2	1				
PAR Paraguay	2014	2014	1	1				
PER Peru	2010	2014	3	2				
PHI Philippines*	1972	2014	5	3				
POL Poland	1924	2014	511	15	6	7	7	20
POR Portugal	1952	2014	12	5				
PRK North Korea	1964	2010	62	5		1	1	2
PUR Puerto Rico*	1984	1998	17	5				
ROU Romania	1928	2014	281	13			1	1
RSA South Africa	1960	2010	11	5				
RUS Russia	1994	2014	616	15	49	40	35	124
SCG Serbia & Montenegro	1998	2006	12	5				
SEN Senegal*	1984	2010	3	1				
SLO Slovenia	1992	2014	158	11	2	4	9	15
SMR San Marino	1976	2014	15	3				
SRB Serbia	2010	2014	15	5				
SUI Switzerland	1924	2014	1,007	15	50	40	48	138
SVK Slovakia	1994	2014	201	12	2	2	1	5
SWE Sweden	1924	2014	902	14	50	40	54	144
SWZ Swaziland	1992	1992	1	1				

Country	From	To	Participants	Sports	Gold	Silver	Bronze	Total
TCH Czechoslovakia	1924	1992	480	11	2	8	15	25
TGA Tonga	2014	2014	1	1				
THA Thailand	2002	2014	3	2				
TJK Tajikistan	2002	2014	2	1				
TLS Timor Leste*	2014	2014	1	1				
TOG Togo*	2014	2014	2	2				
TPE Chinese Taipei	1972	2014	44	8				
TTO Trinidad & Tobago*	1994	2002	4	1				
TUR Turkey	1936	2014	61	3				
UKR Ukraine	1994	2014	198	13	2	1	4	7
URS Soviet Union	1956	1988	473	10	78	57	59	194
URU Uruguay	1998	1998	1	1				
USA United States	1924	2014	1,697	16	96	102	84	282
UZB Uzbekistan	1994	2014	21	3	1			1
VEN Venezuela	1998	2014	5	2				
YUG Yugoslavia	1924	1992	235	10		3	1	4
ZIM Zimbabwe	2014	2014	1	1				
Totals	1924	2014	19,277	702	959	958	948	2,865

*Countries without snow.

Appendix XXVI:
Olympic Sports

Summer Sports	Games	Years	Ctys	Entrants	Men	Women	Most Medals – City	Most Individual Medals
Aeronautics	1	1936	1	1	1	0	1—SUI	1—Hermann Schreiber, SUI
Alpinism	3	1924, 32, 36	6	25	24	1	1—6 nations	1—25 athletes
Archery	15	1900, 04, 08, 20, 72–2012	92	1,028	571	457	34—KOR	10—Hubert Van Innis, BEL
Art Competitions	7	1912–48	51	1,792	1,599	193	24—GER	3—Josef Petersen, DEN 3—Alex Walter Diggelmann, SUI
Athletics	28	1896–2012	223	20,623	14,789	5,831	788—USA	12—Paavo Nurmi, FIN
Badminton	6	1992–2012	66	721	360	361	38—CHN	4— Gao Ling, CHN
Baseball	6	1988–2008	16	762	761	0	5—CUB	4—Pedro Luis Lazo, CUB
Basketball	18	1936–2012	65	3,232	2,390	842	26—USA	5—Teresa Edwards, USA
Beach Volleyball	5	1996–2012	36	321	163	158	11—BRA	3—Misty May-Treanor, USA 3—Kerri Walsh, USA 3—Emanuel, BRA 3—Ricardo, BRA
Boxing	24	1904, 08, 20–2012	172	5,051	5,015	36	110—USA	3—9 athletes
Canoeing	18	1936–2012	94	3,010	2,365	643	77—HUN	12—Birgit Fischer-Schmidt, GDR/GER
Cricket	1	1900	2	24	24	0	1—GBR, MIX	1—24 athletes
Croquet	1	1900	1	10	7	3	7—FRA	2—Gaston Aumoitte, FRA 2—Georges Johin, FRA 2—Chrétien Waydelich, FRA
Cycling	28	1896–2012	140	5,518	4,916	601	97—FRA	7—Chris Hoy, GBR 7—Bradley Wiggins, GBR
Diving	26	1904–2012	80	1,393	796	597	132—USA	8—Dmitry Sautin, EUN/RUS
Equestrianism	24	1900, 1912–2012	71	2,234	1,815	419	60—GER	9—Anky van Grunsven, NED
Fencing	28	1896–2012	99	3,997	3,180	817	123—ITA	13—Edoardo Mangiarotti, ITA

Sport								Most Medals
Football	26	1900–28, 36–2012	90	5,762	5,160	602	7—USA, BRA	4—Christie Pearce-Rampone, USA
Golf	2	1900–04	5	98	88	10	10—USA	2—Chandler Egan, USA
								2—Burt McKinnie, USA
								2—Frank Newton, USA
Gymnastics	28	1896–2012	88	4,005	2,577	1,428	182—URS	18—Larysa Latynina, URS
Handball	12	1936, 72–2012	46	2,479	1,550	929	7—KOR	4—Oh Seong-Ok, KOR
								4—Andrey Lavrov, URS/EUN/RUS
Hockey	22	1908, 20, 28–2012	41	3,594	2,714	880	16—NED	4—Leslie Claudius, IND
								4—Udham Singh, IND
								4—Teun de Nooijer, NED
								4—Lucha Aymar, ARG
Jeu De Paume	1	1908	2	11	11	0	2—GBR	1—Jay Gould, USA
								1—Eustace Miles, GBR
								1—Neville Lytton, GBR
Judo	12	1964, 72–2012	167	2,462	1,796	665	72—JPN	5—Ryoko Tamura-Tani, JPN
Lacrosse	2	1904–08	3	61	60	0	2—CAN	1—60 athletes
Mod. Pentathlon	23	1912–2012	56	822	726	96	22—HUN	7—Pavel Lednyov, URS
Motorboating	1	1908	2	14	13	1	2—GBR	2—John Field-Richards, GBR
								2—Bernard Redwood, GBR
								2—Thomas Thornycroft, GBR
Pelota	1	1900	1	2	2	0	1—ESP	1—Francisco Villota, ESP
								1—José de Amézola, ESP
Polo	5	1900, 08, 20, 24, 36	9	87	87	0	6—GBR	2—Jack, Lord Wodehouse, GBR
								2—Frederick Barrett, GBR
								2—Walter Buckmaster, GBR
								2—Frederick Freake, GBR

Summer Sports	Games	Years	Ctys	Entrants	Men	Women	Most Medals—City	Most Individual Medals
Racquets	1	1908	1	7	7	0	7—GBR	2—John Jacob Astor, GBR; 2—Evan Noel, GBR; 2—Henry Leaf, GBR
Rhythmic Gym.	8	1984–2012	48	494	0	494	8—RUS	2—11 athletes
Roque	1	1904	1	4	4	0	3—USA	1—Charles Jacobus, USA; 1—Smith Streeter, USA; 1—Charles Brown, USA
Rowing	27	1900–2012	92	7,356	6,020	1,335	87—USA	8—Elisabeta Oleniuc-Lipă, ROU
Rugby	4	1900, 08, 20–24	7	155	155	0	2—USA, GBR, FRA	2—7 athletes
Sailing	25	1900, 08–2012	118	4,263	3,739	523	59—USA	5—Ben Ainslie, GBR; 5—Robert Scheidt, BRA; 5—Torben Grael, BRA
Shooting	26	1896–00, 06–24, 28–12	148	4,674	4,019	654	107—USA	11—Carl Osburn, USA
Softball	4	1996–2008	13	367	0	367	4—USA, AUS	4—Laura Berg, USA; 4—Tanya Harding, AUS; 4—Melanie Roche, AUS; 4—Natalie Ward, AUS
Swimming	28	1896–2012	193	8,183	4,814	3,367	520—USA	22—Michael Phelps, USA
Synch. Swimming	8	1984–2012	46	489	0	489	12—JPN	5—Anastasiya Davydova, RUS; 5—Miya Tachibana, JPN; 5—Miho Takeda, JPN
Table Tennis	7	1988–2012	98	666	328	337	47—CHN	5—Wang Nan, CHN; 5—Wang Hao, CHN

Sport		Years						Individual records
Taekwondo	4	2000–2012	98	379	193	186	14—KOR	3—Hadi Saei, IRI 3—Steven Lopez, USA 3—Hwang Gyeong-Seon, KOR
Tennis	15	1896–24, 88–2012	88	1,137	698	439	42—GBR	6—Max Décugis, FRA
Trampolining	4	2000–2012	22	73	38	35	8—CHN	3—Karen Cockburn, CAN
Triathlon	4	2000–2012	48	297	145	152	5—AUS	2—Simon Whitfield, CAN 2—Bevan Docherty, NZL
Tug-Of-War	6	1900–20	13	160	160	0	5—GBR	3—Frederick Humphreys, GBR 3—Edwin Mills, GBR 3—James Shepherd, GBR
Volleyball	13	1964–2012	45	2,287	1,261	1,026	12—URS	4—Inna Ryskal, URS 4—Sergey Tetyukhin, RUS 4—Samuele Papi, ITA
Water Polo	26	1900–04, 08–2012	52	2,449	2,169	280	15—HUN	5—Dezső Gyarmati, HUN
Weightlifting	25	1896, 04–06, 20–2012	148	2,708	2,428	280	62—URS	4—Pyrros Dimas, GRE 4—Ronny Weller, GDR/GER 4—Nikolay Peshalov, BUL/CRO 4—Norb Schemansky, USA
Wrestling	27	1896, 04–2012	129	4,770	4,624	146	125—USA	5—Wilfried Dietrich, GER/FRG
Winter Sports								
Alpine Skiing	19	1936–2014	101	2,735	1,739	996	114—AUT	8—Kjetil André Aamodt, NOR
Biathlon	15	1960–2014	54	1,137	765	372	45—GER	13—Ole Einar Bjørndalen, NOR
Bobsleigh	21	1924–56, 64–2014	54	1,694	1,584	109	31—SUI	7—Bogdan Musiol, GDR/GER
Cross Cty Skiing	22	1924–2014	81	2,402	1,685	717	107—NOR	12—Bjørn Dæhlie, NOR

Winter Sports	Games	Years	Ctys	Entrants	Men	Women	Most Medals—City	Most Individual Medals
Curling	6	1924, 1998–2014	16	349	188	160	10—CAN	2—8 athletes
Figure Skating*	24	1908, 20–2014	55	1,572	747	824	49—USA	4—Gillis Grafström, SWE 4—Yevgeny Plyushchenko, RUS
Freestyle Skiing	7	1992–2014	41	627	359	268	21—USA	3—Kari Traa, NOR
Ice Hockey*	23	1920–2014	34	3,885	3,386	498	20—CAN	5—Jayna Hefford, CAN 5—Hayley Wickenheiser, CAN
Luge	14	1964–2014	49	772	543	228	36—GER	6—Armin Zöggeler, ITA
Military Ski Patrol	1	1924	6	24	24	0	1—SUI, FIN, FRA	1—12 athletes
Nordic Combined	22	1924–2014	31	605	605	0	30—NOR	7—Felix Gottwald, AUT
Short-Track Skating	7	1992–2014	35	444	235	209	42—KOR	8—Apolo Anton Ohno, USA 8—Viktor An, KOR/RUS
Skeleton	6	1928, 48, 2002–14	28	147	101	46	8—USA	2—Aleksandr Tretyakov, RUS 2—Jack Heaton, USA 2—Martins Dukurs, LAT 2—Gregor Stähli, SUI
Ski Jumping	22	1924–2014	37	876	846	30	30—NOR	5—Matti Nykänen, FIN
Snowboarding	5	1998–2014	35	567	328	239	24—USA	3—Kelly Clark, USA
Speed Skating	22	1924–2014	41	1,582	1,054	528	105—NED	9—Claudia Pechstein, GER

*Also held Summer Games.

Appendix XXVII:
Bid Cities

Games of the Olympiad (Summer Games)

Notes	Olympiad	Year	Host City	Host Country	Unsuccessful Bid City	Country
a	I	1896	Athens	GRE	none	
b	II	1900	Paris	FRA	none	
c	III	1904	Chicago	USA	none	
			St. Louis	USA		
d		1906	Rome	ITA		
			Athens	GRE	none	
	IV	1908	London	ENG	Berlin	GER
					Milan	ITA
	V	1912	Stockholm	SWE	none	
e	VI	1916	Berlin	GER	Alexandria	EGY
					Amsterdam	NED
					Brussels	BEL
					Budapest	HUN
					Cleveland	USA
	VII	1920	Antwerp	BEL	Amsterdam	NED
					Atlanta	USA
					Budapest	HUN
					Cleveland	USA
					Havana	CUB
					Lyon*	FRA
					Philadelphia	USA
	VIII	1924	Paris	FRA	Amsterdam	NED
					Barcelona	ESP
					Los Angeles	USA
					Prague	TCH
					Rome	ITA
	IX	1928	Amsterdam	NED	Los Angeles	USA
	X	1932	Los Angeles	USA	none	

Notes	Olympiad	Year	Host City	Host Country	Unsuccessful Bid City	Country
	XI	1936	Berlin	GER	Alexandria	EGY
					Barcelona	ESP
					Budapest	HUN
					Buenos Aires	ARG
					Cologne	GER
					Dublin	IRL
					Frankfurt	GER
					Helsinki	FIN
					Lausanne	SUI
					Nuremberg	GER
					Rio de Janeiro	BRA
					Rome	ITA
f	XII	1940	Tokyo	JPN	none	
			Helsinki	FIN		
f	XIII	1944	London	ENG	Athens	GRE
					Budapest	HUN
					Detroit	USA
					Helsinki	FIN
					Lausanne	SUI
					Montreal	CAN
					Rome	ITA
	XIV	1948	London	ENG	Baltimore	USA
					Lausanne	SUI
					Los Angeles	USA
					Minneapolis	USA
					Philadelphia	USA
	XV	1952	Helsinki	FIN	Amsterdam	NED
					Chicago	USA
					Detroit	USA
					Los Angeles	USA
					Minneapolis	USA
					Philadelphia	USA
	XVI	1956	Melbourne	AUS	Buenos Aires	ARG
g		1956	Stockholm (equestrian only)	SWE	Chicago	USA
					Detroit	USA
					Los Angeles	USA
					Mexico City	MEX
					Minneapolis	USA

Notes	Olympiad	Year	Host City	Host Country	Unsuccessful Bid City	Country
					Philadelphia	USA
					San Francisco	USA
	XVII	1960	Rome	ITA	Brussels	BEL
					Budapest	HUN
					Detroit	USA
					Lausanne	SUI
					Mexico City	MEX
					Tokyo	JPN
	XVIII	1964	Tokyo	JPN	Brussels	BEL
					Detroit	USA
					Vienna	AUT
	XIX	1968	Mexico City	MEX	Buenos Aires	ARG
					Detroit	USA
					Lyon	FRA
	XX	1972	Munich	FRG	Detroit	USA
					Madrid	ESP
					Montreal	CAN
	XXI	1976	Montreal	CAN	Los Angeles	USA
					Moscow	URS
	XXII	1980	Moscow	URS	Los Angeles	USA
	XXIII	1984	Los Angeles	USA	none	
	XXIV	1988	Seoul	KOR	Nagoya	JPN
	XXV	1992	Barcelona	ESP	Amsterdam	NED
					Belgrade	YUG
					Birmingham	ENG
					Brisbane	AUS
					Paris	FRA
	XXVI	1996	Atlanta	USA	Athens	GRE
					Belgrade	YUG
					Manchester	ENG
					Melbourne	AUS
					Toronto	CAN
	XXVII	2000	Sydney	AUS	Beijing	CHN
					Berlin	GER
					Istanbul	TUR
					Manchester	ENG
					Milan*	ITA
					Brasilia*	BRA
					Tashkent*	UZB

Notes	Olympiad	Year	Host City	Host Country	Unsuccessful Bid City	Country
	XXVIII	2004	Athens	GRE	Buenos Aires	ARG
					Capetown	RSA
					Rome	ITA
					Stockholm	SWE
					Istanbul**	TUR
					Lille**	FRA
					Rio de Janeiro**	BRA
					Saint Petersburg**	RUS
					San Juan**	PUR
					Seville**	ESP
	XXIX	2008	Beijing	CHN	Istanbul	TUR
					Osaka	JPN
					Paris	FRA
					Toronto	CAN
					Bangkok**	THA
					Cairo**	EGY
					Havana**	CUB
					Kuala Lumpur**	MAS
					Seville**	ESP
	XXX	2012	London	ENG	Madrid	ESP
					Moscow	RUS
					New York	USA
					Paris	FRA
					Havana**	CUB
					Istanbul**	TUR
					Leipzig**	GER
					Rio de Janeiro**	BRA
	XXXI	2016	Rio de Janeiro	BRA	Chicago	USA
					Madrid	ESP
					Tokyo	JPN
					Baku**	AZE
					Doha**	QAT
					Prague**	CZE
	XXXII	2020	Tokyo	JPN	Istanbul	TUR
					Madrid	ESP
					Rome*	ITA
					Baku**	AZE
					Doha**	QAT

Olympic Winter Games

Notes	Games	Year	Host City	Host Country	Unsuccessful Bid City	Country
	I	1924	Chamonix	FRA	none	
	II	1928	St. Moritz	SUI	Davos	SUI
					Engelberg	SUI
	III	1932	Lake Placid	USA	Bear Mountain	USA
					Denver	USA
					Duluth	USA
					Minneapolis	USA
					Montreal	CAN
					Oslo	NOR
					Yosemite Valley	USA
	IV	1936	Garmisch-Partenkirchen	GER	Montreal	CAN
					St. Moritz	SUI
f		1940	Sapporo	JPN	none	
			St. Moritz	SUI		
			Garmisch-Partenkirchen	GER		
f		1944	Cortina d'Ampezzo	ITA	Montreal	CAN
					Oslo	NOR
	V	1948	St. Moritz	SUI	Lake Placid	USA
	VI	1952	Oslo	NOR	Cortina d'Ampezzo	ITA
					Lake Placid	USA
	VII	1956	Cortina d'Ampezzo	ITA	Colorado Springs	USA
					Lake Placid	USA
					Montreal	CAN
	VIII	1960	Squaw Valley	USA	Garmisch-Partenkirchen	GER
					Innsbruck	AUT
					St. Moritz	SUI
	IX	1964	Innsbruck	AUT	Calgary	CAN
					Lahti	FIN
	X	1968	Grenoble	FRA	Calgary	CAN
					Lahti	FIN
					Lake Placid	USA
					Oslo	NOR
					Sapporo	JPN

Notes	Games	Year	Host City	Host Country	Unsuccessful Bid City	Country
	XI	1972	Sapporo	JPN	Banff	CAN
					Lahti	FIN
					Salt Lake City	USA
h	XII	1976	Denver	USA	Sion	SUI
			Innsbruck	AUT	Tampere	FIN
					Vancouver-Garibaldi	CAN
	XIII	1980	Lake Placid	USA	Vancouver-Garibaldi*	CAN
	XIV	1984	Sarajevo	YUG	Gothenburg	SWE
					Sapporo	JPN
	XV	1988	Calgary	CAN	Cortina d'Ampezzo	ITA
					Falun	SWE
	XVI	1992	Albertville	FRA	Anchorage	USA
					Berchtesgaden	GER
					Cortina d'Ampezzo	ITA
					Falun	SWE
					Lillehammer	NOR
					Sofia	BUL
	XVII	1994	Lillehammer	NOR	Anchorage	USA
					Östersund	SWE
					Sofia	BUL
	XVIII	1998	Nagano	JPN	Aosta	ITA
					Jaca	ESP
					Östersund	SWE
					Salt Lake City	USA
	XIX	2002	Salt Lake City	USA	Östersund	SWE
					Quebec	CAN
					Sion	SUI
					Graz	AUT
					Jaca	ESP
					Poprad-Tatry	SVK
					Sochi	RUS
					Tarvisio	ITA
	XX	2006	Turin	ITA	Sion	SUI
					Helsinki	FIN
					Klagenfurt	AUT
					Poprad-Tatry	SVK
					Zakopane	POL

Notes	Games	Year	Host City	Host Country	Unsuccessful Bid City	Country
	XXI	2010	Vancouver	CAN	Bern*	SUI
					Pyeongchang	KOR
					Salzburg	AUT
					Andorra la Vella	AND
					Harbin	CHN
					Jaca	ESP
					Sarajevo	BIH
	XXII	2014	Sochi	RUS	Pyeongchang	KOR
					Salzburg	AUT
					Almaty	KAZ
					Borjomi	GEO
					Jaca	ESP
					Sofia	BUL
	XXIII	2018	Pyeongchang	KOR	Annecy	FRA
					Munich	GER
	XXIV	2022	to be assigned 31 July 2015		Almaty	KAZ
					Beijing	CHN
					Oslo*	NOR
					Lviv*	UKR
					Krakow*	POL
					Stockholm*	SWE

Notes
*Withdrew prior to final vote.
**Eliminated prior to final vote.
a Athens was selected at the 1st Session of the IOC in 1894.
b Paris was selected for 1900 at the 1st Session of the IOC in 1894.
c Chicago was initially selected for 1904 but allowed St. Louis to hold the Games in conjunction with the St. Louis World's Fair.
d Rome was the initial choice but the eruption of the Mount Vesuvius volcano caused them to relinquish their role as host city.
e Games canceled due to World War I.
f Games canceled due to World War II.
g Australia's strict quarantine laws caused the IOC to select Stockholm for the equestrian events.
h After being awarded the Winter Games, Denver withdrew.

Bibliography

INTRODUCTION

The literature of the Olympic Games is vast and is published in many languages. Every four years (and now every two years), a plethora of books about the Games appears. Many are promotional materials with superficial information put forth by various Olympic sponsors. But there are also quite a few quality works—some by historians and some by talented writers. In this section, we have attempted to list the most useful references for a researcher.

While the Official Reports are of interest, they should not be considered 100 percent accurate—especially the earlier ones. Olympic historians have found many errors and the most accurate information can usually be found on several current websites (e.g., www.sports-reference.com/olympics). Most Official Reports are quite expensive in their bound form, but fortunately copies may be found online at www.la84foundation.org.

In works on the Ancient Olympic Games, the book by Roland Renson, Manfred Lammer, James Riordan, and Dimitrios Chassiotis, eds. *The Olympic Games Through the Ages: Greek Antiquity and Its Impact on Modern Sport* was produced by several leading classics historians and provides a valuable summary of its era. David Young's work *The Olympic Myth of Greek Amateur Athletics* is another written by a classical scholar.

As for attempts at revival, the work by Kostas Georgiadis, *Olympic Revival: The Revival of the Olympic Games in Modern Times*, provides a good analysis of the start of the modern Olympic Games. Francis Burns's opus *Heigh for Cotswold! A History of Robert Dover's Olimpick Games* is an interesting history of an alternative games that continues to this day. Readers fluent in German will find that Karl Lennartz's book *Kenntnisse und Vorstellungen von Olympia und den Olympischen Spielen in der Zeit von 393–1896* is an excellent history as are all of Dr. Lennartz's published writings.

The 24-volume set titled *The Olympic Century: The Official History of the Modern Olympic Movement* provides an excellent comprehensive view of the Modern Olympics. Bill Mallon's individual books on the first seven Modern Olympic Games from 1896 to 1920 provides the greatest in-depth coverage of those Games—far greater than any of the comparable "official reports." Karl Lennartz has produced a book in German on the 1916 Games, which were assigned to Berlin but canceled due to World War I—*Die VI. Olympischen Spiele Berlin 1916.* As would be expected, the 1936 Games has quite a few books written about it. One of the best is by Richard Mandell—*The Nazi Olympics.* Mandell also authored a book on another controversial German Olympic Games—*A Munich Diary: The Olympics of 1972.*

Among the books listed in the "General Sporting Histories of the Olympic Games" section, the two by David Wallechinsky and Jaime Loucky, *The Complete Book of the Olympics* and *The Complete Book of the Winter Olympics*, are essential reference books. Not only do they have results of all sports in all Games, but they provide interesting anecdotes about the Olympians. Other valuable books in that section of the bibliography include Volker Kluge's six-volume set *Winter Olympia Kompakt* and the five volumes on the Summer Games: *Olympische Sommerspiele: Die Chronik I. Athen 1896–Berlin 1936*; *Olympische Sommerspiele: Die Chronik II. London 1948–Tokyo 1964*; *Olympische Sommerspiele: Die Chronik III. Mexico 1968–Los Angeles 1984*; *Olympische Sommerspiele: Die Chronik IV. Seoul 1988–Atlanta 1996*; and *Olympische Sommerspiele: Die Chronik V. Sydney 2000–Athens 2004.*

Richard Espy's *The Politics of the Olympic Games* and Allen Guttmann's *The Olympics: A History of the Modern Games* are both insightful works on Olympic politics. Unfortunately, to fully appreciate many of the histories of national participation at the Olympic Games one needs to be a linguist as many of them are written in the native language of the country. Among the ones in English that are excellent are Harry Gordon's *Australia and the Olympic Games*; Bill Mallon and Ian Buchanan's *Quest for Gold: The Encyclopaedia of American Olympians*; and Ian Buchanan's *British Olympians: A Hundred Years of Gold Medallists.* Baron Pierre de Coubertin's writings must be read in the original French language to be fully appreciated.

Among the biographies of IOC presidents, Allen Guttmann's biography of Avery Brundage *The Games Must Go On: Avery Brundage and the Olympic Movement* and Lord Killanin's autobiography *My Olympic Years* stand out. In the miscellaneous section of this bibliography are two previous bibliographies—one by Karl Lennartz and one by Bill Mallon. Both, though, were written in the 1980s, and since that time quite a few books have appeared. But they remain excellent sources for books written prior to that time. As far as Internet resources go, the most comprehensive one is www.sports-reference.com/olympics.

Within each following section, the books are listed first by Olympic Games, then alphabetically by author, and then chronologically if several books are listed for one author. Also included are dissertations specifically concerned with the Olympic Games or certain aspects of them. In addition, a very few pertinent articles are listed, where no comprehensive book on a subject is available. All transliterated titles are from the native alphabet, using the *Encyclopaedia Britannica* as the source of the transliteration table.

I. OFFICIAL REPORTS

A. The Games of the Olympiad

Current official reports (at least since 1960) are issued in both English and French and usually in the language of the host nation. These are sometimes issued with parallel texts and sometimes as separate editions for each language. COJO is the acronym for Comité d'Organisateur des Jeux Olympiques, the French equivalent for Organizing Committee of the Olympic Games (OCOG).

1896—Athens

Coubertin, Baron de, Timoleon Philemon, Spiridon P. Lambros, and Nikolaos G. Politis, eds. *The Olympic Games 776 B.C.–1896 A.D.; With the Approval and Support of the Central Council of the International Olympic Games in Athens, under the Presidency of H. R. H. the Crown Prince Constantine.* Athens: Charles Beck, 1896. This was issued in various versions, including several in parallel texts, in Greek/ English, Greek/French, Greek/French/English, and German/English. Also, multiple reprints of this first official report have been produced, most notably a 1966 edition with English/French/Greek parallel texts published by the Hellenic Olympic Committee; as well as a German edition, *Die Olympischen Spiele 1896—Offizieller Bericht.* Cologne: Carl-Diem-Institut, 1971; and most recently, with annotations by various historians, *Die Olympischen Spiele 1896 in Athen: Erläuterungen zum Neudruck des Offiziellen Berichtes*, edited by Karl Lennartz. Kassel, Germany: AGON Sportverlag, 1996.

1900—Paris

Merillon, Daniel, ed. *Concours Internationaux d'Exercices Physiques et de Sport: Rapports Publiés sous la Direction de M. D. Merillon, Délégué Général.* 2 vols. Paris: Imprimerie Nationale, 1901 (vol. 1) and 1902 (vol. 2). Strictly speaking, this was a report of the physical culture section of l'Exposition Internationale in Paris in 1900.

1904—St. Louis

Lucas, Charles J. P. *The Olympic Games 1904.* St. Louis, Mo.: Woodward & Tiernan, 1905.
Sullivan, James E., ed. *Spalding's Official Athletic Almanac for 1905: Special Olympic Number, Containing the Official Report of the Olympic Games of 1904.* New York: American Sports Publishing, 1905.

1906—Athens

Savvidis, Panagiotis S., ed. *Leukoma ton en Athenais B'Diethnon Olympiakon Agonon 1906/Jeux Olympiques Internationaux 1906*. Athens: Estia, K. Maisner, N. Kargadouris, 1907.

1908—London

Cook, Theodore Andrea, ed. *The Fourth Olympiad—Being the Official Report of the Olympic Games of 1908 Celebrated in London Under the Patronage of His Most Gracious King Edward VII and by the Sanction of the International Olympic Committee*. London: British Olympic Council, 1909.

1912—Stockholm

Bergvall, Erik, ed. *The Official Report of the Olympic Games of Stockholm 1912 and V. Olympiaden. Officiel redogorelse for olympiska spelen i Stockholm 1912*. Stockholm: Wahlstrom & Widstrand, 1913. Separate editions were published in Swedish and English.

1916—Berlin (scheduled, not held)

COJO Berlin 1916. *Denkschrift zur Vorbereitung der VI. Olympiade 1916, veranstaltet im Deutschen Stadion zu Berlin*. Berlin: Author, n.d.

1920—Antwerp

Verdyck, Alfred, ed. *Rapport officiel des Jeux de la VIIème Olympiade, Anvers 1920*. Brussels: COJO Antwerp 1920, 1922.

1924—Paris

Avé, M. A., ed. *Les Jeux de la VIIIè Olympiade Paris 1924. Rapport officiel du Comité Olympique Français*. Paris: Librairie de France, 1925.

1928—Amsterdam

Rossem, George van, ed. *IXe Olympiade. Officiel gedenkboek van de spelen der IXe Olympiade Amsterdam 1928; The Ninth Olympiad—Being the Official Report of the Olympic Games of 1928 Celebrated at Amsterdam Issued by the Netherlands Olympic Committee*; and *Olympiade Amsterdam 1928. Rapport officiel des Jeux de la IXè Olympiade Amsterdam 1928*. Amsterdam: J. H. de Bussy, 1930. Separate editions were published in Dutch, English, and French.

1932—Los Angeles

Browne, Frederick Granger, ed. *The Games of the Xth Olympiad, Los Angeles, 1932: Official Report*. Los Angeles, Calif.: COJO Los Angeles 1932, 1933.

1936—Berlin

COJO Berlin 1936. *XI Olympiade, Berlin 1936: Amtlicher Bericht; Les XIè Jeux Olympiques, Berlin 1936. Rapport official;* and *The XIth Olympic Games, Berlin 1936—Official Report*. Berlin: W. Limpert, 1937. Separate editions were published in German, French, and English.

1940—Tokyo (scheduled, not held) then Helsinki (scheduled, not held)

COJO Tokyo 1940. *XIIth Olympic Games, Tokyo, 1940. Report of the Organizing Committee on Its Work for the XII. Olympic Games of 1940 in Tokyo Until the Relinquishment*. Tokyo: Isshiki, 1940.

COJO Helsinki 1940. *XII Olympiad Helsinki 1940;* and *Olympische Vorbereitungen für die Feier der 12. Olympiade Helsinki 1940*. Helsinki: Author, 1940. Separate editions were issued in English and German.

1944—London (scheduled, not held)

No report was ever issued.

1948—London

Lord Burghley, ed. *The Official Report of the Organizing Committee for the XIV Olympiad*. London: McCorquodale, 1951.

1952—Helsinki

Kolkka, Sulo, ed. *The Official Report of the Organizing Committee for the Games of the XV Olympiad Helsinki 1952; Le Rapport officiel du comité d'organisateur pour les Jeux Olympiques de la XVè Olympiade Helsinki 1952;* and *XV Olympiakisat Helsingissa 1952. Jarjestelytoimikunnan virallinen kertomus*. Porvoo, Finland: Werner Soderström Osakeyhtio, 1955. Separate editions were published in English and Finnish.

1956—Melbourne

Doyle, E. A., ed. *The Official Report of the Organizing Committee for the Games of the XVI Olympiad, Melbourne 1956*. Melbourne: W. M. Houston, Government Printer, 1958.

1956—Equestrian Games—Stockholm

COJO Stockholm 1956. *Ryttaroolympiaden: The Equestrian Games of the XVIth Olympiad, Stockholm 1956*. Stockholm: Esselte Aktiebolag, 1959. Parallel texts in Swedish and English.

1960—Rome

Giacomini, Romolo, ed. *The Games of the XVII Olympiad, Rome 1960*; *Giochi della XVII Olimpiada Roma 1960*; and *Les jeux de la XVIIè Olympiade, Rome 1960*. 2 vols. Rome: COJO Rome 1960, 1960. Three separate editions published in English, Italian, and French.

1964—Tokyo

COJO Tokyo 1964. *The Games of the XVIII Olympiad, Tokyo 1964: The Official Report of the Organizing Committee*. 2 vols. Tokyo: Author, 1964.

1968—Mexico City

Trueblood, Beatrice, ed. *Mexico 1968: Mémoire officiel des Jeux de la XIX Olympiade/Commemorative Volumes of the Games of the XIX Olympiad*. 4 vols. Mexico City: COJO Mexico City 1968, 1968. Two separate editions were issued, one with parallel texts in French and English and one with parallel texts in Spanish and German. A fifth volume was also issued, which contained entry tickets, programs, and other memorabilia. A supplement was also issued to the second volume.

1972—Munich

Diem, Liselott, and Ernst Knoesel, eds. *Die Spiele: The Official Report of the Organizing Committee for the Games of the XXth Olympiad, Munich 1972*. 3 vols. Munich: ProSport, 1974. Separate editions of volumes 1 and 2 were issued in English, German, and French. Volume 3 (the results) was issued with parallel texts in English, French, and German.

1976—Montreal

Rousseau, Roger, ed. *Games of the XXI Olympiad, Montreal 1976: Official Report*; and *Jeux de la XXIè Olympiade, Montréal 1976—Rapport officiel*. 3 vols. Montreal: COJO Montreal 1976, ca. 1978. Separate editions were issued in English and French.

1980—Moscow

Novikov, I. T., ed. *Games of the XXIInd Olympiad Moscow 1980: Official Report of the Organizing Committee of the Games of the XXIInd Olympiad*; and *Jeux de la*

XXIIè Olympiade Moscou 1980: Rapport officiel du Comité d'organisation des Jeux de la XXIIè Olympiade. 3 vols. Moscow: Fitzkultura i Sport, 1981. Separate editions were issued in English and French.

1984—Los Angeles

Perelman, Richard B., ed. *Official Report of the Games of the XXIIIrd Olympiad Los Angeles, 1984.* 2 vols. Los Angeles: COJO Los Angeles 1984, 1985. Separate editions were issued in French and English.

1988—Seoul

Roh Sang-Kook, Lee Kyong-Hee, and Lee Bong-Jie, eds. *Official Report: Games of the XXIVth Olympiad Seoul 1988.* 2 vols. Seoul: Korean Textbook, 1989. Separate editions were issued in French, English, and Korean.

1992—Barcelona

Cuyàs, Romà, ed. *Official Report: Games of the XXV Olympiad Barcelona 1992.* 4 vols. Barcelona: COJO Barcelona 1992. Separate editions were issued in English, French, Castilian Spanish, and Catalan Spanish. Note that this official report, unlike most of them, did not contain complete results. Volume 4 of the official report listed results, but only the top eight finishers in each event. The results were issued as a separate volume, titled *Games of the XXV Olympiad Barcelona 1992: The Results*, with the same editor and publisher. The results text was issued in parallel texts of English, French, Castilian Spanish, and Catalan Spanish.

1996—Atlanta

Watkins, Ginger T., ed. *The Official Report of the Centennial Olympic Games.* 3 vols. Atlanta, Ga.: Peachtree Publishers, 1997. Separate editions were issued in English, French, Spanish, and German.

2000—Sydney

COJO Sydney 2000. *Official Report of the XXVII Olympiad.* 3 vols. Sydney: Sydney Organizing Committee for the Olympic Games, 2001. Separate editions issued in English and French.

2004—Athens

Organizing Committee for the Olympic Games Athens 2004 (ATHOC). *Official Report of the XXVIII Olympiad, Athens, Greece.* 3 vols. and 3 optical discs. Athens: ATHOC, 2006. Parallel texts in French and English.

2008—Beijing

Beijing Organising Committee for the Games of the XXIX Olympiad (BOCOG). *Official Report of the Beijing 2008 Olympic Games*. 4 vols. and 1 CD and 4 DVDs. Beijing: BOCOG, 2009. Text in English.

2012—London

The London Organising Committee of the Olympic Games and the Paralympic Games. *London 2012 Olympic Games: the Official Report*. Two commemorative books and 1 DVD with official results. London: LOCOG, 2013. Texts in English and French.

B. The Olympic Winter Games

1924—Chamonix

No separate official report of the Chamonix Winter Olympics was ever issued. The report is found at the end of the report for the 1924 Olympic Games in Paris, *Les Jeux de la VIIIè Olympiade Paris 1924: Rapport officiel du Comité Olympique Français*. See above.

1928—St. Moritz

Swiss Olympic Committee. *Rapport général du Comité Exécutif des IIèmes Jeux Olympiques d'Hiver et documents officiels divers*. Lausanne: Author, 1928. Results were not included in this report, but were issued in a separate volume: Swiss Olympic Committee, *Résultats des Concours des IIèmes Jeux Olympiques d'Hiver organisés à St. Moritz*. Lausanne: Author, 1928.

1932—Lake Placid

Lattimer, George M., ed. *Official Report: III Olympic Winter Games, Lake Placid 1932*. Lake Placid, N.Y.: COJO Lake Placid 1932, 1932.

1936—Garmisch-Partenkirchen

COJO Garmisch-Partenkirchen 1936. *IV. Olympische Winterspiele 1936. GarmischPartenkirchen 6. bis 16. Februar: Amtlicher Bericht*. Berlin: Reichssportverlag, 1936.

1940—Sapporo (scheduled, not held) then St. Moritz (scheduled, not held) then Garmisch-Partenkirchen (scheduled, not held)

Diem, Carl, ed. *Vorbereitungen zu den V. Olympischen Winterspiele 1940 GarmischPartenkirchen*. Munich: Knorr und Hirth, 1939. The Games did not take place. They were originally scheduled for Sapporo, Japan, and were later scheduled for St. Moritz, Switzerland, before being rescheduled to Garmisch-Partenkirchen. Sapporo and St. Moritz did not issue reports.

1944—Cortina d'Ampezzo (scheduled, not held)

No report was ever issued.

1948—St. Moritz

Swiss Olympic Committee. *Rapport Général sur les Vès Jeux Olympiques d'Hiver St-Moritz 1948.* Lausanne: Author, 1951.

1952—Oslo

Petersen, Rolf, ed. *VI Olympiske Vinterleker/Olympic Winter Games: Oslo 1952.* English translation by Margaret Wold and Ragnar Wold. Oslo: Kirstes Boktrykkeri, 1956. Parallel texts in English and Norwegian.

1956—Cortina d'Ampezzo

Comitato Olimpico Nazionale Italiano. *VII Giochi Olimpici Invernali/VII Olympic Winter Games: Rapporto ufficiale/Official Report.* Rome: Author, ca. 1957. Parallel texts in Italian and English.

1960—Squaw Valley

Rubin, Robert, ed. *VIII Olympic Winter Games, Squaw Valley, California 1960: Final Report.* Sacramento: California Olympic Commission, 1960. Issued in English only.

1964—Innsbruck

Wolfgang, Friedl, and Berd Neumann, eds. *Offizieler Bericht der IX. Olympischen Winterspiele Innsbruck 1964; Official Report of the IXth Olympic Winter Games, Innsbruck 1964;* and *Rapport du comité d'organisation des IXème Jeux Olympiques d'Hiver 1964.* Vienna: Osterreichischer Bundesverlag, 1967. Separate editions were issued in German, French, and English.

1968—Grenoble

COJO Grenoble 1968. *Xème Jeux Olympiques d'Hiver: Grenoble 1968/Xth Olympic Winter Games Grenoble 1968: Official Report/X. Olympischen Winterspiele*

Grenoble 1968. Amtlicher Bericht. Grenoble: Author, 1968. Parallel texts in French, English, and German.

1972—Sapporo

COJO Sapporo 1972. *Les XI Jeux Olympiques d'Hiver: Sapporo 1972. Rapport official*; and *The 11th Olympic Winter Games: Sapporo 1972: Official Report.* Sapporo: Author, 1972. Separate editions were published in French and English.

1976—Innsbruck

Neumann, Bertl, ed. *Endbericht herausgegeben vom Organisationskomitee der XII. Olympischen Winterspiele Innsbruck 1976/Rapport final publié par le Comité d'Organisation des XIIèmes Jeux Olympiques d'Hiver 1976 à Innsbruck/Final Report Published by the Organizing Committee for the XIIth Winter Olympic Games 1976 at Innsbruck.* Innsbruck: COJO Innsbruck 1976, 1976. Parallel texts in German, French, English, and Russian.

1980—Lake Placid

Madden Robert, and Edward J. Lewi, eds. *Final Report/Rapport Final. XIII Olympic Winter Games/XIII Jeux Olympiques d'Hiver, Lake Placid, NY.* New York: Ed Lewi Associates, 1981. Parallel texts in English and French. Oddly, no results were given in the official report, as is common now, but they were issued separately, with no publishing information given, as *Official Result/Résultats Officiels/Offizielle Ergebnisse.* No real text, but titles were given in English, French, and German.

1984—Sarajevo

COJO Sarajevo 1984. *Final Report Published by the Organising Committee of the XIVth Winter Olympic Games 1984 at Sarajevo/Rapport Final publié par le Comité d'Organisateur des XIVèmes Jeux Olympiques d'Hiver 1984 a Sarajevo/Završni Izvještaj Organizacionoh komiteta XIV zimskih olimipijskih igara Sarajevo, 1984.* Sarajevo: Oslobodjenje, 1985. Parallel texts in English, French, and Serbo-Croatian (but written in the Latin alphabet, thus Croatian as opposed to Serbian, which is written in the Cyrillic alphabet).

1988—Calgary

COJO Calgary 1988. *Rapport officiel des XVes Jeux Olympiques d'hiver/XV Olympic Winter Games Official Report.* Calgary: Author, 1988. Parallel texts in French and English.

1992—Albertville

Blanc, Claudie, and Jean-Marc Eysseric, eds. *Rapport officiel des XVIes Jeux Olympiques d'hiver d'Albertville et de la Savoie/Official Report of the XVI Olympic Winter Games of Albertville and Savoie*. Albertville: COJO Albertville 1992, 1992. Parallel texts in French and English.

1994—Lillehammer

Aune, Tor, Tom Fjellheim, Helge Mjelde, and Linda Verde, eds. *Official Report of the XVII Olympic Winter Games Lillehammer 1994*. 4 vols. Lillehammer: COJO Lillehammer 1994. Separate editions issued in English and French.

1998—Nagano

COJO Nagano 1998. *The XVIII Olympic Winter Games. Official Report*. 3 vols. Nagano: COJO Nagano 1998, 1999. A separate case volume containing a CD-ROM of the report was also issued. Separate editions were issued in English, French, Spanish, German, and Japanese.

2002—Salt Lake City

COJO Salt Lake City 2002. *Salt Lake 2002: Official Report of the XIX Olympic Winter Games*. Salt Lake City, Utah: Salt Lake Organizing Committee, 2002. Separate editions were issued in English and French.

2006—Torino

COJO Torino 2006. *Passion Lives Here: Portrait. XX Giochi Olimpici Invernali—XX Olympic Winter Games—XX Jeux Olympiques d'Hiver. Torino 2006*. Edited by Moira Martin. Torino: Torino Organizing Committee, 2008.

2010—Vancouver

The official report of Vancouver 2010 has a unique format: an official commemorative book published by Wiley, *With Glowing Hearts* and a multimedia set, *Post-Games Report Guide: The Official Report of the Vancouver 2010 Olympic and Paralympic Winter Games*. This set contains an explanatory brochure, two CD-ROMs containing the official results and texts, as well as a commemorative film on DVD, *The Canada that Now Is*. The two volumes are fully bilingual—French and English: Vancouver 2010—Bid Report; Vancouver 2010—Staging the game; Vancouver 2010—Sustainability.

II. ANCIENT OLYMPIC GAMES

Christensen, Paul. *Olympic Victor Lists and Ancient Greek History*. Cambridge: Cambridge University Press, 2007.

Diem, Carl. *Die Olympischen Spiele in Altertum und Gegenwart*. Eulau: n.p., 1933.

Finley, M. I., and H. W. Pleket. *The Olympic Games: The First Thousand Years*. London: Chatto Windus, 1976.

Gardiner, E. Norman. *Athletics of the Ancient World*. Chicago: Ares, 1930.

Hard, Robin. *Olympic Games and Other Greek Athletic Festivals*. London: Routledge, 2006.

Harris, H. A. *Sport in Greece and Rome*. Ithaca, N.Y.: Cornell University Press, 1972.

Matz, David. *Greek and Roman Sport: A Dictionary of Athletes and Events from the Eighth Century B.C. to the Third Century A.D.* Jefferson, N.C.: McFarland, 1991.

Miller, Stephen G. *Ancient Greek Athletics*. New Haven, Conn.: Yale University Press, 2004.

Poliakoff, Michael B. *Competition, Violence, and Culture: Combat Sports in the Ancient World*. New Haven, Conn.: Yale University Press, 1987.

Raschke, Wendy J., ed. *The Archaeology of the Olympics*. Madison: University of Wisconsin Press, 1988.

Renson, Roland, Manfred Lammer, James Riordan, and Dimitrios Chassiotis, eds. *The Olympic Games Through the Ages: Greek Antiquity and Its Impact on Modern Sport*. Athens: Hellenic Sports Research Institute, 1991.

Swaddling, Judith. *The Ancient Olympic Games*. London: British Museum Publications, 1980.

West, Gilbert. *Odes of Pindar, with Several Other Pieces in Prose and Verse, to Which Is Added a Dissertation on the Olympick Games*. London: R. Dodsley, 1753.

Young, David C. *The Olympic Myth of Greek Amateur Athletics*. Chicago: Ares, 1984.

Zarnowski, Frank. *The Pentathlon of the Ancient World*. Jefferson, N.C.: McFarland, 2013.

III. ATTEMPTS AT REVIVAL

Burns, Francis. *Heigh for Cotswold! A History of Robert Dover's Olimpick Games*. Chipping Campden, England: Robert Dover's Games Society, 1981.

Georgiadis, Konstantinos. *Olympic Revival: The Revival of the Olympic Games in Modern Times*. Athens: Ekdotike Athenon, 2003.

Kivroglou, A. "Die Bemühungenn von Ewangelos Sappas um die Wiedereinführung der Olympischen Spiele in Griechenland unter besonderer Berücksichtigung der Spiele von 1859." Unpublished Diplomarbeit, Deutsche Sporthochschule Köln, 1981.

Lennartz, Karl. *Kenntnisse und Vorstellungen von Olympia und den Olympischen Spielen in der Zeit von 393–1896*. Schorndorf: Verlag Karl Hofmann, 1974.

Mullins, Sam. *British Olympians: William Penny Brookes and the Wenlock Games*. London: Birmingham Olympic Council and British Olympic Association, 1986.

Neumüller, B. "Die Geschichte der Much Wenlock Games." Unpublished Diplomarbeit, Deutsche Sporthochschule Köln, 1985.

Redmond, Gerald. *The Caledonian Games in Nineteenth-Century America*. Rutherford, N.J.: Fairleigh Dickinson University Press, 1971.

Rühl, Joachim K. *Die "Olympischen Spiele" Robert Dovers*. Heidelberg: Carl Winter Universitätsverlag, 1975.

Svahn, Åke. "Olympiska Spelen' i Helsingborg 1834 och 1836." *Idrott Historia och Samhalle* (1983): 77–105. Text in Swedish but with an English summary.

Wenlock Olympian Society. *The Olympian Dream—The Life of William Penny Brookes*. Much Wenlock, England: Wenlock Olympian Society, 2010.

Young, David C. "Origins of the Modern Olympics." *International Journal of the History of Sport* 4 (1987): 271–300.

———. *The Modern Olympics: A Struggle for Revival*. Baltimore, Md.: Johns Hopkins University Press, 1996.

IV. WORKS ON SPECIFIC OLYMPIC GAMES

A. All Olympiads

Bulatova, Maria, Sergey Bubka, and Vladimir Platanov. *Olympic Games,* Vol. I *(1896–1972),* Vol. II *(1976–2012)*. Kyiv, Ukraine: NOC of the Ukraine, 2013.

The Olympic Century: The Official History of the Modern Olympic Movement. 24 vols. Los Angeles: World Sport Research & Publications, 1995–2000. Vol. 1, *The Ancient Olympiads & Bridges to the Modern Era: Ancient Olympia 2100 BC to AD 1894*, edited by James Lynch; Vol. 2, *I Olympiad—Athens 1896*, edited by Gary Allison and Dietrich Quanz; Vol. 3, *II Olympiad—Paris 1900 and the Nordic Games*, edited by Carl Posey; Vol. 4, *III Olympiad—St. Louis 1904 and Athens 1906*, edited by Carl Posey; Vol. 5, *IV Olympiad—London 1908 and the International YMCA*, edited by George Constable; Vol. 6, *V & VI Olympiads—Stockholm 1912 and the Inter-Allied Games*, edited by George Daniels; Vol. 7, *VII Olympiad—Antwerp 1920, and Chamonix 1924*, edited by Ellen Phillips; Vol. 8, *VIII Olympiad—Paris 1924 and St. Moritz 1928*, edited by Ellen Phillips; Vol. 9, *IX Olympiad—Amsterdam 1928 and Lake Placid 1932*, edited by Ellen Phillips; Vol. 10, *X Olympiad—Los Angeles 1932 and Garmisch-Partenkirchen 1936*, edited by Ellen Galford; Vol. 11, *The XI, XII, & XIII Olympiads—Berlin 1936 to St. Moritz 1948*, edited by George Constable; Vol. 12, *XIV Olympiad—London 1948 and Oslo 1952*, edited by George Daniels; Vol. 13, *XV Olympiad—Helsinki 1952 and Cortina d'Ampezzo 1956*, edited by Carl Posey; Vol. 14, *XVI Olympiad—Melbourne 1956 and Squaw Valley 1960*, edited by Carl Posey; Vol. 15, *XVII Olympiad—Rome 1960 and Innsbruck 1964*, edited by Ellen Phillips; Vol. 16, *XVIII Olympiad—Tokyo 1964 and Grenoble 1968*, edited by Carl Posey; Vol. 17, *XIX Olympiad—Mexico City 1968 and Sapporo 1972*, edited by George Daniels;

Vol. 18, *XX Olympiad—Munich 1972 and Innsbruck 1976*, edited by George Daniels; Vol. 19, *XXI Olympiad—Montréal 1976 and Lake Placid 1980*, edited by George Constable; Vol. 20, *XXII Olympiad—Moscow 1980 and Sarajevo 1984*, edited by Roberta Conlon; Vol. 21, *XXIII Olympiad—Los Angeles 1984 and Calgary 1988*, edited by Ellen Galford; Vol. 22, *XXIV Olympiad—Seoul 1988 and Albertville 1992*, edited by Ellen Galford; Vol. 23, *XXV Olympiad—Barcelona 1992 and Lillehammer 1994*, edited by George Constable; Vol. 24, *XXVI Olympiad—Atlanta 1996 and Nagano 1998*, edited by Carl Posey. The founder of the series and driving force behind its publication was Gary Allison, head of World Sport Research & Publications and chairman of the 1st Century Project. The publisher of the series was Robert G. Rossi, with associate publishers C. Jay Halzle and James A. Williamson. The series editor was Christian D. Kinney. The senior consultant was Dietrich Quanz. Special consultants to the entire project were Walter Borgers (GER), Ian Buchanan (GBR), Dr. Karl Lennartz (GER), Wolf Lyberg (SWE), and Dr. Norbert Müller (GER). Statistical consultants were Bill Mallon (USA) and Walter Teutenberg (GER). Art editor for the series was Christopher M. Register. There was a series of special contributors and consultants for each volume.

B. Specific Olympic Games

1896

Georgiadis, Konstantinos. "Die Geschichte der ersten Olympischen Spiele 1896 in Athen—ihre Entstehung, Durchführung und Bedeutung." Unpublished Diplomarbeit, Johannes Gutenberg Universität Mainz, 1986/87.

Kardasis, Vasilis. *The Olympic Games in Athens 1896–1906*. Athens: International Sport Publications, 2004.

Kluge, Volker, ed. *1896 Athens: The Pictures of the First Olympiad*. Berlin: Brandenburgisches Verlaghaus, 1996.

Koulouri, Christina. *Athens: Olympic City 1896–1906*. Athens: International Olympic Academy, 2004.

Lennartz, Karl. *Geschichte der Deutschen Reichsaußchußes für Olympische Spiele: Heft I, Die Beteiligung Deutschlands an den Olympischen Spielen 1896 in Athen*. Bonn: Verlag Peter Wegener, 1981.

Lennartz, Karl, and Walter Teutenberg. *Die deutsche Olympia-Mannschaft von 1896*. Frankfurt am Main: Kasseler Sportverlag, 1992.

Mallon, Bill, with Ture Widlund. *The 1896 Olympic Games: Results for All Competitors in All Events, with Commentary*. Jefferson, N.C.: McFarland, 1998.

Mandell, Richard D. *The First Modern Olympics*. Berkeley: University of California Press, 1976.

Smith, Michael Llewellyn. *Olympics in Athens 1896: The Invention of the Modern Olympic Games*. London: Profile Books, 2004.

Tsolakidis, Elias. "Die Olympischen Spiele von 1896 in Athen: Versuch einer Rekonstruktion." Unpublished Diplomarbeit, Deutsche Sporthochschule Köln, 1987.

1900

Bijkerk, Ton. *Nederlandse Deelnemers aan de Tweed Olympische Spelen: Tijdens de Wereldtentoonstelling Parijs 1900*. Haarlem, NED: De Vrieseborch, 2000.

Drevon, André. *Le Jeux Olympiaque Oublié*. Paris: CNRS Editions, 2000.

Lennartz, Karl. *Geschichte des Deutschen Reichsaußchußes für Olympische Spiele: Heft 2, Die Beteiligung Deutschlands an den Olympischen Spielen 1900 in Paris und 1904 in St. Louis*. Bonn: Verlag Peter Wegener, 1983.

Lennartz, Karl, and Walter Teutenberg. *II. Olympische Spiele 1900 in Paris: Darstellung und Quellen*. Berlin: AGON Sportverlag, 1995.

Mallon, Bill. *The 1900 Olympic Games: Results for All Competitors in All Events, with Commentary*. Jefferson, N.C.: McFarland, 1998.

1904

Brownell, Susan. *The 1904 Anthropology Days and Olympic Games: Sport, Race, and American Imperialism*. Critical Studies in the History of Anthropology. Lincoln: University of Nebraska Press, 2008.

Lennartz, Karl. *Geschichte der Deutschen Reichsaußchußes für Olympische Spiele: Heft 2, Die Beteiligung Deutschlands an den Olympischen Spielen 1900 in Paris und 1904 in St. Louis*. Bonn: Verlag Peter Wegener, 1983.

Lucas, Charles J. P. *The Olympic Games 1904*. St. Louis, Mo.: Woodward & Tiernan, 1905.

Mallon, Bill. *A Statistical Summary of the 1904 Olympic Games*. Durham, N.C.: Author, 1981.

———. *The 1904 Olympic Games: Results for All Competitors in All Events, with Commentary*. Jefferson, N.C.: McFarland, 1999.

Matthews, George R. *America's First Olympics: The St. Louis Games of 1904*. Columbia, Mo.: University of Missouri Press, 2005.

1906

Kardasis, Vasilis. *The Olympic Games in Athens 1896–1906*. Athens: International Sport Publications, 2004.

Koulouri, Christina. *Athens: Olympic City 1896–1906*. Athens: International Olympic Academy, 2004.

Lennartz, Karl, and Walter Teutenberg. *Die Olympischen Spiele 1906 in Athen*. Kassel: Kasseler Sportverlag, 1992.

Mallon, Bill. *The 1906 Olympic Games: Results for All Competitors in All Events, with Commentary*. Jefferson, N.C.: McFarland, 1999.

1908

Baker, Keith. *The 1908 Olympics: The First London Games*. Cheltenham, England: SportsBooks, 2008.

Lennartz, Karl, with Ian Buchanan, Volker Kluge, Bill Mallon, and Walter Teutenberg. *Olympische Spiele 1908 in London*. Berlin: AGON Sportverlag, 1999.

Mallon, Bill, and Ian Buchanan. *The 1908 Olympic Games: Results for All Competitors in All Events, with Commentary*. Jefferson, N.C.: McFarland, 2000.

1912

Diem, Carl. *Die olympischen Spiele 1912*. Berlin: Bürger, 1912.

Erseus, Johan. *Solskenolympiaden Stockholm 1912*. Stockholm: Bokforlaget Max Strom, 2012.

Hermelin, [Colonel,] Baron Sven [D. A.], and Erik Peterson. *Den Femte Olympiaden: Olympiska Spelen i Stockholm 1912 i Bild och Ord*. Göteburg: Åhlén & Åkerlund, 1912.

Jonsson, Ake. *Vagledning till Solskenolympiaden*. Stockholm: Klocktornet, 2012.

Lennartz, Karl. *Die Spiele der V. Olympiade 1912 in Stockholm*. Kassel: Agon, 2009.

Mallon, Bill, and Ture Widlund. *The 1912 Olympic Games: Results for All Competitors in All Events, with Commentary*. Jefferson, N.C.: McFarland, 2000.

Yttergren, Leif, and Hans Bolling. *The 1912 Stockholm Olympics*. Jefferson, N.C.: McFarland, 2012.

1916

Lennartz, Karl. *Die VI. Olympischen Spiele Berlin 1916*. Cologne: Barz & Beienburg, 1978.

1920

Lennartz, Karl, Wolf Reinhardt, and Ralph Schluter. *Die Spiele der VII. Olympiade 1920 in Antwerpen*. Kassel: Agon, 2013.

Mallon, Bill. *The Unofficial Report of the 1920 Olympics*. Durham, N.C.: MOST Publications, 1992.

———. *The 1920 Olympic Games: Results for All Competitors in All Events, with Commentary*. Jefferson, N.C.: McFarland, 2001.

Renson, Roland. *The Games Reborn: The VIIth Olympiad Antwerp 1920*. Antwerp: Pandora, 1996. Also published in French as *La VIIiéme Olympiade Anvers 1920: Les Jeux Ressuscités*, in 1995.

1924

Pallière, Johannès. *Les premiers jeux d'hiver de 1924: la grande bataille de Chamonix*. Chambéry: Société Savoisienne d'Histoire et d'Archéologie, 1991.

Vitalien, Pierre. *La mémoire des 1ers jeux Olympiques d'hiver. Chamonix 1924*. Sérignan: Imprimerie Nouvelle Chamonix/Sallanches, 2004.

1928

Lennartz, Karl, and Wolf Reinhardt. *Deutsche Tellnahme an den Spielen der XI Olympiade 1928 in Sankt Moritz und Amsterdam*. Kassel, Germany: Agon, 2011.

1932

Pieroth, Doris H. *Their Day in the Sun: Women of the 1932 Olympics*. Seattle: University of Washington, 1996.

1936

Graham, Cooper. *Leni Riefenstahl and Olympia*. Metuchen, N.J.: Scarecrow Press, 1986.

Hart-Davis, Duff. *Hitler's Games: The 1936 Olympics*. London: Century, 1986.

Hilton, Christopher. *Hitler's Olympics: the 1936 Berlin Olympic Games*. Stoud, England: Sutton Publishing, 2006.

Holmes, Judith. *Olympiad 1936: Blaze of Glory for Hitler's Reich*. New York: Ballantine, 1971.

Kluge, Volker, Karl Lennartz, and Hans-Jochim Teichler. *Autogrammbucher Berlin 1936*. DKB, 2011.

Krüger, Arnd, and William Murray. *The Nazi Olympics: Sport, Politics, and Appeasement in the 1930s*. Urbana and Chicago: University of Illinois Press, 2003.

Large, David Clay. *Nazi Games: The Olympics of 1936*. New York: W.W. Norton, 2007.

Mandell, Richard D. *The Nazi Olympics*. New York: Macmillan, 1971.

Schaap, Jeremy. *Triumph: The Untold Story of Jesse Owens and Hitler's Olympics*. Boston: Houghton Mifflin, 2007.

Walters, Guy. *Berlin Games: How the Nazis Stole the Olympic Dream*. New York: William Morrow, 2006.

1940

Collins, Sandra. *The 1940 Tokyo Games: The Missing Olympics*. New York: Routledge, 2008.

1948

Hampton, Janie. *The Austerity Olympics: When the Games Came to London in 1948*. London: Aurum Press, 2008.

Phillips, Bob. *The 1948 Olympics: How London Rescued the Games*. Cheltenham, England: SportsBooks, 2007.

1956

Lechenperg, Harald. *Olympische Spiele 1956: Cortina, Stockholm, Melbourne*. Munich: Copress-Verlag, 1957.

1960

Lechenperg, Harald. *Olympische Spiele 1960: Squaw Valley, Rome*. Munich: Copress-Verlag, 1960; and Zurich: Schweizer Druckerei und Verlagshaus, 1960. Also published in English as *Olympic Games 1960: Squaw Valley–Rome*. New York: A.S. Barnes, 1960.

Maraniss, David. *Rome 1960: The Summer Olympics that Changed the World*. New York: Simon & Schuster, 2008.

1964

Lechenperg, Harald. *Olympische Spiele 1964: Innsbruck, Tokyo*. Munich: Copress-Verlag, 1964; Zurich: Schweizer Druckerei und Verlagshaus, 1964; and Linz, Austria: Trauner, 1964. Also published in English as *Olympic Games 1964: Innsbruck–okyo*. New York: A.S. Barnes, 1964.

1968

Bass, Amy. *Not the Triumph but the Struggle: The 1968 Olympics and the Making of the Black Athlete*. Minneapolis: University of Minnesota Press, 2002.

Lechenperg, Harald. *Olympische Spiele 1968*. Munich: Copress-Verlag, 1968.

Witherspoon, Kevin. *Before the Eyes of the World: Mexico and the 1968 Olympic Games*. DeKalb: Northern Illinois University Press, 2008.

1972

Groussard, Serge. *The Blood of Israel: The Massacre of the Israeli Athletes: The Olympics, 1972*. New York: Morrow, *1975*.

Klein, Aaron J. *Striking Back: The 1972 Munich Olympics Massacre and Israel's Deadly Response*. New York: Random House, 2005.

Lechenperg, Harald. *Olympische Spiele 1972*. Munich: Copress-Verlag, 1972.

Leebron, Elizabeth Joanne. "An Analysis of Selected United States Media Coverage of the 1972 Munich Olympic Tragedy." Ph.D. thesis, Northwestern University, 1978.

Mandell, Richard D. *A Munich Diary: The Olympics of 1972*. Chapel Hill: University of North Carolina Press, 1991.

Reeve, Simon. *One Day in September*. New York: Arcade Publishing, 2000.

1976

Auf der Maur, Nick. *The Billion Dollar Game: Jean Drapeau and the 1976 Olympics*. Toronto: J. Lorimer, 1977.

Howell, Paul Charles. *The Montreal Olympics: An Insider's View of Organizing a Self-Financing Games*. Montreal: McGill-Queen's University Press, 2009.

Ludwig, Jack. *Five Ring Circus: The Montreal Olympics*. Toronto: Doubleday, 1976.

1980

Barton, Laurence. "The American Olympic Boycott of 1980: The Amalgam of Diplomacy and Propaganda in Influencing Public Opinion." Ph.D. thesis, Boston University, 1983.
Booker, Christopher. *The Games War: A Moscow Journal.* London: Faber & Faber, 1981.
Caraccioli, Tom, and Jerry Caraccioli. *Boycott: Stolen Dreams of the 1980 Moscow Olympic Games.* Washington, D.C.: New Chapter Press, 2008.
Hulme, Derick L., Jr. "The Viability of International Sport as a Political Weapon: The 1980 U.S. Olympic Boycott (United States)." Ph.D. thesis, Fletcher School of Law and Diplomacy (Tufts University), 1988.
——. *The Political Olympics: Moscow, Afghanistan, and the 1980 U.S. Boycott.* New York: Praeger, 1990.
Sarantakes, Nicholas Evan. *Dropping the Torch: Jimmy Carter, The Olympic Boycott and the Cold War.* Cambridge: Cambridge University, 2012.
Wilson, Harold Edwin, Jr. "'Ours Will Not Go.' The U.S. Boycott of the 1980 Olympic Games." Master's thesis, The Ohio State University, Columbus, 1982.

1984

Perelman, Richard B. *Olympic Retrospective: The Games of Los Angeles.* Los Angeles: COJO Los Angeles 1984, 1985.
Reich, Kenneth. *Making It Happen: Peter Ueberroth and the 1984 Olympics.* Santa Barbara, Calif.: Capra Press, 1986.
Shaikin, Bill. *Sport and Politics: The Olympics and the Los Angeles Games.* New York: Praeger, 1988.
Ueberroth, Peter V., with Richard Levin and Amy Quinn. *Made in America: His Own Story.* New York: Morrow, 1985.
Wilson, Harold Edwin, Jr. "The Golden Opportunity: A Study of the Romanian Manipulation of the Olympic Movement During the Boycott of the 1984 Los Angeles Olympic Games." Ph.D. thesis, The Ohio State University, Columbus, 1993.

1988

Kim Un-Yong. *The Greatest Olympics.* Seoul: Si-sa-yong-o-sa, 1990.
King, Frank W. *It's How You Play the Game: The Inside Story of the Calgary Olympics.* Calgary: Script, 1991.
Park She-Jik. *The Seoul Olympics: The Inside Story.* London: Bellew, 1991.
Pound, Richard W. *Five Rings over Korea.* Boston: Little Brown, 1994.

1992

Brunet, Ferrán. *Economy of the 1992 Barcelona Olympic Games.* Barcelona: Centre d'Estudis Olímpics Universitat Autónoma de Barcelona, 1993.

1994

Klausen, Arne Martin, ed. *Olympic Games as Performance and Public Event: The Case of the XVII Winter Olympic Games in Norway*. New York: Berghahn, 1999.

2000

Cashman, Richard. *The Bitter-sweet Awakening: The Legacy of the Sydney 2000 Olympic Games*. Sydney: Walla Walla Press, 2006.

Marichev, Gennadi. *Sydney 2000: The Figures, the Results, the Athletes*. Riga: Demarko Sports Publishing, 2000.

McGeoch, Rod, with Glenda Korporaal. *The Bid: How Australia Won the 2000 Games*. Melbourne: William Heinemann Australia, 1994.

O'Brien, Danny James. *Strategic Business Leveraging of a Mega Sport Event: The Sydney 2000 Olympic Games Experience*. Gold Coast, Qld.: CRC for Sustainable Tourism, 2005.

2002

Romney, Mitt, and Timothy Robinson. *Turnaround: Crisis, Leadership, and the Olympic Games*. Washington, D.C.: Regnery, 2004. Paperback edition in 2007.

2008

Brownell, Susan. *Beijing's Games: What the Olympics Mean to China*. Lanham, Md.: Rowman & Littlefield, 2008.

Close, Pau, David Askew, and Xu Xin. *The Beijing Olympiad: The Political Economy of a Sporting Mega-event*. Abingdon, England/New York: Routledge, 2006.

Xu Guoqi. *Olympic Dreams: China and Sports, 1895–2008*. Cambridge, Mass.: Harvard University Press, 2008.

2012

Lee, Mike. *The Race for the 2012 Olympics: The Inside Story of How London Won the Bid*. London: Virgin, 2006.

Vigor, Anthony, Melissa Mean, and Charlie Tims. *After the Gold Rush: A Sustainable Olympics for London*. London: Institute for Public Policy Research, 2004.

V. GENERAL SPORTING HISTORIES OF THE OLYMPIC GAMES

Andersen, P. Chr., and Vagn Hansen. *Olympiadebogen: De Olympiske Lege 1896–1948*. Copenhagen: Samlererns Forlag, 1948.

Associated Press and Grolier. *The Olympic Story: Pursuit of Excellence.* New York: Franklin Watts, 1979.

Georgiev, Nikolay. *Analyse du programme des Jeux Olympiques d'hiver 1924–1998.* Lausanne: IOC, 1995.

———. *Analyse du programme Olympique 1896–1996.* Lausanne: IOC, 1995.

Gillmeister, Heiner. *Olympisches Tennis: Die Geschichte der olympischen Tennisturniere (1896–1992).* Sankt Augustin: Academia Verlag, 1993.

Greenberg, Stan. *The Guinness Book of Olympics Facts & Feats.* Enfield, Middlesex, England: Guinness, 1983. Second edition issued as *Olympic Games: The Records*, by the same publisher in 1987. Third edition issued as *The Guinness Olympics Fact Book*, by the same publisher in 1991.

———. *Whitaker's Olympic Almanack. The Essential Guide to the Olympic Games.* 2nd ed. London: A. C. Black, 2003.

Gynn, Roger, and David Martin. *The Olympic Marathon.* Champaign, Ill.: Human Kinetics, 2000.

Henry, Bill. *An Approved History of the Olympic Games.* 1st ed., New York: G.P. Putnam, 1948. 2nd ed., New York: G.P. Putnam, 1976. 3rd/4th eds., Sherman Oaks, Calif.: Alfred Publishing, 1981 and 1984. The last three editions were edited by Henry's daughter, Patricia Henry Yeomans.

Kahlich, Endre, László Gy. Papp, and Zoltán Subert. *Olympic Games 1896–1972.* Budapest: Corvina, 1972.

Kaiser, Rupert. *Olympia Almanach: Geschichten, Zahlen, Bilder. 100 Jahre Olympische Spiele.* Kassel, Germany: AGON Sportverlag, 1996.

———. *Olympia Almanach: Geschichten, Zahlen, Bilder. 90 Jahre Olympische Winterspiele.* Kassel, Germany: AGON Sportverlag, 1998.

Kamper, Erich. *Lexikon der Olympischen Winterspiele.* Stuttgart: Union Verlag, 1964. Parallel texts in German, French, English, and Swedish.

———. *Enzyklopädie der Olympischen Spiele.* Dortmund: Harenberg, 1972. Parallel texts in German, French, and English. American edition issued as *Encyclopaedia of the Olympic Games.* New York: McGraw-Hill, 1972.

———. *Lexikon der 12,000 Olympioniken.* Graz, Austria: Leykam-Verlag, 1975. Second edition issued as *Lexikon der 14,000 Olympioniken*, by the same publisher in 1983.

Kamper, Erich, and Bill Mallon. *The Golden Book of the Olympic Games.* Milan: Vallardi, 1993.

Kamper, Erich, and Herbert Soucek. *Olympische Heroen: Portraits und Anekdoten von 1896 bis heute.* Erkrath, Germany: Spiridon Verlag, 1991.

Kluge, Volker. *Die Olympischen Spiele von 1896 bis 1980.* Berlin: Sportverlag, 1981.

———. *Winter Olympia Kompakt.* Berlin: Sportverlag, 1992.

———. *Olympische Sommerspiele: Die Chronik I. Athen 1896–Berlin 1936.* Berlin: Sportverlag, 1997.

———. *Olympische Sommerspiele: Die Chronik II. London 1948–Tokyo 1964.* Berlin: Sportverlag, 1998.

———. *Olympische Sommerspiele: Die Chronik III. Mexico 1968–Los Angeles 1984.* Berlin: Sportverlag, 2000.

———. *Olympische Sommerspiele: Die Chronik IV. Seoul 1988–Atlanta 1996*. Berlin: Sportverlag, 2000.

———. *Olympische Sommerspiele: Die Chronik V. Sydney 2000–Athens 2004*. Berlin: Sportverlag, 2005.

Lord Killanin, and John Rodda, eds. *The Olympic Games*. London: Queen Anne Press, 1976. Second edition published as *The Olympic Games 1984: Los Angeles and Sarajevo*. Salem, N.H.: Michael Joseph, 1983.

Lovett, Charlie. *Olympic Marathon: A Centennial History of the Games' Most Storied Race*. Westport, Conn.: Praeger, 1997.

Mallon, Bill. *The Olympic Record Book*. New York: Garland, 1987.

———. *Olympic Golden Data Retrieval System*. Baltimore, Md.: Datatrace, 2004.

Marichev, Gennadi. *Who Is Who at the Summer Olympics 1896–1992*. 4 vols. Riga: Demarko Sport Publishing, 1996.

———. *Winter Olympics 1924–2002: The Figures, the Results, the Athletes*. Riga: Demarko Sport Publishing, 2002.

Messinesi, Xenophon. *The History of the Olympic Games*. New York/London: Drake, 1976.

Mező, Ferenc. *The Modern Olympic Games*. Budapest: Pannonia Press, 1956. Multiple editions were issued, in English, French, German, Spanish, and Hungarian.

Miller, David. *Athens to Athens: The Official History of the Olympics Games and the IOC, 1904–2004*. Edinburgh and London: Mainstream Publishing, 2003.

The Olympics. Athens to Athens 1896–2004. London: Weidenfeld & Nicolson, 2004.

Petrov, Raiko. *Olympic Wrestling Throughout the Millennia*. Lausanne: FILA, 1993.

Schaap, Richard [Dick]. *An Illustrated History of the Olympics*. Three eds. New York: Alfred A. Knopf, 1963, 1967, 1975. Last two editions list author's name as Dick Schaap.

Shaw, Christopher A. *Five Ring Circus: Myths and Realities of the Olympic Games*. Gabriola Island, B.C.: New Society Publishers, 2008.

Soames, Nicolas, and Roy Inman. *Olympic Judo: History and Techniques*. Wiltshire, England: Crowood Press, 1990.

Wallechinsky, David. *The Complete Book of the Olympics*. 1st ed., Middlesex, England: Penguin Books, 1983. 2nd ed., New York: Viking Penguin, 1988. 3rd ed., London: Aurum, 1991. 4th ed., Boston: Little, Brown, 1996. 5th ed., Woodstock, N.Y.: Overlook Press, 2000. 6th/7th eds., London: Aurum Press, 2004, 2008, 2012. Seventh and eighth editions have Jamie Loucky as coauthor. Probably the best known book, and very complete, in English, on the results of the Olympic Games. Separate editions were published for the Winter Olympics (see below).

———. *The Complete Book of the Winter Olympics*. 1st ed., Boston: Little, Brown, 1993. 2nd/3rd eds., Woodstock, N.Y.: Overlook, 1998, 2001. 4th/5th eds., London: Aurum Press, 2002, 2006, 2010, 2014. Fourth, fifth, sixth, and seventh editions have Jamie Loucky as coauthor.

Wasner, Fritz. *Olympia-Lexikon*. Bielefeld, Germany: Verlag E. Gunglach Aktiengesellschaft, 1939.

Weyand, Alexander M. *Olympic Pageant*. New York: Macmillan, 1952.

zur Megede, Ekkehard. *The Modern Olympic Century 1896–1996*. Berlin: Deutsche Gesellschaft für Leichtathletik-Dokumentation, 1999.

VI. GENERAL POLITICAL AND SOCIOLOGICAL HISTORIES OF THE OLYMPIC GAMES

Chappelet, Jean-Loup, and Brenda Kübler-Mabbott. *International Olympic Committee and the Olympic System (IOC): The Governance of World Sport*. New York/ London: Routledge, 2008.

Clark, Stanley James. "Amateurism, Olympism, and Pedagogy: Cornerstones of the Modern Olympic Movement." Ed.D. thesis, Stanford University, 1975.

Da Costa, Lamartine P. *Olympic Studies. Current Intellectual Crossroads*. Rio de Janeiro: n.p., 2002.

Daniels, Stephanie, and Anita Tedder. *A Proper Spectacle: Women Olympians 1900–1936. Celebrating 100 Years of Women in the Olympics*. Bedfordshire, England: ZeNaNa Press, 2000.

Diem, Carl. *Ewiges Olympia*. Minden: n.p., 1948.

Espy, Richard. *The Politics of the Olympic Games*. Berkeley: University of California Press, 1979.

Findling, John E., and Kimberly D. Pelle. *Historical Dictionary of the Olympic Movement*. Westport, Conn.: Greenwood, 1996 and 2004.

Fuoss, Donald E. "An Analysis of the Incidents in the Olympic Games from 1924 to 1948, with Reference to the Contribution of the Games to International Understanding." Ph.D. thesis, Columbia University, 1952.

Gafner, Raymond, and Norbert Müller. *The International Olympic Committee—One Hundred Years: The Idea—The Presidents—The Achievements*. 3 vols. Lausanne: IOC, 1995.

Girginov, Vassil, ed. *The Olympics: A Critical Reader*. New York: Routledge, 2010.

Graham, Peter J., and Horst Ueberhorst, eds. *The Modern Olympics*. Cornwall, N.Y.: Leisure Press, ca. 1975.

Guttmann, Allen. *The Olympics: A History of the Modern Games*. Urbana: University of Illinois Press, 1992.

Hill, Christopher R. *Olympic Politics: Athens to Atlanta 1896–1996*. 2nd ed. Manchester, England: Manchester University Press, 1996. First edition issued as *Olympic Politics*, by the same publisher in 1992.

Hoberman, John. *Olympic Crisis: Sport Politics and the Moral Order*. New Rochelle, N.Y.: Caratzas, 1986.

Howard, Rachel. *The Truce Story*. Edited by the International Olympic Truce Centre. Athens: Pallis ABEE, 2004.

Jennings, Andrew. *The New Lords of the Rings*. New York: Pocket, 1996. (See Simson and Jennings for the first edition.)

Kanin, David B. *A Political History of the Olympic Games*. Boulder, Colo.: Westview Books, 1981.

Landry, Fernand, Marc Landry, and Magdeleine Yerles, eds. *Sport: The Third Millennium/Le troisième millénaire*. Sainte-Foy, Quebec: Les presses de l'université Laval, 1991. A collection of papers with text in either French or English. Abstracts are provided in both languages.

Leiper, Jean Marion. "The International Olympic Committee: The Pursuit of Olympism, 1894–1970." Ph.D. thesis, University of Alberta (Canada), 1976.

Lenskyj, Helen. *Olympic Industry Resistance: Challenging Olympic Power and Propaganda.* Albany: State University of New York Press, 2008.

Lucas, John. *The Modern Olympic Games.* New York: A.S. Barnes, 1980.

———. *The Future of the Olympic Games.* Champaign, Ill.: Human Kinetics, 1992.

Lyberg, Wolf. *The Book of Facts on the Olympic Winter Games 1924–1992: Part I: The Participants, the Medals, the Spectators.* Lausanne: IOC, 1992.

———. *The History of the IOC Sessions.* 3 vols. Lausanne: IOC, 1994.

———. *Fabulous 100 Years of the IOC: Facts, Figures, and Much, Much More.* Lausanne: IOC, 1996.

———. *The Seventh President of the IOC: Facts and Figures.* Lausanne: IOC, 1997.

Majumdar, Boria, and Sandra S. Collins, eds. *Olympism: From Nationalism to Internationalism.* London/New York: Routledge, 2008.

Messinesi, Xenophon Leon. *A Branch of Wild Olive.* New York: Exposition Press, 1973. Second edition issued as *A History of the* Olympics. New York: Drake Publishers, 1976.

Miller, Geoffrey. *Behind the Olympic Rings.* Lynn, Mass.: H.O. Zimman, 1979.

Multi-Media Partners, Ltd. *Grace & Glory: A Century of Women in the Olympics.* Chicago: Triumph, 1996.

NOK für Deutschland and Kuratorium Olympische Akademie und Olympische Erziehung, eds. *Olympism: The Olympic Idea in Modern Society and Sport/Materialen für den Englischunterricht in der gymnasien Oberstufe.* Stuttgart: n.p., 2004.

Okafor, Udodiri Paul. "The Interaction of Sports and Politics as a Dilemma of the Modern Olympic Games." Ph.D. thesis, The Ohio State University, Columbus, 1979.

Page, James A. *Black Olympian Medalists.* Englewood, Colo.: Libraries Unlimited, 1991.

Platt, Alan R. "The Olympic Games and Their Political Aspects: 1952 to 1972." Ph.D. thesis, Kent State University, 1976.

Plowden, Martha Ward. *Olympic Black Women.* Gretna, La.: Pelican, 1996.

Pound, Dick. *Inside the Olympics: A Behind-the-Scenes Look at the Politics, the Scandals, and the Glory of the Games.* Baltimore, Md.: Wiley, 2004.

Preuss, Holger. *Economics of the Olympic Games: Hosting the Games 1972–2000.* Petersham, NSW: Walla Walla Press, 2000.

———. *The Economics of Staging the Olympics: A Comparison of the Games 1972–2008.* Cheltenham: Elgar, 2004.

Schaffer, Kay, and Sidonie Smith, eds. *The Olympics at the Millennium: Power, Politics, and the Games.* New Brunswick, N.J.: Rutgers University Press, 2000.

Segrave Jeffrey O., and Donald Chu, eds. *The Olympic Games in Transition.* Champaign, Ill.: Human Kinetics, 1988.

Senn, Alfred E. *Power, Politics, and the Olympic Games.* Champaign, Ill.: Human Kinetics, 1999.

Simson, Vyv, and Andrew Jennings. *Lords of the Rings: Power, Money & Drugs in the Modern* Olympics. London: Simon & Schuster, 1991. Published in the United

States as *Dishonored Games: Corruption, Money & Greed at the Olympics*. New York: S.P.I. Books, 1992. (See also Jennings for the second edition.)

Sun Byung-Kee, Lee Sei-Kee, Kim Sung-Kyu, and Kogh Young-Lee, eds. *Olympics and Politics*. Seoul: Hyung-Seul, ca. 1984.

Tait, Robin. "The Politicization of the Modern Olympic Games." Ph.D. thesis, University of Oregon, Eugene, 1984.

Tomlinson, Alan, and Garry Whannel, eds. *Five Ring Circus: Money, Power, and Politics at the Olympic Games*. London: Pluto Press, 1984.

Toohey, Kristine, and Anthony James Veal. *The Olympic Games: A Social Science Perspective*. 2nd ed. Wallingford: CABI Publishing, 2006.

Wenn, Stephen R., and Gerald P. Schaus. *Onward to the Olympics: Historical Perspectives on the Olympic Games*. Waterloo, Ont.: Wilfrid Laurier University Press, 2007.

Young, Kevin, and Kevin B. Wamsley, eds. *Global Olympics: Historical and Sociological Studies of the Modern Games*. Amsterdam/Oxford: JAI Press, 2006.

VII. HISTORIES OF NATIONAL PARTICIPATION AT THE OLYMPIC GAMES

A. Australia

Atkinson, Graeme. *Australian & New Zealand Olympians: The Stories of 100 Great Champions*. Canterbury, Vic.: Five Mile Press, 1984.

Australian Olympic Committee. *The Compendium: Official Australian Olympic Statistics 1896–2002*. St. Lucia: University of Queensland Press, 2003.

Blanch, John, and Paul Jenes. *Australia at the Modern Olympic Games*. Coogee, NSW: John Blanch Publishing, 1984.

Gordon, Harry. *Australia and the Olympic Games*. St. Lucia: University of Queensland Press, 1994.

Howell, Reet, and Maxwell Howell. *Aussie Gold: The Story of Australia at the Olympics*. South Melbourne: Brooks Waterloo, 1988.

Lester, Gary. *Australians at the Olympics: A Definitive History*. Sydney: Lester Townsend Publishing, 1984.

Phillips, Dennis H. *Australian Women at the Olympic Games*. Kenthurst, NSW: Kangaroo Press, 1992.

Poke, Robin, and Kevin Berry. *Olympic Gold: Our Greatest Individual Olympians Since 1896*. Millers Point, Australia: Murdoch, 2012.

B. Bulgaria

Tsigur Petfur Beron. *Olimpiyskite Igry 1896–1980 Shravochnyuk* (transliterated title). Sofia: Meditsina i fizkultura, ca. 1982.

C. Canada

Bryden, Wendy. *The Official Sports History and Record Book: Canada at the Olympic Winter Games*. Edmonton: Hurtig Publishers, 1987.
Cosentino, Frank, and Glynn Leyshon. *Olympic Gold: Canadian Winners of the Summer Games*. Toronto: Holt, Rinehart & Winston, 1975.
———. *Winter Gold: Canada's Winners in the Winter Olympic Games*. Markham, Ont.: Fitzhenry & Whiteside, 1987.
Roxborough, Henry. *Canada at the Olympics*. Three eds. Toronto: Ryerson Press, 1963, 1969, 1975.

D. Cuba

Forbes, Irene, Ana Maria Luján, and Juan Velázquez. *Cubanos en Juegos Olímpicos*. 2nd ed. Havana: Editorial Pueblo y Educación, 2003.

E. Czechoslovakia

Klír, M., Jiří Kössl, and AaM Martíkovi. *Almanach Ceskoslovenskych Olympionikü*. Prague: Stráz, 1987.
Kolář, František a kolektiv. *Kdo byl Kdo. Naši olympionici*. Prague: Nakladatelství Libri, 1999.
Kössl, Jiří, ed. *Cěský Olympijský Výbor. Olympijská knihovnička: Dokumentace K Dějinám Cěského Olympismu*. Prague: Czech Olympic Committee, 1998. Vol. 1, 1891–1918. Vol. 2, 1918–1945. Vol. 3, 1945–1971. Vol. 4, 1971–1998.

F. Estonia

Kivine, P. *Estonikie sportsmeny prisery Olimpiyskikh/Estonian Olympic Medal Winners/Die estnischen Olympiamedaillen-gewinner/Les Médaillés olympiques d'Estonie*. Tallinn: Perioodika, 1980. Parallel texts in Estonian, English, German, and French.

G. France

Charpentier, Henri. *La Grande Histoire des Médaillés Olympiques Français de 1896 à 1988*. Paris: Editions Robert Laffont, ca. 1989.
Lejeune, André. *Les Alsaciens aux Jeux Olympiques—D'Athenes 1896 a Pekin 2008*. Strasbourg, Alsace, France: Association Dialogues Transvosgiens, 2009.
Pellissard-Darrigrand, Nicole. *La Galaxie Olympique d'Hiver*. Biarritz: CNOSF, 1998.
———. *La Galaxie Olympique III: D'Athènes 1896 à Sydney 2000*. Biarritz: Atlantica, 2000.

H. German Democratic Republic

Gilbert, Doug. *The Miracle Machine*. New York: Coward, McCann & Geoghegan, 1980.
Kluge, Volker. *Das große Lexikon der DDR-Sportler*. Berlin: Schwarzkopf & Scwarzkopf, 2001.

I. Germany

NOK für Deutschland von Manfred Lämmer. *Deutschland in der Olympischen Bewegung. Eine Zwischenbilanz*. Frankfurt/Main: NOK für Deutschland, 1999.

J. Great Britain

Buchanan, Ian. *British Olympians: A Hundred Years of Gold Medallists*. London: Guinness, 1991.
Carruthers, Kitty. *British Olympic Heroes—The Best of British Gold Medalists*. London: Stacey International, 2011.
Menary, Steve. *GB United? British Olympic Football and the End of the Amateur Dream*. Worthing, England: Pitch, 2010.

K. Greece

Tarasouleas, At[hanassios]. *Helliniki Simmetokhi Stis Sinkhrones Olympiades* (transliterated title). Athens: Author, 1990.

L. Hungary

Mező, Ferenc. *Golden Book of Hungarian Olympic Champions/Livre d'Or des Champions Olympiques Hongrois*. Budapest: Sport Lap. És Könyvkiadö, 1955. Parallel texts in English and French.
Tamás, Aján, István Szekres, Pál Hencsei, Tibor Ivanics, Ferenc Takács, Lajos Szabó, Vad Desző, and Lászlo Kun. *Magyarok az Olimpai Játékokon: 1896–2000*. Budapest: Magyar Millenium, 2001.

M. India

Ezekiel, Gulu, and K. Arumugam. *Great Indian Olympians*. New Delhi: Field Hockey Publications, 2004. Updated edition with K. Arumugam, 2012.
Sanyal, Saraduni. *Olympic Games and India*. New Delhi: Metropolitan Book, 1970.

N. Ireland

McCarthy, Kevin. *Gold, Silver and Green: The Irish Olympic Journey 1896–1924*. Cork: Cork University Press, 2010.

Murphy, Colm. *The Irish Championships 1885–1922.* Kent, England: self-published, 2010.
Naughton, Lindie, and Johnny Watterson. *Irish Olympians.* Dublin: Blackwater Press, 1992.

O. Israel

Alperovich, Amichai. *Israel in der Olympischen Bewegung.* Sankt Augustin, Germany: Academia, 2012.

P. Latvia

Latvijas Olimpiska–Komiteja. *Latvijas Olimpiska–Ve–sture: No Stokhlmas L–ı dz Soltleiksitijai (The Olympic History of Latvia: From Stockholm to Salt Lake City).* Latvia: Latvijas Olimpiska–Komiteja, 2003.

Q. Luxembourg

Bressler, Henri, Pierre Gricius, and Georges Klepper. *Letzebuerger Olympia Lexikon.* Esch-sur-Alzette, Luxembourg: Schortgen, 2014.

R. The Netherlands

Bijkerk, Ton. *Olympisch Oranje van Athene 1896 tot en met Athene 2004.* Haarlem: De Vrieseborch, 2004. 2nd ed. Baarn: Tirion Uitgevers BV, 2008.
———. *Olympisch Oranje van Athene 1896 tot en met Londen 2012.* Haarlem: Spaar, 2012.
Bijkerk, Ton, and Ruud Paauw. *Gouden Boek van ed Nederlandse Olympiers.* Haarlem: De Vrieseborch, 1996.

S. New Zealand

Atkinson, Graeme. *Australian & New Zealand Olympians: The Stories of 100 Great Champions.* Canterbury, Vic.: Five Mile Press, 1984.

T. Norway

Johnsen, Arnfinn, and Age Dalby. *GULL—101 Portretterav Norske OL-vinnere.* Oslo: Font Forlag, 2013.

U. Poland

Gluszek, Zygmunt. *Polscy Olimpijczycy 1924/1984.* 2nd ed. Warsaw: Sport i Turystyka, 1988. First edition published in 1980 as *Polscy Olimpijczycy 1924/1976.*

Tuszynski, Bogdan. *Polscy Olimpijczycy XX Wieku.* 2 vols. Wrocław: Europa, 2004.
Tuszynski, Bogdan, and Henryk Kurzynski. *Od Chamonix/Paryza do Vancouver—Leksykon olimpijczykow polskidh 1936–2010.* Warsaw: Polski Komitet Olimpijski, 2011.

V. Slovakia

Grexa, Jan, and Lubomir Soucek. *Slovensko v znameni piatich kruhov.* Bratislava, 2007.

W. Slovenia

Levovnik, Tomo, Marko Račić, and Marko Rozman. *1920–1988—Nasi olimpijci.* Ljublana: Grafos, 1992.

X. Soviet Union

Brokhin, Yury. *The Big Red Machine: The Rise and Fall of Soviet Olympic Champions.* New York: Random House, 1977 and 1978.
Khavin, B[oris]. *Vsyo ob Olimpiyskikh Igrakh* (transliterated title). Moscow: Fizkultura i sport, 1979.
Pavlov, S. P. *Olimpiyskaya Entsiklopediya* (transliterated title). Moscow: Fizkultura i sport, 1980.
———. *Olimpiyskaya Komanda SSSR* (transliterated title). Moscow: Fizkultura i sport, 1980.

Y. Sweden

Glanell, Tomas, Gösta Huldtén, et al., eds. *Sverige och OS.* Stockholm: Brunnhages Förlag, 1987.
Pettersson, Ulf, ed. *1896–1980 Guldboken om alla Våra Olympiamästare.* Stockholm: Brunnhages Förlag, 1980.

Z. Ukraine

Zinkewych, Osyp. *Ukrainian Olympic Champions.* 3rd ed. Baltimore, Md.: V. Symonenko Smoloskyp Publishers, 1984.

AA. United States

Bortstein, Larry. *After Olympic Glory: The Lives of Ten Outstanding Medalists.* New York: Frederick Warne, 1978.
Carlson, Lewis H., and John J. Fogarty. *Tales of Gold: An Oral History of the Summer Olympic Games Told by America's Gold Medal Winners.* Chicago: Contemporary, 1987.

Johnson, William O[scar], Jr. *All that Glitters Is Not Gold: An Irreverent Look at the Olympic Games*. New York: Putnam, 1972.

Mallon, Bill, and Ian Buchanan. *Quest for Gold: The Encyclopaedia of American Olympians*. New York: Leisure, 1984.

VIII. BIOGRAPHIES OF IOC PRESIDENTS

A. Demetrios Vikelas

Young, David C. "Demetrios Vikelas: First President of the IOC." *Stadion* (1988): 85–102.

B. Pierre de Coubertin

Boulongne, Yves-Pierre. *La vie et l'œuvre de Pierre de Coubertin*. Ottawa, Que.: Lemeac, 1975.

Durántez, Conrado. *Pierre de Couberrin: The Olympic Humanist*. Lausanne: IOC, 1994.

Durry, Jean. *Le Vrai Pierre de Coubertin*. Paris: Comité français Pierre de Coubertin, 1994.

Éyquem, Marie Thérése. *Pierre de Coubertin. L'Épopée Olympique*. Paris: Calman Lévy, 1966.

Lucas, John Apostal. "Baron Pierre de Coubertin and the Formative Years of the Modern International Olympic Movement 1883–1896." Ed.D. thesis, University of Maryland, College Park, 1962.

MacAloon, John J. *This Great Symbol: Pierre de Coubertin and the Origins of the Modern Olympic Games*. Chicago: University of Chicago Press, 1981.

Müller, Norbert, ed. *Pierre de Coubertin: Textes Choisis*. 3 vols. Zurich: Weidmann, 1986.

Navacelle, Geoffroy de. *Pierre de Coubertin: Sa vie par l'Image*. Lausanne: IOC, 1986.

Wassong, Stephan. *Pierre de Coubertin's American Studies and Their Importance for the Analysis of His Early Educational Campaign*. English translation and web page published by the Amateur Athletic Foundation of Los Angeles at www.aafla .org. German version: *Pierre de Coubertins US–amerikanische Studien und ihre Bedeutung für die Analyse seiner frühen Erziehungskampagne*. Würzburg: n.p., 2002.

C. Henry de Baillet-Latour

Boin, Victor. "Graf Baillet-Latour." *Olympische Rundschau* 17 (1942): 6–11.

Diem, Carl. "Die Beisetzung (Graf Baillet-Latour)." *Olympische Rundschau* 17 (1942): 24.

Polignac, Melchior Marquis de. "Gedanken über Graf Baillet-Latour." *Olympische Rundschau* 17 (1942): 17–22.

D. Johannes Sigfrid Edström

Bratt, K. A. *J. Sigfrid Edström—En Levnadsteckning*. 2 vols. Stockholm: P. A. Nordstedt & Söner, 1950 (Vol. 1) and 1953 (Vol. 2).
Bring, Samuel E., ed. *J. Sigfrid Edström: Vänners hyllning på 75-årsdagen 21 november 1940*. Uppsala: Almqvist & Wicksell, 1940.
Edström, Ruth Randall. *J. Sigfrid Edström*. Viisteris: Vistmanlands Allehanda, 1946.

E. Avery Brundage

Gibson, Richard Lee. "Avery Brundage: Professional Amateur." Ph.D. thesis, Kent State University, 1976.
Guttmann, Allen. *The Games Must Go On: Avery Brundage and the Olympic Movement*. New York: Columbia University Press, 1984.
Schöbel, Heinz. *The Four Dimensions of Avery Brundage*. Translated by Joan Becker. Leipzig, GDR: Offizin Anderson Nexo, 1968.

F. Lord Killanin

Lord Killanin. *My Olympic Years*. London: Secker & Warburg, 1983.

G. Juan Antonio Samaranch

Miller, David. *Olympic Revolution: The Olympic Biography of Juan Antonio Samaranch*. London: Pavilion Books, 1992.

IX. OLYMPIC WORKS BY COUBERTIN

Only books on sport and the Olympic Movement are included, they are listed chronologically.

Coubertin, Pierre de. *L'éducation athlétique*. Paris: Imprimerie de Chaix, 1889.
——. *Notes sur l'Education publique*. Paris: Hachette, 1901.
——. *L'Education des Adolescents au XXe siècle. I: L'Education physique: La Gymnastique utilitaire. Sauvetage—Défense—Locomotion*. Paris: Alcan, 1905.
——. *Une campagne de vingt-et-un ans (1887–1908)*. Paris: Librairie de l'Education Physique, 1909.
——. *Une olympie moderne*. Lausanne: Olympic Review, 1909.
——. *Leçons de Gymnastique Utilitaire. Sauvetage—Défense—Locomotion. A l'Usage des Instituteurs, Moniteurs, Instructeurs militaires, etc*. Paris: Payot, 1916.
——. *Leçons da Pédagogie sportive*. Lausanne: La Concorde, 1921.
——. *Mémoires olympiques*. Lausanne: Bureau international de pédagogie sportive, 1931.

X. MISCELLANEOUS OLYMPIC WORKS

Barker, Philip. *Five Rings Over Britain*. London: Continos, 2012.

———. *The Story of the Olympic Torch*. Gloucestershire: Amberley, 2012.

Barney, Robert K., Stephen R. Wenn, and Scott G. Martyn. *Selling the Five Rings: The International Olympic Committee and the Rise of Commercialism*. Salt Lake City: University of Utah Press, 2002.

Bell, Daniel. *Encyclopedia of International Games*. Jefferson, N.C.: McFarland, 2003.

Billings, Andrew C. *Olympic Media: Inside the Biggest Show on Television*. New York: Routledge, 2007.

Borgers, Walter. *Olympic Torch Relays: 1936–1994*. Berlin: AGON Sportverlag, 1996.

Brittain, Ian. *The Paralympic Games Explained*. New York: Routledge, 2009.

Brown, Daniel James. *The Boys in the Boat*. New York: Viking, 2013.

Bryant, Jennifer O. *Olympic Equestrian: A Century of International Horse Sport*. 2nd ed. Lexington, Ky.: Blood-Horse Publications, 2008.

Buford, Kate. *Native American Son—The Life and Sporting Legend of Jim Thorpe*. New York: Knopf, 2010.

Coe, Sebastian. *Running My Life*. London: Hodder & Stoughton, 2012.

Durántez, Conrado. *The Olympic Flame*. Burlada, Spain: I. G. Castuera, 1998.

Gadoury, Victor, and Romolo Vescovi. *Olympic Medals and Coins: 510 B.C.–1994*. Monaco: Victor Gadoury Publications, 1996.

Gold, John Robert, and Margaret M. Gold. *Olympic Cities: City Agendas, Planning, and the World's Games, 1896–2012*. New York: Routledge, 2007.

Grasso, John, ed. *The Olympic Games Boxing Record Book*. Guilford, N.Y.: International Boxing Research Organization, 1984.

Greensfelder, Jim, Oleg Vorontsov, and Jim Lally. *Olympic Medals: A Reference Guide*. Saratoga, Calif.: GVL Enterprises, 1998.

Heck, Sandra. *Von Spielenden Soldaten und Kampfenden Athleten. Die Genese des Modernen Funfkampfs*. Gottingen, Germany: V&R, 2013.

Hillenbrand, Laura. *Unbroken*. New York: Random House, 2010.

Howe, David. *The Politics of the Paralympic Games*. London: Routledge, 2006.

Jackson, R., and T. McPhail, eds. *The Olympic Movement and the Mass Media: Past, Present, and Future Issues*. Calgary, Alb.: Hurford Enterprises, 1989.

Leigh, Mary Henson. "The Evolution of Women's Participation in the Summer Olympic Games, 1900–1948." Ph.D. thesis, The Ohio State University, Columbus, 1974.

Lennartz, Karl. *Bibliographie: Geschichte der Leibesübungen, Band 5, Olympische Spiele*. 2nd ed. Bonn: Verlag Karl Hofmann, 1983.

Little, Alan. *Tennis and the Olympic Games*. London: Wimbledon Lawn Tennis Museum, 2009.

Mallon, Bill. *The Olympics: A Bibliography*. New York: Garland, 1984.

Menard, Michele. *Coins of the Modern Olympic Games*. Vol. 1. Montréal: Self-published, 1991. (No further volume was ever produced.)

Moragas Spà, Miquel de, Montserrat Llinés, and Bruce Kidd, eds. *Olympic Villages: Hundred Years of Urban Planning and Shared Experiences*. Lausanne: International Olympic Committee, 1997.

Moragas Spà, Miquel de, John MacAloon, and Montserrat Llinés. *Olympic Ceremonies: Historical Continuity and Cultural Exchange*. Lausanne: IOC, 1996.

Moragas Spà, Miquel de, Nancy K. Rivenburgh, and James F. Larson. *Television in the Olympics*. London: John Libbey, 1995.

Müller, Norbert. *One Hundred Years of Olympic Congresses 1894–1994*. Lausanne: IOC, 1994.

Pappas, Nina K. "History and Development of the International Olympic Academy, 1927–1977." Ph.D. thesis, University of Illinois, Champaign, 1978.

Payne, Michael. *Olympic Turnaround: How the Olympic Games Stepped Back from the Brink of Extinction to Become the World's Best Known Brand*. Westport, Conn.: Praeger, 2006.

Stanton, Richard. *The Forgotten Olympic Art Competitions: The Story of the Olympic Art Competitions of the 20th Century*. Victoria, Canada: Trafford, 2000.

Theodoraki, Eleni. *Olympic Event Organization*. Amsterdam/Boston: Butterworth-Heinemann, 2007.

Wallechinsky, David, and Jaime Loucky. *The Book of Olympic Lists*. London: Aurum, 2012.

Welch, Paula Dee. "The Emergence of American Women in the Summer Olympic Games, 1900–1972." Ed.D. thesis, University of North Carolina at Greensboro, 1975.

Wenn, Stephen Robert. "A History of the International Olympic Committee and Television, 1936-1980." Ph.D. thesis, The Pennsylvania State University, State College, 1993.

Wilson, Wayne, and Edward Derse. *Doping in Elite Sport: The Politics of Drugs in the Olympic Movement*. Champaign, Ill.: Human Kinetics, 2000.

XI. INTERNET RESOURCES

ancientolympics.arts.kuleuven.be—overview and background on the Ancient Olympic Games

en.wikipedia.org/wiki/Olympic_Games—starting point for exploring the wealth of Olympic information available on the free Internet encyclopedia Wikipedia

www.aroundtherings.com—newsletter of current Olympic related issues (pay site)

www.gamesbids.com—reviews current status of host city bids

www.insidethegames.com—focuses on the 2012 London Olympics, but gives background on many aspects of the Olympic Movement

www.internationalgames.net—covers the various regional and international sporting events

www.isoh.org—official website of the International Society of Olympic Historians (ISOH)

www.la84foundation.org—digital library containing many interesting Olympic documents, including official reports, magazines, and journals

www.olympedia.org—private site maintained by the OlyMADMen (led by Bill Mallon and Jeroen Heijmans, the co-authors of this book, and Arild Gjerde), their research site for work on the history and statistics of the Olympic Games and Olympic Movement

www.olympic.org—official website of the International Olympic Committee; will also direct users to websites for the various International Federations, National Olympic Committees, and Organizing Committees of the Olympic Games

www.olympic-museum.de—virtual exhibits on artifacts and memorabilia of past Olympics, such as posters, medals, and torches

www.paralympic.org—official website of the International Paralympic Committee

www.sports-reference.com/olympics—website containing complete results of the Olympic Games (all years, all sports, all events, all competitors), compiled by a group of dedicated Olympic historians who refer to themselves as the OlyMAD-Men (including two of the authors of this book)

About the Authors

JOHN GRASSO was born in New York City, raised in Whitestone, New York, educated as an accountant but spent most of his working life in data processing. He moved to Guilford in Central New York State in 1980, has written on several sports, and has traveled extensively—visiting nearly 50 countries and attending nine Olympic Games with his wife, Dorothy, and his two children, Steve Grasso and Dr. Laurel A. Zeisler, and to Sochi 2014 with his grandson, James Hernandez. A sports historian, Grasso, has been a lifetime member of the International Society of Olympic Historians (ISOH) since 1993 and is currently serving his third term as its treasurer (2004–2016). He is also a member of the Association for Professional Basketball Research (APBR), the North American Society for Sport History (NASSH), and the Professional Football Researchers Association (PFRA), and was the founder of the International Boxing Research Organization (IBRO) in 1982.

His published boxing work includes *505 Boxing Questions Your Friends Can't Answer* with Bert R. Sugar; *The 100 Greatest Boxers of All Time* with Bert R. Sugar; *The Olympic Games Boxing Record Book*; and *1984 Ring Record Book and Boxing Encyclopedia* (Olympic Editor). He also contributed boxing essays to the *Biographical Dictionary of American Sports* and to *American National Biography* as well as several columns to *Ring* magazine and *Boxing Illustrated and Wrestling News* magazine. He is also the author of the unpublished history *The New York Golden Gloves 1927–1978*. His basketball work includes the *Historical Dictionary of Basketball*; the section on early professional basketball with Robert Bradley in *Total Basketball*; and two monographs: The *Absurd "Official" Statistics of the 1954–55 NBA Season* and *Olympic Games Basketball Records*. He has also contributed to the last eight editions of *Harvey Pollack's NBA Statistical Yearbook* and to Robert Bradley's *Compendium of Professional Basketball*, 2nd edition.

His eclectic interest in all sports has contributed to him being the author of five volumes in the *Historical Dictionary* sports series—Basketball, Tennis, Football, Boxing, and Wrestling, and the co-author with Eric R. Hartman of the *Historical Dictionary of Bowling*. He is currently a consulting editor for Rowman & Littlefield and is responsible for acquiring new sports titles and working with their authors to help produce the final product.

BILL MALLON, M.D., a former professional golfer, is an orthopedic surgeon whose lifelong interest in the Olympic Games became a second career while he was in medical school at Duke University. This fifth edition is his 25th book on the Olympic Games. With Erich Kamper, he coauthored *The Golden Book of the Olympic Games*, and with the late Ian Buchanan he wrote *Quest for Gold: The Encyclopedia of American Olympians* and several other books, including the first three editions of this book. He is the author of a series of books on the earliest Olympic Games (1896–1920) and is a founding member and past president of the International Society of Olympic Historians and former editor of ISOH's *Journal of Olympic History*. For his contributions to the Olympic Movement, he was awarded the Olympic Order in Silver in 2001. He also serves as the president of the American Shoulder and Elbow Surgeons (ASES) (2014–2015), editor-in-chief of the *Journal of Shoulder and Elbow Surgery*, medical editor of *Golf Digest*, and medical editor of *Orthopaedic Coding Newsletter*.

JEROEN HEIJMANS is an information technology professional from the Netherlands. Fascinated by the Olympics since he was nine years old, he is involved in the OlyMADMen, a group that attempts to collect complete historic results of the Olympic Games (partially available on www.sportsref erence.com/olympics). He has written extensively about the Olympic Games on the Dutch sports history site Sportgeschiedenis.nl and is a member (and the web master) of the International Society of Olympic Historians (ISOH).